Lecture Notes in Computer Science   **12265**

More information about this series at http://www.springer.com/series/7412

Anne L. Martel · Purang Abolmaesumi ·
Danail Stoyanov · Diana Mateus ·
Maria A. Zuluaga · S. Kevin Zhou ·
Daniel Racoceanu · Leo Joskowicz (Eds.)

Medical Image Computing and Computer Assisted Intervention – MICCAI 2020

23rd International Conference
Lima, Peru, October 4–8, 2020
Proceedings, Part V

 Springer

Editors
Anne L. Martel ⓘ
University of Toronto
Toronto, ON, Canada

Danail Stoyanov ⓘ
University College London
London, UK

Maria A. Zuluaga ⓘ
EURECOM
Biot, France

Daniel Racoceanu ⓘ
Sorbonne University
Paris, France

Purang Abolmaesumi ⓘ
The University of British Columbia
Vancouver, BC, Canada

Diana Mateus ⓘ
École Centrale de Nantes
Nantes, France

S. Kevin Zhou ⓘ
Chinese Academy of Sciences
Beijing, China

Leo Joskowicz ⓘ
The Hebrew University of Jerusalem
Jerusalem, Israel

ISSN 0302-9743   ISSN 1611-3349 (electronic)
Lecture Notes in Computer Science
ISBN 978-3-030-59721-4   ISBN 978-3-030-59722-1 (eBook)
https://doi.org/10.1007/978-3-030-59722-1

LNCS Sublibrary: SL6 – Image Processing, Computer Vision, Pattern Recognition, and Graphics

This Springer imprint is published by the registered company Springer Nature Switzerland AG
The registered company address is: Gewerbestrasse 11, 6330 Cham, Switzerland

Preface

The 23rd International Conference on Medical Image Computing and Computer-Assisted Intervention (MICCAI 2020) was held this year under the most unusual circumstances, due to the COVID-19 pandemic disrupting our lives in ways that were unimaginable at the start of the new decade. MICCAI 2020 was scheduled to be held in Lima, Peru, and would have been the first MICCAI meeting in Latin America. However, with the pandemic, the conference and its program had to be redesigned to deal with realities of the "new normal", where virtual presence rather than physical interactions among attendees, was necessary to comply with global transmission control measures. The conference was held through a virtual conference management platform, consisting of the main scientific program in addition to featuring 25 workshops, 8 tutorials, and 24 challenges during October 4–8, 2020. In order to keep a part of the original spirit of MICCAI 2020, SIPAIM 2020 was held as an adjacent LatAm conference dedicated to medical information management and imaging, held during October 3–4, 2020.

The proceedings of MICCAI 2020 showcase papers contributed by the authors to the main conference, which are organized in seven volumes of *Lecture Notes in Computer Science* (LNCS) books. These papers were selected after a thorough double-blind peer-review process. We followed the example set by past MICCAI meetings, using Microsoft's Conference Managing Toolkit (CMT) for paper submission and peer reviews, with support from the Toronto Paper Matching System (TPMS) to partially automate paper assignment to area chairs and reviewers.

The conference submission deadline had to be extended by two weeks to account for the disruption COVID-19 caused on the worldwide scientific community. From 2,953 original intentions to submit, 1,876 full submissions were received, which were reduced to 1,809 submissions following an initial quality check by the program chairs. Of those, 61% were self-declared by authors as Medical Image Computing (MIC), 6% as Computer Assisted Intervention (CAI), and 32% as both MIC and CAI. Following a broad call to the community for self-nomination of volunteers and a thorough review by the program chairs, considering criteria such as balance across research areas, geographical distribution, and gender, the MICCAI 2020 Program Committee comprised 82 area chairs, with 46% from North America, 28% from Europe, 19% from Asia/Pacific/Middle East, 4% from Latin America, and 1% from Australia. We invested significant effort in recruiting more women to the Program Committee, following the conference's emphasis on equity, inclusion, and diversity. This resulted in 26% female area chairs. Each area chair was assigned about 23 manuscripts, with suggested potential reviewers using TPMS scoring and self-declared research areas, while domain conflicts were automatically considered by CMT. Following a final revision and prioritization of reviewers by area chairs in terms of their expertise related to each paper, over 1,426 invited reviewers were asked to bid for the papers for which they had been suggested. Final reviewer allocations via CMT took account of reviewer bidding, prioritization of area chairs, and TPMS scores, leading to allocating about 4 papers per reviewer. Following an initial double-blind review phase by reviewers, area chairs provided a meta-review summarizing key points of reviews and a recommendation for each paper. The program chairs then evaluated the reviews and their scores, along with the recommendation from the area chairs, to directly accept 241 papers (13%) and reject 828 papers (46%); the remainder of the papers were sent for rebuttal by the authors. During the rebuttal phase, two additional area chairs were assigned to each paper using the CMT and TPMS scores while accounting for domain conflicts. The three area chairs then independently scored each paper to accept or reject, based on the reviews, rebuttal, and manuscript, resulting in clear paper decisions using majority voting. This process resulted in the acceptance of a further 301 papers for an overall acceptance rate of 30%. A virtual Program Committee meeting was held on July 10, 2020, to confirm the final results and collect feedback of the peer-review process.

For the MICCAI 2020 proceedings, 542 accepted papers have been organized into seven volumes as follows:

- Part I, LNCS Volume 12261: Machine Learning Methodologies
- Part II, LNCS Volume 12262: Image Reconstruction and Machine Learning
- Part III, LNCS Volume 12263: Computer Aided Intervention, Ultrasound and Image Registration
- Part IV, LNCS Volume 12264: Segmentation and Shape Analysis
- Part V, LNCS Volume 12265: Biological, Optical and Microscopic Image Analysis
- Part VI, LNCS Volume 12266: Clinical Applications
- Part VII, LNCS Volume 12267: Neurological Imaging and PET

For the main conference, the traditional emphasis on poster presentations was maintained; each author uploaded a brief pre-recorded presentation and a graphical abstract onto a web platform and was allocated a personal virtual live session in which they talked directly to the attendees. It was also possible to post questions online allowing asynchronous conversations – essential to overcome the challenges of a global conference spanning many time zones. The traditional oral sessions, which typically included a small proportion of the papers, were replaced with 90 "mini" sessions where all of the authors were clustered into groups of 5 to 7 related papers; a live virtual session allowed the authors and attendees to discuss the papers in a panel format.

We would like to sincerely thank everyone who contributed to the success of MICCAI 2020 and the quality of its proceedings under the most unusual circumstances of a global pandemic. First and foremost, we thank all authors for submitting and presenting their high-quality work that made MICCAI 2020 a greatly enjoyable and successful scientific meeting. We are also especially grateful to all members of the Program Committee and reviewers for their dedicated effort and insightful feedback throughout the entire paper selection process. We would like to particularly thank the MICCAI society for support, insightful comments, and continuous engagement with organizing the conference. Special thanks go to Kitty Wong, who oversaw the entire process of paper submission, reviews, and preparation of conference proceedings. Without her, we would have not functioned effectively. Given the "new normal", none of the workshops, tutorials, and challenges would have been feasible without the true leadership of the satellite events organizing team led by Mauricio Reyes: Erik Meijering (workshops), Carlos Alberola-López (tutorials), and Lena Maier-Hein (challenges). Behind the scenes, MICCAI secretarial personnel, Janette Wallace and Johanne Langford, kept a close eye on logistics and budgets, while Mehmet Eldegez and his team at Dekon Congress and Tourism led the professional conference organization, working tightly with the virtual platform team. We also thank our sponsors for financial support and engagement with conference attendees through the virtual platform. Special thanks goes to Veronika Cheplygina for continuous engagement with various social media platforms before and throughout the conference to publicize the conference. We would also like to express our gratitude to Shelley Wallace for helping us in Marketing MICCAI 2020, especially during the last phase of the virtual conference organization.

The selection process for Young Investigator Awards was managed by a team of senior MICCAI investigators, led by Julia Schnabel. In addition, MICCAI 2020 offered free registration to the top 50 ranked papers at the conference whose primary authors were students. Priority was given to low-income regions and Latin American students. Further support was provided by the National Institutes of Health (support granted for MICCAI 2020) and the National Science Foundation (support granted to MICCAI 2019 and continued for MICCAI 2020) which sponsored another 52 awards for USA-based students to attend the conference. We would like to thank Marius Linguraru and Antonion Porras, for their leadership in regards to the NIH sponsorship for 2020, and Dinggang Shen and Tianming Liu, MICCAI 2019 general chairs, for keeping an active bridge and engagement with MICCAI 2020.

Marius Linguraru and Antonion Porras were also leading the young investigators early career development program, including a very active mentorship which we do hope, will significantly catalyze young and briliant careers of future leaders of our scientific community. In link with SIPAIM (thanks to Jorge Brieva, Marius Linguraru, and Natasha Lepore for their support), we also initiated a Startup Village initiative, which, we hope, will be able to bring in promising private initiatives in the areas of MICCAI. As a part of SIPAIM 2020, we note also the presence of a workshop for Peruvian clinicians. We would like to thank Benjaming Castañeda and Renato Gandolfi for this initiative.

MICCAI 2020 invested significant efforts to tightly engage the industry stakeholders in our field throughout its planning and organization. These efforts were led by Parvin Mousavi, and ensured that all sponsoring industry partners could connect with the conference attendees through the conference's virtual platform before and during the meeting. We would like to thank the sponsorship team and the contributions of Gustavo Carneiro, Benjamín Castañeda, Ignacio Larrabide, Marius Linguraru, Yanwu Xu, and Kevin Zhou.

We look forward to seeing you at MICCAI 2021.

October 2020

Anne L. Martel
Purang Abolmaesumi
Danail Stoyanov
Diana Mateus
Maria A. Zuluaga
S. Kevin Zhou
Daniel Racoceanu
Leo Joskowicz

Organization

General Chairs

Daniel Racoceanu   Sorbonne Université, Brain Institute, France
Leo Joskowicz   The Hebrew University of Jerusalem, Israel

Program Committee Chairs

Anne L. Martel   University of Toronto, Canada
Purang Abolmaesumi   The University of British Columbia, Canada
Danail Stoyanov   University College London, UK
Diana Mateus   Ecole Centrale de Nantes, LS2N, France
Maria A. Zuluaga   Eurecom, France
S. Kevin Zhou   Chinese Academy of Sciences, China

Keynote Speaker Chair

Rene Vidal   The John Hopkins University, USA

Satellite Events Chair

Mauricio Reyes   University of Bern, Switzerland

Workshop Team

Erik Meijering (Chair)   The University of New South Wales, Australia
Li Cheng   University of Alberta, Canada
Pamela Guevara   University of Concepción, Chile
Bennett Landman   Vanderbilt University, USA
Tammy Riklin Raviv   Ben-Gurion University of the Negev, Israel
Virginie Uhlmann   EMBL, European Bioinformatics Institute, UK

Tutorial Team

Carlos Alberola-López   Universidad de Valladolid, Spain
  (Chair)
Clarisa Sánchez   Radboud University Medical Center, The Netherlands
Demian Wassermann   Inria Saclay Île-de-France, France

Challenges Team

Lena Maier-Hein (Chair)	German Cancer Research Center, Germany
Annette Kopp-Schneider	German Cancer Research Center, Germany
Michal Kozubek	Masaryk University, Czech Republic
Annika Reinke	German Cancer Research Center, Germany

Sponsorship Team

Parvin Mousavi (Chair)	Queen's University, Canada
Marius Linguraru	Children's National Institute, USA
Gustavo Carneiro	The University of Adelaide, Australia
Yanwu Xu	Baidu Inc., China
Ignacio Larrabide	National Scientific and Technical Research Council, Argentina
S. Kevin Zhou	Chinese Academy of Sciences, China
Benjamín Castañeda	Pontifical Catholic University of Peru, Peru

Local and Regional Chairs

Benjamín Castañeda	Pontifical Catholic University of Peru, Peru
Natasha Lepore	University of Southern California, USA

Social Media Chair

Veronika Cheplygina	Eindhoven University of Technology, The Netherlands

Young Investigators Early Career Development Program Chairs

Marius Linguraru	Children's National Institute, USA
Antonio Porras	Children's National Institute, USA

Student Board Liaison Chair

Gabriel Jimenez	Pontifical Catholic University of Peru, Peru

Submission Platform Manager

Kitty Wong	The MICCAI Society, Canada

Conference Management

DEKON Group
Pathable Inc.

Program Committee

Ehsan Adeli	Stanford University, USA
Shadi Albarqouni	ETH Zurich, Switzerland
Pablo Arbelaez	Universidad de los Andes, Colombia
Ulas Bagci	University of Central Florida, USA
Adrien Bartoli	Université Clermont Auvergne, France
Hrvoje Bogunovic	Medical University of Vienna, Austria
Weidong Cai	The University of Sydney, Australia
Chao Chen	Stony Brook University, USA
Elvis Chen	Robarts Research Institute, Canada
Stanley Durrleman	Inria, France
Boris Escalante-Ramírez	National Autonomous University of Mexico, Mexico
Pascal Fallavollita	University of Ottawa, Canada
Enzo Ferrante	CONICET, Universidad Nacional del Litoral, Argentina
Stamatia Giannarou	Imperial College London, UK
Orcun Goksel	ETH Zurich, Switzerland
Alberto Gomez	King's College London, UK
Miguel Angel González Ballester	Universitat Pompeu Fabra, Spain
Ilker Hacihaliloglu	Rutgers University, USA
Yi Hong	University of Georgia, USA
Yipeng Hu	University College London, UK
Heng Huang	University of Pittsburgh and JD Finance America Corporation, USA
Juan Eugenio Iglesias	University College London, UK
Madhura Ingalhalikar	Symbiosis Center for Medical Image Analysis, India
Pierre Jannin	Université de Rennes, France
Samuel Kadoury	Ecole Polytechnique de Montreal, Canada
Bernhard Kainz	Imperial College London, UK
Marta Kersten-Oertel	Concordia University, Canada
Andrew King	King's College London, UK
Ignacio Larrabide	CONICET, Argentina
Gang Li	University of North Carolina at Chapel Hill, USA
Jianming Liang	Arizona State University, USA
Hongen Liao	Tsinghua University, China
Rui Liao	Siemens Healthineers, USA
Feng Lin	Nanyang Technological University, China
Mingxia Liu	University of North Carolina at Chapel Hill, USA
Jiebo Luo	University of Rochester, USA
Xiongbiao Luo	Xiamen University, China
Andreas Maier	FAU Erlangen-Nuremberg, Germany
Stephen McKenna	University of Dundee, UK
Bjoern Menze	Technische Universität München, Germany
Mehdi Moradi	IBM Research, USA

Dong Ni	Shenzhen University, China
Marc Niethammer	University of North Carolina at Chapel Hill, USA
Jack Noble	Vanderbilt University, USA
Ipek Oguz	Vanderbilt University, USA
Gemma Piella	Pompeu Fabra University, Spain
Hedyeh Rafii-Tari	Auris Health Inc., USA
Islem Rekik	Istanbul Technical University, Turkey
Nicola Rieke	NVIDIA Corporation, USA
Tammy Riklin Raviv	Ben-Gurion University of the Negev, Israel
Hassan Rivaz	Concordia University, Canada
Holger Roth	NVIDIA Corporation, USA
Sharmishtaa Seshamani	Allen Institute, USA
Li Shen	University of Pennsylvania, USA
Feng Shi	Shanghai United Imaging Intelligence Co., China
Yonggang Shi	University of Southern California, USA
Michal Sofka	Hyperfine Research, USA
Stefanie Speidel	National Center for Tumor Diseases (NCT), Germany
Marius Staring	Leiden University Medical Center, The Netherlands
Heung-Il Suk	Korea University, South Korea
Kenji Suzuki	Tokyo Institute of Technology, Japan
Tanveer Syeda-Mahmood	IBM Research, USA
Amir Tahmasebi	CodaMetrix, USA
Xiaoying Tang	Southern University of Science and Technology, China
Tolga Tasdizen	The University of Utah, USA
Pallavi Tiwari	Case Western Reserve University, USA
Sotirios Tsaftaris	The University of Edinburgh, UK
Archana Venkataraman	Johns Hopkins University, USA
Satish Viswanath	Case Western Reserve University, USA
Hongzhi Wang	IBM Almaden Research Center, USA
Linwei Wang	Rochester Institute of Technology, USA
Qian Wang	Shanghai Jiao Tong University, China
Guorong Wu	University of North Carolina at Chapel Hill, USA
Daguang Xu	NVIDIA Corporation, USA
Ziyue Xu	NVIDIA Corporation, USA
Pingkun Yan	Rensselaer Polytechnic Institute, USA
Xin Yang	Huazhong University of Science and Technology, China
Zhaozheng Yin	Stony Brook University, USA
Tuo Zhang	Northwestern Polytechnical University, China
Guoyan Zheng	Shanghai Jiao Tong University, China
Yefeng Zheng	Tencent, China
Luping Zhou	The University of Sydney, Australia

Mentorship Program (Mentors)

Ehsan Adeli	Stanford University, USA
Stephen Aylward	Kitware, USA
Hrvoje Bogunovic	Medical University of Vienna, Austria
Li Cheng	University of Alberta, Canada
Marleen de Bruijne	University of Copenhagen, Denmark
Caroline Essert	University of Strasbourg, France
Gabor Fichtinger	Queen's University, Canada
Stamatia Giannarou	Imperial College London, UK
Juan Eugenio Iglesias Gonzalez	University College London, UK
Bernhard Kainz	Imperial College London, UK
Shuo Li	Western University, Canada
Jianming Liang	Arizona State University, USA
Rui Liao	Siemens Healthineers, USA
Feng Lin	Nanyang Technological University, China
Marius George Linguraru	Children's National Hospital, George Washington University, USA
Tianming Liu	University of Georgia, USA
Xiongbiao Luo	Xiamen University, China
Dong Ni	Shenzhen University, China
Wiro Niessen	Erasmus MC - University Medical Center Rotterdam, The Netherlands
Terry Peters	Western University, Canada
Antonio R. Porras	University of Colorado, USA
Daniel Racoceanu	Sorbonne University, France
Islem Rekik	Istanbul Technical University, Turkey
Nicola Rieke	NVIDIA, USA
Julia Schnabel	King's College London, UK
Ruby Shamir	Novocure, Switzerland
Stefanie Speidel	National Center for Tumor Diseases Dresden, Germany
Martin Styner	University of North Carolina at Chapel Hill, USA
Xiaoying Tang	Southern University of Science and Technology, China
Pallavi Tiwari	Case Western Reserve University, USA
Jocelyne Troccaz	CNRS, Grenoble Alpes University, France
Pierre Jannin	INSERM, Université de Rennes, France
Archana Venkataraman	Johns Hopkins University, USA
Linwei Wang	Rochester Institute of Technology, USA
Guorong Wu	University of North Carolina at Chapel Hill, USA
Li Xiao	Chinese Academy of Science, China
Ziyue Xu	NVIDIA, USA
Bochuan Zheng	China West Normal University, China
Guoyan Zheng	Shanghai Jiao Tong University, China
S. Kevin Zhou	Chinese Academy of Sciences, China
Maria A. Zuluaga	EURECOM, France

Additional Reviewers

Alaa Eldin Abdelaal
Ahmed Abdulkadir
Clement Abi Nader
Mazdak Abulnaga
Ganesh Adluru
Iman Aganj
Priya Aggarwal
Sahar Ahmad
Seyed-Ahmad Ahmadi
Euijoon Ahn
Alireza Akhondi-asl
Mohamed Akrout
Dawood Al Chanti
Ibraheem Al-Dhamari
Navid Alemi Koohbanani
Hanan Alghamdi
Hassan Alhajj
Hazrat Ali
Sharib Ali
Omar Al-Kadi
Maximilian Allan
Felix Ambellan
Mina Amiri
Sameer Antani
Luigi Antelmi
Michela Antonelli
Jacob Antunes
Saeed Anwar
Fernando Arambula
Ignacio Arganda-Carreras
Mohammad Ali Armin
John Ashburner
Md Ashikuzzaman
Shahab Aslani
Mehdi Astaraki
Angélica Atehortúa
Gowtham Atluri
Kamran Avanaki
Angelica Aviles-Rivero
Suyash Awate
Dogu Baran Aydogan
Qinle Ba
Morteza Babaie

Hyeon-Min Bae
Woong Bae
Wenjia Bai
Ujjwal Baid
Spyridon Bakas
Yaël Balbastre
Marcin Balicki
Fabian Balsiger
Abhirup Banerjee
Sreya Banerjee
Sophia Bano
Shunxing Bao
Adrian Barbu
Cher Bass
John S. H. Baxter
Amirhossein Bayat
Sharareh Bayat
Neslihan Bayramoglu
Bahareh Behboodi
Delaram Behnami
Mikhail Belyaev
Oualid Benkarim
Aicha BenTaieb
Camilo Bermudez
Giulia Bertò
Hadrien Bertrand
Julián Betancur
Michael Beyeler
Parmeet Bhatia
Chetan Bhole
Suvrat Bhooshan
Chitresh Bhushan
Lei Bi
Cheng Bian
Gui-Bin Bian
Sangeeta Biswas
Stefano B. Blumberg
Janusz Bobulski
Sebastian Bodenstedt
Ester Bonmati
Bhushan Borotikar
Jiri Borovec
Ilaria Boscolo Galazzo

Alexandre Bousse
Nicolas Boutry
Behzad Bozorgtabar
Nadia Brancati
Christopher Bridge
Esther Bron
Rupert Brooks
Qirong Bu
Tim-Oliver Buchholz
Duc Toan Bui
Qasim Bukhari
Ninon Burgos
Nikolay Burlutskiy
Russell Butler
Michał Byra
Hongmin Cai
Yunliang Cai
Sema Candemir
Bing Cao
Qing Cao
Shilei Cao
Tian Cao
Weiguo Cao
Yankun Cao
Aaron Carass
Heike Carolus
Adrià Casamitjana
Suheyla Cetin Karayumak
Ahmad Chaddad
Krishna Chaitanya
Jayasree Chakraborty
Tapabrata Chakraborty
Sylvie Chambon
Ming-Ching Chang
Violeta Chang
Simon Chatelin
Sudhanya Chatterjee
Christos Chatzichristos
Rizwan Chaudhry
Antong Chen
Cameron Po-Hsuan Chen
Chang Chen
Chao Chen
Chen Chen
Cheng Chen
Dongdong Chen

Fang Chen
Geng Chen
Hao Chen
Jianan Chen
Jianxu Chen
Jia-Wei Chen
Jie Chen
Junxiang Chen
Li Chen
Liang Chen
Pingjun Chen
Qiang Chen
Shuai Chen
Tianhua Chen
Tingting Chen
Xi Chen
Xiaoran Chen
Xin Chen
Yuanyuan Chen
Yuhua Chen
Yukun Chen
Zhineng Chen
Zhixiang Chen
Erkang Cheng
Jun Cheng
Li Cheng
Xuelian Cheng
Yuan Cheng
Veronika Cheplygina
Hyungjoo Cho
Jaegul Choo
Aritra Chowdhury
Stergios Christodoulidis
Ai Wern Chung
Pietro Antonio Cicalese
Özgün Çiçek
Robert Cierniak
Matthew Clarkson
Dana Cobzas
Jaume Coll-Font
Alessia Colonna
Marc Combalia
Olivier Commowick
Sonia Contreras Ortiz
Pierre-Henri Conze
Timothy Cootes

Luca Corinzia
Teresa Correia
Pierrick Coupé
Jeffrey Craley
Arun C. S. Kumar
Hui Cui
Jianan Cui
Zhiming Cui
Kathleen Curran
Haixing Dai
Xiaoliang Dai
Ker Dai Fei Elmer
Adrian Dalca
Abhijit Das
Neda Davoudi
Laura Daza
Sandro De Zanet
Charles Delahunt
Herve Delingette
Beatrice Demiray
Yang Deng
Hrishikesh Deshpande
Christian Desrosiers
Neel Dey
Xinghao Ding
Zhipeng Ding
Konstantin Dmitriev
Jose Dolz
Ines Domingues
Juan Pedro Dominguez-Morales
Hao Dong
Mengjin Dong
Nanqing Dong
Qinglin Dong
Suyu Dong
Sven Dorkenwald
Qi Dou
P. K. Douglas
Simon Drouin
Karen Drukker
Niharika D'Souza
Lei Du
Shaoyi Du
Xuefeng Du
Dingna Duan
Nicolas Duchateau

James Duncan
Jared Dunnmon
Luc Duong
Nicha Dvornek
Dmitry V. Dylov
Oleh Dzyubachyk
Mehran Ebrahimi
Philip Edwards
Alexander Effland
Jan Egger
Alma Eguizabal
Gudmundur Einarsson
Ahmed Elazab
Mohammed S. M. Elbaz
Shireen Elhabian
Ahmed Eltanboly
Sandy Engelhardt
Ertunc Erdil
Marius Erdt
Floris Ernst
Mohammad Eslami
Nazila Esmaeili
Marco Esposito
Oscar Esteban
Jingfan Fan
Xin Fan
Yonghui Fan
Chaowei Fang
Xi Fang
Mohsen Farzi
Johannes Fauser
Andrey Fedorov
Hamid Fehri
Lina Felsner
Jun Feng
Ruibin Feng
Xinyang Feng
Yifan Feng
Yuan Feng
Henrique Fernandes
Ricardo Ferrari
Jean Feydy
Lucas Fidon
Lukas Fischer
Antonio Foncubierta-Rodríguez
Germain Forestier

Reza Forghani
Nils Daniel Forkert
Jean-Rassaire Fouefack
Tatiana Fountoukidou
Aina Frau-Pascual
Moti Freiman
Sarah Frisken
Huazhu Fu
Xueyang Fu
Wolfgang Fuhl
Isabel Funke
Philipp Fürnstahl
Pedro Furtado
Ryo Furukawa
Elies Fuster-Garcia
Youssef Gahi
Jin Kyu Gahm
Laurent Gajny
Rohan Gala
Harshala Gammulle
Yu Gan
Cong Gao
Dongxu Gao
Fei Gao
Feng Gao
Linlin Gao
Mingchen Gao
Siyuan Gao
Xin Gao
Xinpei Gao
Yixin Gao
Yue Gao
Zhifan Gao
Sara Garbarino
Alfonso Gastelum-Strozzi
Romane Gauriau
Srishti Gautam
Bao Ge
Rongjun Ge
Zongyuan Ge
Sairam Geethanath
Yasmeen George
Samuel Gerber
Guido Gerig
Nils Gessert
Olivier Gevaert

Muhammad Usman Ghani
Sandesh Ghimire
Sayan Ghosal
Gabriel Girard
Ben Glocker
Evgin Goceri
Michael Goetz
Arnold Gomez
Kuang Gong
Mingming Gong
Yuanhao Gong
German Gonzalez
Sharath Gopal
Karthik Gopinath
Pietro Gori
Maged Goubran
Sobhan Goudarzi
Baran Gözcü
Benedikt Graf
Mark Graham
Bertrand Granado
Alejandro Granados
Robert Grupp
Christina Gsaxner
Lin Gu
Shi Gu
Yun Gu
Ricardo Guerrero
Houssem-Eddine Gueziri
Dazhou Guo
Hengtao Guo
Jixiang Guo
Pengfei Guo
Yanrong Guo
Yi Guo
Yong Guo
Yulan Guo
Yuyu Guo
Krati Gupta
Vikash Gupta
Praveen Gurunath Bharathi
Prashnna Gyawali
Stathis Hadjidemetriou
Omid Haji Maghsoudi
Justin Haldar
Mohammad Hamghalam

Bing Han
Hu Han
Liang Han
Xiaoguang Han
Xu Han
Zhi Han
Zhongyi Han
Jonny Hancox
Christian Hansen
Xiaoke Hao
Rabia Haq
Michael Hardisty
Stefan Harrer
Adam Harrison
S. M. Kamrul Hasan
Hoda Sadat Hashemi
Nobuhiko Hata
Andreas Hauptmann
Mohammad Havaei
Huiguang He
Junjun He
Kelei He
Tiancheng He
Xuming He
Yuting He
Mattias Heinrich
Stefan Heldmann
Nicholas Heller
Alessa Hering
Monica Hernandez
Estefania Hernandez-Martin
Carlos Hernandez-Matas
Javier Herrera-Vega
Kilian Hett
Tsung-Ying Ho
Nico Hoffmann
Matthew Holden
Song Hong
Sungmin Hong
Yoonmi Hong
Corné Hoogendoorn
Antal Horváth
Belayat Hossain
Le Hou
Ai-Ling Hsu
Po-Ya Hsu

Tai-Chiu Hsung
Pengwei Hu
Shunbo Hu
Xiaoling Hu
Xiaowei Hu
Yan Hu
Zhenhong Hu
Jia-Hong Huang
Junzhou Huang
Kevin Huang
Qiaoying Huang
Weilin Huang
Xiaolei Huang
Yawen Huang
Yongxiang Huang
Yue Huang
Yufang Huang
Zhi Huang
Arnaud Huaulmé
Henkjan Huisman
Xing Huo
Yuankai Huo
Sarfaraz Hussein
Jana Hutter
Khoi Huynh
Seong Jae Hwang
Emmanuel Iarussi
Ilknur Icke
Kay Igwe
Alfredo Illanes
Abdullah-Al-Zubaer Imran
Ismail Irmakci
Samra Irshad
Benjamin Irving
Mobarakol Islam
Mohammad Shafkat Islam
Vamsi Ithapu
Koichi Ito
Hayato Itoh
Oleksandra Ivashchenko
Yuji Iwahori
Shruti Jadon
Mohammad Jafari
Mostafa Jahanifar
Andras Jakab
Amir Jamaludin

Won-Dong Jang
Vincent Jaouen
Uditha Jarayathne
Ronnachai Jaroensri
Golara Javadi
Rohit Jena
Todd Jensen
Won-Ki Jeong
Zexuan Ji
Haozhe Jia
Jue Jiang
Tingting Jiang
Weixiong Jiang
Xi Jiang
Xiang Jiang
Jianbo Jiao
Zhicheng Jiao
Amelia Jiménez-Sánchez
Dakai Jin
Taisong Jin
Yueming Jin
Ze Jin
Bin Jing
Yaqub Jonmohamadi
Anand Joshi
Shantanu Joshi
Christoph Jud
Florian Jug
Yohan Jun
Alain Jungo
Abdolrahim Kadkhodamohammadi
Ali Kafaei Zad Tehrani
Dagmar Kainmueller
Siva Teja Kakileti
John Kalafut
Konstantinos Kamnitsas
Michael C. Kampffmeyer
Qingbo Kang
Neerav Karani
Davood Karimi
Satyananda Kashyap
Alexander Katzmann
Prabhjot Kaur
Anees Kazi
Erwan Kerrien
Hoel Kervadec

Ashkan Khakzar
Fahmi Khalifa
Nadieh Khalili
Siavash Khallaghi
Farzad Khalvati
Hassan Khan
Bishesh Khanal
Pulkit Khandelwal
Maksym Kholiavchenko
Meenakshi Khosla
Naji Khosravan
Seyed Mostafa Kia
Ron Kikinis
Daeseung Kim
Geena Kim
Hak Gu Kim
Heejong Kim
Hosung Kim
Hyo-Eun Kim
Jinman Kim
Jinyoung Kim
Mansu Kim
Minjeong Kim
Seong Tae Kim
Won Hwa Kim
Young-Ho Kim
Atilla Kiraly
Yoshiro Kitamura
Takayuki Kitasaka
Sabrina Kletz
Tobias Klinder
Kranthi Kolli
Satoshi Kondo
Bin Kong
Jun Kong
Tomasz Konopczynski
Ender Konukoglu
Bongjin Koo
Kivanc Kose
Anna Kreshuk
AnithaPriya Krishnan
Pavitra Krishnaswamy
Frithjof Kruggel
Alexander Krull
Elizabeth Krupinski
Hulin Kuang

Serife Kucur
David Kügler
Arjan Kuijper
Jan Kukacka
Nilima Kulkarni
Abhay Kumar
Ashnil Kumar
Kuldeep Kumar
Neeraj Kumar
Nitin Kumar
Manuela Kunz
Holger Kunze
Tahsin Kurc
Thomas Kurmann
Yoshihiro Kuroda
Jin Tae Kwak
Yongchan Kwon
Aymen Laadhari
Dmitrii Lachinov
Alexander Ladikos
Alain Lalande
Rodney Lalonde
Tryphon Lambrou
Hengrong Lan
Catherine Laporte
Carole Lartizien
Bianca Lassen-Schmidt
Andras Lasso
Ngan Le
Leo Lebrat
Changhwan Lee
Eung-Joo Lee
Hyekyoung Lee
Jong-Hwan Lee
Jungbeom Lee
Matthew Lee
Sangmin Lee
Soochahn Lee
Stefan Leger
Étienne Léger
Baiying Lei
Andreas Leibetseder
Rogers Jeffrey Leo John
Juan Leon
Wee Kheng Leow
Annan Li

Bo Li
Chongyi Li
Haohan Li
Hongming Li
Hongwei Li
Huiqi Li
Jian Li
Jianning Li
Jiayun Li
Junhua Li
Lincan Li
Mengzhang Li
Ming Li
Qing Li
Quanzheng Li
Shulong Li
Shuyu Li
Weikai Li
Wenyuan Li
Xiang Li
Xiaomeng Li
Xiaoxiao Li
Xin Li
Xiuli Li
Yang Li (Beihang University)
Yang Li (Northeast Electric Power
   University)
Yi Li
Yuexiang Li
Zeju Li
Zhang Li
Zhen Li
Zhiyuan Li
Zhjin Li
Zhongyu Li
Chunfeng Lian
Gongbo Liang
Libin Liang
Shanshan Liang
Yudong Liang
Haofu Liao
Ruizhi Liao
Gilbert Lim
Baihan Lin
Hongxiang Lin
Huei-Yung Lin

Jianyu Lin
C. Lindner
Geert Litjens
Bin Liu
Chang Liu
Dongnan Liu
Feng Liu
Hangfan Liu
Jianfei Liu
Jin Liu
Jingya Liu
Jingyu Liu
Kai Liu
Kefei Liu
Lihao Liu
Luyan Liu
Mengting Liu
Na Liu
Peng Liu
Ping Liu
Quande Liu
Qun Liu
Shengfeng Liu
Shuangjun Liu
Sidong Liu
Siqi Liu
Siyuan Liu
Tianrui Liu
Xianglong Liu
Xinyang Liu
Yan Liu
Yuan Liu
Yuhang Liu
Andrea Loddo
Herve Lombaert
Marco Lorenzi
Jian Lou
Nicolas Loy Rodas
Allen Lu
Donghuan Lu
Huanxiang Lu
Jiwen Lu
Le Lu
Weijia Lu
Xiankai Lu
Yao Lu

Yongyi Lu
Yueh-Hsun Lu
Christian Lucas
Oeslle Lucena
Imanol Luengo
Ronald Lui
Gongning Luo
Jie Luo
Ma Luo
Marcel Luthi
Khoa Luu
Bin Lv
Jinglei Lv
Ilwoo Lyu
Qing Lyu
Sharath M. S.
Andy J. Ma
Chunwei Ma
Da Ma
Hua Ma
Jingting Ma
Kai Ma
Lei Ma
Wenao Ma
Yuexin Ma
Amirreza Mahbod
Sara Mahdavi
Mohammed Mahmoud
Gabriel Maicas
Klaus H. Maier-Hein
Sokratis Makrogiannis
Bilal Malik
Anand Malpani
Ilja Manakov
Matteo Mancini
Efthymios Maneas
Tommaso Mansi
Brett Marinelli
Razvan Marinescu
Pablo Márquez Neila
Carsten Marr
Yassine Marrakchi
Fabio Martinez
Antonio Martinez-Torteya
Andre Mastmeyer
Dimitrios Mavroeidis

Jamie McClelland
Verónica Medina Bañuelos
Raghav Mehta
Sachin Mehta
Liye Mei
Raphael Meier
Qier Meng
Qingjie Meng
Yu Meng
Martin Menten
Odyssée Merveille
Pablo Mesejo
Liang Mi
Shun Miao
Stijn Michielse
Mikhail Milchenko
Hyun-Seok Min
Zhe Min
Tadashi Miyamoto
Aryan Mobiny
Irina Mocanu
Sara Moccia
Omid Mohareri
Hassan Mohy-ud-Din
Muthu Rama Krishnan Mookiah
Rodrigo Moreno
Lia Morra
Agata Mosinska
Saman Motamed
Mohammad Hamed Mozaffari
Anirban Mukhopadhyay
Henning Müller
Balamurali Murugesan
Cosmas Mwikirize
Andriy Myronenko
Saad Nadeem
Ahmed Naglah
Vivek Natarajan
Vishwesh Nath
Rodrigo Nava
Fernando Navarro
Lydia Neary-Zajiczek
Peter Neher
Dominik Neumann
Gia Ngo
Hannes Nickisch

Dong Nie
Jingxin Nie
Weizhi Nie
Aditya Nigam
Xia Ning
Zhenyuan Ning
Sijie Niu
Tianye Niu
Alexey Novikov
Jorge Novo
Chinedu Nwoye
Mohammad Obeid
Masahiro Oda
Thomas O'Donnell
Benjamin Odry
Steffen Oeltze-Jafra
Ayşe Oktay
Hugo Oliveira
Marcelo Oliveira
Sara Oliveira
Arnau Oliver
Sahin Olut
Jimena Olveres
John Onofrey
Eliza Orasanu
Felipe Orihuela-Espina
José Orlando
Marcos Ortega
Sarah Ostadabbas
Yoshito Otake
Sebastian Otalora
Cheng Ouyang
Jiahong Ouyang
Cristina Oyarzun Laura
Michal Ozery-Flato
Krittin Pachtrachai
Johannes Paetzold
Jin Pan
Yongsheng Pan
Prashant Pandey
Joao Papa
Giorgos Papanastasiou
Constantin Pape
Nripesh Parajuli
Hyunjin Park
Sanghyun Park

Seyoun Park
Angshuman Paul
Christian Payer
Chengtao Peng
Jialin Peng
Liying Peng
Tingying Peng
Yifan Peng
Tobias Penzkofer
Antonio Pepe
Oscar Perdomo
Jose-Antonio Pérez-Carrasco
Fernando Pérez-García
Jorge Perez-Gonzalez
Skand Peri
Loic Peter
Jorg Peters
Jens Petersen
Caroline Petitjean
Micha Pfeiffer
Dzung Pham
Renzo Phellan
Ashish Phophalia
Mark Pickering
Kilian Pohl
Iulia Popescu
Karteek Popuri
Tiziano Portenier
Alison Pouch
Arash Pourtaherian
Prateek Prasanna
Alexander Preuhs
Raphael Prevost
Juan Prieto
Viswanath P. S.
Sergi Pujades
Kumaradevan Punithakumar
Elodie Puybareau
Haikun Qi
Huan Qi
Xin Qi
Buyue Qian
Zhen Qian
Yan Qiang
Yuchuan Qiao
Zhi Qiao

Chen Qin
Wenjian Qin
Yanguo Qin
Wu Qiu
Hui Qu
Kha Gia Quach
Prashanth R.
Pradeep Reddy Raamana
Jagath Rajapakse
Kashif Rajpoot
Jhonata Ramos
Andrik Rampun
Parnesh Raniga
Nagulan Ratnarajah
Richard Rau
Mehul Raval
Keerthi Sravan Ravi
Daniele Ravì
Harish RaviPrakash
Rohith Reddy
Markus Rempfler
Xuhua Ren
Yinhao Ren
Yudan Ren
Anne-Marie Rickmann
Brandalyn Riedel
Leticia Rittner
Robert Robinson
Jessica Rodgers
Robert Rohling
Lukasz Roszkowiak
Karsten Roth
José Rouco
Su Ruan
Daniel Rueckert
Mirabela Rusu
Erica Rutter
Jaime S. Cardoso
Mohammad Sabokrou
Monjoy Saha
Pramit Saha
Dushyant Sahoo
Pranjal Sahu
Wojciech Samek
Juan A. Sánchez-Margallo
Robin Sandkuehler

Rodrigo Santa Cruz
Gianmarco Santini
Anil Kumar Sao
Mhd Hasan Sarhan
Duygu Sarikaya
Imari Sato
Olivier Saut
Mattia Savardi
Ramasamy Savitha
Fabien Scalzo
Nico Scherf
Alexander Schlaefer
Philipp Schleer
Leopold Schmetterer
Julia Schnabel
Klaus Schoeffmann
Peter Schueffler
Andreas Schuh
Thomas Schultz
Michael Schwier
Michael Sdika
Suman Sedai
Raghavendra Selvan
Sourya Sengupta
Youngho Seo
Lama Seoud
Ana Sequeira
Saeed Seyyedi
Giorgos Sfikas
Sobhan Shafiei
Reuben Shamir
Shayan Shams
Hongming Shan
Yeqin Shao
Harshita Sharma
Gregory Sharp
Mohamed Shehata
Haocheng Shen
Mali Shen
Yiqiu Shen
Zhengyang Shen
Luyao Shi
Xiaoshuang Shi
Yemin Shi
Yonghong Shi
Saurabh Shigwan

Hoo-Chang Shin
Suprosanna Shit
Yucheng Shu
Nadya Shusharina
Alberto Signoroni
Carlos A. Silva
Wilson Silva
Praveer Singh
Ramandeep Singh
Rohit Singla
Sumedha Singla
Ayushi Sinha
Rajath Soans
Hessam Sokooti
Jaemin Son
Ming Song
Tianyu Song
Yang Song
Youyi Song
Aristeidis Sotiras
Arcot Sowmya
Rachel Sparks
Bella Specktor
William Speier
Ziga Spiclin
Dominik Spinczyk
Chetan Srinidhi
Vinkle Srivastav
Lawrence Staib
Peter Steinbach
Darko Stern
Joshua Stough
Justin Strait
Robin Strand
Martin Styner
Hai Su
Pan Su
Yun-Hsuan Su
Vaishnavi Subramanian
Gérard Subsol
Carole Sudre
Yao Sui
Avan Suinesiaputra
Jeremias Sulam
Shipra Suman
Jian Sun

Liang Sun
Tao Sun
Kyung Sung
Chiranjib Sur
Yannick Suter
Raphael Sznitman
Solale Tabarestani
Fatemeh Taheri Dezaki
Roger Tam
José Tamez-Peña
Chaowei Tan
Jiaxing Tan
Hao Tang
Sheng Tang
Thomas Tang
Xiongfeng Tang
Zhenyu Tang
Mickael Tardy
Eu Wern Teh
Antonio Tejero-de-Pablos
Paul Thienphrapa
Stephen Thompson
Felix Thomsen
Jiang Tian
Yun Tian
Aleksei Tiulpin
Hamid Tizhoosh
Matthew Toews
Oguzhan Topsakal
Jordina Torrents
Sylvie Treuillet
Jocelyne Troccaz
Emanuele Trucco
Vinh Truong Hoang
Chialing Tsai
Andru Putra Twinanda
Norimichi Ukita
Eranga Ukwatta
Mathias Unberath
Tamas Ungi
Martin Urschler
Verena Uslar
Fatmatulzehra Uslu
Régis Vaillant
Jeya Maria Jose Valanarasu
Marta Vallejo

Fons van der Sommen
Gijs van Tulder
Kimberlin van Wijnen
Yogatheesan Varatharajah
Marta Varela
Thomas Varsavsky
Francisco Vasconcelos
S. Swaroop Vedula
Sanketh Vedula
Harini Veeraraghavan
Gonzalo Vegas Sanchez-Ferrero
Anant Vemuri
Gopalkrishna Veni
Ruchika Verma
Ujjwal Verma
Pedro Vieira
Juan Pedro Vigueras Guillen
Pierre-Frederic Villard
Athanasios Vlontzos
Wolf-Dieter Vogl
Ingmar Voigt
Eugene Vorontsov
Bo Wang
Cheng Wang
Chengjia Wang
Chunliang Wang
Dadong Wang
Guotai Wang
Haifeng Wang
Hongkai Wang
Hongyu Wang
Hua Wang
Huan Wang
Jun Wang
Kuanquan Wang
Kun Wang
Lei Wang
Li Wang
Liansheng Wang
Manning Wang
Ruixuan Wang
Shanshan Wang
Shujun Wang
Shuo Wang
Tianchen Wang
Tongxin Wang

Wenzhe Wang
Xi Wang
Xiangxue Wang
Yalin Wang
Yan Wang (Sichuan University)
Yan Wang (Johns Hopkins University)
Yaping Wang
Yi Wang
Yirui Wang
Yuanjun Wang
Yun Wang
Zeyi Wang
Zhangyang Wang
Simon Warfield
Jonathan Weber
Jürgen Weese
Donglai Wei
Dongming Wei
Zhen Wei
Martin Weigert
Michael Wels
Junhao Wen
Matthias Wilms
Stefan Winzeck
Adam Wittek
Marek Wodzinski
Jelmer Wolterink
Ken C. L. Wong
Jonghye Woo
Chongruo Wu
Dijia Wu
Ji Wu
Jian Wu (Tsinghua University)
Jian Wu (Zhejiang University)
Jie Ying Wu
Junyan Wu
Minjie Wu
Pengxiang Wu
Xi Wu
Xia Wu
Xiyin Wu
Ye Wu
Yicheng Wu
Yifan Wu
Zhengwang Wu
Tobias Wuerfl

Pengcheng Xi
James Xia
Siyu Xia
Yingda Xia
Yong Xia
Lei Xiang
Deqiang Xiao
Li Xiao (Tulane University)
Li Xiao (Chinese Academy of Science)
Yuting Xiao
Hongtao Xie
Jianyang Xie
Lingxi Xie
Long Xie
Xueqian Xie
Yiting Xie
Yuan Xie
Yutong Xie
Fangxu Xing
Fuyong Xing
Tao Xiong
Chenchu Xu
Hongming Xu
Jiaofeng Xu
Kele Xu
Lisheng Xu
Min Xu
Rui Xu
Xiaowei Xu
Yanwu Xu
Yongchao Xu
Zhenghua Xu
Cheng Xue
Jie Xue
Wufeng Xue
Yuan Xue
Faridah Yahya
Chenggang Yan
Ke Yan
Weizheng Yan
Yu Yan
Yuguang Yan
Zhennan Yan
Changchun Yang
Chao-Han Huck Yang
Dong Yang

Fan Yang (IIAI)
Fan Yang (Temple University)
Feng Yang
Ge Yang
Guang Yang
Heran Yang
Hongxu Yang
Huijuan Yang
Jiancheng Yang
Jie Yang
Junlin Yang
Lin Yang
Xiao Yang
Xiaohui Yang
Xin Yang
Yan Yang
Yujiu Yang
Dongren Yao
Jianhua Yao
Jiawen Yao
Li Yao
Chuyang Ye
Huihui Ye
Menglong Ye
Xujiong Ye
Andy W. K. Yeung
Jingru Yi
Jirong Yi
Xin Yi
Yi Yin
Shihui Ying
Youngjin Yoo
Chenyu You
Sahar Yousefi
Hanchao Yu
Jinhua Yu
Kai Yu
Lequan Yu
Qi Yu
Yang Yu
Zhen Yu
Pengyu Yuan
Yixuan Yuan
Paul Yushkevich
Ghada Zamzmi
Dong Zeng

Guodong Zeng
Oliver Zettinig
Zhiwei Zhai
Kun Zhan
Baochang Zhang
Chaoyi Zhang
Daoqiang Zhang
Dongqing Zhang
Fan Zhang (Yale University)
Fan Zhang (Harvard Medical School)
Guangming Zhang
Han Zhang
Hang Zhang
Haopeng Zhang
Heye Zhang
Huahong Zhang
Jianpeng Zhang
Jinao Zhang
Jingqing Zhang
Jinwei Zhang
Jiong Zhang
Jun Zhang
Le Zhang
Lei Zhang
Lichi Zhang
Lin Zhang
Ling Zhang
Lu Zhang
Miaomiao Zhang
Ning Zhang
Pengfei Zhang
Pengyue Zhang
Qiang Zhang
Rongzhao Zhang
Ru-Yuan Zhang
Shanzhuo Zhang
Shu Zhang
Tong Zhang
Wei Zhang
Weiwei Zhang
Wenlu Zhang
Xiaoyun Zhang
Xin Zhang
Ya Zhang
Yanbo Zhang
Yanfu Zhang

Yi Zhang
Yifan Zhang
Yizhe Zhang
Yongqin Zhang
You Zhang
Youshan Zhang
Yu Zhang
Yue Zhang
Yulun Zhang
Yunyan Zhang
Yuyao Zhang
Zijing Zhang
Can Zhao
Changchen Zhao
Fenqiang Zhao
Gangming Zhao
Haifeng Zhao
He Zhao
Jun Zhao
Li Zhao
Qingyu Zhao
Rongchang Zhao
Shen Zhao
Tengda Zhao
Tianyi Zhao
Wei Zhao
Xuandong Zhao
Yitian Zhao
Yiyuan Zhao
Yu Zhao
Yuan-Xing Zhao
Yue Zhao
Zixu Zhao
Ziyuan Zhao
Xingjian Zhen
Hao Zheng
Jiannan Zheng
Kang Zheng

Yalin Zheng
Yushan Zheng
Jia-Xing Zhong
Zichun Zhong
Haoyin Zhou
Kang Zhou
Sanping Zhou
Tao Zhou
Wenjin Zhou
Xiao-Hu Zhou
Xiao-Yun Zhou
Yanning Zhou
Yi Zhou (IIAI)
Yi Zhou (University of Utah)
Yuyin Zhou
Zhen Zhou
Zongwei Zhou
Dajiang Zhu
Dongxiao Zhu
Hancan Zhu
Lei Zhu
Qikui Zhu
Weifang Zhu
Wentao Zhu
Xiaofeng Zhu
Xinliang Zhu
Yingying Zhu
Yuemin Zhu
Zhe Zhu
Zhuotun Zhu
Xiahai Zhuang
Aneeq Zia
Veronika Zimmer
David Zimmerer
Lilla Zöllei
Yukai Zou
Gerald Zwettler
Reyer Zwiggelaa

Contents – Part V

Cell Segmentation and Stain Normalization

Histopathology Image Analysis

Opthalmology

Biological, Optical, Microscopic Imaging

Channel Embedding for Informative Protein Identification from Highly Multiplexed Images

Salma Abdel Magid[1]([⊠]) ⓘ, Won-Dong Jang[1] ⓘ, Denis Schapiro[2,3] ⓘ,
Donglai Wei[1] ⓘ, James Tompkin[4] ⓘ, Peter K. Sorger[5] ⓘ,
and Hanspeter Pfister[1] ⓘ

[1] School of Engineering and Applied Sciences, Harvard University,
Cambridge, MA, USA
{sabdelmagid,wdjang,donglai,pfister}@g.harvard.edu
[2] Laboratory of Systems Pharmacology, Harvard Medical School, Boston, MA, USA
denis_schapiro@hms.harvard.edu
[3] Klarman Cell Observatory, Broad Institute of MIT and Harvard,
Cambridge, MA, USA
[4] Department of Computer Science, Brown University, Providence, RI, USA
james_tompkin@brown.edu
[5] Department of Systems Biology, Harvard Medical School, Boston, MA, USA
peter_sorger@hms.harvard.edu

Abstract. Interest is growing rapidly in using deep learning to classify biomedical images, and interpreting these deep-learned models is necessary for life-critical decisions and scientific discovery. Effective interpretation techniques accelerate biomarker discovery and provide new insights into the etiology, diagnosis, and treatment of disease. Most interpretation techniques aim to discover spatially-salient regions within images, but few techniques consider imagery with multiple channels of information. For instance, highly multiplexed tumor and tissue images have 30–100 channels and require interpretation methods that work across many channels to provide deep molecular insights. We propose a novel channel embedding method that extracts features from each channel. We then use these features to train a classifier for prediction. Using this channel embedding, we apply an interpretation method to rank the most discriminative channels. To validate our approach, we conduct an ablation study on a synthetic dataset. Moreover, we demonstrate that our method aligns with biological findings on highly multiplexed images of breast cancer cells while outperforming baseline pipelines. Code is available at https://sabdelmagid.github.io/miccai2020-project/.

Keywords: Highly multiplexed imaging · Deep learning · Interpretability

Electronic supplementary material The online version of this chapter (https://doi.org/10.1007/978-3-030-59722-1_1) contains supplementary material, which is available to authorized users.

A. L. Martel et al. (Eds.): MICCAI 2020, LNCS 12265, pp. 3–13, 2020.
https://doi.org/10.1007/978-3-030-59722-1_1

1   Introduction

Highly multiplexed imaging provides data on the spatial distribution of dozens to hundreds of different protein and protein modifications in a tissue. This provides an unprecedented view into the cells and structures that comprise healthy and diseased tissue. As such, highly multiplexed imaging is emerging as a potentially breakthrough technology in translational research and clinical diagnosis. Examples of highly multiplexed imaging technologies include imaging mass cytometry (IMC) [5], multiplexed ion beam imaging (MIBI) [6], co-detection by indexing (CODEX) [3], and cyclic immunofluorescence (CyCIF) [8].

Each image can comprise 30 to 100 unique channels (that each correspond to the detection of a specific protein) with millions of cells, and so computational tools are essential for analysis. To interpret the outputs of computational tools and answer specific research and clinical questions, it is critical to know which image channels are informative. Even though there is research on interpretation techniques for natural images [7,14,15,18], channel- or target-wise importance ranking interpretation techniques for highly multiplexed images do not yet exist.

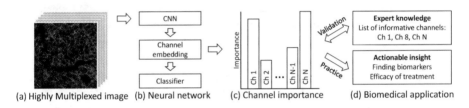

(a) Highly Multiplexed image (b) Neural network   (c) Channel importance   (d) Biomedical application

Fig. 1. Informative channel identification. (a) Given highly multiplexed imaging data, we train (b) a neural network to encode a channel embedding and classify a label (*e.g.*, tumor grade). Then, we measure (c) the classification task channel importance by adopting an interpretation method to the channel embedding. (d) We evaluate our system by comparing the predicted informative channels to expert knowledge, and provide new insights for clinicians and pathologists.

We introduce a novel system to automatically identify informative channels in highly multiplexed tissue images and to provide interpretable and potentially actionable insight for research and clinical applications. The process is illustrated in Fig. 1. What follows is a description of our system for the goal of identifying the most informative channels for assessing the tumor grade of highly multiplexed images [5]. We first encode each channel using the shared weights of a ResNet18 [4] backbone encoder. To obtain an interpretable representation, which we refer to as channel embedding, we use an embedding encoder. Then, we train a classifier to produce a probabilistic prediction for each tumor grade class. Finally, we measure each channel's contribution to the tumor grade classification by applying an interpretation technique, Backprop [18], that backpropagates gradients to the channel embedding. In our experimental results, we demonstrate that our system outperforms conventional algorithms [4,10,20] combined with interpretation techniques [15,18] on the informative channel identification task for assessing tumor grade. Moreover, the informative channels identified by our novel method align with findings from a single cell data analysis [5], even though our approach does not require single cell segmentation.

2   Related Works

Interpretation Techniques for Neural Networks: One category of neural network interpretation is model-agnostic. Backprop [18] and Grad-CAM [15] backpropagate gradients to produce an attention map highlighting important regions in the image. Filter visualization techniques [1,12,21] typically visualize the information extracted from filters. LIME [14], DeepLIFT [17], and SHAP [11] compute the contribution of each feature for a given example. TCAV [7] defines high-level concepts to quantify a model's prediction sensitivity.

Another category is self-interpretable neural networks. SENN [13] trains a self-explaining model, which consists of classification and explanation branches. Zhang *et al.* [22] modify a traditional convolutional neural network (CNN) by adding masking layers followed by convolution layers to force activations to be localized. Building on this work, Zhang *et al.* [23] visualize a CNN's decision making process by learning a decision tree for a pre-trained model. However, these methods are not directly applicable to highly multiplexed input images.

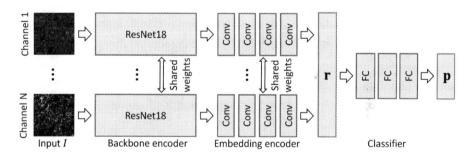

Fig. 2. Our architecture. For an input highly multiplexed image I, we split channels and feed them into ResNet18 [4]. Next, the embedding encoder extracts an interpretable representation $\mathbf{r} = [r_0, \ldots, r_N]$, where N is the number of channels. Both the backbone and embedding encoders share weights across channels. Finally, we adopt three fully-connected layers to estimate class probabilities $\mathbf{p}$.

Frame-Level Action Localization in Videos: Discovering informative channels is similar to localizing frames with target actions in videos. Action localization finds frames of interest in an entire video. CDC [16] predicts per-frame confidence scores using 3D convolutional neural networks. BSN [10] and BMN [9] adopt 2D convolutions to estimate actionness, starting time, and ending time at each frame. These methods can be applicable to informative channel identification by using their per-channel classification as a measure of channel importance.

However, since they perform prediction by classifying one channel at a time, their learned features may not be generalizable and consequently their resulting accuracy may not be sufficient.

3   Proposed Method

To enable the identification of informative channels, we propose a network architecture with a backbone encoder, an embedding encoder, and a classifier (Fig. 2). First, we will introduce the backbone and embedding encoders, which each extract features from each channel independently. For interpretation, we represent each input image channel as a single value r_i. Next, we train a classifier that takes the channel embedding $\mathbf{r}$, which is a concatenation of r_i across channels. The classifier yields predictions, $\mathbf{p}$. Once our network is trained, we apply Backprop [18] to the channel embedding to produce an attention map, which is then used to rank channels in order of importance.

3.1   Channel Embedding

To leverage knowledge from previously-learned image classification tasks and to extract meaningful features from highly multiplexed images, we begin with ResNet18 [4] pretrained on ImageNet [2] as a backbone network. Naive application of ResNet18 does not allow us to identify channels of interest because it weights information across channels through its constituent convolutions (Fig. 3(a)). Even though 3D CNN [20] can suppress this problem by locally weighting channels, it still blends activations across adjacent channels (Fig. 3(b)). Instead, we must extract features from each channel independently. However, doing so will require substantial memory resources (12M parameters per channel). To overcome these problems, we apply the same backbone encoder (shared weights) to each channel individually by modifying the first convolution layer of ResNet18 to accept a single-channel image as opposed to a three-channel (RGB) image (Fig. 3(c)). The last fully connected (FC) layer computes a weighted sum of these independently learned channel embeddings thereby leveraging the power of an independent channel encoding technique while still modeling inter-channel interactions.

For interpretation, applying Backprop [18] to the backbone encoder output yields N 2D tensors, where N is the number of channels. The elements in each 2D tensor represent importance; however, these values are difficult to conceptually interpret. To avoid this issue, we add an embedding encoder that represents each channel as a single value r_i (Fig. 3(d)). The embedding encoder consists of three 3×3 and one 7×7 convolution layers with batch normalization and ReLU. The 3×3 and 7×7 convolution layers have 64 and 1 kernels, respectively. Concatenating the embedding encoder outputs yields a channel embedding $\mathbf{r} = [r_0, \ldots, r_N]$.

To produce a prediction $\mathbf{p}$ for a classification task, we apply a classifier to the channel embedding $\mathbf{r}$. We exploit two FCs with ReLU and one FC with softmax as a classifier. The first two FCs have 200 kernels.

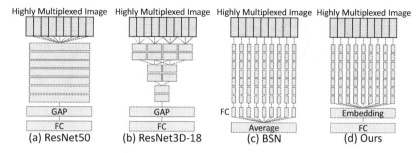

Fig. 3. Architectures of baselines and our network. GAP and FC indicate a global average pooling and a fully connected layer. Unlike other baselines, we convert the input image into a channel embedding and then perform classification.

3.2 Informative Channel Identification

After model training, we apply Backprop [18] to the channel embedding. Specifically, we first convert a given highly multiplexed image into a channel embedding and perform classification. We compute gradients at the channel embedding by backpropagating the gradients of the classification output. Then, we set the importance of each channel as the magnitude of its respective gradient. Unlike other systems using standard classification architectures [4,20], our novel system yields a single value at each channel representing its importance in classification. Note that due to this design choice, our system can be used in a plug-and-play fashion with other interpretation methods [11,14,17] as well. We measure the channel importance of all testing images and then average them across images to measure how informative each channel is for classification.

Alternatively, we can apply a linear regression via a single FC layer to the learned channel embedding. Considering that a simple examination of the coefficients is all that is required, this approach may be easier to interpret. We experimented with this design choice and encountered poor results for both datasets. A single FC layer is not sufficient to model the complex channel interactions. To reduce under-fitting, a non-linear combination of the learned embeddings along with Backprop should be used.

Implementation: We initialize weights in our network with random values except for the pre-trained ResNet18 backbone network. The spatial resolution of the input image I is 224×224 pixels. For data augmentation, we apply horizontal and vertical flips and random cropping. We use an Adam optimizer with a learning rate of 0.0001. The training process iterates for 100 epochs with early stopping while using a batch size of 32 and four Geforce Titan X GPUs.

4 Experimental Results

To validate the design of our model, we conduct an ablation study on a synthetic dataset classification task. To evaluate informative channel identification performance, we define a task in which modern deep neural networks [4,20] achieve

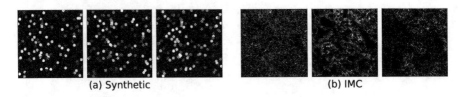

(a) Synthetic   (b) IMC

Fig. 4. Sample channels from (a) synthetic and (b) IMC [5] images.

high accuracy. For a real-world application, we apply our model to a task of predicting tumor grade from a breast cancer dataset generated using IMC [5].

Methods in Comparison: To the best of our knowledge, there is no existing method for informative channel identification. As such, we implement baseline pipelines using modern classifiers, ResNet50 [4], ResNet3D-18 [20], and BSN [10], and model-agnostic interpretation methods, Backprop [15] and GradCAM [18]. We apply the interpretation techniques after training the classifiers to compare them with our system. While ResNet50 and ResNet3D-18 directly predict a class from the image, BSN classifies each channel separately and then aggregates the per-channel predictions to generate a single prediction. For ResNet50 and ResNet3D-18, we use Backprop [18] for interpretation. We convert each channel's attention map into the channel importance by averaging it. For BSN, we adopt GradCAM [15] instead since BSN averages per-channel classification.

4.1 Synthetic Highly Multiplexed Image Classification

According to the single cell analysis of the breast cancer dataset, each channel's pixel intensities follow a bi-modal distribution. We build a synthetic dataset by emulating this highly multiplexed cell imaging environment. This dataset is then used to conduct an ablation study and validate our design choices. The cellular environment is mimicked in these synthetic images by dispersing a random number of circles (cells) of a fixed radius, whose intensities are sampled from bi-modal distributions (representing the signal arising when a target is either present or absent). We randomly choose two modes between $[0.1, 0.3]$ and $[0.7, 0.9]$. Each mode is randomly assigned a frequency of 0.2 or 0.8. We set the variance of intensities as 0.3. We add Gaussian noise to each image. Since our objective is to identify informative channels, we assign two non-overlapping channels to associate with each ground truth. In particular, the two channels assigned to each class are drawn from a class-specific bi-modal distribution, while the intensities in the remaining channels are drawn from a random distribution. An effective model would identify these specific channels assigned to each ground truth during classification. For example, suppose there are 3 classes, A, B, and C, which are assigned the following channel pairs: 4 and 19, 22 and 31, 2 and 17, respectively. Our model when classifying an image from class C must identify channels 2 and 17 and measure their importance. We synthesize 600 training, 300 validation, and 300 test images with 30 channels. Figure 4 visualizes three channels of a synthetic image compared to a real highly multiplexed image [5].

Table 1. Ablation study on the synthetic dataset.

Settings		Scores		
Backbone	Embedding	Accuracy	Recall@6	Recall@10
ResNet18	Independent	98.0	**83.3**	83.3
ResNet18	Shared	99.7	**83.3**	**100.0**
ResNet3D-18	Independent	**100.0**	50.0	66.7
ResNet3D-18	Shared	99.7	33.3	83.3

Evaluation Metric: To evaluate classification performance, we measure accuracy, which is the number of correct predictions divided by the number of total images. For the assessment of informative channel identification, we use Recall@K, which is a recall rate when a model proposes K most informative channels. Since there are six channels (two per class) associated with the classification, we set base K as 6 and expanded K as 10.

Ablation Study: We conduct an ablation study to find the best architecture design. Namely, we consider two choices for the backbone encoder: ResNet18 [4] and ResNet3D-18 [20]. For channel embedding, we consider two approaches: using shared weights across all channels or using independent channel-wise layers. Table 1 lists the scores of each setting. In terms of classification accuracy, all the settings are comparable. However, the purpose of this experiment is to examine the model's ability to identify informative channels rather than classification. For informative channel identification, the ResNet18 + Shared setting achieves the best scores in terms of both Recall@6 and Recall@10. Since the backbone encoder, with 3D convolution layers, mixes information across channels, there is performance degradation in the ResNet3D-18 + Independent setting.

Table 2. Quantitative comparison on the synthetic dataset.

Representation	Method	#Param	Acc	Recall@6	Recall@10
Single prediction	ResNet50 [4]	24M	**100.0**	50.0	66.7
	ResNet3D-18 [20]	33M	**100.0**	50.0	50.0
Channel-wise prediction	BSN [10]	11M	34.7	0.0	0.0
Channel embedding	Ours	12M	99.7	**83.3**	**100.0**

Results: Table 2 compares our system to the baselines. We find that our novel approach significantly outperforms the others in terms of Recall@6 and Recall@10 while achieving similar classification accuracy. This shows that our channel embedding is highly interpretable and effectively represents each channel.

4.2   Tumor Grade Classification

The breast cancer dataset [5] consists of multiplexed images collected using IMC. The images have 39 channels representing a set of proteins that are thought to be important for diagnosis or treatment. For each patient, clinical annotation is available. Here, we focus on identifying tumor grade: grade 1, grade 2, or grade 3. Tumor grade is an indicator of disease progression that is typically scored by a pathologist using only H&E images. We seek to identify the most informative channels among the 39 in the dataset with respect to the prediction of tumor grade. The network input is a multiplexed image and the output is a tumor grade. The dataset contains 723 tissue images from 352 breast cancer patients, and we split them into 506 training images and 217 test images. After training our network, we identify informative channels for predicting tumor grade.

Ground Truth Targets: Quantification of targets in single-cell analysis is correlated with clinical annotations such as tumor grade; however, this requires segmentation to isolate individual cells [5]. In contrast, we predict the tumor grade without using single-cell segmentation. Additionally, we demonstrate that our approach can interpret the importance of individual proteins (channels). We use the single-cell averaged expression of the individual proteins to compare changes between grade 1, grade 2, and grade 3. Further, we use the sum of the absolute fold-change as a ground truth for analysis. Finally, to evaluate the pipelines, we use the same set of targets as those in the Jackson *et al.* study [5].

Table 3. Quantitative results for tumor grading on the breast cancer dataset [5].

Representation	Method	#Param	Acc	Spearman Coeff
Single prediction	ResNet50 [4]	24M	59.9	23.6
	ResNet3D-18 [20]	33M	**68.2**	12.9
Channel-wise prediction	BSN [10]	11M	58.5	41.4
Channel embedding	Ours	12M	65.4	**61.1**

Evaluation Metric: For assessment of classification performance, we report the accuracy. To evaluate each model's informative channel identification, we calculate the Spearman coefficients [19] using the ground truth. The Spearman coefficient measures the correlation between two lists of ranks. To exclude channels with low importance, we only consider the top 15 most informative channels from the ground truth when calculating the Spearman coefficient.

Results: Table 3 compares our system to the baseline pipelines. Our classifier performs better than ResNet50 and BSN. For informative channel identification, our system significantly surpasses the baseline systems in Spearman coefficient. Figure 5 shows the importance of each channel predicted by our pipeline compared to the ground truth. We detect seven of the top 10 ground-truth targets,

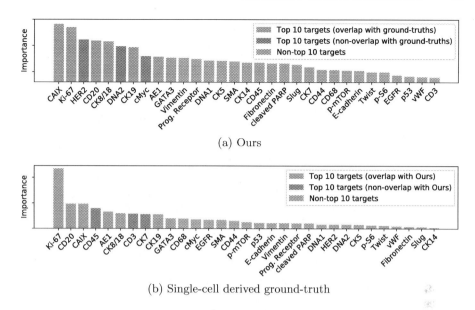

(a) Ours

(b) Single-cell derived ground-truth

Fig. 5. Measured target importance for tumor grade classification on the breast cancer dataset [5], ordered by importance. We highlight the top 10 targets.

which are known proteins associated with tumor progression. One example is Ki-67, which represents a higher proliferation rate with increasing grade. Another example is CAIX, which represents a marker of hypoxia and also increases with a higher grade. Similarly, it was shown that low cytokeratins (like CK8/18, CK19 and anti-pan keratin (AE1)) are correlated with Grade 3 pathology [5].

5   Conclusions and Future Work

We have developed a novel pipeline for channel-wise importance interpretation. Our channel embedding effectively simplifies information in each channel while improving channel-wise interpretability. In the experimental results, we show that our pipeline outperforms existing methods [4,10,20] in terms of classification and informative channel identification for tumor grade prediction [5].

Future work will focus on improving the approach and extending it to other datasets and prediction challenges including (i) biomarker discovery associated with survival time in breast cancer [5], (ii) discovery of cellular features predictive of treatment resistance in metastatic melanoma and other diseases, and (iii) the inclusion of spatial transcriptomic data.

Acknowledgment. Hartland Jackson and Jana Fischer for help with the IMC dataset; This work was supported by NCI (U54-CA225088). Denis Schapiro was supported by an Early Postdoc Mobility fellowship (P2ZHP3_181475). Donglai Wei and Hanspeter Pfister have been partially supported by NSF grant NCS-FO (1835231).

Salma Abdel Magid has been partially supported by Harvard University's Graduate School of Arts and Sciences Graduate Prize Fellowship.

References

1. Bau, D., Zhou, B., Khosla, A., Oliva, A., Torralba, A.: Network dissection: quantifying interpretability of deep visual representations. In: Proceedings of the IEEE Conference on Computer Vision and Pattern Recognition, pp. 6541–6549 (2017)
2. Deng, J., Dong, W., Socher, R., Li, L.J., Li, K., Fei-Fei, L.: ImageNet: a large-scale hierarchical image database. In: 2009 IEEE conference on Computer Vision and Pattern Recognition, pp. 248–255. IEEE (2009)
3. Goltsev, Y., et al.: Deep profiling of mouse splenic architecture with CODEX multiplexed imaging. Cell **174**(4), 968–981 (2018)
4. He, K., Zhang, X., Ren, S., Sun, J.: Deep residual learning for image recognition. In: Proceedings of the IEEE Conference on Computer Vision and Pattern Recognition, pp. 770–778 (2016)
5. Jackson, H.W., et al.: The single-cell pathology landscape of breast cancer. Nature **578**, 1–6 (2020)
6. Keren, L., et al.: A structured tumor-immune microenvironment in triple negative breast cancer revealed by multiplexed ion beam imaging. Cell **174**(6), 1373–1387 (2018)
7. Kim, B., Wattenberg, M., Gilmer, J., Cai, C., Wexler, J., Viegas, F.: Interpretability beyond feature attribution: quantitative testing with concept activation vectors (TCAV). In: International Conference on Machine Learning, pp. 2668–2677 (2018)
8. Lin, J.R., Fallahi-Sichani, M., Chen, J.Y., Sorger, P.K.: Cyclic immunofluorescence (CycIF), a highly multiplexed method for single-cell imaging. Curr. Protoc. Chem. Biol. **8**(4), 251–264 (2016)
9. Lin, T., Liu, X., Li, X., Ding, E., Wen, S.: BMN: Boundary-matching network for temporal action proposal generation. In: Proceedings of the IEEE International Conference on Computer Vision, pp. 3889–3898 (2019)
10. Lin, T., Zhao, X., Su, H., Wang, C., Yang, M.: BSN: Boundary sensitive network for temporal action proposal generation. In: Proceedings of the European Conference on Computer Vision (ECCV), pp. 3–19 (2018)
11. Lundberg, S.M., Lee, S.I.: A unified approach to interpreting model predictions. In: Advances in Neural Information Processing Systems, pp. 4765–4774 (2017)
12. Mahendran, A., Vedaldi, A.: Understanding deep image representations by inverting them. In: Proceedings of the IEEE Conference on Computer Vision and Pattern Recognition, pp. 5188–5196 (2015)
13. Melis, D.A., Jaakkola, T.: Towards robust interpretability with self-explaining neural networks. In: Advances in Neural Information Processing Systems, pp. 7775–7784 (2018)
14. Ribeiro, M.T., Singh, S., Guestrin, C.: "Why should i trust you?": Explaining the predictions of any classifier. In: Proceedings of the 22nd ACM SIGKDD International Conference on Knowledge Discovery and Data Mining, pp. 1135–1144. Association for Computing Machinery, August 2016
15. Selvaraju, R.R., Cogswell, M., Das, A., Vedantam, R., Parikh, D., Batra, D.: Grad-CAM: visual explanations from deep networks via gradient-based localization. In: Proceedings of the IEEE International Conference on Computer Vision, pp. 618–626 (2017)

16. Shou, Z., Chan, J., Zareian, A., Miyazawa, K., Chang, S.F.: CDC: Convolutional-de-convolutional networks for precise temporal action localization in untrimmed videos. In: Proceedings of the IEEE Conference on Computer Vision and Pattern Recognition, pp. 5734–5743 (2017)
17. Shrikumar, A., Greenside, P., Kundaje, A.: Learning important features through propagating activation differences. In: Proceedings of the 34th International Conference on Machine Learning, vol. 70, pp. 3145–3153 (2017)
18. Simonyan, K., Vedaldi, A., Zisserman, A.: Deep inside convolutional networks: visualising image classification models and saliency maps. arXiv preprint arXiv:1312.6034 (2013)
19. Spearman, C.: The Proof and Measurement of Association Between Two Things. Appleton-Century-Crofts, New York (1961)
20. Tran, D., Wang, H., Torresani, L., Ray, J., LeCun, Y., Paluri, M.: A closer look at spatiotemporal convolutions for action recognition. In: Proceedings of the IEEE Conference on Computer Vision and Pattern Recognition, pp. 6450–6459 (2018)
21. Yosinski, J., Clune, J., Bengio, Y., Lipson, H.: How transferable are features in deep neural networks? In: Advances in Neural Information Processing Systems, pp. 3320–3328 (2014)
22. Zhang, Q., Nian Wu, Y., Zhu, S.C.: Interpretable convolutional neural networks. In: Proceedings of the IEEE Conference on Computer Vision and Pattern Recognition, pp. 8827–8836 (2018)
23. Zhang, Q., Yang, Y., Ma, H., Wu, Y.N.: Interpreting CNNs via decision trees. In: Proceedings of the IEEE Conference on Computer Vision and Pattern Recognition, pp. 6261–6270 (2019)

Demixing Calcium Imaging Data in *C. elegans* via Deformable Non-negative Matrix Factorization

Amin Nejatbakhsh[1(✉)], Erdem Varol[1], Eviatar Yemini[2],
Vivek Venkatachalam[3], Albert Lin[4], Aravinthan D. T. Samuel[4],
Oliver Hobert[2], and Liam Paninski[1]

[1] Departments of Neuroscience and Statistics, Grossman Center for the Statistics of Mind, Zuckerman Institute, Center for Theoretical Neuroscience, Columbia University, New York City, NY, USA
mn2822@cumc.columbia.edu
[2] Department of Biological Sciences, Columbia University, New York City, NY, USA
[3] Department of Physics, Northeastern University, Boston, MA, USA
[4] Department of Physics, Harvard University, Cambridge, MA, USA

Abstract. Extracting calcium traces from the neurons of *C. elegans* is an important problem, enabling the study of individual neuronal activity and the large-scale dynamics that govern behavior. Traditionally, non-negative matrix factorization (NMF) methods have been successful in demixing and denoising cellular calcium activity in relatively motionless or pre-registered videos. However, in the case of *C. elegans* or other animal models where motion compensation methods fail to stabilize the effect of even mild motion in the imaging data, standard NMF methods fail to capture cellular footprints since these footprints are variable in time. In this work, we introduce deformable non-negative matrix factorization (dNMF), which models the motion trajectory of the underlying image space using a polynomial basis function. Spatial footprints and neural activity are optimized jointly with motion trajectories in a matrix tri-factorization setting. On simulated data, dNMF is demonstrated to outperform currently available demixing methods as well as methods that account for motion and demixing separately. Furthermore, we display the practical utility of our approach in extracting calcium traces from *C. elegans* microscopy videos. The extracted traces elucidate spontaneous neural activity as well as responses to stimuli. Open source code implementing this pipeline is available at https://github.com/amin-nejat/dNMF

1 Introduction

Recent advances in imaging techniques have enabled the capture of functional neuronal ensembles *in vivo* within a wide variety of animal models [1,5,9,14].

Electronic supplementary material The online version of this chapter (https://doi.org/10.1007/978-3-030-59722-1_2) contains supplementary material, which is available to authorized users.

A crucial step in the study of neuron populations is their segmentation, blind-source separation, and demixing of their calcium signals. Previously, the main approaches to extracting individual neural traces have involved either unsupervised principal component analysis (PCA), independent component analysis (ICA) [10], or semi-supervised region-of-interest (ROI) based segmentation and deconvolution [2]. The evident weaknesses of these approaches are that none of them gracefully handle neuronal ensembles with high-spatial overlap and/or highly-correlated neuronal signals [15]. As a result, non-negative matrix factorization (NMF) based models have been introduced to demix signals from recordings of calcium activity [23]. A primary requisite for this data, in order to permit blind-source separation, is that the imaged ROI remains stationary even, when the animal is awake. Thus satisfying the assumption that the spatial footprints of signal sources remain stationary. This precludes any movement within the ROI.

Recent whole-brain imaging of the model organism *C. elegans* [14] has opened up an exciting new avenue of research. Even during restrained imaging, worms can exhibit highly-nonlinear motion, violating the assumptions that enable NMF-based signal separation. Therefore, common approaches have been to apply motion tracking and simple pixel-averaging methods in two discrete steps [11].

Tracking cells in moving animals has proven to be a challenging machine vision problem [6]. Cell nuclei have similar shapes providing a limited set of unique features to facilitate their tracking. Spatial noise represents a further, inherent limitation, due to the microscopic size of the objects under investigation. Most available microscopy approaches scan the animal in both space and time to achieve volumetric video recordings. Therefore, there are fundamental limits in reaching high-spatiotemporal resolution necessary to resolve unique cell identities and extract their calcium signals.

This problem becomes even harder in the case of *C. elegans* imaging because worms can exhibit nonlinear motion (even when immobilized using popular paralytics). To address this, here we introduce deformable non-negative matrix factorization (dNMF) to jointly model the motion, spatial shapes, and temporal traces of the neurons in a tri-factorization framework. Instead of the two-phase approach of tracking and demixing calcium signals sequentially, we update motion parameters together with updates in the spatial and temporal matrices.

To ensure that our motion model is not over parametrized, we use a small number of parameters that model the worm's motion corresponding to a fixed, spatial representation of the video, matching these to the worm's posture at each time frame. Our framework is general and is suitable for decomposing videos into a set of motion parameters, fixed spatial representations for image components, and temporally varying signals with underlying linear and/or nonlinear motion.

We validate our method on an intensity-varying, particle-tracking simulation and compare it to state-of-the-art calcium-imaging, motion-correction techniques [12] followed by static NMF as well as ROI tracking and averaging [21]. We then demonstrate the ability of our framework to extract calcium traces from all neurons in the head and tail of semi-immobilized *C. elegans* exhibiting nonlinear motion.

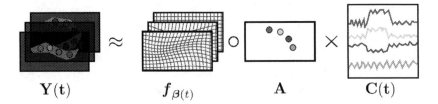

$$\mathbf{Y(t)} \qquad\qquad \boldsymbol{f}_{\beta(t)} \qquad\qquad \mathbf{A} \qquad\qquad \mathbf{C(t)}$$

Fig. 1. Schematic of the deformable non-negative matrix factorization model. The time-series, $\boldsymbol{Y}(t)$, is factorized into time-varying deformation maps, $\boldsymbol{f}_{\beta(t)}$, multiplied by signal spatial footprints $\boldsymbol{A}$, and time-varying intensity coefficients, $\boldsymbol{C}(t)$.

2   Methods

The joint motion correction and signal extraction framework proposed here involves several steps illustrated in Fig. 1. Let $\boldsymbol{Y}_t \in \mathbb{R}^d$ denote the d-pixel vectorized volumetric image at time $t = 1, \dots, T$. We seek to decompose the observations, $\boldsymbol{Y}_t$, into a factorization involving a time-varying deformation term, $\boldsymbol{f}_{\beta_t}$ that acts on a time-invariant canonical representation of k object shapes encoded by $\boldsymbol{A}$. The time-varying spatial signatures, $\boldsymbol{f}_{\beta_t}(\boldsymbol{A}) \in \mathbb{R}^{d \times k}$, are then multiplied by signal carrying coefficients $\boldsymbol{C}_t \in \mathbb{R}^k$. We also encourage model parameters to be "well-behaved" using regularization functions, $\mathcal{R}$. The resulting objective function is:

$$\min_{A,C,\beta} \sum_{t=1}^{T} \left\| \boldsymbol{Y}_t - \boldsymbol{f}_{\beta_t}(\boldsymbol{A})\boldsymbol{C}_t \right\|_2^2 + \mathcal{R}(\boldsymbol{A}, \boldsymbol{C}, \boldsymbol{\beta}) \tag{1}$$

$$\text{s.t. } \boldsymbol{A}, \boldsymbol{C}_{1:T} \geq 0.$$

This formulation differs from standard NMF techniques [8] in that the spatial footprint term consists of a time invariant term, $\boldsymbol{A}$ and a time varying term, $\boldsymbol{f}_{\beta_t}$, which is a differentiable transformation parametrized by β_t, that deforms the canonical representation into the t-th time frame. β_t encapsulates the motion parameters and is usually low dimensional to avoid over-parameterization and overfitting. The regularization $\mathcal{R}(\cdot)$ further constrains the possible choice of spatial footprints, signal coefficients, and spatial deformations. Figure 1 illustrates the model.

2.1   Spatial Component Parametrization: Gaussian Functions

When we have strong prior information about the component shapes we can incorporate that into the model using an appropriate parameterization for the spatial footprints. Neural activity is most commonly imaged using cytosolic or nuclear-localized calcium indicators; nuclear-localized indicators can be reasonably modelled using ellipsoidally-symmetric shape models. Specifically, we observed that the spatial component of the neurons in the videos analyzed here, of *C. elegans* imaged using nuclear-localized calcium indicators, can be well approximated using three-dimensional Gaussian functions. By taking advantage of this observation we can reduce the number of parameters in $\boldsymbol{A}$ from one parameter per pixel per component, to k 3D centers (3 parameters per each neuron) and k covariance matrices (6 parameters per each neuron using the Cholesky parameterization). Formally, we model the footprint of component k using a 3-dimensional Gaussian function with location parameters $\boldsymbol{\mu}_k \in \mathbb{R}^3$ and shape parameters $\boldsymbol{\Sigma}_k \in \mathbb{R}^{3 \times 3}$.

Under this new spatial model for $\boldsymbol{A} = \{\boldsymbol{\mu}_{1:K}, \boldsymbol{\Sigma}_{1:K}\}$, we modify the $\boldsymbol{f}_{\beta_t}$ function to match this parameterization to have $\boldsymbol{f}_{\beta_t}(\boldsymbol{A}) \in \mathbb{R}^{d \times k}$:

$$\boldsymbol{f}_{\beta_t}(\boldsymbol{A})[i,k] \approx \exp\left([\boldsymbol{p}_i - \boldsymbol{\beta}_t \Psi(\boldsymbol{\mu}_k)]^T \boldsymbol{\Sigma}_k^{-1} [\boldsymbol{p}_i - \boldsymbol{\beta}_t \Psi(\boldsymbol{\mu}_k)]\right), \qquad (2)$$

where $\boldsymbol{p}_i$ is the 3D coordinate of the i-th pixel in the image. (Note that non-negativity of the spatial components is enforced automatically here.) Due to the differentiability of $\boldsymbol{f}_{\beta_t}$, it is straightforward to compute gradients with respect to β_t and $\boldsymbol{\Sigma}_k$.

2.2 Regularization: Temporal Continuity and Plausible Deformations

We employ two sets of regularizers to enforce a well-behaved model. To enforce smoothness of the temporal traces and motion trajectories in time we add a regularizer that penalizes discontinuities in the neural trajectories and signal coefficients. Specifically, we encourage the neural centers and signal coefficients at neighboring time points to be close. The regularizer for this purpose is:

$$\mathcal{R}_T(\boldsymbol{C}, \boldsymbol{\beta}) = \lambda_\beta \sum_{t=0}^{T-1} \|\psi(\boldsymbol{\mu}_{1:K})\boldsymbol{\beta}_{t-1} - \psi(\boldsymbol{\mu}_{1:K})\boldsymbol{\beta}_t\|_F^2 + \lambda_C \sum_{t=0}^{T-1} \|\boldsymbol{C}_{t-1} - \boldsymbol{C}_t\|_F^2 .$$
$$(3)$$

In this formulation $\psi(\boldsymbol{\mu}_{1:K})$ is the quadratic transformation of the canonical neural centers. When multiplied by $\boldsymbol{\beta}_{t-1}$ and $\boldsymbol{\beta}_t$ the result will be the neural centers at time $t-1$ and t respectively. The term $\boldsymbol{f}_{\beta_t}$ induces a deformable transformation of the pixel correspondences between time t and the canonical representation $\boldsymbol{A}$.

In order to constrain this transformation to yield physically realistic deformations that respect volumetric changes, we regularize the cost function using the determinant of the Jacobian of the transformation term to encourage the Jacobian to be close to 1 and prevent the deformation from contracting or expanding unrealistically. The Jacobian can be represented as: $\mathcal{J}_\beta(x_1, x_2, x_3)$ with $\mathcal{J}_{ij} = \frac{\partial(\boldsymbol{f}_\beta)_i}{\partial x_j}$. Using the Jacobian, the regularizer is:

$$\mathcal{R}_{\mathcal{J}}(\boldsymbol{\beta}) = \lambda_{\mathcal{J}} \sum_{t=1}^{T} \sum_{i=1}^{j} (\det \mathcal{J}_{\beta_t}(x_i, y_i, z_i) - 1)^2, \qquad (4)$$

where the Jacobian is evaluated on a grid.

2.3   Optimization and Initialization

All the variations of the dNMF cost function are optimized in the following way. To update β and A we use the `autograd` tool and `PyTorch` library to automatically compute gradients of the cost function and `Adam` optimizer to back-propagate the gradients. A forward pass of computation is evaluating the cost function with $\beta_{1:T}$ and A (in the fully parametric case, or $\beta_{1:T}$ (in the Gaussian case) as parameters. Note that for a fixed C, all compartments of the cost function are differentiable with respect to the parameters.

To update C we use multiplicative updates as described in [19]:

$$C_t \leftarrow C_t \odot \frac{f_{\beta_t}^T Y_t + \lambda_C (C_{t-1} + C_{t+1})}{f_{\beta_t}^T f_{\beta_t} C_t + 2\lambda_C C_t}. \tag{5}$$

The key difference between these multiplicative updates from those found in [8] is that the parts of the derivatives of the temporal smoothness regularization terms $2\lambda_C C_t$ and $\lambda_C(C_{t-1} + C_{t+1})$ appear in the denominator and numerator to promote smoothly varying signal.

One key advantage of the *C. elegans* datasets considered here is that we can reliably identify the locations of all cells in the field of view, using methods developed in [22]. Using the location of cells in the initial frame (for example) can tremendously aid the optimization of the objective (1) for two main reasons. First, it serves as a very good initializer for the μ_k parameters for cell spatial footprints mentioned in Sect. 2.1. Second, we know a priori the correct number of cells to be demixed in the FOV. These two factors enable our framework to operate in a **semi-blind** manner towards the deconvolution of neural signals of *C. elegans*, unlike fully blind deconvolution techniques such as e.g. PCA-ICA [10] or CNMF [13].

2.4   Evaluation Metrics and Comparisons

To evaluate the performance of the proposed method as well as the compared methods, we focus on several metrics that shed light both on the signal demixing capabilities of the methods as well as their ability to track objects in time. Namely we focus on two major metrics: **trajectory correlation**, which measures the ability of the deformation model to keep track of the observed motion, and **signal correlation**, which measures the demixing performance by comparing the correlation of demixed signal intensities relative to the ground truth. Specifically, these metrics can be expressed as:

Trajectory correlation:	Signal correlation:
$\rho(\hat{\beta}, \beta) = \dfrac{\sum_{i,j,t}(\hat{\beta}_t^{ij} - \bar{\hat{\beta}})(\beta_t^{ij} - \bar{\beta})}{\sqrt{\sum_{i,j,t}(\hat{\beta}_t^{ij} - \bar{\hat{\beta}})^2}\sqrt{\sum_{i,j,t}(\beta_t^{ij} - \bar{\beta})^2}}$	$\rho(\hat{C}, C) = \dfrac{\sum_{kt}(\hat{C}_{kt} - \bar{\hat{C}})(C_{kt} - \bar{C})}{\sqrt{\sum_{kt}(\hat{C}_{kt} - \bar{\hat{C}})^2}\sqrt{\sum_{kt}(C_{kt} - \bar{C})^2}}$

Using these metrics, we evaluate the signal extraction performance of dNMF against two standard routines in calcium imaging. First, we compare against region of interest (ROI) tracking and pixel averaging within the ROI [21].

This method tracks the positions of cells across time and extracts signal by taking the average pixel intensity value in a pre-defined radial region around the tracking marker. We also compare against the routine of performing motion correction first and then signal extraction through NMF [13]. To replicate this routine in our experiments, we motion correct using Normcorre and then use the Gaussian cell shape parametrization version of NMF that is described in Sect. 2.1. We use this variant of NMF rather than non-parametric variants such as CNMF [13] to bring the comparison against dNMF to an equal footing since dNMF already uses this parametrization that tends to model nuclear shapes well.

2.5   *C. elegans* Video Description

Videos of calcium activity in *C. elegans* were captured via a spinning-disk confocal microscope with resolution (x,y,z)=(0.27,0.27,1.5) microns that correspond pixel dimensions of $(256 \times 128 \times 21)$. Whole-brain calcium activity was measured using the fluorescent sensor GCaMP6s in animals expressing a stereotyped fluorescent color map that permitted class-type identification of every neuron in the worm's brain (NeuroPAL strain OH16230) [22]. Each video was 4 min long and was acquired at approximately 4 Hz. Worms were paralytically immobilized (using tertramisole) in a microfluidic chip capable of delivering chemosensory stimuli (salt and two odors) [4,17]. This setup allows for the controlled delivery of multiple soluble stimuli to the animal with high-temporal precision. See [22] for full experimental details.

3   Results

Simulation Experiments: To evaluate the effectiveness of our algorithm in capturing motion and demixing time-series traces, we simulated the trajectory of a pre-specified number of neurons, with a time-specific trace assigned to each (Fig. 2A-B). The signal for each neuron is modeled as a binary vector with length T and probability p of observing a unit spike, convolved with a decaying exponential kernel. Each trajectory was generated using a randomly sampled quadratic transformation of the point cloud in the previous time frame, starting from a random initial point cloud. Given the mismatch between the simulated trajectories and the modeling assumptions our results suggest that the quadratic transformation is flexible enough to approximate the true trajectories accurately.

We compare the performance of dNMF, Normcorre+NMF, and ROI pixel averaging in a variety of confounding scenarios using the metrics defined in Sect. 2.4. In all simulation experiments, the ROI averaging method is provided with the ground truth cell positions — i.e., we examine the accuracy of this method under the (unrealistically optimistic) assumption that neurons are tracked perfectly, to evaluate the demixing performance of ROI signal extraction without the additional confound of tracking performance.

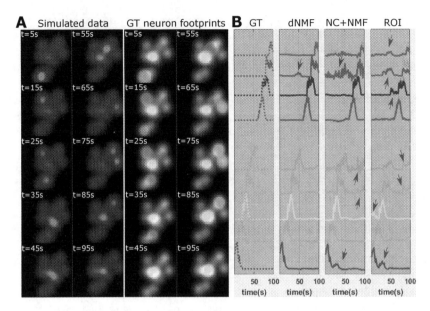

Fig. 2. Demixing calcium signals in simulated videos. A: Neurons are generated as Gaussian shapes and undergo motion and simulated calcium activity in a 100-second long video. Static snapshots of the video are shown (left) and spatial footprints for each cell are assigned unique colors with intensities proportional to calcium activity (right). Note that the spatial footprints of cells are also in motion, tracking the position of the cells. **B:** The ground truth calcium activity for each cell (left) is compared with the neural activity extracted using dNMF (second column), Normcorre [12]+NMF (third column) and ROI tracking and pixel averaging (fourth column). dNMF recovers the ground truth signal well whereas Normcorre+NMF and ROI methods yield significantly more mixed signals (indicated by red arrows) due to the proximity of the cells and the tendency of the spatial footprints of mobile cells to overlap. **C:** The correlation of the recovered signal to the ground truth signal as a function of the image signal-to-noise ratio (SNR). **D:** The correlation of the recovered cell movement trajectories to the ground truth trajectories as a function of trajectory SNR. **E:** The correlation of the recovered signals to the ground truth as a function of the density of independent objects in the FOV. **F:** The correlation of the recovered signals to the ground truth as a function of the density of signaling events (simulating neural excitation) exhibited by the cells. Note that we provided ROI tracking here with access to the ground truth cell centers at all times (explaining why ROI averaging correlation values remain high even in the limit of very high activity density); nonetheless, even with artificially perfect tracking accuracy, mixing of nearby signals remains a significant issue. See MOVIE LINK for further details.(Color figure online)

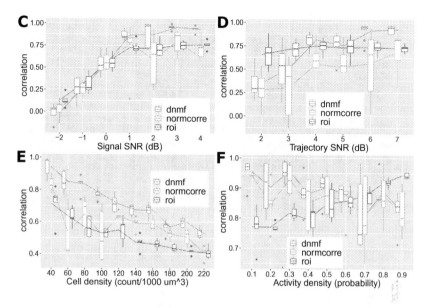

Fig. 2. (*continued*)

In Fig. 2C-F, we explore the performance limits of dNMF, Normcorre+NMF, and ROI pixel averaging as a function of imaging noise and motion variability. Signal SNR is defined by the peak-to-trough difference between the neural activity signals during times of activity. Trajectory SNR is quantified by how well the cells adhere to the motion of all other cells; high trajectory SNR indicates all cells move in unison, resembling a deformable medium, and low trajectory SNR indicates each cell is moving like independent particles. Mathematically, this is proportional to the log ratio of the variance of the average location of the cells versus the variance of the time differences of these locations. It can be seen in Fig. 2D that dNMF is robust to noise but ultimately may introduce errors to demixing and trajectory tracking if the signal and trajectory SNR (Fig. 2D) are too low. Normcorre+NMF does relatively worse than dNMF as a function of signal SNR and trajectory SNR. ROI pixel averaging has the poorest signal recovery performance of the three compared methods as a function of signal SNR. (Note that ROI pixel averaging enjoys a constant trajectory estimation rate in Fig. 2D, since it has access to ground truth cell locations, as discussed above.)

Next, we evaluated the signal extraction performance as a function of the cell density in the FOV. Increased cell density indicates an increased superpositioning of independent signals and therefore a higher degree of signal mixing. dNMF demixing performance degrades as the density of independent objects within the FOV increases (Fig. 2E) but enjoys higher rates of recovery than both Normcorre+NMF and ROI pixel averaging.

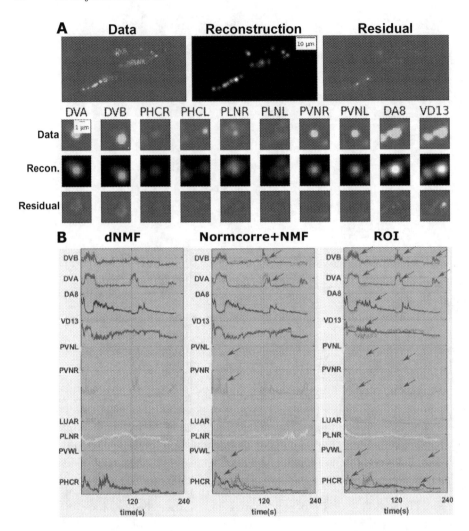

Fig. 3. Demixing neural calcium signal in semi-immobilized *C. elegans* videos. A: A representative z-axis maximum projected frame from a 4-minute long video of GCaMP6s neural activity. We focus on the signal from five pairs of spatially-neighboring neurons in the tail: DVA/DVB, PVNR/PVNL, PVWL/PHCR, PLNR/LUAR, and VD13/DA8. **B:** Calcium signals extracted by dNMF (left), Normcorre [12] + NMF (middle), and ROI tracking and averaging (right). dNMF extracts uncoupled signals that demonstrate independent neural activity. The selected cells were chosen such that the signal recovered by ROI averaging is inconsistent with dNMF (quantified by having correlation smaller than 0.4). Normcorre + NMF partially mixes signals between both PHCR/PVWL and PVNL/PVNR around the 30-second mark and DVB/DVA around the 120-second mark (red arrows), and loses nearly all signal from PLNR, due to motion exhibited by the semi-immobilized animal. ROI averaging produces completely correlated signal (red arrows) between all of the labeled neurons, and loses most of the signal from LUAR and PLNR, due to overlap in their spatial footprints. See MOVIE LINK for further details. (Color figure online)

Finally, we observe that the density of signaling events changes the demixing performance for the three compared methods. In particular, low signal densities (simulating weak excitation) make it harder to track individual cells, which may be dim and therefore hard to detect and track in many frames. dNMF does not suffer in this regime since it combines information across all visible cells to update the tracking model, helping to track dim cells as well.

Demonstration of Demixing in Real *C. elegans* Data: The worm's tail contains several ganglia, with densely-packed neurons, whose spatial footprints often overlap due to insufficient spatial resolution. Additionally, even neurons in separate ganglia can end up in sufficient proximity, due to microfluidic confinement or other imaging-setup induced deformations, such that their spatial footprints overlap. The spatial overlap represents a significant challenge, both for tracking individual neurons and demixing their signal. Figure 3 shows an example of the difficulty present when tracking and demixing neural activity signals from animals with spatially overlapping neural footprints in their recorded images. In this example, ROI tracking loses most of the signal from the LUAR and PLNR neurons and further mixes signals between the DA8/VD13, DVA/DVB, PHCR/PVWL, and PVNL/PVNR neurons. Normcorre+NMF performs better but loses nearly all signals from PLNR while also still mixing signals between the DVA/DVB, PHCR/PVWL, and PVNL/PVNR neurons. In comparison, dNMF recovers strong, independent signals from all ten neurons. Thus dNMF can track and differentiate signals from neurons, even within areas containing multiple spatially-overlapping neural footprints where other comparable algorithms fail.

Conclusion and Future Work: In this paper, we considered the problem of extracting and demixing calcium signals from microscopy videos of *C. elegans*. We developed an extension of NMF, with a nonlinear motion model applied to the spatial cellular footprints, to deform the static image of these cells, modeling the worm's posture at each time frame.

We showed that our method outperforms state-of-the-art models that use a two-step process for motion stabilization/tracking and signal extraction. Finally, we demonstrated the effectiveness of our model by extracting calcium signals from videos of semi-immobilized *C. elegans*.

We have focused here on nuclear-localized calcium imaging in semi-immobilized *C. elegans*. We believe that a similar approach will be useful with other activity sensors [3] and in other preparations, e.g. larval zebrafish [20], Drosophila [16], and Hydra [18]; see, in particular, the recent preprint by [7], who develop improved tracking methods that may nicely complement the dNMF approach. We look forward to exploring these directions further in future work.

References

1. Ahrens, M.B., Orger, M.B., Robson, D.N., Li, J.M., Keller, P.J.: Whole-brain functional imaging at cellular resolution using light-sheet microscopy. Nat. Methods **10**(5), 413–420 (2013)

2. Barbera, G., et al.: Spatially compact neural clusters in the dorsal striatum encode locomotion relevant information. Neuron **92**(1), 202–213 (2016)
3. Chen, Y., et al.: Soma-targeted imaging of neural circuits by ribosome tethering. Neuron **107**, 454–469 (2020)
4. Chronis, N., Zimmer, M., Bargmann, C.I.: Microfluidics for in vivo imaging of neuronal and behavioral activity in Caenorhabditis elegans. Nat. Methods **4**(9), 727–731 (2007)
5. Flusberg, B.A., et al.: High-speed, miniaturized fluorescence microscopy in freely moving mice. Nat. Methods **5**(11), 935–938 (2008)
6. Hirose, O., et al.: SPF-CellTracker: tracking multiple cells with strongly-correlated moves using a spatial particle filter. IEEE/ACM Trans. Comput. Biol. Bioinf. **15**(6), 1822–1831 (2017)
7. Lagache, T., Hanson, A., Fairhall, A., Yuste, R.: Robust single neuron tracking of calcium imaging in behaving hydra. bioRxiv (2020)
8. Lee, D.D., Seung, H.S.: Algorithms for non-negative matrix factorization. In: Proceedings of Advances in Neural Information Processing Systems, pp. 556–562 (2001)
9. Mann, K., Gallen, C.L., Clandinin, T.R.: Whole-brain calcium imaging reveals an intrinsic functional network in Drosophila. Curr. Biol. **27**(15), 2389–2396.e4 (2017)
10. Mukamel, E.A., Nimmerjahn, A., Schnitzer, M.J.: Automated analysis of cellular signals from large-scale calcium imaging data. Neuron **63**(6), 747–760 (2009)
11. Nguyen, J.P., et al.: Whole-brain calcium imaging with cellular resolution in freely behaving Caenorhabditis elegans. Proc. Nat. Acad. Sci. **113**(8), E1074–E1081 (2016)
12. Pnevmatikakis, E.A., Giovannucci, A.: NoRMCorre: an online algorithm for piecewise rigid motion correction of calcium imaging data. J. Neurosci. Methods **291**, 83–94 (2017)
13. Pnevmatikakis, E.A., et al.: Simultaneous denoising, deconvolution, and demixing of calcium imaging data. Neuron **89**(2), 285–299 (2016)
14. Prevedel, R., et al.: Simultaneous whole-animal 3D imaging of neuronal activity using light-field microscopy. Nat. Methods **11**(7), 727–730 (2014)
15. Resendez, S.L., et al.: Visualization of cortical, subcortical and deep brain neural circuit dynamics during naturalistic mammalian behavior with head-mounted microscopes and chronically implanted lenses. Nat. Protoc. **11**(3), 566 (2016)
16. Schaffer, E., Mishra, N., Li, W., et al.: flygenvectors: large-scale dynamics of internal and behavioral states in a small animal. COSYNE (III-19) (2020)
17. Si, G., et al.: Structured odorant response patterns across a complete olfactory receptor neuron population. Neuron **101**(5), 950–962.e7 (2019)
18. Szymanski, J.R., Yuste, R.: Mapping the whole-body muscle activity of hydra vulgaris. Curr. Biol. **29**(11), 1807–1817 (2019)
19. Taslaman, L., Nilsson, B.: A framework for regularized non-negative matrix factorization, with application to the analysis of gene expression data. PLoS ONE **7**(11), 1–7 (2012)
20. Vanwalleghem, G.C., Ahrens, M.B., Scott, E.K.: Integrative whole-brain neuroscience in larval zebrafish. Curr. Opin. Neurobiol. **50**, 136–145 (2018)
21. Venkatachalam, V., et al.: Pan-neuronal imaging in roaming Caenorhabditis elegans. Proc. Nat. Acad. Sci. U.S.A. **113**(8), E1082–E1088 (2016)
22. Yemini, E., et al.: NeuroPAL: a neuronal polychromatic atlas of landmarks for whole-brain imaging in C. elegans, p. 676312. BioRxiv (2019)
23. Zhou, P., et al.: Efficient and accurate extraction of in vivo calcium signals from microendoscopic video data. Elife **7**, e28728 (2018)

Automated Measurements of Key Morphological Features of Human Embryos for IVF

Brian D. Leahy[1,2($\boxtimes$)], Won-Dong Jang[1], Helen Y. Yang[3], Robbert Struyven[1], Donglai Wei[1], Zhe Sun[1], Kylie R. Lee[2], Charlotte Royston[2], Liz Cam[2], Yael Kalma[4], Foad Azem[4], Dalit Ben-Yosef[4,5], Hanspeter Pfister[1], and Daniel Needleman[1,2]

[1] School of Engineering and Applied Sciences, Harvard University, Cambridge, MA 02138, USA
bleahy@seas.harvard.edu
[2] Department of Molecular and Cellular Biology, Harvard University, Cambridge, MA 02138, USA
[3] Harvard Graduate Program in Biophysics, Harvard University, Cambridge, MA 02138, USA
[4] Tel Aviv Sourasky Medical Center, Tel Aviv, Israel
[5] Dept. of Cell and Developmental Biology, Tel Aviv University, Tel Aviv, Israel

Abstract. A major challenge in clinical In-Vitro Fertilization (IVF) is selecting the highest quality embryo to transfer to the patient in the hopes of achieving a pregnancy. Time-lapse microscopy provides clinicians with a wealth of information for selecting embryos. However, the resulting movies of embryos are currently analyzed manually, which is time consuming and subjective. Here, we automate feature extraction of time-lapse microscopy of human embryos with a machine-learning pipeline of five convolutional neural networks (CNNs). Our pipeline consists of (1) semantic segmentation of the regions of the embryo, (2) regression predictions of fragment severity, (3) classification of the developmental stage, and object instance segmentation of (4) cells and (5) pronuclei. Our approach greatly speeds up the measurement of quantitative, biologically relevant features that may aid in embryo selection.

Keywords: Deep learning · Human embryos · In-vitro fertilization

1 Introduction

One in six couples worldwide suffer from infertility [7]. Many of those couples seek to conceive via In-Vitro Fertilization (IVF). In IVF, a patient is stimulated to

B. D. Leahy, W.-D. Jang, H. Y. Yang—These authors contributed equally to this work.

Electronic supplementary material The online version of this chapter (https://doi.org/10.1007/978-3-030-59722-1_3) contains supplementary material, which is available to authorized users.

A. L. Martel et al. (Eds.): MICCAI 2020, LNCS 12265, pp. 25–35, 2020.
https://doi.org/10.1007/978-3-030-59722-1_3

produce multiple oocytes. The oocytes are retrieved, fertilized, and the resulting embryos are cultured *in vitro*. Some of these are then transferred to the mother's uterus in the hopes of achieving a pregnancy; the remaining viable embryos are cryopreserved for future treatments. While transferring multiple embryos to the mother increases the potential for success, it also increases the potential for multiple pregnancies, which are strongly associated with increased maternal morbidity and offspring morbidity and mortality [25]. Thus, it is highly desirable to transfer only one embryo, to produce only one healthy child [29]. This requires clinicians to select the best embryos for transfer, which remains challenging [27].

The current standard of care is to select embryos primarily based on their morphology, by examining them under a microscope. In a typical embryo, after fertilization the two pronuclei, which contain the father's and mother's DNA, move together and migrate to the center of the embryo. The embryo undergoes a series of cell divisions, during the "cleavage stage." Four days after fertilization, the embryo compacts and the cells firmly adhere to each other, at which time it is referred to as a compact "morula." On the fifth day, the embryo forms a "blastocyst," consisting of an outer layer of cells (the trophectoderm) enclosing a smaller mass (the inner-cell mass). On the sixth day, the blastocyst expands and hatches out of the zona pellucida (the thin eggshell that surrounds the embryo) [10]. Clinicians score embryos by manually measuring features such as cell number, cell shape, cell symmetry, the presence of cell fragments, and blastocyst appearance [10], usually at discrete time points. Recently, many clinics have started to use time-lapse microscopy systems that continuously record movies of embryos without disturbing their culture conditions [3,9,30]. However, these videos are typically analyzed manually, which is time-consuming and subjective.

Previous researchers have trained convolutional neural networks (CNNs) to directly predict embryo quality, using either single images or time-lapse videos [26,32]. However, interpretability is vital for clinicians to make informed decisions on embryo selection, and an algorithm that directly predicts embryo quality from images is not interpretable. Worse, since external factors such as patient age [12] and body-mass index [5] also affect the success of an embryo transfer, an algorithm trained to predict embryo quality may instead learn a representation of confounding variables, which may change as IVF practices or demographics change. Some researchers have instead trained CNNs to extract a few identifiable features, such as blastocyst size [18], blastocyst grade [11,19,20], cell boundaries [28], or the number of cells when there are 4 or fewer [17,21]. While extracting identifiable features obviates any problems with interpretability, these works leave out many key features that are believed to be important for embryo quality. Moreover, these methods are not fully automated, requiring the input images to be manually annotated as in the cleavage or blastocyst stage.

Here, we automate measurements of five key morphokinetic features of embryos in IVF by creating a unified pipeline of five CNNs. We work closely with clinicians to choose features relevant for clinical IVF: segmentation of the zona pellucida (Fig. 1a), grading the degree of fragmentation (Fig. 1b), classification of the developmental stage from 1-cell to blastocyst (Fig. 1c), object instance

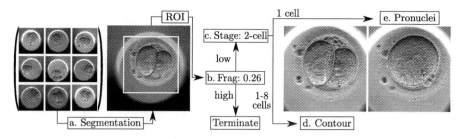

Fig. 1. Instead of performing one task, our unified pipeline extracts multiple features from embryos. We first segment the image to locate the embryo (panel a), colored according to segmentation. The segmentation provides a region-of-interest (ROI, white box) for the other 4 networks, starting with embryo fragmentation (b); the image shown has a predicted fragmentation score of 0.26. If the embryo's fragmentation score is less than 1.5, we classify the developmental stage (c); this image is classified as a 2-cell embryo. We then detect cells in cleavage stage embryos (orange contours in d) and pronuclei in 1-cell embryos (magenta contours in e). (Color figure online)

segmentation of cells in the cleavage stage (Fig. 1d), and object instance segmentation of pronuclei before the first cell division (Fig. 1e). With the exception of zona pellucida segmentation, all these features are used for embryo selection [1, 2, 24, 27]; we segment the zona pellucida both to improve the other networks and because zona properties occasionally inform other IVF procedures [6]. The five CNNs work together in a unified pipeline, combining results to improve performance over individual CNNs trained per task by several percent.

2 Dataset

We train the CNNs using data from the Embryoscope®, the most widely-used system for IVF with standardized, time-lapse microscopy [9]. Embryoscope® images are grayscale, and taken using Hoffman Modulation Contrast microscopy [16], in which the intensity roughly corresponds to refractive index gradients. In our dataset, the Embryoscope® takes an image every 20 min at 7 focal planes, usually at 15 μm increments. The recorded images provide views of the embryo with different amounts of defocus; they do not provide 3D information. The embryos are recorded for 3–5 days, corresponding to 200–350 images at each focal plane (*i.e.*, 1400–2450 images per embryo), although embryos are occasionally removed from the incubation system for clinical procedures. To train the CNNs, we curate a dataset with detailed, frame-by-frame labels for each task.

3 Our Pipeline

For each time-lapse video, we measure 5 morphokinetic features using 5 networks:

Zona Pellucida Segmentation: We first perform semantic segmentation to identify regions of the embryo, segmenting the image into four regions: pixels outside the well, inside the well, the zona pellucida, and the space inside the zona pellucida (the perivitelline space and embryo; Fig. 2, left). We segment the images by using a fully-convolutional network (FCN [23]; based on Resnet101 [15]) to predict a per-pixel class probability for each pixel in the image. We train the FCN with images chosen from 203 embryos at 3,618 time points; we use neither a separate validation set nor early stopping for the zona segmentation.

The zona pellucida segmentation network in our pipeline takes the full 500×500 pixel image as input. We use the segmentation result to crop the images to 328×328, centered around the embryo, as input for the other networks.

Fragmentation Scoring: With the cropped image from the zona pellucida segmentation, we score the embryo's degree of fragmentation using a regression CNN (InceptionV3 [31]). The network takes a single-focus image as input and predicts a fragmentation score of 0 (0% fragments), 1 (<10%), 2 (10–20%), or 3 ($\geq$20%), following clinical practice. We train the network to minimize the L^1 loss on cleavage-stage images of 989 embryos at 16,315 times, each labeled with an integer score from 0–3; we use a validation set of 205 embryos labeled at 3,416 times for early stopping [13]. For each time point in the movie we analyze, we run the CNN on the three middle focal planes and take the average as the final score (Fig. 3, left).

Counting and identifying cells in fragmented embryos is difficult, inhibiting the labeling of train or test data for these embryos. Moreover, since high fragmentation is strongly correlated with low embryo viability [1], in standard clinical practice highly fragmented embryos are frequently discarded. Thus, we only train the rest of the networks on embryos with fragmentation less than 2.

Stage Classification: For low fragmentation embryos, we classify the embryo's developmental stage over time using a classification CNN (ResNeXt101 [33]). The classifier takes the three middle focal planes as input and predicts a 13-element vector of class probabilities, with 9 classes for cleavage-stage embryos (one each for 1–8 cells and one for $\geq$9 cells) and one class each for morula (M), blastocyst (B), empty wells (E), and degenerate embryos (D; Fig. 4, left). To account for inaccuracies in the training data labels, we trained the classifier with a soft loss function modified from the standard cross-entropy loss

$$\log\left(p(\ell|m)\right) = \log\left(\sum_t p(\ell|t)p(t|m)\right) \quad , \tag{1}$$

where t is the true stage of an image, ℓ the (possibly incorrect) label, and m the model's prediction. We measured $p(\ell|t)$ by labeling 23,950 images in triplicate and using a majority vote to estimate the true label t of each image. This soft-loss differs from the regularized loss in [31] by differentially weighting classes; for instance, $p(\ell = 1\text{-cell}|t = 1\text{-cell}) = 0.996$ whereas $p(\ell = 6\text{-cell}|t = 6\text{-cell}) = 0.907$.

Using the measured $p(\ell|t)$, we then trained the network with 341 embryos labeled at 111,107 times, along with a validation set of 73 embryos labeled at 23,381 times for early stopping [13]. Finally, we apply dynamic programming [4] to the predicted probabilities to find the most-likely non-decreasing trajectory, ignoring images labeled as empty or degenerate (Fig. 4, center).

Cell Object Instance Segmentation: For the images identified by the stage classifier as having 1–8 cells, we next perform object instance segmentation on each cell in the image. We train a network with the Mask R-CNN architecture [14] and a ResNet50 backbone [15], using 102 embryos labeled at 16,284 times with 8 or fewer cells; we also use a validation set of 31 embryos labeled at 4,487 times for early stopping [13]. Our instance segmentation model takes as input a single-focus image cropped from the zona segmentation and resized to 500×500. The segmentation model then predicts a bounding box, mask, and confidence score for each detected cell candidate (Fig. 5, left). Both the ground-truth labels and the predicted masks overlap significantly when the embryo has 2–8 cells (Fig. 5, center). We produce a final prediction by running our segmentation model on the three central focal planes; we merge candidates found across focal planes by using the one with the highest confidence score.

Pronucleus Object Instance Segmentation: Finally, in the images identified as 1-cell by the stage classifier, we detect the presence of pronuclei. To do so, we train another object instance segmentation network with the Mask R-CNN architecture [14] and a ResNet50 backbone [15]. We use a training set of 151 embryos labeled at 9,250 times during the 1-cell stage, with a validation set of 33 embryos labeled at 1,982 times for early stopping [13]. Pronuclei are only visible during a portion of the 1-cell stage; correspondingly, about 38% of the training images contain 0, 6% contain 1, and 54% contain 2 pronuclei. The pronuclei detector takes as input a single image, cropped from the zona pellucida segmentation and resized to 500×500, and it predicts a bounding box, mask, and confidence score for each detected candidate (Fig. 6, left). We run the pronuclei detector on the three middle focal planes and merge candidates by using the one with the highest confidence score.

4   Results

We now evaluate our pipeline's performance, demonstrating the effect of each design choice in the models with ablation studies.

Zona Pellucida Segmentation: Our zona pellucida network nearly optimally segments the test set images, taken from 36 embryos at 576 times. The FCN correctly labels image pixels 96.7% of the time, with per-class accuracies between 93–99% (Fig. 2, right). The misclassified pixels arise mostly at region boundaries, roughly corresponding to the few-pixel human labeling inprecision at region boundaries.

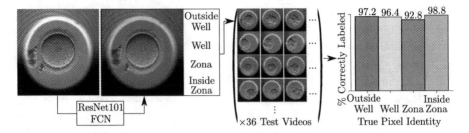

Fig. 2. The zona pellucida network (ResNet101 FCN) performs semantic segmentation on the input image, predicting four class probabilities for each pixel (colored as purple: outside well, pink: inside well, green: zona pellucida, cyan: inside zona). Middle: 12 representative segmentations of 3 embryos from the test set. Right: the per-pixel accuracies of the segmentation on each class in the test set. (Color figure online)

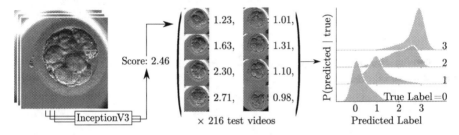

Fig. 3. Left: The fragmentation network (InceptionV3 architecture) scores embryos with a real number from 0–3; the image at left is scored as a fragmentation of 2.46. Center: 8 representative fragmentation scores on the test set, shown as image: score pairs. Right: The distribution of the network's prediction given the ground-truth label on the test set. The green distribution corresponds to images with a ground-truth label of 0; orange those labeled as 1; blue, 2; pink, 3. (Color figure online)

Fragmentation Scoring: The network predicts a score with a mean-absolute deviation of 0.45 from the test labels on the fragmentation test set of 216 embryos labeled at 3,652 times (Fig. 3, right). When distinguishing between low- (<1.5) and high- (≥1.5) fragmentation, the network and the test labels agree 88.9% of the time. Our network outperforms a baseline InceptionV3 by 1.9%; focus averaging and cropping to a region-of-interest each provide a 1–1.5% boost to the accuracy (Table 1).

We suspect that much of the fragmentation network's error comes from imprecise human labeling of the train and test sets, due to difficulties in distinguishing fragments from small cells and due to grouping the continuous fragmentation score into discrete bins. To evaluate the human labeling accuracy, two annotators label the fragmentation test set in duplicate and compare their results. The two annotators have a mean-absolute deviation of 0.37 and are 88.9% consistent in distinguishing low- from high- fragmentation embryos. Thus, the fragmentation CNN performs nearly optimally in light of the labeling inaccuracies.

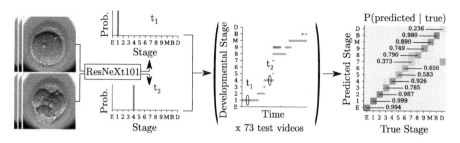

Fig. 4. Left: The stage classification CNN (ResNeXt101) predicts a per-class probability for each image; the two bar plots show the predicted probabilities for the two images. Center: We use dynamic programming to find the most-likely non-decreasing trajectory (orange); the circled times t_1 and t_2 correspond to the predictions at left. Right: The distribution of predictions given the true labels, measured on the test set. (Color figure online)

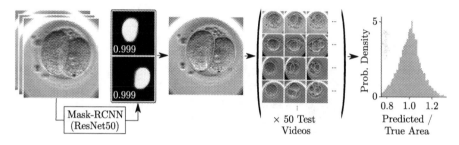

Fig. 5. The cell detection network (Mask-RCNN, ResNet50 backbone) takes an image (left) and proposes candidates as a combined object mask and confidence score from 0–1 (second from left). Center: The boundaries of the object mask represented as the cell's contours (orange, center). Second from right: 12 cell instance segmentations for 4 embryos from the test set (shown as orange contours overlaid on the original image). Right: Histogram of the ratio of predicted to true areas for correctly identified cells in the test set. (Color figure online)

Stage Classification: The stage classifier predicts the developmental stage with a 87.9% accuracy on the test set, consisting of 73 embryos labeled at 23,850 times (Fig. 4, right). The network's accuracy is high but lower than the human labeling accuracy on the test set (94.6%). The network outperforms a baseline ResNeXt101 by 6.7%; both the soft-loss and the dynamic programming each improve the predictions by 2% (Table 1). The stage classifier struggles when there are between 5 and 8 cells (66.9% accuracy for these classes). In contrast, the stage classifier does exceedingly well on images with 1-cell (99.9%), 2-cells (98.7%), empty wells (99.4%), or blastocysts (98.0%; Fig. 4, right). Despite measuring significantly more developmental stages, our stage classifier outperforms previous cell counting networks developed for human embryos [17, 21].

Cell Object Instance Segmentation: We measure the accuracy of the cell instance segmentation network using mean-average precision (mAP) [22], a stan-

Table 1. Effect of design choices for the 4 more difficult tasks, illustrated by removing one modification to the network at a time. Test-set scores are in percent correctly classified (stage, fragmentation) and mean-average precision (blastomere, pronuclei). The best scores are boldfaced. The last row shows the test set scores using all the training data but no input from other networks and no modifications to the network.

Setting	Fragmentation (%)	Stage (%)	Blastomere (mAP)	Pronuclei (mAP)
Full Setting	**88.9**	**87.8**	0.737	**0.680**
Single Focus	87.8	84.8	**0.739**	0.668
No ROI from Zona	87.4	84.9	0.733	0.666
Using 50% Training Data	87.7	85.3	0.718	0.656
No Soft Loss	–	85.3	–	–
No Dynamic Programming	–	86.0	–	–
Single-Task Baselines	87.0	81.1	0.737	0.647
	[31]	[33]	[14]	[14]

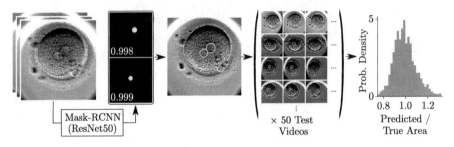

Fig. 6. The pronuclei detection network (Mask-RCNN, ResNet50 backbone) takes an image (left) and proposes candidates as a combined object mask and confidence score from 0–1 (second from left). Center: The boundaries of the object mask represented as the pronuclei contours (magenta, center). Second from right: 12 pronuclei instance segmentations for 4 embryos from the test set (shown as magenta contours overlaid on the original image); the rightmost images illustrate true negatives after the pronuclei have faded. Right: Histogram of the ratio of predicted to true areas for correctly identified pronuclei in the test set. (Color figure online)

dard metric for object instance segmentation tasks. Our network predicts cell masks with a mAP of 0.737 on the test set, consisting of 31 embryos labeled at 4,953 times. The model identifies cells with a precision of 82.8% and a recall of 88.4%, similar to results from other work on fewer images [28]. For correctly-identified candidates, the predicted cell area is within 17% of the true cell area 90% of the time (Fig. 5, right); much of this error arises when cells strongly overlap late in the cleavage stage. Cropping to a region-of-interest provides a marginal improvement to the network's accuracy (Table 1).

Pronucleus Object Instance Segmentation: The pronuclei segmentation network predicts masks with a mAP of 0.680 on the test set of 33 embryos labeled at 2,090 times. The network identifies pronuclei with a precision of 81.4% and a recall of 88.2%. Much of the false positive detections are from vacuoles inside the 1-cell embryo, which look similar to pronuclei. For correctly-identified candidates, the predicted pronuclei area is within 16% of the true pronuclei area 90% of the time (Fig. 6, right). The pronuclei network's mAP outperforms that of a baseline Mask-RCNN by 0.03; averaging across focal planes and cropping to a region-of-interest each improves the mAP by 0.01 (Table 1).

5   Conclusions

Our unified pipeline greatly speeds up the measurement of embryos: running all five networks on a 300-image, five-day movie takes 6 min on a GTX Titan X. In the future, we plan to make this pipeline even faster by combining all five networks with multi-task learning [8]. Since we measure many of the key morphological features used in clinical IVF, our unified pipeline has the potential to reduce the time to grade embryos without sacrificing interpretability. Equally as important, the automatic, high-quality data produced by our pipeline will enable better retrospective chart studies for IVF, improving IVF by informing better clinical practice.

Acknowledgements. We acknowledge M. Venturas and P. Maeder-York for help validating labels and approaches. This work was funded in part by NIH grant 5U54CA225088 and NSF Grant NCS-FO 1835231, by the NSF-Simons Center for Mathematical and Statistical Analysis of Biology at Harvard (award number 1764269), and by the Harvard Quantitative Biology Initiative. DJN and DBY also acknowledge generous support from the Perelson family, which made this work possible.

References

1. Alikani, M., Cohen, J., Tomkin, G., Garrisi, G.J., Mack, C., Scott, R.T.: Human embryo fragmentation in vitro and its implications for pregnancy and implantation. Fertil. Steril. **71**(5), 836–842 (1999)
2. Amir, H., et al.: Time-lapse imaging reveals delayed development of embryos carrying unbalanced chromosomal translocations. J. Assist. Reprod. Genet. **36**(2), 315–324 (2018)
3. Armstrong, S., Bhide, P., Jordan, V., Pacey, A., Marjoribanks, J., Farquhar, C.: Time-lapse systems for embryo incubation and assessment in assisted reproduction. Cochrane Database Syst. Rev. (5), Art. No. CD011320 (2019)
4. Bellman, R.: Dynamic programming. Science **153**(3731), 34–37 (1966)
5. Broughton, D.E., Moley, K.H.: Obesity and female infertility: potential mediators of obesity's impact. Fertil. Steril. **107**(4), 840–847 (2017)
6. Cohen, J., Alikani, M., Trowbridge, J., Rosenwaks, Z.: Implantation enhancement by selective assisted hatching using zona drilling of human embryos with poor prognosis. Hum. Reprod. **7**(5), 685–691 (1992)

7. Cui, W.: Mother or nothing: the agony of infertility. Bull. World Health Organ. **88**, 881 (2010)
8. Dai, J., He, K., Sun, J.: Instance-aware semantic segmentation via multi-task network cascades. In: Proceedings of the IEEE Conference on Computer Vision and Pattern Recognition, pp. 3150–3158 (2016)
9. Dolinko, A.V., Farland, L., Kaser, D., Missmer, S., Racowsky, C.: National survey on use of time-lapse imaging systems in IVF laboratories. J. Assist. Reprod. Genet. **34**(9), 1167–1172 (2017)
10. Elder, K., Dale, B.: In-Vitro Fertilization. Cambridge University Press, Cambridge (2020)
11. Filho, E.S., Noble, J., Poli, M., Griffiths, T., Emerson, G., Wells, D.: A method for semi-automatic grading of human blastocyst microscope images. Hum. Reprod. **27**(9), 2641–2648 (2012)
12. Franasiak, J.M., et al.: The nature of aneuploidy with increasing age of the female partner: a review of 15,169 consecutive trophectoderm biopsies evaluated with comprehensive chromosomal screening. Fertil. Steril. **101**(3), 656–663 (2014)
13. Goodfellow, I., Bengio, Y., Courville, A.: Deep Learning. MIT Press, Cambridge (2016)
14. He, K., Gkioxari, G., Dollár, P., Girshick, R.: Mask R-CNN. In: Proceedings of the IEEE International Conference on Computer Vision, pp. 2961–2969 (2017)
15. He, K., Zhang, X., Ren, S., Sun, J.: Deep residual learning for image recognition. In: Proceedings of the IEEE Conference on Computer Vision and Pattern Recognition, pp. 770–778 (2016)
16. Hoffman, R., Gross, L.: Modulation contrast microscope. Appl. Opt. **14**(5), 1169–1176 (1975)
17. Khan, A., Gould, S., Salzmann, M.: Deep convolutional neural networks for human embryonic cell counting. In: Hua, G., Jégou, H. (eds.) ECCV 2016. LNCS, vol. 9913, pp. 339–348. Springer, Cham (2016). https://doi.org/10.1007/978-3-319-46604-0_25
18. Kheradmand, S., Singh, A., Saeedi, P., Au, J., Havelock, J.: Inner cell mass segmentation in human HMC embryo images using fully convolutional network. In: 2017 IEEE International Conference on Image Processing (ICIP), pp. 1752–1756. IEEE (2017)
19. Khosravi, P., et al.: Deep learning enables robust assessment and selection of human blastocysts after in vitro fertilization. NPJ Digit. Med. **2**(1), 1–9 (2019)
20. Kragh, M.F., Rimestad, J., Berntsen, J., Karstoft, H.: Automatic grading of human blastocysts from time-lapse imaging. Comput. Biol. Med. **115**, 103494 (2019)
21. Lau, T., Ng, N., Gingold, J., Desai, N., McAuley, J., Lipton, Z.C.: Embryo staging with weakly-supervised region selection and dynamically-decoded predictions. arXiv preprint arXiv:1904.04419 (2019)
22. Lin, T.-Y., et al.: Microsoft COCO: common objects in context. In: Fleet, D., Pajdla, T., Schiele, B., Tuytelaars, T. (eds.) ECCV 2014. LNCS, vol. 8693, pp. 740–755. Springer, Cham (2014). https://doi.org/10.1007/978-3-319-10602-1_48
23. Long, J., Shelhamer, E., Darrell, T.: Fully convolutional networks for semantic segmentation. In: Proceedings of the IEEE Conference on Computer Vision and Pattern Recognition, pp. 3431–3440 (2015)
24. Nickkho-Amiry, M., Horne, G., Akhtar, M., Mathur, R., Brison, D.R.: Hydatidiform molar pregnancy following assisted reproduction. J. Assist. Reprod. Genet. **36**(4), 667–671 (2019). https://doi.org/10.1007/s10815-018-1389-9
25. Norwitz, E.R., Edusa, V., Park, J.S.: Maternal physiology and complications of multiple pregnancy. Semin. Perinatol. **29**(5), 338–348 (2005)

26. Petersen, B.M., Boel, M., Montag, M., Gardner, D.K.: Development of a generally applicable morphokinetic algorithm capable of predicting the implantation potential of embryos transferred on day 3. Hum. Reprod. **31**(10), 2231–2244 (2016)
27. Racowsky, C., Stern, J.E., Gibbons, W.E., Behr, B., Pomeroy, K.O., Biggers, J.D.: National collection of embryo morphology data into society for assisted reproductive technology clinic outcomes reporting system: associations among day 3 cell number, fragmentation and blastomere asymmetry, and live birth rate. Fertil. Steril. **95**(6), 1985–1989 (2011)
28. Rad, R.M., Saeedi, P., Au, J., Havelock, J.: A hybrid approach for multiple blastomeres identification in early human embryo images. Comput. Biol. Med. **101**, 100–111 (2018)
29. Practice Committee of the American Society for Reproductive Medicine: Guidance on the limits to the number of embryos to transfer a committee opinion. Fertil. Steril. 107(4), 901 (2017)
30. Rubio, I., et al.: Clinical validation of embryo culture and selection by morphokinetic analysis: a randomized, controlled trial of the embryoscope. Fertil. Steril. **102**(5), 1287–1294 (2014)
31. Szegedy, C., Vanhoucke, V., Ioffe, S., Shlens, J., Wojna, Z.: Rethinking the inception architecture for computer vision. In: Proceedings of the IEEE Conference on Computer Vision and Pattern Recognition, pp. 2818–2826 (2016)
32. Tran, D., Cooke, S., Illingworth, P., Gardner, D.: Deep learning as a predictive tool for fetal heart pregnancy following time-lapse incubation and blastocyst transfer. Hum. Reprod. **34**(6), 1011–1018 (2019)
33. Xie, S., Girshick, R., Dollár, P., Tu, Z., He, K.: Aggregated residual transformations for deep neural networks. In: Proceedings of the IEEE Conference on Computer Vision and Pattern Recognition, pp. 1492–1500 (2017)

A Novel Approach to Tongue Standardization and Feature Extraction

Chenhao Wang[1]([✉]) [iD], Camilla Cattaneo[2] [iD], Jing Liu[3] [iD], Wender Bredie[3] [iD], Ella Pagliarini[2] [iD], and Jon Sporring[1] [iD]

[1] Department of Computer Science, University of Copenhagen, 2100 Copenhagen, Denmark
chenhao.wang@di.ku.dk
[2] Department of Food, Environmental and Nutritional Sciences (DeFENS), University of Milan, 20133 Milan, Italy
[3] Department of Food Science, University of Copenhagen, 1958 Frederiksberg C, Denmark

Abstract. Fungiform papillae are large protrusions on the human tongue and contain many taste-buds. Most are found on the tip and the sides of the tongue, and their distribution varies from person to person. In this paper, we introduce a tongue-based coordinate system to investigate the density and other features of fungiform papillae on the surface of the tongue. A traditional method for estimating the density of fungiform papillae is to count the papillae in either a manually selected area or a predefined grid of areas on the tongue. However, depending on how a person presents his or her tongue in a specific image (such as narrowing, widening, and bending), this can cause visual variations in both the papillae's apparent positions and apparent shapes, which in turn also affects the counts obtained within an area. By transforming the individual tongues into a standardized tongue, our tongue coordinate system minimizes these variations more effectively than current alignment-based methods. We further hypothesize an underlying fungiform papillae distribution for each tongue, which we estimate and use to perform statistical analysis on the different tongue categories. For this, we consider a cohort of 152 persons and the following variables: gender, ethnicity, ability to taste 6-n-propylthiouracil, and texture preference. Our results indicate possible new relations between the distribution of fungiform papillae and some of the aforementioned variables.

Keywords: Tongue mapping · Papillae distribution · Taste perception

1 Introduction

The human tongue is involved in many common activities and is a key contributor to the quality of life. This was shown in a previous study [5], where individuals with common tongue conditions generally reported lower quality-of-life scores than those in the healthy control group. In terms of health, the tongue

© Springer Nature Switzerland AG 2020
A. L. Martel et al. (Eds.): MICCAI 2020, LNCS 12265, pp. 36–45, 2020.
https://doi.org/10.1007/978-3-030-59722-1_4

provides taste perception, which indirectly affects a person's diet and supplies vital information on the state of the food and its nutrients. It is therefore important for us to get a better understanding of our tongue and how we perceive taste.

The study of taste perception typically involves fungiform papillae (FP). These are the small anatomical structures involved in the detection and transduction of oral stimuli [9]. They are located on the anterior two-thirds of the dorsum of the tongue, and together with the much rarer foliate and circumvallate papillae, FP are considered the housing collections of chemosensory cells (taste buds) [1] and are innervated by both gustatory and trigeminal nerve fibers [14]. Due to these double nerve innervations and their reported correlation to the overall taste buds number, FP are often used to infer general taste function, and their counting and measurement often make up the starting point of quantitative research within taste perception. In the past, this process was typically done manually. Considering that a single tongue potentially contains hundreds of papillae, this can be a very tedious and error-prone endeavor.

With recent advancements in computer vision, automatic papillae segmentation has become possible, but the subsequent analysis is still lacking. For example, past studies depended entirely on either basic image alignment [10,12,13] or manual selection [4,7,8] to map and identify the equivalent regions across different tongues for statistical comparison. Given that tongues have natural differences in physical size and their appearances change depending on the tongue's posture, simple image alignment is often not enough. In [3], a more advanced alignment was used by dividing the 2 cm of the tongues equally into 4 by 4 grids. Although this method can model the horizontal variations to some degree, it assumes uniform variations in shape, which is unlikely in our experience. Manually selecting the analysis area, on the other hand, can be very accurate thanks to a human's visual and contextual understanding of the tongue, but the appropriate analysis areas chosen by this approach are limited in size (due to different tongues having different shapes and postures). Examples of such analysis areas are shown in Fig. 1.

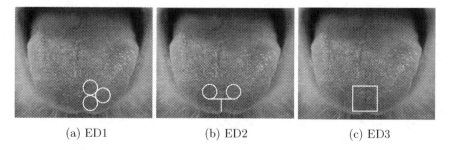

(a) ED1   (b) ED2   (c) ED3

Fig. 1. An example of manually selected regions as defined in [4,7,8].

In this paper, we aim to improve the analysis of fungiform papillae by proposing a more effective method for tongue comparison and FP feature extraction: we define a tongue coordinate system that normalizes the size and shape of an individual tongue, and provide a method for computing heat maps of FP position and FP coverage area, before evaluating whether these heat maps correlate with gender, ethnicity, soft-hard food preference and sensitivity to 6-n-propylthiouracil.

2   Material

The dataset used in this study contains 152 high-resolution tongue images, along with their metadata and corresponding tongue and FP segmentation masks [2]. See Fig. 2 for an example.

(a) The image   (b) The tongue mask   (c) The FP mask

Fig. 2. An example of the data provided for this study.

The tongues' metadata includes information on the participant's gender (29% Male vs 71% Female), ethnicity (49% Chinese vs 51% Danish), Mouth Behaviour (52% Soft vs 48% Firm), and PROP status (18% Non-taster [NT] vs 46% Medium-taster [MT] vs 36% Super-taster [ST]). In this case, Mouth Behaviour refers to the participant's preference for food texture, and PROP describes a participant's taste responsiveness to a specific bitter substance - the 6-n-propylthiouracil (PROP) compound.

For more details on the dataset and how the segmentation masks are produced, we would like to refer the readers to our accompanying paper [2].

3   Methods

In this section, we will describe the construction of our proposed tongue coordinate system, how we use this to standardize individual tongues, and how the heat maps for papillae position and coverage area are produced.

3.1   A New Coordinate System for Tongue Mapping

The human tongue consists of 4 intrinsic and 4 extrinsic muscles which control its shape and position, respectively. In concert, the intrinsic muscles allow for a wide range of tongue shapes, but particularly the transverse muscle seems to be at play for the shape of each tongue. The transverse muscle divides the tongue down the middle, and this division is most often a noticeable valley that goes from the tip to the posterior part of the tongue (i.e. the median lingual sulcus). We call this the midline. For readers who are interested in reading more about the tongue's muscular anatomy, please refer to [11].

Our goal is to define a 2-dimensional tongue coordinate system that is robust to tongue postures. Since the midline is visible in all the images and is often supported by the natural symmetry of the tongue, we will define the tongue's midline as an axis of our coordinate system and use the tongue's tip as its origin. The second axis is defined as the papillae's deviation from the midline, and is constructed by connecting percentage-wise equidistant steps along the tongue's left and right edges with those on the midline. This is illustrated in Fig. 3, and it gives us a non-orthogonal transformation,

$$(u, v) = T_i(x, y), \tag{1}$$

where (x, y) are image coordinates, (u, v) are tongue coordinates, and T_i is the transformation function for image i.

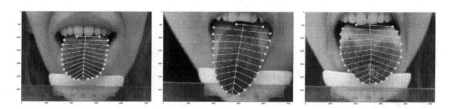

Fig. 3. Visualizations of the coordinate system. The lime green, pink and cyan dots represent points on the left edge, the midline, and the right edge respectively. These points are connected by the deviation lines that represent the u-axis. (Color figure online)

The algorithm used to construct our tongue coordinate system is described below. The algorithm takes the tongue and FP segmentation masks as inputs, see Fig. 2b and c for reference.

1. We pinpoint the tongue's two top-corners, which are located at the posterior of the tongue, by identifying the two points furthest away from the tongue mask's center of mass (excluding the tongue's tip).
2. The tongue and FP mask are rotated such that the line connecting the top-corners, which we call the base-line, is horizontal.

3. The midline of a tongue is computed as the locus of points that are equidistant to the edge of the tongue mask on the horizontal axis. To avoid boundary effects, we disregard the top and bottom 15% of the mask. A spline is then fitted using the remaining points to extrapolate the disregarded region and create a smooth and potentially curved v-axis.

4. The origin of (u, v) is identified as the lowest intersection between the v-axis and the boundary of the tongue mask.

5. We then construct the u-axis by joining percentage-wise equidistant points along v and the left/right edges of the tongue using straight lines, starting at the origin and ending at the two top-corners. We will refer to these straight lines that represent the u-axis as deviation lines. Deviation lines on opposite sides of v are assigned with opposite signs ($+$ and $-$) to distinguish between them.

6. After the coordinate system is constructed as described in steps 1–5, it can be used to transform between image coordinates (x, y) and tongue coordinates (u, v) through nearest-neighbour sampling. Otsu's thresholding is used to read the ruler ticks in each image. Since the ticks 1 mm apart, the pixel-to-centimetre ratio can be calculated by multiplying the mean pixel distance between them by 10. This ratio is used to scale the measurements into real-world units. Any perspective foreshortening in the image is ignored.

3.2 Standardization to Common Reference Tongue

The participants in our image collection stick out their tongues to various lengths. For a uniform comparison, we can only include the area of the tongue, which is visible in all images. The tongue with the shortest visible midline will, therefore, be chosen as the reference tongue.

To project FP between the tongue coordinates of one tongue to the reference tongue, we discard all papillae whose v-coordinates are higher than the length of the reference tongue's midline. The u-coordinates are transformed by proportionally scaling the lengths of equivalent deviation lines. The area parameter of FP also needs to be transformed, and since only the u axis is scaled, the determinant of the Jacobian of this transformation is equal to the same proportionality factor of the deviation lines. Steps of this transformation are illustrated in Fig. 4, and it gives us the projection,

$$(u', v') = P_{ji}(u, v), \tag{2}$$

where P_{ji} is the projection transformation from image i to j.

The full relation between a pixel coordinate on image i to image j is thus,

$$(x', y') = \left(T_j^{-1} \circ P_{ji} \circ T_i\right)(x, y), \tag{3}$$

which is only defined for coordinates (x, y) that are within the projection area defined by P.

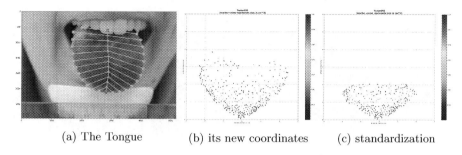

(a) The Tongue   (b) its new coordinates   (c) standardization

Fig. 4. Projection of FP onto new coordinate system. The colours represent the FP's areas. (Color figure online)

3.3   From Point Features to Heat Maps

We presume that there exists an underlying random point process and that the FP detected in each image is a sample of this process. We consider the area each FP covers as a mark. We suspect that the random process is parameterized by gender, ethnicity, mouth behaviour, and PROP status.

To examine this, we estimate the underlying intensity of FP in the reference tongue frame as two heat maps, with and without taking papillae area into account:

1. After a tongue and its FP are transformed onto the reference tongue, we construct an image J in (x, y)-coordinates with the value w assigned to the center of every FP. We use $w = 1$ when ignoring the papillae area, and otherwise $w = a_k$, where a_k is the transformed area of the k'th FP. A value of 0 is assigned to all other pixels in image J.
2. We model the positional uncertainty by normalized convolution,

$$H = \frac{(J \odot M) * K}{M * K}, \tag{4}$$

where H is the resulting heat map, $\odot$ is the Hadamard product, $*$ is the convolution operator, M is the tongue mask and K is 2D Gaussian kernel defined by:

$$K(x, y) = \frac{1}{2\pi\sigma^2} e^{-\frac{\left(x^2 - y^2\right)^2}{2\sigma^2}} \tag{5}$$

Examples of the heat maps produced by our model are shown in Fig. 5.

3.4   Statistical Testing

We test the hypothesized underlying random process by comparing average heat maps for various taster groups. The groups we consider are gender, ethnicity, mouth behaviour, and PROP status.

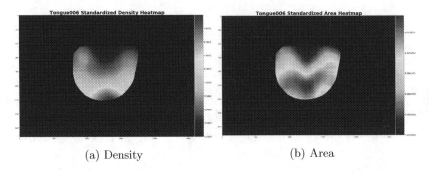

(a) Density   (b) Area

Fig. 5. Example of the density and area heat maps for a tongue. Note that after the normalized convolution, the area heat map shows the amount of papillae coverage, not the papillae size.

More specifically, given two groups $H_i^a \in A$ and $H_i^b \in B$, we estimate the average heat maps and their sum-of-square-differences as test statistics,

$$\bar{H}^a = \frac{1}{|A|} \sum_{i=1}^{|A|} H_i^a, \quad \bar{H}^b = \frac{1}{|B|} \sum_{i=1}^{|B|} H_i^b, \quad D = \sum_{x,y} \left(\bar{H}^a(x,y) - \bar{H}^b(x,y) \right)^2, \quad (6)$$

where $|\cdot|$ is the set-size operator. For a given grouping, we test the null-hypothesis that the two groups have identical means by permutation test: The groups are reshuffled repeatedly into two new groups A' and B' and the histogram of the test statistics D' is calculated and compared with the original test statistics D. If p is the proportion of values in the histogram of D' that are larger than D, then the null-hypothesis is rejected with confidence $1 - p$. We also estimate the power of the test by bootstrapping, where the permutation test is repeated for subsamples of the original groups. This gives a histogram of p values, and when this is clustered near 0, then the null-hypothesis rejection is likely non-spurious. More details on general bootstrapping can be found in [6].

4   Results

We have evaluated our method's ability to minimize the tongue's postural variations against our adaptation of [3] using bounding box image alignment. A test set containing 15 tongues (10% of the entire data set), each with two images in significantly different postures, were standardized and converted to density heat maps using both our method and bounding box image alignment. Since the same tongue always has the same FP distribution regardless of posture, the standardization error can be measured using mean absolute difference between the density heat maps of each posture pair. In the end, our method achieved a lower error than bounding box alignment for 14 out of 15 tongues.

The appropriateness and effectiveness of our method's approach to identifying equivalent regions across different tongues were assessed by comparing its ability to separate taster groups against other existing methods. A series of

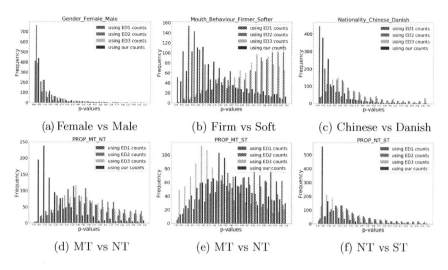

Fig. 6. The histogram of p-values for the manual counts in regions ED1-3, see Fig. 1 and [2], against automated counts on the 2 cm of the standardized tongues. High values concentrated to the left in the histograms implies low p values and are to be preferred.

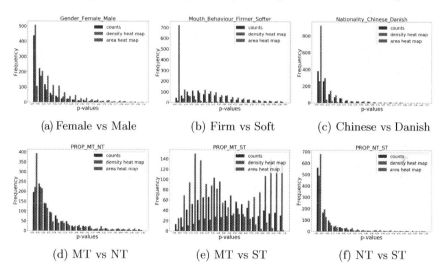

Fig. 7. The histogram of p-values for the count, density-, and area heat maps. High values concentrated to the left in the histograms implies low p values and are to be preferred. Compare with Fig. 6.

bootstrapped permutation tests were performed on FP counts extracted from our standardized tongues, and their results are plotted in Fig. 6 against the results from [2], where FP counts from manually selected regions ED1 - ED3 were used.

The same bootstrapped permutation tests were also repeated for FP density and area heat maps to examine if they are superior to FP counts extracted from the same standardized tongues. The results are shown in Fig. 7.

5   Discussions and Conclusion

The fungiform papillae (FP) play a central role in the taste and the experience of food consumption. Understanding the distribution of FP density and FP area is thus of fundamental importance for the study of food preferences across populations.

In this paper, we have presented a new method for investigating the anatomy of the tongue with a focus on FP. As the same tongue should have identical FP distributions regardless of its appearance in an image, it is essential to represent the papillae in such a way that is robust to participant's constant tongue movements and ever-changing posture. We achieved this elegantly by first transforming the FP onto a tongue coordinate system that is defined by the tongue's shape, before a simple algorithm was applied to project these FP to equivalent positions on a common reference tongue to facilitate cross tongue comparisons. Our experiments have shown that our standardization algorithm is better than state-of-the-art [3].

Furthermore, we compared the FP counts of the entire standardized tongue against the ED1-3 regional counts using bootstrapped permutation tests. We can confirm the apparent difference in the counts between gender (Fig. 6a), and possibly also found a new difference in ethnicity (Fig. 6c) and NT vs ST (Fig. 6f).

The FP density and area heat maps, which took into account the underlying point process associated with papillae distribution, were also used in the comparison between the taster groups. Our results have shown that while FP counts, density heat maps and area heat maps are equally indicative of NT vs ST (Fig. 7f), the area heat maps seem to be overwhelmingly the best choice when examining differences in mouth behaviour (Fig. 7b) and ethnicity (Fig. 7c). The area heat maps, however, did not work as well as the FP counts and density heat maps in terms of the differences in gender (Fig. 7a).

With only 152 participants, the dataset is possibly too small to draw any solid biological conclusion. Nevertheless, the papillae segmentation, our tongue coordinate system, and the density and area heat maps indicated new hitherto unnoticed correlations between the tongue's anatomical features and its taster profile, which are worth exploring further in future studies.

Acknowledgement. This work is supported by The Center for Quantification of Imaging Data from MAX IV (QIM) funded by The Capital Region of Denmark; and also by Arla Foods amba, Viby, Denmark as part of a postdoctoral grant.

References

1. Breslin, P., Huang, L.: Human taste: peripheral anatomy, taste transduction, and coding. Adv. Otorhinolaryngol. **63**, 152–190 (2006). https://doi.org/10.1159/000093760
2. Cattaneo, C., Liu, J., Wang, C., Pagliarini, E., Sporring, J., Bredie, W.L.P.: Comparison of manual and machine learning image processing approaches to determine fungiform papillae on the tongue. bioRxiv (2020). https://doi.org/10.1101/2020.07.05.187658

3. Eldeghaidy, S., et al.: An automated method to detect and quantify fungiform papillae in the human tongue: validation and relationship to phenotypical differences in taste perception. Physiol. Behav. **184**, 226–234 (2018). https://doi.org/10.1016/j.physbeh.2017.12.003

4. Essick, G., Chopra, A., Guest, S., McGlone, F.: Lingual tactile acuity, taste perception, and the density and diameter of fungiform papillae in female subjects. Physiol. Behav. **80**, 289–302 (2003). https://doi.org/10.1016/j.physbeh.2003.08.007

5. Hapa, A., Aksoy, B., Aslan, U., Atakan, N.: Common tongue conditions affect quality of life: an issue to be recognized. Qual. Life Res. **21**, 777–782 (2012). https://doi.org/10.1007/s11136-011-9979-3

6. Maris, E., Oostenveld, R.: Nonparametric statistical testing of EEG- and MEG-data. J. Neurosci. Methods **164**(2007), 177–190 (2007). https://doi.org/10.1016/j.jneumeth.2007.03.024

7. Masi, C., Dinnella, C., Monteleone, E., Prescott, J.: The impact of individual variations in taste sensitivity on coffee perceptions and preferences. Physiol. Behav. **138**, 219–226 (2015). https://doi.org/10.1016/j.physbeh.2014.10.031

8. Nachtsheim, R., Schlich, E.: The influence of 6-n-propylthiouracil bitterness, fungiform papilla count and saliva flow on the perception of pressure and fat. Food Qual. Prefer. **29**(2), 137–145 (2013). https://doi.org/10.1016/j.foodqual.2013.03.011

9. Piochi, M., Dinnella, C., Prescott, J., Monteleone, E.: Associations between human fungiform papillae and responsiveness to oral stimuli: effects of individual variability, population characteristics, and methods for papillae quantification. Chem. Senses **43**(5), 313–327 (2018). https://doi.org/10.1093/chemse/bjy015

10. Piochi, M., et al.: Comparing manual counting to automated image analysis for the assessment of fungiform papillae density on human tongue. Chem. Senses **42**(7), 553–561 (2017). https://doi.org/10.1093/chemse/bjx035

11. Sanders, I., Mu, L.: A three-dimensional atlas of human tongue muscles. Anat. Rec. (Hoboken) **296**(7), 1102–1114 (2013). https://doi.org/10.1002/ar.22711

12. Sanyal, S., O'Brien, S., Hayes, J., Feeney, E.: TongueSim: development of an automated method for rapid assessment of fungiform papillae density for taste research. Chem. Senses **41**(4), 357–365 (2016). https://doi.org/10.1093/chemse/bjw008

13. Valencia, E., et al.: Automatic counting of fungiform papillae by shape using cross-correlation. Comput. Biol. Med. **76**, 168–172 (2016). https://doi.org/10.1016/j.compbiomed.2016.07.002

14. Whitehead, M., Beeman, C., Kinsella, B.: Distribution of taste and general sensory nerve endings in fungiform papillae of the hamster. Am. J. Anat. **173**(3), 185–201 (1985). https://doi.org/10.1002/aja.1001730304

Patch-Based Non-local Bayesian Networks for Blind Confocal Microscopy Denoising

Saeed Izadi$^{(\boxtimes)}$ and Ghassan Hamarneh

School of Computing Science, Simon Fraser University, Burnaby, Canada
{saeedi,hamarneh}@sfu.ca

Abstract. Confocal microscopy is essential for histopathologic cell visualization and quantification. Despite its significant role in biology, fluorescence confocal microscopy suffers from the presence of inherent noise during image acquisition. Non-local patch-wise Bayesian mean filtering (NLB) was until recently the state-of-the-art denoising approach. However, classic denoising methods have been outperformed by neural networks in recent years. In this work, we propose to exploit the strengths of NLB in the framework of Bayesian deep learning. We do so by designing a convolutional neural network and training it to learn parameters of a Gaussian model approximating the prior on noise-free patches given their nearest, similar yet non-local, neighbors. We then apply Bayesian reasoning to leverage the prior and information from the noisy patch in the process of approximating the noise-free patch. Specifically, we use the closed-form analytic *maximum a posteriori* (MAP) estimate in the NLB algorithm to obtain the noise-free patch that maximizes the posterior distribution. The performance of our proposed method is evaluated on confocal microscopy images with real noise Poisson-Gaussian noise. Our experiments reveal the competitive performance of our approach compared to the state-of-the-art.

1 Introduction

Confocal fluorescence microscopy (CFM) has become an indispensable tool in cell biology that provides visualization of living cells and tissues, hence forming the basis for the analysis of their morphological and structural characteristics. Nevertheless, the excitation laser power introduces phototoxic side effects on target cells and even organisms [5]. Consequently, fluorescence microscopy has to be acquired in a low illumination setting, which limits the number of collected photons at the detector plane [17]. Consequently, CFM images are mainly dominated by Poisson noise that renders them less reliable and undermines the biological

---

We use bold capital letters, bold small letters, and regular small letters to denote matrices, vectors, scalars, respectively. Also, $\mathbf{A}^T$ and $\mathbf{A}^{-1}$ indicate transpose and inverse of matrix $\mathbf{A}$.

© Springer Nature Switzerland AG 2020
A. L. Martel et al. (Eds.): MICCAI 2020, LNCS 12265, pp. 46–55, 2020.
https://doi.org/10.1007/978-3-030-59722-1_5

conclusions drawn therefrom [5]. To remedy the problem of low signal-to-noise-ratio (SNR) in CFM, the application of noise reduction methods has become an essential pre-processing step preceding any diagnostics or other biological analyses [2,15].

Until recently, the 'medal' for state-of-the-art image denoising was held by non-local patch-based methods [3,4], which exploit the repetitiveness of patch patterns in the image. To denoise a single patch, a common approach is to retrieve its similar patches within a confined neighborhood followed by an averaging operation over pixel intensities across all neighbors. A Bayesian interpretation of the non-local patch-based schemes was proposed by Lebrun et al. [11], which is based on the assumption that nearest neighbor patches are *i.i.d* samples from a multivariate Gaussian distribution approximating the prior distribution of noise-free samples [11]. Given the prior and the input observation likelihood at hand, a *maximum a posteriori* estimate results in a Wiener filter which is used to infer the denoised patch.

The popularity of deep learning has ignited extensive research aimed at leveraging the capabilities of neural networks for discriminative learning. In the context of denoising, however, a challenging shortcoming of existing discriminative approaches is that their training required noise-free and noisy image pairs. Low-noise images may be collected (in lieu of noise-free images) at the expense of longer acquisition times or more advanced hardware. In the absence of noise-free images, notable progress has been made by relying on the statistical characteristics of noise and the underlying signal, which led to the introduction of self-supervised learning paradigms for denoising that only require single or pairs of noisy images [1,6,8]. Recently, further promising improvements have been achieved by leveraging the Bayesian neural network for pixel-wise probabilistic inference of noise-free values [9,10,14]. However, all of these methods construct posterior probability distributions at the pixel level and using only the surrounding local context while ignoring co-variance between the pixels within patches as well as the valuable source of non-local information across the image.

Summary of Contributions. To circumvent the limitations mentioned above, we make the following contributions: (1) We propose a patch-based extension of the previous probabilistic self-supervised denoising methods that do not require ground truth information; (2) instead of relying on the local context for learning priors, we propose to use the information from multiple non-local patches across the image; (3) we generate similar results to supervised methods even though our method does not observe any noise-free images during training; and (4) our method yields competitive performance compared to previous pixel-wise unsupervised and supervised approaches.

2   Theoretical Background

An observed noisy image $\mathbf{Y}$ can be decomposed into a set of (non)overlapping patches of size $\sqrt{d} \times \sqrt{d}$ denoted by $\mathcal{Y} = \{\mathbf{Y}_i \in \mathbb{R}^{\sqrt{d} \times \sqrt{d}}\}_{i=1}^{N}$. To simplify the following calculations, all patches are further re-arranged into vectors with d

elements. In this setting, an arbitrary patch $\mathbf{y}_i \in \mathbb{R}^d$ from the set $\mathcal{Y}$ can be decomposed as:

$$\mathbf{y}_i = \mathbf{x}_i + \boldsymbol{\eta}_i, \tag{1}$$

where $\mathbf{x}_i$ and $\boldsymbol{\eta}_i \in \mathbb{R}^d$ indicate the underlying noise-free patch and additive noise component, respectively. Patch-based image denoising refers to the task of inspecting the noisy patches $\mathbf{y}_i$ to infer its corresponding noise-free patch $\mathbf{x}_i$. Let $\mathcal{S}_i = \{\mathbf{y}_t\}_{t=1}^{k}$ denote k nearest neighbor patches based on the euclidean similarity. To find the estimate of the denoised patch $\tilde{\mathbf{x}}_i$ in Bayesian framework, we need to induce the posterior distribution over all possible noise-free patches conditioned on the set of nearest neighbors $\mathcal{S}_i$ as well as the observed noisy patch $\mathbf{y}_i$. Then, the optimum noise-free estimate is the one which maximizes the posterior distribution, i.e.:

$$\tilde{\mathbf{x}}_i = \arg\max_{\mathbf{x}_i} p(\mathbf{x}_i | \mathbf{y}_i, \mathcal{S}^i). \tag{2}$$

In the following, we present mathematical derivations for a single patch and omit the subscript i for improved readability. According to the Bayes' rule, Eq. 2 can be transformed to:

$$\tilde{\mathbf{x}} = \arg\max_{\mathbf{x}} p(\mathbf{y}|\mathbf{x}) p(\mathbf{x}|, \mathcal{S}). \tag{3}$$

The term $p(\mathbf{y}|\mathbf{x})$ is the observation likelihood and $p(\mathbf{x}|\mathcal{S})$ captures the prior knowledge we have about a noise-free patch considering its non-local nearest neighbors. We approximate the prior using a multivariate Gaussian distribution $\mathcal{N}(\mathbf{m}_x, \mathbf{C}_x)$ parametrized by $\mathbf{m}_x \in \mathbb{R}^d$ and $\mathbf{C}_x \in \mathbb{R}^{d \times d}$. The maximum likelihood estimates of the prior parameters, over the nearest neighbor patches $\mathbf{y}_t$, are given by Eq. 4 [11]:

$$\overline{\mathbf{m}}_x = \frac{1}{K} \sum_{t=1}^{k} \mathbf{y}_t \quad \text{and} \quad \overline{\mathbf{C}}_x = \frac{1}{k-1} \sum_{t=1}^{k} (\mathbf{y}_t - \overline{\mathbf{m}}_x)(\mathbf{y}_t - \overline{\mathbf{m}}_x)^T. \tag{4}$$

For the generic form of Poisson-Gaussian noise where the observed noisy patch contains both signal-independent and signal-dependent corruption, the noise model is approximated by a heteroscedastic Gaussian model $\mathcal{N}(0, \beta^2 \mathbf{x} + \sigma^2)$ whose variance is a function of the true noise-free measurement $\mathbf{x}$. Symbols $\beta \in \mathbb{R}^d$ and $\sigma \in \mathbb{R}$ refer to the gain of the signal-dependent and standard deviation of the signal-independent noise components, respectively. In this setting, the observation likelihood follows a Gaussian distribution $\mathcal{N}(\mathbf{m}_y, \mathbf{C}_y)$ and its parameters are estimated as:

$$\overline{\mathbf{m}}_x = \overline{\mathbf{m}}_y \quad \text{and} \quad \overline{\mathbf{C}}_y = \overline{\mathbf{C}}_x + \beta^2\, \overline{\mathbf{m}}_x \mathbf{I} + \sigma^2 \mathbf{I}, \tag{5}$$

where $\mathbf{I}$ denotes a diagonal identity matrix. Following [10], we replace the ground truth noise-free patch $\mathbf{x}$ with the predicted prior mean $\overline{\mathbf{m}}_x$ in Eq. 5. With the prior and observation likelihood at hand, a closed-form MAP estimate can be used to infer the denoised patch maximizing the posterior distribution [11]:

$$\tilde{\mathbf{x}} = \overline{\mathbf{m}}_x + \overline{\mathbf{C}}_x \overline{\mathbf{C}}_y^{-1}(\mathbf{y} - \overline{\mathbf{m}}_x). \tag{6}$$

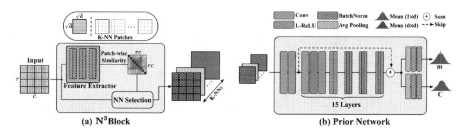

Fig. 1. The overall architecture of our proposed network. (a) architecture for N^3 block, and (b) architecture of prior network

3   Patch-Based Non-local Bayesian Networks

We propose a patch-based non-local Bayesian denoising in the scope of deep neural networks. Original non-local Bayesian denoising approach [11] uses maximum likelihood (ML) estimates in Eq. 4 to approximate the parameters of the assumed multivariate Gaussian prior, however, ML estimates are prone to yielding inaccurate outcomes as they directly manipulate the noisy patch raw intensities in S. To remedy this, we adopt a Bayesian neural network [7] as a learning-based estimator which approximates prior parameters more robustly. In particular, we design a prior network which receives the patches in S and regresses the estimates $\overline{\mathbf{m}}_x$ and $\overline{\mathbf{C}}_x$. With prior and observation likelihood at hand, one can use the MAP estimates to find the optimal approximation of the denoised patch.

3.1   Training

Non-local Similar Patch Search. To form the similar patch set S for a reference patch $\mathbf{y}$, we tailor the nearest neighbor network (N^3Net) proposed by Plötz [13]. In N^3Net, the nearest neighbor selection rule is interpreted as a k-way categorical classification over the candidate patches based on their euclidean similarities derive in a learnable feature space. Therefore, to retrieve k similar patches for $\mathbf{y}$, N^3Net carries out k successive samplings from categorical distribution while discarding the patches already picked for the subsequent rounds. Our proposed framework differs from N^3Net [13] in three aspects: (1) instead of interleaving multiple N^3 blocks across intermediate layers, we employ only an individual N^3 as an initial component of our prior network, (2) in contrast to N^3Net which finds similar patches within the intermediate feature maps, we utilize N^3 block directly in the spatial domain, and (3) N^3Net considers categorical logits for all patches as weights and gives a weighted average of all patches as the aggregated nearest neighbor, however, we discard the aggregation phase and explicitly pick the most likely patch as the k-th nearest neighbor. As depicted in Fig. 1-a, the non-local similar patches are concatenated to across the channel dimension.

Prior Network. Equipped with a set of observed patches $\mathcal{D} = \{\mathbf{Y}\}$, their decomposed patches $\mathcal{Y}$, and non-local similar patches S for every entry in $\mathcal{Y}$, we train a CNN-based prior network, denoted by $f_{prior}(\mathcal{S}; \theta_{prior})$ and parametrized by θ_{prior}, to learn the mapping from non-local similar patches (excluding the observed noisy patch itself) to the Gaussian prior mean and covariance. Mathematically,

$$\overline{\mathbf{m}}_x, \overline{\mathbf{C}}_x = f_{prior}(\mathcal{S}; \theta_{prior}). \tag{7}$$

Our proposed prior network which employs a simple neural architecture possesses two tails at the end of its architecture; either providing the desired estimates $\overline{\mathbf{m}}_x$ and $\overline{\mathbf{C}}_x$ estimates. Since the covariance estimate must strictly fulfill the statistical characteristic of being symmetric and semi-definite, we adopt the notion of Cholesky decomposition and parametrize the covariance matrix as the product of its lower-triangular decomposition matrices, i.e. $\overline{\mathbf{C}}_x = \mathbf{L}_x \mathbf{L}_x^T$. In our implementation, we ensure that $\mathbf{L}_x$ contains positive-valued diagonal entries. During the training, prior network weights are optimized by validating the observation likelihood $\mathcal{N}(\mathbf{m}_y, \mathbf{C}_y)$ on the observed patch $\mathbf{y}$. In other words, we use Eq. 5 to yield estimate $\mathbf{m}_y, \mathbf{C}_y$ and minimize the negative log of observation likelihood over the observed noisy patch to guide the learning in favor of predicting accurate estimates $\overline{\mathbf{m}}_x$ and $\overline{\mathbf{C}}_x$, i.e.:

$$\mathcal{L}(\mathbf{y}, \overline{\mathbf{m}}_y, \overline{\mathbf{C}}_y) = \frac{1}{2}(\mathbf{y} - \overline{\mathbf{m}}_y)^T \overline{\mathbf{C}}_y^{-1}(\mathbf{y} - \overline{\mathbf{m}}_y) + \frac{1}{2}\log |\overline{\mathbf{C}}_y| \tag{8}$$

where $|\cdot|$ indicates the determent to hinder the covariance values become large.

Noise Level Estimation. In Eq. 5, we assume that the noise parameter σ and β are known apriori. However, it is likely to lack this knowledge in real-world denoising situations. To address this, an alternative way is to specify the noise parameter estimation as a part of the optimization procedure and design a network to predict them during the training and inference [7,10]. Specifically, we adopt a CNN to approximate a function $f_{noise}(\mathbf{y}_i; \theta_{noise})$ that regresses the noise parameters estimates $\overline{\sigma}$ and $\overline{\beta}$. In this work, we assume that the σ is fixed across the entire image while β varies across different patches. Following [10], we add a small regularization $-0.1(\sigma + \beta)$ to the loss in favor of explaining the noise as corruption and not the uncertainty about the noise-free measurement.

3.2   Inference

After the prior network is learned, we employ it in a Bayesian inference framing to yield the noise-free estimate of the observed noisy patch. Particularly, we firstly use the trained N^3 block to collect the non-local similar patches which are subsequently piped into the prior network to predict prior estimates. Secondly, we derive the observation likelihood from Eq. 5. As stated earlier, we eventually approximate the noise-free patch $\tilde{\mathbf{x}}$ using the MAP estimate in Eq. 6. An interesting interpretation of Eq. 6 is that the MAP estimates primarily expects $\tilde{\mathbf{x}}$ to equal the $\overline{\mathbf{m}}_x$, and adapts the final estimate by taking into account the influence of the observation likelihood.

Dense Patch Denoising. Patch-based denoising techniques potentially leave block artifacts in the resultant image – no exception for our proposed method.

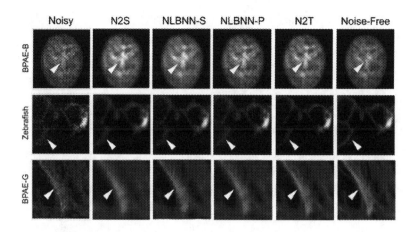

Fig. 2. Qualitative results for three confocal microscopy images

To overcome this, we adopt a dense-strided patch denoising scheme which partitions the image into densely overlapped $\sqrt{d} \times \sqrt{d}$ patches and noise-free estimates for all of them are collected. Afterward, the denoised patches are combined to construct the full-size denoised image by averaging the overlapped regions between denoise patches.

3.3 Network Architecture

For the prior network, we employ the DnCNN [16] architecture with 17 convolution layers and 64 features interleaved with LeakyReLU and batch normalization. As depicted in Fig. 1-b, a skip connection sums the output of the first convolution with the output of the layer before the outputs. As mentioned earlier, two tails receive the extracted features and perform an average pooling with kernel size $\sqrt{d} \times \sqrt{d}$ and stride $\sqrt{d}$ followed by a 1×1 convolution to produce the desired outputs of size $\overline{\mathbf{m}}_x \in \mathbb{R}^d$ and $\overline{\mathbf{C}}_x \in \mathbb{R}^{\frac{d(d+1)}{2}}$. When noise parameters need to be estimated, we use a similar backbone to prior network with 5 convolution layer to build the noise estimator network. Similar to the prior network, the noise estimator network provides two outputs; $\overline{\sigma}$ for the entire image and $\overline{\beta}$ for each patch. In the N^3, we use three convolutions with kernel size 3×3 and 64 features to learn the embedding features for euclidean similarities.

4 Results and Discussion

In this section, we present a detailed performance evaluation of our method and comparison against several unsupervised, self-supervised, and supervised methods for denoising confocal microscopy images corrupted with real noise.

Implementation Detail. As all networks are fully convolutional, we train them all on 90×90 randomly cropped regions in each epoch. For patch-based methods,

Table 1. Quantitative results of NLBNN-P and NLBNN-S against baseline methods in term of PSNR ± SEM and SSIM averaged over noisy images of the held-out FOVs

Dataset	BPAE		Mouse Brain		Zebrafish	
Metric	PSNR↑	SSIM↑	PSNR↑	SSIM↑	PSNR↑	SSIM↑
NLM [3]	34.74	0.9108	36.31	0.9534	28.23	0.7895
BM3D [4]	35.86	0.9338	37.95	0.9637	32.00	0.8854
N2S [1]	36.01	0.9388	37.49	.9574	32.14	0.8889
PN2V [9]	–	–	38.24	–	32.45	–
N2N [12]	36.35	0.9441	38.19	0.9665	32.93	0.9076
DnCNN [16]	36.12	0.9399	38.14	0.9686	32.29	0.9001
NLBNN-S	35.94	0.9388	37.74	0.9611	32.18	0.8986
NLBNN-P	36.02	0.9398	38.12	0.9631	32.48	0.9036

the patch size is set to 5×5 with $k = 8$ nearest neighbors. All networks are trained for 100 epochs with a batch size of 4 using Adam optimizer with default parameters. The initial learning rate is set to $3e^{-4}$ and is halved every 40 epochs. Except for the supervised denoising methods, all networks are trained using only the observed noisy images both as the input and target.

Data. We use confocal images from the fluorescence microscopy dataset released by Zhang et al. [17], which consists of raw images corrupted by real Poisson-Gaussian noise. There are two single-channel confocal sets, namely Mice brain and Zebrafish, and one multi-channel confocal set, i.e. BPAE. Each category also consists of 20 fields of view (FOV). Different samples in each FOV correspond to noisy images of the same scene with a different noise realization. Similar to [9], we use all images from the held-out 19-th FOV for testing with the remaining FOVs used for training. For the multi-channel images, we report the mean scores calculated on Red, Green, and Blue channels separately. Evaluation of more noise levels can be found in the supplementary material.

Comparison Methods. We provide evaluations for two variants of our proposed method: NLBNN-S and NLBNN-P that performs denoising at the pixel-level and patch-level, respectively. We compare these variants against traditional non-local mean (NLM) [3], BM3D [4], Noise2Void (N2S) [1], DnCNN (N2T) [16], Nois2Noise (N2N) [12], and probabilistic Noise2Void (PN2V) [9]. We borrow the scores for NLM, BM3D, N2N from [17] and PN2V from [9].

Qualitative Evaluation. As shown in Fig. 2; it is evident that N2S generates over-smoothed denoised images as it does not leverage observed noisy information during the inference phase. On the other hand, NLBNN-S and NLBNN-P are able to recover finer textures, especially in regions with high contrast. We attribute these improvements to the fact that the MAP estimator used in the NLBNN framework has the flexibility to adaptively combine information from the prior and observation. Between NLBNN variants, we observe that

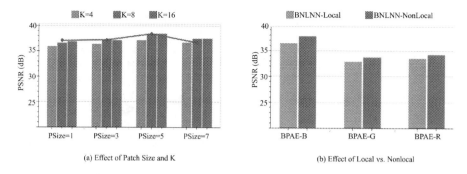

Fig. 3. Analysis of different configurations of the proposed model (Color figure online)

NLBNN-S brings unwanted non-uniform estimates. This is explained by the fact that NLBNN-S performs pixel-wise image manipulation and therefore lacks the implicit prior on generating regularized estimates within a patch. Conversely, NLBNN-P consistently captures the cross-pixel signal dependencies in a patch, leading to smoother results compared to NLBNN-S. Most importantly, Fig. 2 reveals the strength of NLBNN-P to produce denoised images close to the ones obtained by DnCNN [16] even without access to any ground truth data during the training.

Quantitative Evaluation. Table 1 summarizes the performance of our proposed framework against a wider range of state-of-the-art-methods using peak-signal-to-noise-ratio (PSNR) and structural similarity (SSIM) across different confocal subsets. In this table, we observe that BNLCNN-P outperform N2S [1], BM3D [4], and NLM [3] in terms of PSNR over BPAE, ZebraFish and MICE by an average of 0.48 dB, 0.84 dB, and 1.5 dB, respectively. However, it still lags behind the DnCNN [16] and N2N [12] which leverage stronger supervision during the training. Furthermore, our BNLCNN-P achieves competitive results against PN2V [9]. From Table 1, we also notice that classic BM3D, a classic patch-based non-local method, provides competitive performance against strong deep learning-based methods and even outperforms N2S on the Mice Brain set. Finally, we highlight that BNLCNN-P is able to provide superior numerical results against the DnCNN in the ZebraFish set.

Effect of Patch Size and KNN. We examine the effect of patch size and the number k of non-local similar patches using 5-fold validation over the BPAE set while fixing all other parameters. The colored bars in Fig. 3-a show that the denoising performance always improves as we increase the number of retrieved patches from 4 to 8. Further increasing k to 16, however, does not consistently improve performance (it does for patch size 1 but not 3, 5, or 7, wherein PSNR remains almost unchanged). This is not surprising as every additional retrieved patch is gradually less similar to the reference. Therefore, the added computational complexity of retrieving more patches beyond $k = 8$ is unjustifiable. Fixing $k = 8$ and comparing performance across various patch sizes (red poly-line), we note that using patch size 5 outperforms size 1, which motivates using patches instead of pixel-wise predictions. However, performance drops for larger patch size 7 since larger-sized patches are more heterogeneous, and thus finding more similar patches become less probable.

Non-local vs. Local. Next, we study the role of non-local patch retrieval vs. the local patch selection strategy with k and patch size fixed to 8 and 5, respectively. Particularly, we compare the denoising performance of our proposed NLBNN-NonLocal framework against its NLBNN-Local variant in which the $k = 8$ non-local patches are replaced with non-overlapping adjacent (i.e. local) patches. Examining Fig. 3-b, we observe that denoising with non-local patches consistently outperforms denoising with local patches over the BPAE set.

5   Conclusion

We proposed an effective patch-based non-local algorithm for image denoising using the Bayesian reasoning scheme that only requires noisy observations during the training. Given an observed noisy patch, our proposed network leverages a prior network to approximate the parameters of a Gaussian prior about the noise-free counterpart by considering only its non-local nearest neighbor patches. With the prior distribution and the observation likelihood at hand, we use a closed-form MAP estimator to infer the noise-free estimate that maximizes the posterior distribution. In contrast to preceding probabilistic self-supervised methods that adopt pixel-level Bayesian inference, we empirically pointed out the benefits of patch-based Bayesian inference and the merits of self-similarity priors captured via non-local patches. Furthermore, we presented the first attempt to leverage a non-local neural network in an unsupervised image denoising context. Overall, our proposed method both quantitatively and qualitatively outperforms state-of-the-art self-supervised and unsupervised methods.

Acknowledgments. Thanks to the NVIDIA Corporation for the donation of Titan X GPUs used in this research and to the Collaborative Health Research Projects (CHRP) a joint program by Sciences and Engineering Research Council of Canada (NSERC) and the Canadian Institutes of Health Research (CIHR).

References

1. Batson, J., Royer, L.: Noise2Self: blind denoising by self-supervision. In: ICML, vol. 97, pp. 524–533. PMLR (2019)
2. Ben Hadj, S., Blanc-Féraud, L., Aubert, G., Engler, G.: Blind restoration of confocal microscopy images in presence of a depth-variant blur and poisson noise. In: ICCASP, May 2013, pp. 915–919. IEEE (2013)
3. Buades, A., Coll, B., Morel, J.: A non-local algorithm for image denoising. In: CVPR, vol. 2, pp. 60–65. IEEE (2005)
4. Dabov, K., Foi, A., Katkovnik, V., Egiazarian, K.: Image denoising by sparse 3-D transform-domain collaborative filtering. TIP **16**(8), 2080–2095 (2007)

5. Icha, J., Weber, M., Waters, J.C., Norden, C.: Phototoxicity in live fluorescence microscopy, and how to avoid it. BioEssays **39**(8), 1700003 (2017)
6. Izadi, S., et al.: WhiteNNer-blind image denoising via noise whiteness priors. In: ICCV Workshops. IEEE (2019)
7. Kendall, A., Gal, Y.: What uncertainties do we need in Bayesian deep learning for computer vision? In: NeurIPS, pp. 5574–5584. Curran Associates Inc. (2017)
8. Krull, A., Buchholz, T.-O., Jug, F.: Noise2void - learning denoising from single noisy images. In: CVPR. IEEE (2019)
9. Krull, A., Vicar, T., Jug, F.: Probabilistic noise2void: unsupervised content-aware denoising. arXiv preprint arXiv:1906.00651 (2019)
10. Laine, S., Karras, T., Lehtinen, J., Aila, T.: High-quality self-supervised deep image denoising. In: Advances in Neural Information Processing Systems, vol. 32, pp. 6970–6980. Curran Associates Inc. (2019)
11. Lebrun, M., Buades, A., Morel, J.M.: A nonlocal Bayesian image denoising algorithm. SIAM J. Imag. Sci. **6**(3), 1665–1688 (2013)
12. Lehtinen, J.,et al.: Noise2Noise: learning image restoration without clean data. In: Dy, J., Krause, A. (eds.) ICML, vol. 80, pp. 2965–2974. PMLR (2018)
13. Plötz, T., Roth, S.: Neural nearest neighbors networks. In: NeurIPS, pp. 1087–1098. Curran Associates Inc. (2018)
14. Prakash, M., Lalit, M., Tomancak, P., Krull, A., Jug, F.: Fully unsupervised probabilistic noise2void. arXiv preprint arXiv:1911.12291 (2019)
15. Roudot, P., Kervrann, C., Boulanger, J., Waharte, F.: Noise modeling for intensified camera in fluorescence imaging: application to image denoising. In: ISBI, April 2013, pp. 600–603. IEEE (2013)
16. Zhang, K., Zuo, W., Chen, Y., Meng, D., Zhang, L.: Beyond a Gaussian denoiser: residual learning of deep CNN for image denoising. TIP **26**(7), 3142–3155 (2017)
17. Zhang, Y., et al.: A poisson-Gaussian denoising dataset with real fluorescence microscopy images. In: CVPR, June 2019, pp. 11702–11710 (2019)

Attention-Guided Quality Assessment for Automated Cryo-EM Grid Screening

Hong Xu[1(✉)], David E. Timm[2], and Shireen Y. Elhabian[1]

[1] Scientific Computing and Imaging Institute, School of Computing,
University of Utah, Salt Lake City, UT, USA
{hxu,shireen}@sci.utah.edu
[2] Department of Biochemistry, University of Utah, Salt Lake City, UT, USA
david.timm@biochem.utah.edu
http://www.sci.utah.edu, https://medicine.utah.edu/biochemistry,
https://www.cs.utah.edu

Abstract. Cryogenic electron microscopy (cryo-EM) has become an enabling technology in drug discovery and in understanding molecular bases of disease by producing near-atomic resolution (less than 0.4 nm) 3D reconstructions of biological macro-molecules. The imaging process required for 3D reconstructions involves a highly iterative and empirical screening process, starting with the acquisition of low magnification images of the cryo-EM grids. These images are inspected for squares that are likely to contain useful molecular signals. Potentially useful squares within the grid are then imaged at progressively higher magnifications, with the goal of identifying sub-micron areas within circular holes (bounded by the squares) for imaging at high magnification. This arduous, multi-step data acquisition process represents a bottleneck for obtaining a high throughput data collection. Here, we focus on automating the early decision making for the microscope operator, scoring low magnification images of squares, and proposing the first deep learning framework, *XCryoNet*, for automated cryo-EM grid screening. *XCryoNet* is a semi-supervised, attention-guided deep learning approach that provides explainable scoring of automatically extracted square images using limited amounts of labeled data. Results show up to 8% and 37% improvements over a fully supervised and a no-attention solution, respectively, when labeled data is scarce.

Keywords: Cryo-EM · Attention models · Semi-supervised learning

1 Introduction

Cryo-electron microscopy (cryo-EM) has recently emerged as an enabling imaging technology for determining 3D structural information of non-crystalline specimens of biologic macromolecules (a.k.a. single particles) at near-atomic resolution (less than 0.4 nm) [1,2,4,10,17]. Cryo-EM methods are currently the cutting edge of structural biology [1,2,4,10,17], thanks to recent advances in direct

© Springer Nature Switzerland AG 2020
A. L. Martel et al. (Eds.): MICCAI 2020, LNCS 12265, pp. 56–65, 2020.
https://doi.org/10.1007/978-3-030-59722-1_6

electron detector technology [4] and associated software suites for automating data collection [17], data processing and single particle reconstructions [4,5,12,15,18,22]. Cryo-EM enables highly detailed views of biological machinery (proteins, nucleic acids, and their complexes), which in turn advances the understanding of basic biological systems and mechanisms, furthers the knowledge of the underlying molecular mechanisms of human disease, and provides visual structure-based design of therapeutics for treating human disease [3,14]. Nonetheless, data acquisition alone of a single structure on a state-of-the-art electron microscope costs up to several thousand dollars per day for several days. Hence, the use of data collection resources should be optimized to yield the highest quality microscopic information for 3D reconstruction.

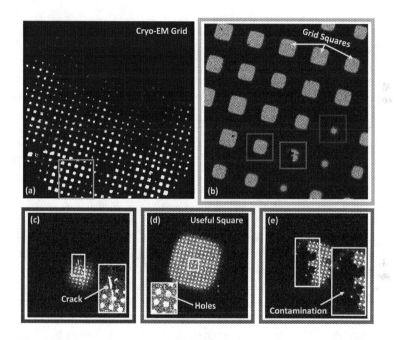

Fig. 1. (a) A 3 mm circular grid imaged by the cryo-EM at 135x magnification. Low magnification views of grids are acquired in equally spaced tiles to cover most of the circular grid. (b) One of the 135x tile images that comprises the grid is shown. Bottom: Three exemplar grid squares are shown (i.e., low magnification targets) extracted from the tile illustrating a crack (c), a useful grid square (d) and a square marred by contamination (e). A microscope operator would scan the grid for promising squares to further image at higher magnifications. This process can be slow and imprecise since the operator must manually closely examine squares and squares can be overlooked in the interest of time.

The grid screening process (imaging & decision making) used to obtain 3D biological information of single particles is a highly iterative, labor intensive process. Screening involves imaging circular grids of fine copper or gold mesh at three or four different levels of magnifications to find the most useful areas for further imaging at the next higher magnification level. At the lowest magnifications, cryo-EM grids are manually screened for square-like features of the metal mesh (a.k.a. grid squares or low-magnification targets) that are the most likely to contain useful microscopic signals, using an informal mental *scoring*, to determine which ones should be further imaged at the next magnification. This process is largely based on empirical trial and error [1]. This *low-magnification target acquisition* process, is illustrated in Fig. 1.

Ideal areas for imaging particles within cryo-EM grids are located in thin vitreous ice within the holes (see Fig. 1(d)) of the carbon film or gold foil present on the grid surface. However, targeting holes with enough particle information for the downstream 3D reconstruction task is frequently foiled by the physical damage of fragile grids, excessive amounts of crystalline ice and hydrophobic contaminants, excessively thick ice that is non-transparent or only partially transparent to the electron beam, and/or excessively thin ice that may not accommodate biomolecules or support their native-structures. In particular, at the lowest magnification, a microscope operator manually determines the overall usefulness/quality of a grid square based on visible *attributes*, such as brightness, squareness, cracking, and contamination, that are indicative of such failure at the highest magnification [17]. However, this arduous, multi-step grid screening process, which entails 3 or 4 multi-scale target acquisition, target scoring, and further imaging subprocesses, represents a bottleneck for obtaining a high throughput of single particle reconstructions [17]. Low-magnification target acquisition, in particular, poses significant manual burden since the microscope operator must manually examine squares, increasing the chance of completely overlooking plenty of useful squares in the interest of time. Furthermore, automating low-magnification target acquisition is the backbone process for picking grid squares for higher magnification acquisitions. Such automation paves the way toward a fully automated grid screening process.

Despite the dramatic impact of the manual burden on imaging throughput, automated grid screening in general, and low-magnification target acquisition in particular, are under-explored problems. Most computational work on cryo-EM focuses on the downstream task of reconstructing particles from already collected high magnification images [17]. Although existing microscope controller software suites have semi-automated ways of finding cryo-EM squares, these methods depend on operator-defined templates or lattices to identify targets of interest, and use transmittance to determine the viability of said targets [9,10,17]. A machine learning based solution for automated low-magnification target acquisition is, however, challenging due to the scarcity and associated cost (monetary, manpower, and expertise) of obtaining labeled data and semantic attributes that are manifested at different levels of image scales. Furthermore, explainable automated selection is required for deploying such a solution in practice.

In this paper, we propose the first deep learning based solution, namely *XCryoNet*, for explainable, automated grid squares scoring for low-magnification target acquisition. To leverage unlabeled data, we borrow ideas from neural network based methods that combine supervised and unsupervised learning by training regularized classifiers using an autoencoder or unsupervised embedding of the data, e.g., [8,13,19]. In particular, we use an autoencoder-like model as a semi-supervised training signal to learn discriminative features from square images that are simultaneously useful for square scoring and reconstruction tasks. This semi-supervised approach exploits the structure assumption, where grid squares with similar image features are likely to have the same score, by forcing an embedding that captures this structure at the latent space of the autoencoder. To capture semantic attributes (e.g., cracking and contamination) that are present at different scales, we propose attribute-specific subnetworks that operate on attention-guided input to score a single attribute while learning attention maps that are relevant to that attribute. Furthermore, this attention mechanism provides a means of interpreting the resulting scoring via identifying regions in the grid square image that trigger the scoring of a specific attribute. Attention maps have been used to allow convolutional networks to capture global features relevant to the supervised task beyond the local receptive fields of convolutional filters [6,20]. These maps have also been used in the context of interpretable identification of thorax disease [6], but under the assumption of a coarse (overall) disease classification that is localized in a single region-of-interest. Another family of interpretable deep networks obtain attention maps through gradient-based visualization of certain convolutional filters [11,16,21]. Nonetheless, such maps are not explicitly learned to reflect attribute-specific interpretations.

We demonstrate that the process of grid screening can be automated in an interpretable way using simple image processing techniques to extract the squares, then using an attention-guided semi-supervised deep network to provide scores representing the quality of said squares.

2 Methods

The proposed *XCryoNet* architecture, illustrated in Fig. 2, automatically scores low-magnification targets (i.e., squares) on a cryo-EM grid using two levels of granularity. Coarse-grained *overall square quality* reflects the perceived overall quality of vitreous ice in a grid square. Fine-grained visible *attributes* (e.g., brightness, squareness, cracking, and contamination) are specific abstract image qualities visible at low magnification indicative of loss of potentially informative microscopic signal at higher magnification levels for 3D reconstructions.

XCryoNet consists of three types of interacting subnetworks (or branches) that are trained end-to-end. First, the *primary* branch aims at solving the primary scoring task for both coarse- and fine-grained qualities. Second, the *attribute* branch aims at solving the scoring task of an individual fine-grained attribute. Third, the *fusion* branch combines features learned from the primary and the attributes branches (via the feature networks) to solve the primary scoring task. Such fusion aggregates features learned by the primary and attribute branches to boost the performance of the primary scoring task. Hereafter, we present the motivations and design choices of these interacting branches.

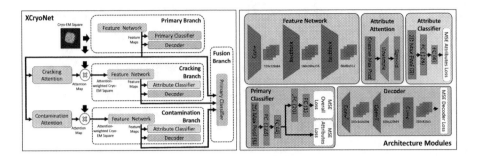

Fig. 2. *XCryoNet* architecture

Attributes and Labeling. Brightness concerns the overall intensity of the square. Squareness is defined by how much the image resembles a square. Cracking is determined by the portion of the surface that has fissures. Contamination is a measure of the portion of the surface covered by artifacts. We encode these attributes into a vector $\mathbf{y} = [y_b, y_s, y_{cr}, y_{co}, y_o]$, where y_b, y_s, y_{cr}, y_{co}, and y_o denote the score of the brightness, squareness, cracking, contamination, and overall quality, respectively and the score $y_* \in \{0, 1, 2, 3, 4\}$.

Primary Branch. The objective of the primary branch is to learn from the global image characteristics to make an informed decision. This branch consists of a feature network, a primary classifier network and a decoder network. The feature network has a convolutional layer and two ResBlocks [7]. The primary classifier network learns an explicit nonlinear functional mapping that infers the overall score directly from the attributes to enforce the dependency of the overall score on the fine-grained attributes. It consists of a pooling layer, two fully connected layers for attribute regression, and two fully connected layers for overall score regression. The decoder network is added after the second ResBlock to account for the scarcity of labeled data by enforcing discriminative features for the scoring task while also being useful for the input reconstruction task. It is comprised of two transpose-convolution layers and one convolution layer.

The primary network is trained by minimizing a supervised loss, $\mathcal{L}_S^p$, that combines the attributes loss, the overall quality loss, and an unsupervised loss, $\mathcal{L}_U^p$, for input reconstruction via the decoder.

$$\mathcal{L}^p(\Theta_p) = \mathcal{L}_S^p(\Theta_p) + \mathcal{L}_U^p(\Theta_p) \tag{1}$$

The supervised attribute loss is defined by

$$\mathcal{L}_S^p(\Theta_p) = \text{MSE}([y_b, y_s, y_{cr}, y_{co}], [\hat{y}_b, \hat{y}_s, \hat{y}_{cr}, \hat{y}_{co}]) + \text{MSE}([y_o], [\hat{y}_o]). \tag{2}$$

where Θ_p are the parameters of the primary network, $\hat{y}_*$ is the prediction for the score value of the y_*, and $\text{MSE}(\mathbf{u}, \mathbf{v})$ is the mean square error between elements of $\mathbf{u}$ and $\mathbf{v}$. The decoder loss is defined by

$$\mathcal{L}_U^p(\Theta_p) = \text{MSE}(\mathbf{I}, \hat{\mathbf{I}}) \tag{3}$$

where $\mathbf{I}$ is the input grid square image and $\hat{\mathbf{I}}$ is the reconstructed image.

Attention Guidance. The primary branch is able to infer global scale attributes (e.g., brightness and squareness), but fails to score attributes with multi-scale presence (e.g., cracking and contamination) in a meaningful manner. Feeding attention-guided squares to attribute branches mitigates the poor cracking and contamination scores by dedicating two subnetworks, the cracking branch and the contamination branch, to the task of scoring individual fine-grained attributes from attention-weighted inputs. The attention-weighted squares are generated by taking the output feature maps from the feature network of the primary branch and distributing the channels evenly among every attribute. In particular, we feed half of the channels to the cracking attention and half to the contamination attention. This separation allows the primary feature network to learn attribute-specific features that are relevant to generating attention maps for each attribute. Not only does this separation produce different feature maps for each branch, but it also allows the attribute branches to serve as regularizers for the primary network to learn to focus on finding the relevant attribute-specific features. Attribute-specific attention-weighted squares are then generated by channel-wise max-pooling the channels corresponding to each attribute, up-sampling to the input size to match the grid square dimension for attention guidance, and a sigmoid function to force a $(0, 1)$−range. The attention-guided grid squares to be fed to the attribute branches are obtained by multiplying the attention map by the grid square image to highlight relevant regions for scoring that attribute.

Attribute Branch. The objective of the attribute branch is to focus on scoring an individual attribute by focusing on areas highlighted by the attention guidance. Attribute branches share a similar architectural design to the primary branch, but instead of regressing on all the attributes, they regresses on a single one. The input of these branches are the attention-weighted grid squares obtained from the primary branch and the attribute attention, and each attribute branch is expected to reconstruct its attention-weighted input using its decoder for semi-supervised learning.

Consider the attribute branch for inferring y_* and let $\mathbf{I}_*$ be its attention-weighted input. Similar to the primary branch loss, the attribute branch is trained using a combination of supervised and unsupervised losses.

$$\mathcal{L}^*(\Theta_*) = \mathcal{L}_S^*(\Theta_*) + \mathcal{L}_U^*(\Theta_*) \tag{4}$$

where $\mathcal{L}_S^*(\Theta_*)$ is the mean square error between y_* and $\hat{y}_*$, and $\mathcal{L}_U^*(\Theta_*)$ is the mean square error between $\mathbf{I}_*$ and $\hat{\mathbf{I}}_*$.

Fusion Branch. The fusion branch combines the feature maps obtained from the primary branch as well as the attribute branches to make a final prediction that leverage both global and multi-scale features. The fusion branch's loss $\mathcal{L}^f(\Theta_f)$ is identical to the supervised loss of the primary branch, $\mathcal{L}^p$.

***XCryoNet* Training.** The training procedure is dissected into three alternating steps. (1) *Primary and attribute training.* The feature, primary/attribute classifiers, and the primary decoder networks are trained by minimizing the supervised losses ($\mathcal{L}_S^p(\Theta_p)$ and $\mathcal{L}_S^*(\Theta_*)$), and the primary decoder loss $\mathcal{L}_U^p(\Theta_p)$. (2) *Attribute autoencoder training.* This procedure freezes the parameters of the whole network except for the encoder (feature) network and decoder network of the attribute branches, and uses the attribute decoder loss $\mathcal{L}_U^*(\Theta_*)$ to back-propagate. The purpose of separating (1) from (2) is such that the decoder output does not influence the construction of the attention-weighted squares. (3) *Fusion training.* Finally, the fusion network parameters are isolated and trained using the fusion loss $\mathcal{L}^f(\Theta_f)$. We train this separately as to properly isolate the individual attribute branches from learning from other attributes.

Fig. 3. Attention maps at epoch 75 for *XCryoNet* with 900 labeled samples and 1500 unlabeled.

3   Results

Our experiments focus on comparing the semi-supervised versus the fully supervised setting for the primary branch (i.e., no attention guidance) and the full *XCryoNet*. A fitting performance metric that allows a quantitative measure of the proximity of the predicted score to the true score is the mean absolute difference between the true scores and the predicted scores $d(y_*, \hat{y}_*) = \frac{1}{n}\sum_{i=0}^{n}|y_* - \hat{y}_*|$. We report the quantitative performance metrics of the various settings and show qualitative results in the form of the attention maps.

Dataset and Preprocessing. The input we work with are 12 MRC/CCP4 2014 files (standard files for cryo-EM image/movie files) along with the microscope parameter files that Thermo-Fisher's EPU software outputs that are used for stitching the individual tiles to fit into a 5×5 montage. The extraction of squares relies on a normalized cross-correlation based template matching with a custom template created according to the pixel intensity distribution of the grid. We acquire 250 640 × 640 images of squares per *grid*, totaling about 3000 for the 12 *grids*. The brightness scores of the extracted squares are set to the mean pixel value of non-zero valued pixels scaled to a score value. The squareness is obtained by applying canny edge detection, then dividing the non-zero pixel area over the total area of a minimum area square scaled to a score value. Finally, the cracking and contamination scores are manually labeled by an experienced microscope operator. These are the squares that are fed to the *XCryoNet*.

Table 1. The quantitative measure of score proximity (lower is better) on held-out (testing) grid squares of the fully supervised (FS) and semi-supervised (SS) versions of the primary and *XCryoNet* with different amount of labeled examples used to train the model. Each network is trained four times for 75 epochs, which were enough for convergence, with random uniformly selected training and test samples; the means and standard deviations among runs are reported.

Method	Supervision |#Labeled|#Unlabeled	Brightness	Squareness	Cracking	Contamination	Overall
Primary	SS|100|1500	1.54 ± .418	1.85 ± .309	1.88 ± .363	1.93 ± .148	2.18 ± .174
Primary	FS|100|0	2.15 ± .719	1.49 ± .265	1.81 ± .061	1.63 ± .394	2.57 ± .443
XCryoNet	SS|100|1500	**0.91 ± .295**	**1.08 ± .245**	**1.35 ± .143**	**1.23 ± .151**	**1.38 ± .386**
XCryoNet	FS|100|0	1.01 ± .290	1.23 ± .442	1.46 ± .154	1.31 ± .567	1.50 ± .340
Primary	SS|500|1500	**0.26 ± .010**	**0.53 ± .022**	0.95 ± .061	0.64 ± .022	0.62 ± .032
Primary	FS|500|0	0.30 ± .025	0.54 ± .021	**0.86 ± .055**	**0.62 ± .037**	0.62 ± .022
XCryoNet	SS|500|1500	0.28 ± .028	0.53 ± .059	0.91 ± .057	0.66 ± .029	0.58 ± .059
XCryoNet	FS|500|0	0.32 ± .034	0.57 ± .033	1.00 ± .064	0.75 ± .043	**0.58 ± .025**
Primary	SS|900|1500	**0.26 ± .024**	0.51 ± .035	0.86 ± .053	0.64 ± .036	0.52 ± .036
Primary	FS|900|0	0.31 ± .021	**0.49 ± .027**	**0.71 ± .033**	**0.62 ± .011**	**0.47 ± .019**
XCryoNet	SS|900|1500	0.36 ± .051	0.55 ± .033	0.87 ± .061	0.62 ± .057	0.51 ± .005
XCryoNet	FS|900|0	0.45 ± .097	0.66 ± .133	1.40 ± .399	0.79 ± .146	0.83 ± .234

Quantitative and Qualitative Results. Table 1 reports $d(y_*, \hat{y}_*)$ for coarse- and fine-grained attributes for fully and semi-supervised settings with and without attention guidance. The experiments were run on an Intel® Core™ i7-6850K @ 3.60 GHz x 12 64 GB DDR4 machine with a GTX 1080 Ti GPU. The fully-supervised primary branch takes 11 min to train for 75 epochs on 100 labeled examples, whereas the semi-supervised primary branch takes an hour and a half with 1500 additional unlabeled examples. In general, the semi-supervised (with 1500 unlabeled examples) runs take from 3 (with 900 labeled examples) to 8 (with 100 labeled examples) times longer than their fully-supervised counterparts. *XCryoNet* takes 4 to 5 times longer to train than just running the primary branch. Test time is almost instantaneous, thanks to the feed-forward architecture of *XCryoNet*. Results shows that as the ratio between labeled and unlabeled data increases, or the amount of labeled signal sufficiently informs the classifier and feature networks, the effect of semi-supervision diminishes. Likewise, the semi-supervised *XCryoNet* can significantly outperform the primary-only setting the scarcer the labeled data becomes. Figure 3 shows examples of generated attention maps for the cracking and contamination attribute branches. These attention maps are able to identify most instances of heavy cracking and contamination, but still struggle to detect more subtle ones. The contamination attention maps highlights the portions of the square without contamination, while the cracking ones highlight the cracks themselves. This is because any dark area within a grid square (which are all supposed to be the same size) is considered to be contamination, so the network must focus on the portion of the grid that is not contaminated to score the contamination attribute accurately.

4 Conclusion

We have presented *XCryoNet*, a semi-supervised, attention-guided deep learning approach that provides interpretable scoring of automatically extracted cryo-EM grid squares using limited amounts of labeled data. Results show that trained *XCryoNets* are able to mimic the mental scoring process of a microscope operator, providing both interpretable attention maps and good scoring performance, even with scarce labeled data. This work represents the first step in fully automating the grid screening process for cryo-EM, which will significantly increase the throughput of high quality reconstructions without the need to waste valuable man-power and research funds.

References

1. Agard, D., Cheng, Y., Glaeser, R.M., Subramaniam, S.: Single-particle cryo-electron microscopy (Cryo-EM): progress, challenges, and perspectives for further improvement, Chap. 2. In: Advances in Imaging and Electron Physics, vol. 185, pp. 113–137. Elsevier (2014). https://doi.org/10.1016/B978-0-12-800144-8.00002-1, http://www.sciencedirect.com/science/article/pii/B9780128001448000021
2. Callaway, E.: The revolution will not be crystallized: a new method sweeps through structural biology. Nature **525**, 172–174 (2015). https://doi.org/10.1038/525172a
3. Ceska, T., Chung, C.W., Cooke, R., Phillips, C., Williams, P.A.: Cryo-EM in drug discovery. Biochem. Soc. Trans. **47**(1), 281–293 (2019)
4. Cheng, Y.: Single-particle Cryo-EM at crystallographic resolution. Cell **161**, 450–457 (2015). https://doi.org/10.1016/j.cell.2015.03.049
5. Grant, T., Rohou, A., Grigorieff, N.: *cis*TEM, user-friendly software for single-particle image processing. eLife **7**, e35383 (2018). https://doi.org/10.7554/eLife.35383
6. Guan, Q., Huang, Y., Zhong, Z., Zheng, Z., Zheng, L., Yang, Y.: Diagnose like a radiologist: attention guided convolutional neural network for thorax disease classification. ArXiv abs/1801.09927 (2018)
7. He, K., Zhang, X., Ren, S., Sun, J.: Deep residual learning for image recognition. In: 2016 IEEE Conference on Computer Vision and Pattern Recognition (CVPR), pp. 770–778 (2016). https://doi.org/10.1109/CVPR.2016.90

8. Kingma, D., Rezende, D., Mohamed, S., Welling, M.: Semi-supervised learning with deep generative models. In: Advances in Neural Information Processing Systems, vol. 4 (2014)

9. Lei, J., Frank, J.: Automated acquisition of cryo-electron micrographs for single particle reconstruction on an FEI Tecnai electron microscope. J. Struct. Biol. **150**(1), 69–80 (2005). https://doi.org/10.1016/j.jsb.2005.01.002. http://www.sciencedirect.com/science/article/pii/S1047847705000225

10. Lyumkis, D.: Challenges and opportunities in cryo-EM single-particle analysis. J. Biol. Chem. **294**(13), 5181–5197 (2019). https://doi.org/10.1074/jbc.REV118. 005602. http://www.jbc.org/cgi/content/short/REV118.005602v1

11. Mahendran, A., Vedaldi, A.: Understanding deep image representations by inverting them, pp. 5188–5196 (2015). https://doi.org/10.1109/CVPR.2015.7299155

12. Punjani, A., Rubinstein, J.L., Fleet, D.J., Brubaker, M.A.: cryoSPARC: algorithms for rapid unsupervised cryo-EM structure determination. Nat. Methods **14**(3), 290–296 (2017). https://doi.org/10.1038/nmeth.4169

13. Ranzato, M., Szummer, M.: Semi-supervised learning of compact document representations with deep networks. In: Proceedings of the 25th International Conference on Machine Learning, pp. 792–799 (2008). https://doi.org/10.1145/1390156. 1390256

14. Renaud, J.P., et al.: Cryo-EM in drug discovery: achievements, limitations and prospects. Nat. Rev. Drug Discov. **17**(7), 471–492 (2018)

15. Scheres, S.H.W.: RELION: implementation of a Bayesian approach to cryo-EM structure determination. J. Struct. Biol. **180**(3), 519–530 (2012). https://doi.org/ 10.1016/j.jsb.2012.09.006. https://pubmed.ncbi.nlm.nih.gov/23000701, 23000701 [pmid]

16. Simonyan, K., Vedaldi, A., Zisserman, A.: Deep inside convolutional networks: visualising image classification models and saliency maps (2013, preprint)

17. Tan, Y.Z., Cheng, A., Potter, C.S., Carragher, B.: Automated data collection in single particle electron microscopy. Microscopy **65**(1), 43–56 (2015). https://doi. org/10.1093/jmicro/dfv369

18. Tegunov, D., Cramer, P.: Real-time cryo-electron microscopy data preprocessing with warp. Nat. Methods **16**(11), 1146–1152 (2019). https://doi.org/10.1038/ s41592-019-0580-y

19. Weston, J., Ratle, F., Collobert, R.: Deep learning via semi-supervised embedding. In: Proceedings of the 25th International Conference on Machine Learning, ICML 2008, pp. 1168–1175. Association for Computing Machinery, New York (2008). https://doi.org/10.1145/1390156.1390303

20. Woo, S., Park, J., Lee, J.-Y., Kweon, I.S.: CBAM: convolutional block attention module. In: Ferrari, V., Hebert, M., Sminchisescu, C., Weiss, Y. (eds.) ECCV 2018. LNCS, vol. 11211, pp. 3–19. Springer, Cham (2018). https://doi.org/10.1007/978-3-030-01234-2_1

21. Zeiler, M.D., Fergus, R.: Visualizing and understanding convolutional networks. In: Fleet, D., Pajdla, T., Schiele, B., Tuytelaars, T. (eds.) ECCV 2014. LNCS, vol. 8689, pp. 818–833. Springer, Cham (2014). https://doi.org/10.1007/978-3-319-10590-1_53

22. Zheng, S.Q., Palovcak, E., Armache, J.P., Verba, K.A., Cheng, Y., Agard, D.A.: MotionCor2: anisotropic correction of beam-induced motion for improved cryo-electron microscopy. Nat. Methods **14**(4), 331–332 (2017). https://doi.org/10. 1038/nmeth.4193. https://pubmed.ncbi.nlm.nih.gov/28250466, 28250466 [pmid]

MitoEM Dataset: Large-Scale 3D Mitochondria Instance Segmentation from EM Images

Donglai Wei[1(✉)], Zudi Lin[1], Daniel Franco-Barranco[2,3], Nils Wendt[4],
Xingyu Liu[5], Wenjie Yin[1], Xin Huang[6], Aarush Gupta[7], Won-Dong Jang[1],
Xueying Wang[1], Ignacio Arganda-Carreras[2,3,8], Jeff W. Lichtman[1],
and Hanspeter Pfister[1]

[1] Harvard University, Cambridge, USA
donglai@seas.harvard.edu
[2] Donostia International Physics Center, Donostia, Spain
[3] University of the Basque Country, Leioa, Spain
[4] Technical University of Munich, Munich, Germany
[5] Shanghai Jiao Tong University, Shanghai, China
[6] Northeastern University, Boston, USA
[7] Indian Institute of Technology Roorkee, Roorkee, India
[8] Ikerbasque, Basque Foundation for Science, Bilbao, Spain

Abstract. Electron microscopy (EM) allows the identification of intra-cellular organelles such as mitochondria, providing insights for clinical and scientific studies. However, public mitochondria segmentation datasets only contain hundreds of instances with simple shapes. It is unclear if existing methods achieving human-level accuracy on these small datasets are robust in practice. To this end, we introduce the *MitoEM* dataset, a 3D mitochondria instance segmentation dataset with two $(30\,\mu m)^3$ volumes from human and rat cortices respectively, 3,600× larger than previous benchmarks. With around 40K instances, we find a great diversity of mitochondria in terms of shape and density. For evaluation, we tailor the implementation of the average precision (AP) metric for 3D data with a 45× speedup. On MitoEM, we find existing instance segmentation methods often fail to correctly segment mitochondria with complex shapes or close contacts with other instances. Thus, our MitoEM dataset poses new challenges to the field. We release our code and data: https://donglaiw.github.io/page/mitoEM/index.html.

Keywords: Mitochondria · EM dataset · 3D instance segmentation

1 Introduction

Mitochondria are the primary energy providers for cell activities, thus essential for metabolism. Quantification of the size and geometry of mitochondria is not

N. Wendt, X. Liu, W. Yin, X. Huang, and A. Gupta—Works are done during internship at Harvard University.

ⓒ Springer Nature Switzerland AG 2020
A. L. Martel et al. (Eds.): MICCAI 2020, LNCS 12265, pp. 66–76, 2020.
https://doi.org/10.1007/978-3-030-59722-1_7

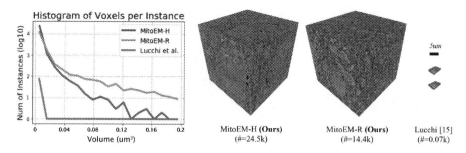

Fig. 1. Comparison of mitochondria segmentation datasets. (Left) Distribution of instance sizes. (Right) 3D image volumes of our MitoEM and Lucchi [20]. Our MitoEM dataset has greater diversity in image appearance and instance sizes.

only crucial to basic neuroscience research, *e.g.*, neuron type identification [26], but also informative to clinical studies, *e.g.*, bipolar disorder [13] and diabetes [35]. Electron microscopy (EM) images have been used to reveal their detailed 3D geometry at the nanometer level with the terabyte scale [22]. Consequently, to enable an in-depth biological analysis, we need high-throughput and robust 3D mitochondria instance segmentation methods.

Despite the advances in the large-scale instance segmentation for neurons from EM images [12], such effort for mitochondria has been overlooked in the field. Due to the lack of a large-scale public dataset, most recent mito-chondria segmentation methods were benchmarked on the EPFL Hippocampus dataset [20] (referred to as *Lucchi* later on), where mitochondria instances are small in number and simple in morphology (Fig. 1). Even for the non-public dataset [1,8], mitochondria instances do not have complex shapes due to the limited dataset size and the non-mammalian tissue. However, in mammal cortices, the complete shape of mitochondria can be sophisticated, where even state-of-the-art neuron instance segmentation methods may fail. In Fig. 2a, we show a mitochondria-on-a-string (MOAS) instance [36], prone to the false split error due to the voxel-level thin connection. We also show multiple instances entan-gling with each other with unclear boundaries, prone to the false merge error in Fig. 2b. Therefore, we need a large-scale mammalian mitochondria dataset to evaluate current methods and foster new researches to address the complex morphology challenge.

To this end, we have curated a large-scale 3D mitochondria instance segmen-tation benchmark, **MitoEM**, which is 3,600× larger than the previous bench-mark [20] (Fig. 1). Our dataset consists of two $30\,\mu m^3$ 3D EM image stacks, one from an adult rat and one from an adult human brain tissue, facilitating large-scale cross-tissue comparison. For evaluation, we adopt the average precision (AP) evaluation metric and design an efficient implementation for 3D volumes to benchmark state-of-the-art methods. Our analysis of model performance sheds light limitations of current automatic instance segmentation methods.

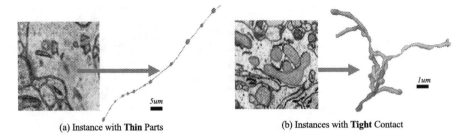

(a) Instance with **Thin** Parts   (b) Instances with **Tight** Contact

Fig. 2. Complex mitochondria in our MitoEM dataset: **(a)** mitochondria-on-a-string (MOAS) [36], and **(b)** dense tangle of touching mitochondria. Those challenging cases are prevalent but not covered by existing labeled datasets.

1.1   Related Works

Mitochondria Segmentation. Most previous segmentation methods are benchmarked on the aforementioned Lucchi dataset [20]. For mitochondria semantic segmentation, earlier works leverage traditional image processing and machine learning techniques [18,19,27,29], while recent methods utilize 2D or 3D deep learning architectures for mitochondria segmentation [4,24]. More recently, Liu et al. [17] showed the first instance segmentation approach on the Lucchi dataset with a modified Mask R-CNN [10], and Xiao et al. [30] obtained the instance segmentation through an IoU tracking approach. However, it is hard to evaluate their robustness in a large-scale setting due to the lack of a proper dataset.

Instance Segmentation for Biomedical Images. Instance segmentation methods in the biomedical domain have been used for the segmenting glands from histology images and neurons from EM images. For gland, state-of-the-art methods [3] train deep learning models to predict both the semantic segmentation mask and the boundary map in a multi-task setting. Additional targets [32] and shape-preserving loss functions [33] are proposed for further improvement.

For neurons, there are two main methodologies. The first one trains 2D or 3D CNNs to predict an intermediate representation such as boundary [6,25,34] or affinity maps [15,28]. Then, clustering techniques such as watershed [7,37] or graph partition [14] transform these intermediate output into a segmentation. Adjacent segments are further agglomerated by a similarity measure using either the intermediate output [9] or a new classifier [11,23,37]. In the other methodology, CNNs are trained recursively to grow the current estimate of a single segmentation mask [12], which is extended to handle multiple objects [21]. Compared to neuron instances, the sparsity of mitochondria instances and the close appearance to other organelles make it hard to directly apply those segmentation methods tuned for neuron segmentation.

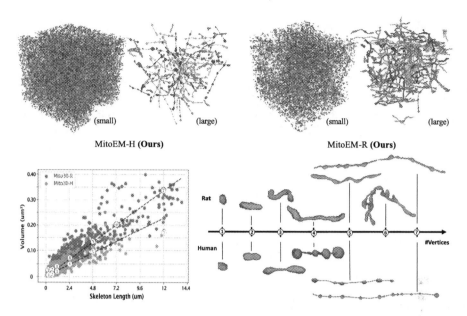

Fig. 3. Visualization of MitoEM-H and MitoEM-R datasets. (Top) 3D meshes of small and large mitochondria, where MitoEM-R has a higher presence of large objects; (Bottom left) scatter plot of mitochondria by their skeleton length and volume; (Bottom right) 3D meshes of the mitochondria at the sampled positions.

2   MitoEM Dataset

Dataset Acquisition. Two tissue blocks were imaged using a multi-beam scanning electron microscope: *MitoEM-H*, from Layer II in the frontal lobe of an adult human and *MitoEM-R*, from Layer II/III in the primary visual cortex of an adult rat. Both samples are imaged at a resolution of $8 \times 8 \times 30\,\mathrm{nm}^3$. After stitching and aligning the images, we cropped a $(30\,\mu\mathrm{m}^3)$ sub-volume, avoiding large blood vessels where mitochondria are absent. To focus on the mitochondria morphology challenge, We made the specific design choice of the dataset size and region, which contains complex mitochondria without introducing much of the domain adaptation problem due to the diverse image appearance.

Dataset Annotation. We facilitated a semi-automatic approach to annotate this large-scale dataset. We first manually annotated a $5\,\mu\mathrm{m}^3$ volume for each tissue, then trained a state-of-the-art 3D U-Net (U3D) model [5] to predict binary masks for unlabeled regions, which are transformed into instance masks with connected-component labeling. Then expert annotator proofread and modify the prediction. With this pipeline, we iteratively accumulated ground truth instance segmentation for the 5, 10, 20, $30\,\mu\mathrm{m}^3$ sub-volumes for each tissue. Considering the complex geometry of large mitochondria, we ordered the labeled instances by volume size and conducted a second round of proofreading with 3D mesh visualization. Finally, we asked three neuroscience experts to go through the dataset to proofread until no disagreement.

Dataset Analysis. The physical size of our two EM volumes is more than *3,600×* larger than the previous Lucchi benchmark [20]. MitoEM-H and MitoEM-R have around 24.5k and 14.4k mitochondria instances, respectively, over *500×* more than that of Lucchi [20]. We show the distribution of instance sizes for both volumes in Fig. 1. Both MitoEM-H and MitoEM-R follow the exponential distribution with different rate parameters. MitoEM-H has more small mitochondria instances, while MitoEM-R has more big ones. To illustrate the diverse morphology of mitochondria, we show all 3D meshes of small objects (<5k voxels) and large objects (>30k voxels) from both tissues (Fig. 3, Top). Despite their differences in species and cortical regions, the mitochondria-on-a-string (MOAS) are common in both volumes, where round balls are connected by ultra-thin tubes. Furthermore, we plot the length versus volume of mitochondria instances for both volumes, where the length of the mitochondria is approximated by the number of voxels in its 3D skeleton (Fig. 3, Bottom left). There is a strong linear correlation between the volume and length mitochondria in both volumes, which is the average thickness of the instance. While the MitoEM-H has more small instances, the MitoEM-R has more large instances with complex morphologies. We sample mitochondria of different length along the regression line and find instances share similar shapes to MOAS in both volumes (Fig. 3, Bottom right).

3   Method

For the 3D mitochondria instance segmentation task, we first introduce the evaluation metric and provide an efficient implementation. Then, we categorize state-of-the-art instance segmentation methods for later benchmarking (Sect. 4).

3.1   Task and Evaluation Metric

Inspired by the video instance segmentation challenge [31], we adapt the COCO evaluation API [16] designed for 2D instance segmentation to our 3D volumetric segmentation. Out of COCO evaluation metrics, we choose AP-75 requiring at least 75% intersection over union (IoU) with the ground truth for a detection to be a true positive. In comparison, AP-95 is too strict even for human annotators and AP-50 is too loose for the high-precision biological analysis.

Efficient Implementation. The original AP implementation for natural image and video datasets is suboptimal for the 3D volume. Two main bottlenecks are the saving/loading of individual masks from an intermediate JSON file, and the IoU computation. For our case, it is storage-efficient to directly input the whole volume, thus removing the overhead for data conversion. For an efficient IoU computation, we first compute the 3D bounding boxes of all the instance segmentation by iterating through each 2D slice in all three dimensions. It reduces

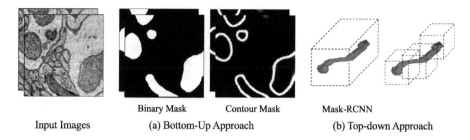

Input Images

Binary Mask **Contour Mask**

(a) Bottom-Up Approach

Mask-RCNN

(b) Top-down Approach

Fig. 4. Instance segmentation methods in two types: bottom-up and top-down.

the complexity to $3N+\mathcal{O}(1)$ compared to $KN+\mathcal{O}(1)$ by naively iterating through all instances, where N is the number of voxels and K is the number of instances. To compute the intersection region with ground truth instances, we only need to do local calculation within the precomputed bounding box. Compared to the previous version on the MitoEM-H dataset, our implementation achieves a **45×** speed-up for 4k instances within a 0.4 Gigavoxel volume.

3.2 State-of-the-Art Methods

We categorize state-of-the-art instance segmentation methods not only from mitochondria literature but also from neuron and gland segmentation (Fig. 4).

Bottom-Up Approach. Bottom-up approaches often use 3D U-Net to predict the binary segmentation mask [25] (U3D-B), affinity map [15] (U3D-A), or binary mask with instance contour [3] (U3D-BC). However, since those predictions are not the instance masks, several post-processing algorithms have been utilized for object decoding. Those algorithms include connected component labeling (CC), graph-based watershed, and marker-controlled watershed (MW). For rigorous evaluation of the state-of-the-art methods, we examine different combinations of model predictions and decode algorithms on our MitoEM dataset.

Top-Down Approach. Methods like Mask-RCNN [10] are not applicable due to the undefined scale of bounding boxes in the EM volume. Previously FFN [12] has shown promising results on neuron segmentation by gradually growing precomputed seeds. We therefore test FFN in the experiments.

4   Experiments

4.1   Implementation Details

For a fair comparison of bottom-up approaches, we use the same residual 3D U-Net [15] for all representations. For training, we use the same data augmentation and learning schedule as in [15]. The input data size is $112 \times 112 \times 112$ for Lucchi and $32 \times 256 \times 256$ for MitoEM due to its anisotropicity. We use weighted BCE loss for the prediction. For the FFN model [12], we only train it on the small Lucchi dataset, which already took 4 hours for label pre-processing. We use the official implementation online and train it until convergence.

Table 1. Mitochondria Segmentation Results on Lucchi Dataset. We show results for (a) previous semantic segmentation methods, (b) a top-down, and (c) bottom-up approaches with different instance decoding methods.

Method	Jaccard↑	AP-75↑
CNN+post [24]	0.907	N/A
Working Set [19]	0.895	N/A
U3D-B [4]	0.889	N/A
GT+dilation-1	0.885	0.881
GT+erosion-1	0.904	0.894

(a) Previous approaches

Method	Jaccard↑	AP-75↑
FFN[12]	0.554	0.230

(b) Top-down approaches

Method		Jaccard↑	AP-75↑
U3D-A	+waterz [9]	0.877	0.802
	+zwatershed [15]		0.801
U2D-B	+CC [25]	0.882	0.760
	+MC [2]		0.521
U3D-B	+CC [5]	0.881	0.769
	+IoU [30]		0.770
	+MW		0.770
U3D-BC	+CC [3]	0.887	0.770
	+IoU		0.771
	+MW		**0.812**

(c) Bottom-up approaches

Table 2. Main benchmark results on the MitoEM dataset. We compare state-of-the-art methods on the MitoEM dataset using AP-75. Following MS-COCO evaluation [16], we report the results for instances of different sizes.

Method		MitoEM-H				MitoEM-R			
		Small	Med	Large	All	Small	Med	Large	All
U3D-A	+zwatershed [37]	**0.564**	0.774	0.615	**0.617**	**0.408**	0.235	**0.653**	0.328
	+waterz [9]	0.454	0.763	0.628	0.572	0.324	0.149	0.539	0.294
U2D-B	+CC [25]	0.408	0.814	**0.711**	0.597	0.104	0.628	0.481	0.355
U3D-B	+CC [5]	0.109	0.497	0.437	0.271	0.017	0.390	0.275	0.208
	+MW	0.439	0.794	0.567	0.561	0.254	0.692	0.397	0.447
U3D-BC	+CC [3]	0.480	0.801	0.611	0.594	0.187	0.551	0.402	0.397
	+MW	0.489	**0.820**	0.618	0.605	0.290	**0.751**	0.490	**0.521**

4.2 Benchmark Results on Lucchi Dataset

We first show previous semantic segmentation results in Table 1a. To evaluate the metric sensitivity to the annotation, we perturb ground truth labels with 1-voxel dilation or erosion, which has similar performance to those from the previous methods. As the annotation is not pixel-level accurate, previous methods have already achieved human-level performance for semantic segmentation.

For the top-down approaches, we tried our best to tune the FFN method without obtaining desirable results (Table 1b). In particular, FFN achieves around 0.7 AP-50 but 0.2 AP-75, showing its weakness in capture object geometry.

For the bottom up approaches (Table 1c), U-Net models with standard training practice achieves on-par results with specifically designed methods [4]. However, the AP-75 instance metric can still reveal the false split and false merge errors in the prediction. All four representations provide similar semantic results and the U3D-BC+MW achieves the best instance decoding result with the help of the additional instance contour information.

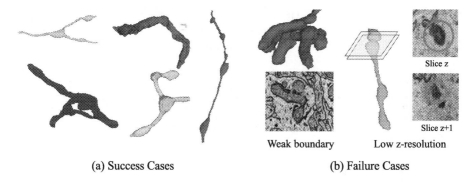

(a) Success Cases   (b) Failure Cases

Fig. 5. Qualitative results on MitoEM. (a) The U3D-BC+MW method can capture complex mitochondria morphology. (b) Failure cases are resulted from ambiguous touching boundaries and highly overlapping cross sections.

4.3   Benchmark Results on MitoEM Dataset

We evaluate previous state-of-the-art methods on our MitoEM dataset. Specifically, both human (MitoEM-H) and rat (MitoEM-R) datasets are partitioned into consecutive `train`, `val` and `test` splits with 40%, 10% and 50% of the total amount of data. We select the hyper-parameters on the `val` split and report the final results on the `test` split. As mitochondria has diverse sizes, we also report the AP-75 results for small, medium and large instances separately with the volume threshold of 5 K and 15K voxels.

As shown in Table 2, all methods perform consistently better on the human tissue (MitoEM-H) than the rat tissue. Besides, marker-controlled watershed (MW) is significantly better than connected-component (CC) and IoU-based tracking (IoU) for processing both binary mask (U3D-B) and binary mask + instance contour (BC). Furthermore, U3D-BC+MW achieves the best performance considering the mean AP-75 scores for both tissues. Our MitoEM posts new challenges for methods which are nearly perfect on the Lucchi dataset.

We show qualitative results of U3D-BC+MW (Fig. 5). Such method successfully captures many mitochondria with non-trivial shapes, but it is still not robust to the ambiguous boundary and overlapping surface. Further improvement can be achieved by considering 3D shape prior of mitochondria.

4.4   Cross-Tissue Evaluation

In this experiment, we examine the cross-tissue performance of the U3D-BC model. That is, we run inference on the MitoEM-Human dataset using the model trained on the MitoEM-Rat dataset, and vice versa. We observe that the MitoEM-R model achieves better performance on the human dataset than the MitoEM-H model, while the MitoEM-H model performs worse than MitoEM-R on the rat dataset (Table 3). Since the rat dataset contains more large objects with complex morphologies, it is reasonable that the models trained on rat datasets generalize better and can handle more challenging instances.

Table 3. Cross-tissue evaluation on MitoEM. The U3D-BC model trained on rat (R model) is tested on human (MitoEM-H), and vice versa. R model generalizes better as the MitoEM-R dataset has higher diversity and complexity.

Method		MitoEM-H (R model)				MitoEM-R (H model)			
		Small	Med	Large	All	Small	Med	Large	All
U3D-BC	+CC [3]	0.533	0.833	0.664	0.650	0.218	0.640	0.354	0.407
	+MW	**0.587**	**0.862**	**0.669**	**0.690**	**0.224**	**0.674**	**0.359**	**0.411**

5 Conclusion

In this paper, we introduce a large-scale mitochondria instance segmentation dataset that reveals the limitation of state-of-the-art methods in the field to deal with mitochondria with complex shape or close contacts with others. Similar to ImageNet for natural images, our densely annotated MitoEM can have various applications beyond its original task, *e.g.*, feature pre-training, 3D shape analysis, and testing approaches on active learning and domain adaptation.

Acknowledgments. This work has been partially supported by NSF award IIS-1835231 and NIH award 5U54CA225088-03.

References

1. Ariadne.ai: Automated segmentation of mitochondria and ER in cortical cells (2018). https://ariadne.ai/case/segmentation/organelles/CorticalCells/. Accessed 7 July 2020
2. Beier, T., et al.: Multicut brings automated neurite segmentation closer to human performance. Nat. Meth. **14**(2), 101–102 (2017)
3. Chen, H., Qi, X., Yu, L., Heng, P.A.: DCAN: deep contour-aware networks for accurate gland segmentation. In: CVPR, pp. 2487–2496. IEEE (2016)
4. Cheng, H.C., Varshney, A.: Volume segmentation using convolutional neural networks with limited training data. In: ICIP, pp. 590–594. IEEE (2017)
5. Çiçek, Ö., Abdulkadir, A., Lienkamp, S.S., Brox, T., Ronneberger, O.: 3D U-Net: learning dense volumetric segmentation from sparse annotation. In: Ourselin, S., Joskowicz, L., Sabuncu, M.R., Unal, G., Wells, W. (eds.) MICCAI 2016. LNCS, vol. 9901, pp. 424–432. Springer, Cham (2016). https://doi.org/10.1007/978-3-319-46723-8_49
6. Ciresan, D., Giusti, A., Gambardella, L.M., Schmidhuber, J.: Deep neural networks segment neuronal membranes in electron microscopy images. In: NeurIPS, pp. 2843–2851 (2012)
7. Cousty, J., Bertrand, G., Najman, L., Couprie, M.: Watershed cuts: minimum spanning forests and the drop of water principle. TPAMI **31**, 1362–1374 (2008)
8. Dorkenwald, S.: Automated synaptic connectivity inference for volume electron microscopy. Nat. Meth. **14**(4), 435–442 (2017)
9. Funke, J.: Large scale image segmentation with structured loss based deep learning for connectome reconstruction. TPAMI **41**(7), 1669–1680 (2018)
10. He, K., Gkioxari, G., Dollár, P., Girshick, R.: Mask R-CNN. In: ICCV, pp. 2961–2969. IEEE (2017)

11. Jain, V., Turaga, S.C., Briggman, K., Helmstaedter, M.N., Denk, W., Seung, H.S.: Learning to agglomerate superpixel hierarchies. In: NeurIPS, pp. 648–656 (2011)

12. Januszewski, M., et al.: High-precision automated reconstruction of neurons with flood-filling networks. Nat. Meth. **15**(8), 605–610 (2018)

13. Kasahara, T., et al.: Depression-like episodes in mice harboring mtDNA deletions in paraventricular thalamus. Mol. Psychiatry **21**(1), 39–48 (2016)

14. Krasowski, N., Beier, T., Knott, G., Köthe, U., Hamprecht, F.A., Kreshuk, A.: Neuron segmentation with high-level biological priors. TMI **37**(4), 829–839 (2017)

15. Lee, K., Zung, J., Li, P., Jain, V., Seung, H.S.: Superhuman accuracy on the SNEMI3D connectomics challenge. arXiv:1706.00120 (2017)

16. Lin, T.-Y., et al.: Microsoft COCO: common objects in context. In: Fleet, D., Pajdla, T., Schiele, B., Tuytelaars, T. (eds.) ECCV 2014. LNCS, vol. 8693, pp. 740–755. Springer, Cham (2014). https://doi.org/10.1007/978-3-319-10602-1_48

17. Liu, J., Li, W., Xiao, C., Hong, B., Xie, Q., Han, H.: Automatic detection and segmentation of mitochondria from SEM images using deep neural network. In: EMBC. IEEE (2018)

18. Lucchi, A., Li, Y., Smith, K., Fua, P.: Structured image segmentation using kernelized features. In: Fitzgibbon, A., Lazebnik, S., Perona, P., Sato, Y., Schmid, C. (eds.) ECCV 2012. LNCS, vol. 7573, pp. 400–413. Springer, Heidelberg (2012). https://doi.org/10.1007/978-3-642-33709-3_29

19. Lucchi, A.: Learning structured models for segmentation of 2-D and 3-D imagery. TMI **34**(5), 1096–1110 (2014)

20. Lucchi, A., Smith, K., Achanta, R., Knott, G., Fua, P.: Supervoxel-based segmentation of mitochondria in EM image stacks with learned shape features. TMI **31**(2), 474–486 (2011)

21. Meirovitch, Y., Mi, L., Saribekyan, H., Matveev, A., Rolnick, D., Shavit, N.: Cross-classification clustering: an efficient multi-object tracking technique for 3-D instance segmentation in connectomics. In: CVPR. IEEE (2019)

22. Motta, A., et al.: Dense connectomic reconstruction in layer 4 of the somatosensory cortex. Science **366**(6469), eaay3134 (2019)

23. Nunez-Iglesias, J., Kennedy, R., Parag, T., Shi, J., Chklovskii, D.B.: Machine learning of hierarchical clustering to segment 2D and 3D images. PLoS ONE **8**, e71715 (2013)

24. Oztel, I., Yolcu, G., Ersoy, I., White, T., Bunyak, F.: Mitochondria segmentation in electron microscopy volumes using deep convolutional neural network. In: IEEE International Conference on Bioinformatics and Biomedicine (2017)

25. Ronneberger, O., Fischer, P., Brox, T.: U-Net: convolutional networks for biomedical image segmentation. In: Navab, N., Hornegger, J., Wells, W.M., Frangi, A.F. (eds.) MICCAI 2015. LNCS, vol. 9351, pp. 234–241. Springer, Cham (2015). https://doi.org/10.1007/978-3-319-24574-4_28

26. Schubert, P.J., Dorkenwald, S., Januszewski, M., Jain, V., Kornfeld, J.: Learning cellular morphology with neural networks. Nat. Commun. **10**, 2736 (2019)

27. Smith, K., Carleton, A., Lepetit, V.: Fast ray features for learning irregular shapes. In: ICCV. IEEE (2009)

28. Turaga, S.C., Briggman, K.L., Helmstaedter, M., Denk, W., Seung, H.S.: Maximin affinity learning of image segmentation. In: NeurIPS, pp. 1865–1873 (2009)

29. Vazquez-Reina, A., Gelbart, M., Huang, D., Lichtman, J., Miller, E., Pfister, H.: Segmentation fusion for connectomics. In: ICCV. IEEE (2011)

30. Xiao, C.: Automatic mitochondria segmentation for EM data using a 3D supervised convolutional network. Front. Neuroanat. **12**, 92 (2018)

31. Xu, N., et al.: YouTube-VOS: a large-scale video object segmentation benchmark. In: ECCV. Springer, Heidelberg (2018)
32. Xu, Y.: Gland instance segmentation using deep multichannel neural networks. Trans. Biomed. Eng. **64**(12), 2901–2912 (2017)
33. Yan, Z., Yang, X., Cheng, K.-T.T.: A deep model with shape-preserving loss for gland instance segmentation. In: Frangi, A.F., Schnabel, J.A., Davatzikos, C., Alberola-López, C., Fichtinger, G. (eds.) MICCAI 2018. LNCS, vol. 11071, pp. 138–146. Springer, Cham (2018). https://doi.org/10.1007/978-3-030-00934-2_16
34. Zeng, T., Wu, B., Ji, S.: DeepEM3D: approaching human-level performance on 3D anisotropic EM image segmentation. Bioinformatics **33**(16), 2555–2562 (2017)
35. Zeviani, M., Di Donato, S.: Mitochondrial disorders. Brain **127**(10), 2153–2172 (2004)
36. Zhang, L., et al.: Altered brain energetics induces mitochondrial fission arrest in Alzheimers disease. Sci. Rep. **6**, 18725 (2016)
37. Zlateski, A., Seung, H.S.: Image segmentation by size-dependent single linkage clustering of a watershed basin graph. arXiv:1505.00249 (2015)

Learning Guided Electron Microscopy with Active Acquisition

Lu Mi[1(✉)], Hao Wang[1], Yaron Meirovitch[1,2], Richard Schalek[2],
Srinivas C. Turaga[3], Jeff W. Lichtman[2], Aravinthan D. T. Samuel[2],
and Nir Shavit[1]

[1] Massachusetts Institute of Technology, Cambridge, MA, USA
lumi@mit.edu
[2] Harvard University, Cambridge, MA, USA
[3] HHMI Janelia Research Campus, Ashburn, VA, USA

Abstract. Single-beam scanning electron microscopes (SEM) are widely used to acquire massive datasets for biomedical study, material analysis, and fabrication inspection. Datasets are typically acquired with uniform acquisition: applying the electron beam with the same power and duration to all image pixels, even if there is great variety in the pixels' importance for eventual use. Many SEMs are now able to move the beam to any pixel in the field of view without delay, enabling them, in principle, to invest their time budget more effectively with non-uniform imaging.

In this paper, we show how to use deep learning to accelerate and optimize single-beam SEM acquisition of images. Our algorithm rapidly collects an information-lossy image (e.g. low resolution) and then applies a novel learning method to identify a small subset of pixels to be collected at higher resolution based on a trade-off between the saliency and spatial diversity. We demonstrate the efficacy of this novel technique for active acquisition by speeding up the task of collecting connectomic datasets for neurobiology by up to an order of magnitude. Code is available at https://github.com/lumi9587/learning-guided-SEM.

Keywords: Electron microscope · Active acquisition · Determinantal point process

1 Introduction

Scanning electron microscopes are widely used for nanometer-scale imaging in diverse applications including structural biology [9,14], materials analysis [22] and semiconductor fabrication [21]. In most cases, an electron beam is applied with the same power and duration to all image pixels. This is fundamentally inefficient since the saliency of each pixel might be heterogeneous.

Electronic supplementary material The online version of this chapter (https://doi.org/10.1007/978-3-030-59722-1_8) contains supplementary material, which is available to authorized users.

A. L. Martel et al. (Eds.): MICCAI 2020, LNCS 12265, pp. 77–87, 2020.
https://doi.org/10.1007/978-3-030-59722-1_8

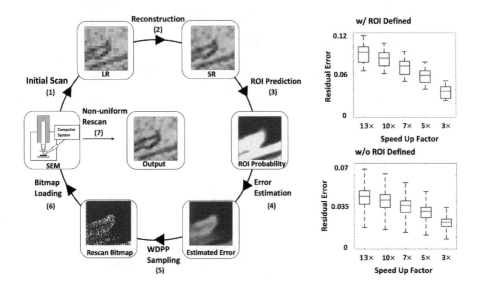

Fig. 1. Left: Overview of our learning guided electron microscope with ROI defined. The SEM firstly performs the initial scan to collect the low-resolution image I_{LR} (1). The reconstruction step is applied to generate a super-resolved image I_{SR} (2). Then the pixel of interest (3) and estimated error (4) is identified. The next step is to implement diversified sampling based on estimated error using weighted determinantal point process (WDPP) (5). Finally a sparse bitmap is sent to SEM (6) to perform rescan (7). See more details in Subsect. 2.1. **Right:** The box plots represent different speedup factors with residual error (L_1 loss) using our active acquisition pipeline on *SNEMI3D*.

In this paper, we design an imaging strategy for a scanning electron microscope (SEM) that mimics the human visual system. The human visual system quickly decides saliency by first using a low-resolution (non-foveal) collection and then applies the high-resolution fovea to dwell on important parts [25]. Most scanning electron microscopes are ideally suited for such active and adaptive image acquisition; their scan generators can instantaneously deflect the beam to any arbitrary position and then stably dwell to acquire each pixel [1,20]. Because of fast beam re-positioning, an arbitrary distribution of pixel locations has negligible impact on scanning time. Therefore, for an image where only 5% of pixels need scanning, one can ideally speed up its acquisition by 20 folds [1,23].

Most images are characterized by two types of saliency: *interest* and *information density*. Conventional SEM ignores both types of saliency and scans the whole image using identical resolution with low efficiency [7]. In this work, we develop a new method to accelerate and optimize SEM acquisition. To do this, we have built an active acquisition algorithm that intelligently budgets the operation of a scanner to focus on regions with high saliency (either high interest or high information density) within an image.

We apply our technology to one critical area using SEM in connectomics, which aims for the reconstruction of synaptic connectivity maps for brain tissue [14,17]. So far, connectomics has only been applied to a small number of specimens because of the enormous burden in acquiring and analyzing datasets that can easily span terabytes and petabytes [13,29]. For example, scanning a cubic millimeter of brain tissue at the resolution needed for connectomics (4 nm × 4 nm × 30 nm per voxel) requires two thousand trillion voxels (2PBs of data). A typical SEM running at one million voxels per second would require 63 years to do this.

Here, we design to accelerate SEM image acquisition for connectomics by exploiting the sparsity of salient pixels in images. The essential goal in connectomics is to map neural circuitry [14,17]. To reconstruct SEM images for neural circuitry [12,18], the structures that contain pixels with high interest are membrane of neurons and objects associated with synapses. All other intracellular objects and extracellular space have low saliency [14]. For typical mammalian tissues, neural membranes account for only 5–10% of the images and synapses account for even less. This sparsity of salient pixels suggests significant potential for speeding up acquisition. In this work, without loss of generality, we define the membrane boundary of individual neurons as the region of interest (ROI), to demonstrate the effectiveness of our pipeline.

In contrast to previous work focusing on image reconstruction and restoration [2,5,6,8,11,16,27,28], or multi-beam approaches that use highly parallelized but expensive microscope systems [4], our work aims to guide widely available single-beam SEMs to collect salient image pixels, thereby reconstructing essential regions at high resolution, as shown in Fig. 1. Our major contributions are:

- We are the first, to our knowledge, to cast the acquisition of electron microscopes as a learning-guided sampling problem and thereby capable to achieve significant speedup.
- We present an effective and principled sampling technique, weighted determinantal point process (WDPP), that optimizes pixel selection based on their saliency and spatial diversity.
- We present a new active-acquisition pipeline for SEM that executes nonuniform pixel-wise scanning, and demonstrate a potential speedup rate of up to an order of magnitude on real-world connectomic datasets.

2   Methodology

In this paper, we formulate a learning-guided sampling problem to speed up SEM acquisition. The goal is to intelligently sample a subset of pixels in a way that balances the following trade-off:

$$\mathcal{C} = \underbrace{|I_{HR} - R(I_{HR} \odot B)|}_{reconstruction\ loss} + \lambda \underbrace{\sum_{i,j} B^{(i,j)}}_{acquisition\ cost} \ .$$

Here I_{HR} denotes a high-resolution image, B is the bitmap with the superscript indexing positions to indicate locations of sampled pixels, $R(\cdot)$ is the reconstruction function, $\odot$ is the Hadamard (element-wise) product, and λ is a hyperparameter balancing the trade-off between reconstruction loss and acquisition cost. Unlike other works [11,16,27,28] focusing on improving $R(\cdot)$ given a low-resolution image $I_{LR} = I_{HR} \odot B$, our work assumes a fixed $R(\cdot)$ and instead tries to find a reasonable bitmap B that can achieve low reconstruction loss with low acquisition cost. We do this via the proposed WDPP sampling technique, which selects pixels based on spatial diversity as well as saliency (quantified as estimated error). In the following, we describe the overview of our active acquisition pipeline, introduce its key components (i.e., binarized error estimation in Subsect. 2.2 and WDPP in Subsect. 2.3) as well as our technical contributions.

2.1 Active Acquisition Pipeline

Below we describe individual steps of the active acquisition pipeline in Fig. 1.

Initial Scan, Reconstruction, and ROI Prediction: As the first step, SEM performs the *initial scan* of a low-resolution image I_{LR} with negligible cost. The next step is to apply a *reconstruction* model R to I_{LR} to generate super-resolved image $I_{SR} = R(I_{LR})$. The model can use either learning-based reconstruction methods or simple interpolation rules such as bicubic. The third step (*ROI Prediction*) is using ROI detector F_{ROI} to predict the saliency score for each pixel. Note that we are interested in two types of tasks in this paper: tasks with and tasks without ROI defined. *ROI Prediction* is not applied for the task without ROI defined. This task only considers regions with high information density as saliency. These steps correspond to (1)–(3) in Fig. 1.

Binarized Error Estimation: The fourth step, shown in (4) of Fig. 1, is to *estimate the prediction error*. For the tasks without ROI defined, the ground truth error is defined as L_1 loss $| I_{HR} - I_{SR} |$; for the tasks with ROI defined, the ground truth error is defined as L_1 loss $| F_{ROI}(I_{HR}) - F_{ROI}(I_{SR}) |$. These errors will be estimated through an efficient and simple learning based method we propose in Subsect. 2.2.

Diversified Sampling: This step, as shown in (5) of Fig. 1, performs WDPP sampling based on the estimated error map from the previous step. The goal is to select K samples contributing the largest estimated error while balancing the spatial diversity at the same time. Details are in Subsect. 2.3.

Bitmap Loading and Rescan: Once the locations of sampled pixels (produced by WDPP) are encoded into bitmaps and loaded into the SEM, the SEM performs rescan based on the sparse bitmap. The final output I_{OUT} is then reconstructed with recollected pixels during rescan as well as pixels in I_{LR} collected in the initial scan.

2.2 Binarized Error Estimation

One key component of the pipeline is our proposed *binarized error estimation*. It is a simple and efficient supervised learning method to estimate pixel-wise error.

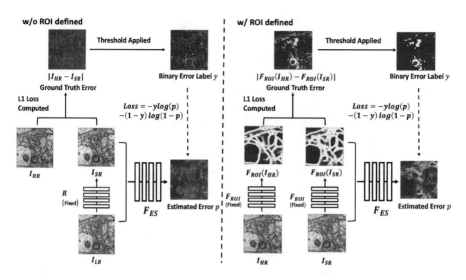

Fig. 2. The overview of our end-to-end learning framework for training the error estimation networks F_{ES}. For the task without ROI defined (**left**), the inputs of F_{ES} are concatenation of I_{SR} and I_{LR}. For the task with ROI defined (**right**), the inputs of F_{ES} are concatenation of $F_{ROI}(I_{SR})$ and I_{SR}. The regression task is reformulated as a binary classification problem after applying a threshold to the ground truth error. ROI detector F_{ROI} and reconstruction model R are fixed during the training of F_{ES}.

As shown in Fig. 2, we first binarize the continuous pixel-wise error using the mean of the error distribution ϵ as the threshold and then train a UNET [24] to perform classification. For the task with ROI defined, our goal is to train a classification network to output the pixel-wise probability (we refer to this probability as *estimated error* in the following text):

$$P(|F_{ROI}(I_{HR}^{(i,j)}) - F_{ROI}(I_{SR}^{(i,j)})| > \epsilon),$$

where the superscript (i, j) indexes positions. For the task without ROI defined, our goal is to predict the probability:

$$P(|I_{HR}^{(i,j)} - I_{SR}^{(i,j)}| > \epsilon).$$

Our preliminary experiments show significant improvement in error estimation compared to directly regressing the error. This is because most pixels in an image have very low error, significantly biasing the model to output low values.

2.3   Diversified Sampling

After the estimated error is acquired, one naive strategy is to rescan K pixels with the highest estimated error. However, due to strong correlation between neighboring pixels, a more cost-effective way is to sample pixels according to both saliency (quantified by estimated error) and spatial diversity. To this end, we formulate the problem as a determinantal point process (DPP) [15].

Moreover, another key contribution in our work is to propose a weighted DPP and construct a proper DPP kernel L balancing saliency and spatial diversity. Specifically, given an image with size of $M \times M$, we construct an $N \times N$ kernel $L = U^\gamma S U^\gamma$, where $N = M^2$ is the total number of pixels in the image, S is a $N \times N$ symmetric matrix indicating location similarity. U is an $N \times N$ diagonal matrix; each diagonal entry u_{ii} indicates pixel i's saliency, which is quantified by the estimated error described in Subsect. 2.2. The exponent, γ, controls the trade-off between saliency and spatial diversity. For pixel i and j, we have

$$L_{ij} = u_{ii}^\gamma S_{ij} u_{jj}^\gamma, \qquad S_{ij} = e^{-[(x_i - x_j)^2 + (y_i - y_j)^2]/\sigma_s^2}, \qquad (1)$$

where σ_s is a hyperparameter. With this new diversified sampling algorithm, our pipeline can select K pixels simultaneously for rescan, while guaranteeing efficiency. The algorithm is shown in Algorithm 1. In brief, conventional DPP sampling promises the diversity of sampled points for each iteration; in the current iteration, DPP finds a point which is diverse from all previous points. In contrast, our proposed WDPP finds a point which strikes a balance between diversity and saliency in each iteration.

Algorithm 1: WDPP Sampling

Input: Location similarity matrix S and diagonalized quality matrix U.
Construct kernel matrix $L = U^\gamma S U^\gamma$.
Compute the eigen-decomposition $(v_n, \lambda_n)_{n=1}^N$ of L.
$J \leftarrow \emptyset$.
for $n = 1, 2, ..., N$ **do**
   | $J \leftarrow J \cup \{n\}$ with prob. $\frac{\lambda_n}{\lambda_n + 1}$.
end
$V \leftarrow \{v_n\}_{n \in J}, Y \leftarrow \emptyset$.
while $|V| > 0$ **do**
   | Select i from y with $Pr(i) = \frac{1}{|V|} \sum_{v \in V} (v^\top e_i)^2$.
   | $Y \leftarrow Y \cup i$.
   | $V \leftarrow V_\perp$, an orthonormal basis for the subspace of V orthogonal to e_i.
end
Output: Y.

---

3   Experiments

In this section, we provide an in-depth analysis of all components in our pipeline. We use two real-world connectomics datasets, *SNEMI3D* [14] from a mouse cortex (with a resolution of $3 \times 3 \times 30$ nm/pixel), and *Human* from a human cerebrum (with a resolution of $4 \times 4 \times 30$ nm/pixel), to evaluate our algorithm. We generate low-resolution images from original images using nearest neighbor with down-sampling rates of ×4, ×8 and ×16.

Table 1. Correlation between ground truth error and error estimated from our method on *SNEMI3D*. Baselines are interest, entropy, infer-transformation, and gradient.

Model	DS rate	Task	**Ours**	Entropy	Interest	Task	**Ours**	Trans	Gradient
Bicubic	× 4	w/ ROI	**0.549**	0.420	0.256	w/o ROI	**0.488**	–	0.323
	× 8		**0.460**	0.306	0.329		**0.437**	–	0.267
	× 16		**0.307**	0.249	0.213		**0.349**	–	0.200
SRGAN	× 4	w/ ROI	0.367	**0.402**	0.252	w/o ROI	**0.599**	0.451	0.347
	× 8		**0.495**	0.262	0.294		**0.514**	0.351	0.215
	× 16		**0.389**	0.111	0.317		**0.461**	0.293	0.136
SRUNET	× 4	w/ ROI	**0.448**	0.416	0.238	w/o ROI	**0.451**	0.399	0.324
	× 8		**0.382**	0.374	0.228		**0.405**	0.311	0.250
	× 16		**0.412**	0.163	0.046		**0.315**	0.203	0.187

3.1 Reconstruction and ROI Detection

We reconstruct I_{SR} from I_{LR} using a UNET. Specifically, we explore two variants of UNET, one trained with an adversarial loss plus an L1 loss (SRGAN) [11] and one trained with only an L1 loss (SRUNET) [24]. Interestingly, we find that whether the adversarial loss improves reconstruction quality depends on I_{HR}'s noise level (see results in Supplementary). Note that reconstruction alone does not guarantee high-quality output, which is why we need adaptive rescan after binarized error estimation and diversified sampling.

For ROI detection, the ROI detector F_{ROI} also uses a UNET. It is trained with I_{HR} as input and human-annotated membrane as ground-truth labels.

3.2 Error Estimation Analysis

The rescan process using estimated error (proposed in Subsect. 2.2) is an effective and efficient way for active acquisition. For the first task without ROI defined, the residual error after reconstruction is $\mid I_{HR} - I_{SR} \mid$, and we use gradient [3] and infer-transformation for uncertainty estimation [19,26] as baselines. For the second task with ROI defined, the residual error after reconstruction is $\mid F_{ROI}(I_{HR}) - F_{ROI}(I_{SR}) \mid$. We use $F_{ROI}(I_{SR})$ (refer to interest in the following text) and its corresponding entropy as baseline.

The first metric is the pixel-wise correlation between the estimated error and ground-truth error. As shown in Table 1, our method can estimate error much more accurately than the baselines (visualizations in Supplementary).

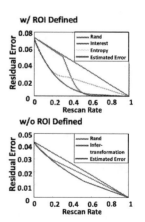

Fig. 3. Sparsification error curves for estimated error (from our method) and baselines on *SNEMI3D*.

This method is also robust to different reconstruction methods and down-sampling rates. The second metric is sparsification error curve [10], which shows how residual error decays as SEM increases the rescan rate. Specifically, we select the top K pixels according to different measurements, e.g., estimated error (our method) and entropy, and set the corresponding ground truth errors of these top K pixels to zero. We then study the decay of error when K increases. Figure 3 shows the results for different methods including random sampling [5,8]. Our method achieves the fastest decay.

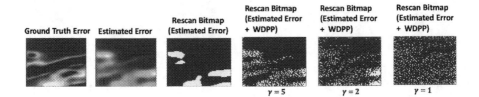

Fig. 4. The effect of γ to balance the trade-off between spatial diversity and saliency for WDPP sampling. All rescan bitmaps contain the same number of samples.

3.3 Sampling with Saliency and Diversity

With the error estimation U, we can then construct the kernel matrix L according to Eq. (1) and run the WDPP sampling algorithm to select pixels for rescan. Figure 4 shows the rescan bitmap produced by WDPP when $\gamma \in \{1, 2, 5\}$. As expected, (1) WDPP can naturally trade off saliency and spatial diversity during sampling; (2) compared to using only error estimation as rescan bitmaps, WDPP can cover larger areas within a sampling budget. Column 4 to 6 in Fig. 5 show the final outputs from SEM following different rescan schemes, i.e., random, estimated error, and estimated error with WDPP, demonstrating WDPP can significantly improve output image quality given a fixed rescan budget.

4   Performance Evaluation

In this section, we evaluate the overall speedup using our active acquisition pipeline, as shown in Fig. 1. The quality of the final output I_{OUT} is compared with I_{HR}. For the task with ROI defined, the residual error is quantified as $| F_{ROI}(I_{HR}) - F_{ROI}(I_{OUT}) |$. For the task without ROI defined, the residual error is quantified as $| I_{HR} - I_{OUT} |$ (evaluations using PSNR and SSIM are shown in Supplementary). We evaluate the initial scan with a down-sampling ratio of $\times 4$; we use different total scan rates (initial scan plus rescan) inversely proportional to the speedup factor, since the total run time of our computational pipeline on a single GPU is a small fraction ($<3\%$) of the SEM imaging time. The results demonstrate that our pipeline can achieve a speedup factor of up to an order of magnitude with relatively small error.

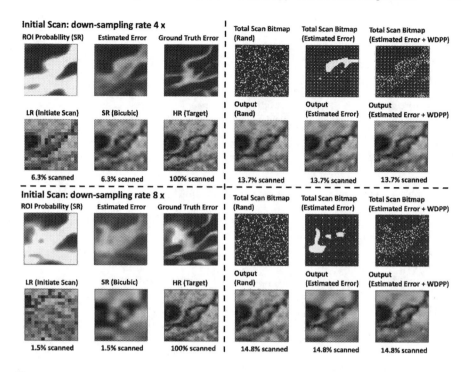

Fig. 5. The final outputs after rescan on *SNEMI3D*. We compare WDPP sampling based on estimated error maps with other baselines, using down-sampling rates of ×4 and ×8 for initial scan. The right part shows different total scan bitmaps and their corresponding outputs using different methods. The total scan bitmaps contain the pixel locations scanned in both initial scan and rescan.

5   Conclusion

We propose a novel and efficient learning-guided sampling algorithm based on learned saliency and spatial diversity. Our active acquisition pipeline demonstrates a potential speedup rate of up to an order of magnitude for SEM in connectomic data collection. In a broader sense, our work addresses research issues across many fields where high-throughput SEM is an essential tool for discovery. Techniques we propose in this work may also be widely used to speed up other imaging systems where sparse scanning can be applied.

Acknowledgement. We would like to thank Remco Schoenmakers and Pengfei Guo for insightful comments and suggestions. This research was supported by the National Science Foundation (NSF) under grants IIS-1607189, CCF-1563880, IOS-1452593 and NSF 1806818.

References

1. Anderson, H.S., Ilic-Helms, J., Rohrer, B., Wheeler, J., Larson, K.: Sparse imaging for fast electron microscopy. In: Computational Imaging XI, vol. 8657, p. 86570C. International Society for Optics and Photonics (2013)
2. Buchholz, T.O., Krull, A., Shahidi, R., Pigino, G., Jékely, G., Jug, F.: Content-aware image restoration for electron microscopy. Meth. Cell Biol. **152**, 277–289 (2019)
3. Dahmen, T.: Feature adaptive sampling for scanning electron microscopy. Sci. Rep. **6**, 25350 (2016)
4. Eberle, A., Mikula, S., Schalek, R., Lichtman, J., Tate, M.K., Zeidler, D.: High-resolution, high-throughput imaging with a multibeam scanning electron microscope. J. Micros. **259**(2), 114–120 (2015)
5. Eldar, Y.C., Kutyniok, G.: Compressed Sensing: Theory and Applications. Cambridge University Press, Cambridge (2012)
6. Fang, L., et al.: Deep learning-based point-scanning super-resolution imaging. bioRxiv, p. 740548 (2019)
7. Flegler, S.L., Flegler, S.L.: Scanning & Transmission Electron Microscopy. Oxford University Press, Oxford (1997)
8. Gan, L.: Block compressed sensing of natural images. In: 2007 15th International Conference on Digital Signal Processing, pp. 403–406. IEEE (2007)
9. Helmstaedter, M., Briggman, K.L., Denk, W.: High-accuracy neurite reconstruction for high-throughput neuroanatomy. Nat. Neurosci. **14**(8), 1081–1088 (2011)
10. Ilg, E.: Uncertainty estimates and multi-hypotheses networks for optical flow. In: Ferrari, V., Hebert, M., Sminchisescu, C., Weiss, Y. (eds.) ECCV 2018. LNCS, vol. 11211, pp. 677–693. Springer, Cham (2018). https://doi.org/10.1007/978-3-030-01234-2_40
11. Isola, P., Zhu, J.Y., Zhou, T., Efros, A.A.: Image-to-image translation with conditional adversarial networks. In: Proceedings of the IEEE Conference on Computer Vision and Pattern Recognition, pp. 1125–1134 (2017)
12. Januszewski, M.: High-precision automated reconstruction of neurons with flood-filling networks. Nat. Meth. **15**, 605–610 (2018)
13. Jarrell, T.A.: The connectome of a decision-making neural network. Science **337**(6093), 437–444 (2012)
14. Kasthuri, N., et al.: Saturated reconstruction of a volume of neocortex. Cell **162**(3), 648–661 (2015)
15. Kulesza, A., Taskar, B., et al.: Determinantal point processes for machine learning. Found. Trends Mach. Learn. **5**(2–3), 123–286 (2012)
16. Ledig, C., et al.: Photo-realistic single image super-resolution using a generative adversarial network. In: Proceedings of the IEEE Conference on Computer Vision and Pattern Recognition, pp. 4681–4690 (2017)
17. Lichtman, J.W., Pfister, H., Shavit, N.: The big data challenges of connectomics. Nat. Neurosci. **17**(11), 1448–1454 (2014)
18. Meirovitch, Y., Mi, L., Saribekyan, H., Matveev, A., Rolnick, D., Shavit, N.: Cross-classification clustering: an efficient multi-object tracking technique for 3-D instance segmentation in connectomics. In: Proceedings of the IEEE Conference on Computer Vision and Pattern Recognition, pp. 8425–8435 (2019)
19. Mi, L., Wang, H., Tian, Y., Shavit, N.: Training-free uncertainty estimation for neural networks. arXiv preprint arXiv:1910.04858 (2019)
20. Mohammed, A.: Scanning electron microscopy (SEM): a review (2018)

21. Newell, T., Tillotson, B., Pearl, H., Miller, A.: Detection of electrical defects with semvision in semiconductor production mode manufacturing. In: 2016 27th Annual SEMI Advanced Semiconductor Manufacturing Conference (ASMC), pp. 151–156. IEEE (2016)

22. Pandey, K., Setua, D., Mathur, G.: Material behaviour: fracture topography of rubber surfaces: an SEM study. Polym. Testing **22**(3), 353–359 (2003)

23. Potocek, P., Trampert, P., Peemen, M., Schoenmakers, R., Dahmen, T.: Sparse scanning electron microscopy data acquisition and deep neural networks for automated segmentation in connectomics. Microsc. Microanal. **26**, 403–412 (2020)

24. Ronneberger, O., Fischer, P., Brox, T.: U-Net: convolutional networks for biomedical image segmentation. In: Navab, N., Hornegger, J., Wells, W.M., Frangi, A.F. (eds.) MICCAI 2015. LNCS, vol. 9351, pp. 234–241. Springer, Cham (2015). https://doi.org/10.1007/978-3-319-24574-4_28

25. Thorpe, S., Fize, D., Marlot, C.: Speed of processing in the human visual system. Nature **381**(6582), 520 (1996)

26. Wang, G., Li, W., Aertsen, M., Deprest, J., Ourselin, S., Vercauteren, T.: Test-time augmentation with uncertainty estimation for deep learning-based medical image segmentation. arXiv preprint arXiv:1807.07356 (2018)

27. Wang, H., et al.: Deep learning enables cross-modality super-resolution in fluorescence microscopy. Nat. Meth. **16**, 103–110 (2019)

28. Weigert, M., et al.: Content-aware image restoration: pushing the limits of fluorescence microscopy. Nat. Meth. **15**(12), 1090 (2018)

29. Yan, G., et al.: Network control principles predict neuron function in the caenorhabditis elegans connectome. Nature **550**(7677), 519 (2017)

Neuronal Subcompartment Classification
and Merge Error Correction

Hanyu Li[1], Michał Januszewski[2], Viren Jain[3], and Peter H. Li[3(✉)]

[1] The University of Chicago, Chicago, IL 60637, USA
[2] Google Research, Zurich, Switzerland
[3] Google Research, Mountain View, CA 94043, USA
phli@google.com

Abstract. Recent advances in 3d electron microscopy are yielding ever larger reconstructions of brain tissue, encompassing thousands of individual neurons interconnected by millions of synapses. Interpreting reconstructions at this scale demands advances in the automated analysis of neuronal morphologies, for example by identifying morphological and functional subcompartments within neurons. We present a method that for the first time uses full 3d input (voxels) to automatically classify reconstructed neuron fragments as axon, dendrite, or somal subcompartments. Based on 3d convolutional neural networks, this method achieves a mean f1-score of 0.972, exceeding the previous state of the art of 0.955. The resulting predictions can support multiple analysis and proofreading applications. In particular, we leverage finely localized subcompartment predictions for automated detection and correction of merge errors in the volume reconstruction, successfully detecting 90.6% of inter-class merge errors with a false positive rate of only 2.7%.

Keywords: Connectomics · 3d neural network · Merge error

1 Introduction

Recent advances in 3d electron microscopy (EM) have enabled synaptic-resolution volumetric imaging of brain tissue at unprecedented scale [1–3]. Semi-automated reconstructions of these volumes yield thousands of neurons and neuronal fragments, interconnected by millions of synapses [4–7]. Together, reconstructed neurons and synapses within each dataset describe a "connectome": a connectivity graph whose structure is anticipated to underlie the computational function of the tissue [8, 9].

Interpreting neural connectivity at this scale is a significant undertaking. One means to enhance interpretability is to use ultrastructural and morphological details of neuronal fragments to distinguish their functional subcompartments. For example, the classical description of "neuronal polarity", i.e. the flow of information within vertebrate neurons,

---

Electronic supplementary material The online version of this chapter (https://doi.org/10.1007/978-3-030-59722-1_9) contains supplementary material, which is available to authorized users.

A. L. Martel et al. (Eds.): MICCAI 2020, LNCS 12265, pp. 88–98, 2020.
https://doi.org/10.1007/978-3-030-59722-1_9

from dendritic subcompartments, into the soma, and out through the axon, remains central to understanding connectivity [10].

Although trained human reviewers can classify many neuronal fragments with respect to subcompartment, the growing scale of connectomic reconstructions demands automated methods. A recent approach to this problem was based on training random forest classifiers on manually defined features extracted from neurite segments and separately detected organelles such as mitochondria or synapses [4, 11]. A later extension improved accuracy by classifying 2d projections of neurites and their organelles with convolutional neural networks (CNNs), a technique called Cellular Morphology Networks (CMNs) [12]. However, an approach based on a full 3d representation of neuron fragments, which retains the maximum morphological and ultrastructural information, has not been previously demonstrated.

Another application for subcompartment predictions is in proofreading, e.g. to correct errors in automated reconstructions. Prior works proposed to detect merge errors through identification of morphologically unlikely cross-shaped fragments [11, 13] or used a 3d CNN trained specifically to detect merge [14] or split errors [15]. Strong biological priors dictate that vertebrate neurons have only one major axonal branch extending from the soma, and that dendritic and axonal subcompartments do not typically intermingle within a neurite [10]. Prior work used these cues to tune agglomeration via sparse subcompartment predictions in a multicut setting, which optimizes over an explicit edge-weighted supervoxel graph [16, 17]. Alternatively, violation of biological priors in subcompartment predictions can be used to detect post-agglomeration reconstruction errors, which can then be flagged for efficient human proof-reading workflows [18], or fully automated error correction.

In the following we (1) present a system for neuronal subcompartment classification based on 3d convolutional neural networks, (2) demonstrate finely localized subcompartment predictions whose accuracy exceeds state-of-the-art, and (3) show how these predictions can be used for high-fidelity detection and correction of agglomeration errors in an automated segmentation.

2   Materials and Methods

2.1   Datasets

We used an automated Flood-Filling Network (FFN) segmentation of a $114 \times 98 \times 96$ µm volume of zebra finch Area X brain tissue acquired with serial blockface EM at a voxel resolution of $9 \times 9 \times 20$ nm [5]. Base FFN supervoxels (SVs) were agglomerated (Fig. 1a) via FFN resegmentation, with additional post-processing applied to the agglomeration graph to reduce merge and split errors [9]. We also used precomputed organelle probability maps for synaptic junctions and vesicle clouds [4] in some experiments.

The agglomerated segmentation was skeletonized via TEASAR [19], and the resulting skeletons were sparsified to a mean inter-node spacing of 300 nm and eroded so that terminal nodes were at least 100 nm from the segment boundary. A subset of the objects in the volume were manually classified by human experts as axon, dendrite, or soma, of which 27 objects were used for training (32.8k axon, 8.4k dendrite, 7.5k soma nodes),

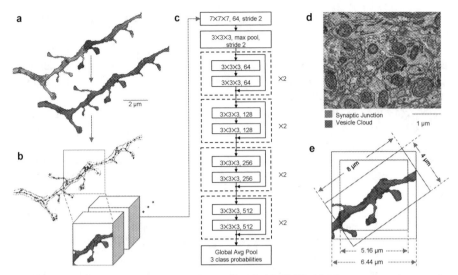

Fig. 1. Neural subcompartment classification with 3d CNN. (a) The segmentation consists of base SVs (top, different colors) that were agglomerated into more complete neuron segments (bottom, solid) [5]. **(b)** Input FOVs are centered at node positions from automated skeletonization of the segmentation mask. **(c)** The classifier architecture is a 3d extension of a ResNet-18 CNN, and outputs probabilities for axon, dendrite, and soma subcompartment classes. **(d)** For some experiments, we provided additional input channels, e.g. the contrast normalized [20] EM image, or precomputed organelle probability maps [4]. **(e)** Illustration of the two primary FOV sizes used in our experiments, approximately 5.16 or 6.44 μm on a side. For comparison, we also illustrate the neurite-aligned $4 \times 4 \times 8$ μm FOV employed by the previous CMN approach [12] (Color figure online).

6 objects for validation (2.6k, 1.0k, 2.0k), and 28 objects for evaluation (29.3k, 38.2k, 32.7k).

Datasets are available from the CMN authors on request [12].

2.2 Classification of Neural Subcompartment with 3d CNNs

Classifier input fields of view (FOVs) were centered at neuron skeleton node locations, with the segment mask extracted from the neuron's agglomerated segmentation (Fig. 1b). However, multiple axonal and dendritic processes from the same neuron sometimes pass close to each other, even if their connection point is far outside the FOV. Therefore, it was beneficial to remove segment mask components in the FOV that were not connected with the component at the center. Disconnected component removal was done at full $9 \times 9 \times 20$ nm resolution, prior to downsampling the block to the network input resolution.

Classifier architectures were derived from the ResNet-18 CNN model [21], with convolution and pooling layers extended to 3d (Fig. 1c). Neuronal morphology was provided to classifiers as a 3d binary segment mask. When additional input channels (EM image, organelle masks; Fig. 1d) were provided, the segment mask was applied to the other channels instead of being provided separately, with areas outside the mask set to zero. Input data was provided at $36 \times 36 \times 40$ nm resolution in blocks of 129 or 161 voxels on a side, for a total field of view of $4.64 \times 4.64 \times 5.16$ or $5.80 \times 5.80 \times 6.44$ μm respectively (Fig. 1e). Network output comprised probabilities for axon, dendrite, and soma subcompartment classes.

For training, the input locations were class balanced by resampling skeleton nodes for underrepresented classes multiple times per epoch. We also applied random 3d rotations to the input as a training data augmentation. Networks were trained via stochastic gradient descent, with learning rate 0.003 and batch size 64 for 1.5M steps. For the best performing network, with two input channels and 6.44 μm field of view, the total number of trainable parameters was 33.2M.

2.3   Automated Detection and Correction of Merge Errors

We applied top-performing subcompartment predictions (Fig. 2) to further improve neuron reconstruction quality by detecting merge errors between different classes. FFN reconstruction biases base SVs (Fig. 1a) to have very few merge errors via an over-segmentation consensus procedure [5], so we focused on errors in SV agglomeration. Once agglomeration errors are identified and localized, they can be fixed efficiently by simply removing the bad agglomeration graph edges, either under human review [18] or automatically.

We used subcompartment predictions to identify all somas and branches, and then to detect and correct two classes of agglomeration errors: axon/dendrite branch merge errors, and soma/neurite merge errors. As ground truth, we manually identified 132 agglomerated neurons that contained merge errors and annotated their bad agglomeration graph edges. This yielded 473 branches, among which there were 83 branch merge errors and 56 soma merge errors. Together these represent a significant fraction of all merge errors identified through an exhaustive screening of the reconstruction.

2.4   Branch Merge Error Correction by Graph Cut Consistency Score

Branch merge errors involve a mis-agglomerated axon and dendrite (Fig. 3a). Intuitively, branches that contain a merge error tend to have lower overall node prediction consistency (defined as weighted mean probability of dominant class type). Removing a bad agglomeration edge should improve the node consistency of the two resulting subgraphs.

The input to our system is the skeleton of the agglomerated neuron with node class predictions, and the neuron's agglomeration graph, where each skeleton node contains information about the base SV it belongs to. The workflow is as follows:

Step 1: Identify soma. If the segment has >200 soma classified nodes, find the SV with the most soma nodes.

Step 2: Separate branches from soma. After removing the primary soma SV, each remaining subgraph of the agglomeration graph is considered a branch if it contains >100 nodes.

Step 3: Compute node weights (optional). Automated skeletonization sometimes over-clusters nodes within thicker objects. Densely clustered nodes can optionally be down-weighted by 1/(node count in 500 nm radius - 2) to discount the nodes in excess of

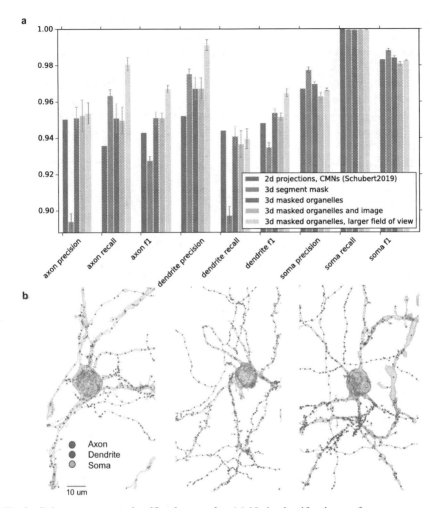

Fig. 2. Subcompartment classification results. (a) Node classification performance on axon, dendrite, and soma labeled examples. **(b)** Skeleton node classifications of three automated neuron reconstructions outside the train, validation, and evaluation sets (Color figure online).

the three expected within each 500 nm of clean path length. Furthermore, neurite nodes proximal to the soma (within 5–10 μm) tend to have inconsistent class predictions. These nodes can also be optionally down-weighted by 0.01, which effectively ignores them except in cases where soma proximal nodes are the only nodes on a branch.

Step 4: Group predictions. Node predictions are aggregated by base SV, to compute weighted mean class probabilities P_{SV} and node count w_{SV} for each SV (Fig. 3b).

Step 5: Compute cut scores. Any cycles are first removed, then edges are traversed from leaf nodes in. At each edge, the branch is conceptually divided into subgraphs G_{leave} and G_{remain}, and the "cut consistency score", a measure of how many nodes belong to

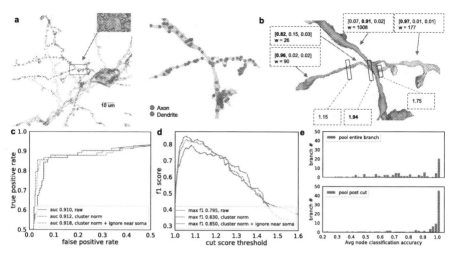

Fig. 3. Correction of branch merge errors via subcompartment prediction. (a) Left, view of an agglomerated segment centered on a branch merge error, with the node predictions for the branch overlaid. Inset shows the EM image and overlaid base SVs for the merge. Right, zoomed in view of the merge error, with base SVs in different colors. (b) Node predictions are aggregated to get class probabilities [axon, dendrite, soma] and weight (node count) per SV. Three SVs are predicted axon, one dendrite, reflecting the merge error. Candidate neuron cuts are annotated with their consistency improvement scores (Eq. 1). (c) ROC plot showing detection performance as the cut score threshold is varied. Separate curves show three variants with different node reweighting (to address node clustering or nodes close to the soma). (d) The f1 of merge detection versus cut score threshold. (e) Branch-wise majority vote pooled class accuracy distribution before (top) and after (bottom) applying suggested cuts (Color figure online).

their respective majority classes post-versus pre-cut, is computed (Fig. 3b):

$$\frac{\max \sum_{SV}^{G_{leave}} P_{SV} w_{SV} + \max \sum_{SV}^{G_{remain}} P_{SV} w_{SV}}{\max \sum_{SV}^{G_{branch}} P_{SV} w_{SV}} \tag{1}$$

Step 6: Detection. The highest predicted cut score is thresholded to determine if the branch contains a merge error, with constraints that G_{leave} and G_{remain} must have different majority class types and their weighted sizes must be >50.

Step 7: Correction (optional). The suggested agglomeration edge is removed, and majority vote pooling is performed within subcomponents. Branch pooled node prediction accuracy is compared pre- and post-cut (Fig. 3e).

2.5 Soma Merge Error Correction by Trajectory of Primary Neurite

The second error mode involves a neurite fragment that is mis-agglomerated with soma (Fig. 4). We observed that these errors can be fixed with a simple heuristic based on branch trajectory relative to the soma surface. The pipeline is as follows:

Steps 1–2: See branch merge detection pipeline above.

Step 3: Distance to soma. For each axon or dendrite node, compute the distance d_s to the nearest soma node.

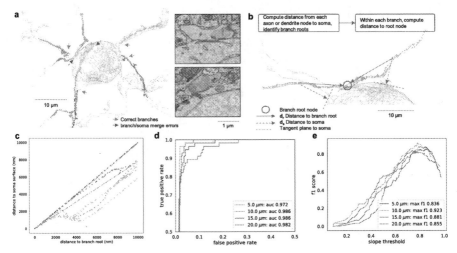

Fig. 4. Correction of soma merge errors. (**a**) Example of a soma with multiple neurite branches, each in a different color. Two of the branches were erroneously agglomerated to the soma. (**b**) For each node along a branch, the distance to the nearest soma node is computed. The distance to the branch root (defined as the branch node closest to the soma) is also computed. (**c**) The soma distance versus branch root distance for the nodes comprising branches from (a), with matching color-coding. The dashed line of slope 0.78 separates the trajectories of correct branches that run primarily radially out from the soma, from the soma merge error branches that run primarily tangential. (**d**) ROC plot showing performance of merge error detection as slope threshold is varied. Separate curves show results with nodes at different distances from the soma included in the analysis. (**e**) The f1 of merge error detection versus slope threshold (Color figure online).

Step 4: Distance to branch root. For each branch, the root is the node with minimum d_s. Compute the distance d_r from each branch node to the root (Fig. 4b).

Step 5: Fit slope. For each branch, compute a linear fit to d_s versus d_r (Fig. 4c) for nodes within a tunable distance to soma. The slope of the fit is then thresholded to determine if a branch is a soma merge error (Fig. 4c–e).

3   Results

3.1   Subcompartment Classification Performance of 3d CNNs

We compared the performance of our 3d CNN classifiers to previous state-of-the-art results from CMNs [12], in terms of class-wise precision, recall, and f1 metrics (Fig. 2a). For each trained 3d CNN, we saved parameter checkpoints throughout the training period and screened them on a small manually labeled validation set. For most models, performance on the validation set approached or exceeded 0.99 on all metrics (not shown), but validation performance was useful for tracking convergence, confirming there was no overfitting to the training set, and for avoiding checkpoints where training temporarily became unstable. We then applied the ten checkpoints with highest validation accuracy to the larger evaluation set to compute the mean and standard deviation for each metric.

Compared with CMNs (Fig. 2a, blue), a network analyzing voxel representation of 3d segment shape alone was competitive (green). Adding vesicle cloud and synaptic junction organelle probability map channels allowed the 3d CNN to exceed state of the art (red). Interestingly, further adding the full EM image channel had negligible impact (yellow). Expanding the field of view for the masked organelles network from 5.16 μm to 6.44 μm yielded the best performing system tested (pink). We also tested expanding the FOV further, increasing the input resolution, increasing the CNN depth, and providing different input channel configurations; see supplemental Table S1.

Of the top ten checkpoints from the best performing model, the median overall node accuracy on the evaluation set was 97.1%, and mean f1 across classes was 0.972. We then used this median checkpoint to predict node classes for reconstructed neurons and fragments throughout the entire volume. Predicted skeletons demonstrate good class consistency within soma and neurites, with some ambiguity at the interface between branch and soma (Fig. 2b). Based on the predictions, the volume contains 3.25 m total axon path length, and 0.79 m dendrite path length, a ratio of 4:1 that is similar to the 5:1 ratio previously reported [12]. However, the total path length here significantly exceeds that previously reported, probably due to differences in skeleton sparsity, so the absolute lengths here should be considered an upper bound.

3.2 Agglomeration Merge Error Detection and Correction

We fed subcompartment predictions back to detect and correct two classes of reconstruction merge errors that occur during SV agglomeration: axon/dendrite branch merges, and soma/neurite merges.

The branch merge error correction system is based on analyzing the predicted subcompartment class consistency of agglomerated segments, with and without candidate cuts applied (Fig. 3a–b). We first considered branch merge error detection performance, and plotted the receiver operating characteristic (ROC) curve by varying the cut score threshold (Fig. 3c–d). In areas with many small SVs, several nearby cut candidates can have equivalent impact, so predicted cuts that fell within four agglomeration graph edges of ground truth cuts were considered correctly detected. The best detection performance was at 1.05 cut score threshold, with f1 of 0.850 (see also Table S2).

Merge error detections can be used to flag the location for human review. We also calculated the node prediction accuracy improvement after directly applying the suggested cut. For the 96 branches with either a predicted merge or ground truth merge, we manually determined their nodewise ground truth class as axon or dendrite, then performed majority vote predicted class pooling before and after applying predicted cuts. Comparing class pooled accuracy pre- and post-cut (Fig. 3e), the mean node prediction accuracy improves from 0.804 to 0.886.

We addressed the second category of agglomeration merge errors, between somas and nearby neurites, by analyzing the trajectory of the branch relative to the somal surface (Fig. 4a–c). We found the best performance is achieved by sampling skeleton nodes within the initial 10 μm from the soma, yielding an f1 of 0.923 at a slope of 0.78 (Fig. 4d–e; see also Table S3).

Combined, branch and soma merge analyses detected 90.6% of merge errors, with a false positive rate of only 2.7%.

4 Conclusions and Discussion

To make volume EM datasets of brain tissue easy to analyze at scale, it is crucial to reduce the data they contain to more compact and semantically meaningful representations. Segmentation and synapse detection provide an important first step in this process. Here we presented a system that can provide further information about the biological identity of neurites by predicting subcompartment types, and feed back to the preceding reconstruction stage through automated correction of agglomeration errors.

We expect this approach to be useful for brain circuit analyses, and to be applicable to diverse datasets. We also anticipate that the approach could be extended to finer grained subcompartment classification. For example, the subcompartment localization of a postsynaptic site on e.g. a dendritic spine, dendritic shaft, soma, or axon initial segment is linked to both the synapse's functional impact as well as the identity of its presynaptic partner [22, 23]. Another related application is in the identification of neuronal subtypes, whose shared structural and functional properties can enhance connectome interpretability by organizing thousands of individual neurons into a reduced complement of conceptual roles [24–26].

The primary advantages of our system are its simplicity, and its ability to capture complete local information about a neurite, resulting in a new state of the art. A fundamental limitation is that processing efficiency drops with increasing field of view as the neurite of interest fills a progressively smaller fraction of the voxels that need to be processed. This limitation could be mitigated by using an alternative representation of sparse 3d data [27–31].

Acknowledgments. We thank Philipp Schubert and Jörgen Kornfeld for sharing detailed CMN results and training data, as well as the EM volume. We thank Jeremy Maitin-Shepard and the anonymous reviewers for comments on the manuscript.

References

1. Zheng, Z., Lauritzen, J.S., Perlman, E., et al.: A complete electron microscopy volume of the brain of adult drosophila melanogaster. Cell **174**, 730–743 (2018)
2. Dorkenwald, S., Turner, N.L., Macrina, T., et al.: Binary and analog variation of synapses between cortical pyramidal neurons. bioRxiv 2019.12.29.890319 (2019)
3. Shan Xu, C., Januszewski, M., Lu, Z., et al.: A connectome of the adult drosophila central brain. bioRxiv 2020.01.21.911859 (2020)
4. Dorkenwald, S., Schubert, P.J., Killinger, M.F., et al.: Automated synaptic connectivity inference for volume electron microscopy. Nat. Methods **14**, 435–442 (2017)
5. Januszewski, M., Kornfeld, J., Li, P.H., et al.: High-precision automated reconstruction of neurons with flood-filling networks. Nat. Methods **15**, 605–610 (2018)
6. Li, P.H., Lindsey, L.F., Januszewski, M., et al.: Automated reconstruction of a serial-section EM drosophila brain with flood-filling networks and local realignment. bioRxiv 605634 (2019)
7. Buhmann, J., Sheridan, A., Gerhard, S., et al.: Automatic detection of synaptic partners in a whole-brain drosophila EM dataset. bioRxiv 2019.12.12.874172 (2019)

8. Dasgupta, S., Stevens, C.F., Navlakha, S.: A neural algorithm for a fundamental computing problem. Science **358**, 793–796 (2017)
9. Kornfeld, J.M., Januszewski, M., Schubert, P.J., et al.: An anatomical substrate of credit assignment in reinforcement learning. bioRxiv 2020.02.18.954354 (2020)
10. Swanson, L.W., Lichtman, J.W.: From Cajal to connectome and beyond. Annu. Rev. Neurosci. **39**, 197–216 (2016)
11. Motta, A., Berning, M., Boergens, K.M., et al.: Dense connectomic reconstruction in layer 4 of the somatosensory cortex. Science **366**(6469) (2019)
12. Schubert, P.J., Dorkenwald, S., Januszewski, M., et al.: Learning cellular morphology with neural networks. Nat. Commun. **10**, 2736 (2019)
13. Meirovitch, Y., Matveev, A., Saribekyan, H., et al.: A multi-pass approach to large-scale connectomics. arXiv [q-bio.QM] (2016)
14. Rolnick, D., Meirovitch, Y., Parag, T., et al.: Morphological error detection in 3D segmentations. arXiv [cs.CV] (2017)
15. Haehn, D., Kaynig, V., Tompkin, J.: Guided proofreading of automatic segmentations for connectomics. In: Proceedings of the IEEE Conference on Computer Vision and Pattern Recognition (2018)
16. Krasowski, N.E., Beier, T., et al.: Neuron segmentation with high-level biological priors. IEEE Trans. Med. Imaging **37**(4), 829–839 (2017)
17. Pape, C., Matskevych, A., et al.: Leveraging domain knowledge to improve microscopy image segmentation with lifted multicuts. Front. Comput. Sci. **1**, 6 (2019)
18. Hubbard, P.M., Berg, S., Zhao, T., et al.: Accelerated EM connectome reconstruction using 3D visualization and segmentation graphs. BioRxiv (2020)
19. Sato, M., Bitter, I., Bender, M.A., et al.: TEASAR: tree-structure extraction algorithm for accurate and robust skeletons. In: Proceedings the Eighth Pacific Conference on Computer Graphics and Applications, pp 281–449 (2000)
20. Zuiderveld, K.: Contrast limited adaptive histogram equalization. In: Heckbert, P.S. (ed.) Graphics Gems IV, pp. 474–485. Academic Press Professional Inc., San Diego (1994)
21. He, K., Zhang, X., Ren, S., Sun, J.: Deep residual learning for image recognition. In: Proceedings of the IEEE Conference on Computer Vision and Pattern Recognition, pp 770–778 (2016)
22. Petilla Interneuron Nomenclature Group, Ascoli, G.A., Alonso-Nanclares, L., et al.: Petilla terminology: nomenclature of features of GABAergic interneurons of the cerebral cortex. Nat. Rev. Neurosci. **9**, 557–568 (2008)
23. Contreras, A., Hines, D.J., Hines, R.M.: Molecular specialization of GABAergic synapses on the soma and axon in cortical and hippocampal circuit function and dysfunction. Front. Mol. Neurosci. **12**, 154 (2019)
24. Jiang, X., Shen, S., Cadwell, C.R., et al.: Principles of connectivity among morphologically defined cell types in adult neocortex. Science **350**, aac9462 (2015)
25. Gouwens, N.W., Sorensen, S.A., Baftizadeh, F., et al.: Toward an integrated classification of neuronal cell types: morphoelectric and transcriptomic characterization of individual GABAergic cortical neurons. bioRxiv 2020.02.03.932244 (2020)
26. Grünert, U., Martin, P.R.: Cell types and cell circuits in human and non-human primate retina. Progress in Retinal and Eye Research, 100844 (2020)
27. Kipf, T.N., Welling, M.: Semi-supervised classification with graph convolutional networks. arXiv [cs.LG] (2016)
28. Qi, C.R., Su, H., Mo, K., Guibas, L.J.: PointNet: deep learning on point sets for 3D classification and segmentation. arXiv [cs.CV] (2016)
29. Riegler, G., Osman Ulusoy, A.: Octnet: learning deep 3d representations at high resolutions. In: Proceedings of the IEEE Conference on Computer Vision and Pattern Recognition (2017)

30. Mescheder, L., Oechsle, M., Niemeyer, M.: Occupancy networks: learning 3d reconstruction in function space. In: Proceedings of the IEEE Conference on Computer Vision and Pattern Recognition (2019)
31. Graham, B., Engelcke, M., Van Der Maaten, L.: 3d semantic segmentation with submanifold sparse convolutional networks. In: Proceedings of the IEEE Conference on Computer Vision and Pattern Recognition, pp. 9224–9232 (2018)

Microtubule Tracking in Electron Microscopy Volumes

Nils Eckstein[1,2(✉)], Julia Buhmann[1,2], Matthew Cook[2], and Jan Funke[1]

[1] HHMI Janelia Research Campus, Ashburn, USA
ecksteinn@janelia.hhmi.org
[2] Institute of Neuroinformatics UZH/ETHZ, Zurich, Switzerland

Abstract. We present a method for microtubule tracking in electron microscopy volumes. Our method first identifies a sparse set of voxels that likely belong to microtubules. Similar to prior work, we then enumerate potential edges between these voxels, which we represent in a candidate graph. Tracks of microtubules are found by selecting nodes and edges in the candidate graph by solving a constrained optimization problem incorporating biological priors on microtubule structure. For this, we present a novel integer linear programming formulation, which results in speed-ups of three orders of magnitude and an increase of 53% in accuracy compared to prior art (evaluated on three $1.2 \times 4 \times 4\,\mu$m volumes of *Drosophila* neural tissue). We also propose a scheme to solve the optimization problem in a block-wise fashion, which allows distributed tracking and is necessary to process very large electron microscopy volumes. Finally, we release a benchmark dataset for microtubule tracking, here used for training, testing and validation, consisting of eight $30 \times 1000 \times 1000$ voxel blocks ($1.2 \times 4 \times 4\,\mu$m) of densely annotated microtubules in the CREMI data set (https://github.com/nilsec/micron).

1 Introduction

Microtubules are part of the cytoskeleton of a cell and crucial for a variety of cellular processes such as structural integrity and intracellular transport of cargo [15]. They are of particular interest for the connectomics community, as they directly follow the morphology of neurons. Tracking of microtubules therefore provides additional structural information that can potentially be leveraged for guided proof-reading of neuron segmentation and aid in the identification of neural subcompartments such as backbones and twigs [17].

Manual tracking of microtubules faces the same limitations as neuron segmentation and synapse annotations. The resolution needed to discern individual structures of interest like neural arbors, synapses, and microtubules can only be achieved with high resolution electron microscopy (EM), which results in

Electronic supplementary material The online version of this chapter (https://doi.org/10.1007/978-3-030-59722-1_10) contains supplementary material, which is available to authorized users.

A. L. Martel et al. (Eds.): MICCAI 2020, LNCS 12265, pp. 99–108, 2020.
https://doi.org/10.1007/978-3-030-59722-1_10

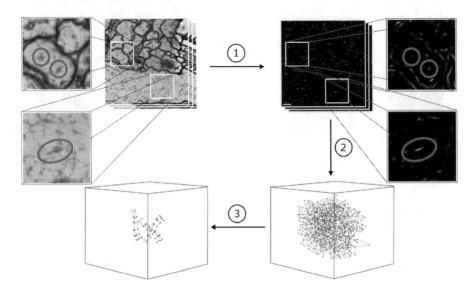

Fig. 1. Overview of the proposed method. **1.** Microtubule scores are predicted via a 3D UNet [16]. Inlets show two microtubules that run perpendicular to the imaging plane (appearing as circles) and one that deviates from a 90° angle of incidence (appearing as a line segment). The corresponding (noisy) microtubule scores show the necessity of post processing. **2.** Candidate microtubule segments are extracted and represented as vertices in a 3D graph, where vertices are connected within a threshold distance. **3.** Final microtubule trajectories are found by solving a constrained optimization problem.

large datasets (several hundred terabytes) even for small model organisms like *Drosophila melanogaster* [22]. With datasets of these sizes, a purely manual analysis becomes impractical. Consequently, the field of connectomics sparked a surge of automatic methods to segment neurons (for recent advances see [7,11,13,14]), annotate synapses [2,3,6,9,10,12,19], and identify other structures of biological relevance such as microtubules [4] or mitochondria [5,6,21]. Large scale automatic reconstruction of microtubules is a particularly challenging problem. With an outer diameter of 24 nm, microtubules are close to the resolution limit of serial section EM[1]. Especially in anisotropic EM volumes, the appearance of microtubules changes drastically depending on their angle of incidence to the imaging plane. Furthermore, they are often locally indistinguishable from other cell organelles (like endoplasmic reticulum) or noise.

Our method for microtubule tracking is based on the formulation proposed in [4], with significant improvements in terms of efficiency and accuracy. Similar to [4], we first predict a score for each voxel to be part of a microtubule. We then identify promising candidate points and possible links between them in a candidate graph as nodes and edges. Finally, we solve a constraint optimization problem incorporating biological priors to find a subset of edges that constitute microtubule tracks (for an overview see Fig. 1).

---

[1] Resolution is around $4 \times 4 \times 40$ nm for ssTEM, and $8 \times 8 \times 8$ nm for FIB-SEM [20].

Our four main contributions are as follows: 1. We propose a new integer linear program (ILP) formulation, which decreases the time needed to solve the constraint optimization by several orders of magnitude. 2. We devise a scheme to solve the resulting optimization problem in a block-wise fashion in linear time, and thus are able to process real-world sized volumes. 3. Our formulation allows tracking of microtubules in arbitrary orientations in anisotropic volumes by introducing a non-maxima suppression (NMS) based candidate extraction method. 4. We improve the voxel-level classifier by training a 3D UNet [7,16] on skeleton annotations, leading to more accurate microtubule scores.

We evaluate our method on a new benchmark comprising 153.6 μm^3 of densely traced microtubules, demonstrating a 53% increase in accuracy (0.517 → 0.789 F1 score) compared to the prior state of the art. Source code and datasets are publicly available at https://github.com/nilsec/micron.

2 Method

2.1 Predictions

Starting from the raw EM input data, we train a 3D UNet [16] to predict a microtubule score $m \in [0,1]$ for each voxel. We generate microtubule scores for training from manually annotated skeletons by interpolating between skeleton markers on a voxel grid followed by Gaussian smoothing. In addition, we train the network to predict spatial gradients of the microtubule score up to second order. This is motivated by the idea that the spatial gradient encodes the local shape of a predicted object. Since microtubule segments have locally line-like shapes this auxiliary task potentially regularises microtubule score predictions.

2.2 Candidate Extraction

Given the predicted microtubule score we perform candidate extraction via two NMS passes, to guarantee that two successive candidates of a single microtubule track are not farther apart than the distance threshold θ_d we will use to connect two candidates with each other. In a first pass, we perform NMS and thresholding with a stride equal to the NMS window size, guaranteeing at least one candidate per NMS window if the maximum is above the threshold. This strategy is problematic if the local maximum lies on the boarder or corner of a NMS window as this produces multiple, in the worst case eight, candidates that are direct neighbors of each other. We remove this redundancy by performing a second NMS pass on the already extracted maxima, providing us with the final set of microtubule segment candidate detections C.

2.3 Constrained Optimization

Following [4], we represent each candidate microtubule segment $i \in C$ as a node in a graph with an associated position $p_i = (x_i, y_i, z_i)$. A priori we do not know which microtubule segments $i \in C$ belong together and form a microtubule. Thus, we connect all microtubule candidates with each other that are below a certain distance threshold θ_d. More formally, we introduce an undirected graph $G = (V, E)$, where $V = C \cup \{S\}$ is the set of microtubule candidate segments C augmented with a special node S and $E \subset V \times V$ is the set of possible links between them. The special node S is used to mark the beginning or end of a microtubule track and is connected to all candidates in C. We further define a set $T = \{(i, j, k) \in V \times C \times V \mid (i, j), (j, k) \in E, i \neq k\}$ of all directly connected triplets on G.

As observed in [4], we can make use of the fact that microtubules do not branch and have limited curvature [8]. We encode these priors as constraints and costs respectively, and solve the resulting optimization problem with an ILP. As outlined in Fig. 2, and in contrast to [4], we formulate consistency and "no-branch" constraints on triplets of connected nodes $(i, j, k) \in T$ only, leading to an orders of magnitude improvement in ILP solve time (see Fig. 4). To this end, we introduce a binary indicator variable $I_{i,j,k} \in \{0, 1\}$ for each $(i, j, k) \in T$ and define selection costs $c_{i,j,k}$ for each triplet by propagating costs c_i on nodes

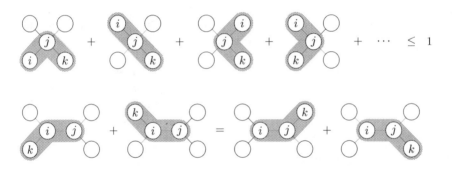

(a) Consistency constraints (top row) and no-branch constraints (bottom row).

$$\min_{I_{i,j,k}} \quad \sum_{i \in V} c_i \cdot I_i + \sum_{(i,j) \in E} c_{i,j} \cdot I_{i,j} + \sum_{(i,j,k) \in T} c_{i,j,k} \cdot I_{i,j,k}$$

s.t.

$$\begin{aligned}
\forall (i,j,k) \in T: & \quad I_i, I_{i,j}, I_{i,j,k} \in \{0, 1\} \\
\forall i \in V: & \quad 2I_i - \sum_{(i,j) \in E} I_{i,j} = 0 \\
\forall (i,j) \in E: & \quad 2I_{i,j} - I_i - I_j \leq 0 \\
\forall (i,j,k) \in T: & \quad 2I_{i,j,k} - I_{i,j} - I_{j,k} \leq 0 \\
& \quad -I_{i,j,k} + I_{i,j} + I_{j,k} \leq 1
\end{aligned}$$

$$\min_{I_{i,j,k}} \quad \sum_{(i,j,k) \in T} c_{i,j,k} \cdot I_{i,j,k}$$

s.t.

$$\begin{aligned}
\forall (i,j,k) \in T: & \quad I_{i,j,k} \in \{0, 1\} \\
\forall j \in V: & \quad \sum_{(i,j,k) \in T} I_{i,j,k} \leq 1 \\
\forall (i,j) \in E: & \quad \sum_{(k,i,j) \in T} I_{k,i,j} - \sum_{(i,j,k) \in T} I_{i,j,k} = 0
\end{aligned}$$

(b) ILP following [4].   (c) Reformulated ILP on triplet indicators.

Fig. 2. Constraint optimization on the candidate graph. We formulate an ILP on binary triplet indicators, which encode the joint selection of two incident candidate edges. The constraints shown in (a) ensure that found tracks are not crossing or splitting. Although mathematically equivalent to the formulation in (b), our formulation (c) is orders of magnitudes more efficient (see Fig. 4).

and $c_{i,j}$ on edges as follows:

$$c_i = \begin{cases} \theta_S \text{ if } i = S \\ \theta_P \text{ else} \end{cases} \quad \begin{aligned} c_{i,j} &= \theta_D \text{ dist}(i,j) + \theta_E \text{ evid}(i,j) + c_i + c_j \\ c_{i,j,k} &= \theta_C \text{ curv}(i,j,k) + c_{i,j} + c_{j,k} \end{aligned}, \quad (1)$$

where θ_S is the cost for beginning/ending a track and $\theta_P < 0$ is the prior on node selection. $\text{dist}(i,j) = \|p_i - p_j\|$ measures the distance between candidates i and j, whereas $\text{evid}(i,j) = \sum_{p \in P_{i,j}} m(p)$ accumulates the predicted evidence for microtubules on all voxels on a line $P_{i,j}$ connecting i and j. $\text{curv}(i,j,k) = \pi - \angle(i,j,k)$ measures deviations of a 180° angle between two pairs of edges, and thus introduces a cost on curvature. The values $\theta_S, \theta_P, \theta_D, \theta_E, \theta_C \in \mathbb{R}$ are free parameters of the method and found via grid search on a validation dataset.

2.4 Blockwise Processing

In order to be able to apply the constraint optimization to arbitrary sized volumes, we decompose the candidate graph spatially into a set of blocks B. For each block $b \in B$, we define a constant-size context region $\bar{b}$, which encloses the block and is chosen to be large enough such that decisions outside the context region are unlikely to change the ILP solution inside the block. We next identify sets $S_i \subset B$ of blocks that are pairwise conflict free, where we define two blocks a and b to be in conflict if a overlaps with $\bar{b}$. All blocks of a subset S_i can then be distributed and processed in parallel. The corresponding ILP for each block $b \in S_i$ is solved within $\bar{b}$, however, assignments of the binary indicators are only stored for indicators corresponding to nodes in b. To obtain consistent solutions across block boundaries, existing indicator assignments from previous runs of conflicting blocks are acknowledged by adding additional constraints to the block ILP. See Fig. 5 and supplement for an illustration.

2.5 Evaluation

To evaluate reconstructed tracks against groundtruth, we resample both reconstruction and groundtruth tracks equidistantly and match nodes based on distance using Hungarian matching. Results are reported in terms of precision and recall on edges, which we consider correct if they connect two matched nodes that are matched to the same track.

3 Results

3.1 Dataset

We densely annotated microtubules in eight $1.2 \times 4 \times 4\,\mu\text{m}$ ($30 \times 1000 \times 1000$ voxel) volumes of EM data in all six CREMI[2] volumes A, B, C, A+, B+, C+ using Knossos [1] and split the data in training (A+, B+, C+), validation (B+$_v$, B$_v$) and test (A, B, C) sets.

___

[2] MICCAI Challenge on Circuit Reconstruction in EM Images, https://cremi.org.

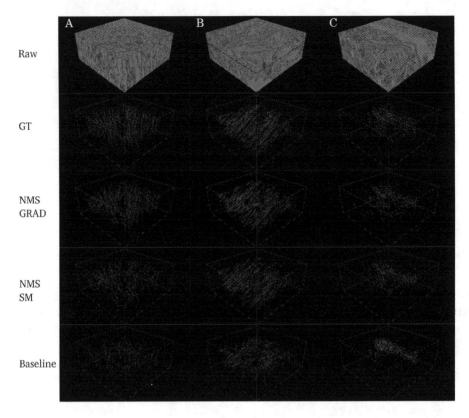

Fig. 3. 3D rendering of raw EM volumes (Raw), manual tracing (GT) and automatically reconstructed microtubules in CREMI volumes A, B, C for our method (NMS_GRAD and NMS_SM) and the considered baseline [4] using validation best ILP parameters (best viewed on screen). (Color figure online)

3.2   Comparison

NMS_* models refer to the model described in the methods section, where NMS_SM uses a 3D UNet predicting microtubule score only, NMS_GRAD additionally predicts spatial gradients of the microtubule score up to second order and NMS_RFC uses a random forest classifier (RFC) instead of a 3D UNet. For each, we first select the best performing UNet architecture (for NMS_RFC we interactively train an RFC using Ilastik [18]) and NMS candidate extraction threshold in terms of recovered candidates on the validation datasets, followed by a grid search over the distance threshold θ_d and ILP parameters for 150 different parameter combinations. For the NMS candidate extraction we use a window size of $1 \times 10 \times 10$ voxels for the first NMS pass to offset the anisotropic resolution of $40 \times 4 \times 4$ nm. For the second NMS pass we use a window size of $1 \times 3 \times 3$ voxels, removing double detections.

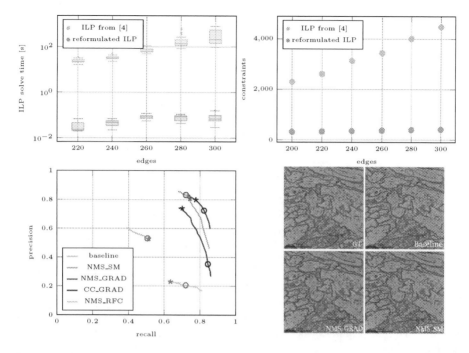

Fig. 4. Top row: comparison of ILP formulations on random candidate graphs in terms of solve time (left) and number of constraints (right). Solve times have been obtained from 54 different ILP parameter configurations $\theta_{S,P,D,E,C}$ on an Intel Xeon(R), 2.40 GHz x 16 CPU processor using the Gurobi optimizer. **Bottom row, left:** Comparison of our method (NMS_SM and NMS_GRAD) to the baseline [4] and two ablation experiments CC_GRAD (NMS replaced with connected component candidate extraction) and NMS_RFC (UNet replaced with RFC). Shown are precision and recall for varying values of the start/end edge prior θ_S averaged over the test datasets A, B, C. The validation and test best are highlighted with circles and stars, respectively. **Bottom row, right:** Qualitative results on sample B (best viewed on screen). (Color figure online)

Baseline refers to an adaptation[3] of the method in [4], that uses an RFC for prediction, z section-wise connected component (CC) analysis on the thresholded microtubule scores for candidate extraction, and a fixed orientation estimate for each microtubule candidate pointing in the z direction[4]. For the baseline we interactively train two (for microtubules of different angles of incidence on the imaging plane) RFCs on training volumes A, B, C using Ilastik [18]. We find the threshold for CC candidate extraction, distance threshold θ_d and ILP parameters via grid search over 242 parameter configurations on the validation set. For an overview see Table 1.

---

[3] We use our ILP formulation, which was necessary to process larger volumes.

[4] Orientation estimate used in [4] (direct communication with authors).

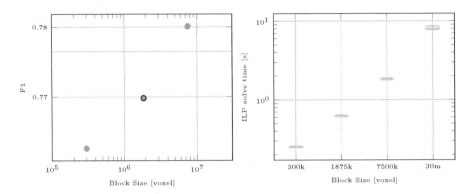

Fig. 5. Left: Accuracy as a function of block size over several orders of magnitude. Shown are the F1 scores, averaged over test data sets A, B and C, using validation best parameters NMS_GRAD. Interestingly, for some sizes, solving the ILP blockwise results in higher F1 scores than solving the ILP to global optimality (blue line). However, it should be noted that the differences in F1 score are minor and likely not significant. The black circle indicates the block size we used for all reported results. **Right**: Box plot of ILP solve time per block as a function of block size. Shown is the wall-clock time needed to solve the ILP for one block, measured for ten runs, on test cube B using validation best parameters NMS_GRAD. Note that in contrast to accuracy, solve time is strongly affected by block size. This implies that we are able to process large volumes by solving the ILP in a blockwise manner, without a significant decrease in accuracy. (Color figure online)

Table 1. Model overview and test best F1 score by data set.

Model	Prediction	Cand. Extr	Edge Score	A	B	C	Avg.
NMS_GRAD	UNet+GRAD	NMS	Evidence	**0.784**	0.827	0.757	**0.789**
NMS_SM	UNet	NMS	Evidence	0.711	**0.828**	**0.785**	0.775
Baseline	RFC	CC	Orientation	0.454	0.547	0.549	0.517
CC_GRAD	UNet+GRAD	CC	Evidence	0.660	0.723	0.537	0.640
NMS_RFC	RFC	NMS	Evidence	0.366	0.375	0.302	0.348

3.3   Test Results

Figure 4 shows that both variants of our proposed model outperform the prior state of the art [4] substantially. Averaged over test data sets A, B, C, we demonstrate a 53% increase in accuracy for NMS_GRAD. Table 1 further shows test best F1 scores for each individual dataset. In accordance with the qualitative results shown in Fig. 3, NMS_GRAD performs substantially better for test set A while NMS_SM is more accurate for volumes B and C. Ablation experiments show that CC candidate extraction leads to overall less accurate reconstructions. Exchanging the UNet with an RFC while retaining NMS candidate extraction seriously harms performance, resulting in large numbers of false positive detections. For extended qualitative results, including reconstruction of micro-tubules in the Calyx, a $76 \times 52 \times 64\,\mu\text{m}$ region of the *Drosophila Melanogaster* brain, see supplement.

4   Discussion

Although some of our improvements in accuracy can be attributed to the use of a deep learning classifier, the presented method relies mostly on an effective way of incorporating biological priors in the form of constraint optimization. In particular our ablation studies (CC_GRAD) show that the strided NMS-based candidate extraction method positively impacts accuracy: Since a single micro-tubule could potentially extend far in the x-y imaging plane, it is not sufficient to represent candidates in one plane by a single node, as done in [4]. The strided NMS detections homogenize the candidate graph and likely allow transferring our method to datasets of different resolutions. A potential downside is poor pre-cision when combined with extremely noisy microtubule score predictions m (see NMS_RFC). In this case NMS on a grid extracts too many candidate segments, and besides structural priors, the only remaining cost we use to extract final microtubule tracks is directly derived from the (noisy) predicted microtubule score m (see Eq. (1)). Note that the baseline does not suffer as much from noisy microtubule scores, because it uses a fixed orientation prior and is thus limited to a subset of microtubules in any given volume. Finally, the reformulation of the ILP and the block-wise processing scheme result in a dramatic speed-up and the ability to perform distributed, consistent tracking, which is required to process petabyte-sized datasets.

Acknowledgements. We thank Tri Nguyen and Caroline Malin-Mayor for code con-tribution; Arlo Sheridan for helpful discussions and Albert Cardona for his contagious enthusiasm and support. This work was supported by Howard Hughes Medical Institute and Swiss National Science Foundation (SNF grant 205321L 160133).

References

1. Boergens, K.M., et al.: Webknossos: efficient online 3d data annotation for connec-tomics. Nat. Methods **14**(7), 691–694 (2017)
2. Buhmann, J., et al.: Synaptic partner prediction from point annotations in insect brains. In: Frangi, A.F., Schnabel, J.A., Davatzikos, C., Alberola-López, C., Fichtinger, G. (eds.) MICCAI 2018. LNCS, vol. 11071, pp. 309–316. Springer, Cham (2018). https://doi.org/10.1007/978-3-030-00934-2_35
3. Buhmann, J., et al.: Automatic detection of synaptic partners in a whole-brain drosophila em dataset. bioRxiv (2019). https://doi.org/10.1101/2019.12.12.874172
4. Buhmann, J.M., Gerhard, S., Cook, M., Funke, J.: Tracking of microtubules in anisotropic volumes of neural tissue. In: 2016 IEEE 13th International Symposium on Biomedical Imaging (ISBI) (2016). https://doi.org/10.1109/isbi.2016.7493275
5. Cheng, H.C., Varshney, A.: Volume segmentation using convolutional neural net-works with limited training data. In: 2017 IEEE International Conference on Image Processing (ICIP), pp. 590–594. IEEE (2017)

6. Dorkenwald, S., et al.: Automated synaptic connectivity inference for volume electron microscopy. Nat. Methods **14**(4), 435–442 (2017)

7. Funke, J., et al.: Large scale image segmentation with structured loss based deep learning for connectome reconstruction. IEEE Trans. Pattern Anal. Mach. Intell., 1 (2018). https://doi.org/10.1109/TPAMI.2018.2835450

8. Gittes, F., Mickey, B., Nettleton, J., Howard, J.: Flexural rigidity of microtubules and actin filaments measured from thermal fluctuations in shape. J. Cell Biol. **120**(4), 923–934 (1993)

9. Heinrich, L., Funke, J., Pape, C., Nunez-Iglesias, J., Saalfeld, S.: Synaptic cleft segmentation in non-isotropic volume electron microscopy of the complete *Drosophila* brain. In: Frangi, A.F., Schnabel, J.A., Davatzikos, C., Alberola-López, C., Fichtinger, G. (eds.) MICCAI 2018. LNCS, vol. 11071, pp. 317–325. Springer, Cham (2018). https://doi.org/10.1007/978-3-030-00934-2_36

10. Huang, G.B., Scheffer, L.K., Plaza, S.M.: Fully-automatic synapse prediction and validation on a large data set. Frontiers Neural Circuits **12**, 87 (2018)

11. Januszewski, M., et al.: High-precision automated reconstruction of neurons with flood-filling networks. Nat. Methods, 1 (2018)

12. Kreshuk, A., Funke, J., Cardona, A., Hamprecht, F.A.: Who is talking to whom: synaptic partner detection in anisotropic volumes of insect brain. In: Navab, N., Hornegger, J., Wells, W.M., Frangi, A.F. (eds.) MICCAI 2015. LNCS, vol. 9349, pp. 661–668. Springer, Cham (2015). https://doi.org/10.1007/978-3-319-24553-9_81

13. Lee, K., Lu, R., Luther, K., Seung, H.S.: Learning Dense Voxel Embeddings for 3D Neuron Reconstruction. arXiv e-prints arXiv:1909.09872, September 2019

14. Lee, K., Zung, J., Li, P., Jain, V., Seung, H.S.: Superhuman accuracy on the snemi3d connectomics challenge. arXiv preprint arXiv:1706.00120 (2017)

15. Nogales, E.: Structural insights into microtubule function. Annu. Rev. Biochem. **69**(1), 277–302 (2000)

16. Ronneberger, O., Fischer, P., Brox, T.: U-net: convolutional networks for biomedical image segmentation. In: Navab, N., Hornegger, J., Wells, W.M., Frangi, A.F. (eds.) MICCAI 2015. LNCS, vol. 9351, pp. 234–241. Springer, Cham (2015). https://doi.org/10.1007/978-3-319-24574-4_28

17. Schneider-Mizell, C.M., et al.: Quantitative neuroanatomy for connectomics in drosophila. eLife **5**, e12059 (2016)

18. Sommer, C., Straehle, C.N., Koethe, U., Hamprecht, F.A., et al.: Ilastik: Interactive learning and segmentation toolkit. In: ISBI, vol. 2, p. 8 (2011)

19. Staffler, B., et al.: Synem, automated synapse detection for connectomics. Elife **6**, e26414 (2017)

20. Takemura, S.y., et al.: Synaptic circuits and their variations within different columns in the visual system of drosophila. Proc. Nat. Acad. Sci. **112**(44), 13711–13716 (2015)

21. Xiao, C., et al.: Automatic mitochondria segmentation for EM data using a 3D supervised convolutional network. Frontiers Neuroanat. **12**, 92 (2018). https://doi.org/10.3389/fnana.2018.00092. https://www.frontiersin.org/article/10.3389/fnana.2018.00092

22. Zheng, Z., et al.: A complete electron microscopy volume of the brain of adult drosophila melanogaster. Cell **174**(3), 730–743 (2018)

Leveraging Tools from Autonomous Navigation for Rapid, Robust Neuron Connectivity

Nathan Drenkow[1], Justin Joyce[1], Jordan Matelsky[1], Jennifer Heiko[2], Reem Larabi[2], Brock Wester[1], Dean Kleissas[1], and William Gray-Roncal[1]([⊠])

[1] The Johns Hopkins University Applied Physics Laboratory,
Laurel, MD 20723, USA
`william.gray.roncal@jhuapl.edu`
[2] The Johns Hopkins University, Baltimore, MD 21218, USA

Abstract. As biological imaging datasets continue to grow in size, extracting information from large image volumes presents a computationally intensive challenge. State-of-the-art algorithms are almost entirely dominated by the use of convolutional neural network approaches that may be difficult to run at scale given schedule, cost, and resource limitations. We demonstrate a novel solution for high-resolution electron microscopy brain image volumes that permits the identification of individual neurons and synapses. Instead of conventional approaches where voxels are labelled according to the neuron or neuron segment to which they belong, we instead focus on extracting the underlying brain graph represented by synaptic connections between individual neurons, while also identifying key features like skeleton similarity and path length. This graph represents a critical step and scaffold for understanding the structure of neuronal circuitry. Our approach, which we call Agents, recasts the segmentation problem to one of path finding between keypoints (i.e., connectivity) in an information sharing framework using virtual agents. We create a family of sensors which follow local decision-making rules that perform computationally cheap operations on potential fields to perform tasks such as avoiding cell membranes and finding synapses. These enable a swarm of virtual agents to efficiently and robustly traverse three-dimensional datasets, create a sparse segmentation of pathways, and capture connectivity information. We achieve results that meet or exceed state-of-the-art performance at a substantially lower computational cost. Agents offers a categorically different approach to connectome estimation that can augment how we extract connectivity information at scale. Our method is generalizable and may be extended to biomedical imaging problems such as tracing the bronchial trees in lungs or road networks in natural images.

Keywords: Connectomics · Neuroscience · Computer vision

© Springer Nature Switzerland AG 2020
A. L. Martel et al. (Eds.): MICCAI 2020, LNCS 12265, pp. 109–118, 2020.
https://doi.org/10.1007/978-3-030-59722-1_11

1   Introduction

Connectomics is the study of structural and functional connections in the nervous system. Recent advances have allowed for large-scale imaging at the nanoscale, providing new capabilities for identifying single cells and their connections within larger brain networks. However, accurately and rapidly estimating these connections is a major bottleneck. Our approach represents a different way to directly map the connectivity between all neurons in a volume, as well as targeted sparse tracing of single neurons.

Current approaches often frame circuit reconstruction as a segmentation problem that aims to label every pixel according to the structure to which it belongs (e.g., `neuron`, `synapse`, `membrane`) [6,7]. Such methods are not optimized for graph generation and typically operate over local sub-volumes due to computational or memory limitations that arise as a result of the large size of neural datasets (e.g., terabytes or petabytes of raw data). Scaling these approaches often leads to accumulated errors (e.g., large-scale merges) and sensitivity to noise (e.g., poor quality or missing data, mis-alignments, ambiguities from imaging artifacts).

In this work we explore a new approach to automated tracing. The state-of-the-art neuron segmentation algorithm, flood-filling networks [4], is reported to take on the order of 4.6 PFLOPs (an immense amount of computation) for a $5200 \times 5200 \times 5120\,\text{nm}$ subvolume. Connectome reconstruction is currently beyond the capabilities of many research groups; further, much of the information produced may be unnecessary to explore initial questions leveraging directed, weighted graphs (e.g., information pathways, typical and pathological circuit patterns).

Our proposed approach seeks to provide a fast, scalable, and CPU-based method for generating neuron connectivity traces in EM volumes as an alternative to current approaches that are more difficult to scale and are driven by expensive GPUs. Our method allows for trade-offs between speed and accuracy, producing coarse models that can be refined over time. Our approach provides both neuron topology and approximate morphology (sometimes referred to as a 'sketch connectome',) but also allows for direct generation of brain network connectivity.

Our tracing method, which we call Agents, is inspired by previous work on dynamic co-fields (DCF) [1,5] which introduced a method for controlling the movement of a mobile autonomous agent swarm through the use of coordination fields. We re-frame the neuron tracing problem as one where autonomous agents trace an EM volume utilizing the outputs of a series of weighted potential fields as local decision making rules to seek out unexplored regions and search for synapses. Dynamic weighting of these fields allows our model to be robust to data defects, one of the current challenges in the field.

We demonstrate the fast, scalable and robust qualities of this agent-based approach for both large-scale connectome generation as well as targeted neuron tracing. We also demonstrate how brain graphs can be directly derived from agent traces. We believe that optimizing for topology instead of morphology provides a more rapid and complementary method for global scene understanding and network reconstruction, compared to current state-of-the-art methods.

2   METHODS

2.1   Overview

Our approach recasts the pixel-level segmentation problem to one of real-time graph extraction using virtual agents. These agents are spawned at putative synapse locations and at regular intervals throughout the volume. At each time step, agents use characteristics of the surrounding 3D space combined with local decision making rules implemented as sensors, each of which contributes updates to the agent's velocity (i.e., direction and speed) illustrated in Fig. 1. Equipped with sensors, agents frequently and efficiently sample information about their own history and their local environment and modify their behavior according to new observations.

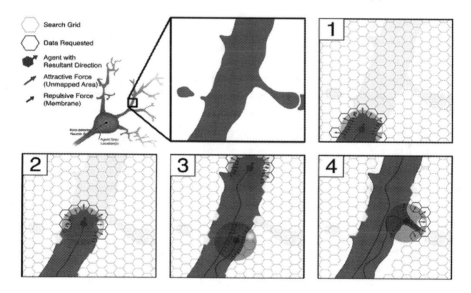

Fig. 1. To trace neurons, image data is re-interpreted as a series of fields which contribute forces that motivate agent behavior. (1–3) Agents are repelled from locations that have already been traversed by other agents. (3) An agent is spawned and is simultaneously attracted to unexplored regions and repelled from membranes. (4) cooperative exploration motivates exploration of small processes in search of synapses.

At the conclusion of an experiment, agents are merged through spatial proximity. These combined location histories result in point sets that each represent pathways in a single neuron. These trajectories are used with the synapses found by the agents to directly form the output graph (i.e., synaptic connections between neurons). The agent-based approach enables parallel cooperative tracing of multiple neurons. Agents can be trivially parallelized across CPU cores and can be easily run on consumer hardware.

2.2 Fields

In the DCF paradigm, coordination fields, F_i, encode contextual information that agents sense and rely on to dictate their behavior. Fields provide a representation of the input space, and sensors perform arithmetic operations on these fields to yield useful decisions. In our EM connectomics application, relevant fields include membrane and synapse maps, agent exploration fields, and boundary maps.

Membrane fields are obtained by performing a cheap segmentation of the EM data (using a U-Net architecture) [9], applying a threshold to the probability maps, and performing a morphological closing operation to remove small gaps. As such, membrane field, F_m, is a binary field such that $F_m(x, y, z) = F_m(\boldsymbol{p}) = 1$ when located on a membrane or 0 when located in free space. Directional Sobel filters applied to the membrane field produce vectors that point away from the edges, and these values are stored in a lookup table. By varying filter sizes, the sensor can be robust to the defects that result from imperfections that remain in the post-processed U-Net output. The synapse field, F_s is obtained by a similar approach, but with an opposite direction to attract agents. Sensors are tuned to minimize accidental membrane crossings, which result in false merges.

Another field type is used to manage boundary crossings; agents that hit a data (sub-volume) boundary can be spawned in the adjacent sub-volume, aiding in merging decisions and facilitating parallelization. This allows agents to scale to arbitrarily large image volumes without a costly and error prone merging step that can adversely affect graph generation. The boundary field, F_b is set to 1 within p voxels of the data volume edges and 0 elsewhere.

An exploration field is maintained by the swarm to account for visited regions; agents will sense locally and move towards unexplored areas. In a distributed framework, agents may broadcast and receive updates from other agents that can be used to update their local field and promote collaborative behavior. The exploration field F_e is updated as $F_e(\boldsymbol{p}) = 1$ for locations $\boldsymbol{p}_i = (x_i, y_i, z_i)$ visited by agents exploring the volume.

2.3 Agents

Agents are virtual entities that are atomically defined by their real-valued position $(\boldsymbol{p})$ and velocity vector $(\boldsymbol{v})$ and are equipped with a set of sensors which allow them to observe their environment. At each time step, every agent modifies its velocity by the weighted sum of the unit vectors returned by each of its sensors and subsequently updates its position by this velocity.

Agents can be throttled by constraining them to a maximum velocity (s_{max}), preventing runoff. Different sets of agents can be given different sets of sensors as well, allowing some to be 'specialists.'

2.4   Sensors

A sensor $S_i(p, F_i; \theta_i)$ receives the current position and appropriate field F_i and is parameterized according to θ_i which may describe the range, direction, or other relevant aspects of the sensing operation. Sensors produce an influence vector v_{F_i} which summarizes the direction in which the agent should move next as determined by the local values of a particular field. For instance, a simple membrane sensor could be implemented according to Eq. 1 relying on the fact that $F_m(p)$ is 1 at membranes and 0 elsewhere:

$$S_m(p_o, F_m; r) = \sum_{p \in \mathcal{P}} -F_m(p)(p - p_o)$$

$$\mathcal{P} = \{p : ||p - p_o||_2 < r\}$$

(1)

Sensors create influence vectors directly from field output, as is the case for the membrane avoidance sensor. Agents can also perform operations on these influence vectors to produce further useful information. For example, taking the vectors orthogonal to the membrane avoidance sensor yields a useful wall follower sensor. Sensors can perform operations on agents, like killing an agent when it hits a wall and spawning a new agent in a new unexplored area of the volume.

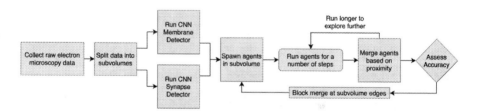

Fig. 2. The agents workflow starts with an image volume, traces neuronal pathways with Agents, and creates output graphs.

2.5   Agent-Based Framework

In our agent-based framework, described in Fig. 2, we combine the co-fields, agents, and sensors as follows: Given a set of fields and sensors, our agent moves according to Eq. 2, where each sensor for each agent retrieves its corresponding influence vector $S_i(p_t, F_i; \theta_i)$, which is scaled by a weight α_i (which can be tuned manually or found via hyperparameter search methods). Each weighted vector is summed and added to the current agent velocity, and this new velocity is used to calculate the agent's next position.

$$v_{t+1} = \sum_i (\alpha_i \cdot S_i(p_t, F_i; \theta_i)) + v_t$$

$$= \sum_i (\alpha_i \cdot v_{F_i}) + v_t$$

(2)

$$\boldsymbol{p}_{t+1} = \boldsymbol{p}_t + s_{max} \cdot \boldsymbol{v}_{t+1} \tag{3}$$

As agents move through image space, agent state information is recorded, including position and velocity histories as well as synapses visited, facilitating exploration. Agent consensus can be used to create confidence maps of neuron segmentation, which can be helpful for tracing coarse neuron morphologies even under suboptimal weight parameters.

2.6   Graph Generation

After exploring an image volume, the connectivity graph can be recovered by fusing agent path histories to determine synapse ownership and connectivity. Paths can be fused by simply considering voxel level overlap; we can extend these ideas to analyze path trajectories and resolve ambiguities. The outputs of the merge are the sets of agent path histories that are connected. By combining these merge sets with the identified synaptic connections, a graph can be created. When synapses are annotated as point annotations denoting the pre- and post-synaptic terminal locations (as is popular in fly data), the merged agents at the pre-synaptic site are connected to the merged agents at the post-synaptic site, creating a directed edge.

3   Experiments and Results

Our approach was primarily tested on the FIB-25 dataset [10]. This data is an approximately 27,000 cubic micron subvolume of a medullar column of a fruit fly (i.e., *Drosophila Melanogaster*). This dataset has been used as a testbed for the development of segmentation algorithms, and it is also the dataset most fairly comparable to published results using state-of-the-art flood-filling networks (FFN) [4]. While other methods have been applied to the FIB-25 dataset, FFN has achieved unparalleled results in raw segmentation quality as well as reductions in merge and split errors during graph generation. As such, this approach forms the primary basis for comparison to our method.

The volumes used in the current experiment were published training and validation volumes from the Janelia FIB-25 dataset ($250 \times 250 \times 250$ and $520 \times 520 \times 520$ voxels in size at a resolution of $8 \times 8 \times 8$ nm). As our comparison method, we used FFN's pretrained weights from the authors. FIB-25 has been segmented by expert researchers who have labelled every voxel of the dataset according to the unique neuron ID to which it belongs. Likewise, the synapses are labelled as pre-synaptic points connected to a series of post-synaptic locations. These together form the data used as ground truth, and these true synapses were used to compare agents and FFN path reconstructions.

Agent tracing runs were conducted using varying numbers of steps and numbers of agents. The results of 19 standardized runs are listed in Fig. 3 and show the relationship between increasing the number of agents and graph quality.

Graph quality was measured based on neural reconstruction integrity (NRI) [8], a metric that measures graph similarity according to the precision and

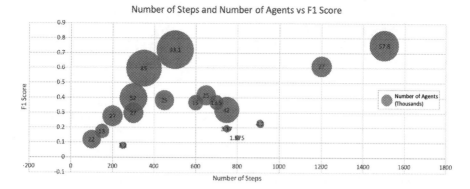

Fig. 3. Increasing the number of agents and increasing the number of steps increase the graph quality of the merged run. We seek to minimize computation expense while ensuring good exploration and therefore neuron representation.

recall of intracellular paths. Incorrect edges (additions or deletions) are penalized and used to create a precision and recall score reflective of graph quality. Additionally, an edge-based precision-recall metric was used that directly calculates scores based on incorrectly found (i.e., false positive) and omitted (i.e., false negative) edges.

For this measurement, we construct line graphs [2]. This representation considers the synapses as nodes, and the edges as paths between synapses. These new graphs are built using the same pre- and post-synaptic synapse points, and reconstructions are compared to the ground truth line graph to determine precision and recall, with each edge representing a detection. These are reported in Table 1. Agents performs on par with state-of-the-art at a fraction of the computational cost and on hardware that allows for large scale parallelization. The tracing results reported in the table are from a run with 1500 steps and about 50,000 agents spawned at synapses and linearly throughout the volume. In preliminary experiments, we have observed that the same weights perform well on other datasets, suggesting that extensive parameter tuning is not required for transfer.

Table 1. Results for experiments run on the FIB-25 dataset

	Graph		NRI			Edge		
	Nodes	Edges	Precision	Recall	f1	Precision	Recall	f1
Ground truth	589	1137	–	–	–	–	–	–
FFN	779	1251	0.767	.709	.737	.692	.790	.738
Agents (ours)	745	1198	.824	.693	.753	.753	.741	.746

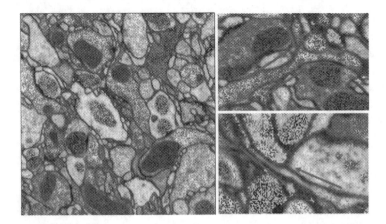

Fig. 4. (Left) A slice of segmentation output, visualized as a 2D cross-section of the merged paths at the conclusion of an agent run. The background is the EM image slice representing the input data, and the dark areas within some of the boundaries are mitochondria, which can be distractors in creating an output graph. (Middle) Agents populate and move along branching passageways, efficiently tracing neuron morphologies (Right) The narrowest passages are difficult for agents to pass through, even with optimized sensor weights. The membrane boundary sensors push agents away from these passages. There is a trade-off between robustness to false gaps that arise as a result of mis-alignments or image processing artifacts and robustly traversing thin pathways. For many workflows, these errors are quick for human annotators to correct

In order to optimize sensor weights, we grid searched the parameter space using gradient descent and our workflow, with NRI as the cost function. Both FFN and our approach were trained and then validated on the aforementioned training and validation sets provided by Janelia. We tuned our error profile to emphasize graph splits over merges, since the workflows of many high-throughput connectomics projects prefer to quickly stitch together path fragments rather than break up erroneous objects. This operating point is achieved by adjusting the $alpha_i$'s increase the weight of some sensors while decreasing the weight of others in order to cause agents to segment more conservatively or aggressively.

4   Discussion and Conclusions

Agent-based path tracing is complementary to that of existing dense segmentation approaches and can provide crucial context for voxel-accurate dense measurements in targeted regions using a coarse-to-fine approach. We emphasize that this approach is different than the conventional methods used to estimate connectome graphs and offers an attractive alternative for rapidly, cheaply, and robustly creating connectivity maps. As datasets grow in size, processing these volumes can be a major challenge for research groups, and this technique allows users to focus less on perfect alignment and sample preparation, and avoid some of the more common challenges associated with scalability. This method is also easily parallelizable across CPUs and requires no GPU resources as is commonplace amongst state-of-the-art approaches like FFN. The far cheaper cost of CPU cores relative to GPUs allows our method to be parallelized on computer clusters to segment a large volume very quickly and at low cost.

For some applications, detailed morphology is critical, and this technique will require post-processing to produce dense maps; although this has been addressed in other work [3]. We observe that our Agents method reaches many, but not all small processes; tortuous spine necks can be challenging as seen in Fig. 4; processes that appear disconnected in adjacent slices may also be troublesome. Future work will explore more powerful sensing strategies and post-processing (e.g., learning) approaches to address these scenarios, as well as transfer to other datasets. Agents can be extended naturally to other graph reconstruction challenges such as those in magnetic resonance imaging, CLARITY, Array Tomography and X-ray microtomography (XRM). Overall, we believe that this technique will work in concert with existing methods and allow scientists to more rapidly understand the underlying connectivity in their large, high-resolution datasets.

Acknowledgements. This material is based upon work supported by the Office of the Director of National Intelligence (ODNI), Intelligence Advanced Research Projects Activity (IARPA), via IARPA Contract No. 2017-17032700004-005 under the MICrONS program. The views and conclusions contained herein are those of the authors and should not be interpreted as necessarily representing the official policies or endorsements, either expressed or implied, of the ODNI, IARPA, or the U.S. Government. The U.S. Government is authorized to reproduce and distribute reprints for Governmental purposes notwithstanding any copyright annotation therein. Research reported in this publication was also supported by the National Institute of Mental Health of the National Institutes of Health under Award Numbers R24MH114799 and R24MH114785. The content is solely the responsibility of the authors and does not necessarily represent the official views of the National Institutes of Health. This work was completed with the support of the CIRCUIT initiative www.circuitinstitute.org, and JHU/APL Internal Research Funding.

References

1. Chalmers, R., Scheidt, D., Neighoff, T., Witwicki, S., Bamberger, R.: Cooperating unmanned vehicles. In: AIAA 1st Intelligent Systems Technical Conference, p. 6252 (2004)
2. Gray Roncal, W., et al.: An automated images-to-graphs framework for high resolution connectomics. Front. Neuroinform. **9**, 20 (2015). https://doi.org/10.3389/fninf.2015.00020. https://www.frontiersin.org/article/10.3389/fninf.2015.00020
3. Helmstaedter, M., et al.: Connectomic reconstruction of the inner plexiform layer in the mouse retina. Nature **500**(7461), 168 (2013). https://doi.org/10.1038/nature12346
4. Januszewski, M., et al.: High-precision automated reconstruction of neurons with flood-filling networks. Nat. Methods **15**(8), 605–610 (2018)
5. Mamei, M., Zambonelli, F., Leonardi, L.: Cofields: a physically inspired approach to motion coordination. IEEE Pervasive Comput. **3**(2), 52–61 (2004)

6. Nunez-Iglesias, J., Kennedy, R., Plaza, S.M., Chakraborty, A., Katz, W.T.: Graph-based active learning of agglomeration (gala): a python library to segment 2d and 3d neuroimages. Front. Neuroinform. **8**, 34 (2014)
7. Parag, T., et al.: Anisotropic em segmentation by 3d affinity learning and agglomeration (2017). arXiv preprint arXiv:1707.08935
8. Reilly, E.P., et al.: Neural reconstruction integrity: a metric for assessing the connectivity accuracy of reconstructed neural networks. Front. Neuroinform. **12**, 74 (2018)
9. Ronneberger, O., Fischer, P., Brox, T.: U-net: convolutional networks for biomedical image segmentation. In: Navab, N., Hornegger, J., Wells, W., Frangi, A. (eds.) MICCAI 2015. LNCS, vol. 9351, pp. 234–241. Springer, Cham (2015). https://doi.org/10.1007/978-3-319-24574-4_28
10. Takemura, S., et al.: Synaptic circuits and their variations within different columns in the visual system of drosophila. Proc. Nat. Acad. Sci. **112**(44), 13711–13716 (2015)

Statistical Atlas of *C. elegans* Neurons

Erdem Varol[1(✉)], Amin Nejatbakhsh[1], Ruoxi Sun[1], Gonzalo Mena[3],
Eviatar Yemini[2], Oliver Hobert[2], and Liam Paninski[1]

[1] Departments of Neuroscience and Statistics, Grossman Center for the Statistics
of Mind, Zuckerman Institute, Center for Theoretical Neuroscience,
Columbia University, New York, USA
ev2430@columbia.edu
[2] Department of Biological Sciences, Columbia University, New York, USA
[3] Department of Statistics and Data Science Initiative, Harvard University,
Cambridge, USA

Abstract. Constructing a statistical atlas of neuron positions in the
nematode *Caenorhabditis elegans* enables a wide range of applications
that require neural identity. These applications include annotating gene
expression, extracting calcium activity, and evaluating nervous-system
mutations. Large complete sets of neural annotations are necessary to
determine canonical neuron positions and their associated confidence
regions. Recently, a transgene of *C. elegans* ("NeuroPAL") has been
introduced to assign correct identities to all neurons in the worm via
a deterministic, fluorescent colormap. This strain has enabled efficient
and accurate annotation of worm neurons. Using a dataset of 10 worms,
we propose a statistical model that captures the latent means and covariances
of neuron locations, with efficient optimization strategies to infer
model parameters. We demonstrate the utility of this model in two
critical applications. First, we use our trained atlas to automatically
annotate neuron identities in *C. elegans* at the state-of-the-art rate. Second,
we use our atlas to compute correlations between neuron positions,
thereby determining covariance in neuron placement. The code to replicate
the statistical atlas is distributed publicly at https://github.com/
amin-nejat/StatAtlas.

1 Introduction

Imaging-based atlases of human and animal brains have enabled the principled
and standardized means of hypothesis testing in a wide variety of domains [3, 7,
10, 12, 13, 15, 20]. Common procedures that atlases enable are the registration of
population samples to a common space [23], discriminating pattern differences
across samples [2], segmentation into regions of interest [4], and regularizing

Electronic supplementary material The online version of this chapter (https://
doi.org/10.1007/978-3-030-59722-1_12) contains supplementary material, which is
available to authorized users.

© Springer Nature Switzerland AG 2020
A. L. Martel et al. (Eds.): MICCAI 2020, LNCS 12265, pp. 119–129, 2020.
https://doi.org/10.1007/978-3-030-59722-1_12

complex Bayesian models [17]. Importantly, atlases enable the formation of large-scale population studies due to their ability to gather high-dimensional data into a commensurate space.

C. elegans is a widely studied model organism with a simple nervous system that consists of 302 neurons in the adult hermaphrodite [21]. Its simplicity and stereotypy have enabled highly-reproducible experimental settings which have been crucial in elucidating neuroscientific hypotheses. Furthermore, to date, *C. elegans* is the only animal whose connectome is completely mapped [6,9,21]. Despite this atlas of connectivity, attempts at quantifying the variability of the neuron positions therein has been limited, capturing only a partial subset of these neurons [20]. This is due to the limited number of samples available from electron micrograph reconstructions and an inability to identify neural identities via position alone [22]. The recent introduction of NeuroPAL, a strain for complete neural identification in *C. elegans*, has enabled efficient and precise annotation of neuron positions in multiple worms.

Using a NeuroPAL dataset, encompassing all head and tail neurons from 10 worms, we propose a latent multivariate statistical model that captures the canonical positions and covariances of *C. elegans* neurons. The observed neurons were captured by fluorescent volumetric imaging. These were then modeled as a multivariate sample, drawn from a latent distribution subjected to a random affine transformation. Given this statistical model, we infer the canonical means and covariances of all neurons present in the head and tail of the worm, yielding a novel positional statistical atlas. To improve our statistical atlas with additional, incompletely annotated worms, we propose a semi-supervised approach for cell-identification. As shown in [22], using our trained atlas, we can automatically identify neurons in out-of-sample worms with more than 86% accuracy in the head and 94% accuracy in the tail. These accuracies represent the current state of the art, improving the accuracies reported in [11] and [20]. Furthermore, we demonstrate an additional application of our atlas to obtain a correlation analysis of neural positions, which sheds light on the structural organization of neurons and their potential connections to genetic lineages.

2   Data and Pre-processing

To construct the statistical atlas of *C. elegans* neurons, we used volumetric images of both heads and tails from 10 worms (strain OH15262). All worms were imaged on a Zeiss LSM 880 confocal with 32 detector channels and the following laser lines: 405 nm, 488 nm, 561 nm, and 633 nm. Volumetric resolution was approximately (X,Y,Z): 0.2 μm × 0.2 μm × 0.8 μm. Images were acquired with four color channels, corresponding to the NeuroPAL fluorophores: mTagBFP2, CyOFP1, mNeptune2.5, and TagRFP-T [22]. See Fig. 1 for a representative maximum intensity projection from a head sample. The volumetric images were subsequently annotated by an expert to denote the approximate center for each neuron and its corresponding identity. In total, 240 neurons were annotated in each worm, 195 from the head and 45 from tail. The remaining neurons from the midbody were not imaged for this study.

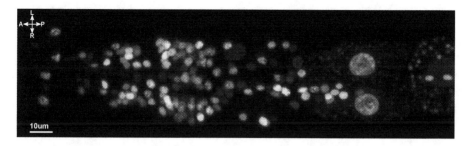

Fig. 1. Deterministic coloring of *C. elegans* neurons, in a NeuroPAL strain, enables the complete neural identification across a population of worms. See [22] for details.

3   Method

Due to variability in illumination and the pose of the worm when imaged, observed neuron positions and their exact color balance may vary across imaged worms. This presents a significant challenge when attempting to obtain correspondence between worms to infer the identities of neurons. Therefore, to normalize the random variability that occurs across different worms, prior to identifying neurons in any given microscopy image, we estimate a statistical atlas of neuron positions and colors.

The approach we take resembles the joint expectation-maximization alignment of point sets technique of [8], with several important differences discussed below. The dataset we are modeling consists of a collection of point sets: each worm corresponds to one point set, with each point in the set corresponding to the position and color of a single detected neuron. We model each of these positions and colors as samples from a statistical atlas that is common across worms. Each neuron i has a corresponding mean and covariance in this atlas, denoted as $\boldsymbol{\mu}_i$ and $\boldsymbol{\Sigma}_i$, respectively. After drawing all the positions and colors for a given worm j we apply a random affine transformation (parametrized by a matrix $\boldsymbol{\beta}_j$ and translation vector $\boldsymbol{\beta}_j^0$). Finally, since the order of neurons in each point set is arbitrary, we scramble the identities of the neurons with a random permutation, parameterized by a permutation matrix $\boldsymbol{P}_j$. This generative model is summarized in Fig. 2. See also [3] for a related model (without the alignment term, and with an inference approach that differs from the methods we describe below).

We build on the methods in [8] to infer the parameters of this generative model (i.e., the means and covariances of the statistical atlas, the random transformations, and the random permutations), in a completely unsupervised fashion, using a three-way expectation-maximization procedure. However, in our dataset, we have access to fully annotated neuron detections. We take advantage of this supervised data to simplify the inference problem.

Now we can describe our model in detail. Neuron positions are three-dimensional, and there are three color channels in this dataset (given our three neuron-specific fluorophore channels, we discard the panneuronal TagRFP-T

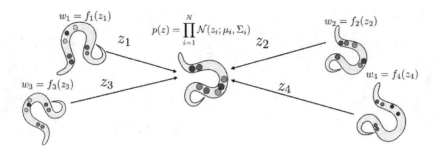

Fig. 2. Schematic of the generative model of neuron position and color expression. First we draw a position and color for each neuron i from a distribution with mean $\boldsymbol{\mu}_i$ and covariance $\boldsymbol{\Sigma}_i$; then, to create the observed data $\mathbf{w}_{i,j}$ (the color and position of the i-th neuron of the j-th worm) we apply a random affine transformation and a random permutation encoded by $f(\cdot)$.

channel as uninformative); therefore, if we use $\mathbf{w}_{i,j}$ to denote the appended position and color vector of the i-th neuron in worm j (as output by the detection step described in the previous section), then $\mathbf{w}_{i,j} \in \mathbb{R}^6$. Each of these observed $\mathbf{w}_{i,j}$ vectors has a corresponding latent vector $\boldsymbol{z}_{i,j}$ in the aligned atlas space. We model this latent vector as a Gaussian,

$$\boldsymbol{z}_{i,j} \sim \mathcal{N}(\boldsymbol{\mu}_i, \boldsymbol{\Sigma}_i), \tag{1}$$

with means $\boldsymbol{\mu}_i \in \mathbb{R}^6$ and covariances $\boldsymbol{\Sigma}_i \in \mathbb{S}_+^6$ that do not depend on the worm index j. We model the covariance $\boldsymbol{\Sigma}_i$ with block structure of the form $\boldsymbol{\Sigma}_i = \begin{bmatrix} \Sigma_{\text{position}}^i & \mathbf{0} \\ \mathbf{0} & \Sigma_{\text{color}}^i \end{bmatrix}$, since position and each color are independently varying.

Now the latent vectors $\boldsymbol{z}_{i,j}$ in the atlas space and observed data $\mathbf{w}_{i,j}$ extracted from the imaged worm j are connected by a worm-specific random affine transformation and permutation. We denote the intermediate affine-transformed variables as $\boldsymbol{x}_{i,j}$:

$$\boldsymbol{x}_{i,j} = \boldsymbol{z}_{i,j}\boldsymbol{\beta}_j + \boldsymbol{\beta}_j^0, \tag{2}$$

with $\boldsymbol{\beta}_j$ a 6×6 matrix (with a similar block structure as $\boldsymbol{\Sigma}_i$) and $\boldsymbol{\beta}_j^0 \in \mathbb{R}^6$. then we obtain $\mathbf{w}_{i,j}$ by scrambling the labels via the permutation p_j (corresponding to a permutation matrix $\mathbf{P}_j$):

$$\boldsymbol{w}_{i,j} = \boldsymbol{x}_{p_j(i),j}. \tag{3}$$

The summary of the generative process is illustrated in Fig. 2 by combining the permutation operation and the transformation together as a latent function $f(\cdot)$. Note that this model permits partial and variable observations of neurons across different animals if we allow the permutation matrix to be unbalanced (not square), indicating the existence of neurons that are not observed in individual animals.

Given these modeling assumptions, for a dataset of m worms and n_j detected neurons in each worm, we can express the likelihood as:

$$P(\boldsymbol{w}|\boldsymbol{\mu},\boldsymbol{\Sigma},\boldsymbol{P},\boldsymbol{\beta},\boldsymbol{\beta}^0) = \prod_{j=1}^{m}\prod_{i=1}^{n_j} \frac{e^{-(1/2)(\boldsymbol{w}_{i,j}-\boldsymbol{\mu}_{p_{i,j}}\boldsymbol{\beta}_j-\boldsymbol{\beta}_j^0)(\boldsymbol{\beta}_j\boldsymbol{\Sigma}_{p_{i,j}}\boldsymbol{\beta}_j^T)^{-1}(\boldsymbol{w}_{i,j}-\boldsymbol{\mu}_{p_{i,j}}\boldsymbol{\beta}_j-\boldsymbol{\beta}_j^0)^T}}{(2\pi)^{d/2}\det((\boldsymbol{\beta}_j\boldsymbol{\Sigma}_{p_{i,j}}\boldsymbol{\beta}_j^T))^{1/2}}$$

(4)

Since the term $\sum_j\sum_i(1/2)\log\det((\boldsymbol{\beta}_j\boldsymbol{\Sigma}_{p_{i,j}}\boldsymbol{\beta}_j^T)$ is permutation invariant, we can write it as $\sum_j\sum_i(1/2)\log\det((\boldsymbol{\beta}_j\boldsymbol{\Sigma}_i\boldsymbol{\beta}_j^T)$ and thus the maximum likelihood estimate (MLE) for our generative model involves optimizing the negative log-likelihood:

$$\underset{\boldsymbol{P},\boldsymbol{\beta},\boldsymbol{\beta}^0,\boldsymbol{\mu},\boldsymbol{\Sigma}}{\text{minimize}} \sum_{j=1}^{m}\sum_{i=1}^{n_j}(\boldsymbol{w}_{i,j}-\boldsymbol{\mu}_{p_{i,j}}\boldsymbol{\beta}_j-\boldsymbol{\beta}_j^0)(\boldsymbol{\beta}_j\boldsymbol{\Sigma}_{p_{i,j}}\boldsymbol{\beta}_j^T)^{-1}(\boldsymbol{w}_{i,j}-\boldsymbol{\mu}_{p_{i,j}}\boldsymbol{\beta}_j-\boldsymbol{\beta}_j^0)^T)$$
$$+ \log\det((\boldsymbol{\beta}_j\boldsymbol{\Sigma}_i\boldsymbol{\beta}_j^T)$$

(5)

3.1   Optimization

To infer the parameters of the generative model, we take an iterative block-coordinate descent approach, similar to [8]: we fix $(\boldsymbol{P},\boldsymbol{\beta},\boldsymbol{\beta}_0)$ (with $\boldsymbol{P}$ abbreviating the collection of permutations $\boldsymbol{P}_j$ for all worms j, and similarly for $\boldsymbol{\beta},\boldsymbol{\beta}_0$) and solve for $(\boldsymbol{\mu},\boldsymbol{\Sigma})$, then fix $(\boldsymbol{\mu},\boldsymbol{\Sigma})$ and solve for $(\boldsymbol{P},\boldsymbol{\beta},\boldsymbol{\beta}_0)$. Below are the update steps for each of these blocks.

Inference of the Statistical Atlas Parameters $\boldsymbol{\mu},\boldsymbol{\Sigma}$: Let $\boldsymbol{P}_j \in \mathcal{P}^{n\times n}$ denote the permutation matrix, $\boldsymbol{W}_j = [\mathbf{w}_{1,j}^T \ldots \mathbf{w}_{n,j}^T]^T \in \mathbb{R}^{n\times d}$ denote the row stacked features of the neurons of the jth worm, and let $\boldsymbol{\mu} = [\boldsymbol{\mu}_1^T \ldots \boldsymbol{\mu}_n^T] \in \mathbb{R}^{n\times d}$ denote the row stacked neuron means. The generative model can be written in matrix form as: $\boldsymbol{W}_j = \boldsymbol{P}_j\boldsymbol{\mu}\boldsymbol{\beta}_j + 1\boldsymbol{\beta}_j^0 + \boldsymbol{E}$ where $\boldsymbol{E}_i \sim \mathcal{N}(0,\boldsymbol{\beta}_j\boldsymbol{\Sigma}_{P_{i,j}}\boldsymbol{\beta}_j^T)$ denotes the row stacked uncertainty terms.

Since $\boldsymbol{P}_j^T\boldsymbol{P}_j = \mathbf{I}$ because $\boldsymbol{P}$ is a permutation matrix and assuming that $\boldsymbol{\beta}_j$ is a non-degenerate transformation, its inverse exists and can be used to write the system as: $\boldsymbol{P}_j^T\boldsymbol{W}_j\boldsymbol{\beta}_j^{-1} - 1\boldsymbol{\beta}_j^0\boldsymbol{\beta}_j^{-1} = \boldsymbol{\mu} + \boldsymbol{V}$ where $\boldsymbol{V}_i \sim \mathcal{N}(0,\boldsymbol{\Sigma}_i)$ is a term to quantify uncertainty.

This equation can be used to infer $\boldsymbol{\mu}$ and $\boldsymbol{\Sigma}$ in closed form by computing the first and second moments of $\boldsymbol{V}$:

$$\boldsymbol{\mu}^* = \frac{1}{m}\sum_{j=1}^{m}\boldsymbol{P}_j^T\boldsymbol{W}_j\boldsymbol{\beta}_j^{-1} - 1\boldsymbol{\beta}_j^0\boldsymbol{\beta}_j^{-1}$$

(6)

$$\boldsymbol{\Sigma}_i^* = \frac{1}{m}\sum_{j=1}^{m}(\boldsymbol{P}_{j,i}^T\boldsymbol{W}_j\boldsymbol{\beta}_j^{-1} - \boldsymbol{\beta}_j^0\boldsymbol{\beta}_j^{-1} - \boldsymbol{\mu}_i)^T(\boldsymbol{P}_{j,i}^T\boldsymbol{W}_j\boldsymbol{\beta}_j^{-1} - \boldsymbol{\beta}_j^0\boldsymbol{\beta}_j^{-1} - \boldsymbol{\mu}_i)$$

(7)

Inference of the Transformation Terms $\boldsymbol{\beta},\boldsymbol{\beta}_0$: We can infer the transformation and translation terms $\boldsymbol{\beta},\boldsymbol{\beta}_0$ by solving a weighted linear regression problem

---

Algorithm 1. Train statistical neuron atlas

Input: $\{\mathbf{w}_{i,j}\}$ (colors and positions) and $\{\boldsymbol{P}_{i,j}\}$ (neuron correspondences) for $j = 1, \ldots, m$ worms in a training set and $i = 1, \ldots, n$ neurons, ϵ (convergence tolerance)

Initalization $k < \frac{n}{2}$ (number of outliers)

Select random worm $j \sim \text{Unif}[m]$

Set means as neuron centers of worm j:$\boldsymbol{\mu}_i^0 \leftarrow \mathbf{w}_{i,j}$ for $i = 1, \ldots, n$

Set covariances as identity: $\boldsymbol{\Sigma}_i^0 \leftarrow \boldsymbol{I}_6$ for $i = 1, \ldots, n$

1: **while** Not converged **do**
2:      $t \leftarrow t + 1$
3:      **for** j=1,...,n **do**
4:          Solve alignment of jth worm to atlas $\{\boldsymbol{\mu}, \boldsymbol{\Sigma}\}$ using equations 9 and 10
5:      **end for**
6:      Update $\boldsymbol{\mu}^t, \boldsymbol{\Sigma}^t$ using equations 6
7:      Check convergence $\|\boldsymbol{\mu}^t - \boldsymbol{\mu}^{t-1}\|_F \leq \epsilon$ and $\|\boldsymbol{\Sigma}^t - \boldsymbol{\Sigma}^{t-1}\|_F \leq \epsilon$
8: **end while**
9: **return** Statistical atlas of neuron colors and positions $\{\boldsymbol{\mu}^t, \boldsymbol{\Sigma}^t\}$.

---

with a Mahalanobis norm for each neuron quantified by the covariance terms, $\boldsymbol{\Sigma}_i$:

$$\underset{\boldsymbol{\beta}_j^{-1}, \boldsymbol{\beta}_j^0 \boldsymbol{\beta}_j^{-1}}{\text{minimize}} \sum_{i=1}^{n_j} (\boldsymbol{P}_{j,i}^T \boldsymbol{W}_j \boldsymbol{\beta}_j^{-1} - \boldsymbol{\beta}_j^0 \boldsymbol{\beta}_j^{-1} - \boldsymbol{\mu}_i) \boldsymbol{\Sigma}_i^{-1} (\boldsymbol{P}_{j,i}^T \boldsymbol{W}_j \boldsymbol{\beta}_j^{-1} - \boldsymbol{\beta}_j^0 \boldsymbol{\beta}_j^{-1} - \boldsymbol{\mu}_i)^T. \tag{8}$$

This system admits a fixed point iteration that yields the global minimum [8]. First, the closed form solution for $\boldsymbol{\beta}_j^0 \boldsymbol{\beta}_j^{-1}$ is given by:

$$\boldsymbol{\beta}_j^0 \boldsymbol{\beta}_j^{-1*} = \left(\sum_{i=1}^{n} (\boldsymbol{P}_{j,i}^T \boldsymbol{W}_j \boldsymbol{\beta}_j^{-1} - \boldsymbol{\mu}_i) \boldsymbol{\Sigma}_i^{-1} \right) \left(\sum_{i=1}^{n} \boldsymbol{\Sigma}_i^{-1} \right)^{-1} \tag{9}$$

To analytically solve for $\boldsymbol{\beta}_j^{-1}$, we use the fact that $\text{vec}(ABC) = (C^T \otimes A)\text{vec}(B)$ where $\text{vec}(\cdot)$ denotes the vectorization operation and $\otimes$ denotes Kronecker product. This yields the following vectorized closed form update for $\boldsymbol{\beta}_j^{-1}$:

$$\text{vec}(\boldsymbol{\beta}_j^{-1*})$$
$$= \left(\sum_{i=1}^{n} (\boldsymbol{\Sigma}_i^{-1} \otimes (\boldsymbol{P}_{j,i}^T \boldsymbol{W}_j)^T (\boldsymbol{P}_{j,i}^T \boldsymbol{W}_j)) \right)^{-1} \left(\sum_{i=1}^{n} \text{vec}((\boldsymbol{P}_{j,i}^T \boldsymbol{W}_j)^T (\boldsymbol{\beta}_j^0 \boldsymbol{\beta}_j^{-1} + \boldsymbol{\mu}_i) \boldsymbol{\Sigma}_i^{-1}) \right) \tag{10}$$

Permutation Inference: Lastly, we can solve for the doubly-stochastic matrix, $\boldsymbol{P}_j$ by setting up a $n \times n_j$ transport matrix $\boldsymbol{D}$ where

$$\boldsymbol{D}_{u,v} = (\boldsymbol{\mu}_u \boldsymbol{W} \boldsymbol{\beta}_j + \boldsymbol{\beta}_j^0 - \boldsymbol{W}_{j,v}) \boldsymbol{\Sigma}_u^{-1} (\boldsymbol{\mu}_u \boldsymbol{W} \boldsymbol{\beta}_j + \boldsymbol{\beta}_j^0 - \boldsymbol{W}_{j,v})^T \tag{11}$$

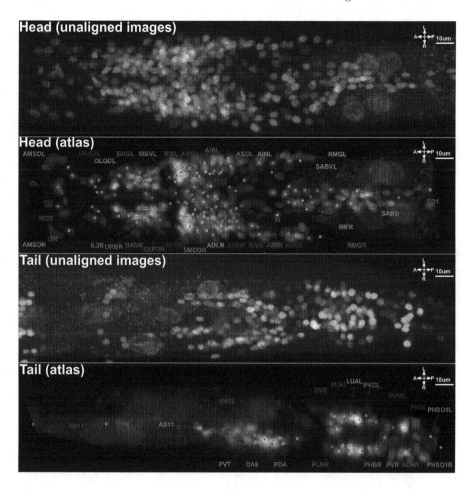

Fig. 3. The construction of the statistical atlas of *C. elegans* neurons in the head and tail is demonstrated by contrasting the superposition of unaligned images of the 10 NeuroPAL worms (top row for head, third row for tail) with the superposition of aligned images to the converged atlas (second row for head, fourth row for tail). The canonical neuron positions and their NeuroPAL colors are represented as colored dots. A limited selection of neurons are annotated to avoid overcrowding in the figure. Note that the nerve ring (the hollow space in the head, one-third distance from the anterior) and the empty boundaries separating many of the worm ganglia, are distinct in the aligned images while indistinguishable in the unaligned images. See [22] Fig. 2 for further details.

and obtaining P_j through the solving the entropic optimal transport problem [16] using the Sinkhorn-Knopp algorithm [18] which minimizes the following objective:

$$P_j^* = \arg\min_{p \in \mathcal{P}} \sum_{u,v} p_{u,v} D_{u,v} - \gamma p_{u,v} \log p_{u,v} \tag{12}$$

Further details of permutation inference for neuron identification can be found in [14].

3.2 Statistical Atlas of Neuron Positions and Colors

If we have access to several annotated worms, meaning that we have access to both the neural detections W and their corresponding identities, P, we can infer the transformation terms $\{\beta, \beta_0\}$ as well as the parameters of the statistical atlas $\{\mu, \Sigma\}$ using the procedure outlined in Algorithm 1.

In words, Algorithm 1 operates in the following way. First, the targeted inference parameters are initialized using the neuron centers and colors for a random worm. Then, the remaining worms are affinely aligned to the hypothetical atlas by solving the linear system for $\{\beta_j, \beta_j^0\}$ in Eq. 10. The means and covariances of the aligned neurons are then used to update the atlas parameters of μ and Σ. This procedure is iteratively repeated until convergence. See Fig. 3 for an illustration.

4 Applications

Automatic/Semi-automatic Neuron Identification: Automated neural detection and identification in *C. elegans* [1,11,19] enable neural-level hypotheses and facilitate large-scale, high-throughput analyses across worm populations. These features include neural activity traces, measuring the presence and intensity of fluorescent biomarkers under various experimental conditions, and assessment of mutant-driven neural displacements from canonical positioning. To infer neural identity, we use the trained statistical atlas's positional means as a source point cloud, computing the Mahalanobis distance of out-of-sample worm neurons using the atlas covariances in Eq. (11). We then employ the iterative closest point algorithm [5] using iterative updates of Eqs. (9), (10) and (12) to match atlas neurons to the out-of-sample neurons. As discussed in [22], this procedure yields a leave-one-worm-out automatic neuron identification accuracy of 88% with 86% in the head and 94% in the tail, with most misidentifications occurring in the dense ventral and retrovesicular ganglia (Fig. 4A). This result is superior to the previously reported automatic neuron identification accuracy in [20]. Note that in this study, Toyoshima et al. use a larger set of animals (311 worms), but only partial coverage of the head neurons (on average 80% of 196 head neurons) and of these, the accuracy of the first rank identity is 62%. We further incorporate a semi-supervised approach (described in the supplementary), wherein the user can provide a number of annotations, thus improving algorithmic accuracy to over 95% for both the head and tail using 20 and 4 manual annotations, respectively (Fig. 4C-D).

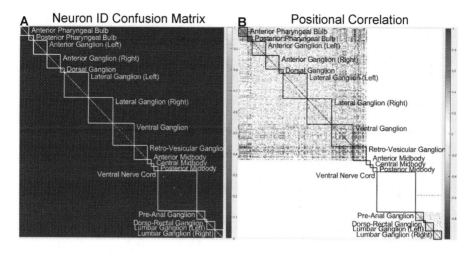

Fig. 4. A: Neuron identification accuracy confusion matrix, organized by ganglia, **B:** Positional-displacement correlations of neurons after their alignment to the atlas space.

Positional Correlation: Using the 10 annotated worm samples, we align all animals to the common statistical atlas space. We then perform a correlation analysis between pairs of neurons using the displacement vectors of individual worms' neurons relative to their corresponding means. Analyzing the top correlation for each pair of neurons, we obtain Fig. 4B. The blockwise patterns displayed here demonstrate that there is a strong intra-ganglion correlation of neuron placements in both the anterior and posterior pharyngeal bulbs.

Conclusion and Future Directions: In this paper, we proposed a statistical framework to estimate an atlas of neuron positions in *C. elegans* using images of 10 annotated NeuroPAL worms [22]. We demonstrated two important applications of this atlas, automatically identifying neurons in unlabelled worms and partially explaining the positional correlations between the placement of neurons.

The proposed statistical atlas of *C. elegans* neurons has a wide variety of applications in addition to the ones demonstrated above. Such atlases can quickly be derived for all larval developmental stages, including dauer and male worms. These atlases could then be used to model neural repositioning throughout development. Automatic segmentation of neurons and neural activity (or dynamic changes in biomarker intensities), extracted from time-series data, are two other prominent directions of research that will be beneficial to the computational neuroscience community. The current atlas used an affine alignment model since the worms that were studied exhibited a straight posture. To extend this to freely-moving worms, one can generalize the alignment model to include higher-order deformations that account for postural variability. Lastly, analysis of color alterations as well as cell losses and/or duplications in mutant worms, combined with inferences from the invariant lineage, could be used to model lineal mutant effects consistent with the observed disruptions, thus elucidating genes involved in patterning the nervous system.

Acknowledgment. The authors acknowledge the following funding sources. Paninski Lab: NSF NeuroNex Award DBI-1707398, The Gatsby Charitable Foundation, NIBIB R01 EB22913, DMS 1912194, Simons Foundation Collaboration on the Global Brain. Hobert Lab: Howard Hughes Medical Institute, NIH (5T32DK7328-37, 5T32DK007328-35, 5T32MH015174-38, and 5T32MH015174-37), Venkatachalam Lab: Burroughs Wellcome Fund Career Award at the Scientific Interface.

References

1. Aerni, S.J., et al.: Automated cellular annotation for high-resolution images of adult caenorhabditis elegans. Bioinformatics **29**(13), i18–i26 (2013)
2. Ashburner, J., Friston, K.J.: Voxel-based morphometry-the methods. Neuroimage **11**(6), 805–821 (2000)
3. Bubnis, G., Ban, S., DiFranco, M.D., Kato, S.: A probabilistic atlas for cell identification (2019). arXiv preprint arXiv:1903.09227
4. Cabezas, M., Oliver, A., Lladó, X., Freixenet, J., Cuadra, M.B.: A review of atlas-based segmentation for magnetic resonance brain images. Comput. Methods Programs Biomed. **104**(3), e158–e177 (2011)
5. Chetverikov, D., Svirko, D., Stepanov, D., Krsek, P.: The trimmed iterative closest point algorithm. In: Object Recognition Supported by User Interaction for Service Robots, vol. 3, pp. 545–548. IEEE (2002)
6. Cook, S.J., et al.: Whole-animal connectomes of both caenorhabditis elegans sexes. Nature **571**(7763), 63–71 (2019)
7. Dickie, D.A., Shenkin, S.D., et al.: Whole brain magnetic resonance image atlases: a systematic review of existing atlases and caveats for use in population imaging. Front. Neuroinf. **11**, 1 (2017)
8. Evangelidis, G.D., Horaud, R.: Joint alignment of multiple point sets with batch and incremental expectation-maximization. IEEE Trans. Pattern Anal. Mach. Intell. **40**(6), 1397–1410 (2018)
9. Jarrell, T.A., et al.: The connectome of a decision-making neural network. Science **337**(6093), 437–44 (2012)
10. Jones, A.R., Overly, C.C., Sunkin, S.M.: The allen brain atlas: 5 years and beyond. Nat. Rev. Neurosci. **10**(11), 821–828 (2009)
11. Kainmueller, D., Jug, F., Rother, C., Myers, G.: Active graph matching for automatic joint segmentation and annotation of *C. elegans*. In: Golland, P., Hata, N., Barillot, C., Hornegger, J., Howe, R. (eds.) MICCAI 2014. LNCS, vol. 8673, pp. 81–88. Springer, Cham (2014). https://doi.org/10.1007/978-3-319-10404-1_11
12. Lein, E.S., Hawrylycz, M.J., et al.: Genome-wide atlas of gene expression in the adult mouse brain. Nature **445**, 168–176 (2007)
13. Mazziotta, J., Toga, A., et al.: A probabilistic atlas and reference system for the human brain: international consortium for brain mapping (ICBM). Philos. Trans. R. Soc. Lond. Ser. B Biol. Sci. **356**(1412), 1293–322 (2001)
14. Mena, G., Varol, E., Nejatbakhsh, A., Yemini, E., Paninski, L.: Sinkhorn permutation variational marginal inference. In: Symposium on Advances in Approximate Bayesian Inference, pp. 1–9 (2020)

15. Oh, S.W., et al.: A mesoscale connectome of the mouse brain. Nature **508**(7495), 207–214 (2014)
16. Peyré, G., Cuturi, M., et al.: Computational optimal transport. Found. Trends Mach. Learn. **11**(5–6), 355–607 (2019)
17. Saxena, S., et al.: Localized semi-nonnegative matrix factorization (locanmf) of widefield calcium imaging data. bioRxiv, p. 650093 (2019)
18. Sinkhorn, R., Knopp, P.: Concerning nonnegative matrices and doubly stochastic matrices. Pac. J. Math. **21**(2), 343–348 (1967)
19. Tokunaga, T., et al.: Automated detection and tracking of many cells by using 4D live-cell imaging data. Bioinformatics **30**(12), i43–i51 (2014)
20. Toyoshima, Y., et al.: Neuron id dataset facilitates neuronal annotation for whole-brain activity imaging of C. elegans. BMC Biol. **18**(1), 1–20 (2020)
21. White, J.G., Southgate, E., Thomson, N.J., Brenner, S.: The structure of the nervous system of the nematode caenorhabditis elegans. Philos. Trans. R. Soc. Lond. B Biol. Sci. **314**(1165), 1–340 (1986)
22. Yemini, E., et al.: Neuropal: a neuronal polychromatic atlas of landmarks for whole-brain imaging in C. elegans. BioRxiv. p. 676312 (2019)
23. Zitova, B., Flusser, J.: Image registration methods: a survey. Image Vis. Comput. **21**(11), 977–1000 (2003)

Probabilistic Joint Segmentation and Labeling of *C. elegans* Neurons

Amin Nejatbakhsh[1(✉)], Erdem Varol[1], Eviatar Yemini[2], Oliver Hobert[2], and Liam Paninski[1]

[1] Departments of Neuroscience and Statistics, Grossman Center for the Statistics of Mind, Center for Theoretical Neuroscience, Zuckerman Institute, Columbia University, New York, USA
`mn2822@cumc.columbia.edu`
[2] Department of Biological Sciences, Columbia University, New York, USA

Abstract. Automatic identification and segmentation of the neurons of *C. elegans* enables evaluating nervous system mutations, positional variability, and allows us to conduct high-throughput population studies employing many animals. A recently introduced transgene of *C. elegans*, named "NeuroPAL" has enabled the efficient annotation of neurons and the construction of a statistical atlas of their positions. Previous atlas-based segmentation approaches have modeled images of cells as a mixture model. The expectation-maximization (EM) algorithm and its variants are used to find the (local) maximum likelihood parameters for this class of models. We present a variation of the EM algorithm called Sinkhorn-EM (sEM) that uses regularized optimal transport Sinkhorn iterations to enforce constraints on the marginals of the joint distribution of observed variables and latent assignments in order to incorporate our prior information about cell sizes into the cluster-data assignment proportions. We apply our method to the problem of segmenting and labeling neurons in fluorescent microscopy images of *C. elegans* specimens. We show empirically that sEM outperforms vanilla EM and a recently proposed 3-step (filter, detect, identify) labeling approach. Open source code implementing this method is available at https://github.com/amin-nejat/SinkhornEM.

1 Introduction

hole-brain functional imaging of *Caenorhabditis elegans* has been recently introduced to enable the measurement of neural activity at unprecedented temporal and spatial resolution [10]. Obtaining a complete measurement of neuron positioning and activity enables the study of a wide range of hypotheses including the identification of brainwide dynamic networks involved in action sequences

Electronic supplementary material The online version of this chapter (https://doi.org/10.1007/978-3-030-59722-1_13) contains supplementary material, which is available to authorized users.

© Springer Nature Switzerland AG 2020
A. L. Martel et al. (Eds.): MICCAI 2020, LNCS 12265, pp. 130–140, 2020.
https://doi.org/10.1007/978-3-030-59722-1_13

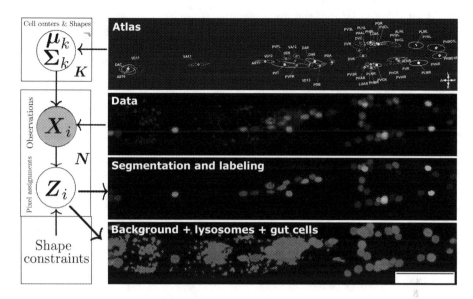

Fig. 1. Segmentation and labeling of fluorescently-colored neurons, in image volumes of NeuroPAL worms, using the proposed method. Left: The graphical model of the probabilistic inference procedure employed to identify and segment neurons. Right: The model uses the atlas from [14] as a prior to assign latent neuron identities to each observed pixel, subject to constraints on the total mass assigned to each cell. (Color figure online)

and decisions, decoding of nervous system responses to repulsive and attractive stimuli from distinct modalities, and monitoring of neural identity to reveal neural-fate alterations in the presence of gene mutations [14]. However, a significant analysis bottleneck is the segmentation and identification of all imaged neurons. Automated segmentation and identification of *C. elegans* neurons would enable high-throughput experiments for many applications.

There have been many recent works towards segmenting and labeling cells and in particular, neurons. Several methods address the cell labeling problem directly without segmenting their shapes [1,7,12,13]. Broadly, current algorithms for cell labeling can be categorized into two classes: the first and more common approach is to split the labeling problem into multiple steps. These steps include a filtering step to eliminate background components and non-cellular objects. The second step is to detect potential locations of the cells. This step is prone to the false detection of non-cellular objects, depending on how accurate the filtering and detection steps are. The final step to label the cells is to run a point matching algorithm to find the correspondences between the cells and their features in an atlas and the set of detected cells. A very recent work in this class of models [5] trains an atlas of the pairwise distances between the neurons, and finds the correspondence between the points such that the pairwise distances match the atlas. The second approach for cell labeling is to directly model the pixels as the observations of a model with cell centers as unobserved variables. The goal in these models is to classify pixels and to infer the unobserved cell centers simultaneously. An example of this paradigm is demonstrated in [9], where the authors consider a subset of well separated and large non-neuronal cells for segmentation and annotation.

A novel transgenic strain of *C. elegans* called "NeuroPAL" (a Neuronal Poly-chromatic Atlas of Landmarks) has introduced differential fluorescent coloring of neurons to resolve all unique neural identities [14]. This has enabled the con-struction of a complete statistical atlas of neuron positions and colors. Here, we present a novel statistical pipeline for joint segmentation and labeling of neural identities in NeuroPAL images. We formulate the segmentation problem as a posterior inference over the latent variables of a mixture model and show that the neural labeling arises naturally from our formulation. We further present a novel technique to constrain the posterior distribution in the expectation-maximization (EM) algorithm to enforce prior knowledge about cell sizes using the Sinkhorn-Knopp algorithm [11].

Our experimental results illustrate that the resulting "Sinkhorn EM" (**sEM**) approach outperforms vanilla EM (**vEM**) both in terms of segmentation quality as well as neuron identification accuracy. We further show that we outperform the multi-step method for neural identification developed in [14].

2   Methods

2.1   Probabilistic Model

First we introduce notation. Let N represent the total number of pixel observa-tions in our multi-colored volumetric image. Each observed pixel in the volume is in the form of a 4-D tensor where the first 3 dimensions are spatial coordinates x, y, z and the 4th dimension corresponds to the different color channels. To facilitate notation within our probabilistic model, we represent the set of pixels as N tuples $\boldsymbol{X}_i = (\boldsymbol{l}_i, \boldsymbol{c}_i) \in \mathbb{R}^{3+C}$ where C is the total number of color channels. The first part of this tuple, $\boldsymbol{l}_i = (x_i, y_i, z_i) \in \mathbb{R}^3$, corresponds to the location of pixel i. The next part of this tuple, $\boldsymbol{c}_i = (c_i^1, \ldots, c_i^C)$, is a vector indicating the color intensity of pixel i in all channels. Next, we model these pixel tuples as random variables drawn from a mixture model.

Let $\boldsymbol{\theta}$ denote the set of parameters of the mixture distribution that these observations are assumed to be drawn from. Since we are trying to segment images comprising of neurons as well as non-neuronal background components, we model this mixture in terms of K components that correspond to neurons that we are trying to segment and B components that capture the background. Given these N pixel observations, $\boldsymbol{X} = \{\boldsymbol{X}_1, \ldots, \boldsymbol{X}_N\}$ and distribution parameters, $\boldsymbol{\theta}$, we model the data using the following joint probabilistic mixture model:

$$P(\boldsymbol{X}, \boldsymbol{\theta}) = P(\boldsymbol{\theta}) \prod_{i=1}^{N} P(\boldsymbol{X}_i | \boldsymbol{\theta}) = P(\boldsymbol{\theta}) \prod_{i=1}^{N} \sum_{l=1}^{K+B} \pi_l P_l(\boldsymbol{X}_i | \boldsymbol{\theta}). \tag{1}$$

Here π_l denotes the membership weights for the lth component and $P_l(\boldsymbol{X}_i|\boldsymbol{\theta})$ denotes the likelihood of the ith pixel given the lth component. Next, we explicitly model the distributions of neurons and the background. We model pixel observations of neurons as multivariate normal distributed in both position and color, i.e. we expect to observe pixels corresponding to the neuron VA11 (the solo magenta neuron roughly one-third from the left-side of Fig. 1) in the general vicinity of where neuron VA11 is positioned and in colors close to the stereotypical color of the neuron VA11. Furthermore, the *C. elegans* nuclei imaged here are roughly ellipsoidal, which make Gaussian modeling plausible. On the other hand, we model background components to be positioned uniformly throughout the volume but with multivariate-normal distributed colors; i.e., lysosomes (indicated by the green speckles in Fig. 1) could be positioned arbitrarily but usually are in a shade of green. The likelihood of this model can be expressed as:

$$\sum_{l=1}^{K+B} \pi_l P_l(\boldsymbol{X}_i|\boldsymbol{\theta}) \tag{2}$$

$$= \underbrace{\sum_{k=1}^{K} \pi_k^n \mathcal{N}((\boldsymbol{l}_i, \boldsymbol{c}_i)|\boldsymbol{\mu}_k^n, \boldsymbol{\Sigma}_k^n)}_{\text{Neurons}} + \underbrace{\sum_{j=1}^{B} \pi_j^b \mathcal{U}(\boldsymbol{l}_i|\boldsymbol{l}_{\min}, \boldsymbol{l}_{\max})\mathcal{N}(\boldsymbol{c}_i|\boldsymbol{\mu}_j^b, \boldsymbol{\Sigma}_j^b)}_{\text{Background components}}.$$

Here $\mathcal{N}(\cdot)$ is a multivariate normal distribution, and $\mathcal{U}(\cdot)$ is a multi-dimensional uniform distribution defined in a hyper-cube that ranges from $\boldsymbol{l}_{\min}$ to $\boldsymbol{l}_{\max}$ where $\boldsymbol{l}_{\min}$ denotes the lower bound of pixel coordinates and $\boldsymbol{l}_{\max}$ denotes the upper bound.

The multivariate Gaussian distributions to model neurons are parametrized by $\boldsymbol{\theta}^n = \{\boldsymbol{\beta}, \boldsymbol{\mu}_{1:K}^n, \boldsymbol{\Sigma}_{1:K}^n\}$ where $\boldsymbol{\beta} \in \mathbb{R}^{4\times3}$ denotes an affine transformation of the observed neuron positions from their stereotypical position (encoded by an atlas for example). $\boldsymbol{\mu}_k^n \in \mathbb{R}^{3+C}$ denotes the stereotypical position and color of the kth neuron and $\boldsymbol{\Sigma}_k^n \in \mathbf{S}_{++}^{3+C}$ denotes its covariance. Background components are modeled similarly with respect to color, but are permitted to occupy any position in the volume. Namely, $\boldsymbol{\theta}^b = \{\boldsymbol{\mu}_{1:B}^b, \boldsymbol{\Sigma}_{1:B}^b\}$ where $\boldsymbol{\mu}_j^b \in \mathbb{R}^C$ and $\boldsymbol{\Sigma}_j^b \in \mathbf{S}_{++}^C$ denote the mean and covariance of the jth background component color.

The prior distribution of our model is a multivariate normal distribution that encodes the canonical locations and colors of the neurons aligned to the image using the affine transformation term $\boldsymbol{\beta}$. We use the atlas described in [14] and shown in Fig. 1:

$$P(\boldsymbol{\theta}) = \mathcal{N}(\boldsymbol{\mu}_{1:K}|\boldsymbol{\beta}\boldsymbol{\mu}_{1:K}^a, \boldsymbol{\beta}\boldsymbol{\Sigma}_{1:K}^a\boldsymbol{\beta}^T), \tag{3}$$

where the super-script a denotes the atlas parameters, here the mean $\boldsymbol{\mu}^a$ and the covariance $\boldsymbol{\Sigma}^a$ of a Multivariate Normal distribution. Here we assume the existence of an affine transformation matrix that roughly aligns the atlas to the image. The $\boldsymbol{\beta}$ is fit using a few landmark cells and is updated further through iterations using the update rules discussed in the supplementary.

Given the set of N pixel observations $\boldsymbol{X} = \{\boldsymbol{X}_1, \ldots, \boldsymbol{X}_N\}$, we seek to find the maximum a posteriori (MAP) estimate of the parameters given the observations. In other words, our objective is to maximize the following log-posterior:

$$\mathcal{L}(\boldsymbol{\theta}) = \log P(\boldsymbol{\theta}|\boldsymbol{X}) = \log P(\boldsymbol{\theta}) + \sum_{i=1}^{N} \log P(\boldsymbol{X}_i|\boldsymbol{\theta}) + C', \tag{4}$$

where C' is a constant with respect to $\boldsymbol{\theta}$ that can be ignored optimizing the cost with respect the parameters.

2.2   Optimization

Vanilla EM Algorithm: To find the local MAP estimate of the model parameters, a common strategy is to introduce a latent assignment variable Z that assigns each observation to one of the mixture components. We then maximize the expected complete log likelihood where the expectation is taken under the posterior distribution of the assignment variable.

$$P(\boldsymbol{X}, \boldsymbol{\theta}|Z = l) = P(\boldsymbol{X}|\boldsymbol{\theta}_l)P(\boldsymbol{\theta}) \tag{5}$$

$$Q(\boldsymbol{\theta}|\boldsymbol{\theta}_t) = \mathbb{E}_{P(Z|\boldsymbol{X},\boldsymbol{\theta}_t)}[\log P(\boldsymbol{X}, \boldsymbol{\theta}, Z)] \tag{6}$$

Here $\boldsymbol{\theta}_t$ denotes the estimate of model parameters at the tth iterate. This function lower bounds $\mathcal{L}(\boldsymbol{\theta})$ and maximizing it improves $\mathcal{L}(\boldsymbol{\theta})$ in each iteration [6], yielding the vanilla[1] Expectation-Maximization (**vEM**) algorithm:

$$\textbf{vEM:} \begin{cases} \textbf{E-step:} & \text{update } \boldsymbol{\gamma} \text{ by evaluating } Q(\boldsymbol{\theta}|\boldsymbol{\theta}_t) \\ \textbf{M-step:} & \text{solve } \boldsymbol{\theta}_{t+1} = \arg\max_{\boldsymbol{\theta}} Q(\boldsymbol{\theta}|\boldsymbol{\theta}_t) \end{cases} \tag{7}$$

The E-step consists of computing a term $\boldsymbol{\gamma}$ known as the **responsibility matrix** with $\gamma_{l,i} = P(Z_i = l|\boldsymbol{X}_i, \boldsymbol{\theta})$. For each pixel, this variable defines a probability space over the mixture components and provides a soft assignment of the pixels to components. For example, for a fixed row, $\gamma_{l,:}$ denotes the distribution of the lth component across space of pixels, roughly encoding the spatial extent and shape of the lth object. Conversely, the ith column of γ, $\gamma_{:,i}$ denotes the membership of the ith pixel amongst the k components. The analytical derivation of the EM parameter updates for the mixture model in (1) is included in the supplementary material.

Once we optimize the objective introduced in the previous section, the responsibility matrix and parameter estimates can then be used to drive the segmentation and neuron labeling, respectively. Namely, we can use responsibility matrix terms, $\gamma_{l,i}$, to infer whether the ith pixel is occupied by the kth neuron, or the bth background component. Additionally, we can infer the neuron positions and colors with the $\boldsymbol{\mu}_k^n$ estimates. Lastly, $\boldsymbol{\Sigma}_k^n$ can inform us about the neuron shapes and color variability.

---

[1] We add the term "vanilla" to disambiguate the standard EM meta-algorithm from the proposed variant described later in the text.

Sinkhorn EM Algorithm: By definition, the rows of the responsibility matrix, $\gamma_{l,:}$, must sum to one, in order to be a bonafide probability. In other words, the lth component must exist somewhere within the image. However, in **vEM** (7), the only way to control the row sum of this matrix is through the constraints on component proportions or distribution-specific component parameters (such as constraining covariance eigenvalues to stay within a range for the Gaussian distribution). Both of these types of constraints effectively act as regularization on the responsibility matrix, γ. However, in practice, it is common that responsibilities for a component can collapse to zero through the mode collapse phenomenon [2]. This effectively prevents the segmentation of the lth object from the image, leading to false negatives.

In image segmentation, there often exists some information about the size of each component to be segmented. In our application of neuron segmentation, we have an estimation of how many pixels a neuron should occupy. To incorporate this information into the EM algorithm, we can explicitly constrain the row sum of the responsibility matrix, γ, to match the desired number of pixels (or weights), while keeping the column sum normalized to one. Specifically, in each iteration of EM algorithm, we aim to find a matrix $\hat{\gamma}$ that is close to γ while satisfying $\sum_l \gamma_{l,i} = 1$ and $\sum_i \gamma_{l,i} = \alpha_l$ where α_l encodes the proportion of pixels that the lth object must occupy. This procedure we describe has been explored by Sinkhorn and Knopp in [11] in what is known as the *matrix balancing algorithm*. In each iteration of EM, We use Sinkhorn's algorithm, to efficiently approximate $\hat{\gamma}$ by iteratively normalizing the row and column of γ matrix to sum to the pre-determined marginals α_l (Fig. 1). We term the resulting algorithm "Sinkhorn Expectation Maximization" (**sEM**) and study its empirical performance in comparison with **vEM** in the following sections.

3   Results

More formally, **sEM** deviates from **vEM** in the evaluation of the responsibilities. Instead of evaluating the expectation of the complete log likelihood, we base our algorithm on the recent finding that the E-step can be modified to be cast as an entropic optimal transport problem. Mena et al. in [8] have shown that this modification of the E-step still yields a monotonic increase in the log-posterior function and enjoys better convergence properties. We perform the iterations:

$$\textbf{Sinkhorn EM}: \begin{cases} \textbf{E-step:} & \text{update } \hat{\gamma} \text{ by solving:} \\ \hat{\gamma} = \underset{\gamma \in \Pi(\alpha, \frac{1}{N})}{\arg\min} \sum_{i,l} -\log P_l(X_i, \theta)\gamma_{l,i} + \mathcal{H}(\gamma | \alpha \otimes \frac{1}{N}) \\ \textbf{M-step:} & \text{solve } \theta_{t+1} = \underset{\theta}{\arg\max}\, Q(\theta | \theta_t) \end{cases}$$

$$(8)$$

Here $\boldsymbol{\alpha} = (\alpha_1, \ldots, \alpha_{K+B})$ is a vector that encapsulates our desired component proportions, $\mathbf{1}$ denotes a vector of ones with length N, $\Pi(\boldsymbol{V}_1, \boldsymbol{V}_2)$ is the set of all matrices with marginals equal to vectors $\boldsymbol{V}_1$ and $\boldsymbol{V}_2$, and $\mathcal{H}(\boldsymbol{\gamma} | \boldsymbol{A})$ is the relative entropy between probability measures γ, $\boldsymbol{A}$ which in our case simplifies

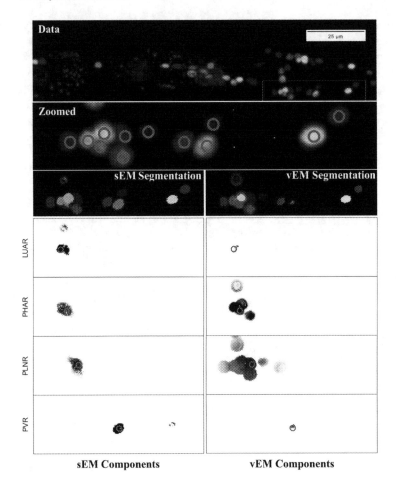

Fig. 2. Qualitative comparison of sEM and vEM segmentation maps. A maximum intensity projection of the volumetric NeuroPAL image is shown in the Data panel. To show the segmentation performance we zoom in on the Right Lumbar Ganglion (Zoomed panel; red rectangle in Data panel). Green circles represent expert annotations. Segmentation panels show the probabilistic segmentation of the components (γ_l). Each component is shown in its inferred color (μ_l^n) using both algorithms; **sEM** provides segmentation maps that are sharper and more cell-like, with more visible boundaries and less spread. Components panels show example per-component probabilistic segmentation maps (γ_l), with darker pixels having posterior assignment probabilities closer to one for each component. Red dots are the centers inferred by both algorithms. vEM tends to miss some components (LUAR, PVR) and spreads its mass to irrelevant regions for some other components (PHAR, PLNR). (Color figure online)

to $\sum_{l,i} \gamma_{l,i} \log \gamma_{l,i}$. As noted above, the E-step here can be solved by Sinkhorn iterations, the details of which can be found in the supplementary material.

Datasets: We ran the proposed algorithm on a *C. elegans* dataset consisting of images of 10 heads and 10 tails from the NeuroPAL strain. The images were captured using a spinning-disk confocal microscope with resolution $(x, y, z) = (0.27, 0.27, 1.5)\,\mu$. There were three color channels encoding red, green, and blue fluorescence excitation. Each head and tail image roughly consists of about 190 and 40 neurons, respectively, which were annotated by an expert who determined their positions. Processing and annotation details are described in [14]. Note that the only ground truth available were point markers that denoted the neuron centers. Complete ground truth segmentation of the cell shapes was not provided.

Compared Methods: We compare our algorithm, **sEM**, with a method that is designed specifically toward neural identification in NeuroPAL strains of *C. elegans* [14]. The neuron identification algorithm in [14], termed **CELL-ID**, employs a 3 (or 2) step process of filtering, detection, and identification. We hereafter refer to detect+identify version of this method as **CELL-ID (2)** and the filter+detect+identify version as **CELL-ID (3)**. The filtering steps here involve heuristic methods and the detection system uses a greedy matching pursuit algorithm. Lastly, the neuron identification is done by a variant of the iterative closest point algorithm [3].

Additionally, we compare with the segmentation and labeling performance of **vEM** as described in Eq. 7. Due to a lack of ground truth, we evaluated the segmentation results qualitatively by visualizing the spread and sharpness of the segmentation maps.

Neuron Identification: For each worm image, we first spatially smoothed it using a small 3D Gaussian filter (width $0.5\,\mu$m in each dimension). We then removed the low-intensity background pixels using a small threshold to ensure that only dark background pixels are removed (70-th percentile).

Each of **sEM** and **vEM** outputs the cell centers, colors, and shapes (in terms of 3D covariance matrices) as well as a γ matrix that includes neuron-specific probabilistic segmentation maps. **CELL-ID** on the other hand only outputs the centers and identities of neurons. The cell centers are used to quantify the accuracy of **sEM** in comparison to **vEM** and **CELL-ID** $(2)/(3)$. For each method, the accuracy is computed by counting the number of mixture components that are within a radius of $3\,\mu$ from their true location (annotated by an expert), dividing this by the total number of neurons. We detail the quantitative neuron identification results in Fig. 3A–B. In Fig. 3A, we show the neuron identification accuracy for the four compared methods. Due to the higher density of neurons in the head, the accuracies of all methods tended to be lower in the head than in the tail. However, **sEM** displayed significantly higher accuracies than all compared methods, with about 72% accuracy in the head and 89% in the tail. Similarly, Fig. 3B demonstrates that the distance of the cell centers inferred by **sEM** is less than $3\,\mu$ away from the expert annotations, on average, roughly corresponding to the average diameter of neurons.

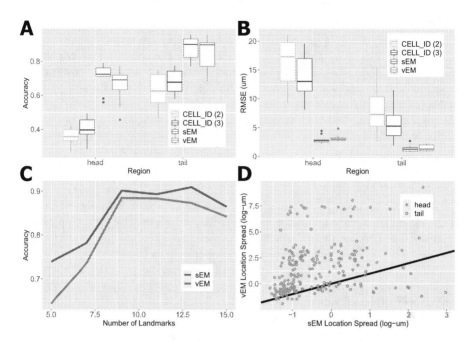

Fig. 3. Quantitative evaluations for neuron identification and segmentation sharpness. A: Comparison of neuron identification accuracy between **sEM**, **vEM**, **CELL-ID** (2) (detect+id) [14], and **CELL-ID** (3) (filter+detect+id); **sEM** accuracy is significantly higher than all other methods in the head, and slightly better than **vEM** in the tail. Both **vEM** and **sEM** outperform the multi-step **CELL-ID** approach. **B:** Root Mean Squared Error (RMSE) between the inferred neural locations and their expert annotated location; similar to **A**, **vEM** and **sEM** outperform **CELL-ID**, and **sEM** achieves lower RMSE than **vEM** in both head and tail. **C:** Average accuracy of **sEM** and **vEM** as a function of randomly chosen landmark cells; **sEM** slightly outperforms **vEM** and the accuracy increases as we use more landmark cells for the initial alignment. **D:** Median spatial spread of the neuron segmentation maps resulting from **sEM** and **vEM**. Here each dot indicates the spread of a particular neuron, with median taken across the population of worms. **vEM** spreads its mass for each component more than **sEM**, resulting in lower confidence in segmentation assignments. This is visually observed in Fig. 2 where the segmentation maps of **sEM** are more localized and sharper than those from **vEM**.

Robustness to Initialization and the Number of Landmark Cells: To evaluate the robustness of **sEM** and **vEM** to the selection of landmark cells, we did the following experiment: For $\kappa \in \{5, 7, 9, 11, 13\}$ we randomly selected a set of κ cells. Both sEM and vEM were run such that these positions and the identity of these cells were used as landmark cells for computing the initial alignment, β, that transforms the neuron positions from their atlas-based locations. The average accuracy increases with more landmark cells (Fig. 3C), but the best results are obtained if the landmark cells accurately portray the posture of the worm.

We further evaluated the robustness of our algorithm to initialization. Instead of initializing the centers and colors using an atlas, we initialized them using a random subset of the points selected uniformly from the observed pixels. Although initialized randomly, the effect of the atlas as a prior on the cell centers and colors led both **sEM** and **vEM** to converge quickly toward the actual cell locations, with accuracies reaching 80% (std $= 0.07$) for **sEM** and 79% (std $= 0.1$) with **vEM**.

Segmentation Quality: The probabilistic segmentation maps are used to qualitatively evaluate **sEM** and **vEM**. In Fig. 2, we observe that **sEM** provides sharper and more localized segmentation maps for neurons with boundaries that are more visible and more similar to the presumed borders. To quantify these sharpness attributes, we computed the spatial spread of the segmentations for the lth neuron by computing the spatial variance of using the following formula:

$$\textbf{Location spread}(l) = \text{Var}_{l_i \sim \gamma_{i,l}}(\boldsymbol{l}_i), \tag{9}$$

where we compute the variance of the lth neuron's map by using the γ matrix as weights. Note that $\boldsymbol{l}_i$ denotes the coordinates of the ith pixel. We then compared this metric between **vEM** and **sEM** across all neurons of the head and tail (Fig. 3D). The results show that while both methods perform similarly in the tail, **sEM** yields significantly sharper and more localized segmentation maps in the denser head images.

Our results show that in addition to the theoretical properties examined in [8], another advantage of **sEM** over **vEM** in the context of image segmentation with shape or size priors, is that mode collapse is prevented due to matrix balancing on γ (see **vEM** components of LUAR and PVR in Fig. 2).

Conclusion: In this paper, we studied the problem of probabilistic cell segmentation and labeling in the nematode *C. elegans*, exploiting a spatial+color atlas of neurons developed in [14]. We formulated the segmentation problem as a mixture model and incorporated additional constraints on cell sizes using an efficient Sinkhorn iterative approach. The resulting Sinkhorn Expectation-Maximization approach led to significant improvements compared to previous analysis approaches developed for this type of data.

Several important directions for future work remain open. First, our preliminary affine alignment requires some (modest) user input to label a few cells; it would be preferable to use a fully-automatic alignment approach. We may also achieve further improvements with a non-affine registration model or a more detailed atlas that models correlations in the locations of nearby cells [4]. We could also incorporate further shape constraints on the probabilistic segmentation terms γ_l here; for example, enforcing spatial locality constraints could help eliminate multimodal segmentation of nearby cells with similar colors. Finally, the methods developed here should apply to a wide variety of other worm datasets from a variety of developmental stages. We hope to pursue these directions in the near future.

References

1. Aerni, S.J., et al.: Automated cellular annotation for high-resolution images of adult caenorhabditis elegans. Bioinformatics (Oxford, Engl.) **29**(13), i18–i26 (2013). 23812982[pmid]
2. Archambeau, C., Lee, J.A., Verleysen, M., et al.: On convergence problems of the em algorithm for finite Gaussian mixtures. In: ESANN, vol. 3, pp. 99–106 (2003)
3. Besl, P.J., McKay, N.D.: Method for registration of 3-d shapes. In: Sensor fusion IV: control paradigms and data structures, vol. 1611, pp. 586–606. International Society for Optics and Photonics (1992)
4. Bubnis, G., Ban, S., DiFranco, M.D., Kato, S.: A probabilistic atlas for cell identification. arXiv:1903.09227 (2019)
5. Chaudhary, S., Lee, S.A., Li, Y., Patel, D.S., Lu, H.: Automated annotation of cell identities in dense cellular images. bioRxiv (2020)
6. Dempster, A.P., Laird, N.M., Rubin, D.B.: Maximum likelihood from incomplete data via the EM algorithm. J. Roy. Stat. Soc.: Ser. B (Methodol.) **39**(1), 1–22 (1977)
7. Hirose, O., Kawaguchi, S., et al.: SPF-CellTracker: tracking multiple cells with strongly-correlated moves using a spatial particle filter. IEEE/ACM Trans. Comput. Biol. Bioinf. **15**(6), 1822–1831 (2018)
8. Mena, G., Nejatbakhsh, A., Varol, E., Niles-Weed, J.: Sinkhorn EM: an expectation-maximization algorithm based on entropic optimal transport. arXiv:2006.16548 (2020)
9. Qu, L., et al.: Simultaneous recognition and segmentation of cells: application in C. elegans. Bioinformatics (Oxford, Engl.) **27**(20), 2895–2902 (2011). 21849395[pmid]
10. Schrödel, T., Prevedel, R., Aumayr, K., Zimmer, M., Vaziri, A.: Brain-wide 3d imaging of neuronal activity in caenorhabditis elegans with sculpted light. Nat. Methods **10**(10), 1013 (2013)
11. Sinkhorn, R., Knopp, P.: Concerning nonnegative matrices and doubly stochastic matrices. Pac. J. Math. **21**(2), 343–348 (1967)
12. Tokunaga, T., et al.: Automated detection and tracking of many cells by using 4d live-cell imaging data. Bioinformatics (Oxford, Engl.) **30**(12), i43–i51 (2014). 24932004[pmid]
13. Toyoshima, Y., Wu, S., Kanamori, M., Sato, H., Jang, M.S., Oe, S., Murakami, Y., et al.: An annotation dataset facilitates automatic annotation of whole-brain activity imaging of C. elegans. bioRxiv (2019)
14. Yemini, E., et al.: NeuroPAL: a neuronal polychromatic atlas of landmarks for whole-brain imaging in C. elegans. bioRxiv (2019)

Segmenting Continuous but Sparsely-Labeled Structures in Super-Resolution Microscopy Using Perceptual Grouping

Jiabing Li[(✉)], Camille Artur, Jason Eriksen, Badrinath Roysam,
and David Mayerich

University of Houston, Houston, USA
jiabingli601@hotmail.com

Abstract. Super Resolution (SR) microscopy leverages a variety of optical and computational techniques for overcoming the optical diffraction limit to acquire additional spatial details. However, added spatial details challenge existing segmentation tools. Confounding features include protein distributions that form membranes and boundaries, such as cellular and nuclear surfaces. We present a segmentation pipeline that retains the benefits provided by SR in surface separation while providing a tensor field to overcome these confounding features. The proposed technique leverages perceptual grouping to generate a tensor field that enables robust evolution of active contours despite ill-defined membrane boundaries.

Keywords: Super resolution · Segmentation · Perceptual grouping · Tensors · Contours

Super resolution (SR) microscopy [24] encompasses a set of imaging techniques that overcome the diffraction limit [8] of traditional microscopes. SR imaging enables high-resolution microscopy, enabling biologists to probe tissue structure at the nanometer scale. In recent years, a number of novel approaches have been employed to circumvent the diffraction limit, including expansion microscopy (ExM) [2,5], stimulated emission depletion microscopy (STED) [25], photo activation localization microscopy (PALM) [9], stochastic optical reconstruction microscopy (STORM) [19] and structured illumination microscopy (SIM) [7].

SR provides greater spatial detail, enabling differentiation of individual protein clusters and separating tightly packed membranes (Fig. 1). While these additional features provide important details for understanding tissue structure, they challenge automated segmentation algorithms. For example, cellular and nuclear membranes are often identified by labeling embedded proteins, resulting in non-continuous punctate boundaries (Fig. 1). Algorithms commonly used for traditional microscopy, such as the FARSIGHT Toolkit [1] produce over-segmented

© Springer Nature Switzerland AG 2020
A. L. Martel et al. (Eds.): MICCAI 2020, LNCS 12265, pp. 141–150, 2020.
https://doi.org/10.1007/978-3-030-59722-1_14

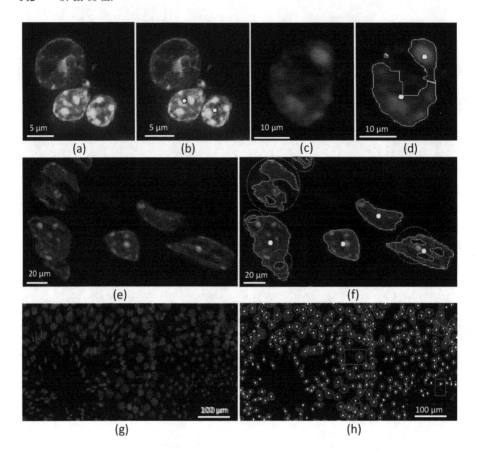

Fig. 1. FARSIGHT segmentation results on mouse brain(a, b, e, f) and kidney(c, b) histological nuclear staining using STED (a, b), using ExM (c, d, g, h), and high-resolution confocal microscopy (e, f).

results. Other challenges include (1) heterogeneous cell shapes, (2) contrast disparities, and (3) overlapping/clustered cells and nuclei. **In general, enhanced resolution provides additional spatial detail while making surfaces less clearly defined.**

In this paper, we propose a novel segmentation method *localization-reinforced perceptual grouping* (LRPG) that constructs a tensor-based [10] representation of the image and then refines this field leveraging perceptual grouping methods [15]. The resulting tensor field forms the basis for a more robust SR segmentation. Our approach maintains the coherence of punctate surfaces as well as the desired benefits of surface separability provided by SR imaging. Performance is tested on SR images acquired using expansion microscopy (ExM) [2] and stimulated emission depletion (STED) [25]. Performance benchmarks are compared to the current state-of-the-art in cell and nuclear segmentation, including FARSIGHT [1], modular interactive nuclear segmentation (MINS) [13], and TIMING 2.0 [14].

Our perceptually-based approach improves the performance of active contours, such as level set, and provides a significant benefit over existing algorithms for SR images.

1   Localization-Reinforced Perceptual Grouping

Our proposed LRPG framework is shown as Fig. 2, which includes four main steps: cell centroid detection, tensor voting, level set evolution, and watershed segmentation. We first identify cell positions using iterative voting [20], which requires an initial estimate of cell radius. We then calculate and refine a tensor field used to guide contours through high-frequency features in the image. This refinement is based on optimizing the angular discrepancy between the primary tensor direction and cell centroids. Cell contours are identified using a level set method evolved from the set of centroids and guided by the refined tensor field. Finally, watershed method is applied to separate connected cells.

1.1   Cell Seeds Detection

A GPU-based iterative voting method [20] is used to quickly calculate candidate points representing cell positions. We initialize the voting using the image gradient and apply iterative voting. The voting fields are refined to produce a set of candidate seeds (Fig. 3). A threshold is specified across the entire voting data to select candidate cell positions. Note that iterative voting requires an estimate of the cell radius as input. Since cell sizes can cover a wide range, we apply scale-space sampling using multiple iterative voting with different radius parameters. The voting images are added together and smoothed with a Gaussian filter ($\sigma = 5$) to merge multi-detected cell positions. Finally, a single iterative voting step is applied to this final image to extract the set of final cell centroids.

1.2   Localization Reinforced Tensor Voting

Tensor voting [12,16,17] is an algorithm for identifying "salient" structures in multi-dimensional data. This approach uses local features to reinforce global structure [6]. We leverage this approach to (1) reconstruct cell contours, and (2) extract refined tensor field flow as force flow for level set segmentation and gradient flow for watershed segmentation.

A Canny edge detector [21] is applied to identify candidate contour features defining cell boundaries. These contours are encoded using ball tensors when construct original tensor field and then iteratively refined using tensor voting [16]. After each voting iteration, the tensor field is decomposed into eigenvalues λ_1, λ_2 and their corresponding eigenvectors e_1, e_2 [10,17], which is defined as:

$$T = \lambda_1 e_1 e_1^T + \lambda_2 e_2 e_2^T = (\lambda_1 - \lambda_2)e_1 e_1^T + \lambda_2(e_1 e_1^T + e_2 e_2^T), \quad (1)$$

where $(\lambda_1 - \lambda_2)e_1 e_1^T$ describes a stick tensor T_S and $\lambda_2(e_1 e_1^T + e_2 e_2^T)$ describes a ball tensor T_B. Each feature is characterized by its curve saliency ($\lambda_1 -$

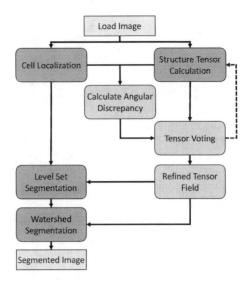

Fig. 2. Pipeline of localization-reinforced perceptual grouping. Input image are processed into four main steps: cell seeds extraction, cell saliency feature extraction from tensor voting, binary mask extraction from level set segmentation and final using seeds based watershed methods to segment every single cell.

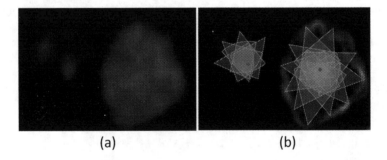

Fig. 3. Iterative voting for cell seeds identification [20]. (a) Input image. (b) Calculate the gradient of the input image and each non-zero point of the gradient image can be a voter. Then calculate voting area of voter and integrate all votes from voters. Local maximum algorithm is applied to extract cell positions candidates.

λ_2) with orientation e_1, and point saliency λ_2 with no preferred orientation (Fig. 4(a)). We apply a threshold (usually 0.05) on curve feature $(\lambda_1 - \lambda_2)$ to remove useless contour sides. Salient cell contours are then reconstructed by iterative tensor voting (Fig. 5).

We then implement a novel localization-reinforced tensor voting method to generate and refine a field for contour evolution. A new field $\mathbf{S}(x, y)$ is generated by calculating the structure tensor at each point. We then calculate the angular discrepancy $R(x, y)$ between cell centroids and principal eigenvectors $\mathbf{e}_1(x, y)$

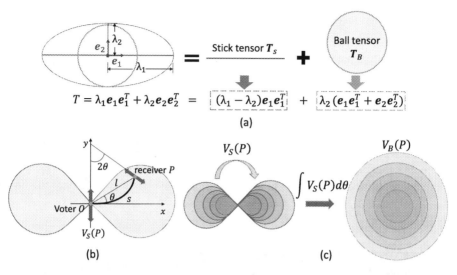

Fig. 4. (a) Tensor decomposition into a stick tensor and ball tensor. (b) Stick tensor voting field calculation. O is the voter and P is a receiver, s is the arc length, and l is OP length, θ is the angle between the tangent to the osculating circle at the voter and the line going through the voter and receiver. Voting value is based on saliency decay function: $V_S(l, \theta, \sigma) = e^{\frac{s^2 + ck^2}{\sigma^2}}$,, where $s = \frac{\theta l}{sin\theta}, k = \frac{2sin\theta}{l}$. Voting value is zero if θ larger than $\pi/4$. (c) Ball voting field is an integration of stick tensor voting field.

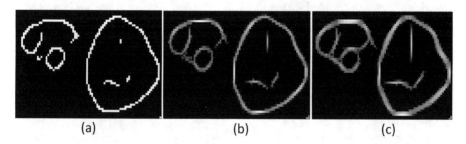

Fig. 5. Cell contours reconstruction from iterative tensor voting. (a) Original cell curve after applying a Canny detector. (b) Cell contours after one time tensor voting. (c) Cell contours after two times tensor voting.

of $\mathbf{S}(x, y)$ by computing their dot product with the gradient of the centroid's Euclidean distance field $\mathbf{D}(x, y)$:

$$R(x, y) = \left| \frac{\mathbf{e}_1(x, y) \cdot \nabla \mathbf{D}(x, y)}{||\mathbf{e}_1(x, y) \cdot \nabla \mathbf{D}(x, y)||} \right| \tag{2}$$

The angular discrepancy $R(x, y)$ can be thought of as a scalar value to quantify each tensor's reliability. Then we set a threshold t_r on R to force unreliable voters' value to zero (our experiments use $t_r = 0.8$).

Then for each voting iteration, the total number of votes received at a pixel i is given by:

$$T_{n+1} = T_n + R \sum_{i\varepsilon\omega} V(i), \qquad (3)$$

where the $V(i)$ means the total voting at pixel i integrated from neighbor voters. We repeat the step of localization reinforced tensor voting until most (usually 90%) tensors are recognized as reliable tensors, which means small angular discrepancy with seeds. Finally, we decompose the final refined tensor field T_N to extract eigen vector e_{1N} as cell contours expansion flow. After the localization reinforced tensor voting, we can see the original messed tensor field (Fig. 6(c)) becomes the refined tensor field (Fig. 6(d)), in which most tensors are aligned to point to seeds. Most importantly, the tensor field still keeps the original cell shapes.

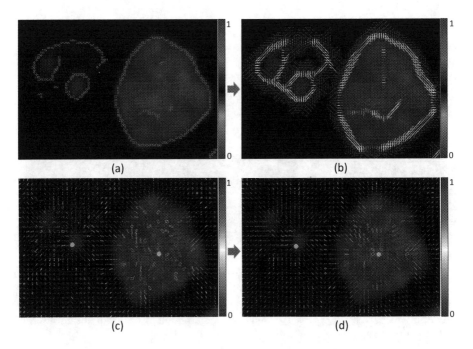

Fig. 6. Tensor field refining. (a) Original encoded tensor field of Canny edge using ball tensor. (b) Cell contours tensor field after iterative tensor voting. (c) Original mess tensor field encoding using image gradient. (d) Refined tensor field after localization reinforced tensor voting. Color bars indicate tensor reliability. (Color figure online)

1.3 Level Set Contour Evolution

Level set methods [18,22] are commonly used to solve curve evolution problems with potential topological changes, such as splitting and merging. This approach calculates the evolution of an embedded (2D) curve within a higher-dimensional (3D) space. The curve is initialized as a point at each cell centroid and propagated along a velocity field specified by the refined tensor field using Euler integration to solve the resulting partial differential equation (PDE) [4,11]. Iterative voting provides high confidence cell centroids used as initial contours. The eigenvector $\mathbf{e}_1(x, y)$ provides the outward gradient flow and $\nabla I'$ provides an additional inward force. The level set contour moves outward following $\mathbf{e}_1$ until balanced by the inward force to achieve a minimum energy state.

Our level set based on refined tensor field performs significantly better than a traditional level set approach based on gradient. Due to the velocity field design, traditional level set evolution often stops at local minima. Since refined tensor field provide continue flow from cell centers to cell boundaries, it can help level set evolution propagate over dim signal part to real cell boundaries.

1.4   Watershed Segmentation

Watershed algorithm [23] is used to separate connected cells. Due to too many local minima problem in traditional gradient-descent algorithms, watershed often results in over-segmentation [3]. From the refined tensor field, we can extract the smoothing gradient field to filter out local minima. So it can fix over-segmentation efficiently (Fig. 8). To prove that, we reconstruct image I' using the Poisson Reconstruction method [26]. In Fig. 7(a), we can see that the reconstructed cell has the highest intensity in its center with intensity decreasing gradually from center to boundaries. The gradient from I' could remove the impact of noise and quantization errors in watershed. It also can be seen as a refined cell distance field keeping the original cell shape. Combining extracted binary mask from level set, seeds from iterative vote and refined tensor field as gradient flow, watershed yields good results for segmenting every single cell.

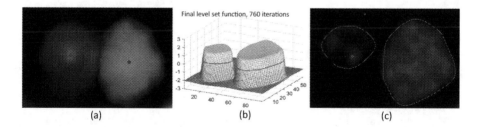

(a)   (b)   (c)

Fig. 7. Level set active contour movement till inward and outward balance, extract minimum energy line as final reconstructed cell contour. (a) Poisson reconstructed image from refined tensor field. (b) Final level set function after 760 iterations; (c) Final segmentation contour from level set evolution.

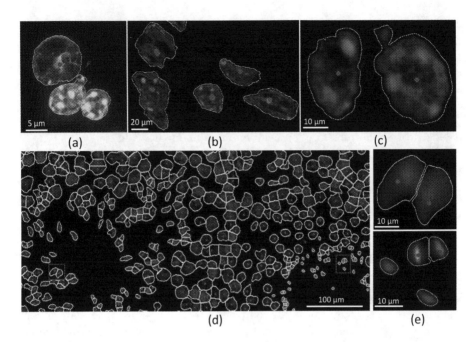

Fig. 8. Segmentation results. (a) Mouse brain STED image. (b) Mouse brain confocal image. (c) Mouse kidney expansion microscopy. (d–e) Mouse testicle expansion microscopy.

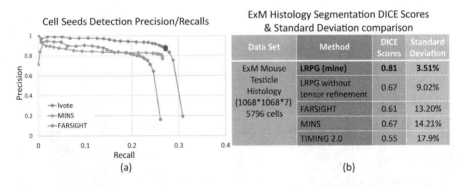

Fig. 9. Analysis of segmentation results on ExM testicle images ($1068 \times 1068 \times 7$ pixels, 5,796 cells in total). (a) Precision-Recall curve comparison of seeds detection using iterative voting, FARSIGHT and MINS. (b) Segmentation DICE scores and standard deviation comparison.

2   Results Analysis

We quantified the results on seven ExM mouse testicle images ($1068 * 1068$) with 5796 cells in total. Seeds identification results are compared with MINS [13] and FARSIGHT [1] using precision-recall curves (Fig. 9a). Segmentation results are quantified using DICE scores (Fig. 9b). LRPG yields significantly better results when segmenting sparsely-labeled cells with punctate features, where other methods over-segment the nuclei (Fig. 8a–c). LRPG also performs better when segmenting heterogeneous cells with a wide range sizes and contrasts (Fig. 9d–e).

3   Conclusion and Future Work

The proposed perceptual grouping approach is highly parallel and is extendable to higher-dimensional images, as well as multiplex imaging. Potential future directions include a GPU-based implementation to enable the practical segmentation of large images.

Acknowledgement. This work is funded in part by the National Institutes of Health/National Heart, Lung, and Blood Institute (NHLBI) #R01HL146745, the Cancer Prevention and Research Institute of Texas (CPRIT) #RR140013, the National Science Foundation I/UCRC BRAIN Center #1650566, and the National Institutes of Health Training Grant #T15LM007093.

References

1. Al-Kofahi, Y., Lassoued, W., Lee, W., Roysam, B.: Improved automatic detection and segmentation of cell nuclei in histopathology images. IEEE Trans. Biomed. Eng. **57**(4), 841–852 (2010)
2. Artur, C., Womack, T., Eriksen, J.L.J., Mayerich, D., Shih, W.C.: Hyperspectral expansion microscopy. In: 2017 IEEE Photonics Conference (IPC), pp. 23–24, October 2017
3. Beucher, S.: Watershed, hierarchical segmentation and waterfall algorithm. In: Serra, J., Soille, P. (eds.) Mathematical Morphology and Its Applications to Image Processing. Computational Imaging and Vision, vol. 2, pp. 69–76. Springer, Dordrecht (1994). https://doi.org/10.1007/978-94-011-1040-2_10
4. Chan, T.F., Shen, J., Vese, L.: Variational PDE models in image processing. Not. AMS **50**(1), 14–26 (2003)
5. Chen, F., Tillberg, P.W., Boyden, E.S.: Expansion microscopy. Science **347**(6221), 543–548 (2015)
6. Guy, G., Medioni, G.: Inferring global perceptual contours from local features. Int. J. Comput. Vis. **20**(1), 113–133 (1996). https://doi.org/10.1007/BF00144119
7. Heintzmann, R., Huser, T.: Super-resolution structured illumination microscopy. Chem. Rev. **117**(23), 13890–13908 (2017)
8. Huang, B., Babcock, H., Zhuang, X.: Breaking the diffraction barrier: super-resolution imaging of cells. Cell **7**(143), 1047–1058 (2010)
9. Huang, B., Bates, M., Zhuang, X.: Super resolution fluorescence microscopy. Annu. Rev. Biochem. **78**, 993–1016 (2009)
10. Jörgens, D., Moreno, R.: Tensor voting: current state, challenges and new trends in the context of medical image analysis. In: Hotz, I., Schultz, T. (eds.) Visualization and Processing of Higher Order Descriptors for Multi-Valued Data. MV, pp. 163–187. Springer, Cham (2015). https://doi.org/10.1007/978-3-319-15090-1_9

11. Li, C., Xu, C., Gui, C., Fox, M.D.: Distance regularized level set evolution and its application to image segmentation. IEEE Trans. Image Process. **19**(12), 3243–3254 (2010)

12. Loss, L., Bebis, G., Nicolescu, M., Skurikhin, A.: An iterative multi-scale tensor voting scheme for perceptual grouping of natural shapes in cluttered backgrounds. Comput. Vis. Image Underst. **113**(1), 126–149 (2009)

13. Lou, X., Kang, M., Xenopoulos, P., Muñoz-Descalzo, S., Hadjantonakis, A.K.: A rapid and efficient 2D/3D nuclear segmentation method for analysis of early mouse embryo and stem cell image data. Stem Cell Rep. **2**(3), 382–397 (2014)

14. Lu, H., et al.: TIMING 2.0: high-throughput single-cell profiling of dynamic cell-cell interactions by time-lapse imaging microscopy in nanowell grids. Bioinformatics **35**, 706–708 (2018)

15. Luo, J., Guo, C.E.: Perceptual grouping of segmented regions in color images. Pattern Recogn. **36**(12), 2781–2792 (2003)

16. Mordohai, P., Medioni, G.: Tensor voting: a perceptual organization approach to computer vision and machine learning. **2**(1), 1–136 (2006). Morgan & Claypool Publishers

17. Moreno, R., Garcia, M.A., Puig, D., Julià, C.: On adapting the tensor voting framework to robust color image denoising. In: Jiang, X., Petkov, N. (eds.) CAIP 2009. LNCS, vol. 5702, pp. 492–500. Springer, Heidelberg (2009). https://doi.org/10.1007/978-3-642-03767-2_60

18. Osher, S., Fedkiw, R.: Level Set Methods and Dynamic Implicit Surfaces, vol. 153. Springer, Heidelberg (2006). https://doi.org/10.1007/b98879

19. Rust, M.J., Bates, M., Zhuang, X.: Sub-diffraction-limit imaging by stochastic optical reconstruction microscopy (STORM). Nat. Methods **3**(10), 793–796 (2006)

20. Saadatifard, L., Abbott, L.C., Montier, L., Ziburkus, J., Mayerich, D.: Robust cell detection for large-scale 3D microscopy using GPU-accelerated iterative voting. Front. Neuroanat. **12**, 28 (2018)

21. Sahir, S.: Canny Edge Detection Step by Step in Python - Computer Vision, January 2019

22. Sethian, J.A.: Level Set Methods and Fast Marching Methods: Evolving Interfaces in Computational Geometry, Fluid Mechanics, Computer Vision, and Materials Science, vol. 3. Cambridge University Press, Cambridge (1999)

23. Shen, J., Jin, X., Zhou, C., Wang, C.C.L.: Gradient based image completion by solving the Poisson equation. Comput. Graph. **31**, 119–126 (2007)

24. Shtengel, G., et al.: Interferometric fluorescent super-resolution microscopy resolves 3D cellular ultrastructure. Proc. Nat. Acad. Sci. **106**(9), 3125–3130 (2009)

25. Vicidomini, G., Bianchini, P., Diaspro, A.: STED Super-resolved microscopy. Nat. Methods **15**(3), 173–182 (2018)

26. Willett, R.M., Harmany, Z.T., Marcia, R.F.: Poisson image reconstruction with total variation regularization. In: 2010 IEEE International Conference on Image Processing, pp. 4177–4180, September 2010. https://doi.org/10.1109/ICIP.2010.5649600

DISCo: Deep Learning, Instance Segmentation, and Correlations for Cell Segmentation in Calcium Imaging

Elke Kirschbaum[1,2](✉), Alberto Bailoni[1], and Fred A. Hamprecht[1]

[1] Interdisciplinary Center for Scientific Computing (IWR), Heidelberg University, 69120 Heidelberg, Germany
{alberto.bailoni,fred.hamprecht}@iwr.uni-heidelberg.de
[2] Amazon Research, 72076 Tübingen, Germany
elkeki@amazon.com

Abstract. Calcium imaging is one of the most important tools in neurophysiology as it enables the observation of neuronal activity for hundreds of cells in parallel and at single-cell resolution. In order to use the data gained with calcium imaging, it is necessary to extract individual cells and their activity from the recordings. We present DISCo, a novel approach for the cell segmentation in calcium imaging videos. We use temporal information from the recordings in a computationally efficient way by computing correlations between pixels and combine it with shape-based information to identify active as well as non-active cells. We first learn to predict whether two pixels belong to the same cell; this information is summarized in an undirected, edge-weighted graph which we then partition. Evaluating our method on the Neurofinder public benchmark shows that DISCo outperforms all existing models trained on these datasets.

Keywords: Calcium imaging · Cell segmentation · Neuro imaging analysis

1 Introduction

Calcium imaging is a microscopy technique that allows the observation of the activity of large neuronal populations at single-cell resolution [3,8,13]. This makes it one of the most important tools in neurophysiology since it enables the study of the formation and interaction of neuronal networks in the brain. The data recorded with calcium imaging is a sequence of images that shows multiple cells at fixed locations and with varying luminosity. The extraction of

---

E. Kirschbaum—This work was done while E.K. was at 1.

Electronic supplementary material The online version of this chapter (https://doi.org/10.1007/978-3-030-59722-1_15) contains supplementary material, which is available to authorized users.

© Springer Nature Switzerland AG 2020
A. L. Martel et al. (Eds.): MICCAI 2020, LNCS 12265, pp. 151–162, 2020.
https://doi.org/10.1007/978-3-030-59722-1_15

the individual cell locations from the calcium imaging videos is a fundamental but yet unsolved problem in the analysis of this data [16].

In order to encourage the development of new tools for the cell segmentation in calcium imaging videos, and to enable a meaningful comparison of different approaches, the Neurofinder public benchmark [2] was initiated. The Neurofinder challenge consists of 19 calcium imaging videos with ground truth cell annotations for training, and of nine test videos with undisclosed ground truth. Both, training and test set, can be clustered into five dataset series (named 00, 01, 02, 03, and 04) which were recorded under different conditions and differ also in labeling technique and whether the ground truth annotations also contain inactive cells. Details on the five groups of datasets can be found in [30].

In this paper, we present *DISCo*, a novel approach using *D*eep learning, *I*nstance *S*egmentation, and *Co*rrelations for the cell segmentation in calcium imaging videos. DISCo combines the advantages of a deep learning model with a state-of-the-art instance segmentation algorithm, allowing the direct extraction of cell instances. Additionally, we use temporal context from the calcium imaging videos by computing segment-wise correlations between pixels. This temporal information is combined with shape-based information, which is a huge advantage of DISCo compared to methods that solely rely on the one or the other. This enables us to achieve a very good overall performance using only a single model on all Neurofinder datasets. Moreover, when training individual networks on the five dataset series (submission called DISCos), we are able to outperform all other methods trained on the Neurofinder datasets.

2   Related Work

For the extraction of cells from calcium imaging data most existing algorithms are based on non-negative matrix factorization (NMF) [6,9,11,12,24–26], clustering [14,30], dictionary learning [5,7,20,23], and deep learning [17,28]. In the Neurofinder leaderboard the currently top scoring methods are STNeuroNet and 3dCNN [28], followed by HNCcorr [30] combined with Conv2D [10], UNet2DS [17], as well as Sourcery and Suite2P [21] together with Donuts [20]. UNet2DS and Conv2D use deep learning models with so-called *summary images* as input. These summary images contain for each pixel the mean projection over time, which means that all temporal information of the calcium imaging videos is lost. As a consequence, these approaches are not competitive on datasets which contain many active neurons, like the dataset series 01, 02 and 04 of the Neurofinder challenge. In contrast to this, the method HNCcorr is able to detect the active cells in the dataset series 01, 02 and 04 fairly well, while it performs rather poorly on the other datasets. The reason for this is that HNCcorr uses a clustering algorithm based on the distance of pixels in *correlation space*. In this correlation space pixels from cells with a changing signal should be well separated from background pixels, but pixels from cells with weak or constant activity will not be distinguishable from background. In order to overcome this problem and to achieve competitive average F1-scores in the Neurofinder challenge, HNCcorr and Conv2D were combined by using the first for the dataset series 01, 02 and 04 and the latter for the series 00 and 03 [30]. The same holds true for the NMF-based methods Sourcery and Suite2P which need to be complemented by the shape-based algorithm Donuts in order to achieve decent average F1-scores. In contrast to this, the deep learning models STNeuroNet and its developmental stage 3dCNN are able to achieve good F1-scores on all test datasets with a single method using a 3D convolutional neural network (CNN) on the calcium imaging video. Since such models can become computationally very costly, especially for videos consisting of several thousand frames like the ones in the Neurofinder challenge, the models are only run on short temporal batches of the video and to gain the cell locations for the whole video, the outputs from the different batches have to be merged in the post-processing. Moreover, like all leading methods using deep learning, STNeuroNet and 3dCNN only provide a foreground-background prediction and also need post-processing to extract individual cell instances. STNeuroNet was trained with additional data and with manually refined ground truth. In contrast to this, 3dCNN uses only the datasets and ground truth provided in the Neurofinder challenge. Though the 3dCNN submission consists of a single method, it uses separately trained networks for each of the five Neurofinder dataset series.

3 Method

DISCo extracts temporal information from the calcium imaging videos by computing segment-wise correlations between pixels. This temporal information is combined with shape-based information from a summary image and transformed to affinities between pixels by a deep neural network. Finally, the affinities are used by a state-of-the-art instance segmentation algorithm to extract and separate individual cells.

More specifically, DISCo starts by splitting the video temporally into segments on which the correlations between pixels are computed as described in Sect. 3.1. Computing the correlations on multiple segments means that the temporal dimension of the video tensor is reduced, but is not completely removed. Hence, we use a small 3D CNN to aggregate the information from the different segments. In addition, a summary image is computed by taking for each pixel the mean projection over the whole video. The summary image is combined with the aggregated information from the segment-wise correlations to provide the second network with temporal and shape-based information. The second network maps this input to affinities between pixels in a highly non-linear fashion. The details of the two networks and how they are jointly trained are given in Sect. 3.2. In the final step, an undirected, edge-weighted graph is constructed from the predicted affinities and the individual cells are directly extracted and separated by partitioning this signed graph. In addition to the pixel-wise affinities, the neural network also provides a foreground-background prediction which is used in the instance segmentation algorithm to directly exclude background pixels from the graph before the clustering, reducing false merges of cells and background. The details of the instance segmentation algorithm are described in Sect. 3.3.

The complete model is also summarized in Fig. 1 and a PyTorch implementation of the proposed method is available on GitHub.[1]

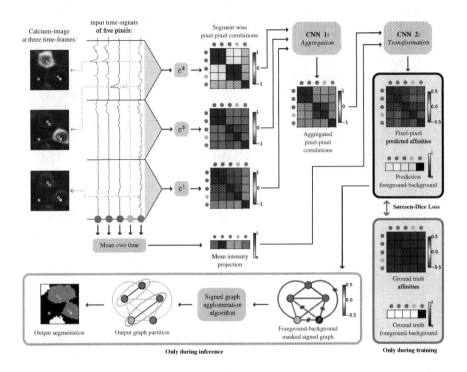

Fig. 1. DISCo workflow. For five exemplary pixel signals from the Neurofinder training set we show how they are processed by DISCo. First, the signals are split into temporal segments and segment-wise correlations between the pixels are computed. Next, the information from the segments is aggregated by a first CNN. These aggregated correlations are complemented by a mean intensity projection over time for each pixel. This combination of temporal and spatial information is processed by a second CNN which outputs affinities between pixels and a foreground-background prediction. Both CNNs are trained end-to-end. The predicted affinities are used by a graph partitioning algorithm to gain the final instance segmentation.

3.1   Temporal Information from Correlations

Since the fluorescence dynamics of cells and those of background pixels differ drastically, using the temporal context from calcium imaging videos is a huge benefit for the detection of cells. Moreover, without temporal information it is difficult to separate touching or overlapping cells correctly. For this reason,

---

[1] https://github.com/EKirschbaum/DISCo.

we use the temporal information from the calcium imaging videos in form of correlations.

Consider a video $\mathbf{X} \in \mathbb{R}^{T \times P \times Q}$ with T time frames and $P \times Q$ pixels. We define the vector $\mathbf{x}_{pq}$ to be the signal of pixel (p, q) of length T with $\mathbf{x}_{pq}(t) = \mathbf{X}_{tpq}$. For two pixels (p, q) and (p', q') the Pearson correlation coefficient [22] between their signals is

$$c(\mathbf{x}_{pq}, \mathbf{x}_{p'q'}) := \frac{\langle \mathbf{x}_{pq} - \bar{\mathbf{x}}_{pq}, \mathbf{x}_{p'q'} - \bar{\mathbf{x}}_{p'q'} \rangle}{\|\mathbf{x}_{pq} - \bar{\mathbf{x}}_{pq}\|_2 \cdot \|\mathbf{x}_{p'q'} - \bar{\mathbf{x}}_{p'q'}\|_2}, \tag{1}$$

where $\bar{\mathbf{x}}_{..}$ denotes the mean of the signal $\mathbf{x}_{..}$ over time and $\langle \cdot, \cdot \rangle$ is the dot product. The Pearson correlation coefficient measures the linear correlation between the two signals and is 1 for perfectly correlated signals, 0 for non-correlated signals and -1 for anti-correlated signals. In theory it might seem beneficial to use other measures that can also take into account non-linear associations between signals, like e.g. the distance correlation [31]. In practice, however, we found the Pearson correlation to be the better choice, since it can be computed faster and very efficiently even for large images and long time series. This allows us to compute the correlations online during the network training, which enables a broader range of data augmentation steps. Instead of computing the correlations between two pixels over the whole temporal extent of the video, we first split the video into $N = 10$ segments and then compute the correlations segment-wise. The correlation between two pixels during the n-th segment is then given by

$$c^n(\mathbf{x}_{pq}, \mathbf{x}_{p'q'}) := c(\mathbf{x}_{pq}^n, \mathbf{x}_{p'q'}^n) \tag{2}$$

with $\mathbf{x}_{..}^n$ being the n-th segment of the time series $\mathbf{x}_{...}$. The segment-wise computation of correlation coefficients was also proposed in [19] in form of the *scaled correlation* to remove correlation components slower than those defined by the used scale. Note that although Pearson correlation coefficients are a measure of linear association, their computation is non-linear and hence $c_s \neq c$ for $N > 1$. In contrast to this scaled correlation, which takes the mean over the segments, we use a CNN to aggregate the information of the different segments. As shown in Sect. 4 this provides more information for the transformation network and results in a better segmentation.

Inspired by the idea of the correlation space used in [30], we compute the correlations not only between a pixel and its direct neighbors, but to a broader neighborhood. For each pixel, we compute the correlation to $C = 15$ other pixels with a distance up to three pixels away. This size of neighborhood empirically showed to provide enough information for the network. Thus, the output of the correlation computations are $N = 10$ stacks of size $C \times P \times Q$, where each channel contains the correlations for all $P \times Q$ pixels to one of the $C = 15$ considered neighbors.

3.2 Deep Neural Network

The used deep neural network consists of two parts which are trained together end-to-end. The first CNN with 3D convolutions aggregates the information of the segment-wise correlations. The output of this network is combined with a summary image and passed to the second network, which is a standard 2D U-Net architecture[2] [27]. The outputs of this network are the predicted affinities between pixels together with a foreground-background prediction. The details of the network architectures as well as the input and output structures are provided in the supplementary.

The two networks were trained jointly by applying the Sørensen Dice loss [4, 29] on the output of the second network. The correlations and summary images were normalized channel-wise to zero mean and unit variance. For training, we converted the ground truth cell annotations into affinities between pixels and to foreground-background labels. The affinities are computed by first assigning all pixels belonging to a cell with a unique label. For two pixels i and j with assigned labels L_i and L_j the affinity a_{ij} between them is

$$a_{ij} = \begin{cases} 1 & \text{if } L_i = L_j \\ 0 & \text{if } L_i \neq L_j \end{cases} \qquad . \qquad (3)$$

We applied the Sørensen Dice loss [4,29] to all output channels because it has been successfully used to learn affinities [32] and because it can deal with the large class-imbalance that exists between foreground and background in the Neurofinder datasets.

In order to find suitable hyperparameters for the network training, we split every video of the Neurofinder training set spatially into 75% training and 25% validation set. We tested different parameter settings and used the validation loss to determine the best setting. Afterwards, we used this set of hyperparameters to train the networks on the complete videos of the training set. The used hyperparameters can be found in the supplementary. For the submission named DISCo we used all Neurofinder datasets, while for DISCos we trained and evaluated on each of the five dataset series individually.

Since the Neurofinder training data consists of only 19 videos, data augmentation is essential for successful network training. We used data augmentation both in the temporal and the spatial dimensions of the videos as follows: Before computing the correlations we performed max-pooling over time on the videos. For training, we varied the temporal length of the max-pooling kernel between three and nine frames. For inference, we fixed the length of the max-pooling kernel to five frames. At train time, we also cut the video randomly into ten segments which were additionally shuffled before computing the correlations. In the spatial dimensions of the videos we used random flips and rotations. Additionally, we trained only on random crops of the image plane of size 128×128 pixels. We assured that each crop used for training contained at least one cell.

---

[2] We used the U-Net implementation provided in Inferno 0.3.0 with depth five, see https://github.com/inferno-pytorch/inferno.

3.3   Instance Segmentation

For the final step of extracting the actual cell instances, we use the Generalized Algorithm for Signed graph Partitioning (GASP) [1]. In contrast to Hochbaum's normalized cut (HNC) model used in HNCcorr [30] and the watershed algorithm used for post-processing in the models Conv2D [10] and STNeuroNet [28], GASP neither requires a threshold for stopping the partitioning nor seeds nor a predefined number of clusters.

GASP is designed for the task of partitioning a signed graph $\mathcal{G} = (V, E, W)$ with nodes V, edges E and edge weights W. In our case, the nodes V correspond to the pixels in the image plane of the calcium imaging video and the structure for the edges is pre-defined as shown in the supplementary. Since cells in calcium imaging videos are usually relatively small, we only connected pixels up to a distance of five pixels to enable the correct separation of small and especially adjacent cells. The weights $w_{ij} \in \mathbb{R}$ for the edges $e_{ij} \in E$ are gained from the predicted affinities $a_{ij} \in [0, 1]$ according to $w_{ij} = a_{ij} - 0.5$. An edge with high positive edge weight indicates the tendency of the nodes to be merged together in the same cluster, while a strong negative weight corresponds to a strong tendency of the two nodes to be separated.

The GASP algorithm starts with each node in its own cluster and then iteratively merges *adjacent* clusters. Adjacent means that two clusters S_u and S_v have at least one connecting edge $e_{ij} \in E$ from a node i in cluster S_u to a node j in cluster S_v and that the interaction between the two clusters $\mathcal{W}(S_u, S_v)$ is positive. We have used the *linkage criterion* $\mathcal{W}$ defined by

$$\mathcal{W}(S_u, S_v) = \sum_{e \in E_{uv}} \frac{w_e}{|E_{uv}|}, \tag{4}$$

with $E_{uv} \subset E$ denoting all edges connecting S_u and S_v. We prefer the average linkage over sum [15, 18] and absolute maximum linkage [32] because it has been shown to be extremely robust and at the same time outperformed other criteria in instance segmentation tasks on biological and street-scene images [1]. The GASP algorithm automatically stops as soon as $\mathcal{W}(S_u, S_v) \leq 0$ for all clusters S_u and S_v.

In order to avoid false merges of cells and background and to remove all background instances from the final result, we exclude all edges to background pixels from the graph before performing the partitioning. The decision whether a pixel is assigned to the background is based on the foreground-background prediction of the network. All pixels for which the background prediction is higher than the value for the foreground/cell prediction are excluded from the graph. This step slightly improved the results and made the instance segmentation step much faster since the graph to partition becomes smaller when excluding all background pixels. As a last step, in order to remove also tiny background segments, we used a simple threshold to exclude all instances with a size smaller than 25 pixels from the final result.

4   Experiments and Results

We trained the networks for DISCo on the publicly available Neurofinder training set with the hyperparameters shown in the supplementary and as described in Sect. 3.2. The results are evaluated on the Neurofinder test set with the segmentation quality measured by computing the average F1-score over the nine videos in the test set.[3]

DISCo significantly outperforms methods which are solely based on summary images like UNet2DS and Conv2D (two-sided Wilcoxon test as described in [28], p-value ≤ 0.05) and also performs much better than those only relying on correlations like HNCcorr, as shown in Table 1 (rows highlighted in gray). Furthermore, when training and evaluating individual networks for the five different dataset series 00, 01, 02, 03, and 04 (submission named DISCos), our model even outperforms all other methods trained on the Neurofinder datasets (see Table 1).

Table 1. Neurofinder leaderboard: methods trained only on the Neurofinder datasets. We show an excerpt of the Neurofinder leaderboard containing the top methods trained on the original Neurofinder training set. Methods using a single model on all five dataset series are highlighted in gray. We show the F1-score for each of the nine test datasets. The sorting is based on the average F1-score over all test datasets (ØF1). DISCo outperforms the other methods when applying a single model to all datasets and when training and evaluating individual models on the five dataset series (submission named DISCos).

Method	ØF1	F1-scores on individual test datasets								
		00		01		02		03	04	
DISCos[a]	**0.67**	0.64	0.71	0.61	0.56	0.82	0.77	0.55	0.53	0.82
3dCNN[a]	0.66	0.63	0.72	0.63	0.54	0.63	0.56	0.89	0.55	0.78
DISCo	**0.63**	0.61	0.73	0.59	0.54	0.60	0.65	0.55	0.55	0.83
HNCcorr + Conv2D[b]	0.62	0.55	0.61	0.53	0.56	0.75	0.68	0.81	0.38	0.68
Sourcery[b]	0.58	0.45	0.53	0.62	0.45	0.72	0.56	0.84	0.39	0.69
UNet2DS	0.57	0.64	0.70	0.56	0.46	0.49	0.41	0.89	0.33	0.64
Suite2P + Donuts[b]	0.55	0.45	0.53	0.49	0.39	0.60	0.52	0.84	0.47	0.66
. . .										
HNCcorr	0.49	0.29	0.33	0.53	0.56	0.75	0.68	0.23	0.38	0.68
. . .										
Conv2D	0.47	0.54	0.61	0.27	0.27	0.42	0.38	0.84	0.29	0.60

[a]Network models trained and evaluated on each of the five different dataset series individually.

[b]Combination of two methods, one applied to datasets 01, 02, 04, the other to datasets 00, 03.

---

[3] Leaderboard of the Neurofinder challenge at http://neurofinder.codeneuro.org. Accessed: 2020-03-05. We do not discuss the submissions Mask R-CNN and human-label since we have no information on the used models and training procedures.

To find out how beneficial it is to use both, correlations and summary images, we trained DISCo with different inputs: summary images and segment-wise correlations (as proposed in Sect. 3); summary images and correlations over the whole video length; only summary images; and only correlations.

The results in Table 2 show that the combination of summary images and correlations over segments clearly outperforms the models only trained on summary images and only on correlations. This holds true when training only a single model on all datasets (see Table 2) but also when training on each of the five dataset series individually (the results for DISCos are shown in the supplementary). Comparing the results for the segment-wise correlations and the correlations over the whole video length, the difference is not that big, but still the model using segment-wise correlations performs slightly better.

Table 2. Lesion study. We show the results on the Neurofinder test set for the DISCo model with different kinds of input (top) and methods to aggregate the information from the segments (bottom). The most informative input is the combination of segment-wise correlations and summary images and the best aggregation method is a CNN.

| Input/Aggregation model | ∅F1 | F1-scores on individual test datasets | | | | |
		00	01	02	03	04
Segment-wise correlations + summary image	**0.63**	0.61	0.73	0.59	0.54	0.60	0.65	0.55	0.55	0.83
Correlations (whole video) + summary image	0.62	0.47	0.70	0.62	0.53	0.74	0.67	0.55	0.50	0.83
Only correlations	0.50	0.32	0.42	0.45	0.41	0.68	0.62	0.36	0.50	0.77
Only summary image	0.49	0.51	0.59	0.51	0.38	0.51	0.37	0.54	0.31	0.65
CNN	**0.63**	0.61	0.73	0.59	0.54	0.60	0.65	0.55	0.55	0.83
Mean (scaled correlation)	0.61	0.52	0.72	0.58	0.51	0.68	0.63	0.55	0.50	0.78
Max	0.60	0.58	0.71	0.55	0.51	0.60	0.58	0.56	0.48	0.82
Max, min, mean, std, sum	0.62	0.49	0.72	0.60	0.54	0.69	0.70	0.54	0.47	0.79

An alternative to using a CNN to aggregate the information from the ten segments into a single input for the second network would be to use the scaled correlation [19]. However, in Table 2 we show that using only the mean over the segments performs much worse than using the aggregation network. This is also the case when taking the maximum over the segments instead of the mean. Only when we use a combination of several statistics, namely maximum, minimum, mean, standard deviation, and sum, the model performs almost as good as the model using the CNN.

In the supplementary, we also investigate the performance of DISCos with different neighborhoods for the computation of the correlations, different numbers of temporal segments N, and different structures for the graph partitioned with GASP.

The results on the test videos are very heterogeneous. Since also the competing methods perform highly heterogeneous, we assume that one reason for this lies in the huge heterogeneity among the datasets in the Neurofinder challenge, which strongly differ in recording quality, number of training examples and used labeling technique. This might explain why e.g. DISCos clearly out-performs 3dCNN on the videos 02.0 and 02.1, and on the other hand 3dCNN performs much better on the video 03.0, while the scores of the other test videos are comparable for both methods. One reason why dataset 03 seems to be par-ticularly challenging for our method might lie in the extreme noisiness of these videos. This might result in inconclusive correlation values which would explain why the HNCcorr algorithm struggle particularly with this dataset, too.

5   Summary and Conclusion

We have presented a new approach for cell segmentation in calcium imaging videos. We use a deep learning model, but in contrast to previous work we nei-ther restrict ourselves purely on shape-based summary images as input nor use computationally expensive 3D CNNs directly on the calcium imaging videos. Instead, we propose a computationally efficient framework that achieves top scores on the Neurofinder benchmark. As input to our network model we use a combination of correlations between pixels and summary images, which allows us to detect active cells as well as cells with weak or almost constant signals. Impor-tantly, computing the correlations segment-wise provides more fine-grained tem-poral information than correlations over the whole length of the video. Another novelty compared to other methods for cell segmentation in calcium imaging videos is that the used deep learning model does not only provide a foreground-background prediction, but additionally predicts affinities between pixels. This allows us to directly apply an instance segmentation method on the network output to extract the individual cells.

Acknowledgements. We gratefully acknowledge partial financial support by DFG SFB 1134 ›Functional Ensembles‹ and DFG HA 4364/9-1.

References

1. Bailoni, A., Pape, C., Wolf, S., Beier, T., Kreshuk, A., Hamprecht, F.A.: A gener-alized framework for agglomerative clustering of signed graphs applied to instance segmentation. arXiv preprint (2019)
2. CodeNeuro: neurofinder public benchmark (2016). http://neurofinder.codeneuro. org. Accessed 05 Mar 2020
3. Denk, W., Strickler, J.H., Webb, W.W.: Two-photon laser scanning fluorescence microscopy. Science **248**, 73–76 (1990)
4. Dice, L.R.: Measures of the amount of ecologic association between species. Ecology **26**, 297–302 (1945)
5. Diego, F., Hamprecht, F.A.: Learning multi-level sparse representations. In: NIPS (2013)
6. Diego, F., Hamprecht, F.A.: Sparse space-time deconvolution for calcium image analysis. In: NIPS (2014)
7. Diego, F., Reichinnek, S., Both, M., Hamprecht, F.A.: Automated identification of neuronal activity from calcium imaging by sparse dictionary learning. In: IEEE International Symposium on Biomedical Imaging (ISBI) (2013)

8. Flusberg, B.A., et al.: High-speed, miniaturized fluorescence microscopy in freely moving mice. Nat. Methods (2008)

9. Friedrich, J., Zhou, P., Paninski, L.: Fast online deconvolution of calcium imaging data. PLoS Comput. Biol. **13**, e1005423 (2017)

10. Gao, S.: Conv2D (2016). https://github.com/iamshang1/Projects/tree/master/Advanced_ML/Neuron_Detection. Accessed 19 Jul 2019

11. Giovannucci, A., et al.: Caiman an open source tool for scalable calcium imaging data analysis. eLife **8**, e38173 (2019)

12. Giovannucci, A., et al.: Onacid: online analysis of calcium imaging data in real time. In: NIPS (2017)

13. Helmchen, F., Denk, W.: Deep tissue two-photon microscopy. Nat. Methods (2005)

14. Kaifosh, P., Zaremba, J.D., Danielson, N.B., Losonczy, A.: SIMA: python software for analysis of dynamic fluorescence imaging data. Front. Neuroinform. **8**, 80 (2014)

15. Keuper, M., Levinkov, E., Bonneel, N., Lavoué, G., Brox, T., Andres, B.: Efficient decomposition of image and mesh graphs by lifted multicuts. In: IEEE International Conference on Computer Vision (ICCV), Proceedings (2015)

16. Kirschbaum, E., et al.: LeMoNADe: learned motif and neuronal assembly detection in calcium imaging videos. In: International Conference on Learning Representations (ICLR), Proceedings (2018)

17. Klibisz, A., Rose, D., Eicholtz, M., Blundon, J., Zakharenko, S.: Fast, simple calcium imaging segmentation with fully convolutional networks. In: International Workshop on Deep Learning in Medical Image Analysis and Multimodal Learning for Clinical Decision Support (DLMIA and ML-CDS), held in conjunction with MICCAI (2017)

18. Levinkov, E., Kirillov, A., Andres, B.: A comparative study of local search algorithms for correlation clustering. In: Roth, V., Vetter, T. (eds.) GCPR 2017. LNCS, vol. 10496, pp. 103–114. Springer, Cham (2017). https://doi.org/10.1007/978-3-319-66709-6_9

19. Nikolić, D., Mureşan, R.C., Feng, W., Singer, W.: Scaled correlation analysis: a better way to compute a cross-correlogram. Eur. J. Neurosci. **35**, 742–762 (2012)

20. Pachitariu, M., Packer, A.M., Pettit, N., Dalgleish, H., Hausser, M., Sahani, M.: Extracting regions of interest from biological images with convolutional sparse block coding. In: NIPS (2013)

21. Pachitariu, M., et al.: Suite2p: beyond 10,000 neurons with standard two-photon microscopy. bioRxiv preprint (2017)

22. Pearson, K.: Notes on regression and inheritance in the case of two parents. Proc. Roy. Soc. Lond. **58**, 240–242 (1895)

23. Petersen, A., Simon, N., Witten, D.: Scalpel: extracting neurons from calcium imaging data. Ann. Appl. Stat. **12**, 2430 (2018)

24. Pnevmatikakis, E.A., et al.: A structured matrix factorization framework for large scale calcium imaging data analysis. arXiv preprint (2014)

25. Pnevmatikakis, E.A., Paninski, L.: Sparse nonnegative deconvolution for compressive calcium imaging: algorithms and phase transitions. In: NIPS (2013)

26. Pnevmatikakis, E.A., et al.: Simultaneous denoising, deconvolution, and demixing of calcium imaging data. Neuron **89**, 285–299 (2016)

27. Ronneberger, O., Fischer, P., Brox, T.: U-net: convolutional networks for biomedical image segmentation. In: Navab, N., Hornegger, J., Wells, W., Frangi, A. (eds.) MICCAI 2015. LNCS, vol. 9351, pp. 234–241. Springer, Cham (2015). https://doi.org/10.1007/978-3-319-24574-4_28

28. Soltanian-Zadeh, S., Sahingur, K., Blau, S., Gong, Y., Farsiu, S.: Fast and robust active neuron segmentation in two-photon calcium imaging using spatiotemporal deep learning. Proc. Natl. Acad. Sci. **116**, 8554–8563 (2019)

29. Sørensen, T.J.: A method of establishing groups of equal amplitude in plant sociology based on similarity of species content and its application to analyses of the vegetation on danish commons. Biol. Skar **5**, 1–34 (1948)

30. Spaen, Q., Asín-Achá, R., Chettih, S.N., Minderer, M., Harvey, C., Hochbaum, D.S.: HNCcorr: a novel combinatorial approach for cell identification in calcium-imaging movies. eNeuro (2019)

31. Székely, G.J., Rizzo, M.L., Bakirov, N.K.: Measuring and testing dependence by correlation of distances. Ann. Stat. **35**, 2769–2794 (2007)

32. Wolf, S., et al.: The mutex watershed: efficient, parameter-free image partitioning. In: Ferrari, V., Hebert, M., Sminchisescu, C., Weiss, Y. (eds.) ECCV 2018. LNCS, vol. 11208, pp. 571–587. Springer, Cham (2018). https://doi.org/10.1007/978-3-030-01225-0_34

Isotropic Reconstruction of 3D EM Images with Unsupervised Degradation Learning

Shiyu Deng[1], Xueyang Fu[1(✉)], Zhiwei Xiong[1], Chang Chen[1], Dong Liu[1], Xuejin Chen[1], Qing Ling[2], and Feng Wu[1]

[1] University of Science and Technology of China, Hefei, China
xyfu@ustc.edu.cn
[2] Sun Yat-sen University, Guangzhou, China

Abstract. The isotropic reconstruction of 3D electron microscopy (EM) images with low axial resolution is of great importance for biological analysis. Existing deep learning-based methods rely on handcrafted downscaled training data, which does not model the real degradation accurately and thus leads to unsatisfying performance in practice. To address this problem, we propose a universal and unsupervised framework to simultaneously learn the real axial degradation and the isotropic reconstruction of 3D EM images. First, we train a degradation network using unpaired low-resolution (LR) and high-resolution (HR) slices, both of which are from real data, in an adversarial manner. Then, the degradation network is further used to generate realistic LR data from HR labels to form paired training data. In this way, the generated degraded data is consistent with the real axial degradation process, which guarantees the generalization ability of subsequent reconstruction networks to the real data. Our framework has the flexibility to work with different existing reconstruction methods. Experiments on both simulated and real anisotropic EM images validate the superiority of our framework.

Keywords: Isotropic reconstruction · Unsupervised learning · EM image

1 Introduction

Three dimensional electron microscopy (EM) imaging reveals biological information at a scale of nanometer, which makes it possible for ultrastructural analysis. It is desirable to have a consistent resolution across all dimensions, both for visualization and for biological analysis tasks. In practice, however, most EM techniques such as serial section Transmission EM (ssTEM) and block-face scanning EM fail to obtain the desired high axial resolution [17]. Generally, the axial (z) resolution is of one magnitude lower compared with the lateral (x, y) resolution. Although Focused Ion Beam Scanning EM (FIB-SEM) can achieve 8–10 nm resolution in all the x, y, z directions, it takes an unaffordable long time

© Springer Nature Switzerland AG 2020
A. L. Martel et al. (Eds.): MICCAI 2020, LNCS 12265, pp. 163–173, 2020.
https://doi.org/10.1007/978-3-030-59722-1_16

to image a large volume sample [8]. Therefore, it is of great demand to replace the time-consuming imaging with an effective reconstruction method to obtain high-quality isotropic 3D EM images.

To increase the resolution along the axial direction of 3D EM images, traditional interpolation methods are widely used due to their straightforward operations. Although these methods are simple and efficient, they usually result in images with severe volume artifacts, which hinders the subsequent processing and analysis [27]. Recently, deep learning-based methods have achieved significant improvements on both natural images restoration [2,3,12,15,23] and biomedical images analysis [5,18]. There also emerge a few works aiming to recover isotropic EM images with the deep learning framework. As a representative, Heinrich et al. [10] compared two 3D convolutional neural networks (CNNs), which are trained in a supervised manner on artificially down-scaled isotropic FIB-SEM images for 3D EM super-resolution. Their results indicate that inferring high-resolution (HR) structures from low-resolution (LR) EM images is possible. However, the isotropic ground truth images of the same category are not always available, and these supervised 3D CNNs may not generalize well to EM images that are drastically different from the training data in content. This domain shift issue poses a common challenge for existing supervised CNNs-based methods.

Along the other line, Weigert et al. [20,21] proposed a self-supervised deep learning method to restore isotropic fluorescence volumes from anisotropic optical acquisitions, where the restoration process is modeled as a combination of a super-resolution problem on sub-sampled data and a deconvolution problem to counteract the microscopy induced optical point spread function (PSF). Most importantly, they introduced the concept of self super-resolution, i.e., training and testing on the same anisotropic volumetric data. Similar ideas have also been explored for isotropic reconstruction of magnetic resonance images in [4,27,28]. Although self-supervised methods do not require isotropic ground truth training data, which may cause potential domain shift issues, these methods require prior knowledge of the PSF. In practice, however, this degradation is unknown and could be drastically different from the handcrafted designed ones, which again restricts the generalization ability of the above methods in real scenarios.

Theoretically, the real degradation along the axial direction can be exactly learned by CNNs trained on realistic axial HR-LR pairs. Nevertheless, this kind of axial HR-LR pairs are difficult to acquire, which makes supervised learning not feasible. In this paper, inspired by unpaired learning for natural image processing [1,22,29,30], we propose a framework with unsupervised degradation learning for isotropic reconstruction of 3D EM images. Different from those methods on 2D natural images, we design our framework for the 3D volume. Specifically, our framework contains a degradation model and a reconstruction model. To train the degradation model, we adopt unpaired HR lateral and LR axial images from a single, anisotropic 3D EM volume as training data. We assume that the biological structure in the 3D volume conforms to an isotropic distribution (i.e. the cell body is spherical). In this way, using the unpaired training strategy, the trained

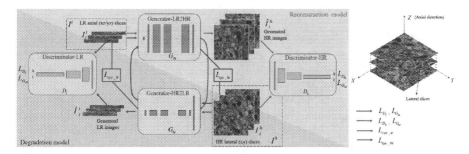

Fig. 1. Overview of our framework. G_{hl} aims to generate LR image $\hat{I}_j^l$ from the real HR image I_j^h; G_{lh} aims to restore HR image $\hat{I}_i^h$ from the real LR image I_i^l. The generated LR image $\hat{I}_j^l$ and real LR image I_i^l are used to train the discriminator D_l; the generated HR image $\hat{I}_i^h$ and real HR image I_j^h are used to train the discriminator D_h.

model can generate down-scaled slices that are close to those from the real axial degradation. The generated LR images paired with original HR images are further fed into the reconstruction model to learn the reconstruction function. This makes our framework easy to train and can be directly applied to anisotropic data. Thus, neither the domain shift issue in previous supervised methods nor the mismatch of the degradation in previous self-supervised methods will exist, which greatly improves the generalization ability of our framework in practice. Experiments demonstrate notably improved numerical and perceptual results of our framework over existing solutions, and a state-of-the-art neuron segmentation method is evaluated on the reconstructed isotropic volume, which further validate the superiority of our framework on the subsequent analysis. Moreover, the proposed framework is agnostic to the reconstruction network backbones, and a wide range of super-resolution networks can be plugged in. Furthermore, the proposed framework can be readily applied to isotropic reconstruction of other 3D biomedical images.

This paper has the following contributions: 1) We propose a universal and unsupervised framework, in which both the real axial degradation and the reconstruction can be jointly learned, for isotropic reconstruction of 3D EM images. 2) We prove that the generalization ability of our framework can be guaranteed since neither external training data nor degradation assumptions are needed. 3) Within our framework, users can arbitrarily choose the restoration method, which increase the flexibility of our framework. Experiments on both simulated and real anisotropic EM data validate the superiority of our framework.

2 Methodology

Overall Architecture. As shown in Fig. 1, our framework includes a degradation model and a reconstruction model, both of which consist of a generator and a discriminator. In the degradation model, we use unpaired HR lateral (xy) and LR axial (xz/yz) slices from an anisotropic 3D EM volume to train the generator, which aims to simulate the real degradation process and generate LR images. In the reconstruction model, the generator aims to restore HR images from LR axial (xz/yz) slices. The two discriminators try to distinguish between real or generated images, and the two generators try to fool the corresponding discriminator. Therefore, the discriminators and generators are jointly trained in an adversarial manner. In this way, the trained generator is able to capture the true data distribution [7], which enables it to produce realistic LR images as new training data.

Specifically, given an anisotropic 3D EM volume I, we denote the LR axial slices as I^l, and the HR lateral slices as I^h. The degradation model and the reconstruction model learn the mappings between I^l and I^h. As shown in Fig. 1, using the jth HR image I_j^h as input, the generator G_{hl} down-scales it into an LR image $\hat{I}_j^l$. Similarly, using the ith LR image I_i^l as input, the generator G_{lh} super-resolves it into an HR image $\hat{I}_i^h$. The generated LR image $\hat{I}_j^l$ and real LR image I_i^l are used to train the discriminator D_l, while $\hat{I}_i^h$ and I_j^h are used to train the discriminator D_h. In addition, as shown by the green and blue circles, we also add cycle-consistent losses to force the backward mapping to bring the generated image back to the original for stable training. At the testing phase, only G_{lh} is used for super-resolving I_i^l. Since our framework is able to receive unpaired images from different sources as training data, neither the domain shift issue in previous supervised methods nor the mismatch of the degradation in previous self-supervised methods will exist.

Network Implementation. The degradation model consists of the generator G_{hl} and the discriminator D_l. The generator G_{hl} uses ResNet [9] as the backbone structure. Specifically, we first adopt an average pooling layer to down-scale the input resolution 10 times along the vertical (y) direction, followed by 9 residual blocks to generate the LR image. Similar to [15], we remove the batch normalization. We set the kernel size as 3×3, and each convolution layer includes 64 filters. For the discriminator D_l, we stack 4 stride convolution layers, which followed by Leaky ReLU activation, along the horizontal (x) direction. The kernel size is set to 3×7 to adapt to the resolution of input images.

The reconstruction model consists of G_{lh} and D_h. The generator G_{lh} increases the resolution of an input image 10 times along the vertical direction. To guarantee the restoration quality, universal super-resolution networks can be used as G_{lh}. To be simple and effective, by default, the generator G_{lh} contains a linear interpolation in the front of the network, and 9 residual blocks are then used to learn the non-linear mapping for HR detail restoration. We refer to this Default ReConstruction network as *DRCNet*. For the discriminator D_h, we adopt the architecture of PatchGAN [14,30] to relieve the computation burden.

Loss Function. We adopt adversarial losses to guide the training of both HR to LR mapping and LR to HR mapping. Specifically, we use a least-squares loss [16]. For the HR to LR mapping: $I^h \rightarrow I^l$, we formulate the objective as

$$\mathcal{L}_{G_{hl}} = \mathbb{E}_{I_j^h \sim P(I^h)} \|D_l(G_{hl}(I_j^h)) - 1\|_2. \tag{1}$$

For the discriminator D_l, we have

$$\mathcal{L}_{D_l} = \mathbb{E}_{I_i^l \sim P(I^l)} \|D_l(I_i^l) - 1\|_2 + \mathbb{E}_{I_j^h \sim P(I^h)} \|D_l(G_{hl}(I_j^h))\|_2. \tag{2}$$

Similarly, for the LR to HR mapping: $I^l \rightarrow I^h$, we have

$$\mathcal{L}_{G_{lh}} = \mathbb{E}_{I_i^l \sim P(I^l)} \|D_h(G_{lh}(I_i^l)) - 1\|_2. \tag{3}$$

For the discriminator D_h, we have

$$\mathcal{L}_{D_h} = \mathbb{E}_{I_j^h \sim P(I^h)} \|D_h(I_j^h) - 1\|_2 + \mathbb{E}_{I_i^l \sim P(I^l)} \|D_h(G_{lh}(I_i^l))\|_2. \tag{4}$$

According to [30], using only adversarial losses cannot guarantee that the learned function maps an individual input I_i^l to the desired I_i^h, thus cycle-consistent losses are further applied. As illustrated by the green circle in Fig. 1, each real LR image x_i and generators G_{lh}, G_{hl} should satisfy: $I_i^l \rightarrow G_{lh}(I_i^l) \rightarrow G_{hl}(G_{lh}(I_i^l)) \approx I_i^l$. As shown by the blue circle, each real HR image I_j^h and generators G_{lh}, G_{hl} should satisfy: $I_j^h \rightarrow G_{hl}(I_j^h) \rightarrow G_{lh}(G_{hl}(I_j^h)) \approx I_j^h$. The cycle consistent loss is

$$\begin{aligned}\mathcal{L}_{cyc} &= \mathcal{L}_{cyc\_lr} + \mathcal{L}_{cyc\_hr} \\ &= \mathbb{E}_{I_i^l \sim P(I^l)} \|G_{hl}(G_{lh}(I_i^l) - I_i^l\|_1 + \mathbb{E}_{I_j^h \sim P(I^h)} \|G_{lh}(G_{hl}(I_j^h) - I_j^h\|_1.\end{aligned} \tag{5}$$

For the two generators, we minimize the following objective

$$\mathcal{L}_G = \alpha \mathcal{L}_{G_{hl}} + \beta \mathcal{L}_{G_{lh}} + \eta \mathcal{L}_{cyc}, \tag{6}$$

where α, β, η are positive values. To train discriminator D_h and D_l, we minimize

$$\mathcal{L}_D = \mathcal{L}_{D_l} + \mathcal{L}_{D_h}. \tag{7}$$

3   Experiments

We evaluate our framework on two popular EM data sets, FIB-25 [19] and Cremi [11], which can be used as simulated anisotropic images and real anisotropic images, respectively. We employ the Adam optimizer [13] with $\beta_1 = 0.5$, $\beta_2 = 0.999$. The initial learning rate of generators is set to 2×10^{-4} and then decreases by a factor of 0.98 for every epoch. The discriminators are trained with fixed learning rate of 10^{-4}. We implement the proposed framework with PyTorch by using a Titan XP GPU.

Table 1. Quantitative (PSNR/SSIM) comparisons on the axial (xz/yz) slices of FIB-25 dataset. Bold is the best and italic is the second best performance. Note that 'Cubic' is the ideal case where the exactly matched degradation is used for supervised training.

Method	Interp	DRCNet				Isonet-2			
		Take	Gau	Ours	Cubic	Take	Gau	Ours	Cubic
xz	25.93	22.97	25.98	*26.58*	**26.85**	22.91	25.96	*26.56*	**26.81**
	0.652	0.523	0.643	*0.678*	**0.696**	0.560	0.648	*0.679*	**0.692**
yz	25.93	23.00	25.99	*26.57*	**26.86**	22.87	26.01	*26.58*	**26.83**
	0.644	0.518	0.635	*0.670*	**0.688**	0.551	0.642	*0.672*	**0.685**

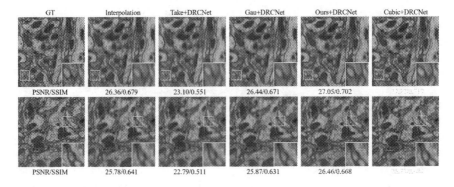

Fig. 2. Visual comparisons on FIB-25 dataset. Best viewed in electronic format.

Evaluation on Simulated Anisotropic Images. To investigate whether the degradation network can learn the correct degradation process, we conduct experiments on simulated anisotropic images. Different from most existing EM data sets, FIB-25 [19] contains isotropic data from the drosophila brain obtained with the FIB-SEM technique. We use a sub-volume ($500 \times 500 \times 500$) from the FIB-25 data set for our experiments. We simulate anisotropic ssTEM images by down-sampling the isotropic images by a factor of 10 along the axial direction using cubic down-sample operation at first, which results in an anisotropic 3D volume with a resolution of $500 \times 500 \times 50$. To verify the effectiveness of our framework, we adopt two reconstruction networks (DRCNet and Isonet-2 [20]) in the experiments. Each reconstruction network is trained in two ways: one is trained in an unsupervised manner using our framework, and the other is trained in a supervised manner using the lateral slices paired with their artificially down-scaled ones. For our unsupervised training, the axial (xz/yz) slices (with a resolution of 500×50) and the lateral (xy) slices (with a resolution of 500×500) of the simulated anisotropic volume are used as training data. For the supervised training, we generate three training data sets to represent different kinds of degradation assumptions. Specifically, the HR ground-truth lateral slices are down-scaled by taking every 10th row, down-scaled using the cubic down-sample operation or firstly blur by a gaussian kernel and then down-scaled

Table 2. Segmentation results on the restored isotropic images. Lower is better.

Table 3. Quantitative comparisons on stimulated degraded images.

Method	Interp	DRCNet			
		Take	Gau	Ours	Cubic
VOI	5.88	6.03	5.87	**4.98**	5.08

Method	Take	Gau	Ours
PSNR	22.68	29.35	**36.55**
SSIM	0.716	0.929	**0.984**

by taking-slice operation. Then, these three kinds of paired HR-LR data are used to train the reconstructed network in a supervised manner. After training, the network models corresponding to different degradation processes can be obtained. At the testing phase, for all methods, *only* the axial (xz/yz) slices of the cubic down-sample simulated anisotropic volume are used as testing images.

Table 1 shows PSNR and SSIM results of the above methods. The words 'Take' means training on taking-slices degradation assumption, 'Gau' means training on gaussian+taking-slices degradation assumption, 'Ours' means training with our framework, and 'Cubic' means training on cubic degradation assumption (ideal case). As can been seen, our unsupervised framework achieves comparable results with the ideal supervised method 'Cubic'. This is because our framework can provide training data, which conforms to the correct degradation process, to the reconstruction network. In contrast, the performance of the networks trained on data with mismatched degradation assumptions, i.e., 'Take' and 'Gau', are even worse than the direct cubic interpolation. This is caused by the degradation mismatch between training and testing data, which is a common problem in self-supervised learning. As shown in Fig. 2, the results produced by our framework are visually close to 'Cubic', which is consistent with quantitative assessments. To prove that our framework can learn the correct degradation process, we further calculate the PSNR/SSIM between the cubic down-sampled LR xz/yz slices and those LR xz/yz images generated by our framework. As shown in Table 3, our framework achieves the highest scores, which indicates that our framework is able to generate more realistic LR images.

To validate the effectiveness of our framework in the subsequent analysis tasks, we further conduct segmentation experiments. We use a state-of-the-art neuron segmentation method [6]. First, we train the segmentation network on the isotropic ground truth, and then use the trained model to evaluate on different restored isotropic volumes. We show the results of variation of information (VOI) in Table 2. Our framework achieves the best performance, which is even better than 'Cubic' since the adversarial loss we use could benefit segmentation.

Evaluation on Real Anisotropic Images. To evaluate our framework on real anisotropic images, we conduct experiments on the Cremi [11] dataset, which contains EM data of drosophila brain with anisotropic resolution. We use a volume of $1250 \times 1250 \times 125$ for our experiments, where all the lateral (xy) slices and axial (xz/yz) slices are used as training data. As shown in Fig. 3, even when the real degradation is unknown, using our framework

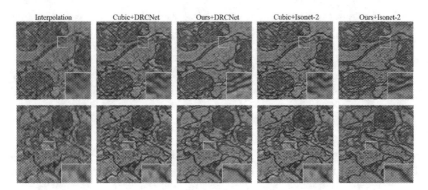

Interpolation   Cubic+DRCNet   Ours+DRCNet   Cubic+Isonet-2   Ours+Isonet-2

Fig. 3. Visual comparisons on Cremi dataset.

Table 4. Quantitative (PSNR/SSIM) comparisons on the lateral (xy) slices of Cremi dataset. Bold is the best and italic is the second best performance.

Method	DRCNet	Isonet-1	Isonet-2	VDSR	EDSR	RDN	RCAN	Interp
Cubic	23.00	23.16	22.95	23.02	22.80	22.66	22.69	23.31
								0.625
	0.624	0.624	0.626	0.623	0.609	0.608	0.609	
Ours	26.06	24.25	26.04	25.81	26.30	*26.53*	**26.74**	
	0.693	0.650	0.694	0.686	0.697	*0.708*	**0.715**	

(Ours+DRCNet, Ours+Isonet-2) can still generate promising results as it learns the real degradation. While directly using cubic interpolation fails to recover HR details. Other two methods, Cubic+DRCNet and Cubic+IsoNet-2, which are trained on the assumption of cubic degradation, introduce unrealistic artifacts. This is because the real degradation is not consistent with the artificial one it assumes. In other words, only the learned reconstruction network with accurate degradation modeling can generalize well to real anisotropic images.

To further validate the effectiveness of our framework, we also conduct experiments on the lateral slices of Cremi dataset. Since it is difficult to acquire large amount of isotropic images paired with its real anisotropic ones, we use our framework to generate anisotropic images from real axial degradation. We first generate LR images by performing the degradation network of 'Ours+DRCNet' that previously trained on all the lateral (xy) slices of Cremi dataset. These generated LR images are close to real data. Then, we divide these LR images into a training set and a test set. Finally, we fine-tune our framework with different reconstruction networks on the training set. We select above mentioned DRC-Net, Isonet-1 [20], Isonet-2 [20] and other four deep learning-based SR methods: VDSR [12], EDSR [15], RDN [25,26], RCAN [24]. These SR networks are trained with and without our framework, respectively. We modify the pixel shuffle layer to do up-sample operation in a single direction. As shown in Table 4, due to the degradation mismatch, using SR networks does not produce satisfactory results. While adopting our framework improves performance, i.e., the values in the second row are significantly higher than those in the first row. This means the users can choose any reconstruction network according to the actual situation.

4 Conclusions

In this paper, we propose an effective framework for isotropic restoration of 3D EM images. We achieve this goal by simultaneously learning the degradation and reconstruction processes in an unsupervised manner. Since our framework requires neither external paired training data nor degradation assumptions, it is easy to implement in most practical applications. In the absence of paired data, our framework still shows encouraging performance. Experiments have demonstrated that even though the reconstruction network is trained with unpaired data in our framework, its reconstruction performance is still close to the performance obtained by training with pre-collected paired data.

Acknowledgment. This work was supported in part by Key Area R&D Program of Guangdong Province with grant No. 2018B030338001, the Fundamental Research Funds for the Central Universities under Grant WK2380000002, and the Natural Science Foundation of China (NSFC) under Grant 61901433.

References

1. Bulat, A., Yang, J., Tzimiropoulos, G.: To learn image super-resolution, use a gan to learn how to do image degradation first. In: Ferrari, V., Hebert, M., Sminchisescu, C., Weiss, Y. (eds.) ECCV 2018. LNCS, vol. 11210, pp. 185–200. Springer, Cham (2018). https://doi.org/10.1007/978-3-030-01231-1_12

2. Chen, C., Xiong, Z., Tian, X., Zha, Z.J., Wu, F.: Camera lens super-resolution. In: Proceedings of the IEEE Conference on Computer Vision and Pattern Recognition, pp. 1652–1660 (2019)

3. Chen, C., Xiong, Z., Tian, X., Zha, Z.J., Wu, F.: Real-world image denoising with deep boosting. IEEE Trans. Pattern Anal. Mach. Intell. (2019)

4. Chen, Y., Shi, F., Christodoulou, A.G., Xie, Y., Zhou, Z., Li, D.: Efficient and accurate mri super-resolution using a generative adversarial network and 3d multi-level densely connected network. In: Frangi, A., Schnabel, J., Davatzikos, C., Alberola-López, C., Fichtinger, G. (eds.) MICCAI 2018. LNCS, vol. 11070, pp. 91–99. Springer, Cham (2018). https://doi.org/10.1007/978-3-030-00928-1_11

5. Çiçek, Ö., Abdulkadir, A., Lienkamp, S.S., Brox, T., Ronneberger, O.: 3d u-net: learning dense volumetric segmentation from sparse annotation. In: Ourselin, S., Joskowicz, L., Sabuncu, M., Unal, G., Wells, W. (eds.) MICCAI 2016. LNCS, vol. 9901, pp. 424–432. Springer, Cham (2016)

6. Funke, J., et al.: Large scale image segmentation with structured loss based deep learning for connectome reconstruction. IEEE Trans. Pattern Anal. Mach. Intell. **41**(7), 1669–1680 (2018)

7. Goodfellow, I., et al.: Generative adversarial nets. In: Advances in Neural Information Processing Systems, pp. 2672–2680 (2014)

8. Hayworth, K.J., et al.: Ultrastructurally smooth thick partitioning and volume stitching for large-scale connectomics. Nat. Methods **12**(4), 319 (2015)
9. He, K., Zhang, X., Ren, S., Sun, J.: Deep residual learning for image recognition. In: IEEE Conference on Computer Vision and Pattern Recognition, pp. 770–778 (2016)
10. Heinrich, L., Bogovic, J.A., Saalfeld, S.: Deep learning for isotropic super-resolution from non-isotropic 3d electron microscopy. In: International Conference on Medical Image Computing and Computer-Assisted Intervention, pp. 135–143 (2017)
11. Funke, J., Saalfeld, S.: D.B.S.T.E.P.: cremi.org. http://cremi.org/
12. Kim, J., Kwon Lee, J., Mu Lee, K.: Accurate image super-resolution using very deep convolutional networks. In: IEEE Conference on Computer Vision and Pattern Recognition, pp. 1646–1654 (2016)
13. Kingma, D.P., Ba, J.: Adam: a method for stochastic optimization. arXiv preprint arXiv:1412.6980 (2014)
14. Ledig, C., et al.: Photo-realistic single image super-resolution using a generative adversarial network. In: IEEE Conference on Computer Vision and Pattern Recognition, pp. 4681–4690 (2017)
15. Lim, B., Son, S., Kim, H., Nah, S., Mu Lee, K.: Enhanced deep residual networks for single image super-resolution. In: IEEE Conference on Computer Vision and Pattern Recognition Workshops, pp. 136–144 (2017)
16. Mao, X., Li, Q., Xie, H., Lau, R.Y., Wang, Z., Paul Smolley, S.: Least squares generative adversarial networks. In: IEEE International Conference on Computer Vision, pp. 2794–2802 (2017)
17. Mikula, S.: Progress towards mammalian whole-brain cellular connectomics. Front. Neuroanat. **10**, 62 (2016)
18. Ronneberger, O., Fischer, P., Brox, T.: U-net: convolutional networks for biomedical image segmentation. In: Navab, N., Hornegger, J., Wells, W., Frangi, A. (eds.) MICCAI 2015. LNCS, vol. 9351, pp. 234–241. Springer, Cham (2015). https://doi.org/10.1007/978-3-319-24574-4_28
19. Takemura, S., et al.: Synaptic circuits and their variations within different columns in the visual system of drosophila. Natl. Acad. Sci. **112**(44), 13711–13716 (2015)
20. Weigert, M., Royer, L., Jug, F., Myers, G.: Isotropic reconstruction of 3d fluorescence microscopy images using convolutional neural networks. In: International Conference on Medical Image Computing and Computer-Assisted Intervention, pp. 126–134 (2017)
21. Weigert, M., et al.: Content-aware image restoration: pushing the limits of fluorescence microscopy. Nat. Methods **15**(12), 1090 (2018)
22. Yuan, Y., Liu, S., Zhang, J., Zhang, Y., Dong, C., Lin, L.: Unsupervised image super-resolution using cycle-in-cycle generative adversarial networks. In: IEEE Conference on Computer Vision and Pattern Recognition Workshops, pp. 701–710 (2018)
23. Zhang, K., Zuo, W., Chen, Y., Meng, D., Zhang, L.: Beyond a gaussian denoiser: residual learning of deep cnn for image denoising. IEEE Trans. Image Process. **26**(7), 3142–3155 (2017)
24. Zhang, Y., Li, K., Li, K., Wang, L., Zhong, B., Fu, Y.: Image super-resolution using very deep residual channel attention networks. In: Ferrari, V., Hebert, M., Sminchisescu, C., Weiss, Y. (eds.) ECCV 2018. LNCS, vol. 11211, pp. 286–301. Springer, Cham (2018). https://doi.org/10.1007/978-3-030-01234-2_18
25. Zhang, Y., Tian, Y., Kong, Y., Zhong, B., Fu, Y.: Residual dense network for image super-resolution. In: IEEE Conference on Computer Vision and Pattern Recognition, pp. 2472–2481 (2018)

26. Zhang, Y., Tian, Y., Kong, Y., Zhong, B., Fu, Y.: Residual dense network for image restoration. IEEE Trans. Pattern Anal. Mach. Intell. (2020)
27. Zhao, C., Carass, A., Dewey, B.E., Prince, J.L.: Self super-resolution for magnetic resonance images using deep networks. In: IEEE 15th International Symposium on Biomedical Imaging (ISBI 2018), pp. 365–368 (2018)
28. Zhao, C., et al.: A deep learning based anti-aliasing self super-resolution algorithm for MRI. In: Frangi, A.F., Schnabel, J.A., Davatzikos, C., Alberola-López, C., Fichtinger, G. (eds.) MICCAI 2018. LNCS, vol. 11070, pp. 100–108. Springer, Cham (2018). https://doi.org/10.1007/978-3-030-00928-1_12
29. Zhao, T., Zhang, C., Ren, W., Ren, D., Hu, Q.: Unsupervised degradation learning for single image super-resolution. arXiv preprint arXiv:1812.04240 (2018)
30. Zhu, J.Y., Park, T., Isola, P., Efros, A.A.: Unpaired image-to-image translation using cycle-consistent adversarial networks. In: IEEE International Conference on Computer Vision, pp. 2223–2232 (2017)

Background and Illumination Correction for Time-Lapse Microscopy Data with Correlated Foreground

Tingying Peng[1,2(✉)], Lorenz Lamm[1], Dirk Loeffler[3], Nouraiz Ahmed[3],
Nassir Navab[2,4], Timm Schroeder[3], and Carsten Marr[1]

[1] Helmholtz Zentrum München–German Research Center for Environmental Health,
Institute of Computational Biology, 85764 Neuherberg, Germany
`tingying.peng@tum.de`
[2] Computer Aided Medical Procedures (CAMP), Technical University of Munich,
Munich, Germany
[3] Department of Biosystems Science and Engineering (D-BSSE), ETH Zurich, 4058
Basel, Switzerland
[4] Computer Aided Medical Procedures (CAMP), Johns Hopkins University,
Baltimore, USA

Abstract. Due to the inherent imperfections in the optical path,
microscopy images, particularly fluorescence microscopy images, are
often skewed by uneven illumination and hence have spurious intensity variation, also known as shading or vignetting effect. Besides spatial intensity inhomogeneity, time-lapse microscopy imaging further suffers from background variation in time, mostly due to photo-bleaching
of the background medium. Moreover, the temporal background variation is often experiment-specific and hence cannot be easily corrected,
in contrast to shading, where a prospective calibration method can be
used. Existing retrospective illumination correction methods, ranging
from simple multi-image averaging to sophisticated optimisation based
methods such as CIDRE and BaSiC, all assume that the foreground of
all images is uncorrelated between each other. However, this assumption
is violated in e.g. long-term time-lapse microscopy imaging of adherent
stem cells, in which a strong foreground correlation is observed from
frame to frame. In this paper, we propose a new illumination and background correction method for time-lapse imaging, based on low-rank and
sparse decomposition. We incorporate binary segmentation masks that
inform the weighting scheme of our reweighted L_1 norm minimisation
about foreground vs background pixels in the image. This yields a better separation of the low-rank and sparse component, hence improving the estimation of illumination profiles. Experiments on both simulated and real time-lapse data demonstrate that our approach is superior to existing illumination correction methods and improves single cell
quantification.

© Springer Nature Switzerland AG 2020
A. L. Martel et al. (Eds.): MICCAI 2020, LNCS 12265, pp. 174–183, 2020.
https://doi.org/10.1007/978-3-030-59722-1_17

1   Introduction

A powerful tool to study stem cell differentiation is time-lapse microscopy, which enables continuous monitoring of individual cells over days [1]. Using fluorescent molecular markers, continuous long-term time-lapse fluorescence microscopy imaging can capture the dynamics of changing cellular properties over time and provide insights into the molecular mechanisms of lineage choice, resolving fundamental questions in stem cell biology [2]. However, like all optical microscopy data, time-lapse fluorescence microscopy images suffer from uneven illumination due to an imperfect optical path, also known as shading or vignetting, which is reflected as an attenuation of the brightness intensity from the centre of the optical axis to the edges [3]. Besides the spatial shading effect, time-lapse movies often exhibit a temporal baseline drift due to photo-bleaching of the background medium, which further skews the quantification of single cell molecular properties.

Among existing illumination correction methods, CIDRE [4] and BaSiC [5] build upon physical models of microscopy image formation and extract the shared illumination profiles from multiple images that are captured with the same microscopy settings. In this way, their estimations are usually more reliable than single-image based algorithms, e.g. "rolling ball background subtraction" in ImageJ [6] and can be used for fluorescence image quantification [7]. However, one fundamental assumption of CIDRE and BaSiC is that the foreground of every image should be uncorrelated between frames. This assumption, unfortunately, is not valid for many biomedical time-lapse data. For example, most long-term time-lapse movies of adherent stem cells, e.g. embryonic stem cells, have a strong frame-to-frame correlation, as cells have low mobility and newly divided cells stick to each other (see Fig. 3a). In such cases, CIDRE and BaSiC would consider the consistently higher image intensities in these locations as a local increase in the illumination, and background and illumination correction would fail.

In our paper, we propose a new illumination and background correction method for time-lapse microscopy movies, particularly useful for movies with correlated foregrounds where existing correction methods fail. Like BaSiC [5], our new method is based on low-rank and sparse decomposition. Yet, we separate the contribution of foreground and background in the decomposition by using binary segmentation masks and push the correlated foreground to the sparse component, yielding a more reliable estimation of the illumination profiles in the low-rank component. We evaluate our new method on both simulated and real time-lapse data and demonstrate that it is superior to existing illumination correction methods and improves single cell quantification.

2   Method

Figure 1 shows an overview of our proposed time-lapse image correction based on low-rank and sparse decomposition, where binary segmentation masks that inform foreground and background absent is incorporated in the iterative reweighted L_1-norm minimization of the sparse component. We explain each step of our correction method with detailed mathematic derivations in the subsequent sections.

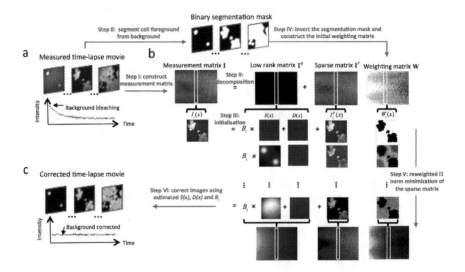

Fig. 1. Schematic of our proposed time-lapse image correction based on low-rank and sparse decomposition where the segmentation mask is incorporated in the iterative reweighted l1-norm minimization of the sparse component. (a) A time-lapse movie corrupted by both uneven illumination in space and photobleaching in time. (b) Estimation of flat-field $S(x)$, dark-field $D(x)$ and time-varying background B_i, using the inverted segmentation mask as the initial weighting matrix to down-weight the contribution of the foreground and up-weight the contribution of the background (see Method for detailed explanation). (c) The corrected time-lapse movie that both spatial intensity inhomogeneity and background bleaching over time are removed.

2.1 Physical Model of Microscopy Image Formation

The physical process of image formation can be approximated as a linear function [8] that relates a measured image, $I^{\mathrm{meas}}(x)$ at location x, to its uncorrupted true correspondence, $I^{\mathrm{true}}(x)$, as:

$$I^{\mathrm{meas}}(x) = I^{\mathrm{true}}(x) \times S(x) + D(x) \tag{1}$$

where the multiplicative term $S(x)$ represents the change in effective illumination across an image, known as flat-field; the additive term $D(x)$, known as dark-field, is dominated by camera offset and thermal noise, which are present even if no light is incident on the sensor. For a time-lapse microscopy image sequence, the illumination-corrected image $I_i^{\mathrm{true}}(x)$ of the ith frame can be further decomposed into the sum of a spatially-constant baseline signal, B_i, representing the bleaching of the background medium and the spatially varying foreground fluorescence signal of cells, $F_i(x)$. Hence the full model for a time-lapse microscopy movie becomes:

$$I_i^{\text{meas}}(x) = (B_i + F_i(x)) \times S(x) + D(x) \tag{2}$$

2.2   Low-Rank and Sparse Decomposition

We convert each frame, $I_i^{\text{meas}}(x)$ into a column vector $\vec{I}_i^{\text{meas}}$ (from now on, we denote the same variable in image space with (x) and as vector without (x)). Hence, we construct the measurement matrix as:

$$\vec{I}^{\text{meas}} = [\vec{I}_1^{\text{meas}}, ..., \vec{I}_n^{\text{meas}}]$$
$$\vec{I}_i^{\text{meas}} = B_i \times \vec{S} + \vec{D} + \vec{F}_i$$

The sum of the first two terms forms a *rank 2* matrix, $\vec{I}^B = \vec{B} \otimes \vec{S} \oplus \vec{D}$ ($\otimes$ and $\oplus$ denote column-wise multiplication and addition, respectively), as all images share the same flat-field S and dark-field D. The residual matrix, $\vec{I}^F$, stands for the foreground fluorescence signals of real biological relevance. In BaSiC [5], the residual matrix is assumed to be *sparse*. This sparse assumption, however, no longer holds for late time points of long-term time-lapse movies of dividing cells, when the generated cells occupy most of image domain (as shown in Fig. 3a). To solve this problem, we invert segmentation masks of foreground pixels as a weighting matrix $\vec{W}_s$ for $\vec{I}^F$. The weighted foreground matrix is assumed to be sparse, thus leading to the constraint optimization problem:

$$\min_{\vec{B},\vec{S},\vec{D}} \|\vec{W}^S \circ \vec{I}^F\|_0$$
$$\text{subject to } \vec{I} = \vec{I}^B + \vec{I}^F, \vec{I}^B = \vec{B} \otimes \vec{S} \oplus \vec{D}, \tag{3}$$

where $\circ$ denotes the element-wise Hadamard product and $\|\|_0$ denotes the L_0-norm, that is, the number of non-zero elements in $\vec{W}^S \circ \vec{I}^F$.

2.3   Reweighted L_1-Norm Minimization for the Sparse Component

In previous low-rank and sparse decomposition literature [9], the minimization of a L_0-norm is mostly replaced by the L_1-norm. Yet, we find for our problem, L_1-norm minimization only work well when the foreground component is *very sparse*, i.e. occupying less than 5% of all image pixels. To overcome this limitation, we use a reweighted L_1-norm minimization, which approximates better the L_0-norm when the component is *less sparse*. Additionally, we impose smooth regularisation on $S(x)$ and $D(x)$ by promoting the sparseness of their Fourier-transformed coefficients. So the complete objective function is written as:

$$\min_{\vec{B},\vec{S},\vec{D}} \{\|\vec{W} \circ \vec{I}^F\|_1 + \lambda_s \|\mathcal{F}(S(x))\|_1 + \lambda_d \|\mathcal{F}(D^R(x))\|_1 + \lambda_d \|D^R(x)\|_1\}$$
$$\text{subject to } \vec{I} = \vec{I}^B + \vec{I}^F, \vec{I}^B = \vec{B} \otimes \vec{S} \oplus \vec{D}, \vec{D} = D^z + \vec{D}^R, D^z \in [0, \min(\vec{I})] \tag{4}$$

where the dark-field $D(x)$ is decomposed into the sum of its mean D^Z and the residual $D^R(x)$. W is the weighting matrix which balances the penalty of large coefficients and small coefficients. We initialise W_0 to be W_s and update it using

$$\vec{W}^{k+1} = \frac{1}{\vec{I}^{F,k}/\vec{I}^{B,k} + \epsilon} \circ \vec{W}_s, \tag{5}$$

where the parameter $\epsilon > 0$ is introduced to provide stability.

In each iteration, we simultaneously minimise the L_1-norm of matrices in both the image and Fourier spaces respectively. We utilise the Linearized augmented Lagrangian method (LADM) [10], like the one used in robust PCA in [11]). In practice, the dark-field $D(x)$ is usually low and can often be neglected. Moreover, for time-lapse image sequence, the contribution of $D(x)$ can also be accounted by B_i as $D(x)$ is usually flat (since it represents the camera offset, which is a scalar). Therefore, we set $D(x)$ to be zero in our experiments.

2.4   Simulation of Synthetic Time-Lapse Microscopy Images

To evaluate our correction algorithm, we generate synthetic images using the following procedure:

Step I: We generate a shading-free time-lapse image sequence using the fluorescence simulation tool from [12]. To mimic stem cell divisions, we initialise the simulation with two stem cells in time frame 1 and increase the cell population by one cell at each subsequent time frame. Many important stem cell types, e.g. embryonic or blood stem cells, and their differentiated progeny do not move much (see e.g. [13]). This results in a high between-frame correlation, where existing retrospective illumination corrections fail. To simulate low cell mobility, we use a high probability of cell clustering and thus force the newly generated cells do not leave their birthplace. We simulate each image with a size of 256x256 pixels and two channels, one for fluorescently labeled nuclei and one for fluorescently labeled cytoplasm. The maximum cell density (proportional to the area occupied by the cell foreground) at the end of the movie for the nuclei and the cytoplasm channel are 37.2% and 83.7%, respectively.

Step II: We simulate the shading effect by corrupting the simulated shading-free images with a preset multiplicative flat-field $S(x)$ (dark-field $D(x)$ is negligible as explained in the previous section). In order to make our simulation as realistic as possible, we use $S(x)$ obtained prospectively from a concentrated dye solution. Additionally, we simulate the background bleaching as an exponentially decaying function. The simulated image sequence is shown in Fig. 2a.

Step III: We quantify the error between the estimated flat-field S^{est} and the ground-truth S^{gt} as Γ^S, defined as:

$$\Gamma^S = \frac{\sum \|S^{est} - S^{gt}\|_1}{\sum \|S^{gt} - 1\|_1} \tag{6}$$

3   Results and Discussion

3.1   Evaluation on Synthetic Data

We first evaluate our algorithm on synthetic data, where the ground-truth segmentation mask is used to initialise the weights W_s, and the ground-truth flat-field $S(x)$ and background B_i are available to quantify our estimation error. We compare our algorithm with two other popular image correction methods, CIDRE [4] and BaSiC [5]. As shown in Fig. 2b, the estimated flat-field $S(x)$ of our proposed method agrees well with the ground-truth in both nuclei and cytoplasm channels (error < 3%), suggesting our method is robust to different cell densities. In comparison, BaSiC performs relatively well in the nuclei channel (error = 6.5%), but it completely fails in the cytoplasm channel (error > 600%), where the foreground is getting crowded. CIDRE, as another competitive method, performs poorly in both nuclei and cytoplasm channels (error > 100% for both channels), illustrating that CIDRE should not be applied to images with strong foreground correlation. Besides a more accurate estimation of $S(x)$, our proposed method recovers the ground-truth background intensities, B_i, better than BaSiC, particularly in the cytoplasm channel. CIDRE, unfortunately, does not have an option to estimate time-varying background.

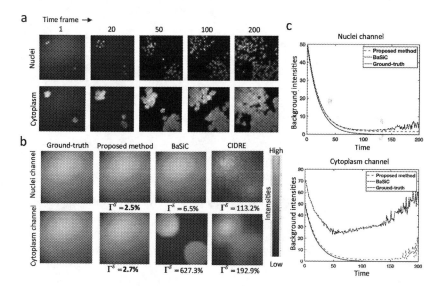

Fig. 2. Our proposed method outperforms CIDRE and BaSiC on synthetic data. (a) simulated time-lapse microscopy movie of two channels: fluorescently labeled nuclei (top) and cytoplasm (bottom). (b) Our estimated flat-field $S(x)$ agrees better with the ground-truth than two other competitive methods, CIDRE and BaSiC. Γ^S quantify the estimation error (see Methods). (c) Our proposed method recovers the ground-truth time-varying background intensities better than BaSiC, particularly in the cytoplasm channel (CIDRE cannot estimate time-varying background).

We further investigate the critical role of incorporating the binary segmentation mask in our reweighting L_1-norm minimisation. As shown in Fig. 3a, updating the weighting matrix without using segmentation masks does not recover the ground-truth flat-field $S(x)$ in the low-rank component. On the other hand, using binary segmentation masks as the weighting matrix alone also fail to reconstruct the true $S(x)$, as shown in the decomposition results of iteration 1 on Fig. 3b. Yet the combination of the two, i.e. updating weighting matrix using the inverted sparse component from the previous iteration as well as segmentation masks according to Eq. (5) , we can guide the low-rank component to quickly converge to the ground-truth flat-field $S(x)$ in subsequent iterations.

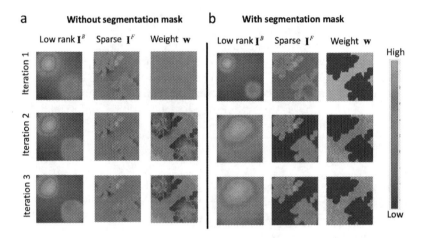

Fig. 3. Reweighting sparse component without (a) and with segmentation mask (b).

3.2   Evaluation on Real Data

Blood stem cells were isolated and sorted as previously described [14]. Time-lapse experiments were conducted at 37 degree, 5% O_2, 5% CO_2 on μ-slide VI0,4 channels slides (IBIDI). Images were acquired using a Nikon-Ti Eclipse equipped with a linear encoded motorized stage, Orca Flash 4.0 V2 (Hamamatsu), Spectra X fluorescent light source (Lumencor) and "The Cube" (Life Imaging Service) temperature control system. Time interval of fluorescent image acquisition is around 20 min, which was chosen to minimize phototoxicity. Images were acquired using a 10x CFI Plan Apochromat λ objective (NA 0.45). Exemplary images of the collected time-lapse image sequence is shown in Fig. 4a.

We obtain binary segmentation masks by thresholding fluorescence intensities of each frame followed by simple morphological dilations (Fig. 4a). It is worth to point out that the segmentation masks we obtained with such a simple method are not highly accurate. Yet, it is sufficient for our proposed algorithm for illumination correction. This is a key advantage of our algorithm that we do not need **perfect segmentation**. Instead, **rough segmentation** that achieves over 50% accuracy guarantees our low-rank component to converge to background rather than foreground. As shown in Fig. 4b, our proposed method (left) infers considerably smoother flat-field $S(x)$ compared to BaSiC (middle), where artefacts are present (indicated by black arrows). To better visualise the discrepancy between the two methods, we also plot the absolute difference of their estimated $S(x)$ (Fig. 4b right). The two estimations only differ in some hot-spot locations where new cells are generated and clustered (see Fig. 4a). This would lead to an over-correction of fluorescence intensities in these locations, hence removing true cellular signal of biological relevance. Additionally, BaSiC also tends to overestimate background from time frame 300 onwards, which could lead to further over-correction.

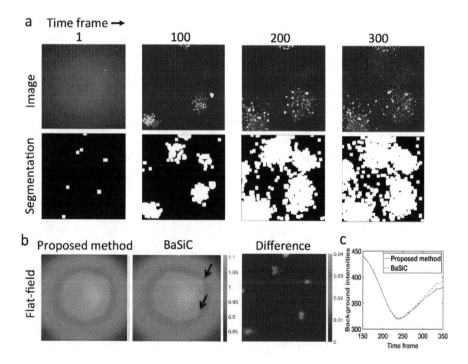

Fig. 4. Evaluation the proposed method on a real time-lapse microscopy movie of blood stem cells. (a) Top: exemplary images of time-lapse microscopy movie. Bottom: the corresponding rough segmentation masks. (b) Our estimated flat-field $S(x)$ is more smooth than that from BaSiC, where artefacts are indicated by black arrows. (c) BaSiC estimates higher blackground intensities than our proposed method at time frames 300 onwards, which indicates that BaSiC struggles to find the true background at frames with high cell density.

4   Conclusion

We propose a novel illumination and background correction method for time-lapse microscopy movies, based on low-rank and sparse decomposition. Particularly targeting movies with a strong foreground correlation, we propose a new weighting scheme that is initialised by binary segmentation masks that infer absent foreground vs. background in the L_1-norm minimisation of the sparse component. In this way, we preserve desirable separation of low-rank and sparse components even when cells become crowded in the late time points of a movie. Notably, we require only a rough segmentation for our method, which could be easily achieved by simple intensity threshold methods with minimum additional effort. We would also like to emphasise that our proposed method is the only one that applies to movies with correlated foreground. We will also develop our method into a user-friendly software tool that a large biological community can benefit from.

5   Novelty

We developed a novel weighting scheme for reweighted L1 norm minimisation of the sparse component, thus improving the quality of low-rank and sparse decomposition in general. Based on the improved decomposition, we propose a novel illumination and background correction method, which is the only method that works for time-lapse microscopy data with correlated foreground.

References

1. Etzrodt, M., Endele, M., Schroeder, T.: Quantitative single-cell approaches to stem cell research. Cell Stem Cell **15**(5), 546–58 (2014). http://www.ncbi.nlm.nih.gov/pubmed/25517464
2. Skylaki, S., Hilsenbeck, O., Schroeder, T.: Challenges in long-term imaging and quantification of single-cell dynamics. Nat. Biotechnol. **34**(11), 1137–1144 (2016). http://www.nature.com/doifinder/10.1038/nbt.3713
3. Goldman, D.B.: Vignette and exposure calibration and compensation. IEEE Trans. Pattern Anal. Mach. Intell. **32**(12), 2276–2288 (2010). http://ieeexplore.ieee.org/articleDetails.jsp?arnumber=5432200
4. Smith, K., et al.: CIDRE: An illumination-correction method for optical microscopy. Nat. Methods **12**(5), 404–406 (2015). http://www.nature.eaccess.ub.tum.de/nmeth/journal/vaop/ncurrent/full/nmeth.3323.html
5. Peng, T., et al.: A BaSiC tool for background and shading correction of optical microscopy images. Nat. Commun. **8**(1), 1–7 (2017). www.nature.com/naturecommunications
6. Collins, T.J.: ImageJ for microscopy. BioTechniques **43**(1 Suppl), 25–30 (2007). http://www.ncbi.nlm.nih.gov/pubmed/17936939
7. Lefebvre, J., Delafontaine-Martel, P., Lesage, F.: A Review of intrinsic optical imaging serial blockface histology (ICI-SBH) for whole rodent brain imaging. Photonics **6**(2), 66 (2019), https://www.mdpi.com/2304-6732/6/2/66

8. Likar, B., Maintz, J.B., Viergever, M.A., Pernuš, F.: Retrospective shading correction based on entropy minimization. J. Microsc. **197**(3), 285–295 (2000). https://pubmed.ncbi.nlm.nih.gov/10692132/

9. Peng, Y., Ganesh, A., Wright, J., Xu, W., Ma, Y.: RASL: Robust alignment by sparse and low-rank decomposition for linearly correlated images. IEEE Trans. Pattern Anal. Mach. Intell. **34**(11), 2233–46 (2012). http://www.ncbi.nlm.nih.gov/pubmed/22213763

10. Lin, Z., Chen, M., Ma, Y.: The augmented lagrange multiplier method for exact recovery of corrupted low-rank matrices. In: NIPS (2011)

11. Candès, E., Li, X., Ma, Y., Wright, J.: Robust principal component analysis ? J. ACM (JACM) (2011). http://dl.acm.org/citation.cfm?id=1970395

12. Lehmussola, A., Ruusuvuori, P., Selinummi, J., Huttunen, H., Yli-Harja, O.: Computational framework for simulating fluorescence microscope images with cell populations. IEEE Trans. Med. Imag. **26**(7), 1010–1016 (2007). https://pubmed.ncbi.nlm.nih.gov/17649914/

13. Filipczyk, A., et al.: Network plasticity of pluripotency transcription factors in embryonic stem cells. Nat. Cell Biol. **17**(10), 1235–1246 (2015). https://www.nature.com/articles/ncb3237

14. Loeffler, D., et al.: Asymmetric lysosome inheritance predicts activation of haematopoietic stem cells. Nature **573**(7774), 426–429 (2019). https://www.nature.com/articles/s41586-019-1531-6

Joint Spatial-Wavelet Dual-Stream Network for Super-Resolution

Zhen Chen[1], Xiaoqing Guo[1], Chen Yang[1], Bulat Ibragimov[2],
and Yixuan Yuan[1(✉)]

[1] Department of Electrical Engineering, City University of Hong Kong, Kowloon,
Hong Kong, China
`yxyuan.ee@cityu.edu.hk`
[2] University of Copenhagen-DIKU, Copenhagen, Denmark

Abstract. Super-Resolution (SR) techniques can compensate for the
missing information of low-resolution images and further promote
experts and algorithms to make accurate diagnosis decisions. Although
the existing pixel-loss based SR works produce high-resolution images
with impressive objective metrics, the over-smoothed contents that lose
high-frequency information would disturb the visual experience and the
subsequent diagnosis. To address this issue, we propose a joint Spatial-
Wavelet super-resolution Network (SWD-Net) with collaborative Dual-
stream. In the spatial stage, a Refined Context Fusion (RCF) is proposed to iteratively rectify the features by a counterpart stream with
compensative receptive fields. After that, the wavelet stage enhances
the reconstructed images, especially the structural boundaries. Specifically, we design the tailor-made Wavelet Features Adaptation (WFA) to
adjust the wavelet coefficients for better compatibility with networks and
Wavelet-Aware Convolutional blocks (WAC) to exploit features in the
wavelet domain efficiently. We further introduce the wavelet coefficients
supervision together with the traditional spatial loss to jointly optimize
the network and obtain the high-frequency enhanced SR images. To evaluate the SR for medical images, we build a benchmark dataset with
histopathology images and evaluate the proposed SWD-Net under different settings. The comprehensive experiments demonstrate our SWD-Net
outperforms state-of-the-art methods. Furthermore, SWD-Net is proven
to promote medical image diagnosis with a large margin. The source code
and dataset are available at https://github.com/franciszchen/SWD-Net.

Keywords: Super-resolution · Wavelet domain · Convolutional neural
networks

1 Introduction

Super-Resolution (SR) is a fundamental problem in low-level vision, and single-
image SR refers to reconstructing High-Resolution (HR) images from their corresponding Low-Resolution (LR) inputs. By introducing extra pixels, SR techniques compensate for the missing information of low-resolution images. Existing

© Springer Nature Switzerland AG 2020
A. L. Martel et al. (Eds.): MICCAI 2020, LNCS 12265, pp. 184–193, 2020.
https://doi.org/10.1007/978-3-030-59722-1_18

works have proven that pretrained SR networks can promote the performance in recognition and detection tasks [17,18]. In the field of medical images, Srivastav *et al.* [20] integrated a progressive SR network to append high-frequency features for the surgeon pose estimation during surgery, which brought a 6.5% increase of the percentage of correct keypoints (PCK).

In recent years, various deep learning based SR methods have been developed in the medical image community [9,12,15,23,27]. Particularly, Zhao *et al.* [27] proposed a channel splitting network with a residual branch and a dense branch to extract hierarchical features of magnetic resonance images. Li *et al.* [12] proposed a two-stage network supervised by gradient sensitive loss as well as traditional MSE loss to super-resolve the arterial spin labeling. Khan *et al.* [9] employed SR techniques on the Hilbert transformed data to enhance the ultrasound imaging. Mukherjee *et al.* [15] proposed a mechanism to train the SR network with intermediate-resolution sub-tasks for histopathology images.

Although existing SR networks supervised by pixel-loss in image space have achieved impressive objective metrics, including PSNR and SSIM [25], their predictions suffer from the over-smoothed contents and blurred edges, which hamper visual comprehension of image details. This problem is especially pronounced for medical image diagnosis where the loss of important image details induced by over-smoothing and blurring would disturb the decision making by both experts and algorithms. A reasonable solution is to reconstruct the high-frequency details explicitly. Following this idea, some SR works adopted wavelet techniques, which can decompose images into low-frequency components and high-frequency details [6,8,14]. Huang *et al.* [8] proposed the Wavelet-SRNet with specific-level Wavelet Packet Transformation (WPT), which predicted each sub-band coefficients of SR images with an independent subnet. The MWCNN [14] combined multi-level WPT and U-Net structure with improved down/upsampling and feature fusion. But these works only conducted the SR tasks in wavelet domain and ignored the information in image space. Besides, specific modules are required to construct networks in the wavelet domain more effectively, which may further improve the efficiency of usage on scarce medical data.

Moreover, most existing SR networks are constructed with a single backbone path [2,5,10,13,26], which may not be optimal for capturing multi-scale contextual information. Recently, a repeated fusion of multi-scale branches achieved superior performance in high-level tasks [21]. Similar architectures with multi-branch extracting contextual information at different scales, are also suitable for SR tasks. Through recursive fusions of multi-branch, each branch is enhanced by multi-scale features of other branches. However, the fusion by adding different branches directly [21] would lose important information, which is inappropriate in SR tasks. To address this issue, a tailor-made fusion module is devised to distill the significant context for SR reconstruction.

In this paper, we propose a Spatial-Wavelet Dual-stream Network (SWD-Net) integrated with Refined Context Fusion (RCF) to accomplish the SR task. Supervised by the spatial loss and wavelet loss, SWD-Net is able to recover high-resolution images with clear structural boundaries. To fully exploit the

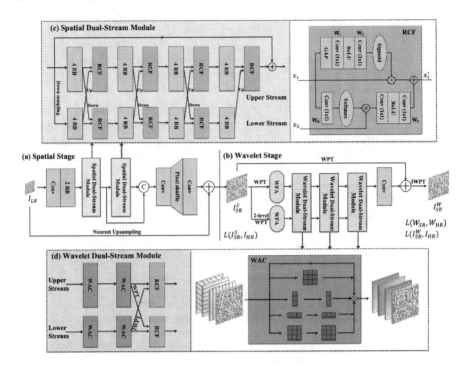

Fig. 1. The framework of SWD-Net. SWD-Net consists of two stages, spatial stage and wavelet stage. The activation functions, PReLU, are omitted in the diagram. (a) The spatial stage. (b) The wavelet stage. (c) Spatial dual-stream module and Refined Context Fusion (RCF). The channel of each stream is set as 32. (d) Wavelet dual-stream module with Wavelet-Aware Convolutional blocks (WAC). The channel of the upper stream is set as 24 and the channel of the lower stream is set as 96, which is compatible with wavelet packet transformation. Better viewed in colors. (Color figure online)

capability of networks in the wavelet domain, we design the Wavelet Features Adaptation (WFA) to adjust the wavelet coefficients into an appropriate range and Wavelet-Aware Convolutional blocks (WAC) to efficiently extract contextual information in wavelet domain. Additionally, we build a benchmark SR dataset in histopathology domain, named HistoSR.

2   SWD-Net

Our SWD-Net is built using the dual-stream architecture and consists of sequential spatial stage and wavelet stage to recover the SR image $I_{SR}^W \in \mathbb{R}^{sH \times sW}$ from the LR image $I_{LR} \in \mathbb{R}^{H \times W}$, where H and W represent the height and width, respectively, and s is the scale factor in the SR task. In the spatial stage, SWD-Net takes I_{LR} as an input, and produces a preliminary SR image I_{SR}^S with a posterior upsampling layer. In the wavelet stage, SWD-Net conducts multi-level

WPT on I_{SR}^S and enhances the high-frequency details with explicit loss in wavelet domain, and generates the final SR image I_{SR}^W. The framework of SWD-Net is illustrated in Fig. 1.

2.1   Spatial Stage

The SWD-Net first executes a 3×3 convolutional layer and two ResBlocks [7] to convert the input I_{LR} into feature maps. Then, SWD-Net is implemented with two spatial dual-stream modules, and their output feature maps are concatenated to provide multi-scale information for SR reconstruction. After a bottleneck, the pixel-shuffle upsampling [19] enlarges the feature maps into the targeted resolution, followed by a convolutional layer converting the features into image domain. Besides, a global skip connection with nearest interpolation is added to produce a preliminary SR prediction I_{SR}^S.

As shown in Fig. 1(a), the spatial dual-stream module consists of the upper stream and the lower stream. The input feature maps and the downsampled counterpart are delivered to the upper stream and the lower stream, respectively. Particularly, each stream is constructed with four repeated groups of four ResBlocks and a RCF, as well as a local skip connection. The stacked Res-Blocks of two streams extract the features at different scales. Specifically, the upper stream contains more details, while the lower stream focuses on structures. With necessary down/upsampling to adjust the resolution, RCF rectifies and exchanges the knowledge of these two streams iteratively.

Refined Context Fusion (RCF) Previous work conducted the fusion of multi-scale features by adding them directly [21]. However, the information loss induced by this operation may damage the performance in low-level tasks. Fusion with global context is an efficient solution [4]. For the SR task, we design the RCF to refine and fuse the contextual features of two streams. The workflow of RCF is shown in Fig. 1(c), where x_1 and x_2 are feature maps of the current stream and the counterpart one, respectively. The output of RCF, x_1', is computed as follows:

$$x_1' = x_1 \cdot \sigma(\mathbf{W}_2 \cdot \delta\left(\mathbf{W}_1 \cdot \mathbf{GAP}(x_1)\right)) + \mathbf{W}_v \sum_{j=1}^{hw} \frac{\exp\left(\mathbf{W}_k x_1^j\right)}{\sum_{m=1}^{hw} \exp\left(\mathbf{W}_k x_1^m\right)} x_2^j, \quad (1)$$

where σ stands for Sigmoid function, δ refers to PReLU function, $\mathbf{GAP}$ represents global average pooling, each $\mathbf{W}$ represents the parameters of 1×1 conv layers, h and w are the height and width of inputs. The first term adaptively modifies x_1 with the gate mechanism, while the second term rectifies x_2 using the spatial context of x_1. By adding these two terms together, RCF is able to utilize the context of x_1 and x_2 more comprehensively.

2.2   Wavelet Stage

In the wavelet stage, we first conduct 1-level WPT and 2-level WPT on I_{SR}^S and deliver these wavelet coefficients to the dual-stream structure. To adjust the ranges of wavelet coefficients, we apply a WFA module to each stream before convolution operations. Then, these adapted features are processed by three stacked wavelet dual-stream modules. In each module, two WACs are stacked at both the upper stream and the lower stream. Before RCF exchanges the information, we apply the WPT or IWPT on each stream to convert features into the compatible wavelet-level. Finally, a global skip connection is adopted in the 1-level WPT domain, and the IWPT transforms the feature maps into the final SR image, I_{SR}^W. The details of the wavelet stage and wavelet dual-stream module are demonstrated in Fig. 1(b) and (d), respectively. Subsequently, we introduce the details of WPT, WFA and WAC modules in turn.

Integrating WPT into Network. Multi-level 2D WPT is accomplished with 2D Discrete Wavelet Transformation (DWT) on each produced sub-band recursively [16]. Particularly, DWT utilizes four filters, $\mathbf{f}_{LL}$, $\mathbf{f}_{LH}$, $\mathbf{f}_{HL}$ and $\mathbf{f}_{HH}$ to convolve with an image or a feature map $\mathbf{x}$, and downsamples by 2 times to obtain the four sub-bands $\mathbf{x}_{LL}$, $\mathbf{x}_{LH}$, $\mathbf{x}_{HL}$ and $\mathbf{x}_{HH}$. The Inverse WPT (IWPT) can trace back the WPT procedure with inverted steps. We implement WPT using Haar wavelet, where the four filters as follows:

$$\mathbf{f}_{LL} = \frac{1}{2}\begin{bmatrix} 1 & 1 \\ 1 & 1 \end{bmatrix}, \mathbf{f}_{LH} = \frac{1}{2}\begin{bmatrix} -1 & -1 \\ 1 & 1 \end{bmatrix}, \mathbf{f}_{HL} = \frac{1}{2}\begin{bmatrix} -1 & 1 \\ -1 & 1 \end{bmatrix}, \mathbf{f}_{HH} = \frac{1}{2}\begin{bmatrix} 1 & -1 \\ -1 & 1 \end{bmatrix}. \quad (2)$$

At a given spatial location, $\mathbf{x}_{LL}$ gives the general information of $\mathbf{x}$, and $\mathbf{x}_{LH}$, $\mathbf{x}_{HL}$ and $\mathbf{x}_{HH}$ provides the horizontal, vertical and diagonal structural information, respectively.

Wavelet Features Adaptation (WFA). Existing works conducted convolutional layers on the results of DWT/WPT directly [6,14]. However, among the wavelet coefficients of an image, the coefficients of the average sub-band are positive, while the ranges of other three sub-bands are symmetry about zero. The range bias in channel-wise may lead the network to ignore the coefficients with small values. Thus, we propose the WFA to balance the wavelet coefficients of different channels before convolutional layers, which is implemented as:

$$x' = x \cdot tanh(\mathbf{W}_4 \cdot \delta\left(\mathbf{W}_3 \cdot \mathbf{GAP}(x)\right)), \quad (3)$$

where x' and x are the output and input feature maps of the WFA respectively, δ refers to PReLU function, $\mathbf{W}_3$ and $\mathbf{W}_4$ are 1×1 convolutional layers and $\mathbf{GAP}$ represents global average pooling. In this way, WFA converts the wavelet coefficients into similar ranges, which can stabilize the training process.

Wavelet-Aware Convolutional blocks (WAC). We design the WAC to upgrade the capability of convolutional neural networks (CNNs) under wavelet transform. The WAC is constructed with four convolutional paths, as demonstrated in Fig. 1(d). For the sub-band $\mathbf{x}_{LL}$, a 3×3 conv is utilized to process the low-frequency information. To efficiently expand the receptive field in horizontal and vertical directions, we adopt two spatial separable filters, 3×1 or 1×3, with same direction in a row, which effectively extracts the context of $\mathbf{x}_{LH}$ and

$\mathbf{x}_{HL}$ with minimum parameters. For the diagonal structural details in $\mathbf{x}_{HH}$, we further stack two 3×3 convolutional layers to capture the high-frequency information. A local skip connection is introduced to guarantee the back-propagation of gradients. Finally, different structural features generated by these paths are added together, which is more efficient than the concatenation used in Inception module [22]. Compared with simply stacking convolutional layers, WAC can capture the contextual information in wavelet domain more efficiently.

2.3 Weighted Spatial and Wavelet Loss Function

Generally, our network is an end-to-end mapping from LR images to SR images. To preserve high-frequency details, we optimize the gap between the predicted SR images and ground truth HR images, not only in spatial domain but also in wavelet domain. Given a training set $\left\{ \left(I_{LR}^{(i)}, I_{HR}^{(i)} \right) \right\}_{i=1}^{N}$, the loss function is calculated as follows:

$$
\begin{aligned}
L &= \lambda_1 L(I_{SR}^S, I_{HR}) + \lambda_2 L(I_{SR}^W, I_{HR}) + \lambda_3 L(W_{SR}, W_{HR}) \\
&= \frac{1}{N} \sum_{i=1}^{N} (\lambda_1 \left\| I_{SR}^{S(i)} - I_{HR}^{(i)} \right\|_1 + \lambda_2 \left\| I_{SR}^{W(i)} - I_{HR}^{(i)} \right\|_1 + \lambda_3 \left\| W_{SR}^{(i)} - W_{HR}^{(i)} \right\|_1),
\end{aligned}
\tag{4}
$$

where $I_{SR}^{W(i)}$ and $I_{SR}^{S(i)}$ are the i-th SR predictions of the wavelet stage and spatial stage respectively, $W_{SR}^{(i)}$ and $W_{HR}^{(i)}$ are the wavelet coefficients of the final prediction and HR image respectively, and λ_1, λ_2 and λ_3 are the weights to balance each loss. Specifically, the first term supervises the spatial stage of SWD-Net to achieve better convergence of the SR training. The second term encourages the final SR prediction consistent with ground truth in image space. Additionally, the third term supervises SWD-Net to recover details of different wavelet sub-bands, where the high-frequency details are preserved explicitly.

3   Experiment

3.1   HistoSR Dataset and Training Strategy

The whole-slide images (WSIs) have revealed advantages in tumors grading and detection of lung cancer nodules, glomeruli, or vessels [1]. However, high magnification WSIs scanners are typically very expensive. With SR techniques, the images acquired by low magnification scanners can be processed into the same resolution as well as similar quality [15], which are widely available and comparatively inexpensive. To facilitate this, we built a HistoSR dataset for SR on histopathology. Camelyon16 dataset provides 400 high-quality H&E stained WSIs of sentinel lymph node sections [3]. We random cropped patches from Camelyon16 WSIs and built the SR dataset by downsampling. With the labels of Camelyon16 dataset, we kept the ratio of tumor patches and normal patches

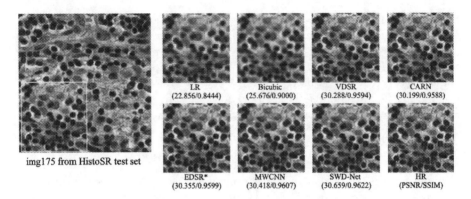

Fig. 2. Qualitative comparison of our SWD-Net with VDSR [10], CARN [2], MWCNN [14] and EDSR* [13] on HistoSR dataset with bicubic degradation.

as 1 : 1. The dataset provides a $2\times$ zoom-in from 96×96 patch at $10\times$ magnification (at 0.972 microns per pixel) to 192×192 patch at $20\times$ magnification (at 0.486 microns per pixel). The HistoSR dataset provides two versions with different degradation kernels. Specifically, the bicubic kernel is the common choice and retains neighboring information, while the nearest one discards the pixels directly. In this way, the nearest version provides a more difficult case to comprehensively evaluate various algorithms. Each version of HistoSR dataset contains 30, 000 image pairs in training set and 5, 000 image pairs in test set.

The SR models were optimized using Adam [11] with the batch size of 24. The learning rate was initialized as 1×10^{-4} and halved after every 100 epochs until convergence. The weight decay was set 5×10^{-4}. The λ_1, λ_2 and λ_3 were set as 0.1, 0.1 and 1, respectively. To further integrate the well-trained SR models with diagnosis networks, we implemented the SR training with RGB channels. For the diagnosis experiment, a classifier and the pretrained SR model were further fine-tuned using Adam with cross-entropy. The batch size was 16, and the learning rate was initialized as 1×10^{-4} and halved after every 20 epochs.

3.2   Super-Resolution with Different Degradation Kernels

We compared our SWD-Net with several state-of-the-art algorithms [2,10,13,14] on two degradation versions of HistoSR dataset. These networks were optimized using the training set of HistoSR dataset, and then evaluated on the test set of HistoSR dataset. For a fair comparison, we employed the EDSR baseline model [13], denoted as EDSR*, because both EDSR* and two streams of SWD-Net contain 64 filters at each layer. As shown in Table 1, SWD-Net achieves superior performance in both cases, especially the nearest one. It is worth noting that MWCNN outperforms EDSR* in the nearest degradation case. We suppose that the reconstruction in wavelet domain may have advantages in more difficult scenarios. By combining spatial domain and wavelet domain together, our SWD-Net outperforms MWCNN with 0.272 dB using only 12.9% parameters

Table 1. SR performance on HistoSR dataset in terms of PSNR (in dB) and SSIM. Best and second best results are **highlighted** and <u>underlined</u>.

Methods	Bicubic degradation		Nearest degradation	
	PSNR	SSIM	PSNR	SSIM
Bicubic	28.399	0.8859	25.143	0.8281
VDSR [10]	32.378	0.9481	30.524	0.9295
CARN [2]	32.393	0.9477	30.815	0.9316
EDSR* [13]	<u>32.676</u>	<u>0.9502</u>	31.181	0.9360
MWCNN [14]	32.498	0.9486	<u>31.266</u>	<u>0.9369</u>
SWD-Net	**32.769**	**0.9510**	**31.538**	**0.9397**

Table 2. Ablation study of SWD-Net on HistoSR with bicubic degradation.

Ablation Methods	PSNR	SSIM
w/o wavelet stage	32.674	0.9502
w/o RCF	32.713	0.9503
w/o WFA	32.723	0.9505
w/o WAC	32.721	0.9505
SWD-Net	**32.769**	**0.9510**

Table 3. The promotion of SR methods on tumor recognition task.

Methods	Accuracy	F1 score
Original	84.51%	0.8428
Bicubic	85.09%	0.8484
VDSR [10]	86.63%	0.8648
CARN [2]	87.26%	0.8714
SWD-Net	**87.73%**	**0.8762**

of MWCNN. In Fig. 2, we demonstrate the details of the reconstructed images. This shows that SWD-Net generates high-quality SR predictions, with structural boundaries consistent with ground truth to the best extent.

To demonstrate the capability of our RCF, WFA and WAC, we conducted ablation experiments on the bicubic version of HistoSR. As for the w/o WAC case, we replaced each WAC with two successive convolutional layers with more channels to guarantee the amount of parameters unchanged. As shown in Table 2, each of RCF, WFA and WAC individually contributes about 0.05 dB to PSNR. In addition, the spatial stage of SWD-Net performs on par with EDSR*. On this basis, the wavelet stage further brings a gain of about 0.1 dB in terms of PSNR.

3.3 Super-Resolution for Diagnosis

To evaluate the promotion of SR methods on diagnosis tasks, we further conducted the tumor recognition on PCam dataset [24]. PCam dataset provides $262,144$ color images for training and $32,768$ images for testing, and each image is annotated with a binary label indicating presence of metastatic tissue. We chose ResNet-18 as the baseline classifier [7]. The improvements induced by various SR methods are shown in Table 3. SR methods introduce extra domain knowledge and achieve superior gain over bicubic interpolation. It is clear that our SWD-Net brings the maximum performance rise, with a 3.22% increase in accuracy. This supports the fact that SWD-Net can recover more discriminative details that promote the diagnosis algorithm.

4   Conclusion

In this work, we propose a SWD-Net to solve the shortcomings of spatial domain SR by introducing the wavelet domain reconstruction. The dual-stream structure with RCF efficiently extracts and rectifies the multi-scale features to generate high-resolution images. The well-designed WFA and WAC further enhance the performance of SWD-Net. Experiments demonstrate that SWD-Net not only outperforms the state-of-the-art methods in SR tasks, but also promotes the diagnosis algorithms with a large margin. In the future, we are going to improve diagnosis frameworks integrated with SWD-Net.

References

1. Aeffner, F., et al.: Introduction to digital image analysis in whole-slide imaging: a white paper from the digital pathology association. J. Pathol. Inform. **10**, 9 (2019)
2. Ahn, N., Kang, B., Sohn, K.A.: Fast, accurate, and lightweight super-resolution with cascading residual network. In: Proceedings of the European Conference on Computer Vision (ECCV), pp. 252–268 (2018)
3. Bejnordi, B.E., et al.: Diagnostic assessment of deep learning algorithms for detection of lymph node metastases in women with breast cancer. JAMA **318**(22), 2199–2210 (2017)
4. Cao, Y., Xu, J., Lin, S., Wei, F., Hu, H.: Gcnet: Non-local networks meet squeeze-excitation networks and beyond. In: Proceedings of the IEEE International Conference on Computer Vision Workshops (2019)
5. Du, C., et al.: Orientation-aware deep neural network for real image super-resolution. In: Proceedings of the IEEE Conference on Computer Vision and Pattern Recognition Workshops (2019)
6. Guo, T., Seyed Mousavi, H., Huu Vu, T., Monga, V.: Deep wavelet prediction for image super-resolution. In: Proceedings of the IEEE Conference on Computer Vision and Pattern Recognition Workshops, pp. 104–113 (2017)
7. He, K., Zhang, X., Ren, S., Sun, J.: Deep residual learning for image recognition. In: Proceedings of the IEEE Conference on Computer Vision and Pattern Recognition, pp. 770–778 (2016)
8. Huang, H., He, R., Sun, Z., Tan, T.: Wavelet-srnet: A wavelet-based CNN for multi-scale face super resolution. In: ICCV, pp. 1689–1697 (2017)
9. Khan, S., Huh, J., Ye, J.C.: Deep learning-based universal beamformer for ultrasound imaging. In: Shen, D., et al. (eds.) MICCAI 2019. LNCS, vol. 11768, pp. 619–627. Springer, Cham (2019). https://doi.org/10.1007/978-3-030-32254-0_69
10. Kim, J., Kwon Lee, J., Mu Lee, K.: Accurate image super-resolution using very deep convolutional networks. In: Proceedings of the IEEE Conference on Computer Vision and Pattern Recognition, pp. 1646–1654 (2016)
11. Kingma, D.P., Ba, J.: Adam: A method for stochastic optimization. In: Proceedings of the 3rd International Conference on Learning Representations (ICLR) (2015)

12. Li, Z., et al.: A two-stage multi-loss super-resolution network for arterial spin labeling magnetic resonance imaging. In: Shen, D., et al. (eds.) MICCAI 2019. LNCS, vol. 11766, pp. 12–20. Springer, Cham (2019). https://doi.org/10.1007/978-3-030-32248-9_2

13. Lim, B., Son, S., Kim, H., Nah, S., Mu Lee, K.: Enhanced deep residual networks for single image super-resolution. In: Proceedings of the IEEE Conference on Computer Vision and pattern recognition workshops, pp. 136–144 (2017)

14. Liu, P., Zhang, H., Zhang, K., Lin, L., Zuo, W.: Multi-level wavelet-cnn for image restoration. In: CVPR Workshops. pp. 773–782 (2018)

15. Mukherjee, L., Bui, H.D., Keikhosravi, A., Loeffler, A., Eliceiri, K.W.: Super-resolution recurrent convolutional neural networks for learning with multi-resolution whole slide images. J. Biomed. Optics **24**(12), 126003 (2019)

16. Peyré, G.: A Wavelet Tour of Signal Processing: The Sparse Way. Academic Press, USA (2009)

17. Sajjadi, M.S., Scholkopf, B., Hirsch, M.: Enhancenet: Single image super-resolution through automated texture synthesis. In: Proceedings of the IEEE International Conference on Computer Vision, pp. 4491–4500 (2017)

18. Shermeyer, J., Van Etten, A.: The effects of super-resolution on object detection performance in satellite imagery. In: Proceedings of the IEEE Conference on Computer Vision and Pattern Recognition Workshops (2019)

19. Shi, W., et al.: Real-time single image and video super-resolution using an efficient sub-pixel convolutional neural network. In: Proceedings of the IEEE Conference on Computer Vision and Pattern Recognition, pp. 1874–1883 (2016)

20. Srivastav, V., Gangi, A., Padoy, N.: Human pose estimation on privacy-preserving low-resolution depth images. In: Shen, D., et al. (eds.) MICCAI 2019. LNCS, vol. 11768, pp. 583–591. Springer, Cham (2019). https://doi.org/10.1007/978-3-030-32254-0_65

21. Sun, K., Xiao, B., Liu, D., Wang, J.: Deep high-resolution representation learning for human pose estimation. In: Proceedings of the IEEE Conference on Computer Vision and Pattern Recognition, pp. 5693–5703 (2019)

22. Szegedy, C., Vanhoucke, V., Ioffe, S., Shlens, J., Wojna, Z.: Rethinking the inception architecture for computer vision. In: Proceedings of the IEEE Conference on Computer Vision and Pattern Recognition, pp. 2818–2826 (2016)

23. Upadhyay, U., Awate, S.P.: A mixed-supervision multilevel GAN framework for image quality enhancement. In: Shen, D., et al. (eds.) MICCAI 2019. LNCS, vol. 11768, pp. 556–564. Springer, Cham (2019). https://doi.org/10.1007/978-3-030-32254-0_62

24. Veeling, B.S., Linmans, J., Winkens, J., Cohen, T., Welling, M.: Rotation equivariant CNNs for digital pathology. In: Frangi, A.F., Schnabel, J.A., Davatzikos, C., Alberola-López, C., Fichtinger, G. (eds.) MICCAI 2018. LNCS, vol. 11071, pp. 210–218. Springer, Cham (2018). https://doi.org/10.1007/978-3-030-00934-2_24

25. Wang, Z., Bovik, A.C., Sheikh, H.R., Simoncelli, E.P.: Image quality assessment: From error visibility to structural similarity. IEEE Trans. Image Process. **13**(4), 600–612 (2004)

26. Zhang, Y., Li, K., Li, K., Wang, L., Zhong, B., Fu, Y.: Image super-resolution using very deep residual channel attention networks. In: Proceedings of the European Conference on Computer Vision (ECCV), pp. 286–301 (2018)

27. Zhao, X., Zhang, Y., Zhang, T., Zou, X.: Channel splitting network for single MR image super-resolution. IEEE Trans. Image Process. **28**(11), 5649–5662 (2019)

Towards Neuron Segmentation
from Macaque Brain Images:
A Weakly Supervised Approach

Meng Dong, Dong Liu[✉], Zhiwei Xiong, Xuejin Chen, Yueyi Zhang,
Zheng-Jun Zha, Guoqiang Bi, and Feng Wu

University of Science and Technology of China, Hefei, China
dongeliu@ustc.edu.cn

Abstract. The advance of microscopic imaging technology has enabled
the observation of primate brain in its entirety and at single-neuron
resolution. It is then an urgent need to develop means for automated
analyses of these brain images, e.g. neuron segmentation. Deep learning is
demonstrated an appealing approach for segmentation of natural images,
but the success of deep learning is highly dependent on the large-scale
and well-built training data that are costly to collect. In this paper, we
take a step towards the goal of neuron segmentation from primate brain
images, using a weakly supervised approach. We build – to our best
knowledge – the first dual-channel three-dimensional image dataset of
macaque brain for neuron segmentation. We propose two kinds of "weak"
labels, i.e. central points and rough masks, to prepare training data with
an affordable cost. Accordingly, we design a weakly supervised learning
method for neuron instance segmentation where instances can be easily
extracted from the predicted peak-shape probability maps. Experimental
results have shown the effectiveness of our approach. We also verify the
efficiency of the proposed method on a public nuclei dataset. Our dataset
and code have been published at https://braindata.bitahub.com/.

Keywords: Instance segmentation · Macaque brain · Weakly
supervised learning

1 Introduction

Understanding the form and structure of primate brain contributes to unrav-
eling the mystery of brain. However, conducting morphological analyses of primate brain images at whole-brain scale and single-neuron resolution is still a
great challenge for both data collecting and image analyzing. Many existing
works have explored such high-resolution brain atlas of small non-primates such

Electronic supplementary material The online version of this chapter (https://
doi.org/10.1007/978-3-030-59722-1_19) contains supplementary material, which is
available to authorized users.

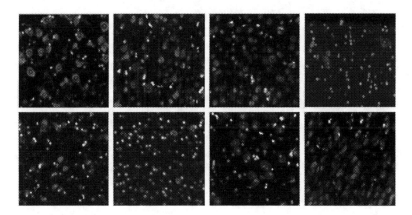

Fig. 1. Examples of our dual-channel macaque brain images. Soma and dendrite roots are stained with NeuroTrace (red), and nuclei are stained with DAPI (green). (Color figure online)

as drosophilas and mice. However, primates have a much more complex brain mechanism which is closer to human. Thus investigating primate brains is more important yet more challenging. For the first time, we collect dual-channel volumetric images of rhesus macaque brain using fluorescent staining and VISoR microscope imaging techniques. These techniques have been reported in [11] for mice. The resolution is high enough to identify each neuron or even nuclei, which enables analyses such as detection and segmentation.

Instance segmentation is an informative pixel-level image analysis task, because the acquired classification and individual information can serve for further higher-level tasks including counting, classification, and tracking. Li et al. [5] present a classic segmentation method based on gradient flow tracking, but this method may have difficulty in handling textured blob objects or irregular shapes. Popular deep learning-based approaches perform well on instance segmentation tasks for natural images, but most of them demand precise labels, e.g. pixel-wise accurate masks, which are quite expensive to label manually. Such labor-intensive labeling is almost impossible for our macaque brain data for two reasons. First, the data volume is huge, as a single whole-brain volume occupies around 200 TB. Second, the cells are observed in volumetric images, and they appear small and crowded. Thus we want to explore a cost effective approach. Since training an instance segmentation model requires both instance information and appearance information, we propose two types of "weak" labels including central points and rough masks, which can provide both kinds of information but save considerable labeling cost than the pixel-wise masks. Then our target is to achieve instance segmentation on our macaque brain data with the proposed weak labels.

Weakly supervised instance segmentation for biomedical images has attracted growing attention. Instead of relying on pixel-wise labeling, more and more methods are introduced for segmentation with bounding boxes [3], points [2,7,8,12] or mixed labels [9,14]. Dong et al. [3] borrow the idea of peak response mapping

(PRM) from [16] to find visual cues for instances, and use an improved Otsu algorithm as post-processing to segment instance masks. Nishimura et al. [7] also realize instance segmentation by propagating the response of a detection network, while they take graph-cut as post-processing. Besides [7], there are increasing studies on weakly supervised instance segmentation with point labels only [2,8,12]. Yoo et al. [12] propose a training method for nuclei segmentation, and they utilize a Pseudo-Edge-Net to help recognize nuclei edges. In [2,8], the authors generate pixel-wise labels from point labels first, then train a segmentation model with the pixel-wise labels. Also, Chamanzar et al. [2] train a multi-task model for mutual promotion. Qu et al. improve [8] with mixed labels [9], where a few full-mask labels are added for the instances with high uncertainty. Zhao et al. [14] utilize both bounding boxes and a small proportion of full instance masks to train a 3D Mask R-CNN for instance segmentation.

In the above works, the PRM-based methods [3,7] rely on carefully designed post-processing procedures, and the PRM operation is time-consuming since it is conducted for every instance and the total number of instances can be huge. Other methods like [2,8,12] directly treat the connected components in segmentation results as instance masks, thus merge errors are common especially for crowded instances. We address these challenging problems with a novel weakly supervised instance segmentation method, where the model first learns to predict a peak-shape probability map and then instance masks can be extracted from the map. Our main contributions can be summarized as below:

- We build the first dual-channel three-dimension image dataset of macaque brain at single-neuron resolution for instance segmentation. The data have weak labels for training set and full instance masks for testing set.
- We propose two kinds of weak labels, including central points for instance supervision and rough masks for appearance supervision. Both kinds of labels can be obtained with an affordable cost.
- We design a weakly supervised instance segmentation method, where a peak-shape probability map can be learned with proper loss functions and used to achieve instance segmentation with simple instance extraction steps.

2   Method

2.1   Efficient Annotation Methods for Macaque Brain Data

The Raw Macaque Brain Data. Our macaque brain data are captured from an adult male rhesus macaque aged 10. Two kinds of fluorescent are used to label cell structures, NeuroTrace and DAPI (c.f. the red and green channels in Fig. 1). NeuroTrace can label the ribosome-related substances which are concentrated on the soma and dendrite roots, while DAPI can label DNA to indicate the nuclei regions. The images are acquired with an advanced volumetric imaging technique [11] at whole-brain scale. The voxel size is $2.5 \times 1.0 \times 1.0 \, \mu m^3$. The whole-brain data have around 250 sections and occupy up to 200 TB. The data we used for instance segmentation only cover a tiny proportion.

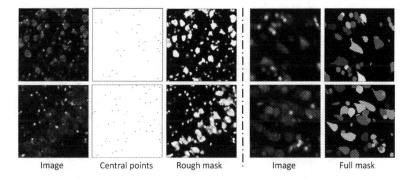

Image   Central points   Rough mask   Image   Full mask

Fig. 2. Examples of our labeled macaque brain dataset for instance segmentation. The training set has central points and rough masks. The test set has full instance masks.

Table 1. Statistics of our macaque brain dataset

	Image size	No. Images	No. Cells
Training set	$64 \times 256 \times 256$	100	130234
Testing set	$32 \times 128 \times 128$	3	597

Two Kinds of Weak Labels. From Fig. 2, we can see that the neuron distribution in our macaque brain data is extremely dense. Also, the neuron sizes are in a large range and the majority of neurons are quite small. It is challenging to manually label such small and crowded neurons from volumetric images for segmentation purpose. As for the two channels, firstly, the red channel shows the whole appearance of soma and part of dendrites, but it is hard to distinguish neuron instances in crowded cases; Secondly, the green channel shows the nuclei regions, most of which are smaller and have more regular shapes. Thus we choose to use two types of weak labels to take advantage of the two channels. The first one is central points. We use Imaris to automatically detect nuclei with 'spots' from the green channel. Spots provide central-point coordinates. After using Imaris, we load the detected spots into ImageJ and manually correct the errors using CellCounter plugin. The second kind of weak label is rough masks, the probability map for foreground class. We use an interactive tool – Ilastik [1] to perform pixel binary classification with manual scribbles on two-channel images. Ilastik trains Random Forest classifiers with some handcrafted features. This procedure is fast, because once a classifier is trained, it can be applied to other images in a batch process. However, the classification performance is not always satisfactory for all images. So the Ilastik results are regarded as rough labels. Figure 2 shows two training images with the proposed weak labels. The rough masks are not accurate and lack instance information. On the contrary, the central points offer relatively accurate instance information but have no appearance knowledge. Therefore, both kinds of weak labels can work together as complementary supervision for instance segmentation. Finally, for testing purpose we

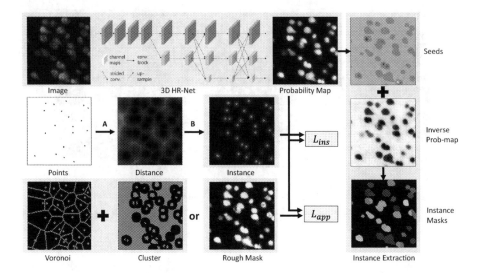

Fig. 3. Overview of our proposed approach. The 3D HR-Net is trained to predict a peak-shape probability map to minimize instance loss (L_{ins}) and appearance loss (L_{app}). Instance label is generated from central points in two steps (A is distance transformation, and B is continuous mapping). Voronoi and Cluster labels are similar to those in [8]. The instance extraction step is taken during inference only.

manually label several images with full masks using ITK-SNAP [13]. The statistics of our labeled macaque brain dataset are shown in Table 1.

2.2 Instance Segmentation with Weak Labels

We design a novel strategy for instance segmentation with the proposed weak labels. The approach may be extended to incorporate other methods for further improvement. Figure 3 presents the overview of our method. Considering the small neuron size of macaque brain data, we choose the high-resolution network (HR-Net) [10] as the backbone. Note that we use a 3D version of HR-Net and simplify the structure to save calculations. We propose two losses with specifically designed labels to guide the network to predict a peak-shape probability map. In inference, we design an instance extraction process to generate the final results.

Two Loss Functions. To utilize both instance and appearance information from the two kinds of weak labels, we propose to train the 3D HR-Net with multi-loss supervision. Note that our method aims to predict peak-shape probability maps that have both instance and appearance knowledge. Such maps can be learned with an instance loss L_{ins} and an appearance loss L_{app}:

$$Loss = L_{ins} + \lambda \cdot L_{app}, P_{iv} = \frac{1}{1 + \alpha \cdot d_v} \tag{1}$$

$$L_{ins} = \frac{1}{N} \sum_v \left(-P_{iv} \cdot \log(\hat{P}_v) - (1 - P_{iv}) \cdot \log(1 - \hat{P}_v) \right) \qquad (2)$$

$$L_{app} = \frac{1}{N} \sum_v \left(-P_{av} \cdot \log(\hat{P}_v) - (1 - P_{av}) \cdot \log(1 - \hat{P}_v) \right) \qquad (3)$$

where P_{iv} is the continuous value at voxel v in the map of instance labels, which are generated from the central points by two steps (see Fig. 3). We first apply distance transformation to the points, then the instance map is calculated with a mapping in (1) where d_v is distance and α controls the gradient of peaks ($\alpha = 0.8$ by default in our experiments). The distance transformation can help separate nearby instances, and the mapping aims to produce a continuous peak-shape map for instance supervision. $\hat{P}_v$ is the predicted probability at voxel v. P_{av} in (3) is the value at voxel v in the map of class labels, which may be deduced from Voronoi, cluster labels, or our rough masks. Note that Voronoi and cluster labels are discrete values while our rough mask labels are continuous probabilities that are given by Ilastik. The Ilastik results are not accurate enough, so we choose to keep the probabilities instead of thresholding. Finally, we use cross entropy function to guide network to learn from both instance and class labels. λ in (1) is a loss weight to balance the two losses ($\lambda = 0.5$ by default in our experiments).

Instance Extraction. During reference, given the predicted probability map P, local maximums are first detected as instance seeds, and voxels with probabilities lower than a given threshold are set as background seeds. Then a watershed algorithm is performed over the inverse probability map ($\max(P) - P$). Finally, the connected components are regarded as the segmented instances masks.

3 Experiments

We conduct experiments on our macaque brain data as well as a nuclei dataset called Multi-Organ [4] to verify the effectiveness of our method. We compare with a competitive method [8] that uses point labels for instance segmentation.

Macaque Brain Dataset. For training, we crop the original training set into 4,500 smaller blocks of the size $20 \times 128 \times 128$ with proper overlap. 1,000 blocks are randomly selected as validation data. The input images are normalized on their two channels individually. All the models are trained with a batch size of 8 on four GeForce GTX 1080Ti GPUs for 15 epochs. During inference, the probability map is first normalized into the range of [0, 255]. The size of the maximum filter and the threshold of background seeds are 10 and 50 respectively. We take F1 score and Dice$_{obj}$ to evaluate the performance. For both metrics, three IoU thresholds are used to judge true positives. F1 score can reflect object-level accuracy while Dice$_{obj}$ cares more about instance-mask quality. The Dice$_{obj}$ is averaged over all segmented masks.

Table 2. Results of F1 score and Dice_{obj} with three IoU thresholds on our macaque brain dataset. R-Masks means rough masks, and Mixed denotes Points and R-Masks.

Method	Label	IoU 0.3		IoU 0.4		IoU 0.5	
		F1	Dice_{obj}	F1	Dice_{obj}	F1	Dice_{obj}
Points [8]	Points	0.5824	0.4296	0.4042	0.3230	0.2586	0.2191
Points [8]+Our L_{ins}		0.7224	0.4757	0.5789	0.4018	0.3899	0.2853
Ours w/o L_{app}	Points	0.6313	0.4127	0.4545	0.3161	0.1963	0.1486
Ours w/o L_{ins}	R-Masks	0.4853	0.5207	0.4374	0.4859	0.3613	0.4196
Ours	Mixed	**0.8219**	**0.6377**	**0.7500**	**0.6006**	**0.6610**	**0.5453**

Table 3. Results on the Multi-Organ dataset. Results of the first three methods are reported in [9]. The best results among the methods using point labels only are in bold.

Method	Label	Pixel-level		Object-level	
		Acc	F1	Dice_{obj}	AJI
DIST [6]	Full masks	-	0.7623	-	0.5598
CIA-Net [15]		-	-	-	0.6205
Full masks		0.9194	0.8100	0.6763	0.3919
Mixed [9] (rand)	Mixed	0.9111	0.7753	0.7280	0.5106
Mixed [9] (un)		0.9114	0.7748	0.7323	0.5297
Points [8] w/o CRF	Points	0.9052	0.7745	0.7231	0.5045
Points [8] w/ CRF		0.9071	0.7776	**0.7270**	0.5097
Ours w/o CRF		0.9070	0.7804	0.7238	0.5179
Ours w/ CRF		**0.9081**	**0.7821**	0.7237	**0.5202**

To compare with [8], we also generate reasonable Voronoi and cluster labels using points from 2D images. Because both the image formats and the distribution of objects differ a lot between our macaque data and the nuclei data [8], we make some customizations (see supplementary material) when generating these two labels according to the guidance in [8]. The results are shown in Table 2. The first three rows (denoted by r1, r2, r3) demand point labels only, but they produce different ground truth (GT) from points and use different loss functions. r1 uses appearance loss whose GT is Voronoi and cluster labels; r3 uses instance loss whose GT is instance label; and r2 combines the losses and GT of r1 and r3, where the loss weights are $L_{ins} : L_{vor} : L_{clu} = 1 : 0.5 : 0.5$. Compared with [8], adding instance loss does not incur additional labeling cost, but the results especially F1 scores are improved a lot. To further understand the benefits of the two losses, we check the performance of the models trained with L_{ins} only or L_{app} only. With only L_{ins} as supervision, the model has fair results in F1 score but worse Dice_{obj}, i.e. it can identify instances well but the segmented masks are not accurate. The results of the models trained with L_{app} only are just on the

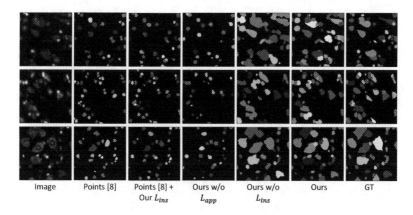

Image	Points [8]	Points [8] + Our L_{ins}	Ours w/o L_{app}	Ours w/o L_{ins}	Ours	GT

Fig. 4. Visual results on our macaque brain dataset.

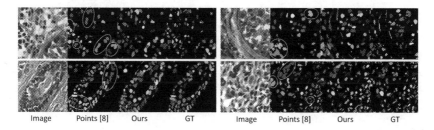

Image	Points [8]	Ours	GT	Image	Points [8]	Ours	GT

Fig. 5. Visual results on the Multi-Organ dataset. Note the regions with yellow circles.

contrary. These experiment results demonstrate the effectiveness of our method on the macaque brain dataset.

Although our best results are partially due to additional labels, the required extra labeling cost could be safely ignored compared with labeling the points. As discussed in Sect. 2.1, the points require manually checking the instances one by one through 2D images to determine a proper location in 3D space. The rough masks, on the contrary, are automatically produced in batch by a pixel classifier, where we only need to draw some scribbles on a few 2D images to train the classifier. The drawing procedure is simple for human labeling, thus, the labeling time is still dominated by the points labeling. We believe that it makes sense to achieve the improvement with such tiny extra labeling cost.

Multi-organ Nuclei Data. This dataset is largely different from our macaque brain data, but they [8] also tackle instance segmentation with points annotation on it. The comparison with [8] on this dataset can demonstrate the generalization ability of our approach. We use the training data and follow the settings in [8] for fair comparison. We keep the original Voronoi and cluster labels, and add our instance labels where α is set to 0.2 and the loss weights are set to $L_{ins} : L_{vor} : L_{clu} = 1 : 0.5 : 0.5$. For the instance extraction step, the size of the maximum filter is 25 and the threshold of background seeds is 50. Besides, we apply a second local maximum detection step with a smaller filter size of 5 to merge the false peaks of the same instance. Table 3 presents the experiment results. Note that different methods in comparison use full-mask, mixed, or points only labels. Augmenting our L_{ins} and instance extraction, the performance of [8] is improved a lot without extra labeling cost. The improved results are even comparable with [9] which requires extra precise labeling. The F1 and AJI of ours without CRF are still better than [8] with CRF, and are comparable with [9]. These results verify the effectiveness and generalization ability of our method.

Visualization. Figure 4 presents some visual results of the five methods in Table 2. We can see that the method [8] cannot segment the full masks of neurons, because the adopted k-means method for generating cluster labels is not robust enough to handle diverse cells. The merge errors are common. When adding our instance loss, merge errors reduce. We remark that training with both instance loss and appearance loss makes a better tradeoff between instance detection and appearance segmentation. Figure 5 shows the results on Multi-Organ dataset, where yellow circles denote merge errors. With our instance loss, neuron instances are better distinguished and the segmented masks are closer to the ground truth.

4   Conclusion

In this paper, we build a dual-channel volumetric image dataset of macaque brain for neuron instance segmentation. We propose two kinds of weak labels to provide instance and appearance supervision with an affordable labeling cost. Accordingly, we design two losses to fully utilize the weak labels to guide the network to predict a peak-shape probability map, from which instance masks can be easily obtained with our instance extraction process. In addition, our losses and instance extraction process can be combined with other methods to further improve the performance without extra labeling cost.

Acknowledgments. This work is supported in part by Key Area R&D Program of Guangdong Province with grant No. 2018B030338001, and the Fundamental Research Funds for the Central Universities under Grant WK2380000002.

References

1. Berg, S., et al.: ilastik: Interactive machine learning for (bio) image analysis. Nat. Methods **16**, 1–7 (2019)
2. Chamanzar, A., Nie, Y.: Weakly supervised multi-task learning for cell detection and segmentation (2019). arXiv preprint arXiv:1910.12326
3. Dong, M., et al.: Instance segmentation from volumetric biomedical images without voxel-wise labeling. In: MICCAI, pp. 83–91 (2019)

4. Kumar, N., et al.: A dataset and a technique for generalized nuclear segmentation for computational pathology. IEEE TMI **36**(7), 1550–1560 (2017)
5. Li, G., et al.: 3D cell nuclei segmentation based on gradient flow tracking. BMC Cell Biol. **8**(1), 40 (2007)
6. Naylor, P., et al.: Segmentation of nuclei in histopathology images by deep regression of the distance map. IEEE TMI **38**(2), 448–459 (2018)
7. Nishimura, K., Ker, D.F.E., Bise, R.: Weakly supervised cell instance segmentation by propagating from detection response. In: Shen, D., et al. (eds.) MICCAI 2019. LNCS, vol. 11764, pp. 649–657. Springer, Cham (2019). https://doi.org/10.1007/978-3-030-32239-7_72
8. Qu, H., et al.: Weakly supervised deep nuclei segmentation using points annotation in histopathology images. In: MIDL, pp. 390–400 (2019)
9. Qu, H., et al.: Nuclei segmentation using mixed points and masks selected from uncertainty. In: ISBI (2020)
10. Sun, K., et al.: High-resolution representations for labeling pixels and regions (2019). arXiv preprint arXiv:1904.04514
11. Wang, H., et al.: Scalable volumetric imaging for ultrahigh-speed brain mapping at synaptic resolution. Nat. Sci. Rev. **6**(5), 982–992 (2019)
12. Yoo, I., et al.: Pseudoedgenet: Nuclei segmentation only with point annotations. In: MICCAI, pp. 731–739 (2019)
13. Yushkevich, P.A., et al.: User-guided 3D active contour segmentation of anatomical structures: Significantly improved efficiency and reliability. Neuroimage **31**(3), 1116–1128 (2006)
14. Zhao, Z., et al.: Deep learning based instance segmentation in 3D biomedical images using weak annotation. In: MICCAI, pp. 352–360 (2018)
15. Zhou, Y., Onder, O.F., Dou, Q., Tsougenis, E., Chen, H., Heng, P.-A.: CIA-Net: Robust nuclei instance segmentation with contour-aware information aggregation. In: Chung, A.C.S., Gee, J.C., Yushkevich, P.A., Bao, S. (eds.) IPMI 2019. LNCS, vol. 11492, pp. 682–693. Springer, Cham (2019). https://doi.org/10.1007/978-3-030-20351-1_53
16. Zhou, Y., et al.: Weakly supervised instance segmentation using class peak response. In: CVPR, pp. 3791–3800 (2018)

3D Reconstruction and Segmentation of Dissection Photographs for MRI-Free Neuropathology

Henry F. J. Tregidgo[1]([✉]), Adrià Casamitjana[1], Caitlin S. Latimer[2],
Mitchell D. Kilgore[2], Eleanor Robinson[1], Emily Blackburn[3],
Koen Van Leemput[4,5], Bruce Fischl[4], Adrian V. Dalca[4,6],
Christine L. Mac Donald[7], C. Dirk Keene[2], and Juan Eugenio Iglesias[1,4,6]

[1] Centre for Medical Image Computing, University College London, London, UK
h.tregidgo@ucl.ac.uk
[2] Department of Pathology, University of Washington, Seattle, WA, USA
[3] Queen Square Institute of Neurology, University College London, London, UK
[4] Martinos Center for Biomedical Imaging, MGH and Harvard Medical School,
Boston, USA
[5] Department of Health Technology, DTU, Lyngby, Denmark
[6] Computer Science and Artificial Intelligence Laboratory, MIT, Cambridge, USA
[7] Department of Neurological Surgery, University of Washington, Seattle, WA, USA

Abstract. Neuroimaging to neuropathology correlation (NTNC) promis-es to enable the transfer of microscopic signatures of pathology to *in vivo* imaging with MRI, ultimately enhancing clinical care. NTNC traditionally requires a volumetric MRI scan, acquired either *ex vivo* or a short time prior to death. Unfortunately, *ex vivo* MRI is difficult and costly, and recent *premortem* scans of sufficient quality are seldom available. To bridge this gap, we present methodology to 3D reconstruct and segment full brain image volumes from brain dissection photographs, which are routinely acquired at many brain banks and neuropathology departments. The 3D reconstruction is achieved via a joint registration framework, which uses a reference volume other than MRI. This volume may represent either the sample at hand (e.g., a surface 3D scan) or the general population (a probabilistic atlas). In addition, we present a Bayesian method to segment the 3D reconstructed photographic volumes into 36 neuroanatomical structures, which is robust to nonuniform brightness within and across photographs. We evaluate our methods on a dataset with 24 brains, using Dice scores and volume correlations. The results show that dissection photography is a valid replacement for *ex vivo* MRI in many volumetric analyses, opening an avenue for MRI-free NTNC, including retrospective data. The code is available at https://github.com/htregidgo/DissectionPhotoVolumes.

© Springer Nature Switzerland AG 2020
A. L. Martel et al. (Eds.): MICCAI 2020, LNCS 12265, pp. 204–214, 2020.
https://doi.org/10.1007/978-3-030-59722-1_20

1   Introduction

A crucial barrier to the study of neurodegenerative diseases (e.g., Alzheimer's disease and its mimics [3,17]) is the lack of reliable *premortem* biomarkers, as definitive diagnoses can only be obtained via neuropathology. To overcome this, neuroimaging to neuropathology correlational (NTNC) science seeks to establish imaging phenotypes that correlate with gold standard pathological diagnoses, in order to port these signatures to *in vivo* imaging as biomarkers. One candidate for NTNC is *in vivo* or *ex vivo* MRI. Reliable matching of histology and *in vivo* MRI requires a *premortem* scan acquired a short time before death. Unfortunately, these are difficult to obtain for precisely the most interesting individuals – asymptomatic, early-stage cases. This problem can be overcome with *ex vivo* MRI, which has been successfully used in NTNC (e.g., [7,13]), but is also challenging to perform: it requires scanning and sample preparation expertise that is not present at many research centres, cannot easily be done on the frozen tissue required in many genetics analyses, and is expensive.

Meanwhile, a wealth of information exists in brain banks that is hidden in existing images from routine dissection photography. Here we present algorithms to 3D reconstruct and segment imaging volumes from this underutilised modality, enabling morphometric NTNC studies without MRI at almost no cost.

Related Work: Building 3D images from dissection photographs requires alignment of a stack of 2D photographs into a 3D consistent volume via image registration [15,27]. Registration of image pairs is a well-studied problem but, to the best of our knowledge, literature on joint registration of dissection photographs for 3D reconstruction is nonexistent. The closest related work is a method for volumetric reconstruction from printed films of MRI [9], which is not suitable for our task, as it requires a reference MRI volume (which we wish to avoid).

One step further removed is 3D histology reconstruction [20]. Despite the peculiarities of histological data in terms of contrast, resolution, and sectioning distortions, many of the challenges we face in this work are similar. Without an additional reference, recovering the 3D shape of a 2D stack of images is a heavily underconstrained problem. A common approach is to iteratively align each 2D image to its neighbours, possibly with an outlier rejection strategy [31]. This approach yields smooth volumes but can result in straightening of curved structures (often known as "banana effect" [30]), and accumulation of errors along the stack (*z-shift*, [19]). These can both be overcome with a reference MRI scan [1,2] – a requirement which, again, we are trying to avoid.

For brain segmentation, the neuroimaging literature has long been dominated by multi-atlas segmentation (MAS), Bayesian segmentation and, more recently, deep convolutional neural networks (CNNs). MAS [11,23] nonlinearly registers several labelled atlases to a target scan, deforms the corresponding segmentations, and merges these warped label maps into a robust estimate of the segmentation with a label fusion algorithm. Segmentation CNN architectures [12,14,16], best represented by the ubiquitous U-Net [24], yield state-of-the-art accuracy and runtimes (seconds). Being supervised methods, MAS and CNNs share the

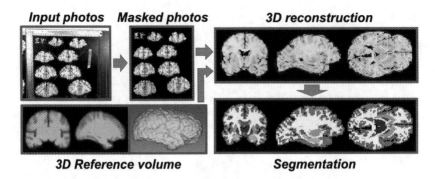

Fig. 1. Diagram of the proposed processing pathway for dissection photography. Photographs are coarsely corrected for pixel size and perspective; arranged into a volume; registered to each other and a reference surface mask; and automatically segmented.

disadvantage that performance quickly decreases when the training and test domains do not match. Despite progress in data augmentation [33] and transfer learning [26], manual labels are often needed for every new segmentation task.

Bayesian segmentation with probabilistic atlases uses a generative model combining a supervised prior model of anatomy (the atlas) and a model of image formation (likelihood). Segmentation is then posed as a Bayesian inference problem, estimating the most probable hidden segmentation that generated the observed image, given the atlas. A subset of Bayesian segmentation methods [4,21,29,32] use an unsupervised likelihood model, usually a Gaussian mixture model (GMM) whose parameters are estimated specifically for each volume to segment, making the segmentation adaptive to different contrasts.

Contribution: The contribution of this paper is twofold. First, we propose a joint registration algorithm for reconstruction of 3D imaging volumes from stacks of dissection photographs, requiring only a reference mask. This mask can be "hard", e.g., measured directly with a 3D surface scanner [10], or "soft", e.g., a probabilistic atlas of the whole brain; neither of these require MRI acquisition. Second, we present a Bayesian algorithm to segment 3D reconstructed stacks of photographs into 36 brain structures. We have designed an unsupervised likelihood term that models photography-specific artifacts, readily adapting to photographic hardware and brain fixation differences, thus making our publicly available code immediately usable with data from any institution.

2   Methods

2.1   General Workflow

The workflow of our framework is outlined in Fig. 1. The inputs of the algorithm are dissection photographs of brain slices, and a reference volume R describing the exterior shape of the brain. In addition, the user provides two inputs. First, three landmarks on the photographs (e.g., on rulers which are commonly used in dissection photographs), which we use for coarse pixel size calibration and perspective correction. Second, segmentations for the different slices, which isolate tissue from background and encode the order of the slices. These can often be obtained with minimal interaction – we use a simple GMM [34] requiring one click per slice. The resulting slices and masks are ordered manually and arranged into sets of stacked slices $S = \{S_n\}$, and corresponding masks $M = \{M_n\}$.

2.2   3D Reconstruction from Dissection Photographs

Let $\{\Phi_n\}$ be a set of 2D affine geometric transforms for the brain slices, which brings them into alignment. These transforms correct for slice displacement and rotation, as well as perspective distortion. Then, $S_n[\boldsymbol{x}; \Phi_n]$ and $M_n[\boldsymbol{x}; \Phi_n]$ denote a resampling of slice n and its corresponding mask, to a discretised grid given by $\boldsymbol{x}$, where the in-plane coordinates have been transformed according to the parameters in Φ_n. Similarly, we define a 3D rigid transform for the reference volume R that brings it into alignment with the stack of slices, such that $R[\boldsymbol{x}; \Psi]$ is a resampling of R parameterised by the 3D transform in Ψ. If the reference R is hard and directly represents the target shape, we also include an additional scaling in the direction of slicing (typically the anterior-posterior axis, for coronal slices) to account for deviations from the nominal slice thickness; with a soft atlas as reference, this is not possible. We jointly register the reference volume and the slices by maximising the following objective function $\mathcal{F}$:

$$\mathcal{F}(\Psi, \{\Phi_n\}) = \alpha \mathcal{D}(M[\boldsymbol{x}; \{\Phi_n\}], R[\boldsymbol{x}; \Psi]) + \beta \frac{1}{N_s} \sum_{n=1}^{N_s-1} \mathcal{C}(S_n[\boldsymbol{x}; \Phi_n], S_{n+1}[\boldsymbol{x}; \Phi_{n+1}])$$

$$(1)$$

$$+ \gamma \frac{1}{N_s} \sum_{n=1}^{N_s-1} \mathcal{D}(M_n[\boldsymbol{x}; \Phi_n], M_{n+1}[\boldsymbol{x}; \Phi_{n+1}]) - \nu \frac{1}{N_s} \sum_{n=1}^{N_s} f(\Phi_n),$$

where N_s is the number of slices, $\mathcal{D}$ is the Dice score, $\mathcal{C}$ is the normalised cross correlation, f is a regulariser, and $\{\alpha, \beta, \gamma, \nu\}$ are relative weights for each term.

Equation 1 corrects for overall shape by encouraging a high Dice similarity coefficient between $M[\boldsymbol{x}; \{\Phi_n\}]$ and R, i.e., the 3D reconstructed mask and the reference volume. Smoothness within the reconstructed photography volume $S[\boldsymbol{x}; \{\Phi_n\}]$ is encouraged with two terms: the normalised cross correlation between successive slices in S, and the Dice coefficient between the corresponding masks. The final term, $f(\Phi_n)$, is a regulariser used to constrain the 2D spatial transforms not to be excessively scaled or sheared, which is particularly useful for the first and last slices in the stack, as they often contain little tissue.

The registration is solved in a hierarchical fashion using two levels with increasing complexity, combined with a multi-scale approach, to help avoid local maxima and increase convergence speed. At the first level, we limit the registration to correcting for slice displacement and rotation only, which is achieved by constraining each Φ_n to be rigid rather than affine. At this level, no regularisation is needed. At the second level, we use the full model (i.e., affine $\{\Phi_n\}$). Undue scaling or shearing is avoided at this level by penalising transformations that excessively modify the area of a pixel, with $f(\Phi_n) = |\log|\Phi_n||$ in Eq. 1.

Optimisation is performed at three levels of resolution (1/4, 1/2 and 1) with the L-BFGS algorithm [5,18]. The 2D transforms are initialised by aligning the centres of gravity (COGs) of the masks, and the 3D transform by matching the COG of the 3D mask with the COG of the initialised stack. Model parameters were set via visual inspection on a separate dataset. If the reference R is soft, we set $\alpha = 10$, $\beta = 1$, $\gamma = 2$, $\nu = 0.1$. If R is hard (i.e., measured directly), we give it a higher weight in the reconstruction ($\alpha = 50$) and regularise less ($\nu = 0.05$).

2.3   Segmentation

The ultimate purpose of the photographic volumes is for morphometric analyses, most of which require image segmentation. Since our goal is to make our code available to other researchers, supervised CNNs or MAS may not be appropriate as they may not generalise well to photographs of brains that have been fixed with potentially very different protocols. Instead, we propose a Bayesian algorithm with an unsupervised likelihood that includes a model of artefacts specific to photography, and thus adapts to cases fixed and imaged with any protocol.

Specifically, we maximise the probability of a 3D label map L given the image data D using Bayes' rule $p(L|D) \propto p(D|L)p(L)$. Both the prior and the likelihood have an associated set of parameters, θ_L and θ_D, respectively, with prior distributions $p(\theta_L)$ and $p(\theta_D)$. The prior $p(L|\theta_L)$ is a publicly available probabilistic atlas of anatomy [21] with $K = 36$ neuroanatomical classes, encoded as a tetrahedral mesh endowed with a deformation model [28]. Each voxel of the segmentation is assumed to be an independent sample of the discrete distribution defined by the deformed atlas at the location of the voxel.

The likelihood $p(D|L, \theta_D)$ combines a GMM with a model for brightness variations. Specifically, each of the K classes has an associated set of GMM parameters (weights, means, covariances), such that the intensity of a voxel is assumed to be a sample of the GMM associated with its label. These intensities are further corrupted by a slice-specific, smooth, multiplicative field (henceforth "brightness field"), which we assume to be a linear combination of smooth basis functions allowing bilinear variation in plane, independently for each slice.

It is typical in Bayesian segmentation to first compute point estimates of the model parameters $(\hat{\theta}_L, \hat{\theta}_D)$ by maximising $p(\theta_L, \theta_D|D)$, and then to estimate the segmentation as the maximum of $p(D|L, \hat{\theta}_D)p(L|\hat{\theta}_L)$. Let $\boldsymbol{\Gamma} = \{\boldsymbol{\Gamma}_k\}_{k=1}^{K}$ be the GMM parameters of the different classes, $\boldsymbol{C}$ the matrix of brightness field coefficients (with 3 rows and as many columns as basis functions), and $\boldsymbol{x}$ the atlas mesh position, such that $\theta_D = (\boldsymbol{\Gamma}, \boldsymbol{C})$ and $\theta_L = \boldsymbol{x}$. Then, taking the logarithm of $p(\theta_L, \theta_D | D)$ yields the following objective function for the model parameters:

$$\left\{\hat{\boldsymbol{x}}, \hat{\boldsymbol{\Gamma}}, \hat{\boldsymbol{C}}\right\} = \underset{\boldsymbol{x},\boldsymbol{\Gamma},\boldsymbol{C}}{\arg\max} \sum_{i=1}^{N} \log \left(\sum_{k=1}^{K} p_i(\boldsymbol{d}_i | \boldsymbol{\Gamma}, \boldsymbol{C}, k) p_i(k|\boldsymbol{x}) \right) + \log p(\boldsymbol{x}) + \log p(\boldsymbol{C}),$$

$$(2)$$

where d_i is the vector with the log-transformed RGB intensities of voxel i and N is the number of voxels; a flat prior is assumed for $\boldsymbol{\Gamma}$. The likelihood term is:

$$p_i(\boldsymbol{d}_i | k, \boldsymbol{C}, \boldsymbol{\Gamma}) = \sum_{g=1}^{G_k} w_{k,g} \mathcal{N}(\boldsymbol{d}_i - \boldsymbol{C}\boldsymbol{\phi}_i | \boldsymbol{\mu}_{k,g}, \boldsymbol{\Sigma}_{k,g}),$$

where G_k is the number of components of the GMM of class k; $w_{k,g}$ is the weight of component g of class k; $\mathcal{N}$ is the Gaussian distribution; $\boldsymbol{\phi}_i$ is a vector with the values of the brightness field basis functions at voxel i; and $\boldsymbol{\mu}_{k,g}, \boldsymbol{\Sigma}_{k,g}$ are the mean vector and covariance matrix associated with component g of class k.

Segmentation is achieved by maximising Eq. 2 with coordinate ascent. We numerically optimise θ_L with L-BFGS, initialised with an affine transform computed by registering the atlas to R with a robust approach [22]. We optimise θ_D with the Generalised EM algorithm [8]. GEM involves iteratively: (i) constructing a lower bound of the objective function that touches it at the current estimate of the parameters, which amounts to a soft classification of each voxel (E step); and (ii) improving this bound to update θ_D (generalised M step). Upon convergence, the probabilistic segmentation $p(D|L, \hat{\theta}_D)p(L|\hat{\theta}_L)$ is given by the soft classification of the final E step. We implement this optimisations by adapting routines from the public SAMSEG repository [21]. All parameters (number of Gaussians G_k, mesh stiffness, etc.) are set to default SAMSEG values.

3 Experiments and Results

3.1 Datasets

We used a dataset consisting of dissection photography and matched *ex vivo* MRI for 24 cases, including only the cerebrum (i.e., no cerebellum or brainstem). Photographs were acquired of slices cut in the coronal plane with 4 mm thickness, using a 35 Megapixel camera. After initial perspective and pixel size adjustments, the calibrated photos were resampled to a pixel size of 0.1 mm. The *ex vivo* MRI were acquired using a FLAIR sequence with 0.8 mm isotropic resolution.

To evaluate the algorithms, we used two sets of reference segmentations. The first set consists of sparse manual delineations made on one slice photograph per volume. The slices were chosen to be close to the mid-coronal plane, while maximising visibility of seven representative subcortical structures: lateral ventricle, thalamus, caudate, putamen, pallidum, hippocampus and amygdala. The second set consists of dense segmentations of 36 brain structures, estimated from the FLAIR scans using SAMSEG [21]. Leaving aside two cases in which SAMSEG

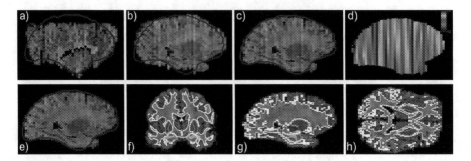

Fig. 2. Demonstration of 3D reconstruction and segmentation with a hard reference. The stack of slices (a) is aligned by COG (b) and registered (c). A brightness correction (d) is calculated and applied to generate a corrected volume (e). Orthogonal views are shown of resulting segmentation labels (f-h). The surface of the reference is represented with red and blue contours (initialised and registered, respectively).

failed, we used these segmentations as a silver standard to evaluate the methods using every available voxel. Moreover, the cerebral tissue labels from these segmentations were also used to simulate a 3D surface scan (which in the future we plan to achieve with an inexpensive device) for hard reconstruction. We also tested a version with a soft reference, using the LPBA40 atlas [25].

3.2   Experimental Setup

Two volumes were reconstructed, using hard and soft references respectively, for each case in the dataset. Reconstructions were computed at 0.5 mm in-plane resolution, and segmented using the Bayesian method in Sect. 2.3. Since direct evaluation of registration error is very difficult, we used two measures of segmentation quality as surrogates. First, Dice scores were calculated against manual delineation of cerebral cortex, white matter, and the seven subcortical structures listed in Sect. 3.1. The evaluation was then extended to the whole brain by computing the correlation (and associated p value) between the volumes of the nine structures, derived from the *ex vivo* MRI and from the 3D reconstructed photographic volumes with our method.

3.3   Results

Figure 2 shows representative images from each stage in the registration and segmentation process, using a hard reference. The proposed procedure successfully aligns the photographs to the reference surface and estimates a brightness field that clearly increases the homogeneity of the image intensities, enabling accurate segmentation. Further qualitative results are shown in Figs. 3(a-c), which compare the manual delineations with our automated segmentations, using both the hard and soft references. The corresponding quantitative results (Dice scores)

Table 1. Correlation coefficient (r) and associated p values for the volumes derived from the *ex vivo* MRI with SAMSEG and from the photographs with our method.

Structure	Wh.Ma.	Cortex	Lat.Vent.	Thal.	Caud.	Put.	Pallid.	Hippo.	Amyg
r (hard)	0.80	0.92	0.73	0.78	0.79	0.77	0.63	0.45	0.82
p (hard)	$< 10^{-4}$	$< 10^{-8}$	$< 10^{-3}$	$< 10^{-4}$	$< 10^{-4}$	$< 10^{-4}$	< 0.005	< 0.05	$< 10^{-5}$
r (soft)	0.80	0.84	0.73	0.77	0.81	0.77	0.70	0.28	0.71
p (soft)	$< 10^{-4}$	$< 10^{-4}$	$< 10^{-3}$	$< 10^{-4}$	$< 10^{-5}$	$< 10^{-4}$	$< 10^{-3}$	< 0.2	$< 10^{-3}$

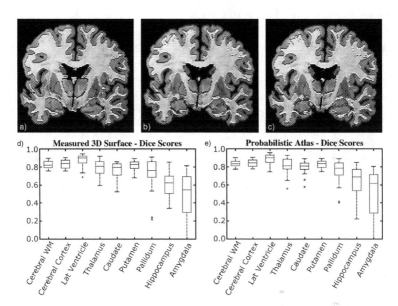

Fig. 3. Comparison of manual labelling with proposed automated method. (a) Manual tracing. (b) Bayesian segmentation with hard reference. (c) With soft reference. (d) Box plots for Dice scores of hard reference using 24 coronal slices. (e) For soft reference.

are shown in Figs. 3(d-e). The segmentations are quite accurate for most structures, except for the hippocampus and amygdala, whose interface is difficult to separate in this particular coronal plane. The method also commits minor mistakes that are common in Bayesian segmentation, e.g., including the claustrum in the putamen. But overall, the Dice scores are competitive (above 0.8 for many structures), which is very encouraging given that they are computed from photographs. Particularly high scores are achieved for the cerebral cortex, since there is no extracerebral tissue in the images.

While Dice scores on a single slice are informative, in order to show that measured trends from photo volumes are transferable to clinical imaging modalities it is crucial to test whether the volumes computed with our method on thick slices correlate well with the volumes derived from the isotropic MRI. For this reason we compare the silver standard volumes derived from the *ex vivo* MRI, with the volumes given by our proposed method. Table 1 shows the correlation coefficients and associated p values for the nine representative structures of interest. The results are consistent with the Dice scores on the sparse slices, showing strong correlations and significance for all structures except for the pallidum and the hippocampus. The pallidum is notoriously difficult to segment, even in MRI, due its low contrast. The hippocampus seems to be particularly affected by the large slice thickness in our reconstructed photography volumes.

4   Discussion and Conclusion

We have presented the first algorithm for the construction of registered dissection photography volumes using only an external boundary shape as reference. For this proof of concept study we tested our methods on 24 cases, and assessed accuracy and sensitivity using Dice scores and correlations to silver standard volumes, respectively. The results are promising, both with the hard and the soft reference, and pave the way for inexpensive, large-scale NTNC studies – even retrospectively, using the soft version.

Future work will follow several directions. First, we will more thoroughly validate the methods, using additional cases, metrics, and manually traced images. We also plan to extend our method to slices with uneven thickness, and explore imputation algorithms (e.g., [6]) to increase the resolution of the 3D reconstructed scans. Access to super-resolved isotropic volumes is expected to enhance the quality of the segmentations (e.g., for the hippocampus), and also has the potential to enable other volumetric analyses that underperform with insufficient resolution (e.g., registration, cortical thickness). These additional analyses will likely benefit from a hard external reference: while drifts in the 3D reconstruction towards an average shape due to the probabilistic atlas do not seem to penalise segmentation, we hypothesise that using a 3D surface scan (an increasingly inexpensive technology) like the one in Fig. 1 will increase the precision of cortical measurements and registration, and enable the discovery of new imaging markers to study neurodegenerative diseases.

Acknowledgements. Work primarily supported by ARUK (ARUK-IRG2019A-003) and the ERC (677697). Additional support provided in part by: the BRAIN Initiative (U01-MH117023); NIH (P50-AG005136, U01-AG006781, 5U01-MH093765); NIMH; NIBIB (P41-EB015896, 1R01-EB023281, R01-EB006758, R21-EB018907, R01-EB019956); NIA (1R56-AG064027, 1R01-AG064027, 5R01-AG008122, R01-AG016495); NIDDK (1-R21-DK-108277-01); NINDS (R01-NS0525851, R21-NS072652, R01-NS070963, R01-NS083534, 5U01-NS086625, 5U24-NS10059103, R01-NS105820, R01-NS112161); HU00011920008 subaward to CMD; the Nancy and Buster Alvord Endowment; the EU H2020 (Marie Sklodowska-Curie grant 765148); Shared Instrumentation Grants 1S10RR023401, 1S10RR019307, 1S10RR023043. BF has a financial interest in CorticoMetrics, managed by MGH and Partners HealthCare. Authors would also like to thank L. Keene, K. Kern, A. Keen and E. Melief for their assistance with data acquisition.

References

1. Adler, D.H., Pluta, J., Kadivar, S., Craige, C., Gee, J.C., et al.: Histology-derived volumetric annotation of the human hippocampal subfields in postmortem MRI. NeuroImage **84**, 505–523 (2014)
2. Amunts, K., Lepage, C., Borgeat, L., Mohlberg, H., Dickscheid, T., et al.: Bigbrain: an ultrahigh-resolution 3D human brain model. Science **340**(6139), 1472–1475 (2013)
3. Armstrong, R.A., Lantos, P.L., Cairns, N.J.: Overlap between neurodegenerative disorders. Neuropathology **25**(2), 111–124 (2005)
4. Ashburner, J., Friston, K.: Unified segmentation. NeuroImage **26**(3), 839–51 (2005)
5. Byrd, R.H., Lu, P., Nocedal, J., Zhu, C.: A limited memory algorithm for bound constrained optimization. SIAM J. Sci. Comput. **16**(5), 1190–1208 (1995)
6. Dalca, A.V., Bouman, K.L., Freeman, W.T., Rost, N.S., Sabuncu, M.R., Golland, P.: Medical image imputation from image collections. IEEE Trans. Med. Imag. **38**(2), 504–514 (2019)
7. Dawe, R.J., Bennett, D.A., Schneider, J.A., Arfanakis, K.: Neuropathologic correlates of hippocampal atrophy in the elderly: A clinical, pathologic, postmortem MRI study. PLOS ONE **6**(10), 1–13 (2011)
8. Dempster, A.P., Laird, N.M., Rubin, D.B.: Maximum likelihood from incomplete data via the EM algorithm. J. R. Stat. Soc.: Series B (Methodological) **39**(1), 1–22 (1977). https://doi.org/10.1111/j.2517-6161.1977.tb01600.x
9. Ebner, M., Chung, K.K., Prados, F., Cardoso, M.J., Chard, D.T., et al.: Volumetric reconstruction from printed films: Enabling 30 year longitudinal analysis in MR neuroimaging. NeuroImage **165**, 238–250 (2018)
10. Geng, J.: Structured-light 3D surface imaging: A tutorial. Adv. Opt. Photon. **3**(2), 128–160 (2011)
11. Iglesias, J.E., Sabuncu, M.R.: Multi-atlas segmentation of biomedical images: A survey. Med. Image Anal. **24**(1), 205–219 (2015)
12. Kamnitsas, K., Ledig, C., Newcombe, V., Simpson, J., Kane, A., et al.: Efficient multi-scale 3D CNN with fully connected CRF for accurate brain lesion segmentation. Med. Image Anal. **36**, 61–78 (2017)
13. Kotrotsou, A., Schneider, J.A., Bennett, D.A., Leurgans, S.E., Dawe, R.J., et al.: Neuropathologic correlates of regional brain volumes in a community cohort of older adults. Neurobiol. Aging **36**(10), 2798–2805 (2015)
14. Litjens, G., Kooi, T., Bejnordi, B.E., Setio, A.A.A., Ciompi, F., et al.: A survey on deep learning in medical image analysis. Med. Image Anal. **42**, 60–88 (2017)
15. Maintz, J., Viergever, M.A.: A survey of medical image registration. Med. Image Anal. **2**(1), 1–36 (1998)
16. Milletari, F., Navab, N., Ahmadi, S.A.: V-Net: Fully convolutional neural networks for volumetric medical image segmentation. In: 3D Vision (3DV), pp. 565–571 (2016)
17. Nelson, P.T., Dickson, D.W., Trojanowski, J.Q., Jack, C.R., Boyle, P.A., et al.: Limbic-predominant age-related TDP-43 encephalopathy (LATE): Consensus working group report. Brain **142**(6), 1503–1527 (2019)
18. Nocedal, J., Wright, S.: Numerical optimization. Springer Science & Business Media (2006)
19. Pichat, J., Iglesias, E., Nousias, S., Yousry, T., Ourselin, S., Modat, M.: Part-to-whole registration of histology and MRI using shape elements. In: ICCV Workshops (2017)

20. Pichat, J., Iglesias, J.E., Yousry, T., Ourselin, S., Modat, M.: A survey of methods for 3D histology reconstruction. Med. Image Anal. **46**, 73–105 (2018)
21. Puonti, O., Iglesias, J.E., Leemput, K.V.: Fast and sequence-adaptive whole-brain segmentation using parametric bayesian modeling. NeuroImage **143**, 235–249 (2016)
22. Reuter, M., Rosas, H.D., Fischl, B.: Highly accurate inverse consistent registration: A robust approach. NeuroImage **53**(4), 1181–1196 (2010)
23. Rohlfing, T., Brandt, R., Menzel, R., Maurer Jr., C.R.: Evaluation of atlas selection strategies for atlas-based image segmentation with application to confocal microscopy images of bee brains. NeuroImage **21**(4), 1428–1442 (2004)
24. Ronneberger, O., Fischer, P., Brox, T.: U-Net: Convolutional networks for biomedical image segmentation. In: Navab, N., Hornegger, J., Wells, W.M., Frangi, A.F. (eds.) MICCAI 2015. LNCS, vol. 9351, pp. 234–241. Springer, Cham (2015). https://doi.org/10.1007/978-3-319-24574-4_28
25. Shattuck, D.W., Mirza, M., Adisetiyo, V., Hojatkashani, C., Salamon, G., et al.: Construction of a 3D probabilistic atlas of human cortical structures. NeuroImage **39**(3), 1064–1080 (2008)
26. Shin, H.C., Roth, H.R., Gao, M., Lu, L., Xu, Z., et al.: Deep convolutional neural networks for computer-aided detection: CNN architectures, dataset characteristics and transfer learning. IEEE Trans. Med. Imaging **35**(5), 1285–1298 (2016)
27. Sotiras, A., Davatzikos, C., Paragios, N.: Deformable medical image registration: A survey. IEEE Trans. Med. Imaging **32**(7), 1153–1190 (2013)
28. Van Leemput, K.: Encoding probabilistic brain atlases using bayesian inference. IEEE Trans. Med. Imaging **28**(6), 822–837 (2009)
29. Van Leemput, K., Maes, F., Vandermeulen, D., Suetens, P.: Automated model-based tissue classification of MR images of the brain. IEEE Trans. Med. Imaging **18**(10), 897–908 (1999)
30. Yang, Z., Richards, K., Kurniawan, N.D., Petrou, S., Reutens, D.C.: MRI-guided volume reconstruction of mouse brain from histological sections. J. Neurosci. Methods **211**(2), 210–217 (2012)
31. Yushkevich, P.A., Avants, B.B., Ng, L., Hawrylycz, M., Burstein, P.D., Zhang, H., Gee, J.C.: 3D mouse brain reconstruction from histology using a coarse-to-fine approach. In: Pluim, J.P.W., Likar, B., Gerritsen, F.A. (eds.) WBIR 2006. LNCS, vol. 4057, pp. 230–237. Springer, Heidelberg (2006). https://doi.org/10.1007/11784012_28
32. Zhang, Y., Brady, M., Smith, S.: Segmentation of brain MR images through a hidden Markov random field model and the expectation-maximization algorithm. IEEE Trans. Med. Imaging **20**(1), 45–57 (2001)
33. Zhao, A., Balakrishnan, G., Durand, F., Guttag, J.V., Dalca, A.V.: Data augmentation using learned transforms for one-shot medical image segmentation. In: CVPR (2019)
34. Zivkovic, Z.: Improved adaptive Gaussian mixture model for background subtraction. In: Proceedings of the 17th International Conference on Pattern Recognition, ICPR 2004, vol. 2, pp. 28–31 (2004)

DistNet: Deep Tracking by Displacement Regression: Application to Bacteria Growing in the *Mother Machine*

Jean Ollion[1,2(✉)] [ID] and Charles Ollion[3] [ID]

[1] Laboratoire Jean -Perrin UMR 8237, Sorbonne Université, Paris, France
[2] SABILAb, Paris, France
`jean.ollion@polytechnique.org`
[3] Heuritech, Paris, France
`charles.ollion@gmail.com`,
`https://sabilab.github.io/`

Abstract. The *mother machine* is a popular microfluidic device that allows long-term time-lapse imaging of thousands of cells in parallel by microscopy. It has become a valuable tool for single-cell level quantitative analysis and characterization of many cellular processes such as gene expression and regulation, mutagenesis or response to antibiotics. The automated and quantitative analysis of the massive amount of data generated by such experiments is now the limiting step. In particular the segmentation and tracking of bacteria cells imaged in phase-contrast microscopy—with error rates compatible with high-throughput data—is a challenging problem.

In this work, we describe a novel formulation of the multi-object tracking problem, in which tracking is performed by a regression of the bacteria's displacement, allowing simultaneous tracking of multiple bacteria, despite their growth and division over time. Our method performs jointly segmentation and tracking, leveraging sequential information to increase segmentation accuracy.

We introduce a Deep Neural Network (DNN) architecture taking advantage of a self-attention mechanism which yields extremely low tracking error rate and segmentation error rate. We demonstrate superior performance and speed compared to state-of-the-art methods. Our method is named DiSTNet which stands for DISTance+DISplacement Segmentation and Tracking Network.

While this method is particularly well suited for *mother machine* microscopy data, its general joint tracking and segmentation formulation could be applied to many other problems with different geometries.

Keywords: Multi-object tracking · Deep neural networks · Self-attention

Electronic supplementary material The online version of this chapter (https://doi.org/10.1007/978-3-030-59722-1_21) contains supplementary material, which is available to authorized users.

© Springer Nature Switzerland AG 2020
A. L. Martel et al. (Eds.): MICCAI 2020, LNCS 12265, pp. 215–225, 2020.
https://doi.org/10.1007/978-3-030-59722-1_21

1   Introduction

1.1   Context

Single-cell study has become a focus of research in numerous fields of biology during the past decades [5,6,15]. In particular, time-lapse microscopy has been extensively used to investigate cellular processes dynamically and non-invasively in single cells [14]. It is now being increasingly used in combination with microfluidic devices that allow both high-throughput data collection at the single-cell level and a precise spatiotemporal control of the environment [13]. Among those devices, the *mother machine*, developed by Wang et al. in 2010 [27], is one of the most popular. It contains thousands of parallel dead-end microchannels in which cells grow in single file (See Fig. 1). Cells can grow and divide inside the microchannels for hundreds of generations, allowing the imaging of 10^5–10^6 individual cells per experiment. *Mother machine* devices are being increasingly used for single-cell studies on bacteria to investigate various subjects, such as gene expression and regulation [3,9,18], mutagenesis and evolution [21,22] or single cell response to antibiotics [1,2]. The massive amount of data generated by long-term imaging of cells growing in the *mother machine* (typically several hundred gigabytes worth of images per experiment) needs to be processed automatically, in particular methods for automatic segmentation and tracking of cells with very low error rate are needed.

In this work, we focus on segmentation and tracking of bacteria growing in microchannels observed with phase-contrast, a very common imaging technique. The term tracking refers to the matching of the observed bacteria between two successive frames, as shown with colored arrows in Fig. 1-B.

Tracking of bacteria growing in the *mother machine* faces three major challenges: (1) cell growth induces changes in bacteria morphology; (2) bacteria can divide; (3) due to cell growth, bacteria located at the open-end of microchannels are pushed out by other bacteria, thus their next observation is sometimes outside or partly outside the image.

Studying some biological processes such as mutagenesis require very fine statistics in order to detect rare events as in [22]. To achieve this, one need to analyse massive datasets with typically 10^6–10^7 observations of bacteria, at a very low segmentation and tracking error rate, typically less than 0.01%, in order to limit manual curation time.

1.2   Related Work

Multi-object tracking is a challenging task well studied within the computer vision community. Multi-object detection and tracking are usually considered as separated processes [4,12], where object detection on natural images have much improved, see e.g. Faster-RCNN [20]. Tracking then relies on finding similarities between detections—usually a combination of the semantics (deep features), shape and velocity of the detected objects—and matching them over the successive frames [28,29]. A few studies perform both tasks in a single pass, such as TrackNet [10], which derives from the Faster-RCNN architecture. While the method yields promising results, it remains very complex and the authors admit that the simultaneous detection and tracking problem is still at its infancy. Moreover, these methods do not take into account specific aspects of context of bacteria growing in microchannels, such as bacteria division.

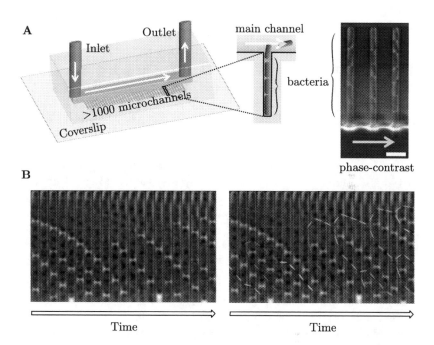

Fig. 1. *Escherichia coli* bacteria growing in the *mother machine*. A: left pane: the *mother machine* microfluidic chip; right pane: corresponding phase-contrast microscopy images; scale bar: 5 μm; white arrows represent the flow of growing medium. B: Kymographs showing phase-contrast images of bacteria growing in a single microchannel; images from successive frames are displayed next to one another; cells are going out through the open end located at the lower part of the images. The right pane displays outlines of segmented bacteria and tracking links as coloured lines, each colour representing one generation.

Several methods have been developed specifically for this problem, most of them perform segmentation and/or tracking with a combination of pre-defined classical computer vision operations [9,19,24,25] and are thus very difficult to tune for datasets generated on different imaging setups and/or strains. A recent software, DeLTA [11], uses DNN both for segmentation and tracking. Segmentation is performed first, using the original U-Net approach [23] the tracking is performed by another U-Net-like neural network, which predicts the next cell(s) for each cell. The authors report an error rate of 1%, which can be too high for some applications in which rare events are studied for instance.

2   Method

2.1   Problem Formulation

The main contribution of this work is to track bacteria by performing a regression of their displacement between two successive frames. This formulation contrasts with previous tracking systems, as the detection and tracking are performed simultaneously and in one pass for all bacteria. This is motivated by the following:

- **Global consistency:** we expect this method to have more coherent results, i.e. less conflicting predictions compared to a method that make one prediction per bacterium, because tracking is done simultaneously for all bacteria.
- **Speed:** This method is faster because one prediction by image is needed instead of one for the detection, then a second one per bacterium for the tracking.
- **Simplicity:** Our method enables to jointly train a single model, which is derived straightforwardly from a U-Net architecture, and could be adapted easily to different problem settings or backbone networks. In contrast, tracking methods involving two steps and several models induce more hyperparameters and complexity. Note that adapting to models such as Faster R-CNN (not covered in this study) would require further developments.

Model Description. As bacteria grow in a single file in the microchannels, prediction of the displacement along the axis of microchannel (further called Y-axis) is sufficient. We achieve this by predicting, for each bacteria observed frame F the displacement along the Y-axis between its center and the center of the same bacteria observed at frame $F - 1$ (See Fig. 2-(i)). Formally, we predict a map $m_{x,y}$ which has the same spatial dimensions as the frame F, defined as follows:

$$m_{x,y} = \begin{cases} c^F(B) - c^{F-1}(B), & \text{if } (x, y) \text{ inside bacterium } B \\ 0, & \text{otherwise} \end{cases} \quad (1)$$

where $c^F(B)$ is the Y-coordinate of the center of bacterium B at frame F.

Tracking at a given frame F is then simply achieved by moving each bacteria observed at a frame F by the opposite value of their predicted displacement and associating them to the most overlapping bacterium at frame $F - 1$. We make a prediction of the previous observation of the bacteria and not of the next, because bacteria can divide but not merge and thus each bacteria can be associated to at most one single bacteria observed at the previous frame.

Another important aspect of our method is that we perform segmentation jointly with tracking by a regression of the euclidean distance map (EDM), Fig. 2-(c–d). Segmentation by regression of the EDM has been proposed before [7, 8,16]: in contrast to the original U-Net formulation that focuses on cell contours, it detects the interior of the cells. It is likely to be more robust in cases where cell contours are less visible, which happens very often in the case of bacteria growing in microchannels when they are in close contact to one another or to the border of the microchannel (See Fig. 1). A previous study suggests that this formulation pushes the neural network to learn some notion of objects [16], which may also benefit to tracking. Individual cells are then easily segmented using a classical watershed transform as in [16]. As EDM corresponds to the distance to background (in pixels unit), the watershed is naturally restricted to predicted EDM ≥ 1. To limit over-segmentation, segmented regions in contact with each other where merged when the EDM value at their interface was over a threshold.

The network also predicts a category: background, dividing cells, cell not linked to a previous cell, other cells (non dividing and linked to a cell at previous frame), as exemplified in Fig. 2-(e–h). When a cell is predicted as having no previous cell—such as the bottom cell in Fig. 2-(d)—it is not linked to any cell in the tracking procedure.

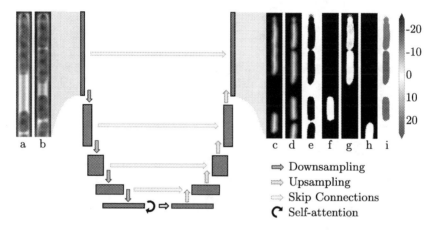

Fig. 2. DistNet based on U-Net architecture. Each blue block corresponds to a 2D multi-channel feature map. The network has an encoder-decoder structure. The encoder reduces spatial dimensions and increases the number of channels at each contraction (red arrows). The decoder reduces the number of channels at each up-sampling level, and restores spatial dimensions using both feature maps of the previous level (green arrows) and of the corresponding level in the encoder (yellow arrows). Our modified version of U-Net contains a self-attention layer at the last contraction level (see section S1 for mathematical details). Inputs are couples of successive grayscale images (a: previous frame, b: current frame). The upper bacteria in (a) divides in (b). Outputs are: EDM predictions for the previous (c) and current frame (d); category prediction (e): background, (f): cell that do not divide and are associated to a cell at the previous frame, (g): cells that divided, (h): cells that are not associated to a cell at the previous frame); (i): prediction of bacteria Y-displacement between the two frames, in pixels and within an image of height 256. (Color figure online)

2.2   Network Architecture

While U-Net-like architectures are efficient to integrate local semantic information to take precise decision at the pixel level [23] (See Fig. 2), we posit that they lack understanding of global structure. This is not particularly a problem for semantic segmentation as a rather restricted context might be enough to provide the necessary object boundaries information. However, in the context of tracking objects with potential division or displacement, some decisions must be made at the global image level, so that no contradictory information emerge from two different local contexts - for instance a very large bacteria dividing into two should have coherent global behavior, rather than independent prediction for each of the local bacteria.

In order to integrate global context, and following recent success in natural language processing, graph-based machine learning as well as many other fields, we incorporated a self-attention layer similar to the ones found in the *Transformer* architecture [26] instead of the last convolution of the encoder network. This layer enables the DNN to combine information from the whole image, while a convolution only mixes information locally. The description of the layer is detailed in section S1.

As a reference, we compared this strategy to a previously proposed one that consists in stacking hourglass models (i.e. encoder-decoder architectures) [17]. This model is referred to as stacked hourglass model.

3   Experiments

3.1   Training

We created a training dataset (referred to as DST) of 65344 images from 3 different *E. Coli* strains acquired on the same setup (from [22]). We used BACM-MAN software [19] to generate labels and curate them manually. In order to limit over-fitting and increase generalization to different domains (experimental setups, strains or mutants), we performed a data augmentation step with both classical and specifically designed transformations described in section S3. Model architectures are detailed in section S2.

3.2   Evaluation

We created two evaluation datasets composed of images of randomly chosen microchannels from several experiments performed with different imaging setups and/or strands using the same procedure as for DST. The first one (referred to as DSE1) corresponds to experiments where bacteria have similar aspect to those of DST (8 different experiments including 3 different strands and 2 different setups, 51000 observations of bacteria within 12600 frames). Images of DST and DSE1 were chosen among distinct microchannels. The second one (referred to as DSE2) to experiments where bacteria have an aspect that differs substantially from DST (3 experiments including 3 different setups and strands, 8760 observations of bacteria within 1680 frames). DSE2 is composed of images from publicly available datasets published along with software for *mother machine* analysis [9,11,24]. We excluded frames with important anomalies on bacteria morphology.

We analysed 3 types of segmentation errors: false positive (predicted bacteria with no corresponding ground truth bacteria), false negative (ground truth bacteria with no corresponding prediction) and division errors (DE). The latter occur when a division is detected too early or too late. As the exact frame at which a cell divides is sometimes hard to discern visually, we added a tolerance of one frame, i.e. we counted an error if a division was detected at least two frames before or two frames after the ground truth division frame. Matching between ground truth cells and predicted cells was done using a maximum overlap criterion, and insignificant effect is observed when using a IoU-based criterion instead. We did not use metrics that estimate the overlap with ground truth such as IoU because exact cell contours are difficult to obtain, which makes these metrics less informative. We also analysed tracking errors, which occur when a link is predicted between two bacteria and that the corresponding bacteria in the ground truth are not linked. Note that the links that differ between ground truth and prediction as a consequence of a DE are not considered as tracking errors as long as linked bacteria remain in the same lineage. We excluded bacteria that were partially out of the images (i.e. going out of the microchannels) with a length lower than 40 pixels, because they are often excluded from analysis, in an automated way.

4   Results

We compared the performance of our method to two baselines: segmentation and tracking performed by BACMMAN [19] and DeLTA softwares. DeLTA models were also trained on the same dataset as our model with the same data augmentation scope. Table 1 shows the percentage of errors on dataset DSE1: both self-attention and stacked hourglass models perform better than the two baselines for segmentation and tracking. Importantly both models achieve very low error rates, lower than 0.005% for tracking and of 0.03% for segmentation. The Self-attention network displays slightly better performances than the stacked hourglass network in terms of accuracy and speed, and has less parameters. The percentages of segmentation and tracking errors of DeLTA on DSE1 are compatible with those reported by the authors [11]. The higher number of tracking errors made by DeLTA is mainly due to contradictory predictions that happen when the same next cell is predicted for two different cells.

In order to estimate the generalization capacity of our network, we performed an evaluation on dataset DSE2, which contains bacteria displaying a different aspect from DST. Percentage of errors are shown in Table 2. We observe a significant drop of performances for all methods, to 7–8% for the baseline methods and 1% for our method. Although 1% is too high an error rate for analysis of rare events on large datasets, it can be acceptable for other types of analysis. We were able to recover performances on a dataset composed of images from

Table 1. Percentage of errors on dataset DSE1 (cells with similar aspect to the training set). Last column shows inference time in seconds for 1000 frames, on CPU (2 Intel Core i7-4790 K 4 GHz) / GPU (GeForce RTX 2080 Ti).

Method/Model	Tracking links	Segmentation errors			Total	Execution time
		Division	False −	False +		
BACMMAN	0.14	0.63	0.036	0.0076	0.82	23/NA
DeLTA	0.57	0.069	0.0018	0.069	0.71	249/6
Stacked hourglass	0.0021	0.025	0.0038	0	0.031	126/5
Self-attention	0.0042	0.019	0.0019	0	0.025	100/3

[11] (which have different aspect from DST) by a fine-tuning procedure with a training dataset as little as 3% of the size of DST. This also shows that the chosen hyper-parameters are valid for an independent dataset.

Table 2. Percentage of errors on dataset DSE2 (cells with different aspect from the training set).

Method/Model	Tracking links	Segmentation errors			Total
		Division	False −	False +	
BACMMAN	0.84	0.59	6.6	0	8.1
DeLTA	6.3	1.1	0.20	0.022	7.6
Stacked hourglass	0.27	0.64	0.11	0	1.0
Self-attention	0.30	0.57	0.068	0	0.93

To test whether our model was leveraging sequential information for segmentation or not, we trained a model with a similar architecture to the self-attention model that performed segmentation of a single frame through regression of the EDM. We found 3 times more division errors on DSE1, which suggests that to segment bacteria at a given frame, our models are able to use information contained in the previous frame.

To better understand the contribution of the main design choices of the self-attention network, we performed ablation experiments that are presented in section S4 and summarized in Table S1. They mainly show that the self-attention layer is very useful for tracking and not especially for segmentation, except that it helps to detect empty microchannels.

In order to get insights into the way the DNN uses the attention layer for tracking, we studied the attention weights in section S5. We mainly show that attention effectively allows to integrate global context, and is mainly focused on edges of cells rather than on their interior.

5   Conclusion

In this study we present a novel formulation of the multi-object tracking problem using DNN. In contrast with most existing methods, tracking is done through a single DNN step, allowing significant speed improvement. Moreover it performs jointly segmentation and tracking, allowing to leverage sequential information for segmentation. To support this formulation, we introduced a DNN architecture based on U-Net modified by incorporating a self-attention layer.

We applied successfully this method to the problem of bacteria growing in the *mother machine*, and achieved error rates lower than 0.005% for tracking and of 0.03% for segmentation, outperforming current state-of-the-art methods, and making this method well-suited for high-throughput data analysis.

The simplicity of our formulation and our model allows to adapt it easily to other problems with other geometry or other objects to be detected, and to implement it using other DNN architectures. DistNet is publicly available: we provide source code[1] as well as a module for Bacmman software[2] and a tutorial for fine-tuning that includes a ready-to-use notebook[3].

Acknowledgements. We thank Lydia Robert for kindly providing us with the datasets, as well as Thomas Robert for the useful comments on the manuscripts. We would also like to thank the reviewers, in particular reviewer 2 for the constructive critical comments that helped us improve the manuscript.

References

1. Bamford, R.A., Smith, A., Metz, J., Glover, G., Titball, R.W., Pagliara, S.: Investigating the physiology of viable but non-culturable bacteria by microfluidics and time-lapse microscopy. BMC Biol. **15**(1), 121 (2017)
2. Bergmiller, T., et al.: Biased partitioning of the multidrug efflux pump AcrAB-TolC underlies long-lived phenotypic heterogeneity. Science **356**(6335), 311–315 (2017)
3. Brenner, N., Braun, E., Yoney, A., Susman, L., Rotella, J., Salman, H.: Single-cell protein dynamics reproduce universal fluctuations in cell populations. Eur. Phys. J. E **38**(9), 1–9 (2015). https://doi.org/10.1140/epje/i2015-15102-8
4. Chen, S., Xu, Y., Zhou, X., Li, F.: Deep learning for multiple object tracking: a survey. IET Comput. Vis. **13** (2019). https://doi.org/10.1049/iet-cvi.2018.5598
5. Davie, K., et al.: A single-cell transcriptome atlas of the aging drosophila brain. Cell **174**(4), 982–998 (2018)
6. Elowitz, M.B., Levine, A.J., Siggia, E.D., Swain, P.S.: Stochastic gene expression in a single cell. Science **297**(5584), 1183–1186 (2002)
7. Graham, S., et al.: Hover-net: Simultaneous segmentation and classification of nuclei in multi-tissue histology images (2018). arXiv preprint arXiv:1812.06499

---

[1] https://github.com/jeanollion/distnet.

[2] https://github.com/jeanollion/bacmman/wiki/DistNet.

[3] https://github.com/jeanollion/bacmman/wiki/FineTune-DistNet.

8. Heinrich, L., Funke, J., Pape, C., Nunez-Iglesias, J., Saalfeld, S.: Synaptic cleft segmentation in non-isotropic volume electron microscopy of the complete drosophila brain. In: International Conference on Medical image computing and computer assisted intervention, pp. 317–325. Springer (2018)

9. Kaiser, M., et al.: Monitoring single-cell gene regulation under dynamically controllable conditions with integrated microfluidics and software. Nat. Commun. **9**(1), 212 (2018)

10. Li, C., Dobler, G., Feng, X., Wang, Y.: Tracknet: simultaneous object detection and tracking and its application in traffic video analysis (2019). arXiv preprint arXiv:1902.01466

11. Lugagne, J.B., Lin, H., Dunlop, M.J.: Delta: automated cell segmentation, tracking, and lineage reconstruction using deep learning. BioRxiv, p. 720615 (2019)

12. Luo, W., et al.: Multiple object tracking: a literature review (2014). arXiv preprint arXiv:1409.7618

13. Mehling, M., Tay, S.: Microfluidic cell culture. Curr. Opin. Biotechnol. **25**, 95–102 (2014)

14. Muzzey, D., van Oudenaarden, A.: Quantitative time-lapse fluorescence microscopy in single cells. Ann. Rev. Cell Dev. **25**, 301–327 (2009)

15. Navin, N., et al.: Tumour evolution inferred by single-cell sequencing. Nature **472**(7341), 90 (2011)

16. Naylor, P., Laé, M., Reyal, F., Walter, T.: Segmentation of nuclei in histopathology images by deep regression of the distance map. IEEE Trans. Med. Imag. **38**(2), 448–459 (2018)

17. Newell, A., Yang, K., Deng, J.: Stacked hourglass networks for human pose estimation. In: Leibe, B., Matas, J., Sebe, N., Welling, M. (eds.) ECCV 2016. LNCS, vol. 9912, pp. 483–499. Springer, Cham (2016). https://doi.org/10.1007/978-3-319-46484-8_29

18. Norman, T.M., Lord, N.D., Paulsson, J., Losick, R.: Memory and modularity in cell-fate decision making. Nature **503**(7477), 481 (2013)

19. Ollion, J., Elez, M., Robert, L.: High-throughput detection and tracking of cells and intracellular spots in mother machine experiments. Nat. Protoc. **14**(11), 3144–3161 (2019)

20. Ren, S., He, K., Girshick, R., Sun, J.: Faster R-CNN: towards real-time object detection with region proposal networks. In: Advances in Neural Information Processing Systems, pp. 91–99 (2015)

21. Robert, L., Ollion, J., Elez, M.: Real-time visualization of mutations and their fitness effects in single bacteria. Nat. Protoc. **14**(11), 3126–3143 (2019)

22. Robert, L., Ollion, J., Robert, J., Song, X., Matic, I., Elez, M.: Mutation dynamics and fitness effects followed in single cells. Science **359**(6381), 1283–1286 (2018)

23. Ronneberger, O., Fischer, P., Brox, T.: U-Net: convolutional networks for biomedical image segmentation. In: Navab, N., Hornegger, J., Wells, W.M., Frangi, A.F. (eds.) MICCAI 2015. LNCS, vol. 9351, pp. 234–241. Springer, Cham (2015). https://doi.org/10.1007/978-3-319-24574-4_28

24. Sachs, C.C., et al.: Image-based single cell profiling: high-throughput processing of mother machine experiments. PloS one **11**(9), e0163453 (2016)

25. Smith, A., Metz, J., Pagliara, S.: Mmhelper: an automated framework for the analysis of microscopy images acquired with the mother machine. Sci. Rep. **9**(1), 1–12 (2019)

26. Vaswani, A., et al.: Attention is all you need. In: Advances in Neural Information Processing Systems, pp. 5998–6008 (2017)

27. Wang, P., et al.: Robust growth of escherichia coli. Curr. Biol. **20**(12), 1099–1103 (2010)
28. Yu, F., Li, W., Li, Q., Liu, Yu., Shi, X., Yan, J.: POI: multiple object tracking with high performance detection and appearance feature. In: Hua, G., Jégou, H. (eds.) ECCV 2016. LNCS, vol. 9914, pp. 36–42. Springer, Cham (2016). https:// doi.org/10.1007/978-3-319-48881-3_3
29. Zhang, L., Li, Y., Nevatia, R.: Global data association for multi-object tracking using network flows. In: 2008 IEEE Conference on Computer Vision and Pattern Recognition, pp. 1–8. IEEE (2008)

A Weakly Supervised Deep Learning Approach for Detecting Malaria and Sickle Cells in Blood Films

Petru Manescu[1]([⊠]), Christopher Bendkowski[1], Remy Claveau[1], Muna Elmi[1], Biobele J. Brown[2], Vijay Pawar[1], Mike J. Shaw[1], and Delmiro Fernandez-Reyes[1,2]([⊠])

[1] Faculty of Engineering Sciences, Department of Computer Science,
University College London, London, UK
{p.manescu,delmiro.fernandez-reyes}@ucl.ac.uk
[2] Department of Pediatrics, College of Medicine, University of Ibadan,
University College Hospital, Ibadan, Nigeria

Abstract. Machine vision analysis of blood films imaged under a brightfield microscope could provide scalable malaria diagnosis solutions in resource constrained endemic urban settings. The major bottleneck in successfully analyzing blood films with deep learning vision techniques is a lack of object-level annotations of disease markers such as parasites or abnormal red blood cells. To overcome this challenge, this work proposes a novel deep learning supervised approach that leverages weak labels readily available from routine clinical microscopy to diagnose malaria in thick blood film microscopy. This approach is based on aggregating the convolutional features of multiple objects present in one hundred high resolution image fields. We show that this method not only achieves expert-level malaria diagnostic accuracy without any hard object-level labels but can also identify individual malaria parasites in digitized thick blood films, which is useful in assessing disease severity and response to treatment. We demonstrate another application scenario where our approach is able to detect sickle cells in thin blood films. We discuss the wider applicability of the approach in automated analysis of thick blood films for the diagnosis of other blood disorders.

Keywords: Weak supervision · Malaria · Sickle cells · Blood films · Microscopy

1 Introduction

Assessment of the ubiquitous Giemsa-stained Thick Blood Film (TBF) by a trained microscopist remains the gold-standard diagnostic tool in regions of the world where malaria is endemic [1]. The TBF is often accompanied by a Blood Film Smear (BFS), also called Thin Blood Film, which is not always fully examined. Assessment of both

---

P. Manescu and D. Fernandez-Reyes—Equal contribution.

Electronic supplementary material The online version of this chapter (https://doi.org/10.1007/978-3-030-59722-1_22) contains supplementary material, which is available to authorized users.

TBF and BFS provides valuable information that facilitate malaria and hematology care pathways in resource constrained settings. Despite being treatable, malaria remains a major global health challenge with over 219 million cases worldwide leading to almost half-million deaths annually [1], mostly among children. Fast and reliable diagnostic testing scalable to large urban endemic regions is urgently needed. However, human visual inspection of the TBF by a malaria pathologist is time-consuming (particularly in low-parasitemia or negative cases), subject to errors associated with human-fatigue and cognitive load in busy clinical microscopy services and relies on the availability of trained personnel. Advances in digital pathology could provide automated or assisted solutions to facilitate malaria and hematology clinical pathways in large urban malaria regions as well as supporting peri-urban and rural regions lacking pathologists.

In recent years, computer vision techniques have been developed in an attempt to automatically detect malaria parasites in digitized microscopic images of TBFs based on image processing and supervised machine learning [2, 3]. Convolutional Neural Networks (ConvNets) have shown promise in identifying malaria parasites in TBF [4–6]. Nevertheless, the challenges in using these techniques are two-fold: Firstly, they rely on thousands, if not millions, of object-level manual annotations to train deep learning models to differentiate objects of interest (parasites) from distractors (staining artefacts, platelets, etc.). These annotations are difficult to obtain since they require the expertise of teams of trained microscopists to assess thousands of digitized Fields of View (FoVs). Secondly, automated diagnosis, which requires inspection of up to a hundred FoVs, is unreliable in cases with a low parasite count due to the inherent false positive rate of supervised deep learning detection models. Recently, weakly supervised approaches have been successfully applied to identify cancerous regions in digital histopathology images [7–10] More specifically, they classify and segment microscopy images using only whole image level annotations [11]. However, in the context of high-magnification blood film analysis, image level annotations are not easily available. Nevertheless, sample-level annotations, which translate into a set of images (FoVs) associated with a single label (e.g. clinical diagnosis of malaria confirmed by microscopy) are far easier to obtain.

Here we propose a weakly-supervised deep learning approach entitled Multiple Objects Features Fusion (MOFF) to diagnose malaria in one hundred high resolution TBF FoVs. Our method does not necessitate any hard object-level annotations for training (full supervision) but relies only the clinical-microscopy diagnosis of the sample (weak supervision with labels provided by routine clinical-microscopy). The method is also able to detect individual parasites in images, which is useful for estimating the severity of the disease and the response to treatment. To show the versatility of our approach, we also present an extension of the MOFF method for detection of sickle Red Blood Cells (RBCs) in the BFS, illustrating its broader value for extraction of clinically important data from the ubiquitous blood film. Since MOFF does not rely on a complex annotation system or availability of human-expert pathologists to annotate at the object-level, our approach has significant potential for deployment in resource constrained settings for a variety of diagnostic applications.

2   Multiple Objects Feature Fusion (MOFF) Learning

Potential objects of interest (O_i) (e.g. parasites, distractors) are identified and extracted from all captured FoVs (Fig. 1). For this region proposal phase, we chose a segmentation approach based on binary thresholding and morphological operations to extract regions of interest (ROIs) around objects of 2–4 μm in diameter (parasite-like objects) in TBF FoV [2]. Depending on the task, other modalities such as selective search [12] or cell segmentation techniques [13] (Supplementary material) can be employed during this phase. These O_i are next passed as the input of a ConvNet classification model whose output is the diagnosis of the sample provided by the clinical microscopist (e.g. malaria positive). The flattened feature vectors (F_v^i) output by the convolutional layers (*conv*) of the model are fused into one single feature vector which is next passed through the fully connected (FC) layers to predict the clinical diagnosis (C_d):

$$C_d(O_1, O_2, \ldots, O_N) = \sigma_L\left(\ldots\left(\sigma_1\left(f_{fusion}\left(F_v^1, F_v^2, \ldots, F_v^N\right)\cdot W_1 + b_1\right)\ldots\right)W_L + b_L\right) \quad (1)$$

where N is the number of input images, L is the number of FC layers, W_k, b_k, σ_k are the corresponding weights, biases and activations of each FC layer, $F_v^i = conv(O_i)$ and f_{fusion} is the feature fusion rule. More specifically:

$$f_{fusion}^{i=1\ldots N}\left(F_v^i\right) = \underset{1\leq i\leq N}{\mathrm{agg}}\left(\zeta_{j=1\ldots n_f}^i\right) \quad (2)$$

With n_f, the number of individual features (ζ_j^i) in each F_v^i, and *agg*, the aggregation modality (for example *average* or max*).

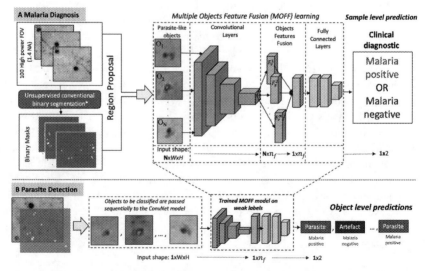

Fig. 1. Multiple objects features fusion (MOFF) learning approach applied to malaria diagnosis and parasite detection. *For details, see supplementary material.

2.1 Sample-Level Prediction

Given the large number of images which must to be analyzed per sample, the object proposal phase outputs a large number (thousands) of proposed object images. Due to GPU memory constraints, during the training phase, for each iteration N_o a randomly selected subset of object images from each sample are passed through the network. This works as an augmentation technique since a different subset of object images are selected from each sample during each epoch. The architecture allows a variable number of input object images because the ConvNet feature vectors are fused. During the test (prediction) phase, all the extracted object images for each sample are passed through the network in subsets of N_T ($N_T \gg N_o$) and a final predicted C_d is reached following a majority voting rule. The feature vector fusion before the FC layers has the additional benefit of reducing the GPU memory requirements and computational effort. This allows a large enough number of object images to be passed through the network during both training ($N_o > 100$) and testing ($N_T > 500$) which is essential in cases where parasites (or any other object of interest) are sparsely distributed in the samples.

2.2 Object-Level Detection

The MOFF model is trained to distinguish between those ROIs which contain parasites, when assessing TBF or sickle red blood cells when analyzing BFS, and those ROIs which do not, without specifically relying on object-level annotations. Once a sample has been classified as positive, the individual objects extracted by the segmentation algorithms are passed *one-by-one* through the trained model. The feature fusion step does not affect the inference since the number of F_v is equal to one (Fig. 1 B). Consequently, an object image gets classified as malaria positive (or sickle RBC positive) if it contains a malaria parasite (or morphologically abnormal RBCs).

3 Experiments

3.1 Data Sets

Clinical Malaria Microscopy. Malaria parasites (MPs) were detected and counted by human-expert microscopists in thick blood films stained with Giemsa at our clinics at the University College Hospital (UCH) in the city of Ibadan, Nigeria. A patient was declared malaria negative if no parasites were detected in 100 high magnification (100x) TBF FoVs. The corresponding films were next digitized (Sect. 3.2) and used to train and evaluate our MOFF model (Table 1).

Sickle Cell Disease Diagnosis. Hemoglobin electrophoresis [14] is routinely used to obtain the haemoglobin phenotype (C_d labels) and test patients for Sickle Cell Disease (SCD) in our clinics. Giemsa-stained thin blood smears were prepared and digitized for a group of patients (Table 1).

Ethical Statement. The internationally recognized ethics committee at the Institute for Advanced Medical Research and Training (IAMRAT) of the College of Medicine, University of Ibadan (COMUI) approved this research with permit numbers: UI/EC/10/0130,

UI/EC/19/0110. Parents and/or guardians of study participants gave informed written consent in accordance with the World Medical Association ethical principles for research involving human subjects.

3.2 Image Acquisition and Pre-processing

Images were captured with custom built brightfield microscope fitted with a 100X/1.4NA objective lens, a motorized x-y sample positioning stage and a color camera. For each thick blood film sample, we used random sampling to automatically select and capture 100 non-overlapping FoVs, each covering an area of 166 μm × 142 μm. For blood film smears, between 10 and 20 FoVs containing 1500–4000 RBCs were manually captured. Given the limited depth of field of the high numerical aperture objective lens, a focal series (z-stack) of 14 planes with a separation of 0.5 μm was acquired to capture the entire thickness of the blood film (typically ~ 3 to 6 μm) for each FoV. Each z-stacks was then projected onto a single (xy) plane using a wavelet-based Extended Depth of Field (EDoF) algorithm [15].

Table 1. Number of patient samples used to train and evaluate our approach.

	Malaria, Thick blood film (TBF)[a]		Sickle cell, Blood film smear (BFS)[b]	
	Negative	Positive	Negative	Positive
Train	85	84	34	37
Test	70	60	35	35
Total	155	144	69	72

[a] TBF dataset available at https://doi.org/10.5522/04/12173568.
[b] BFS dataset available at https://doi.org/10.5522/04/12407567.

3.3 Model Training

The weights of the convolutional layers of the MOFF model were initialized with weights from a VGG-19 model [16] pre-trained on the ImageNet dataset [17]. A window of 64 × 64 pixels (4.2 μm × 4.2 μm) around the centroid of each segmented object was chosen for generating the object images for the malaria problem. Images of individual RBCs corresponding to their bounding boxes as output by the segmentation step were scaled to 128 × 128 pixels and used as input object images for the sickle cell anemia diagnosis. Geometrical transformation such as random rotations and random flips were applied to the object images from each sample in the training set. N_o was set to 200 whereas N_T to 1000. Stochastic gradient descent with a learning rate of 0.0003 and a cross entropy loss function were applied to optimize the model weights during 100 epochs. No object-level labels were used. We compared two feature fusion strategies: *max* and *average*[1].

---

[1] Code available at https://github.com/UCL/FASt-MAL-MOFF.

4   Results

We evaluated our diagnostic prediction for malaria and SCD against the clinical diagnostic on the test samples in Table 1. The object-level detection of the MOFF models, for both parasites and sickle cells, was evaluated on a subset of images manually annotated by expert clinical microscopists.

4.1   Malaria Diagnosis and Parasite Detection

We compared the accuracy of our weakly supervised malaria diagnostic approach with an existing supervised approach [4]. This latter approach relies on an object detector to detect individual parasites in high power FoVs as suggested in [18] and diagnoses a sample as positive if the number of detected parasites exceeds a certain threshold determined using the negative samples in the training set as described in [4]. The object detector was trained on a separate annotated set of similar FoVs [19].

Table 2. Evaluation of automated malaria diagnosis in thick blood films. Parasitemia levels in (MP/100 FoVs) stratified as *Low*: up to 10; *Medium*: >10 to 100; *High*: >100

Method	Type	Specificity	Sensitivity			
			Low	Medium	High	Overall
Mehanian et al. [4] (Reported)	Full supervision	>.90	–	–	–	.87
Torres et al. [5] (Reported)	Full supervision	.85	–	–	–	.72
Mehanian et al. [4] (Our test set)[1]	Full supervision	**.95**	0	.23	.81	.66
MOFF-avg (Our test set)	Weak supervision	**.95**	.50	.62	.80	.75
MOFF-max (Our test set)	Weak supervision	.93	**.75**	**.92**	**.94**	**.93**

Our MOFF learning approach outperforms the Mehanian et al. diagnosis method[2] [4] (which is based on supervised parasite detection) on our test dataset in terms sensitivity for a specificity higher than .90 (Table 2), especially in samples with a low parasite count (as reported by the pathologists on the field). Both, Mehanian et al. [4] or Torres et al. [5] have not provided publicly accessible images for us to be able to test our MOFF method on their datasets. However, both the specificity and sensitivity of our weakly supervised method are equal or higher than those reported by these works (Table 2). The *max* feature fusion strategy outputs a better sensitivity (.93) compared to the *average* one (.75) at the expense of a slightly lower specificity (.93 to .95).

---

[2] Implemented slightly different than in the original paper as original code was not available.

Table 3. Malaria parasite (object-level) detection accuracy

Method	Type	Precision	Recall	F1-Score
R-FCN	Full supervision	.92	.57	.70
MOFF-avg	Weak supervision	.89	.52	.66
Faster R-CNN	Full supervision	.70	.58	.64
MOFF-max	Weak supervision	.64	.65	.64

The trained MOFF model's ability to detect individual objects was evaluated on a test dataset of 33 FoV containing 300 manually annotated parasites by an expert clinical microscopist. We compared the outcome with that of two state-of-the art fully supervised object detectors [20, 21] trained to identify parasites on a separate dataset (159 FoV with 2287 manually annotated parasites1). Surprisingly, without being trained on any object-level annotations, the performance of our MOFF model in terms of parasite detection is close to that of the fully supervised object detectors (Table 3). Figure 2 shows an example of parasites (red) and distractors (blue) identified by the weakly supervised MOFF in a test FoV from a malaria positive sample.

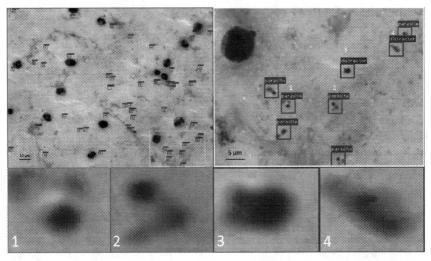

Fig. 2. MOFF parasite detection on a test high magnification FoV (100x 1.4NA). Red boxes indicate objects classified as parasites. Blue boxes indicate objects classified as distractors. (Color figure online)

4.2 Sickle Cell Detection in Blood Film Smears

Recent approaches for automatic analysis of BFS [22, 23] including sickle cell disease (SCD) detection [24] still rely on fully supervised machine learning approaches which require large amounts of cell-level manual annotations. In contrast, our weakly supervised MOFF approach was able to provide a diagnosis (Table 4) together with an abnormal RBC count (Fig. 3) without having to rely on any individual cell labels. As for malaria diagnosis, the *max* fusion strategy outputs a higher accuracy than the average one in detecting SCD (Table 4). The *max* fusion strategy was also significantly more precise in detecting abnormal RBCs associated with sickle cell anemia than the *average* fusion strategy at the expense of a slight decrease in recall (Table 5, test set of 5 FoVs containing 233 manually labelled sickle RBCs).

Table 4. MOFF sickle cell disease detection accuracy

Method	Specificity	Sensitivity	Accuracy
MOFF-max	.86	.97	.91
MOFF-avg	.89	.74	.80

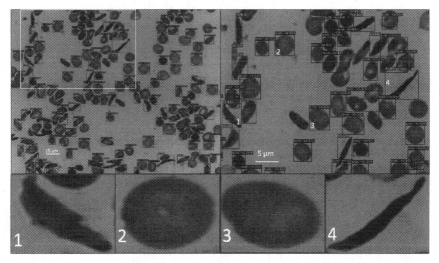

Fig. 3. Abnormal RBC detection using MOFF. Red boxes indicate RBCs identified as sickle cells. Blue boxes indicate RBCs identified as non-sickle (Color figure online)

Table 5. Abnormal RBC detection accuracy using MOFF

Method	Precision	Recall	F1-Score
MOFF-max	.86	.69	.77
MOFF-avg	.56	.74	.64

Figure 3 shows that the MOFF model trained with weak labels is able to differentiate between sickle RBCs (red boxes) and normal RBCs (blue boxes) in BFS.

5 Discussion

We have demonstrated a weakly supervised deep learning method that is able to diagnose malaria in TBF and detect sickle cells in BFS by analyzing multiple FoVs. The method, which is based on the fusion of the convolutional features of multiple objects, was successful in identifying individual objects associated with the two disorders (malaria parasites and sickle cells). The MOFF approach has successfully overcome the challenge that the markers of the conditions (malaria parasites or abnormal RBCs) are often sparse (not present in every image). Results indicate that the maximum fusion strategy performs better which can be explained by the fact that, in most of the samples, the number of malaria parasites (or sickle RBCs) is much lower than the number of artefacts (or normal RBCs) and therefore a max-fusion would better signal the presence of a small number of markers in a large pool of candidate objects. Whereas most weakly supervised approaches use image-level labels to detect specific objects inside the image our approach uses sample-level labels associated with multiple image fields knowing that the malaria parasites, or sickle RBCs might not be present in every image of the sample. Although we have restricted our analysis to binary classification ('diseased' or 'healthy'), our method could readily be adapted to multiple classes and extended to identify other types of blood disorders.

References

1. World Health Organization: World Malaria Report (2018)
2. Arco, J., Górriz, J., Ramírez, J., Álvarez, I., Puntonet, C.: Digital image analysis for automatic enumeration of malaria parasites using morphological operations. Exp. Syst. Appl. **42**, 3041–3047 (2015)
3. Rosado, L., Da Costa, J., Elias, D., Cardoso, J.: Automated detection of malaria parasites on thick blood smears via mobile devices. Procedia Comput. Sci. **90**, 138–144 (2016)
4. Mehanian, C., et al.: Computer-automated malaria diagnosis and quantitation using convolutional neural networks. In: Proceedings of the IEEE International Conference on Computer Vision (2017)
5. Torres, K., et al.: Automated microscopy for routine malaria diagnosis: a field comparison on Giemsa-stained blood films in Peru. Malaria J. **17**, 1–11 (2018)
6. Yang, F., Poostchi, M., Yu, H., et al.: Deep learning for smartphone-based malaria parasite detection in thick blood smears. IEEE J. Biomed. Health Inf. **24**(5), 1427–1438 (2019)
7. Couture, H.D., Marron, J.S., Perou, C.M., Troester, M.A., Niethammer, M.: Multiple instance learning for heterogeneous images: training a CNN for histopathology. In: MICCAI (2018)
8. Jia, Z., Huang, X., Eric, I., Chang, C., Xu, Y.: Constrained deep weak supervision for histopathology image segmentation. IEEE Trans. Med. Imaging **36**(11), 2376–2388 (2017)
9. Courtiol, P., et al.: Deep learning-based classification of mesothelioma improves prediction of patient outcome. Nat. Med. **25**(10), 1519–1525 (2019)
10. Campanella, G., Hanna, M., Geneslaw, L., et al.: Clinical-grade computational pathology using weakly supervised deep learning on whole slide images. Nat. Med. **25**, 1301–1309 (2019)
11. Kraus, O.Z., Ba, J.L., Frey, B.J.: Classifying and segmenting microscopy images with deep multiple instance learning. Bioinformatics **32**(12), i52–i59 (2016)
12. Uijlings, J.R.R., Van De Sande, K.E.A., Gevers, T., Smeulders, A.W.M.: Selective search for object recognition. Int. J. Comput. Vis. **104**(2), 154–171 (2013)

13. Das, D.K., Mukherjee, R., Chakraborty, C.: Computational microscopic imaging for malaria parasite detection: a systematic review. J. Microsc. **1**, 1–19 (2015)
14. Naik, R.P., Haywood Jr., C.: Sickle cell trait diagnosis: clinical and social implications. Hematology Am. Soc. Hematol. Educ. Program. **2015**(1), 160–167 (2015)
15. Forster, B., Van De Ville, D., Berent, J., Sage, D., Unser, M.: Complex wavelets for extended depth-of-field: a new method for the fusion of multichannel microscopy images. Microsc. Res. Tech. **65**, 33–42 (2004)
16. Simonyan, K., Zisserman, A.: Very deep convolutional networks for large-scale image recognition (2015)
17. Deng, J., Dong, W., Socher, R., et al.: ImageNet: a large-scale hierarchical image database. In: CVPR (2009)
18. Yang, F., Yu, H., et al.: Parasite detection in thick blood smears based on customized faster-RCNN on smartphones. Lister Hill National Center for Biomedical Communications (2019)
19. Manescu, P., Shaw, M., et al.: Giemsa Stained Thick Blood Films for Clinical Microscopy Malaria Diagnosis with Deep Neural Networks Dataset. University College London (2020). Dataset. https://doi.org/10.5522/04/12173568.v1
20. Dai, J., Li, Y., He, K., Sun, J.: R-FCN: object detection via region-based fully convolutional networks. In: Advances Neural Information Processing System, pp. 379–387 (2016)
21. Ren, S., He, K., Girshick, R., Sun, J.: Faster R-CNN: towards real-time object detection with region proposal networks. IEEE Trans. Pattern Anal. Mach. Intell. **39**(6), 1137–1149 (2017)
22. Mundhra, D., Cheluvaraju, B., Rampure, J., Dastidar, T.R.: Analyzing microscopic images of peripheral blood smear using deep learning. In: Deep Learning in Medical Image Analysis and Multimodal Learning for Clinical Decision Support (2017)
23. Sadafi, A., et al.: Multiclass deep active learning for detecting red blood cell subtypes in brightfield microscopy. In: Shen, D., et al. (eds.) MICCAI 2019. LNCS, vol. 11764, pp. 685–693. Springer, Cham (2019). https://doi.org/10.1007/978-3-030-32239-7_76
24. Xu, M., Papageorgiou, D.P., Abidi, S.Z., Dao, M., Zhao, H., Karniadakis, G.E.: A deep convolutional neural network for classification of red blood cells in sickle cell anemia. PLoS Comput. Biol. **13**(10), e1005746 (2017)

Imaging Scattering Characteristics of Tissue in Transmitted Microscopy

Mihoko Shimano[1(✉)], Yuta Asano[1], Shin Ishihara[2], Ryoma Bise[3], and Imari Sato[1,2]

[1] National Institute of Informatics, Tokyo, Japan
{miho,asanoy,imarik}@nii.ac.jp
[2] Tokyo Institute of Technology, Tokyo, Japan
ishihara.s.aj@m.titech.ac.jp
[3] Kyushu University, Fukuoka, Japan
bise@ait.kyushu-u.ac.jp

Abstract. Scattering property plays a very important role in optical imaging and diagnostic applications, such as analysis of cancerous process and diagnosis of dysplasia or cancer. The existing methods focused on removing scattering components in order to visualize the spatial distribution of the reflection and absorption properties. We propose a novel method for estimating the spatial distribution of scattering property by measuring a set of intensities of the direct scattered light with each angle for each point. Our key contribution is to decompose the captured light into the direct scattered light with each angle by using varying spatial frequency of illumination patterns that can control the range of the scattered angle. By applying the method to observe a spatially inhomogeneous translucent object, we can extract the map of the angular distribution of scattering. To the best of our knowledge, this is the first method to enable visualizing a spatial map of scattering property using a conventional transmitted microscope setup. Experimental results on synthetic data and real complex materials demonstrate the effectiveness of our method for the estimation of scattering distribution.

Keywords: Scattering · Transmitted microscopy · Computational photography · Image decomposition · Illumination · Direct-global separation · Medical and biological imaging

1 Introduction

Scattering is one of the essential optical characteristics in addition to direct reflection and absorption. Recently, scattering characteristics including the angular distribution of scattering play an important role in optical imaging and diagnostic applications such as detection of a cell, analysis of cancerous process and diagnosis of dysplasia or cancer [4–6]. Therefore, it has great potential for biomedical image analysis to visualize the scattering properties that cannot be visualized in the conventional microscopy method.

© Springer Nature Switzerland AG 2020
A. L. Martel et al. (Eds.): MICCAI 2020, LNCS 12265, pp. 236–245, 2020.
https://doi.org/10.1007/978-3-030-59722-1_23

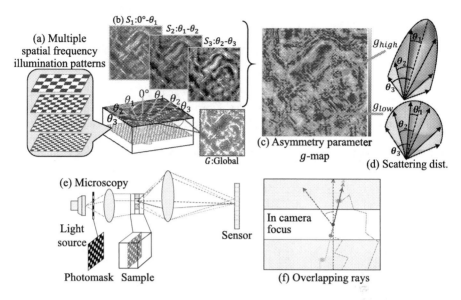

Fig. 1. Overview of our method: (a) Illumination patterns, (b) Example of the angular distribution of scattering (pig skin), (c) Asymmetry parameter g-map, (d) Scattering distributions, (e) Microscopy set up and (f) Overlapping rays.

Scattering is a phenomenon that particles in tissue are exposed to light and re-emit light in different directions with different intensity as shown in Fig. 1(d). In this paper, we call the distribution of intensities in different angles of scattering light rays as scattering property. For example, the figures in Fig. 1(d) show the two intensity distributions under different scattering properties. The upper distribution is an example of forward scattering where the intensities at the area of a smaller angle (*e.g.*, θ_1) are high and the intensity drastically decreases with the larger angle (*e.g.*, θ_2, θ_3). In contrast, the bottom one has more isotropic intensities. In order to measure this scattering property, it is required to measure the distribution of intensities of multiple light rays. Narasimhan *et al.* [8] proposed a technique for measuring scattering property by observing the angular distribution of light scattered in a homogeneous liquid. Although their technique works for liquids, it cannot handle spatially inhomogeneous objects.

On the other hand, in transmitted light microscopy, which has been widely used in the biomedical research field, the captured light consists of the light rays that have traveled along different paths with scattering and reaches to an image sensor with overlapping various scattered light coming from different points in the tissue. It is known that the high amount of light scattering in biological tissues tends to make images blur [4,7,11].

Many methods have been proposed to remove such various scattered light for improving visualization. For example, in a reflected scene, Nayar *et al.* [9] proposed a method that separates the reflecting light at the surface (direct components) from scattering (global components) by using high-frequency illumination.

It has been extended for separating desired components: inner slice images [14], inter-reflection and subsurface scattering [13], and others [1,2,10]. Several methods were adapted for transmitted scenes by using high-frequency illumination concept for obtaining absorption properties [3,12,15]. However, these previous works for light separation basically focus on visualizing the absorption or reflection properties. Although their methods separate scattering light from the various different points, these cannot measure the scattering property at each point.

In this paper, we propose a novel method for estimating the distribution of intensities in different angles of scattering light in transmitted light microscopy by using multiple spacial frequency illumination patterns. Our key contribution is that the range of the scattering angle can be controlled by the frequency of binary checkered illumination pattern (*i.e.*, the size of a lit/unlit area), where the white patch is lit, and the black is unlit in Fig. 1(a). For example, the light at the sensor position contains the widely spreading light rays when the checker size is large (low-frequency), whereas it contains the narrow spreading light rays when the size is small (high-frequency). On the basis of this phenomenon, we estimate the images for each angle range (*e.g.*, S_1 for $0°-\theta_1$, S_2 for $\theta_1-\theta_2$ in Fig. 1(b)). The set of the estimated images represents the scattering property (the distribution of intensities in different angles) at each point, and we can also visualize the map of an asymmetry parameter g (Fig. 1(c)) that represents the angular distribution with a common scattering model (Henyey-Greenstein phase function). To best of our knowledge, this is the first work that enables the decomposition of the captured light into the direct scattered light with each angle for visualizing the spatial distribution of scattering property using a typical transmitted microscope setup. The experimental results on synthetic data and real complex materials demonstrate the effectiveness of our method for estimating scattering property.

2   Scattered Light Separation Method

2.1   Investigating Overlapped Various Scattered Light

When we capture a scattered tissue by transmitted microscopy, a measured signal at an image sensor contains various scattered light coming from different points in the tissue. In this section, we investigate what types of light rays reach an image sensor together in transmitted microscopy and the problem of the assumption of the previous work [12].

Figures 1(e)(f) show an illustration of the light rays in transmitted microscopy. Let us consider light rays that pass through a point of interest (e.g., the red point in Fig. 1(f)) in camera focus and reach the same sensor as shown in Fig. 1(e). The light rays that reach the same sensor p can be classified into four types: 1) directly transmitted light without scattering $T(p)$ (dotted black arrow); 2) single scattered light from the target depth $S_R(p, x)$ is scattered only at point x and thereafter reaches the sensor without scattering (the solid and dotted red arrows); 3) single scattered light from a different depth $M_{SR}(p, x)$ (the orange arrow); and 4) multiply scattered light $M_{MR}(p, x)$ that is scattered more than once and consequently overlaps the above three types (the cyan arrow). The image intensity $L(\boldsymbol{p})$ captured at pixel $\boldsymbol{p}$ is defined as the sum of these four types of light as follows:

$$
\begin{aligned}
L(\boldsymbol{p}) &= D(\boldsymbol{p}) + G(\boldsymbol{p}) \\
&= T(\boldsymbol{p}) + \sum_{R \in \mathbf{R}(p)} S_R(\boldsymbol{p}, \boldsymbol{x}) + \sum_{R \in \mathbf{R}(p)} M_{SR}(\boldsymbol{p}, \boldsymbol{x}) + \sum_{R \in \mathbf{R}(p)} M_{MR}(\boldsymbol{p}, \boldsymbol{x}), \quad (1)
\end{aligned}
$$

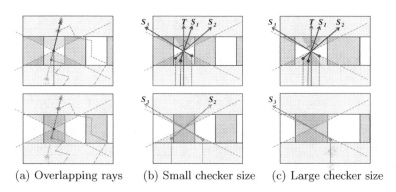

(a) Overlapping rays   (b) Small checker size   (c) Large checker size

Fig. 2. Illustration of (a) overlapping rays in the cases of lit point (top in red), and an unlit point (bottom in red); (b) (c) single scattered light at different angles. The white region is lit, and the dark gray region is unlit. (Color figure online)

where we call the first and second terms the direct components $D(\boldsymbol{p})$, and the other two terms as the global components $G(\boldsymbol{p})$. In contrast to [12] in which only rays in the same direction(solid arrows)are considered, we consider various single scattered light rays captured at the same pixel $\boldsymbol{p}$ (both the solid and dotted arrows). We denote the set of paths of such light rays as $\mathbf{R}(\boldsymbol{p})$, one such ray as R, and $S_R(\boldsymbol{p}, \boldsymbol{x})$ as the intensity of the single scattered light on R that reaches pixel $\boldsymbol{p}$.

2.2 Separating Direct Single Scattered Light with Each Angle

Our aim is to separate the scattered light depending on its direction and visualize the spatial map of angular distribution of scattered light considering the above direct scattered light with each angle from a target depth. Our method uses the multiple frequencies of binary checkered illumination patterns for this purpose. We first explain the intensities in the case using a fixed size pattern.

Figure 1(e) shows the setup of the microscopy and high-frequency binary checkered pattern. The checkered pattern is set between the light source and the illumination focus lens, where the white patch is lit, and the dark gray is unlit in Figs. 2. Let us consider for capturing an area of interest that is in focus of both the camera and the high-frequency checkered pattern illumination. By moving the checker pattern, we can capture two types of images; the lit or the unlit area of interest. The top panels in Fig. 2(a) show cases when the point of interest (the red point) is lit. The corresponding intensity contains both direct (red arrow) and global components (cyan and orange arrows). The bottom panels in Fig. 2(a) show when the point of interest (red point) is unlit. In this case, the light contains only global components (cyan and orange arrows) since there are no light rays that are scattered at the point of interest and they reach the same sensor. The intensities when the point of interest is lit or unlit can be formulated as [12]:

$$L^+(\boldsymbol{p}) = T(\boldsymbol{p}) + \sum_{R \in \mathbf{R}(\boldsymbol{p})} \alpha_R S_R(\boldsymbol{p}, \boldsymbol{x}) + \frac{1}{2}\left(\sum_R M_{SR}(\boldsymbol{p}, \boldsymbol{x}) + \sum_R M_{MR}(\boldsymbol{p}, \boldsymbol{x})\right), \quad (2)$$

$$L^-(\boldsymbol{p}) = \sum_{R \in \mathbf{R}(\boldsymbol{p})} (1 - \alpha_R) S_R(\boldsymbol{p}, \boldsymbol{x}) + \frac{1}{2}\left(\sum_R M_{SR}(\boldsymbol{p}, \boldsymbol{x}) + \sum_R M_{MR}(\boldsymbol{p}, \boldsymbol{x})\right), \quad (3)$$

where α_R and $1 - \alpha_R$ indicate the ratios of the lit area and unlit area in the focused area (the green areas in Fig. 2).

Next, let us consider how the angles of the light rays in $\mathbf{R}(\boldsymbol{p})$ change with the size of the binary checkered pattern. Figures 2(b) and (c) show small checker and large checker cases. Here, we define the diagonal axis to the focus plane (vertical axis in the figure) as $0°$, and the horizontal axis as $90°$. For example, S_1 is the smaller angle light than S_2. When the point of interest is lit in both cases, the intensity $L(\boldsymbol{p})$ captured at pixel $\boldsymbol{p}$ is the sum of $T(\boldsymbol{p})$ and the intensity of single scattered light with every angle (S_1, S_2, S_3) from the lit area in the target depth (green area). However, the amount of light of a specific angle may change when the pattern size changes since the ratio between the lit and unlit area along the angle in the focused depth (green area). We explain the details of this phenomenon using Fig. 2. In the small size case (Fig. 2(b)), the light rays with the small angle that are scattered in the orange area (e.g., S_1), travel through only a lit area in the target depth (i.e., the ratio of the lit area is 1). The light rays with the wider angle which are scattered at the points outside the orange area (e.g., S_2, S_3) travel through both a lit and unlit area in the target depth (i.e., the ratio of the lit area is smaller than 1). In contrast, in the large size case (Fig. 2(c)), the light rays that are scattered thorough the yellow area (e.g., S_2) travel through only a lit area (i.e., the ratio is 1). It indicates the amount of light rays that are scattered in the yellow region is different between these two cases.

Similarly, when the point of interest is unlit as shown in the top figures in Fig. 2, the range of angles of the rays depends on the size of the checker pattern. When the checker size is larger, the range of the light angles becomes the narrower, in which it contains the wider angles to the diagonal axis (e.g., S_3) but dose not contain the smaller angle (e.g., S_2) since the neighbor lit area is farther from the point of interest when the pattern becomes large.

Based on this observation, we use K illumination patterns to divide the angles into K groups (e.g., the orange area, yellow area, ...) from 0 degrees to angle of the green line that depends on the optical lens property. We define the ratio of the lit and unlit in the region of the i-th angle (e.g., the yellow area) for pattern k as a_{ki}, a'_{ki}, in which $a_{ki} + a'_{ki} = 1$. These ratios can be computed on the basis of the setup of microscopy and illumination patterns. The sum of intensities of the k-th group with a certain angle range is denoted by $S_k\{S_k|k=1,\ldots,K\}$. Then, Eq. 3 can be written as follows:

$$
\boldsymbol{L}(\boldsymbol{p})=\boldsymbol{A}\boldsymbol{X}(\boldsymbol{p}),\quad
\begin{bmatrix}
L_1^+(\boldsymbol{p})\\
L_1^-(\boldsymbol{p})\\
\vdots\\
L_k^+(\boldsymbol{p})\\
L_k^-(\boldsymbol{p})\\
\vdots\\
L_K^+(\boldsymbol{p})\\
L_K^-(\boldsymbol{p})
\end{bmatrix}
=
\begin{bmatrix}
a_{11} & a_{12} & a_{13} & \cdots & a_{1K} & \frac{1}{2}\\
a_{11}' & a_{12}' & a_{13}' & \cdots & a_{1K}' & \frac{1}{2}\\
\vdots & \vdots & \vdots & \vdots & \vdots & \vdots\\
a_{k1} & a_{k2} & a_{k3} & \cdots & a_{kK} & \frac{1}{2}\\
a_{k1}' & a_{k2}' & a_{k3}' & \cdots & a_{kK}' & \frac{1}{2}\\
\vdots & \vdots & \vdots & \vdots & \vdots & \vdots\\
a_{K1} & a_{K2} & a_{K3} & \cdots & a_{KK} & \frac{1}{2}\\
a_{K1}' & a_{K2}' & a_{K3}' & \cdots & a_{KK}' & \frac{1}{2}
\end{bmatrix}
\begin{bmatrix}
T(\boldsymbol{p})+S_1(\boldsymbol{p})\\
S_2(\boldsymbol{p})\\
\vdots\\
S_k(\boldsymbol{p})\\
\vdots\\
S_K(\boldsymbol{p})\\
G(\boldsymbol{p})
\end{bmatrix},\quad(4)
$$

where $\boldsymbol{L}(\boldsymbol{p})$ is a vector that consists of the intensities in the lit (L^+) and unlit (L^-) case for K patterns and $\boldsymbol{A}$ is a matrix of coefficients a_{ki} and a_{ki}'. $\boldsymbol{X}(\boldsymbol{p})$ is a row vector of single scattered light with k-th angle and $G(\boldsymbol{p})$. Since the direction of $T(\boldsymbol{p})$ is parallel to incident illumination as explained above, $T(\boldsymbol{p})$ is included in the first element of $\boldsymbol{X}(\boldsymbol{p})$ as $T(\boldsymbol{p})+S_1(\boldsymbol{p})$.

In practice, a set of intensities at each pixel is recorded by shifting the k-th illumination pattern and selecting the maximum and minimum intensity for each point, denoted as $L_k^{max}(\boldsymbol{p})$ and $L_k^{min}(\boldsymbol{p})$, respectively. Here, when the pixel takes the maximum/minimum value, the pixel can be considered as placed at the center of the lit/unlit area. Thus, we set $L_k^+(\boldsymbol{p})=L_k^{max}(\boldsymbol{p})$, and $L_k^-(\boldsymbol{p})=L_k^{min}(\boldsymbol{p})$. Given $\boldsymbol{L}(\boldsymbol{p})$ and $\boldsymbol{A}$, $\boldsymbol{X}(\boldsymbol{p})$ can be estimated by minimizing the mean square error $\|\boldsymbol{L}(\boldsymbol{p})-\boldsymbol{A}\boldsymbol{X}(\boldsymbol{p})\|^2$. This estimation is applied for every pixels.

2.3   Estimation of the Scattering Asymmetry Parameter g

In order to visualize the scattering property by a single image, we also estimate a scattering parameter g, which can represent the distribution of scattering light, from the estimated intensity of direct single scattered light with each angle for each point. It is known that the intensity of scattered light on a particular angle θ, which is the angle between the incident light direction and the scattered light direction, can be modeled by a phase function $P(\theta;g)$. For this phase function, we use Henyey-Greenstein phase function, which has been widely used to fit to biological scattering data. It is defined as follows:

$$
P(\theta)=\frac{1}{4\pi}\frac{1-g^2}{(1+g^2-2g\cos\theta)^{\frac{3}{2}}},\tag{5}
$$

where the shape of the scattering distribution becomes isotropic when $g=0$, and it becomes forward scattering when g is near 1, and backward scattering when g is near -1. We estimate the asymmetry parameter g by using the obtained intensities with each angle S_k.

3   Experimental Results

3.1   Quantitative Evaluation Using Synthetic Data

We first determined that the proposed method works well at separating direct single scattered light depending on the scattering angle and estimating the asymmetry parameter g by using synthetic data. In this simulation, we followed the setup of the real microscope used in the experimental evaluation discussed in the next section. We changed the checker pattern pitch from 4 to 31 pixels at 3-pixel intervals and prepared a total of ten types of input images for each data. We evaluated the proposed method on seven different scenes with the asymmetry parameter g varying from 0.3 to 0.9 in 0.1 intervals since the range of g is usually in $[0.5, 0.9]$ in a real material. The similarity of the separated direct single scattered light was calculated by using the cosine similarity: $\frac{S_k \cdot \bar{S}_k}{\|S_k\| \|\bar{S}_k\|}$, where S_k means the vector of estimated direct single scattered light components $\{S_1, S_2, ..., S_{10}, G\}$, and $\bar{S}_k$ means the simulated ground truth vector. Table 1 shows a summary of the experimental results indicating that the proposed method accurately estimated g under various conditions.

3.2   Qualitative Evaluation Using Real Materials

Next, we qualitatively validated our method by examining recovered scattered light images of real-world materials.

Measurement System and Setup: The experimental setup consisted of a microscope (BX53, Olympus) with a halogen lamp, a light source with several bandpass filters, a high-frequency checker pattern filter, and a camera (GS3-U3-41C6NIR, FLIR). For the high-frequency checker pattern filter, we used a photomask with four binary checker patterns, in which the photomask was set between a field diaphragm and a condenser lens as shown in Fig. 1(e). The checker pattern ranged in checker size from 7×7 to 16×16 µm (interval of 3 µm). An XYZ-axes motorized stage (KXT04015-LC, Suruga Seiki) was used to shift the photomask.

Estimation of Scattered Light with Each Angle and g: We examined many solid tissues (*e.g.*, apple, pork, chicken, ham in milk and others in supplement materials) to show the effectiveness of our method for visualizing the scattering angle distribution in spatially inhomogeneous structures.

In each image, the angles of the direct scattered light were separated into four ranges, and, thus, the intensities for each angle and global component could be estimated ($T + S_1$, S_2, S_3, S_4, and G) as shown in Fig. 3. The right column shows the g-map calculated from the decomposed intensities for each angle. 'Original' indicates the original image captured by transmitted microscopy without illumination patterns.

Table 1. Estimation results using synthetic data (Global Component $G = 100$, almost the same scale as other S_k components)

g_{gt}	0.3	0.4	0.5	0.6	0.7	0.8	0.9
g_{est}		0.3070	0.4088	0.4999	0.5978	0.7130	0.8213	0.9286
S_k Similarity	0.9999	0.9999	0.9999	0.9999	0.9997	0.9997	0.9997

As shown in Fig. 3 (Apple), although the two orange boxes in the original image seem similarly blurred, the intensities of these areas in S_4 are different. In the figures of (Pork), there are also significantly different appearances between the original image and $S1$ in the orange rectangle areas. We can distinguish the sharp structures of fibers in $S1$, and the intensities in the orange box decrease as the angle becomes larger. This indicates that the fibers are predominantly forward scattering. In the figures of (Chicken1), we can see concentric circles in the orange box. In S_1 in this area, the intensities at the center of the circle are high, and as the angle becomes wider, the high intensity area moves to the periphery of the circle. This indicates that the scattering property may be able to be used to represent the structure of the tissue.

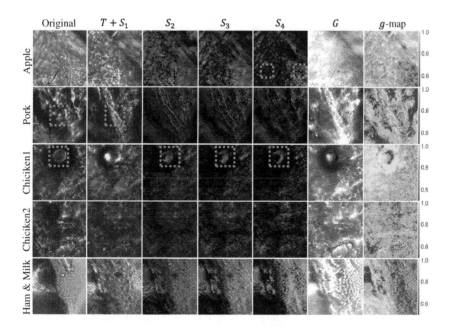

Fig. 3. Results for real images.

Next, we measured the target slices at different depths in the same area in order to demonstrate the efficacy of our method for revealing inhomogeneous structures along the depth direction. The results on two different depths are shown in Fig. 3 (Chicken1) and (Chicken2). The separated scattering images at each depth recovered different structures of appearances. We also examined a controlled setup in which milk was filled on ham and the boundary area of a piece of ham was captured (*i.e.*, the boundary of the two materials could be observed in the area). These two materials could be separated in g-map and the g value of each material was similar to the value that was measured in a simple substance. The experimental results validated the accuracy of our method.

The experimental results show an ability for representing optical characteristics that cannot be obtained from the original image even though the original images are blurred. This capability has the potential to be used in detection and diagnosis of dysplasia and cancer [4–6]. The supplemental material contains more results of g-map and the extinction coefficients.

4 Conclusion

We proposed a novel method for imaging the spatial distribution of the scattering properties of tissue in transmitted light microscopy by using multiple high-frequency illumination patterns. The proposed method can estimate the scattering property that represents the angular distribution of light rays scattered at a point. It is founded upon the observation that the range of such angle can be controlled by varying the spatial frequency of a binary checkered illumination pattern. The effectiveness of the separation technique was confirmed in numerical evaluations and in experiments observing real materials. In particular, the experimental results suggest that this technique can represent important optical characteristics of materials that are blurry in the conventional microscopy images but are distinguishable through their scattering properties.

Acknowledgements. This work was supported by JSPS KAKENHI Grant Number JP19J40303 to M.S.

References

1. Achar, S., Nuske, S.T., Narasimhan, S.G.: Compensating for motion during direct-global separation. In: IEEE International Conference on Computer Vision (2013)
2. Fuchs, C., Heinz, M., Levoy, M., Seidel, H.P., Lensch, H.P.A.: Combining confocal imaging and descattering. Comput. Graph. Forum **27**, 1245–1253 (2008)
3. Kuniyoshi, F., Funatomi, T., Kubo, H., Sawada, Y., Kato, Y., Mukaigawa, Y.: Visibility enhancement by integrating refocusing and direct-global separation with contact imaging. Int. J. Comput. Vis. **127**(8), 1162–1174 (2019)
4. LDrezek, R., et al.: Light scattering from cervical cells throughout neoplastic progression: influence of nuclear morphology, DNA content, and chromatin texture. J. Biomed. Opt. **8**(1), 7–16 (2003). https://doi.org/10.1117/1.1528950
5. Lin, X., Wan, N., Weng, L., Zhou, Y.: Light scattering from normal and cervical cancer cells. Appl. Opt. **56**, 3608 (2017). https://doi.org/10.1364/AO.56.003608

6. Lovat, L., et al.: 4919 a novel optical biopsy technique using elastic scattering spectroscopy for dysplasia and cancer in barrett's esophagus. Gastrointest. Endosc. **51**, AN227 (2000). https://doi.org/10.1016/S0016-5107(00)14616-4

7. Moscoso, M., Keller, J., Papanicolaou, G.: Depolarization and blurring of optical images by biological tissue. J. Opt. Soc. Am. A Opt. Image Sci. Vis. **18**, 948–60 (2001). https://doi.org/10.1364/JOSAA.18.000948

8. Narasimhan, S., Gupta, M., Donner, C., Ramamoorthi, R., Nayar, S., Jensen, H.W.: Acquiring scattering properties of participating media by dilution. ACM Trans. Graph. **25**(3), 1003–1012 (2006)

9. Nayar, S.K., Krishnan, G., Grossberg, M.D., Raskar, R.: Fast separation of direct and global components of a scene using high frequency illumination. ACM Trans. Graph. **25**(3), 935–944 (2006)

10. Nishino, K., Subpa-asa, A., Asano, Y., Shimano, M., Sato, I.: Variable ring light imaging: capturing transient subsurface scattering with an ordinary camera. In: Ferrari, V., Hebert, M., Sminchisescu, C., Weiss, Y. (eds.) ECCV 2018. LNCS, vol. 11215, pp. 624–639. Springer, Cham (2018). https://doi.org/10.1007/978-3-030-01252-6_37

11. Ntziachristos, V.: Going deeper than microscopy: the optical imaging frontier in biology. Nat. Methods **7**(8), 603–614 (2010). https://doi.org/10.1038/nmeth.1483

12. Shimano, M., Bise, R., Zheng, Y., Sato, I.: Separation of transmitted light and scattering components in transmitted microscopy. In: Descoteaux, M., Maier-Hein, L., Franz, A., Jannin, P., Collins, D.L., Duchesne, S. (eds.) MICCAI 2017. LNCS, vol. 10434, pp. 12–20. Springer, Cham (2017). https://doi.org/10.1007/978-3-319-66185-8_2

13. Subpaasa, A., Zheng, Y., Ono, N., Sato, I.: Light transport component decomposition using multi-frequency illumination. In: IEEE International Conference on Image Processing (2017)

14. Tanaka, K., Mukaigawa, Y., Kubo, H., Matsushita, Y., Yagi, Y.: Recovering inner slices of layered translucent objects by multi-frequency illumination. IEEE Trans. Pattern Anal. Mach. Intell. **39**(4), 746–757 (2017)

15. Tanaka, K., Mukaigawa, Y., Matsushita, Y., Yagi, Y.: Descattering of transmissive observation using parallel high-frequency illumination. In: International Conference on Computational Photography (2013)

Attention Based Multiple Instance Learning for Classification of Blood Cell Disorders

Ario Sadafi[1,2,3], Asya Makhro[4], Anna Bogdanova[4], Nassir Navab[2,5], Tingying Peng[1,2], Shadi Albarqouni[2,6], and Carsten Marr[1($\boxtimes$)]

[1] Helmholtz Zentrum Müchen - German Research Center for Environmental Health, Institute of Computational Biology, Munich, Germany
carsten.marr@helmholtz-muenchen.de
[2] Computer Aided Medical Procedures, Technical University of Munich, Munich, Germany
[3] Helmholtz AI, Helmholtz Center Munich, Munich, Germany
[4] Red Blood Cell Research Group, Institute of Veterinary Physiology, Vetsuisse Faculty and the Zurich Center for Integrative Human Physiology, University of Zurich, Zurich, Switzerland
[5] Computer Aided Medical Procedures, Johns Hopkins University, Baltimore, USA
[6] Computer Vision Lab (CVL), ETH Zurich, Zurich, Switzerland

Abstract. Red blood cells are highly deformable and present in various shapes. In blood cell disorders, only a subset of all cells is morphologically altered and relevant for the diagnosis. However, manually labeling of all cells is laborious, complicated and introduces inter-expert variability. We propose an attention based multiple instance learning method to classify blood samples of patients suffering from blood cell disorders. Cells are detected using an R-CNN architecture. With the features extracted for each cell, a multiple instance learning method classifies patient samples into one out of four blood cell disorders. The attention mechanism provides a measure of the contribution of each cell to the overall classification and significantly improves the networks classification accuracy as well as its interpretability for the medical expert.

Keywords: Multiple instance learning · Attention · Red blood cells

1 Introduction

Historically, classification of hereditary hemolytic anemias, a particular class of blood disorders, is based on the abnormal shape of red blood cells. Sickle cell disease, spherocytosis, ovalocytosis, stomatocytosis: these types of anemia refer directly to the changes in cell shape, whereas genetic causes of the disease were identified later [7,8,14]. All but one (sickle cell disease) of the above-mentioned

---

T. Peng, S. Albarqouni, and C. Marr—Shared senior authorship.

A. L. Martel et al. (Eds.): MICCAI 2020, LNCS 12265, pp. 246–256, 2020.
https://doi.org/10.1007/978-3-030-59722-1_24

disorders are structural diseases of the red blood cell membrane caused by muta-tions in genes coding for the cytoskeletal proteins spectrin, ankyrin and band 3 protein, as well as protein 4.2 [7] making cells look like flowers, stars, hedgehogs, cups, droplets or spheres [2]. Characteristic changes in morphology are hallmarks of diseases caused by abnormalities in hemoglobin structure as for sickle cell dis-ease and thalassemia. Somewhat more subtle are the changes in shape of red blood cells of patients harboring mutated glycolytic enzymes [9] or ion channels (like the Gardos channel or the PIEZO1 channel [18]). Independent of the cause and class of hereditary anemia, not all red blood cells but a fraction of them (often as large as 5–10% of the total cell population) are abnormally shaped. This makes diagnosis based on shape changes alone difficult, and additional tests are currently required. Furthermore, detection of abnormal shapes suffers from the subjective view of a human observer, a skillful, but possibly biased expert that may only process several hundreds of cells per patient. Instead, machine learning approaches are required and have been showing to outperform human experts in a number of clinical tasks. Classification of skin cancer at the derma-tologist level proposed by Esteva et al. [6], human level recognition of blast cells by Matek et al. [15] or an AI system for breast cancer screening developed by McKinney et al. [16] are just some of the various cases machine learning excels experts. Introduction of an unbiased computer-based assessment of red blood cell shapes and their abundance in a blood sample may open new possibilities for diagnostics, assessment of disease severity, and monitoring of treatment success for the patients with rare anemias.

Multiple instance learning (MIL) is used in medical image computation when all of the instances from a patient must be taken into account and no specific label exists for each of the instances. For example, Campanella et al. [3] propose a method to whole slide pathology image classification with the MIL. Here, each whole slide image is weakly labeled as healthy or cancerous, but no specific label exists for every small image patch. Similarly, Ozdemir et al. [17] suggest a method based on MIL to classify lung cancer CT scans. In a slightly different work, Conjeti et al. [5] suggest a method of hashing for medical image retrieval based on MIL and the auxiliary branch for the vanishing gradient problem known to impede MIL approaches. While these approaches perform on a patch level, none of them is able to identify single cells that are often crucial for the diagnosis.

To this end, we propose a method based on weak patient labels and atten-tion based MIL to classify patient blood samples into disease classes. Cells are extracted from images by an R-CNN architecture previously trained on a single cell detection task and feature maps of the backbone ResNet are passed to the proposed method. Without any cellwise labeling, the model manages to detect landmark cells for every disease in an unsupervised way by giving them the highest attention.

2 Methodology

A patients blood sample may consist of several bright-field images (see Dataset for a detailed description) and each image contains several instances/single red blood cells (see Fig. 1). A previously trained R-CNN architecture is used to find instances and extract their features (see Fig. 2). Based on these features, we propose to classify a sample into one of four diseases taking into account the features of all of the instances present in the input. Additionally, an attention score improves performance and interpretability of the method to medical experts for further verification. The proposed approach consists of three main blocks: (i) the multiple instance learning, (ii) an auxiliary single instance classifier and (iii) the attention mechanism (see Fig. 1).

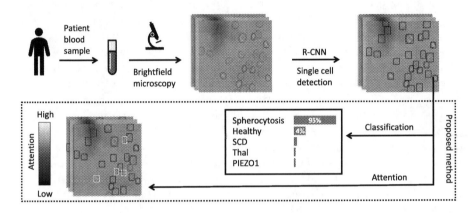

Fig. 1. Overview of the proposed method. Bright-field images of blood samples are acquired with a microscope. Using a previously trained R-CNN, all cells are detected from each image. Looking at all of the cells our proposed approach classifies the sample and provides a cell-wise attention score for better interpretability.

More formally, our objective is a model f that classifies a blood sample containing several instances into one of the classes $c_i \in C$ and generates a score $a_k \in A$ denoting the contribution of each instance in the final decision:

$$c_i, a_k = f(B), \tag{1}$$

where $B = \{I_1, \ldots, I_N\}$ is the bag of instances and each instance I_i is a tensor of the size $256 \times 14 \times 14$.

2.1   Preprocessing: Single Cell Detection

Any off the shelf detection algorithm can be used for detecting single cells in the images. We are using a modified Mask R-CNN architecture [10] with ResNet [11] backbone that generates the features. For every detected cell the relevant features are extracted with RoI aligning and used as an instance I given as the input to our method. The Mask R-CNN was trained on a separate dataset from [20], consisting of 208 microscopic images with each containing 30–40 red blood

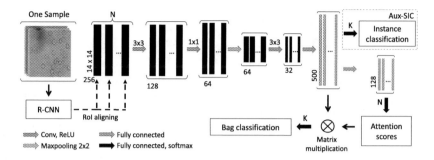

Fig. 2. Architecture of the proposed method. The R-CNN extracts features from the input images and detects the red blood cells. Based on the detected cells a bag of cell features in all of the images is formed after RoI aligning. Passing through convolutional and fully connected layer and attention pooling a feature vector is shaped for the bag and classified. An auxiliary single instance classification (Aux-SIC) branch helps the training during the first steps. N is the number of instances in a bag and K the total number of classes.

cells (total of >7000 single cells) annotated by a biomedical expert. The Mask R-CNN achieves a mean average precision (mAP) of 0.91 which is accurate enough for our application. In order to prevent cumbersome cell by cell annotation for segmentation which is not required in this approach, we limited the Mask R-CNN to a binary classification and disabled the mask head. This way, annotation of data for single cell extraction is limited to bounding boxes around the cells that does not require any special expertise and can be performed by anyone with minimum training.

2.2   Single Instance Classification

Single instance classification (SIC) is the most intuitive approach for classification of samples. In our case, each instance is passed through several convolutional layers and a embedding feature vector h for every instance in the bag is generated (Fig. 2). SIC is a CNN architecture that classifies each instance embedding based on the weak labels of the bag. At inference time, a majority voting is employed to determine the class of a given sample based on the single cells' classification results:

$$\mathcal{L}_{\mathrm{SIC}}(\theta, \psi) = \frac{1}{N} \sum_{i=1}^{N} \mathrm{CE}(c_i, \hat{c}_i), \tag{2}$$

where $\hat{c}_i = f_{\mathrm{SIC}}(h_i; \psi)$, CE is the cross entropy loss, and

$$h_i = f_{\mathrm{EMB}}(I_i, \theta) : I_i \in B \tag{3}$$

with c_i being the label for each cell i based on the bag label. ψ and θ are learned model parameters.

2.3 Multiple Instance Learning

In contrast to supervised methods where for every given instance one tries to find a target variable $\hat{c} \in C$, multiple instance learning (MIL) tries to find the target variable $\hat{c}$ based the input which is a set of instances $B = \{I_1, \ldots, I_N\}$. There are two approaches to implement MIL: instance level and embedding level approaches. We use the embedding level approach to formulate the MIL problem. As defined in Eq. 3, the function f_{EMB} maps every instance into a low dimensional space h and a single representation for the whole bag z is generated using a MIL pooling method. A bag level classifier classifies z into one of the classes. A few MIL pooling methods exist. One popular method is max pooling [1] where maximization is used to generate the bag level representation:

$$z_m = \max_{k=1\ldots N} \{h_{km}\}. \tag{4}$$

The MIL approach can be formulated as follows:

$$\mathcal{L}_{MIL}(\theta, \phi) = CE(c, \hat{c}), \tag{5}$$

where $\hat{c} = f_{MIL}(\{h_1, \ldots, h_N\}, \{\alpha_1, \ldots, \alpha_N\}; \phi)$, where α is the attention score (see Sect. 2.4), and ϕ represents learned model parameters.

2.4 Attention Mechanism

An attention mechanism is widely used in various deep learning tasks from semantic segmentation [4] to conversational question answering [23]. Ilse et al. [13] proposed an attention mechanism where a weighted average is calculated over the instance embeddings and these weights are learned by the neural network. If $H = \{h_1, \ldots, h_N\}$ is a bag of instance embeddings, attention based MIL pooling is defined as:

$$z = \sum_{k=1}^{N} \alpha_k h_k, \tag{6}$$

where

$$\alpha_k = \frac{\exp\{w^T \tanh(V h_k^T)\}}{\sum_{j=1}^{N} \exp\{w^T \tanh(V h_j^T)\}}. \tag{7}$$

V and w are parameters that are learned during the training. This attention scores α_k help the interpretability of the trained model by discovering the contribution of each instance in the drawn conclusion and acting as a similarity measure for comparison between the instances.

2.5 Overall Objective Function

One of the difficulties of MIL is sparse and vanishing gradients due to instance pooling. Here, we propose a dynamic loss function that incorporates the MIL loss along with the auxiliary SIC branch during the training using a decaying coefficient defined as follows:

$$\mathcal{L}(\theta, \phi, \psi) = (1 - \beta^{\mathrm{E}})\mathcal{L}_{\mathrm{MIL}} + \beta^{\mathrm{E}}\mathcal{L}_{\mathrm{SIC}}, \tag{8}$$

where β is a hyper-parameter, and E is the epoch index.

3   Experiments

We validated the proposed method on a dataset of bright-field microscopy images of human blood cell genetic disorders. We designed an ablation study as follows: (i) single instance classification (SIC), (ii) multiple instance learning (MIL) with maxpooling, (iii) MIL with maxpooling and the auxiliary SIC branch, and (iv) MIL with attention pooling and auxiliary SIC branch.

Dataset. All images are obtained by an Axiocam mounted on Axiovert 200m Zeiss microscope with a 100x objective. No preprocessing is done and cells are not stained. The data consists of patient samples acquired at different time points, or in different kinds of solutions. In each sample there are 4–12 images and each image contains 12–45 cells. The dataset contains four genetic morphological disorders: Thalassemia (3 patients, 25 samples), sickle cell disease (9 patients, 56 samples), PIEZO1 mutation (8 patients, 44 samples) and hereditary spherocytosis (13 patients, 89 samples). Also we have a healthy control group (26 individuals, 137 samples). We did patient-wise train and test split for a fair test set selection.

Patients previously diagnosed with hereditary spherocytosis were enrolled in the CoMMiTMenT-study (http://www.rare-anaemia.eu/). This study was approved by the Medical Ethical Research Board of the University Medical Center Utrecht, the Netherlands, under reference code 15/426M and by the Ethical Committee of Clinical Investigations of Hospital Clinic, Spain (IDIBAPS) under reference code 2013/8436. Genetic cause of the disease was identified by the research group of Richard van Wijk, University Medical Center Utrecht, the Netherlands. The healthy subjects study was approved by the ethics committees of the University of Heidelberg, Germany, (S-066/2018) and of the University of Berne, Switzerland (2018-01766), and was performed according to the Declaration of Helsinki.

Implementation Details. The proposed method consists of three components: multiple instance embedding, auxiliary SIC, attention & bag classifier. Figure 2 shows the architecture of the method.

The multiple instance embedding is a multi-layer convolutional neural network used for embedding features extracted by the R-CNN. It consists of five convolutional layers, a dropout layer with probability of 0.1 after the first convolution, a maxpooling layer and a fully connected layer that creates the representative 1-D embedding feature vector. These layers are common between both SIC and MIL branches and remain trainable by both branches.

An auxiliary single instance classifier looks at every instance embedding and tries to classify it with a fully connected layer. We chose a β equal to 0.5 to have a decaying contribution of this auxiliary branch during the training. Starting with a high contribution at the beginning and gradually reaching zero towards the end of the training.

Table 1. Comparison of the proposed method (MIL + att. + SIC) with other baselines. Mean and standard deviation for accuracy, weighted F1 score and average of area under ROC curve of all classes for five runs is shown.

Method	Accuracy	F1 score	AU ROC
SIC	0.50 ± 0.01	0.46 ± 0.01	0.743 ± 0.005
MIL + max	0.46 ± 0.04	0.33 ± 0.05	0.644 ± 0.049
MIL + max + SIC	0.70 ± 0.01	0.69 ± 0.11	0.916 ± 0.005
MIL + att. + SIC	$\mathbf{0.79 \pm 0.04}$	$\mathbf{0.78 \pm 0.01}$	$\mathbf{0.960 \pm 0.003}$

In the attention and bag classifier the matrix of embedded instance representations (H) is multiplied by the attention matrix. The attention matrix is dynamically generated based on H. After the multiplication bag classifier, a fully connected layer with softmax, does the final MIL classification.

Training. We decided to use threefold cross validation. Three different, independent models are trained based on each fold and performances are averaged. The models are trained by AMSGrad variation of Adam optimizer [19] with a learning rate of 0.0005 and the weight decay coefficient of 10^{-5}. Training continues for a maximum of 150 epochs with an early stopping if the MIL loss drops below a specific threshold (0.005) for five consecutive epochs. The same training parameters are used across all conducted experiments. Further details about hyper parameters and implementation details can be found in our repository under https://github.com/marrlab/attMIL.

Evaluation Metrics. Accuracy, macro F1 score and average area under the ROC and precision recall curves are used for comparison between different approaches.

Baselines. SIC is the baseline for our approach. We compare the results with a MIL without the designed auxiliary SIC branch and a MIL with a maxpooling method to our approach.

3.1   Ablation Study

All of the experiments were run for five times and the average metric with standard deviation is reported. For each of the experiments we report the accuracy, weighted F1 score and area under the ROC curve in Table 1. Additionally, in Fig. 3, the area under precision recall curve for all five classes is reported.

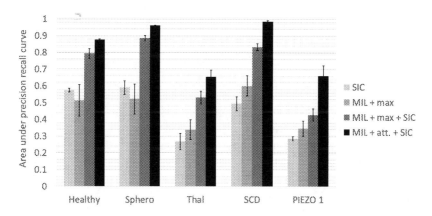

Fig. 3. Area under precision recall curve for all experiments and every class is demonstrated. We show mean and standard deviation of five runs.

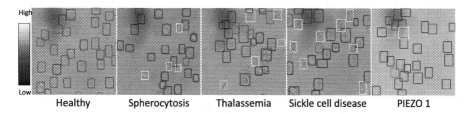

Fig. 4. Exemplary whole slide images with attention values, demonstrated with colored bounding boxes. White has the highest attention score while blue and dark blue are the lowest. (Color figure online)

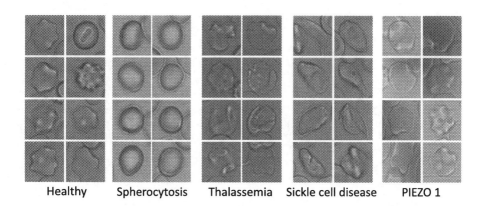

Fig. 5. Eight exemplary single cells per class with highest attention.

3.2   Qualitative Assessment and Interpretability

The attention mechanism allows us to have a qualitative evaluation of the model. Showing the cells contributing most to the classification can be beneficial for clinical adaptability of the model as it provides the experts with some explanation of the decisions made by the neural network. If cells receiving a high attention are known to be important for a specific morphological disorder, not only the model has learned them in an unsupervised manner but this also proves that the model actually knows what is relevant and what is not. Figure 4 shows cell attention in an exemplary image from samples belonging to each of the five classes.

Further, we extracted the top eight cells of a sample from every class in the dataset having the highest attention (Fig. 5). Cells are clearly morphologically different. It is interesting to note that for the healthy control class, cells that look a little bit odd received highest attentions as they might be flags for some disorders, although in the end they are not different enough to make the whole sample considered as a disorder. Note that the attention of healthy cells is generally lower than cells from disease samples (Fig. 4).

4   Conclusion

Our proposed approach based on MIL improves the performance of classification of the genetic blood disorders. The attention mechanism is effective both in terms of accuracy and interpretability of classification. The model automatically learns about diagnostic cells in the samples giving them a high attention. These results are promising and have great potential for decision support and clinical applications in terms of diagnosing blood diseases and training of medical students.

Possible future works can include uncertainty estimation of the classification [22], including an active learning framework [21] and using extra features in the attention. Additionally, detailed analysis on the shape of the cells receiving high attention might be informative about the underlying pathological mechanisms and severity of the disease manifestation. This might allow stratifying patients and targeted treatments in terms of personalized medicine, which is especially important for rare anemias such as spherocytosis and xerocytosis, but also for hemolytic anemia with poor response to conventional treatment [12].

Acknowledgments. C.M. and A.S. have received funding from the European Research Council (ERC) under the European Unions Horizon 2020 research and innovation programme (Grant agreement No. 866411). C.M. was supported by the BMBF, grant 01ZX1710A-F (Micmode-I2T). S.A. is supported by the PRIME programme of the German Academic Exchange Service (DAAD) with funds from the German Federal Ministry of Education and Research (BMBF).

References

1. Amores, J.: Multiple instance classification: review, taxonomy and comparative study. Artif. Intell. **201**, 81–105 (2013)

2. Bessis, M.: Corpuscles: Atlas of Red Blood Cell. Springer, Heidelberg (1974). https://doi.org/10.1007/978-3-642-65657-6

3. Campanella, G.: Clinical-grade computational pathology using weakly supervised deep learning on whole slide images. Nat. Med. **25**(8), 1301–1309 (2019)

4. Chen, L.C., Yang, Y., Wang, J., Xu, W., Yuille, A.L.: Attention to scale: scale-aware semantic image segmentation. In: The IEEE Conference on Computer Vision and Pattern Recognition (CVPR) (2016)

5. Conjeti, S., Paschali, M., Katouzian, A., Navab, N.: Deep multiple instance hashing for scalable medical image retrieval. In: Descoteaux, M., Maier-Hein, L., Franz, A., Jannin, P., Collins, D.L., Duchesne, S. (eds.) MICCAI 2017. LNCS, vol. 10435, pp. 550–558. Springer, Cham (2017). https://doi.org/10.1007/978-3-319-66179-7_63

6. Esteva, A., et al.: Dermatologist-level classification of skin cancer with deep neural networks. Nature **542**(7639), 115–118 (2017)

7. Gallagher, P.G.: Red cell membrane disorders. Hematology Am. Soc. Hematol. Educ. Program **2005**(1), 13–18 (2005). ASH Education Program Book

8. Gallagher, P.: Update on the clinical spectrum and genetics of red blood cell membrane disorders. Curr. Hematol. Rep. **3**(2), 85–91 (2004)

9. Grace, R.F., Glader, B.: Red blood cell enzyme disorders. Pediatr. Clin. **65**(3), 579–595 (2018)

10. He, K., Gkioxari, G., Dollár, P., Girshick, R.: Mask R-CNN. In: Proceedings of the IEEE International Conference on Computer Vision, pp. 2961–2969 (2017)

11. He, K., Zhang, X., Ren, S., Sun, J.: Deep residual learning for image recognition. In: Proceedings of the IEEE Conference on Computer Vision and Pattern Recognition, pp. 770–778 (2016)

12. Huisjes, R., et al.: Density, heterogeneity and deformability of red cells as markers of clinical severity in hereditary spherocytosis. Haematologica **105**(2), 338–347 (2020)

13. Ilse, M., Tomczak, J.M., Welling, M.: Attention-based deep multiple instance learning. arXiv preprint arXiv:1802.04712 (2018)

14. Distelmaier, L., Dührsen, U., Dickerhoff, R.: Sichelzellkrankheit. Der Internist **61**(7), 754–758 (2020). https://doi.org/10.1007/s00108-020-00822-z

15. Matek, C., Schwarz, S., Spiekermann, K., Marr, C.: Human-level recognition of blast cells in acute myeloid leukaemia with convolutional neural networks. Nat. Mach. Intell. **1**(11), 538–544 (2019)

16. McKinney, S.M.: International evaluation of an ai system for breast cancer screening. Nature **577**(7788), 89–94 (2020)

17. Ozdemir, O., Russell, R.L., Berlin, A.A.: A 3D probabilistic deep learning system for detection and diagnosis of lung cancer using low-dose CT scans. arXiv preprint arXiv:1902.03233 (2019)

18. Picard, V., et al.: Clinical and biological features in PIEZO1-hereditary xerocytosis and Gardos channelopathy: a retrospective series of 126 patients. Haematologica **104**(8), 1554–1564 (2019)

19. Reddi, S.J., Kale, S., Kumar, S.: On the convergence of ADAM and beyond. In: International Conference on Learning Representations (2018)

20. Sadafi, A., et al.: Multiclass deep active learning for detecting red blood cell subtypes in brightfield microscopy. In: Shen, D., et al. (eds.) MICCAI 2019. LNCS, vol. 11764, pp. 685–693. Springer, Cham (2019). https://doi.org/10.1007/978-3-030-32239-7_76

21. Settles, B., Craven, M., Ray, S.: Multiple-instance active learning. In: Advances in Neural Information Processing Systems, pp. 1289–1296 (2008)

22. Wang, X., et al.: UD-MIL: uncertainty-driven deep multiple instance learning for OCT image classification. IEEE J. Biomed. Health Inform. (2020)
23. Zhu, C., Zeng, M., Huang, X.: SDNet: Contextualized attention-based deep network for conversational question answering. arXiv preprint arXiv:1812.03593 (2018)

A Generative Modeling Approach for Interpreting Population-Level Variability in Brain Structure

Ran Liu[1]([✉]), Cem Subakan[2], Aishwarya H. Balwani[1], Jennifer Whitesell[3], Julie Harris[3], Sanmi Koyejo[4], and Eva L. Dyer[1,5]

[1] School of Electrical and Computer Engineering, Georgia Institute of Technology, Atlanta, USA
rliu361@gatech.edu
[2] Mila - Quebec Artificial Intelligence Institute, Montreal, Canada
[3] Neuroanatomy Division, Allen Institute for Brain Science, Seattle, USA
[4] Department of Computer Science, University of Illinois at Urbana Champaign, Urbana, USA
[5] Department of Biomedical Engineering, Georgia Institute of Technology, Atlanta, USA

Abstract. Understanding how neural structure varies across individuals is critical for characterizing the effects of disease, learning, and aging on the brain. However, disentangling the different factors that give rise to individual variability is still an outstanding challenge. In this paper, we introduce a deep generative modeling approach to find different modes of variation across many individuals. Our approach starts with training a variational autoencoder on a collection of auto-fluorescence images from a little over 1,700 mouse brains at 25 μm resolution. We then tap into the learned factors and validate the model's expressiveness, via a novel bidirectional technique that makes structured perturbations to both, the high-dimensional inputs of the network, as well as the low-dimensional latent variables in its bottleneck. Our results demonstrate that through coupling generative modeling frameworks with structured perturbations, it is possible to probe the latent space of the generative model to provide insights into the representations of brain structure formed in deep networks.

Keywords: Variational autoencoder · Interpretable deep learning · Brain architecture and neuroanatomy

1 Introduction

Understanding how disease, learning, or aging impact the structure of the brain is made difficult by the fact that neural structure varies across individuals [6,15].

Electronic supplementary material The online version of this chapter (https://doi.org/10.1007/978-3-030-59722-1_25) contains supplementary material, which is available to authorized users.

A. L. Martel et al. (Eds.): MICCAI 2020, LNCS 12265, pp. 257–266, 2020.
https://doi.org/10.1007/978-3-030-59722-1_25

Thus, there is a need for better ways to model individual variability that provide accurate detection of structural changes when they occur. Traditional approaches for modeling variability [5,6] require extensive domain knowledge to produce handcrafted features e.g., volumetric covariance descriptors over pre-specified regions of interest (ROIs) [14,20]. However, in high-resolution datasets where micron-scale anatomical features can be resolved, it is unclear i) which features best describe changes of interest across many brains, and ii) how to extract these features directly from images. Thus, unsupervised data-driven solutions for discovering variability across many brains are critical moving forward.

In this work, we introduce a deep learning model and strategy for interpreting population-level variability in high-resolution neuroimaging data (Fig. 1). Our model is a regularized variant of the variational autoencoder (VAE) called the β-VAE [3,8], and consists of an *encoder* and a *decoder* which work together to first distill complex images into a low dimensional latent space and next, expand this low-dimensional representation to generate high resolution images. Therefore, to gain insight into what the complete model has learned from the data, we take a *bi-directional* approach to characterizing how latent components are both, impacted by perturbations to specific regions in the input, via the encoder, and consequently impact specific regions of the generated output, via the decoder. Our work provides new strategies for understanding how different brain regions are mapped to latent variables within the network, an important step towards building an interpretable deep learning model that gives insight into how changes in different brain regions may contribute to population-level differences.

We applied this method to a collection of roughly 1,700 mouse brain images at 25 μm resolution from different individuals in the Allen Mouse Connectivity Atlas. By tuning the regularization strength in the β-VAE, we found that it is possible to both generate plausible brain imagery, as well as denoise images in the dataset that are corrupted by a number of artifacts. Our investigation into the latent space of this model also revealed a number of interesting findings; First, we found that information contained within the latent space is often asymmetric, with artifacts and noise being stored in one direction and biologically meaningful variance observed across many individuals in a separate direction within the same latent factor. Second, we found that multiple latent factors appear to generate outputs that vary within specific brain areas and thus have localized impact on generated outputs. Our results demonstrate that the proposed approach can be used to systematically find latent factors that are tuned to specific ROIs, and that generative modeling approaches can be used to reveal informative components of individual variability.

The contributions of this paper include: (i) the creation and specification of a β-VAE that can model high-resolution structural brain images, (ii) a bi-directional approach for revealing relationships between brain regions and latent factors in a deep generative network, and (iii) demonstration that structured perturbations to both image inputs and the latent space can reveal biologically meaningful variability.[1]

---

[1] Code and visualization can be found at: https://nerdslab.github.io/brainsynth/

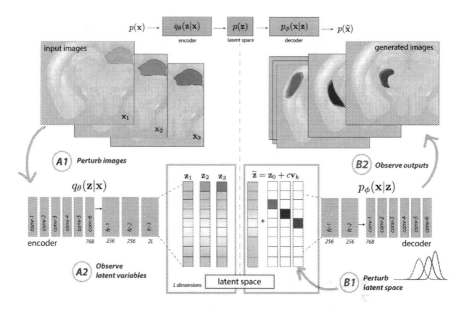

Fig. 1. *Visualization of our bi-directional approach for analyzing variational autoencoders trained to generate brain imagery.* On the left, we show a specific ROI being manipulated in a collection of input images (A1) and how this perturbation might result in a distinct shift in the latent representations (A2) formed from these inputs. On the right, we show the reverse process, where we perturb the latent space (B1) and observe the generated output images (B2).

2   Methods

2.1   Model Details

Low-dimensional models are used throughout machine learning to represent complex data with only a small set of latent variables. In deep learning, a bottleneck, i.e., layer with small width inside the neural network, often enforces a low-dimensional modeling of data. The VAE couples an autoencoder architecture [9,18] with a variational objective, thus providing a probabilistic view towards the generation of new high-dimensional data samples [10,17]. Much like regular autoencoders, VAEs embed information from the image space $\mathcal{X}$ into a latent space $\mathcal{Z}$ with latent dimension L via an encoder, and transform elements from the latent space into those in the image space via a decoder. The relationship between the encoder, decoder, and latent space can be written as:

$$\text{Encoder}: q(\mathbf{z}|\mathbf{x})p(\mathbf{x}) \mapsto p(\mathbf{z}), \quad \text{Decoder}: q(\mathbf{x}|\mathbf{z})p(\mathbf{z}) \mapsto q(\hat{\mathbf{x}}), \qquad (1)$$

where $p(\mathbf{x})$ denotes our dataset's distribution over the high-dimensional image space, $q(\mathbf{z}|\mathbf{x})$ and $q(\mathbf{x}|\mathbf{z})$ are, respectively, the distribution of the estimated encoder and estimated decoder, and $p(\mathbf{z})$ is the assumed prior on latent variables[2].

To train a good encoder (θ) and decoder (ϕ), the VAE aims to maximize the following objective:

$$\mathcal{L}(\theta, \phi; \mathbf{x}, \mathbf{z}) = \mathbb{E}_{q_\phi(\mathbf{z}|\mathbf{x})}[\log p_\theta(\mathbf{x}|\mathbf{z})] - \beta D_{KL}(q_\phi(\mathbf{z}|\mathbf{x})\|p(\mathbf{z})). \tag{2}$$

The first term measures the likelihood of the reconstructed samples and the second term measures the KL-divergence between the estimated posterior distribution $q_\phi(\mathbf{z}|\mathbf{x})$ and the assumed prior distribution. When $\beta = 1$, the model simplifies to a vanilla-VAE, whereas when β is a free parameter, the resulting model is referred to as the β-VAE [8]. Increasing the value of β encourages a certain degree of clustering, whereas lowering it encourages dispersion of similar elements in the latent space. Thus, by tuning β correctly, the model can learn to disentangle latent factors [3,8].

In our experiments, we used a β-VAE with a deep convolutional structure mimicking the DC-GAN architecture [16] (Fig. 1). Our encoder had seven convolutional layers followed by three fully connected layers and used the ReLU activation function throughout. The same structure was mirrored for the decoder. The learning rate and batch size were set to 2e−4 and 64 respectively, resulting in a training time of roughly 4 h on an Nvidia Titan RTX. After performing a grid search ($\beta = 1$–20, $L = 4$–20), we selected $L = 8$ and $\beta = 3$ as our model hyper-parameters since they exhibited performance that was relatively stable (i.e., these parameters produced an inflection point in evaluation metrics). The vanilla VAE's performance also exhibits an inflection point at the same latent dimension, which further confirmed that this choice holds for different amounts of regularization. In contrast, PCA continues to decrease its approximation error with higher dimensions; however, high-variance artifacts and other sources of noise are very quickly incorporated into the model when the bottleneck size increases beyond 30 dimensions.

2.2 Bi-directional Latent Space Analysis

As images in our dataset are spatially aligned to an atlas, understanding how different regions of the pixel space are mapped to latent variables within the network can be a critical first step in building an interpretable model that gives insight into how different brain regions may contribute to population-level differences. To do this, we present a bi-directional approach to investigate the interaction between the image space and the β-VAE's latent space (see Fig. 1). By understanding how the encoder and decoder work together to represent spatial changes in the data, we can build a more informed look into how brain structure can be modeled effectively within deep networks [11,21].

In one direction, we can map a latent variable's *receptive field* (left, Fig. 1), i.e. which pixels in the input space impact each latent factor's activations. If

---

[2] For simplicity, the prior is typically assumed to be Gaussian, $\mathbf{z} \sim \mathcal{N}(0, \boldsymbol{I})$.

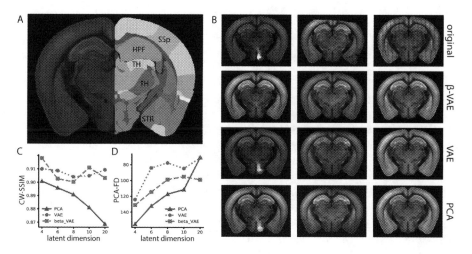

Fig. 2. *Evaluation of image synthesis and denoising performance.* **(A)** The left half of the image shows the average brain template and on the right, we display simplified annotations for different regions of interest, including somatosensory cortex (SSp), hippocampal formation (HPF), striatum (STR), and parts of the thalamus (TH). **(B)** Examples of corrupted images with physical sectioning and grid-like artifacts along the top row. Below, we display the reconstructions obtained using a β-VAE, VAE, and PCA. The CW-SSIM and PCA-based FD scores for all three models are compared in **(C)** and **(D)**, respectively. (Color figure online)

changing the content of a region of the input image does not impact a specific unit, then the manipulated region is not in the unit's receptive field. To model this perturbation, let $\widetilde{\mathbf{x}} = \mathbf{x}_0 + w\mathbf{p}_\ell$ denote the perturbed input image, where $\mathbf{x}_0$ is the original image, $\mathbf{p}_\ell$ is a region specific (spatially localized ROI) perturbation, and w is the perturbation weight. By designing these perturbations to examine the responses of the units to changes in specific brain regions of interest, we can study the regional specificity of different units.

In the other direction, we can map a latent variable's *projective field* (right, Fig. 1), or the parts of space that a latent variable affects when a new image is generated. To make this precise, let $\mathbf{v}_k$ be a canonical basis vector with a one in the kth entry and zeros otherwise, c denote the interpolation weight, and $\mathbf{z}_0$ be the distribution mean. To generate an output image, we will first define the latent representation as $\widetilde{\mathbf{z}} = \mathbf{z}_0 + c\mathbf{v}_k$, and then pass this representation through the decoder to generate an image. We can use this synthesis approach to estimate the spatial extent of each factor's projective field by producing outputs across a range of different interpolation weights and then computing the variance of each pixel in the generated images.

3 Results

3.1 Dataset and Pre-processing

To build a generative model of brain structure, we utilized registered images from 1,723 individuals within the Allen Institute for Brain Science's (AIBS) Mouse Connectivity Atlas [13].[2] The connectivity atlas consists of 3D image volumes acquired using serial 2-photon tomography (STP) collected from whole mouse brains (0.35 μm × 0.35 μm × 100 μm resolution, 1 TB per experiment). Rather than using the fluorescence signal obtained from the viral tracing experiments (green channel), we obtained the auto-fluorescence signal acquired from each of the injected brains (red channel), which captures brain structure and information about overall cell density and axonal projection patterns. Our models were trained on 2D coronal sections extracted from near the middle of the brain (slice 286 out of 528) in each of the individuals in our dataset. This particular coronal slice was selected because it reveals key brain areas, including the hippocampus (HPF), regions of thalamus (TH), and parts of striatum (STR) (Fig. 2A). The images were then downsampled from 0.35 μm to 25 μm, and centre-cropped to produce an image of size 320 × 448. In order to mitigate the effects of leakage of fluorescence signal, we pre-processed the data by adjusting each image's overall brightness to the dataset's average brightness and then set high intensity pixels 3.8 times over the average to this maximum value.

3.2 Evaluations and Comparisons

To evaluate the image generation capability of our β-VAE model, we compared its performance with a vanilla-VAE and PCA. We first sought to examine each model by seeing how it performed when supplied with images containing three different types of artifacts: (i) corrupted bright areas due to leakage from the fluorescence signal's green channel, (ii) physical sectioning artifacts (missing data), and (iii) grid artifacts from scanning (Fig. 2B, Supplementary Material Sect. 1). In these and other examples, we found that the β-VAE did the best job of removing artifacts from data while still preserving relevant biological variance. The ability of the β-VAE to reject artifacts is particularly pronounced in the case of classes (i, ii), where both PCA and VAE fail to reject the signal leaking into the channel of interest and cannot recover missing data. We observe that the β-VAE tends to learn a more accurate distribution over the dataset, while the vanilla-VAE overfits to the noise, and PCA does not deviate much from the mean in terms of its structural details.

To quantify the quality of images generated by the different models, we computed two metrics used to evaluate generative model outputs viz. the complex wavelet structural similarity (CW-SSIM) [19] (Supplementary Material Subsect. 1.1), and the PCA-based Frechet distance (PCA-FD) [7,12] (Supplementary Material Sect. 1.2). When studying these metrics for different bottleneck

---

[2] The MCA is accessible through the Allen Institute's Python-based SDK [1] (http://connectivity.brain-map.org/).

sizes, we found that both for the β-VAE and the vanilla-VAE, latent dimensions in the range $L = 8$–10 produced stable performance (where scores plateau) before decreasing in accuracy. Analysis of the CW-SSIM scores along with visual inspection of the generated images, revealed that PCA is unable to capture high-dimensional textural details for low dimensions and quickly begins to represents artifacts and noise when the size of the latent space is increased. The PCA-FD scores, on the other hand, suggest that both VAE models capture more variability across the data and better match the overall global distribution of population-level variance. However, the β-VAE appears to successfully capture variability without reconstructing artifacts due to the explicit regularization that we utilized in training. These results provide initial evidence that regularization, in this case with a β-VAE model, is helpful for striking a balance between denoising, representing fine scale structures, and capturing the data's global distributional properties.

3.3   Interpreting the Latent Factors

After confirming that our model can generate high quality images and denoise data, we next explored its interpretability with the bi-directional analysis method described in Sect. 2.2 (Fig. 1). We first examined the *projective field* of each latent factor. In this case, our goal was to produce three heatmaps to reveal which parts of the image space are impacted by changing a specific latent factor with either a (i) a small negative, (ii) small positive, or (iii) a large interpolation weight. Sorting the interpolations in this way allows us to generate three images that can be stacked into different channels of a color image to visualize the impact of all three types of perturbations on the image domain jointly (Fig. 3A). Upon further inspection of the images that resulted from this analysis (Supplementary Material Sect. 4), we observed that localized noise artifacts (type i) were synthesized at the extrema of the interpolation space. Interestingly, we observed asymmetries in the representations: Type (i) artifacts, while not usually recovered by the decoder, were more likely recapitulated when moving far into the space of negative interpolation weights (Supplementary Material Sect. 4). In contrast, small interpolation weights appeared to highlight biologically meaningful variance that aligns with key ROIs including the barrel fields of somatosensory cortex, hippocampus, and retrosplenial areas in cortex. These results provide initial evidence that VAE models can be used to decompose biological variability in complex data, even in the presence of different types of noise and artifacts.

We next asked whether we could understand properties about each unit's *receptive field*. To do so, we selected a set of high-quality images without obvious artifacts, applied masks to remove all content from different ROIs, and then modulated their intensity with perturbation weights w. We fed these perturbed images into the encoder (Supplementary Material Sect. 2), computed the latent representations, and fit a Gaussian to the resulting latent codes across all image examples ($n = 832$) (Fig. 3C, Supplementary Material Sect. 3). The results of this perturbation analysis revealed multiple units that are strongly modulated by changes in some brain regions but not others, and that exhibit localized receptive

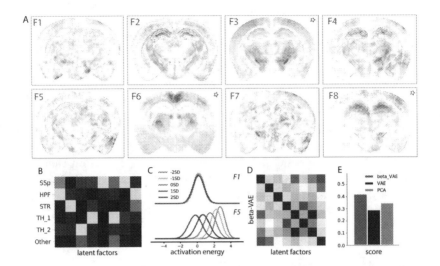

Fig. 3. *Model interpretation.* **(A)** A visualization of how changing a latent factor impacts the generated output images. Here, cyan and magenta represent the pixel level variance in images generated from interpolation weights in the quartile above and below average, respectively, and yellow represents pixels that vary with high interpolation weights. For all factors, the interpolation weight is varied from $[-7, 7]$ with a step size of 0.005. **(B)** For each ROI, we compute the KL-divergence between each factor's response to extreme ROI specific perturbations (blue is low impact, yellow is high impact). **(C)** We show how perturbing the image brightness in HPF region impacts the activation distribution for two factors (F1, F5). **(D)** The covariance of the impact matrix in (B) measures the similarity between how different latent variables impact specific ROIs. **(E)** The disentanglement score for PCA, the VAE, and β-VAE provide a measure of how uncorrelated factors are in terms of their impact on specific brain regions. (Color figure online)

fields. We found that perturbations to the hippocampus (HPF) impacted almost all of the latent variables, and striatum also has wide reaching impacts. This seems to align with the fact that variability in these areas is more complex and thus it is necessary to encode this variance over multiple factors.

The impact of perturbing a specific ROI on a latent factor could be further quantified by computing the KL-divergence between the activation distributions for two extreme perturbations (strong negative or positive scaling of missing data in ROI). We computed this *impact score* for all 6 brain ROIs and all 8 latent factors in the trained network (displayed as a 6×8 matrix in Fig. 3B, further visualized in Fig. 3C). This matrix quantifies the impact that missing information from a ROI has on activations in each latent variable in the model. One interesting result from our analysis is that, in some cases, the receptive field and projective field may not be spatially aligned (see Factor 8, HPF). Our results reveal that receptive and projective fields can be asymmetric, and thus it is critical to map input-output relationships from the image space to the latent space and back again.

To quantify the separability or *disentanglement* of a model's latent space relative to known brain structures, we examined whether regional perturbations impact different factors in unique ways. We thus computed the covariance between each latent factor's impact scores to reveal their similarity and defined the disentanglement score s as a measure of how far this matrix is from diagonal, where $s = Tr(\mathbf{A})/(\sum_{ij} \mathbf{A}_{ij} - Tr(\mathbf{A}))$ and $\mathbf{A}$ denotes the covariance matrix of interest. A comparison between the β-VAE, VAE, and PCA in terms of their scores revealed that the β-VAE achieved the best disentanglement among three models (Fig. 3E). This provides evidence that the β-VAE model can capture variance across a few key brain areas while also providing good separation across different latent factors. In contrast, the vanilla-VAE appears to have factors with much lower disentanglement. PCA on the other hand, provides better disentanglement due to its orthogonality constraints but still doesn't separate brain areas as well as the β-VAE model.

4   Discussion

This work presents a novel data-driven approach for learning population-level differences across high-resolution microscopy images collected from many individuals. Our key contribution is a new method for interpreting factors that drive variance in a deep generative model for brain image synthesis.

In our current study, we used a β-VAE model because of its simplicity and flexibility; however, there are other interpretable VAE variants that have been proposed to facilitate disentanglement [3, 4, 21] that we could apply our approach to. As our interpretability approach is quite general, one could also potentially use it to visualize and interpret latent representations and/or biomarkers found in other instances of representation learning in neuroscience [2] and medical imaging [15]. Moving forward, interpretability approaches that can probe and model collective responses across many units will be important for revealing complex interactions between features, as well as inspiring new approaches for modeling variability in large high-dimensional datasets.

Acknowledgements:. This work was supported by NSF award number IIS-1755871 (ELD, AHB), an Alfred P. Sloan Fellowship (ELD, RL), and NIH Award No. 1R24MH114799-01 (ELD).

References

1. Allen Institute for Brain Science: Allen Mouse Brain Connectivity Atlas. connectivity.brain-map.org (2011)
2. Balwani, A.H., Dyer, E.L.: A deep feature learning approach for mapping the brain's microarchitecture and organization. bioRxiv (2020)
3. Burgess, C.P., et al.: Understanding disentangling in β-VAE. arXiv preprint arXiv:1804.03599 (2018)

4. Chen, T.Q., Li, X., Grosse, R.B., Duvenaud, D.K.: Isolating sources of disentanglement in variational autoencoders. In: Advances in Neural Information Processing Systems, pp. 2610–2620 (2018)
5. DuPre, E., Spreng, R.N.: Structural covariance networks across the life span, from 6 to 94 years of age. Netw. Neurosci. **1**(3), 302–323 (2017)
6. Hafkemeijer, A.: Differences in structural covariance brain networks between behavioral variant frontotemporal dementia and Alzheimer's disease. Hum. Brain Mapp. **37**(3), 978–988 (2016)
7. Heusel, M., Ramsauer, H., Unterthiner, T., Nessler, B., Hochreiter, S.: GANs trained by a two time-scale update rule converge to a local Nash equilibrium. In: Advances in Neural Information Processing Systems, pp. 6626–6637 (2017)
8. Higgins, I., et al.: β-VAE: learning basic visual concepts with a constrained variational framework. In: International Conference on Learning Representations, vol. 2, no. 5, p. 6 (2017)
9. Hinton, G.E., Salakhutdinov, R.R.: Reducing the dimensionality of data with neural networks. Science **313**(5786), 504–507 (2006)
10. Kingma, D.P., Welling, M.: Auto-encoding variational Bayes. arXiv preprint arXiv:1312.6114 (2013)
11. Locatello, F., et al.: Challenging common assumptions in the unsupervised learning of disentangled representations. In: International Conference on Machine Learning, pp. 4114–4124 (2019)
12. Lucic, M., Kurach, K., Michalski, M., Gelly, S., Bousquet, O.: Are GANs created equal? A large-scale study. In: Advances in Neural Information Processing Systems, pp. 700–709 (2018)
13. Oh, S.W.: A mesoscale connectome of the mouse brain. Nature **508**(7495), 207 (2014)
14. Pagani, M., Bifone, A., Gozzi, A.: Structural covariance networks in the mouse brain. NeuroImage **129**, 55–63 (2016)
15. Prescott, J.W.: Quantitative imaging biomarkers: the application of advanced image processing and analysis to clinical and preclinical decision making. J. Digit. Imaging **26**(1), 97–108 (2013)
16. Radford, A., Metz, L., Chintala, S.: Unsupervised representation learning with deep convolutional generative adversarial networks. arXiv preprint arXiv:1511.06434 (2015)
17. Rezende, D.J., Mohamed, S., Wierstra, D.: Stochastic backpropagation and approximate inference in deep generative models. In: International Conference on Machine Learning, pp. 1278–1286 (2014)
18. Rifai, S., Vincent, P., Muller, X., Glorot, X., Bengio, Y.: Contractive auto-encoders: explicit invariance during feature extraction. In: International Conference on Machine Learning, pp. 833–840 (2011)
19. Sampat, M.P., Wang, Z., Gupta, S., Bovik, A.C., Markey, M.K.: Complex wavelet structural similarity: a new image similarity index. IEEE Trans. Image Process. **18**(11), 2385–2401 (2009)
20. Vandenberghe, M.E.: High-throughput 3D whole-brain quantitative histopathology in rodents. Sci. Rep. **6**, 20958 (2016)
21. Zhao, S., Song, J., Ermon, S.: InfoVAE: balancing learning and inference in variational autoencoders. Proc. AAAI Conf. Artif. Intell. **33**, 5885–5892 (2019)

Processing-Aware Real-Time Rendering for Optimized Tissue Visualization in Intraoperative 4D OCT

Jakob Weiss[1]([envelope])(iD), Michael Sommersperger[1,4], Ali Nasseri[2], Abouzar Eslami[3], Ulrich Eck[1], and Nassir Navab[1,4]

[1] Technical University of Munich, Munich, Germany
jakob.weiss@tum.de
[2] Klinikum Rechts der Isar, Augenklinik, Munich, Germany
[3] Carl Zeiss Meditec AG, Munich, Germany
[4] Johns Hopkins University, Baltimore, USA

Abstract. Intraoperative Optical Coherence Tomography (iOCT) has advanced in recent years to provide real-time high resolution volumetric imaging for ophthalmic surgery. It enables real-time 3D feedback during precise surgical maneuvers. Intraoperative 4D OCT generally exhibits lower signal-to-noise ratio compared to diagnostic OCT and visualization is complicated by instrument shadows occluding retinal tissue. Additional constraints of processing data rates upwards of 6 GB/s create unique challenges for advanced visualization of 4D OCT. Prior approaches for real-time 4D iOCT rendering have been limited to applying simple denoising filters and colorization to improve visualization.

We present a novel real-time rendering pipeline that provides enhanced intraoperative visualization and is specifically designed for the high data rates of 4D iOCT. We decompose the volume into a static part consisting of the retinal tissue and a dynamic part including the instrument. Aligning the static parts over time allows temporal compounding of these structures for improved image quality. We employ a translational motion model and use axial projection images to reduce the dimensionality of the alignment. A model-based instrument segmentation on the projections discriminates static from dynamic parts and is used to exclude instruments from the compounding. Our real-time rendering method combines the compounded static information with the latest iOCT data to provide a visualization which compensates instrument shadows and improves instrument visibility.

We evaluate the individual parts of our pipeline on pre-recorded OCT volumes and demonstrate the effectiveness of our method on a recorded volume sequence with a moving retinal forceps.

Keywords: Advanced intraoperative visualization · Optical Coherence Tomography · Real-time volumetric processing

Electronic supplementary material The online version of this chapter (https://doi.org/10.1007/978-3-030-59722-1_26) contains supplementary material, which is available to authorized users.

© Springer Nature Switzerland AG 2020
A. L. Martel et al. (Eds.): MICCAI 2020, LNCS 12265, pp. 267–276, 2020.
https://doi.org/10.1007/978-3-030-59722-1_26

Fig. 1. Challenges and our solution to 4D iOCT rendering: Straightforward DVR *(left)* is not sufficient for good visualization and advanced color schemes [17] *(middle)* do not cope well with noise and artifacts. Our novel method *(right)* reduces noise and artifacts and extends the field of view. All images were rendered with the same opacity transfer function. See Supplementary Material for a high-resolution version.

1 Introduction

Intraoperative Optical Coherence Tomography (iOCT) in ophthalmology has seen dramatic technical advances in imaging speed and quality in recent years. Technological advances such as the application of swept-source lasers [8], spectral splitting [7] and linear velocity spiral scanning [3] have made continuous 4D intraoperative OCT imaging feasible at high resolution and volume rates. State of the art systems are able to sample with volume rates of up to 24.2 Hz at a resolution of $330 \times 330 \times 595$ voxels [9]. Ehlers et al. [4] have shown the effectiveness of 2D iOCT in clinical practice in a large scale study, however clinical studies on 4D OCT do not yet exist. Still, 4D OCT is expected to improve spatial visualization during complex and precise maneuvers. Potential applications include robotics [18] or even retinal surgery under exclusive OCT guidance [9] which can greatly reduce adverse effects associated with the endoilluminators required for traditional fundus view surgery. With data rates surpassing 6 GB/s, 4D iOCT is a uniquely challenging modality for advanced processing in an intraoperative setting. OCT-only surgery is currently challenged also by higher noise level compared to diagnostic OCT, instrument shadows hiding relevant anatomical structures and a limited field of view.

In this work, we propose a real-time processing and rendering pipeline to improve instrument visibility by combining volumes temporally. A semantic segmentation step allows to discern static retinal tissue, which is then used to register subsequent volumes and selectively mitigate instrument shadows. We propose an adaptive visualization that makes the involved processing steps apparent to the viewer.

To improve quality in diagnostic OCT, repeated scanning of B-scans is employed to reduce noise by averaging [1,15]. Because this approach would reduce volume rates to impractical speeds, a similar solution is to average subsequent volumes, however this requires some form of motion compensation. Previous works on OCT motion compensation are focused on motion during acquisition of a single volume [10] or on registering diagnostic OCT volumes acquired at different visits for progression analysis. 3D SIFT features [12] have been used for full 3D registration but many approaches use 2D projections generated from volumes to perform separate alignment across dimensions using ICP [13], SIFT [6] or SURF [14]. To the best of our knowledge, there is no published research on solving the problem with the additional constraints of real-time processing and a potentially moving surgical instrument.

Metallic instruments pose an additional challenge to iOCT visualization, causing total loss of signal below the instrument due to the metal blocking the light. This shadows relevant retinal tissue below the instrument, causing "holes" in the 3D rendering. Special OCT-compatible instruments have been proposed [5], but are not yet translated to clinical practice. Effective visualization of iOCT volumes is not trivial due to the aforementioned problems, which is why straightforward methods like direct volume rendering (DVR) with intensity-based transfer functions perform badly (c.f. Fig. 1, *left*). Viehland et al. [16] introduced a DVR method for OCT that was extended by Draelos et al. [2] to add colorization along the axial direction. Both however rely on spatial filtering with Gaussian and median filters to reduce noise prior to rendering. Recently, Weiss et al. [17] introduced a layer-aware volume rendering in which a layer segmentation was used to anchor a color map to improve perception (c.f. Fig. 1, *middle*). In this work, our aim is to show the feasibility of advanced real-time processing and visualization for 4D iOCT. Our novel real-time processing and rendering method combines temporal information and mitigates instrument opacity (c.f. Fig. 1, *right*).

Our contributions are the following: We introduce a fast registration and compositing method that temporally combines the static parts within the OCT view. This is supported by a learning-based instrument segmentation in 2D projection images. We then propose a processing-aware rendering method that optimizes tissue visibility by inpainting shadowed areas, ensuring interpretability of the view through sensible color mapping.

2   Methods

Our visualization was built around the two goals of reducing imaging noise over time and using data from previous frames to fill in the gaps produced by instrument shadowing. The approach is based on the notion that with 4D iOCT, retinal tissue is imaged many times while remaining relatively unchanged. Therefore, we discriminate the retinal tissue to align it over time and use the aggregated information to improve our visualization. Due to the high data rates and time constraints we rely on processing 2D projection images instead of 3D volumes.

Our novel method consists of several steps (see Fig. 2): To initialize our algorithm, a larger reference volume is acquired to prime our compounding volume I_c and establish a reference. For each newly acquired volume I_a and once for the reference volume, we generate a set of 2D projection images and use a learning-based approach to find a tissue mask M_t by segmenting instruments in 2D. The

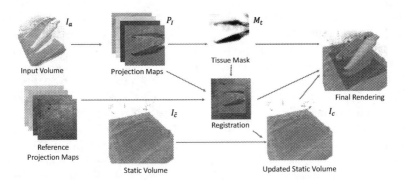

Fig. 2. Our processing pipeline for a single new acquired volume. Reference projection maps are generated from an overview scan at acquisition start.

masked projection images are then used to register the I_a to I_c. The registration together with M_t allows us to maintain an updated representation of the static retinal tissue while excluding the instrument and shadows. Finally, our enhanced rendering selectively combines the two volumes to provide an responsive visualization. We leverage the instrument mask and projection images to combine I_c and I_a on the fly during rendering and adapt the rendering parameters, encoding the reliability of the information through color.

2.1   Axial Projection Images

Axial projection images are a class of 2D images that we generate from projecting every A-scan in the volume to a single corresponding value. Averaging projections have been used extensively in the past [6,13,14] as so-called *Enface* images. We generalize them to new functions which create 2D feature maps $P(x, y)$ with different characteristics that we use for alignment and instrument segmentation:

$$P_{\text{avg}}(x, y) = \frac{1}{N} \sum_z I(x, y, z), \tag{1a}$$

$$P_{\text{max}}(x, y) = \max_z I(x, y, z), \tag{1b}$$

$$P_{\text{argmax}}(x, y) = \arg\max_z I(x, y, z), \tag{1c}$$

$$P_{\text{centr}}(x, y) = \sum_z z I(x, y, z) / \sum_z I(x, y, z) \tag{1d}$$

where N is the number of samples in one A-scan.

Note that while *Average* and *Maximum* encode intensity features, *Argmax* and *Centroid* provide positional information while they can still be computed simultaneously in a single iteration over the A-Scan voxels.

2.2   Learning-Based Instrument Segmentation

A tissue mask M_t is obtained from the 2D projections by training a simple and lightweight segmentation model. We use the pytorch-based fast.ai library to train a UNet variant[1] that uses a ResNet18-based encoder that was pretrained on ImageNet connected to a decoder with skip connections to perform subsequent upsampling. All four available projection images are provided as input features to the network to maximize accuracy.

2.3   Registration

To combine the sequence of volumes, it is required to know for every voxel the corresponding location in the compounded volume. During a surgery, the imaged region can change over time due to systematic changes of the galvo offsets, but also due to relative movement of the patient's eye.

Motion Model. With the eye anaesthetized and fixed in the eye socket, rotations generally only occur during brief, intentional adjustments of the view by the surgeon. During precise manipulation in which our OCT image guidance is used, the surgeon actively stabilizes the eye and thus we adjust one d.o.f. less than [14]. Due to our exponential averaging, only the most recent few volumes influence the displayed result. Analyzing DS3 (see Sect. 3) using offline volumetric registration confirms that axial rotation is negligible in our data set as rotation between consecutive volumes is below $0.5°$. We approximate the motion as a pure translational change in the OCT coordinate system. Two corresponding positions in reference and acquired volume p_r, p_a are related by $p_r = p_a + t_a$. We further decompose the translation t_a can be decomposed into the transverse translation (t_x, t_y) (mainly caused by rotational movement of the eye around its center) and the axial translation t_z (typically caused by inadvertent pressure on the trocars pushing the eye into or out of the eye socket).

Transverse Alignment. Because the transverse alignment (t_x, t_y) is aligned with the layout of the generated projection images P_r, P_a, we can find the best alignment using template matching with normalized cross correlation (NCC) as a metric. To find the transverse alignment, we compute the location of maximum NCC between P_r and P_a using M_t to mask instrument pixels in the template.

Axial Alignment. To find the axial alignment t_z, we use the P_{argmax} images in the region where the two images overlap based on (t_x, t_y). We compute the average distance across the overlap region O while taking into account the tissue mask M_t of the current image:

$$t_z = \sum_{p \in O} M_t(p) \left(P_{r,\text{argmax}}(p) - P_{a,\text{argmax}}(p)\right) / \sum_{p \in O} M_t(p) \qquad (2)$$

---

[1] https://docs.fast.ai/vision.models.unet.html.

2.4 Compounding

With a known transformation we can integrate the new volume I_a in our compounded representation I_c of the static scene:

$$I_c(p) = \omega(p)I_a(p + t_a) + (1 - \omega(p))I_{\bar{c}}(p) \tag{3}$$

for every voxel position p in I_c where $\omega = \omega_0 M_t(p)$ and ω_0 is a integration weighting parameter used to control the amount of exponential averaging over time. The update conditionally integrates new data for A-Scans where M_t is not set while retaining data from the previous compounded volume $I_{\bar{c}}$ otherwise. Using the M_t in the integration weighting masks out A-scans containing the instrument while averaging the retinal tissue.

2.5 Rendering

To provide a well interpretable rendering that makes the user apparent of the reliability of the shown data, we use an adaptive colorization that extends the color map by Weiss [17]. Our goal is to emphasize which parts of the volume are from the last acquired volume and visually set apart data that has been inpainted from previous data. Thus, we differentiate three semantic regions within our volumes: *(a)* data that has been recently updated or is sampled directly from I_a, *(b)* data that has been inpainted from the I_c with no correspondence in I_a and *(c)* areas around the instrument. When determining the sample intensity I_s for a raymarch step position p_s, we combine I_c and I_a using an instrument predicate κ_i and a recency predicate κ_r defined as:

$$\kappa_i(p) = \neg M_t(p) \wedge |p_z - P_{\mathrm{ArgMax}}(p)| < d_i, \tag{4a}$$

$$\kappa_r(p) = M_t(p) \wedge I_a(p) > I_c(p). \tag{4b}$$

In A-scans that contain an instrument, we combine the intensities of both volumes with a max operation. The max operation ensures visibility of both instrument and inpainted tissue in areas of signal loss:

$$I_s(p_s) = \begin{cases} I_c(p_s) & \text{if } \kappa_s(p) \\ max(I_c(p_s), I_a(p_s)) & \text{otherwise.} \end{cases} \tag{5}$$

The recency predicate therefore marks sampled locations in which I_s was influenced by the most recently acquired volume, either because it was incorporated into the compounding (Eq. 3) or used directly (Eq. 5). In tissue regions, we apply the same layer colorization $C_{\mathrm{LAB}}(I, \delta^*(p))$ as [17]. We compensate for the lack of a layer segmentation by instead using P_{argmax} to align the axial color mapping to the retinal structure. Furthermore, the colorization is only applied for pixels that have not been inpainted from the compounded volume, using a grayscale colormap for this data instead. For instrument areas, we use a fixed color C_i to further enhance instrument visibility and contrast to the surrounding tissue (Fig. 1).

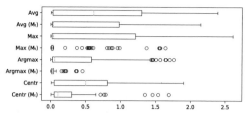

Table 1. Comparison of projection images in terms of their registration performance using M_t (errors in mm).

Projection	Avg error	RMSE	Std dev
Average	0.5379	0.6743	0.6516
Maximum	0.1394	0.2034	0.3329
Argmax	**0.0426**	**0.0583**	**0.0675**
Centroid	0.2128	0.2985	0.2817

Fig. 3. Registration error (in mm) without using a tool mask compared to the registration error using M_t.

$$C_s(p_s) = \begin{cases} C_i & \text{if } \kappa_i(p_s) \\ (I_s, I_s, I_s) & \text{if } \neg\kappa_r(p_s) \\ C_{\text{LAB}}(I_s, \delta^*(p)) & \text{otherwise.} \end{cases} \tag{6}$$

3 Results

As state of the art 4D iOCT systems are not readily available, the three data sets used in this work were instead recorded with a RESCAN 700 (Carl Zeiss Meditec) iOCT system (27 kHz A-Scan rate) which acquires volumes of $512 \times 128 \times 1024$ resolution at non-interactive rates. **DS1** consists of projection images from 605 retinal OCT scans containing a range of different instruments and situations in human or porcine eyes. We generated projection images as described in Sect. 2.1, resample them to 128×128 px and manually labeled the instruments. **DS2** consists of $3 \times 3 \times 2.9$ mm^3 OCT volumes from 6 enucleated porcine eyes with removed anterior segment. On a fixated eye, a $6 \times 6 \times 2.9$ mm^3 reference volume and grids of 5×5 volumes were acquired with 0.25 mm offset in x/y dimensions by changing the OCT acquisition offset. In three eyes, a 23G vitreoretinal forceps was used, in the remaining three a 27G injection needle. **DS3** is a sequence of 67 volumes from an enucleated porcine eye with intact anterior segment. The first volume is acquired at $6 \times 6 \times 2.9$ mm^3 while the following are recorded with $3 \times 3 \times 2.9$ mm^3 field of view. A surgical instrument (23G retinal forceps) was moved between acquisitions to create a simulated 4D OCT sequence that shows instrument and retina motion as described in Sect. 2.3.

Registration. To evaluate our registration approach, we use the known relative offsets between volumes in **DS2**. We use the reference volume of each eye and register each of the 25 grid volumes to it using our approach. Figure 3 shows the registration error $e_r = \sqrt{d_x^2 + d_y^2}$ of the offsets d_x, d_y after registration for different projection images. The results show that using M_t dramatically improves the registration. Overall the *argmax* image performed best with an average offset error of 0.0426 mm, RMSE of 0.0583 mm and median error of 0.025 mm.

Instrument Segmentation. We train our segmentation model on **DS1** with a batch size of 64 and random data split of 80% training and 20% validation set. To overcome the problems related to limited size of our data set and to enhance the generalization of our segmentation model we augment with vertical and horizontal flipping, random rotation up to $10°$ and random cropping to zoom up to a maximum scaling factor of 1.5. We use cross-entropy as our loss function and train with a learning rate of 0.01 and the AdamW [11] optimizer ($\beta_1 = 0.9$, $\beta_2 = 0.99$). Our model converged after 95 epochs and has a validation accuracy of 99.34% and 85.33% for retina and instrument classes, respectively.

Table 2. Average processing time in ms for volumes at source and resampled resolution.

	Project	Segment	Register	Compound	Render	**Total**	**FPS**
$512 \times 128 \times 1024$	1.92	7.41	11.91	7.61	19.00	**47.85**	**20.90**
$330 \times 330 \times 595$	1.81	6.68	20.80	8.49	9.13	**46.91**	**21.32**

Real-Time Processing. Our real-time visualization system was implemented in C++. We use the OpenCL-accelerated template matching implementation of OpenCV and TensorRT[2] to optimize and execute our trained model on the GPU. Projection image generation, volume compounding and rendering leverage the GPU using OpenGL. We evaluated computational performance by looping **DS3** (see Supplementary Video) with data preloaded to the GPU to simulate GPU reconstruction as in [9]. To compare our implementation to the data rates of a state of the art SS-OCT device, we resample our input data to a matching resolution of $330 \times 330 \times 595$. Table 2 shows the average results on the original and resampled data sets on our evaluation system (Intel Core i7-8700K @3.7 GHz, NVidia Titan Xp). The total processing time dictates both maximum frame rate of our setup and minimum latency from acquisition to display. Our achieved 21.32 frames per second is close to 24.2 Hz volume rate reported by [9].

4   Discussion and Conclusions

We presented the first end-to-end real-time pipeline to process and visualize 4D OCT data while mitigating instrument shadowing. Our adaptive visualization makes this processing and enhancement visible to the viewer and aids interpretation of the shown data. We demonstrated the feasibility of such a pipeline, achieving real-time processing speeds close to the state of the art imaging systems. Our evaluation reveals potential for future improvements for the registration approach. The implementation is based on off-the-shelf solutions for template matching and 2D image segmentation. Our matching errors are in the order

---

[2] https://developer.nvidia.com/tensorrt.

of several px which leads to potentially oversmoothed results. Because the focus of this work was to introduce the general concept and benefits of temporal alignment in 4D OCT, we consider the evaluation and development of more robust registration solutions as future work. A further interesting challenge is how to mitigate deformations that are caused for example by tool-tissue interactions. With the current approach, these deformations are smoothed over time as the compounded volume I_c gets updated. A higher value for ω_0 can improve responsiveness in these cases at the cost of lower denoising, thus more fine-grained adaptations of $\omega(p)$ could be developed in future extensions.

4D iOCT is not yet widely available but has already attracted much interest within its community. In this work, we developed a novel visualization and tested it on simulated 4D iOCT on porcine eyes. The described approach is currently being integrated into a state-of-the-art 4D iOCT imaging system. Once the integrated system has received ethical approval, it will be able to supply data with moving instruments within human eyes and thus enable further investigations into the clinical benefits of our advanced processing and visualization.

Data Set and Code Availability. The data sets and code used in this study are available upon request from the corresponding author.

Acknowledgements. This work was partially supported by U.S. National Institutes of Health under grant number 1R01EB025883-01A1 as well as the Federal Ministry of Education and Research of Germany (BMBF) in the framework of Software Campus 2.0 (FKZ 01IS17049). The authors acknowledge NVidia Corporation for donating the GPU used in the experiments.

References

1. Baumann, B., et al.: Signal averaging improves signal-to-noise in OCT images: but which approach works best, and when? Biomed. Opt. Exp. **10**(11), 5755 (2019). https://doi.org/10.1364/boe.10.005755
2. Bleicher, I.D., Jackson-Atogi, M., Viehland, C., Gabr, H., Izatt, J.A., Toth, C.A.: Depth-based, motion-stabilized colorization of microscope-integrated optical coherence tomography volumes for microscope-independent microsurgery. Transl. Vis. Sci. Technol. **7**(6), 1 (2018). https://doi.org/10.1167/tvst.7.6.1
3. Carrasco-Zevallos, O.M., Viehland, C., Keller, B., McNabb, R.P., Kuo, A.N., Izatt, J.A.: Constant linear velocity spiral scanning for near video rate 4D OCT ophthalmic and surgical imaging with isotropic transverse sampling. Biomed. Opt. Exp. **9**(10), 5052 (2018). https://doi.org/10.1364/BOE.9.005052
4. Ehlers, J.P., et al.: The DISCOVER study 3-year results. Ophthalmology **125**(7), 1014–1027 (2018). https://doi.org/10.1016/j.ophtha.2017.12.037
5. Ehlers, J.P., Uchida, A., Srivastava, S.K.: Intraoperative optical coherence tomography-compatible surgical instruments for real-time image-guided ophthalmic surgery. Br. J. Ophthalmol. **101**(10), 1306–1308 (2017). https://doi.org/10.1136/bjophthalmol-2017-310530
6. Gan, Y., Yao, W., Myers, K.M., Hendon, C.P.: An automated 3D registration method for optical coherence tomography volumes. In: 2014 36th Annual International Conference of the IEEE Engineering in Medicine and Biology Society, pp. 3873–3876 (2014). https://doi.org/10.1109/EMBC.2014.6944469

7. Ginner, L., Blatter, C., Fechtig, D., Schmoll, T., Gröschl, M., Leitgeb, R.: Wide-field OCT angiography at 400 KHz utilizing spectral splitting. Photonics **1**(4), 369–379 (2014). https://doi.org/10.3390/photonics1040369

8. Grulkowski, I., et al.: Retinal, anterior segment and full eye imaging using ultrahigh speed swept source OCT with vertical-cavity surface emitting lasers. Biomed. Opt. Exp. **3**(11), 2733 (2012)

9. Kolb, J.P.: Live video rate volumetric OCT imaging of the retina with multi-MHz A-scan rates. PLoS ONE **14**(3), e0213144 (2019). https://doi.org/10.1371/journal.pone.0213144

10. Kraus, M.F., et al.: Motion correction in optical coherence tomography volumes on a per A-scan basis using orthogonal scan patterns. Biomed. Opt. Exp. **3**(6), 1182–1199 (2012). https://doi.org/10.1364/BOE.3.001182

11. Loshchilov, I., Hutter, F.: Decoupled weight decay regularization. In: International Conference on Learning Representations (2019)

12. Niemeijer, M., Garvin, M., Lee, K., Ginneken, B., Abramoff, M., Sonka, M.: Registration of 3D spectral OCT volumes using 3D SIFT feature point matching. In: Proceedings of SPIE - The International Society for Optical Engineering (February 2009). https://doi.org/10.1117/12.811906

13. Niemeijer, M., Lee, K., Garvin, M.K., Abrmoff, M.D., Sonka, M.: Registration of 3D spectral OCT volumes combining ICP with a graph-based approach. In: Haynor, D.R., Ourselin, S. (eds.) Medical Imaging 2012: Image Processing, vol. 8314, pp. 378–386. International Society for Optics and Photonics, SPIE (2012). https://doi.org/10.1117/12.911104

14. Pan, L., Guan, L., Chen, X.: Segmentation guided registration for 3D spectral-domain optical coherence tomography images. IEEE Access **7**, 138833–138845 (2019). https://doi.org/10.1109/ACCESS.2019.2943172

15. Szkulmowski, M., Wojtkowski, M.: Averaging techniques for OCT imaging. Opt. Exp. **21**(8), 9757 (2013)

16. Viehland, C., et al.: Enhanced volumetric visualization for real time 4D intraoperative ophthalmic swept-source OCT. Biomed. Opt. Exp. **7**(5), 1815–1829 (2016). https://doi.org/10.1364/BOE.7.001815

17. Weiss, J., Eck, U., Nasseri, M.A., Maier, M., Eslami, A., Navab, N.: Layer-aware iOCT volume rendering for retinal surgery. In: Kozlíková, B., Linsen, L., Vázquez, P.P., Lawonn, K., Raidou, R.G. (eds.) Eurographics Workshop on Visual Computing for Biology and Medicine. The Eurographics Association (2019). https://doi.org/10.2312/vcbm.20191239

18. Zhou, M., et al.: Towards robotic-assisted subretinal injection: a hybrid parallel-serial robot system design and preliminary evaluation. IEEE Trans. Ind. Electro. **0046**(c), 1 (2019). https://doi.org/10.1109/tie.2019.2937041

Cell Segmentation and Stain Normalization

Boundary-Assisted Region Proposal Networks for Nucleus Segmentation

Shengcong Chen[1] , Changxing Ding[1(✉)] , and Dacheng Tao[2]

[1] School of Electronic and Information Engineering,
South China University of Technology, Guangzhou 510641, China
`chxding@scut.edu.cn`
[2] UBTECH Sydney AI Centre, School of Computer Science, Faculty of Engineering,
The University of Sydney, Darlington, NSW 2008, Australia

Abstract. Nucleus segmentation is an important task in medical image analysis. However, machine learning models cannot perform well because there are large amount of clusters of crowded nuclei. To handle this problem, existing approaches typically resort to sophisticated hand-crafted post-processing strategies; therefore, they are vulnerable to the variation of post-processing hyper-parameters. Accordingly, in this paper, we devise a Boundary-assisted Region Proposal Network (BRP-Net) that achieves robust instance-level nucleus segmentation. First, we propose a novel Task-aware Feature Encoding (TAFE) network that efficiently extracts respective high-quality features for semantic segmentation and instance boundary detection tasks. This is achieved by carefully considering the correlation and differences between the two tasks. Second, coarse nucleus proposals are generated based on the predictions of the above two tasks. Third, these proposals are fed into instance segmentation networks for more accurate prediction. Experimental results demonstrate that the performance of BRP-Net is robust to the variation of post-processing hyper-parameters. Furthermore, BRP-Net achieves state-of-the-art performances on both the Kumar and CPM17 datasets. The code of BRP-Net will be released at https://github.com/csccsccsccsc/brpnet.

Keywords: Nucleus segmentation · Multi-task learning · Instance segmentation

1 Introduction

Nucleus segmentation is a crucial task in computational pathology, as it provides rich spatial and morphometric information regarding nuclei. However, automatic nucleus segmentation remains challenging. This is for a number of reasons: first, a large amount of nucleus clusters exist, which results in crowded and

Electronic supplementary material The online version of this chapter (https://doi.org/10.1007/978-3-030-59722-1_27) contains supplementary material, which is available to authorized users.

© Springer Nature Switzerland AG 2020
A. L. Martel et al. (Eds.): MICCAI 2020, LNCS 12265, pp. 279–288, 2020.
https://doi.org/10.1007/978-3-030-59722-1_27

overlapping nuclei; second, the boundary of nuclei in out-of-focus images tends to be blurry, which increases the difficulty associated with separating crowded instances; third, both nucleus appearance and shape exhibit dramatic variation, which makes the segmentation task more difficult.

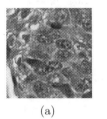 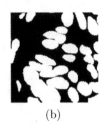 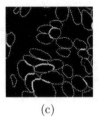

(a)   (b)   (c)

Fig. 1. An example that illustrates the essential difference between the semantic segmentation task and the instance boundary detection task. (a) original image; (b) ground-truth for semantic segmentation; (c) ground-truth for nucleus boundary. The boundaries that separates two overlapping instances, i.e. pixels colored in green in (c), cannot be directly inferred from the semantic segmentation results in (b).

Many approaches to nucleus segmentation have been proposed. One popular scheme is based on the use of boundary detection [1–3]. These approaches subtract instance boundaries from semantic segmentation results and then employ complex post-processing rules to obtain specific instances. In order to obtain the instance boundaries, DCAN [1] adopted two decoders for U-Net, one for semantic segmentation and another for instance boundary detection. No interactions take place between the two decoders. To make use of their correlation, BES-Net [2] and CIA-Net [3] further introduced uni-directional and bi-directional information transmission, respectively, which means one decoder obtains extra features from the other one. There are two key downsides of the above approaches. First, as they adopt a shared encoder for both tasks, they consequently underestimate the essential differences between tasks in feature learning; for example, the boundaries in Fig. 1(c) that separate two overlapping instances cannot be directly inferred from the semantic segmentation results in Fig. 1(b). Second, because these approaches adopt complex post-processing rules, their performance is sensitive to the variation of post-processing hyper-parameters.

Another popular strategy used to separate crowded instances is the distance-based approach [4,5]. For example, DIST [4] predicted the distance between each foreground pixel and its nearest background pixel, while HoVer-Net [5] enriched prediction by considering distances in both the horizontal and vertical directions. Subsequently, these works apply the watershed algorithm to the predicted distance maps to obtain instances. However, one downside of this approach is that the watershed algorithm may be sensitive to the noise in the distance maps. Finally, clustering-based methods predict the spatial location of the associated instance for each foreground pixel [6]. These instances are separated by clustering the predicted location coordinates.

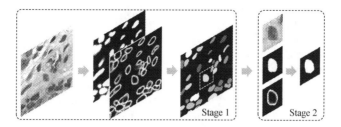

Fig. 2. Overview of BRP-Net. BRP-Net comprises two stages: one stage to obtain instance proposals and another for proposal-wise segmentation.

In this paper, we propose a novel framework for nucleus segmentation, referred to as Boundary-assisted Region Proposal Network (BRP-Net). Similar to Mask R-CNN [7], BRP-Net comprises two stages: one stage to obtain instance proposals and another for proposal-wise segmentation. In the first stage, we implement the boundary detection-based scheme to obtain instance proposals. This can be contrasted with Mask R-CNN [7], which predicts rectangular proposals directly from feature maps. As was demonstrated in [16], crowded instances result in bounding boxes with significant overlap; this means a single bounding box can be associated with multiple instances, consequently affecting the optimization quality of the network. Moreover, we further propose the Task-aware Feature Encoding (TAFE) network, which efficiently extracts high-quality features for semantic segmentation and instance boundary detection tasks. TAFE aids BRP-Net in robustly obtaining instance proposals. The second stage refines the segmentation result for each proposal, which enables BRP-Net to be robust to the variation of post-processing hyper-parameters in TAFE. Extensive experiments are conducted on two publicly available nucleus segmentation datasets, from which we can conclude that BRP-Net consistently achieves state-of-the-art performance on both datasets.

2   Method

The overall framework of BRP-Net is presented in Fig. 2. This framework includes two stages: one for obtaining instance proposals and another for proposal-wise segmentation. The first stage adopts a similar pipeline to CIA-Net [3], and the second one aims to refine the segmentation results of the first stage in a proposal-wise manner.

2.1   Region Proposal Generation

We adopt a boundary detection-based scheme to obtain high-quality region proposals. Following the post-processing rules outlined in [1,3], instance boundaries are subtracted from the predictions of semantic segmentation. Subsequently, connected component analysis is applied to produce instance proposals. Extant approaches have integrated semantic segmentation and instance boundary detection tasks into one model [1–3]; however, as they adopt a shared encoder for both tasks, they may underestimate their essential differences regarding feature learning, as is analyzed in Sect. 1. One intuitive solution would be adopting independent encoders for the two tasks. However, this strategy increases the model complexity and also completely ignores their correlation. Accordingly, we propose a novel Task-aware Feature Encoding (TAFE) network capable of efficiently extracting high-quality features for each of these tasks.

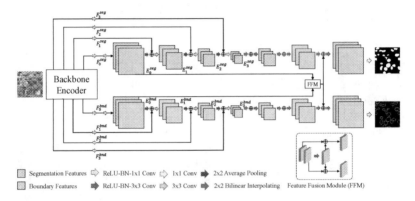

Fig. 3. Architecture details of TAFE. The number of channels in F_i is set to 256 consistently. Feature maps produced by both encoders are fused in FFMs to make use of their correlation. For simplicity, only one FFM is shown and the other two FFMs are ignored in this figure. (Best viewed in color). (color figure online)

Figure 3 presents the architecture of TAFE. First, nucleus images are fed into a single backbone encoder to extract feature maps that are $\{1, 1/2, 1/4, 1/8\}$ of the original image size. The structure of the backbone encoder is provided in the supplementary file. Subsequently, each of them is passed through one unshared 1×1 convolutional layer to obtain F_i^{seg} and F_i^{bnd}. F_i^{seg} and F_i^{bnd} are fed into Task-specific Encoders (TSE), which are designed for the semantic segmentation and instance boundary detection tasks, respectively. In each encoder, feature maps after down-sampling are merged with an F_i of the same size via element-wise summation. The merged features are then passed through one 3×3 convolutional layer to generate E_i. Similar to CIA-Net [3], deep supervision is applied and the auxiliary classifiers take E_i as inputs. Moreover, inspired by the Information Aggregation Modules [3], we propose the light-weight Feature Fusion Modules (FFMs), which is based on residual learning to aggregate information in E_i^{seg} and E_i^{bnd}. In the experimentation section, we demonstrate the superiority of FFMs. FFMs are helpful for making use of the correlation as well as reserving the differences between both tasks. Outputs of each FFM are fed into two shallow decoders via element-wise summation. The two decoders are used for the semantic segmentation task and the instance boundary detection task. Each decoder contains three BN-ReLU-Conv layers.

2.2   Proposal-Wise Segmentation

The first stage of BRP-Net, i.e. TAFE, adopts hand-crafted post-processing rules to obtain instance proposals. Accordingly, the quality of proposals is affected by post-processing hyper-parameters. To address this problem, we propose a second stage for BRP-Net to facilitate more robust segmentation.

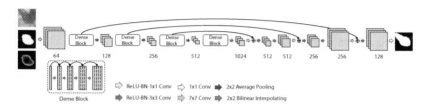

Fig. 4. The two networks in the proposal-wise segmentation stage adopt the same architecture. Each layer in the network includes one dense block that consists of four 3×3 convolutional layers. Growth rates of the four dense blocks are set to 16, 32, 64, and 128, respectively. The number below each group of feature maps denotes the number of channels. (Best viewed in color). (color figure online)

We crop one square patch containing each proposal with a minimal margin of 12 pixels on each side. Because the patches vary dramatically in size, we group them into small and large patches with a threshold of S_S according to their length. Then, small and large patches are resized to $S_S \times S_S$ and $S_L \times S_L$, respectively. Finally, we train one network for the small and another for the large patches. These two networks have the same architecture, the details of which are illustrated in Fig. 4. Inputs to the model include the patch, and the probability maps that are predicted by the semantic segmentation and boundary detection tasks in the first stage. To relieve the influence of background, elements in the probability maps that fall outside of the dilated proposal are set to zero. The dilation rate is set to 2 pixels.

During training, each proposal is matched to a ground-truth instance depending on their Intersection over Union (IoU). For proposals with an IoU larger than τ, their label maps are set with reference to the matched ground-truth instance; otherwise, the proposals are considered to be false-positive predictions. Therefore, all elements in their label maps are set to zero (denoting background).

2.3   Inference

During the inference process, nucleus images are fed into BRP-Net. Semantic segmentation and instance boundary detection results are produced by TAFE. Then, post-processing operations in [1,3] are implemented to obtain instance proposals. Finally, patches containing these proposals are extracted and respectively fed into proposal-wise segmentation networks for robust instance segmentation.

3   Experiments

We conduct experiments on two publicly available datasets. The first is a multi-organ nucleus dataset [8,9], referred to as Kumar, which contains 30 Hema-toxylin and Eosin ($H\&E$) stained images with resolution of 1000×1000. They are divided into a training set of 16 images and a testing set of 14 images according to the same protocol used in previous works [3,5,6,8]. In the testing set, 8 images are from 4 organs in the training set (seen organ), and the remained 6 images are from 3 organs that do not appear in the training set (unseen organ). The second dataset is Computational Precision Medicine Dataset (CPM17) [10], which contains 32 images for training and 32 images for testing.

Evaluation metrics for the two datasets are different. In the Kumar dataset, the main metric is the Average Jaccard Index (AJI) [8]. We also report the F1-Score to measure the instance detection performance. In CPM17, we use the same metrics as used in [10], i.e. the DICE coefficient (DICE 1) and Ensemble Dice (DICE 2). DICE 1 measures the overall overlap between the predictions and the ground truth, and DICE 2 measures the average overlap between the predictions and their matched ground truth instances. Besides, in order to better compare with one state-of-the-art work [5], we also report AJI in the experiments.

3.1   Implementation Details

We first perform stain normalization [12] to reduce the color differences between the stained images. In the next step, we normalize each image by subtracting the mean and dividing by the standard deviation of the training set. Training data are augmented by random cropping, flipping, color jittering, blurring and elastic transformation. We crop images to a size of 256×256 pixels before using them as the input of BRP-Net.

In a similar way to CIA-Net [3], we adopt DenseNet [13] as TAFE's back-bone encoder and initialize its parameters using a single pretrained model[1]. We also adopt both the Smooth Truncated Loss [3] and Soft Dice Loss [17] for the optimization of both tasks in TAFE. Weight of the Soft Dice Loss is set to 0.5. We use the AdamW [14] optimizer for training. The number of training epochs is set to 600. The learning rate is initially set to 0.0003, and decreases according to the cosine annealing schedule [14]. The learning rate decreases to zero in 40 epochs and is then reset. At each restart, the new start learning rate is set to be one half of the previous rate, while the new period lasts for twice as long as the previous one.

Finally, S_S and S_L are set to be 48 and 176 pixels, respectively. The two thresholds are selected to ensure the ratio between the numbers of small and large patches are around 2:1. Training settings for the proposal-wise segmentation networks are similar to those of TAFE. But we use Focal Loss [15] for optimization and the training lasts for only ten epochs. The learning rate is

---

[1] The pretrained model can be downloaded from https://download.pytorch.org/models/densenet121-a639ec97.pth.

set to 0.0003 initially, and decreases according to the cosine annealing schedule without restart.

3.2   Ablation Study

Table 1. Performance comparisons between the baseline, baseline+FFMs, and TAFE.

Network	AJI (%)			F1-Score (%)		
	Seen	Unseen	All	Seen	Unseen	All
Baseline	61.15	62.58	61.76	82.99	84.08	83.46
Baseline+FFMs	61.41	63.39	62.26	82.35	**84.90**	83.44
TAFE	**61.96**	**63.84**	**62.77**	82.81	84.34	83.47

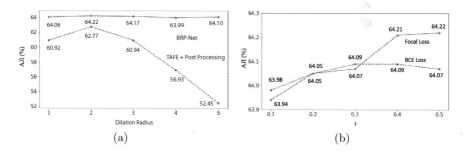

(a)   (b)

Fig. 5. Evaluation on different settings for BRP-Net. (a) The influence of different dilation radii in the post-processing step of TAFE. (b) The choice of IoU thresholds τ and different loss functions for the second stage of BRP-Net.

Effectiveness of TAFE. We compare the performance of TAFE with a baseline network that is similar to existing boundary detection-based methods [3]. In brief, it shares encoder for the semantic segmentation and instance boundary detection tasks. The two tasks still own respective decoders equipped with IAMs. For fair comparison, the baseline has the same number of parameters as TAFE. Table 1 presents the performance of TAFE and baseline. We also equip IAMs with the same residual learning scheme as FFMs and report the performance of baseline again, which is referred to as 'baseline+FFMs' in the table. Architecture details of both the baseline and 'baseline+FFMs' are provided in the supplementary file. It can be seen from our results that TAFE achieves higher AJI performance on both the seen and unseen organ datasets. It is also clear that the residual learning scheme in FFMs is helpful. This may be because this scheme better highlights the differences between the two tasks, as illustrated in Fig. 3. The comparison justifies the effectiveness of TAFE and the FFM modules.

Evaluation on Post-Processing Settings in TAFE. Existing boundary detection-based methods are sensitive to the post-processing hyper-parameters, particularly the dilation radius for recovering the subtracted instance boundaries [1,3]. We conduct experiments to evaluate the influence of different dilation radii on both TAFE and the entire BRP-Net pipeline. Results are presented in Fig. 5(a). It can be found that due to the proposal-wise segmentation stage, BRP-Net is highly robust to the value of dilation radius. By contrast, the performance of single-stage method is less stable.

Table 2. Quantitative comparisons between BRP-Net and existing methods.

(a) Comparisons on the Kumar database [8].

Network	AJI (%)			F1-Score (%)		
	seen	unseen	all	seen	unseen	all
CNN3 [8]	51.54	49.89	50.83	82.26	83.22	82.67
DIST [4]	55.91	56.01	55.95	–	–	–
Mask R-CNN [7]	59.78	55.31	57.86	81.07	82.91	81.86
CIA-Net [3]	61.29	63.06	62.05	82.44	84.58	83.36
HoVer-Net [5]	–	–	61.80	–	–	–
Spa-Net [6]	62.39	63.40	62.82	82.81	84.51	83.53
BRP-Net (ours)	**63.07**	**65.75**	**64.22**	**83.46**	**85.26**	**84.23**

(b) Comparisons on CPM17 database [10]

Network	Dice 1 (%)	Dice 2 (%)	AJI (%)
DRAN [10]	86.2	70.3	68.3
HoVer-Net [5]	86.9	–	70.5
Micro-Net [11]	85.7	**79.6**	–
BRP-Net (ours)	**87.7**	79.5	**73.1**

Evaluations on Settings for Proposal-Wise Segmentation. We evaluate the influence of IoU thresholds τ and different loss functions on the second stage of BRP-Net. Experimental results are presented in Fig. 5(b). It is shown that the performance of BRP-Net is generally robust to the value of τ, as well as that focal loss [15] slightly outperforms cross-entropy loss. According to the evaluation results, we select focal loss for training and set τ as 0.5 for the second stage.

3.3   Comparisons with State-of-the-art Methods

Comparisons between BRP-Net and state-of-the-art methods on the Kumar database are reported in Table 2(a). It can be seen that BRP-Net achieves both the highest AJI and the highest F1-Score among all the methods. In particular, BRP-Net outperforms the previous best method, i.e. SPA-Net, by 0.68%, 2.35%, and 1.40% on the seen organ, unseen organ, and all testing data, respectively. We also provide qualitative comparisons in the supplementary file.

We further conduct comparisons on CPM17 database [10] and summarize the results in Table 2(b). From the results, we can see that BRP-Net continues to achieves state-of-the-art performance. Its performance in Dice 1 and AJI outperforms existing approaches by 0.8% and 2.6%, respectively. The above comparisons demonstrate the effectiveness of BRP-Net.

4 Conclusion

In this paper, we propose the Boundary-assisted Region Proposal Network (BRP-Net) for nucleus segmentation. BRP-Net contains one stage designed for obtaining instance proposals and a second stage for proposal-wise segmentation. To separate crowded nuclei, we adopt a boundary detection-based scheme for the first stage. We further propose a novel Task-specific Feature Encoding network with Feature Fusion Modules to achieve this goal. The second stage is further introduced to segment proposals of various size, and enables BRP-Net to be robust to the variation of post-processing hyper-parameters in the first stage. Finally, BRP-Net achieves strong performance on both the Kumar and CPM17 datasets.

Acknowledgement. Changxing Ding is the corresponding author. This work was supported by NSF of China under Grant 61702193, the Science and Technology Program of Guangzhou under Grant 201804010272, the Program for Guangdong Introducing Innovative and Entrepreneurial Teams under Grant 2017ZT07X183, the Fundamental Research Funds for the Central Universities of China under Grant 2019JQ01, the Guangzhou Key Laboratory of Body Data Science under Grant 201605030011, and the Australian Research Council Project FL-170100117.

References

1. Chen, H., Qi, X., Yu, L., Heng, P.A.: DCAN: deep contour-aware networks for accurate gland segmentation. In: Proceedings of the IEEE Conference on Computer Vision and Pattern Recognition, pp. 2487–2496 (2016)
2. Oda, H., et al.: BESNet: boundary-enhanced segmentation of cells in histopathological Images. In: Frangi, A.F., Schnabel, J.A., Davatzikos, C., Alberola-López, C., Fichtinger, G. (eds.) MICCAI 2018. LNCS, vol. 11071, pp. 228–236. Springer, Cham (2018). https://doi.org/10.1007/978-3-030-00934-2_26
3. Zhou, Y., Onder, O.F., Dou, Q., Tsougenis, E., Chen, H., Heng, P.-A.: CIA-Net: robust nuclei instance segmentation with contour-aware information aggregation. In: Chung, A.C.S., Gee, J.C., Yushkevich, P.A., Bao, S. (eds.) IPMI 2019. LNCS, vol. 11492, pp. 682–693. Springer, Cham (2019). https://doi.org/10.1007/978-3-030-20351-1_53

4. Naylor, P., Laé, M., Reyal, F., Walter, T.: Segmentation of nuclei in histopathology images by deep regression of the distance map. IEEE Trans. Med. Imaging **38**(2), 448–459 (2018)

5. Graham, S., et al.: Hover-Net: simultaneous segmentation and classification of nuclei in multi-tissue histology images. Med. Image Anal. **58**, 101563 (2019)

6. Alemi Koohbanani, N., Jahanifar, M., Gooya, A., Rajpoot, N.: Nuclear instance segmentation using a proposal-free spatially aware deep learning framework. In: Shen, D., et al. (eds.) MICCAI 2019. LNCS, vol. 11764, pp. 622–630. Springer, Cham (2019). https://doi.org/10.1007/978-3-030-32239-7_69

7. He, K., Gkioxari G., Dollár P., Girshick R.: Mask r-cnn. In: Proceedings of the IEEE International Conference on Computer Vision, pp. 2980–2988 (2017)

8. Kumar, N., Verma, R., Sharma, S., Bhargava, S., Vahadane, A., Sethi, A.: A dataset and a technique for generalized nuclear segmentation for computational pathology. IEEE Trans. Med. Imaging **36**(7), 1550–1560 (2017)

9. Kumar, N., et al.: A multi-organ nucleus segmentation challenge. IEEE Trans. Med. Imaging. https://doi.org/10.1109/TMI.2019.2947628

10. Vu, Q.D., et al.: Methods for segmentation and classification of digital microscopy tissue images. Front. Bioeng. Biotechnol. **7**, 53 (2019)

11. Raza, S.E.A., et al.: Micro-Net: a unified model for segmentation of various objects in microscopy images. Med. Image Anal. **52**, 160–173 (2019)

12. Macenko, M., Niethammer, M., Marron, J.S., et al.: A method for normalizing histology slides for quantitative analysis. In: Proceedings of IEEE International Symposium on Biomedical Imaging, pp. 1107–1110 (2009)

13. Huang, G., Liu, Z., van der Maaten, L., Weinberger, K.Q.: Densely connected convolutional networks. In: Proceedings of the IEEE conference on Computer Vision and Pattern Recognition, pp. 4700–4708 (2017)

14. Loshchilov, I., Hutter, F.: Fixing weight decay regularization in adam (2017). arXiv preprint arXiv:1711.05101

15. Lin, T.Y., Goyal, P., Girshick, R., He, K., Dollár, P.: Focal loss for dense object detection. In: Proceedings of the IEEE International Conference on Computer Vision, pp. 2980–2988 (2017)

16. Ding, H., Qiao, S., Shen, W., Yuille, A.: Shape-aware feature extraction for instance segmentation (2019). arXiv preprint arXiv:1911.11263

17. Milletari, F., Navab, N., Ahmadi, S.A.: V-net: fully convolutional neural networks for volumetric medical image segmentation. In: International Conference on 3D Vision (3DV), pp. 565–571. IEEE (2016)

BCData: A Large-Scale Dataset and Benchmark for Cell Detection and Counting

Zhongyi Huang[1], Yao Ding[2], Guoli Song[3], Lin Wang[1], Ruizhe Geng[1], Hongliang He[1], Shan Du[4], Xia Liu[5], Yonghong Tian[3,6], Yongsheng Liang[7], S. Kevin Zhou[3,8], and Jie Chen[1,3(✉)]

[1] School of Electronic and Computer Engineering, Peking University, Shenzhen, China
[2] University of Chinese Academy of Sciences, Beijing, China
[3] Peng Cheng Laboratory, Shenzhen, China
chenj@pcl.ac.cn
[4] Shenzhen Hospital, University of Chinese Academy of Sciences, Shenzhen, China
[5] The Second People's Hospital of Shenzhen, Shenzhen, China
[6] School of Electronics Engineering and Computer Science, Peking University, Beijing, China
[7] Harbin Institute of Technology Shenzhen Graduate School, Shenzhen, China
[8] Institute of Computing Technology, Chinese Academy of Sciences, Beijing, China

Abstract. Breast cancer is a main malignant tumor for women and the incidence is trending to ascend. Detecting positive and negative tumor cells in the immunohistochemically stained sections of breast tissue to compute the Ki-67 index is an essential means to determine the degree of malignancy of breast cancer. However, there are scarcely public datasets about cell detection of Ki-67 stained images. In this paper, we introduce a large-scale Breast tumor Cell Dataset (BCData) for cell detection and counting, which contains 1,338 images with 181,074 annotated cells belonging to two categories, i.e., positive and negative tumor cells. (We state that our dataset can only be used for non-commercial research.) Our dataset varies widely in both the distributing density of tumor cells and the Ki-67 index. We conduct several cell detection and counting methods on this dataset to set the first benchmark. We believe that our dataset will facilitate further research in cell detection and counting fields in clustering, overlapping, and variational stained conditions. Our dataset is available at https://sites.google.com/view/bcdataset

Keywords: Breast tumor cell dataset · Cell detection · Cell counting

Electronic supplementary material The online version of this chapter (https://doi.org/10.1007/978-3-030-59722-1_28) contains supplementary material, which is available to authorized users.

1   Introduction

Breast cancer is one of the most common malignant tumors affecting women [14]. In clinical practice, to determine the severity of the cancer, pathologists select several regions of interest (ROIs) from the Ki-67 stained whole slide images (WSIs) and approximate the positive rate of tumor cells, which is called Ki-67 proliferation index (hereinafter referred to as Ki-67 index) [4]. Ki-67 index is a significant index to evaluate the degree of the cell proliferation and the malignancy of breast cancer. However, due to the dense distribution of cells and heavy burden of diagnosis, it is always hard for pathologists to count tumor cells precisely. Indeed, Ki-67 index estimated by pathologists cannot avoid artificial subjectivity and randomness, which may lead to very inconsistent diagnosis results. To improve diagnostic efficiency and reduce the burden on pathologists, we explore how to obtain an accurate Ki-67 index by cell detection and counting.

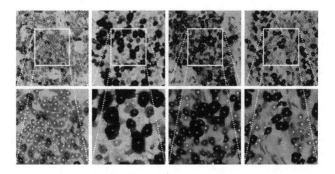

Fig. 1. Sample images in the BCData dataset. These images are ROIs selected by pathologists from the WSIs. The red and the green marks indicate the locations of the positive and the negative tumor cells, respectively. (Color figure online)

Cell or nuclei detection (hereinafter referred to as cell detection for simplicity) is a hot topic in medical image analysis. Some previous works mainly focus on hand-crafted features or/and traditional machine learning methods [1,12,13]. Recently, more and more models based on deep learning have been applied to cell detection for their high performance [2,3,5,7,8,10,16,17,19–23,25]. However, deep models tend to rely on large amounts of data, otherwise they are prone to problems such as overfitting. But unfortunately, existing related datasets are always small in scale of cases or annotated objects due to the expensive labeling cost of medical images, and few of publicly available cell detection datasets are based on Ki-67 staining. For example, Kainz et al. [8] only contains 11 samples with 4,205 cells annotated. Although dataset in [18] contains more than 600 samples, there are only about 1,000 cells annotated. Hence, such datasets are unsuited for some dense cell detection tasks. Lempitsky et al. [9] had synthesized a relatively large cell dataset, but it is still not authentic enough to be applied to medical practice. Furthermore, existing publicly available datasets such as [16,17] are always based on only few cases, so the sample diversity cannot be guaranteed. Moreover, some datasets such as [5] are heretofore unavailable to the public.

Table 1. Comparisons of related center-point cell/nuclei detection datasets. The 'AO' denotes the annotated objects. The 'MC' denotes whether the datasets contain multi classes or not. The 'PA' denotes whether the dataset is publicly available or not.

Dataset	# Images	# AO	# Cases	Resolution	MC	Real	Year	PA
SyntCell [9]	200	35,192	-	256×256	✗	✗	2010	✓
HeLa [1]	22	2,229	UNK	400×400	✗	✓	2012	✓
AMIDA13 [18]	606	1,083	23	$2,000 \times 2,000$	✗	✓	2013	✓
BM [8]	11	4,205	8	$1,200 \times 1,200$	✗	✓	2015	✓
UW [16]	100	29,756	9	500×500	✗	✓	2016	✓
PSU [17]	120	25,462	12	612×452	✗	✓	2019	✓
mIHC [5]	175	20,477	6	UNK	✓	✓	2019	✗
BCData (Ours)	1,338	181,074	394	640×640	✓	✓	2020	✓

To advance the research in evaluating Ki-67 index, we introduce a dataset named BCData, a large-scale breast tumor cell dataset for Ki-67 cell detection and counting. An organized and detailed comparison between existing cell detection datasets and our dataset is shown in Table 1. The BCData covers 394 WSIs, 1,338 ROIs, and 181,074 annotated tumor cells. Some annotated samples are shown in Fig. 1. Our dataset is similar to the real-world scenarios and has the following features: 1) the distributing density of tumor cells is diverse; 2) the rate of positive tumor cells is varied; 3) tumor cells vary in size and shape with vague boundary. To validate the application and research value of the proposed dataset, we report performance of some cell detection and counting algorithms on the BCData. The results indicate that the dataset is a valuable research topic. In summary, our main contributions are as follows:

– We collect and annotate a large-scale dataset for cell detection and counting.
– We design an exquisite and unified labeling pipeline carefully to ensure the quality of annotations. To our knowledge, our BCData is the largest publicly available annotated cell detection and counting dataset about tumor cells under Ki-67 stained images from breast cancer patients at present.
– We carry out benchmark experiments on our dataset for further research.

2   Our Dataset

2.1   Data Collection

We entrust pathologists to collect the Ki-67 stained sections of breast tissue from the database center of the hospital. All the WSIs are scanned by a Motic BA600-4 scanner at 40× magnification with the pixel resolution of 0.2239 μm/pixel. All the data are anonymised for privacy protection.

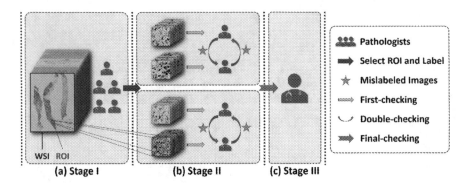

Fig. 2. The designed labeling pipeline. In stage I, we invite five pathologists to select ROIs from the WSIs and annotate the category and center coordinate of each tumor cell within the ROIs. In stage II, we further invite another four pathologists to cross-validate the annotations under a majority voting system. In stage III, a senior expert makes the final decision on the annotations. (Color figure online)

2.2 Data Annotation

We invite ten professional pathologists to annotate our dataset. It is well known that medical image annotation is a task of high ambiguity and subjectivity, so these ten pathologists develop a unified and rigorous labeling standard and pipeline through discussion before annotation. The designed labeling pipeline is shown in Fig. 2. We divide the annotation process into three stages, and the ten pathologists are divided into three teams corresponding to these three stages (five for stage I, four for stage II, and one for stage III). In addition, since it can be argued that whether a particular weakly stained cell is deemed positive or not, the pathologists reached a consensus that this kind of cell is regarded as positive before annotation. As for the non-malignant but Ki-67 positive cells, the pathologists came to an agreement that there is no need to label them in that the calculation of the Ki-67 index has nothing to do with non-tumor cells. We introduce the three labeling stages in detail below.

In stage I, the five pathologists select several ROIs with 640×640 resolution from the WSIs and label each tumor cell with a mark near the center of it. These marks fall into two categories (positive and negative). Therefore, from the marks on the ROIs, we can tell the coordinates and categories of the tumor cells. Once the labeling process is completed, we crop all the labeled ROIs with marks from the WSIs to obtain a series of patch images with annotations.

In stage II, we divide the annotated ROIs obtained from stage I into four groups evenly and assign them to the four pathologists in stage II for review. Each pathologist is responsible for one group of these images. Moreover, the four pathologists are separated into two pairs for double-checking. One pathologist in a pair is responsible for first-checking, including reviewing the images and screening out the region that is mislabeled (if there is one), while the other in the same pair is responsible for double-checking. If the other pathologist also considers it mislabeled, then it will be revised. This designed checking flow is motivated by a choosing-two-from-the-three voting mechanism. The pathologists in stage I stand for one vote, while the two pathologists in pairs in stage II stand for one vote, respectively. Finally, all revised images are submitted to the chief and expert pathologist in stage III for final-checking.

Table 2. Details about the separation of our dataset. The 'Pos.' and the 'Neg.' denote the positive and the negative tumor cells, respectively.

Set	# Pos. Cell	# Neg. Cell	# Total Cell	# Images
Train	33,058	60,780	93,838	803
Validation	7,701	14,103	21,804	133
Test	21,864	43,568	65,432	402
Total	62,623	118,451	181,074	1,338

2.3 Data Split

Our dataset contains 1,338 images from 394 cases (WSIs) with 181,074 labeled tumor cells. We divide our dataset into training, validation, and testing set at a ratio of approximately 6:1:3. More details are shown in Table 2. Since different ROIs may come from the same case, we guarantee that the ROI images from the same case are divided into the same set when splitting our dataset.

2.4 Discussion

The challenges of our dataset are three folds. Firstly, the size, shape, and other appearances of the tumor cells vary widely owing to the characteristics of tumor cells and different staining conditions, as shown in Fig. 1. Secondly, the tumor cell density (the number of tumor cells in each ROI) and the Ki-67 index of each ROI is diverse. Thirdly, some non-tumor cells in ROIs can also affect the performance of the detectors due to the similarity between the tumor and non-tumor cells in size, shape, color, etc.

3 Benchmark

3.1 Cell Detection

In cell center point detection, one of the most popular and effective pipelines is to generate cell distribution probability maps based on point annotation and then use some models to learn the probability map. During inference, the coordinates of cells are obtained by taking the local maximum under the pre-defined threshold and window size on the probability map predicted by the model. We also adopt this pipeline in our benchmark, and more details are given below.

Ground Truth Generation. To generate the ground truth cell distribution probability map, we use a similar method as Zhang et al. [24]. Since there are two categories of tumor cells in our dataset, we generate one probability map for each kind of cell, respectively. The Gaussian kernel convolution [24] is necessary because the center coordinate values of cells are sparse in the ground truth map, so it is difficult for models to regress the raw coordinates directly.

Probability Map Learning. To learn the mapping from the input images to the probability map, we employ the Congested Scene Recognition Network (CSRNet) [11] and our modified version as our benchmarks. CSRNet is a classical network in the field of crowd counting. It uses the head of VGG nets [15] to extract the features of the image (called frontend). Then, it applies a series of dilated convolutions to expand the receptive field (called backend). In this paper, we change the backbone of VGG nets to ResNet-50 [6]. CSRNet has been proved to have excellent performance on the probability or density map prediction in crowd counting tasks, so we adopt it as one of our baseline models.

However, it is worth noting that the output of the original CSRNet is eight times lower resolution than the input. Therefore, it is not precise enough when we use it as the prediction of the probability map of cell distribution directly. Especially when the cell distribution is very dense, it is hard to distinguish the different probability peaks. Therefore, we add transpose convolution layers after its backend so that the final output probability map can be identical to the resolution of the input (called U-CSRNet in this paper). Our experiment results show the effectiveness of this simple but powerful operation.

We modify the output of CSRNet and U-CSRNet from one channel to two channels to represent the two kinds of tumor cells, respectively. As for the training loss, we adopt the Euclidean distance to estimate the distance between ground truth map and the predicted map.

3.2 Cell Counting

For the counting task, there are two kinds of methods as below.

Counting by Detection. It is straightforward that we can obtain the counts of the two kinds of tumor cells by summing the detected objects, so we adopt it as one of the methods for the cell counting task in our dataset.

Counting by Integrating the Probability Map. Recently, the crowd counting task has attracted more and more attention in the computer vision community. The latest algorithms of crowd counting usually model the crowd distribution as a density map and design models to learn it. During inference, the count of crowd can be obtained by integrating the predicted density map [9,24]. Since the principle we generate our ground truth probability maps in Sect. 3.1 is the same as that in [9,24], we can actually regard our probability map as a kind of density map. Therefore, we can obtain the counting of the tumor cells by integrating the predicted probability maps in Sect. 3.1. We refer the readers to [9,24] for more details about this kind of counting methods.

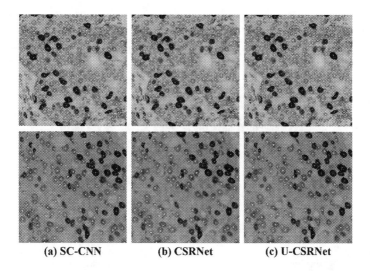

(a) SC-CNN   **(b) CSRNet**   **(c) U-CSRNet**

Fig. 3. The qualitative cell detection results. The circles represent the ground truth areas while the filled dots represent the predicted coordinates (red and green denote the positive and negative tumor cells, respectively). (Color figure online)

Table 3. The quantitative cell detection results. The 'P', 'R', and 'F1' denotes the Precision, Recall, and F1 Score, respectively. The '↑' indicates that the higher the value, the better the performance.

Methods	Positive tumor cells			Negative tumor cells			Average		
	P↑	R↑	F1↑	P↑	R↑	F1↑	P↑	R↑	F1↑
SC-CNN [16]	0.7704	0.8280	0.7982	0.7335	0.8292	0.7784	0.7519	0.8286	0.7883
CSRNet [11]	0.8241	0.8338	0.8289	0.8094	0.8189	0.8142	0.8167	0.8264	0.8215
U-CSRNet	0.8690	0.8573	0.8631	0.8435	0.8596	0.8515	0.8563	0.8585	0.8573

4 Experiment

4.1 Cell Detection

Evaluation Metrics. We use Precision, Recall and F1 Score to evaluate the detection performance in accordance with Sirinukunwattana et al. [16]. A predicted point is regarded as true positive if it is within the region of a ground truth point with a predefined radius (we set it to 10 pixels in our experiment). Centers that have been detected more than once are considered as false positive.
Results. We employ the detection methods introduced in Sect. 3.1 to detect the tumor cells. The quantitative results are shown in Table 3. We can see that the modified U-CSRNet outperforms its initial version CSRNet and SC-CNN [16]. Some qualitative results are shown in Fig. 3 for comparisons.

Table 4. The quantitative cell counting results. The 'detection' inside the braces denotes the results are obtained from the detection results directly. The 'integrating' denotes the results are obtained by integrating the probability maps. The 'MP', 'MN', and 'MA' denote the MAE of positive cells, negative cells, and the average value, respectively. The '↓' indicates that the lower the value, the better the performance.

Methods	MP↓	MN↓	MA↓
SC-CNN [16] (detection)	9.182	20.600	14.891
CSRNet [11] (integrating)	9.236	24.898	17.067
CSRNet [11] (detection)	7.736	14.117	10.927
U-CSRNet (integrating)	10.040	18.092	14.066
U-CSRNet (detection)	6.883	14.194	10.539

4.2 Cell Counting

Evaluation Metrics. For the counting task, we adopt the mean absolute error (MAE) as our metric, which is defined as

$$MAE^{cate} = \frac{1}{N} \sum_{i=1}^{N} \left| c_i^{cate} - \hat{c}_i^{cate} \right|, \tag{1}$$

where c_i^{cate} and $\hat{c}_i^{cate}$ are the ground truth and predicted cell counts of image i, respectively. N is the total number of images. The corner mark $cate$ at the top right means the category of the tumor cells. The metric is nearly the same as the one in the crowd count task, except that it counts different categories separately. We also calculate the mean of MAE of different categories for comparisons.

   Results. We employ the two methods described in Sect. 3.2 in the cell counting task, and the results are shown in Table 4. We can see that counting by detection in our dataset is superior to counting by integrating the probability maps. The reason is that the center points of the tumor cells are relatively distinguishable, and counting by detection can preserve more location information.

Table 5. Cell nuclei detection results on PSU Dataset. The 'Prior Info?' denotes whether the method needs additional prior information from experts.

Methods	Precision↑	Recall↑	F1 Score↑	Prior Info?
SP-CNN [17]	0.854	0.871	0.863	Yes
TSP-CNN [17]	0.874	0.911	0.892	Yes
SSAE [21]	0.665	0.634	0.649	No
NP-CNN [17]	0.746	0.859	0.799	No
SR-CNN [19]	0.797	0.805	0.801	No
SC-CNN [16]	0.821	0.830	0.825	No
U-CSRNet	0.913	0.903	0.908	No

4.3 Comparison Experiments on Open Dataset: PSU Dataset

To demonstrate the effectiveness of our cell detection benchmark (U-CSRNet), we conduct comparison experiments on an open cell nuclei detection dataset named PSU Dataset [17]. The experiment results are shown in Table 5. We can see that our benchmark outperforms many state-of-the-art cell or nuclei detection methods in F1 score. In addition, it is worth mentioning that SP-CNN and TSP-CNN in [17] need to provide the model with additional expert prior knowledge in addition to the original annotations, while our benchmark does not need any additional prior information.

5 Conclusion

We collect and annotate a dataset from immunohistochemical sections of breast cancer for cell detection and counting. The dataset contains two kinds of tumor cells varying in shape, size, color, etc., and therein exists situation of overlapping, making it challenging to detect and count. Furthermore, we evaluate several detection and counting methods on the dataset. We hope that this work will help stimulate further research on cell detection and counting.

Acknowledgements. This work is supported by the Nature Science Foundation of China (No. 62081360152, No. 61972217), Natural Science Foundation of Guangdong Province in China (No. 2019B1515120049, 2020B1111340056).

References

1. Arteta, C., Lempitsky, V., Noble, J.A., Zisserman, A.: Learning to detect cells using non-overlapping extremal regions. In: Ayache, N., Delingette, H., Golland, P., Mori, K. (eds.) MICCAI 2012. LNCS, vol. 7510, pp. 348–356. Springer, Heidelberg (2012). https://doi.org/10.1007/978-3-642-33415-3_43

2. Chen, H., Dou, Q., Wang, X., Qin, J., Heng, P.A.: Mitosis detection in breast cancer histology images via deep cascaded networks. In: AAAI (2016)

3. Cireşan, D.C., Giusti, A., Gambardella, L.M., Schmidhuber, J.: Mitosis detection in breast cancer histology images with deep neural networks. In: Mori, K., Sakuma, I., Sato, Y., Barillot, C., Navab, N. (eds.) MICCAI 2013. LNCS, vol. 8150, pp. 411–418. Springer, Heidelberg (2013). https://doi.org/10.1007/978-3-642-40763-5_51

4. Dhall, D., et al.: Ki-67 proliferative index predicts progression-free survival of patients with well-differentiated ileal neuroendocrine tumors. Hum. Pathol. **43**(4), 489–495 (2012)

5. Hagos, Y.B., Narayanan, P.L., Akarca, A.U., Marafioti, T., Yuan, Y.: ConCORDe-Net: cell count regularized convolutional neural network for cell detection in multiplex immunohistochemistry images. In: Shen, D., et al. (eds.) MICCAI 2019. LNCS, vol. 11764, pp. 667–675. Springer, Cham (2019). https://doi.org/10.1007/978-3-030-32239-7_74

6. He, K., Zhang, X., Ren, S., Sun, J.: Deep residual learning for image recognition. In: CVPR, pp. 770–778 (2016)

7. Hou, L., et al.: Sparse autoencoder for unsupervised nucleus detection and representation in histopathology images. Pat. Recog. **86**, 188–200 (2019)
8. Kainz, P., Urschler, M., Schulter, S., Wohlhart, P., Lepetit, V.: You should use regression to detect cells. In: Navab, N., Hornegger, J., Wells, W.M., Frangi, A.F. (eds.) MICCAI 2015. LNCS, vol. 9351, pp. 276–283. Springer, Cham (2015). https://doi.org/10.1007/978-3-319-24574-4_33
9. Lempitsky, V., Zisserman, A.: Learning to count objects in images. In: NeurIPS, pp. 1324–1332 (2010)
10. Li, C., Wang, X., Liu, W., Latecki, L.J., Wang, B., Huang, J.: Weakly supervised mitosis detection in breast histopathology images using concentric loss. Med. Image Anal. **53**, 165–178 (2019)
11. Li, Y., Zhang, X., Chen, D.: CSRNet: dilated convolutional neural networks for understanding the highly congested scenes. In: CVPR, pp. 1091–1100 (2018)
12. Ram, S., Rodriguez, J.J.: Size-invariant detection of cell nuclei in microscopy images. IEEE Trans. Med. Imaging **35**(7), 1753–1764 (2016)
13. Rojas-Moraleda, R., et al.: Robust detection and segmentation of cell nuclei in biomedical images based on a computational topology framework. Med. Image Anal. **38**, 90–103 (2017)
14. Siegel, R.L., Miller, K.D., Jemal, A.: Cancer statistics, 2019. CA: A Cancer J. Clin. **69**(1), 7–34 (2019)
15. Simonyan, K., Zisserman, A.: Very deep convolutional networks for large-scale image recognition. In: ICLR (2015)
16. Sirinukunwattana, K., Raza, S.E.A., Tsang, Y.W., Snead, D.R., Cree, I.A., Rajpoot, N.M.: Locality sensitive deep learning for detection and classification of nuclei in routine colon cancer histology images. IEEE Trans. Med. Imaging **35**(5), 1196–1206 (2016)
17. Tofighi, M., Guo, T., Vanamala, J.K., Monga, V.: Prior information guided regularized deep learning for cell nucleus detection. IEEE Trans. Med. Imaging **38**, 2047–2058 (2019)
18. Veta, M., et al.: Assessment of algorithms for mitosis detection in breast cancer histopathology images. Med. Image Anal. **20**(1), 237–248 (2015)
19. Xie, Y., Xing, F., Kong, X., Su, H., Yang, L.: Beyond classification: structured regression for robust cell detection using convolutional neural network. In: Navab, N., Hornegger, J., Wells, W.M., Frangi, A.F. (eds.) MICCAI 2015. LNCS, vol. 9351, pp. 358–365. Springer, Cham (2015). https://doi.org/10.1007/978-3-319-24574-4_43
20. Xie, Y., Xing, F., Shi, X., Kong, X., Su, H., Yang, L.: Efficient and robust cell detection: a structured regression approach. Med. Image Anal. **44**, 245–254 (2018)
21. Xu, J., et al.: Stacked sparse autoencoder (SSAE) for nuclei detection on breast cancer histopathology images. IEEE Trans. Med. Imaging **35**(1), 119–130 (2015)
22. Xue, Y., Bigras, G., Hugh, J., Ray, N.: Training convolutional neural networks and compressed sensing end-to-end for microscopy cell detection. IEEE Trans. Med. Imaging **38**, 2632–2641 (2019)
23. Yellin, F., Haeffele, B.D., Roth, S., Vidal, R.: Multi-cell detection and classification using a generative convolutional model. In: CVPR, pp. 8953–8961 (2018)
24. Zhang, A., Shen, J., Xiao, Z., Zhu, F., Zhen, X., Cao, X., Shao, L.: Relational attention network for crowd counting. In: ICCV, pp. 6788–6797 (2019)
25. Zhou, Y., Dou, Q., Chen, H., Qin, J., Heng, P.A.: SFCN-OPI: detection and fine-grained classification of nuclei using sibling FCN with objectness prior interaction. In: AAAI (2018)

Weakly-Supervised Nucleus Segmentation Based on Point Annotations: A Coarse-to-Fine Self-Stimulated Learning Strategy

Kuan Tian[1], Jun Zhang[1], Haocheng Shen[1], Kezhou Yan[1], Pei Dong[1], Jianhua Yao[1], Shannon Che[2], Pifu Luo[2(✉)], and Xiao Han[1(✉)]

[1] Tencent AI Lab, Shenzhen, Guangdong, China
haroldhan@tencent.com
[2] KingMed Diagnostics Co., Ltd., Guangzhou, Guangdong, China
Siweipathology@qq.com

Abstract. Nucleus segmentation is a fundamental task in digital pathology analysis. However, it is labor-expensive and time-consuming to manually annotate the pixel-level full nucleus masks, while it is easier to make point annotations. In this paper, we propose a coarse-to-fine weakly-supervised framework to train the segmentation model from only point annotations to reduce the labor cost of generating pixel-level masks. Our coarse-to-fine strategy can improve segmentation performance progressively in a self-stimulated learning manner. Specifically, to generate coarse segmentation masks, we employ a self-supervision strategy using clustering to perform the binary classification. To avoid trivial solutions, our model is sparsely supervised by annotated positive points and geometric-constrained negative boundaries, via point-to-region spatial expansion and Voronoi partition, respectively. Then, to generate fine segmentation masks, the prior knowledge of edges in the unadorned image is additionally utilized by our proposed contour-sensitive constraint to further tune the nucleus contours. Experimental results on two public datasets show that our model trained with weakly-supervised data (i.e., point annotations) achieves competitive performance compared with the model trained with fully supervised data (i.e., full nucleus masks). The code is made publicly available at https://github.com/tiankuan93/C2FNet.

Keywords: Nucleus segmentation · Weakly-supervised learning · Point-based supervision

1 Introduction

The recent success of deep learning approaches for image segmentation in natural image analysis is generally supported by large-scale fully annotated datasets.

K. Tian and J. Zhang—These authors contribute equally to this paper.

© Springer Nature Switzerland AG 2020
A. L. Martel et al. (Eds.): MICCAI 2020, LNCS 12265, pp. 299–308, 2020.
https://doi.org/10.1007/978-3-030-59722-1_29

Although several deep-learning-based nucleus segmentation methods have been proposed [8,9,11,12], it is still challenging to segment nuclei from pathological images, due to limited training data with full nucleus masks. Generally, it is labor-expensive and time-consuming to perform the full mask annotation. Alternatively, it is much easier to annotate the nuclei with points.

Currently, there are a few studies that focus on the problem of segmenting nuclei with point supervision. To train nucleus segmentation model with only point annotations, extra supervised information, including geometric diagram and clustering labels have been employed [2–4]. For example, Qu et al. [3] proposed a weakly-supervised method for nucleus segmentation based on point annotation in H&E histopathology images, which extracts pixel-level labels by using the Voronoi diagram and k-means clustering algorithm. Then, Chamanzar et al. [4] further modified this method to detect and segment nuclei in immunohistochemistry (IHC) images by using local pixel clustering in every Voronoi sub-region and repel encoding. However, these methods do not pay attention to the nucleus boundary. Differently, Nishimura et al. [2] proposed to a postprocessing method to segment the individual nucleus with graph-cut after obtaining the nucleus region map. Generally, it is difficult to rectify the large bias by independent post-processing. Therefore, Yoo et al. [5] extended a blob generation method (training with point supervision) [1] for nucleus segmentation with an auxiliary network, in which an auxiliary network helps the segmentation network to recognize nucleus boundaries. For the same purpose, Qu et al. [3] employed a dense CRF loss for model refinement in nucleus segmentation.

Accordingly, we would like to develop a method that can integrate the benefits of using pixel clustering and boundary attention. In this paper, we propose a coarse-to-fine framework that can improve the segmentation performance progressively in a self-stimulated learning manner. Specifically, to generate coarse segmentation masks, we employ a self-supervision strategy using clustering to perform the binary classification. To avoid trivial solutions, our model is sparsely supervised by annotated positive points and geometric-constrained negative boundaries, via point-to-region spatial expansion and Voronoi partition. Then, to generate fine segmentation masks, the prior knowledge of edges in the unadorned image is additionally utilized by our proposed contour-sensitive constraint to further tune the nucleus contours. By doing so, both coarse information (i.e., the roughly mask generated by stimulated learning from point annotation) and contour information (i.e., the contour obtained by unadorned image) can be progressively integrated into the learning model in the whole framework, by utilizing our rectified supervisions. Experiments show that our model trained with weakly-supervised data achieves competitive performance compared with the model trained with fully supervised data on MoNuSeg and TNBC datasets.

2   Method

As shown in Fig. 1, our method has two major stages for training the fully convolutional networks (FCN). The first stage obtains the initial coarse nucleus

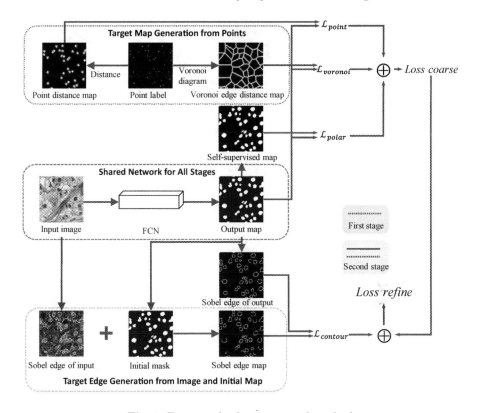

Fig. 1. Framework of our proposed method.

masks for all training data with self-supervised learning and estimated *distance* maps. The second stage further refines the FCN with an additional contour constraint. In the application stage, our FCN model can directly perform the inference with the well trained FCN.

2.1 Coarse Segmentation Estimation

Our target is to generate coarse segmentation masks in the first training stage. Intuitively, we can perform binary classification with clustering via self-supervised learning (i.e., deep clustering [6]). However, typical clustering has the problem of trivial solutions. An optimal decision boundary is to assign all pixels to a single class. While point annotations provide us necessary positive pixels that are too sparse and one class only. Therefore, we would like to transform the point annotations to more informative supervision maps in the first place. With the generated supervision maps, we can train an FCN model end-to-end to obtain the coarse segmentation masks.

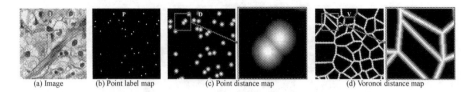

(a) Image   (b) Point label map   (c) Point distance map   (d) Voronoi distance map

Fig. 2. Sparse supervision maps for segmentation.

Maps for Supervision. We denote the image as $\mathbf{I}$ and the positive point annotation map as $\mathbf{P}$. We intend to generate two distance maps that focus on reliable positive and negative pixels, respectively.

1) We propose a *point distance map* (i.e., $\mathbf{D}$) focusing on positive pixels with high confidence. We assume that the annotated point for each nucleus is near the center of the nucleus. Then, we perform a distance filter to point annotations to dilate the dot to a local region with decreasing response, which is considered reliable nucleus supervision, as shown in Fig. 2(c). Mathematically, each element $d_{i,j}$ (i and j are the coordinates in the image space) in $\mathbf{D}$ is calculated as

$$d_{i,j} = max(0, 1 - \alpha\sqrt{(i-m)^2 + (j-n)^2})) \tag{1}$$

where m and n are the coordinates of the nearest positive point in the positive point annotation map $\mathbf{P}$, and α is a scaling parameter to control the scale of distribution. Note that, a Gaussian-like filter could also be employed in our application to obtain the point distance map.

2) We propose another *Voronoi edge distance map* (i.e., $\mathbf{V}$) focusing on negative pixels with high confidence. Since most nuclei are convex and have the shape of ellipse, the Voronoi diagram, according to a given set of points, is an ideal partition of a plane into blocks. Therefore, we employ the Voronoi diagram to obtain the partition edges that are further dilated with the rapidly decreasing response using a distance filter (Eq. 1). This Voronoi edge distance map is utilized to describe reliable negative pixels, as shown in Fig. 2(d).

First Stage Sparsely Supervised Learning. To perform the self-supervised learning, we employ the polarization loss to guide the update of the weights (i.e., $\mathbf{W}$) in the FCN (denoted as f). Denote the output segmentation map as $\mathbf{S}$, with the probability value from 0 to 1, the polarization loss is calculated as

$$\mathcal{L}_{polar}(\mathbf{W}) = \| (f(\mathbf{I}) - H(\mathbf{S}\text{-}\mathbf{0.5})) \|_F^2, \tag{2}$$

where the H(Heaviside step function) operation rectified the output segmentation map to the binary mask to realize the self-supervised learning. Note that, we do not require the function H to be differentiable, since we employ this function for generating the pseudo segmentation mask.

Besides, we calculate two *sparse* losses, named $\mathcal{L}_{point}$ and $\mathcal{L}_{voronoi}$, to guide the update of $\mathbf{W}$. Since the two maps only focus on partial positive and negative

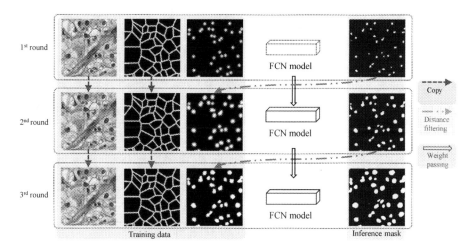

Fig. 3. Point-to-region coarse segmentation method.

pixels. The pixels without responses are the unknown pixels that should not be involved in calculating the loss. Therefore, the losses are sparsely calculated according to the following equations:

$$\mathcal{L}_{point}(\mathbf{W}) = \| \; ReLU(\mathbf{D}) \cdot (f(\mathbf{I}) - \mathbf{D}) \; \|_F^2, \tag{3}$$

$$\mathcal{L}_{voronoi}(\mathbf{W}) = \| \; ReLU(\mathbf{V}) \cdot (f(\mathbf{I}) - \mathbf{0}) \; \|_F^2, \tag{4}$$

where $\cdot$ is the pixel-wise product, and the ReLU operation here is to extract the reliable weight mask for sparse loss calculation. By doing this, $\mathcal{L}_{point}$ only focuses on the assured positive pixels, and $\mathcal{L}_{voronoi}$ only focuses on the assured negative pixels.

Generally, it is difficult to directly obtain satisfactory segmentation masks by training with such sparse constraints. While we could receive initial segmentation maps that are the expansion of our point annotations. Therefore, we iteratively train the segmentation model with the expanded point distance maps, which are updated by the latest trained model. The *point distance map* (i.e., $\mathbf{D}$) is updated according to Eq. 1, where the point annotation map $\mathbf{P}$ is replaced with the estimated segmentation mask (i.e., $\mathbf{S}_c$) from previous training round. The operation repeats two additional times to achieve reliable segmentation masks. As shown in Fig. 3, the silhouette of the nucleus gradually becomes clear by multiple training rounds. Note that, we employ the same Voronoi edge distance map for three iterations. Importantly, because the nuclei differ significantly in size in different images, it is a good idea to use the same size disk (up to the nucleus scale) as the nucleus area. Small nuclei will provide *wrong reliable* positive pixels. Therefore, we gradually fit the coarse segmentation that is more suitable for nuclei of different sizes.

2.2   Contour Refinement

The contours of nuclei in coarse segmentation are not accurate. We propose to use an additional contour-sensitive constraint to refine the contours.

Contour Map for Supervision. For the observation that the colors of nucleus pixels are often different from the surrounding background pixels. We can extract the apparent contour (not necessary to be the complete contours for nuclei) of the input images as an additional supervision. Specifically, we first employ a Sobel operator to detect edges from the original images. Not surprisingly, there are lots of noisy edges in the edge map (i.e., $\mathbf{E}$), as shown in Fig. 4(b). Then, we refine the edge map by the coarse segmentation mask (i.e., $\mathbf{S}_c$), obtained in the *first stage*, to eliminate the unnecessary Sobel edges. The refined edge map (i.e., $\mathbf{E}_r$) is obtained as

$$\mathbf{E}_r = (dilation(\mathbf{S}_c, k) - erosion(\mathbf{S}_c, k))\&\mathbf{E}, \tag{5}$$

where $\&$ is the pixel-wise AND operator, and $dilation(\cdot, k)$ and $erosion(\cdot, k)$ are the morphological operations of image dilation and erosion in k pixels, respectively. Sample images can be found in Fig. 4.

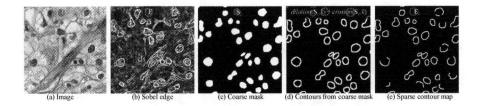

(a) Image   (b) Sobel edge   (c) Coarse mask   (d) Contours from coarse mask   (e) Sparse contour map

Fig. 4. Supervision maps for contour refinement.

Second Stage Sparsely-Supervised Learning. To implement the supplement boundary supervision, we propose an additional contour-sensitive loss (i.e., $\mathcal{L}_{contour}$) to the existing losses to fine-tune the nucleus contours. Similarly, we also perform the supervision sparsely using our generated contour map. The contour-sensitive loss is defined as

$$\mathcal{L}_{contour}(\mathbf{W}) = \| ReLU(\mathbf{E}_r) \cdot (sobel(f(\mathbf{I})) - \mathbf{E}_r) \|_F^2, \tag{6}$$

Note that, the sobel operation is differentiable, and thus $\mathbf{W}$ can be optimized by backpropagation.

2.3   Implementation Details

During the whole training process, the segmentation model is a unified FCN of LinkNet [7], while different synergistic tasks with corresponding losses is applied to the same model output. Our model is implemented based on Keras with Tensorflow backend. The scaling parameter α is set to 0.05. The parameter k for morphological operations is set to 5.

In our weakly-supervised framework, we initialized the network with pre-trained parameters from an natural image segmentation dataset. Because of the lack of training samples, random cropping, scaling, rotation, flipping, brightness, and gamma transformation are utilized for data augmentation. We randomly crop the input image into the size of 512×512 for training the model. For every coarse segmentation iteration, we employ $\mathcal{L}_{point}$, $\mathcal{L}_{voronoi}$, and $\mathcal{L}_{polar}$ with weights of 1.0, 0.1, 0.1, respectively, to train network in 200 epochs. While in the contour estimation stage, we update the network by introducing an additional loss of $\mathcal{L}_{contour}$, to refine the model in 50 epochs. And the final loss weights are 0.01, 0.01, 0.01, 1.0, respectively. We employ Adam optimizer with a learning rate of 0.001 for both stages.

3   Experiments

3.1   Datasets

We evaluate our proposed weakly-supervised framework on two independent nucleus segmentation datasets: MoNuSeg [8] and TNBC [9]. MoNuSeg consists of 30 images of size 1000×1000, which are selected from the TCGA website of different cancer types from multiple hospitals. And TNBC is comprised of 50 images of size 512×512, which are extracted from slides of a cohort of Triple Negative Breast Cancer (TNBC) patients, scanned with Philips Ultra Fast Scanner 1.6RA. Both MoNuSeg and TNBC have pixel-level mask annotations. Therefore we can generate the points annotation for the training set by calculating the central point (with a random bias) of each nucleus mask. We adopt tenfold cross-validation for evaluation.

3.2   Evaluation Metrics

We use four metrics for evaluation, including two pixel-level criteria (i.e., pixel-level IoU and F1 score) and two object-level criteria (i.e., object-level Dice coefficient [10] and Aggregated Jaccard Index (AJI) [8]). The detailed definitions of these metrics are provided in [3,8]. Note that, the pixel-level F1 score is also known as the pixel-level Dice coefficient.

3.3   Results and Comparison

We compare our method with three weakly-supervised methods [1,3,5]. It should be noted that results from [3] are obtained by running the provided code, while

Table 1. Ten-fold validation results on MoNuSeg and TNBC datasets

MoNuSeg

Methods	Pixel-level		Object-level	
	IoU	F1 score	Dice	AJI
Issam et al. [1]	0.5710 ± 0.02	-	-	-
Yoo et al. [5]	0.6136 ± 0.04	-	-	-
Qu et al. [3]	0.5789 ± 0.06	0.7320 ± 0.05	0.7021 ± 0.04	$\mathbf{0.4964 \pm 0.06}$
Our method	$\mathbf{0.6239 \pm 0.03}$	$\mathbf{0.7638 \pm 0.02}$	$\mathbf{0.7132 \pm 0.02}$	0.4927 ± 0.04
Fully supervised	0.6494 ± 0.04	0.7859 ± 0.02	0.7358 ± 0.03	0.5169 ± 0.05

TNBC

Methods	Pixel-level		Object-level	
	IoU	F1 score	Dice	AJI
Issam et al. [1]	0.5504 ± 0.04	-	-	-
Yoo et al. [5]	0.6038 ± 0.03	-	-	-
Qu et al. [3]	0.5420 ± 0.04	0.7008 ± 0.04	0.6931 ± 0.04	0.5181 ± 0.05
Our method	$\mathbf{0.6393 \pm 0.03}$	$\mathbf{0.7510 \pm 0.04}$	$\mathbf{0.7413 \pm 0.03}$	$\mathbf{0.5509 \pm 0.04}$
Fully supervised	0.6950 ± 0.03	0.8022 ± 0.03	0.7881 ± 0.02	0.6233 ± 0.03

Table 2. Comparison of different iterations

MoNuSeg

Iteration	Pixel-level		Object-level	
	IoU	F1 score	Dice	AJI
First-stage-r1	0.2315 ± 0.05	0.3710 ± 0.06	0.3771 ± 0.06	0.2164 ± 0.04
First-stage-r2	0.4198 ± 0.06	0.5864 ± 0.06	0.5741 ± 0.05	0.3727 ± 0.05
First-stage-r3	0.5244 ± 0.03	0.6860 ± 0.02	0.6497 ± 0.03	0.4348 ± 0.05
First-stage-r4	0.5080 ± 0.04	0.6704 ± 0.03	0.6175 ± 0.04	0.3907 ± 0.06
Second-stage-r1	$\mathbf{0.6239 \pm 0.03}$	$\mathbf{0.7638 \pm 0.02}$	$\mathbf{0.7132 \pm 0.02}$	$\mathbf{0.4927 \pm 0.04}$

TNBC

Iteration	Pixel-level		Object-level	
	IoU	F1 score	Dice	AJI
First-stage-r1	0.3426 ± 0.05	0.5053 ± 0.06	0.4984 ± 0.06	0.3303 ± 0.05
First-stage-r2	0.4836 ± 0.08	0.6417 ± 0.08	0.6403 ± 0.05	0.4412 ± 0.07
First-stage-r3	0.5424 ± 0.06	0.6662 ± 0.07	0.6568 ± 0.05	0.4523 ± 0.05
First-stage-r4	0.4362 ± 0.09	0.5895 ± 0.10	0.5664 ± 0.10	0.3450 ± 0.09
Second-stage-r1	$\mathbf{0.6393 \pm 0.03}$	$\mathbf{0.7510 \pm 0.04}$	$\mathbf{0.7413 \pm 0.03}$	$\mathbf{0.5509 \pm 0.04}$

results for [1,5] are obtained from related paper [5]. Furthermore, we train a fully supervised model to illustrate the upper limit of our method. As shown in Table 1, in comparison with all weakly-supervised methods, our method almost achieves the best segmentation performance (except AJI on MoNuSeg set) on two datasets in terms of all evaluation criteria. Moreover, our method can achieve a competitive result compared with the fully supervised model.

To illustrate the effect of the point-to-region stage and contour-refine stage, Table 2 lists the results of each iteration. In the point-to-region stage, the accuracies of the first three iterations are gradually increased, while the fourth iteration decreases the performance. This is because when the positive segmentation results gradually reach the nucleus scale (even larger scale), certain negative pixels will be introduced into the positive point distance map according to Eq. 1, thus leading to unreliable positive map. However, the last row of Table 2 shows that after the contour-refinement stage, the segmentation model can better fit the nucleus edges, thereby further improving the effectiveness of the segmentation model.

4 Conclusion

In this paper, we propose a weakly-supervised segmentation framework based on point annotations. First, we train a sparse segmentation model through multiple iterations, and then we propose to use the additional contour-sensitive loss for contour refinement. In the experiments, our method can obtain a superior segmentation performance compared with the state-of-the-art weakly-supervised methods using point supervision. It suggests the effectiveness of our proposed coarse-to-fine learning framework.

References

1. Laradji, I.H., Rostamzadeh, N., Pinheiro, P.O., Vazquez, D., Schmidt, M.: Where are the blobs: counting by localization with point supervision. In: Ferrari, V., Hebert, M., Sminchisescu, C., Weiss, Y. (eds.) ECCV 2018. LNCS, vol. 11206, pp. 560–576. Springer, Cham (2018). https://doi.org/10.1007/978-3-030-01216-8_34
2. Nishimura, K., Ker, D.F.E., Bise, R.: Weakly supervised cell instance segmentation by propagating from detection response. In: Shen, D., et al. (eds.) MICCAI 2019. LNCS, vol. 11764, pp. 649–657. Springer, Cham (2019). https://doi.org/10.1007/978-3-030-32239-7_72
3. Qu, H., Wu, P., Huang, Q., et al.: Weakly supervised deep nuclei segmentation using points annotation in histopathology images. In: International Conference on Medical Imaging with Deep Learning, pp. 390–400 (2019)
4. Chamanzar, A., Nie, Y.: Weakly supervised multi-task learning for cell detection and segmentation. arXiv preprint arXiv:1910.12326 (2019)
5. Yoo, I., Yoo, D., Paeng, K.: PseudoEdgeNet: nuclei segmentation only with point annotations. In: Shen, D., et al. (eds.) MICCAI 2019. LNCS, vol. 11764, pp. 731–739. Springer, Cham (2019). https://doi.org/10.1007/978-3-030-32239-7_81

6. Hershey, J.R., Chen, Z., Le Roux, J., et al.: Deep clustering: discriminative embeddings for segmentation and separation. In: 2016 IEEE International Conference on Acoustics, Speech and Signal Processing (ICASSP). IEEE, pp. 31–35 (2016)
7. Chaurasia, A., Culurciello, E.: Linknet: exploiting encoder representations for efficient semantic segmentation. In: 2017 IEEE Visual Communications and Image Processing (VCIP). IEEE, pp. 1–4 (2017)
8. Kumar, N., Verma, R., Sharma, S., et al.: A dataset and a technique for generalized nuclear segmentation for computational pathology. IEEE Trans. Med. Imaging **36**(7), 1550–1560 (2017)
9. Naylor, P., Lae, M., Reyal, F., et al.: Segmentation of nuclei in histopathology images by deep regression of the distance map. IEEE Trans. Med. Imaging **38**(2), 448–459 (2018)
10. Sirinukunwattana, K., Snead, D.R.J., Rajpoot, N.M.: A stochastic polygons model for glandular structures in colon histology images. IEEE Trans. Med. Imaging **34**(11), 2366–2378 (2015)
11. Sadanandan, S.K., Ranefall, P., Le Guyader, S., et al.: Automated training of deep convolutional neural networks for cell segmentation. Sci. Rep. **7**(1), 1–7 (2017)
12. Hatipoglu, N., Bilgin, G.: Cell segmentation in histopathological images with deep learning algorithms by utilizing spatial relationships. Med. Biol. Eng. Comput. **55**(10), 1829–1848 (2017)

Structure Preserving Stain Normalization of Histopathology Images Using Self Supervised Semantic Guidance

Dwarikanath Mahapatra[1(✉)], Behzad Bozorgtabar[2,3,4],
Jean-Philippe Thiran[2,3,4], and Ling Shao[1,5]

[1] Inception Institute of Artificial Intelligence, Abu Dhabi, UAE
{dwarikanath.mahapatra,ling.shao}@inceptioniai.org
[2] Signal Processing Laboratory 5, EPFL, Lausanne, Switzerland
{behzad.bozorgtabar,jean-philippe.thiran}@epfl.ch
[3] Department of Radiology, Lausanne University Hospital, Lausanne, Switzerland
[4] Center of Biomedical Imaging, Lausanne, Switzerland
[5] Mohamed bin Zayed University of Artificial Intelligence, Abu Dhabi, UAE

Abstract. Although generative adversarial network (GAN) based style transfer is state of the art in histopathology color-stain normalization, they do not explicitly integrate structural information of tissues. We propose a self-supervised approach to incorporate semantic guidance into a GAN based stain normalization framework and preserve detailed structural information. Our method does not require manual segmentation maps which is a significant advantage over existing methods. We integrate semantic information at different layers between a pre-trained semantic network and the stain color normalization network. The proposed scheme outperforms other color normalization methods leading to better classification and segmentation performance.

Keywords: GANs · Semantic guidance · Color normalization · Digital pathology

1 Introduction

Increased digitization of pathology slides has enhanced the importance of digital histopathology in the medical imaging community. Staining is an important part of pathological tissue preparation where, e.g., Hematoxylin and Eosin dyes alter intensity of tissue elements - nuclei turns dark purple while other structures become pink. Tissue structures become distinguishable facilitating manual or automated analysis. Color variation of the same structure is observed due to differences in staining protocols from different centers, different dye manufacturers and scanner characteristics. Consequently, this leads to inconsistent diagnosis and limits the efficacy of automated methods. Hence there is a need for stain color normalization to have uniform appearance of dye-stained regions.

A. L. Martel et al. (Eds.): MICCAI 2020, LNCS 12265, pp. 309–319, 2020.
https://doi.org/10.1007/978-3-030-59722-1_30

We propose to integrate self-supervised semantic guidance with GANs for better structure preservation after stain normalization.

Two widely explored categories for stain normalization methods are color matching [23], and stain-separation [14,18]. Since these methods rely on template images it leads to mismatch and poor performance when the template is not representative of the dataset The third category comprises machine learning approaches [12] which sub-divide an input image into multiple tissue regions using a sparse autoencoder, and independently normalize each region. Recent works solve stain normalization as a style-transfer problem using Generative adversarial networks(GANs) [4]. GANs have found many applications in medical image analysis [13,32] such as image super-resolution [19], registration [22], segmentation [21,34] and augmentation [5,20] to name a few. Unpaired Image-to-Image Translation with CycleGANs were used in [26] to facilitate style transfer across two domains. These methods do not require a reference image and achieve high visual agreement with images from the target domain. Gupta et. al. in [10] leverage GAN based image-image translation for augmenting histopathology images to improve segmentation accuracy. Other variants include use of prior latent variables and auxiliary networks [33], and auxiliary inputs [35].

Previous works have demonstrated the effectiveness of cycle GANs in stain normalization, thus eliminating the tedious task of selecting a reference stain. However, as pointed out in [8] shape outlines of translated objects may change which leads to sub optimal performance. Gadermayr [8] used two different pipelines to overcome this pitfall. While their results are effective, the pipeline itself is tedious. Vahadane et al. [30] propose a structure preserving normalization method using non negative matrix factorization but do not explicitly use semantic information. Lahiani et al. [16] introduce a perceptual embedding loss to reducing tiling artifacts in reconstructed whole slide images (WSI).

Self-supervised learning requires formulating a proxy (or pretext) task which can be solved on the same dataset and using the trained network to perform self supervised tasks such as segmentation or depth estimation [9]. Some examples in the field of medical image analysis include surgical video re-colorization as a pretext task for surgical instrument segmentation [25], rotation prediction for lung lobe segmentation and nodule detection [29] and use disease bounding box localization for cardiac MR image segmentation [2].

Contributions: Since medical image analysis influences diagnostic decisions it is helpful to preserve information about finer structures for semantic guidance. Inclusion of segmentation information requires detailed annotations of the image which is extremely cumbersome for WSIs. Our primary contribution is a color stain normalization method that uses semantic guidance through self supervised features. We build our model using cyclic GANs [22,36] as they are an effective choice for transferring image appearances across domains. Semantic guidance is incorporated using a pre-trained semantic segmentation network trained on a different dataset. Semantic information in the form of segmentation feature maps from multiple levels is injected into the stain normalization network. Since

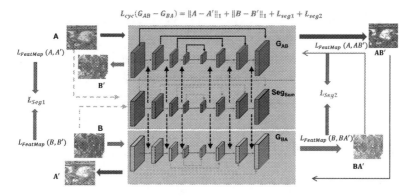

$$\mathcal{L}_{cyc}(G_{AB} - G_{BA}) = \|A - A'\|_1 + \|B - B'\|_1 + L_{seg1} + L_{seg2}$$

Fig. 1. Workflow of our proposed stain colour normalization method using CycleGANs. Semantic guidance is injected from the corresponding layers of Seg_{Sem} into the generators G_{AB}, G_{BA} and help preserve important cellular structures in normalization.

we use self supervised segmentation maps we do not need manual annotations during training or test stages which makes it easy to deploy for novel test cases.

Our paper makes the following contributions: 1) we integrate self-supervised features for stain normalization using semantic guidance from a pre-trained network; 2) self supervised segmentation feature maps allow us to use our method despite unavailability of manual segmentation maps. Our proposed method beats the state of the art stain normalization methods when the normalized images are used for classification and segmentation tasks. Different from [16], 1) we explicitly use semantic information to capture geometric and structural patterns for image normalization; 2) use pixel adaptive convolutions; and 3) match fine grained segmentation maps of normalized images.

2   Method

We denote the set of training images as I_{Tr}, their labels (manual segmentation masks or disease class) as L_{Tr}, and the trained model (segmentation or classification) as M_{Tr}. Given a set of test images I_{Test} our objective is to segment/classify them using the pre-trained model M_{Tr}. To successfully do that we : 1) color normalize the test images using our proposed method SegCN-Net; and 2) apply pre-trained M_{Tr}.

Figure 1 depicts the workflow of our proposed stain normalization method. There are three different networks, G_{AB} (the generator network in red), Seg_{Sem} (the pre-trained segmentation network in yellow providing semantic guidance), and G_{BA} (the generator network in green). All three networks are based on a UNet architecture [24] to facilitate easy integration of semantic information during training and test phases. G_{AB} transforms A to look like an image from domain B while G_{BA} performs the reverse translation to maintain cycle consistency. Images from A and B are passed through Seg_{Sem} and the information from different layers of Seg_{Sem} is fused with the corresponding layer of G_{AB} and G_{BA} to facilitate integration of semantic guidance.

2.1   Semantic Guidance Through Self Supervised Learning

Our self-supervised approach does not define any pretext task but focuses on using pre-trained networks for semantic guidance in stain normalization. Semantic features for guiding the stain normalization task come from the pre-trained segmentation network Seg_{Sem} shown in Fig. 1. Seg_{Sem}'s pre-trained weights guide the feature learning process of the two generators without the need for further finetuning.

The translation invariance property of standard convolution makes it content-agnostic and poses certain limitations such as, despite reducing number of parameters it may lead to sub-optimal learning of feature representations. Additionally, spatially-shared filters globally average loss gradients over the entire image and the learned weights can only encode location-specific information within their limited receptive fields. Content-agnostic filters find it difficult to distinguish between visually similar pixels of different regions (e.g. dark areas due to artifacts or tissues) nor learn to identify similar objects of different appearance (e.g. same tissue structure with different shades as in our problem).

Pixel-adaptive convolutions [28] can address the above limitations where the feature representations encoded in the semantic network helps to distinguish between confounding regions, and are defined as

$$\mathbf{v}'_i = \sum_{j \in \Omega(i)} K(\mathbf{f}_i, \mathbf{f}_j) \mathbf{W} \left[\mathbf{p}_i - \mathbf{p}_j \right] \mathbf{v}_j + b \tag{1}$$

where $\mathbf{f}$ are the features from the semantic network that guide the pixel adaptive convolutions, $\mathbf{p}$ are pixel co-ordinates, $\mathbf{W}$ is the convolutional weights of kernel size k, Ω_i is a $k \times k$ convolution window around pixel i, $\mathbf{v}$ is the input and b is the bias term. For each feature map, we apply a 3×3 and a 1×1 convolution layer followed by Group Normalization [31] and exponential linear units (ELU) non-linearities [7]. The resulting semantic feature maps are fused with the corresponding layers of G_{AB} and G_{BA}, and used as guidance on their respective pixel-adaptive convolutional layers. K is a standard Gaussian kernel defined by

$$K(\mathbf{f}_i, \mathbf{f}_j) = \exp\left(-\frac{1}{2}(\mathbf{f}_i - \mathbf{f}_j)^T \Sigma_{ij}^{-1} (\mathbf{f}_i - \mathbf{f}_j) \right) \tag{2}$$

where Σ_{ij}^{-1} is the covariance matrix between feature vectors $\mathbf{f}_i, \mathbf{f}_j$ and formulated as a diagonal matrix $\sigma^2 \cdot I_D$, where σ is an additional learnable parameter for each filter. Standard convolution is a special case when $K(\mathbf{f}_i, \mathbf{f}_j) = 1$.

To capture semantic information across multiple scales we extract the feature maps after each convolution stage to get a set of maps with varying dimension due to max pooling operations, whose values are normalized to $[0, 1]$. For a given pair of images we calculate the mean squared error between f_s - corresponding multi scale feature maps. Thus, the feature map loss between a and $\hat{a}$ is

$$L_{FeatMap}(a,\hat{a}) = \sum_{s=1}^{S} \sqrt{\frac{(f_s(a) - f_s(\hat{a}))^2}{N}} \tag{3}$$

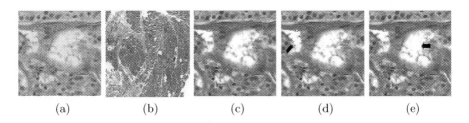

(a)	(b)	(c)	(d)	(e)

Fig. 2. Color normalization results: (a) Domain A image; (b) Domain B image; Domain A transformed to Domain B using: (c) proposed $SegCN - Net$; (d) [8]; (e) [35]. Areas of structure inconsistency are shown by black arrows. (Color figure online)

2.2 Color Normalization Using Semantic Guidance

Cycle GANs transform an image from domain A to B, and the reverse translation from B to A should generate the original input image. In forward cycle consistency, an image from domain A is translated to domain B by generator G_{AB} expressed as $a\hat{b} = G_{AB}(a)$. Image $a\hat{b}$ is translated back to domain A by G_{BA} to get $\hat{a} = G_{BA}(a\hat{b})$. Similarly, the original and reconstructed images from B should also match. Thus the overall cycle consistency loss is,

$$L_{cycle}(G_{AB}, G_{BA}) = E_a \|a - G_{BA}(G_{AB}(a))\|_1 + \|b - G_{AB}(G_{BA}(b))\|_1 + L_{Seg}, \tag{4}$$

$$L_{Seg} = \overbrace{L_{FeatMap}(a,\hat{a}) + L_{FeatMap}(b,\hat{b})}^{L_{Seg1}} + \overbrace{L_{FeatMap}(a,a\hat{b}) + L_{FeatMap}(b,b\hat{a})}^{L_{Seg2}} \tag{5}$$

We impose the additional constraint that the fine grained segmentation maps of images should match, not just of the reverse transformed images $a,\hat{a}$ and $b,\hat{b}$) but also between the outputs of each generator and the corresponding original images, i.e. between $a,a\hat{b}$ and $b\hat{a},b$. L_{Seg2} is specifically designed to preserve structural information between images of domain A, B in stain normalization.

Discriminator D_B is employed to distinguish between real image b and generated image $a\hat{b}$ where the adversarial loss in forward cycle, L_{adv}, is

$$L_{adv}(G_{AB}, D_B, A, B) = E_b \log D_B(b) + E_a \log \left[(1 - D_B(G_{AB}(a)))\right]. \tag{6}$$

There also exists a corresponding $L_{adv}(G_{BA}, D_A, B, A)$ to distinguish between real image a and generated image $b\hat{a}$ Thus the final objective function is

$$L = L_{adv}(G_{AB}, D_B, A, B) + L_{adv}(G_{BA}, D_A, B, A) + L_{cyc}(G_{AB}, G_{BA}) \tag{7}$$

Network Architecture. All the networks $(G_{AB}, G_{BA}, Seg_{Sem})$ are based on a UNet architecture [24] with a ResNet backbone. Each convolution block has 3 layers of convolution layers (all using the pixel adaptive convolutions and ELU) followed by a 2×2 maxpooling step of stride 2. Skip connections exist between the stages of the contracting and expanding path. 3×3 kernels are used with adequate padding to maintain image dimensions. There are four convolution blocks in both paths.

3   Experimental Results

3.1   Evaluation Set up for Classification

Our proposed color normalization method is SegCN-Net (segmentation based color normalization network), and evaluate it's performance as a pre-processing step. CAMELYON16 [3] and CAMELYON17 [6] public datasets are used having WSIs for classification and segmentation of breast cancer metastases. CAMELYON16 has images from 2 independent medical centers while CAMELYON17's images come from 5 centers. We train SegCN-Net on CAMELYON16 and evaluate on transformed images of CAMELYON17. Domain A consists of images from Center 1 of CAMELYON16 ($C1_{16}$), while Domain B has images from $C2_{16}$. $100,000$ patches of 256×256 were extracted from each domain, and we train all models using a NVIDIA Titan X GPU having $12\,GB$ RAM, Adam optimiser [15] with a learning rate of 0.002. Xavier initialization was used and training took $42\,h$ for 150 epochs with batch size 16.

For evaluation, images from the different centers of CAMELYON17 were split into training/validation/test in $50/30/20\%$ to obtain the following split: $C1_{17}$:37/22/15, $C2_{17}$: 34/20/14, $C3_{17}$: 43/24/18, $C4_{17}$: 35/20/15, $C5_{17}$: 36/20/15. For our first baseline, we train 5 different ResNet50 [11] with batch size 32, Adam optimizer learning rate of 0.001 for 70 epochs (denoted as $\mathbf{ResNet}_{NoNorm}$) on images from $C1_{17}$–$C5_{17}$ using the split described before, but without normalization. We apply SegCN-Net on images from different centers of CAMELYON17 to color normalize them and train ResNet50 networks with similar settings as $ResNet_{NoNorm}$ using the data split of $C1_{17}$–$C2_{17}$. The results (using area under curve (AUC) as the performance metric) are reported in Table 1 under SegCN-Net. We replace our stain normalization method with other competing methods, such as [8,18,23,30,35] and perform the same set of classification experiments with the performance summarized in Table 1.

[30] aims to preserve structure information through templates while [35] employ stain color matrix matching. Since they do not explicitly use segmentation information, SegCN-Net performs better than both methods. The method by [8] actually does better than others because of the use of segmentation information, but requires labeled segmentation maps. SegCN-Net's superior performance shows that use of self supervised segmentation can be leveraged when manual segmentation maps are not available. Figure 2 shows the stain normalized images of different methods. The advantage of SegCN-Net in preserving structural information is indicated by the black arrows where the glandular structure

is deformed from the original image in [35], and to a lesser extent in [8]. Thus the advantages of our semantic guidance based stain normalization is obvious.

Table 1. Classification results in terms of AUC measures for different stain normalization methods on the CAMELYON17 dataset. p values are with respect to SegCN-Net.

Method	Center 1	Center 2	Center 3	Center 4	Center 5	Average	p
$ResNet_{C17noNorm}$	0.8068	0.7203	0.7027	0.8289	0.8203	0.7758	0.0001
Reinhard [23]	0.7724	0.7934	0.8041	0.8013	0.7862	0.7915	0.0001
Macenko [18]	0.7148	0.7405	0.8331	0.7412	0.7436	0.7546	0.0001
CycleGAN	0.9010	0.7173	0.8914	0.8811	0.8102	0.8402	0.002
Vahadane [30]	0.9123	0.7347	0.9063	0.8949	0.8223	0.8541	0.003
Zhou [35]	0.9381	0.7614	0.7932	0.9013	0.9227	0.8633	0.013
Gadermayr [8]	0.9487	0.8115	0.8727	0.9235	0.9351	0.8983	0.013
SegCN-Net	**0.9668**	**0.8537**	**0.9385**	**0.9548**	**0.9462**	**0.9320**	-
Ablation Study Results							
SegCN-Net$_{Conv}$	0.9331	0.8255	0.9148	0.9259	0.9181	.9035	0.0008
SegCN-Net$_{Seg\ Only}$	0.9376	0.7974	0.8942	0.9187	0.9012	0.8898	0.0001
SegCN-Net$_{C17Rand}$	0.9624	0.8403	0.9267	0.9478	0.9391	0.9232	0.34
SegCN-Net$_{Glas}$	0.9762	0.8627	0.9509	0.9677	0.9588	0.9432	0.042

3.2 Ablation Studies

Table 1 summarizes the performance of the following variants of our method:

1. SegCN-Net$_{Conv}$ - $SegCN - Net$ using standard convolutions instead of pixel adaptive convolutions.
2. SegCN-Net$_{Seg}$ - SegCN-Net using only the final segmentation masks without the intermediate feature map. This evaluates the relevance of using a single segmentation map without semantic guidance at each layer.
3. SegCN-Net$_{C17Rand}$ - SegCN-Net tested on all normalized images of C17 with random selection of train/val/split. The results are an average of 10 runs and investigate possible bias in data split.

In the original approach Seg_{Sem} was pre-trained on the MS-COCO dataset [17]. In a variant of our proposed method we use a network pre-trained on the Glas segmentation challenge dataset [27] which has segmentation masks of histological images, and use it for classification of the test images from CAMELYON17. The results are shown in Table 1 under SegCN-Net$_{Glas}$.

SegCN-Net$_{Glas}$ shows better classification performance than SegCN-Net, and the difference in results at $p = 0.042$ is significant as semantic guidance is obtained from a network trained on histology images while SegCN-Net used natural images. Although natural images provide some degree of semantic guidance by learning edge features, Seg_{Sem} trained on histopathology images provides domain specific guidance and hence leads to better performance. Since such a annotated dataset is not always available for medical images, we show that semantic guidance from a network trained on natural images significantly improves upon the state of art method for stain color normalization.

SegCN-Net$_{C17Rand}$ performance is close to SegCN-Net without any statistically significant difference, indicating that SegCN-Net is not biased on the test set. SegCN-Net$_{Seg\ Only}$ shows inferior performance compared to SegCN-Net, which indicates that multistage semantic guidance is much better than a single segmentation map. However SegCN-Net$_{Seg\ Only}$ still performs slightly better than [8] indicating the advantages of including segmentation information for structure preserving color normalization.

Table 2. Segmentation results on the GLas Segmentation challenge for $SegCN - Net$, [8,35] and the top ranked method. HD is in mm. Best results per metric in bold.

	$SegCN - Net$		Glas Rank 1		[8]		[35]	
	Part A	Part B	Part A	Part B	Part A	Part B	Part A	Part B
F1	**0.9351**	**0.7542**	0.912	0.716	0.926	0.728	0.922	0.729
DM	**0.9212**	**0.8054**	0.897	0.781	0.909	0.798	0.892	0.785
HD	**42.276**	**143.286**	45.418	160.347	44.243	157.643	47.012	161.321

3.3   Segmentation Results

We apply our method on the public GLAS segmentation challenge [27] which has manual segmentation maps of glands in 165 $H\&E$ stained images derived from 16 histological sections from different patients with stage $T3$ or $T4$ colorectal adenocarcinoma. We normalize the images using SegCN-Net (using MS-COCO images for semantic guidance), train a UNet with residual convolution blocks and apply on the test set. The performance metrics - Dice Metric (DM), Hausdorff distance (HD), F1 score (F1)- for SegCN-Net, [8,35] and the top ranked method [1] are summarized in Table 2. [35]'s performance comes close to the top ranked while [8] outperforms both of them, and SegCN-Net gives the best results across all three metrics. This shows that stain normalization in general does a good job of standardizing image appearance which in turn improves segmentation results. SegCN-Net performs best due to integration of segmentation information through self supervised semantic guidance.

3.4   Color Constancy Results:

Similar to [33] we report results for normalized median intensity, which measures color constancy of images, for the same dataset and obtained the following values:

SegCN-Net - Standard Deviation (SD) = 0.011, Coefficient of Variation (CV) = 0.021, which is better than Zanjani et al. [33] - $SD = 0.0188, CV = 0.0209$.

As reported in [16] we calculate values for complex wavelet structural similarity index (CWSSIM) between real and generated images. CWSSIM $\in [0, 1]$ with higher values indicating better match and is robust to small translations and rotations. Mean CWSSIM values of SegCN-Net is 0.82, which is higher than CycleGAN (0.75), [16] (0.77) and other baseline methods.

4 Conclusion

We have proposed a histopathology image stain color normalization approach using cycle GANs that integrates semantic guidance from self supervised segmentation feature maps. Our semantic guidance approach facilitates inclusion of segmentation information without the need for manually segmented maps that are very difficult to obtain. Experimental results on public datasets show our approach outperforms state of the art normalization methods when evaluated for classification and segmentation. Ablation studies also show the importance of semantic guidance. Although semantic guidance is obtained from the MS-COCO dataset of natural images, we also demonstrate that when domain specific guidance is used the results improve even further. This has potential in improving performance of medical image analysis tasks where annotations are not readily available.

References

1. Glas segmentation challenge results. https://warwick.ac.uk/fac/sci/dcs/research/tia/glascontest/results/. Accessed 30 Jan 2020
2. Bai, W., et al.: Self-supervised learning for Cardiac MR image segmentation by anatomical position prediction. In: Shen, D., et al. (eds.) MICCAI 2019. LNCS, vol. 11765, pp. 541–549. Springer, Cham (2019). https://doi.org/10.1007/978-3-030-32245-8_60
3. Bejnordi, B.E., Veta, M., van Diest, P.J., van Ginneken, B., Karssemeijer, N., Litjens, G., van der Laak, J.: Diagnostic assessment of deep learning algorithms for detection of lymph node metastases in women with breast cancer. JAMA **318**(22), 2199–2210 (2017)
4. BenTaieb, A., Hamarneh, G.: Adversarial stain transfer for histopathology image analysis. IEEE Trans. Med. Imaging **37**(3), 792–802 (2018)
5. Bozorgtabar, B., et al.: Informative sample generation using class aware generative adversarial networks for classification of chest Xrays. Comput. Vis. Image Underst. **184**, 57–65 (2019)
6. Bándi, P., et al.: From detection of individual metastases to classification of lymph node status at the patient level: The CAMELYON17 challenge. IEEE Trans. Med. Imaging **38**(2), 550–560 (2019)
7. Clevert, D.A., Unterthiner, T., Hochreiter, S.: Fast and accurate deep network learning by exponential linear units (ELUs). In: Proceedings of ICLR (2016)

8. Gadermayr, M., Appel, V., Klinkhammer, B.M., Boor, P., Merhof, D.: Which way round? a study on the performance of stain-translation for segmenting arbitrarily dyed histological images. In: Frangi, A.F., Schnabel, J.A., Davatzikos, C., Alberola-López, C., Fichtinger, G. (eds.) MICCAI 2018. LNCS, vol. 11071, pp. 165–173. Springer, Cham (2018). https://doi.org/10.1007/978-3-030-00934-2_19

9. Guizilini, V., Hou, R., Li, J., Ambrus, R., Gaidon, A.: Semantically-guided representation learning for self-supervised monocular depth. In: Proceedings of ICLR, pp. 1–14 (2020)

10. Gupta, L., Klinkhammer, B.M., Boor, P., Merhof, D., Gadermayr, M.: GAN-based image enrichment in digital pathology boosts segmentation accuracy. In: Shen, D., et al. (eds.) MICCAI 2019. LNCS, vol. 11764, pp. 631–639. Springer, Cham (2019). https://doi.org/10.1007/978-3-030-32239-7_70

11. He, K., Zhang, X., Ren, S., Sun, J.: Deep residual learning for image recognition. In: Proceedings of CVPR (2016)

12. Janowczyk, A., Basavanhally, A., Madabhushi, A.: Stain normalization using sparse autoencoders (STANOSA): application to digital pathology. Comput. Med. Imaging Graph **57**, 50–61 (2017)

13. Kazeminia, S., et al.: Gans for medical image analysis. In: arXiv preprint arXiv:1809.06222 (2018)

14. Khan, A., Rajpoot, N., Treanor, D., Magee, D.: A nonlinear mapping approach to stain normalization in digital histopathology images using image-specific color deconvolution. IEEE Trans. Biomed. Eng. **61**(6), 1729–1738 (2014)

15. Kingma, D.P., Ba, J.: Adam: a method for stochastic optimization. In: arXiv preprint arXiv:1412.6980 (2014)

16. Lahiani, A., Navab, N., Albarqouni, S., Klaiman, E.: Perceptual embedding consistency for seamless reconstruction of Tilewise style transfer. In: Shen, D., et al. (eds.) MICCAI 2019. LNCS, vol. 11764, pp. 568–576. Springer, Cham (2019). https://doi.org/10.1007/978-3-030-32239-7_63

17. Lin, T.-Y., et al.: Microsoft COCO: common objects in context. In: Fleet, D., Pajdla, T., Schiele, B., Tuytelaars, T. (eds.) ECCV 2014. LNCS, vol. 8693, pp. 740–755. Springer, Cham (2014). https://doi.org/10.1007/978-3-319-10602-1_48

18. Macenko, M., et al.: A method for normalizing histology slides for quantitative analysis. In: IEEE International Symposium on Proceedings of Biomedical Imaging: From Nano to Macro, ISBI 2009, pp. 1107–1110 (2009)

19. Mahapatra, D., Bozorgtabar, B., Hewavitharanage, S., Garnavi, R.: Image super resolution using generative adversarial networks and local saliency maps for retinal image analysis. In: Descoteaux, M., Maier-Hein, L., Franz, A., Jannin, P., Collins, D.L., Duchesne, S. (eds.) MICCAI 2017. LNCS, vol. 10435, pp. 382–390. Springer, Cham (2017). https://doi.org/10.1007/978-3-319-66179-7_44

20. Mahapatra, D., Bozorgtabar, B., Shao, L.: Pathological retinal region segmentation from oct images using geometric relation based augmentation. In: Proceedings of IEEE CVPR, pp. 9611–9620 (2020)

21. Mahapatra, D., Bozorgtabar, B., Thiran, J.-P., Reyes, M.: Efficient active learning for image classification and segmentation using a sample selection and conditional generative adversarial network. In: Frangi, A.F., Schnabel, J.A., Davatzikos, C., Alberola-López, C., Fichtinger, G. (eds.) MICCAI 2018. LNCS, vol. 11071, pp. 580–588. Springer, Cham (2018). https://doi.org/10.1007/978-3-030-00934-2_65

22. Mahapatra, D., Ge, Z.: Training data independent image registration using generative adversarial networks and domain adaptation. Pattern Recogn. **100**, 1–14 (2020)

23. Reinhard, E., Adhikhmin, M., Gooch, B., Shirley, P.: Color transfer between images. IEEE Comput. Graph. Appl. **21**(5), 34–41 (2001)
24. Ronneberger, O., Fischer, P., Brox, T.: U-Net: convolutional networks for biomedical image segmentation. In: Navab, N., Hornegger, J., Wells, W.M., Frangi, A.F. (eds.) MICCAI 2015. LNCS, vol. 9351, pp. 234–241. Springer, Cham (2015). https://doi.org/10.1007/978-3-319-24574-4_28
25. Ross, T., et al.: Gexploiting the potential of unlabeled endoscopic video data with self-supervised learning. Int. J. Comput. Assist. Radiol. Surg. **13**, 925–933 (2018)
26. Shaban, M.T., Baur, C., Navab, N., Albarqouni, S.: StainGAN: stain style transfer for digital histological images. arXiv preprint arXiv:1804.01601 (2018)
27. Sirinukunwattana, K., et al.: Gland segmentation in colon histology images: the GlaS challenge contest. Med. Imaging Anal. **35**, 489–502 (2017)
28. Su, H., Jampani, V., Sun, D., Gallo, O., Learned-Miller, E., Kautz, J.: Pixel-adaptive convolutional neural networks. In: Proceedings of IEEE CVPR, pp. 11166–11175 (2019)
29. Tajbakhsh, N., et al.: Surrogate supervision for medical image analysis: effective deep learning from limited quantities of labeled data. In: Proceedings of IEEE ISBI, pp. 1251–1255 (2019)
30. Vahadane, A., et al.: Structure-preserving color normalization and sparse stain separation for histological images. IEEE Trans. Med. Imaging **35**(8), 1962–1971 (2016)
31. Wu, Y., He, K.: Group normalization. In: Ferrari, V., Hebert, M., Sminchisescu, C., Weiss, Y. (eds.) ECCV 2018. LNCS, vol. 11217, pp. 3–19. Springer, Cham (2018). https://doi.org/10.1007/978-3-030-01261-8_1
32. Yi, X., Walia, E., Babyn, P.: Generative adversarial network in medical imaging: a review. Med. Imaging Anal. **58**, 101552 (2019)
33. Zanjani, F.G., Zinger, S., Bejnordi, B.E., van der Laak, J.A.: Histopathology stain-color normalization using deep generative models. In: Proceedings of Medical Imaging with Deep Learning (2018)
34. Zhao, M., et al.: Craniomaxillofacial Bony structures segmentation from MRI with deep-supervision adversarial learning. In: Frangi, A.F., Schnabel, J.A., Davatzikos, C., Alberola-López, C., Fichtinger, G. (eds.) MICCAI 2018. LNCS, vol. 11073, pp. 720–727. Springer, Cham (2018). https://doi.org/10.1007/978-3-030-00937-3_82
35. Zhou, N., Cai, D., Han, X., Yao, J.: Enhanced cycle-consistent generative adversarial network for color normalization of H&E stained images. In: Shen, D., et al. (eds.) MICCAI 2019. LNCS, vol. 11764, pp. 694–702. Springer, Cham (2019). https://doi.org/10.1007/978-3-030-32239-7_77
36. Zhu, J., Park, T., Isola, P., Efros, A.: Unpaired image-to-image translation using cycle-consistent adversarial networks. In: arXiv preprint arXiv:1703.10593 (2017)

A Novel Loss Calibration Strategy for Object Detection Networks Training on Sparsely Annotated Pathological Datasets

Hansheng Li[1], Xin Han[1], Yuxin Kang[1], Xiaoshuang Shi[2], Mengdi Yan[1],
Zixu Tong[1], Qirong Bu[1], Lei Cui[1(✉)], Jun Feng[1], and Lin Yang[1]

[1] School of Information Science and Technology, Northwest University,
Xi'an 710127, Shaanxi, China
{leicui,fengjun,linyang}@nwu.edu.cn
[2] Biomedical Engineering, University of Florida, Gainesville, USA

Abstract. Recently, object detection frameworks based on Convolutional Neural Networks (CNNs) have become powerful methods for various tasks of medical image analysis; however, they often struggle with most pathological datasets, which are impossible to annotate all the cells. Obviously, sparse annotations may lead to a seriously miscalculated loss in training, which limits the performance of networks. To address this limitation, we investigate the internal training process of object detection networks. Our core observation is that there is a significant density difference between the regression boxes of the positive instances and negative instances. Our novel Boxes Density Energy (BDE) focuses on utilizing the densities of regression boxes to conduct loss-calibration, which is dedicated to reducing the miscalculated loss, meanwhile to penalizing mispredictions with a relatively more significant loss. Thus BDE can guide networks to be trained along the right direction. Extensive experiments have demonstrated that, BDE on the sparsely annotated pathological dataset can significantly boost the performance of networks, and even with 1.0–1.5% higher recall than networks trained on the fully annotated dataset.

1 Introduction

Many excellent object detection frameworks based on Convolutional Neural Networks (CNNs) have been proposed and persistently improved in recent years [1–8]. Meanwhile, medical image analysis methods based on these architectures are also booming [9–11]. It is worth noting that the tremendous success of object detection depends on the availability of a large corpus of fully annotated instances (such as object bounding boxes) in training images, which means that every positive instance in each training image must be annotated [12].

However, for pathological images, as shown in Fig. 1, it usually requires to annotate hundreds of cells even for a small patch sampled from the whole slide

---

J. Feng and L. Yang—Joint corresponding authors.

© Springer Nature Switzerland AG 2020
A. L. Martel et al. (Eds.): MICCAI 2020, LNCS 12265, pp. 320–329, 2020.
https://doi.org/10.1007/978-3-030-59722-1_31

image, which is an expensive and laborious task. Additionally, more than hundreds of images are required to train a detector, which makes it is impossible to annotate all the cells but only a few cells per training image. Hence, the sparsely annotated datasets (SAD) are normal in the field of pathology, i.e., the only feasible way is to train detection networks on the pathological SAD. However, due to numerous unannotated positive instances are mistaken for background in the SAD, seriously miscalculated loss appears during training, thereby restricting the performance of the commonly used object detection networks.

Recently, several pseudo-annotations based approaches have been proposed to address the training problem caused by SAD [12–17]. In general, they firstly train a detection network using the available instance-level annotations. Then, the pre-trained model generates pseudo-annotations, which are merged with original annotations to iteratively update the network. For example, Niitani et al. [16] utilize the Open Images Dataset v4 (OID) to train a model to generate annotations, and then they sample pseudo-annotations using assumptions like "a car should contain a tire". However, such assumptions in the pathological field are unknown. Yan et al. [13] and Inoue et al. [17] employ a subset of a dataset with full annotations to obtain a pre-trained model and then generate pseudo-annotations. In addition, several loss function weighting schemes have been proposed for the category imbalance problem [18,19], but they will impose a relatively greater loss on correct predictions that lack corresponding annotations, which makes them invalid in the SAD.

As our best knowledge, there is no solution to the SAD training problem in medical and pathological datasets currently. Meanwhile, these pseudo-annotations based approaches are not suitable for the pathological SAD training problem, due to their successes owe to salient features of instances in natural images, while pathological images usually contain more fine-grained features. Thus, in the pathological field, these multi-stage approaches may lead to the superfluous false-positive instances in pseudo-annotations as the iteration continues. Further, their techniques are concluded unreliable [16]. Therefore, it is extremely crucial to solve the pathological SAD training problem in an end-to-end manner.

In this paper, we firstly identify the training problem caused by the SAD, as all we know, it is the first time we formalize the SAD training problem. Then, we explore the training process of object detection networks and observe the significant density difference between the regression boxes of the positive instances and negative instances. After that, we propose a loss-calibration strategy correlated with densities of regression boxes to address the SAD training problem, namely Boxes Density Energy (BDE). Specifically, BDE utilizes the information of densities to reduce the miscalculated loss, meanwhile to penalize mispredictions with a relatively more significant loss. So that, networks can be trained along the right direction in an end-to-end manner.

We conduct experiments on the MITOS-ATYPIA-14 dataset, besides, we evaluate our BDE on the sparse MITOS-ATYPIA-14, which is artificially created by randomly deleting labels in images. We observe BDE extended networks

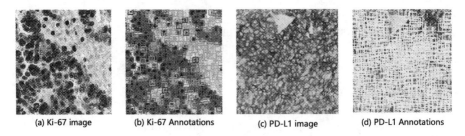

(a) Ki-67 image   (b) Ki-67 Annotations   (c) PD-L1 image   (d) PD-L1 Annotations

Fig. 1. Examples to illustrate the difficulties of full annotations on pathological images. (a) Ki-67 image on 40x magnification scale. (b) Positive tumor cells, necrotic cells, and lymphocytes are annotated with red boxes, blue boxes, and green boxes, respectively. (c) Programmed cell death-ligand 1 (PD-L1) image on 40x magnification scale. (d) Positive tumor cells are annotated with yellow boxes. (Color figure online)

achieve 5.0–7.7% and 4.8–6.8% recall improvements on the sparse and intact MITOS-ATYPIA-14 dataset, respectively. These results illustrate the effectiveness and potential of BDE on pathological detection tasks.

2   Methodology

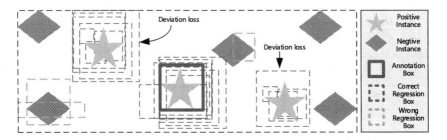

Fig. 2. The deviation-loss in the sparsely annotated dataset.

2.1   Sparsely Annotated Datasets Problem: Deviation-Loss

Generally, object detection networks have two sibling output layers to produce regression boxes (b) with probability distribution (p) to locate and identify positive instances. For a regression box indexed by k, the probability distribution is generated by a classification sibling layer with softmax-activation and is represented as p_k. The regression sibling layer outputs four offsets to generate the location of regression box $b_k = (x_k, y_k, w_k, h_k)$, which represents the central x-coordinate, central y-coordinate, the width and height of the regression box, respectively. Typically, there are often hundreds of regression boxes in one image during network training.

The original loss of object detection networks consists of the classification loss L_{cls} and bounding-box regression loss L_{loc}:

$$L\,(p, u, b, v) = L_{cls}(p, u) + L_{loc}\,(b, v)\,, \tag{1}$$

where u indicates the class ground-truths of regression boxes, we assume u_k represents a one-hot label for a regression box indexed by k. The k-box is assigned with a positive one-hot label $(u_k \neq 0)$, when its Intersection Over Union (IoU) with any instance annotation higher than a threshold, otherwise a background $(u_k = 0)$. Besides, v indicates the annotated bounding-boxes. L_{cls} usually is a cross-entropy loss, and can be formulated as:

$$L_{cls}(p, u) = \sum_k -\,[u_k \cdot \log{(p_k)}]\,, \tag{2}$$

where N is number of regression boxes. Meanwhile, the bounding-box regression loss usually can be approximatively represented as:

$$L_{loc}\,(b, v) = \sum_k smooth_{L_1}\,(b_k - v_k)\,, \tag{3}$$

in which,

$$smooth_{L_1}(x) = \begin{cases} 0.5x^2 & if\,|x| < 1 \\ |x| - 0.5\ otherwise. \end{cases} \tag{4}$$

On the fully annotated dataset, the total loss of L (Eq. 1) can accurately measure the margins between p and u, b and v. However, the annotations of pathological datasets are often incredibly sparse, which leads to u and v transformed into "untrustworthy" ground-truths (all unannotated positive instances are mistaken for background). Thus, L_{cls} and L_{loc} may seriously deviate from the real value, which we name as deviation-loss, as shown in Fig. 2. Moreover, the deviation-loss confuses the training of networks, leading to the limited performance of object detection networks trained on a sparsely annotated pathological dataset.

2.2   Boxes Density Energy

The Boxes Density Energy (BDE) is proposed to encourage the correct regression boxes of unannotated instances to ignore the adverse effect of the deviation-loss. The core observation is that during network training, there are always numerous surrounding regression boxes for positive instances, but few isolate regression boxes for negative instances, as shown in Fig. 3. The observation inspires us to model the density of all boxes to correlate with the loss value. In other words, those boxes that are more clustered with each other are calibrated to smaller losses. In comparison, those more isolated boxes are calibrated to more significant losses.

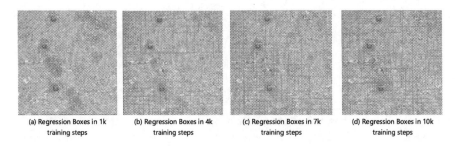

(a) Regression Boxes in 1k
training steps
(b) Regression Boxes in 4k
training steps
(c) Regression Boxes in 7k
training steps
(d) Regression Boxes in 10k
training steps

Fig. 3. The variation of regression boxes' densities during training on MITOS-ATYPIA-14 dataset. Regression boxes are colored in green, and manual annotations are colored in red. (Color figure online)

The Process of Boxes Density Energy. The overall process of Boxes Density Energy (BDE) is shown in Fig. 4. (a) There is a sparsely annotated image is used as the training samples, and each instance is surrounded by some regression boxes that we regard as a cluster. (b) Boxes Density: the average distance. (c) Boxes Energy: The average distance divided by the maximum distance among all boxes. (d) There is a tremendous deviation-loss in the original total loss. (e) The BDE loss is obtained by using the original loss to multiply the Boxes Energy. Finally, the deviation loss in the original loss is eliminated, and networks can be trained along the right direction.

Boxes Density. We utilize the average distance between each box as a measure of density, which indicates the denser boxes have smaller average distances than isolating ones. The average distance of a box indexed by i can be represented as:

$$\text{Density}(b_i) = \frac{1}{N} \sum_{j}^{N} D(b_i, b_j), \tag{5}$$

here N is the number of boxes, D is the Manhattan distance (considering the less computational cost), while other distance measures such as Euclidean distance are also feasible. D in this paper is defined as follows:

$$D(b_i, b_j) = |x_i - x_j| + |y_i - y_j|, \tag{6}$$

here, the x_i and y_i indicate the x-coordinate and y-coordinate of the center point of the box indexed by i. Additionally, the average distance can distinguish the density effectively. For example, we treat regression boxes around an instance as a group, and assume that we have k groups $\{G_1, \ldots, G_j, \ldots G_k\}$, meanwhile there are $\{m_1, \ldots, m_j, \ldots, m_k\}$ boxes in the corresponding group. For simplicity, we assume that the distance within a group is 0, the distance among groups are all d, the total number of boxes is N, which means $N = \sum_{l=1}^{k} m_l$. Hence, the average distance of every box in group j is

$$\text{Density}(b_i) = \frac{0 \times m_j + (N - m_j) \times d}{N} = d \times (1 - \frac{m_j}{N}). \tag{7}$$

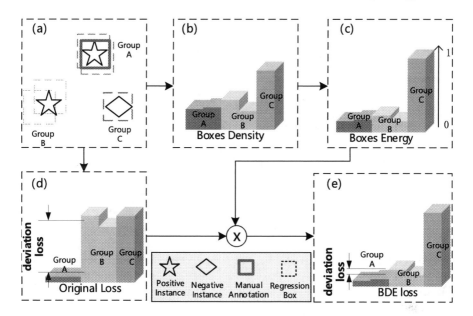

Fig. 4. The process of Boxes Density Energy

Equation 7 suggests that the larger (denser) m_j in j-group has a smaller average distance. Thus, the average distance is a suitable way to measure the density.

Boxes Energy. Boxes Energy is converted from the Boxes Density using the Eq. 8, in which the $\max(D(b))$ represents the maximum distance among all boxes. Boxes Energy ranges from 0 to 1, then can be utilized as a weight of L_{cls} and L_{loc}. After that, the deviation loss is alleviated by calibrating the original loss.

$$\text{Energy}(b_i) = \frac{\text{Density}(b_i)}{\max(D(b))}. \tag{8}$$

Boxes Density Energy Loss. From now on, we have Boxes Energy to calibrate the original loss and decrease the deviation-loss. In detail, the classification loss calculated by Eq. 2 is changed to

$$L_{cls}^{BDE}(p, u) = \sum_k \left[1_{u_k=0} \left(Energy\left(b_k \right) \right) + 1_{u_k \neq 0} \right] \cdot \left[-u_k \cdot \log \left(p_k \right) \right], \tag{9}$$

where u_k is zero, it indicates the one-hot label of the box indexed by k is a background. Similarly, the bounding-box regression loss (Eq. 3) is modified to

$$L_{loc}^{BDE}(b, v, u) = \sum_k \left[1_{u_k=0} \left(Energy\left(b_k \right) \right) + 1_{u_k \neq 0} \right] \cdot \left[\text{smooth}_{L_1} \left(b_k - v_k \right) \right]. \tag{10}$$

Meanwhile, the total loss is improved from Eq. 1 to

$$L^{BDE}\left(p, u, b, v \right) = L_{cls}^{BDE}(p, u) + L_{loc}^{BDE}\left(b, v \right). \tag{11}$$

Finally, networks can be trained along the right direction on the SAD when BDE is conducted. For example, if the box indexed by k is mistaken for background (u_k is zero) due to SAD, but has a small $Energy(b_k)$, then, the original deviation-loss is calibrated by the term of $Energy(b_k)$.

3 Experiments

We utilize the Feature Pyramid Network (FPN) [2] as the baseline to detect mitosis on the MITOS-ATYPIA-14 dataset. We have fully considered the most convenient annotation process for pathologists: (1) Annotate only one instance per image. (2) Annotate only key points for convenience. In this section, we simulate these processes and verify the effectiveness of our approach. We firstly randomly delete annotations until there is only one in per training image. Meanwhile, in MITOS-ATYPIA-14 dataset, each mitosis is annotated with a key point, then we generate bounding boxes around the key points automatically. Besides, experiments conducted on this dataset, we can verify the detection performance of BDE on small positive instances (smaller than 32×32 pixels).

3.1 Dataset

Description and Implementation Details. There are 393 patches with a resolution of 1663×1485 pixels that contain mitosis in the dataset of MITOS-ATYPIA-14. Pathologists have annotated each mitosis as far as possible with a key point, and we generate 32×32 bounding boxes centered on all key points. Patches are resized to 800×800 pixels and fed into the FPN. The number of training steps is 10k. The learning rate is initially set to 0.001 and is divided by 10 at 0.5k and 0.75k steps, and 4-fold cross-validation is used in our experiments.

Fully and Sparsely Annotated Dataset. We refer to the original data as a fully annotated dataset, although the full annotations are not guaranteed. Meanwhile, we refer an extremely sparse dataset as sparsely annotated dataset, which is artificially created by randomly deleting annotations until there is only one in per training image. We only conduct the sparse operations on the training dataset, and the test dataset is intact.

3.2 Results

Results of the Fully Annotated Dataset. Table 1 lists the recall and average precision (AP) results on the fully annotated dataset.

- **Recall results.** FPN-res50 and FPN-resnet101 achieve 89.8% and 87.4% average recall, respectively. While FPN-res50-BDE and FPN-res101-BDE achieve 94.6% and 94.2%, exceeding that of FPN by 4.8% and 6.8%. The performance degradation of the FPN-res101 is due to increased parameters, but the training sample is small.

Table 1. The recall and average precision (AP) results on the fully annotated dataset

Method	Fold1		Fold2		Fold3		Fold4		Avg. Recall	Avg. AP
	Recall	AP	Recall	AP	Recall	AP	Recall	AP		
FPN-res50	80.2	41.8	89.4	46.9	95.8	44.6	93.6	60.7	89.8	**48.5**
FPN-res50-BDE	90.6	40.7	93.3	42.3	99.4	43.2	95.0	59.1	**94.6**	46.3
FPN-res101	77.1	44.6	86.5	42.6	92.8	37.9	93.1	64.2	87.4	**47.3**
FPN-res101-BDE	93.8	35.9	90.4	44.6	98.8	40.3	94.0	63.3	**94.2**	46.0

Table 2. The recall and average precision (AP) results on the sparsely annotated dataset

Method	Fold1		Fold2		Fold3		Fold4		Avg. Recall	2Avg. AP
	Recall	AP	Recall	AP	Recall	AP	Recall	AP		
FPN-res50	69.8	34.5	81.7	32.9	94.6	37.4	88.1	55.9	83.6	40.2
FPN-res50-BDE	88.5	41.8	89.4	37.1	95.8	40.2	91.3	60.1	**91.3**	**44.8**
FPN-res101	72.9	33.8	81.7	23.9	90.4	31.0	88.5	55.2	83.4	36.0
FPN-res101-BDE	81.0	36.0	86.5	33.9	95.2	41.0	90.8	62.0	**88.4**	**43.2**

- **AP results.** Compared with FPN, the results of the average AP of FPN-BDE are slightly reduced. However, due to full annotations are not guaranteed, recall is the objective evaluation for our strategy.

Results of Sparsely Annotated dataset. Table 2 lists the recall and average precision (AP) results on the sparsely annotated dataset.

- **Recall results.** FPN-res50-BDE achieves 91.3% average recall, exceeding that of the FPN-res50 (83.6%) by 7.7%, meanwhile, compared with FPN-res101 (83.4%), FPN-res101-BDE (88.4%) achieves improvements of 5.0%. Additionally, we observe that the results of FPN-BDE (91.3%/88.4%) in the context of the sparsely annotated dataset even exceed the results of FPN (89.8%/87.4%) which are trained on fully dataset.
- **AP results.** The AP results of using BDE also improve a lot on the sparsely annotated dataset. FPN-res50-BDE achieves 44.8% average AP, exceeding that of the FPN-res50 (40.2%) by 4.6%, meanwhile, compared with FPN-res101 (36.0%), FPN-res101-BDE achieves improvements of 7.2%.

4   Conclusion

In this paper, we firstly identify and formalize the limitation of object detection networks trained on sparsely annotated pathological datasets. In order to address the limitation, we propose a novel loss-calibration strategy, namely Boxes Density Energy (BDE), which is utilized to make the object detection networks trained well on the sparsely annotated pathological datasets. Extensive experiments demonstrated the strength of BDE to significantly improve the performance of networks trained on the sparsely annotated pathological datasets. Thus BDE might enable faster and better development of accurate pathological detection methods.

Acknowledgements. This work was supported by the National Key Research and Development Program of China under grant 2017YFB1002504.

References

1. Ren, S., He, K., Girshick, R., Sun, J.: Faster R-CNN: towards real-time object detection with region proposal networks. In: Advances in Neural Information Processing Systems, pp. 91–99 (2015). https://doi.org/10.1109/tpami.2016.2577031
2. Lin, T.Y., Dollár, P., Girshick, R., He, K., Hariharan, B., Belongie, S.: Feature pyramid networks for object detection. In: Proceedings of the IEEE Conference on Computer Vision and Pattern Recognition, pp. 2117–2125 (2017). https://doi.org/10.1109/cvpr.2017.106
3. Ghiasi, G., Lin, T.Y., Le, Q.V.: NAS-FPN: learning scalable feature pyramid architecture for object detection. In: Proceedings of the IEEE Conference on Computer Vision and Pattern Recognition, pp. 7036–7045 (2019). https://doi.org/10.1109/cvpr.2019.00720
4. Zhong, Z., Jin, L., Zhang, S., Feng, Z.: DeepText: a unified framework for text proposal generation and text detection in natural images. arXiv preprint arXiv:1605.07314 (2016)
5. Kong, T., Yao, A., Chen, Y., Sun, F.: HyperNet: towards accurate region proposal generation and joint object detection. In: Proceedings of the IEEE Conference on Computer Vision and Pattern Recognition, pp. 845–853 (2016). https://doi.org/10.1109/cvpr.2016.98
6. Guo, C., Fan, B., Zhang, Q., Xiang, S., Pan, C.: AugFPN: improving multi-scale feature learning for object detection. arXiv preprint arXiv:1912.05384 (2019)
7. Qin, Z., et al.: ThunderNet: towards real-time generic object detection on mobile devices. In: Proceedings of the IEEE International Conference on Computer Vision, pp. 6718–6727 (2019). https://doi.org/10.1109/iccv.2019.00682
8. Zhou, J., Ma, C., Xiong, J., Meng, D.: HR-NET: a highly reliable message-passing mechanism for cluster file system. In: 2011 IEEE Sixth International Conference on Networking, Architecture, and Storage, pp. 364–371. IEEE (2011). https://doi.org/10.1109/nas.2011.21
9. Schmidt, U., Weigert, M., Broaddus, C., Myers, G.: Cell detection with star-convex polygons. In: Frangi, A.F., Schnabel, J.A., Davatzikos, C., Alberola-López, C., Fichtinger, G. (eds.) MICCAI 2018. LNCS, vol. 11071, pp. 265–273. Springer, Cham (2018). https://doi.org/10.1007/978-3-030-00934-2_30
10. Sadafi, A., et al.: Multiclass deep active learning for detecting red blood cell subtypes in brightfield microscopy. In: Shen, D., et al. (eds.) MICCAI 2019. LNCS, vol. 11764, pp. 685–693. Springer, Cham (2019). https://doi.org/10.1007/978-3-030-32239-7_76

11. Zhou, Y., Chen, H., Xu, J., Dou, Q., Heng, P.-A.: IRNet: instance relation network for overlapping cervical cell segmentation. In: Shen, D., et al. (eds.) MICCAI 2019. LNCS, vol. 11764, pp. 640–648. Springer, Cham (2019). https://doi.org/10.1007/978-3-030-32239-7_71

12. Xu, M., et al.: Missing labels in object detection. In: The IEEE Conference on Computer Vision and Pattern Recognition (CVPR) Workshops (2019)

13. Yan, Z., Liang, J., Pan, W., Li, J., Zhang, C.: Weakly-and semi-supervised object detection with expectation-maximization algorithm. arXiv preprint arXiv:1702.08740 (2017)

14. Zhang, X., Wei, Y., Feng, J., Yang, Y., Huang, T.S.: Adversarial complementary learning for weakly supervised object localization. In: Proceedings of the IEEE Conference on Computer Vision and Pattern Recognition, pp. 1325–1334 (2018). https://doi.org/10.1109/cvpr.2018.00144

15. Zhang, X., Wei, Y., Kang, G., Yang, Y., Huang, T.: Self-produced guidance for weakly-supervised object localization. In: Ferrari, V., Hebert, M., Sminchisescu, C., Weiss, Y. (eds.) ECCV 2018. LNCS, vol. 11216, pp. 610–625. Springer, Cham (2018). https://doi.org/10.1007/978-3-030-01258-8_37

16. Niitani, Y., Akiba, T., Kerola, T., Ogawa, T., Sano, S., Suzuki, S.: Sampling techniques for large-scale object detection from sparsely annotated objects. In: Proceedings of the IEEE Conference on Computer Vision and Pattern Recognition, pp. 6510–6518 (2019). https://doi.org/10.1109/cvpr.2019.00667

17. Inoue, N., Furuta, R., Yamasaki, T., Aizawa, K.: Cross-domain weakly-supervised object detection through progressive domain adaptation. In: Proceedings of the IEEE Conference on Computer Vision and Pattern Recognition, pp. 5001–5009 (2018). https://doi.org/10.1109/cvpr.2018.00525

18. Lin, T.Y., Goyal, P., Girshick, R., He, K., Dollár, P.: Focal loss for dense object detection. In: Proceedings of the IEEE International Conference on Computer Vision, pp. 2980–2988 (2017). https://doi.org/10.1109/iccv.2017.324

19. Li, B., Liu, Y., Wang, X.: Gradient harmonized single-stage detector. In: Proceedings of the AAAI Conference on Artificial Intelligence, pp. 8577–8584 (2019). https://doi.org/10.1609/aaai.v33i01.33018577

Histopathological Stain Transfer Using Style Transfer Network with Adversarial Loss

Harshal Nishar[1], Nikhil Chavanke[1,2], and Nitin Singhal[1(✉)]

[1] Aira Matrix, Mumbai, India
{harshal.nishar,nitin.singhal}@airamatrix.com,nikhilchavanke21@gmail.com
[2] Indian Institute of Technology, Bombay, India
https://airamatrix.com/

Abstract. Deep learning models that are trained on histopathological images obtained from a single lab and/or scanner give poor inference performance on images obtained from another scanner/lab with a different staining protocol. In recent years, there has been a good amount of research done for image stain normalization to address this issue. In this work, we present a novel approach for the stain normalization problem using fast neural style transfer coupled with adversarial loss. We also propose a novel stain transfer generator network based on High-Resolution Network (HRNet) which requires less training time and gives good generalization with few paired training images of reference stain and test stain. This approach has been tested on Whole Slide Images (WSIs) obtained from 8 different labs, where images from one lab were treated as a reference stain. A deep learning model was trained on this stain and the rest of the images were transferred to it using the corresponding stain transfer generator network. Experimentation suggests that this approach is able to successfully perform stain normalization with good visual quality and provides better inference performance compared to not applying stain normalization.

Keywords: Stain normalization · Histopathological image analysis · Neural style transfer · Genrative Adversarial Network (GAN)

1 Introduction

Histopathological whole slide images (WSI) are generated by scanning tissue images using microscopic scanners. Hematoxylin and Eosin (H&E) stain is the most commonly used stain for these tissue images. Computer aided histopathological image analysis has gained a significant momentum, and there is an increasing use of supervised deep learning (DL) classification and segmentation models for the same. However, histopathological images obtained from one lab differ significantly from other labs, as every lab has a different staining protocol (Fig. 1). Same tissue slides that are scanned using different scanners may also

© Springer Nature Switzerland AG 2020
A. L. Martel et al. (Eds.): MICCAI 2020, LNCS 12265, pp. 330–340, 2020.
https://doi.org/10.1007/978-3-030-59722-1_32

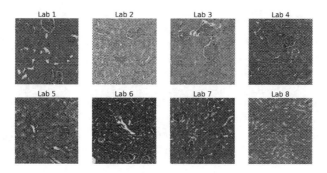

Fig. 1. Sample patches taken from WSI images of H&E stained tissues of Wistar rat kidney obtained from 8 different laboratories.

generate different looking images due to difference in color calibration. Despite great generalization ability of DL models, stain variation can pose a serious problem for DL models which are generally trained using images sourced from one or few labs. Various image stain normalization techniques have been proposed to solve this stain variation problem. Experimentation has shown that stain normalization can improve the accuracy of DL models [4]. Recently few approaches have been proposed using deep generative neural networks for image stain normalization which have shown promising results [2,8,17]. Building onto that, we present an image to image transformation network, called stain transfer generator network, based on High-Resolution Network (HRNet) [18] architecture to transform images from one stain to another.

Contributions. 1. We propose to use neural style transfer with addition of adversarial loss for image stain normalization. To the best of our knowledge, this is the first work which couples neural style transfer with GAN based framework for histopathological stain normalization 2. We suggest a simple yet effective modification to HRNet: a direct skip connection from input to output. This helps in faster training and improved convergence of stain transfer generator network. 3. We have tested the proposed method on data obtained from 8 different labs.

2   Existing Approaches for Stain Normalization

Histogram matching of RGB channnels of input image with corresponding channel of reference image is the simplest approach, but it requires similar distribution of various tissue components. Reinhard et al. [15] uses global image mean and standard deviation in LAB color space for image normalization. Such global methods do not consider local variation in color distribution and hence lead to inaccurate color mapping. If applied on local image patches then there is no consistency in transformed patches across the WSI. Bejnordi [1] uses color and shape based pixel classification into dye types and matches class specific mean and standard deviation.

Color deconvolution [16] based stain separation methods have been proposed, which separate images into H and E stain components and apply normalization on each of them separately. A pioneering work in automatic color deconvolution matrix computation uses non-negative matrix factorization for stain unmixing [13]. Recent work by Vahadane et al. [19] uses sparse non-negative matrix factorization (SNMF) for this task. Any stain separation method transforms three channel color image into image having two dimensional basis with each basis vector representing H and E color component. In all the reconstructed images, we have observed red color of RBCs getting wrongly transformed to pink color of cytoplasm. Loss of such vital color information can cause significant degradation of DL models which depend on RBC features. Also, this method does not classify whether the component belongs to H stain or E stain automatically.

Recently, some authors have used deep learning to solve stain color normalization problem. In [11], image patch is divided into several classes using K-means clustering on features obtained from trained auto-encoders and histogram matching is done on each cluster to match image stain. Zanjani et al. [8], uses deep convolutional GMM to do image clustering and then applies cluster-wise color transfer. Performance of cluster based color matching techniques depends heavily on clustering accuracy and even slight misclassification of cluster can introduce severe degradation. Some approaches use grayscale image colorization using GAN for stain normalization [3,20,21]. If we could obtain complete color information from grayscale images, then it would have been easier to train deep learning models directly on the grayscale images and save significant computation time and the need for stain normalization. However, segmentation of some features invariably need color images and hence grayscale image colorization cannot be helpful there. In [2], authors have jointly trained GAN based stain transformation network along with classifier. CycleGANs have also been used for image stain normalization [17], additionally authors in [5,6] proposed to use identity loss in addition to cycle consistency loss. In [18], authors have used deep convolutional features for pairing reference image patches with input image patch and then compute a global color transformation matrix.

3   Proposed Method

The problem of histopathological image stain normalization can be formulated as follows:

Let R corresponds to a set of reference stain images, P be a set of input stain images and T be a set of transformed images. We want to find a transformation $\mathcal{G} : P \to T$ such that $\mathcal{S}(T, R)$ is minimum and $\mathcal{C}(\mathcal{G}(p), p)$ is minimum $\forall\, p \in P$ Here $\mathcal{S}(.)$ is stain style similarity measure which defines the similarity between two sets of stains and $\mathcal{C}(.)$ is content similarity measure between input image and transformed image.

This is a highly ill-posed problem where a concrete similarity measure is also not available. Our approach to solve this problem is inspired from neural style transfer [7] where a pre-trained neural network is used as a feature extractor for style as well as content features. The original neural style transfer method follows iterative optimization approach to transfer each of the input images to desired style on the fly, making it very slow. Instead, here a stain transfer generator CNN is trained using a small set of paired input and reference stain images. Training a neural network to do this task is similar to fast neural style transfer proposed by Johnson et al. [12].

3.1 Loss Definition

Let p be input image, r be reference image and t be transformed image (the output of stain transfer generator network), then content and style loss is computed as follows:

Content Loss is computed from the content features(F_{ij}^l) obtained by passing the input image p and the transformed image r through a pre-trained CNN (eg. VGG16 or VGG19). Here F_{ij}^l corresponds to the features from the ith feature map of the lth layer of the CNN at the jth location.

$$\mathcal{L}_{content}^l(p,t) = \frac{1}{2}\sum_{ij}(F_{ij}^l(p) - F_{ij}^l(t))^2 \tag{1}$$

Style Loss is computed from the style representation (G^l) obtained by passing the reference image r and the transformed image t through a pre-trained CNN (eg. VGG16 or VGG19). Style representations are the Gram matrices of CNN features at each layers. Each element of a Gram matrix at location ik is given by the inner product of the vectorized i^{th} and k^{th} feature maps:

$$G_{ik}^l = \sum_j F_{ij}^l F_{kj}^l \tag{2}$$

Style loss corresponding to each layer l is given below where N_l is total number of feature maps and M_l is the size of the feature map at layer l:

$$\mathcal{E}^l(r,t) = \frac{1}{N_l M_l}\sum_{ik}(G_{ik}^l(r) - G_{ik}^l(t))^2 \tag{3}$$

Total style loss is computed as the weighted sum of the style loss for each layer

$$\mathcal{L}_{style}(r,t) = \sum_l \omega_l \mathcal{E}^l(r,t) \tag{4}$$

Further, we propose to add an adversarial loss to the above loss, thus making our network a generative adversarial network. Generative adversarial network first proposed by Goodfellow et al. [9] has been extensively used in image to image translation tasks due to its ability to generate new images appearing as if they have been drawn from the reference domain.

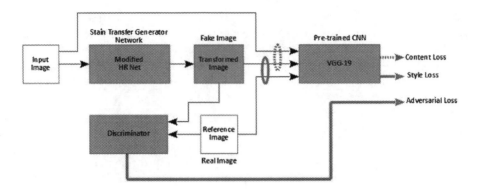

Fig. 2. Block diagram showing how each of the training losses are computed.

To compute adversarial loss an additional network called discriminator ($\mathcal{D}$) has to be trained such that it distinguishes between original reference stain images and fake images generated using stain transfer generator network.

Discriminator Loss is computed as follows:

$$\mathcal{L}_{dis} = log(1 - \mathcal{D}(r)) + log(\mathcal{D}(t)) \tag{5}$$

Adversarial Loss: The generator has to generate images that are similar to reference stain images so that the discriminator can not distinguish them from the real samples drawn from reference stain images. For this purpose, we need to minimize the adversarial loss defined as follows:

$$\mathcal{L}_{adv} = log(1 - \mathcal{D}(t)) \tag{6}$$

Total Generator Loss is computed as a weighted combination of content loss, style loss and adversarial loss, where each of the weighting factors (λ_a, λ_c and λ_s) are model hyper-parameters.

$$\mathcal{L}_{gen} = \lambda_a \mathcal{L}_{adv} + \lambda_c \mathcal{L}_{content} + \lambda_s \mathcal{L}_{style} \tag{7}$$

To train the stain transfer generator network, the discriminator loss ($\mathcal{L}_{dis}$) and the total generator loss ($\mathcal{L}_{gen}$) are iteratively minimized. While training the discriminator, the generator weights are frozen and vice versa while training the generator, the discriminator weights are frozen. However, the weights of the pre-trained CNN network, which is used only as a deep feature extractor, must be kept constant throughout the training process. Figure 2 is a block diagram of the complete system that illustrates how various generator losses are computed.

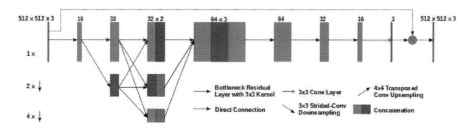

Fig. 3. Stain transfer generator network architechure (Modified HRNet).

3.2   Generator Network Architecture

In the artistic style transfer, retention of the minute details in the transformed image is not very important. But the stain transfer generator network must retain the high resolution content features in the transformed image. Hence instead of ResNet based style transfer network proposed by Johnson et al, our stain transfer generator architecture is based on High-Resolution Net (HRNet). HRNet has been shown to retain rich high resolution representations, which helps in maintaining the quality of histopathological images. As a major modification to HRNet, a direct skip connection from input to output has been added. Figure 3 shows full generator network architecture with feature map size at each layers. Let p be the input image and $\mathcal{G}$ be the stain transfer generator network then,

$$\mathcal{G}(p) = p + \mathcal{G}'(p) \tag{8}$$

Intuition behind the skip connection is that, in the worst case scenario, the stain transfer generator network should at least return the original content image. Due to a direct skip connection, the network has to learn only the residue transformation instead of the actual transformation. This residual learning is much faster and gives better convergence. The proposed stain transfer generator network learns good transformation with as little as 20 paired training images and 50 epochs of training.

3.3   Implementation Details

WSIs are divided into non-overlapping patches of 512×512 pixels at 10x magnification. Around 20 patches from each input stain is paired to reference stain patch based on content similarity. In stain transfer generator network, all convolutional layers except last one are followed by batch-normalization and ReLU activation. The discriminator follows architectural guidelines given in DCGAN [14] and uses instance-normalization instead of batch-normalization. Also, our discriminator implementation is 16×16 PatchGAN [10] and hence it classifies 16×16 patch of an image as real or fake. The generator learning rate is kept at 1e$-$3 and the discriminator learning rate is kept at 1e$-$5. For training, we have used Adam optimizer and batch size of 4. Content features are taken from second convolutional layer of VGG19 (conv2_2) pre-trained on ImageNet dataset. For style loss, weight of each layer is kept constant 1.

4   Experimentation

Throughout the experimentation, lab 1 (see Fig. 1) is selected as a reference stain and other images are transformed to this stain. To check the effectiveness of our proposed method, we have compared the stain transfer performance in 4 different settings: 1. Neural style transfer using generator network proposed in [12] (NST) 2. Neural style transfer with addition of adversarial loss (NST_AD) 3. Neural style transfer using modified HRNet (NST_HRNet) and 4. Neural style transfer with adversarial loss and modified HRNet (NST_AD_HRNet). All the models are trained with their best hyper-parameters. It has been observed that NST gave good results with Lab 3 but very poor results with Lab 2. NST_AD has generated images looking like reference stain but has distortions. NST_HRNet has good results with both lab 2 and lab 3 with minute content details preserved. NST_AD_HRNet has generated best results for both the labs, with images looking very close to the reference stain (Fig. 4).

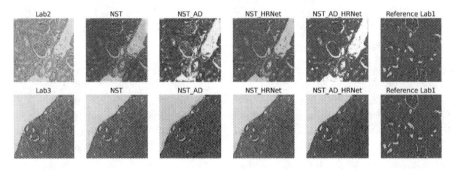

Fig. 4. This figure shows output of style transfer network with different configuration. Original 512×512 image patches from lab 2 and lab 3 are shown at leftmost side.

For result comparison with other well-known approaches (Reinhard [15], Vahadane [19], Zanjani [8] and StainGAN [17]), we use publicly available ICPR2014 Mitosis dataset[1] in which the same tissue slides are scanned using two different scanners (Aperio and Hamamatsu). Hamamatsu scanner is taken as reference and Aperio scanner images are transformed to it. In Fig. 5, we can see that Vahadane's method makes red RBCs pinkish as we had discussed previously. Zanjani's DCGMM produces good output but has sharpened texture and brighter colors as compared to actual reference images. Also, due to large textural variations in kidney images, DCGMM does not produce good clusters

---

[1] https://mitos-atypia-14.grand-challenge.org/Dataset/.

and gives poor stain normalized output. StainGAN produces decent output for mitosis images, however, for kidney images it produces images that look like reference stain but with significant textural distortions. We have observed that some of the image similarity measures like SSIM and PSNR are quite misleading and do not indicate true perceptual similarity between images, hence we have used deep features based perceptual similarity measure by Zhang et al. [22], which has been shown to perform significantly better perceptually than other measures. On this measure, the performance of the proposed approach is only 3% poorer than StainGAN and 20% better than Zanjani's approach (Tabel 1). While CycleGAN based StainGAN took more than 72 h to train, the proposed network got trained in less than 2 h. Also, our generator network did not suffer from training instability generally observed with GAN. See supplementary material available at https://github.com/harshalnishar/MICCAI2020 for the comparison on kidney data from all the labs.

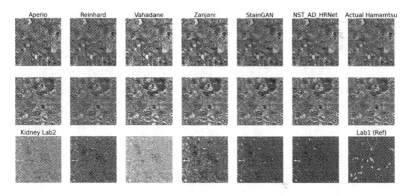

Fig. 5. Comparison of the proposed approach with the other approaches and with the reference. First two rows show results for mitosis dataset and last row shows results for lab 2 from our kidney dataset.

Table 1. Comparison with deep features based perceptual similarity distance measure (lower is better)

Method	Reinhard	Vahadane	Zanjani	StainGAN	NST_AD_HRNet
Mean distance	0.325	0.205	0.191	0.148	0.153
Std. div.	0.129	0.156	0.080	0.111	0.107

To validate the effectiveness of the proposed approach in improving the accuracy of a pre-existing DL model on new unseen stain images, testing has been done on 7 different stains. We have trained a ResNet50-FCN based Glomeruli segmentation network on image patches taken from lab 1. Color based data augmentations were applied on training data. For lab 2 to lab 8, we trained corresponding stain transfer generator network to transform each of them to lab 1. Table 2 shows the performance of segmentation model with and without proposed stain normalization. There is a significant improvement in model performance due to the proposed stain normalization for all the labs.

Table 2. Mean dice score for segmentation model with and without proposed stain normalization.

Lab	Lab 2	Lab 3	Lab 4	Lab 5	Lab 6	Lab 7	Lab 8
Without normalization dice	0.183	0.754	0.804	0.718	0.805	0.593	0.641
With normalization dice	0.437	0.904	0.815	0.900	0.899	0.787	0.771

5   Conclusion

In this paper we presented a novel, fast and effective stain color normalization technique for H&E stained histopathological images. The proposed method was compared with other well known techniques and gave superior stain normalization performance. Due to a direct skip connection from input to output, stain transfer generator network can be trained quickly and with very few paired training images. This helps in quick adaptation of existing deep learning models for a differently stained data. The proposed method was tested on data obtained from 8 different labs and was able to transform each of them to the reference stain without any distortions in the original content. We believe this work can be extended to staining dyes other than H&E and can also be used for domain adaptation like transforming images from H&E to PAP stain.

References

1. Bejnordi, B.E., et al.: Stain specific standardization of whole-slide histopathological images. IEEE Trans. Med. Imaging **35**, 404–415 (2016)
2. Bentaieb, A., Hamarneh, G.: Adversarial stain transfer for histopathology image analysis. IEEE Trans. Med. Imaging **37**(3), 792–802 (2018). https://doi.org/10.1109/TMI.2017.2781228
3. Cho, H., Lim, S., Choi, G., Min, H.: Neural stain-style transfer learning using gan for histopathological images (2017)
4. Ciompi, F., et al.: The importance of stain normalization in colorectal tissue classification with convolutional networks. In: IEEE 14th International Symposium on Biomedical Imaging, pp. 160–163 (2017)
5. de Bel, T., Hermsen, M., Kers, J., van der Laak, J., Litjens, G.: Stain-transforming cycle-consistent generative adversarial networks for improved segmentation of renal histopathology. In: Cardoso, M.J., et al. (eds.) Proceedings of The 2nd International Conference on Medical Imaging with Deep Learning. Proceedings of Machine Learning Research, vol. 102, pp. 151–163. PMLR, London, United Kingdom, 08–10 Jul 2019 (2019). http://proceedings.mlr.press/v102/de-bel19a.html

6. Gadermayr, M., Appel, V., Klinkhammer, B.M., Boor, P., Merhof, D.: Which way round? a study on the performance of stain-translation for segmenting arbitrarily dyed histological images. In: Frangi, A.F., Schnabel, J.A., Davatzikos, C., Alberola-López, C., Fichtinger, G. (eds.) MICCAI 2018, vol. 11071, pp. 165–173. Springer International Publishing, Cham (2018). https://doi.org/10.1007/978-3-030-00934-2_19

7. Gatys, L.A., Ecker, A.S., Bethge, M.: Image style transfer using convolutional neural networks. In: IEEE Conference on Computer Vision and Pattern Recognition (CVPR), pp. 2414–2423, June 2016. https://doi.org/10.1109/CVPR.2016.265

8. Ghazvinian Zanjani, F., Zinger, S., de With, P.H.N.: Deep convolutional gaussian mixture model for stain-color normalization of histopathological images. In: Frangi, A.F., Schnabel, J.A., Davatzikos, C., Alberola-López, C., Fichtinger, G. (eds.) MICCAI 2018. LNCS, vol. 11071, pp. 274–282. Springer, Cham (2018). https://doi.org/10.1007/978-3-030-00934-2_31

9. Goodfellow, I., et al.: Generative adversarial nets. In: Ghahramani, Z., Welling, M., Cortes, C., Lawrence, N.D., Weinberger, K.Q. (eds.) Advances in Neural Information Processing Systems,vol. 27, pp. 2672–2680. Curran Associates, Inc. (2014). http://papers.nips.cc/paper/5423-generative-adversarial-nets.pdf

10. Isola, P., Zhu, J.Y., Zhou, T., Efros, A.A.: Image-to-image translation with conditional adversarial networks. In: IEEE Conference on Computer Vision and Pattern Recognition (CVPR), pp. 5967–5976 (2016)

11. Janowczyk, A., Basavanhally, A., Madabhushi, A.: Stain normalization using sparse autoencoders (StaNoSA): application to digital pathology. Comput. Med. Imaging Graph. **57**, 50–61 (2016). https://doi.org/10.1016/j.compmedimag.2016.05.003

12. Johnson, J., Alahi, A., Fei-Fei, L.: Perceptual losses for real-time style transfer and super-resolution. In: Leibe, B., Matas, J., Sebe, N., Welling, M. (eds.) ECCV 2016. LNCS, vol. 9906, pp. 694–711. Springer, Cham (2016). https://doi.org/10.1007/978-3-319-46475-6_43

13. Rabinovich, A., Agarwal, S., Laris, C., Price, J.H., Belongie, S.J.: Unsupervised color decomposition of histologically stained tissue samples. In: Thrun, S., Saul, L.K., Schölkopf, B. (eds.) Advances in Neural Information Processing Systems, vol. 16, pp. 667–674. MIT Press (2004). http://papers.nips.cc/paper/2497-unsupervised-color-decomposition-of-histologically-stained-tissue-samples.pdf

14. Radford, A., Metz, L., Chintala, S.: Unsupervised representation learning with deep convolutional generative adversarial networks (2015)

15. Reinhard, E., Adhikhmin, M., Gooch, B., Shirley, P.: Color transfer between images. IEEE Comput. Graph. Appl. **21**(5), 34–41 (2001). https://doi.org/10.1109/38.946629

16. Ruifrok, A.C., Johnston, D.A., et al.: Quantification of histochemical staining by color deconvolution. Anal. Quant. Cytol. Histol. **23**(4), 291–299 (2001)

17. Shaban, M.T., Baur, C., Navab, N., Albarqouni, S.: Staingan: stain style transfer for digital histological images. In: IEEE 16th International Symposium on Biomedical Imaging, pp. 953–956, April 2019. https://doi.org/10.1109/ISBI.2019.8759152

18. Sun, K., Xiao, B., Liu, D., Wang, J.: Deep high-resolution representation learning for human pose estimation. In: IEEE Conference on Computer Vision and Pattern Recognition (CVPR) (2019)

19. Vahadane, A., et al.: Structure-preserving color normalization and sparse stain separation for histological images. IEEE Trans. Med. Imaging **35**, 1962–1971 (2016)

20. Yuan, E., Suh, J.: Neural stain normalization and unsupervised classification of cell nuclei in histopathological breast cancer images. CoRR abs/1811.03815 (2018). http://arxiv.org/abs/1811.03815

21. Zanjani, F.G., Zinger, S., Bejnordi, B.E., van der Laak, J., de With, P.H.N.: Stain normalization of histopathology images using generative adversarial networks. In: IEEE 15th International Symposium on Biomedical Imaging, pp. 573–577 (2018)
22. Zhang, R., Isola, P., Efros, A.A., Shechtman, E., Wang, O.: The unreasonable effectiveness of deep features as a perceptual metric. In: CVPR (2018)

Instance-Aware Self-supervised Learning for Nuclei Segmentation

Xinpeng Xie[1], Jiawei Chen[2], Yuexiang Li[2(✉)], Linlin Shen[1], Kai Ma[2], and Yefeng Zheng[2]

[1] Computer Vision Institute, Shenzhen University, Shenzhen, China
llshen@szu.edu.cn
[2] Tencent Jarvis Lab, Shenzhen, China
vicyxli@tencent.com

Abstract. Due to the wide existence and large morphological variances of nuclei, accurate nuclei instance segmentation is still one of the most challenging tasks in computational pathology. The annotating of nuclei instances, requiring experienced pathologists to manually draw the contours, is extremely laborious and expensive, which often results in the deficiency of annotated data. The deep learning based segmentation approaches, which highly rely on the quantity of training data, are difficult to fully demonstrate their capacity in this area. In this paper, we propose a novel self-supervised learning framework to deeply exploit the capacity of widely-used convolutional neural networks (CNNs) on the nuclei instance segmentation task. The proposed approach involves two sub-tasks (i.e., scale-wise triplet learning and count ranking), which enable neural networks to implicitly leverage the prior-knowledge of nuclei size and quantity, and accordingly mine the instance-aware feature representations from the raw data. Experimental results on the publicly available MoNuSeg dataset show that the proposed self-supervised learning approach can remarkably boost the segmentation accuracy of nuclei instance—a new state-of-the-art average Aggregated Jaccard Index (AJI) of 70.63%, is achieved by our self-supervised ResUNet-101. To our best knowledge, this is the first work focusing on the self-supervised learning for instance segmentation.

Keywords: Self-supervised learning · Nuclei instance segmentation · Histopathological images

1 Introduction

Nuclei instance segmentation provides not only location and density information but also rich morphology features (e.g., magnitude and the cytoplasmic ratio) for the tumor diagnosis and related treatment procedures [1]. To this end, many

---

X. Xie—This work was done when Xinpeng Xie was an intern at Tencent Jarvis Lab.
J. Chen—Equal contribution.

© Springer Nature Switzerland AG 2020
A. L. Martel et al. (Eds.): MICCAI 2020, LNCS 12265, pp. 341–350, 2020.
https://doi.org/10.1007/978-3-030-59722-1_33

researches have been proposed to establish automated systems for accurate nuclei segmentation. For examples, Xie et al. [14] utilized Mask R-CNN to directly localize and segment the nuclei instances in histopathological images. Oda et al. [9] proposed a deep learning method called Boundary-Enhanced Segmentation Network (BESNet) to segment cell instances from pathological images. The proposed BESNet had similar architecture to U-Net but utilized two decoders to enhance cell boundaries and segment entire cells, respectively. Inspired by [9], Zhou et al. [15] proposed a multi-level information aggregation module to fuse the features extracted by the two decoders of BESNet. The proposed framework, namely Contour-aware Informative Aggregation Network (CIA-Net), achieved an excellent accuracy of nuclei instance segmentation and won the first prize on the Multi-Organ-Nuclei-Segmentation (MoNuSeg) challenge. Although deep learning based approaches achieve outstanding segmentation accuracy for nuclei instances, they share a common challenge for further improvements—the deficiency of annotated data. Due to the wide existence and large morphological variances of nuclei, the annotating of nuclei instances requires experienced physicians to repetitively investigate the histopathological images and carefully draw the contours, which is extremely laborious and expensive. Therefore, the performance of deep learning based approaches suffers from the limited quantity of annotated histopathological images.

Self-supervised learning, as a solution to loose the requirement of manual annotations for neural networks, attracts increasing attentions from the community. The pipeline usually consists of two steps: 1) pre-train the network model on a proxy task with a large unlabeled dataset; 2) fine-tune the pre-trained network for the specific target task with a small set of annotated data. Recent studies have validated the effectiveness of self-supervised learning on multiple tasks of medical image processing such as brain area segmentation [13], brain tumor segmentation [17] and organ segmentation [16]. However, few studies focused on the topic of instance segmentation, which is a totally different area from the semantic segmentation [11]. The neural network performing instance segmentation needs to identify not only the object category but also the object instance for each pixel belonging to. Therefore, the self-supervised learning approach is required to implicitly learn to be self-aware of object instance from the raw data for more accurate nuclei segmentation.

In this paper, we propose an instance-aware self-supervised learning approach to loose the requirement of manual annotations in deep convolutional neural networks. The proposed self-supervised proxy task involves two sub-tasks (i.e., scale-wise triplet learning and count ranking), which enforce the neural network to autonomously learn the prior-knowledge of nuclei size and quantity by deeply exploiting the rich information contained in the raw data. The publicly available MoNuSeg dataset is adopted to evaluate the improvements yielded by the proposed proxy task. The experimental results demonstrate that our self-supervised learning approach can significantly boost the accuracy of nuclei instance segmentation—a new state-of-the-art average Aggravated Jaccard Index (AJI) of 70.63% is achieved by the self-supervised ResUNet-101.

2   Method

In this section, the proposed instance-aware self-supervised proxy tasks are introduced in details.

2.1   Image Manipulation

Multiple example learning (e.g., pair-wise and triplet learning), which aims to learn an embedding space that captures dissimilarity among data points, is adopted to encourage neural networks to implicitly learn the characteristics of nuclei instances (i.e., nuclei size and quantity). An example of generating triplet samples for a given histopathological image is shown in Fig. 1.

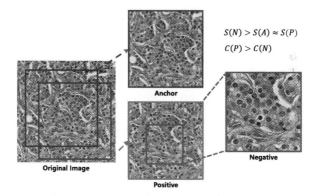

Fig. 1. Image manipulation of a histopathological image. The $S(.)$ and $C(.)$ represent the average nuclei size and the number of nuclei of generated samples (i.e., anchor A, positive P, and negative N), respectively. The two equations reflect heuristic relationship among the samples.

Nuclei Size. Specifically, as presented in Fig. 1, for a histopathological image of 1000×1000 pixels from the MoNuSeg dataset, we first crop a patch with 768×768 pixels (i.e., the red square) as the anchor. Next, we generate a positive sample containing nuclei with similar sizes to the anchor patch by cropping an adjacent patch (i.e., the blue square) with the same size (768×768 pixels) from the histopathological image. To better embed the information of nuclei size into self-supervised learning, a negative sample containing nucleus with larger sizes is generated—a sub-patch (i.e., the green square) random cropped from the positive sample and resized to 768×768 pixels. To increase the diversity of negative samples, the scale of green square is randomly selected from a pool $\{512 \times 512, 256 \times 256, 128 \times 128, 64 \times 64\}$ for each triplet. The anchor, positive and negative samples form a standard triplet data, which is used for the proxy task in self-supervised learning.

Nuclei Quantity. The positive and negative samples not only contain nuclei with different sizes (S), but also different quantities of nuclei (C)—the number of nuclei in negative samples is always lower than that of positive samples. Therefore, we propose to adopt a pair-wise count ranking metric to reflect the difference of nuclei quantity during self-supervised learning.

2.2   Self-supervised Approach with Triplet Learning and Ranking

With the triplet samples (i.e., anchor A, positive P, and negative N), we formulate two self-supervised proxy tasks to pre-train the neural networks for nuclei instance segmentation. The pipeline of the proposed proxy task is illustrated in Fig. 2, which consists of three shared-weight encoders supervised by two losses—scale-wise triplet loss and count ranking loss. As aforementioned, the scale-wise triplet learning and count ranking aim to extract features related to knowledge of nuclei size and quantity, respectively. The shared-weight encoders embed the triplet samples into a latent feature space (Z), which can be formulated as: $E_A : A \rightarrow z_a$, $E_P : P \rightarrow z_p$, $E_N : N \rightarrow z_n$, where z_a, z_p, and z_n are 128-d features.

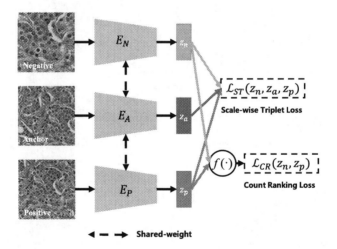

Fig. 2. The pipeline of the proposed self-supervised proxy tasks. The knowledge of nuclei size and quantity is implicitly captured by the scale-wise triplet learning and pair-wise count ranking, respectively.

Proxy Task 1: Scale-Wise Triplet Learning. The triplet learning [12] encourages samples from the same class to be closer and pushes apart samples from different classes in the embedding space. The proposed approach labels the samples cropped in the same scale with the same class, while treating samples in different scales as different classes. Therefore, the scale-wise triplet loss ($\mathcal{L}_{ST}$) for the embedded triplet features (z_a, z_p, z_n) can be formulated as:

$$\mathcal{L}_{ST}\left(z_a, z_p, z_n\right) = \sum \max\left(0,\ d\left(z_a, z_p\right) - d\left(z_a, z_n\right) + m_1\right) \tag{1}$$

where m_1 is a margin (which is empirically set to 1.0); $d(.)$ is the squared L_2 distance between two features. Regularized by the triplet loss, the network narrows down the perceptional distance between anchor and positive samples in the feature space and enlarge the semantic dissimilarity (i.e., nuclei size) between the anchor and negative samples.

Proxy Task 2: Count Ranking. Based on aforementioned observation—the positive sample always contains more nuclei than the negative one, we propose a pair-wise count ranking loss ($\mathcal{L}_{CR}$) to enforce the network to identify the sample containing a larger crowd of nuclei. A mapping function f is first applied to the embedded features (z_p, z_n) to arrive at a scalar value whose relative rank is known. And in our experiment, f is implemented by a fully convolution layer. Then, the loss function for the embedded features (z_p, z_n) can be defined as:

$$\mathcal{L}_{CR} = \sum \max(0, f(z_n) - f(z_p) + m_2) \tag{2}$$

where m_2 is a margin (which is empirically set to 1.0). The well-trained network is implicitly regularized to be aware of the nuclei quantity. To further illustrate this, the features extracted from last deconvolution layer are visualized as the nuclei density maps in Fig. 3. It can be observed that the density maps of negative samples cropped from positive samples are ordered and sparse, which demonstrate the relative rank created by the mapping function f and the effectiveness of our count ranking loss.

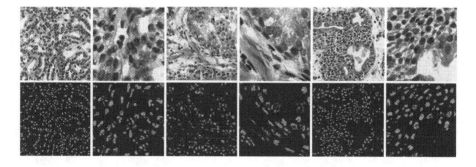

Fig. 3. Density maps of samples containing different quantities of nuclei. The even columns on top represents the negative samples cropped from the positive samples (odd columns). The neural network realizes the variation of nucleus quantity between the positive and negative samples, and activates dense areas in the positive one.

Objective. With the previously defined scale-wise triplet loss $\mathcal{L}_{ST}$ and count ranking loss $\mathcal{L}_{CR}$, the full objective $\mathcal{L}$ for our self-supervised approach is summarized as:

$$\mathcal{L} = \mathcal{L}_{ST} + \mathcal{L}_{CR}. \tag{3}$$

Fine-Tuning on Target Task. The recently proposed one-stage framework [2] is adopted to perform nuclei instance segmentation. The framework has a U-shape architecture [10], which classifies each pixel to three categories (i.e., nuclei body, nuclei boundary and background). We pre-train the encoder of one-stage framework with the proposed proxy tasks to extract instance-aware feature representations and then transfer the pre-trained weights to the target task with a randomly initialized decoder. The widely-used ResNet-101 [4] is adopted as the backbone of the encoder. Henceforth, the one-stage framework adopted in this study is referred as ResUNet-101.

3   Experiments

The proposed instance-aware self-supervised learning approach is evaluated on the publicly available MoNuSeg dataset to demonstrate its effectiveness on improving segmentation accuracy of nuclei instance.

Table 1. AJI (%) for models finetuned with different amounts of labeled data on the MoNuSeg 2018 test set.

ResUNet-101	AJI(%)				
	100%	70%	50%	30%	10%
Train-from-scratch	65.29	60.33	51.45	44.32	43.58
ImageNet pre-trained	65.83	62.60	53.54	48.57	48.31
SSL (Ours)	**70.63**	68.87	62.34	60.31	55.01

3.1   Datasets

MoNuSeg 2018 Dataset [7]. The dataset consists of diverse H&E stained tissue images captured from seven different organs (e.g., breast, liver, kidney, prostate, bladder, colon and stomach), which were collected from 18 institutes. The dataset has a public training set and a public test set. The training set contains 30 histopathological images with hand-annotated nuclei, while the test set consists of 14 images. The resolution of the histopathological images is 1000×1000 pixels. In our experiments, we separate the public training set to training and validation sets according to the ratio of 80:20. To evaluate the segmentation accuracy of nuclei instance, we adopt the Aggregated Jaccard Index (AJI) [7] as the metric. The AJI [7] is proved to be a more suitable metric to evaluate the segmentation performance at the object level, which involves matching per ground truth nucleus to one segmented necleus by maximizing the Jaccard index.

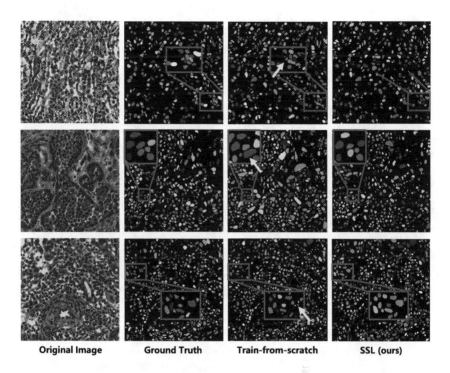

      Original Image   **Ground Truth**   **Train-from-scratch**   **SSL (ours)**

Fig. 4. The nuclei instance segmentation results produced by ResUNet-101 train-from-scratch and self-supervised learning (SSL) pre-trained, respectively.

3.2 Performance Evaluation

We first evaluate the improvement yielded by the proposed self-supervised learning proxy tasks to the performance of instance segmentation. The nuclei instance segmentation results of ResUNet-101 trained with different strategies are presented in Fig. 4. It can be observed that pre-trained ResUNet-101 produces more plausible segmentation of nuclei instances, especially for the overlapping nuclei marked by yellow arrows, compared to the one trained from scratch. For further evaluation, the AJIs of the two approaches and our self-supervised learning framework finetuned with different amounts of labeled data are evaluated and presented in Table 1. Due to the gap between natural and medical images, the ImageNet pre-trained weights yield marginal improvement (e.g., +0.54% with 100% annotations) to train-from-scratch. It can be observed that our self-supervised learning proxy tasks significantly and consistently improve the AJI under all conditions, especially with the extremely small quantity (e.g., 10%) of annotations, i.e., +11.43% higher than train-from-scratch.

Table 2. AJI (%) for ResUNet-101 trained with different strategies and the top-5 approaches on the MoNuSeg 2018 test set.

Training strategy (ResUNet-101)		MoNuSeg 2018 leaderboard	
Train-from-scratch	65.29	Navid Alemi	67.79
ImageNet pre-trained	65.83	Yunzhi	67.88
Jigsaw puzzles [8]	66.68	Pku.hzq	68.52
RotNet [3]	67.61	BUPT.J.LI	68.68
ColorMe [6]	67.94	CIA-Net [15]	69.07
SSL (Ours)	**70.63**		

For comprehensive quantitative analysis, ResUNet-101 trained with different strategies, including state-of-the-art self-supervised learning approaches [3,6,8], is evaluated and the results are presented in Table 2. The accuracy of the top-5 teams on MoNuSeg 2018 Segmentation Challenge leaderboard[1] are also involved for comparison. As shown in Table 2, the proposed self-supervised learning pre-trained model significantly boosts the accuracy of nuclei instance segmentation (+5.34%), compared with train-from-scratch. We believe that the improvement comes from the prior knowledge of nuclei size and quantity that is learned implicitly in the self-supervised proxy tasks, since our approach outperforms all the listed self-supervised methods, which do not take the instance-related knowledge into consideration. Our self-supervised pre-trained ResUNet-101 is also observed to surpass the winner on the leaderboard (i.e., CIA-Net [15]), which leads to a new state-of-the-art, i.e., 70.63%, on the MoNuSeg test set. It is worthwhile to mention that our framework has a much lower computational complexity and fewer network parameters, compared to the CIA-Net, which utilizes DenseNet [5] as the encoder and has two decoders for nuclei body and boundary, respectively.

Ablation Study. To assess the accuracy improvement yielded by each component of our self-supervised learning proxy tasks, we conduct an ablation study. The experimental results are presented in Table 3. Compared to train-from-scratch, fine-tuning from the $\mathcal{L}_{ST}$-only and $\mathcal{L}_{CR}$-only pre-trained weights improves the segmentation accuracy by +4.35% and +4.80%, respectively. Since jointly pre-training on the two sub-tasks (i.e., $\mathcal{L}_{ST}$ and $\mathcal{L}_{CR}$) increases the diversity of feature representation learned by neural networks, it provides the highest improvement, i.e., +5.34%.

Validation on Another Dataset. The evaluation results on the Computational Precision Medicine (CPM) dataset can be found in Table 4.

---

[1] https://monuseg.grand-challenge.org/Results/.

Table 3. Performance produced by different self-supervised proxy tasks on the MoNuSeg 2018 test set.

Setup	ResUnet	$+\mathcal{L}_{ST}$	$+\mathcal{L}_{CR}$	$+\mathcal{L}_{ST}+\mathcal{L}_{CR}$
AJI (%)	65.29	69.64	70.09	**70.63**

Table 4. Dice score (%) and AJI (%) on the Computational Precision Medicine (CPM) dataset*. A 5-fold cross validation is conducted. Apart from the AJI, we also evaluate the Dice score, which proposed by the CPM competition. An average Dice of 86.36% is achieved by our self-supervised ResUNet-101, which is comparable to the winner of CPM 2018 competition (i.e., 87.00%).

	Fold 1	Fold 2	Fold 3	Fold 4	Fold 5	Average
Dice score						
Train-from-scratch	85.29	83.99	84.12	82.89	86.05	84.47
SSL (Ours)	86.54	85.18	85.84	86.08	88.14	**86.36**
AJI						
Train-from-scratch	74.43	72.79	72.80	71.03	75.60	73.33
SSL (Ours)	76.34	74.56	75.37	75.84	78.83	**76.19**

* https://wiki.cancerimagingarchive.net/pages/viewpage.action?
pageId=37224869

4   Conclusion

In this paper, we proposed an instance-aware self-supervised learning framework for nuclei segmentation. The proposed proxy consists of two sub-tasks (i.e., scale-wise triplet learning and count ranking), which enable the neural network to implicitly acquire the knowledge of nuclei size and quantity. The proposed self-supervised learning proxy tasks were evaluated on the publicly available MoNuSeg dataset and a new state-of-the-art AJI (i.e., 70.63%) was achieved.

Acknowledgement. This work is supported by the Natural Science Foundation of China (No. 91959108 and 61702339), the Key Area Research and Development Program of Guangdong Province, China (No. 2018B010111001), National Key Research and Development Project (2018YFC2000702) and Science and Technology Program of Shenzhen, China (No. ZDSYS201802021814180).

References

1. Chang, H., et al.: Invariant delineation of nuclear architecture in glioblastoma multiforme for clinical and molecular association. IEEE Trans. Med. Imaging **32**(4), 670–682 (2013)
2. Cui, Y., Zhang, G., Liu, Z., Xiong, Z., Hu, J.: A deep learning algorithm for one-step contour aware nuclei segmentation of histopathology images. Med. Biol. Eng. Comput. **57**, 2027–2043 (2019)

3. Gidaris, S., Singh, P., Komodakis, N.: Unsupervised representation learning by predicting image rotations. In: International Conference on Learning Representations (2018)
4. He, K., Zhang, X., Ren, S., Sun, J.: Deep residual learning for image recognition. In: IEEE Conference on Computer Vision and Pattern Recognition, pp. 770–778 (2016)
5. Huang, G., Liu, Z., van der Maaten, L., Weinberger, K.Q.: Densely connected convolutional networks. In: IEEE Conference on Computer Vision and Pattern Recognition, pp. 4700–4708 (2017)
6. Li, Y., Chen, J., Zheng, Y.: A multi-task self-supervised learning framework for scopy images. In: IEEE International Symposium on Biomedical Imaging (2020)
7. Naylor, P., Lae, M., Reyal, F., Walter, T.: Segmentation of nuclei in histopathology images by deep regression of the distance map. IEEE Trans. Med. Imaging **38**(2), 448–459 (2018)
8. Noroozi, M., Favaro, P.: Unsupervised learning of visual representations by solving jigsaw puzzles. In: Leibe, B., Matas, J., Sebe, N., Welling, M. (eds.) ECCV 2016. LNCS, vol. 9910, pp. 69–84. Springer, Cham (2016). https://doi.org/10.1007/978-3-319-46466-4_5
9. Oda, H., et al.: BESNet: boundary-enhanced segmentation of cells in histopathological images. In: International Conference on Medical Image Computing and Computer Assisted Intervention, pp. 228–236 (2018)
10. Ronneberger, O., Fischer, P., Brox, T.: U-net: convolutional networks for biomedical image segmentation. In: International Conference on Medical Image Computing and Computer Assisted Intervention, pp. 234–241 (2015)
11. Ruiz-Santaquiteria, J., Bueno, G., Deniz, O., Vallez, N., Cristobal, G.: Semantic versus instance segmentation in microscopic algae detection. Eng. Appl. Artif. Intell. **87**, 103271 (2020)
12. Schroff, F., Kalenichenko, D., Philbin, J.: A unified embedding for face recognition and clustering. In: IEEE Conference on Computer Vision and Pattern Recognition, pp. 815–823 (2015)
13. Spitzer, H., Kiwitz, K., Amunts, K., Harmeling, S., Dickscheid, T.: Improving cytoarchitectonic segmentation of human brain areas with self-supervised siamese networks. In: International Conference on Medical Image Computing and Computer Assisted Intervention, pp. 663–671 (2018)
14. Xie, X., Li, Y., Zhang, M., Shen, L.: Robust segmentation of nucleus in histopathology images via Mask R-CNN. In: Brainlesion: Glioma, Multiple Sclerosis, Stroke and Traumatic Brain Injuries, pp. 428–436 (2018)
15. Zhou, Y., Onder, O.F., Dou, Q., Tsougenis, E., Chen, H., Heng, P.A.: CIA-Net: robust nuclei instance segmentation with contour-aware information aggregation. In: International Conference on Information Processing in Medical Imaging, pp. 682–693 (2019)
16. Zhou, Z., et al.: Models genesis: generic autodidactic models for 3D medical image analysis. In: International Conference on Medical Image Computing and Computer Assisted Intervention, pp. 384–393 (2019)
17. Zhuang, X., Li, Y., Hu, Y., Ma, K., Yang, Y., Zheng, Y.: Self-supervised feature learning for 3D medical images by playing a Rubik's cube. In: International Conference on Medical Image Computing and Computer Assisted Intervention, pp. 420–428 (2019)

StyPath: Style-Transfer Data Augmentation for Robust Histology Image Classification

Pietro Antonio Cicalese[1,2]($\boxtimes$), Aryan Mobiny[1], Pengyu Yuan[1], Jan Becker[3], Chandra Mohan[2], and Hien Van Nguyen[1]

[1] Department of Electrical Engineering, University of Houston, Houston, TX, USA
[2] Department of Biomedical Engineering, University of Houston, Houston, TX, USA
pcicalese@uh.edu
[3] Institute of Pathology, University Hospital of Cologne, Cologne, Germany

Abstract. The classification of Antibody Mediated Rejection (AMR) in kidney transplant remains challenging even for experienced nephropathologists; this is partly because histological tissue stain analysis is often characterized by low inter-observer agreement and poor reproducibility. One of the implicated causes for inter-observer disagreement is the variability of tissue stain quality between (and within) pathology labs, coupled with the gradual fading of archival sections. Variations in stain colors and intensities can make tissue evaluation difficult for pathologists, ultimately affecting their ability to describe relevant morphological features. Being able to accurately predict the AMR status based on kidney histology images is crucial for improving patient treatment and care. We propose a novel pipeline to build robust deep neural networks for AMR classification based on StyPath, a histological data augmentation technique that leverages a light weight style-transfer algorithm as a means to reduce sample-specific bias. Each image was generated in 1.84 ± 0.03 s using a single GTX TITAN V gpu and pytorch, making it faster than other popular histological data augmentation techniques. We evaluated our model using a Monte Carlo (MC) estimate of Bayesian performance and generate an epistemic measure of uncertainty to compare both the baseline and StyPath augmented models. We also generated Grad-CAM representations of the results which were assessed by an experienced nephropathologist; we used this qualitative analysis to elucidate on the assumptions being made by each model. Our results imply that our style-transfer augmentation technique improves histological classification performance (reducing error from 14.8% to 11.5%) and generalization ability.

Keywords: Pathology · Style-transfer · CNN classifier · Data augmentation · Inter-observer agreement

Electronic supplementary material The online version of this chapter (https://doi.org/10.1007/978-3-030-59722-1_34) contains supplementary material, which is available to authorized users.

A. L. Martel et al. (Eds.): MICCAI 2020, LNCS 12265, pp. 351–361, 2020.
https://doi.org/10.1007/978-3-030-59722-1_34

1   Introduction

Low intra and inter observer reproducibility in the analysis of histologic features has been a persistent concern amongst pathologists across various tissue types and diseases. Although concordance is generally within an acceptable range for diagnosis, the clinical adoption of certain scoring parameters has been hindered by disagreement between observers and insufficient empirical evidence. This has a negative impact on the reproducibility of any given histological diagnosis and thus complicates the path to both consistent and effective treatment, and the design of multicentric pharmaceutical studies. The degree of disagreement observed has been the topic of several publications; varying levels of experience, the number of scoring parameters, cutoff values, and the type of stains used to assess a biopsy have all been associated with variable diagnosis [6,13,15,23]. Discrepancies in staining quality within and between pathology labs have also been implicated as a cause for variability, with variations in stain intensity being associated with poor diagnostic performance [2]. The effect of this apparent stain bias is similar to the texture and context bias we observe when training Convolutional Neural Networks (or CNNs), which negatively impacts the generalization ability of the model.

Geirhos *et al.* showed that CNNs trained on the ImageNet dataset are heavily biased towards texture and fail to match human performance in the silhouette and edge classification tasks [10]. These models can therefore appear to yield exceptional performance in real world applications, when they are actually depending on a single cue for classification. This poses a significant challenge in histological diagnosis tasks where each biopsy has unique texture and color characteristics, which may have a negative impact on performance and the model's ability to generalize. This issue is also exacerbated by the relatively small sample sizes of histology datasets; whereas large datasets are less likely to yield models with sample specific bias, a small dataset is likely to yield models with poor generalization ability. We believe that by combining texture and color information from various training samples, we could reduce this texture bias while increasing the classifier shape bias, ultimately yielding a more robust model. Our contributions are as follows:

- We propose a sample and condition agnostic style-transfer data augmentation technique to improve histological training performance with a small glomerular-level Antibody Mediated Rejection (AMR) dataset. Our technique depends on both the moderated transfer of spatial relationships and style, yielding a more diverse training population that retains the desired target concepts.
- We use Bayesian inference to compensate for the ignorance of the model (due to the small dataset size) and to estimate a more reliable measure of performance. Our technique improves upon the prediction accuracy of the baseline model at a lower computational cost relative to similar techniques.
- Qualitative analysis and visual inspection by an experienced nephropathologist are provided to demonstrate that the StyPath augmented models are

more robust, capturing information that would have otherwise been missed by the baseline model.

Related Works. The issue of histological stain normalization has been addressed by various research groups in both the medical and computer science communities. Adam *et al.* proposed a single feature schema in the qualitative scoring of polyomavirus BK (BKV) nephropathy immunohistochemistry (IHC) slides and stain protocol standardisation practices as a means to reduce the inter-observer variance associated with differing stain intensities [2]. This solution is limited by the difficulty associated with novel scoring parameter adoption and the cost incurred by pathology labs to standardize their equipment and procedures. These kinds of limitations have ultimately led various groups to develop *in silico* stain normalization techniques that could be used to improve upon quantitative histological image analysis. In the hemotoxylin and eosin (H&E) data normalization task, Macenko *et al.* proposed a deconvolution technique which effectively separates the hemotoxylin and eosin stains to then generate their respective normalized components [14]. Bejnordi *et al.* developed a whole-slide image color standardizer that combines color and spatial information to categorize each pixel in a slide scan as a stain component [3]. Bug *et al.* proposed a style-transfer normalization algorithm which transfers pathology lab profiles between samples without altering spatial relationships [5]. Interestingly, Tellez *et al.* evaluated all three of these stain normalization techniques and showed that they had a largely negligible (or even negative) effect on CNN classification performance while adding a significant computational cost, prompting them to favor other stain augmentation techniques [22]. It is important to note that the style-transfer algorithm they evaluated only transfers the color profiles between pathology labs, remaining largely agnostic to the sources of variability present within each lab and stained section. Shaban *et al.* and BenTaieb *et al.* also proposed conditional stain transfer techniques that utilized adversarial networks to generate new samples for each target domain [4,20]. While powerful, these techniques require explicitly defined domain labels; this prevents the techniques from capturing important variations that may be present within each predefined condition set. We were interested in developing a sample and condition agnostic style-transfer augmentation procedure that could be applied to any histological dataset to address all sources of stain variability. We also propose the moderated transfer of spatial relationships between samples; while prior techniques avoided altering the morphological appearance of each image, we hypothesized that slight image alterations through the style-transfer algorithm could be beneficial to the generalization capabilities of a model, especially when trained with a small dataset.

2   Methodology

AMR Dataset Generation and Annotation. A total of 86 (38 non-AMR and 48 AMR, chronic active AMR, or chronic AMR) blood group ABO- compatible kidney transplant biopsies were randomly selected for processing and analysis, each fulfilling the minimum sample criteria (≥ 7 glomeruli, ≥ 1 artery). Each paraffin embedded section was cut at $2\,\text{mm}$ and stained with periodic acid-Schiff (PAS) in the same pathology lab over the span of two years. For each section, micrographs were taken from all non-globally sclerosed glomeruli that were at least four levels apart at a resolution of 1024×768 pixels. All segmented glomerular images were then annotated by an experienced nephropathologist using the Labelbox platform; label choices were given as either AMR, non-AMR, or inconclusive, yielding 1503 conclusively labeled glomerular images (1001 non-AMR and 502 AMR) [1].

Style-Transfer. One can think of the style-transfer algorithm as a means to generate artificial images that combine the high-level semantic representation of one image with the low-level perceptual representation of another image. The semantic image (i.e. the content image) represents the objects that will be depicted in the generated image, while the perceptual image (i.e. the style image) characterizes simpler information (such as color and texture). The ability to generate these artificial images depends on the extraction and manipulation of feature maps from the filters of the selected layers of a CNN [9]. An input image $\mathbf{x}$ is effectively encoded in each layer of a CNN by the filter responses to image $\mathbf{x}$, which allows us to extract various representations of the image depending on the layer. Feature maps from deeper layers of a CNN characterize complex concepts (such as cells and glomeruli) while those from shallow layers characterize simple concepts (such as edges and color). We say that a layer l with N_l unique filters therefore has N_l unique feature maps of dimensions M_l^{hw}, corresponding to the height multiplied by the width of each feature map. We can then say that the filter responses within a given layer l can be stored in a matrix $F_l \in R^{N_l \times M_l^{hw}}$ where F_l^{ij} corresponds to the activation of the ith filter at position j in layer l.

Suppose that we have a given content image $\mathbf{x}_{cont}$ and an output image $\mathbf{x}_{out}$; we define their respective feature responses in a given layer l as F_l^{cont} and F_l^{out}, respectively. We can then define the squared-error content loss λ^{cont} for a given layer l following

$$\lambda_l^{cont}(\mathbf{x}_{cont}, \mathbf{x}_{out}) = \frac{1}{2} \sum_{ij} (F_l^{ij,out} - F_l^{ij,cont})^2. \tag{1}$$

We can thus define the derivative of the squared-error loss between each set of feature representations for a given layer l following

$$\frac{d\lambda_l^{cont}}{dF_l^{ij,out}} = \begin{cases} (F_l^{ij,out} - F_l^{ij,cont}), & F_l^{ij,out} > 0 \\ 0, & F_l^{ij,out} < 0 \end{cases}, \tag{2}$$

which can then be used to compute the content gradient with respect to image $\mathbf{x}_{out}$. We then generate a Gram matrix which takes the correlation between various filter responses as a means to capture the style of the desired style image $\mathbf{x}_{sty}$. The generated Gram matrix is given by $G_l \in R^{N_l \times M_l^h \times M_l^w}$, where G_l^{ij}

represents the inner product between the vectorised feature map i and j in a given layer l at position k. We define G_l^{ij} following

$$G_l^{ij} = \sum_k F_l^{ik} F_l^{jk}, \tag{3}$$

which we then use to match the style between $\mathbf{x}_{out}$ and $\mathbf{x}_{sty}$ by minimising the mean-squared distance between their respective Gram matrices. Let $G_l^{ij,out}$ and $G_l^{ij,sty}$ represent the Gram matrices from a given layer l of $\mathbf{x}_{out}$ and $\mathbf{x}_{sty}$, respectively. We then say that the contribution of layer l to the total style loss is given by

$$\lambda_l^{sty} = \frac{1}{4(N_l)^2(M_l^{hw})^2} \sum_{ij} (G_l^{ij,out} - G_l^{ij,sty})^2, \tag{4}$$

while total style loss is given by

$$\lambda^{sty}(\mathbf{x}_{sty}, \mathbf{x}_{out}) = \sum_{l=0}^{L} w_l \lambda_l^{sty}, \tag{5}$$

with w_l corresponding to weighting factors of the contribution of each layer to the total loss (which we simply set equal to one divided by the number of active layers). We can then compute the derivative of λ_l^{sty} following

$$\frac{d\lambda_l^{sty}}{dF_l^{ij}} = \begin{cases} \frac{1}{(N_l)^2(M_l^{hw})^2}(F_l^{ij})^T(G_l^{ij,out} - G_l^{ij,sty}) & F_l^{ij} > 0 \\ 0 & F_l^{ij} < 0 \end{cases}, \tag{6}$$

thus allowing us to compute the style gradient with respect to $\mathbf{x}_{out}$. Finally, to generate the style-transfer samples, we simply minimize both λ^{cont} and λ^{sty} following

$$\lambda^{tot}(\mathbf{x}_{cont}, \mathbf{x}_{sty}, \mathbf{x}_{out}) = \alpha\lambda^{cont}(\mathbf{x}_{cont}, \mathbf{x}_{out}) + \lambda^{sty}(\mathbf{x}_{sty}, \mathbf{x}_{out}), \tag{7}$$

where α is used to scale down the content loss, allowing us to control the stylization of the generated image.

Approximate Bayesian Inference via MC-Dropout. Training a standard neural network parameterized by its weights is equivalent to generating a maximum likelihood estimation (MLE) of the network parameters, which yields a single set of parameters [11]. Such a model generates point estimates for each testing sample it classifies and ignores any model uncertainty that may be present in the proper weight values. In medical applications, this can eventually mislead the physician into believing that a model is confident about a prediction that may actually be a lucky guess [7]. Model uncertainty, also known as epistemic uncertainty, is most prevalent when a model is trained using a small sample set, where irrelevant information may be abused by the model to improve performance [7,16]. It would therefore be more informative to generate a model that provides a probabilistic estimate of its predictions, which can then be used to estimate the model's level of uncertainty. This can be accomplished by generating a Bayesian Neural Network (BNN) model; it is possible to generate a prior distribution over the network's parameters, outputting a probability distribution which can be used to estimate class posterior probabilities for each testing sample [18]. One can then integrate over the class posterior probabilities to produce a predictive posterior distribution over the class membership probabilities, and measure dispersion over the predictive posterior to generate uncertainty estimates. However, BNN models are computationally intractable, which has prompted various groups to develop methods to approximate Bayesian inference. To generate such a model, Gal *et al.* proved that a feed-forward neural network with a given number of layers and non-linearities can be equivalent to approximate variational inference in the deep Gaussian Process model when dropout is applied to all units [8]. We can therefore use Monte Carlo (MC) dropout at test time to yield a Bernoulli distribution over the weights of a CNN to generate an approximation of the posterior distribution without having to train additional parameters [17]. Through this technique, we can therefore quantitatively measure a more accurate estimate of each model's performance and describe their ability to generalize during the testing phase.

Grad-CAM Visualization. Being able to visualize and interpret the classification criteria being used by a CNN is critical to both confirming the assumptions being made by the classifier and learning from the classifiers decisions. Selvaraju *et al.* showed that visual explanations for each model prediction could be generated by using gradient information flowing into the last convolutional layer of a CNN, capturing the semantic information being used to classify a given sample [19]. These extracted Gradient-weighted Class Activation Maps (Grad-CAMs) could thus be used to depict a high-level representation of the classifiers decision making process. To further understand how both the baseline and Sty-Path augmented models drew their conclusions, we chose to generate Grad-CAM representations of each testing set prediction, which were then assessed by an experienced nephropathologist.

3   Results and Discussion

Style-Transfer Hyper Parameters. We elected to use the original VGG19 network during the style-transfer sample generation phase due to its light-weight yet powerful contextual representation ability [21]. Following Gatys *et al.*, we take the output of the fourth convolutional layer for content and the outputs of convolutional layers one through five for style [9]. We chose to initialize $\mathbf{x}_{out}$ to be an exact copy of $\mathbf{x}_{cont}$, allowing us to retain high content image fidelity while reducing the number of iterations needed to produce a meaningful output (100 iterations to generate each sample, as shown in Fig. 1). This allowed us

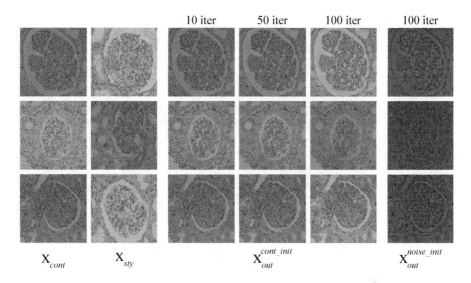

Fig. 1. Comparison of content and random initialization results. We note that output images initialized as the content image retain their morphological characteristics while capturing color and texture from the style image within 100 iterations. Output images initialized as noise appear distorted and discolored, failing to retain content fidelity.

to generate each image in 1.84 ± 0.03 s using a single GTX TITAN V gpu and pytorch, making it faster than other popular data augmentation techniques. This also helps soften the transfer of spatial relationships, allowing only slight structural modifications to occur that do not alter the desired target concept. We elected to use an α value of 2×10^{-4} following visual inspection of the generated samples by an experienced nephropathologist; this ensured that the generated samples retained the morphological characteristics of their respective content image while capturing the texture and color characteristics of their respective style image. When generating each $\mathbf{x}_{out}$, we selected one content and style image at random from the training set, irrespective of their associated label or section of origin. The generated style-transfer images were assigned the label of their corresponding content image and then appended to the training set before each augmented training experiment.

Bayesian Classification Analysis. During the classification task, we used the DenseNet-121 architecture pre-trained on the ImageNet dataset [12]. Both the original and StyPath augmented sample sets were resized to 256×256 pixels prior to being passed to each model; each classifier was trained for 200 epochs, using a batch size of 10, a drop rate of 0.1 in all bottleneck blocks, and a learning rate of 10^{-4}. Online augmentation was performed in all experiments for fair comparison between models; images had a 50% chance of being flipped horizontally, being flipped vertically, having up to 30% of their x and y axis cropped, and being rotated in either direction by up to $90°$. Each testing fold in our five fold cross validation scheme consisted of original glomerular images; no images derived from the same section could be present in both the training and testing set folds. We gradually added an equal amount of randomly selected AMR and non-AMR style-transfer images to each training set to identify where performance saturated. We note that the baseline model achieves a weighted Bayesian classification accuracy of 85.2% while the StyPath augmented model saturates around 88.5% (after adding 300 style-transfer samples to each class, as shown in Fig. 2a). To confirm that StyPath's performance increase had saturated, we also evaluated the model after adding 10000 style-transfer samples to each class, which yielded a Bayesian classification accuracy of 88.2%.

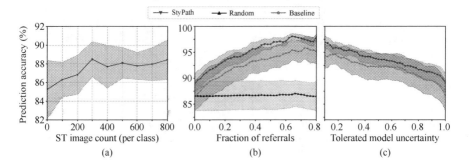

Fig. 2. Quantitative comparison of the baseline and StyPath augmented model performance. We note that the Bayesian performance of StyPath saturates after adding 300 Style-Transfer (ST) samples per class (a). When removing samples based on their uncertainty estimates, we note that the StyPath augmented model outperforms the baseline model while varying less across all five folds (b and c).

Epistemic Uncertainty Analysis. We then filtered samples based on their normalized epistemic uncertainty values; we observe that the StyPath augmented model consistently outperforms the baseline model while its performance varies significantly less across all folds (as shown in Fig. 2b and c). This result implies that StyPath augmented models have improved generalization ability, suggesting that the information being used by the model is more descriptive of the target concept.

Qualitative Analysis Using Grad-CAM. We note that certain StyPath augmented model predictions caused the Grad-CAM activations to shift, widen, or narrow down to diagnostic features present in the glomeruli, correcting erroneous baseline model predictions (as shown in Fig. 3, columns 1 through 5). While some failure cases indicate that the StyPath augmented model missed the desired concept (Fig. 3, columns 8 and 9), the initial label (non-AMR) of Fig. 3, column 6

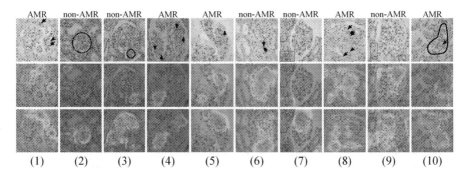

Fig. 3. Comparison of baseline (second row) and StyPath augmented (third row) Grad-CAM activations. Columns (1) through (5) represent success cases where the StyPath augmented prediction is correct and the baseline model prediction is incorrect, while columns (6) through (10) represent failure cases where the StyPath augmented prediction is incorrect and the baseline model prediction is correct. Black arrows in the original image (top row, labeled) are indicative of glomerulitis, mononuclear cells/infiltrates, and split glomerular basement membranes, while black and red outlines characterize regions of interest and misleading areas, respectively (Color figure online).

was put into question upon observing the StyPath augmented Grad-CAM activation; the model detects an accumulation of intracapillary mononuclear cells that are indicative of glomerulitis (and thus AMR). We observe that the baseline model correctly classifies Fig. 3, column 7 as non-AMR by counter intuitively focusing on an area of dense infiltrates in the periglomerular interstitium, which is not descriptive of non-AMR. Although the sample is misclassified, the StyPath augmented model instead focuses on the glomerular tuft, indicating that it detected the correct region of interest. We also note that generally, collapsed glomerular images seemed to pose a challenge for both the nephropathologist and the classifier, with both baseline and StyPath augmented models failing to focus on the areas indicative of AMR (Fig. 3, column 10).

4   Conclusions

We present a novel histological data augmentation technique called StyPath, which generates new histological samples through the sample and condition agnostic transfer of both spatial relationships and style. We use Bayesian inference to evaluate the technique and show that it improves both the performance and generalization ability of the classifier at a low computational cost. We then generated Grad-CAM representations of both the baseline and StyPath augmented models for assessment by an experienced nephropathologist. This assessment showed that the augmented model tended to focus on morphologically relevant information which ultimately improved its classification accuracy. Our future works aim to compare the performance of StyPath to other SOTA techniques on larger multi-conditional datasets.

Acknowledgments. This research was supported by the National Science Foundation (NSF-IIS 1910973).

References

1. Labelbox: labelbox (2020). https://labelbox.com
2. Adam, B., et al.: Banff initiative for quality assurance in transplantation (bifquit): reproducibility of polyomavirus immunohistochemistry in kidney allografts. Am. J. Transplant. **14**(9), 2137–2147 (2014)
3. Bejnordi, B.E., et al.: Stain specific standardization of whole-slide histopathological images. IEEE Trans. Med. Imaging **35**(2), 404–415 (2015)
4. BenTaieb, A., Hamarneh, G.: Adversarial stain transfer for histopathology image analysis. IEEE Trans. Med. Imaging **37**(3), 792–802 (2017)
5. Bug, D., et al.: Context-based normalization of histological stains using deep convolutional features. In: Cardoso, M.J., et al. (eds.) DLMIA/ML-CDS -2017. LNCS, vol. 10553, pp. 135–142. Springer, Cham (2017). https://doi.org/10.1007/978-3-319-67558-9_16
6. Dasari, S., Chakraborty, A., Truong, L., Mohan, C.: A systematic review of inter-pathologist agreement in histologic classification of lupus nephritis. Kidney Int. Rep. **4**(10), 1420–1425 (2019)
7. Gal, Y., Ghahramani, Z.: Bayesian convolutional neural networks with Bernoulli approximate variational inference. arXiv preprint arXiv:1506.02158 (2015)
8. Gal, Y., Ghahramani, Z.: Dropout as a Bayesian approximation: Representing model uncertainty in deep learning. In: International Conference on Machine Learning, pp. 1050–1059 (2016)
9. Gatys, L.A., Ecker, A.S., Bethge, M.: A neural algorithm of artistic style. arXiv preprint arXiv:1508.06576 (2015)
10. Geirhos, R., Rubisch, P., Michaelis, C., Bethge, M., Wichmann, F.A., Brendel, W.: Imagenet-trained cnns are biased towards texture; increasing shape bias improves accuracy and robustness. arXiv preprint arXiv:1811.12231 (2018)
11. Goodfellow, I., Bengio, Y., Courville, A.: Deep Learning. MIT press, Cambridge (2016)
12. Iandola, F., Moskewicz, M., Karayev, S., Girshick, R., Darrell, T., Keutzer, K.: Densenet: implementing efficient convnet descriptor pyramids. arXiv preprint arXiv:1404.1869 (2014)
13. Koelzer, V.H., et al.: Tumor budding in colorectal cancer revisited: results of a multicenter interobserver study. Virchows Arch. **466**(5), 485–493 (2015). https://doi.org/10.1007/s00428-015-1740-9
14. Macenko, M., et al.: A method for normalizing histology slides for quantitative analysis. In: 2009 IEEE International Symposium on Biomedical Imaging: From Nano to Macro, pp. 1107–1110. IEEE (2009)
15. Martin, B., et al.: Interobserver variability in the h&e-based assessment of tumor budding in pt3/4 colon cancer: does it affect the prognostic relevance? Virchows Arch. **473**(2), 189–197 (2018)
16. Mobiny, A., Nguyen, H.V., Moulik, S., Garg, N., Wu, C.C.: Dropconnect is effective in modeling uncertainty of Bayesian deep networks. arXiv preprint arXiv:1906.04569 (2019)
17. Mobiny, A., Singh, A., Van Nguyen, H.: Risk-aware machine learning classifier for skin lesion diagnosis. J. Clin. Med. **8**(8), 1241 (2019)

18. Neal, R.M.: Bayesian Learning for Neural Networks. Lecture Notes in Statistics, vol. 118. Springer Science & Business Media, New York (2012). https://doi.org/10.1007/978-1-4612-0745-0

19. Selvaraju, R.R., Cogswell, M., Das, A., Vedantam, R., Parikh, D., Batra, D.: Grad-cam: visual explanations from deep networks via gradient-based localization. In: Proceedings of the IEEE International Conference on Computer Vision, pp. 618–626 (2017)

20. Shaban, M.T., Baur, C., Navab, N., Albarqouni, S.: Staingan: stain style transfer for digital histological images. In: 2019 IEEE 16th International Symposium on Biomedical Imaging (ISBI 2019), pp. 953–956. IEEE (2019)

21. Simonyan, K., Zisserman, A.: Very deep convolutional networks for large-scale image recognition. arXiv preprint arXiv:1409.1556 (2014)

22. Tellez, D., et al.: Quantifying the effects of data augmentation and stain color normalization in convolutional neural networks for computational pathology. Med. Image Anal. **58**, 101544 (2019)

23. Wilhelmus, S., et al.: Interobserver agreement on histopathological lesions in class III or IV lupus nephritis. Clin. J. Am. Soc. Nephrol. **10**(1), 47–53 (2015)

Multimarginal Wasserstein Barycenter for Stain Normalization and Augmentation

Saad Nadeem[1]([✉]), Travis Hollmann[2], and Allen Tannenbaum[3]

[1] Department of Medical Physics, Memorial Sloan Kettering Cancer Center,
New York, USA
nadeems@mskcc.org
[2] Department of Pathology, Memorial Sloan Kettering Cancer Center,
New York, USA
[3] Departments of Computer Science and Applied Mathematics,
Stony Brook University, Stony Brook, USA

Abstract. Variations in hematoxylin and eosin (H&E) stained images (due to clinical lab protocols, scanners, etc) directly impact the quality and accuracy of clinical diagnosis, and hence it is important to control for these variations for a reliable diagnosis. In this work, we present a new approach based on the multimarginal Wasserstein barycenter to normalize and augment H&E stained images given one or more references. Specifically, we provide a mathematically robust way of naturally incorporating additional images as intermediate references to drive stain normalization and augmentation simultaneously. The presented approach showed superior results quantitatively and qualitatively as compared to state-of-the-art methods for stain normalization. We further validated our stain normalization and augmentations in the nuclei segmentation task on a publicly available dataset, achieving state-of-the-art results against competing approaches.

Keywords: Wasserstein Barycenter · Stain normalization

1 Introduction

Histology is founded on the study of microscopic images to diagnose cell structures and arrangements for which staining is a critical part of the tissue preparation process. In particular, certain staining agents (mainly hematoxylin and eosin) transform the transparent tissue samples to become more distinguishable. Hematoxylin dyes the nuclei a dark purple color while eosin dyes other structures a pink color. A major problem is that results from the staining are inconsistent and prone to variability due to many factors including differing lab

Electronic supplementary material The online version of this chapter (https:// doi.org/10.1007/978-3-030-59722-1_35) contains supplementary material, which is available to authorized users.

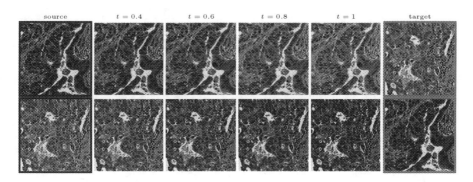

Fig. 1. Traditional ($N = 2$) Wasserstein Barycenter. The source color distribution is interpolated towards the target color distribution in the Lab color space.

protocols, inter-patient variabilities, differences in raw materials, and variations in the slide scanners. These inconsistencies may cause major problems not only for pathologists, but may also degrade the performance of computer-aided diagnosis systems.

It is well-known that for downstream applications such as nuclei segmentation, stain normalization and augmentation are essential [5,16]. In fact, augmentation might be more important than normalization, as pointed out by [10]. Color jitter or random HSV shifts was identified as an important step for the top contenders of the MonuSeg competition [6]. Due to the coming telemedicine revolution, there will be a strong requirement for either matching to a reference distribution or incorporating stain invariant approaches using stain augmentation or training on diverse datasets.

Tellez *et al.* [16] showed that for certain specific tasks, stain augmentation (adding color jitters in HSV or HED color space), with and without normalization, may also improve performance while making the resultant models more robust; nuclei segmentation was not explored as one of the tasks in the latter paper. Further as shown in [10], deep learning stain normalization/transfer approaches, such as StainGAN [14], are not particularly suitable for nuclei segmentation task given the lack of training data representing enough samples from same tissue, institution, preparation protocols, etc. Stain invariant models learnt via novel stain augmentation approaches can help achieve better performance. The work of Vahadane *et al.* [17] has been the predominant choice in the past for stain normalization in the nuclei segmentation tasks.

To deal with some of the aforementioned issues, *we introduce a new approach for simultaneous H&E stain normalization and augmentation based on the multimarginal Wasserstein barycenter approach*. Specifically, the novelty of the paper lies in first introducing the traditional Wasserstein barycenter approach for stain normalization/augmentation (Fig. 1), and then introducing the multimarginal version [1,9] to overcome the limitations of the traditional approach in this context (Fig. 2). Note that the traditional Wasserstein barycenter (1 source and 1 reference), although widely employed in computer vision, to the best of

our knowledge has never been used for stain normalization/augmentation and
the more general multimarginal Wasserstein barycenter (1 source and multiple
references) has hardly ever been used in computer vision or medical imaging
communities. For more accurate stain normalization, the multimarginal version
allows one to incorporate additional distributions by utilizing one or more intermediate reference images (Fig. 2). The resultant interpolations span a broad
spectrum of stain variations allowing for simultaneous stain normalization and
augmentation.

With respect to the pipeline, we convert given source and target images from
RGB to the Lab color space, interpolate between the given color distributions
using the Wasserstein barycenter, and then convert back to the RGB space.
The Lab color space was chosen based on its general effectiveness (decorrelated
color channels, etc.) in color transfer applications; see Reinhard and Pouli [13]
and the references therein. Finally, we quantified our results on stain normalization with respect to a publicly available dataset and obtained state-of-the-art
results. Similarly, we augment and normalize stain images in a publicly available
nuclei segmentation dataset and again achieved state-of-the-art results using our
method.

2   Background on Wasserstein Distance

We first very briefly review some basic material on optimal mass transport
(OMT) theory and the Wasserstein distance that we will need in the sequel.
We refer the reader to [19] for a more detailed development of the subject and
references.

Consider two probability measures μ_0, μ_1 on $\mathbb{R}^n$. In the original formulation
of OMT due to Gaspard Monge [18,19], one seeks a transport map

$$T \; : \; \mathbb{R}^n \rightarrow \mathbb{R}^n \; : \; x \mapsto T(x)$$

which specifies where the initial mass $\mu_0(dx)$ at x should be transported in
order match the final distribution. This means that $T_\sharp \mu_0 = \mu_1$ where μ_1 is the
"push-forward" of μ_0 under T:

$$\mu_1(B) = \mu_0(T^{-1}(B))$$

for every Borel set B in $\mathbb{R}^n$. Moreover, given the transportation cost $c(x,y)$, the
map should minimize

$$\int_{\mathbb{R}^n} c(x, T(x)) d\mu_0(x). \tag{1}$$

In this paper, we will only consider the case $c(x,y) = \|x - y\|^2$. To ensure finite
cost, we will assume that μ_0 and μ_1 lie in the space of probability densities with
finite second moments, denoted by $P_2(\mathbb{R}^n)$.

The dependence of the transportation cost on T is highly nonlinear and a
minimum may not exist for general costs c. In order to handle this problem,
Leonid Kantorovich proposed a relaxed formulation [18,19], in which one seeks

a joint distribution $\pi \in \Pi(\mu_0, \mu_1)$ on $\mathbb{R}^n \times \mathbb{R}^n$, referred to as a *coupling* of μ_0 and μ_1, i.e., the marginals along the two coordinate directions should coincide with μ_0 and μ_1, respectively. More precisely, in this setting, we consider

$$K := \inf_{\pi \in \Pi(\mu_0, \mu_1)} \int_{\mathbb{R}^n \times \mathbb{R}^n} \|x - y\|^2 d\pi(x, y). \tag{2}$$

For the case where μ_0, μ_1 are absolutely continuous with respect to the Lebesgue measure, it is a standard result that OMT (2) has a unique solution [18,19]. This is of the form

$$\pi = (\mathrm{Id} \times T)_\sharp \mu_0,$$

where Id stands for the identity map, and T is the unique minimizer of (1). One may also show that the unique optimal transport T is the gradient of a convex function ω, i.e.,

$$y = T(x) = \nabla \omega(x). \tag{3}$$

Wasserstein Metric: The square root of the optimal cost formally defines a Riemannian metric on $P_2(\mathbb{R}^n)$, known as the Wasserstein metric W_2 [18,19], i.e., $W_2(\mu_0, \mu_1) := \sqrt{K}$ with K in (2).

Naturally $P_2(\mathbb{R}^n)$ is a geodesic space: a geodesic between μ_0 and μ_1 is of the form

$$\mu_t = (T_t)_\sharp \mu_0, \quad T_t(x) = (1 - t)x + tT(x). \tag{4}$$

A geodesic path is also known as *displacement interpolation* [8]. It holds that

$$W_2(\mu_s, \mu_t) = (t - s)W_2(\mu_0, \mu_1), \quad 0 \le s < t \le 1. \tag{5}$$

μ_t also solves the Wasserstein barycenter problem in the case of two probability measures as we will now describe below.

3 Wasserstein Barycenter

We follow the theory described in [1,9] to which we refer the interested reader to all the relevant references. We follow the notation and set-up from Sect. 2. In the case of images of interest in the present work, we take $n = 2$ or $n = 3$ in $P_2(\mathbb{R}^n)$.

Then the ***Wasserstein barycenter*** of N probability measures $\mu_1, \ldots, \mu_N \in P_2(\mathbb{R}^n)$ is the minimizer of the functional

$$f(\mu) = \sum_{i=1}^N \lambda_i W_p^p(\mu_i, \mu), \quad \lambda_i \ge 0, \quad \sum_{i=1}^N \lambda_i = 1. \tag{6}$$

This is a special case of the Multimarginal Optimal Transport (MOMT) problem [1,9].

The case $N = 2$ is classical due to McCann [8] has been sketched in Sect. 2. For our purposes for stain normalization and augmentation in histological data,

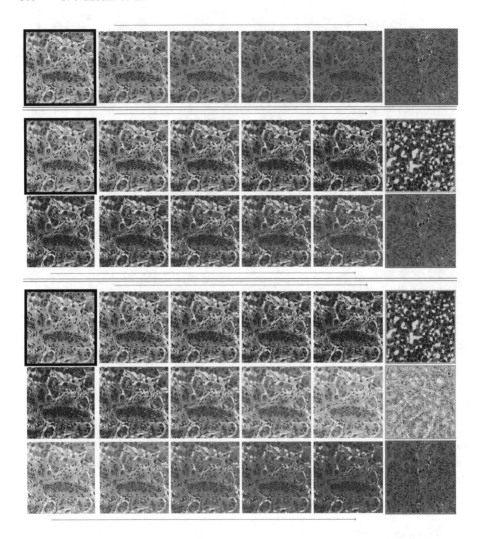

Fig. 2. Multimarginal Wasserstein Barycenter with 1, 2, and 3 reference images, i.e., $N = 2,3$ or 4 in (6). The images with blue borders are input/source images, the ones with green are the (intermediate) references and the red ones are the final reference/target images. Reference images can be from the same or different domains. Ideally in the multimarginal case, one of the intermediate references should have some background. (Color figure online)

we may regard μ_1 as the source distribution and μ_2 as the reference distribution. Then for $t \in [0,1]$, we can consider minimizing the family of functionals

$$f_t(\mu) = (1-t)W_2^2(\mu_1, \mu) + tW_2^2(\mu_2, \mu),$$

and hence get a continuous family of interpolations which form a geodesic in the space of probability distributions as described in Sect. 2. See Eq. (4).

In the present work, we also employ one source distribution μ_1 and either $1, 2$ or 3 reference distributions μ_i ($2 \leq i \leq 4$). For $N \geq 3$ in (6), i.e., two or more references, we use the term "multimarginal OMT," to emphasize the fact that we are considering more than two measures. For the application to images, one can always normalize to make sure that the total mass (intensity) is 1. Further in the examples below (see Sect. 4), we choose $\lambda_i = 1/N$, $1 \leq i \leq N$. Let μ_{opt} denote the optimal solution of (6), that is, the barycenter. Notice that taking μ_1 and μ_{opt} as the marginals, we also find the optimal transport map $T_{\#}\mu_1 = \mu_{opt}$. We also set the parameter $m = N - 2$, which is the number of intermediate reference images. Thus, $m = 0$ refers to the usual Wasserstein barycenter computed with respected to a reference and a source, with no intermediate reference images.

Computation of Wasserstein Barycenters: There are a number of algorithms for the computation of the multimarginal Wasserstein barycenter; see the very recent paper [11] and the references therein. In our implementation, we used the approach developed in Cuturi and Doucet [3], which we briefly sketch.

In the latter work, the authors propose (sub)gradient descent framework based on a modification of the functional (6); see in particular Sect. 4 of [3]. Because of the computational complexity, they first smooth the Wasserstein distance via an entropic regularizer. This allows them to employ the *Sinkhorn algorithm* [2], which is an iterative rescaling descent procedure that converges to the desired regularized distance. The procedure of [3] leads to a strictly convex objective function whose gradients can be computed in a fast, efficient manner. We employed the algorithm for the case in which we want the barycenter for N distributions ($N = 2, 3$ or 4) where N is the total number of masses in the weighted sum defining the Wasserstein barycenter (Eq. 6). As mentioned above, $m = N - 2$ is the number of intermediate reference images.

4   Experiments and Results

We implemented our algorithm using the Python Optimal Transport (POT) library[1] which include GPU-accelerated versions of Sinkhorn regularization. We used Nvidia GeForce RTX 2080 Ti for our experiments. Pytorch framework was used for StainGAN[2] and CNN3[3] implementations. We evaluated our approach against Reinhard *et al.* [12], Macenko *et al.* [7], Khan *et al.* [4], Vahadne *et al.* [17], and StainGAN [14].

4.1   Stain Normalization Evaluation

We used MITOS-ATYPIA'14 challenge dataset for evaluating our stain normalization. The dataset includes same tissue sections scanned by two different

[1] https://github.com/rflamary/POT.

[2] https://github.com/xtarx/StainGAN.

[3] https://github.com/neerajkumarvaid/Nuclei_Segmentation.

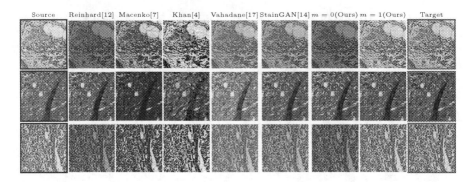

Fig. 3. Multimarginal Wasserstein Barycenter comparison with state of the art methods on MITOS-ATYPIA'14 challenge dataset. The blue bordered image is the input image and the two red bordered images are the references (with the one above being the intermediate reference). m is the number of intermediate references (in traditional Wasserstein barycenter $m = 0$; there is no intermediate reference). (Color figure online)

Table 1. Stain Normalization Comparison (Mean ± Standard Deviation) on MITOS-ATYPIA'14 challenge dataset using Structural Similarity Index (SSIM) [20], Feature Similarity Index (FSIM) [21]. The time is the total time taken for normalizing all 500 images.

Methods	SSIM	FSIM	Time (sec)
Reinhard [12]	0.55 ± 0.13	0.63 ± 0.07	**6.76**
Macenko [7]	0.51 ± 0.08	0.62 ± 0.09	59.40
Khan [4]	0.62 ± 0.18	0.65 ± 0.08	1994.87
Vahdane [17]	0.63 ± 0.11	0.65 ± 0.06	502.04
StainGAN [14]	0.68 ± 0.23	0.69 ± 0.06	69.12
$m = 0$ (Ours)	0.59 ± 0.32	0.67 ± 0.08	254.06
$m = 1$ (Ours)	$\mathbf{0.73 \pm 0.06}$	$\mathbf{0.75 \pm 0.11}$	384.28

scanners (Aperio-A and Hamamatsu-H) with total 424 X20 A-H frame pairs, 300 training and 124 testing. Images from scanner A are normalized and matched against the real corresponding images from H (ground truth). As in StainGAN [14], 10,000 random (256×256) patches from 300 training frames were used for training (26 epochs with the regularization parameter $\lambda = 10$, learning rate 0.0002, Adam optimizer with a batch size of 4) and 500 patches from 124 testing data used for evaluation. The visual and quantitative comparisons are shown in Fig. 3 and Table 1, respectively. For the traditional case (one reference and source), our results are very similar to Reinhard *et al.* [12] since they also do color matching in Lab space, but our results improve drastically given two reference images. The references in our case span patches with different amounts of background visible. We also tested with different reference images and we show that we get a tighter bound as long as the references contain different amounts of background visibility; see the supplementary material for the box plots of SSIM for different references.

4.2   Nuclei Segmentation

We also evaluate our stain augmentation/normalization in the nuclei segmentation settings. Specifically, we test our approach on MoNuSeg challenge dataset [6]. Previous works [6,10] have already shown that stain normalization improves performance for nuclei segmentation tasks. As mentioned in the Introduction, Tellez *et al.* [16] demonstrated that for several key specific tasks, stain augmentation improves performance and robustifies the resultant models. Very importantly, deep learning stain normalization/transfer approaches, e.g., StainGAN [14], are not particularly suitable for nuclei segmentation task given the lack of

Table 2. Nuclei Segmentation comparisons using Aggregated Jaccard Index on same MoNuSeg test dataset as reported in [6] for direct comparison (with images from 4 organs –Breast, Liver, Kidney and Prostate– also included in the training data and 3 others–Bladder, Colon and Stomach– not included in training). For the same underlying architecture (CNN3 [6]) denoted by C, different combinations of the following are explored: Vahadane Stain Normalization (V), geometric augmentation (G) via rigid (rotation and flipping) and affine transformations, color jitter via random HSV/HED shifts (J), stain augmentation via direct perturbations of H&E color channels (A) as introduced by Tellez et al. [15] (α_i and β_i were similarly taken from two uniform distributions), and finally our stain normalization (SN) and augmentation (SA). For SN, we just include the final interpolation and for SA we include all the interpolations.

Organ	Image	C+V [6]	C+SN	C+G+J+A	C+G+SN+SA
Breast	1	0.4974	0.5211	0.4532	0.5325
	2	0.5796	0.5726	0.4830	0.5815
Liver	1	0.5175	0.5462	0.6134	0.5598
	2	0.5148	0.5829	0.5918	0.6013
Kidney	1	0.4792	0.4812	0.5815	0.5648
	2	0.6672	0.7187	0.6924	0.7414
Prostate	1	0.4914	0.5305	0.5491	0.6270
	2	0.3761	0.4017	0.3191	0.5296
Bladder	1	0.5465	0.5634	0.5510	0.6475
	2	0.4968	0.5016	0.4489	0.5267
Colon	1	0.4891	0.5108	0.4904	0.5318
	2	0.5692	0.6179	0.5879	0.6263
Stomach	1	0.4538	0.5318	0.4823	0.6408
	2	0.4378	0.4520	0.3912	0.6551
Overall		0.5083	0.5381	0.5168	0.5976

training (source-target image pair) data; see [10] for the details. The work of Vahadane *et al.* [17] has been one of the main methodologies for stain normalization in nuclei segmentation.

Here we explore the effects of using different combinations of stain normalization and augmentation approaches for the same underlying architecture (CNN3), geometric augmentation and post-processing approaches [6]. We used the same architecture and hyperparameters as reported in Kumar *et al.* [6]. After training and validation, the Aggregated Jaccard Index was computed on the same test set as in [6] for direct comparison. To drive the stain normalization and augmentation, in our approach we used 4 reference images, one from each organ present in the training dataset; images from 4 organs were used for training and testing and images from 3 additional organs were included just in the test set (Table 2).

5   Conclusions and Future Work

In the paper, we presented a new multimarginal Wasserstein barycenter method for H&E stain normalization and augmentation given one or more references. The method achieved superior performance in stain normalization and nuclei segmentation tasks because of the use of the intermediate references in the multimarginal setting. This allows one to incorporate additional distributions that can give physically more realistic interpolations (hence augmentation) as well as normalization. Since the normalization is done in the color distribution space and is not dependent on the number of pixels, the method can easily be scaled to whole slide images. In the future, we will also explore incorporating our Wasserstein barycenter formulation as a deep learning loss function.

Acknowledgements. This study was supported by AFOSR grants (FA9550-17-1-0435, FA9550-20-1-0029), NIH grant (R01-AG048769), MSK Cancer Center Support Grant/Core Grant (P30 CA008748), and a grant from Breast Cancer Research Foundation (grant BCRF-17-193).

References

1. Agueh, M., Carlier, G.: Barycenters in the Wasserstein space. SIAM J. Math. Anal. **43**(2), 904–924 (2011)
2. Cuturi, M.: Sinkhorn distances: lightspeed computation of optimal transport. In: Advances in Neural Information Processing Systems, pp. 2292–2300 (2013)
3. Cuturi, M., Doucet, A.: Fast computation of Wasserstein Barycenters. In: ICML 2014: Proceedings of 31st International Conference on Machine Learning, vol. 32, pp. 685–693 (2014)
4. Khan, A.M., Rajpoot, N., Treanor, D., Magee, D.: A nonlinear mapping approach to stain normalization in digital histopathology images using image-specific color deconvolution. IEEE Trans. Biomed. Eng. **61**(6), 1729–1738 (2014)
5. Kumar, N., et al.: A multi-organ nucleus segmentation challenge. IEEE Trans. Med. Imaging **39**, 1380–1391 (2019)

6. Kumar, N., Verma, R., Sharma, S., Bhargava, S., Vahadane, A., Sethi, A.: A dataset and a technique for generalized nuclear segmentation for computational pathology. IEEE Trans. Med. Imaging **36**(7), 1550–1560 (2017)

7. Macenko, M., et al.: A method for normalizing histology slides for quantitative analysis. In: IEEE International Symposium on Biomedical Imaging: From Nano to Macro, pp. 1107–1110 (2009)

8. McCann, R.: A convexity principle for interacting gases. Adv. Math. **128**(1), 153–179 (1997)

9. Pass, B.: Multi-marginal optimal transport: theory and applications. ESAIM Math. Model. Numer. Anal. **49**(6), 1771–1790 (2015)

10. Pontalba, J.T., Gwynne-Timothy, T., David, E., Jakate, K., Androutsos, D., Khademi, A.: Assessing the impact of color normalization in convolutional neural network-based nuclei segmentation frameworks. Front. Bioeng. Biotechnol. **7**, 300 (2019)

11. Puccetti, G., Rüschendorf, L., Vanduffel, S.: On the computation of Wasserstein barycenters. J. Multivar. Anal. **176**, 104581 (2020)

12. Reinhard, E., Adhikhmin, M., Gooch, B., Shirley, P.: Color transfer between images. IEEE Comput. Graph. Appl. **21**(5), 34–41 (2001)

13. Reinhard, E., Pouli, T.: Colour spaces for colour transfer. In: Schettini, R., Tominaga, S., Trémeau, A. (eds.) CCIW 2011. LNCS, vol. 6626, pp. 1–15. Springer, Heidelberg (2011). https://doi.org/10.1007/978-3-642-20404-3_1

14. Shaban, M.T., Baur, C., Navab, N., Albarqouni, S.: Staingan: stain style transfer for digital histological images. In: International Symposium on Biomedical Imaging, pp. 953–956 (2019)

15. Tellez, D., et al.: Whole-slide mitosis detection in H&E breast histology using PHH3 as a reference to train distilled stain-invariant convolutional networks. IEEE Trans. Med. Imaging **37**(9), 2126–2136 (2018)

16. Tellez, D., et al.: Quantifying the effects of data augmentation and stain color normalization in convolutional neural networks for computational pathology. Med. Image Anal. **58**, 101544 (2019)

17. Vahadane, A., et al.: Structure-preserving color normalization and sparse stain separation for histological images. IEEE Trans. Med. Imaging **35**(8), 1962–1971 (2016)

18. Villani, C.: Topics in Optimal Transportation. No. 58, American Mathematical Society, Providence (2003)

19. Villani, C.: Optimal Transport: Old and New. Grundlehren der mathematischen Wissenschaften, vol. 338. Springer, Heidelberg (2008). https://doi.org/10.1007/978-3-540-71050-9

20. Wang, Z., Bovik, A.C., Sheikh, H.R., Simoncelli, E.P.: Image quality assessment: from error visibility to structural similarity. IEEE Trans. Image Process. **13**(4), 600–612 (2004)

21. Zhang, L., Zhang, L., Mou, X., Zhang, D.: Fsim: a feature similarity index for image quality assessment. IEEE Trans. Image Process. **20**(8), 2378–2386 (2011)

Corruption-Robust Enhancement of Deep Neural Networks for Classification of Peripheral Blood Smear Images

Songtao Zhang[1], Qingwen Ni[1], Bing Li[2], Shan Jiang[1], Wenyu Cai[3], Hang Chen[1], and Lin Luo[1,4(✉)]

[1] College of Engineering, Peking University, Beijing, China
luol@pku.edu.cn
[2] MDS and MPN Centre, Institute of Haematology and Blood Diseases Hospital, Chinese Academy of Medical Sciences and Peking Union Medical College, Tianjin, China
[3] Department of Pathology, Institute of Haematology and Blood Diseases Hospital, Chinese Academy of Medical Sciences and Peking Union Medical College, Tianjin, China
[4] IE-School, Southern University of Science and Technology, Shenzhen, China

Abstract. Deep learning emerges as a promising technology for automated peripheral blood smear analysis and hematologic diagnosis. A big challenge to deep learning model is the accuracy drop when facing image corruptions caused by different smear preparation and digitalization operations. In order to serve the real applications of peripheral blood analysis, a practical deep learning classifier needs to be robust against a wide range of corruptions. In this paper, we first investigate the comprehensive corruption types for peripheral blood smear image and establish the benchmark dataset Smear-C simulating the real physical cause factors. Then we propose a novel method SmearRobust which can easily fit into the existing neural networks and improve the robustness. Experimental results show that SmearRobust can significantly enhance the robustness upon Smear-C dataset. Furthermore, the proposed corruption simulation algorithms and the robust learning method can be potentially applied to bone marrow smear and general pathology areas.

Keywords: Peripheral blood · Deep learning · Corruption · Robustness

1 Introduction

Morphologic analysis of peripheral blood smear (PB Smear) images plays an important role in diagnostic assessment. Specifically, differential counting of

Electronic supplementary material The online version of this chapter (https://doi.org/10.1007/978-3-030-59722-1_36) contains supplementary material, which is available to authorized users.

© Springer Nature Switzerland AG 2020
A. L. Martel et al. (Eds.): MICCAI 2020, LNCS 12265, pp. 372–381, 2020.
https://doi.org/10.1007/978-3-030-59722-1_36

white blood cell (WBC) subtypes is critical in determining many hematologic diseases, such as leukemia, lymphoma, and dysplasia [21]. The cells are usually examined under a microscope and counted by hematologists, which is a labor-intensive, time-consuming procedure and suffers from observer bias. Although automated hematology techniques such as flow cytometry [12] and image processing methods [5] are used to solve the problems, they still have limitations in analyzing the morphologic variance of cells.

Deep learning algorithm coupled with digital pathology imaging emerges as a highly promising technology for automated pathology analysis [3,4,6,13,16, 18,21]. One major limitation of current deep learning approaches is the lack of robustness to accommodate slight image variances. Unlike human vision system, deep neural networks can be easily confused by the contextual corruptions such as illumination changes, snow and rain, motion blur, pepper noise, etc. [1,17]. Hyndrycks et al. proposed a benchmark corruption dataset to quantitatively assess classifier robustness on natural images [10], and an AugMix algorithm to resist the corruptions [11].

Corruptions in pathological images come from operational variance. E.g. smears may be manually prepared by different technicians and digitized by different imaging devices. It is critical for deep learning algorithms to be robust against those corruptions in order to support general clinical use. Stain normalization is a data-preprocessing step to mitigate the staining variance [7]. However, there are many other corruption types in pathology, especially for hematology, which is hard for preprocessing to resolve. The root cause of pathological corruption has not been well investigated, neither has a method been proposed to tackle with these problems by directly improving the deep learning model.

In this paper, we establish the benchmark dataset Smear-C based on the comprehensive corruption types of PB Smear, and then propose a novel method SmearRobust which can enhance the resistance to corruptions and easily fit into the existing training pipelines of neural networks. To our best knowledge, this is the first in-depth work modeling the corruptions with the physical cause factors along the whole procedure of smear preparation and digitization. The corruption simulation algorithms and the robust learning method proposed here can be further developed to adapt to bone marrow smear and general pathological images.

2   Modeling of Corruptions

A typical process of PB Smear images includes two main stages (shown in Fig. 1): Smear Preparation and Slide Imaging. **Smear Preparation** is to make a physical smear, which further includes the spreading and staining steps. After blood specimen collection, smear is prepared by spreading a drop of blood. Then the smear is dried, fixed and stained to facilitate the microscopic examination of blood cell types [15]. **Slide Imaging** is to digitize a physical slide into a whole slide image. Smear is scanned as adjacent tiles with the whole slide scanners (usually with 100× oil immersion objective lens), and then the tiles are digitally assembled into a large-scale image.

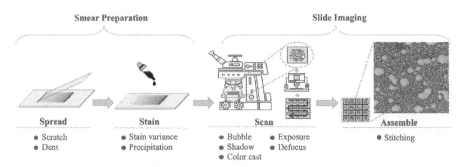

Fig. 1. Typical process of producing Peripheral Blood Smear images contains two procedures: Smear preparation and Slide imaging (Color figure online)

Corruptions in Smear Preparation include *Scratch*, *Dent*, Stain variance (*Acidity, Alkalinity, Under-stained*) and *Precipitation*, as shown in Fig. 2. *Scratch* and *Dent* are usually caused by scratching on the surface of smear when spreading blood or wiping the immersion oil from the smear. Stain variance, which includes *Acidity, Alkalinity* and *Under-stained*, are very common. Wrights stain is the most used, which is sensitive to PH value as methylene blue showing a greater intensity with increasing alkalinity, whereas eosin is more intense with increasing acidity. *Acidity* is the case that the buffer or stain is too acid, as the result the color of the smear appears red-orange and pale blue. *Alkalinity* means the buffer or stain is too alkaline, and the color of the smear appears blue purple. *Under-stained* is caused by insufficient staining time, lower room temperature and weak stain solution, and it results in an overall light color. *Precipitation* appears as dark impurities on the slide, which comes from inadequate washing of the blood smear or incomplete dissolution of the dyes. Note some cases may be mitigated by quality control. Here we try to cover the comprehensive corruption types as a foundation.

Corruptions in Slide Imaging include *Bubble, Shadow, Color cast*, Exposure (*Underexposure, Overexposure*), Defocus (*Foreground defocus, Background defocus, Overall defocus*) and *Stitching*. *Bubble* and *Shadow* is caused by the bubbles and dust in immersion oil between the sample and objective. *Color cast* is influenced by the spectrum of the LED light source. *Overexposure* and *Underexposure* could be caused by the imaging setup, and the latter one also appears with the lumen decay of LED, which is attributed to the high temperature and the degradation of the driver. Defocus is contributed by three factors, and they are (i) cells are usually located in different planes, (ii) the error of autofocusing, (iii) the depth of focus is only several hundred nanometers for a NA 1.4 objective. And there are three types of defocus in Slide Imaging. *Foreground, Background,* and *Overall defocus* is the case that the target cell, the other cells and all of the cells are defocused, respectively. *Stitching* is caused by the unevenness of the illumination or the setup of the camera, which influence the intensity of image

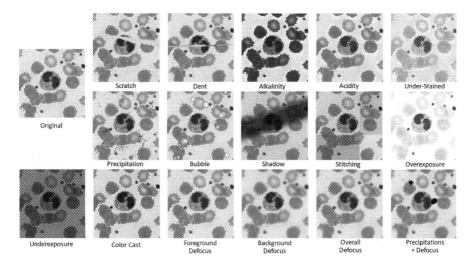

Fig. 2. Original image and corruption types (Color figure online)

especially at the margin of each field of view (FOV). Then, a grad-like stitching will exist on the whole slide image. Compound Corruptions is the case that multiple corruptions occur together along the whole process. For example, *Precipitation + Defocus* means that all cells are defocused, and only precipitation is in focus, which caused by the error of the autofocusing.

Simulation of the corruptions is based on the physical causes. We divide the corruptions into three categories: Coverage (*Scratch, Dent, Precipitation, Bubble* and *Shadow*), Color (*Stain variance, Color cast, Exposure* and *Stitching*), and *Defocus*. Coverage effects are simulated by generating a mask to overlay on the original image, and the severity of corruptions can be realized by controlling the density and scale. Color effects are simulated different severity by enhancing/reducing the RGB intensity with artificial ratios. Among them, *Stitching* only affects in subarea of the experimental image. Defocus effects are simulated quantitatively based on a scalar-based diffraction model, Born and Wolf approximation [2,14], with the experimental parameters. And the details can be found in the supplementary material.

3 Robustness Enhancement Method

We propose a robustness enhancement algorithm called SmearRobust which adopts an AugMix-inspired augmentation policy [8,11], and a special transformation to adapt to smear scenarios, as illustrated in Fig. 3. In order to force the network to learn consistent features between the augmented data and the original one, we add a Contrastive Loss component to the overall loss function.

3.1   Mixing Augmentations of Data

We adopt the AugMix augmentation policy which mixes several chains of augmentation operations and then combines the mixed results and merges into the original image. The elementary augmentation operations, which are disjoint from the corruptions encountered in test dataset, consist of *equalize posterize, rotate, solarize, shear_x, shear_y, translate_x* and *translate_y*. The policy contains three augmentation chains, and each is constructed with one to three randomly selected augmentation operations. The resulting images from the three augmentation chains are mixed with coefficients randomly sampled from a $Dirichlet(\alpha, \ldots, \alpha)$ distribution. The mixing result of the three augmentation chains and the original image are combined through a second random convex combination sampled from a $Beta(\alpha, \alpha)$ distribution. $AugMixT$ is used to denote the above transformation of AugMix.

3.2   Random Block Color Jitter

When looking at the Smear-C corruptions, the structure-related and color-related corruption types hold a large portion, e.g., *Shadow, Stain variance, Exposure,* etc. Recent studies prove that a model which captures the local features can better accommodate structural variation [20]. Therefore, we propose a simple and straightforward image transformation called Random Block Color Jitter (RBCJ) aiming to address both types of corruptions. RBCJ introduces both color and structural inconsistency to an image without affecting the local features. In details, an image is randomly split into k uneven blocks horizontally, with an empirical k = 9. Then the same random split operation is conducted vertically. The resulting image is divided into k*k blocks. For each block area, we apply a random color jitter. RBCJ is applied on the image as the final step after $AugMixT$ is performed. An instance of the overall transformation policy is shown in Fig. 3.

3.3   Objective Function with Contrastive Loss

After the AugMixT and RBCJ, an input image can represent certain variety compared to the original while still possessing most of the morphological features and local details. In order to force the model to learn those robust representations, we add a Contrastive Loss component which formulates the feature shifts between the original image and the AugMixT-RBCJ transformed image using a mean square error in the latent space. The overall objective function can be formulated as follow:

$$ContrastiveLoss(F; x, y) = \|f(RBCJ(x_{AugMixT})) - f(x)\|_2^2 \qquad (1)$$

$$L_{total}(F; x, y) = L(F; RBCJ(x_{AugMixT}), y) + \lambda * ContrastiveLoss(F; x, y) \quad (2)$$

where $f(\cdot)$ denotes the mapping of logits layer, and $\|\cdot\|_2^2$ denotes the squared Euclidean norm. $L(F; RBCJ(x_{AugMixT}), y)$ denotes the cross entropy loss. λ is set to 1 in our experiment.

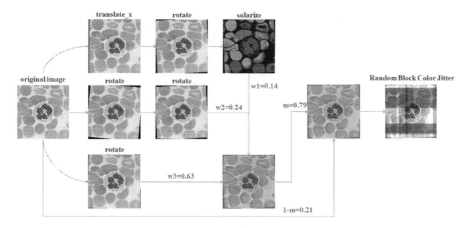

Fig. 3. An illustration of augmentation policy of AugMix and RBCJ. Randomly separated block with color jitter and the composition of randomly sampled basic operations are applied to the original image. (Color figure online)

4 Experiment

4.1 Dataset

There are a total of 16013 WBC images in the final dataset captured from PB Smear of 169 healthy people. All of images had a size of 1024 × 1224 pixels. The images include 7 categories: i. Segmented neutrophil, ii. Band neutrophil, iii. Lymphocyte, iv. Monocyte, v. Basophils, vi. Eosinophil and vii. others. Each image is labeled by 5 hematologists with criteria consensus before starting the task. We split the dataset in ratio of 7:3 to form the training set and testing set. The Smear-C dataset includes 16 different types of corruptions, and all applied to the testing set with common severity.

4.2 Baselines

We first evaluate the popular CNN architectures as robustness baselines. VGG16, Resnet18, Resnet50, Resnet101, DenseNet121 are selected for training on the original images. Results on original test images versus those on the proposed corruption dataset Smear-C are reported in the leftmost 5 columns of Table 1. For most the selected classifiers, the accuracy numbers on corruptions decrease severely (under 50%) on *Alkalinity, Acidity, Under-stained, Shadow, Stitching, Underexposure, Overexposure* and *Color cast*. Accuracy on other corruption types also drops in certain degrees.

4.3 SmearRobust Method

To evaluate the robustness of SmearRobust method against corruptions, we compare it with the baseline method of Normal Training and a state-of-the-art

Table 1. Accuracy values of different corruptions and architectures. Augmix and our method use the Resnet50 as the basic classifier.

	Vgg16	Resnet18	Resnet101	Densenet121	Resnet50	AugMix	Ours
Original	88.47	89.18	88.33	89.12	88.41	86.41	85.6
Scratch	69.58	79.31	75.12	80.83	71.51	73.28	72.78
Dent	72.25	81.28	78.33	82.39	78.16	79.97	80.71
Alkalinity	62.52	8.29	10.92	4.27	2.38	60.63	81.28
Acidity	27.01	6.28	5.09	5.62	1.11	66.34	83.09
Understained	17.32	34.73	11	10.22	36.49	42.53	82.64
Precipitation	82.96	77.87	84.44	86.95	83.46	84.11	83.99
Bubble	81.36	82.92	78.65	83.99	79.93	80.87	79.43
Shadow	40.6	39.94	23.4	23.56	34.32	73.11	77.13
Stitching	4.19	25.78	18.02	1.15	16.22	40.85	50.21
Overexpousure	29.31	33.78	29.68	37.15	1.15	82.06	81.24
Underexposure	17.32	34.73	11	10.22	36.49	81.4	83.78
Color cast	30.01	14.86	24.14	12.89	18.92	82.01	83.13
Foreground defocus	83.78	85.92	85.06	86.7	82.39	85.63	81.98
Background defocus	87.77	89.24	87.27	88.88	87.81	85.59	84.85
Overall defocus	83.66	85.96	84.28	86.62	82.14	85.89	82.51
Precipitations+Defocus	80.83	83.99	81.24	84.36	80.67	84.69	80.46
Average accuracy	54.40	54.06	49.23	49.11	49.57	74.31	**79.33**

method AugMix. Normal Training is the training from scratch. AugMix uses random and diverse augmentations and a Jensen-Shannon Divergence consistency loss [11]. Here we use Resnet50 as the basic classifier, SGD with Nesterov momentum set to 0.9, and a cosine learning rate schedule. The learning rate and epochs trained with SmearRobust, AugMix and Normal Training are 0.01, 0.1, 0.1 and 150, 150, 100, respectively. All the experiments achieved the best performance on the original test data with the above training parameters. Results are shown in the rightmost 3 columns of Table 1. The average accuracy over all corruptions is simply used as the robustness measurement. Performance gains are widely observed across most corruption types, especially in the Stain-related ones of *Under-stained*, *Alkalinity* and *Acidity*. Overall, SmearRobust achieves average accuracy of 79.33% on Smear-C, which outperforms the 74.31% for AugMix-enhanced and the 49.57% for Normal Training.

We further test the generality of SmearRobust on 5 common CNN architectures. All of the models demonstrate accuracy gain, as shown in Table 2. Results prove that SmearRobust can effectively strengthen the robustness of networks against the most of the corruptions across all of the five architectures.

4.4   Visualization of Salience Map

We further investigate the features that the models captured through visualization of the salience maps [20]. A salience map is used to show the sensitivity of network to each pixel of an input image. We use Grad [19] to generate the

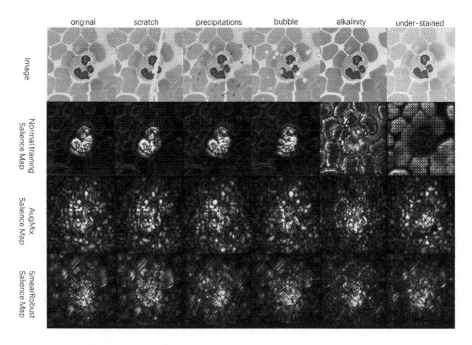

Fig. 4. Salience maps of the models trained with Normal Training and our method on corrupted images

Table 2. A comparison of the average accuracy over different corruptions using different network architecture trained with Normal Training, AugMix and our method.

	Vgg16	Resnet18	Resnet50	Resnet101	Densenet121
Normal Training	54.40	54.06	49.57	49.23	49.11
AugMix	77.4	79.16	74.31	71.72	79.81
Ours	**81.8**	**81.18**	**79.33**	**76.9**	**82.69**

salience maps on our Smear-C dataset. As illustrated in Fig. 4, the normally-trained model captures the contour features of the cell and even slightly shows the structural features within the cell, which may make it lose certain capability of generalization against structure variation. In contrast, the model trained with our SmearRobust captures more local details all over the image. It is noticeable that no matter what corruption types are tested, the salient areas bear close similarity, which demonstrates the consistency of the captured features.

5   Conclusion

We introduced our work on constructing the Smear-C corruption dataset and the SmearRobust algorithm that can resist corruptions. Smear-C provides comprehensive PB Smear corruptions simulated with configurable physical models.

SmearRobust algorithm is proved to effectively raise neural networks' robustness. The combination of Smear-C and SmearRobust has made a important step of automated pathology diagnosis to bridge the gap between the clinical diagnosis in practice and the lab-tested algorithm under ideal setups. The same methodology of Smear-C can be applied to construct general histopathological corruption benchmarks, while additional types like Tissue fold and Venetian blind artifacts should be considered. In the Future, we plan to extend Smear-C to include bone marrow smear corruptions (e.g. Cell pileup) and enhance the robustness metrics. Self-supervised learning is also considered to discover the intrinsic features of smear images and improve SmearRobust. The metrics and the refined Smear-Robust are to be tested on diversed data obtained from different scanners.

Acknowledgements. This research was supported in part by the National Natural Science Foundation of China (61705252), Natural Science Foundation of Jiangsu Province (BK20170388), the Foundation of Shenzhen Science and Technology Innovation Committee (JCYJ20180507181527806, JCYJ20170817105131701) and Beijing Innovation Center for Engineering Science and Advanced Technology, Peking University. And we gratefully acknowledge the reviews and suggestions from Dr. Jianfeng Yao and Dr. Shiqiang Qu from Institute of Haematology and Blood Diseases Hospital, Tianjin, China.

References

1. Azulay, A., Weiss, Y.: Why do deep convolutional networks generalize so poorly to small image transformations? JMLR **20**(184), 1–25 (2019)
2. Boas, D.A., Pitris, C., Ramanujam, N.: Handbook of Biomedical Optics, 1st edn. CRC Press, Boca Raton (2011)
3. Bejnordi, B.E., Veta, M., Van Diest, P.J., et al.: Diagnostic assessment of deep learning algorithms for detection of lymph node metastases in women with breast cancer. JAMA **318**(22), 2199–2210 (2017)
4. Campanella, G., Hanna, M.G., Geneslaw, L., et al.: Clinical-grade computational pathology using weakly supervised deep learning on whole slide images. Nat. Med. **25**(8), 1301–1309 (2019)
5. Ceelie, H., Dinkelaar, R.B., van Gelder, W.: Examination of peripheral blood films using automated microscopy; evaluation of Diffmaster Octavia and Cellavision DM96. J. Clin. Pathol. **60**(1), 72–79 (2007)
6. Chandradevan, R., Aljudi, A.A., Drumheller, B.R., et al.: Machine-based detection and classification for bone marrow aspirate differential counts: initial development focusing on nonneoplastic cells. Lab. Invest. **100**, 98–109 (2020)
7. Ciompi, F., Geessink, O., Bejnordi, B.E., et al.: The importance of stain normalization in colorectal tissue classification with convolutional networks. In: International Symposium on Biomedical Imaging (ISBI), pp. 160–163. IEEE (2017)
8. Cubuk, E.D., Zoph, B., Mane, D., et al.: AutoAugment: learning augmentation strategies from data. In: Proceedings of the IEEE Conference on Computer Vision and Pattern Recognition, pp. 113–123 (2019)
9. Goodfellow, I., Bengio, Y., Courville, A.: Deep Learning. MIT Press, Cambridge (2016)

10. Hendrycks, D., Dietterich, T.G.: Benchmarking neural network robustness to common corruptions and perturbations. In: ICLR (2019)
11. Hendrycks, D., Mu, N., Cubuk, E.D., et al.: AugMix: a simple data processing method to improve robustness and uncertainty. In: ICLR (2020)
12. Janossy, G., Jani, I.V., Bradley, N.J., et al.: Affordable CD4+-T-cell counting by flow cytometry: CD45 gating for volumetric analysis. Clin. Vaccine Immunol. $9(5)$, 1085–1094 (2002)
13. Nirmal Jith, O.U., Harinarayanan, K.K., Gautam, S., Bhavsar, A., Sao, A.K.: DeepCerv: deep neural network for segmentation free robust cervical cell classification. In: Stoyanov, D., et al. (eds.) OMIA/COMPAY - 2018. LNCS, vol. 11039, pp. 86–94. Springer, Cham (2018). https://doi.org/10.1007/978-3-030-00949-6_11
14. Kirshner, H., Sage, D., Unser, M.: 3D PSF models for fluorescence microscopy in ImageJ, p. 154, Strasbourg, French Republic (2011)
15. Lee, S.H., Erber, W.N., Porwit, A., et al.: ICSH guidelines for the standardization of bone marrow specimens and reports. Int. J. Lab. Hematol. $230(5)$, 349–364 (2008)
16. Matek, C., Schwarz, S., Spiekermann, K., et al.: Human-level recognition of blast cells in acute myeloid leukaemia with convolutional neural networks. Nat. Mach. Intell. 1, 538–544 (2019)
17. Recht, B., Roelofs, R., Schmidt, L., et al.: Do CIFAR-10 classifiers generalize to CIFAR-10? arXiv preprint arXiv:1806.00451 (2018)
18. Sadafi, A., et al.: Multiclass deep active learning for detecting red blood cell subtypes in brightfield microscopy. In: Shen, D., et al. (eds.) MICCAI 2019. LNCS, vol. 11764, pp. 685–693. Springer, Cham (2019). https://doi.org/10.1007/978-3-030-32239-7_76
19. Selvaraju, R.R., Cogswell, M., Das, A., Vedantam, R., et al.: Grad-CAM: visual explanations from deep networks via gradient-based localization. In: IEEE International Conference on Computer Vision, pp. 618–626 (2017)
20. Song, C., He, K., Lin, J., et al.: Robust local features for improving the generalization of adversarial training. In: ICLR (2020)
21. Wang, Q., Bi, S., Sun, M., et al.: Deep learning approach to peripheral leukocyte recognition. PLoS ONE $14(6)$, e0218808 (2019)

Multi-field of View Aggregation and Context Encoding for Single-Stage Nucleus Recognition

Tian Bai[1], Jiayu Xu[1], and Fuyong Xing[2(✉)]

[1] College of Computer Science and Technology, Jilin University, Changchun, China
`baitian@jlu.edu.cn`
[2] Department of Biostatistics and Informatics, University of Colorado Anschutz
Medical Campus, Aurora, USA
`fuyong.xing@cuanschutz.edu`

Abstract. Automated nucleus/cell recognition is a very challenging task, especially for differentiating tumor nuclei from non-tumor nuclei in Ki67 immunohistochemistry (IHC) stained images. Convolutional neural networks and their variants have been recently introduced to identify different types of nuclei and have achieved state-of-the-art performance. However, previous nucleus recognition approaches do not explicitly encode contextual information in the images, which can be very helpful for network representation learning. In this paper, we propose a novel multi-field-of-view context encoding method for single-stage nuclei identification in Ki67 IHC stained images. Specifically, we learn a deep structured regression model that takes multi-field of views of images as input and conducts feature aggregation on the fly for representation learning; then, we design a context encoding module to explicitly explore the multi-field-of-view contextual information and enhance the model's representation power. In order to further improve nucleus recognition, we also introduce a novel deep regression loss that can emphasize specific channels of the prediction map with category-aware channel suppression. The proposed method can be learned in an end-to-end, pixel-to-pixel manner for single-stage nucleus recognition. We evaluate our method on a large-scale pancreatic neuroendocrine tumor image dataset, and the experiments demonstrate the superior performance of our method in nucleus recognition.

Keywords: Nucleus recognition · Nucleus classification · Context encoding · Ki67 · Microscopy image analysis · Pathology image analysis

1 Introduction

Individual nucleus or cell recognition is an important yet challenging task in microscopy image analysis, such as identification of immunopositive tumor,

Electronic supplementary material The online version of this chapter (https://doi.org/10.1007/978-3-030-59722-1_37) contains supplementary material, which is available to authorized users.

immunonegative tumor and non-tumor nuclei/cells in Ki67 immunohistochemistry (IHC) stained images. Convolutional neural networks (CNNs) have been applied to nucleus/cell recognition in different types of histopathology and microscopy images, leading to improved performance compared to traditional machine learning methods [2,15,18]. However, these methods identify different categories of nuclei either in a sliding window manner, which is computationally expensive for large-sized images, or using a multi-stage data processing pipeline, which introduces an additional step and leads to potentially inefficient image analysis.

Fully convolutional networks (FCNs) [10] and their variants such as U-Net-like neural networks [14], which allow direct pixel-to-pixel mappings, have recently attracted considerable attention in nucleus/cell recognition. Not only do these techniques avoid the computationally inefficient sliding window strategy, but they also enable simultaneous nucleus localization and classification, i.e., single-stage nucleus recognition [6,12,21,25,26]. However, none of these methods explicitly explore contextual information, which can enhance networks' representation power and improve object recognition [1,9,22]. In digital pathology, contextual information from neighboring nuclei or surrounding regions is helpful for nucleus classification [11]. In addition, when pathologists determine nucleus categories in histopathology images, it is not uncommon for them to study the spatial configuration of nuclei in low-resolution images and meanwhile inspect cellular morphology such as the shape and size in high-resolution images [17]. Thus, it is valuable to take into consideration multi-field of views of the images with different resolutions for nucleus recognition.

In this paper, we propose a novel multi-field-of-view context encoding method for single-stage nucleus recognition. In order to take advantage of multi-resolution images, we introduce a deep structured regression model that can learn feature representations from multi-field-of-view images at different resolutions. Then we incorporate a context encoding module into the model, explicitly exploring multi-field-of-view contextual information and capturing global feature statistics so as to avoid isolation of individual pixel prediction from global context. Finally, we present a new deep regression loss specifically for nucleus recognition, which is able to highlight desired channels of the prediction map by suppressing the other channels. In this way, it can reduce the effects of other nucleus types when learning parameters for a specific nucleus category. To the best of our knowledge, this is the first work explicitly exploiting multi-field-of-view, deep contextual information for nucleus recognition in microscopy images.

2   Methodology

Figure 1 shows an overview of the proposed method, which consists of two major modules: feature aggregation and context encoding. With multiple U-Net-like networks (here we use two fully residual convolutional network (FRCN) architectures [20]), the feature aggregation module takes multi-field-of-view, multi-resolution images as input and conducts feature aggregation on the fly via a

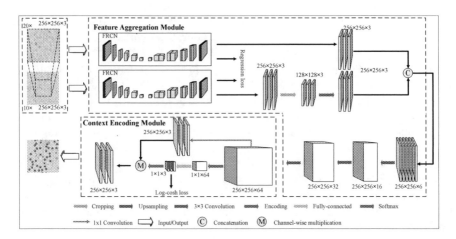

Fig. 1. An overview of the proposed method. The feature aggregation module takes as input 20×- and 10×-magnification images and produces aggregated feature presentations, which are fed into the context encoding module for nucleus recognition. The FRCN represents a U-Net-like network architecture [20]. The size of input images can be arbitrary (here using $256 \times 256 \times 3$ for illustration). The connections with different colors represent distinct operations. Here we use Ki67 IHC stained images as an example and aim to identify three types of nuclei: immunopositive tumor, immunonegative tumor and non-tumor. (Color figure online)

set of stacked convolutional layers. Next, the context encoding module explores the aggregated features and learns to leverage global contextual information for robust prediction of nucleus recognition, with selectively highlighting class-dependent feature maps.

2.1   Multi-field-of-View Feature Aggregation

High-resolution histopathology images usually exhibit detailed information such as shapes and sizes of individual nuclei, while low-resolution images deliver a wide range of patterns of nucleus distributions. In practice, pathologists often differentiate different types of nuclei based on both nucleus appearance and distributions, especially for classification of tumor and non-tumor nuclei in Ki67 IHC stained images [21]. Thus, instead of relying on a single input image, the feature aggregation module learns robust representations from images with different spatial resolutions and fields of view. In our application, we use two distinct resolutions of images.

Let $X_{20\times} \in \mathbb{R}^{W \times H \times C}$ and $X_{10\times} \in \mathbb{R}^{W \times H \times C}$ be the input images of the feature aggregation module, where W, H, and C are the width, height and channel of images respectively. $X_{20\times}$ and $X_{10\times}$ represent microscopy images captured at 20× and 10× magnifications respectively, as shown in Fig. 1. Here $X_{20\times}$ is the target image, where individual nuclei need to be identified. For each input image, we use a recent state-of-the-art nucleus localization neural network, FRCN [20], to extract M feature maps, where M is the number of nucleus categories. With the auxiliary regressors (see Sect. 2.3), each of these feature maps is actually a heat map of the likelihood of each category of nucleus in the input image. Because $X_{10\times}$ has a larger field of view than $X_{20\times}$, we crop the central region of each feature map of $X_{10\times}$ (the dashed-line box in the $10\times$ image in Fig. 1) and then upsample the cropped region to have the same size as the heat maps of $X_{20\times}$. Note that the cropped feature maps are generated based on a broader field of view in $X_{10\times}$, i.e., regions outside the dashed-line box, such that more spatial information can be exploited for feature learning. Finally, we aggregate the (upsampled) feature maps of $X_{10\times}$ and $X_{20\times}$ with a channel-wise concatenation followed by a set of stacked convolutional operations, which learn more abstract representations for the subsequent global context encoding.

2.2   Contextual Information Encoding

In histopathology images, tumor nuclei are typically adjacent to other tumor nuclei, while non-tumor nuclei often appear in other regions such as stroma and glandular areas [11,21]. Inspired by [23], we build a context encoding module on top of the feature aggregation module to explore rich contextual information and capture global feature statistics. Our modeling is significantly different from [23], because (1) we learn orderless global representations and describe the feature distribution from multi-field-of-view, multi-resolution images that exhibit more rich and flexible contextual information, and (2) we regularize the context encoding with regression of the number of each type of nucleus in the input images, instead of prediction of the presence of object categories.

Our context encoding module consists of an encoding layer [23,24], a fully-connected layer, a 1×1 convolutional layer and a Softmax layer (see Fig. 1). By interpreting the input feature map $F \in \mathbb{R}^{W_F \times H_F \times C_F}$ as a set of C_F-dimensional feature descriptors $\{f_i\}_{i=1}^{W_F \times H_F}$, the encoding layer learns an inherent codebook of K codewords $\{d_k\}_{k=1}^{K} \in \mathbb{R}^{C_F \times K}$ and a set of smooth factors. The inherent codebook is learned from the descriptor distributions and used to produce feature representations, while the smooth factors enable soft-weight assignment for feature encoding and make the model differentiable [23,24]. The output of the encoding layer is a fixed-length representation, which describes global feature distributions based on the codebook. This is different from the traditional bag-of-words (BoW) model that first generates a codebook and then conducts feature encoding [4,5]. Instead, the encoding layer simultaneously learns the codebook and feature representations in an end-to-end manner such that feature encoding can benefit from labeled data and produce global representations. The fully-connected layer followed by a Softmax layer learns a set of scaling factors, and these factors can be used to selectively highlight category-dependent feature maps (e.g., immunopositive tumor versus immunonegative tumor nuclei) via a channel-wise multiplication between the factors and the output of 1×1 convolutional operation on the input feature map F [7]. The multiplication result serves as the output map of the context encoding module. This scaling strategy can enhance network representation's discriminative power and facilitate the final nucleus recognition.

Given a loss function for nucleus recognition such as mean squared error (MSE) [21], we can train the entire model using the standard backpropagation algorithm. However, this training strategy learns a network by calculating per-pixel loss separately and might not understand the global context [23]. To address this problem, we introduce an additional loss to explicitly regularize the context encoding and enforce the entire model to understand the global scene and exploit contextual information for better nucleus recognition. Specifically, we add a side regressor on top of the context encoding module (see Fig. 1) to predict the number of each category of nucleus in the input images. Unlike natural image data that often contain only a single or several target objects per image, a histopathology image can have thousands or even more mixed-type nuclei such that predicting the existence of nucleus categories might not be sufficient to assist with understanding the context. In this paper, we use a log hyperbolic cosine (log-cosh) loss to estimate the numbers of different types of nuclei in each target training image $X_{20\times}^i$, $i = 1, 2, \ldots, N$, where N is the number of training images, and regularize the training of the context encoding module as follows:

$$\mathcal{L}_{lc} = \frac{1}{N_b \times M} \sum_{i=1}^{N_b} \sum_{m=1}^{M} \log(\cosh(\frac{\hat{p}_m^i - p_m^i}{z_m})), \tag{1}$$

where N_b is the number of training images within each batch, $\hat{p}_m^i$ represents the predicted number of the m-th category of nucleus in $X_{20\times}^i$, and p_m^i is the corresponding gold standard, which can be obtained from the training images. z_m is the average gold-standard number of the m-th type of nucleus over all the training images, and it is used to normalize the estimation error so as to alleviate the effects of the potential unbalanced data distribution of different-type nuclei. Compared with the standard MSE loss, this log-cosh function is not significantly affected by occasionally incorrect estimations. Note that this function only predicts the number of nuclei in the target images, i.e., $\{X_{20\times}^i\}_{i=1}^N$, and it would be discarded during model testing.

2.3   Nucleus Recognition Loss

Nucleus recognition is formulated as a category-aware structured regression problem. Let multi-resolution input training images (here using $20\times, 10\times$) and corresponding gold-standard labels be $\{(X_{20\times}^i, Y_{20\times}^i)\}_{i=1}^N$ and $\{(X_{10\times}^i, Y_{10\times}^i)\}_{i=1}^N$, where $Y_{20\times}^i \in \mathbb{R}^{W \times H \times M}$ and $Y_{10\times}^i \in \mathbb{R}^{W \times H \times M}$ are the labels for $X_{20\times}^i$ and $X_{10\times}^i$, respectively. $Y_{20\times}^i$ is an M-channel proximity map with continuous, non-negative values and one channel corresponds to one type of nucleus: $Y_{20\times}^i(w, h, m) = (e^{\gamma(1 - \frac{D_{20\times}^i(w,h,m)}{\tau})} - 1)/(e^\gamma - 1)$ when $0 \leq D_{20\times}^i(w, h, m) \leq \tau$ and $Y_{20\times}^i(w, h, m) = 0$ otherwise. $D_{20\times}^i$ is the Euclidean distance between pixel (w, h) and its closest annotated nucleus for the m-th category. $\tau = 10$ is a threshold to define the central region of each nucleus and $\gamma = 3$ controls the decay of proximity values. Each pixel in $Y_{20\times}^i$ measures the proximity to the center of its closest nucleus with the same type [21]. A similar definition is applied to $Y_{10\times}^i$. With these training data, our goal is to learn a structured regressor that maps the target images into the label space for individual nucleus recognition. This can be achieved by adding a convolutional layer on top of the context encoding module to conduct an end-to-end, pixel-to-pixel mapping for desired predictions. In our application, we directly use the output of the context encoding module as the prediction, $\hat{Y}_{20\times}^i$, which is an M-channel map for each target input image, $X_{20\times}^i$.

We learn the structured regressor with a novel weighted MSE loss. Compared with standard MSE losses that assign equal weights to all pixels in each image, a weighted MSE is able to highlight the central region of nuclei and thus to prevent a trivial solution that simply predicts zeros for all pixels [20, 21]. However, these weighted MSE functions [20, 21] calculate the loss for each nucleus category separately and do not take into consideration the effects of other nucleus classes during model training. Thus, a single pixel might have responses in more than one channels of the prediction map. Intuitively, each pixel should exhibit a non-zero value in only one channel to facilitate nucleus localization. To this end, we propose a novel weighted MSE loss for structured regression learning, which is able to explicitly suppress other channels when dealing with a specific channel:

$$\mathcal{L}_{nr} = \frac{1}{Z} \sum_{i=1}^{N_b} \sum_{w=1}^{W} \sum_{h=1}^{H} \sum_{m=1}^{M} (\lambda_1^i + \lambda_2^i)(Y_{20\times}^i(w,h,m) - \hat{Y}_{20\times}^i(w,h,m))^2, \quad (2)$$

where $Z = 2N_b \times W \times H \times M$. $\lambda_1^i = \alpha(\eta Y_{20\times}^i(w,h,m) + \bar{Y}_{20\times}^i(m))$, where $\bar{Y}_{20\times}^i(m)$ represents the mean value of $Y_{20\times}^i$ on the m-th channel and $\alpha \in [0,1]$, $\eta \in [0,1]$ are weighting parameters. $\lambda_2^i = (1-\alpha)\sum_{j=1}^{M-1}(\eta \tilde{Y}_{20\times}^{i,j}(w,h,m) + \bar{\tilde{Y}}_{20\times}^{i,j}(m))$, where $\tilde{Y}_{20\times}^{i,j}$ is generated by rolling $Y_{20\times}^i$ by a j offset along the channel dimension. λ_2^i is used to penalize the undesired responses on certain channels of the prediction $\hat{Y}_{20\times}^i$. For instance, suppose that $\lambda_2^i = 0$ and the image $X_{20\times}^i$ has only the m-th class of nuclei. In this scenario, $Y_{20\times}^i$ has non-zero values only on the m-th channel and zeros for all the others; thus, $\lambda_1^i = 0$ for all the channels except the m-th channel in Eq. (2) and $\hat{Y}_{20\times}^i$ may exhibit responses on the not-m-th channel, which are not desirable. This will challenge nucleus localization because a single pixel might exhibit responses in multiple channels of the prediction map. However, with introducing $\lambda_2^i \neq 0$ that always holds for the presence of nuclei in $X_{20\times}^i$, the responses on undesired channels of $\hat{Y}_{20\times}^i$ are explicitly suppressed so as to encourage the model to predict values on the m-th channel of $\hat{Y}_{20\times}^i$. Therefore, the proposed MSE loss not only effectively handles unbalanced pixel distributions in the images (i.e., background versus nuclei) with $\{\lambda_1^i\}_{i=1}^{N_b}$, but also dynamically penalizes undesired predictions with $\{\lambda_2^i\}_{i=1}^{N_b}$.

We apply this loss $\mathcal{L}_{nr}$ to the output of the context encoding module for model learning. In order to assist with learning this very deep network, we add an auxiliary regressor to the output layer of each FRCN architecture in Fig. 1.

Table 1. Comparison with recent state-of-the-art deep models in terms of precision (P), recall (R), and F_1 score. For each metric, the highest and second-highest values are highlighted with bold and underlines, respectively.

Methods	Immunopositive tumor			Immunonegative tumor			Non-tumor		
	P	R	F_1	P	R	F_1	P	R	F_1
FCN-8s [10]	0.793	0.536	0.640	0.802	0.696	0.745	0.517	0.301	0.381
U-Net [14]	0.638	0.470	0.541	0.835	0.729	0.778	0.633	0.618	0.625
FCRNA [19]	0.774	0.552	0.616	0.809	0.619	0.701	0.398	0.581	0.473
FCRNB [19]	0.805	0.541	0.647	0.814	0.593	0.686	0.375	0.632	0.471
FRCN [20]	<u>0.872</u>	0.584	0.700	**0.877**	0.754	0.811	0.606	0.543	0.573
SFCN-OPI [26]	0.814	<u>0.839</u>	<u>0.826</u>	0.781	**0.852**	0.815	<u>0.788</u>	**0.832**	**0.809**
AWMF-CNN [17]	0.784	0.536	0.637	0.845	0.755	0.797	0.720	0.811	0.763
MapDe [13]	0.834	0.742	0.785	<u>0.875</u>	0.771	<u>0.820</u>	**0.813**	0.682	0.742
Ours	**0.935**	**0.856**	**0.894**	0.873	<u>0.821</u>	**0.846**	0.757	<u>0.814</u>	<u>0.784</u>

This strategy can combat the problem of gradient vanishing [16,17]. We use the definition in Eq. (2) to calculate the losses for these two auxiliary regressors, $\mathcal{L}_{20\times}$ with $\{(X_{20\times}^i, Y_{20\times}^i)\}_{i=1}^{N_b}$ and $\mathcal{L}_{10\times}$ with $\{(X_{10\times}^i, Y_{10\times}^i)\}_{i=1}^{N_b}$ for each batch. Note that calculation of $\mathcal{L}_{20\times}$ and $\mathcal{L}_{10\times}$ do not rely on the context encoding. Our full objective is $\mathcal{L} = \mathcal{L}_{lc} + \mathcal{L}_{nr} + \mathcal{L}_{20\times} + \mathcal{L}_{10\times}$. Note that the auxiliary regressors are discarded during model testing.

3   Experiments

3.1   Datasets and Implementation Details

We evaluate the proposed method on 203 Ki67 IHC stained pancreatic neuroendocrine tumor (NET) tissue microarray images with a maximum magnification of 20×, each corresponding to one case. Each image contains hundreds of nuclei and has a size of $1000 \times 1000 \times 3$. The dataset has three categories of nuclei: immunopositive tumor (2809), immunonegative tumor (145087) and non-tumor (37877), with 185773 nuclei in total. We randomly split the dataset into training, validation and test sets with a ratio of 6:2:2. We follow [15,21,26] to use precision, recall and F_1 score to evaluate the performance of nucleus recognition.

We train the entire model from scratch using the Adam algorithm [8] with parameters: $\beta_1 = 0.9$, $\beta_2 = 0.999$, learning rate $= 0.0001$, batch size $= 4$, and number of epochs $= 250$. We use the exponential linear unit activation [3]. During training, we conduct data augmentation with random cropping, flipping, rotation, shifting, shearing and zooming. The training stops if the performance on the validation set does not improve for successive 10 epochs. We set $\alpha = 0.75$, $\eta = 0.2$ in Eq. (2) and multiply the labels by a constant 5 to facilitate model training [20].

3.2 Model Evaluation

Comparison with State-of-the-Art Methods. Table 1 shows the comparison of the proposed method with several recent deep learning models, such as FCN-8s [10], U-Net [14], FCRNA/FCRNB [19], FRCN [20], SFCN-OPI [26], AWMF-CNN [17] and MapDe [13]. We note that the proposed method achieves the best or second-best performance in almost all the metrics. In particular, our method significantly outperforms the others in all the metrics for identification of immunopositive tumor nuclei, probably because most of these nuclei exhibit different colors or spatial configuration from the other nuclei. Additionally, our method provides slightly superior or very competitive performance with other methods for other types of nuclei. Qualitative results of nucleus recognition are provided in Figure S1 of the Supplementary Material.

Ablation Study. To evaluate the contribution of each component in the proposed method, we conduct the following ablation studies with different settings: (a) whether using multi-resolution input images $\{X_{20\times}^i, X_{10\times}^i\}_{i=1}^N$ or a single-resolution image $\{X_{20\times}^i\}_{i=1}^N$, (b) whether using the context encoding module and (c) whether using channel suppression, i.e., whether $\{\lambda_2^i = 0\}_{i=1}^{N_b}$ in Eq. (2). Table 2 lists the nucleus recognition performance for these settings. We note that the proposed method provides the highest F_1 score, a unary evaluation metric for nucleus recognition, for tumor nuclei. In addition, the joint usage of multi-resolution image input and context encoding is very helpful for immunopositive tumor and non-tumor nuclei, while using context encoding with channel suppression is particularly beneficial for immunopositive tumor and immunonegative tumor nuclei.

Table 2. Ablation study for different settings of the proposed method in terms of precision (P), recall (R), and F_1 score. (a), (b), and (c) denote using multi-resolution image input, context encoding and channel suppression, respectively. Baseline means using none of (a), (b) and (c). For each metric, the highest and second-highest values are highlighted with bold and underlines, respectively.

Methods	Immunopositive tumor			Immunonegative tumor			Non-tumor		
	P	R	F_1	P	R	F_1	P	R	F_1
Baseline	0.872	0.584	0.700	<u>0.877</u>	0.754	0.811	0.606	0.543	0.573
(a)	0.781	0.739	0.761	0.849	0.722	0.780	0.745	0.688	0.715
(b)	0.835	**0.862**	0.848	0.789	**0.834**	0.811	0.681	0.774	0.725
(c)	0.858	0.717	0.781	0.834	0.767	0.799	0.702	0.749	0.724
(a, b)	0.917	0.820	0.866	**0.892**	0.739	0.808	**0.818**	0.791	**0.804**
(a, c)	0.813	0.750	0.780	0.825	0.796	0.810	<u>0.793</u>	0.744	0.768
(b, c)	**0.945**	0.813	<u>0.874</u>	0.861	0.805	<u>0.832</u>	0.744	<u>0.805</u>	0.773
(a, b, c)	<u>0.935</u>	<u>0.856</u>	**0.894**	0.873	<u>0.821</u>	**0.846**	0.757	**0.814**	<u>0.784</u>

Parameter Sensitivity Analysis. The proposed method has two important parameters, the number of codewords K in the encoding layer and the α in Eq. (2). The left panel of Fig. 2 displays the F_1 score with $K = 0$, 8, 16, and 32, where $K = 0$ denotes the case using global average pooling, and we find $K = 16$ yields the best performance for identification of all the three categories of nuclei. The right panel of Fig. 2 shows the effects of α in Eq. (2), and we note that $\alpha > 0.65$ is better than $\alpha \leq 0.65$, demonstrating the importance of $\{\lambda_1^i\}_{i=1}^{N_b}$. In particular, the F_1 score grows at the beginning and then decreases after $\alpha > 0.7$ for the classes of immunopositive and immunonegative tumor nuclei, and this suggests the necessity of $\{\lambda_2^i\}_{i=1}^{N_b}$ in Eq. (2).

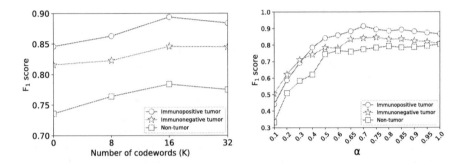

Fig. 2. F_1 score with respect to different numbers of codewords K in the encoding layer (left) and the α in Eq. (2) (right). $K = 0$ means using global average pooling.

4   Conclusion

We propose a novel multi-field-of-view context encoding method for single-stage nucleus recognition. It learns and aggregates feature representations from multi-field-of-view, multi-resolution images and then explicitly encodes the contextual information in the aggregated features. Additionally, it designs a new deep regression loss, which can suppress undesired responses in the prediction for robust nucleus recognition. Extensive experiments on a large-scale Ki67 IHC stained pancreatic NET image dataset demonstrate the effectiveness of our method.

References

1. Bell, S., Zitnick, C.L., Bala, K., Girshick, R.: Inside-outside net: detecting objects in context with skip pooling and recurrent neural networks. In: 2016 IEEE Conference on Computer Vision and Pattern Recognition (CVPR), pp. 2874–2883 (2016)
2. Cireşan, D.C., Giusti, A., Gambardella, L.M., Schmidhuber, J.: Mitosis detection in breast cancer histology images with deep neural networks. In: Mori, K., Sakuma, I., Sato, Y., Barillot, C., Navab, N. (eds.) MICCAI 2013. LNCS, vol. 8150, pp. 411–418. Springer, Heidelberg (2013). https://doi.org/10.1007/978-3-642-40763-5_51

3. Clevert, D.A., Unterthiner, T., Hochreiter, S.: Fast and accurate deep network learning by exponential linear units (ELUs). In: International Conference on Learning Representations (ICLR), pp. 1–14 (2016)
4. Csurka, G., Dance, C.R., Fan, L., Willamowski, J., Bray, C.: Visual categorization with bags of keypoints. In: ECCV Workshop on Statistical Learning in Computer Vision, pp. 1–22 (2004)
5. Fei-Fei, L., Perona, P.: A Bayesian hierarchical model for learning natural scene categories. In: 2005 IEEE Computer Society Conference on Computer Vision and Pattern Recognition (CVPR), vol. 2, pp. 524–531 (2005)
6. Graham, S., et al.: Hover-Net: simultaneous segmentation and classification of nuclei in multi-tissue histology images. Med. Image Anal. **58**, 101563 (2019)
7. Hu, J., Shen, L., Sun, G.: Squeeze-and-excitation networks. In: 2018 IEEE/CVF Conference on Computer Vision and Pattern Recognition (CVPR), pp. 7132–7141 (2018)
8. Kingma, D.P., Ba, J.L.: Adam: a method for stochastic optimization. In: International Conference on Learning Representations (ICLR), pp. 1–15 (2015)
9. Liu, L., et al.: Deep learning for generic object detection: a survey. Int. J. Comput. Vis. **128**, 261–318 (2020). https://doi.org/10.1007/s11263-019-01247-4
10. Long, J., Shelhamer, E., Darrell, T.: Fully convolutional networks for semantic segmentation. In: 2015 IEEE Conference on Computer Vision and Pattern Recognition (CVPR), pp. 3431–3440 (2015)
11. Nguyen, K., Bredno, J., Knowles, D.A.: Using contextual information to classify nuclei in histology images. In: 2015 IEEE 12th International Symposium on Biomedical Imaging (ISBI), pp. 995–998 (2015)
12. Qu, H., et al.: Joint segmentation and fine-grained classification of nuclei in histopathology images. In: 2019 IEEE 16th International Symposium on Biomedical Imaging (ISBI), pp. 900–904 (2019)
13. Raza, S.E.A., et al.: Deconvolving convolutional neural network for cell detection. In: 2019 IEEE 16th International Symposium on Biomedical Imaging (ISBI), pp. 891–894 (2019)
14. Ronneberger, O., Fischer, P., Brox, T.: U-Net: convolutional networks for biomedical image segmentation. In: Navab, N., Hornegger, J., Wells, W.M., Frangi, A.F. (eds.) MICCAI 2015. LNCS, vol. 9351, pp. 234–241. Springer, Cham (2015). https://doi.org/10.1007/978-3-319-24574-4_28
15. Sirinukunwattana, K., Raza, S.E.A., Tsang, Y.W., Snead, D.R.J., Cree, I.A., Rajpoot, N.M.: Locality sensitive deep learning for detection and classification of nuclei in routine colon cancer histology images. IEEE Trans. Med. Imag. **35**(5), 1196–1206 (2016)
16. Szegedy, C., et al.: Going deeper with convolutions. In: 2015 IEEE Conference on Computer Vision and Pattern Recognition (CVPR), pp. 1–9 (2015)
17. Tokunaga, H., Teramoto, Y., Yoshizawa, A., Bise, R.: Adaptive weighting multi-field-of-view CNN for semantic segmentation in pathology. In: 2019 IEEE/CVF Conference on Computer Vision and Pattern Recognition (CVPR), pp. 12589–12598 (2019)
18. Wang, S., Yao, J., Xu, Z., Huang, J.: Subtype cell detection with an accelerated deep convolution neural network. In: Ourselin, S., Joskowicz, L., Sabuncu, M.R., Unal, G., Wells, W. (eds.) MICCAI 2016. LNCS, vol. 9901, pp. 640–648. Springer, Cham (2016). https://doi.org/10.1007/978-3-319-46723-8_74
19. Xie, W., Noble, J.A., Zisserman, A.: Microscopy cell counting with fully convolutional regression networks. In: The 1st Workshop on Deep Learning in Medical Image Analysis, pp. 1–8 (2015)

20. Xie, Y., Xing, F., Shi, X., Kong, X., Su, H., Yang, L.: Efficient and robust cell detection: a structured regression approach. Med. Image Anal. **44**, 245–254 (2018)
21. Xing, F., Cornish, T.C., Bennett, T., Ghosh, D., Yang, L.: Pixel-to-pixel learning with weak supervision for single-stage nucleus recognition in Ki67 images. IEEE Trans. Biomed. Eng. **66**(11), 3088–3097 (2019)
22. Zeng, X., et al.: Crafting GBD-Net for object detection. IEEE Trans. Pattern Anal. Mach. Intell. **40**(9), 2109–2123 (2018)
23. Zhang, H., et al.: Context encoding for semantic segmentation. In: 2018 IEEE/CVF Conference on Computer Vision and Pattern Recognition (CVPR), pp. 7151–7160 (2018)
24. Zhang, H., Xue, J., Dana, K.: Deep TEN: texture encoding network. In: 2017 IEEE Conference on Computer Vision and Pattern Recognition, pp. 2896–2905 (2017)
25. Zhang, M., Li, X., Xu, M., Li, Q.: RBC semantic segmentation for sickle cell disease based on deformable U-Net. In: Frangi, A.F., Schnabel, J.A., Davatzikos, C., Alberola-López, C., Fichtinger, G. (eds.) MICCAI 2018. LNCS, vol. 11073, pp. 695–702. Springer, Cham (2018). https://doi.org/10.1007/978-3-030-00937-3_79
26. Zhou, Y., Dou, Q., Chen, H., Qin, J., Heng, P.A.: SFCN-OPI: detection and fine-grained classification of nuclei using sibling FCN with objectness prior interaction. In: The Thirty-Second AAAI Conference on Artificial Intelligence (AAAI), pp. 2652–2659 (2018)

Self-supervised Nuclei Segmentation in Histopathological Images Using Attention

Mihir Sahasrabudhe[1,2], Stergios Christodoulidis[3], Roberto Salgado[4,5],
Stefan Michiels[3,6], Sherene Loi[4], Fabrice André[3], Nikos Paragios[1,7],
and Maria Vakalopoulou[1,2,3(✉)]

[1] Université Paris-Saclay, CentraleSupélec, Mathématiques et Informatique pour la
Complexité et les Systèmes, 91190 Gif-sur-Yvette, France
maria.vakalopoulou@centralesuplec.fr
[2] Inria Saclay, 91190 Gif-sur-Yvette, France
[3] Institut Gustave Roussy, 94800 Villejuif, France
[4] Division of Research, Peter MacCallum Cancer Centre, Melbourne, Australia
[5] Department of Pathology, GZA-ZNA Hospitals, 2050 Antwerp, Belgium
[6] Service de Biostatistique et d'Epidémiologie, Gustave Roussy, CESP U108,
Université ParisSud, Université Paris Saclay, Villejuif, France
[7] Therapanacea, 75014 Paris, France

Abstract. Segmentation and accurate localization of nuclei in histopathological images is a very challenging problem, with most existing approaches adopting a supervised strategy. These methods usually
rely on manual annotations that require a lot of time and effort from
medical experts. In this study, we present a self-supervised approach
for segmentation of nuclei for whole slide histopathology images. Our
method works on the assumption that the size and texture of nuclei
can determine the magnification at which a patch is extracted. We show
that the identification of the magnification level for tiles can generate
a preliminary self-supervision signal to locate nuclei. We further show
that by appropriately constraining our model it is possible to retrieve
meaningful segmentation maps as an auxiliary output to the primary
magnification identification task. Our experiments show that with standard post-processing, our method can outperform other unsupervised
nuclei segmentation approaches and report similar performance with
supervised ones on the publicly available MoNuSeg dataset. Our code
and models are available online (https://github.com/msahasrabudhe/
miccai2020_self_sup_nuclei_seg) to facilitate further research.

Keywords: Pathology · Whole slide images · Nuclei segmentation ·
Deep learning · Self-supervision · Attention models

1 Introduction

Histology images are the gold standard in diagnosing a considerable number
of diseases including almost all types of cancer. For example, the count of

© Springer Nature Switzerland AG 2020
A. L. Martel et al. (Eds.): MICCAI 2020, LNCS 12265, pp. 393–402, 2020.
https://doi.org/10.1007/978-3-030-59722-1_38

nuclei on whole-slide images (WSIs) can have diagnostic significance for numerous cancerous conditions [20]. The proliferation of digital pathology and high-throughput tissue imaging leads to the adoption in clinical practice of digitized histopathological images that are utilized and archived every day. Such WSIs are acquired from glass histology slides using dedicated scanning devices after a staining process. In each WSI, thousands of nuclei from various types of cell can be identified. The detection of such nuclei is crucial for the identification of tissue structures, which can be further analyzed in a systematic manner and used for various clinical tasks. Presence, extent, size, shape, and other morphological characteristics of such structures are important indicators of the severity of different diseases [6]. Moreover, a quantitative analysis of digital pathology is important, to understand the underlying biological reasons for diseases [21].

Manual segmentation or estimation of nuclei on a WSI is an extremely time consuming process which suffers from high inter-observer variability [1]. On the other hand, data-driven methods that perform well on a specific histopathological datasets report poor performance on other datasets due again to the high variability in acquisition parameters and biological properties of cells in different organs and diseases [13]. To deal with this problem, datasets integrating different organs [4,13] based on images from The Cancer Genome Atlas (TCGA) provide pixelwise annotations for nuclei from variety of organs. Yet, these datasets provide access to only a limited range of annotations, making the generalization of these techniques ambiguous and emphasizing the need for novel segmentation algorithms without relying purely on manual annotations.

To this end, in this paper, we propose a self-supervised approach for nuclei segmentation without requiring annotations. The contributions of this paper are threefold: (i) we propose using scale classification as a self-supervision signal under the assumption that nuclei are a discriminative feature for this task; (ii) we employ a fully convolutional attention network based on dilated filters that generates segmentation maps for nuclei in the image space; and (iii) we investigate regularization constraints on the output of the attention network in order to generate semantically meaningful segmentation maps.

2   Related Work

Hematoxylin and eosin (H&E) staining is one of the most common and inexpensive staining schemes for WSI acquisition. A number of different tissue structures can be identified in H&E images such as glands, lumen (ducts within glands), adipose (fat), and stroma (connective tissue). The building blocks of such structures are a number of different cells. During the staining process, hematoxylin renders cell nuclei dark blueish purple and the epithelium light purple, while eosin renders stroma pink. A variety of standard image analysis methods are based on hematoxylin in order to extract nuclei [2,24] reporting very promising results, albeit evaluated mostly on single organs. A lot of research on the segmentation of nuclei in WSI images has been presented over the past few decades. Methodologies that integrate thresholding, clustering, watershed algorithms, active contours, and variants along with a variety of pre- and post-processing techniques

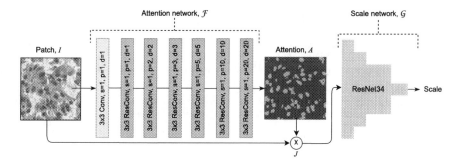

Fig. 1. A diagram of our approach. Each patch I is fed to the attention network $\mathcal{F}$ generating an attention map A. The "attended" image J is then given to the scale classification network $\mathcal{G}$. Both networks are trained in an end-to-end fashion. s, p, and d for convolution blocks refer to stride, padding, and dilation. (Color figure online)

have been extensively studied [8]. A common problem among the aforementioned algorithmic approaches is the poor generalization across the wide spectrum of tissue morphologies introducing a lot of false positives.

To counter this, a number of learning-based approaches have been investigated in order to better tackle the variation over nuclei shape and color. One group of learning-based methods includes hand-engineered representations such as filter bank responses, geometric features, texture descriptors or other first order statistics paired with a classification algorithm [12,18]. Recent success of deep learning-based methods and the introduction of publicly available datasets [4,13] formed a second learning-based group of supervised approaches. In particular, [13] summarises some of these supervised approaches that are developed for multi-organ nuclei segmentation, most of them based on convolutional neural networks. Among them the best performing method proposes a multi-task scheme based on an FCN [14] architecture using a ResNet [9] backbone encoder with one branch to perform nuclei segmentation and a second one for contour segmentation. Yet, the emergence of self-supervised approaches in computer vision [5,17] has not successfully translated to applications in histopathology. In this paper, we proposed a self-supervised method for nuclei segmentation exploiting magnification level determination as a self-supervision signal.

3   Methodology

The main idea behind our approach is that given a patch extracted from a WSI viewed at a certain magnification, the level of magnification can be ascertained by looking at the size and texture of the nuclei in the patch. By extension, we further assume that the nuclei are enough to determine the level of magnification, and other artefacts in the image are not necessary for this task.

Contrary to several concurrent computer vision pipelines which propose to train and evaluate models by feeding images sampled at several scales in order for them to learn multi-scale features [9] or models which specifically train for scale equivariance [23], we posit learning a scale-*sensitive* network which specifically trains for discriminative features for correct scale classification[1]. Given a set of WSIs, we extract all tissue patches (tiles) from them at a fixed set of magnifications $\mathcal{C}$. We consider only these tiles, with the "ground-truth" knowledge for each tile being at what magnification level it was extracted. Following our earlier reasoning, if nuclei in a given tile $I \in \mathbb{R}^{3 \times H \times W}$ are enough to predict the level of magnification, we assume that there exists a corresponding attention map A, so that $A \odot I$ is also enough to determine the magnification, where $\odot$ represents element-wise multiplication, and $A \in [0, 1]^{1 \times H \times W}$ is a single channel attention image that focuses on the nuclei in the input tile (Fig. 1).

We design a fully-convolutional feature extractor $\mathcal{F}$ to predict the attention map A from the patch I. Our feature extractor consists of several layers of convolution operations with a gradual increase in the dilation of the kernels so as to incorporate information from a large neighborhood around every pixel. This feature extractor $\mathcal{F}$ regresses a confidence map $\mathbf{a} = \mathcal{F}(I) \in \mathbb{R}^{1 \times H \times W}$, which is activated by a compressed and biased sigmoid function so that $A = \sigma(\mathbf{a})$. In order to force the attention map to focus only on parts of the input patch, we apply a sparsity regularizer on A. This regularizer follows the idea and implementation of a concurrent work on unsupervised separation of nuclei and background [10]. Sparsity is imposed by picking the η-th percentile value in the confidence map $\mathbf{a}$ for all images in the batch, and choosing a threshold τ equal to the average of this percentile over an entire training batch. Formally,

$$\tau = \frac{1}{B} \sum_{b=1}^{B} \mathbf{a}_b^{(\eta)}, \tag{1}$$

where $\mathbf{a}_b^{(\eta)}$ represents the $\left(\frac{\eta}{100} \cdot HW\right)$-th largest value in the confidence map $\mathbf{a}_b$ for the b-th image in the training batch of B images. The sigmoid is then defined as $\sigma(x) = \frac{1}{1+\exp(-r(x-\tau))}$. It is compressed in order to force sharp transitions in the activated attention map, the compression being determined by r. We use $r = 20$ in our experiments.

The "attended" image $J = A \odot I$ is now enough for magnification or scale classification. We train a scale classification network $\mathcal{G}$, which we initialize as a ResNet-34 [9], to predict the magnification level for each input tile J. The output of this network is scores for each magnification level, which is converted to probabilities using a softmax activation. The resulting model (Fig. 1) is trainable in an end-to-end manner. We use negative log-likelihood to train the scale classification network $\mathcal{G}$, and in turn the attention network $\mathcal{F}$—

$$\mathcal{L}_{\text{scale}}(\hat{\mathbf{p}}, l) = -\log \hat{p}_l; \quad \hat{p}_i = [\text{softmax}(\hat{\mathbf{s}})]_i; \quad \hat{\mathbf{s}} = \mathcal{G}(J); \quad 1 \leq i \leq N_{\mathcal{C}}, \tag{2}$$

where l is the scale ground-truth, and $N_{\mathcal{C}} = |\mathcal{C}|$.

---

[1] Note that the terms *scale* (in the context of computer vision) and *magnification* (in the context of histopathology) are semantically equivalent and used interchangeably.

3.1   Smoothness Regularization

We wish A to be semantically meaningful and smooth with blobs focusing on nuclei instead of having high frequency components. To this end, we incorporate a smoothness regularizer on the attention maps. The smoothness regularizer attempts simply to reduce the high frequency component that might appear in the attention map because of the compressed sigmoid. We employ a standard smoothness regularizer based on spatial gradients defined as

$$\mathcal{L}_{\text{smooth}} = \frac{1}{(H-1)(W-1)} \sum_{i,j} \|A_{i+1,j} - A_{i,j}\|_1 + \|A_{i,j+1} - A_{i,j}\|_1 . \quad (3)$$

3.2   Transformation Equivariance

Equivariance is a commonly used constraint on feature extractors for imposing semantic consistency [3,22]. A feature extractor f is equivariant to a transformation g if g is replicated in the feature vector produced by f, i.e., $f(g(\mathbf{x})) = g(f(\mathbf{x}))$, for an image $\mathbf{x}$. In the given context, we want the attention map obtained from $\mathcal{F}$ to be equivariant to a set $\mathcal{T}$ of certain rigid transforms. We impose equivariance to these transformations through a simple mean squared error loss on A. Formally, we define the equivariance constraint as

$$\mathcal{L}_{\text{equiv}} = \frac{1}{HW} \|\sigma\left(t\left(\mathcal{F}\left(I\right)\right)\right) - \sigma\left(\mathcal{F}\left(t\left(I\right)\right)\right)\|_2^2 , \quad (4)$$

for a transformation $t \in \mathcal{T}$. We set $\mathcal{T}$ to include horizontal and vertical flips, matrix transpose, and rotations by 90, 180, and 270°, as well as bilinear downsampling by a factor of 2. Each training batch uses a random $t \in \mathcal{T}$.

3.3   Training

The overall model is trained in an end-to-end fashion, with $\mathcal{L}_{\text{scale}}$ being the guiding self-supervision loss. For models incorporating all constraints, i.e., smoothness, sparsity, and equivariance, the total loss is

$$\mathcal{L}_{\text{total}} = \mathcal{L}_{\text{scale}} + \mathcal{L}_{\text{smooth}} + \mathcal{L}_{\text{equiv}}. \quad (5)$$

We refer to a model trained with all these components together as $\mathsf{M}_{\text{proposed}}$. We also test models without one of these losses to demonstrate how each loss contributes to the learning. More specifically, we define the following models:

1. $\mathsf{M}_{\neg\text{smooth}}$: does not include $\mathcal{L}_{\text{smooth}}$.
2. $\mathsf{M}_{\neg\text{equiv}}$: does not include $\mathcal{L}_{\text{equiv}}$.
3. $\mathsf{M}_{\neg\text{sparse}}$: does not include a sparsity regularizer on the attention map. In this case, the sigmoid is simply defined as $\sigma(x) = \frac{1}{1+\exp(-x)}$.
4. $\mathsf{M}_{\neg\text{WSI}}$: a model which does not sample images from WSIs, but instead from a set of pre-extracted patches (see Sect. 4.1).

We set the sparsity parameter η empirically in order to choose the 93-rd percentile value for sparsity regularization. This is equivalent to assuming that, on an average, 7% of the pixels in a tile represent nuclei.

3.4 Post Processing, Validation, and Model Selection

In order to retrieve the final instance segmentation from the attention image we employ a post processing pipeline that consists of 3 consequent steps. Firstly, two binary opening and closing morphological operations are sequentially performed using a coarse and a fine circular element ($r = 2$, $r = 1$). Next, the distance transform is calculated and smoothed using a Gaussian blur ($\sigma = 1$) on the new attention image and the local maxima are identified in a circular window ($r = 7$). Lastly, a marker driven watershed algorithm is applied using the inverse of the distance transform and the local maxima as markers.

As our model does not explicitly train for segmentation of nuclei, we require a validation set to determine which model is finally best-suited for our objective. To this end, we record the Dice score between the attention map and the ground truth on the validation set (see Sect. 4.1) at intermediate training epochs, and choose the epoch which performs the best. We noticed that, in general, performance increases initially on the validation, but flattens after $\sim$30 epochs.

4 Experimental Setup and Results

4.1 Dataset

For the purposes of this study we used the MoNuSeg database [13]. This dataset contains thirty 1000×1000 annotated patches extracted from thirty WSIs from different patients suffering from different cancer types from The Cancer Genomic Atlas (TCGA). We downloaded the WSIs corresponding to patients included in the training split and extracted tiles of size 224×224 from three different magnifications, namely $10\times$, $20\times$, and $40\times$. For each extracted tile, we perform a simple thresholding in the HSV color space to determine whether the tile contains tissue or not. Tiles with less then 70% tissue cover are not used. Furthermore, a stain normalization step was performed using the color transfer approach described in [19]. Finally, a total of 1 125 737 tiles from the three aforementioned scales were selected and paired with the corresponding magnification level. The MoNuSeg train and test splits were employed, while the MoNuSeg train set was further split into training and validation as 19 and 11 examples, respectively. The annotations provided by MoNuSeg on the validation set were utilized for determining the four post processing parameters (Sect. 3.4) and for the final evaluation. For the model $M_{\neg WSI}$, which does not use whole slide images, we use the MoNuSeg patches instead for training, using the same strategy to split training and validation. We further evaluated the performance of our model that was trained on the MoNuSeg training set on the TNBC [15] and CoNSeP [7] datasets.

4.2 Implementation

We use the PyTorch [16] library for our code. We use the Adam [11] optimizer in all our experiments, with an initial learning rate of 0.0002, a weight decay of 0.0001, and $\beta_1 = 0.9$. We use a batch size of 32, 100 minibatches per epoch, and

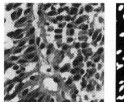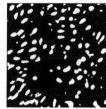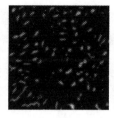

Fig. 2. Input, intermediate results and output of the post processing pipeline. From left to right: the input image; the attention map obtained from $M_{proposed}$ after the post-processing; the distance transform together with local maxima over-imposed in red; and the final result after the marker driven watershed. (Color figure online)

randomly crop patches of size 160×160 from training images to use as inputs to our models. Furthermore, as there is a high imbalance among the number of tiles for each of the magnification level (images are about 4 times more in number for a one step increase in the magnification level), we force a per-batch sampling of images that is uniform over the magnification levels, i.e., each training batch is sampled so that images are divided equally over the magnification levels. This is important to prevent learning a biased model.

4.3   Results

To highlight the potentials of our method we compare its performance with supervised and unsupervised methods on the MoNuSeg testset presented in [13]. In particular, in Table 1 we summarize the performance of three supervised methods (CNN2, CNN3 and Best Supervised) and two completely unsupervised methods (Fiji and CellProfiler) together with different variations of our proposed method. Our method outperforms the unsupervised methods, and it reports similar performance with CNN2 [13] and CNN3 [13] on the same dataset. While it reports lower performance than the best supervised method from [13], our formulation is quite modular and able to adapt multi-task schemes similar to the one adapted by the winning method of [13].

On the TNBC and CoNSeP datasets, our method is strongly competitive among the unsupervised methods. We should emphasize that these results have been obtained without retraining on these datasets. The CoNSeP dataset consists mainly of colorectal adenocarcinoma which is under-represented in the training set of MoNuSeg, proving very good generalization of our method.

Moreover, from our ablation study (Table 1), it is clear that all components of the proposed model are essential. Sparsity is the most important as by removing it, the network regresses an attention map that is too smooth and not necessarily concentrating on nuclei, thus being semantically meaningless. Qualitatively, we observed that $\mathcal{L}_{smooth}$ allows the network to focus on only on nuclei by removing attention over adjacent tissue regions, while $\mathcal{L}_{equiv}$ further refines the attention maps by imposing geometric symmetry. Finally, in Fig. 2 the segmentation map for one test image is presented. Results obtained from the $M_{proposed}$

Table 1. Quantitative results of the different benchmarked methods on three different public available datasets. AJI, AHD, and ADC stand for Aggregated Jaccard Index, Average Hausdorff Distance, and Average Dice Coefficient, respectively. Methods marked with † are supervised.

Test dataset	Method	AJI [13]	AHD	ADC
MoNuSeg test	CNN2 [13]†	0.3482	8.6924	0.6928
	CNN3 [13]†	0.5083	7.6615	**0.7623**
	Best Supervised [13]†	**0.691**	–	–
	CellProfiler [13]	0.1232	9.2771	0.5974
	Fiji [13]	0.2733	8.9507	0.6493
	$M_{\neg sparse}$	0.0312	13.1415	0.2283
	$M_{\neg smooth}$	0.1929	8.8166	0.4789
	$M_{\neg WSI}$	0.3025	8.2853	0.6209
	$M_{\neg equiv}$	0.4938	8.0091	0.7136
	$M_{proposed}$	**0.5354**	**7.7502**	**0.7477**
TNBC [15]	U-Net [7]†	0.514	–	0.681
	SegNet+WS [7]†	0.559	–	**0.758**
	HoverNet [7]†	**0.590**	–	0.749
	CellProfiler	0.2080	–	0.4157
	$M_{proposed}$	0.2656	–	0.5139
CoNSeP [7]	SegNet [7]†	0.194	–	**0.796**
	U-Net [7]†	**0.482**	–	0.724
	CellProfiler [7]	0.202	–	0.434
	QuPath [7]	0.249	–	0.588
	$M_{proposed}$	0.1980	–	0.587

attention network together with the nuclei segmentation after the performed post-processing are summarised.

5   Conclusion

In this paper, we propose and investigate a self-supervised method for nuclei segmentation of multi-organ histopathological images. In particular, we propose the use of the scale classification as a guiding self-supervision signal to train an attention network. We propose regularizers in order to regress attention maps that are semantically meaningful. Promising results comparable with supervised methods tested on the publicly available MoNuSeg dataset indicate the potentials of our method. We show also via. experiments on TNBC and ConSeP that our model generalizes well on new datasets. In the future, we aim to investigate the integration of our results within a treatment selection strategy. Nuclei presence is often a strong bio-marker as it concerns emerging cancer treatments (immunotherapy). Therefore, the end-to-end integration coupling histopathology and treatment outcomes could lead to prognostic tools as it concerns treatment response. Parallelly, other domains in medical imaging share concept similarities with the proposed concept.

References

1. Andrion, A., et al.: Malignant mesothelioma of the pleura: interobserver variability. J. Clin. Pathol. **48**(9), 856–860 (1995)
2. Boyle, D.P., et al.: The prognostic significance of the aberrant extremes of p53 immunophenotypes in breast cancer. Histopathology **65**(3), 340–352 (2014)
3. Cohen, T.S., Weiler, M., Kicanaoglu, B., Welling, M.: Gauge equivariant convolutional networks and the icosahedral CNN. arXiv preprint arXiv:1902.04615 (2019)
4. Gamper, J., Alemi Koohbanani, N., Benet, K., Khuram, A., Rajpoot, N.: PanNuke: an open pan-cancer histology dataset for nuclei instance segmentation and classification. In: Reyes-Aldasoro, C.C., Janowczyk, A., Veta, M., Bankhead, P., Sirinukunwattana, K. (eds.) ECDP 2019. LNCS, vol. 11435, pp. 11–19. Springer, Cham (2019). https://doi.org/10.1007/978-3-030-23937-4_2
5. Gidaris, S., Singh, P., Komodakis, N.: Unsupervised representation learning by predicting image rotations. arXiv preprint arXiv:1803.07728 (2018)
6. Gleason, D.F.: Histologic grading of prostate cancer: a perspective. Hum. Pathol. **23**(3), 273–279 (1992)
7. Graham, S., et al.: HoVer-Net: simultaneous segmentation and classification of nuclei in multi-tissue histology images. Med. Image Anal. **58**, 101563 (2019)
8. Gurcan, M.N., Boucheron, L.E., Can, A., Madabhushi, A., Rajpoot, N.M., Yener, B.: Histopathological image analysis: a review. IEEE Rev. Biomed. Eng. **2**, 147–171 (2009)
9. He, K., Zhang, X., Ren, S., Sun, J.: Deep residual learning for image recognition. In: Proceedings of the IEEE Conference on Computer Vision and Pattern Recognition, pp. 770–778 (2016)
10. Hou, L., et al.: Sparse autoencoder for unsupervised nucleus detection and representation in histopathology images. Pattern Recognit. **86**, 188–200 (2019)
11. Kingma, D.P., Ba, J.: Adam: a method for stochastic optimization. arXiv preprint arXiv:1412.6980 (2014)
12. Kong, H., Gurcan, M., Belkacem-Boussaid, K.: Partitioning histopathological images: an integrated framework for supervised color-texture segmentation and cell splitting. IEEE Trans. Med. Imaging **30**(9), 1661–1677 (2011)
13. Kumar, N., Verma, R., Sharma, S., Bhargava, S., Vahadane, A., Sethi, A.: A dataset and a technique for generalized nuclear segmentation for computational pathology. IEEE Trans. Med. Imaging **36**(7), 1550–1560 (2017)
14. Long, J., Shelhamer, E., Darrell, T.: Fully convolutional networks for semantic segmentation. In: Proceedings of the IEEE Conference on Computer Vision and Pattern Recognition, pp. 3431–3440 (2015)
15. Naylor, P., Laé, M., Reyal, F., Walter, T.: Segmentation of nuclei in histopathology images by deep regression of the distance map. IEEE Trans. Med. Imaging **38**(2), 448–459 (2018)
16. Paszke, A., et al.: Automatic differentiation in PyTorch (2017)
17. Pathak, D., Agrawal, P., Efros, A.A., Darrell, T.: Curiosity-driven exploration by self-supervised prediction. In: Proceedings of the IEEE Conference on Computer Vision and Pattern Recognition Workshops, pp. 16–17 (2017)

18. Plissiti, M.E., Nikou, C.: Overlapping cell nuclei segmentation using a spatially adaptive active physical model. IEEE Trans. Image Process. **21**(11), 4568–4580 (2012)

19. Reinhard, E., Adhikhmin, M., Gooch, B., Shirley, P.: Color transfer between images. IEEE Comput. Graphics Appl. **21**(5), 34–41 (2001)

20. Ruan, M., et al.: Predictive value of tumor-infiltrating lymphocytes to pathological complete response in neoadjuvant treated triple-negative breast cancers. Diagn. Pathol. **13**(1), 66 (2018)

21. Rubin, R., Strayer, D.S., Rubin, E., et al.: Rubin's Pathology: Clinicopathologic Foundations of Medicine. Lippincott Williams & Wilkins, Philadelphia (2008)

22. Thewlis, J., Bilen, H., Vedaldi, A.: Unsupervised learning of object landmarks by factorized spatial embeddings. In: Proceedings of the IEEE International Conference on Computer Vision, pp. 5916–5925 (2017)

23. Worrall, D., Welling, M.: Deep scale-spaces: equivariance over scale. In: Advances in Neural Information Processing Systems (2019)

24. Yi, F., Huang, J., Yang, L., Xie, Y., Xiao, G.: Automatic extraction of cell nuclei from H&E-stained histopathological images. J. Med. Imaging **4**(2), 027502 (2017)

FocusLiteNN: High Efficiency Focus Quality Assessment for Digital Pathology

Zhongling Wang[1], Mahdi S. Hosseini[2,3]($^{(\boxtimes)}$), Adyn Miles[3],
Konstantinos N. Plataniotis[3], and Zhou Wang[1]

[1] University of Waterloo, Waterloo, ON N2L 3G1, Canada
{zhongling.wang,zhou.wang}@uwaterloo.ca
[2] Huron Digital Pathology, St. Jacobs, ON N0B 2N0, Canada
[3] University of Toronto, Toronto, ON M5S 1A1, Canada
{mahdi.hosseini,adyn.miles}@mail.utoronto.ca, kostas@ece.utoronto.ca
https://github.com/icbcbicc/FocusLiteNN

Abstract. Out-of-focus microscopy lens in digital pathology is a critical bottleneck in high-throughput Whole Slide Image (WSI) scanning platforms, for which pixel-level automated Focus Quality Assessment (FQA) methods are highly desirable to help significantly accelerate the clinical workflows. Existing FQA methods include both knowledge-driven and data-driven approaches. While data-driven approaches such as Convolutional Neural Network (CNN) based methods have shown great promises, they are difficult to use in practice due to their high computational complexity and lack of transferability. Here, we propose a highly efficient CNN-based model that maintains fast computations similar to the knowledge-driven methods without excessive hardware requirements such as GPUs. We create a training dataset using FocusPath which encompasses diverse tissue slides across nine different stain colors, where the stain diversity greatly helps the model to learn diverse color spectrum and tissue structures. In our attempt to reduce the CNN complexity, we find with surprise that even trimming down the CNN to the minimal level, it still achieves a highly competitive performance. We introduce a novel comprehensive evaluation dataset, the largest of its kind, annotated and compiled from TCGA repository for model assessment and comparison, for which the proposed method exhibits superior precision-speed trade-off when compared with existing knowledge-driven and data-driven FQA approaches.

Keywords: Digital pathology · Out-of-focus · Focus Quality Assessment · Whole Slide Image (WSI) · Deep learning

Electronic supplementary material The online version of this chapter (https://doi.org/10.1007/978-3-030-59722-1_39) contains supplementary material, which is available to authorized users.

A. L. Martel et al. (Eds.): MICCAI 2020, LNCS 12265, pp. 403–413, 2020.
https://doi.org/10.1007/978-3-030-59722-1_39

1   Introduction

The problem of out-of-focus microscopy lens in digital pathology is a huge bottle-neck in existing high throughput Whole Slide Image (WSI) scanning platforms, making them difficult to be integrated in clinical workflows. WSI scans (aka digital slides) are required to be manually inspected for Focus Quality Assessment (FQA) on the pixel-level, which is (a) highly tedious and time consuming; and (b) subjective to an individual scoring that often causes inter/intra-variability issues. Both knowledge-driven and data-driven approaches have been developed to automate this process.

Data-Driven FQAs. Recent developments involve supervised training of CNNs on the image patch labels of a given focus dataset of WSIs, where the network is either adopted from a pre-designed architecture followed by some minor adjustments [2,12] or tailored from the scratch [16,17,22]. The selection of training dataset can also be divided into two categories of either synthetically generating out-of-focus (defocus) images by convolving in-focus patches with artificial blur kernel with different grades (i.e. classes) [2,12,22], or scanning tissue slides in different focal planes (z-levels) to generate real blur classes [17]. Existing open source software solutions such as CellProfiler [15] and HistoQC [11] adopt variants of such models for FQA of WSIs. The high computational complexity and the lack of transferability are the main drawbacks of these models.

Knowledge-Based FQAs. Numerous methods have been developed in the literature based on a wide variety of domain knowledge, including human visual system models [7,9], microscopic optics models [8], signal processing models [5,13], and natural image statistics models [1,14]. For more information, please refer to [8] and references therein. Although these methods may have low computational cost, their precision performances are relatively low compared to data-driven solutions, as will be shown later.

How Existing Models are Limited? Despite great performances of data-driven approaches such as Convolutional Neural Network (CNN) in deep learning [2,2,12,12], they have not been integrated into high throughput scanners for QC control purposes due to two main reasons. First, the computational complexity of data-driven solutions is often too high to process GigaByte WSIs. We explain this in example as follows. Despite the FQA models take few seconds to process a patch from WSI that are fast enough, the story is quite different for high-throughput scanning systems. Depending on the vendors, several hundreds of glass slides can be mount in scanners (e.g. Philips Ultra Fast Scanner accepts 300 slides of 1" x 3" and Huron TissueScope-iQ accepts 400). In clinical settings, all scans should be completed during the night hours (less than 12 h time frame) to be ready for diagnosis for the next day. Each slide is usually scanned at $0.5\,\mu\text{m}$/pixel @20X magnification, containing $\sim$1 cm $\times$ 1 cm tissue which translates to 25,000 $\times$ 25,000 digital WSI, yielding $\sim$2,500 patches of 1024$\times$1024 (50% overlap). Assuming two models are used for assessment, i.e. M1: DenseNet-10 and M2: FocusLiteNN (our proposed model), the time taken for two models to complete the task is

$$M1: \ 2,500(\text{patches/WSI}) \times 300(\text{WSI}) \times 0.355 \ \text{s/patch} = 73.96 \ \text{h}$$
$$M2: \ 2,500(\text{patches/WSI}) \times 300(\text{WSI}) \times 0.017 \ \text{s/patch} = 3.54 \ \text{h}$$

Clearly, the speed gain from model M2 over M1 is obvious. The limitation in computational resources becomes equally important as the precision when choosing FQA models for GigaByte WSI processing [4,20]. The second limitation is the lack of transferability of CNNs which becomes a barrier to process WSIs across different tissue stains and scanner variations.

Contributions. Our aim in this paper is to address the challenges in data-driven FQAs. In particular, (a) we build a highly-efficient extremely light weight CNN-based model i.e. FocusLiteNN[1] that maintains fast computations similar to the knowledge driven methods without excessive hardware requirements such as GPUs. The database used for training plays a crucial role, for which we suggest a training dataset using FocusPath [9] which encompasses diverse tissue slides across nine different stain colors. We hypothesise that the stain diversity greatly helps the model to learn diverse color spectrum and tissue structures. (b) For algorithm evaluation and comparison, we introduce a novel comprehensive evaluation dataset that is annotated and compiled from TCGA repository. Comprehensive experiments and analysis are conducted that demonstrate the superior precision-speed compromise of the proposed approach.

2   FocusLiteNN: Extremely Light-Weight CNN for FQA

The main idea of our model design here is to reduce the layer complication in deep learning for FQA in digital pathology, while still being able to benefit from machine learning framework to adapt data distribution for generalization. We build a simple data-driven model, called FocusLiteNN, which includes only one convolution layer (very shallow) for feature transformation. Such shallow design is based on the assumption that out-of-focus blur in digital pathology can be characterized using a relatively simple model since (a) the distortion process is taken place in a well controlled environment (within the WSI scanner); and (b) focus information is mainly encoded in the low-level (edge) information rather than high-level (semantic) information.

Let us assume that the sharpness level is uniform within a small enough mosaic patch $\mathbf{X} \in \mathbb{R}^{H \times W \times 3}$ extracted from a WSI scan. The idea is to first convolve the image patch with a kernel set $\boldsymbol{\Phi} \in \mathbb{R}^{h \times w \times 3 \times N}$ and then apply a non-linear pooling function to predict the sharpness of the input patch

$$y = p_{\text{NL}} \left(\sum_{k=1}^{3} \boldsymbol{\Phi}_k * \mathbf{X_k} + \mathbf{b} \right) \tag{1}$$

---

[1] Codes and models are available at https://github.com/icbcbicc/FocusLiteNN.

where, $\mathbf{\Phi}_k \in \mathbb{R}^{h \times w \times N}$ is the convolution kernel for kth input channel. Here, $\mathbf{X_k} \in \mathbb{R}^{H \times W}$ is kth channel of input patch and $\mathbf{b} \in \mathbb{R}^N$ is a bias vector. $y \in \mathbb{R}$ is the predicted score of $\mathbf{X}$. The 2D convolution operator $*$ is applied with a stride of 5 and p_{NL} is a non-linear pooling function which maps a 2D response to an overall sharpness score $y \in \mathbb{R}$. We set the kernel size to $h = w = 7$ for all experiments. The use of pooling function p_{NL} is also critical: by adding non-linearity to the model, it greatly enhances the approximation capability of the simple model. We defined it as

$$p_{\mathrm{NL}}(\mathbf{x}) = \mathbf{w_1} \cdot \min(\mathbf{x}) + \mathbf{w_2} \cdot \max(\mathbf{x}) + w_3 \tag{2}$$

where, $\mathbf{x} \in \mathbb{R}^{\frac{H-h+7}{5} \times \frac{W-w+7}{5} \times N}$ are the responses produced by convolution and $\mathbf{w_1} \in \mathbb{R}^N, \mathbf{w_2} \in \mathbb{R}^N, w_3 \in \mathbb{R}$ are trainable parameters. The use of channel-wise 2D max and min in p_{NL} makes the model capable of capturing extreme kernel responses. We refer the model in (1) as N-kernel mode of FocusLiteNN. Here we demonstrate the kernel response in FocusLiteNN (1-kernel) for each color channel in Fig. 1. The filter responses are shown for both spatial representation (aka impulse response) i.e. $\phi(x_1, x_2)$, magnitude frequency response $|\hat{\phi}(\omega_1, \omega_2)|$ and phase frequency response $\angle\hat{\phi}(\omega_1, \omega_2)$. Note that the filter responses are mainly significant along the perpendicular axes (i.e. horizontal and vertical) rather than rotational angles.

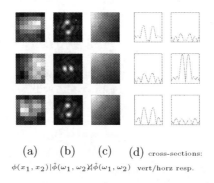

(a)   (b)   (c)   (d) cross-sections:

$\phi(x_1, x_2) |\hat{\phi}(\omega_1, \omega_2)| \angle\hat{\phi}(\omega_1, \omega_2)$ vert/horz resp.

Fig. 1. Filter responses of 1-kernel mode FocusLiteNN, shown for (a) spatial representation, (b) frequency amplitude, (c) unwrapped frequency phase; and (d) cross-sections (vertical/horizontal) for frequency amplitudes. (Color figure online)

3   Selection of Dataset

The development of data-driven FQA in digital pathology heavily relies on the selection of dataset for training. While the CNN models perform very well on training dataset, the ultimate question is how well the models can be transferred to other dataset for evaluation? This is of paramount importance in digital pathology where the models should be capable of (a) accurately predicting focus scores on the slides regardless of tissue structures and staining protocols; and (b) accounting for color disparities that could cause by WSI scanner variations and tissue preparation in different pathology labs.

3.1   FocusPath for CNN Training

The FocusPath[2] dataset [9] contains 8,640 patches of 1024×1024 image extracted from nine different stained slides. The WSIs are scanned by Huron TissueScope LE1.2 [3] using 40X optics lens @0.25 µm/pixel resolution. Each patch is associated with different focal plane (i.e. absolute z-level score) ranging from $\{0, \cdots, 14\}$ corresponding to the ground-truth class for focus level. The statistical distribution of color stains in FocusPath is shown in Fig. 2a and the patch examples are shown in Fig. 2b for different variations of focus levels.

Since the FocusPath includes diverse color stains compiled with different tissue structures, this makes the dataset well suited for developments of data-driven FQA models. Furthermore, we hypothesize that the diversity of color stains greatly helps generalize the CNN training to different tissues structures and color spectrum–no color augmentation is required such as in [18].

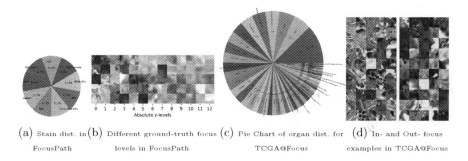

(a) Stain dist. in FocusPath   (b) Different ground-truth focus levels in FocusPath   (c) Pie Chart of organ dist. for TCGA@Focus   (d) In- and Out- focus examples in TCGA@Focus

Fig. 2. (a)–(b) FocusPath dataset [9] containing 8,640 image patches distributed among nine different tissue stains and annotated in 15 different focus levels. (c)–(d) The TCGA@Focus dataset containing 14,371 image patches compiled with both in- and out-focus labels. (Color figure online)

3.2   TCGA@Focus–An Evaluation Benchmark

A dataset of 1000 WSIs was selected from The Cancer Genome Atlas (TCGA) repository in SVS format gathered from 52 organ types provided by the National Cancer Institute (NCI)/National Institutes of Health (NIH) [19]. The statistical distribution of the number of slides per organ site is shown in Fig. 2c. Note that

---

[2] The data is available at https://zenodo.org/record/3926181.

the diversity of the organ types here is important to include wide spectrum of tissue textures and color information caused by variations in staining and WSI scans. Our goal here was to annotate two different categories of "*in-focus*" and "*out-focus*" regions-of-interests (ROI) within each slide corresponding to the binary ground truth scores of "1" and "0", respectively. The patch examples of each category are shown in Fig. 2d for different organ types. The compiled dataset is called TCGA@Focus[3] and contains 14,371 image patches in total, where 11,328 patches are labeled in-focus and 3,043 patches out-focus.

4   Experiments

Model Selection and Evaluation. We adopt five different categories in knowledge based methods for the experiments using (1) human visual system: Synthetic-MaxPol [7], and HVS-MaxPol-1/HVS-MaxPol-2 [9], (2) microscopy lens modeling: FQPath [8], (3) natural image statistics: MLV [1], SPARISH [14]; and (4) signal processing based: GPC [13] and LPC [5]. For data-driven methods we select a diverse range of CNN models in terms architecture complexity using EONSS [21] with four conv layers developed for the purpose of Image Quality Assessment (IQA), as well as DenseNet-13 [10] (eight conv layers) and variations of ResNet [6] (8, 48, and 99 conv layers) developed for computer vision applications. We evaluate selected FQA models in terms of statistical correlation and classification performance as well as computational complexity on the FocusPath and TCGA@Focus datasets. At the end, we also show the heat maps generated by these models on a sample image.

Implementation Details. All CNNs are re-trained on the FocusPath dataset with the same pre-processing techniques, optimizer and loss function. The Focus-Path dataset is randomly split into a train (60%) - validation (20%) - test (20%). The validation subset is used to determine the hyper-parameters. Training and testing are repeated in 10 folds of splits and the average performance is reported. All models are transferred to TCGA@Focus dataset for evaluation. The input dimensions for all CNNs are set to $235 \times 235 \times 3$. During testing, we densely sample the original patches with a stride of 128×128 and the average score is taken as the overall sharpness. Adam optimizer is utilized for all models. For FocusLiteNN, the learning rate is set to 0.01 with decay interval of 60 epochs. For other models, the learning rate is set to 0.001 with decay interval of 40 epochs. Each model is trained for 120 epochs to ensure convergence. The Pearson Linear Correlation Coefficient (PLCC) is used as the loss function for all models. PLCC bounds the loss value between -1 and 1, which helps to stabilize the training process.

Performance Evaluation. The metrics used to evaluate the performances are Spearman's Rank Correlation Coefficient (SRCC), PLCC, Area Under the Curve of the Receiver Operating Characteristic curve (ROC), Area Under the Curve

---

[3] The data is available at https://zenodo.org/record/3910757.

Table 1. SRCC, PLCC, ROC-AUC, PR-AUC performance of 16 FQA models on FocusPath dataset and TCGA@Focus dataset.

Type	Model	FocusPath				TCGA@Focus		Size	Time (sec)
		SRCC	PLCC	ROC	PR	ROC	PR		
Data-driven based	FocusLiteNN (1-kernel)	0.8766	0.8668	0.9468	0.9768	0.9310	0.8459	**148**	**0.017**
	FocusLiteNN (2-kernel)	0.8782	0.8686	0.9481	0.9770	**0.9337**	0.8499	299	0.019
	FocusLiteNN (10-kernel)	0.8931	0.8857	0.9542	0.9802	0.9322	**0.8510**	1.5K	0.019
	EONSS [21]	0.9009	0.8951	0.9540	0.9799	0.9000	0.8473	123K	0.063
	DenseNet-13 [10]	**0.9253**	**0.9197**	**0.9662**	0.9849	**0.9386**	**0.8646**	193K	0.355
	ResNet-10 [6]	**0.9278**	**0.9232**	**0.9671**	**0.9853**	0.9292	**0.8559**	4.9M	0.334
	ResNet-50 [6]	**0.9286**	**0.9244**	**0.9676**	**0.9855**	**0.9364**	0.8144	24M	1.899
	ResNet-101 [6]	0.9242	0.9191	0.9644	**0.9840**	0.9320	0.8447	43M	2.655
Knowledge based	FQPath [8]	0.8395	0.8295	0.9375	0.9739	0.7483	0.6274	N.A	0.269
	HVS-MaxPol-1 [9]	0.8044	0.8068	0.9400	0.9743	0.7118	0.5622	N.A	0.257
	HVS-MaxPol-2 [9]	0.8418	0.8330	0.9434	0.9757	0.7861	0.6721	N.A	0.458
	Synthetic-MaxPol [7]	0.8243	0.8139	0.9293	0.9707	0.6084	0.4617	N.A	0.841
	LPC [5]	0.8375	0.8321	0.9223	0.9681	0.5576	0.4564	N.A	7.510
	GPC [13]	0.7851	0.7602	0.9095	0.9604	0.4519	0.2830	N.A	0.599
	MLV [1]	0.8623	0.8528	0.9414	0.9758	0.8235	0.6943	N.A	0.482
	SPARISH [14]	0.3225	0.3398	0.7724	0.8875	0.7293	0.6414	N.A	4.853

of the Precision Recall Curve (PR). SRCC measures the monotonicity between the predicted sharpness score and the absolute z-level, while PLCC measures the linear correlation between them. When measuring ROC and PR on the FocusPath dataset, we first binarize the z-levels by considering all patches with absolute z-level 0, 1, 2 as sharp and those equal or larger than 2 as blurry. The results are shown in Table 1. On the FocusPath dataset, the overall performance of DenseNet-13 [10], ResNet-10 [6], ResNet-50 [6] and ResNet-101 [6] in all 6 metrics are the best and are similar to each other. Assuming that the testing subset of FocusPath is drawn from the same distribution as of the training subset, this observation shows that those data-driven based models with more parameters can fit the distribution of training data better. ResNet-50, the best performer among deep CNN based models, outperforms the 10-kernel model, the best performer among shallow CNN based models, by 3.5% in SRCC and 2% in ROC. To visualize the statistical correlation of all models, the scatter plots of the predicted scores versus z-levels on the FocusPath testing subset are shown in the first row of Fig. 3. We can see that the monotonicity and linearity between the prediction and ground truth are best preserved in deep CNN base models.

All models are also evaluated on the TCGA@Focus dataset to study the transferability performance where no training is involved. Here, DenseNet-13 [10] achieves the highest scores on both ROC-AUC and PR-AUC. While the overall performance of the deep CNN based models are still in the top tier, the gap between them and the shallow CNNs are getting smaller compared with the performance difference on FocusPath dataset: ResNet-50 only outperforms the FocusLiteNN (10-kernel) model by 0.4% in terms of ROC. Distribution of the predicted scores on the TCGA@Focus dataset and their ground truth labels as well as the classification thresholds for all models are also shown in the second and third rows of Fig. 3.

Computational Complexity Analysis. The testing image is $1024 \times 1024 \times 3$ 8-bit in the FocusPath dataset. Two experiments are conducted, the first one is ROC-AUC on the TCGA@Focus dataset versus CPU time (Fig. 3 last row left). To fairly compare the computational complexity, all models are running on an Intel i9-7920X @ 2.90 GHz with 32 GB memory. Image reading time is excluded from the CPU time, but the pre-processing time for each model, such as dense sampling, is measured. The Monte Carlo simulation is done for 100 times and the average is reported. The second experiment is ROC-AUC on the TCGA@Focus dataset versus number of model parameters (Fig. 3 last row right). We count the number of trainable parameters of the data-driven models and plot the numbers against their performance. We can clearly see that the 1-kernel model outperforms others by a large margin in terms of both CPU time and model size: it outperforms the second fast model EONSS [21] by 3.4% in terms of ROC-AUC, but consuming only 27% of its CPU time with 0.1% of its model size.

Heat Map Visualization. To better visualize the model outputs, we generate heat maps for each model, as shown in Fig. 3 (further heatmaps are provided in Supplementary Materials Fig. 1). For all models, we densely sample 235×235 patches from the WSI scan with a stride of 128×128 for scoring and interpolated accordingly. These scores are then mapped to colors and overlaid on the grayscale version of the scan. The most blurry parts are in the upper left corner, lower right corner, and in the circle in the middle. The vertical strip taken up $\frac{1}{3}$ of the space is in focus. In Fig. 3 the third row, we showed the relative blurriness level within a scan by normalizing the scores to the range 0 to 1 before color mapping. Knowledge based models and FocusLiteNN prefer to predict the entire scan as more blurry even for in focus part. Deep CNN-based models such as EONSS [21], ResNet [6] and DenseNet [10] are less aggressive and can identify in focus regions, which are more perceptually accurate. To demonstrate the absolute blurriness level of a scan, we train the FocusLiteNN (1-kernel), ResNet-10 [6] and EONSS [21] with MSE loss on the FocusPath dataset. The predicted scores correspond to absolute z-levels in the FocusPath dataset. The results are shown in the first row of Supplementary Materials Fig. 1.

5   Conclusion

We propose a highly efficient CNN-based automated FQA approach, aiming to accelerate the clinical workflow in WSI scanning. Reaching the performance of more complex models with fewer parameters is one of our main contributions. We use FocusPath to create a training dataset with diverse tissue slides and stain colors, which helps the model to learn diverse color spectrum and tissue structures. We introduce a novel comprehensive evaluation dataset annotated and compiled from TCGA repository, the largest of its kind for assessing and comparing FQA

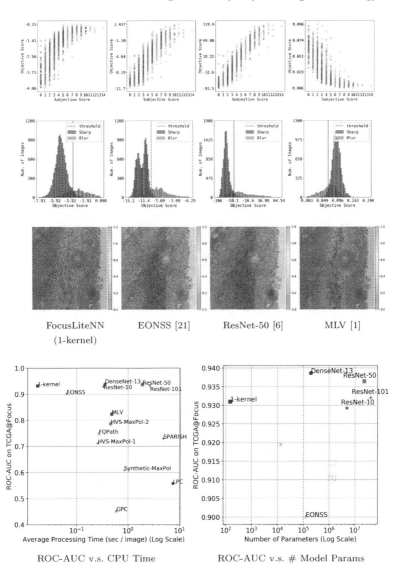

Fig. 3. Evaluation results for 4 models. **First row:** scatter plots of absolute z-level versus predicted scores on FocusPath dataset. **Second row:** histogram of objective scores on TCGA@Focus. **Third row:** normalized heat maps. Higher score indicate more blurriness. **Forth row:** average Processing Time versus ROC-AUC and model size versus ROC-AUC on TCGA@Focus Dataset. Please refer to the Supplementary Materials (Fig. 2) for the complete results of 16 models. (Color figure online)

models. Our test results show that the proposed model demonstrates superior precision-speed trade-off when compared with existing knowledge-driven and data-driven FQA approaches. A somewhat surprising finding in our study is that even when we trim down our CNN model to the minimal 1-kernel size, it still maintains a highly competitive performance and transferability. In conclusion, our proposed FocusLiteNN surpasses (by a large margin) all SOTA models in terms of speed, and yet achieves competitive performance with best accuracy model i.e. DenseNet-13.

Acknowledgements. The authors would like to greatly thank *Huron Digital Pathology* (St. Jacobs, ON N0B 2N0, Canada) for the support of this research work.

References

1. Bahrami, K., Kot, A.C.: A fast approach for no-reference image sharpness assessment based on maximum local variation. IEEE Signal Process. Lett. **21**(6), 751–755 (2014)
2. Campanella, G., Rajanna, A.R., Corsale, L., Schüffler, P.J., Yagi, Y., Fuchs, T.J.: Towards machine learned quality control: a benchmark for sharpness quantification in digital pathology. Comput. Med. Imaging Graph. **65**, 142–151 (2018)
3. Dixon, A.E.: Pathology slide scanner. US Patent 8,896,918, 25 Nov 2014
4. Gupta, A., et al.: Deep learning in image cytometry: a review. Cytometry Part A **95**(4), 366–380 (2019)
5. Hassen, R., Wang, Z., Salama, M.M.A.: Image sharpness assessment based on local phase coherence. IEEE Trans. Image Process. **22**(7), 2798–2810 (2013)
6. He, K., Zhang, X., Ren, S., Sun, J.: Deep residual learning for image recognition. In: 2016 IEEE Conference on Computer Vision and Pattern Recognition (CVPR), pp. 770–778 (2016). https://doi.org/10.1109/CVPR.2016.90
7. Hosseini, M.S., Plataniotis, K.N.: Image sharpness metric based on MaxPol convolution kernels. In: 2018 25th IEEE International Conference on Image Processing (ICIP), pp. 296–300 (2018). https://doi.org/10.1109/ICIP.2018.8451488
8. Hosseini, M.S., Brawley-Hayes, J.A., Zhang, Y., Chan, L., Plataniotis, K.N., Damaskinos, S.: Focus quality assessment of high-throughput whole slide imaging in digital pathology. IEEE Trans. Med. Imaging **39**(1), 62–74 (2019)
9. Hosseini, M.S., Zhang, Y., Plataniotis, K.N.: Encoding visual sensitivity by MaxPol convolution filters for image sharpness assessment. IEEE Trans. Image Process. **28**(9), 4510–4525 (2019)
10. Huang, G., Liu, Z., van der Maaten, L., Weinberger, K.Q.: Densely connected convolutional networks. In: 2017 IEEE Conference on Computer Vision and Pattern Recognition (CVPR), pp. 2261–2269 (2017). https://doi.org/10.1109/CVPR.2017.243
11. Janowczyk, A., Zuo, R., Gilmore, H., Feldman, M., Madabhushi, A.: HistoQC: an open-source quality control tool for digital pathology slides. JCO Clin. Cancer Inform. **3**, 1–7 (2019)
12. Kohlberger, T., et al.: Whole-slide image focus quality: automatic assessment and impact on AI cancer detection. J. Pathol. Inform. **10**, 39 (2019)
13. Leclaire, A., Moisan, L.: No-reference image quality assessment and blind deblurring with sharpness metrics exploiting Fourier phase information. J. Math. Imaging Vis. **52**(1), 145–172 (2015)

14. Li, L., Wu, D., Wu, J., Li, H., Lin, W., Kot, A.C.: Image sharpness assessment by sparse representation. IEEE Trans. Multimedia **18**(6), 1085–1097 (2016)
15. McQuin, C., et al.: CellProfiler 3.0: next-generation image processing for biology. PLoS Biol. **16**(7), e2005970 (2018)
16. Pinkard, H., Phillips, Z., Babakhani, A., Fletcher, D.A., Waller, L.: Deep learning for single-shot autofocus microscopy. Optica **6**(6), 794–797 (2019)
17. Senaras, C., Niazi, M.K.K., Lozanski, G., Gurcan, M.N.: DeepFocus: detection of out-of-focus regions in whole slide digital images using deep learning. PLoS ONE **13**(10), e0205387 (2018)
18. Stacke, K., Eilertsen, G., Unger, J., Lundström, C.: A closer look at domain shift for deep learning in histopathology. arXiv preprint arXiv:1909.11575 (2019)
19. Tomczak, K., Czerwińska, P., Wiznerowicz, M.: The Cancer Genome Atlas (TCGA): an immeasurable source of knowledge. Contemp. Oncol. **19**(1A), A68 (2015)
20. Topol, E.J.: High-performance medicine: the convergence of human and artificial intelligence. Nat. Med. **25**(1), 44–56 (2019)
21. Wang, Z., Athar, S., Wang, Z.: Blind quality assessment of multiply distorted images using deep neural networks. In: Karray, F., Campilho, A., Yu, A. (eds.) ICIAR 2019. LNCS, vol. 11662, pp. 89–101. Springer, Cham (2019). https://doi.org/10.1007/978-3-030-27202-9_8
22. Yang, S.J., et al.: Assessing microscope image focus quality with deep learning. BMC Bioinform. **19**(1), 77 (2018)

Histopathology Image Analysis

Pairwise Relation Learning
for Semi-supervised Gland Segmentation

Yutong Xie[1], Jianpeng Zhang[1], Zhibin Liao[2,3], Johan Verjans[2,3],
Chunhua Shen[2], and Yong Xia[1,4(✉)]

[1] National Engineering Laboratory for Integrated Aero-Space-Ground-Ocean Big
Data Application Technology, School of Computer Science and Engineering,
Northwestern Polytechnical University, Xi'an 710072, China
yxia@nwpu.edu.cn
[2] The University of Adelaide, Adelaide, Australia
[3] South Australian Health and Medical Research Institute, Adelaide, Australia
[4] Research & Development Institute of Northwestern Polytechnical University
in Shenzhen, Shenzhen 518057, China

Abstract. Accurate and automated gland segmentation on histology
tissue images is an essential but challenging task in the computer-aided
diagnosis of adenocarcinoma. Despite their prevalence, deep learning
models always require a myriad number of densely annotated training
images, which are difficult to obtain due to extensive labor and associated expert costs related to histology image annotations. In this paper,
we propose the pairwise relation-based semi-supervised (PRS^2) model for
gland segmentation on histology images. This model consists of a segmentation network (S-Net) and a pairwise relation network (PR-Net). The
S-Net is trained on labeled data for segmentation, and PR-Net is trained
on both labeled and unlabeled data in an unsupervised way to enhance
its image representation ability via exploiting the semantic consistency
between each pair of images in the feature space. Since both networks
share their encoders, the image representation ability learned by PR-Net
can be transferred to S-Net to improve its segmentation performance.
We also design the object-level Dice loss to address the issues caused by
touching glands and combine it with other two loss functions for S-Net.
We evaluated our model against five recent methods on the GlaS dataset
and three recent methods on the CRAG dataset. Our results not only
demonstrate the effectiveness of the proposed PR-Net and object-level
Dice loss, but also indicate that our PRS^2 model achieves the state-of-
the-art gland segmentation performance on both benchmarks.

Keywords: Gland segmentation · Semi-supervised learning · Pairwise
relation learning

Y. Xie and J. Zhang contributed equally to this work. The work was partially done
while the co-first authors were visiting The University of Adelaide.

A. L. Martel et al. (Eds.): MICCAI 2020, LNCS 12265, pp. 417–427, 2020.
https://doi.org/10.1007/978-3-030-59722-1_40

1   Introduction

Quantitative measurement of glands on histology tissue images is an effective means to assist pathologists in diagnosing the malignancy of adenocarcinoma [6]. Manual annotation of glands requires specialized knowledge and intense concentration, and is often time-consuming. Automated gland segmentation avoids many of these issues and provides pathologists an unprecedented ability to reliably characterise and quantify glands. Although being increasingly studied to improve its accuracy, efficiency and objectivity [7,16,19], this task remains challenging mainly due to (1) inadequate training data with pixel-wise dense annotations and (2) small gaps and adhesive edges between adjacent glands.

Currently, most available gland segmentation methods are based on deep convolutional neural networks (DCNNs) [2,7,13,16,18,19]. Chen *et al.* [2] presented a deep contour-aware network that harnesses multi-scale features to separate glands from the background and also employs the complementary information of contours to delineate each gland. Qu et al. [13] proposed a full resolution convolutional neural network to improve the gland localization and introduced a variance constrained cross-entropy loss to advance the shape similarity of glands. Yan et al. [19] developed a shape-aware adversarial learning model for simultaneous gland segmentation and contour detection. Although superior to the performance of previous solutions, the performance of these DCNN-based gland segmentation methods depends heavily on a substantial number of training images with pixel-wise labels, which are difficult to obtain due to the tremendous efforts and costs tied to the dense annotations of histology images.

To alleviate the burden of data annotation, semi-supervised segmentation models have been developed to jointly use labeled and unlabeled data for co-training [17]. Recent semi-supervised learning (SSL) methods are usually based on consistency regularization [12]. Specifically, unlabeled data are exploited according to the smoothness assumption that certain perturbations of an input should not significantly vary the prediction [4,9,10,12,20]. Nevertheless, these methods only measure the consistency between different perturbations of an input image. In fact, different images may contain the same kind of foreground objects (e.g., glands). The objects on two images may share consistent representations in the feature space as long as they have the same semantic label. We advocate that such pairwise consistency should be explored to establish an unsupervised way to learn generalized feature representation from unlabeled data.

In this paper, we propose the pairwise relation-based semi-supervised (PRS^2) model for gland segmentation on histology tissue images. This model is composed of a supervised segmentation network (S-Net) and an unsupervised pairwise relation network (PR-Net). The PR-Net is trained to boost its ability to learn both semantic consistency and image representation via exploiting the semantic consistency between each pair of images in the feature space. Since the encoders of S-Net and PR-Net share parameters, the ability learned by PR-Net can be transferred to S-Net to improve its segmentation performance. Meanwhile, we employ the object-level Dice loss to impose additional constraints on each individual gland, and thus addresses the issues caused by touching glands. The

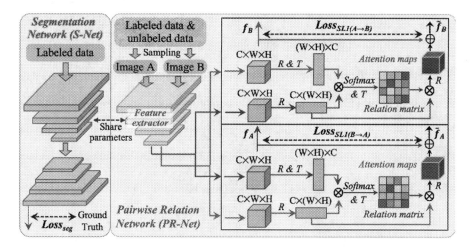

Fig. 1. Diagram of the proposed PRS^2 model.

object-level Dice was originally proposed in [14] as a performance metric, but not as a loss function. We transform it as a loss and combine this loss with the pixel-level cross-entropy loss and global-level Dice loss to form a multi-level loss for S-Net. We evaluate the proposed PRS^2 model on the GlaS Challenge dataset and CRAG dataset and achieve superior performance over several recently published gland segmentation models.

The contributions include: (1) proposing the pairwise relation interaction to exploit the semantic consistency between each pair of images in the feature space, enabling the model to learn semantic consistency and image representation in an unsupervised way; (2) transforming the object-level Dice evaluation metric as a loss and employing it to address the issues caused by touching glands; and (3) constructing the PRS^2 model that achieves the state-of-the-art gland segmentation performance on two benchmarks.

2   Method

The proposed PRS^2 model has two major modules: the S-Net for supervised gland segmentation and PR-Net for unsupervised semantic relation learning (see Fig. 1). Let the labeled training set with M images be denoted by $\boldsymbol{X}^L$, the unlabeled training set with N images be denoted by $\boldsymbol{X}^U$, and the whole training image set be denoted by $\boldsymbol{X} = \boldsymbol{X}^L \cup \boldsymbol{X}^U$. The pipeline of this model can be summarized in two steps. First, the S-Net is trained on $\boldsymbol{X}^L$ for an initialization. Since the encoders of both networks share the same architecture and parameters, the encoders PR-Net is also initialized in this step. Then, both the S-Net and the PR-Net are jointly fine-tuned on $\boldsymbol{X}$ with the parameter-sharing mechanism.

S-Net: We use the DeepLabv3+ model [3] pretrained on PASCAL VOC 2012 dataset [5] as S-Net. To adapt DeepLabv3+ to our task, we replace the last convolutional layer, which is task specific, with a convolutional layer that contains two output neurons to predict glands and background. The weights in this layer are randomly initialized, and the activation is set to the softmax function.

We design the following multi-level segmentation loss $\mathcal{L}_{seg}$ for S-Net, defined as follows

$$\mathcal{L}_{seg} = \mathcal{L}_{ce} + \mathcal{L}_{Dice} + \mathcal{L}_{objDice}, \tag{1}$$

where $\mathcal{L}_{ce}$ is the cross-entropy loss that optimizes pixel-level accuracy, $\mathcal{L}_{Dice}$ is the Dice loss that optimizes the overlap between the prediction and ground truth, and $\mathcal{L}_{objDice}$ is the object-level Dice loss. Combining the first two losses is commonly used in many medical image segmentation applications and achieves remarkable success [15, 21]. However, gland segmentation requires not only to segment the glands from background, but also to separate each individual gland from others. The latter requirement is quite challenging due to the existence of touching glands. To address this challenge, we propose the object-level Dice loss as follows

$$\mathcal{L}_{objDice} = \frac{1}{2} \left[\sum_{i=1}^{n} \frac{|\boldsymbol{S}_i|}{\sum_{k=1}^{n} |\boldsymbol{S}_k|} \mathcal{L}_{Dice}(\boldsymbol{G}_i, \boldsymbol{S}_i) + \sum_{j=1}^{m} \frac{|\tilde{\boldsymbol{G}}_j|}{\sum_{k=1}^{m} |\tilde{\boldsymbol{G}}_k|} \mathcal{L}_{Dice}(\tilde{\boldsymbol{G}}_j, \tilde{\boldsymbol{S}}_j) \right], \tag{2}$$

where $\boldsymbol{S}_i$ is the ith segmented gland, $\boldsymbol{G}_i$ is the ground truth gland that maximally overlaps $\boldsymbol{S}_i$, $\tilde{\boldsymbol{G}}_j$ is the jth ground truth gland, and $\tilde{\boldsymbol{S}}_j$ is the segmented gland that maximally overlaps $\tilde{\boldsymbol{G}}_j$. The m and n denote the total number of ground truth glands and segmented glands for an input image, respectively. In this definition, the first term measures how well each segmented gland overlaps its corresponding ground truth, whereas the second term measures how well each ground truth gland overlaps its corresponding segmented gland. This loss function considers the instance-level discrepancy between a segmentation result and its ground truth, and thus is able to help S-Net learn more discriminatory feature representations for gland segmentation.

PR-Net: The PR-Net exploits the semantic consistency between each pair of images for unsupervised pairwise relation learning. It is a composition of three modules: (1) an image pair input layer, (2) an encoder $\mathcal{F}(\cdot)$ for feature extraction, and (3) a pairwise relation module (PRM). The input layer accepts a pair of images $(\boldsymbol{x}_A, \boldsymbol{x}_B)$, which are randomly sampled from the whole training set $\boldsymbol{X}$, as input. The encoder shares the identical architecture and parameters with the encoder of S-Net (i.e., modified aligned Xception), whose output can be formally presented as follows

$$\boldsymbol{f}_A = \mathcal{F}(\boldsymbol{x}_A; \boldsymbol{\Theta}) \in \mathbb{R}^{C \times H \times W}, \boldsymbol{f}_B = \mathcal{F}(\boldsymbol{x}_B; \boldsymbol{\Theta}) \in \mathbb{R}^{C \times H \times W}, \tag{3}$$

where $\boldsymbol{\Theta}$ denotes the parameters of the encoder, and C, H and W denote respectively the number of channels, height, and width of the encoded feature representation.

The PRM is proposed to highlight the targets of the same semantic class but located on two images. To this end, we first calculate the consistency relation matrix $\mathbb{C}$ from $\boldsymbol{f}_B$ to $\boldsymbol{f}_A$ as follows

$$\mathbb{C}_{B \rightarrow A} = \text{softmax}(R(\boldsymbol{f}_A)^T \cdot R(\boldsymbol{f}_B))^T \in \mathbb{R}^{(H \times W) \times (H \times W)}, \tag{4}$$

where $R(\cdot)$ represents a reshape function which collapses the H and W dimensions into a single dimension with $H \times W$ elements, and the softmax function normalizes the elements in the second dimension. The $\mathbb{C}_{(B \rightarrow A)_{i,j}}$ measures the consistency ith flattened 'pixel' (in the feature representation space) of $\boldsymbol{f}_B$ to jth 'pixel' of $\boldsymbol{f}_A$, where a larger $\mathbb{C}_{(B \rightarrow A)_{i,j}}$ indicates a higher semantic consistency between these two 'pixels'.

Next, we perform a matrix multiplication between $R(\boldsymbol{f}_B)$ and $\mathbb{C}_{B \rightarrow A}$ to obtain the attention map $\mathbb{M}$ of $\boldsymbol{f}_A$, formulated as

$$\mathbb{M}_A = R^{-1}\big(R(\boldsymbol{f}_B) \cdot \mathbb{C}_{B \rightarrow A}\big) \in \mathbb{R}^{C \times H \times W}, \tag{5}$$

where R^{-1} is a reverse operation of R, each element in $\mathbb{M}_A$ can be considered as a weighted sum of $\boldsymbol{f}_B$ over all positions, where the weights are determined by $\mathbb{C}_{B \rightarrow A}$. Finally, we add $\mathbb{M}_A$ to the feature map $\boldsymbol{f}_A$ via an element-wise summation to obtain the target-highlighted feature maps $\tilde{\boldsymbol{f}}_A$, show as follows

$$\tilde{\boldsymbol{f}}_A = \mathbb{M}_A + \boldsymbol{f}_A, \tag{6}$$

Similarly, the $\tilde{\boldsymbol{f}}_B$ can be calculated as

$$\tilde{\boldsymbol{f}}_B = \mathbb{M}_B + \boldsymbol{f}_B, \tag{7}$$

Both target-highlighted feature maps $\tilde{\boldsymbol{f}}_A$ and $\tilde{\boldsymbol{f}}_B$ have the merit of consistency relation information between $\boldsymbol{f}_A$ and $\boldsymbol{f}_B$, and thus can serve as the targets of PR-Net to enforce the model to increase the semantic consistency for any pair of image feature maps. Hence, the loss function of PR-Net can be expressed as

$$\mathcal{L}_{PR} = \underbrace{\mathcal{L}_{SL1}\Big(\sigma(\tilde{\boldsymbol{f}}_A), \sigma(\boldsymbol{f}_A)\Big)}_{\mathcal{L}_{SL1}(B \rightarrow A)} + \underbrace{\mathcal{L}_{SL1}\Big(\sigma(\tilde{\boldsymbol{f}}_B), \sigma(\boldsymbol{f}_B)\Big)}_{\mathcal{L}_{SL1}(A \rightarrow B)}, \tag{8}$$

where $\mathcal{L}_{SL1}$ is the smooth $L1$ loss, and $\sigma(\cdot)$ is the sigmoid function. Both $\tilde{\boldsymbol{f}}_A$ and $\tilde{\boldsymbol{f}}_B$, served as the target signals, do not perform back-propagation in each iteration. We also randomly select a pair of images and visualize their corresponding channel-wise sum of $\sigma(\boldsymbol{f})$ as well as $\sigma(\tilde{\boldsymbol{f}})$ in Fig. 2 to show the superiority of $\tilde{\boldsymbol{f}}$.

Optimization of PRS² Model: the total loss of the proposed PRS² model is defined as the weighted sum of multi-level segmentation loss $\mathcal{L}_{seg}$ and unsupervised semantic consistency loss $\mathcal{L}_{PR}$ such that

$$\mathcal{L}_{total} = \mathcal{L}_{seg} + \alpha \mathcal{L}_{PR}, \tag{9}$$

where α is a weighting factor that controls the contribution of unsupervised loss and is empirically set to 0.05. We adopt the Adam algorithm [11] with a batch

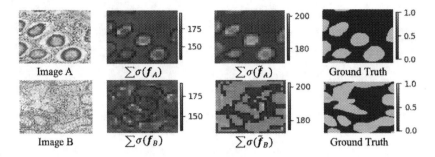

Fig. 2. A pair of images and the corresponding channel-wise sum of $\sigma(f)$ and $\sigma(\tilde{f})$

size of 5 and 10 to train S-Net and PR-Net, respectively, and also set 20% of the training set as a validation set to monitor the performance of both networks. The initial learning rate is set to 1e−4 in the initialization step and 5e−5 in the fine-tuning step.

3   Experiments and Results

Materials: We adopted the 2015 MICCAI Gland Segmentation (GlaS) challenge dataset [14] and colorectal adenocarcinoma gland (CRAG) dataset [1,7] to evaluate the proposed PRS^2 model. The GlaS dataset contains 85 training and 80 test images (60 in Part A; 20 in Part B). The CRAG dataset has 173 training and 40 test images. When evaluating PRS^2 on the GlaS test set, the CRAG training set was considered as unlabeled training data, and vice versa.

Evaluation Metrics: On the GlaS dataset, three metrics officially suggested by the GlaS Challenge [14] were calculated to assess the segmentation performance, including the object-level Dice (Obj-D) that represents the accuracy of delineating each individual gland, the object-level F1 score (Obj-F) that evaluates the accuracy of detecting each gland, and the object-level Hausdorff distance (Obj-H) that measures the shape similarity between each segmented gland and its ground truth. Meanwhile, all competing segmentation models were ranked according to each of these three metrics, and the sum of three ranking scores is calculated to measure the overall performance of each model. Note that a lower ranking score indicates better segmentation performance.

Implementation Details: In the training stage, we followed the suggestion in [16] to randomly crop patches from each training image as the input of both S-Net and PR-Net. The patch size was set to 416×416 on the GlaS dataset and 512×512 on the CRAG dataset. When training PRS^2 model, we resized CRAG patches to 416×416 if the labelled samples are from GlaS dataset, or resized GlaS patches to 512×512 if the labelled samples are from CRAG dataset. To further enlarge the training dataset, we employed the online data augmentation,

Table 1. Gland segmentation performance of the proposed PRS^2 model and recently published models on both GlaS and CRAG datasets. M and R denote metric value and ranking score, respectively. Note that the performance on the GlaS dataset is the average performance on test data part A and part B

Datasets	Methods	Obj-D		Obj-F		Obj-H		Rank sum
		M (%)	R	M (%)	R	M	R	
GlaS dataset	DCAN	83.9	8	81.4	8	102.9	8	24
	MILD-Net	87.5	6	87.9	5	73.7	6	17
	SADL	87.3	7	88.9	3	76.7	7	17
	Rota-Net	88.4	5	87.2	6	68.4	5	16
	FullNet	88.5	4	88.9	3	63.0	4	11
	DSE	89.9	2	**89.4**	1	55.9	2	5
	SS	89.6	3	86.9	7	62.8	3	13
	Our PRS^2	**90.6**	1	89.0	2	**55.1**	1	**4**
CRAG dataset	DCAN	79.4	5	73.6	5	218.8	5	15
	MILD-Net	87.5	4	82.5	3	160.1	4	11
	DSE	88.9	2	83.5	2	120.1	2	6
	SS	87.6	3	81.6	4	145.0	3	10
	Our PRS^2	**89.2**	1	**84.3**	1	**113.1**	1	**3**

which includes random rotation, shear, shift, zooming, and horizontal/vertical flip, and color normalization. In the test stage, test time augmentations including cropping, horizontal/vertical flip and rotation, were also utilized to improve the robustness of segmentation. As a result, each segmentation result is the average of the results obtained on the original image and its three types of augmented copies. Moreover, the morphological opening using a square structure element with a size of 10×10 was finally performed to smooth segmentation results.

Results on Two Datasets: On the GlaS dataset, we compared the proposed PRS^2 model to five recently published gland segmentation models, including the deep contour-aware network (DCAN) [2], the minimal information loss dilated network (MILD-Net) [7], the shape-aware adversarial learning (SADL) model [19], the rotation equivariant network (Rota-Net) [8], the full resolution convolutional neural network (FullNet) [13], and the deep segmentation-emendation (DSE) model [16]. On the CRAG dataset, we compared our model to three models, i.e., DCAN, MILD-Net, and DSE. The performance of these models was given in Table 1. Note that the performance of all competing models was adopted in the literature, and the performance on the GlaS dataset is the average performance on test data part A and part B. Finally, we also compared our model to a typical semi-supervised (SS) method on both datasets, i.e., using a trained S-Net to generate segmentation predictions of unlabelled data and using a CRF-like approach to generate the proxy labels for fine-tuning the S-Net.

It shows that our model achieves the highest Obj-D, second highest Obj-F, and lowest Obj-H on the GlaS dataset. Comparing to the DSE model that performs the second best, our model improves the Obj-D by 0.7% and the Obj-H by 0.8. On the CRAG dataset, it reveals that our model achieves the highest Obj-D, highest Obj-F, and lowest Obj-H, improving the Obj-D, Obj-F and Obj-H from 88.9%, 83.5% and 120.1, which were achieved by the second best model, to 89.2%, 84.3% and 113.1, respectively. The results on both datasets indicate that the proposed PRS^2 model is able to produce more accurate for segmentation of glands and its performance is relatively robust.

4 Discusses

Trade-Off Between Labeled and Unlabeled Data: A major advantage of our PRS^2 model is to use the unlabeled images to facilitate model training, leading to (1) less requirement of densely annotated training data or (2) improved segmentation performance when the labeled training dataset is small. To validate this, we kept the test set and unlabeled training set unchanged and randomly selected 20% and 50% labeled training images, respectively, to perform the segmentation experiments on both datasets again. As a control, we also used those selected labeled training images to train S-Net in a fully-supervised manner. The segmentation performance of our PRS^2 model and S-Net was shown in Fig. 3, from which three conclusions can be drawn. First, the segmentation performance of both models improves as the number of labeled training images increases. Second, using both labeled the unlabeled images, our model outperforms the fully-supervised S-Net steadily no matter how many labeled training images were used. More important, it is interesting that our model trained with 50% labeled images can achieve a comparable performance with the fully-supervised S-Net trained with 100% training data on both datasets. Similarly, it reveals that our model trained with 20% labeled images can achieve a comparable performance with the S-Net trained with 50% training data. It suggests that our model provides the possibility of using unlabeled data to replace almost half of labeled training images while maintaining the segmentation performance.

Multi-level Segmentation Loss: To demonstrate the performance gain resulted from the proposed multi-level segmentation loss, we also attempted to train the S-Net with different loss functions, including $\mathcal{L}_{Dice}$, $\mathcal{L}_{ce}$ and $\mathcal{L}_{Dice}+\mathcal{L}_{ce}$. The results in Table 2 reveals that (1) using the combination of Dice and cross-entropy loss can produce higher Obj-F than using the Dice loss or cross-entropy loss alone, and (2) the superior performance of our multi-level loss over the combination of Dice and cross-entropy loss confirms the effectiveness of using the object-level Dice loss to pose constraints to each individual gland.

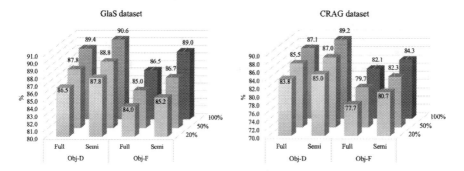

Fig. 3. Obj-D and Obj-F values achieved on two datasets by our semi-supervised PRS^2 model and fully-supervised S-Net, when 20%, 50% and 100% labeled training images

Table 2. Gland segmentation performance of S-Net obtained on two datasets when using different loss functions

Loss functions	GlaS dataset			CRAG dataset		
	Obj-D	Obj-F	Obj-H	Obj-D	Obj-F	Obj-H
$\mathcal{L}_{Dice}$	86.5	86.2	75.3	84.7	78.9	174.9
$\mathcal{L}_{ce}$	88.4	86.1	65.5	86.7	77.8	139.5
$\mathcal{L}_{ce} + \mathcal{L}_{Dice}$	88.7	86.0	66.5	86.3	80.3	157.3
$\mathcal{L}_{ce} + \mathcal{L}_{Dice} + \mathcal{L}_{objDice}$ (**Ours**)	**89.4**	**86.5**	**64.1**	**87.1**	**82.1**	**138.6**

Complexity: Two parameter-sharing DCNNs in our PRS^2 model are trained using the open source Pytorch software packages. In our experiments, it took about 12 h to train our PRS^2 model (2 h for the initialization step and 10 h for the fine-tuning step) and less than 1 s to segment each test image on a server with 4 NVIDIA GTX 2080 Ti GPUs and 128 GB Memory.

5   Conclusion

In this paper, we propose the PRS^2 model for gland segmentation on histology tissue images, which consists of a supervised segmentation network with a newly designed loss and an unsupervised PR-Net that boosts its image representation ability via exploiting the semantic consistency between each pair of images in the feature space. Our results indicate that this model outperforms five recent methods on the GlaS dataset and three recent methods on the CRAG dataset. Our ablation study suggests the effectiveness of proposed loss and PR-Net. Although our model is built upon the specific application of gland segmentation, the pairwise relation-based semi-supervised strategy itself is generic and can potentially be applied to other deep model-based medical image segmentation tasks to reduce the requirement of densely annotated training images.

Acknowledgment. Yutong Xie, Jianpeng Zhang, and Yong Xia were supported in part by the National Natural Science Foundation of China under Grants 61771397, in part by the Science and Technology Innovation Committee of Shenzhen Municipality, China, under Grants JCYJ20180306171334997, and in part by Innovation Foundation for Doctor Dissertation of Northwestern Polytechnical University under Grants CX202010.

References

1. Awan, R., et al.: Glandular morphometrics for objective grading of colorectal adenocarcinoma histology images. Sci. Rep. **7**(1), 16852 (2017)

2. Chen, H., Qi, X., Yu, L., Heng, P.A.: DCAN: deep contour-aware networks for accurate gland segmentation. In: IEEE International Conference on Computer Vision (ICCV), pp. 2487–2496 (2016)

3. Chen, L.-C., Zhu, Y., Papandreou, G., Schroff, F., Adam, H.: Encoder-decoder with atrous separable convolution for semantic image segmentation. In: Ferrari, V., Hebert, M., Sminchisescu, C., Weiss, Y. (eds.) ECCV 2018. LNCS, vol. 11211, pp. 833–851. Springer, Cham (2018). https://doi.org/10.1007/978-3-030-01234-2_49

4. Cui, W., et al.: Semi-supervised brain lesion segmentation with an adapted mean teacher model. In: Chung, A.C.S., Gee, J.C., Yushkevich, P.A., Bao, S. (eds.) IPMI 2019. LNCS, vol. 11492, pp. 554–565. Springer, Cham (2019). https://doi.org/10.1007/978-3-030-20351-1_43

5. Everingham, M., Van Gool, L., Williams, C.K., Winn, J., Zisserman, A.: The pascal visual object classes (VOC) challenge. Int. J. Comput. Vision **88**(2), 303–338 (2010)

6. Gazdar, A., Maitra, A.: Adenocarcinomas. In: Brenner, S., Miller, J.H. (eds.) Encyclopedia of Genetics, pp. 9–12. Academic Press, New York (2001). https://doi.org/10.1006/rwgn.2001.1540. http://www.sciencedirect.com/science/article/pii/B0122270800015408

7. Graham, S., et al.: MILD-Net: minimal information loss dilated network for gland instance segmentation in colon histology images. Med. Image Anal. **52**, 199–211 (2019)

8. Graham, S., Epstein, D., Rajpoot, N.: Rota-Net: rotation equivariant network for simultaneous gland and lumen segmentation in colon histology images. In: Reyes-Aldasoro, C.C., Janowczyk, A., Veta, M., Bankhead, P., Sirinukunwattana, K. (eds.) ECDP 2019. LNCS, vol. 11435, pp. 109–116. Springer, Cham (2019). https://doi.org/10.1007/978-3-030-23937-4_13

9. Jeong, J., Lee, S., Kim, J., Kwak, N.: Consistency-based semi-supervised learning for object detection. In: Advances in Neural Information Processing Systems (NeurIPS), pp. 10758–10767 (2019)

10. Ke, Z., Wang, D., Yan, Q., Ren, J., Lau, R.W.: Dual student: breaking the limits of the teacher in semi-supervised learning. In: IEEE International Conference on Computer Vision (ICCV), pp. 6728–6736 (2019)

11. Kingma, D.P., Ba, J.: Adam: a method for stochastic optimization. In: International Conference on Learning Representations (ICLR) (2015)

12. Oliver, A., Odena, A., Raffel, C.A., Cubuk, E.D., Goodfellow, I.: Realistic evaluation of deep semi-supervised learning algorithms. In: Advances in Neural Information Processing Systems (NeurIPS), pp. 3235–3246 (2018)

13. Qu, H., Yan, Z., Riedlinger, G.M., De, S., Metaxas, D.N.: Improving nuclei/gland instance segmentation in histopathology images by full resolution neural network and spatial constrained loss. In: Shen, W., et al. (eds.) MICCAI 2019. LNCS, vol. 11764, pp. 378–386. Springer, Cham (2019). https://doi.org/10.1007/978-3-030-32239-7_42

14. Sirinukunwattana, K., et al.: Gland segmentation in colon histology images: the glas challenge contest. Med. Image Anal. **35**, 489–502 (2017)

15. Wong, K.C.L., Moradi, M., Tang, H., Syeda-Mahmood, T.: 3D segmentation with exponential logarithmic loss for highly unbalanced object sizes. In: Frangi, A.F., Schnabel, J.A., Davatzikos, C., Alberola-López, C., Fichtinger, G. (eds.) MICCAI 2018. LNCS, vol. 11072, pp. 612–619. Springer, Cham (2018). https://doi.org/10.1007/978-3-030-00931-1_70

16. Xie, Y., Lu, H., Zhang, J., Shen, C., Xia, Y.: Deep segmentation-emendation model for gland instance segmentation. In: Shen, D., et al. (eds.) MICCAI 2019. LNCS, vol. 11764, pp. 469–477. Springer, Cham (2019). https://doi.org/10.1007/978-3-030-32239-7_52

17. Xie, Y., Zhang, J., Xia, Y.: Semi-supervised adversarial model for benign-malignant lung nodule classification on chest CT. Med. Image Anal. **57**, 237–248 (2019)

18. Xu, Y., et al.: Gland instance segmentation using deep multichannel neural networks. IEEE Trans. Biomed. Eng. **64**(12), 2901–2912 (2017)

19. Yan, Z., Yang, X., Cheng, K.: Enabling a single deep learning model for accurate gland instance segmentation: a shape-aware adversarial learning framework. IEEE Trans. Med. Imaging 1 (2020). https://doi.org/10.1109/TMI.2020.2966594

20. Zhai, X., Oliver, A., Kolesnikov, A., Beyer, L.: S4L: self-supervised semi-supervised learning. In: IEEE International Conference on Computer Vision (ICCV), pp. 1476–1485 (2019)

21. Zhang, J., Xie, Y., Zhang, P., Chen, H., Xia, Y., Shen, C.: Light-weight hybrid convolutional network for liver tumour segmentation. In: International Joint Conference on Artificial Intelligence (IJCAI), pp. 10–16 (2019)

Ranking-Based Survival Prediction on Histopathological Whole-Slide Images

Donglin Di[1] , Shengrui Li[1] , Jun Zhang[2] , and Yue Gao[1(✉)]

[1] BNRist, THUIBCS, KLISS, School of Software, Tsinghua University,
Beijing, China
gaoyue@tsinghua.edu.cn
[2] Tencent AI Lab, Shenzhen, Guangdong, China

Abstract. Survival prediction for patients based on gigapixel histopathological whole-slide images (WSIs) has attracted increasing attention in recent years. Previous studies mainly focus on the framework of predicting the survival hazard scores based on one individual WSI for each patient directly. These prediction methods ignore the relative survival differences among patients, *i.e.*, the ranking information, which is important for a regression task. Under such circumstances, we propose a ranking-based survival prediction method on WSIs – RankSurv, which takes the ranking information into consideration during the learning process. First, a hypergraph representation is introduced to conduct hazard prediction on each WSI respectively, which is able to learn the high-order correlation among different patches in the WSI. Then, a ranking-based prediction process is conducted using pairwise survival data. Experiments are conducted on three public carcinoma datasets (*i.e.*, LUSC, GBM, and NLST). Quantitative results show that the proposed method significantly outperforms state-of-the-art methods on all three datasets, which demonstrates the effectiveness of the proposed ranking-based survival prediction framework.

Keywords: Survival prediction · WSI · Ranking · Hypergraph

1 Introduction

In recent years, survival prediction on gigapixel histopathological whole-slide images (WSIs) [22] has become a hot task in the medical imaging field [14,19–21]. This task aims at modeling the survival duration, which elapses from the beginning of follow-up to a certain event of interest (*e.g.*, biological death) that occurs, directly from histopathological WSIs.

Previous studies mainly address the survival prediction task by conducting a regression model on the WSI for each patient directly [14,19,20], while ignoring the relative ranking order among these patients. Besides the prediction on each individual data directly, it is noted that the ranking order plays an even more important role when comparing different data [1]. The ranking order information

© Springer Nature Switzerland AG 2020
A. L. Martel et al. (Eds.): MICCAI 2020, LNCS 12265, pp. 428–438, 2020.
https://doi.org/10.1007/978-3-030-59722-1_41

among the group is more essential to differentiate the targets compared with the single values for each individual.

The key challenges lie in two aspects. First, how to better represent the WSI targeting on hazard prediction based on single WSI directly. Second, how to incorporate the ranking order information in the survival prediction process.

To tackle the above issues, we propose a ranking-based survival prediction method on WSIs – RankSurv, which takes the ranking information into consideration during the learning process. First, a hypergraph representation is introduced to conduct hazard prediction on each WSI respectively, which is able to learn the high-order correlation among different patches in the WSI. Then, a ranking-based prediction process is conducted using pairwise survival data.

We have conducted experiments on three public medical datasets (*i.e.*, LUSC, GBM, and NLST). Experimental results and comparisons show that our method achieves significant and consistent improvement compared with state-of-the-art methods.

The main contributions of this paper are summarized as follows:

- Different from traditional survival prediction methods using individual WSI, we propose a ranking-based survival prediction framework, which can take the ranking order information into consideration and lead to better performance.
- To better investigate each WSI, we propose a hypergraph representation method for hazard prediction on one WSI, which is able to learn the high-order correlation among different patches in the WSI.
- The proposed method consistently outperforms state-of-the-art methods by a large margin. Specifically, it achieves the prediction accuracy of 66.08%, 66.27%, and 68.20% on the C-index metric, which are respectively, 5.98%, 7.49% and 7.33% relative improvements on the LUSC, GBM, and NLST datasets over the state-of-the-art.

2 Ranking-Based Survival Prediction

As shown in Fig. 1, we design a framework called Ranking-based Survival Prediction Network (RankSurv), which consists of three stages: "Preprocessing", "Hazard prediction using hypergraph representation" and "Survival rank prediction" to predict the survival hazard score as well as pairwise ranking results in an end-to-end manner. The first stage extracts raw patch-level features of patches sampled from the input original WSI data. After that, we feed the patch-level features to the hazard prediction stage based on a hypergraph regression model to fine-tune the representation and predict the hazard score. Finally, we design a ranking-specific back-propagation mechanism to take advantage of the supervision from pairwise ranking loss. We will go through each step in detail.

2.1 Preprocessing

Given a set of WSIs from M patients with their corresponding labels, *i.e.* the input data can be represented as: $\mathbb{D}_{in} = \{C_1, C_2, ..., C_M\}, M \geq 2$,

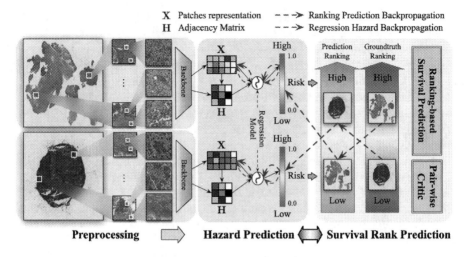

Fig. 1. Pipeline of our Ranking-based Survival Prediction Network (RankSurv). Firstly, we sample patches from the raw images and utilize a backbone model to extract raw patch-level features. Then the hypergraph signal matrix $\mathbf{X}$ and the hyperedges incidence matrix $\mathbf{H}$ are generated. After training by several hypergraph spectral convolutional layers, the regression module leverages the representation and masters the skills to predict the risk of given WSIs. In addition to the hazard prediction back-propagation, the third stage further fine-tunes the pairwise ranking and reach better representation and performance.

$C_i = \langle I_i, t_i, \delta_i \rangle, i \in [1, M]$, where I_i stands for the i_{th} image, t_i and δ_i indicate the observation time and survival status, respectively. The observation time t_i is either a survival time (T_{event}) or a right-censored time (T_{censor}) for each case. The δ_i represents the survival status for the i_{th} patient in a binary value, where 1 represents the uncensored case, and 0 represents the censored case.

The first stage of the framework extracts the base visual features from a given $\mathbb{D}_{in}$. We randomly sample K (*e.g.*, 2000) patches from each of the images after scaling-down, masking, splitting informative tissues or cells by adopting the OTSU algorithm [16], which could avoid certain noise regions like blood, blank or erosion. Then, the primary patch-level visual features $X = \{x_1, x_2, ..., x_M\}, x_i \in \mathbb{R}^{K \times F}$ are generated by the backbone pre-trained model from ImageNet [17], where x_i denotes the i_{th} case's feature map, and the F denotes the length of each patch feature vector. This preprocessing strategy is motivated by [22], and the raw features extracted from the pre-trained model have already verified to be suitable for the stratification of intricate tissue patterns [2].

2.2 Hazard Prediction Using Hypergraph Representation

As shown in Fig. 1, we feed the raw patch representation X, extracted from the former preprocessing, to predict the survival hazard score. There are several choices to learn the fine-tuned survival-specific representation, such as CNN-based model [22], GCN-based model [14] and FCN-based model [19]. In addition to these baselines above, we further propose to utilize the hypergraph structure [6,7,10] to represent the hierarchy information. The strategy of the hypergraph spectral convolution layer in our hazard prediction stage plays a crucial role in the training process. Since there is no unique mathematical definition of translation on the hypergraph from the *spatial* perspective, we propose the *spectral* hypergraph convolution for survival prediction basing on [6]. The hypergraph consists of N hyperedges, and each hyperedge associates $\mathcal{K}$ entries constructed by the K-nearest neighbor method with the Euclidean distance, and the nodes in which are set to 1 and others are 0, so the incidence matrix $\mathbf{H} \in \mathbb{R}^{\mathbf{N} \times \mathbf{k}}$ is built. The hyperedge provides an aisle that enables the most similar $\mathcal{K}$ patches to be integrated and homogenized so that the hierarchy grouping pattern could be learned beyond pairwise graph structure. Figure 1 illustrates that a spectral convolution layer is fed with two matrices, a node feature matrix $\mathbf{X}$ and a hypergraph incidence matrix $\mathbf{H}$. The hypergraph convolutional layer is illustrated briefly in the formulation 1:

$$\mathbf{X}^{(l+1)} = \sigma \left(\mathbf{D}_v^{-1/2} \mathbf{H} \mathbf{W} \mathbf{D}_e^{-1} \mathbf{H}^\top \mathbf{D}_v^{-1/2} \mathbf{X}^{(l)} \mathbf{\Theta}^{(l)} \right) \tag{1}$$

where $\mathbf{X}^{(l)} \in \mathbb{R}^{\mathbf{N} \times \mathbf{C}}$ is a signal with N nodes and C dimensions that fed in layer l, $\mathbf{X}^{(l+1)}$ is the output of layer l, σ denotes the nonlinear activation function like $ReLU(\cdot)$, and $\mathbf{\Theta}^{(l)}$ denotes a learnable parameter in the layer l. After several layers of spectral convolution, the N hyperedges could stand for the N patterns of pathogenic factors. The final learned patch-level features $\mathbf{X_n} \in \mathbb{R}^{\mathbf{N} \times \mathbf{C_n}}$ are obtained for survival prediction. After squeezing $\mathbf{X_n}$ into $X \in \mathbb{R}^{1 \times C_n}$, the first-step survival hazard score can be predicted temporally using a fully connected layer. And the back-propagation process of regression hazard scale is supervised by the observation time t_i (denoted as the blue dotted arrow).

2.3   Survival Rank Prediction

The most insightful module in our framework is the last but vital stage, *i.e.*, supervising the back-propagation of ranking prediction at a higher level. The situation that the model cannot distinguish two close cases is the most likely reason causing the mistake of comparison. We here introduce a Bayesian-based strategy, called Bayesian Concordance Readjust (BCR), to further fine-tune the ranking prediction. Let $\mathcal{H}_i$ and $\mathcal{H}_j$ denote the hazard scores of i_{th} and j_{th} cases from $\mathbb{D}_{in}$, and $\widehat{\mathcal{H}}_i$, $\widehat{\mathcal{H}}_j$ denote their corresponding predicted hazard scores, respectively. Note that the fine-tuned feature maps $\mathcal{F}_i$ and $\mathcal{F}_j$ generated from the second hazard prediction stage. The basic Concordance index (C-index) [9] is widely adopted as a measure of goodness of fit for binary outcomes in a logistic regression model, and defined as follows:

$$\mathcal{C}_{index}(\mathbb{D}_{in}) = \frac{1}{\mathcal{M}} \sum_{i:\delta_i=1} \sum_{j:T_i<T_j} \mathcal{I}[(T_i, X_i) < (T_j, X_j)] \tag{2}$$

where $\mathcal{M}$ is the number of comparable pairs, $\mathcal{I}[.]$ denotes the indicator function, and T is the actual observation. The value of C-index ranges from 0 to 1 and the larger C-index value means the better prediction performance of the model and vice versa. Specifically, 0 is the worst condition, 1 is the best, and 0.5 is the value as a random guess. Note that the indicator matrix of C-index has a unique characteristic, as illustrated in the following formulation 3:

$$\mathcal{I}(X_i, X_j) + \mathcal{I}(X_j, X_i) = 1 \tag{3}$$

which means the target function for this task has to fit this characteristic, *i.e.*, $F(X_i, X_j) = 1 - F(X_j, X_i)$.

Different from this standard calculation process, we design the Bayesian optimization criterion to make the concordance index learnable and supervisable. The purpose of formulation is trying to maximize the pairwise ranking for all cases, *i.e.*, maximizing the $P(\Theta|\mathbb{D}_{in})$, in the formulation 4.

$$P(\Theta|\widetilde{\mathbb{D}_{in}}) = \frac{P(\Theta)P(\widetilde{\mathbb{D}_{in}}|\Theta)}{P(\widetilde{\mathbb{D}_{in}})} \propto P(\Theta)P(\widetilde{\mathbb{D}_{in}}|\Theta) := \widetilde{\mathcal{I}(\mathbb{D}_{in})} \tag{4}$$

where Θ represents the parameter vector of the prediction model, and $\widetilde{\mathbb{D}_{in}}$ denotes the latent representations for input data $\mathbb{D}_{in}$. The WSI prediction and ranking in each pair of data are independent with each other. Therefore, the purpose of the model is rewritten to optimize the following formulation 5:

$$\mathcal{C}_{index}(\mathbb{D}_{in}) = \mathcal{I}(\mathbb{D}_{in}) \odot \widetilde{\mathcal{I}(\mathbb{D}_{in})} \tag{5}$$

The above survival-specific likelihood function $P(\widetilde{\mathbb{D}_{in}}|\Theta)$ can be calculated as the formulation 6.

$$P(\widetilde{\mathbb{D}_{in}}|\Theta) := \sum_{i,j \in \mathbb{D}_{in}} F(i,j) \tag{6}$$

And the target function F is defined as follows:

$$F(i,j) = \delta(\widehat{X_{ij}}(\Theta)), \delta(x) := \frac{1}{1 + e^{-x}} \tag{7}$$

where $\widehat{X_{ij}}(\Theta)$ can be any anti-symmetric operation satisfying $\widehat{X_{ij}}(\Theta) = -\widehat{X_{ji}}(\Theta)$. In our model, $\widehat{X_{ij}}(\Theta) := \mathbb{W} \cdot (X_i(\Theta) - X_j(\Theta))^T$, where $\mathbb{W}^{1 \times C_n}$ is a linear weight vector and $X_i(\Theta) \in \mathbb{R}^{1 \times C_n}$ is the squeezed output from the last layer. And the other component is a general prior density $P(\Theta)$, following a normal distribution with zero mean and variance-covariance matrix Σ_Θ:

$$P(\Theta) \sim N(0, \Sigma_\Theta) \tag{8}$$

Therefore, the BCR loss function is designed as

$$Loss = -\log\left(\delta(\mathbb{W} \cdot (X_i - X_j)^T)\right) \tag{9}$$

In this way, the final predictions are generated by the target function F.

3   Experiments

3.1   Datasets

We mainly evaluate the proposed method on three datasets, including two lung cancer datasets (*i.e.*, LUSC and NLST) and a brain carcinoma dataset (*i.e.*, GBM) from the generic cancer patient dataset TCGA [11]. These three datasets are used in two modes. On the one hand, we follow the experimental settings of previous methods [14,20,22], *i.e.*, randomly selecting same scale of the WSIs from the corresponding three datasets for the training and evaluation. The datasets used in this mode are called the "Subset" datasets. On the other hand, we train and evaluate the proposed method with its competitors on the complete data from these three datasets. We denote the datasets used in this mode as the "Whole" datasets. In our implementation, five-fold cross-validation is employed to investigate the optimal parameter setting within the randomly selected training datasets. To verify the stability of the proposed method, we run the experiments five times for each set of parameter settings and compare their mean performance (Table 1).

Table 1. Dataset statistics.

Datasets	Cancer type	Subset		Whole		Quality	Avg. size
		No. patient	No. WSI	No. patient	No. WSI		
TCGA	LUSC	463	535	504	1612	Medium	0.72 GB
TCGA	GBM	365	491	617	2053	Low	0.50 GB
NLST	ADC & SCC	263	425	452	1225	High	0.74 GB

3.2   Evaluation Metric

We adopt the C-index [9] to evaluate the survival prediction performance of each model. Besides, the Receiver Operating Characteristic (ROC) [5] is adopted as another evaluation criterion. Specifically, we divide the sample according to real recorded survival time into a high group and low group, representing a good prognosis and poor prognosis, respectively. The hazard of each sample generated by ranking prediction is treated as a classification criterion. As shown in Fig. 2, the Area Under Curve (AUC) represents the overall accuracy of the regression under different thresholds. Similar to C-index, the larger AUC value means the better prediction performance of the model and vice versa.

3.3   Methods for Comparison

In our experiments, the following state-of-the-art methods are compared: (**1**), DeepConvSurv [21] proposed the first CNN-based survival prediction model. It directly takes sampled patches as input from the WSIs for training a CNN. (**2**), WSISA [22] proposed another CNN-based prediction model, which includes several separate stages to train several DeepConvSurv models independently. **(3)**, GCN [13] is a general graph convolutional network based model. We use it as an extra baseline for the survival prediction task, taking the sampled patches as input to build up the graph structure. **(4)**, DeepGraphSurv [14] employs spectral GCN to take the topological relationships into consideration. Its regression model employs the Cox regression model [3]. **(5)**, Multi-instance Learning for Survival Prediction (MILSurv) [19] proposed a model considering multiple slides from one patient and predict on the global representations.

Table 2. The comparison results of all the methods. ("†" denotes the significance testing, *p-value* < 0.001.)

Methods	Datasets					
	Subset dataset			Whole dataset		
	LUSC	GBM	NLST	LUSC	GBM	NLST
DeepConvSurv [21]	0.5784	0.5231	0.5144	0.4962	0.5008	0.4933
GCN [13]	0.6280	0.5901	0.6687	0.5923	0.6044	0.5910
DeepGraphSurv [14]	0.6606	0.6215	0.7066	0.5964	0.5877	0.6212
WSISA [22]	0.6380	0.5760	0.6539	0.6076	0.5789	0.5836
MILSurv [19]	-	0.6570	0.6780	0.6235	0.6165	0.6354
RankSurv	**0.6791**†	**0.6722**†	**0.7183**†	**0.6608**†	**0.6627**†	**0.6820**†

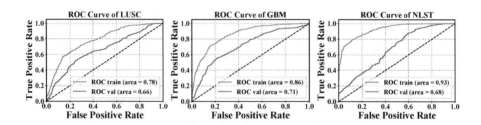

Fig. 2. The ROC curves of our proposed RankSurv method on three datasets.

3.4   Implementation

The first step is sampling patches from original WSIs, where we adopt a public toolbox called "openslide" released in [8]. After loading the raw WSI, we generate the background mask on one level. By utilizing the OTSU [16] thresholding algorithm, we set the size of the patch as 256 pixels × 256 pixels and collect 2000 patches randomly from separated objects region. Visual features are extracted for each patch from pre-trained ResNet-34 on ImageNet [4], whose dimension is $x_0 \in \mathbb{R}^{1 \times 512}$. The hypergraph node matrix $\mathbf{X} = (x_0, x_1, ...x_{2000})^\top$ is built up by vertical stacking, so that the dimension of which is $\mathbf{X_n} \in \mathbb{R}^{2000 \times 512}$.

The extracted features $\mathbf{X_n} \in \mathbb{R}^{2000 \times 128}$ from the last hypergraph layer are squeezed into $\mathbf{X_s} \in \mathbb{R}^{1 \times 128}$. We first take advantage of a fully connected layer with a sigmoid activation function to implement hazard regression and then further learn ranking information as shown in Fig. 1.

Our model is trained on each dataset with 80% as training data and 20% as validation data, by randomly separating. Note that since we propose a pair-wise ranking loss, the strategy of sampling the pairs in training is to iterate over all data pairs, $i.e.$, $\frac{N^2}{2}$, where N denotes the number of cases in the training set. The learning rate is set to 0.0001. For hypergraph network, $\mathcal{K}$ ($i.e.$, K-NN) in the hyperedge generation procedure is set as 9 and the number of hypergraph convolutional layers is set as 2.

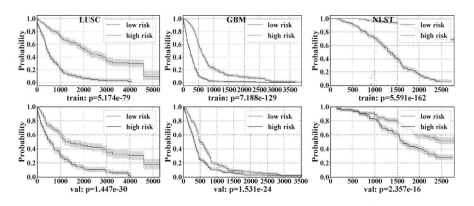

Fig. 3. The KM-estimation curves of our proposed RankSurv method on three datasets.

3.5 Results and Discussions

The comparison results of all methods are summarized in Table 2. Note that the reported results for all baseline methods on the full-scale datasets are based on our implementations since all baseline methods, except the GCN [13], did not release their source codes. Based on the quantitative results shown in Table 2, we have the following observations: Considering the real situation, patients may only focus on whether their current disease is serious or not. Therefore, it is also tempting to adopt a logistic regression to divide prognosis into a high group and low group. Significantly, we find our RankSurv behave well in this task. Thus we get the following AUC curve on three datasets, as shown in the Fig. 2. Further, to capture the over-all prognosis difference between high-risk group and low-risk group, we refer to the univariate KM-estimation [12], as shown in Fig. 3. All samples are divided into high/low groups based on the result of hazard prediction through RankSurv. It can be observed that our result is reliable both from p-values and the significant differences in probability curves between the two groups.

Table 3. Experimental comparison of different settings for our method.

Methods	Subset dataset			Whole dataset		
Hazard prediction + Survival rank	LUSC	GBM	NLST	LUSC	GBM	NLST
1 DeepGraphSurv [14] + Our method	0.6613	0.6322	0.6814	0.6173	0.6137	0.6286
2 Our method + -	0.6592	0.6579	0.6773	0.6487	0.6489	0.6570
3 Our method + RankNet [1]	0.6652	0.6680	0.6900	0.6552	0.6538	0.6628
4 RankSurv	**0.6791**	**0.6722**	**0.7183**	**0.6608**	**0.6627**	**0.6820**
Hazard prediction + Loss function	LUSC	GBM	NLST	LUSC	GBM	NLST
5 Our method + Cox [3]	0.6183	0.6012	0.6200	0.6020	0.5933	0.6185
6 Our method + BoostCI [15]	0.6244	0.6196	0.6279	0.6143	0.6022	0.6230
7 Our method + EnCox [18]	0.6437	0.6328	0.6472	0.6319	0.6235	0.6439
8 RankSurv	**0.6791**	**0.6722**	**0.7183**	**0.6608**	**0.6627**	0.6820

To evaluate the effectiveness of different components in our proposed framework, we have alternated the settings for the hazard prediction, the survival rank procedures and the loss function. The experimental results are shown in Table 3, where the following settings are used: replacing the hazard prediction using hypergraph representation by DeepGraphSurv [14] (line 1); removing the survival rank prediction procedure (line 2); replacing the proposed survival rank prediction by RankNet [1], which is a commonly used ranking method (line 3) and the whole method RankSurv (line 4). For interpreting the usefulness of the proposed loss function (BCR), we replace BCR by traditional cox partial likelihood loss (Cox) [3] (line 5), BoostCI [15] (line 6), and EnCox [18] (line 7), respectively. The following observations can be made from the results: **(1)** The introduced hazard prediction using hypergraph representation can achieve better performance compared with that of using DeepGraphSurv [14]. **(2)** The use of ranking information can improve the performance (the results in line 3 and line 4 are better than the results in line 2). **(3)** The proposed rank prediction method is better than RankNet [1] (the result in line 3). **(4)** The proposed loss function (BCR) outperforms existing classical methods significantly (line 8 is much better than lines 5, 6, and 7), which also demonstrates that considering the rank information is very effective and efficient.

4   Conclusion

In this paper, we propose a ranking-based survival prediction method (RankSurv) on WSIs. This method takes the relative ranking order information among different patients into consideration. In this method, a hypergraph representation is introduced to conduct hazard prediction on each WSI respectively, and then a ranking-based prediction process is conducted using pairwise survival data. Experiments on three public carcinoma datasets and comparisons with the state-of-the-art methods show superior prediction results of our proposed method. We have also investigated the effectiveness of different components in the proposed framework, and the ranking-based survival prediction framework shows better performance compared with that of using just each data individually.

References

1. Burges, C.J.: From ranknet to lambdarank to lambdaMART: an overview. Learning **11**(23–581), 81 (2010)
2. Bychkov, D., et al.: Deep learning based tissue analysis predicts outcome in colorectal cancer. Sci. Rep. **8**(1), 1–11 (2018)
3. Cox, D.R.: Regression models and life-tables. J. Roy. Stat. Soc.: Ser. B (Methodol.) **34**(2), 187–202 (1972)
4. Deng, J., Dong, W., Socher, R., Li, L.J., Li, K., Fei-Fei, L.: ImageNet: a large-scale hierarchical image database. In: CVPR, pp. 248–255. IEEE (2009)
5. Fawcett, T.: An introduction to roc analysis. Pattern Recogn. Lett. **27**(8), 861–874 (2006)
6. Feng, Y., You, H., Zhang, Z., Ji, R., Gao, Y.: Hypergraph neural networks. In: AAAI, vol. 33, pp. 3558–3565 (2019)
7. Gao, Y., Wang, M., Tao, D., Ji, R., Dai, Q.: 3-D object retrieval and recognition with hypergraph analysis. IEEE Trans. Image Process. **21**(9), 4290–4303 (2012)
8. Goode, A., Gilbert, B., Harkes, J., Jukic, D., Satyanarayanan, M.: OpenSlide: a vendor-neutral software foundation for digital pathology. J. Pathol. Inform. **4** (2013)
9. Heagerty, P.J., Zheng, Y.: Survival model predictive accuracy and ROC curves. Biometrics **61**(1), 92–105 (2005)
10. Jiang, J., Wei, Y., Feng, Y., Cao, J., Gao, Y.: Dynamic hypergraph neural networks. In: IJCAI, pp. 2635–2641. AAAI Press (2019)
11. Kandoth, C.: Mutational landscape and significance across 12 major cancer types. Nature **502**(7471), 333 (2013)
12. Kaplan, E.L., Meier, P.: Nonparametric estimation from incomplete observations. J. Am. Stat. Assoc. **53**(282), 457–481 (1958)
13. Kipf, T.N., Welling, M.: Semi-supervised classification with graph convolutional networks. In: ICLR (2017)
14. Li, R., Yao, J., Zhu, X., Li, Y., Huang, J.: Graph CNN for survival analysis on whole slide pathological images. In: Frangi, A.F., Schnabel, J.A., Davatzikos, C., Alberola-López, C., Fichtinger, G. (eds.) MICCAI 2018. LNCS, vol. 11071, pp. 174–182. Springer, Cham (2018). https://doi.org/10.1007/978-3-030-00934-2_20
15. Mayr, A., Schmid, M.: Boosting the concordance index for survival data-a unified framework to derive and evaluate biomarker combinations. PLoS One **9**(1), e84483 (2014)
16. Otsu, N.: A threshold selection method from gray-level histograms. IEEE Trans. Syst. Man Cybern. **9**(1), 62–66 (1979)
17. Simonyan, K., Zisserman, A.: Very deep convolutional networks for large-scale image recognition. arXiv:1409.1556 (2014)
18. Yang, Y., Zou, H.: A cocktail algorithm for solving the elastic net penalized Coxs regression in high dimensions. Stat. Interface **6**(2), 167–173 (2013)
19. Yao, J., Zhu, X., Huang, J.: Deep multi-instance learning for survival prediction from whole slide images. In: Shen, D., et al. (eds.) MICCAI 2019. LNCS, vol. 11764, pp. 496–504. Springer, Cham (2019). https://doi.org/10.1007/978-3-030-32239-7_55

20. Yao, J., Zhu, X., Zhu, F., Huang, J.: Deep correlational learning for survival prediction from multi-modality data. In: Descoteaux, M., Maier-Hein, L., Franz, A., Jannin, P., Collins, D.L., Duchesne, S. (eds.) MICCAI 2017. LNCS, vol. 10434, pp. 406–414. Springer, Cham (2017). https://doi.org/10.1007/978-3-319-66185-8_46
21. Zhu, X., Yao, J., Huang, J.: Deep convolutional neural network for survival analysis with pathological images. In: BIBM, pp. 544–547. IEEE (2016)
22. Zhu, X., Yao, J., Zhu, F., Huang, J.: WSISA: making survival prediction from whole slide histopathological images. In: CVPR, pp. 7234–7242 (2017)

Renal Cell Carcinoma Detection and Subtyping with Minimal Point-Based Annotation in Whole-Slide Images

Zeyu Gao[1,2], Pargorn Puttapirat[1,2], Jiangbo Shi[1,2], and Chen Li[1,2(✉)]

[1] School of Computer Science and Technology, Xi'an Jiaotong University,
Xi'an 710049, Shaanxi, China
`gzy4119105156@stu.xjtu.edu.cn`, `cli@xitu.edu.cn`
[2] National Engineering Lab for Big Data Analytics, Xi'an Jiaotong University,
Xi'an 710049, Shaanxi, China

Abstract. Cancerous region detection and subtyping in whole-slide images (WSIs) are fundamental for renal cell carcinoma (RCC) diagnosis. The main challenge in the development of automated RCC diagnostic systems is the lack of large-scale datasets with precise annotations. In this paper, we propose a framework that employs a semi-supervised learning (SSL) method to accurately detect cancerous regions with a novel annotation method called Minimal Point-Based (Min-Point) annotation. The predicted results are efficiently utilized by a hybrid loss training strategy in a classification model for subtyping. The annotator only needs to mark a few cancerous and non-cancerous points in each WSI. The experiments on three significant subtypes of RCC proved that the performance of the cancerous region detector trained with the Min-Point annotated dataset is comparable to the classifiers trained on the dataset with full cancerous region delineation. In subtyping, the proposed model outperforms the model trained with only whole-slide diagnostic labels by 12% in terms of the testing f1-score. We believe that our "detect then classify" schema combined with the Min-Point annotation would set a standard for developing intelligent systems with similar challenges.

Keywords: Detection · Subtyping · Min-Point annotation

1 Introduction

Renal cell carcinoma (RCC) accounts for more than 90% in the kidney cancer cases. While it contains roughly ten histologic and molecular subtypes [1], the three including Clear cell (cc), papillary (p), and chromophobe (ch) are major [2]. RCC diagnosis is critical and generally consists of a histologic subtype and a grade. Each subtype could yield dramatically different prognoses, treatment strategies, and survival outcomes [3–5]. Similarly, the five-year overall survival outcome varies from 32% to 91% for ccRCC with different grades [2]. Tumor grading, either with the Fuhrman's [6] or the ISUP grading system [7],

© Springer Nature Switzerland AG 2020
A. L. Martel et al. (Eds.): MICCAI 2020, LNCS 12265, pp. 439–448, 2020.
https://doi.org/10.1007/978-3-030-59722-1_42

are developed based on the visual inspection of cancerous cells hence identifying cancerous regions is critical [8–10]. These situations have led us to focus on the development of accurate cancerous region detection and subtyping in RCC.

Deep learning is a method of choice for such problem. It requires an extraordinary amount of manually labeled data as seen in the Camelyon 2016 [11] and TUPAC 2016 [12] datasets. Nevertheless, keep annotating large-scale datasets for other types of cancer is very expensive. Existing works rely on complete and precise annotations to develop cancer region detection. To reduce annotation efforts, we propose a novel annotation method called Min-Point annotation that only requires annotators to minimally annotate points on cancerous and non-cancerous regions of WSI.

Regarding the Min-Point annotation, we adopt a semi-supervised learning (SSL) strategy for cancer region detection. SSL has been proven to be effective in utilizing unlabeled data, thus reducing the need for large-scale annotations in natural images [13–15] and medical images [16–18]. The proposed detection framework utilizes a holistic SSL approach called MixMatch. Berthelot D et al. [19] has unified current SSL approaches to form a new algorithm which obtains the state-of-the-art results on several natural image datasets. Our work takes WSIs with Min-Point annotation as the training data to build the initial classifier. Then, a relatively larger set of the unlabeled WSIs called the 'extension set' is used to fine-tune the model, resulting in the final classifier. After that, based on the detected cancerous regions, we propose a hybrid loss to train a robust deep learning subtype classifier. The proposed approach is different from [20] since the latter only trains the classifier with the diagnoses provided by The Cancer Genome Atlas (TCGA), ignoring the negative effects of non-cancerous regions in WSIs and being unable to give evidential outputs.

In this paper, our main contributions are as the following. (1) We introduce a cancer region detection framework for RCC with a novel annotation method called Min-Point annotation, combining with the technique proposed in [19]. The proposed model can be applied to other large-scale unlabeled datasets with minimal modifications. (2) We propose a subtyping framework for RCC based on detected cancerous regions by formulating a hybrid loss for the RCC subtype classifier. (3) Our experiments on three major subtypes of RCC from TCGA prove the effectiveness of the proposed framework. The cancer region detection model is only trained with a relatively small set of the labeled data and a large set of unlabeled data when compared to those required by fully-supervised models trained on the manually annotated dataset. Our subtype classifier has 12% better f1-score than the baseline. As an extra feature, the framework can provide evidential information along with its classification output.

2   Proposed Framework

2.1   Minimal Point-Based Annotation

Typically, the development of a cancer region detection model requires datasets where annotators must provide accurate boundaries of all cancer regions

Table 1. The average annotation times of Min-Point annotation and Complete Region annotation for each annotator. P1 and P2 stand for two pathologists, T1–T4 as four well-trained annotators.

Annotation times (sec)	P1	P2	Mean		
Minimal Point-based annotation	17.2	14.8	16.0		
Annotation times (sec)	T1	T2	T3	T4	Mean
Complete region annotation	386.1	430.3	302.2	407.5	381.5

(a)   (b)

Fig. 1. The Minimal Point-Based annotations (a) consist of positive points (yellow) and negative points (green) which indicate cancerous and non-cancerous regions. The complete region annotation (b) consist of one or multiple enclosed regions with precise perimeters on cancerous regions and non-cancerous region outside. (Color figure online)

(complete region annotation) as shown in Fig. 1(b). To achieve precise perimeters, annotators need to zoom in and out between high and low magnification and outline the regions carefully. This type of activity is time consuming, and has to be done by domain experts. With Min-Point annotation, experts such as pathologists would only need to add a few points scattered on both cancerous and non-cancerous regions of WSI at low magnification by OpenHI [21] as shown in Fig. 1(a). The number of the points could be as few as five to ten. According to our annotation experience, Min-Point annotation can reduce the annotation time to roughly one-twentieth when compared to the complete annotation. The comparison of annotation times is shown in Table 1.

The minimally annotated dataset was used to generate labeled and unlabeled data. The labeled patches including cancerous and non-cancerous patches were created based on annotated points positioned at the center. The unlabeled patches were extracted by the sliding window strategy with a background filter. Following the experience of pathologists, the original size of a patch was 2000 × 2000 pixels at 40x magnification, then, the patches were resized to 224 × 224 pixels for training.

2.2   SSL Model for Cancer Region Detection

With Min-Point annotation, insufficient training data is expected. This is where we would exploit valuable information from large amounts of unlabeled data. SSL becomes a natural choice. The SSL approach which combines multiple methods called MixMatch proposed in [19] has proven to be effective in leveraging

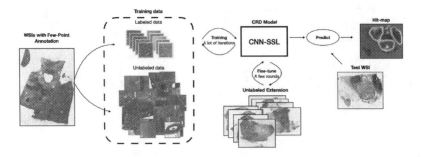

Fig. 2. The proposed semi-supervised cancer region detection framework

unlabeled data. We adopt this approach and integrate it into the proposed framework. First, Berthelot D et al. augment the labeled and unlabeled data with crop, rotate and flip operation, specifically K augmentations is used on unlabeled data. Then, they use a classification model to get a "guess" label, which performs a sharpening [22] to lower the entropy for each augmented unlabeled data. After that, MixUp [23] is utilized for both labeled and unlabeled samples. Finally, a combined loss for SSL is minimized for model training.

Let D_l and D_u be the set of labeled and unlabeled data, D_l' and D_u' be the set of augmented labeled and unlabeled data, respectively. C stands for the numbers of classes, $H(p, q)$ is the cross-entropy between two distributions and p_{pred}, q_{pred} represents the probability vectors of the model outputs. The combined loss function is as the following:

$$D_l', D_u' = MixMatch(D_l, D_u) \tag{1}$$

$$L = \frac{1}{|D_l'|} \sum_{x,p \in D_l} H(p, p_{pred}) + \lambda \frac{1}{C |D_u'|} \sum_{u,q \in D_u'} \|q - q_{pred}\|_2^2 \tag{2}$$

Notice that λ controls the importance of unlabeled data loss. In our experiment, we increase λ linearly to its maximum over the training process. Since the model is unstable at the beginning, then becomes more discriminative as the iterations continue. In the fine-tuning phase, we want the model to learn more knowledge from the other part of unlabeled data (the extension set), so we set λ as a constant. The data in the extension set is completely unlabeled, and it is hard for the model to learn valuable knowledge from this data. Still, if the model is already discriminative, the unlabeled data could help to increase its robustness. The overall cancer region detection framework, as shown in Fig. 2, includes (1) labeled and unlabeled image patches generate from minimally annotated WSIs for training, (2) training of a convolutional neural network with SSL strategy (CNN-SSL) and (3) involving an extension dataset consist of unlabeled data to fine-tune the CNN-SSL model.

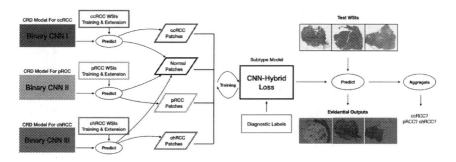

Fig. 3. Proposed subtyping framework

2.3   Hybrid Loss for Subtyping

After cancerous regions are recognized, they could be used for subtyping. Tabibu S et al. [20] treat the subtyping as a three-class classification problem (ccRCC vs. pRCC vs. chRCC) without considering the non-cancerous regions. Since there is not much difference between non-cancerous tissues among different subtypes, labeling these normal tissues as corresponding subtypes will have an adverse impact on both training and prediction of the model. We consider the non-cancerous regions as an additional "normal" class to form a four-class classification (normal vs. ccRCC vs. pRCC vs. chRCC), as shown in Fig. 3. The binary CNN I, II, III are cancer region detection models for ccRCC, pRCC, chRCC, respectively. After predicting the labels of each patch, an evidential result can be presented to pathologists, and then the subtype label can be obtained by aggregation operation. In our experiment, we use majority voting to form the final decision without considering the predicted normal patches.

Regarding the discarded predicted normal patches, we strengthen the constraint on the misclassified patches between subtypes, i.e., we increase the loss value of patches classified to other subtypes to achieve a better subtyping performance. For example, a patch from ccRCC WSI is classified as pRCC or chRCC. If this patch is classified as normal or ccRCC, it would be unchanged. In doing so, the penalty for cross-subtypes false is increased by using the hybrid loss, which consists of a standard cross-entropy loss and a novel subtype loss. Each patch was assigned a subtype based on the diagnostics of the corresponding WSI.

There are two labels for each patch x, one is a four-class label y, the other is a three-class label z. Let D be the set of training data, $p_{pred} = [p_0, p_1, ..., p_C]$ stands for the output probabilities of C classes, class 0 indicates normal class. We transform p_{pred} to a subtype probability vector s_{pred} as (3). Then, the hybrid loss function is defined as (4) where p, s represent one-hot codes of y, z, respectively. μ is a hyperparameter. As $\mu \to 0$, the loss function will return to traditional cross-entropy loss, raising μ encourages the model to increase the penalties for misclassification between different subtypes and reduce the sensitivity to some noise about "normal" and "cancer" class. In our experiment, we set $\mu = 5$.

Table 2. Statistics for all datasets. Bold numbers represent the number of labeled patches for each cancer region detection dataset.

WSIs (Patches)	Training	Extension	Validation	Test	Total
ccRCC detection	20 (**200**,19999)	58 (59216)	10 (11201)	35 (35286)	123
pRCC detection	15 (**150**,13585)	48 (45953)	5 (4361)	20 (14953)	88
chRCC detection	5 (**50**,6192)	25 (25058)	5 (5093)	10 (10593)	45
Subtyping	171 (170003)	–	20 (20655)	65 (60832),463	654

$$s_{pred} = \begin{cases} s_i = p_i & \text{if } i \neq z \\ s_i = p_i + p_0 & \text{if } i = z \end{cases} \tag{3}$$

$$L = \frac{1}{|D|} \left(\sum_{x,p,s \in D} H\left(p, p_{pred}\right) + \mu H(s, s_{pred})) \right) \tag{4}$$

3 Experiment

3.1 Datasets

A total of 654 WSIs (299, 254, 101 for three subtypes) of RCC from TCGA were used. All selected slides were scanned at 40x magnification. Three sets of data (D_{ccRCC}, D_{pRCC}, D_{chRCC}) were created for cancer region detection. Two pathologists were asked to annotate 10 points (5 cancerous, 5 non-cancerous) on each WSIs for training. Training sets consisted of a few labeled, a large number of unlabeled patches and a relatively larger unlabeled set (extension set) was used for fine-tuning. For subtyping, dataset $D_{subtype}$ consist of three cancer region detection models were used to generate predicted labels from training and extension sets of D_{ccRCC}, D_{pRCC}, D_{chRCC}. The test set of subtyping consists of two parts: $Test_{patch}$ containing 60832 labeled patches from 65 WSIs for the patch-level results (4-class) evaluation and $Test_{wsi}$ which is the original data (463 WSIs) from TCGA with diagnostic labels for the slide-level (3-class) evaluation. The details of these datasets are shown in Table 2.

Additionally, four trained annotators were invited to make a complete region annotation on 256 WSIs (123, 88, 45 WSIs for three subtypes). We equally separated all WSIs into 4 sets. After completion of each set, the annotation would be verified by another annotator, and then used to generate the region-based annotated data. This data was used to train the fully-supervised model and evaluate the performance of each model.

3.2 Implementation and Results

The Resnet-34 architecture [24] and the backbone pre-trained on image-net were used for all models in the experiment. Source code of our work is available at: https://gitlab.com/BioAI/RCC_DS.

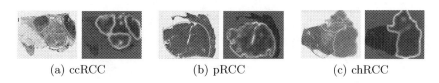

(a) ccRCC   (b) pRCC   (c) chRCC

Fig. 4. Predicted heat maps of WSIs for three subtypes of RCC. Region-based annotation on the left and predicted heat maps on the right

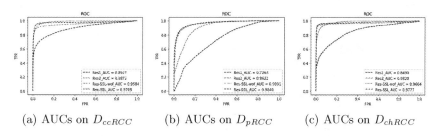

(a) AUCs on D_{ccRCC} (b) AUCs on D_{pRCC} (c) AUCs on D_{chRCC}

Fig. 5. AUC results of $Model_{Res1}$, $Model_{Res2}$, $Model_{Res-SSL-wof}$ and $Model_{Res-SSL}$ on three datasets, D_{ccRCC}, D_{pRCC} and D_{chRCC}.

Cancer Region Detection. Three baseline models ($Model_{Res1}$, $Model_{Res2}$, $Model_{Res-SSL-wof}$) tested on D_{ccRCC}, D_{pRCC}, D_{chRCC} were used for performance comparison against the proposed framework ($Model_{Res-SSL}$). $Model_{Res1}$ is a Resnet-34 trained on labeled data of training set only. $Model_{Res2}$ is a Resnet-34 trained on segmentation annotated training and extension set, this model is a fully supervised model. $Model_{Res-SSL-wof}$ is a Resnet-34 trained by SSL strategy on training set without fine-tuning. We trained all models with the same optimizer, Adam, with an initial learning rate of 0.001. The learning rate was decreased automatically by the *ReduceLROnPlateau* function with a factor of 10 in Pytorch. All models were trained until convergence, $Model_{Res1}$, $Model_{Res2}$ took 50 epochs, $Model_{Res-SSL-wof}$, $Model_{Res-SSL}$ spent 200–300 epochs, and for $Model_{Res-SSL}$, it cost 5 extra epochs for fine-tuning. We used the cross-entropy loss for training $Model_{Res1}$ and $Model_{Res2}$.

On three datasets, the performance of models shows similar patterns, as illustrated in Fig. 5. $Model_{Res1}$ shows the worst performance since only a few annotated data is available to the model. And due to the effect of fine-tuning, $Model_{Res-SSL}$ outperforms $Model_{Res-SSL-wof}$ by about 0.15 AUC on D_{ccRCC} and D_{chRCC}, 0.55 AUC on D_{pRCC}. Also, we can see from the results that AUC values of $Model_{Res-SSL}$ and $Model_{Res2}$ are comparable, and gaps between the two models are within ± 0.1 AUC. Figure 4 shows predicted heat maps of three cases from different datasets by $Model_{Res-SSL}$.

Subtyping. For subtyping task, three models were tested. $Model_{CE-4class}$ and $Model_{HB-4class}$ are two Resnet-34 models trained by generated labels with cross-entropy and hybrid loss, respectively. $Model_{CE-3class}$ is a Resnet-34 model

Table 3. Subtyping results

Model	WSI-wise			Patch-wise
	Precision	Recall	F1-Score	F1-Score
Res-CE-3class	0.78	0.82	0.79	–
Res-CE-4class	0.86	0.89	0.87	**0.88**
Res-HB-4class	**0.89**	**0.92**	**0.91**	0.87

Table 4. The confusion matrix of $Model_{CE-4class}/Model_{HB-4class}$ on $Test_{patch}$. Bold numbers indicate reduction of misclassified patches between the two models.

	normal	ccRCC	pRCC	chRCC
normal	24279/24639	427/259	209/54	55/18
ccRCC	1408/2342	16445/16269	1177/**471**	95/**43**
pRCC	2116/3454	154/**23**	7759/6693	179/**38**
chRCC	332/612	89/**10**	516/**81**	5592/5826

trained by diagnostic labels only. All models have the same training process with the models in the previous section.

As shown in Table 3, $Model_{CE-4class}$ outperforms $Model_{CE-3class}$ by 8% on $Test_{wsi}$ in terms of f1-score. We hold ignorance for the normal region accountable for adverse effects on subtyping results. In $Model_{HB-4class}$, the f1-score is 4% more than $Model_{CE-4class}$ on WSI-wise data, proving the effectiveness of the proposed hybrid loss. Also in Table 4, the number of misclassified patches between different subtypes was reduced, but more cancerous patches were classified as normal. Note that predict labels of WSIs are aggregated by patch-level results, except normal class. That is why using hybrid loss causes the model performs a slightly worse on $Test_{patch}$ (Patch-wise in Table 3), but better on the final subtyping result.

4   Conclusion

Pathologists should not be further burdened by annotation tasks while developing intelligence systems. Streamlined annotation strategies and methods to leverage unlabeled data for digital pathology is urgently needed. In this paper, we introduce a framework with a novel annotation method (Minimal Point-Based annotation) for RCC cancer region detection. It only needs pathologists to select a few points on a limited number of WSIs. This can dramatically reduce annotation efforts over the traditional annotation method. An SSL-based approach for training CNN model can be applied to the annotated data. Our results prove that cancer region detection accuracy of the proposed framework is competitive with a fully supervised learning approach on three major subtypes of RCC. We also propose a subsequent work for RCC subtyping where the results show that merely using diagnostic labels and ignoring normal regions for RCC subtype classification is irrational. The proposed framework with hybrid loss has significantly improved accuracy. Our future work will be focusing on developing a clinical-grade diagnostic system for RCC.

Acknowledgements. This work has been supported by National Key Research and Development Program of China (2018YFC0910404); National Natural Science Foundation of China (61772409); The consulting research project of the Chinese Academy of Engineering (The Online and Offline Mixed Educational Service System for "The Belt and Road" Training in MOOC China); Project of China Knowledge Centre for Engineering Science and Technology; The innovation team from the Ministry of Education (IRT_17R86); and the Innovative Research Group of the National Natural Science Foundation of China (61721002). The results shown here are in whole or part based upon data generated by the TCGA Research Network: https://www.cancer.gov/tcga.

References

1. Hsieh, J.J., et al.: Renal cell carcinoma. Nat. Rev. Dis. Primers **3**, 17009 (2017)
2. Ljungberg, B., et al.: EAU guidelines on renal cell carcinoma: 2014 update. Eur. Urol. **67**(5), 913–924 (2015)
3. Soyer, P., Dufresne, A.-C., Klein, I., Barbagelatta, M., Hervé, J.M., Scherrer, A.: Renal cell carcinoma of clear type: correlation of CT features with tumor size, architectural patterns, and pathologic staging. Eur. Radiol. **7**(2), 224–229 (1997). https://doi.org/10.1007/s003300050140
4. Delahunt, B., Eble, J.N.: Papillary renal cell carcinoma: a clinicopathologic and immunohistochemical study of 105 tumors. Mod. Pathol. Off. J. U. S. Canad. Acad. Patholo. **10**(6), 537–544 (1997)
5. Megumi, Y., Nishimura, K.: Chromophobe cell renal carcinoma. Urol. Int. **61**(3), 172–174 (1998)
6. Fuhrman, S.A., Lasky, L.C., Limas, C.: Prognostic significance of morphologic parameters in renal cell carcinoma. Am. J. Surg. Pathol. **6**(7), 655–663 (1982)
7. Delahunt, B., et al.: The international society of urological pathology (ISUP) grading system for renal cell carcinoma and other prognostic parameters. Am. J. Surg. Pathol. **37**(10), 1490–1504 (2013)
8. Golatkar, A., Anand, D., Sethi, A.: Classification of breast cancer histology using deep learning. In: Campilho, A., Karray, F., ter Haar Romeny, B. (eds.) ICIAR 2018. LNCS, vol. 10882, pp. 837–844. Springer, Cham (2018). https://doi.org/10.1007/978-3-319-93000-8_95
9. Kong, B., Sun, S., Wang, X., Song, Q., Zhang, S.: Invasive cancer detection utilizing compressed convolutional neural network and transfer learning. In: Frangi, A.F., Schnabel, J.A., Davatzikos, C., Alberola-López, C., Fichtinger, G. (eds.) MICCAI 2018. LNCS, vol. 11071, pp. 156–164. Springer, Cham (2018). https://doi.org/10.1007/978-3-030-00934-2_18
10. Le, H., Samaras, D., Kurc, T., Gupta, R., Shroyer, K., Saltz, J.: Pancreatic cancer detection in whole slide images using noisy label annotations. In: Shen, D., et al. (eds.) MICCAI 2019. LNCS, vol. 11764, pp. 541–549. Springer, Cham (2019). https://doi.org/10.1007/978-3-030-32239-7_60
11. Bejnordi, B.E., et al.: Diagnostic assessment of deep learning algorithms for detection of lymph node metastases in women with breast cancer. JAMA **318**(22), 2199–2210 (2017)

12. Veta, M., et al.: Predicting breast tumor proliferation from whole-slide images: the TUPAC16 challenge. Med. Image Anal. **54**, 111–121 (2019)
13. Tarvainen, A., Valpola, H.: Mean teachers are better role models: weight-averaged consistency targets improve semi-supervised deep learning results. In: Advances in Neural Information Processing Systems 30, pp. 1195–1204. Curran Associates, Inc. (2017)
14. Sajjadi, M., Javanmardi, M., Tasdizen, T.: Regularization with stochastic trans-formations and perturbations for deep semi-supervised learning. In: Advances in Neural Information Processing Systems 29, pp. 1163–1171. Curran Associates, Inc. (2016)
15. Rasmus, A., Berglund, M., Honkala, M., Valpola, H., Raiko, T.: Semi-supervised learning with ladder networks. In: Advances in Neural Information Processing Sys-tems 28, pp. 3546–3554. Curran Associates, Inc. (2015)
16. Xu, K., Su, H., Zhu, J., Guan, J.S., Zhang, B.: Neuron segmentation based on CNN with semi-supervised regularization. In: The IEEE Conference on Computer Vision and Pattern Recognition (CVPR) Workshops, June 2016
17. Bai, W., et al.: Semi-supervised learning for network-based cardiac MR image segmentation. In: Descoteaux, M., Maier-Hein, L., Franz, A., Jannin, P., Collins, D.L., Duchesne, S. (eds.) MICCAI 2017. LNCS, vol. 10434, pp. 253–260. Springer, Cham (2017). https://doi.org/10.1007/978-3-319-66185-8_29
18. Cheplygina, V., de Bruijne, M., Pluim, J.P.: Not-so-supervised: a survey of semi-supervised, multi-instance, and transfer learning in medical image analysis. Med. Image Anal. **54**, 280–296 (2019)
19. Berthelot, D., et al.: MixMatch: a holistic approach to semi-supervised learning. In: Advances in Neural Information Processing Systems 32, pp. 5049–5059. Curran Associates, Inc. (2019)
20. Tabibu, S., Vinod, P., Jawahar, C.: Pan-renal cell carcinoma classification and survival prediction from histopathology images using deep learning. Sci. Rep. **9**(1), 1–9 (2019)
21. Puttapirat, P., et al.: OpenHI: open platform for histopathological image annota-tion. Int. J. Data Min. Bioinform. **22**(4), 328–349 (2019)
22. Goodfellow, I., Bengio, Y., Courville, A.: Deep Learning. MIT Press, Cambridge (2016)
23. Zhang, H., Cissé, M., Dauphin, Y.N., Lopez-Paz, D.: mixup: Beyond empirical risk minimization. CoRR abs/1710.09412 (2017). http://arxiv.org/abs/1710.09412
24. He, K., Zhang, X., Ren, S., Sun, J.: Deep residual learning for image recognition. In: The IEEE Conference on Computer Vision and Pattern Recognition (CVPR), June 2016

Censoring-Aware Deep Ordinal Regression for Survival Prediction from Pathological Images

Lichao Xiao[1], Jin-Gang Yu[1,2(✉)], Zhifeng Liu[1], Jiarong Ou[1], Shule Deng[1], Zhenhua Yang[1], and Yuanqing Li[1,2]

[1] School of Automation Science and Engineering, South China University of Technology, Guangzhou 510641, China
`jingangyu@scut.edu.cn`
[2] Pazhou Lab, Guangzhou 510335, China

Abstract. Survival prediction is a typical task in computer-aided diagnosis with many clinical applications. Existing approaches to survival prediction are mostly based on the classic Cox model, which mainly focus on learning a hazard or survival function rather than the survival time, largely limiting their practical uses. In this paper, we present a Censoring-Aware Deep Ordinal Regression (CDOR) to directly predict survival time from pathological images. Instead of relying on the Cox model, CDOR formulates survival prediction as an ordinal regression problem, and particularly introduces a censoring-aware loss function to train the deep network in the presence of censored data. Experiment results on publicly available dataset demonstrate that, the proposed CDOR can achieve significant higher accuracy in predicting survival time.

Keywords: Survival prediction · Pathological images · Ordinal regression

1 Introduction

Survival prediction refers to the task of modeling the time at which a certain biological event of interest (e.g., death of cancer patients) occurs. It can be clinically used to test significant risk factors influencing survival time [8], to assist clinicians in making early decisions on treatment or healthcare, *etc.* Many medical data, such as CT images, MRIs, pathological images, molecular data, genomic data, and so forth, can be utilized to make survival prediction, among which pathological images are popular mainly due to the very high-resolution, the relative low cost and the informativeness. Some representative pathological images are visualized in Fig. 1 for intuition.

Recent approaches to survival prediction from pathological images usually integrate image analysis models, most typically convolutional neural network

A. L. Martel et al. (Eds.): MICCAI 2020, LNCS 12265, pp. 449–458, 2020.
https://doi.org/10.1007/978-3-030-59722-1_43

Survival time: 2493 days   Survival time: 1236 days   Survival time: 609 days   Survival time: 4695 days

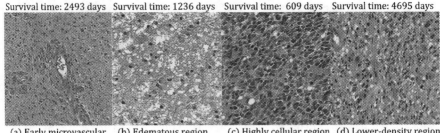

(a) Early microvascular   (b) Edematous region   (c) Highly cellular region   (d) Lower-density region
proliferation

Fig. 1. Some representative pathological image patches of patients with gliomas.

(CNN), into the well-known Cox proportional hazard model [2]. Zhu *et al.* [18] proposed the so-called DeepConvSurv which exploits a CNN to predict the risk function in the Cox model. Mobadersany *et al.* [9] utilized a similar CNN-based method to carry out a comprehensive study on predicting cancer outcomes from histology and genomics. Zhu *et al.* [19] proposed a two-stage framework which can automatically select survival-discriminative patches from whole slide histopathological images and further make survival prediction. Bo *et al.* [14] integrated a Capsule network with Cox loss. Yao *et al.* [17] took advantages of deep multiple instance learning to encode the patterns underlying the clusters of patches into a predicted risk. These Cox-based approaches predict a risk function, which are effective in tasks like testing significant factors affecting survival time. However, in other clinical applications where the survival time (rather than the risk) is desired, for instance, assisting clinicians to make planning for optimized and personalized treatments, these methods are limited. The major reason is that, the derivation of survival time in the Cox model involves accurate estimation of the baseline hazard function (see Sect. 2.1), which is practically very challenging. Very recently, some authors [15,16] attempted other ways of predicting survival time, without using the Cox framework, which directly predicts survival time based on a multi-task CNN. However, they solely ignored censored data, which is fundamental and of critical importance to survival prediction.

In this paper, we present a novel approach, called Censoring-Aware Deep Ordinal Regression (CDOR), for survival prediction from pathological images. Different from prior works, we aim to directly predict survival time from pathological images in the presence of censored observation data. Inspired by the intrinsically similar task of age estimation from face images [1,7,10], an active research topic in the community of computer vision, we formulate survival prediction as an ordinal regression problem [12], which converts regression into a series of ordered subtasks of binary classification. To allow the original ordinal regression to deal with censored data, a censoring-aware loss function is introduce to guide the model training, leading to the Censoring-Aware Deep Ordinal Regression (CDOR). Compared to Cox-based approaches, the proposed CDOR is able to predict the absolute survival time with significantly higher accuracy, since it takes different mechanism to achieve survival prediction without the necessity of estimating a baseline hazard model. In addition, the ordinal regression in CDOR enables us to well cope with the orderness and the non-stationary property underlying survival data, leading to its superior performance. Comprehensive experiments are carried out on the publicly available TCGA-GM dataset to predict the survival time of patients with gliomas, which demonstrate the effectiveness of the proposed CDOR.

2 Method

2.1 Problem Definition and Motivation

Let us denote by a quadruplet $(\boldsymbol{x}, \tau, \delta)$ an observation over a patient, where $\boldsymbol{x}$ is a feature vector, τ the observation time and δ a censoring indicator. The observation time $\tau \in \mathbb{R}^+$ is the time being of making this observation. We are concerned with the survival time $t \in \mathbb{R}^+$, the time being when the event of interest (typically death) of the patient occurs (both t and τ are relative to a certain origin of time). There inherently exist two possibilities when making such an observation, which is the so-called censoring problem [11]: the patient had already died, or the patient was still alive. In the former case, we have $t = \tau$ and $\delta = 0$, called an uncensored observation (data). And in the latter case, we assign $\delta = 1$, but the survival time t is unknown at the observation time τ, called a censored observation (data).

Given a set of observations $\mathcal{X} = \{(\boldsymbol{x}_i, \tau_i, \delta_i)\}_{i=1}^{|\mathcal{X}|}$, conventional survival analysis mostly use the Cox model, central to which is to learn a hazard function $h(t|\boldsymbol{x}) = h_0(t) \exp(\boldsymbol{\beta}^\mathsf{T} \boldsymbol{x})$, where $h_0(t)$ is the baseline hazard, $\boldsymbol{\beta}$ is the vector of regression parameters, and $\gamma(\boldsymbol{x}) = \boldsymbol{\beta}^\mathsf{T} \boldsymbol{x}$ is called a risk function. Previous methods mainly focus on estimating the risk function $\gamma(\boldsymbol{x})$ in order to enable such tasks as comparatively testing significant risk factors affecting survival, where the baseline hazard $h_0(t)$ is not necessitated. As aforementioned, these method are however limited in case that the absolute survival time is desired, because the accurate estimation of $h_0(t)$ is very challenging. Towards this end, we formulate the task of survival prediction as to learn from $\mathcal{X}$ a model $t = f(\boldsymbol{x})$ which directly predicts the survival time t according to the feature vector $\boldsymbol{x}$, rather than a risk function $\gamma(\boldsymbol{x})$.

2.2 Censoring-Aware Deep Ordinal Regression for Survival Prediction

One straightforward way to formulate survival prediction may be multi-label classification or metric regression (directly predicting a real-valued output for survival time). However, these strategies are unable to capture the underlying properties of the problem. Specifically, multi-label classification cannot take into account the order in survival time, and metric regression is likely to fail as well because the mapping from pathological images to survival time is highly non-stationary, which is very difficult to be encoded by the use of a single regressor. Survival prediction by nature is very similar to the task of age estimation from face images [1,7,10], which is an active research topic in the community of computer vision. One of the most representative solutions to age estimation is the so-called ordinal regression. By discretizating the target variable $t \in \mathbb{R}$ (survival time in our work) into K intervals, denoted by $\{T_1, ..., T_K\}$ with $T_1 < T_2 < \cdots < T_K$ being ordered interval boundaries, ordinal regression then transforms the regression problem into a series of K binary classification problems where the k-th classifier predicts if $t > T_k$ or not.

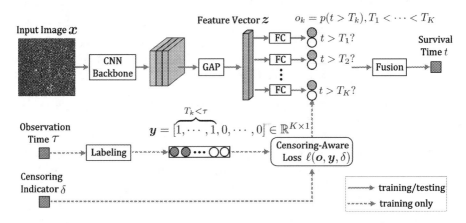

Fig. 2. Overview of Censoring-Aware Deep Ordinal Regression (CDOR) for survival prediction.

Inspired by its great success in age estimation, we adapt ordinal regression to our task of survival prediction. But unfortunately, this is non-trivial since the original ordinal regression for age estimation is unable to cope with censored data, while the censoring problem is of critical importance to survival prediction. For this purpose, we propose to introduce a censoring-aware loss into ordinal regression to enable the handling of censored data, leading to the Censoring-Aware Deep Ordinal Regression (CDOR).

An overview of CDOR is shown in Fig. 2. The input $x \in \mathbb{R}^{H \times W \times C}$, which is an $H \times W$ patch cropped from a whole slide of C-channel pathological image, is first fed into a CNN backbone, followed by a global average pooling (GAP) layer, to obtain a feature vector $z \in \mathbb{R}^{C \times 1}$. Then K binary classification heads are connected to the feature vector in parallel through one fully-connected (FC) layer for each, where the k-th head predicts the probability of the survival time t being larger than T_k, denoted by $o_k = p(t > T_k)$. Each head consists of two output nodes scored by o_k and $1 - o_k$ respectively. Finally, these classifier scores are fused to get the predicted survival time t by $t = \sum_{k=1}^{K} o_k(T_k - T_{k-1})$, where we let $T_0 = 0$. In the training stage, the observation time τ and the censoring indicator δ associated to x are taken to get the label and establish the censoring-aware loss.

Censoring-Aware Loss. As stated above, at the core of CDOR is the censoring-aware loss, which allows CDOR to deal with censored data. As shown in Fig. 2, the observation time τ is first converted to a label vector $y = [y_1, ..., y_K]^\mathsf{T}$ simply by setting $y_k = 1$ if $T_k < \tau$ and $y_k = 0$ otherwise. Let us denote by $o = [o_1, ..., o_K]^\mathsf{T}$ the predictions of the K classifiers. If the training sample is uncensored ($\delta = 0$), the loss can be established as usual by using cross-entropy

$$\ell(o, y) = -\sum_{k=1}^{K} [y_k \log(o_k) + (1 - y_k) \log(1 - o_k)]. \tag{1}$$

And if the training sample is censored ($\delta = 1$), only those classifiers indexed by $\{k | y_k = 1\}$ are partially involved in establishing the loss

$$\ell(o, y) = -\sum_{\{k | y_k = 1\}} [y_k \log(o_k) + (1 - y_k) \log(1 - o_k)]. \tag{2}$$

The intuition underlying Eq. (2) is that, the ground truth labels y_k's for classifiers with $T_k > \tau$ ($y_k = 0$ in this case according to our labeling scheme) cannot be determined if the training sample is censored (see Sect. 2.1 for details), which should be excluded from the loss. However, the classifiers with $T_k < \tau$ ($y_k = 1$) should still be included since their labels are informative, which is actually important to the effectiveness of our method (see Sect. 3.3 for comparison).

Given all these, the censoring-aware loss over an individual training sample can be written in a compact form as

$$\ell(o, y, \delta) = -\sum_{k=1}^{K} [(1 - \delta) + \delta y_k] [y_k \log(o_k) + (1 - y_k) \log(1 - o_k)]. \tag{3}$$

Further, for a set of training samples $\mathcal{X} = \{(x_i, \tau_i, \delta_i)\}_{i=1}^{N}$, let us denote by $o_i = [o_{1i}, o_{2i}, \cdots, o_{Ki}]^\mathsf{T}$ and $y_i = [y_{1i}, y_{2i}, \cdots, y_{Ki}]^\mathsf{T}$ the prediction vector and the label vector for the i-th sample respectively, and denote $O = [o_1, \cdots, o_N]$, $Y = [y_1, \cdots, y_N]$, and $\delta = [\delta_1, \cdots, \delta_N]^\mathsf{T}$, the total censoring-aware loss over $\mathcal{X}$ is given by

$$\mathcal{L}(O, Y, \delta) = \frac{1}{N} \sum_{i=1}^{N} \ell(o_i, y_i, \delta_i)$$

$$= -\frac{1}{N} \sum_{i=1}^{N} \sum_{k=1}^{K} [(1 - \delta_i) + \delta_i y_{ki}][y_{ki} \log(o_{ki}) + (1 - y_{ki}) \log(1 - o_{ki})]. \tag{4}$$

Discretization of Survival Time. The discretization of survival time in CDOR requires the choice of K interval boundaries $\{T_1, ..., T_K\}$. One natural way is to partition the entire time interval $[T_{\min}, T_{\max}]$ ($T_{\min}$ and $T_{\max}$ are the minimal and maximal follow-up times respectively and usually $T_1 = T_{\min}$, $T_K = T_{\max}$) into K equal intervals (referred to as "EqualInt"). However, such a strategy is practically not effective due to the fact that, the observation (survival) time is usually not uniformly distributed over a training set, which will lead to unbalance among the numbers of training samples for the K classifiers and consequently degradation in performance. Hence, we adopt a different discretization strategy in our work, *i.e.*, we partition the intervals such that each interval contains an equal number of training samples (referred to as "EqualFreq"). Notably, the discretization strategy may largely influence the performance in practice (see Sect. 3.3 for comparison).

Table 1. Quantitative results of survival time prediction by various methods.

Methods	SCNN [9]		DCS [18]		MR	CDOR
	Expect	Thresh	Expect	Thresh		
MAE	1012.1	424.5	602.1	439.1	551.7	**321.2**
C-index	0.727	0.725	**0.748**	0.731	0.593	0.737

3   Experiments and Results

3.1   Experimental Settings

Dataset. To evaluate the proposed CDOR method, we follow [9] to adopt the gliomas data from The Cancer Genome Atlas (TCGA) Lower-Grade Glioma (LGG) and Glioblastoma (GBM) projects, termed as **TCGA-GM**. The TCGA-GM dataset contains 1,505 patches with the resolution of 1024×1024 pixels manually cropped from 1,061 whole slide pathological images, which were captured from 769 patients with gliomas. The numbers of uncensored and censored patients are 321 and 295 in the training set, and 67 and 86 in the testing set.

Performance Measures. As the exact survival time is concerned in our work, **C-index** [4], which may be the most commonly-used performance measure in survival analysis, is inappropriate because it can only pair-wisely measure the consistency of relative order between prediction and ground truth, rather than the accuracy in absolute values. To this end, we use the **Mean Absolute Error (MAE)** as the major measure for quantitative evaluation. Specifically, for the patient with the observation time τ, the censoring indicator δ and the predicted survival time t, the absolute error $\Delta = (\tau - t)\mathbb{I}_{t<\tau} + (1-\delta)(t-\tau)\mathbb{I}_{t\geq\tau}$ where $\mathbb{I}$ is an indicator function. And MAE is the absolute error averaged over all patients in the testing set. Notice that this absolute error is defined at the patient level. The patient-level survival time is obtained by averaging those predicted on the patches belonging to the same patient.

Implementation Details. We use ResNet-18 [5] pre-trained on ImageNet as the backbone. In the training phase, the model is trained for 20 epochs with Adam optimizer [6]. The learning rate starts with 0.0001 and decays by a factor of 5 after every 5 epochs. The batch size is set to be 96. Our experiments were conducted on a workstation with two Nvidia Titan XP GPUs with totally 24 GB memory. Our method is implemented with MXNet.

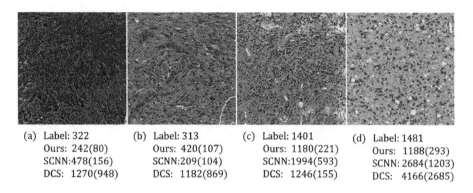

(a) Label: 322
    Ours: 242(80)
    SCNN:478(156)
    DCS: 1270(948)

(b) Label: 313
    Ours: 420(107)
    SCNN:209(104)
    DCS: 1182(869)

(c) Label: 1401
    Ours: 1180(221)
    SCNN:1994(593)
    DCS: 1246(155)

(d) Label: 1481
    Ours: 1188(293)
    SCNN: 2684(1203)
    DCS: 4166(2685)

Fig. 3. Some representative results of survival time prediction obtained by various methods.

3.2 Comparison with Existing Methods

To our knowledge, no previous method is able to predict the absolute survival time like ours. In order to enable our comparative study, we consider two methods based on Cox model, termed as **SCNN** [9] and **DCS** [18]. They were chosen mainly for three reasons: (1) they are very impactful in the literature; (2) they are based on deep learning like ours; (3) they perform survival analysis at the patch level like ours, rather than WSIs. However, these method were originally developed for predicting the risk function $\gamma(\boldsymbol{x})$. To make our comparison possible, we need to convert the predicted $\gamma(\boldsymbol{x})$ into a survival time t. Fortunately, this can be conveniently achieved by using an off-the-shelf Python package called *lifelines* [3]. For clarity, we outline the main procedures as follows: (1) estimating the baseline hazard function $h_0(t)$ and the baseline cumulative hazard $H_0(t) = \int_0^t h_0(u)du$; (2) computing the cumulative hazard $H(t) = H_0(t)\exp(\gamma(\boldsymbol{x}))$; (3) computing the survival function $S(t) = \exp(-H(t))$; (4) obtaining the survival time t by taking the expectation (termed as "Expect") of or thresholding (termed as "Thresh") $S(t)$ (Two functions named *"predict_expectation"* and *"predict_percentile"* in *lifelines*). For SCNN [9], we use the source codes released by the authors. And for

DCS [18], no source code is publicly available, but fortunately we can manage to implement the method following the very clear presentation in [18]. Additionally, we also include metric regression as another baseline, termed as **MR**, which directly predicts a real-valued survival time using an end-to-end CNN regressor.

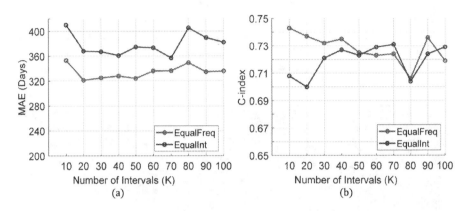

Fig. 4. Comparison of discretization strategies in terms of (a) MAE and (b) C-Index.

Quantitative results of survival time prediction by various methods are reported in Table 1. As can be observed, our CDOR performs significantly better than SCNN [9] and DCS [18] in terms of MAE and comparably in terms of C-index. The advantage of our method is mainly attributed to that we deploy an effective mechanism to directly predict the survival time. By contrast, the Cox-based methods predict the risk, and have to estimate the baseline hazard function in order to derive the survival time, for which it is practically difficult to get accurate results. The lack of a reasonable baseline hazard function does not influence the prediction of relative order [13], which gives reason to their comparable C-index to ours. Also notice that the survival times of SCNN [9] and DCS [18] rely much on how to post-processing the survival function (The results for "Thresh" in Table 1 are the optimal obtained by the threshold of 0.7), making them difficult for practical uses. Our CDOR performs far better than MR which straightforwardly predicts the survival time by a single regressor, validating the effectiveness of the special regression mechanism in CDOR. Some representative pathological images and the corresponding survival times predicted by various methods are further demonstrated in Fig. 3 for intuitive comparison, where our CDOR can obtain more favorable results.

3.3 Validation of Key Components

To further validate the effectiveness of our CDOR, we compare with the variants of some key components.

Discretization Strategy. We compare two discretization strategies, namely "EqualInt" and "EqualFreq" (see Sect. 2.2), with the results in terms of both

MAE and C-index presented in Fig. 4. It can be observed that, EqualFreq adopted by CDOR performs better than EqualInt. Additionally, EqualFreq is not sensitive to the number of intervals K, and we set $K = 20$ throughout our experiments in this paper.

Censoring-Aware Loss. We construct a variant of the censoring-aware loss in Eq. (3) by $\ell(\boldsymbol{o}, \boldsymbol{y}, \delta) = -\sum_{k=1}^{K}(1 - \delta)\left[y_k \log(o_k) + (1 - y_k)\log(1 - o_k)\right]$, which uses uncensored data only in computing the loss. The results obtained by this variant and our censoring-aware loss are 434.7 and 321.2 respectively in terms of MAE, and 0.559 and 0.737 respectively in terms of C-index, which demonstrates our censoring-aware loss performs far better.

4   Conclusion

We have presented a novel approach called Censoring-Aware Deep Ordinal Regression (CDOR) for survival prediction from pathological images. CDOR formulates survival prediction as an ordinal regression problem, and further introduces a censoring-aware loss function to guide the model training in order to cope with censored data. Experiments of survival time prediction for patients with gliomas on the publicly available TCGA-GM dataset have demonstrated that, the proposed CDOR is able to predict the absolute survival time with significantly higher accuracy. Comparative study with the variants of key components in CDOR have performed to further validate its effectiveness. In our future work, we will test our method with more clinical data of different types of diseases.

Acknowledgement. This work was supported by the National Natural Science Foundation of China under Grant 61703166 and Grant 61633010, the National Key Research and Development Program of China under Grant 2017YFB1002505, the Guangdong Natural Science Foundation under Grant 2014A030312005, the National Key Basic Research Program of China (973 Program) under Grant 2015CB351703, the Guangzhou Science and Technology Program under Grant 201904010299, and the Fundamental Research Funds for the Central Universities, SCUT, under Grant 2018MS72.

References

1. Chen, S., Zhang, C., Dong, M., Le, J., Rao, M.: Using ranking-CNN for age estimation. In: Proceedings of the IEEE Conference on Computer Vision and Pattern Recognition, pp. 5183–5192 (2017)
2. Cox, D.R.: Regression models and life-tables. J. Roy. Stat. Soc.: Ser. B (Methodol.) **34**(2), 187–202 (1972)
3. Davidson-Pilon, C.: lifelines: survival analysis in Python. J. Open Source Softw. **4**(40), 1317 (2019)
4. Harrell, F.E., Califf, R.M., Pryor, D.B., Lee, K.L., Rosati, R.A.: Evaluating the yield of medical tests. J. Am. Med. Assoc. **247**(18), 2543–2546 (1982)

5. He, K., Zhang, X., Ren, S., Sun, J.: Deep residual learning for image recognition. In: Proceedings of the IEEE Conference on Computer Vision and Pattern Recognition, pp. 770–778 (2016)
6. Kingma, D.P., Ba, J.: Adam: a method for stochastic optimization. arXiv preprint arXiv:1412.6980 (2014)
7. Li, K., Xing, J., Su, C., Hu, W., Zhang, Y., Maybank, S.: Deep cost-sensitive and order-preserving feature learning for cross-population age estimation. In: Proceedings of the IEEE Conference on Computer Vision and Pattern Recognition, pp. 399–408 (2018)
8. Liu, J., et al.: An integrated TCGA pan-cancer clinical data resource to drive high-quality survival outcome analytics. Cell **173**(2), 400–416 (2018)
9. Mobadersany, P., et al.: Predicting cancer outcomes from histology and genomics using convolutional networks. Proc. Nat. Acad. Sci. **115**(13), E2970–E2979 (2018)
10. Niu, Z., Zhou, M., Wang, L., Gao, X., Hua, G.: Ordinal regression with multiple output CNN for age estimation. In: Proceedings of the IEEE Conference on Computer Vision and Pattern Recognition, pp. 4920–4928 (2016)
11. Reddy, C.K., Li, Y., Aggarwal, C.: A review of clinical prediction models. Healthc. Data Anal. **36**, 343–378 (2015)
12. Schölkopf, B., Platt, J.C., Hoffman, T.: Ordinal regression by extended binary classification. In: Advances in Neural Information Processing Systems, pp. 865–872 (2007)
13. Steck, H., Krishnapuram, B., Dehing-Oberije, C., Lambin, P., Raykar, V.C.: On ranking in survival analysis: bounds on the concordance index. In: Advances in Neural Information Processing Systems, pp. 1209–1216 (2008)
14. Tang, B., Li, A., Li, B., Wang, M.: CapSurv: capsule network for survival analysis with whole slide pathological images. IEEE Access **7**, 26022–26030 (2019)
15. Tang, Z., et al.: Pre-operative overall survival time prediction for glioblastoma patients using deep learning on both imaging phenotype and genotype. In: Shen, D., et al. (eds.) MICCAI 2019. LNCS, vol. 11764, pp. 415–422. Springer, Cham (2019). https://doi.org/10.1007/978-3-030-32239-7_46
16. Tang, Z., et al.: Deep learning of imaging phenotype and genotype for predicting overall survival time of glioblastoma patients. IEEE Trans. Med. Imaging **39**, 2100–2109 (2020)
17. Yao, J., Zhu, X., Huang, J.: Deep multi-instance learning for survival prediction from whole slide images. In: Shen, D., et al. (eds.) MICCAI 2019. LNCS, vol. 11764, pp. 496–504. Springer, Cham (2019). https://doi.org/10.1007/978-3-030-32239-7_55
18. Zhu, X., Yao, J., Huang, J.: Deep convolutional neural network for survival analysis with pathological images. In: IEEE International Conference on Bioinformatics and Biomedicine, pp. 544–547 (2016)
19. Zhu, X., Yao, J., Zhu, F., Huang, J.: WSISA: making survival prediction from whole slide histopathological images. In: Proceedings of the IEEE Conference on Computer Vision and Pattern Recognition, pp. 7234–7242 (2017)

Tracing Diagnosis Paths on Histopathology WSIs for Diagnostically Relevant Case Recommendation

Yushan Zheng[1][✉], Zhiguo Jiang[1,2], Haopeng Zhang[1,2], Fengying Xie[1,2], and Jun Shi[3]

[1] Beijing Advanced Innovation Center for Biomedical Engineering, Beihang University, Beijing 100191, China
yszheng@buaa.edu.com
[2] Image Processing Center, SA, Beihang University, Beijing 102206, China
[3] School of Software, Hefei University of Technology, Hefei 230601, China

Abstract. Telepathology has enabled the remote cancer diagnosis based on digital pathological whole slide images (WSIs). During the diagnosis, the behavior information of the pathologist can be recorded by the platform and then archived with the digital cases. The diagnosis path of the pathologist on a WSI is valuable information since the image content within the path is highly correlated with the diagnosis report of the pathologist. In this paper, we proposed a novel diagnosis path network (DPathNet). DPathNet utilizes the diagnosis paths of pathologists on the WSIs as the supervision to learn the pathology knowledge from the image content. Based on the DPathNet, we develop a novel approach for computer-aided cancer diagnosis named session-based histopathology image recommendation (SHIR). SHIR summaries the information of a WSI while the pathologist browsing the WSI and actively recommends the relevant cases within similar image content from the database. The proposed approaches are evaluated on a gastric dataset containing 983 cases within 5 categories of gastric lesions. The experimental results have demonstrated the effectiveness of the DPathNet to the SHIR task and the supervision of the diagnosis path is sufficient to train the DPathNet. The MRR and MAP of the proposed SHIR framework are respectively 0.741 and 0.777 on the gastric dataset.

Keywords: Digital pathology · Gastric cancer · Recommendation

1 Introduction

With the development of whole slide imaging and digital pathology, the biopsy sections have been well archived and the artificial intelligent methods for

Electronic supplementary material The online version of this chapter (https://doi.org/10.1007/978-3-030-59722-1_44) contains supplementary material, which is available to authorized users.

histopathological whole slide image analysis are widely developed [1,4]. There are two remarkable research interests in recent studies on histopathological image analysis (HIA). The one is to develop weak-supervision [2] frameworks to relieve the annotation load of the pathologists [7]. Another is to utilize the resource of digital pathology platforms to enrich the information [9] of auxiliary diagnosis. With the increasing application of the telepathology system, abundant diagnosed cases have been accumulated. The cases contain not only the WSIs but also valuable data including the diagnosis report, meta information, user behavior data, etc. These data are potential to develop CAD applications that are both light-annotated and informative.

One notable information in the telepathology platform is the browse path on the WSI during the diagnosis, which can be automatically recorded by the digital platform without disturbing the pathologists. Theoretically, the pathologist should have reviewed the conclusive regions related to a specific disease before making the diagnosis. Therefore, the diagnosis path on the WSI and the diagnosis result should be highly correlated. This hypothesis motivated us to build a deep neural network to learn the relationship between image content under the diagnosis path and the label of the WSI, and verify whether this type of weak supervision is sufficient to learn pathology knowledge and build computer-aided cancer diagnosis system.

In this paper, we propose a novel deep learning framework to learn pathology knowledge based on the path of diagnosis on WSIs. Furthermore, we proposed a novel approach for computer-aided diagnosis named session-based histopathology image recommendation (SHIR). As shown in Fig. 1, the application is designed to monitor the pathologist's browse path on the WSI during diagnosis and actively query the telepathology database to recommend historical cases within relevant path and image content. The similar cases are fed to the pathologist to provide assistant information. We have conducted experiments to verify the proposed method and compared it with related methods [15,18,20] on a large scale gastric dataset. The experimental results have demonstrated the supervision of the diagnosis path is sufficient to train a qualified model for histopathological image analysis, and the proposed SHIR is promising to develop systems for computer-aided cancer diagnosis.

The contribution of this paper is two-fold. 1) We proposed a novel DPath-Net, which utilized the browse paths on the WSIs as the supervision to learn the pathology knowledge from WSIs. The training of DPathNet does not rely on the pixel-level or image-level annotations. The annotation workload is much lighter than that in traditional methods. 2) We introduced the technique of session-based recommendation [10,17] into the domain of histopathological image analysis and developed the session-based histopathology image recommendation (SHIR). The data for training and application of the SHIR can be automatically formed by the telepathology platform without disturbing the diagnosis of pathologists.

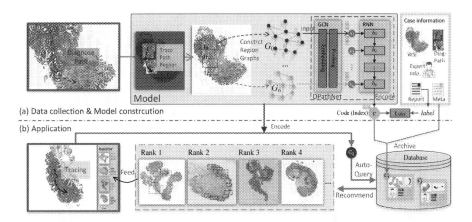

Fig. 1. The framework of the proposed recommendation approach. (a) presents the flowchart of the model construction, where the ROIs in the diagnosis path are numbered and the features of ROIs are extracted using GCNs, then the sequence of features are fed into an RNN to obtain the code of the path. (b) illustrates an application instance, where the diagnosis path is encoded using the trained model and then the relevant cases are recommended based on similarity measurement.

2   Related Works

Recommendation is an important task in online services (e.g. e-commerce, media streaming), which traces the browsing history of a customer and feeds back the relevant items to the customer for reference. In the domain of histopathological image analysis, the most related existing application is content-based histopathological image retrieval (CBHIR) [9,11,12,22]. CBHIR can provide more interpretable information than the traditional applications, e.g. segmentation, detection, to the pathologists [5,6,13,21]. However, CBHIR requires the pathologists manually selecting a region of interest (ROI) as the query instance and the retrieval does not consider the regions the pathologists have already viewed. In comparison, the proposed recommendation framework can continuously analyze the intention of the pathologists throughout the diagnosis and actively feed back the relevant cases to pathologists. The application is more informative and convenient than the CBHIR.

In the aspect of machine learning techniques, graph convolution networks (GCNs) and recurrent neural networks (RNNs) are introduced into the domain of histopathology image analysis in recent years and have proven effective in the tasks of large histopathology image encoding and recognition. Li et al. [8] utilized graphs for survival analysis based on WSI. Zheng et al. [20] applied a GCN to encode the sub-regions on the WSI for CBHIR. Campanella et al. [2] employed RNNs to combine the information of key patches in the feature space and Yan et al. [18] used RNNs to model the adjacency of patches for histopathological image classification. In our method, GCN is utilized to encode the ROIs in the diagnosis path and RNN is employed to mine the pathology information based on the features of the sequential ROIs.

3   Method

The proposed SHIR framework is illustrated in Fig. 1, where the DPathNet is the main component in the framework. The feature extraction for ROIs within the path and the encoding of the sequential browsing information are the main tasks of DPathNet, which will be detailed in this section.

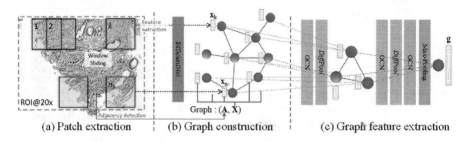

(a) Patch extraction   (b) Graph construction   (c) Graph feature extraction

Fig. 2. The flowchart of region feature extraction, where (a) displays an ROI in a diagnosis path and the window sliding strategy on the region, (b) illustrates the items for graph construction, and (c) is structure of the GCN for graph feature extraction.

3.1   ROI Feature Extraction

The features to represent image regions within the diagnosis path are extracted based on GCNs following Zheng et al. [20]. As shown in Fig. 2, an ROI is divided into patches using a sliding window and the patches are fed into a CNN to extract patch features. The CNN structure is the EfficientNet [14] for its good performance in image classification tasks. The resolution to extract the features is $0.48\,\mu\text{m}/\text{pixel}$ (under $20\times$ lens). Letting $\mathbf{x}_k \in \mathbb{R}^d$ denote the CNN feature of the k-th patch, the graph for the ROI is defined as $G = (\mathbf{A}, \mathbf{X})$, where $\mathbf{A} \in \{0,1\}^{n_p \times n_p}$ is the 4-neighborhood adjacency matrix for the n_p patches in the ROI and $\mathbf{X} = [\mathbf{x}_1, ..., \mathbf{x}_{n_p}] \in \mathbb{R}^{d \times n_p}$ is the feature matrix of the graph[1]. Next, the graph is fed into a hierarchical GCN structures with DiffPool modules [19] to extract the graph feature. The process is represented in brief as $\mathbf{g} = \mathcal{F}_{graph}(\mathbf{A}, \mathbf{X})$ in this paper and the details for the graph feature extraction please refer to the *Supplemental Material*.

---

[1] The blank patches are filtered in the construction of the graph.

3.2 Diagnosis Path Encoding

The encoding of the path is based on an RNN. In this paper, we selected the Gated Recurrent Units (GRU)[3] to build the RNN. Here, the features of the sequential ROIs are represented as $S = \{\mathbf{g}_1, \mathbf{g}_2, ..., \mathbf{g}_n\}$. Letting S be the input of the RNN, the inference of the GRU at time $t = 1, 2, .., n$ is defined as

$$\mathbf{z}_t = \sigma(\mathbf{W}_z \mathbf{g}_t + \mathbf{U}_z \mathbf{h}_{t-1}), \mathbf{r}_t = \sigma(\mathbf{W}_r \mathbf{g}_t + \mathbf{U}_r \mathbf{h}_{t-1}),$$
$$\tilde{\mathbf{h}} = \tanh(\mathbf{W}\mathbf{g}_t + \mathbf{U}(\mathbf{r}_t \odot \mathbf{h}_{t-1})), \mathbf{h}_t = (1 - \mathbf{z}_t) \odot \mathbf{h}_{t-1} + \mathbf{z}_t \odot \tilde{\mathbf{h}}, \tag{1}$$

where $\mathbf{z}_t$ and $\mathbf{r}_t$ are respectively the update gate and the reset gate, the notations involving $\mathbf{W}$ and $\mathbf{U}$ are trainable parameters, $\odot$ represents the Hadamard product, and $\mathbf{h}_t$ is the activation at time t ($\mathbf{h}_0 = \mathbf{0}$). Correspondingly, $\mathbf{h}_n$ is the final output of the RNN.

3.3 Training and Recommendation

The recommendation based on the DPathNet faces the following four issues. 1) The explicit label for each ROI in the path is unavailable in the practical application of SHIR. Therefore, the training of the DPathNet can only utilize the labels of paths. 2) The WSI occasionally contains multiple lesions and thereby the corresponding path is multi-labeled. It determines the network is inappropriate to be trained using class-exclusive loss functions, e.g. cross-entropy. 3) The scale of the recommendation database is growing during the work of the telepathology platform. Therefore, the model should be scalable to the size of the database. 4) The recommendation system is expected to be real-time. The efficiency of the model should be considered.

To simultaneously solve the above issues, we built an encoding layer $\mathbf{c} = \tanh(\mathbf{W}_h \mathbf{h}_n + \mathbf{b}_h)$ at the end of DPathNet to convert the RNN outputs $\mathbf{h}_n$ as binary-like codes, then trained the model using a triplet loss function and finally realized the recommendation based on similarity matching. Specifically, the loss function is defined by the negative log triplet label likelihood [16], which is formulated as

$$L = -\frac{1}{M} \sum_{m=1}^{M} \log \sigma(\frac{1}{2} \mathbf{c}_{a_m}^T \mathbf{c}_{p_m} - \frac{1}{2} \mathbf{c}_{p_m}^T \mathbf{c}_{n_m} - \alpha)$$
$$+ \lambda \frac{1}{M} \sum_{m=1}^{M} \sum_{k \in \{a_m, p_m, b_m\}} \|\mathbf{c}_k - \mathbf{u}_k\|_2^2, \tag{2}$$

where $(\mathbf{c}_{a_m}, \mathbf{c}_{p_m}, \mathbf{c}_{n_m})$ denotes the code of (anchor, relevant, irrelevant) paths for the m-th triplet, M is the number of training paths, α is defined as the margin in the triplet loss, $\sigma(\cdot)$ is the sigmoid function to generate the probability, and $\mathbf{u}_k = sign(\mathbf{c}_k)$ is the binarization code of $\mathbf{c}_k$. The GCN and the RNN in the DPathNet are jointly trained by integrated backward propagation. The gradient optimization algorithm was mini-batch Stochastic Gradient Descent (SGD) with momentum.

The recommendation is achieved by the binary code **u** with the similarity measurement based on Hamming distance [11,20]. The cases having the most similar binary codes to the path at a certain time are returned as the recommendation results for the time.

4   Experiment

4.1   Experimental Settings

To study the feasibility and effectiveness of the SHIR approach, we collected a gastric WSI dataset containing 983 gastric cases. One conclusive WSI was selected from each case to build the WSI dataset. We invited pathologists to make diagnoses for the WSIs on the digital pathology platform[2]. The browsing paths of the pathologists were recorded by the platform during the diagnoses and then supplied for this research. Specifically, the screens *focused* on by the pathologists above 10× lenses (0.96 μm/pixel) were recorded to the sequential path data. A screen is recognized as *focused* when the display rendering is completed after all the tiles within the screen are downloaded from the cloud. Owning to the second level cache mechanism of the browsing system, small movement and zoom or the revisit to a certain screen will not trigger the rendering and thereby will not repeatedly recorded to the path.

To comprehensively evaluate the proposed model and assess the corresponding full-supervision methods, we invited experts to annotate the exact lesion regions associated to the path and categorize the annotations into 5 types of gastric pathology (including *Low-grade intraepithelial neoplasia* (LGIN), *High-grade intraepithelial neoplasia* (HGIN), *Adenocarcinoma* (A.), *Mucinous adenocarcinoma* (MA), and *Signet-ring cell carcinoma* (SRCC)). The paths were labeled following the priority A.=MA=SRCC>HGIN>LGIN according to the annotation of ROIs in the path. A path was assigned multiple labels if and only it contained more than one malignant tumors (A.,MA, and SRCC), and otherwise, it was assigned a single label. The lengths of the paths range from 1 to 61 with an average number of 10.20. The total number of focused views (i.e., ROIs) is 10030. Several instances from the dataset are presented in Fig. 3.

The WSIs in the dataset are divided into subsets as $(\mathcal{D}_{train}, \mathcal{D}_{val}, \mathcal{D}_{test})$ in number of $(550, 138, 295)$ cases. $\mathcal{D}_{train}$ was used to train the DPathNet and regarded as the recommendation database in the experiment, $\mathcal{D}_{val}$ was used to tune the hyper-parameters involved in the model, and $\mathcal{D}_{test}$ was used as the query set and to assess of the final performance of the SHIR framework. A pair of paths were considered as relevant in both the training and in the evaluation phases if the intersection set of their labels is nonempty and as irrelevant otherwise. The precision for recommending N items (P@N), mean reciprocal rank (MRR) and mean average precision (MAP) for the recommendation were the metrics. The EfficientNet-b0 structure pre-trained on the ImageNet was employed to extract the patch features. The size of patches is 224×224 to fit the input size

---

[2] https://gallery.motic.com.

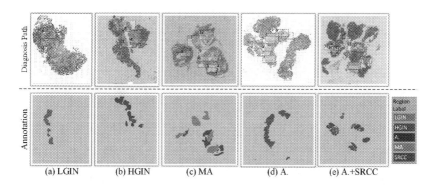

Fig. 3. Display of the gastric database, where the first row displays the diagnosis paths (the regions are numbered in chronological order) traced by telepathology platform, the second row provides the annotations with the notes on the right, and the path labels are provided under the annotations.

of EfficientNet. The hyper-parameters for the GCN model were set referring to [20]. The naive RNN module and LSTM were also evaluated besides GRU.

All the algorithms were implemented in python with torch and run on a computer with 2 CPUs of Intel Xeon E5-2630 and 4 GPUs of Nvidia Geforce 2080Ti. The parameters in the DPathNet are jointly trained by integrated backward propagation. The mini-batch data for each step of training was generated by weighted sampling to ensure a balanced distribution of category labels. The paths in a mini-batch were padded to the maximum path length in the batch. More details please refer to the source code at https://github.com/Zhengyushan/dpathnet.

4.2 Results and Discussion

The performance of the proposed recommendation framework is presented in Table 1, where the results for the binary-category (malignancy *vs.* benign) recommendation task are also compared. To quantitatively assess the gap of the path-level supervision from the pixel-wise annotation, we made full use of the pixel-wise annotation to pre-train the EfficientNet and the GCN by image patch and ROI classification tasks, respectively, and then fine-tuned the GCN during the training of the DPathNet. The corresponding results (noted by *Pixel* in Table 1) were considered as the upper boundary of the recommendation problem. Table 1 shows that the DPathNet within GRU module achieves an MAP of 0.777 for the 5-category recommendation task (0.921 for the binary task), which is 0.015 (0.014) to the networks trained by pixel-level annotations. The results have indicated 1) The proposed DPathNet is effective in the SHIR task and is promising to build automatic learning systems for telepathology platforms. 2) The path-level (i.e., the WSI-level) supervision is basically sufficient to train the DPathNet. The workload of manual annotation of the pathologist can be entirely relieved at the cost of less than 2% decrease of the recommendation accuracy.

Table 1. Comparison of the recommendation metrics for different levels of supervision. Please refer to the text for detail.

Methods	Label type	Binary task				5-category task			
		P@5	P@20	MRR	MAP	P@5	P@20	MRR	MAP
DPathNet w/ RNN	*Pixel*	0.919	0.910	0.937	0.938	0.736	0.736	0.760	0.784
DPathNet w/ LSTM		0.906	0.903	0.912	0.931	0.749	0.752	0.775	0.792
DPathNet w/ GRU		0.909	0.912	0.922	0.937	0.755	0.749	0.773	0.784
DPathNet w/ RNN	*WSI*	0.860	0.864	0.874	0.898	0.626	0.629	0.696	0.659
DPathNet w/ LSTM		0.887	0.889	0.888	0.921	0.691	0.684	0.725	0.760
DPathNet w/ GRU		0.892	0.897	0.911	0.924	0.716	0.707	0.741	0.777

Table 2. Comparison of the recommendation metrics for relevant approaches and the proposed method. Please refer to the text for detail.

Methods	Binary task				5-category task			
	P@5	P@20	MRR	MAP	P@5	P@20	MRR	MAP
Jimenez-del-Toro et al. [15]	0.795	0.811	0.883	0.818	0.632	0.622	0.692	0.655
Yan et al. [18]	0.859	0.849	0.904	0.862	0.678	0.664	0.726	0.702
Zheng et al. [20]	0.834	0.858	**0.915**	0.881	0.654	0.659	0.721	0.712
DPathNet (Ours)	**0.892**	**0.897**	0.911	**0.924**	**0.716**	**0.707**	**0.741**	**0.777**

Then, we compared the proposed method with 3 related works [15,18,20]. The method [15] studies WSI retrieval. We adopted the algorithm in [15] to achieve diagnosis path recommendation. Yan et al. [18] utilized an RNN to classify histopathological images and Zheng et al. [20] applied GCNs to encoding sub-regions on the WSI. In this experiment, we trained the networks in the two methods based on the ROI labels to extracted ROI features. Meanwhile, we adapted the patch-based similarity measurement proposed in [15] to these ROI features to realize the recommendation. The results are given in Table 2. Overall, the proposed DPathNet performed significantly better than the compared methods. The supervision (ROI label) in [18] and [20] is stronger than that in DPathNet but the two methods do not consider the sequential information of ROIs in the diagnosis path. Therefore, the results of the two methods cannot surpass DPathNet. In comparison, DPathNet has modeled the sequential information using an RNN structure. The high level of pathology knowledge for lesion recognition has been learned from the context relationship within the diagnosis path, and thereby delivered better recommendation performance. The average time for a step of recommendation when a new screen was appended to the path was 474.84 ms, which is promising to develop near real-time applications.

Figure 4 illustrates 3 recommendation instances of the proposed SHIR framework. Generally, the recommendation for lesion types A. and SRCC are acceptable. The accuracy for the type HGIN occasionally confused with the LGIN and A. in its present version, which needs to be improved in future work.

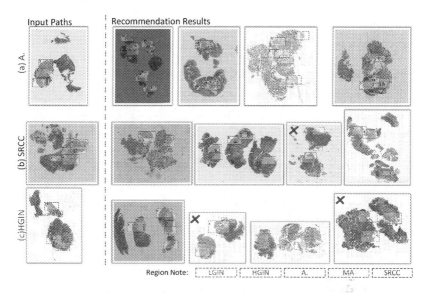

Fig. 4. The illustration of recommendation results, where first column displays 3 instances in the testing set with the path label provided on the left, the top recommendation results for each instance is are displayed on the right, and the incorrect results (irrelevant to the input one) are marked by red cross. (Color figure online)

5   Conclusion

The browse paths of pathologists on the whole slide images are valuable information, which is highly correlated with the diagnosis of cancer cases yet can be easily recorded by the digital pathology platform. In this paper, we developed a novel DPathNet to model the path information on the WSI. Meanwhile, we proposed a novel computer-aided cancer diagnosis framework named session-based histopathological image recommendation (SHIR) based on the DPathNet. The experiments have shown that the DPathNet has successfully learned the pathology knowledge by only using the diagnosis paths, for which the workload of manually annotation can be significantly relieved. The results on the gastric dataset indicates that the DPathNet is a promising to develop SHIR system for telepathology platform.

Acknowledgment. This work was partly supported by the National Natural Science Foundation of China (Grant No. 61901018, 61771031, and 61906058), partly by China Postdoctoral Science Foundation (No. 2019M650446) and partly by Motic-BUAA Image Technology Research Center.

References

1. Bejnordi, B.E., Veta, M., Van Diest, P.J., Van Ginneken, B., Karssemeijer, N., Litjens, G., Van Der Laak, et al.: Diagnostic assessment of deep learning algorithms for detection of lymph node metastases in women with breast cancer. JAMA **318**(22), 2199–2210 (2017)
2. Campanella, G., et al.: Clinical-grade computational pathology using weakly supervised deep learning on whole slide images. Nat. Med. **25**(8), 1301–1309 (2019)
3. Cho, K., van Merriënboer, B., Gulcehre, C., Bahdanau, D., Bougares, F., Schwenk, H., Bengio, Y.: Learning phrase representations using RNN encoder-decoder for statistical machine translation. In: Proceedings of the 2014 Conference on Empirical Methods in Natural Language Processing (EMNLP), pp. 1724–1734 (2014)
4. Hollon, T.C., Pandian, B., Adapa, A.R., Urias, E., Save, A.V., Khalsa, S.S.S., Eichberg, D.G., D'Amico, R.S., Farooq, Z.U., Lewis, S., et al.: Near real-time intraoperative brain tumor diagnosis using stimulated raman histology and deep neural networks. Nat. Med. **26**(1), 52–58 (2020)
5. Hu, D., Zheng, Y., Zhang, H., Sun, S., Xie, F., Shi, J., Jiang, Z.: Informative retrieval framework for histopathology whole slides images based on deep hashing network. In: 2020 IEEE 17th International Symposium on Biomedical Imaging (ISBI), pp. 244–248 (2020)
6. Kalra, S., Tizhoosh, H., Choi, C., Shah, S., Diamandis, P., Campbell, C.J., Pantanowitz, L.: Yottixel - An image search engine for large archives of histopathology whole slide images. Med. Image Anal. **65**, 101757 (2020)
7. Van der Laak, J., Ciompi, F., Litjens, G.: No pixel-level annotations needed. Nat. Biomed. Eng. **3**(11), 855–856 (2019)
8. Li, R., Yao, J., Zhu, X., Li, Y., Huang, J.: Graph CNN for survival analysis on whole slide pathological images. In: Frangi, A.F., Schnabel, J.A., Davatzikos, C., Alberola-López, C., Fichtinger, G. (eds.) MICCAI 2018. LNCS, vol. 11071, pp. 174–182. Springer, Cham (2018). https://doi.org/10.1007/978-3-030-00934-2_20
9. Li, Z., Zhang, X., Müller, H., Zhang, S.: Large-scale retrieval for medical image analytics: A comprehensive review. Med. Image Anal. **43**, 66–84 (2018)
10. Liu, Q., Zeng, Y., Mokhosi, R., Zhang, H.: Stamp: Short-term attention/memory priority model for session-based recommendation. In: Proceedings of the 24th ACM SIGKDD International Conference on Knowledge Discovery & Data Mining, pp. 1831–1839 (2018)
11. Peng, T., Boxberg, M., Weichert, W., Navab, N., Marr, C.: Multi-task learning of a deep k-nearest neighbour network for histopathological image classification and retrieval. In: Shen, D., Liu, T., Peters, T.M., Staib, L.H., Essert, C., Zhou, S., Yap, P.-T., Khan, A. (eds.) MICCAI 2019. LNCS, vol. 11764, pp. 676–684. Springer, Cham (2019). https://doi.org/10.1007/978-3-030-32239-7_75
12. Sapkota, M., Shi, X., Xing, F., Yang, L.: Deep convolutional hashing for low-dimensional binary embedding of histopathological images. IEEE J. Biomed. Health Inform. **23**(2), 805–816 (2018)
13. Shi, X., Sapkota, M., Xing, F., Liu, F., Cui, L., Yang, L.: Pairwise based deep ranking hashing for histopathology image classification and retrieval. Pattern Recogn. **81**, 14–22 (2018)
14. Tan, M., Le, Q.: Efficientnet: Rethinking model scaling for convolutional neural networks. In: International Conference on Machine Learning, pp. 6105–6114 (2019)

15. Jimenez-del-Toro, O., Otálora, S., Atzori, M., Müller, H.: Deep multimodal case-based retrieval for large histopathology datasets. In: Wu, G., Munsell, B.C., Zhan, Y., Bai, W., Sanroma, G., Coupé, P. (eds.) Patch-MI 2017. LNCS, vol. 10530, pp. 149–157. Springer, Cham (2017). https://doi.org/10.1007/978-3-319-67434-6_17

16. Wang, X., Shi, Y., Kitani, K.M.: Deep supervised hashing with triplet labels. In: Lai, S.-H., Lepetit, V., Nishino, K., Sato, Y. (eds.) ACCV 2016. LNCS, vol. 10111, pp. 70–84. Springer, Cham (2017). https://doi.org/10.1007/978-3-319-54181-5_5

17. Wu, S., Tang, Y., Zhu, Y., Wang, L., Xie, X., Tan, T.: Session-based recommendation with graph neural networks. In: Proceedings of the AAAI Conference on Artificial Intelligence, vol. 33, pp. 346–353 (2019)

18. Yan, R., et al.: Breast cancer histopathological image classification using a hybrid deep neural network. Methods **173**, 52–60 (2019)

19. Ying, Z., You, J., Morris, C., Ren, X., Hamilton, W., Leskovec, J.: Hierarchical graph representation learning with differentiable pooling. In: Advances in Neural Information Processing Systems, pp. 4800–4810 (2018)

20. Zheng, Y., Jiang, B., Shi, J., Zhang, H., Xie, F.: Encoding histopathological WSIs using GNN for scalable diagnostically relevant regions retrieval. In: Shen, D., Liu, T., Peters, T.M., Staib, L.H., Essert, C., Zhou, S., Yap, P.-T., Khan, A. (eds.) MICCAI 2019. LNCS, vol. 11764, pp. 550–558. Springer, Cham (2019). https://doi.org/10.1007/978-3-030-32239-7_61

21. Zheng, Y., et al.: Histopathological whole slide image analysis using context-based CBIR. IEEE Trans. Med. Imag. **37**(7), 1641–1652 (2018)

22. Zheng, Y., et al.: Size-scalable content-based histopathological image retrieval from database that consists of WSIS. IEEE J. Biomed. Health Inform. **22**(4), 1278–1287 (2018)

Weakly Supervised Multiple Instance Learning Histopathological Tumor Segmentation

Marvin Lerousseau[1,2]($\boxtimes$), Maria Vakalopoulou[1,2], Marion Classe[1,3], Julien Adam[3], Enzo Battistella[1,2], Alexandre Carré[1], Théo Estienne[1,2], Théophraste Henry[1], Eric Deutsch[1], and Nikos Paragios[4]

[1] Paris-Saclay University, Gustave Roussy, Inserm, 94800 Villejuif, France
[2] Paris-Saclay University, CentraleSupélec, 91190 Gif-sur-Yvette, France
`marvin.lerousseau@centralesupelec.fr`
[3] Gustave Roussy, Pathology Department, 94800 Villejuif, France
[4] TheraPanacea, 75014 Paris, France

Abstract. Histopathological image segmentation is a challenging and important topic in medical imaging with tremendous potential impact in clinical practice. State of the art methods rely on hand-crafted annotations which hinder clinical translation since histology suffers from significant variations between cancer phenotypes. In this paper, we propose a weakly supervised framework for whole slide imaging segmentation that relies on standard clinical annotations, available in most medical systems. In particular, we exploit a multiple instance learning scheme for training models. The proposed framework has been evaluated on multi-locations and multi-centric public data from The Cancer Genome Atlas and the PatchCamelyon dataset. Promising results when compared with experts' annotations demonstrate the potentials of the presented approach. The complete framework, including 6481 generated tumor maps and data processing, is available at https://github.com/marvinler/tcga_segmentation.

Keywords: Weakly supervised learning · Histopathological segmentation · Multiple instance learning · Tumor segmentation

1 Introduction

In digital pathology, whole slide images (WSI) are considered the golden standard for primary diagnosis [13,16]. The use of computer-assisted image analysis tools is becoming a mainstream for automatic quantitative or semi-quantitative analysis for pathologists, including the discovery of novel predictive biomarkers [12]. However, a lot of challenges remain to be addressed for machine learning methods because to the high variability of quality of tissue preparation and digital acquisition, and in tissue phenotype. A central objective in digital pathology

© Springer Nature Switzerland AG 2020
A. L. Martel et al. (Eds.): MICCAI 2020, LNCS 12265, pp. 470–479, 2020.
https://doi.org/10.1007/978-3-030-59722-1_45

is the accurate identification of cell or tissue of interest. For instance, computational staining of tumor tissue could be used for slide screening in order to increase the efficiency of pathologists. Automatically computed tumor maps could identify regions of interest for whole slide image classification [5], or be combined with automatic detection of lymphocytes [15] to further characterize the tumor and immune micro-environment for predicting treatment response [3].

Traditionally, image segmentation is tackled by leveraging pixel-wise or patch-wise ground-truth annotations [9]. This is highly problematic in digital pathology due to the colossal size of WSIs with respect to the biological components, implying that the annotation process is considerably time-consuming. Moreover, the high variance of clinical samples contributes on the deficiency of generalization, as illustrated in [4] where the front-runner solution of the CAMELYON16 challenge [2] has reportedly 4 times higher classification errors on the same task for in-house data from the same location.

A standard multiple instance learning (MIL) scheme [8] deals with classifying an entity (bag) from its constituents (instances). The MIL paradigm is particularly suited to histopathological image analysis due to its ability on reasoning on subsets of data (patches) that is often a computational necessity in histopathology. The general approach of MIL consists in learning a model that embeds each instance of a bag into a latent space. Then, the collection (usually of fixed size) of instances latent vectors is forwarded into an aggregating function which outputs the predicted bag probability, using different principles such as max-pooling [8], support vector machine [1], or even attention-based neural networks [11]. Recent large-scale histopathological studies provides promising classification solutions based on the MIL scheme [4–6]. Such approaches generally indicate whether a slide is non-neoplastic (normal), or the predicted subtype of apparent tumor tissue without accurately identifying the tumoral regions in the slide.

There are two ways to interpret multiple instance learning: MIL for classifying bags (or slides), or MIL for training an instance classifier model, apparent to bag segmentation. In particular, studies such as [4–6] use max-pooling MIL and its relaxed formulation [18] to first train an instance model, and then investigate various ways to combine instance predictions into a slide prediction. These works demonstrate that MIL schemes provide powerful formulations for the WSI classification, by reaching AUC for tumor versus normal slide classification higher than 0.99. However, these studies lack extensive evaluation for a more detailed MIL-driven segmentation performance since slide-based classification measures could lead to erroneous assessment regarding instance-level performance.

In this paper, we propose a weakly supervised segmentation scheme that is able to generate tumor segmentation models using annotations from the conventional clinical practice of pathologists' assessment. The contributions of this paper are: (i) a generic meta-algorithm, generating labels from WSI binary values intended to train detailed WSI segmentation models, (ii) a training scheme providing instance-level predictions, trained only with binary WSI annotations, (iii) the release of 6481 automatically generated tumor maps for publicly available slides of The Cancer Genome Atlas (TCGA), an order of magnitude above previous released WSI tumor maps.

2   Weakly Supervised Learning for Tissue-Type Segmentation in Histopathological Images

Contextually, we consider a set $S = \{S_i\}$ of training whole slide images, where each slide S_i is associated with a label $T_i = \{0, 1\}$ where 1 refers to tumor and 0 to normal. More precisely, $T_i = 0$ indicates that there is no apparent tissue in the slide, and $T_i = 1$ indicates that some tissue is tumorous. The goal is to learn a tumor segmentation model, or a patch classifier, using only those binary annotations. To train a model in a fully supervised setup, a batch of patches $\{p_s\}$ is randomly sampled from a WSI along with their annotations computed beforehand. However, such microscopic annotations are impractical to obtain when the number of whole slides images is in the hundreds or thousands, which is necessary for good generalization. To deal with this limitation, the aim of the proposed framework is to generate a set of proxy patch-level ground truth labels by exploiting properties from the available global T_i labels.

By construction, a WSI with $T_i = 0$ indicates that all extracted patches are of normal class (0). In that case, a proxy-label filled with 0 provides perfect instance annotations, equivalent to a fully supervised learning scheme. However, in slides with $T_i = 1$, tumor tissue could possibly be in any extent on the S_i. Alternatively, a WSI with $T_i = 1$, normal tissue can theoretically cover no pixel up to the entire region in the slide except one pixel. We integrate this property by proposing a training scheme in which two parameters α and β are used for each training slide of $T_i = 1$ in the following deterministic process:

- assign a label 1 to the patches ensuring at least $\alpha\%$ are of class 1
- assign a label 0 to the patches ensuring at least $\beta\%$ are of class 0
- discard other patches from the computation of the loss signal

In such a setup, $\alpha\%$ represents the minimum assumed relative area of tumor tissue in the WSI, and similarly for $\beta\%$ with the normal tissue extent. Because the explicit process is deterministic, the framework is identified by the values of α and β. Noteworthy, (α, β) such that $(\alpha + \beta) > 100\%$ would produce contradictory proxy labels for $100 - (\alpha + \beta)\% > 0$ instances, which could impede training by diminishing the signal-to-noise ratio. Therefore, the possible space of these two parameters can be defined as $\mathbb{F} = \{(\alpha, \beta); \alpha > 0, \beta \geq 0, \alpha + \beta \leq 1\}$.

Formally, given a loss function L (e.g. binary cross-entropy), the formulated framework aims at minimizing the following empirical risk on S:

$$c_0 \cdot \sum_{\substack{S_i \in S; \\ T_i = 0}} \underbrace{\left[\sum_{p_s \sim S_i} L(f(p_s), 0) \right]}_{R_{\mathrm{FP}}}$$

$$+ c_1 \cdot \sum_{\substack{S_i \in S; \\ T_i = 1}} \left[\underbrace{\sum_{\substack{p_s \sim S_i; \\ p_s \in P(f(p_s); \alpha, 100)}} L(f(p_s), 1)}_{R_\alpha} + \underbrace{\sum_{\substack{p_s \sim S_i; \\ p_s \in P(f(p_s); 0, \beta)}} L(f(p_s), 0)}_{R_\beta} \right]$$

where $P(f(p_s); p_{\min}, p_{\max})$ is defined as the subset of patches $f(p_s)$ for which the predicted probability lies within the $p_{\min}th$ and the $p_{\max}th$ percentiles of the predictions $f(p_s)$, c_0 and c_1 are constants for batch averaging and class imbalance for both classes, and T_i refers to the binary ground-truth of S_i. Minimizing this empirical risk will guide models into recalling enough positive tumoral patches (R_α) per slide but not too much (R_β) while maintaining a low level of false positive in negative slides R_{FP}. The formulated approach is generic, in the sense that it can be used to train a large scope of machine learning models, including neural networks, with patch-based or pixel-wise predictions, and it can be coupled with most usual loss functions. It produces trained segmentation models, readily available to produce heatmaps without intervention of the formulated pipeline nor $\alpha\%$ and $\beta\%$ parameters.

3   Implementation Details and Dataset

3.1   Framework Setup and Architecture Details

We perform a benchmark of a representative population of the framework parameters space $\mathbb{F}$. Specifically, $\mathbb{F}$ is sampled starting from 0 with increment of 0.2 (or 20%) for both α and β (e.g. $(0,0)$, $(0, 0.2)$, $(0, 0.4)$ and so on), resulting in $\frac{6 \cdot 7}{2} = 21$ configurations. Of those, the 6 configurations with $\alpha = 0$ are discarded, as this would imply that the framework provides only 0 labels contradicting with the $T_i = 1$ assumption of our empirical risk formulation. At the end only 15 sampled configurations had been used.

Each configuration is used to train a ResNet50 architecture [10], which has been extensively used for histopathology image analysis in a multitude of tasks [14], and can be used without the global average pooling layer to yield 13×13 outputs per 224 pixel-wide input image. Pre-training is used with initialization on a well-performing snapshot on ImageNet [7]. At each epoch, each training slide is sampled once. Upon sampling, a batch size of 150 patches of size 224×224 are randomly sampled at 20x magnification in the tissue region of a WSI. Data augmentation is used independently on each image, with random rotations and flips while also applying channel-wise standard scaling from training averages and variances, and color jitter. The model is then concurrently inferred on the 150 patches of the batch, and a proxy-vector is constructed with the formulated pipeline as illustrated for 10 patches in Fig. 1. Specifically, the

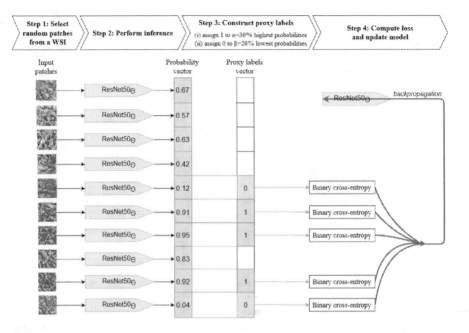

Fig. 1. Illustration of the processing of a batch of 10 patches from a positive WSI. A unique ResNet50 model with parameters θ is inferred on all images of the batch. For a given configuration of (α, β) (here, $(0.3, 0.2)$), these predictions are first used to create a proxy image-wise labels vector, then combined with the proxy label to compute batch error for further parameters θ update with backpropagation.

$\lfloor 150 \times \alpha \rfloor$ patches of highest probabilities are associated with a proxy value of 1, and the $\lfloor 150 \times \beta \rfloor$ patches of lowest probabilities with a proxy value of 0. A masking vector of size 150 is concurrently filled such that patches with no attributed label are discarded. The proxy vector is then coupled with the model's 150 predictions minus the discarded ones, in order to compute patch-wise binary cross-entropy loss which is then averaged and retro-propagated across all the non masked predictions. The error signal is used to tune model parameters using Adam optimizer with learning rate of 10^{-4} and default momentum parameters. c_0 and c_1 are set to 1. Each configuration is trained for 20 epochs on 2 V100 NVIDIA GPU, for a training time of ~ 16 h, or a total benchmark training time of ~ 240 h. The code is implemented with pytorch 1.5.0 and torchvision 0.4.0 on python3.6.

3.2   Dataset

The dataset consists of 6481 flash-frozen whole slide images from TCGA, issued from kidney (2334), bronchus and lung (2168) and breast (1979) WSIs locations. These locations were selected on TCGA as the first 3 indexed, while no slide filtering nor slide selection has been performed to be coherent with standard clinical practices. This dataset was divided in training, validation and testing sets on a case basis, with 65%, 15%, and 20% of cases respectively. For the rest of the paper this testing set is denoted as "In-distribution". Each selected configuration is trained using the training set, with hyper-parameters optimized on the validation set. Then, their performance is assessed on the testing set. For extensive quantitative performance assessment, expert pathologists annotated 130 slides from this testing set (45 breast, 40 kidney, 45 bronchus and lung), thus measuring in-distribution generalization. Annotations were computed at 20x magnification by a junior pathologist on a in-house annotation tool by contouring tumor tissue regions which were then filled, and were modified until validation by a senior pathologist.

The same protocol was applied on additional slides extracted from locations which are not used in the previous cohort. Specifically, 35 WSIs from colon, 35 from ovary and 30 from corpus uteri are pixel-wise annotated and used to measure generalization performance of models to unseen tissue environments, which we denote as the "Out-of-location" testing set. We pinpoint that these annotations were not used during training nor validation, but only to assess testing segmentation performance of the produced models. For training, we use diagnostic labels extracted directly from TCGA, for which each slide name contain a code indicating the type of specimen (e.g. "Solid Tissue Normal" or "Primary Solid Tumor")[1]. Notably, normal slides are explicitly discerned from slide with apparent pathological tissue. In such context, each slide is associated with a binary value indicating whether tumor tissue is apparent in the slide, or whether the slide is of normal tissue only. To further compare with results from the community, we infer all models on the PatchCamelyon dataset [17]. The dataset consists in 96×96 patches extracted from formalin-fixed, paraffin-embedded (FFPE) tissues from sentinel lymph nodes at 10x magnification. In PatchCamelyon, images are labeled as 1 if their 32×32 center region contains at least 1 pixel of tumor cell, otherwise 0. To accommodate with the 224×224 input at 20x magnification of the learned models, these images were bi-linearly upsampled twice and padded with 0. This testing set is particularly challenging for the benchmarked models, since they are not trained on FFPE slides, which are visually highly different from flash-frozen ones. Besides, the trained models did not include any tissue extracted from sentinel lymph nodes, highlighting the generalization challenge of the proposed framework.

4   Results and Discussion

For performance assessment, all 15 trained ResNet50 models are inferred on the testing slides. The resulting heatmaps are compared to segmentations maps provided by the pathologists. All configurations are found to converge to sup-random In-distribution performance, except for the two extreme configurations ($\alpha = 1, \beta = 0$) and $(0.2, 0.8)$, as displayed in Table 1. The average In-distribution AUC is 0.675 ± 0.132, with optimal AUC of 0.804 for ($\alpha = 0.2, \beta = 0.2$).

---

[1] https://gdc.cancer.gov/resources-tcga-users/tcga-code-tables/sample-type-codes.

Precision and recall are extracted after threshold selection on validation set and displayed in Fig. 2. The α parameter seems to influence the recall at the expense of precision. Upon performance introspection by location, all configurations report the worse performance for the location bronchus and lung, with twice as much AUC error compared to kidney and breast locations. Concerning the Out-of-distribution cohort, the average AUC is 0.679 ± 0.154, which is close to In-distribution performance, although lower when omitting bronchus and lung location from the latter. There is no evident pattern for configurations that yield improved Out-of-location results.

Table 1. Pixelwise AUC for the 15 (α, β) framework configurations on the hold-out testing set (In-distribution) and the testing set from locations unseen in training (Out-of-location). Grey results take background into account, black ones are computed by completely discarding background from performance computation.

$\alpha =$	0.2					0.4				0.6			0.8		1.0
$\beta =$	0	0.2	0.4	0.6	0.8	0	0.2	0.4	0.6	0	0.2	0.4	0	0.2	0
In-distribution	.786	.804	.749	.681	.566	.720	.726	.767	.685	.766	.758	.650	.589	.619	.256
	.964	.952	.960	.930	.874	.967	.953	.959	.935	.957	.960	.940	.946	.946	.926
Out-of-location	.866	.732	.709	.583	.257	.783	.710	.762	.658	.790	.787	.673	.785	.695	.404
	.984	.974	.972	.958	.917	.980	.972	.978	.966	.981	.980	.968	.980	.970	.933

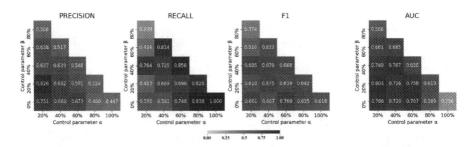

Fig. 2. Quantitative results for the 15 benchmarked configurations on the hold-out testing set (In-distribution) from bronchus and lung, kidney, and breast locations. Each subplot (4 in total) displays a pixelwise measure, as indicated in its sup-title, for each configuration in a matrix format. AUC: area under the ROC curve.

Some visual representations of two different samples testing are presented on Fig. 3. In particular, in the figure we present the WSI image together with the pixel-wise annotations of the pathologist. Moreover, different segmentation maps depending on the configuration are also presented. It can observed that there are 3 or 4 configurations that are close to the expert's annotations. These configurations are in line with our quantitative results. Additional post-processing strategies would potentially boost the performance of our framework.

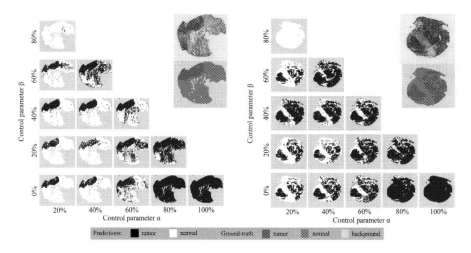

Fig. 3. Unfiltered predicted tumor maps on hold-out testing samples for the 15 bench-marked framework configurations. 2 WSI and their corresponding results are displayed in a matrix-format. The red and green images are the ground-truth.

To test the generalization of our method, we performed also experiments on the PatchCamelyon dataset [17]. In particular we found the most of the configurations (12 out of the 15) reporting quite low AUC, between 0.428 and 0.612. However, 3 configurations are found to generalize to some extent, that is $(\alpha = 0.2, \beta = 0)$ with 0.672 AUC, $(0.2, 0.2)$ with 0.802, and $(0.4, 0)$ with 0.758. Although these results are far from report AUC of 0.963 obtained with fully supervised models specifically trained on this dataset [17], the results suggest the presented framework could provide models which can grasp generic discriminative cancer features from multiple types of slides in broad biological context.

5   Conclusion and Future Works

In this paper we propose a weakly supervised model which provides segmentation maps of WSIs, trained only with binary annotations over the entire WSIs. From our experiments we saw that usually 3 to 4 configurations are expected to yield respectively high precision, high recall, and high overall performance for WSIs of different organs and tumor coverage. The findings in this paper highlight the potential of weakly supervised learning in histopathological image segmentation, which is known to be heavily impeded by the annotation bottleneck. With the complete open-source releases of both the complete WSI pre-processing pipeline, the presented training framework, as well as the inference pipeline, the presented approach can be used off-the-shelf for pan-cancer tumor segmentation using the entire 18k flash-frozen WSI of TCGA, or other type of tissue segmentation such as necrosis or stromal tissue. The public release of 6481 automatically generated tumor maps, with an expected AUC above 0.932, should lower the barrier of entry to pathomics by bypassing tumor annotation efforts. All code and results can be found at https://github.com/marvinler/tcga_segmentation.

There are many ways to fine-tune a segmentation model using the formulated framework, such as with more appropriate deep learning architectures or with more extensive hyper-parameters optimization. We believe the most impactful future works will revolve around the proxy-generation labels from more sophisticated slide labels which would yield higher information while remaining fast to obtain, essentially trading annotation time for performance.

References

1. Andrews, S., Tsochantaridis, I., Hofmann, T.: Support vector machines for multiple-instance learning. In: Advances in Neural Information Processing Systems, pp. 577–584 (2003)
2. Bejnordi, B.E., Veta, M., Van Diest, P.J., Van Ginneken, B., Karssemeijer, N., Litjens, G., Van Der Laak, J.A., Hermsen, M., Manson, Q.F., Balkenhol, M., et al.: Diagnostic assessment of deep learning algorithms for detection of lymph node metastases in women with breast cancer. Jama 318(22), 2199–2210 (2017)
3. Binnewies, M., Roberts, E.W., Kersten, K., Chan, V., Fearon, D.F., Merad, M., Coussens, L.M., Gabrilovich, D.I., Ostrand-Rosenberg, S., Hedrick, C.C., et al.: Understanding the tumor immune microenvironment (time) for effective therapy. Nat. Med. 24(5), 541–550 (2018)
4. Campanella, G., Hanna, M.G., Geneslaw, L., Miraflor, A., Silva, V.W.K., Busam, K.J., Brogi, E., Reuter, V.E., Klimstra, D.S., Fuchs, T.J.: Clinical-grade computational pathology using weakly supervised deep learning on whole slide images. Nat. Med. 25(8), 1301–1309 (2019)
5. Campanella, G., Silva, V.W.K., Fuchs, T.J.: Terabyte-scale deep multiple instance learning for classification and localization in pathology (2018). arXiv preprint arXiv:1805.06983
6. Coudray, N., Ocampo, P.S., Sakellaropoulos, T., Narula, N., Snuderl, M., Fenyö, D., Moreira, A.L., Razavian, N., Tsirigos, A.: Classification and mutation prediction from non-small cell lung cancer histopathology images using deep learning. Nat. Med. 24(10), 1559 (2018)
7. Deng, J., Dong, W., Socher, R., Li, L.J., Li, K., Fei-Fei, L.: ImageNet: a large-scale hierarchical image database. In: 2009 IEEE Conference on Computer Vision and Pattern Recognition, pp. 248–255. IEEE (2009)
8. Dietterich, T.G., Lathrop, R.H., Lozano-Pérez, T.: Solving the multiple instance problem with axis-parallel rectangles. Artif. Intell. 89(1–2), 31–71 (1997)
9. Guo, Y., Liu, Y., Georgiou, T., Lew, M.S.: A review of semantic segmentation using deep neural networks. Int. J. Multimedia Inf. Retrieval 7(2), 87–93 (2017). https://doi.org/10.1007/s13735-017-0141-z
10. He, K., Zhang, X., Ren, S., Sun, J.: Deep residual learning for image recognition. In: Proceedings of the IEEE Conference on Computer Vision and Pattern Recognition, pp. 770–778 (2016)
11. Ilse, M., Tomczak, J.M., Welling, M.: Attention-based deep multiple instance learning (2018). arXiv preprint arXiv:1802.04712
12. Janowczyk, A., Madabhushi, A.: Deep learning for digital pathology image analysis: A comprehensive tutorial with selected use cases. J. Pathol. Inform. 7, 29 (2016)

13. Jara-Lazaro, A.R., Thamboo, T.P., Teh, M., Tan, P.H.: Digital pathology: Exploring its applications in diagnostic surgical pathology practice. Pathology **42**(6), 512–518 (2010)
14. Mormont, R., Geurts, P., Marée, R.: Comparison of deep transfer learning strategies for digital pathology. In: Proceedings of the IEEE Conference on Computer Vision and Pattern Recognition Workshops, pp. 2262–2271 (2018)
15. Saltz, J., et al.: Spatial organization and molecular correlation of tumor-infiltrating lymphocytes using deep learning on pathology images. Cell Reports **23**(1), 181–193 (2018)
16. Stathonikos, N., Veta, M., Huisman, A., van Diest, P.J.: Going fully digital: Perspective of a dutch academic pathology lab. J. Pathol. Inform. **4**, 15 (2013)
17. Veeling, B.S., Linmans, J., Winkens, J., Cohen, T., Welling, M.: Rotation equivariant CNNs for digital pathology. In: Frangi, A.F., Schnabel, J.A., Davatzikos, C., Alberola-López, C., Fichtinger, G. (eds.) MICCAI 2018. LNCS, vol. 11071, pp. 210–218. Springer, Cham (2018). https://doi.org/10.1007/978-3-030-00934-2_24
18. Zhu, W., Lou, Q., Vang, Y.S., Xie, X.: Deep multi-instance networks with sparse label assignment for whole mammogram classification. In: Descoteaux, M., Maier-Hein, L., Franz, A., Jannin, P., Collins, D.L., Duchesne, S. (eds.) MICCAI 2017. LNCS, vol. 10435, pp. 603–611. Springer, Cham (2017). https://doi.org/10.1007/978-3-319-66179-7_69

Divide-and-Rule: Self-Supervised Learning for Survival Analysis in Colorectal Cancer

Christian Abbet[1]([✉]), Inti Zlobec[4], Behzad Bozorgtabar[1,2,3],
and Jean-Philippe Thiran[1,2,3]

[1] Signal Processing Laboratory 5, EPFL, Lausanne, Switzerland
{christian.abbet,behzad.bozorgtabar,jeanphilippe.thiran}@epfl.ch
[2] Department of Radiology, Lausanne University Hospital, Lausanne, Switzerland
[3] Center of Biomedical Imaging, Lausanne, Switzerland
[4] TRU – Translational Research Unit, Bern, Switzerland

Abstract. With the long-term rapid increase in incidences of colorectal cancer (CRC), there is an urgent clinical need to improve risk stratification. The conventional pathology report is usually limited to only a few histopathological features. However, most of the tumor microenvironments used to describe patterns of aggressive tumor behavior are ignored. In this work, we aim to learn histopathological patterns within cancerous tissue regions that can be used to improve prognostic stratification for colorectal cancer. To do so, we propose a self-supervised learning method that jointly learns a representation of tissue regions as well as a metric of the clustering to obtain their underlying patterns. These histopathological patterns are then used to represent the interaction between complex tissues and predict clinical outcomes directly. We furthermore show that the proposed approach can benefit from linear predictors to avoid overfitting in patient outcomes predictions. To this end, we introduce a new well-characterized clinicopathological dataset, including a retrospective collective of 374 patients, with their survival time and treatment information. Histomorphological clusters obtained by our method are evaluated by training survival models. The experimental results demonstrate statistically significant patient stratification, and our approach outperformed the state-of-the-art deep clustering methods.

Keywords: Self-supervised learning · Histology · Survival analysis · Colorectal cancer

1 Introduction

Colorectal cancer is the third leading cause of cancer-related mortality worldwide. Five-year survival rates are low, at 60%. Although standard histopathological of cancer reporting based on features such as staging and grading identifies

Electronic supplementary material The online version of this chapter (https://doi.org/10.1007/978-3-030-59722-1_46) contains supplementary material, which is available to authorized users.

© Springer Nature Switzerland AG 2020
A. L. Martel et al. (Eds.): MICCAI 2020, LNCS 12265, pp. 480–489, 2020.
https://doi.org/10.1007/978-3-030-59722-1_46

patients with a potentially worse outcome to therapy, there is still an urgent need to improve risk stratification. Pathologists typically limit their reporting of colorectal cancers to approximately ten features, which they describe as single elements in their report (e.g., depth of invasion, pT; lymph node metastasis, etc.). However, the histopathological (H&E) slide is a "snapshot" of all occurring tumor-related processes, and their interactions may hold a wealth of information that can be extracted to help refine prognostication. These slides can then be digitized and used as input for computational algorithms to help support pathologists in their decision-making. The distribution of tissue types within the slide, the proximity of cell types or tissue components, and their spatial arrangement throughout the tissue can identify new patterns not previously detectable to the human eye alone.

Few studies have performed unsupervised clustering of whole slide images (WSIs) based on patch descriptors. They have been used to address the problem of image segmentation [16] or latent space clustering [4,6]. Among DL-based survival models, a recent study [13] used a supervised CNN for end-to-end classification of tissues to predict the survival of patients with colorectal cancer. Similar to our approach, several recent works have proposed unsupervised methods [14,17,22] for slide-level survival analysis. In [22], one of the first unsupervised approaches, DeepConvSurv has been proposed for survival prediction based on WSIs. More recently, DeepGraphSurv [14] has been presented to learn global topological representations of WSI via graphs. However, they heavily relied on noisy compressed features from a pre-trained VGG network. Recently, self-supervised representation learning methods [2,8,23] have been proposed to utilize the pretext task for extracting generalizable features from the unlabeled data itself. Therefore, the dataset does not need to be manually labeled by qualified experts to solve the pretext task.

Contributions. In this work, we propose a new approach to learn histopathological patterns through self-supervised learning within each WSI. Besides, we present a novel way to model the interaction between tumor-related image regions for survival analysis and tackle the inherent overfitting problem on tiny patient sets. To this end, we take advantage of a well-characterized, retrospective collective of 374 patients with clinicopathological data, including survival time and treatment information. H&E slides were reviewed, and at least one tumor slide per patient was digitized. To accelerate research we have made our code and trained models publicly available on GitHub[1].

2   Method

We first introduce our self-supervised image representation (Sect. 2.2) for the cancerous tissue area identified by our region of interest (RoI) detection scheme (Sect. 2.1). Then, we propose our deep clustering scheme and baseline algorithms

---

[1] https://github.com/christianabbet/DnR.

in Sect. 2.3 and Sect. 2.4, respectively. The clustering approach's usefulness is assessed by conducting survival analysis (Sect. 2.5) to measure if the learned clusters can contribute to disease prognostication. Finally, we discuss our implementation setup and experimental results in Sect. 3.

2.1 RoI Detection

Our objective is to learn discriminative patterns of unhealthy tissues of patients. However, WSI does not include information about the cancerous regions or the location of the tumor itself. Therefore, we seek a transfer learning approach for the classification of histologic components of WSIs. To do so, we choose to use the dataset presented in [12] to train a classifier to discriminate relevant areas. The dataset is composed of 100 K examples of tissue from CRC separated into nine different classes. For our task, we choose to retain three classes: lymphocytes (LYM), cancer-associated stroma (STR), and colorectal adenocarcinoma epithelium (TUM) that show the discriminative evidence for the class-of-interest and have been approved by the pathologist. Note that the presence of a large number of lymphocytes around the tumor is an indication of the immune reaction and, therefore, possibly linked to a higher survival score. We first train our classifier with the ResNet-18 backbone [9]. Then we use the stain normalization approach proposed in [15] to match the color space of the target domain and prevent the degradation of the classifier on transferred images. An example of RoI estimation is presented in Fig. 1. Such a technique allows us to discard a large part of the healthy tissue regions.

2.2 Self-Supervised Representation Learning

In this paper, we propose a self-supervised transfer colorization scheme to learn a more meaningful feature representation of the tissues and reduce the requirement for intensive tissue labeling. Unsupervised learning methods such as autoencoder trained by minimizing reconstruction error tend to ignore the underlying structure of the image as the model usually learns the distribution of the color space. To avoid this issue, we use colorization learning as a proxy task. As the input image, we convert the original unlabeled image through mapping function $\zeta(x)$ to a two-channel image (hematoxylin and eosin) that describes the nuclei and amount of extracellular material, respectively. To sidestep the memory bottleneck, we represent the WSI as a set of adjacent/overlapping tiles (image patches) $\{x_i \in \mathcal{X}\}_{i=1}^N$.

We define a function $\zeta : \mathcal{X} \to \mathcal{X}^{HE}$ that converts the input images to their HE equivalent [15,18]. Then, we train a convolutional autoencoder (CAE) to measure the per-pixel difference between transformed image(s) and input image(s) using MSE loss:

$$\min_{\phi,\psi} \mathcal{L}_{\mathrm{MSE}} = \min_{\phi,\psi} \|x - \psi \circ \phi \circ \zeta(x)\|_2^2. \tag{1}$$

The encoder $\phi : \mathcal{X}^{HE} \to \mathcal{Z}$ is a convolutional neural network that maps an input image to its latent representation $\mathcal{Z}$. The decoder $\psi : \mathcal{Z} \to \mathcal{X}$ is an upsampling convolutional neural network that reconstructs the input image given

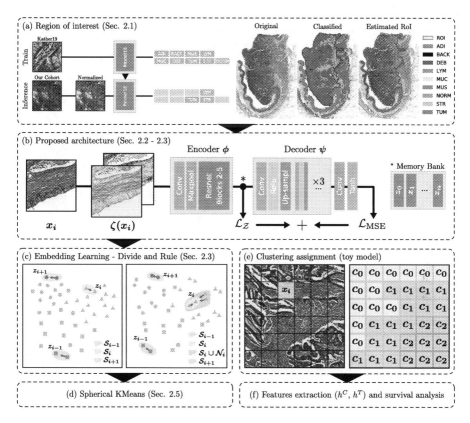

Fig. 1. The pipeline of the proposed approach. Estimation of the region of interest (a), learning of the embedding space (b–c), fitting of the cluster, assignment of all patient patches, and survival analysis (d–f).

a latent space representation. As a result, we use a single input branch to take into account the tissue's structural aspect.

2.3 Proposed Divide-and-Rule Approach

The principle behind our self-supervised learning approach is to represent image patches based on their spatial proximity in the feature space, meaning any two adjacent image patches (positive pairs) are more likely to be close to each other in the feature space $\mathcal{Z}$ than two distant patches (negative pairs). Such characteristics are met for overlapping patches as they share similar histomorphological patterns. We let $\mathcal{S}_i$ denote the set of patches that overlap with patch i spatially. Besides, we can assume that image patches in which their relative distances are smaller than a proximity threshold in the feature space should share common patterns. We define $\mathcal{N}_i$ as the set of top-k patches that achieve the lowest cosine distance to the embedding z_i of the image patch i.

Firstly, we initialize the network parameters using the self-supervised reconstruction loss in Eq. 1. Then, for each patch embedding i, we label its overlapping set of patches $\mathcal{S}_i$ as similar patches (positive pairs). Otherwise, we consider any distant patches as a negative pair, whose embeddings should be scattered. Motivated by [19], we use a variant of the cross-entropy to compute the instance loss (Eq. 2):

$$\mathcal{L}_{\text{Divide}} = - \sum_{i \in \mathcal{B}_{\text{inst}}} \log \left(\sum_{j \in S_i} p\left(j \mid i\right) \right), \quad p\left(j \mid i\right) = \frac{\exp\left(z_j^{\top} z_i / \tau\right)}{\sum_{k=1}^{N} \exp\left(z_k^{\top} z_i / \tau\right)}. \tag{2}$$

where $\tau \in \,]0, 1]$ is the temperature parameter and $\mathcal{B}_{\text{inst}}$ denotes the set of samples in the mini-batch.

Secondly, we jointly optimize the training of network with reconstruction loss and a Rule loss $\mathcal{L}_{\text{Rule}}$ that takes into account the similarity of different images in the feature space (Eq. 3). We gradually expand the vicinity of each sample to select its neighbor samples. If samples have high relative entropy, they are dissimilar and should be considered as individual classes, $z \in \mathcal{B}_{\text{inst}}$. On the contrary, if samples have low relative entropy with their neighbors, they should be tied together, $z \in \mathcal{Z} \backslash \mathcal{B}_{\text{inst}}$. In practice, the entropy acts as a threshold to decide a boundary between close and distant samples and is gradually increased during training such that we go from easy samples (low entropy) to hard ones (high entropy). Finally, the proposed training loss, $\mathcal{L}_{\text{DnR}}$, joins the above losses with a weighting term λ (see Eq. 4):

$$\mathcal{L}_{\text{Rule}} = - \sum_{i \in \mathcal{Z} \backslash \mathcal{B}_{\text{inst}}} \log \left(\sum_{j \in \mathcal{S}_i \cup \mathcal{N}_i} p\left(j \mid i\right) \right). \tag{3}$$

$$\min_{\phi, \psi} \mathcal{L}_{\text{DnR}} = \min_{\phi, \psi} \mathcal{L}_{\text{MSE}} + \lambda \min_{\phi} [\mathcal{L}_{\text{Divide}} + \mathcal{L}_{\text{Rule}}]. \tag{4}$$

Dictionary Learning. Measuring similarities between samples requires the computation of features in the entire dataset for each iteration. The complexity grows as a function of the number of samples in the dataset. To avoid this, we use a memory bank, where we keep track and update the dictionary elements as in [19,23].

2.4   Algorithm Baselines

Deep Clustering Based on Spatial Continuity (DCS). As our first baseline, we leverage an inherent spatial continuity of WSIs. Spatially adjacent image patches (tiles) are typically more similar to each other than distant image patches in the slide and therefore should have similar feature representation $\mathcal{Z}$. Hence, we force the model to adopt such behavior by minimizing the distance between feature representations of a specific tile z_i and its overlapping tiles $\mathcal{S}_i$.

Deep Cluster Assignment (DCA). The downside of the first baseline is that in some cases, two distant image patches may be visually similar, or there may exist some spatially close patches that are visually different. This introduces noise in the optimization process. To tackle this issue, we can impose cluster membership as in [17].

Deep Embedded Clustering (DEC). Unlike the second baseline, the objective of our last baseline is not only to determine the clusters but also to learn a meaningful representation of the tiles. Therefore, we consider to jointly learn deep feature representation (ϕ, ψ) and image clusters U. The optimization is performed through the joint minimization of reconstruction loss and the KL divergence to gradually anneal cluster centers by fitting the model to an auxiliary distribution (see [20] for details).

2.5   Survival Analysis

Clustering and Assignment. The learned embedding space is assumed to be composed of a limited number of homogeneous clusters. We fit spherical KMeans clustering (SPKM) [21] to the learned latent space with K clusters. As a result, every patch within a patient slide will be assigned to a cluster, $c_k = \arg\min_{k \in \{0...K-1\}} \mathrm{SPKM}(x_i, \mu_k)$.

Our objective is to model the interaction between tumor-related image regions (neighbor patches and clusters). To do so, we define a patient descriptor $h = [h^C, h^T] \in \mathbb{R}^{N \times (K+K^2)}$ as:

$$h_k^C = p(s = k) \quad \text{and} \quad h_{j \to k}^T = p(s = k \mid N(s) = j), \tag{5}$$

where s is a patch, h_k^C denotes the probability that a patch belongs to cluster k and h_k^T is the probability transition between a patch and its neighbors $N(s)$ (i.e. local interactions between clusters within the slide).

Survival. Survival analysis is prone to overfitting as we usually rely on a small patient set and a large number of features. To counter this issue, we first apply forward variable selection [10] using log partial likelihood function with tied times [5], $\mathcal{L}_{ll}$, and likelihood-ratio (LR) test to identify the subset of relevant covariates:

$$\mathrm{LR} = -2[\mathcal{L}_{ll}(\beta^{\mathrm{new}} \mid h^{\mathrm{new}}) - \mathcal{L}_{ll}(\beta^{\mathrm{prev}} \mid h^{\mathrm{prev}})]. \tag{6}$$

Here $(h, \beta)^{\mathrm{prev}}$ and $(h, \beta)^{\mathrm{new}}$ are the previous and new estimated set of covariates, respectively. To validate that the selected covariates do not overfit the patient data, we use leave-one-out cross-validation (LOOCV) on the dataset and predict linear estimators [3] as $\hat{\eta}_i = h_i \cdot \beta^{-i}$ and $\hat{\eta} = (\hat{\eta}_1, \hat{\eta}_2, \dots \hat{\eta}_N)$ to compute C-Index [7]. Here, β^{-i} is estimated on the whole patient set minus patient i.

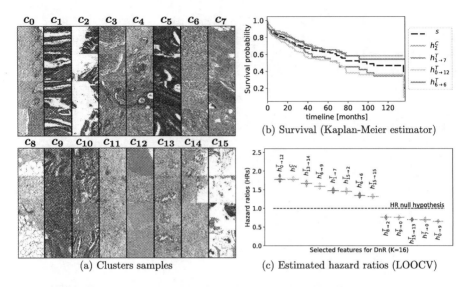

(a) Clusters samples

(b) Survival (Kaplan-Meier estimator)

(c) Estimated hazard ratios (LOOCV)

Fig. 2. Comparison of estimated clusters representation. (a) Survival results and estimated hazard ratios over LOOCV (b–c). For Kaplan-Meier estimators, we choose a subset of curves that do not overlap too much for better visualization.

3   Experimental Results

Dataset. We use a set of 660 in-house unlabeled WSIs of CRC stained with hematoxylin and eosin (H&E). The slides are linked to a total of 374 unique patients diagnosed with adenocarcinoma. The dataset was filtered such that we exclude cases of mucinous adenocarcinoma in which their features are considered independent with respect to standard adenocarcinoma. A set of histopathological features (HFs) is associated with each patient entry (i.e. depth of invasion, pT, etc.). The survival time is defined as the period between resection of the tissue (operation) and the event occurrence (death of the patient). We denote $\mathcal{D}^S$ as the dataset that contains slides images and $\mathcal{D}^{S \cap HF}$ as the dataset that contains both information of the HFs and slides for each patient. Note that $|\mathcal{D}^{S \cap HF}| < |\mathcal{D}^S|$ as some patients have missing HFs and were excluded.

Experimental Settings. We use ResNet-18 for the encoder where the input layer is updated to support 2 input channels. The latent space has dimensions $d = 512$. The decoder is a succession of convolutional layers, ReLUs, and up-samplings (bicubic). The model was trained with the reconstruction loss $\mathcal{L}_{\text{MSE}}$ for 20 epochs with early stopping. We use Adam optimizer $\beta = (0.9, 0.999)$ and learning rate, $lr = 1\text{e}{-}3$. Then, we add $\mathcal{L}_{\text{Divide}}$ for an additional 20 epochs with $\lambda = 1\text{e}{-}3$ and $\tau = 0.5$. Finally, we go through 3 additional rounds using $\mathcal{L}_{\text{Rule}}$ while raising the entropy threshold between each round.

Table 1. Multivariate survival analysis for the proposed approach and baselines. K and N_{feat} denote the number of clusters and the number of features that achieve statistical relevance when performing forward selection ($p < 0.05$). n denotes the number of patient in each set. Brier and Concordance Index are indicators of the performance.

Method	K	N_{feat}	$\mathcal{D}^{S \cap HF}$ ($n = 253$)		$\mathcal{D}^S$ ($n = 374$)	
			Brier [1]	C-Index [7]	Brier	C-Index
Histo. features (HFs)		8	0.2896	0.6076***	–	–
DCS	8	3	0.2840	0.5398+	0.2848	0.5562**
DCA† [17]	8	2	0.2887	0.5452**	0.2850	0.5555***
DEC† [20]	8	4	0.2884	0.6089**	0.2830	0.5765**
DnR w/o $\mathcal{L}_{Divide}$, $\mathcal{L}_{Rule}$	8	3	0.2870	0.6070*	0.2824	0.6040***
DnR w/o $\mathcal{L}_{Rule}$	8	3	0.2828	0.5951**	0.2840	0.5919***
DnR (ours)	8	4	0.2854	0.6107*	0.2832	0.6243***
DCS	16	9	0.2934	0.6073	0.2879	0.6464***
DCA† [17]	16	7	0.2827	0.6246+	0.2852	0.6322**
DEC† [20]	16	7	**0.2758**	0.6410**	0.2763	0.6426***
DnR w/o $\mathcal{L}_{Divide}$, $\mathcal{L}_{Rule}$	16	5	0.2819	0.6364*	0.2795	0.6324***
DnR w/o $\mathcal{L}_{Rule}$	16	10	0.3006	0.6207+	0.2934	0.6468***
DnR (ours)	16	13	0.2849	**0.6736****	**0.2725**	**0.6943*****

† Autoencoder is replaced with the self-supervised objective function.
+ $p < 0.1$; * $p < 0.05$; ** $p < 0.01$; *** $p < 0.001$ (log-rank test).

Clustered Embedding Space. We fit SPKM with $K = 8$ and $K = 16$. The sampled tiles for each cluster are presented in Fig. 2. Clusters demonstrate different tumor and stroma interactions (c_0, c_1, c_5, c_9), inflammatory tissues (c_6), muscles and large vessels (c_7), collagen and small vessels (c_8), blood and veins (c_{11}) or connective tissues (c_{12}). Some clusters do not directly represent the type of tissue but rather the positioning information such as c_2, which describe the edge of the WSI.

Ablation Study and Survival Analysis Results. We build our survival features (Eq. 5) on top of the predicted clusters, and their contribution is evaluated using Eq. 6. In Table 1, we observe that our model outperforms previous approaches by a safe 5% margin on C-Index [7]. The second step of the learning (DnR w/o $\mathcal{L}_{Rule}$) tends to decrease the prediction score. Such behavior is to be expected as the additional term ($\mathcal{L}_{Divide}$) will scatter the data and focus on self instance representation. When $\mathcal{L}_{Rule}$ is then introduced, the model can restructure the embedding by linking similar instances. Also, we observe an augmentation in features, N_{feat}, that achieve statistical relevance for prognosis as we go through our learning procedure (for $K = 16$), which proves that our proposed framework can model more subtle patches interactions. We show in Fig. 2

the distribution of hazard ratios for all models (from LOOCV) and the Kaplan-Meier estimator [11] for a subset of the selected covariates. In the best case, we identify 13 features that contribute to the survival outcome of the patients. For example, the interaction between blood vessels and tumor stroma ($h_{1 \to 7}^T$) is linked to a lower survival outcome. A similar trend observed in the relation between tumor stroma and connective tissues ($h_{0 \to 12}^T$).

4   Conclusion

We have proposed a self-supervised learning method that offers a new approach to learn histopathological patterns within cancerous tissue regions. Our model presents a novel way to model the interactions between tumor-related image regions and tackles the inherent overfitting problem to predict patient outcome. Our method surpasses all previous baseline methods and histopathological features and achieves state-of-the-art results, i.e., in C-Index without any data-specific annotation. Ablation studies also show the importance of different components of our method and the relevance of combining them. We envision the broad application of our approach for clinical prognostic stratification improvement.

References

1. Brier, G.W.: Verification of forecasts expressed in terms of probability. Mon. Weather Rev. **78**(1), 1–3 (1950)
2. Chen, T., Kornblith, S., Norouzi, M., Hinton, G.: A simple framework for contrastive learning of visual representations. arXiv preprint arXiv:2002.05709 (2020)
3. Dai, B., Breheny, P.: Cross validation approaches for penalized Cox regression. arXiv preprint arXiv:1905.10432 (2019)
4. Dercksen, K., Bulten, W., Litjens, G.: Dealing with label scarcity in computational pathology: a use case in prostate cancer classification. arXiv preprint arXiv:1905.06820 (2019)
5. Efron, B.: The efficiency of Cox's likelihood function for censored data. J. Am. Stat. Assoc. **72**(359), 557–565 (1977)
6. Fouad, S., Randell, D., Galton, A., Mehanna, H., Landini, G.: Unsupervised morphological segmentation of tissue compartments in histopathological images. PLoS ONE **12**(11), e0188717 (2017)
7. Harrell Jr., F.E., Lee, K.L., Mark, D.B.: Multivariable prognostic models: issues in developing models, evaluating assumptions and adequacy, and measuring and reducing errors. Stat. Med. **15**(4), 361–387 (1996)
8. He, K., Fan, H., Wu, Y., Xie, S., Girshick, R.: Momentum contrast for unsupervised visual representation learning. In: Proceedings of the IEEE/CVF Conference on Computer Vision and Pattern Recognition, pp. 9729–9738 (2020)
9. He, K., Zhang, X., Ren, S., Sun, J.: Deep residual learning for image recognition. In: Proceedings of the IEEE Conference on Computer Vision and Pattern Recognition, pp. 770–778 (2016)
10. Hosmer Jr., D.W., Lemeshow, S., May, S.: Applied Survival Analysis: Regression Modeling of Time-to-Event Data, vol. 618. Wiley, Hoboken (2011)

11. Kaplan, E.L., Meier, P.: Nonparametric estimation from incomplete observations. J. Am. Stat. Assoc. **53**(282), 457–481 (1958)
12. Kather, J.N., Halama, N., Marx, A.: 100,000 histological images of human colorectal cancer and healthy tissue, April 2018. https://doi.org/10.5281/zenodo.1214456
13. Kather, J.N., et al.: Predicting survival from colorectal cancer histology slides using deep learning: a retrospective multicenter study. PLoS Med. **16**(1), e1002730 (2019)
14. Li, R., Yao, J., Zhu, X., Li, Y., Huang, J.: Graph CNN for survival analysis on whole slide pathological images. In: Frangi, A.F., Schnabel, J.A., Davatzikos, C., Alberola-López, C., Fichtinger, G. (eds.) MICCAI 2018. LNCS, vol. 11071, pp. 174–182. Springer, Cham (2018). https://doi.org/10.1007/978-3-030-00934-2_20
15. Macenko, M., et al.: A method for normalizing histology slides for quantitative analysis. In: 2009 IEEE International Symposium on Biomedical Imaging: From Nano to Macro, pp. 1107–1110, June 2009
16. Moriya, T., et al.: Unsupervised pathology image segmentation using representation learning with spherical k-means. In: Medical Imaging 2018: Digital Pathology, vol. 10581, p. 1058111. International Society for Optics and Photonics (2018)
17. Muhammad, H., et al.: Unsupervised subtyping of cholangiocarcinoma using a deep clustering convolutional autoencoder. In: Shen, D., et al. (eds.) MICCAI 2019. LNCS, vol. 11764, pp. 604–612. Springer, Cham (2019). https://doi.org/10.1007/978-3-030-32239-7_67
18. Vahadane, A., et al.: Structure-preserving color normalization and sparse stain separation for histological images. IEEE Trans. Med. Imaging **35**(8), 1962–1971 (2016)
19. Wu, Z., Xiong, Y., Yu, S.X., Lin, D.: Unsupervised feature learning via nonparametric instance discrimination. In: Proceedings of the IEEE Conference on Computer Vision and Pattern Recognition, pp. 3733–3742 (2018)
20. Xie, J., Girshick, R., Farhadi, A.: Unsupervised deep embedding for clustering analysis. In: International Conference on Machine Learning, pp. 478–487 (2016)
21. Zhong, S.: Efficient online spherical k-means clustering. In: Proceedings of 2005 IEEE International Joint Conference on Neural Networks, vol. 5, pp. 3180–3185. IEEE (2005)
22. Zhu, X., Yao, J., Zhu, F., Huang, J.: WSISA: making survival prediction from whole slide histopathological images. In: Proceedings of the IEEE Conference on Computer Vision and Pattern Recognition, pp. 7234–7242 (2017)
23. Zhuang, C., Zhai, A.L., Yamins, D.: Local aggregation for unsupervised learning of visual embeddings. In: Proceedings of the IEEE International Conference on Computer Vision, pp. 6002–6012 (2019)

Microscopic Fine-Grained Instance Classification Through Deep Attention

Mengran Fan[1], Tapabrata Chakraborti[1], Eric I-Chao Chang[2], Yan Xu[2,3], and Jens Rittscher[1(✉)]

[1] Department of Engineering Science, Institute of Biomedical Engineering, University of Oxford, Oxford, UK
mengran.fan@eng.ox.ac.uk, tapabrata.chakraborty@eng.ox.ac.uk, jens.rittscher@eng.ox.ac.uk
[2] Microsoft Research, Beijing, China
echang@microsoft.com, xuyan04@gmail.com
[3] Department of Biology and Medicine, Beihang University, Beijing, China

Abstract. Fine-grained classification of microscopic image data with limited samples is an open problem in computer vision and biomedical imaging. Deep learning based vision systems mostly deal with high number of low-resolution images, whereas subtle details in biomedical images require higher resolution. To bridge this gap, we propose a simple yet effective deep network that performs two tasks simultaneously in an end-to-end manner. First, it utilises a gated attention module that can focus on multiple key instances at high resolution without extra annotations or region proposals. Second, the global structural features and local instance features are fused for final image level classification. The result is a robust but lightweight end-to-end trainable deep network that yields state-of-the-art results in two separate fine-grained multi-instance biomedical image classification tasks: a benchmark breast cancer histology dataset and our new fungi species mycology dataset. In addition, we demonstrate the interpretability of the proposed model by visualising the concordance of the learned features with clinically relevant features.

Keywords: Medical image classification · Deep attention mechanism

1 Introduction

Fine-grained image classification, which focuses on distinguishing subtle visual differences between classes, is an open problem in biomedical image analysis. Deep learning has led to a remarkable progress in fine-grained classification on large-scale natural images [14,21,23]. Despite the important advances in computer vision, it is usually challenging to achieve the same success on specific biomedical image classification tasks [20,22]. To sum up, current methods mainly face three challenges. Due to the cost of data acquisition and the limited availability of specimens, well-organised medical datasets in medical usually tend to

© Springer Nature Switzerland AG 2020
A. L. Martel et al. (Eds.): MICCAI 2020, LNCS 12265, pp. 490–499, 2020.
https://doi.org/10.1007/978-3-030-59722-1_47

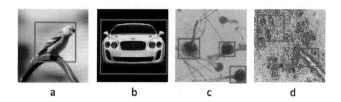

Fig. 1. Classification challenges in biomedical imaging. Compared to large-scale datasets on natural images (a-b), well-organised biomedical datasets (c-d) tend to be small and require expensive human expert annotations. Secondly, while we typically expect one centre-aligned instance (red box) in natural images, there are often multiple discriminative instances (red boxes) in biomedical images, which poses another challenge for feature learning. Finally, interpretability needs to be considered when developing a reliable medical image analysis system.

be small, which limits the representation ability of deep networks. The main reason is that the current state-of-the-art convolutional neural networks (CNN) are capable of extracting semantically meaningful features on large-scale datasets. When training data is limited deep networks may overfit and may bias the classification result on confounding background clutter.

Especially when working on the microscopic scale, multiple instances (e.g. glands, vessels, or crypts) need to be considered. This seriously restricts the adaptation of existing methods in the fine-grained classification of natural images. For instance, we randomly select samples (Fig. 1 (a) - (b)) from the most popular fine-grained datasets in computer vision (CUB-200-2001 [16] and Stanford Cars [11]), where there is mostly one centre-aligned instance in an image. Although a large number of strategies have been proposed to detect the discriminative parts (e.g., head, belly for birds) in such images, the size and layout of the detected components are almost identical for each image. In comparison to natural images, biomedical images (Fig. 1 (c) - (d)) may have a wide variety of discriminative instances (regions) with different sizes and densities, leading to more complicated structural information and a larger within-class variation. This motivates the need for investigating methods for building comprehensive and discriminative feature representations that can be applied in this domain. Thirdly, apart from the accurate prediction, the interpretability also plays a crucial role in a reliable medical image classification system [19]. In this work, we propose a novel attention-based classification network that is capable of jointly localising discriminative instances and enhancing consistent fine-grained feature learning in an end-to-end fashion. The main contributions of this paper are: (1) A lightweight gated attention module where the most discriminative instances can be localised simultaneously without requiring any part annotations or redundant region proposals. (2) A multi-task learning scheme that dynamically controls the weights of member modules and enforces the network to learn consistent instance-level features. (3) Improved interpretability of learned features when compared with features used by human experts for decision making.

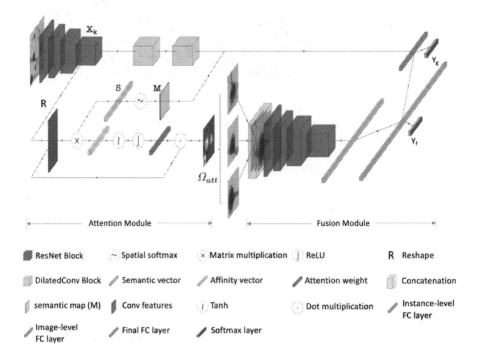

Fig. 2. Framework for the proposed multiple instance fine-grained classification pipeline. The proposed network consists of two main modules: the attention module and the feature fusion module. The details of the attention module and definition of the variables are explained in Sect. 2.1. In the fusion module, we threshold the attention map to generate a binary mask, crop these patches from the input image, resize them to a predefined size and feed them into a shared CNN model. Finally, we concatenate all instance-level features with image-level features for final prediction. The predictions in the inference stage are also conducted in this way.

2   Methodology

We propose a novel fine-grained multi-instance classification scheme (Fig. 2) that consists of two main modules: (i) a novel gated attention mechanism for discriminative instances localisation; and (ii) a feature fusion strategy that consolidates the global and local features to facilitate the final predictions.

2.1   Gated Attention Module

In natural images, noisy background or irrelevant regions are highly variable and can be therefore naturally discarded by deep neural networks. However, for medical datasets with limited training samples, this is more difficult to achieve. Here, we propose a gated attention mechanism that is aimed to filter out the confounding channels and localise the most discriminative instances without extra part supervision or redundant region proposals. As shown in Fig. 2, the module first summarises a $2D$ semantic map $S \in \mathbb{R}^{H \times W}$ from the input convolutional feature maps $X \in \mathbb{R}^{C \times H \times W}$. Furthermore, we use the high-level semantic information to filter out the confounding channels based on the pairwise correspondences between each input channel and the generated semantic map, thus suppressing the irrelevant background and localising the most discriminative instances.

Semantic Modelling. Since spatial attention weights computed for each query position are almost the same for different tasks [3], we extract a global spatial attention map from the input features, which are shared by all query positions within an image. For multi-level semantics understanding, we first apply two dilated convolution blocks [4] to the output of the feature extractor X_k. The set of multi-scale features are compressed by computing the sum of all channels $M = \sum_{k=1}^{C} W^T X_k$ where W^T is the weights of dilated blocks. This channel compression rests on the assumption that if the region is activated on most channels, the region tends to be more discriminative and to have higher likelihood of being part of the object of interest. The final semantic map S is generated by applying a spatial softmax layer that performs the softmax operation over all feature points in the aggregated map M, resulting in a probability distribution that roughly indicates the regions of the most discriminative instances:

$$S_{i,j} = \frac{\exp(M_{i,j})}{\sum_{l=1}^{H} \sum_{k=1}^{W} \exp(M(l,k))} \tag{1}$$

Gated Mechanism. To measure the discriminability of each channel, we capture the spatial correspondence scores via conducting matrix multiplication over X^T and S, where X^T is the original convolutional feature maps with the shape of $c \times hw$. For example, X_k is the kth channel of the input feature maps, containing its specific semantic responses. So $X_k^T S$ is the importance coefficient that indicates the semantic representation power of this channel. Our method is different from traditional channel-based self-attention mechanisms [6,23] that usually directly capture the pairwise inter-channel dependencies by calculating $X^T X$. In order to enhance the specific semantics, we summarise a global high-level semantic map and use it as a template to quantify the representation capability of each channel by $X^T S$. Therefore, we apply such a mechanism to obtain the $1D$ coefficient vector $X^T S \in \mathbb{R}^{C \times 1}$ rather than $X^T X \in \mathbb{R}^{C \times C}$.

To filter out the confounding channels, the hyperbolic tangent ($tanh$) and ReLU activation functions are used to normalise the discriminability coefficient among all channels. As a result, a set of gated weights is obtained, selects channels that look at the most discriminative regions. In particular, the gated weight is approximately 1 for the most informative channels, and approximately 0 for the channels highlighting the irrelevant background (Fig. 3). The gated activation layer can also be regarded as a filter which enforces the model to ignore the confounding channels and pay attention to more informative channels. Consequently, to let the attention module focus on multiple instances, we model the final attention map as a gated average of the outputs of the original channels.

$$\Omega_{att} = \frac{1}{C} \sum_{k=1}^{C} (X_k^T \odot ReLU(\tanh(X_k^T \otimes S))) \qquad (2)$$

2.2 Multi-task Loss Function

Different from traditional two-stage frameworks consisting of two separate networks, the multi-task loss aims to enable the model to jointly learn multi-instance localisation and image classification in an end-to-end fashion. Specifically, our network is optimised by a global attention loss and a final fusion loss:

$$\mathcal{L} = \lambda L_{\mathcal{G}}(Y_g, Y^\star) + (1 - \lambda)(L_{\mathcal{F}}(Y_f, Y^\star)) \qquad (3)$$

where $L_{\mathcal{G}}$ and $L_{\mathcal{F}}$ are standard cross entropy losses with respect to the outputs of the global image-level network Y_g and the proposed multi-instance fusion network Y_f, respectively. $Y^\star$ represents the ground truth label and the parameter λ is initialised as 1 and gradually decreased during training. As a result, the network initially focuses on extracting global image-level features, and increases the contribution of discriminative instance-level features during training.

3   Evaluation

All input images were resized to 224×224, and a Resnet-18 was used to extract global image-level information from down-sampled images. After instance localisation, extracted patches were scaled to 336×336, and fed to a Resnet-50 for final image-level prediction. Other CNN architectures could be used instead. To improve training efficiency, pre-trained weights from the ImageNet dataset were used for initialisation. Mini batch size was set to 16. We used the stochastic gradient descent (SGD) optimiser with an initial learning rate of 0.05 that was multiplied by 0.1 after every 50 epochs. The initial weight score λ in the loss function is 1, and reduced by 0.1 after every 20 training epochs. The publicly available MXNet library was used to implement the model, training was performed on two NVIDIA GeForece 1080 Ti GPUs.

Evaluation and Performance Analysis On New Fungi Species Dataset. To the best of our knowledge, this is the first attempt for bringing deep learning based approaches to fungal species identification. 2151 microscopy images from 59 patients were collected in collaboration with the Peking Union Medical College Hospital. In this dataset, we particularly focus on five most common species involved in human disease: (1)Aspergillus fumigatus, (2)Aspergillus flavus, (3)Aspergillus niger, (4)Aspergillus terreus and (5)Aspergillus nidulans. We provide quantitative results and compare it with recent competing methods. We also benchmark the performance of the novel gated attention mechanism with other attention schemes. For all experiments, we randomly split the samples in each class in a ratio of $1 : 3$ for constructing testing and training sets.

Table 1. Results on Fungi species dataset.

Methods	Accuracy
Resnet-50 [8]	0.907
Residual attention [17]	0.867
Attend & Rectify [14]	0.871
Trilinear attention [23]	0.883
NTS Network [21]	0.914
Our method	**0.951**

Table 2. Comparison of attention mechanisms.

Attention mechanisms	Accuracy
Spatial attention [18]	0.859
Channel-wise attention [23]	0.883
Dual attention [6]	0.901
Squeeze-Excitation attention [9]	0.939
Global Context attention [3]	0.937
Our Gated Attention	**0.951**

Table 3. Results on breast cancer dataset.

Methods	Accuracy	Methods	Accuracy
Vgg19 [10]	0.925	Inception-v3 [10]	0.913
DenseNet-161 [10]	0.940	Model Fusion [13]	0.925
AlexNet [12]	0.813	ResNet-152 [2]	0.830
RFSVM-All [2]	0.930	Ensemble [15]	0.825
Refined Ensemble [15]	0.875	Two-stage network [7]	0.850
Hybrid deep network [20]	0.913	**Our method**	**0.970**

Quantitative Comparison With Competing Methods. We evaluated the effectiveness of the proposed method by comparing it with several state-of-the-art fine-grained classification methods. All of the compared methods were trained with the same backbone network and computing environment. From the comparison shown in Table 1, we observe that our method achieves the best performance when compared with other fine-grained classification methods.

Evaluation of Gated Attention Mechanism. To measure the effectiveness of our gated attention module we compared it with other existing attention mechanisms but using the same sampling strategy, feature fusion scheme and loss function. We only modified the attention-based instance localisation module in the baseline model, and investigate the performance of different attention mechanisms. Table 2 shows the results of integrating different attention modules in our classification framework, and Fig. 3 depicts a visualisation example of each step in our gated attention module. Our gated attention mechanism not only outperforms all other attention modules but it also suppresses the confounding information, demonstrating the effectiveness and localisation ability.

Evaluation on Breast Cancer Histology Images. The BreAst Cancer Histology images (BACH) benchmark dataset [1] is used to investigate the method's ability for histology images. This dataset consists of 400 high-resolution (2018 × 1356) Hematoxylin and eosin stained microscopy images, with an even distribution over four classes. Each image is labeled as one of four types: 1) normal, 2) benign, 3) in situ carcinoma and 4) invasive carcinoma, according to the

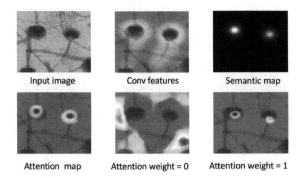

Fig. 3. Visualization of the gated attention module for one sample image. The top row shows the input image, original convolutional feature map and the corresponding semantic map (defined in Eq. 1). The bottom row shows the final attention map and two representative channels with the lowest and highest attention.

predominant tissue type. We randomly perform a $75\% - -25\%$ split for training and testing. Table 3 shows the classification results on breast cancer histology images. We compared the best classification accuracy over several advanced methods in the case of the 400 images provided by the challenge organizer. Our approach achieves the best classification performance with 0.970, showing that our network can be effectively applied to the classification tasks of histology images.

Interpretability and Alignment With Clinical Background. By analysing the concordance of the learned attention maps with well established visual clues used by human experts we evaluate their interpretability. The reader can easily appreciate the importance of this in addition to accuracy in results. **Fungal species:** In clinical practice, key criteria [5,24] are a range of morphological features associated with the structure of conidial heads, especially the colour, size and shape of vesicles (Fig. 4 (b)). Figure 4 (a) shows the sample images and corresponding attention maps of each specie. Our attention maps consistently highlight the relevance of these vesicle patterns. **Breast cancer:** A normal healthy breast duct is made up of layers of inner epithelial cells, outer myoepithelial cells and a basement membrane (see Fig. 5 (b)). In the case of *in situ* carcinomas, the proliferating cancer cells are restrained inside the basement membrane, whereas the cancer cells break out of the walls and invade the surrounding breast tissue in invasive cases. Thus, the intactness of the basement membrane is diagnostic relevance. To evaluate the effectiveness of learned features, bounding box annotations were generated by an expert pathologist on 100 test images. Overall, 72% of the bounding boxes are covered by our network and selected examples of *in situ* carcinomas are shown in Fig. 5 (a).

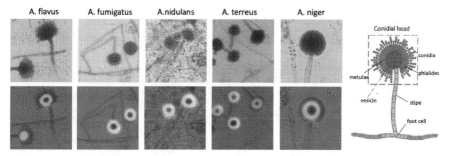

(a) Visualization of the attention maps in different classes.   (b) Schematic representation

Fig. 4. Clinical alignment on fungi dataset. Clinicians mainly rely on the morphology assessment of conidial heads, especially vesicles (shown in (b)), to differentiate Aspergillus species. The attention maps (shown in (a)) generated by the proposed network consistently match the guideline for clinical decision making.

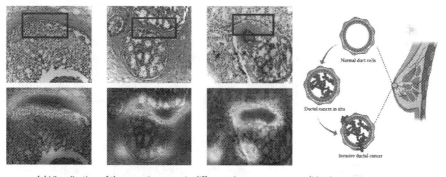

(a) Visualization of the attention maps in different classes.   (b) Schematic representation

Fig. 5. Clinical alignment on breast cancer dataset. The first row in (a) shows the examples of *in situ* carcinomas with bounding box annotations. The attention maps shown in the second row consistently focus on the membrane boundaries, covering the human annotations .

4   Conclusion

We present a simple yet effective end-to-end deep architecture that addresses the problem of fine-grained multi-instance classification from biomedical images at high resolution. It achieves this by first using a lightweight gated attention mechanism that detects multiple key instances and then combining the global structure and local instance features for a final image level classification. The proposed network is evaluated on a new fungi species classification dataset and a publicly available breast cancer dataset and achieves state-of-the-art performance. We also demonstrate in details the scope of our method as an interpretable model by showing the strong alignment of the learned features with well documented visual clues used by human subject matter experts.

Acknowledgement. MF received financial support from the Arthritis Therapy Programme (A-TAP) funded by the Kennedy Trust. JR and TC are supported by the EPSRC SeeBiByte Programme Grant (EP/M013774/1). TC is also supported by the Oxford CRUK Cancer Centre.

References

1. Aresta, G., Araújo, T., Kwok, S., Chennamsetty, S.S., Safwan, M., Alex, V., Marami, B., Prastawa, M., Chan, M., Donovan, M., et al.: Bach: Grand challenge on breast cancer histology images. Med. Image Anal. **56**, 122–139 (2019)
2. Cao, H., Bernard, S., Heutte, L., Sabourin, R.: Improve the performance of transfer learning without fine-tuning using dissimilarity-based multi-view learning for breast cancer histology images. In: Campilho, A., Karray, F., ter Haar Romeny, B. (eds.) ICIAR 2018. LNCS, vol. 10882, pp. 779–787. Springer, Cham (2018). https://doi.org/10.1007/978-3-319-93000-8_88
3. Cao, Y., Xu, J., Lin, S., Wei, F., Hu, H.: GCNet: Non-local networks meet squeeze-excitation networks and beyond (2019). arXiv preprint arXiv:1904.11492
4. Chen, L.C., Papandreou, G., Kokkinos, I., Murphy, K., Yuille, A.L.: DeepLab: Semantic image segmentation with deep convolutional nets, atrous convolution, and fully connected CRFs. IEEE Trans. Pattern Anal. Mach. Intell. **40**(4), 834–848 (2017)
5. Diba, K., Kordbacheh, P., Mirhendi, S., Rezaie, S., Mahmoudi, M.: Identification of aspergillus species using morphological characteristics. Pakistan J. Med. Sci. **23**(6), 867 (2007)
6. Fu, J., et. al.: Dual attention network for scene segmentation. In: Proceedings of the IEEE Conference on Computer Vision and Pattern Recognition, pp. 3146–3154 (2019)
7. Golatkar, A., Anand, D., Sethi, A.: Classification of breast cancer histology using deep learning. In: Campilho, A., Karray, F., ter Haar Romeny, B. (eds.) ICIAR 2018. LNCS, vol. 10882, pp. 837–844. Springer, Cham (2018). https://doi.org/10.1007/978-3-319-93000-8_95
8. He, K., Zhang, X., Ren, S., Sun, J.: Deep residual learning for image recognition. In: Proceedings of the IEEE Conference on Computer Vision and Pattern Recognition, pp. 770–778 (2016)
9. Hu, J., Shen, L., Sun, G.: Squeeze-and-excitation networks. In: Proceedings of the IEEE Conference on Computer Vision and Pattern Recognition, pp. 7132–7141 (2018)
10. Kohl, M., Walz, C., Ludwig, F., Braunewell, S., Baust, M.: Assessment of breast cancer histology using densely connected convolutional networks. In: Campilho, A., Karray, F., ter Haar Romeny, B. (eds.) ICIAR 2018. LNCS, vol. 10882, pp. 903–913. Springer, Cham (2018). https://doi.org/10.1007/978-3-319-93000-8_103
11. Krause, J., Stark, M., Deng, J., Fei-Fei, L.: 3d object representations for fine-grained categorization. In: Proceedings of the IEEE International Conference on Computer Vision Workshops, pp. 554–561 (2013)
12. Nawaz, W., Ahmed, S., Tahir, A., Khan, H.A.: Classification of breast cancer histology images using ALEXNET. In: Campilho, A., Karray, F., ter Haar Romeny, B. (eds.) ICIAR 2018. LNCS, vol. 10882, pp. 869–876. Springer, Cham (2018). https://doi.org/10.1007/978-3-319-93000-8_99

13. Rakhlin, A., Shvets, A., Iglovikov, V., Kalinin, A.A.: Deep convolutional neural networks for breast cancer histology image analysis. In: Campilho, A., Karray, F., ter Haar Romeny, B. (eds.) ICIAR 2018. LNCS, vol. 10882, pp. 737–744. Springer, Cham (2018). https://doi.org/10.1007/978-3-319-93000-8_83

14. Rodríguez, P., Gonfaus, J.M., Cucurull, G., XavierRoca, F., Gonzalez, J.: Attend and rectify: A gated attention mechanism for fine-grained recovery. In: Proceedings of the European Conference on Computer Vision (ECCV), pp. 349–364 (2018)

15. Vang, Y.S., Chen, Z., Xie, X.: Deep learning framework for multi-class breast cancer histology image classification. In: Campilho, A., Karray, F., ter Haar Romeny, B. (eds.) ICIAR 2018. LNCS, vol. 10882, pp. 914–922. Springer, Cham (2018). https://doi.org/10.1007/978-3-319-93000-8_104

16. Wah, C., Branson, S., Welinder, P., Perona, P., Belongie, S.: The caltech-ucsd birds-200-2011 dataset. Technical Report CNS-TR-2011-201 (2011)

17. Wang, F., Jiang, M., Qian, C., Yang, S., Li, C., Zhang, H., Wang, X., Tang, X.: Residual attention network for image classification. In: Proceedings of the IEEE Conference on Computer Vision and Pattern Recognition, pp. 3156–3164 (2017)

18. Wang, X., Girshick, R., Gupta, A., He, K.: Non-local neural networks. In: Proceedings of the IEEE Conference on Computer Vision and Pattern Recognition, pp. 7794–7803 (2018)

19. Weese, J., Lorenz, C.: Four challenges in medical image analysis from an industrial perspective. Med. Image Anal. 33, 44–49 (2016)

20. Yan, R., et. al.: Breast cancer histopathological image classification using a hybrid deep neural network. Methods 173, 52–60 (2019)

21. Yang, Z., Luo, T., Wang, D., Hu, Z., Gao, J., Wang, L.: Learning to navigate for fine-grained classification. In: Proceedings of the European Conference on Computer Vision (ECCV), pp. 420–435 (2018)

22. Zhang, J., Xie, Y., Wu, Q., Xia, Y.: Medical image classification using synergic deep learning. Med. Image Anal. 54, 10–19 (2019)

23. Zheng, H., Fu, J., Zha, Z.J., Luo, J.: Looking for the devil in the details: Learning trilinear attention sampling network for fine-grained image recognition. In: Proceedings of the IEEE Conference on Computer Vision and Pattern Recognition, pp. 5012–5021 (2019)

24. Zulkifli, N.A., Zakaria, L.: Morphological and molecular diversity of aspergillus from corn grain used as livestock feed. HAYATI J. Biosci. 24(1), 26–34 (2017)

A Deformable CRF Model for Histopathology Whole-Slide Image Classification

Yiqing Shen[1,4] and Jing Ke[2,3(✉)]

[1] School of Mathematical Sciences, Shanghai Jiao Tong University, Shanghai, China
shenyq@sjtu.edu.cn
[2] Department of Computer Science and Engineering, Shanghai Jiao Tong University, Shanghai, China
kejing@sjtu.edu.cn
[3] School of Computer Science and Engineering, University of New South Wales, Sydney, Australia
[4] Zhiyuan College, Shanghai Jiao Tong University, Shanghai, China

Abstract. To detect abnormality from histopathology images in a patch-based convolutional neural network (CNN), spatial context is an important cue. However, whole-slide image (WSI) is characterized by high morphological heterogeneity in the shape and scale of tissues, hence a simple visual span to a larger context may not well capture the information associated with the central patch or disease of interest. In this paper, we propose a Deformable Conditional Random Field (DCRF) model to learn the offsets and weights of neighboring patches in a spatial-adaptive manner. Additionally, rather than using regularly tessellated or overlapped patches, we localize patches with more powerful feature representations by the adaptively adjusted offsets in a WSI. Both the employment of DCRF for better feature extraction from spatial sampling patches, as well as utilization of the auto-generated patches as training input, can achieve performance improvement in the target task. This model is feasible to the widespread annotation strategies in histopathology images, either with a contoured region of interest (ROI) or patch-wise multi-tissue labels. The proposed model is validated on the patient cohorts from The Cancer Genome Atlas (TCGA) dataset and the Camelyon16 dataset for performance evaluation. The experimental results demonstrate the advantage of the proposed model in the classification task, by the comparison against the baseline models.

Keywords: Deformable conditional random field · Auto-labelling · Spatial correlation · Whole-slide image

1 Introduction

Pathology practically relies on the accurate interpretation of microscope samples to correctly diagnose patients and guide decision making [1]. Recently, when

© Springer Nature Switzerland AG 2020
A. L. Martel et al. (Eds.): MICCAI 2020, LNCS 12265, pp. 500–508, 2020.
https://doi.org/10.1007/978-3-030-59722-1_48

glass slides could be digitized into whole slide images (WSIs) with high resolution, digital pathology has become widely adopted in the diagnostic tasks and research applications. The growing adoption of tissue specimens in WSI has made digital pathology a very popular application area by deep learning techniques, and there is growing evidence that histopathological features and even biomarker information can be extracted by deep learning. Some applications have demonstrated promising performance results in a variety of diagnostic tasks such as survival prediction, cancer metastasis detection, tumor grading, and histologic classification [2–5].

However, different from other medical disciplines like computed tomography (CT) or magnetic resonance imaging (MRI), WSI often undergoes high-resolution digitization to be gigabyte images. Instead of using the whole image as input, image patches are used for feature extraction to train a deep learning model, attributable to the limited computational and memory resources in the computing environment [6]. As a result, the patch-based analysis faces two significant challenges. One problem is that, in many applications, spatial context is ignored that the network is trained with independent patch images and that is hazardous to the performance in diagnostic tasks. To be contrast with clinical practice, in light of the characterization of morphology within a tissue sample, pathologists often view the adjacent areas of suspicious tissue before making a decision, in particular when the complete morphology features extraction of a particular tissue-of-interest is larger than a patch size. A couple of solutions have been proposed by the incorporation of bidirectional spatial correlation from left-top to right-bottom neighbors [4,15] or adaptive multiple magnifications [7–9]. The other problem is the routine tessellation method for patch annotation. Currently, patch-level annotations are widely used for its strong supervision as every training patch is assigned a class label. Currently, several practical annotation strategies are widely adopted in the ground truth labeling. A simple and direct approach is to make use of all the patches, with overlapping or non-overlapping patterns. To reduce the excessive computational and memory cost in the deep learning training, another popular method is the random sampling of a proportion of patches from WSIs. To further decrease the workload from pathologists, a popular solution is to contour and label an irregular region while cropping patches within the inner area. In some research, active learning is also employed in annotation [10]. However, none of these annotation approaches consider learning an adaptively adjusted offset when picking up a patch to label. To be more specific, the most representative samples may not be cropped and used in training.

To address the two issues mentioned above, we proposed a framework to identify the patches with better feature representations in the target diagnostic task, described in Fig. 1. We also design a method to create more representative and well-labeled datasets with an adaptive capture of irregular-offset patches, which are spatially close to the central annotated patch. We can gain more performance improvement with the generated datasets. To the best of our knowledge, this novel approach has never been proposed explicitly in any existing methods.

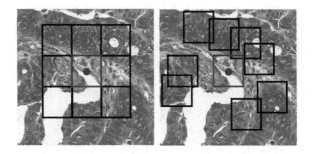

Fig. 1. Incorporate spatial context for the central patch prediction (marked by green color). The left image uses a routine tessellated 9-patch grid, and the right image demonstrates feature extraction from the adaptively located patches learned from the proposed deformable CRF framework. (Color figure online)

2   Methodology

We propose a deformable conditional random field (DCRF) model to learn the offsets and weights of the most representative patches in a spatial-adaptive manner. Furthermore, the learned offsets from deformable CRF can adaptively locate representative patches for the training stage. The main workflow of the deformable CRF model is shown in Fig. 2. The rest of the section is organized as follows. In Sect. 2.1, we describe the DCRF model constructed with three blocks, including an offset-adjust to learn the adjustable offsets, a convolutional neural network (CNN) block for feature extraction and a fully-connected conditional random field [12,13] block to aggregate spatial correlations and organizations among a grid of patches. We introduce the adjustive sample strategy to pick up better associated neighboring patches to improve the performance in training in Sect. 2.2.

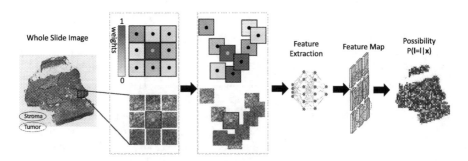

Fig. 2. The workflow of the proposed DCRF model for patch-wise tumor prediction in a WSI.

2.1   Deformable Conditional Random Field

We present the overall architecture of the model in Fig. 3. Denote a regular grid of the fixed size input patches as $\mathbf{x} = \{\mathbf{x}(\mathbf{p}_i)\}_{i=1}^{N}$, $\mathbf{p}_i$ is the center of tile $\mathbf{x}(\mathbf{p}_i)$, and N is the number of patches in a grid e.g., $N = 3 \times 3 = 9$. As the mapping from patches to their center coordinates is one-to-one, we can describe a patch by its center position.

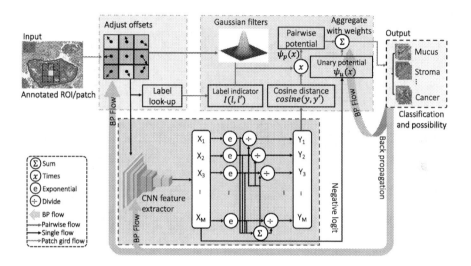

Fig. 3. The overall architecture of DCRF, constructed of three blocks: an offset-adjust block marked by yellow, a CNN block in blue to obtain M-dimension embedding feature vectors and a CRF block in green. (Color figure online)

Then we can rewrite the grid as $\mathbf{x} = \{\mathbf{x}(\mathbf{p}_0 + \Delta\mathbf{p}_i)|\Delta\mathbf{p}_i \in \mathcal{G}\}_{i=1}^{N}$, with $\mathbf{p}_0 + \Delta\mathbf{p}_i = \mathbf{p}_i$, where $\mathbf{p}_0$ is the center coordinate of the emphasized patch in the grid. For example, a 3×3 grid of $r \times r$ patches is shown in Fig. 2, with $\mathcal{G} = \{-r, 0, r\} \times \{-r, 0, r\}$, and r is valued by 224. For a clear notation, we will use '$\Delta\mathbf{p}_i$' instead of '$\mathbf{p}_0 + \Delta\mathbf{p}_i$' in the rest of paper. We augment feature representativeness of the regular grid $\mathcal{G}$ with additional offset $\delta\mathbf{p}_i$ corresponding to $\Delta\mathbf{p}_i \in \mathcal{G}$, for a better measurement of the configuration $\mathbf{l}$ under the condition $\mathbf{p}$. Offsets of patches will be adjusted by adding a bias to each patch in the grid, central patch exclusive, for a better adaption to the visual context. Offsets are trained by the standard back-propagation algorithm. The grid adjusted to the new position by offsets δ is then described as $\mathbf{x}^{\delta} = \{\mathbf{x}(\Delta\mathbf{p}_i + \delta\mathbf{p}_i)|\Delta\mathbf{p}_i \in \mathcal{G}\}_{i=1}^{N}$. To save effort from labeling on multiple image patches of $r \times r$ in size, pathologists can alternatively provide the annotations on a lower granularity of a larger size. We denote the random variable associated regular label grid of (i.e., none additional offsets) $\mathbf{x}$ as $\mathbf{l} = \{l(\mathbf{p}_i)\}_{i=1}^{N}$.

Based on the one-to-one mapping from the centre coordinate $\mathbf{p}$ to the patch $\mathbf{x}$, we can characterize random filed $(\mathbf{l}, \mathbf{x})$ via the conditional distribution of $(\mathbf{l}, \mathbf{p})$

with a Gibbs distribution as follows:

$$P(\mathbf{l} = l|\mathbf{x}) = P(\mathbf{l} = l|\mathbf{p}) = \frac{1}{Z(\mathbf{p})} exp(-\mathbb{E}(l, \mathbf{p})) \qquad (1)$$

where $\mathbb{E}(l, \mathbf{p})$ is the energy function and $Z(\mathbf{p})$ is the normalization function to make $P(\cdot)$ into a validate probability distribution. In a fully-connected pairwise conditional random filed model, proposed in [14], the energy function can be depicted by:

$$\mathbb{E}(l, \mathbf{p}) = \sum_{\Delta\mathbf{p}\in\mathcal{G}} \psi_u(l(\Delta\mathbf{p})) + \frac{1}{2} \sum_{\Delta\mathbf{p}\neq\Delta\mathbf{p}'\in\mathcal{G}} \psi_p(l(\Delta\mathbf{p}), l(\Delta\mathbf{p}')) \qquad (2)$$

Regarding the patches are updated by the learned offsets in the an offset-adjust block, the energy will be:

$$\mathbb{E}(l, \mathbf{p}) = \sum_{\Delta\mathbf{p}\in\mathcal{G}} \psi_u(l(\Delta\mathbf{p}+\delta\mathbf{p})) + \frac{1}{2} \sum_{\Delta\mathbf{p}\neq\Delta\mathbf{p}'\in\mathcal{G}} \psi_p(l(\Delta\mathbf{p}+\delta\mathbf{p}), l(\Delta\mathbf{p}'+\delta\mathbf{p}')) \quad (3)$$

where $\delta\mathbf{p}$ is the offset associated with $\Delta\mathbf{p}$. $\psi_u(\cdot)$ is the unary potential to measure the cost of patch $\mathbf{x}(\Delta\mathbf{p} + \delta\mathbf{p})$ taking the label $l(\Delta\mathbf{p} + \delta\mathbf{p})$. It is defined to be the probability output before the *softmax* layer in the neural network. $\psi_p(\cdot, \cdot)$ is the pairwise potential to measure the spatial correlations between two patches. In the proposed model, it is defined as follows.

$$\psi_p(l(\Delta\mathbf{p} + \delta\mathbf{p}), l(\Delta\mathbf{p}' + \delta\mathbf{p}')) = \overbrace{w_{(\Delta\mathbf{p}+\delta\mathbf{p},\Delta\mathbf{p}'+\delta\mathbf{p}')}}^{\text{trainable weight}} \cdot \overbrace{\mathbb{I}(\Delta\mathbf{p} + \delta\mathbf{p}, \Delta\mathbf{p}' + \delta\mathbf{p}')}^{\text{label indicator}} \cdot$$
$$\underbrace{exp(-\frac{\|\delta\mathbf{p}\|^2 + \|\delta\mathbf{p}'\|^2}{2\sigma^2})}_{\text{Gaussian filter}} \cdot (1 - \underbrace{\frac{Y(\Delta\mathbf{p} + \delta\mathbf{p}) \cdot Y(\Delta\mathbf{p}' + \delta\mathbf{p}')}{\|Y(\Delta\mathbf{p} + \delta\mathbf{p})\|\|Y(\Delta\mathbf{p}' + \delta\mathbf{p}')\|}}_{\text{Cosine distance}}) \qquad (4)$$

$w_{(\Delta\mathbf{p}+\delta\mathbf{p},\Delta\mathbf{p}'+\delta\mathbf{p}')}$ is the learned weight for the spatial correlations between patches within the grid. In the proposed model, we set $w_{(\Delta\mathbf{p}+\delta\mathbf{p},\Delta\mathbf{p}'+\delta\mathbf{p}')} = w_{(\Delta\mathbf{p}'+\delta\mathbf{p}',\Delta\mathbf{p}+\delta\mathbf{p})}$ for all $\Delta\mathbf{p}, \Delta\mathbf{p}' \in \mathcal{G}$ and their associated offsets to reduce the amount of learning parameters. These weights can be well correlated with the spatial distance in a WSI, and acquired through the standard back-propagation (BP) training [13,15]. $\mathbb{I}(\cdot)$ is the indicator function, and it is set to 1, if and only if $l(\Delta\mathbf{p} + \delta\mathbf{p}) = l(\Delta\mathbf{p}' + \delta\mathbf{p}')$, otherwise to 0. The restriction of the value range is obtained by the variable σ in a Gaussian filter. To be more specific, a larger σ enables a larger value range of offsets. The cosine distance is employed to measure the spatial correlation between patches in the grid. $Y(\cdot)$ denotes the M-dimension embedding feature vector obtained by CNN block via the patch $\mathbf{x}(\cdot)$. We employ the cross entropy loss function with the probability in Eq. (1).

A float-valued $\delta\mathbf{p}_i$ will inevitably use bilinear interpolation to construct the value of $\mathbf{x}$, and eventually cost excessive computational time. To address this issue, we set all $\delta\mathbf{p}_i$ to be integer-valued. It can be learned through an end-to-end back propagation algorithm by computing the gradient of the loss function concerning the offsets $\{\delta\mathbf{p}\}$. Denote the loss function with respect to $\Delta\mathbf{p} + \delta\mathbf{p}$ as $\mathcal{L}(\Delta\mathbf{p} + \delta\mathbf{p})$, we can use the following approximation as the gradient.

$$
\frac{\partial \mathcal{L}(\Delta\mathbf{p} + \delta\mathbf{p})}{\partial \delta\mathbf{p}_x} \approx \frac{1}{2}(\mathcal{L}(\Delta\mathbf{p}_x + \delta\mathbf{p}_x - 1, \Delta\mathbf{p}_y + \delta\mathbf{p}_y) + \\
\mathcal{L}(\Delta\mathbf{p}_x + \delta\mathbf{p}_x + 1, \Delta\mathbf{p}_y + \delta\mathbf{p}_y)) - \mathcal{L}(\Delta\mathbf{p} + \delta\mathbf{p}) \tag{5}
$$

where $\Delta\mathbf{p} = (\Delta\mathbf{p}_x, \Delta\mathbf{p}_y)$, $\delta\mathbf{p} = (\delta\mathbf{p}_x, \delta\mathbf{p}_y) \in \mathbb{R}^2$. Consequently, the calculation of $\frac{\partial \mathbf{x}(\Delta\mathbf{p}+\delta\mathbf{p})}{\partial \delta\mathbf{p}_y}$ is available in the same fashion.

2.2 DCRF to Generalize Samples of Adaptively Adjusted Offsets

In order to achieve better performance in the classification task, we implement the DCRF model to adaptively locate the most representative samples into training dataset. First, we pre-train the CNN feature extractor block and the CRF block in the DCRF. Each region of interest (ROI), covering N patches $\{\mathbf{x}_i\}_{i=1}^N$, will be processed by our model to output a group of adjusted offsets of the target patches, marked with the label l. To be more specific, DCRF can pick up the most suitable offset $\mathcal{D}^*$ associated with the grid of N patches from all the potential candidates $\mathcal{D}$ in the ROI, restricted with a searching region. The selection process is formulated by the following maximum processing.

$$
\mathcal{D}^* = \arg \min_{\delta\mathbf{p} \in \mathcal{D}} P(\mathbf{l} = l | \mathbf{p} + \delta\mathbf{p}) \tag{6}
$$

Then the selected representative patches in the grid will be $\{\mathbf{x}(\Delta\mathbf{p}_i + \delta\mathbf{p}_i) | \delta\mathbf{p}_i \in \mathcal{D}\}$.

3 Experiments and Results

3.1 Experimental Datasets

The experiments are performed on hematoxylin and eosin (H&E) stained whole-slide images from The Cancer Genome Atlas (TCGA) [16] for gastric (stomach) adenocarcinoma and colorectal cancer detection, including three subsets of: i) TCGA-STAD (n = 432 samples), ii) TCGA-COAD (n = 460 samples), iii) TCGA-READ (n=171 samples), and the Camelyon16 (n = 400 samples) for automated detection of metastases in lymph node sections. On TCGA datasets, we classified patches into 3-classes, namely loose non-tumor tissue, dense non-tumor tissue, and tumor tissue class. We employ ResNet-18, ResNet-34 [17] and DenseNet [18] as feature extractors for their high accuracy in classification tasks compared with other models empirically. On each dataset, we set 70% samples for training, 15% for validation and 15% for evaluation. ResNet-18, ResNet-34 and DenseNet are pre-trained on ImageNet. We use 224×224 pixels as the input size of the patches to leverage the pre-trained ResNet-18, ResNet-34 and DenseNet, at the magnification of 20× to retain the high resolutions.

3.2 Evaluations of DCRF

The proposed DCRF is evaluated in the inference stage. We employ the models of ResNet-18, ResNet-34 [17] and DenseNet [18] as the baseline and carry out the tumor detection task on the benchmark datasets for performance evaluations. The proposed DCRF outperforms other classical classification and spatial correlation methods [13] in terms of accuracy and free-response receiver operating characteristic (FROC) score improvement in Table 1. It demonstrates an improved information extraction from precisely located neighboring patches-of-interests.

We choose ResNet [17] and DenseNet [18] as a backbone for their outstanding performance on histopathology, as well as there compact architectures and non-costly training, which have been proved in the previous works [11] and [13]. Nevertheless, our performance improvement is completely architecture-independent, which is expected to be effective to any state-of-art CNN structure as a backbone.

All experiments are carried out on the state-of-art deep learning device NVIDIA Tesla V100 GPU device. The model is implemented on Pytorch. All the hyper-parameters were set as follows: $\beta_1 = 0.9, \beta_2 = 0.999, learning\ rate = 10^{-5}$ for the Adam optimizer, scheduler which reduces the *learning rate* by 5% each 5 epochs if the validation does not improve, $M = 2048$ as dimension of the embedding feature vectors, the grid size $N = 3 \times 3 = 9$, $\sigma = 56$ in Eq. (4) and 784×784 as the spatial restriction for training each grid of nine patches. Our initial pattern is exactly based on a 3×3 patches structure, and the network is trained to relocate the 9 patches which shows a better representation. Moreover, it is flexible to be extended to any $n \times n$ grid of patches for spatial correlation extraction.

Table 1. A performance comparison evaluated on four cohorts of patient datasets. Our proposed model shows the improvement in the classification accuracy and the FROC score.

Method	Camelyon16		TCGA-STAD [16]		TCGA-COAD [16]		TCGA-READ [16]	
	Accuracy	FROC	Accuracy	FROC	Accuracy	FROC	Accuracy	FROC
ResNet-18 [17]	92.42	0.7825	86.61	0.7353	87.72	0.7555	87.61	0.7745
ResNet-34 [17]	92.51	0.7444	87.03	0.7232	89.10	0.7410	87.93	0.7720
DenseNet [18]	93.20	0.7531	86.95	0.7243	90.23	0.7514	87.98	0.7752
ResNet-18+NCRF [13]	92.96	0.7934	88.30	0.7341	88.93	0.7700	88.40	0.7832
ResNet-34+NCRF [13]	93.38	0.7704	89.24	0.7367	90.05	0.7651	88.99	0.7817
ResNet-18+DCRF	94.11	**0.8111**	92.31	**0.7763**	92.71	**0.7830**	91.47	0.8017
ResNet-34+DCRF	94.55	0.8003	93.45	0.7702	**93.42**	0.7721	92.85	**0.8020**
DenseNet+DCRF	**94.68**	0.8010	**93.98**	0.7754	93.37	0.7804	**92.94**	0.8003

3.3 Representative Patches Auto-Generated from DCRF

We also compare our auto-selected patches by the proposed DCRF with the routine tessellated patches in the training stage for performance evaluation. Using a smaller amount of the auto-selected patches by the proposed method, we achieve a higher accuracy with the lower generalization error, and additionally, obtain a faster convergence. The performance chart is shown in Fig. 4.

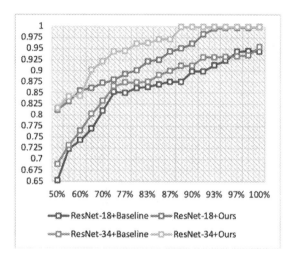

Fig. 4. AUC comparison chart of the number of patches used for training. We get a training dataset of 11977 patches in total. The performance chart demonstrates the effectiveness of the adoption of patches sampled by the DCRF model.

4 Conclusion

In this paper, we present a deformable conditional random field model to incorporate spatial context from patch-of-interest by adding adaptive offsets to patches in a grid. By "teaching" the network where to "see", the target-spatial-aware system can improve the performance in the batch-based diagnostic tasks on WSIs by convolutional neural networks. Moreover, with the framework, we can produce more representative patches for the training stage. These auto-annotated strategy has demonstrated its capability in a better classification performance with a less quantity of samples and training time. In the following work, we will apply the model to multiple caner types of WSIs for further improvement.

References

1. Zarella, M.D., Bowman, D., et al.: A practical guide to whole slide imaging: A white paper from the digital pathology association. Arch. Pathol. Lab. Med. **143**(2), 222–234 (2019)

2. Kather, J.N., Krisam, J., et al.: Predicting survival from colorectal cancer histology slides using deep learning: A retrospective multicenter study. PLoS Med. **16**(1), e1002730 (2019)

3. Bejnordi, B.E., Veta, M., et al.: Diagnostic assessment of deep learning algorithms for detection of lymph node metastases in women with breast cancer. JAMA **318**(22), 2199–2210 (2017)

4. Li, Y., Ping, W.: Cancer metastasis detection with neural conditional random field (2018). arXiv preprint arXiv:1806.07064

5. Coudray, N., Ocampo, P.S., et al.: Classification and mutation prediction from non-small cell lung cancer histopathology images using deep learning. Nat. Med. **24**(10), 1559–1567 (2018)

6. Hou, L., Samaras, D., et al.: Patch-based convolutional neural network for whole slide tissue image classification. In: Proceedings of the IEEE Conference on Computer Vision and Pattern Recognition, pp. 2424–2433 (2016)

7. Tokunaga, H., Teramoto, Y., et al.: Adaptive weighting multi-field-of-view CNN for semantic segmentation in pathology. In: Proceedings of the IEEE Conference on Computer Vision and Pattern Recognition, pp. 12597–12606 (2019)

8. Kong, B., Wang, X., Li, Z., Song, Q., Zhang, S.: Cancer metastasis detection via spatially structured deep network. In: Niethammer, M., Styner, M., Aylward, S., Zhu, H., Oguz, I., Yap, P.-T., Shen, D. (eds.) IPMI 2017. LNCS, vol. 10265, pp. 236–248. Springer, Cham (2017). https://doi.org/10.1007/978-3-319-59050-9_19

9. Yan, J., Li, C., Li, Y., et al.: Adaptive discrete hypergraph matching. IEEE Trans. Cybern. **48**(2), 765–779 (2017)

10. Yang, L., Zhang, Y., Chen, et al.: Suggestive annotation: A deep active learning framework for biomedical image segmentation. In: International Conference on Medical Image Computing and Computer-Assisted Intervention, pp. 399–407 (2017)

11. Kather, J.N., Pearson, A.T., et al.: Deep learning can predict microsatellite instability directly from histology in gastrointestinal cancer. Nat. Med. **25**(7), 1054–1056 (2019). https://doi.org/10.1038/s41591-019-0462-y

12. Zanjani, F.G., Zinger, S.: Cancer detection in histopathology whole-slide images using conditional random fields on deep embedded spaces. In: Medical Imaging: Digital Pathology, vol. 10581 (2018). https://doi.org/10.1117/12.2293107

13. Li, Y., Ping, W.: Cancer metastasis detection with neural conditional random field (2018). arXiv:1806.07064

14. Krähenbühl, P., Koltun, V.: Efficient inference in fully connected CRFs with Gaussian edge potentials. In: Advances in Neural Information Processing Systems, pp. 109–117 (2011)

15. Zheng, S., Jayasumana, S., et al.: Conditional random fields as recurrent neural networks. In: Proceedings of the IEEE International Conference on Computer Vision, pp. 1529–1537 (2015)

16. The Cancer Genome Atlas (TCGA) dataset. https://portal.gdc.cancer.gov

17. He, K., Zhang, X., Ren, S., et al.: Deep residual learning for image recognition. In: Proceedings of the IEEE Conference on Computer Vision and Pattern Recognition, pp. 770–778 (2016)

18. Iandola F., Moskewicz M., Karayev S., et al.: Densenet: Implementing efficient convnet descriptor pyramids (2014). arXiv preprint arXiv:1404.1869

Deep Active Learning for Breast Cancer Segmentation on Immunohistochemistry Images

Haocheng Shen[1], Kuan Tian[1], Pei Dong[1], Jun Zhang[1], Kezhou Yan[1], Shannon Che[2], Jianhua Yao[1], Pifu Luo[2], and Xiao Han[1(✉)]

[1] AI Lab, Tencent, Shenzhen, China
haroldhan@tencent.com
[2] KingMed Diagnostics Co., Ltd., Guangzhou, China

Abstract. Immunohistochemistry (IHC) plays an essential role in breast cancer diagnosis and treatment. Reliable and automatic segmentation of breast cancer regions on IHC images would be of considerable value for further analysis. However, the prevalent fully convolutional networks (FCNs) suffer from difficulties in obtaining sufficient annotated training data. Active learning, on the other hand, aims to reduce the cost of annotation by selecting an informative and effective subset for labeling. In this paper, we present a novel deep active learning framework for breast cancer segmentation on IHC images. Three criteria are explicitly designed to select training samples: *dissatisfaction, representativeness* and *diverseness. Dissatisfaction*, consisting of both pixel-level and image-level dissatisfaction, focuses on selecting samples that the network does not segment well. *Representativeness* chooses samples that can mostly represent all the other unlabeled samples and *diverseness* further makes the chosen samples different from those already in the training set. We evaluate the proposed method on a large-scale in-house breast cancer IHC dataset and demonstrate that our method outperforms the state-of-the-art suggestive annotation (SA) [1] and representative annotation (RA) [5] on two test sets and achieves competitive or even superior performance using 40% of training data to using the full set of training data.

Keywords: IHC images · Active learning · Segmentation

1 Introduction

Immunohistochemistry (IHC) plays an essential role in breast cancer diagnosis and treatment, e.g., evaluating the severity and prognosis or choosing the therapeutic methods. Reliable and automatic segmentation of breast cancer regions on IHC images would be of considerable value for further analysis, such as nuclei counting and positive-stained nuclei percentage calculation. However, the task is challenging due to large diversity of nuclei size, appearance and staining procedure. Figure 1 shows six IHC cases with different nuclei staining grades: negative

© Springer Nature Switzerland AG 2020
A. L. Martel et al. (Eds.): MICCAI 2020, LNCS 12265, pp. 509–518, 2020.
https://doi.org/10.1007/978-3-030-59722-1_49

(left two), weakly positive (middle two) and strongly positive (right two), where the red lines show the manually delineated cancer regions.

Fully convolutional networks (FCNs) have achieved promising performance on several biomedical image segmentation tasks [1,10,13,14]. However, obtaining sufficient training data for FCNs is time-consuming and labor expensive. Although annotating small datasets is tractable, it becomes extremely costly for large-scale datasets, especially for medical data, which requires experts' domain knowledge. Active learning [1–5] aims to alleviate the burden of manual annotation by selecting the most informative and effective subset for labeling. Meanwhile, the network is expected to be sufficiently accurate by training on this subset. Recently, Yang et al. [1] introduced a suggestive annotation (SA) method for glands segmentation using ensemble FCNs. By combining image uncertainty and similarity, SA is able to find the difficult and representative samples and obtain the competitive segmentation results using only 50% of training data. Zheng et al. [5] proposed a representative annotation (RA) approach, which is an extension of SA by first training a variational auto-encoder (VAE) [6] for unsupervised feature extraction, followed by a combination of the classical clustering and the max-cover approaches for sample selection.

In this paper, we extend SA [1] from three perspectives: firstly, instead of using ensemble FCNs, we apply a Bayesian network for estimating the image uncertainty, which is more resource and computational friendly; secondly, in addition to the uncertainty estimation from pixel-level entropy, we introduce a new image-level estimation to reflect the overall image segmentation satisfaction and combine both pixel-level and image-level estimation as a new ranking method for unlabeled images; thirdly, besides selecting the representative samples in [1], we design an extra selection criterion called diverseness, making the samples in the training set as diverse as possible, which could potentially strengthen the generalization capability of the network. We evaluate the proposed method on a large-scale in-house breast cancer IHC dataset and demonstrate that our method outperforms SA [1] and RA [5] on two test sets and achieves competitive or even better performance using 40% of training data compared with using the full set of training data.

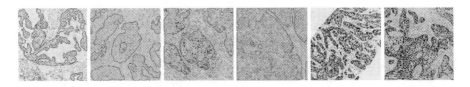

Fig. 1. Six breast IHC exemplars: negative (left two), weakly positive (middle two) and strongly positive (right two). The red lines show the manually delineated cancer regions. (Color figure online)

2   Methodology

We design three sample selection criteria: *dissatisfaction, representativeness* and *diverseness*. To select a subset consisting of k images, we firstly select $K(K > k)$ samples by dissatisfaction to form a candidate set S_c, then the set S_r ($S_r \subseteq S_c$) having the largest representativeness is built. In the end, S_r is further refined by diverseness criterion to form the set S_d ($S_d \subseteq S_r$), which is then added into the training set. This procedure is repeated for m iterations as needed.

2.1   Dissatisfaction

Pixel-Level Dissatisfaction. This can be easily interpreted as pixel-level uncertainty, which can be modeled by Monte-Carlo (MC) dropout [7]. Dropout is commonly applied during training to prevent over-fitting. When it is activated during testing and the input image I is feed-forwarded T times through the network, each time with a different and random dropout mask, this procedure can be viewed as an approximation of a Bayesian neural network [7,9]. To this end, MC sampling of the models generates T samples of predicted probability maps $\{p_1, \ldots p_T\}$, and the final probability map $\hat{p}$ is estimated as the average over all the MC probability maps: $\hat{p} = \frac{1}{T} \sum_{i=1}^{T} p_i$. After getting $\hat{p}$, we can use the normalized entropy as a measurement of pixel-level uncertainty as follows:

$$H = - \sum_{c \in C} \hat{p}^c \log(\hat{p}^c) / \log(|C|) \tag{1}$$

where $\hat{p}^c$ is the softmax output for class c and C is the set of classes ($C = \{0, 1\}$ in our case). Note that H is an uncertainty map and in the range of $[0, 1]$. Intuitively, pixels with low uncertainty (i.e. low entropy) receive high confident predictions. On the other hand, the predictions of pixels with high uncertainty are either sensitive to the altering neuron connectivity or consistently equivalent to random guess (e.g., pixels with a probability of 0.5 have the largest uncertainty).

Image-Level Dissatisfaction. Pixel-level dissatisfaction emphasizes pixel prediction confidence, which cannot reflect the overall image segmentation accuracy. Therefore we introduce image-level dissatisfaction. Dice coefficient is a widely used measurement for evaluating segmentation accuracy [1,8,9]. High Dice values stand for good segmentations while low values may indicate segmentation failures. In active learning setting, it would be more useful to select samples which the network does not perform well rather than the ones that already produce reasonable results. However, the real Dice coefficients cannot be exactly calculated during the sample selection phase as no ground truth mask is available. We borrow the idea from Roy et al. [10] which proposed to use the intersection over union (IoU) over all the T MC samples as a proxy for Dice coefficient and demonstrated that they are highly correlated. Specifically, the value of IoU is between $[0, 1]$ and computed as:

$$IoU = \frac{|q_1 \cap q_2 \cap \cdots \cap q_T|}{|q_1 \cup q_2 \cup \cdots \cup q_T|} \tag{2}$$

where $q_{i(i=1,...,T)}$ is the binary mask after thresholding the probability map p_i. As we can see, the image-level dissatisfaction takes the overall segmentation quality into consideration rather than focusing on each pixel's prediction confidence.

The dissatisfaction ranking score s for each image can be calculated as the combination of pixel-level s_{pix} and image-level s_{img} dissatisfaction measurement as follows:

$$s = s_{pix} - \lambda \cdot s_{img} = \frac{1}{N} \sum_{i=1}^{N} h_i - \lambda \cdot IoU \qquad (3)$$

where N is the number of pixels in the image and h_i represents the normalized entropy of pixel i in H. λ is the trade-off weight balancing the two dissatisfaction measurements. After obtaining s for each image, we select top K images based on highest ranking scores to form the candidate set S_c.

We choose LinkNet [8] as the segmentation model due to its superior performance and less computational and memory requirement. LinkNet has an encoder-decoder based architecture where it adopts ResNet18 [12] as the encoder and skip connection between each encoder and decoder block similar to Unet [13]. For Bayesian LinkNet, we insert a dropout layer after every encoder and decoder block with a rate r.

2.2   Representativeness

To maximize the effectiveness of the annotated data and avoid delineating redundant images which have similar appearance or feature, the selected images need to be representative among the large set of unlabeled images. In other words, it would be useful for the selected images to include patterns or features for as many unannotated images as possible. Yang et al. [1] propose to mine representative samples based on image similarity: the representativeness of the selected subset S_r for all the unannotated images set S_u is formulated as $F(S_r, S_u) = \sum_{I_j \in S_u} f(S_r, I_j)$ where $f(S_r, I_j) = \max_{I_i \in S_r} sim(I_i, I_j)$ and $sim(\cdot, \cdot)$ is the similarity estimation between image I_i and I_j. This can be explained that for each image $I_j \in S_u$, it is represented by its most similar image in S_r using the similarity measurement, and $F(S_r, S_u)$ is the sum of such the most similarity representation for all the images in S_u. Thus, the problem can be converted to $S_r = \arg\max F(S_r, S_u)$.

Finding S_r that maximizes $F(S_r, S_u)$ is a generalized maximum set cover (max-cover) problem [11] and is NP-hard. In this paper, we take the same strategy in [1] to solve this NP-hard problem by applying the approximation greedy method [11]: we iteratively add $I_i \in S_c$ that maximizes $F(S_r \cup I_i, S_u)$ over S_r, until S_r contains the pre-set number of images. It is worth noting that because of the max operation in $f(\cdot, \cdot)$, adding an image which is identical to an image in S_r cannot increase $F(S_r, S_u)$, thus it will be less likely to be selected.

To calculate the similarity estimation between I_i and I_j, similar to [1], we extract the output of the last encoder block as the high level feature and calculate the channel-wise mean as the image descriptors, denoted as d_i and d_j, and *cosine* similarity is used as the measurement: $sim(I_i, I_j) = d_i \cdot d_j^\top / (\|d_i\| \cdot \|d_j\|)$.

2.3   Diverseness

Besides selecting samples which well-represent the unannotated image set S_u, it is also necessary to select samples that are diverse enough. For example, in our case, we would like the training IHC images to be different from each other as much as possible, covering a large range of nuclei types, tissue types and image staining styles, rather than focusing on some specific image character- istics. This could potentially prevent over-fitting and strengthen the general- ization capability of the network. Although the max operation in f described above in Sect. 2.2 can guarantee that the images with similar appearance are less likely to be chosen in the same iteration, they may still be possibly chosen in the next iteration. To this end, we propose to refine S_r by further select- ing the samples which are dissimilar with those already in the current training set S_t. Analogously, we calculate the diverseness of the selected subset S_d for S_t as $D(S_d, S_t) = \sum_{I_j \in S_t} f'(S_d, I_j)$ where $f'(S_d, I_j) = \max_{I_i \in S_d} dis(I_i, I_j)$ and $dis(\cdot, \cdot)$ is the dissimilarity estimation between image I_i and I_j. In this paper, we simply define $dis(I_i, I_j) = 1 - sim(I_i, I_j)$.

Similarly, finding the most diverse subset of samples can be converted to $S_d = \arg\max D(S_d, S_t)$, which can be solved by the greedy method [11] as described in Sect. 2.2.

3   Evaluation

The proposed framework was implemented in Tensorflow. We used $T = 10$ MC samples and set the dropout rate to $r = 0.8$. The trade-off weight λ was set to 0.1 experimentally. The segmentation model was trained for 10,000 steps using mean square error loss, which produced better segmentation results than cross entropy loss in our experiments. The initial learning rate was set to 10^{-2} and gradually decreased to 10^{-5}. These settings were kept the same for all the experiments.

We evaluated the proposed method on a large in-house breast cancer IHC dataset. The training set contains a total of 2767 estrogen receptor (ER), pro- gesterone receptor (PR) and Ki67 staining images. Among them, 2154 images are extracted from hot spot areas in whole slide tissue images (WSIs) from more than 200 patients collected from four centers and 613 images are captured from microscopic views. Two held-out test sets are used: TestA with 306 images and TestB with 368 images. Note TestB is from a center that is not covered in the training set. There is no overlap of patients between training and test sets. All the images are resized to have $0.848\,\mu\mathrm{m}$/pixel, which is equivalent to $10\times$ objec- tive magnification of a normal microscope. The images were manually annotated by junior pathologists first, then rectified and verified by senior pathologists.

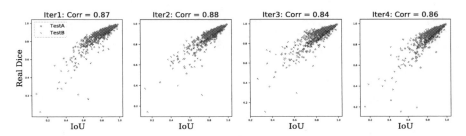

Fig. 2. Scatter plot and correlation *Corr* of the real Dice and the IoU between MC samples for different training iterations using 10%–40% of training data. (Color figure online)

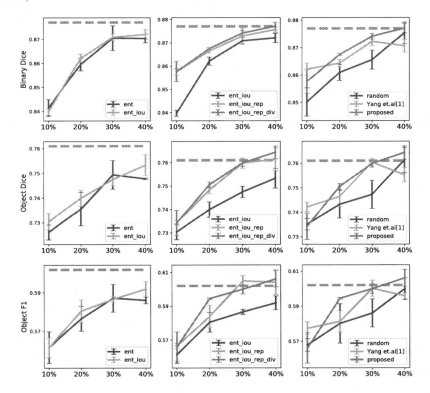

Fig. 3. Performance curves of different methods over annotation budgets on TestA. The dashed blue line are the results using full training data.

To simulate the active learning process, the annotations of the training samples were kept hidden unless the proposed method selects the samples. We set the annotation budget from 10% to 40% of the overall labeled images. We train a model using 50 randomly selected training images with labels as a start point.

We compute the correlation coefficient *Corr* between the real Dice coefficient and the IoU between MC samples firstly. To calculate the real Dice, we threshold

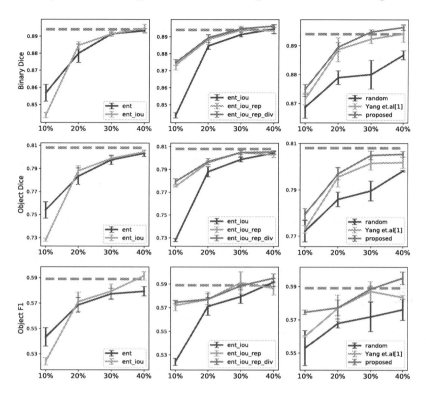

Fig. 4. Performance curves of different methods over annotation budgets on TestB. The dashed blue line are the results using full training data.

the average probability map $\hat{p}$ over all MC samples as the final prediction, which is then compared with the ground truth mask. The scatter plots and $Corr$ values over different training iterations are shown in Fig. 2. Each dot represents one image, with unique colors for each test set. It can be seen that, regardless of training iteration, the real Dice and the IoU are highly positively correlated, with $Corr$ values in the range of 0.84–0.88. Thus, it is reasonable to use the IoU (Eq. 2) as the proxy of Dice to select the image-level unsatisfactory samples (e.g., the ones with low IoU values).

To evaluate the effectiveness of the proposed active learning framework, we plot the performance curves over different annotation budgets on TestA and TestB shown in Fig. 3 and Fig. 4, respectively. We adopt three evaluation metrics: binary Dice (B-$Dice$), object-level Dice (O-$Dice$) and object-level F1 (O-$F1$). B-$Dice$ is the Dice coefficient for overall binary predictions while O-$Dice$ and O-$F1$ take individual objects into consideration [14]. All the experiments are repeated three times to report the mean and standard deviation of the performance. The dashed lines indicate the performance using full training data.

We firstly compare using pixel-level dissatisfaction only (ent) with the proposed combination of pixel-level and image-level dissatisfaction (ent_iou) (left column of Fig. 3 and Fig. 4). It can be seen that although no obvious difference exists between *ent_iou* and *ent* for *B-Dice* on two sets, *ent_iou* gives improvements for *O-F1* on both sets and *O-Dice* on TestA as well. In addition, using dissatisfaction criterion alone underperforms compared with full data training (the dash lines) on TestA. Keeping adding difficult samples for training would harm the generalization capability of the network as it may cause over-fitting or introduce noisy labels during training.

Then, we investigate the effectiveness of successionally adding representativeness (*ent_iou_rep*) and diverseness (*ent_iou_rep_div*) criterion (middle column of Fig. 3 and Fig. 4). It shows that adding representativeness is consistently better than using dissatisfaction only for both sets and TestA benefits more than TestB. This could be explained that as the center of TestA is covered by the training set, selecting representative samples could make the learned feature more general and generalize better to TestA. While for a new center TestB, different staining styles from the training set could be one possible reason for the relatively small improvements. Adding diverseness can further give slight improvement for both sets, especially when the annotation budget increased from 30% to 40%. We attribute this to as the number of training samples increases, the diverseness of training samples matters more. From Fig. 3 and Fig. 4, the proposed method (*ent_iou_rep_div*) can achieve competitive or even better performance using only 40% of the training data compared to using full of them.

Table 1. The average performance of different methods over training iterations and †
indicates statistical significance using paired t-test.

Method	TestA			TestB		
	O-F1(%)	O-Dice (%)	B-Dice (%)	O-F1 (%)	O-Dice (%)	B-Dice (%)
entropy	$57.8 \pm 0.2^\dagger$	$73.9 \pm 0.2^\dagger$	$86.0 \pm 0.1^\dagger$	$56.7 \pm 0.4^\dagger$	$78.4 \pm 0.3^\dagger$	$88.0 \pm 0.2^\dagger$
entropy_iou	$58.0 \pm 0.1^\dagger$	$74.3 \pm 0.1^\dagger$	$86.1 \pm 0.0^\dagger$	$56.6 \pm 0.0^\dagger$	$78.0 \pm 0.0^\dagger$	$87.9 \pm 0.0^\dagger$
entropy_iou_rep	59.0 ± 0.0	75.1 ± 0.1	$86.7 \pm 0.1^\dagger$	58.2 ± 0.5	$79.3 \pm 0.2^\dagger$	$88.7 \pm 0.2^\dagger$
random	$58.3 \pm 0.6^\dagger$	$74.7 \pm 0.4^\dagger$	$86.3 \pm 0.3^\dagger$	$56.7 \pm 0.4^\dagger$	$78.6 \pm 0.2^\dagger$	$87.8 \pm 0.2^\dagger$
SA [1]	58.9 ± 0.2	75.1 ± 0.1	$86.7 \pm 0.1^\dagger$	$57.5 \pm 0.2^\dagger$	$79.3 \pm 0.2^\dagger$	$88.6 \pm 0.2^\dagger$
Proposed	$\mathbf{59.2 \pm 0.3}$	$\mathbf{75.2 \pm 0.2}$	$\mathbf{86.9 \pm 0.1}$	$\mathbf{58.4 \pm 0.2}$	$\mathbf{79.7 \pm 0.1}$	$\mathbf{88.9 \pm 0.1}$

Lastly, we compare the proposed method with 1) random selection, 2) SA by Yang et al. [1] and 3) RA by Zheng et al. [5]. The comparison with random selection and SA are shown in the right column of Fig. 3 and Fig. 4 and Table 1. We replace the ensemble FCNs in SA with Bayesian LinkNet to produce the uncertainty maps for a fair comparison. It can be observed that our method and SA outperform random selection for all the metrics, especially when the annotation budget is relatively smaller (e.g., 20% or 30%). Moreover, the larger standard deviations indicate that random selection is not stable. The proposed method also outperforms SA for two test sets. It is worth noting that there is a performance drop in SA when the annotation budget increased from 30% to 40%. This phenomenon is also found in [5] and is mainly because that the max-cover method [11] used by SA is NP-hard, thus using the greedy approximation algorithm makes the performance degrade when the size of the data increases. On the contrary, the diverseness criterion in our proposed method can alleviate this problem by preserving valuable and diverse samples, especially when the size of training set becomes large. The average quantitative segmentation results of different methods over training iterations (using 10%–40% of training data) are presented in Table 1. It shows that our proposed method outperforms all other methods in all metrics on both test sets. Most of the improvements are statistical significant (p-value < 0.05, indicated by †) using paired t-test, especially on TestB from an unseen center.

We further evaluate RA [5] on our datasets. As RA has no iteration process and only trains the model once, we compare RA with our method by selecting 40% training data. Unlike using the clustering method to include diverseness implicitly in RA, our method has a diverseness score to ensure the diversity of samples explicitly. The experiments show that our proposed method are 1.3%, 1.7%, 2.7% higher than RA [5] on TestA and 1.5%, 1.4%, 2.2% higher on TestB for *B-Dice*, *O-Dice*, *O-F1*, respectively, demonstrating the effectiveness of our sample selection criteria.

4   Conclusion

In this paper, we present a new active learning framework for breast cancer segmentation on IHC images. With the designed three sample selection criteria, our method can significantly relieve manual annotation burden while not compromise the segmentation accuracy. Note that our method is not constrained to IHC images, and future work would evaluate our method in other image domains.

References

1. Yang, L., Zhang, Y., Chen, J., Zhang, S., Chen, D.Z.: Suggestive annotation: a deep active learning framework for biomedical image segmentation. In: Descoteaux, M., Maier-Hein, L., Franz, A., Jannin, P., Collins, D., Duchesne, S. (eds.) MICCAI 2017. LNCS, vol. 10435, pp. 399–407. Springer, Cham (2017). https://doi.org/10.1007/978-3-319-66179-7_46
2. Aghdam, H.H., Gonzalez-Garcia, A., Weijer, J.V.D., Lpez, A.M.: Active learning for deep detection neural networks. In: Proceedings of the IEEE International Conference on Computer Vision (ICCV), pp. 3672–3680 (2019)
3. Lubrano di Scandalea, M., Perone, C.S., Boudreau, M., Cohen-Adad, J.: Deep active learning for axon-myelin segmentation on histology data. arXiv preprint arXiv:1907.05143 (2019)
4. Konyushkova, K., Sznitman, R., Fua, P.: Geometry in active learning for binary and multi-class image segmentation. Comput. Vis. Image Underst. **182**, 1–16 (2019)
5. Zheng, H.: Biomedical image segmentation via representative annotation. Proc. AAAI Conf. Artif. Intell. **33**, 5901–5908 (2019)
6. Kingma, D.P., Welling, M.: Auto-encoding variational Bayes. arXiv preprint arXiv:1312.6114 (2013)

7. Gal, Y., Ghahramani, Z.: Dropout as a Bayesian approximation: representing model uncertainty in deep learning. In: International Conference on Machine Learning (ICML), pp. 1050–1059 (2016)
8. Chaurasia, A., Culurciello, E.: LinkNet: exploiting encoder representations for efficient semantic segmentation. In: IEEE Visual Communications and Image Processing, pp. 1–4 (2017)
9. Jungo, A., Reyes, M.: Assessing reliability and challenges of uncertainty estimations for medical image segmentation. In: Shen, D., et al. (eds.) MICCAI 2019. LNCS, vol. 11765, pp. 48–56. Springer, Cham (2019). https://doi.org/10.1007/978-3-030-32245-8_6
10. Roy, A.G., Conjeti, S., Navab, N., Wachinger, C.: Bayesian QuickNAT: model uncertainty in deep whole-brain segmentation for structure-wise quality control. NeuroImage **195**, 11–22 (2019)
11. Feige, U.: A threshold of ln n for approximating set cover. J. ACM **45**(4), 634–652 (1998)
12. He, K., Zhang, X., Ren, S., Sun, J.: Deep residual learning for image recognition. In: Proceedings of the IEEE Conference on Computer Vision and Pattern Recognition (CVPR), pp. 770–778 (2016)
13. Ronneberger, O., Fischer, P., Brox, T.: U-Net: convolutional networks for biomedical image segmentation. In: Navab, N., Hornegger, J., Wells, W.M., Frangi, A.F. (eds.) MICCAI 2015. LNCS, vol. 9351, pp. 234–241. Springer, Cham (2015). https://doi.org/10.1007/978-3-319-24574-4_28
14. Sirinukunwattana, K., Pluim, J.P., Chen, H., et al.: Gland segmentation in colon histology images: the GlaS challenge contest. Med. Image Anal. **35**, 489–502 (2017)

Multiple Instance Learning with Center Embeddings for Histopathology Classification

Philip Chikontwe[1], Meejeong Kim[2], Soo Jeong Nam[2], Heounjeong Go[2,3], and Sang Hyun Park[1(✉)]

[1] Department of Robotics Engineering, DGIST, Daegu, South Korea
{philipchicco,shpark13135}@dgist.ac.kr
[2] Department of Pathology, Asan Medical Center, Seoul, South Korea
[3] Department of Pathology, University of Ulsan College of Medicine, Seoul, South Korea

Abstract. Histopathology image analysis plays an important role in the treatment and diagnosis of cancer. However, analysis of whole slide images (WSI) with deep learning is challenging given that the duration of pixel-level annotations is laborious and time consuming. To address this, recent methods have considered WSI classification as a Multiple Instance Learning (MIL) problem often with a multi-stage process for learning instance and slide level features. Currently, most methods focus on either instance-selection or instance prediction-aggregation that often fails to generalize and ignores instance relations. In this work, we propose a MIL-based method to jointly learn both instance- and bag-level embeddings in a single framework. In addition, we propose a center loss that maps embeddings of instances from the same bag to a single centroid and reduces intra-class variations. Consequently, our model can accurately predict instance labels and leverages robust hierarchical pooling of features to obtain bag-level features without sacrificing accuracy. Experimental results on curated colon datasets show the effectiveness of the proposed methods against recent state-of-the-art methods.

1 Introduction

In the current age of digitizing glass slides into histopathology images using whole-slide image (WSI) scanners, histopathology images play a vital role as a gold standard for cancer diagnosis in clinical settings. However, given the sheer volume of a single WSI (i.e. $100k$ pixels), effective analysis is considered both laborious and time consuming. Moreover, due to the high computational costs and the bias of subjective judgments among observers, automated and accurate analysis of WSIs promises improved diagnostics and better treatment strategies.

In particular, deep learning has become a popular solution and has yielded remarkable results when sufficiently labeled training data is provided. However, pixel level annotations are difficult and costly to acquire. Thus, multiple instance learning (MIL) based training of neural networks [2,5,9,12,13,20] presents a

© Springer Nature Switzerland AG 2020
A. L. Martel et al. (Eds.): MICCAI 2020, LNCS 12265, pp. 519–528, 2020.
https://doi.org/10.1007/978-3-030-59722-1_50

unique solution to alleviate these challenges towards final WSI diagnosis without precise annotations. Though, due to the ambiguity of instance labels in MIL, learning robust instance embeddings is also challenging.

To address this, recent methods [4,7,10,19,23,25] often adopt a two-stage approach that includes (1) learning an instance encoder based on sampled regions from the WSI to obtain a prediction score or low dimensional feature, and (2) learning an aggregation model that uses the learned instance encoder to integrate instance level information for slide-level prediction. Though successful in some problem settings, this approach often fails when learning based on noisy labels and is worsened in the second stage of aggregation since features are not representative of the true labels. Therefore, an end-to-end framework that exploits both instance- and bag-level representations is beneficial. Also, providing interpretable results that follow standard pathology workflows can further aid experts to make informed decisions on diagnosis and treatment options. In this work, we propose a model that consists of top-k instance selection, instance- and bag-representation learning, as well as a center embedding module that reduces intra-class variations during learning via a center loss [21].

In addition, instance- and bag-losses with respect to the slide labels are also used to update the entire model. By this process, our model can improve feature representation and also use the instance level information to regularize bag level features. Moreover, instead of a decoupled feature aggregation step as in previous methods [2,9], our model consists of a bag module that creates a bag level feature via pyramidal feature aggregation. We consider a bag of k instances as a single input with k channels. Thus, we apply several convolution operations via the proposed bag module to obtain a single representation that considers key semantic information from earlier layers of our model. Consequently, we obtain a robust embedding that is effective for classification. On the other hand, despite using noisy labels in a MIL scenario, both instance and bag loss in our method enable features from different classes to be apart while center loss clusters features of the same class towards corresponding centers. Lastly, apart from the use of a bag classifier for diagnosis prediction, we also propose a *soft*-assignment method [22] to assign aggregated slide-level embeddings to the learned centers for final diagnosis. The benefit of using a *soft*-assignment is empirically shown in our experiments. Our main contributions are summarised as follows:

- We propose an end-to-end model for weakly supervised histopathology classification able to assign correct instance and bag labels.
- We show that center loss can improve bag feature learning and also reduce ambiguity in instance labels.
- By jointly considering instance based-MIL (i.e. accurate instance level predictions) and embedding-based MIL, our method shows improved classification performance with reduced false positives.
- Experimental results on two datasets further show that our approach is comparable in performance to methods that learn separate bag-level classifiers and use attention mechanisms for instance selection.

1.1 Related Works

We consider two categories of approaches in recent literature that use MIL for medical image analysis i.e. (a) methods that use MIL for tile selection [2,3,7, 11,24], and (b) those that use unsupervised learning with MIL to learn instance embeddings [13,15,18].

MIL in Histology. MIL methods have been proposed for histopathology [2,4,5,7,8,10,24,25]. Li et al. [9] proposed a key instance learning using hard negative mining based on adaptive attention. However, attention based methods such as [8] may overfit when the number of slides is limited and fail to learn useful representations due to the bias of negative samples. More recently, Campanella et al. [2] proposed a two-step MIL method with impressive results on a large dataset using a recurrent neural network (RNN) for feature aggregation. However, RNNs are inherently difficult to train and have limited applicability. Although previous studies [8,9] show considerable improvements by using attention and its related variants, most methods propose multi-stage learning schemes that decouple instance level learning and instance aggregation, which inturn makes clinical deployment non trivial. To address these challenges, we propose a MIL method that jointly learns instance and bag embeddings in a single framework, showing the benefit of robust representative and separable features for classification.

Unsupervised Methods with MIL. In this setting, recent methods [13,15,18, 22] aim to learn representative features across tissue heterogeneity enabling WSI regression such as survival analysis [24,25] since MIL may fail when instances in a slide are assigned noisy labels. Tellez et al. [18] proposed neural compression for WSIs based on unsupervisedly learnt instance encoders using contrastive self pre-training before classification. Lu et al. [13] proposed contrastive predicting coding (CPC) as pre-training for histology and combined it with MIL to achieve improved results. To address survival analysis, Muhammad et al. [15] proposed to cluster instances with a reconstruction based objective. However, in most cases, to learn effective slide clusters from instance embeddings, iterative methods such as K-means are required to initialize centers and require complex cluster re-assignment strategies. In this work, we address this with a center loss capable to clustering features based on a mini-batch without the requirement of iterating the entire dataset.

2 Methods

Given a WSI dataset $\mathcal{D} = \{S_1, \ldots, S_n\}$ where each S_i is a whole slide image with its label $y_i \in \{0, 1\}$. For each $S_i \in \mathcal{D}$ with m instances $S_i = \{s_{i1}, s_{i2}, \ldots, s_{im}\}$ s.t $m \leq M$, sampled from non-background regions with M denoting the total number of instances in a slide. Our goal is to assign the correct label y_i to each slide. In this setting, only slide level labels are available during training, where

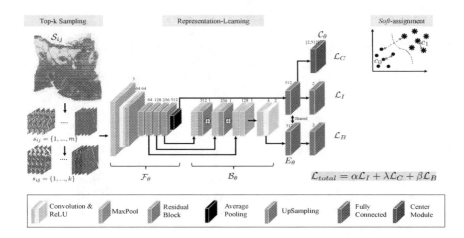

Fig. 1. Overview of the proposed framework. For a given slide, we first sample k instances at the start of each training epoch based on top predicted probabilities per slide via the instance module (i.e. $\mathcal{F}_\theta$ through $\mathcal{L}_I$ branch with shared embedding module E_θ). Top-k instances are feed through $\mathcal{F}_\theta$ to obtain embeddings with k channels via the bag module $\mathcal{B}_\theta$. Following, we feed the bag- and instance-embeddings to E_θ then the classification modules (bag and instance) to obtain final predictions and update the model.

1 means positive and 0 negative. Formally, MIL must satisfy the constraints: if S_i is negative, then all instances in S_i should be negative i.e. $y_i = 0, \forall(y_{ij}) = 0$, where y_{ij} are instance labels. If S_i is positive, then at least one instance should be positive, i.e. $y_i = 1, \sum y_{ij} \geq 1$.

To this end, we develop a convolutional neural network (CNN) model able to perform both instance level discrimination and slide level classification in an end-to-end framework. In particular, our method consists of (1) top-k instance selection (2) instance- and bag-representation learning, and (3) *soft*-assignment based inference with learned centers. Figure 1 shows the overall framework.

Top-k Instance Selection. We implement a neural network $\mathcal{F}_\theta(\cdot)$ to transform an instance from i-th slide(bag) into a low dimensional embedding $g_{ij} = \mathcal{F}_\theta(s_{ij})$ via the instance branch ($\mathcal{L}_I$ path in Fig. 1) with a shared embedding module E_θ, followed by a classification module that outputs the positiveness of an instance $p_{ij} = \mathcal{H}_I(g_{ij})$ i.e. $\mathcal{H}_I$ is binary classifier. Then, instance level probabilities $\{p_{i1}, \ldots, p_{im}\}$ from all bags are sorted to obtain top-k instances per slide for training i.e. we form a $\mathcal{D}_k \subset \mathcal{D}$. Note that in this procedure, parameters θ of $\mathcal{F}$, $\mathcal{B}$, and E as well as other modules are not updated or stored.

Instance Level Learning. In each training phase, for a given instance input $s_{ij} \in \mathcal{D}_k$ we obtain embeddings g_{ij} after global average pooling via $\mathcal{F}_\theta$. Each instance is assigned its corresponding bag-level label y and is used to compute the instance loss $\mathcal{L}_I$ given the prediction $\hat{y}$ after g_{ij} is feed to E_θ and an instance classifier $\mathcal{H}_\mathcal{I}$ using cross-entropy. Formally, instance loss is presented as follows.

$$\mathcal{L}_I = -\sum y_{ij} \log p_{ij} \tag{1}$$

Pyramidal Bag-Level Learning. In addition to g_{ij}, three features maps from the earlier blocks of $\mathcal{F}_\theta$ are used for bag-level learning in $\mathcal{B}_\theta$. We feed each feature map to a series of convolutional blocks with input sizes $\{512, 256, 128\}$ corresponding to the feature map size and obtain reduced features each with a single channel. Next, we upsample the maps using linear interpolation to match the size at the previous block and concatenate with the previous feature map to form a single spatial map with k channels that is used to obtain the final flattened feature z_i. Following, z_i is passed to our shared embedding module E then the bag classifier $\mathcal{H}_\mathcal{B}(z_i)$. Bag predictions $\hat{y}$ are used to evaluate bag loss $\mathcal{L}_B(\hat{y}, y_i)$ using cross-entropy, formally:

$$\mathcal{L}_B = -\sum y_i \log \hat{y}. \tag{2}$$

In addition, to improve the discriminative power of the deep features; a center loss is proposed. It characterizes intra-class variations by learning embeddings that minimize the distance of instances from the same bag. Formally, center loss is expressed as:

$$\mathcal{L}_C = \frac{1}{2} \sum_{i=1}^{u} \| g_{ij} - c_{y_i} \|_2^2 . \tag{3}$$

In Eq.(3), c_{y_i} denotes the y_{ij}th class center's deep features with same dimension as g_{ij} and u is the mini-batch size. In this work, class centers are parameterized by the center module $\mathcal{C}_\theta(\cdot)$ initialized from a standard normal distribution and trained jointly with $\mathcal{L}_C$ and $\mathcal{L}_B$. Intuitively, instance-embeddings from the same bag should have similar features that can cluster to similar points in the embedding space. The class centers are updated based on instance-embeddings in a mini-batch rather than the entire training set which would be impractical for large datasets. The final loss function is defined as:

$$\mathcal{L} = \alpha\mathcal{L}_I + \lambda\mathcal{L}_C + \beta\mathcal{L}_B, \tag{4}$$

where λ, α and β balance the losses.

***Soft*-Assignment Based Inference.** In the testing stage, given a bag embedding obtained via $\mathcal{B}$, our goal is to assign the correct label $\hat{y}$ as the final diagnosis. To achieve this, we infer that instance-embeddings of the same bag should be matched to a single centroid that represents the bag-label. Given a bag-level embedding $z_i = \mathcal{B}\{g_{i1}, \ldots, g_{ik}\}$ for slide $\mathcal{S}_i$, we assign z_i to the learned centroid c_{y_i} using the students t-distribution [14] as a kernel to measure the similarity between the two points as:

$$q_i = \frac{(1 + \| z_i - c_{y_i} \|^2 / \varphi)^{-\frac{\varphi+1}{2}}}{\sum_{i'} (1 + \| z_i - c_{y_{i'}} \|^2 / \varphi)^{-\frac{\varphi+1}{2}}} \tag{5}$$

where q_i can be considered as the probability of assigning z_i to a class center and φ are the degrees of freedom of the Students distribution.

3   Experiments and Results

Dataset and Settings. We conduct experiments on two colectoral cancer (CRC) WSI datasets collected at Anonymous medical center with different scanning conditions i.e. Dataset I and II. The datasets involve Hematoxylin and Eosin stained (H&E) slides of normal and malignant tissues scanned at x40 magnification using different scanners. CRC is the third most prevalent cancer in humans and common cause of death in both male and females. In this work, malignant slides involve microsatellite instable (MSI) [1] CRC which is a molecular phenotype due to defective DNA mismatch repair system. Expert pathologists curated and detected the presence of MSI using Immunohistochemical analysis (IHC) and PCR-based amplication. Determination of MSI status in CRC has prognostic and therapeutic implications.

Dataset I consists of 173 WSI (59 normal & 114 MSI) whereas set II has 193 (85 normal & 108 MSI) WSIs. We follow a 40%-10%-50% split to create nonoverlapping sets for training, validation and testing, respectively. For each WSI, we applied the Otsu method [17] to filter-out non tissue regions after conversion to HSV color space. Patch candidate locations were selected randomly for extraction per slide during training and validation, respectively. During training and inference, we set top-k instance selection to 50 and used instances with 256×256 size. A ResNet-34 [6] was finetuned and used as the feature extraction model $\mathcal{F}_\theta(\cdot)$. In addition, Fully Connected (FC) layers was employed for both the instance and bag classifiers $\mathcal{H}_\mathcal{I}$ and $\mathcal{H}_\mathcal{B}$. The feature dimension of the embeddings and center module was set to 512. The entire framework was trained end-to-end with a learning rate of $1e-4$ for 40 epochs. We empirically set the loss hyperparameters $\lambda = 0.01$, $\alpha = 1.0$ and $\beta = 0.01$, respectively.

Comparison Methods. In this work, we compare the proposed method with the recent state-of-the-art method in [2][1], we term this method as 'CampanellaMILRNN'. In addition, we also evaluated against DeepAttenMIL [8][2] and TwoStageMIL [16][3] methods. For a fair comparison, the same backbone $\mathcal{F}_\theta(\cdot)$ is used in all cases. Both CampanellaMILRNN and TwoStageMIL use a two-stage learning procedure i.e. (1) instance level learning and (2) slide-level aggregation. DeepAttenMIL uses an end-to-end approach with permutation invariant pooling based on the attention mechanism.

---

[1] We used the publicly available implementations: https://github.com/MSKCC-Computational-Pathology/MIL-nature-medicine-2019.

[2] https://github.com/AMLab-Amsterdam/AttentionDeepMIL.

[3] https://github.com/ImagingLab/ICIAR2018.

Table 1. Evaluation of the proposed methods on Dataset I with $k = 50$. 'bag' implies the use of the bag classifier and 'soft' means with soft-assignment during testing.

Method	F1Score	Precision	Recall	Accuracy
CampanellaMIL [2]	76.8	84.46	79.49	79.49
CampanellaMIL+RNN [2]	80.16	85.98	82.05	82.05
DeepAttenMIL [8]	85.95	86.03	85.90	85.90
TwoStageMIL [16]	65.21	80.41	71.79	71.79
Ours (w/o center loss)	86.93	87.2	87.18	87.18
Ours (w/all loss + bag)	86.77	87.58	87.18	87.18
Ours (w/all loss + soft)	**92.36**	**92.54**	**92.31**	**92.31**

Quantitative Results. Tables 1 and 2 shows the performance of the proposed method against recent approaches. Among the comparison methods, the proposed solution with a *soft*-assignment based inference achieved the best result. Since 'CampanellaMIL' considers the probability of the top-most instance as the final slide classification, it performed poorly. Moreover, when our method was evaluated using bag classification only, we note consistent improvements over other methods i.e. +9.97% over CampanellaMIL's method, whereas our assignment based approach showed +15.56%. Notably, DeepAttenMIL was the best among the compared methods showing the benefit of attention based aggregation. Though no attention was used in our method, we report better performance. This leads us to believe performance of our model can further increase if attention is applied in our bag module.

In most cases, soft-assignment shows to be a good alternative over bag classifiers. We argue that since the learned centers capture the maximum information among similar instance embeddings; soft inference can be more robust than using a bag classifier in some settings. Results on dataset II also show that our method has the best performance. Though the RNN-based aggregation was the best among others on this set, our method showed a +1.28% improvement. Given previous methods emphasize decoupling of instance and bag level learning, evidence serves to show that there is no clear advantage in separating the two procedures and supports our initial objective of a single framework. Further, the majority of methods showed high performance on dataset II compared to the first. Due to the difference in scanning protocols used in preparation, performance may vary. However, note that no color normalization methods were used in pre-processing since we follow the standard protocol introduced in [2] that did use recent normalization techniques.

Qualitative Results. In Fig. 2, we present qualitative results of our method in two aspects (1) top-k patches that the model samples per slide-class, and (2) effectiveness of the learned model in interpretability via segmentation. In clinical workflows, it is beneficial to view which regions the model focuses on when

Table 2. Evaluation of the proposed methods on Dataset *II* with $k = 50$. 'bag' implies the use of the bag classifier and 'soft' means with soft-assignment during testing.

Method	F1Score	Precision	Recall	Accuracy
CampanellaMIL [2]	92.06	93.13	92.31	92.31
CampanellaMIL + RNN [2]	97.41	97.53	97.44	97.44
DeepAttenMIL [8]	93.65	94	93.59	93.59
TwoStageMIL [16]	89.55	89.89	89.74	89.74
Ours (w/o center loss)	93.43	94.17	93.59	93.59
Ours (w/all loss + bag)	97.41	97.53	97.44	97.44
Ours (w/all loss + soft)	**98.71**	**98.74**	**98.72**	**98.72**

making a decision to aid experts. Thus, we visually validate the effectiveness of the proposed methods by collecting the top-$k = 5$ patches with both high and low positiveness predicted by the instance classifier. Notably, the lowest predicted instances all correspond to actual normal tissues whereas those with high probability are regions of highly malignant nuclei clustered together. This shows that our model can accurately separate ambiguous labels in each slide. In addition, we performed patch-wise classification on entire slides using the trained model to obtain a heatmap that is thresholded and shows regions of high tumor probability. Notably, predictions correctly match expert annotations. This is attributed to the sampling step that accurately selects suspicious instances in each phase and avoids false negatives. The results validate our initial assertions and show that our method has a good trade-off between learning instance and bag features.

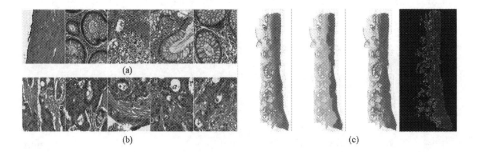

Fig. 2. Top-k examples and segmentation. (a) Instances with lowest probability (least-positiveness) (b) Instance with highest probability (positiveness) (c) Patch-based segmentation results of the proposed method: From left to right, WSI, WSI ground-truth annotation and predicted malignant regions. (Green) Normal regions w/o muscle and irrelevant tissues (Red) Suspicious tumor regions. (Color figure online)

4   Conclusion and Future Work

In this work, we presented a novel framework for histopathology slide classification in a multiple instance learning (MIL) setting. Two key concepts are introduced: (a) an end-to-end framework for both instance and bag level learning with a center loss that minimizes intra-class distances in the embedding space. (b) we proposed a *soft*-assignment based inference method for bag-level prediction. The proposed method was validated on two Colectoral cancer (CRC) datasets with overall improved performance over recent state-of-the-art methods. More importantly, the benefit of using a center loss is evident in the discriminative and generalized nature of learnt embeddings. Future works will explore multi-class multi-instance settings as well as the applicability of this method in WSI tumor grading.

Acknowledgment. This work was supported by the National Research Foundation of Korea (NRF) grant funded by the Korean Government (MSIT) (No. 2019R1C1C1008727), and the Grant of Artificial Intelligence Bio-Robot Medical Convergence Technology funded by the Ministry of Trade, Industry and Energy, the Ministry of Science and ICT, and the Ministry of Health and Welfare (No. 20001533).

References

1. Boland, C.R., Goel, A.: Microsatellite instability in colorectal cancer. Gastroenterology **138**(6), 2073–2087 (2010)
2. Campanella, G.: Clinical-grade computational pathology using weakly supervised deep learning on whole slide images. Nat. Med. **25**(8), 1301–1309 (2019)
3. Chen, H., et al.: Rectified cross-entropy and upper transition loss for weakly supervised whole slide image classifier. In: Shen, D., et al. (eds.) MICCAI 2019. LNCS, vol. 11764, pp. 351–359. Springer, Cham (2019). https://doi.org/10.1007/978-3-030-32239-7_39
4. Cosatto, E., et al.: Automated gastric cancer diagnosis on h and e-stained sections; training a classifier on a large scale with multiple instance machine learning. In: Medical Imaging 2013: Digital Pathology, vol. 8676, p. 867605. International Society for Optics and Photonics (2013)
5. Hashimoto, N., et al.: Multi-scale domain-adversarial multiple-instance CNN for cancer subtype classification with non-annotated histopathological images. arXiv preprint arXiv:2001.01599 (2020)
6. He, K., Zhang, X., Ren, S., Sun, J.: Deep residual learning for image recognition. In: Proceedings of the IEEE Conference on Computer Vision and Pattern Recognition, pp. 770–778 (2016)
7. Hou, L., Samaras, D., Kurc, T.M., Gao, Y., Davis, J.E., Saltz, J.H.: Patch-based convolutional neural network for whole slide tissue image classification. In: Proceedings of the IEEE Conference on Computer Vision and Pattern Recognition, pp. 2424–2433 (2016)
8. Ilse, M., Tomczak, J.M., Welling, M.: Attention-based deep multiple instance learning. arXiv preprint arXiv:1802.04712 (2018)

9. Li, M., Wu, L., Wiliem, A., Zhao, K., Zhang, T., Lovell, B.: Deep instance-level hard negative mining model for histopathology images. In: Shen, D., et al. (eds.) MICCAI 2019. LNCS, pp. 514–522. Springer, Cham (2019). https://doi.org/10.1007/978-3-030-32239-7_57

10. Li, S.: Multi-instance multi-scale CNN for medical image classification. In: Shen, D., et al. (eds.) MICCAI 2019. LNCS, vol. 11767, pp. 531–539. Springer, Cham (2019). https://doi.org/10.1007/978-3-030-32251-9_58

11. Li, W., Nguyen, V.-D., Liao, H., Wilder, M., Cheng, K., Luo, J.: Patch transformer for multi-tagging whole slide histopathology images. In: Shen, D., et al. (eds.) MICCAI 2019. LNCS, vol. 11764, pp. 532–540. Springer, Cham (2019). https://doi.org/10.1007/978-3-030-32239-7_59

12. Lin, Y., Zhang, H.: Regularized instance embedding for deep multi-instance learning. Appl. Sci. **10**(1), 64 (2020)

13. Lu, M.Y., Chen, R.J., Wang, J., Dillon, D., Mahmood, F.: Semi-supervised histology classification using deep multiple instance learning and contrastive predictive coding. arXiv preprint arXiv:1910.10825 (2019)

14. van der Maaten, L., Hinton, G.: Visualizing data using t-SNE. J. Mach. Learn. Res. **9**, 2579–2605 (2008)

15. Muhammad, H., et al.: Unsupervised subtyping of cholangiocarcinoma using a deep clustering convolutional autoencoder. In: Shen, D., et al. (eds.) MICCAI 2019. LNCS, vol. 11764, pp. 604–612. Springer, Cham (2019). https://doi.org/10.1007/978-3-030-32239-7_67

16. Nazeri, K., Aminpour, A., Ebrahimi, M.: Two-stage convolutional neural network for breast cancer histology image classification. In: Campilho, A., Karray, F., ter Haar Romeny, B. (eds.) ICIAR 2018. LNCS, vol. 10882, pp. 717–726. Springer, Cham (2018). https://doi.org/10.1007/978-3-319-93000-8_81

17. Otsu, N.: A threshold selection method from gray-level histograms. IEEE Trans. Syst. Man Cybern. **9**(1), 62–66 (1979)

18. Tellez, D., Litjens, G., van der Laak, J., Ciompi, F.: Neural image compression for gigapixel histopathology image analysis. IEEE Trans. Pattern Anal. Mach. Intell. (2019)

19. Wang, X.: Weakly supervised deep learning for whole slide lung cancer image analysis. IEEE Trans. Cybern. **50**, 3950–3962 (2019)

20. Wang, X., Yan, Y., Tang, P., Bai, X., Liu, W.: Revisiting multiple instance neural networks. Pattern Recogn. **74**, 15–24 (2018)

21. Wen, Y., Zhang, K., Li, Z., Qiao, Y.: A discriminative feature learning approach for deep face recognition. In: Leibe, B., Matas, J., Sebe, N., Welling, M. (eds.) ECCV 2016. LNCS, vol. 9911, pp. 499–515. Springer, Cham (2016). https://doi.org/10.1007/978-3-319-46478-7_31

22. Xie, J., Girshick, R., Farhadi, A.: Unsupervised deep embedding for clustering analysis. In: International Conference on Machine Learning, pp. 478–487 (2016)

23. Xu, G., et al.: CAMEL: a weakly supervised learning framework for histopathology image segmentation. In: Proceedings of the IEEE International Conference on Computer Vision, pp. 10682–10691 (2019)

24. Yao, J., Zhu, X., Huang, J.: Deep multi-instance learning for survival prediction from whole slide images. In: Shen, D., et al. (eds.) MICCAI 2019. LNCS, vol. 11764, pp. 496–504. Springer, Cham (2019). https://doi.org/10.1007/978-3-030-32239-7_55

25. Zhu, X., Yao, J., Zhu, F., Huang, J.: WSISA: making survival prediction from whole slide histopathological images. In: Proceedings of the IEEE Conference on Computer Vision and Pattern Recognition, pp. 7234–7242 (2017)

Graph Attention Multi-instance Learning for Accurate Colorectal Cancer Staging

Ashwin Raju[1], Jiawen Yao[1], Mohammad MinHazul Haq[1],
Jitendra Jonnagaddala[2], and Junzhou Huang[1(✉)]

[1] Department of Computer Science and Engineering,
The University of Texas at Arlington, 76019 Arlington, TX, USA
jzhuang@uta.edu

[2] School of Public Health and Community Medicine, University of New South Wales,
Sydney, Australia

Abstract. Colorectal Cancer (CRC) is one of the most common cancer diagnosed in humans. Outcomes vary significantly among patients with different tumor status. Accurate staging of colorectal cancer for personalized treatment is thus highly desired. Whole slide pathological images (WSIs) serves as the gold standard for Tumour Node Metastasis (TNM) staging. However, TNM staging for colorectal cancer relies on labor-intensive manual discriminative patch labeling, which is not suitable and scalable for large-scale WSIs TNM staging. Though various methods have been proposed to select key image patches to perform staging, they are unable to consider the structure of tissue types in biopsy samples which is a key evidence for determining tumor status. In this paper, we propose a Graph Attention Multi-instance Learning (Graph Attention MIL) with texture features, which encodes a spatial structure between patches and jointly predicts the TNM staging. We evaluated our proposed method on a large cohort of colorectal cancer dataset. The proposed framework improves the performance over the existing state-of-the-art methods indicating the future research towards graph based learning for TNM staging.

Keywords: Colorectal cancer · Graph Attention Multi-instance learning · TNM staging

1 Introduction

Colorectral Cancer (CRC), a cancer that affects colon or rectum, is one of the most common cancer diagnosed in both women and men. The survival rate for patients with Stage I to Stage IV cancer drops from 90% to 10% and therefore early prognosis and diagnosis of CRC is critical [1]. Histopathologic diagnosis

Electronic supplementary material The online version of this chapter (https://doi.org/10.1007/978-3-030-59722-1_51) contains supplementary material, which is available to authorized users.

of CRC involves visual inspection of WSIs to analyse the anatomical extent of tumor cancers. However, with the increase in colorectal cancer cases and the limitation of expert pathologists, the diagnostic burden for pathologists have increased over the years. In the recent years, computational methods have been developed to aid the pathologists to diagnose CRC and Lung cancer with limited supervision [3,7,20,23,25]. However, the pathologist needs to label each tissue partition [7] or manually annotate Region Of Interests (ROIs) [11] from each tissue partition. These approaches require the presence of expert pathologist to annotate each WSIs.

Weakly-supervised learning provides an important and possible solution for solving less dense annotations in medical imaging [2,15,21,29]. To explore the WSIs with only the access of image-level labels, several frameworks have been proposed [10,13,14,24,29]. Tellez et al. [14] proposed a two step pipeline, where an encoder is used to compress the WSIs into a low resolution spatial representation in the first step and in the second step, a CNN is trained on these representations to predict different staging at image level. Their proposed two step pipeline is time consuming as the second step has to slide through the pathological image (WSI) to create the lower resolution spatial representation. Li et al. [10] proposed a Patch Transformer to predict multiple tags for WSIs. The patch Transformer extracts patch characteristics considering global context of the WSIs. The learned patch characteristics can be used to predict the different staging of CRC. Yao et al. [24] proposed deep multi-instance learning method where each instance is considered as a pool of clustered features from each tissue type and the instances together represent the WSI. The bag of instances are then used to predict the outcome of the WSI. Even though both approaches [10,24] have practical merits to consider the important patches for predicting the staging, they do not consider the spatial relationship between patches, which is very crucial for identifying tumor stage in CRC. Figure 1 shows different staging of cancer based on tumor position. The tumor stage increases as the tumor grows from submucosa to all the way through subserosa. The staging of CRC based on Tumor in TNM [17] relies on the size and the relative position of tumor with respect to other tissue partitions.

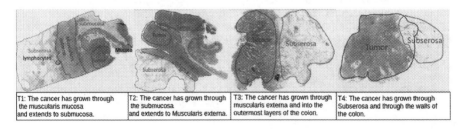

Fig. 1. Gigapixel Whole Slide Histopatholigcal Images of different TNM staging (best viewed in color). (Color figure online)

In this paper, we address the problem by considering the spatial relationship of tumor with other tissue partitions by introducing a novel Graph Attention Multi-instance learning network where multiple graphs, with each graph having nodes representing different tissues acts as an instance. The multiple instances for a WSI form a bag which aids to predict the tumor stage. We represent the node in the graph as the texture feature of an image patch. Different from the previous state-of-the-art methods, our proposed framework considers the spatial relationship between different texture features. To summarize our motivations, we introduce a texture feature extraction method to encode texture for an image patch and cluster similar texture features together. We then introduce a novel Graph Attention Multi-instance learning network to predict the tumor stage by considering a bag of multiple graphs with spatial relationship between tissues invoked in each graph. Extensive experiments verify the effectiveness of our proposed framework on a large cohort of CRC.

2   Methodology

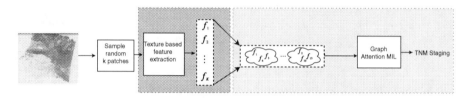

Fig. 2. Overview of our pipeline. Given a WSI, we randomly sample k patches and extract texture features for each patch. The texture features are grouped into multiple graphs and each graph has features from all clusters. Here the cloud represents a graph. The Graph Attention Multi-instance learning is used to predict the tumor stage. (Best viewed in color). (Color figure online)

We denote the WSI dataset $\mathcal{D}_\ell = \{X_i, Y_i\}$, with X_i denoting the WSI and $Y_i \in \{0, 1, 2, 3\}$ indicating different tumor stages. Given the rich information of a WSI, generally in range $(10^6 \times 10^6)$, we first extract random M tissue patches at 20X (0.5 microns per pixel) objective magnification with image size fixed to $224 \times 224 \times 3$. We then create a set of bags $B = \{B_1, B_2, ..., B_n\}$, where B_n contains randomly sampled M tissue patches for X_n. The training objective is to correctly classify the tumor stage with the given B_n from X_n. The overview of our proposed two step pipeline is outlined in Fig. 2. The first step is a texture extractor, which projects input raw image patches into a low-dimensional space. Motivated from [26,27], we propose a texture based clustering auto encoder to cluster similar features into same cluster. Different from [24], where a pre-trained VGG model from ImageNet is used to extract the features, we propose a texture auto encoder to extract the textures from each patch as proposed by [27] and force the textures to be invariant to different augmentation of the same patch. The reason for using texture based encoding is because texture features encode domain specific information from the image patch. In step 2, the extracted texture features for B_i is used for our Graph Attention Multi-instance learning network to classify image level label for a WSI X_i. We explain each step in more details in the further sections.

Texture Feature Extraction. The goal here is to learn a feature representation for a given image patch. We focus on texture based feature representation which encodes orderless visual patterns of an image. Furthermore, we want the texture features for similar image patches to be close to each other and for dissimilar image patches far away from each other. To achieve this we use two main components, 1) Texture encoding network. 2) Cluster embedding network. Texture encoding network [27], uses a novel *learnable residual encoding layer*, which learns an inherent dictionary and domain specific information for a given image patch. The cluster embedding network, clusters similar textures by using a Siamese network to train a binary classification task, where similar textures are assigned the same class and dissimilar patches are assigned a different class. The Siamese network shown in Fig. 3 under Step I depicts how texture features are clustered and when trained till convergence the texture features are clustered like the Embedding space shown in Fig. 3 under step I. We denote the image $P_i \in \mathbb{R}^{H \times W \times 3}$ as a randomly sampled patch from the WSI and use ResNet50 [4] as an encoder to extract feature map $E_i \in \mathbb{R}^{\frac{H}{R} \times \frac{W}{R} \times C}$, where R indicates the downsampling factor and C is the number of features. We remap the feature map E_i back to the image resolution using the decoder proposed by [12]. We follow the deep texture encoder network [27] to encode the visual descriptors

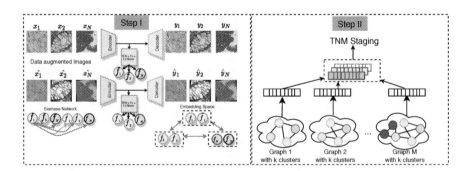

Fig. 3. Step I of our architecture performs clustering of texture features. The siamese network in step I brings the patch P_i and data augmented patch $\mathcal{T}(P_i)$ to be same and the patch P_i and patch P_j to be different in the embedding space. Step II of our architecture contains many small graphs, where each graph contains random subset of patches from all C clusters. The feature pooled from each graph are represented as instance from the graph to perform attention multi-instance learning to predict the tumor Stage.

$E_i = \{e_1, .., e_N\}$, where N is the number of spatial locations in the feature map, to a fixed length representation $F = \{f_1, .., f_K\}$, where K indicates the number of texture features.

The textures of same image under different data augmentation should be close to each other and should be spread-out for different images. Inspired from [26], we apply data augmentation $\mathcal{T}(.)$ to slightly modify the image patch. For an instance i, where the original image P_i and data augmented image $\mathcal{T}(P_i)$, denoted by $\hat{P}_i$ with their corresponding $\mathcal{L}_2$ normalized texture features f_i and $\hat{f}_i$ should be classified into instance i, and for other instances, $j \neq i$ shouldn't be classified into instance i. We train a Siamese network as proposed by [26] to achieve this objective.

Following the texture feature extraction, we assign cluster labels for each texture feature. Assigning the labels to each texture feature for a WSI aids to stratify the random patches so that each graph in our Graph Attention Multi-instance learning network can have different distribution of tissue types. In order to assign a label for similar image patches, we take use of tissue wise annotated CRC dataset [3] which we call as reference dataset and randomly sample 100 patches from each tissue from their training dataset. The reference dataset is used only to assign a label for image patches. For a given l_2 normalized texture feature f_i and $F \in \mathbb{R}^{M \times D}$, where M denotes all the l_2 normalized texture features from reference dataset [3] and D indicates the dimension of feature, we assign the cluster label by applying weighted kNN proposed by [18] with k set to 1. Figure 4 shows the result of our texture features that has been assigned to different cluster labels. Our clustering approach based on texture features is dataset invariant and can be visually seen in Fig. 4.

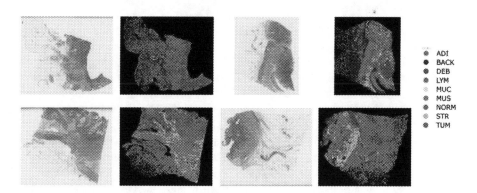

Fig. 4. Clustering overview. Each pixel in the colormap represents a texture feature and representing different tissue types provided by [3].

To optimize step I, we use mean squared error to minimize the distance between predicted pixel and ground truth pixel. To optimize texture feature embedding in step I, we use the loss function mentioned by [26]. The overall loss function is defined as:

$$L_{step1} = L_{mse} + \lambda_1 L_{texture} \tag{1}$$

where L_{mse} is applied for each image in the batch, $L_{texture}$ as defined by [26] is applied for texture features in the batch.

Graph Attention Multi-Instance Learning. Once the patches have been clustered into different tissue types as shown in Fig. 4, the next step is to use the texture features F from the patches randomly sampled from the WSI to predict the tumor stage. The goal is to learn the relationship between the features from each WSI jointly to predict the tumor stage. Graph Convolutional Network (GCN) provides a good direction to consider information exchange between nodes and the spatial structure of medical imaging data [9,22,28]. In our work, we incorporate spatial information of different tissue features in the form of graph learning. We decompose each WSI into multiple graphs and each graph has features from all the cluster labels with approximately equal number of patches from each cluster. The multiple graphs are treated as multiple instances in a bag and the bag for each WSI is used to predict the tumor stage using attention attention multi-instance learning (MIL) as depicted in Fig. 3 (step II). We use Adaptive GraphSage proposed by [28] to create a graph of nodes where nodes present texture features extracted from the image patches. The reason for using Adaptive GraphSage over other graph networks is because the ability to learn the embedding feature between nodes more effectively as mentioned in [28].

To construct the adjacency matrix for our graph we follow [28]. Formally, the adjacency matrix can be written as:

$$A_{ij} = \begin{cases} 1 & \text{if } j \in KNN(i) \text{ and } D(i,j) < d \\ 0 & \text{Otherwise} \end{cases} \tag{2}$$

where $D(.)$ is the euclidean distance, d is the manually selected threshold, KNN is the K nearest neighbour to the patch i. Based on the empirical analysis, here we set the threshold for d as 0.4. We follow the architecture proposed by [28], where the nodes are represented as texture features and the adjacency matrix defined from Eq. (2) to create multiple graphs with shared weights. We use k graphs, where k is set 7 based on the experiments and each graph contains randomly sampled features from C clusters from a WSI. Here we set C as 9 based on the reference dataset [3].

To extract texture feature from a graph $\mathcal{G}_i$, we use the concatenation of max operation and mean operation on the node embeddings [8]. The feature pooling (FP) operation can be defined as:

$$FP = \frac{1}{N} \sum_{i=1}^{N} x_i \| \max_{i=1}^{N} x_i \tag{3}$$

where N is the number of nodes and x_i is the output embedding feature for each node in the graph network. From multiple graphs, we extract features

$\{FP_1, FP_2, ..., FP_k\}$, where FP_k represents feature from the graph $\mathcal{G}_k$. We consider the set of features as an instances in a bag and train an attention MIL [5] to predict the tumor stage. The learnable attention weights in the MIL gives more importance to instances in the bag which are responsible for predicting the tumor stage. The output from the attention MIL yields a feature vector which is connected to a linear classifier to predict the tumor stages. To optimize Graph Attention Multi-instance learning, we minimize the loss function as follows:

$$L_{step2} = \frac{1}{M} \sum_{i=1}^{M} H\left(p_i, q_i\right) \tag{4}$$

where M is the number of WSIs and $H(.)$ is the weighted cross entropy loss between ground truth p_i and prediction q_i.

3 Experiments

Dataset Description and Baselines. The data we used, Molecular and Cellular Oncology (MCO) study [6,16], is a collection of imaging, specimen, clinical and genetic data from over 1,500 Australian individuals who underwent curative resection for colorectal cancer from 1994 to 2010. To evaluate our models, we split the total dataset containing $1,345$ WSIs with 115, 202, 698 and 330 stage I to stage IV cancer WSIs into 70%, 10%, 20% for training, validation and testing, respectively. Each WSI has been annotated with a image level label representing the tumor stage by the expert pathologist. We extracted 1000 random patches at 20X magnification from each WSI, covering approximately 82% of tissue area. In total, $1,345,000$ patches (more than 1 million) patches were extracted from the dataset. We build several baselines for comparisons. To evaluate results from directly using down-sampled WSIs, we treat the WSI as a reduced image resolution with size (2048×2048) and then train a image classification model. We also compare with other state-of-the-art models for WSIs classification and survival prediction task and accordingly modify them for colorectal cancer staging. The comparison method includes Tellez et al. [14], Gupta et al. [3] and Yao et al. [24]. We also perform ablation study on our proposed architecture in step II with graph CNN proposed by [28].

Results and Discussions. For training step I, we used Adam optimizer with learning rate set to 0.003 and reduced the learning rate for every 20 epochs. We used random horizontal and vertical flipping, random crop, random rotation and Gaussian noise as transformation operation $\mathcal{T}(.)$ in step I. For training step II, we used Adam optimizer with learning rate set to 0.0003.

Table 1 shows the performance of our proposed method with other comparison methods. The baseline method trained on reduced resolution with (2048×2048) achieves the 53.6% which demonstrates down-sampled WSIs is not useful for staging. The reason is due to the reduced resolution loses much

Table 1. Performance comparison of the proposed method and other existing related methods using mean accuracy and mean F1 scores are tabulated.

Model	Accuracy	F1
Baseline	53.6	50.9
Tellez et al. [14]	63.2	62.8
Yao et al. [24]	66.8	65.2
Gupta et al. [3]	71.5	60.8
Yao et al. [24] with our step I	74.5	72.5
Cell graph [28] with 200 patches	69.7	67.2
Cell graph [28] with 1000 patches	79.8	77.4
Proposed	**81.1**	**79.8**

information and many details from the original WSI. Tellez et al. with contrastive network, uses a time consuming encoding step to predict the image level label whereas our proposed method extracts random patches from the WSI to predict the image level label. Gupta et al. [3] uses a labelled patch level label to train a patch level classifier and uses a network similar to step II proposed by Tellez et al. to predict image level label. The step II of Gupta et al. is as time consuming as Tellez et al. Yao et al. [24] used kmeans clustering on 1D features extracted from pre-trained VGG model whereas our proposed step I trains to bring similar patches closer and dissimilar patches far from each other.

From the Table 1, we can see the model [24] with using k-means to cluster features performs 0.668 on our test dataset whereas when replaced k-means with our clustering method the performs increases by 9%. The reason for the improvement in the performance is using texture based feature extraction and Siamese network to make similar features close to each other and dissimilar features far from each other. However, both the models does not perform better than our proposed method, the reason is DeepMIL [24] does not consider relationship between node features to predict the image level label. To predict tumor stage, the spatial relationship between features is important. We also compared with step II architecture with a single graph proposed by [28], to show that our proposed multi graph Attention MIL can perform better than a single Graph network. The single graph with 1000 patches from the features extracted from the step I of our pipeline achieves 0.7987 but is computationally slower as the time complexity for graph CNN is $O(n^3)$ [19], where n is the number of nodes in the graph. We also compared with 200 patches using a single graph, however it yields a lower accuracy than the single graph with 1000 patches. We have showed the confusion matrix of our proposed method and the cell graph with 1000 patches in the supplementary material.

Our proposed method uses multiple graphs with each graph having randomly sampled features from the 1000 patches for each WSI. Each graph also has features from every tissue types represented by [3]. The time complexity of each graph is less than a single graph and multiple graphs are considered to be instances in a bag to predict the tumor stage. For fair comparison, we use the same Adaptive GraphSage architecture as [28]. From the table 1, our proposed method achieves best performance when compared to other compared methods.

4   Conclusion

We proposed a novel Graph Attention Multi-instance learning framework to learn the spatial relationship between image patches. Here we also demonstrate that the Graph network using textures result in a better performance when evaluated with other previous state-of-the-art methods. Future research will focus on how our proposed method can also be used on different task such as predicting Overall survival rate of an patient.

Acknowledgments. This work was partially supported by US National Science Foundation IIS-1718853, the CAREER grant IIS-1553687 and Cancer Prevention and Research Institute of Texas (CPRIT) award (RP190107).

References

1. https://www.cancer.net/cancer-types/colorectal-cancer/statistics (2019)
2. Chen, H., et al.: Anatomy-aware Siamese network: exploiting semantic asymmetry for accurate pelvic fracture detection in x-ray images (2020)
3. Gupta, P., et al.: Prediction of colon cancer stages and survival period with machine learning approach. Cancers $11(12)$, 2007 (2019)
4. He, K., Zhang, X., Ren, S., Sun, J.: Deep residual learning for image recognition. In: Proceedings of the IEEE Conference on Computer Vision and Pattern Recognition, pp. 770–778 (2016)
5. Ilse, M., Tomczak, J.M., Welling, M.: Attention-based deep multiple instance learning. arXiv preprint arXiv:1802.04712 (2018)
6. Jonnagaddala, J., et al.: Integration and analysis of heterogeneous colorectal cancer data for translational research, p. 387 (2016)
7. Kather, J.N., et al.: Predicting survival from colorectal cancer histology slides using deep learning: a retrospective multicenter study. PLoS Med. $16(1)$, e1002730 (2019)
8. Lee, J., Lee, I., Kang, J.: Self-attention graph pooling. arXiv preprint arXiv:1904.08082 (2019)
9. Li, R., Yao, J., Zhu, X., Li, Y., Huang, J.: Graph CNN for survival analysis on whole slide pathological images. In: Frangi, A.F., Schnabel, J.A., Davatzikos, C., Alberola-López, C., Fichtinger, G. (eds.) MICCAI 2018. LNCS, vol. 11071, pp. 174–182. Springer, Cham (2018). https://doi.org/10.1007/978-3-030-00934-2_20
10. Li, W., Nguyen, V.D., Liao, H., Wilder, M., Cheng, K., Luo, J.: Patch transformer for multi-tagging whole slide histopathology images. In: Shen, D., Liu, T., Peters, T.M., Staib, L.H., Essert, C., Zhou, S., Yap, P.T., Khan, A. (eds.) Medical Image Computing and Computer Assisted Intervention - MICCAI 2019. LNCS, vol. 11764, pp. 532–540. Springer, Cham (2019)

11. Morkūnas, M., Treigys, P., Bernatavičienė, J., Laurinavičius, A., Korvel, G.: Machine learning based classification of colorectal cancer tumour tissue in whole-slide images. Informatica **29**(1), 75–90 (2018)
12. Muhammad, H., et al.: Unsupervised subtyping of cholangiocarcinoma using a deep clustering convolutional autoencoder. In: Shen, D., et al. (eds.) MICCAI 2019. LNCS, vol. 11764, pp. 604–612. Springer, Cham (2019). https://doi.org/10.1007/978-3-030-32239-7_67
13. Shapcott, C.M., Rajpoot, N., Hewitt, K.: Deep learning with sampling for colon cancer histology images. Front. Bioeng. Biotechnol. **7**, 52 (2019)
14. Tellez, D., van der Laak, J., Ciompi, F.: Gigapixel whole-slide image classification using unsupervised image compression and contrastive training (2018)
15. Wang, Y., et al.: Weakly Supervised Universal Fracture Detection in Pelvic X-Rays. In: Shen, D., et al. (eds.) MICCAI 2019. LNCS, vol. 11769, pp. 459–467. Springer, Cham (2019). https://doi.org/10.1007/978-3-030-32226-7_51
16. Ward, R.L., Hawkins, N.J.: Molecular and cellular oncology (MCO) study tumour collection. UNSW Aust. (2015). https://doi.org/10.4225/53/5559205bea135
17. Wu, J.S.: Rectal cancer staging. Clin. Colon Rectal Surg. **20**(03), 148–157 (2007)
18. Wu, Z., Xiong, Y., Yu, S.X., Lin, D.: Unsupervised feature learning via non-parametric instance discrimination. In: Proceedings of the IEEE Conference on Computer Vision and Pattern Recognition, pp. 3733–3742 (2018)
19. Wu, Z., Pan, S., Chen, F., Long, G., Zhang, C., Yu, P.S.: A comprehensive survey on graph neural networks. arXiv preprint arXiv:1901.00596 (2019)
20. Xu, J., et al.: Multi-tissue partitioning for whole slide images of colorectal cancer histopathology images with deeptissue net. In: Reyes-Aldasoro, C.C., Janowczyk, A., Veta, M., Bankhead, P., Sirinukunwattana, K. (eds.) ECDP 2019. LNCS, vol. 11435, pp. 100–108. Springer, Cham (2019). https://doi.org/10.1007/978-3-030-23937-4_12
21. Yan, C., Yao, J., Li, R., Xu, Z., Huang, J.: Weakly supervised deep learning for thoracic disease classification and localization on chest x-rays. In: Proceedings of the 2018 ACM International Conference on Bioinformatics, Computational Biology, and Health Informatics, pp. 103–110 (2018)
22. Yao, J., Cai, J., Yang, D., Xu, D., Huang, J.: Integrating 3D geometry of organ for improving medical image segmentation. In: Shen, D., et al. (eds.) MICCAI 2019. LNCS, vol. 11768, pp. 318–326. Springer, Cham (2019). https://doi.org/10.1007/978-3-030-32254-0_36
23. Yao, J., Wang, S., Zhu, X., Huang, J.: Imaging biomarker discovery for lung cancer survival prediction. In: Ourselin, S., Joskowicz, L., Sabuncu, M.R., Unal, G., Wells, W. (eds.) MICCAI 2016. LNCS, vol. 9901, pp. 649–657. Springer, Cham (2016). https://doi.org/10.1007/978-3-319-46723-8_75
24. Yao, J., Zhu, X., Huang, J.: Deep multi-instance learning for survival prediction from whole slide images. In: Shen, D., et al. (eds.) MICCAI 2019. LNCS, vol. 11764, pp. 496–504. Springer, Cham (2019). https://doi.org/10.1007/978-3-030-32239-7_55
25. Yao, Jiawen., Zhu, Xinliang., Zhu, Feiyun, Huang, Junzhou: Deep correlational learning for survival prediction from multi-modality data. In: Descoteaux, M., et al. (eds.) MICCAI 2017. LNCS, vol. 10434, pp. 406–414. Springer, Cham (2017). https://doi.org/10.1007/978-3-319-66185-8_46
26. Ye, M., Zhang, X., Yuen, P.C., Chang, S.F.: Unsupervised embedding learning via invariant and spreading instance feature. In: Proceedings of the IEEE Conference on Computer Vision and Pattern Recognition, pp. 6210–6219 (2019)

27. Zhang, H., Xue, J., Dana, K.: Deep TEN: texture encoding network. In: Proceedings of the IEEE Conference on Computer Vision and Pattern Recognition, pp. 708–717 (2017)
28. Zhou, Y., Graham, S., Koohbanani, N.A., Shaban, M., Heng, P.A., Rajpoot,N.: CGC-net: cell graph convolutional network for grading of colorectal cancer histology images. In: Proceedings of the IEEE International Conference on Computer Vision Workshops (2019)
29. Zhu, X., Yao, J., Zhu, F., Huang, J.: WSISA: making survival prediction from whole slide Histopathological images. In: CVPR., pp. 7234–7242 (2017)

Deep Interactive Learning: An Efficient Labeling Approach for Deep Learning-Based Osteosarcoma Treatment Response Assessment

David Joon Ho[1]($\boxtimes$), Narasimhan P. Agaram[1], Peter J. Schüffler[1],
Chad M. Vanderbilt[1], Marc-Henri Jean[1], Meera R. Hameed[1],
and Thomas J. Fuchs[1,2]

[1] Department of Pathology, Memorial Sloan Kettering Cancer Center,
New York, NY 10065, USA
hod@mskcc.org

[2] Weill Cornell Graduate School for Medical Sciences, New York, NY 10065, USA

Abstract. Osteosarcoma is the most common malignant primary bone tumor. Standard treatment includes pre-operative chemotherapy followed by surgical resection. The response to treatment as measured by ratio of necrotic tumor area to overall tumor area is a known prognostic factor for overall survival. This assessment is currently done manually by pathologists by looking at glass slides under the microscope which may not be reproducible due to its subjective nature. Convolutional neural networks (CNNs) can be used for automated segmentation of viable and necrotic tumor on osteosarcoma whole slide images. One bottleneck for supervised learning is that large amounts of accurate annotations are required for training which is a time-consuming and expensive process. In this paper, we describe Deep Interactive Learning (DIaL) as an efficient labeling approach for training CNNs. After an initial labeling step is done, annotators only need to correct mislabeled regions from previous segmentation predictions to improve the CNN model until the satisfactory predictions are achieved. Our experiments show that our CNN model trained by only 7 h of annotation using DIaL can successfully estimate ratios of necrosis within expected inter-observer variation rate for non-standardized manual surgical pathology task.

Keywords: Computational pathology · Interactive learning · Osteosarcoma

1 Introduction

Osteosarcoma is the most common bone cancer occurring in adolescents with a second smaller peak in older adults [16]. Pre-operative chemotherapy followed by

---

D.J. Ho and N.P. Agaram—The first two authors contributed equally.

M.R. Hameed and T.J. Fuchs—The last two authors contributed equally.

© Springer Nature Switzerland AG 2020
A. L. Martel et al. (Eds.): MICCAI 2020, LNCS 12265, pp. 540–549, 2020.
https://doi.org/10.1007/978-3-030-59722-1_52

surgery is a standard treatment for osteosarcoma. The ratio of necrotic tumor to overall tumor post neoadjuvant chemotherapy is a well-known prognostic factor and correlates with patients' survival [13,19]. Thus, for patients with localized disease who have undergone complete resection, if the ratio of tumor necrosis is greater than 90%, the 5-year survival is higher than 80%. Currently, the ratio of tumor necrosis is manually estimated by pathologists by microscopic review of multiple glass slides from respected specimens.

Computational pathology has provided automated and reproducible techniques to analyze digitized histopathology images [10], especially with convolutional neural networks (CNNs) [22]. Arunachalam showed a patch-level classification CNN composed of three convolutional layers and two fully-connected layers could be used to identify viable tumor, necrotic tumor, and non-tumor in osteosarcoma [1]. For more accurate analysis, fully convolutional networks were developed for a pixel-wise classification, also known as semantic segmentation [15]. U-Net segmenting subcellular structures in microscopy images was described in [18]. More recently, Deep Multi-Magnification Network (DMMN) was introduced for multi-class tissue segmentation of histopathology images by looking at patches in multiple magnifications and has shown outstanding segmentation performance in breast cancer [12].

Performance of these supervised machine learning methods highly depends on the amount and quality of annotations. Public datasets with annotations are generally available for common cancer types such as breast [2,7] and have been widely used for training CNNs [14,24]. For rare cancers such as osteosarcoma, fresh manual annotations by pathologists with specialized expertise are required. Such annotations require a lot of time from busy professionals and thus optimizing for reduced burden is paramount. To reduce annotation time, interactive learning has been developed. Interactive learning allows annotators to "interact" with a machine learning model by correcting predictions of the model to improve its performance until the predictions are satisfied [8,20]. An interactive segmentation toolkit for biomedical images, known as ilastik, was introduced in [4,21]. Here, random forest classifiers [6] were used for segmentation. QuPath [3] was developed to interactively analyze giga-pixel whole slide images where segmentation was also done based on random forest classifiers [6].

In this paper, we propose Deep Interactive Learning (DIaL) by integrating the concept of interactive learning into deep learning framework for multi-class tissue segmentation of histopathology images and treatment response assessment for osteosarcoma. To evaluate our segmentation model, we estimate the necrosis ratio in case-level by counting the number of pixels predicted as viable tumor and necrotic tumor by the segmentation model and compare with the ratio from pathology reports. We observe our CNN model can estimate the necrosis ratio within expected inter-observer variation rate for non-standardized manual surgical pathology task. Note that the total labeling time took approximately 7 h with DIaL.

2   Proposed Method

It is necessary to manually label osteosarcoma whole slide images (WSIs) to supervise a segmentation convolutional neural network (CNN) for automated treatment response assessment. Labeling WSIs exhaustively would be ideal but it needs tremendous labeling time. Partial labeling approaches are introduced to reduce labeling time [5,12], but challenging or rare morphological features can be missed. We propose Deep Interactive Learning (DIaL) to efficiently annotate both characteristic features and challenging features on WSIs to have outstanding segmentation performance. Our block diagram is shown in Fig. 1. First of all, initial annotation is partially done mainly on characteristic features of classes. During DIaL, training a CNN, segmentation prediction, and correction on mislabeled regions are repeated to improve segmentation performance until segmentation predictions on training images are satisfied by the annotators. Note that challenging or rare features would be labeled during the correction step. When training the CNN is finalized, the CNN is used to segment viable tumor and necrotic tumor on testing cases to assess treatment responses.

2.1   Initial Annotation

Initial annotation on characteristic features of each class is done to train an initial CNN model. In this work, annotators label 7 morphologically distinct classes, shown in Fig. 2: viable tumor, necrosis with bone, necrosis without bone, normal bone, normal tissue, cartilage, and blank. Note initial annotation is partially done on training images.

2.2   Deep Interactive Learning

During initial annotation, challenging or rare features may not be included in the training set which can lead to mislabeled predictions. These challenging features can be added into the training set through Deep Interactive Learning (DIaL) by repeating training/finetuning, segmentation, and correction. These three steps are repeated until annotators are satisfied with segmentation predictions on training images.

Initial Training. We need an initially trained model to annotate mislabeled regions with challenging features. WSIs are too large to be processed at once. Thus, the labeled regions are extracted into 256×256 pixels patches only when more than 1% of pixels in the patch are annotated. To balance the number of pixels between classes, patches containing rare classes are deformed to produce additional patches by elastic deformation [9,18]. Here, we define a class is rare if the number of pixels in the class is less than 70% of the maximum number of pixels among classes. After patch extraction and deformation are done, some cases are separated for validating the CNN model where approximately 20%

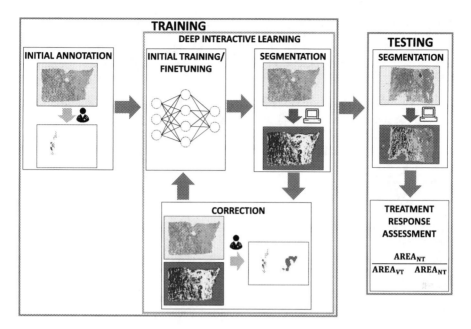

Fig. 1. Block diagram of the proposed method. First of all, initial annotation is done on training whole slide images (WSIs) where characteristic features of each class are partially annotated. The annotated regions are used to train a Deep Multi-Magnification Network [12]. Segmentation is done on the same training WSIs to correct any mislabeled regions containing challenging or rare features. These corrected regions are added to the training set to finetune the model. This training-segmentation-correction iteration, denoted as Deep Interactive Learning (DIaL), is repeated until segmentation predictions are satisfied by annotators. The final model is used to segment testing WSIs to assess treatment responses.

of pixels in each class are separated. We use a Deep Multi-Magnification Network (DMMN) [12] for multi-class tissue segmentation where the model looks at patches in multiple magnifications for accurate predictions. Specifically, the DMMN is composed of three half-channeled U-Nets, U-Net-20×, U-Net-10×, and U-Net-5×, where input patches of these U-Nets are in 20×, 10×, and 5× magnifications, respectively, with size of 256×256 pixels centered at the same location. Intermediate feature maps in decoders of U-Net-10× and U-Net-5× are center-cropped and concatenated to a decoder of U-Net-20× to enrich feature maps. The final prediction patch of the DMMN is generated in size of 256×256 pixels in 20× magnification. To train our model initialized by [11], we use weighted cross entropy as our loss function where a weight for class c, w_c, is defined as $w_c = 1 - \frac{p_c}{\sum_{c=1}^{C} p_c}$, where $C = 7$ is the total number of classes and p_c is the number of pixels in class c. Note that unlabeled regions do not contribute to the training process. During training, random rotation, vertical and horizontal flip, and color jittering are used as data augmentation. Stochastic gradient descent

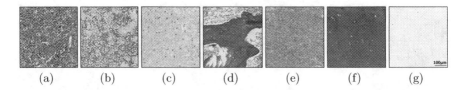

(a)	(b)	(c)	(d)	(e)	(f)	(g)

Fig. 2. A convolutional neural network we designed in this paper can predict 7 classes: (a) viable tumor, (b) necrosis with bone, (c) necrosis without bone, (d) normal bone, (e) normal tissue, (f) cartilage, and (g) blank. Our goal is to accurately segment viable tumor and necrotic tumor on osteosarcoma whole slide images for automated treatment response assessment.

(SGD) optimizer with a learning rate of 5×10^{-5}, a momentum of 0.99, and a weight decay of 10^{-4} is used for 30 epochs. In each epoch, a model is validated by mean Intersection-Over-Union (mIOU) and the model with the highest mIOU is selected as an output model.

Segmentation. After training a model is done, all training WSIs are processed to evaluate unlabeled regions. A set of patches with size of 256×256 pixels in $20\times$, $10\times$, and $5\times$ magnifications centered at the same location is processed using the DMMN. Note that zero-padding is done on the boundary of WSIs. Patch-wise segmentation is repeated in x and y-directions with a stride of 256 pixels until the entire WSI is processed.

Correction. Characteristic features are annotated during initial annotation, but challenging or rare features may not be included. During the correction step, these challenging features that the model could not predict correctly are annotated to be included in the training set to improve the model. In this step, the annotators look at segmentation predictions and correct any mislabeled regions. If the predictions are satisfied throughout training images, the model is finalized.

Finetuning. Assuming the previous CNN model has already learned most features of classes, we finetune the previous model to improve segmentation performance. Corrected regions are extracted into patches and included in the training set to improve the CNN model. Additional patches are generated by deforming the extracted patches to give a higher weight on challenging or rare features to emphasize these features to be learned during finetuning. SGD optimizer and weighted cross entropy with the updated weights are used during training, and we reduced a learning rate to be 5×10^{-6} and the number of epochs to be 10 not to perturb parameters of the CNN model too much from the previous model. Note validation cases can be selected again to utilize the majority of corrected cases for the optimization.

2.3 Treatment Response Assessment

The final CNN model segments viable tumor and necrotic tumor on testing WSIs. Note necrotic tumor is a combination of necrosis with bone and necrosis without bone. The ratio of necrotic tumor to overall tumor in case-level estimated by a deep learning model, R^{DL}, is defined as

$$R^{DL} = \frac{p_{NT}}{p_{VT} + p_{NT}} \tag{1}$$

where p_{VT} and p_{NT} are the number of pixels of viable tumor and necrotic tumor in a case, respectively.

3 Experimental Results

Our hematoxylin and eosin (H&E) stained osteosarcoma dataset is digitized in $20\times$ magnification by two Aperio AT2 scanners at Memorial Sloan Kettering Cancer Center where microns per pixel (MPP) for one scanner is 0.5025 and MPP for the other scanner is 0.5031. The osteosarcoma dataset contains 55 cases with 1578 whole slide images (WSIs) where the number of WSIs per case ranges between 1 to 109 with mean of 28.7 and median of 22, and the average width and height of the WSIs are 61022 pixels and 41518 pixels, respectively. We used 13 cases for training and the other 42 cases for testing. Note 8 testing cases do not contain the necrosis ratio on their pathology reports, so they were excluded for evaluation. Two annotators (N.P.A. and M.R.H.) selected 49 WSIs from 13 training cases and independently annotated them without case-level overlaps. The pixel-wise annotation was performed on an in-house WSI viewer, allowing measuring the time taken for annotation. The annotators labeled three iterations using Deep Interactive Learning (DIaL): initial annotation, first correction, and second correction. They annotated 49 WSIs in 4 h, 37 WSIs in 3 h, and 13 WSIs in 1 h during the initial annotation, the first correction, and the second correction, respectively. The annotators also exhaustively labeled the entire WSI which took approximately 1.5 h. An example of exhaustive annotation and annotation with DIaL is shown in Fig. 3. With the same given time, the annotators would be able to exhaustively annotate only 5 WSIs without DIaL. The annotators can annotate more diverse cases with DIaL. The number of pixels annotated and deformed are shown in Fig. 4(a). The implementation was done using PyTorch [17] and an Nvidia Tesla V100 GPU is used for training and segmentation. Initial training and finetuning took approximately 5 days and 2 days, respectively. Segmentation of one WSI took approximately $20 \sim 25$ min.

For evaluating our segmentation model, 1044 WSIs from 34 cases were segmented to estimate the necrosis ratio. Note all WSIs were segmented as if pathologists look at all glass slides under the microscope to assess the necrosis ratio. To numerically evaluate the estimated necrosis ratio, we compared with the ratio from pathology reports written by experts. Here, the error rate, E, is defined as

$$E = \frac{1}{N} \sum_{i=1}^{N} |R_i^{PATH} - R_i^{DL}| \tag{2}$$

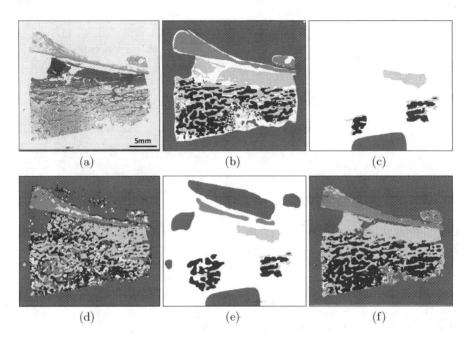

Fig. 3. An example of Deep Interactive Learning (DIaL). (a) An original training whole slide image, (b) an exhaustive annotation, (c) an initial annotation, (d) the first prediction from a CNN trained by the initial annotation, (e) the first correction where more regions for necrosis with bone, normal tissue, and blank are labeled to correct the first prediction, (f) the second prediction from a CNN finetuned from the initial model with double-weighted first correction, satisfied by annotators. The annotators spent approximately 1.5 h to exhaustively label one whole slide image. With DIaL, the annotators are able to efficiently label characteristic features and challenging features on more diverse cases at the same given time. In this experiment, two annotators initially annotated 49 images in 4 h and corrected 37 images in 3 h. Note viable tumor, necrosis with bone, necrosis without bone, normal bone, normal tissue, cartilage, and blank are labeled in red, blue, yellow, green, orange, brown, and gray, respectively. White regions in (b), (c), and (e) are unlabeled regions. (Color figure online)

where R_i^{PATH} is the ratio from a pathology report and R_i^{DL} is the ratio estimated by a deep learning model for the i-th case, and $1 \leq i \leq N$ where $N = 34$ is the number of testing cases. Figure 4(b) shows the error rates for our models. Model1, Model2a, Model2b, Model3 denote an initially-trained model, a finetuned model from Model1 with single-weighted first correction, a finetuned model from Model1 with double-weighted first correction, and a finetuned model from Model2b with double-weighted second correction, respectively. Note we tried both single-weighted correction including only extracted correction patches and double-weighted correction including both extracted correction patches and their corresponding deformed patches during the finetuning step. We observed that the error rate decreases after the first correction, especially with a higher weight on correction patches to emphasize challenging features. We selected

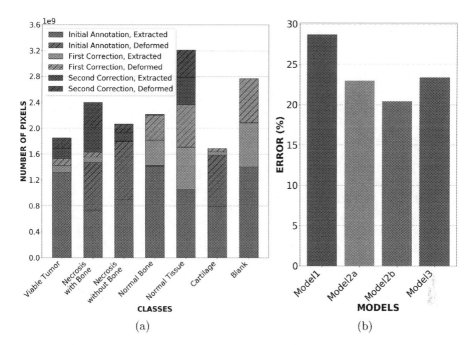

Fig. 4. (a) The number of pixels in a training set for each class. During initial annotation, elastic deformation [9,18] is used on patches containing necrosis with bone, necrosis without bone, and cartilage to balance the number of pixels between classes. Elastic deformation is used on all correction patches to give a higher weight on them. (b) Error rates of Model1, trained by initial annotation alone, Model2a, finetuned from Model1 with single-weighted first correction, Model2b, finetuned from Model1 with double-weighted first correction, and Model3, finetuned from Model2b with double-weighted second correction. Our final model, Model2b, achieves the error rate of 20% considered as an expected inter-observer variation rate [23].

Model2b as our final model because the error rate stopped reducing after the second correction. Our final model, trained by only 7 h of annotations done by DIaL, was able to achieve the error rate of 20%. A 20% inter-observer error rate is generally acceptable for non-standardized tasks in surgical pathology such as assessment of percentage of tumor cells has been overestimated by pathologists up to 20% in certain instances [23]. While this cannot be directly transferred to necrosis estimation we have used this data to show that the model is able to achieve this error rate.

The task of manual quantification of the necrosis ratio done by pathologists is challenging because one must make an estimate across multiple glass slides that may differ substantially in the ratio of necrosis. We are convinced that our objective and reproducible deep learning model estimating the necrosis ratio within expected inter-observer variation rate can be superior to manual interpretation.

4   Conclusion

We presented Deep Interactive Learning (DIaL) for an efficient annotation to train a segmentation CNN. With 7 h of labeling, we achieved a CNN segmenting viable tumor and necrotic tumor on osteosarcoma whole slide images. Our experiments showed that the CNN model can successfully estimate the necrosis ratio known as a prognostic factor for patients' survival for osteosarcoma in an objective and reproducible way. In the future, we plan for patient stratification based on patients' survival data using our deep learning model.

5   Acknowledgments/Disclosures

This work was supported by the Warren Alpert Foundation Center for Digital and Computational Pathology at Memorial Sloan Kettering Cancer Center and the NIH/NCI Cancer Center Support Grant P30 CA008748. T.J.F. is the Chief Scientific Officer, co-founder and equity holder of Paige.AI. P.J.S. is a lead machine learning scientist, co-founder and equity holder of Paige.AI. C.M.V. is a consultant for Paige.AI. D.J.H. and T.J.F. have intellectual property interests relevant to the work that is the subject of this paper. MSK has financial interests in Paige.AI. and intellectual property interests relevant to the work that is the subject of this paper.

References

1. Arunachalam, H.B., et al.: Viable and necrotic tumor assessment from whole slide images of osteosarcoma using machine-learning and deep-learning models. PLoS ONE **14**(4), e0210706 (2019)
2. Bandi, P., et al.: From detection of individual metastases to classification of lymph node status at the patient level: the CAMELYON17 challenge. IEEE Trans. Med. Imaging **38**(2), 550–560 (2019)
3. Bankhead, P., et al.: QuPath: open source software for digital pathology image analysis. Sci. Rep. **7**, 16878 (2017)
4. Berg, S., et al.: ilastik: interactive machine learning for (bio)image analysis. Nat. Methods **16**, 1226–1232 (2019)
5. Bokhorst, J.M., et al.: Learning from sparsely annotated data for semantic segmentation in histopathology images. In: Proceedings of the International Conference on Medical Imaging with Deep Learning, pp. 84–91 (2019)
6. Breiman, L.: Random forests. Mach. Learn. **45**(1), 5–32 (2001)
7. Ehteshami Bejnordi, B., et al.: Diagnostic assessment of deep learning algorithms for detection of lymph node metastases in women with breast cancer. JAMA **318**(22), 2199–2210 (2017)
8. Fails, J.A., Olsen, D.R.: Interactive machine learning. In: Proceedings of the International Conference on Intelligent User Interfaces, pp. 39–45 (2003)
9. Fu, C., et al.: Nuclei segmentation of fluorescence microscopy images using convolutional neural networks. In: Proceedings of the IEEE International Symposium on Biomedical Imaging, pp. 704–708 (2017)

10. Fuchs, T.J., Buhmann, J.M.: Computational pathology: challenges and promises for tissue analysis. Comput. Med. Imaging Graph. **35**(7), 515–530 (2011)

11. Glorot. X., Bengio, Y.: Understanding the difficulty of training deep feedforward neural networks. In: Proceedings of the International Conference on Artificial Intelligence and Statistics, pp. 249–256 (2010)

12. Ho, D.J., et al.: Deep multi-magnification networks for multi-class breast cancer image segmentation. arXiv preprint, arXiv:1910.13042 (2019)

13. Huvos, A.G., Rosen, G., Marcove, R.C.: Primary osteogenic sarcoma: pathologic aspects in 20 patients after treatment with chemotherapy en bloc resection, and prosthetic bone replacement. Arch. Pathol. Lab. Med. **101**(1), 14–18 (1977)

14. Lee, B., Paeng, K.: A robust and effective approach towards accurate metastasis detection and pN-stage classification in breast cancer. In: Proceedings of the International Conference on Medical Image Computing and Computer-Assisted Intervention, pp. 841–850 (2018)

15. Long, J., Shelhamer, E., Darrell, T.: Fully convolutional networks for semantic segmentation. In: Proceedings of the IEEE Conference on Computer Vision and Pattern Recognition, pp. 3431–3440 (2015)

16. Ottaviani, G., Jaffe, N.: The epidemiology of osteosarcoma. Pediatric and Adolescent Osteosarcoma **152**, 3–13 (2009)

17. Paszke, A., et al.: PyTorch: an imperative style, high-performance deep learning library. In: Proceedings of the Neural Information Processing Systems, pp. 8024–8035 (2019)

18. Ronneberger, O., Fischer, P., Brox, T.: U-Net: convolutional networks for biomedical image segmentation. In: Proceedings of the International Conference on Medical Image Computing and Computer-Assisted Intervention, pp. 234–241 (2015)

19. Rosen, G., et al.: Preoperative chemotherapy for osteogenic sarcoma: selection of postoperative adjuvant chemotherapy based on the response of the primary tumor to preoperative chemotherapy. Cancer **49**(6), 1221–1230 (1982)

20. Schüffler, P.J., Fuchs, T.J., Ong, C.S., Wild, P., Buhmann, J.M.: TMARKER: a free software toolkit for histopathological cell counting and staining estimation. J. Pathol. Inform. **4**(2), S2 (2013)

21. Sommer, C., Straehle, C., Koethe, U., Hamprecht, F. A.: ilastik: interactive learning and segmentation toolkit. In: Proceedings of the IEEE International Symposium on Biomedical Imaging, pp. 230–233 (2011)

22. Srinidhi, C. L., Ciga, O., Martel, A. L.: Deep neural network models for computational histopathology: a survey. arXiv preprint, arXiv:1912.12378 (2019)

23. Viray, H., et al.: A prospective, multi-institutional diagnostic trial to determine pathologist accuracy in estimation of percentage of malignant cells. Arch. Pathol. Lab. Med. **137**(11), 1545–1549 (2013)

24. Wang, D., Khosla, A., Gargeya, R., Irshad, H., Beck, A. H.: Deep learning for identifying metastatic breast cancer. arXiv preprint, arXiv:1606.05718 (2016)

Modeling Histological Patterns for Differential Diagnosis of Atypical Breast Lesions

Akash Parvatikar[1]([✉]), Om Choudhary[1], Arvind Ramanathan[2],
Olga Navolotskaia[3], Gloria Carter[3], Akif Burak Tosun[4], Jeffrey L. Fine[3],
and S. Chakra Chennubhotla[1,4]

[1] Department of Computational and Systems Biology, University of Pittsburgh,
Pittsburgh, USA
{akp47,opc3,chakracs}@pitt.edu
[2] Data Science and Learning, Argonne National Laboratory, Lemont, IL, USA
ramanathana@anl.gov
[3] Department of Pathology, UPMC Magee-Womens Hospital, Pittsburgh, USA
{navolotskaiao,finejl}@upmc.edu, cartgj@mail.magee.edu
[4] SpIntellx Inc., Pittsburgh, USA
{burak,chakra}@spintellx.com

Abstract. Our goal in this paper is to build parametric models for a dictionary of histological patterns that aid in the differential diagnosis of atypical breast lesions and evaluate the inferential power of these hand-crafted features. Diagnosis of high-risk atypical breast lesions is challenging and remains a critical component of breast cancer screening, presenting even for experienced pathologists a more difficult classification problem than the binary detection task of cancer *vs* not-cancer. Following guidelines in the WHO classification of the tumors of the breast (an essential reference for pathologists, clinicians and researchers) and in consultation with our team of breast sub-specialists ($N = 3$), we assembled a visual dictionary of sixteen histological patterns (e.g., cribriform, picket-fence), a subset that pathologists frequently use in making complex diagnostic decisions of atypical breast lesions. We invoke parametric models for each pattern using a mix of *unary*, *binary* and *ternary* features that account for morphological and architectural tissue properties. We use 1441 ductal regions of interest (ROIs) extracted automatically from 93 whole slide images (WSIs) with a computational pathology pipeline. We collected diagnostic labels for all of the ROIs: normal and columnar cell changes (CCC) as low-risk benign lesions ($= 1124$), and flat epithelium atypia (FEA) and atypical ductal hyperplasia (ADH) as high-risk benign lesions ($= 317$). We generate likelihood maps for each dictionary pattern across a given ROI and integrate this information to determine a diagnostic label of high- or low-risk. Our method has comparable classification accuracies to the pool of breast pathology sub-specialists. Our

Electronic supplementary material The online version of this chapter (https://doi.org/10.1007/978-3-030-59722-1_53) contains supplementary material, which is available to authorized users.

study enables a deeper understanding of the discordance among pathologists in diagnosing atypical breast lesions.

Keywords: Atypical breast lesions · Visual feature dictionary ·
Parametric models · Computational pathology

1   Introduction

Benign breast lesion diagnoses account for approximately a million cases annually [1]. The patients are subjected to additional screening procedures depending upon the relative risk associated with the diagnostic subtypes of the benign lesions (e.g., high-risk is associated with atypical hyperplasia) [2,3]. Over half of the patients diagnosed with atypical hyperplasia, which is histologically further classified into atypical ductal hyperplasia (ADH) and atypical lobular hyperplasia (ALH), contract breast cancer within 10 years of screening, thereby demanding an accurate diagnosis of these precursor lesions.

On the contrary, a recent clinical study showed significant levels of disagreement in differential diagnosis of cases with atypia (48–56%) resulting in *overinterpretation* (subjecting patients to unnecessary medical procedures) and *underinterpretation* (subjecting patients to no treatment) [4]. The underlying difficulty in classifying atypia from benign lesions stems from the fact that diagnostically relevant histopathological patterns overlap in the spectrum of low- to high-risk lesions, complicating the decision making process (Fig. 1). In the interest of patient management, it is convenient to stratify patients into "low-/high-risk" categories based on their histological evidence and associated risk-factor [3].

Our Approach: Following guidelines in the WHO classification of the tumors of the breast [5] (an essential reference for pathologists, clinicians and researchers) and in consultation with our team of breast pathology sub-specialists ($N = 3$), we assembled a visual dictionary of a *subset* of histological patterns that aid pathologists in undertaking differential diagnoses of atypical breast lesions (Fig. 1). Our goal in this differential diagnostic study is to build parametric models for each pattern using a mix of unary, binary and ternary features that account for cytological (nuclear shape and orientation, lumen shape), architectural (intraductal), and spatial-extent details of low- and high-risk lesions.

Prior Work: Previously, we have approached this problem in an unsupervised manner by simply encoding cytological properties of nuclear atypia and integrating them with the spatial distribution of the nuclei in relationship to stroma and lumen components of breast tissue (i.e., architectural patterns) [6]. Measured in terms of *recall* of high-risk lesions, *the classification performance reported here (0.76) is a significant improvement over our previous approach (0.69).* Although there are studies in the machine classification of breast tumors [7–10], many of these do not include diagnostically challenging ADH cases nor provide directions for a *computational* understanding of the structural changes in the breast tissue triggered by atypia and other malignancies. To the best of our knowledge, our work in analytically modeling a visual pattern dictionary that traditionally defines the standards on tumor classification/nomenclature for pathologists worldwide is the first of its kind.

2   Methodology

2.1   Segmenting Ducts, Lumen and Nuclei

We designed a new algorithm for segmenting ducts, lumen and nuclei on large scale WSIs. To start with, WSI images stored in RGB format are color deconvolved into their respective stain intensities namely, hematoxylin and eosin by using the color deconvolution plugin in ImageJ [11]. The stain colors are further normalized with a reference dataset to standardize color variations for downstream processing (see supplementary material for more details). To ease the computational burden of detecting ducts in a WSI, we build a Gaussian pyramid of the hematoxylin intensity WSI. The hematoxylin intensity image at the coarsest level of the pyramid is broken into non-overlapping superpixels (area = 300 pixels), which are sets of connected pixels with similar intensity values, using simple linear iterative clustering (SLIC) algorithm [12]. The innovative steps of our algorithm are in assigning probabilities for the presence of a duct given a pair of nearby superpixels ("context-ML") and further identifying all those superpixels that are "moderate-to-heavily" stained as the ones inside a duct ("stain-ML"). Using the superpixels identified as initial guesses, we perform a region-based active contour segmentation [13] that separates foreground (ducts/lumen) from the background (rest of the image). For hematoxylin and eosin stained images, the cost-function for the active contour is driven by the difference in the mean of the hematoxylin stain in the foreground and background regions. For example, two superpixels that have a high probability of being inside a duct have roughly the same stain ("moderate to heavy stain") and their boundaries are merged iteratively by the active contour optimization. Often ducts appear as "clusters" and to segment these we run the region-based active contour on the *probability* map returned by the context and stain-ML models. The probability maps impute non-zero probabilities to ducts and regions bridging them, and a region-based active contour model run on the probability map is more successful in delineating a cluster of ducts.

   To identify lumen we use context- and stain-based ML models to select image regions that are not part of the ducts – non-tissue areas on the WSI, connective tissue areas and lumen. We perform connected-component analysis to select and exclude large components, likely to correspond to non-tissue and connective tissue areas. The remaining components highlight lumen regions that lie inside ducts and are verified visually in our training images. To identify and segment nuclei inside a duct, we first select parts of image lying inside a duct, then use ImageJ to threshold intensities and finally run watershed to delineate the nuclear boundaries (see supplementary material for more details).

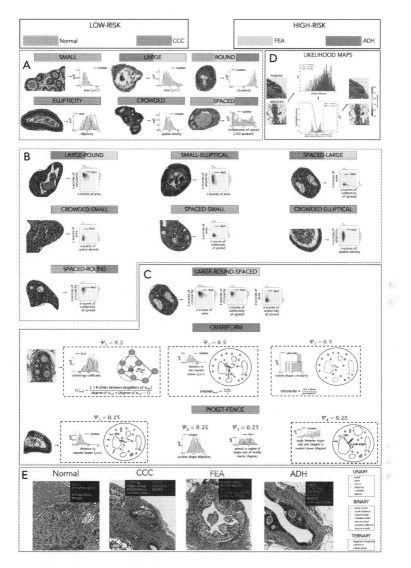

Fig. 1. Parametric models of histological patterns in the form of (A) unary, (B) binary and (C) ternary features. (D) Computing likelihood scores to reveal (E) dominant patterns in representative images of low- and high-risk lesions. (Color figure online)

2.2   Building Parametric Models of Histological Patterns

We invoke parametric models for histological patterns using a mix of *unary*, *binary* and *ternary* features as shown in Fig. 1. The colorbars over each feature in Fig. 1 indicate the lesion where the feature is most likely to be found, e.g., large and round nuclei are often found in high-risk lesions, small and elliptical nuclei in low-risk lesions, and cribriform pattern tends to be exclusive to ADH.

Unary Features: In consultation with the breast pathologists on our team, we selected a spectrum of morphological features on the basis of size, shape, and spatial spread around each nucleus. Nuclear size (quantified using area) is known to provide diagnostic cues in pathological grading [14–17], with groups of small and large nuclei having a propensity to belong to low-risk and high-risk lesions respectively [18]. To build analytical models of *small* and *large*, we first construct a histogram of nuclear areas obtained from an ensemble of ROIs showing prototypical example regions within a duct containing small and large nuclei (Fig. 1A) and model this histogram with a Gamma distribution (see supplementary material for a listing of all the model parameters derived in this section).

Next, nuclear shape has been identified as diagnostically meaningful, e.g., CCC lesion shows dominant elliptical nuclei [19]. We quantitate this feature with *roundness* measured as $(4\pi \times area)/perimeter^2$ and *ellipticity* given by the ratio of length of minor-axis to the length of major-axis. Roundness ranges from 0 (irregular star-like appearance) to 1 (perfect circle), while ellipticity characterizes the "flatness" of an object with lower values denoting highly elliptical nuclei (Fig. 1A). In each case, because of the intrinsic heterogeneity of these measurements, we consider a spatial neighborhood around each nucleus, and model the distributions of roundness with a Gamma distribution and ellipticity with a 2-component mixture of Gaussians (MoG) model (Fig. 1A).

Finally, several studies have shown that studying the spatial organization of nuclei provides insights into the abnormalities of cells which might eventually lead to malignancy. For instance, the nuclei arrangement in a CCC lesion frequently exhibits crowding and/or overlapping [20,21].

However, for cases belonging to high-risk atypical lesions (FEA and ADH) the nuclei tends to be uniform and evenly-spaced [20,22]. To quantify "crowding" around each nucleus, its average distance to 10 nearest nuclei is computed. An analytical model of *crowdedness* is constructed by considering local ROIs within a duct where clusters of nuclei show significant crowding behavior and then computing its spatial density. To capture evenly spaced/uniform dispersion pattern around a nucleus, we start by placing a regular grid of size 3×3 centered at a reference nucleus and measure the density of 20 neighboring nuclei by counting the population of nuclei in each grid cell as described in [23]. We then compare this observed population against expected number of nuclei under the *complete spatial randomness* hypothesis which asserts the occurrence of points (here nuclei) within grids in a random fashion analogous to a Poisson point process using a χ^2-test statistic and acquiring the corresponding p-value using the χ^2 distribution table. Larger the p-value, greater is the likelihood of observing a uniform/evenly spaced dispersion of nuclei around the reference nucleus.

Binary Features: Although, the unary features show some inferential strength (indicated by the color bars on top of each feature in Fig. 1), a pathologist typically makes an informed decision by paying attention to the pairwise combinations of such features. For instance, a CCC lesion (low-risk) exhibits crowded and elliptical nuclei arrangement. A high-risk lesion tends to display a greater likelihood of large-round, spaced-large, and spaced-round nuclei. A lesion showing majority regions of small nuclei coupled with crowded and/or spaced behavior is representative of a normal duct. In our study, we considered 7 such binary features obtained from pairwise combinations of unary features which is shown in panel Fig. 1B. We take z-scores for each unary feature, and model the joint distribution of z-scores from the feature pair with a two-component, two-dimensional mixture of Gaussian distribution.

Ternary Features: Some of the diagnostically relevant histological patterns are best represented by a combination of more than two unary features. *I. Large-Round-Spaced*: We take z-scores from each feature, i.e., large, round and spaced, and build a three-component, three-dimensional mixture of Gaussian model using ground-truth examples. *II. Cribriform*: This pattern is characterized by polarization of epithelial cells within spaces formed by "almost" circular multiple lumen (>2) which are 5–6 cells wide and whose appearance closely resembles to "holes in Swiss cheese". This complex architectural pattern can be identified by analytically modeling three sub-features: *clustering coefficient*, distance of the nucleus from two nearest lumen, and circularity of the lumen (computed using ImageJ) adjacent to the nucleus. The polarization of epithelial cells around lumen is characterized by clustering-coefficient and is computed by following the method described in [24] and is illustrated in the second row of Fig. 1C. A group of nuclei occupying the spacing between two lumen has a tendency to show cribriform pattern around them. Thus, we measure the average distance between each nucleus to the nearest two lumen and model its distribution using gamma function (see middle row of Fig. 1C). The final likelihood for cribriform pattern is obtained from the weighted sum of the likelihood scores of sub-features. We performed grid search on the mixing coefficients to learn that the likelihood scores from the three sub-features should be mixed in the proportion of 0.2, 0.5, and 0.3 respectively. *III. Picket-Fence*: This pattern is recognized from a group of crowded elliptical nuclei oriented perpendicular to the basement membrane (lumen). The analytical model of this high-order visual feature can be obtained by constructing parametric models of four simple sub-features: distance of a nucleus to nearest lumen, nuclear ellipticity, a spread in the angle of major-axis of 10 nearby nuclei, and its local angle with respect to the basement membrane as shown in the last row of Fig. 1C. Since, each sub-feature contributes equally to observing this ternary feature, we chose to assign a mixing coefficient of 0.25 in combining the likelihood scores from the four sub-features to determine the presence of a picket-fence pattern.

2.3   Computing Likelihood Scores to Assigning Diagnostic Labels

Computing Likelihood Scores: As discussed in the previous section, the parametric models for the histological patterns are probability distributions. For example, a cytological feature like nuclear ellipticity for a given nucleus inside a ROI can be assigned a probability value under the mixture of Gaussian model for the template ($\mathcal{G}_t$) image derived in Fig. 1A. However, accurate measurements of ellipticity values are greatly influenced by the precision with which nuclei boundaries are segmented. This naturally leads to heterogeneity in the estimates of ellipticity. To account for this heterogeneity, we chose to compare the neighborhood around the reference nucleus to the neighborhood in the template image. In particular, we model the ellipticity values in the neighborhood of the reference nucleus with a new mixture of Gaussian model ($\mathcal{G}_n$), just like in Fig. 1A, and then compare model parameters of $\mathcal{G}_n$ with $\mathcal{G}_t$ as shown in Fig. 1D. We used two different distance measures for comparing the model parameters: *Kullback-Leibler divergence* for mixture of Gaussians and *two-sample Kolmogorov Smirnov test* for unimodal Gamma distributions. Small distances imply greater evidence for the pattern. We turn the distances into a likelihood score by an inverted S-function as shown in Fig. 1D. This process is carried out in a similar fashion for every feature present in the visual dictionary.

Strategy for Differential Diagnosis: We adopt a non-linear strategy here, similar to what expert pathologists do, in that we find sub-regions within ROI by non-maxima suppression (threshold value of 0.85 on the likelihood scores) where the evidence for one or more of the unary, binary or ternary feature is dominating. Figure 1E provides a visual illustration of the likelihood maps of dominant patterns in representative images of low- and high-risk lesions. Low-risk lesions show dominant islands of *round, small, spaced,* and *spaced-small* in a normal ROI and *elliptical, round, spaced-small, crowded-small,* and *picket-fence* neighborhoods in a CCC ROI. In comparison, high-risk lesions show dominant regions of *spaced-large,* and *spaced-round* in a FEA labeled ROI and compelling strengths for *large* and *cribriform* patterns along with traces of *crowded* and *spaced* in ADH labeled ROI. These patterns validate the canonical forms shown in Fig. 1A–C.

Having identified dominant unary, binary and ternary feature regions, we use 3 descriptive statistics: median value of the likelihood scores of all the nuclei found in each sub-region, median number of nuclei found in each sub-region and the number of sub-regions.

This is calculated for each one of the unary, binary and ternary features (total = 16), thereby obtaining a 48 column feature vector for a single image. We computed feature vectors for all 1441 labeled duct ROIs which resulted in 834×48 size feature map used to train the classifier and 607×48 data matrix for testing. To analyze the benefit of including binary and ternary features we further slice the 48 column feature vector to be suitable for three scenarios: unary (U) only, unary and binary (U-B), and unary, binary, and ternary features (U-B-T). Due to inherent training and testing class imbalance, which reflects the real-world prevalence statistics of atypical lesions, we upsampled high-risk examples using SMOTE technique [25].

Prior to classifying the lesions, we pay close attention to the presence of cribriform pattern, a symbolic visual primitive of ADH (a high-risk) category [22,26,27]. ROIs predicted to show cribriform pattern are classified as high-risk, if the number of nuclei forming the cribriform sub-region is greater than 8 (hyperparameter optimized over the training data). The reduced dataset, devoid of cribriform, is tested for each of the scenarios (U, U-B, and U-B-T) with logistic regression (LR), support vector machine (SVM), random forest (RF), and gradient boosted classifier algorithms. The best model was chosen by optimizing the parameters using GridSearchCV based on precision, recall, and F-scores and then performed a tenfold stratified cross-validation to check for overfitting. In optimizing the hyperparameters, the operating point was selected to value recall over precision reflecting the clinical decision objective where a false negative outcome is penalized higher than a false positive.

3   Results and Discussion

Table 1. Performance measures with U, U-B and U-B-T feature sets and comparison with other baseline strategies (including majority classification and average single expert pathologist assessment) and deep-learning models.

	Baseline		Comparisons			U	U-B	U-B-T
Models	Majority	Expert	Lenet	Overfeat	Alexnet		LR	
Recall	0	**0.77**	0.23	0.31	0.4	0.56	0.59	**0.76**
Specificity			0.88	0.84	0.86	0.64	0.69	0.63
TN			475	451	462	345	373	336
FN			54	48	42	31	29	17

Dataset: We used 1441 ductal ROIs extracted automatically from a computational pathology pipeline (see Subsect. 2.1) from 93 WSIs which were scanned at $0.5\,\mu m$/pixel resolution at 20× magnification captured using Aperio ScanScope XT microscope. Among these, the *training* set constituting 834 ROIs were diagnostically labeled by a single sub-specialist pathologist (SP1), while a consensus diagnosis was achieved for the remaining 607 *testing* set ROIs with a pool of 3 breast pathology sub-specialists (SP1, SP2, and SP3). The diagnostic labels include: "Normal", "CCC", "FEA", or "ADH", which were further regrouped into two classes: low-risk (Normal and CCC) and high-risk (FEA and ADH). While the training set comprised of 587 low-risk and 247 high-risk examples, the test set included 537 low-risk and only 70 high-risk cases, leading to the issue of class-imbalance and the choice of *recall* of high-risk lesions as a performance metric for the classification strategy. We are reporting recall to emphasize correct detection of high-risk lesions, as the consequence of misdiagnoses (false negative) implies increased chance of developing cancer for lack of providing early treatment. The concordance among the 3 pathologists in labeling the test set was moderate (Fleiss' kappa score of ≈0.55 [6]).

Results: Table 1 shows the outcome of the differential diagnosis strategy that we implemented using the three feature sets: U, U-B, and U-B-T. The average performance of the three pathologists informs the baseline with single expert pathologist [6]. We tested with Logistic Regression (LR), Random Forest, and SVM with SMOTE and cross-validation parameter scanning. LR performed the best. SVM and Random Forest misclassified high-risk images containing large/round/spaced nuclei (a high-risk feature, see Fig. 1) as low-risk. This resulted in lower recall compared to LR, which was successful in capturing these features. Additionally, we tested approaches with deep learning: Lenet [28], Alexnet [29], and Overfeat [30]. For training deep learning networks the ROIs obtained from duct segmentation were downscaled to 512 × 512 and the class imbalance was handled by performing data augmentation through rotations and reflections. Further, these class-balanced batches were trained using 3 networks for 3,000 epochs.

Discussion: We find progressive improvement in the performance from U to U-B to U-B-T feature sets, achieving highest recall of 0.76 which outperforms the majority classification (obtained by assigning all cases to the majority label of low-risk, thereby having a recall of 0) and has a comparable performance to the assessment made by single breast pathology sub-specialist (SP1). Our approach with ∼150 parameters (see supplementary material) is readily amenable to explainability which cannot be delivered by current deep learning (DL) methods (∼10–50 million parameters and large training data). To the best of our knowledge, there are no widely reported DL methods for borderline of atypical breast lesions, but an abundance of these algorithms for cancer vs no-cancer datasets. To further promote research in the use of DL for borderline cases, we chose to continue working with the same set of networks as used in our previous work [6], with one exception of incorporating improved duct segmentation component (see supplementary material). The average computation time to obtain likelihood scores and return a diagnostic label is 1 min for an image with 1000 nuclei on a single 2.4 GHz processor. In some low-risk examples, the accurate identification of class specific histological patterns (e.g. small, crowded-small) is missed due to the under-segmentation of overlapping nuclei resulting in a wrong classification (false positive). However, we observed that U-B-T features (best recall) misclassified 24% of the high-risk images as low-risk (false negative). Upon investigation, we found that majority of the wrongly classified images had rigid cellular bars and micropapillae (club-shaped lumina) architecture, two additional distinguishing characteristics of ADH [5] not included in the dictionary for the present study. As future work, we anticipate successful inclusion and analytical modeling of the missing patterns from the WHO breast cancer resource, to further reduce the number of false positives and false negatives. Our strategy has the potential to extend to other organ systems and act as a surrogate in the case review and quality assurance discussions for reducing discordance between pathologists.

Acknowledgments. The grant NIH-NCI U01CA204826 to SCC supported this work. The work of AP and OC was partially supported by the sub-contracts 9F-60178 and 9F-60287 from Argonne National Laboratory (ANL) to the University of Pittsburgh from the parent grant DE-AC02-06CH1135 titled, Co-Design of Advanced Artificial

Intelligence Systems for Predicting Behavior of Complex Systems Using Multimodal Datasets, from the Department of Energy to ANL.

References

1. Figueroa, J.D., et al.: Standardized measures of lobular involution and subsequent breast cancer risk among women with benign breast disease: a nested case-control study. Breast Cancer Res. Treat. **159**(1), 163–172 (2016)
2. Santen, R.J.: Benign breast disease in women. In: Endotext [Internet]. MDText.com, Inc. (2018)
3. Dyrstad, S.W., et al.: Breast cancer risk associated with benign breast disease: systematic review and meta-analysis. Breast Cancer Res. Treat. **149**(3), 569–575 (2015)
4. Elmore, J.G., et al.: Diagnostic concordance among pathologists interpreting breast biopsy specimens. JAMA **313**(11), 1122–1132 (2015)
5. Lakhani, S.R.: WHO Classification of Tumours of the Breast. International Agency for Research on Cancer (2012)
6. Tosun, A.B., et al.: Histological detection of high-risk benign breast lesions from whole slide images. In: Descoteaux, M., Maier-Hein, L., Franz, A., Jannin, P., Collins, D.L., Duchesne, S. (eds.) MICCAI 2017. LNCS, vol. 10434, pp. 144–152. Springer, Cham (2017). https://doi.org/10.1007/978-3-319-66185-8_17
7. Mercan, E., et al.: Assessment of machine learning of breast pathology structures for automated differentiation of breast cancer and high-risk proliferative lesions. JAMA Netw. Open **2**(8), e198777 (2019)
8. Bejnordi, B.E., et al.: Context-aware stacked convolutional neural networks for classification of breast carcinomas in whole-slide histopathology images. J. Med. Imaging (Bellingham) **4**(4), 044504 (2017)
9. Li, H., et al.: Quantitative nuclear histomorphometric features are predictive of Oncotype DX risk categories in ductal carcinoma in situ: preliminary findings. Breast Cancer Res. **21**(1), 114 (2019)
10. Dong, F., et al.: Computational pathology to discriminate benign from malignant intraductal proliferations of the breast. PLoS ONE **9**(12), e114885 (2014)
11. Schindelin, J., et al.: Fiji: an open-source platform for biological-image analysis. Nat. Meth. **9**(7), 676–682 (2012)
12. Achanta, R., et al.: SLIC superpixels compared to state-of-the-art superpixel methods. IEEE Trans. Pattern Anal. Mach. Intell. **34**(11), 2274–2282 (2012)
13. Chan, T.F., et al.: Active contours without edges. IEEE Trans. Image Process. **10**(2), 266–277 (2001)
14. Pienta, K.J., et al.: Correlation of nuclear morphometry with progression of breast cancer. Cancer **68**(9), 2012–2016 (1991)
15. Cui, Y., et al.: Nuclear morphometric features in benign breast tissue and risk of subsequent breast cancer. Breast Cancer Res. Treat. **104**(1), 103–107 (2007)
16. Kashyap, A., et al.: Study of nuclear morphometry on cytology specimens of benign and malignant breast lesions: a study of 122 cases. J. Cytol. **34**(1), 10 (2017)
17. Narasimha, A., et al.: Significance of nuclear morphometry in benign and malignant breast aspirates. Int. J. Appl. Basic Med. Res. **3**(1), 22 (2013)
18. Mommers, E.C.M., et al.: Prognostic value of morphometry in patients with normal breast tissue or usual ductal hyperplasia of the breast. Int. J. Cancer **95**(5), 282–285 (2001)

19. Yamashita, Y., et al.: Does flat epithelial atypia have rounder nuclei than columnar cell change/hyperplasia? A morphometric approach to columnar cell lesions of the breast. Virchows Arch. **468**(6), 663–673 (2016)
20. Logullo, A.F., et al.: Columnar cell lesions of the breast: a practical review for the pathologist. Surg. Exp. Pathol. **2**(1), 1–8 (2019)
21. Pinder, S.E., et al.: Non-operative breast pathology: columnar cell lesions. J. Clin. Pathol. **60**(12), 1307–1312 (2007)
22. Allison, K.H., et al.: Histological features associated with diagnostic agreement in atypical ductal hyperplasia of the breast: illustrative cases from the B-Path study. Histopathology **69**(6), 1028–1046 (2016)
23. Sergio R., et al.: pysal/pointpats: pointpats 2.1.0 (2019). https://doi.org/10.5281/zenodo.3265637
24. Zhou, N., et al.: Large scale digital prostate pathology image analysis combining feature extraction and deep neural network. arXiv:1705.02678 (2017)
25. Chawla, N.V., et al.: SMOTE: synthetic minority over-sampling technique. J. Artif. Intell. Res. **16**, 321–357 (2002)
26. Ely, K.A., et al.: Core biopsy of the breast with atypical ductal hyperplasia: a probabilistic approach to reporting. Am. J. Surg. Pathol. **25**(8), 1017–1021 (2001)
27. Chen, L., et al.: Diagnostic upgrade of atypical ductal hyperplasia of the breast based on evaluation of histopathological features and calcification on core needle biopsy. Histopathology **75**(3), 320–328 (2019)
28. LeCun, Y., et al.: LeNet-5, convolutional neural networks, vol. 20, no. 5 (2015). http://yann.lecun.com/exdb/lenet
29. Krizhevsky, A., et al.: Imagenet classification with deep convolutional neural networks. In: NeurIPS, pp. 1097–1105 (2012)
30. Sermanet, P., et al.: OverFeat: integrated recognition, localization and detection using convolutional networks. In: ICLR, CBLS (2014)

Foveation for Segmentation of Mega-Pixel Histology Images

Chen Jin[1(✉)], Ryutaro Tanno[1,2], Moucheng Xu[1], Thomy Mertzanidou[1], and Daniel C. Alexander[1]

[1] Centre for Medical Image Computing, Department of Computer Science, University College London, London, UK
chen.jin@ucl.ac.uk
[2] Healthcare Intelligence, Microsoft Research Cambridge, Cambridge, UK

Abstract. Segmenting histology images is challenging because of the sheer size of the images with millions or even billions of pixels. Typical solutions pre-process each histology image by dividing it into patches of fixed size and/or down-sampling to meet memory constraints. Such operations incur information loss in the field-of-view (FoV) (i.e., spatial coverage) and the image resolution. The impact on segmentation performance is, however, as yet understudied. In this work, we first show under typical memory constraints (e.g., 10G GPU memory) that the trade-off between FoV and resolution considerably affects segmentation performance on histology images, and its influence also varies spatially according to local patterns in different areas (see Fig. 1). Based on this insight, we then introduce *foveation module*, a learnable "dataloader" which, for a given histology image, adaptively chooses the appropriate configuration (FoV/resolution trade-off) of the input patch to feed to the downstream segmentation model at each spatial location (Fig. 1). The foveation module is jointly trained with the segmentation network to maximise the task performance. We demonstrate, on the Gleason2019 challenge dataset for histopathology segmentation, that the foveation module improves segmentation performance over the cases trained with patches of fixed FoV/resolution trade-off. Moreover, our model achieves better segmentation accuracy for the two most clinically important and ambiguous classes (Gleason Grade 3 and 4) than the top performers in the challenge by 13.1% and 7.5%, and improves on the average performance of 6 human experts by 6.5% and 7.5%.

1 Introduction

The histology images are ultra-high resolution microscope images from Hematoxylin and Eosin-stained biopsy, which form the primary source of information

Electronic supplementary material The online version of this chapter (https://doi.org/10.1007/978-3-030-59722-1_54) contains supplementary material, which is available to authorized users.

© Springer Nature Switzerland AG 2020
A. L. Martel et al. (Eds.): MICCAI 2020, LNCS 12265, pp. 561–571, 2020.
https://doi.org/10.1007/978-3-030-59722-1_54

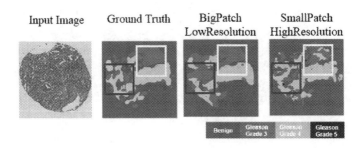

Fig. 1. A 4-class Gleason grade segmentation example under two trade-off configurations: "BigPatch-LowResolution" with patch size of 5000^2 pixels and downsampling rate of 0.2 and "SmallPatch-HighResolution" with patch size of 2000^2 pixels and downsampling rate of 0.5.

for cancer detection, grading and treatment planning. However manual analysis of histology images is expensive and prone to false negative detection due to their enormous size (up to $100,000^2$ pixels), motivating the development of accurate automated methods. Deep learning (DL) based approaches have been recently adopted to improve the segmentation of high-resolution images in recent years. However, modern DL methods cannot operate on mega(giga)-pixel histology images, given the limited GPU memory constraints. To mitigate this issue, histology images are typically dissected into smaller patches and/or down-sampled to fit into the available GPU memory [1]. To exploit all the available GPU memory thus requires one to trade off field of view (FoV), i.e. spatial extent of context, against resolution, i.e. level of image detail. Tuning this trade-off exhaustively is expensive [2], and as a result, it is commonly set by crude developer intuition.

A considerable amount of work has attempted to alleviate the issue of subjectivity in tuning this trade-off by learning to merge multi-scale information, in both medical imaging [3] and computer vision [4,5]. These works optimise model performance by exploiting the information from multi-scale sources. Specifically, they learn feature representations from multiple parallel networks, then aggregate learnt multiple scale representations before making the final prediction. DeepMedic [3] is one pioneering example in this category, having two parallel networks and applied to brain lesion segmentation. Another is [6], which is designed to work specifically with histopathology images. In general computer vision, the authors of [5] boost the learning efficiency of multi-scale information by enforcing global and local streams to interactively exchange information with each other. On the other hand, Chen *et al.* [4] perform multi-scale feature aggregation via an attention mechanism, which weights the prediction score from multi-scale parallel networks. However, these approaches: 1) construct multiple parallel networks, which can be computationally expensive; 2) typically use limited (2 or 3) manually selected scales; 3) need to to rely on specific choices of neural network architecture.

Our Contributions: In this work, we first demonstrate empirically on a public histology segmentation dataset that the choice of the input patch configuration (i.e., FoV/resolution trade-off) considerably influences the segmentation performance on different classes. Secondly, motivated by this finding, we then propose *foveation module*, a data-driven "data loader" that learns to provide the segmentation network with the most informative patch configuration for each location in a ultra-high-resolution image. The foveation module can be trained jointly in an end-to-end fashion with the segmentation network to optimise the task performance. The inspiration for our method roots from the ways in which pathologist segment high-resolution images — starting from a low-resolution bird's-eye view of the whole image[1], the annotators navigate their gaze through different locations and zoom in to the right extent to collect both local and contextual information. The magnification scale is controlled by, what is called, *foveation* (i.e., the process of adjusting the focal length of the eye, the distance between the lens and fovea). We also note that our work bears some similarity with the recent approach proposed by Katharopoulos *et al.* [7] in which attention weights are learned over the mega-pixel histology image to sample patches from a small informative sub-locations for the downstream classification task. However, our work differs from theirs in that we aim to select the best patch configuration at every spatial location for the downstream segmentation task, while their method tries to select the most informative subset of all spatial locations for the classification task. We evaluate the benefits of our foveation module on the Gleason2019 challenge dataset, where we show it boosts segmentation performance with little extra computational cost.

2 Methods

In this section, we first perform empirical analysis to illustrate the impact of the patch FoV/resolution trade-off on the histology segmentation performance and its spatial variation across the image. Motivated by this finding, we then propose *foveation module*, a module that learns to provide the segmentation network with the most informative patch configuration for each location in an ultra-high-resolution histology image.

2.1 Effects of Patch Configuration on Histology Segmentation

The first part of our work is a comprehensive empirical analysis, investigating a key question: "How does the FoV/resolution of training input patches affect the final segmentation performance?". To this end, we validate our method on a multi-class segmentation dataset: the Gleason2019 Challenge[2] which contains 322 histology images of average size $\approx 5000 \times 5000$ pixels. Each image is labelled by a subset of 6 annotators (all experts). Each pixel is labelled into one from four classes (Benign, Gleason Grade 3, 4, 5). Preprocessing for empirical analysis: A subset of 298 training examples have been used in the first part of our work. We

---

[1] Screen display or human vision typically have lower resolutions than that of the ultra-high resolution images of interest in this work.

[2] https://gleason2019.grand-challenge.org.

fuse 6 annotations into 1 using pixel-level probabilistic analysis by STAPLE [8]. Each image is paired with 1 STAPLE fused annotation as gold standard. Pre-processing for foveation experiments: we extract central part of input images $\mathbf{x}$ of size 4400^2 from the original histology images to ensure the constant size of input image. We randomly split 298 images into a training subset (268) and a testing subset (30).

Then, we perform three sets of experiments: 1) the first investigates the impact of FoV only; 2) the second investigates the impact of resolution; and 3) the last studies the combination of the FoV and resolution (i.e. the FoV/resolution trade-off). To study the impact of the FoV, we divide the original 5000^2 images into 256^2, 512^2, 768^2 patches, respectively. It is noted all sampled patches share the same original resolution. In the second set of experiments, we downsample the original 5000^2 images using four different downsampling rates of 0.03, 0.06, 0.12 and 0.22, respectively. To examine the trade-off between FoV and resolution, we first fix our memory limit at 10G. Then we divide the original images into 1100^2, 2000^2, 3000^2, 4000^2, 5000^2, respectively, to create five sets of patches, which share the same resolution. Afterwards, we further perform down-sampling on each set of the five sets of patches, with different downsampling rates all to an identical size of 1100^2. We illustrate the results of the total three sets of experiments in blue curves in Fig. 2(a). In Fig. 2(a), the red star repre-sents the trade-off which has the best mean performance of the 4 classes across all of the experiments. Meanwhile, the trade-offs of best performances for each class across all of the experiments, are also highlighted in different shaped marks (see Legends in Fig. 2(a)). It is clear that there is no single "best fit" sampling size for best mean performance and best performances for each class, simulta-neously. We also show visual results of the best segmentation for each class in Fig. 2(b). As visually illustrated in Fig. 2(b), each trade-off is only optimal for each pattern at each spatial location. This shows that the standard sampling strategy is not optimal overall. This motivates our novel Foveation module to learn to sample the most optimal training patches, which will be introduced in the following section.

2.2   Foveation Module

The inspiration for our method is to combine information from multiple scales and locations, as the fovea of the eye does that automatically adjusting the focal length according to different regions of interests via simply a glimpse over the scene. Our method consists of two components (see Fig. 3 for a schematic); (1) *Foveation module* that takes a low-resolution version of a mega-pixel input image and generates importance weights over a set of patches with varying spa-tial FoV/resolution at different pixel locations, (2) *Segmentation network* that processes the input patches based on the outputs of the foveation module, and estimates the corresponding segmentation probabilities. This segmentation net-work can be any existing models.

For each mega-pixel image $\mathbf{x} \in \mathbb{R}^{H \times W \times C}$ where H, W, C denote the height, width and channels respectively, we compute its lower resolution version $\mathbf{x}_{lr} \in$

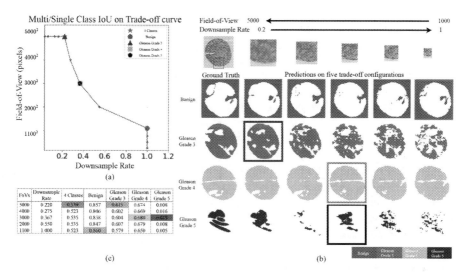

Fig. 2. Quantitative (left) and qualitative (right) evidence of different optimal FoV/resolution trade-offs for different classes. (a): The best patch configuration (i.e., FoV/resolution trade-off) for segmentation performance overall and for individual classses are highlighted. (b): A visual illustration of the class-wise variation of the best patch configuration. Here the size of FoV decreases from left to right and Down-sampling rate increases from left to right. In each row, the best segmentation result among the five trade-off configurations is highlighted, which corresponds to the trade-off configuration in Left. (c): The corresponding segmentation performance measured in *intersection over union* (IoU) are reported.

$\mathbb{R}^{h \times w \times C}$. The resolution of $\mathbf{x}_{\mathrm{lr}}$ is empirically determined based on performance. We also define a "patch-extractor" function $PE(\mathbf{x}, i) = \{\mathbf{p}_1^{(i)}(\mathbf{x}), ..., \mathbf{p}_D^{(i)}(\mathbf{x})\}$ that extracts a set of D patches of varying field-of-view/resolution (but the same number of pixels to tackle the FoV-resolution trade-off when the input patch size is fixed due to limited memory) from the full resolution image $\mathbf{x}$ centered at the corresponding i^{th} pixel in $\mathbf{x}_{\mathrm{lr}}$ (see Fig. 3 for a set of examples). *Foveation module*, F_θ, parametrised by θ, takes the low-resolution image $\mathbf{x}_{\mathrm{lr}}$ as the input and generates the probability distributions $F_\theta(\mathbf{x}_{\mathrm{lr}}) \in [0, 1]^{h \times w \times D}$ over patches $PE(\mathbf{x}, i)$ at respective spatial locations $i \in \{1, ..., wh\}$ in $\mathbf{x}_{\mathrm{lr}}$.

Based on the outputs of the foveation module, at each location i, we compute the input patch by taking the weighted average of the extracted patches of varying resolutions/sizes:

$$\mathbf{p}^{(i)}(\mathbf{x}) := \sum_{d=1}^{D} f_d^{(i)}(\mathbf{x}_{\mathrm{lr}}) \cdot \mathbf{p}_d^{(i)}(\mathbf{x}) \tag{1}$$

where $f_d^{(i)}(\mathbf{x}_{\mathrm{lr}})$ denotes the value of $F_\theta(\mathbf{x}_{\mathrm{lr}})$ at i^{th} pixel, and quantifies the "importance" of the dth patch at that location. The importance weights $[f_1^{(i)}(\mathbf{x}_{\mathrm{lr}}), ..., f_D^{(i)}(\mathbf{x}_{\mathrm{lr}})]$ sum up to one. The weighted average of the multiple patches based on the estimated probabilities ensures the full differentiability of the objective function with respect to θ. This approach can be viewed as the mean approximation of the "stochastic hard" attention employed in [7], similar to the approach in [9] and the "deterministic soft" attention in [10]. We then subsequently feed this input patch to *segmentation network*, $S_\phi(\mathbf{p}^{(i)}(\mathbf{x}))$, parametrised by ϕ to estimate the segmentation probabilities within the spatial extent covered by the patch with the smallest field of view in $PE(\mathbf{x}, i)$. During training, the parameters $\{\theta, \phi\}$ of both the foveation module and the segmentation network are jointly learned to minimise the segmentation specific loss function (e.g., cross entropy) by performing stochastic gradient descent. We extract patches at different locations and process them separately, which can be computationally expensive. For computational efficiency, for each mega-pixel image $\mathbf{x}$, we randomly select a subset of pixels (locations) from its low resolution counterpart $\mathbf{x}_{\mathrm{lr}}$, compute the corresponding input patches according to Eq. (1), feed them to the segmentation network and compute the losses. At inference time, we segment the whole mega-pixel image $\mathbf{x}$ by aggregating predictions $S_\phi(\mathbf{p}^{(i)}(\mathbf{x}))$ at different locations i. We open-source the code at https://github.com/lxasqjc/Foveation-for-Segmentation-of-Mega-pixel-Histology-Images.

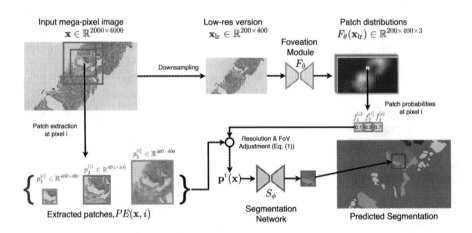

Fig. 3. Architecture schematic.

3   Network Architectures and Implementation Details

Training: For all experiments, we employ the same training scheme unless otherwise stated. We optimize parameters using Adam [11] with initial learning rate of $2e10^{-5}$ and $\beta = 0.9$ and train for 50 epochs. We apply batches size of 2. For patch extractor we extract a set of 5 patches at field-of-view $\{1100^2, 2000^2, 2900^2, 3800^2, 4400^2\}$ pixels and apply a down-sampling factor of $\{1, 0.55, 0.38, 0.29, 0.25\}$ to have identical 1100^2 pixels in extracted patches.

Architectures: The Foveation module was defined as a light weighted CNN architecture (0.1M parameter) comprised of 3 convolution layers, each with 3'–3 kernels follower by BatchNorm and Relu. The number of kernels in each respective layer is $\{40, 40, 5\}$. A softmax layer is added at the end. All convolution layers are initialised following He initialization [12]. The Segmentation module was defined as a deep CNN architecture (66M parameter) referring to HRNetV2-W48 in [13] (details provided in the original literature). The segmentation network is initialized with HRNetV2-W48 pre-trained on Imagenet dataset as provided by the author [13].

4   Results

In this section, we 1) qualitatively inspect the learnt spatial distribution of the FoV/Resolution Trade-off; 2) quantitatively compare our method with seven baselines, average expert and top Gleason2019 challenge performers; 3) provide visual results of our segmentation performance against the set of six baselines.

For one input image $\mathbf{x}$, based on the output of foveation module $F_\theta(\mathbf{x}_{\mathrm{lr}})$, we calculate the weighted average patch size over all localtions, and refer to as Average Patch Size Map (APSM). In Fig. 4, we pick one validation image as input and plot its APSM at three different epochs. As shown in Fig. 4, as training progresses, the average patch sizes at regions with small patterns (e.g. nuclei) shrink, while the average patch sizes at regions with large patterns (e.g. glands or background) expand. The observation evidenced that our method can learn the spatial distribution the FoV/Resolution Trade-off.

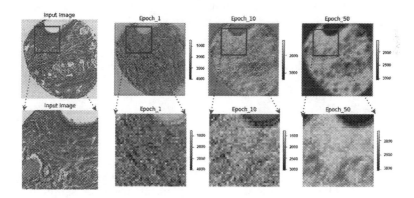

Fig. 4. The evolution of the learned weighted average patch size during training for one validation image. The brighter the colour, the higher the resolution and smaller patch.

To quantitatively evaluate our method we perform comparisons with three groups of baselines: Group 1) five one-hot baselines which force the probability distributions from foveation module $F_\theta(\mathbf{x}_{\mathrm{lr}})$ to be fixed one-hot vectors, thus selecting only one scale per baseline from the given set of 5 patches with varying FoV/resolution. A uniform random one-hot baseline that at each location randomly selects one from the given set of 5 patches with varying FoV/resolution, referred to as Baseline-Random. And an average baseline that assigns equal probability $f_d^{(i)}$ of 1/5 over the set of 5 patches with varying FoV/resolution, referred to as Baseline-Average; Group 2) average expert baseline measure the 6 annotators' performance taking STAPLE fused golden standard as ground truth; Group 3) top 2 results of the Gleason2019 challenge leaderboard https:// gleason2019.grand-challenge.org/Results/ ranked by overall all classes average segmentation accuracy. We also collect highest segmentation accuracy of each classes as a third Single-Class-Best case for comparison. We quantify segmentation performance of group 1 and group 2 by Intersection over Union (mIoU). We quantify segmentation performance of group 3 via pixel accuracy for each class, to be consistent and comparable against results released on the leaderboard. It is worth noting that for all results we remove the "Gleason Grade 5" class in evaluation, as it is under represented - only 2% pixels in the given dataset.

We first compare our method against the baseline approaches in Group 1. The results are shown in Table 1. Our method achieved better segmentation performance (mIoU/IoU) over the 7 one-hot baselines described above in i) overall four class average, ii) benign class and iii) class Grade 4. The performance is also comparable with the best of class Grade 3. The results show that our method combines the advantages of different FoV/Resolution trade-off over the five baselines. This point is also qualitatively illustrated in Fig. 5. The results against the baseline of Group 2 are shown in last row of Table 1, where our model improves on the average performance of 6 human experts by 6.5% and 7.5% for the two most clinically important and ambiguous classes (Gleason Grade 3 and 4), and gives comparable performance for overall average and the Benign class. Group 3 results are shown in Table 2, where our model achieves better segmentation accuracy against the top performers in the challenge for the two most clinically important and ambiguous classes (Gleason Grade 3 and 4) by 13.1% and 7.5%.

5   Discussion

Motivated by our observation that the FoV/resolution trade-off varies widely, we introduced a new theoretically grounded algorithm for simultaneously learning the spatial distribution of the trade-off and training a segmentation network that exploits it. Our method is simple to implement, requiring simply the addition of a"patch-extractor" and a light weighted foveation module (CNN). Our approach is complementary to a wide range of existing "multi-resolution" segmentation architectures. In this work we used HRNetV2, a SoTA very deep multi-scale architecture and enhanced it with the proposed foveation module. Experiments on the Gleason2019 challenge segmentation data set show superior performance over single "best fit" trade-offs, average expert performance, and challenge leaderboard top results, especially for the two most clinically important and ambiguous classes (Gleason Grade 3 and 4). For the typically easy Benign

Table 1. Mean IoU (column 2) and IoU (column 3–5) on Gleason2019 Histology dataset. row 2–6: 5 one-hot baselines; row 7: uniform random one-hot baselines; row 8: average baseline; row 9: our result with foveation approach; row 10: average expert baseline.

Baselines	Overall	Benign	Grade 3	Grade 4
Baseline-1100^2	0.520	0.810	0.618	0.650
Baseline-2000^2	0.525	0.805	0.644	0.653
Baseline-2900^2	0.530	0.810	**0.649**	0.661
Baseline-3800^2	0.505	0.764	0.614	0.640
Baseline-4400^2	0.460	0.675	0.556	0.610
Baseline-random	0.487	0.722	0.586	0.638
Baseline-average	0.493	0.788	0.522	0.660
Ours	**0.533**	**0.824**	0.630	**0.678**
Average expert	0.569	0.839	0.564	0.603

Table 2. Quantitative comparision to Gleason2019 challenge leaderboard results measured by single class pixel accuracy

Experiment	Benign	Grade 3	Grade 4
Ours	88.3	**83.8**	**78.1**
Overall Top1	**95.9**	2.24	16.5
Overall Top2	83.0	52.7	54.0
Single-class-best	95.9	70.7	70.6

class, the performance of our approach is slightly lower but still competitive to the challenge leaderboard top results, and the variation compared to other classes is anticipated: a) Table 1 shows our method outperforms all seven baselines on the Benign class and is comparable (1% difference) to average expert performance; b) Table 2 shows that our Benign-class performance is similar to the leading published.

We acknowledge the noisy nature of the dataset used to demonstrate our approach, however we believe that it is a good example to illustrate its robustness. The noise in the annotations is due to minor pattern variations between adjacent Gleason classes that leads to high variation in experts' performance in Table 1 and Fig. 1 (in supplementary material). Our method shown promising results on Gleason2019 Tissue microarrays (also TMAs) images, we would expect it to perform well on WSI and more generic non-medical ultra-high resolution image dataset too and would test in future work.

In the current implementation, all scales are searched equally, which means that all local patterns/classes are treated equally. This does not account well for class imbalance. In the Gleason challenge, as in many medical image segmentation tasks, rare classes can be overlooked unless explicitly emphasised during

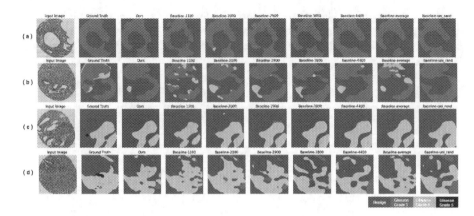

Fig. 5. Qualitative comparison of our method versus the seven baselines on four example validation images

training. Therefore a key focus for future is to add a weighting mechanism taking care imbalanced classes.

Acknowledgements. We sincerely acknowledge: Marnix Jansen for inspirational pathological advice. Hongxiang Lin for the insightful discussions. C.J., T.M. and D.A. acknowledge funding by the EPSRC grants EP/R006032/1, EP/M020533/1, the CRUK/EPSRC grant NS/A000069/1, and the NIHR UCLH Biomedical Research Centre.

References

1. Srinidhi, C.L., Ciga, O., Martel, A.L.: Deep neural network models for computational histopathology: asurvey. arXiv preprint arXiv:1912.12378 (2019)
2. Seth, N., Akbar, S., Nofech-Mozes, S., Salama, S., Martel, A.L.: Automated segmentation of DCIS in whole slide images. In: Reyes-Aldasoro, C.C., Janowczyk, A., Veta, M., Bankhead, P., Sirinukunwattana, K. (eds.) ECDP 2019. LNCS, vol. 11435, pp. 67–74. Springer, Cham (2019). https://doi.org/10.1007/978-3-030-23937-4_8
3. Kamnitsas, K., et al.: Efficient multi-scale 3D CNN with fully connected CRF for accurate brain lesion segmentation. Med. Image Anal. **36**, 61–78 (2017)
4. Chen, L.-C., Yang, Y., Wang, J., Xu, W., Yuille, A.L.: Attention to scale: scale-aware semantic image segmentation. In: Proceedings of the IEEE Conference on Computer Vision and Pattern Recognition, pp. 3640–3649 (2016)
5. Chen, W., Jiang, Z., Wang, Z., Cui, K., Qian, X.: Collaborative global-local networks for memory-efficient segmentation of ultra-high resolution images. In: Proceedings of the IEEE Conference on Computer Vision and Pattern Recognition, pp. 8924–8933 (2019)
6. Li, Y., Junmin, W., Qisong, W.: Classification of breast cancer histology images using multi-size and discriminative patches based on deep learning. IEEE Access **7**, 21400–21408 (2019)

7. Katharopoulos, A., Fleuret, F.: Processing megapixel images with deep attention-sampling models. arXiv preprint arXiv:1905.03711 (2019)
8. Warfield, S.K., Zou, K.H., Wells, W.M.: Simultaneous truth and performance level estimation (staple): an algorithm for the validation of image segmentation. IEEE Trans. Med. Imaging **23**(7), 903–921 (2004)
9. Ilse, M., Tomczak, J.M., Welling, M.: Attention-based deep multiple instance learning. arXiv preprint arXiv:1802.04712 (2018)
10. Xu, K., et al.: Show, attend and tell: Neural image caption generation with visual attention. In: International Conference on Machine Learning, pp. 2048–2057 (2015)
11. Kingma, D.P., Ba, J.: Adam: a method for stochastic optimization. arXiv preprint arXiv:1412.6980 (2014)
12. He, K., Zhang, X., Ren, S., Sun, J.: Delving deep into rectifiers: surpassing human-level performance on imagenet classification. In: Proceedings of the IEEE International Conference on Computer Vision, pp. 1026–1034 (2015)
13. Sun, K., et al.: High-resolution representations for labeling pixels and regions. arXiv preprint arXiv:1904.04514 (2019)

Multimodal Latent Semantic Alignment for Automated Prostate Tissue Classification and Retrieval

Juan S. Lara[1]([✉]), Victor H. Contreras O.[1], Sebastián Otálora[2],
Henning Müller[2], and Fabio A. González[1]

[1] Departamento de Ingeniería de Sistemas e Industrial, Universidad Nacional de
Colombia, Bogotá, Colombia
julara@unal.edu.co
[2] Institute of Information Systems, HES-SO, University of Applied Sciences
and Arts Western Switzerland, Sierre, Switzerland

Abstract. This paper presents an information fusion method for the automatic classification and retrieval of prostate histopathology whole-slide images (WSIs). The approach employs a weakly-supervised machine learning model that combines a bag-of-features representation, kernel methods, and deep learning. The primary purpose of the method is to incorporate text information during the model training to enrich the representation of the images. It automatically learns an alignment of the visual and textual space since each modality has different statistical properties. This alignment enriches the visual representation with complementary semantic information extracted from the text modality. The method was evaluated in both classification and retrieval tasks over a dataset of 235 prostate WSIs with their pathology report from the TCGA-PRAD dataset. The results show that the multimodal-enhanced model outperform unimodal models in both classification and retrieval. It outperforms state–of–the–art baselines by an improvement in WSI cancer detection of 4.74% achieving 77.01% in accuracy, and an improvement of 19.35% for the task of retrieving similar cases, obtaining 64.50% in mean average precision.

Keywords: Multimodal fusion · Histopathology images · Prostate cancer

1 Introduction

Prostate cancer (PCa) is the fourth most common cancer worldwide with 1.2 million new cases in 2018 and it has the second-highest incidence of all cancers in men [17]. Currently, the Gleason score (GS) is the standard grading system used to determine the aggressiveness of PCa and determine treatment. Typical scores range from 6 to 10 and cases with higher values are more likely to grow and spread fast [12]. The gold standard for the diagnosis of PCa is the inspection of biopsies

© Springer Nature Switzerland AG 2020
A. L. Martel et al. (Eds.): MICCAI 2020, LNCS 12265, pp. 572–581, 2020.
https://doi.org/10.1007/978-3-030-59722-1_55

or tissue samples. Thanks to the recent improvements in digital microscopy, the diagnosis is increasingly made through the visual inspection of high-resolution scans of a tissue sample or a Whole-Slide Image (WSI) [2]. Digital pathology is focused on the management of this kind of data. Collections of WSIs and related information like pathology reports can be accessed and stored using Picture Archiving and Communication Systems (PACS). This preserves the data in the long term providing a valuable clinical information source. Computer-Assisted Diagnosis (CAD) is one the most studied tasks in digital pathology. It generally covers tasks such as the automatic classification or grading of a disease, segmentation of regions of interest, mitosis and necrosis detection, image retrieval, among others [9].

Databases of medical images usually contain additional text data that is often not used by CAD systems [8]. There are diagnostic reports, clinical and related metadata that can be used to improve the performance of current CAD systems. Text usually contains semantic content that complements the information in the images. However, a current challenge is related to the appropriate combination of the image and the text information, specially, considering that these modalities originate from different sources and therefore have different statistical properties [1]. Multimodal fusion is an approach that aims to combine the information from different modalities or information sources. Its application in the medical domain is an active research area [3,10] and it has not been fully explored for the analysis of multimodal prostate histopathology data. Related studies show that an appropriate combination of the image and text modalities provides a better overall performance in comparison with single modal approaches. For instance, Jimenez-del-Toro et al. [8] proposed a multimodal retrieval method that combines deep learning with rank fusion, their results show that multimodal queries outperform both image and text in the retrieval of prostate tissue cases. In the same manner, Contreras et al. [6] proposed a method that combines the data in an early representation level besides the rank fusion, showing that there is joint information that can be exploited at different fusion levels.

One of the main disadvantages of these methods is that they are unfeasible in certain scenarios where a pathologist may only have an image, because, these approaches also require multimodal inputs during the prediction or retrieval of new cases. This motivates a fusion strategy that enhances the independent representations of each modality instead of enhancing a joint and combined representation. In this regard, some strategies have been proposed for the analysis of histopathology data: Caicedo et al. [2] proposed a non-negative matrix factorization method for the multimodal indexing of multiple organ tissues, it aims to induct a shared latent space for all modalities through an iterative optimization process that independently reconstructs a modality in each step. Cheerla et al. [5] proposed an unsupervised deep multimodal representation for pancancer prognosis prediction, it combines information from clinical data, genomics, microRNA and WSIs, using deep representation learning and a loss function based on siamese networks. These approaches show the feasibility of a new kind of weakly-supervised multimodal fusion that can be used to enrich the representation of the histopathology images and can be explored in the analysis of PCa.

Besides the fusion strategy, a multimodal system requires an appropriate representation of the images. In this matter, deep learning has become the state of the art in many applications of computer vision, digital pathology and the automatic analysis of prostate tissue images. Specifically, models like the Convolutional Neural Networks (CNNs) can learn high-level representations from the raw images without requiring hand–crafted feature extraction and with minimal preprocessing. Since WSIs are large images, the CNNs are usually trained to identify patch-level patterns and the information is summarized for the global prediction through a majority vote, bag-of-features or ensembles [7,11,14]. There is evidence that CNN-based CAD systems are comparable to international pathology experts in prostate cancer detection and grading [14]. Nonetheless, the integration of semantic information in deep learning models for the automatic analysis of prostate images still remains a challenge.

This work addresses the problem of cancer detection and similar case retrieval using multimodal histopathology data from prostate WSIs and their diagnostic reports. To this end, we present Multimodal Latent Semantic Alignment (M-LSA), a model to simultaneously learn an embedded representation for the WSIs and their associated text content, it is trained using a weakly-supervised approach that uses text information to enhance the representation of the images. The method exploits the complementary information of visual and text modalities, which leads to a better classification and retrieval performance as shown by the experimental evaluation. The remainder of this document is organized as follows: Sect. 2 presents M-LSA, showing details about the information fusion

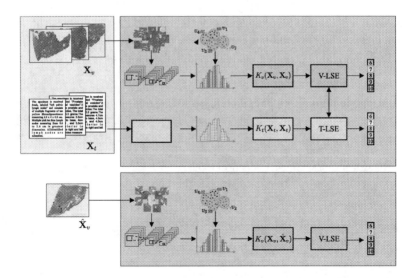

Fig. 1. Overview of the training and prediction phases of the proposed method for the automatic classification of prostate WSIs.

strategy and the representation techniques; Sect. 3 describes the experimental evaluation used to assess the effects of the weak semantic supervision in classification and retrieval tasks; Sect. 4 presents the experimental results and the analysis; Sect. 5 shows the conclusions.

2 Overview of Multimodal Latent Semantic Alignment

An overview of the method is shown in Fig. 1. During the training phase, the method incorporates weakly-supervised information from the diagnostic reports to enhance an embedded representation of the WSIs. This enhanced representation is used during the prediction phase to obtain a GS estimation using only the information from the images. The WSIs are represented using a Bag-of-Visual Words (BoVW) approach and the text content is represented using a Bag-of-Words (BoW). These representations are embedded and aligned using an information fusion strategy that is described in the following subsections.

2.1 Data Representation

As shown in Fig. 1, the training data are composed of pairs of annotated WSIs and their diagnostic reports. We represent these multimodal data as a term frequency – inverse document frequency (TF-IDF) matrix for each modality. In this way, the representation of the text content is straightforward. The text preprocessing consists of stop-word removal during the text vocabulary T construction. We use the TF-IDF weighting schema because it benefits the information fusion strategy providing numerical stability while increasing the importance of unique terms and attenuating the common ones.

For the images, a codebook or visual vocabulary V is constructed to represent a WSI as a Bag-of-Visual-Words (BoVW). The BoVW contains a distribution $P(V = v_i | \mathcal{I} = I_j)$ of certain visual words v_i in an image I_j. To compute this, 2000 non overlapping patches of size 256×256 are selected from each WSI using the blue ratio as filtering criteria (for obtaining mainly cancer areas that are most severe) [4] as it is done in [7]. Then, a feature representation of the patches is computed using the GoogLeNet CNN architecture that was pre-trained for the binary classification of the GS, we use this network because it has demonstrated to outperform other architectures in the automatic diagnostic of prostate tissues [7]. Each patch is described with the feature vector that outputs the last average pooling layer of GoogLeNet, which is commonly used for feature extraction. The codebook is constructed using K-means over the CNN descriptors. More precisely, a visual word is a cluster in the CNN representation space and a visual document is constructed by assigning each patch descriptor to their closest centroid. As shown in Fig. 1, this procedure allows to compute the BoVW by counting the number of patches in each cluster. In addition, TF-IDF is also used to weight the distribution of the visual words.

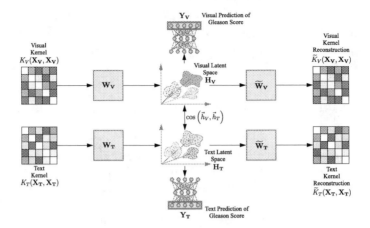

Fig. 2. Conceptual diagram of the multimodal information fusion strategy.

2.2   Information Fusion

An overall description of the information fusion strategy is shown in Fig. 2. This strategy uses a reformulation of kernel matrix factorization that allows to solve the problem through gradient-based optimization techniques as originally proposed in [15, 16]. The main idea of the strategy is to take advantage of the reformulation and include certain constraints that incorporate supervised and weakly-supervised semantic information. This can be seen as a extension of the original embedding learning problem, in which the goal is not only to find a low-dimensional latent space but to learn an aligned latent space for each modality that also contains information about the GS.

The information fusion strategy requires to compute two kernel matrices: on the one hand, a matrix $K_V(\mathbf{X_V}, \hat{\mathbf{X}}_\mathbf{V})$ is calculated applying a visual kernel function K_V on the TF-IDF representations $X_v \in \mathbb{R}^{N \times |V|}$ of the training WSIs (N is the number of observations and $|V|$ is the visual codebook size) and a matrix $\hat{\mathbf{X}}_\mathbf{V}$ that can be the visual training or the test TF-IDF representations. On the other hand, a matrix $K_T(\mathbf{X_T}, \hat{\mathbf{X}}_\mathbf{T})$ is calculated using the equivalent text matrices and functions. The main purpose of the kernel functions is to capture the complex nature of each modality to obtain a simpler representation, i.e., the data is transformed into a feature space where linear relations are more likely to be found. In this case, the feature spaces of each modality, $X_i \in \{V, T\}$, are mapped into a latent space $\mathbf{H_i}$ of dimension L, through a linear transformation $K_i(\mathbf{X_i}, \hat{\mathbf{X}}_\mathbf{i})\mathbf{W_i}$ that uses a weight matrix $\mathbf{W_i}$ that must be learned.

The complete loss function is presented in Eq. 1, it combines the three following errors: (1) each space is linearly projected using a weight matrix $\widetilde{\mathbf{W}}_\mathbf{i}$ to obtain a reconstruction of each kernel $\widetilde{K}_i(\mathbf{X_i}, \hat{\mathbf{X}}_\mathbf{i})$. This allows to estimate a reconstruction error $\overset{1}{\mathcal{J}}_i$, which is the mean squared error between the input and the output of each i modality and was derived using the kernel trick in [15]. This error is the basis of matrix factorization and is a non-supervised way to learn latent factors; (2) an artificial neural network (ANN) with a softmax activation output is used to obtain the predictions $\widetilde{\mathbf{Y}}_\mathbf{i}$ of the GS. These predictions are used to calculate the *categorical cross-entropy* $\overset{2}{\mathcal{J}}_i$, which is used as an estimate of how different the predictions to one-hot encodings are of the GS ground truth $\mathbf{Y}_\mathbf{i}$; (3) the cosine similarity $cos(\boldsymbol{h_1}, \boldsymbol{h_2})$ is computed between latent vectors of each modality $\boldsymbol{h_1} \in \mathbf{H_1}$ and $\boldsymbol{h_2} \in \mathbf{H_2}$. It measures the degree of alignment between the visual and text latent spaces, and allows to calculate an alignment error $\overset{3}{\mathcal{J}}$. The alignment term promotes the learning of close latent spaces, this allows the mutual enrichment of the visual and textual latent representations.

$$\overset{1}{\mathcal{J}}_i = \frac{1}{2} \sum_{\boldsymbol{x}_j \in \mathbf{X_i}} \left(1 - 2K(\boldsymbol{x}_j, \mathbf{X_i})\widetilde{K}_i(\boldsymbol{x}_j, \mathbf{X_i})^T + \widetilde{K}_i(\boldsymbol{x}_j, \mathbf{X_i})K(\mathbf{X_i}, \mathbf{X_i})\widetilde{K}_i(\boldsymbol{x}_j, \mathbf{X_i})^T\right)$$

$$\overset{2}{\mathcal{J}}_i = - \sum_{\boldsymbol{y}_j \in \mathbf{Y_i}, \tilde{\boldsymbol{y}}_j \in \widetilde{\mathbf{Y_i}}} \langle \boldsymbol{y}_j, \log \tilde{\boldsymbol{y}}_j \rangle \qquad \overset{3}{\mathcal{J}} = \frac{1}{2} \sum_{\boldsymbol{h_1} \in \mathbf{H_1}, \boldsymbol{h_2} \in \mathbf{H_2}} (\cos(\boldsymbol{h_1}, \boldsymbol{h_2}) - 1)^2$$

$$\mathcal{J} = \alpha_1 \overset{1}{\mathcal{J}}_V + \alpha_2 \overset{1}{\mathcal{J}}_T + \beta_1 \overset{2}{\mathcal{J}}_V + \beta_2 \overset{2}{\mathcal{J}}_T + \gamma \overset{3}{\mathcal{J}}$$

$$(1)$$

3   Experimental Settings

TCGA-PRAD Dataset: The dataset is comprised of images and diagnostic reports from prostate cancer tissue with Gleason scores between 6 and 10. The data are available via The Cancer Genome Atlas (TCGA), which is a publicly available large collection of digital pathology and other data that contains a set of 500 cases of prostate adenocarcinoma (PRAD). We use a subset with 235 cases as suggested in our baseline [7,8]. The dataset was divided into the same baseline partitions for cross-validation: 141 cases for training, 48 for validation and 46 for testing.

Cancer Detection Performance: The proposed method is evaluated on the automatic classification of low (GS 6 and 7) and high (GS 8, 9 and 10) grades, as this stratification changes the treatment decision. Our aim is to evaluate the effects of the semantic enhancement. For this reason, two versions of the proposed model are trained: (1) A visual latent semantic embedding *V-LSE*, which is a version of the proposed model that does not include the alignment, i.e., it is a model that is only trained using the WSIs. (2) *M-LSA*, which is a V-LSE model that is enhanced using the semantic information of the reports during training and is evaluated as shown in Fig. 1. In this case we evaluate the performance in terms of classification accuracy, that is the metric used in similar studies [7,11].

Image Retrieval Performance: In this case, the models are trained to classify the five different categories of GS and the softmax outputs are used as an indexer.

A single experiment consists of a simulated query, i.e., an example image is taken from the test set and the softmax outputs are calculated. Finally, these outputs are compared to the training set and using the cosine similarity with all the test cases a ranking is constructed. Similar to our baseline studies [6,8], a case is relevant to the query if they share the same GS. The performance in this case is evaluated in terms of Mean Average Precision (MAP), GM-MAP, and precision at top 10 (P@10) and 30 (P@30) retrieved results.

Hyperparameter Selection: The validation set is used to determine an appropriate combination of hyperparameters. We use a random search due to the large number of combinations. The model's weights are estimated through the Adam optimization algorithm ($lr = 10^{-3}, \beta_1 = 10^{-1}, \beta_1 = 10^{-2}$) using the training set and a combination of hyperparameters is selected using the validation loss as criteria. The loss parameters are configured as follows: $\beta_1 = \beta_2 = 5$, $\alpha_1 = \alpha_2 = \gamma = 1$; the visual codebook size $|V|$ is explored in a range between 100 and 1000; the latent dimension L is explored between 10 and 100; the activation functions of the ANNs are explored between relu, sigmoid and linear; the ANNs have two hidden layers and the number of units in each layer is explored in a range between 16 and 256; a dropout probability of 0.2 is added to the ANN weights for regularization; finally, some common kernels for histogram-based representations such as the linear, cosine, χ^2 and RBF are evaluated. The last two kernels have an additional hyper-parameter γ that must be determined, the range of the visual χ^2 kernel is $\gamma_V \in [10^{-3}, 10]$, the range for the text χ^2 kernel is $\gamma_T \in [10^{-4}, 10^{-1}]$, the range for the visual RBF kernel is $\gamma_V \in [10^{-2}, 100]$ and the range for the text RBF kernel is $\gamma_T \in [10^{-3}, 10]$. There are a total of 16 possible kernel combinations, for each one 100 random combinations of hyper-parameters are used. The generated parameters for the visual modality are also used to train the V-LSE.

4   Results and Analysis

Table 1 presents the results for cancer detection. The proposed method is compared with similar studies that use comparable evaluation strategies on the same dataset. In the first baseline study [7] a GoogLeNet is used to represent the patches and to summarize the information through a majority vote. V-LSE is able to achieve an equivalent performance. This behaviour is reasonable considering that we are using the same CNN for the representation and a unimodal model should achieve a similar performance. The second baseline study [13] presents a modified AlexNet architecture and summarizes using a majority vote. The authors specify that they included more training data. Thus, an important advantage of M-LSA is that it achieves a similar performance including text content instead of more training data. This means it can obtain better performance when limited training data are available. In addition, the weak supervision allows to find a better visual latent representation through the automatic incorporation of text content. There is no need to assign additional local labels to model a visual vocabulary as it is usually done in similar approaches.

Table 1. Comparison with state-of-the art methods in cancer detection.

Method	Accuracy
GoogLeNet [7]	73.52
Modified AlexNet [13]	76.90
V-LSE	74.02
M-LSA	**77.01**

The weak supervision allows to find a more appropriate feature space that may not be found using the image content only, the results show that M-LSA outperforms V-LSE in cancer detection, achieving the best performance using a RBF kernel for both modalities, whereas V-LSE achieves it using a linear kernel. Likewise, compared to the linear alignment case of M-LSA, the RBF kernel achieves an accuracy improvement of 2.25%, which shows the advantage of a non-linear alignment, specially, the importance of the kernel functions lies in their capacity to transform the representations to a feature space in which it is more likely to align the embeddings from different modalities. This is important considering that the representations learnt in a deep neural network may not share linear relations with other modalities, thus, the kernel methods are valuable to model the complex nature of multimodal data.

The retrieval results are shown in Table 2, presenting a comparison with the state-of-the-art retrieval methods that have been used to search PCa cases on the same dataset. It can be noticed that the semantic enhanced M-LSA model outperforms other image retrieval approaches. It is important to highlight that M-LSA only uses an image as query, whereas other multimodal retrieval approaches require a multimodal query during the testing phase, which may not be suitable in realistic environments with new and uncertain cases where pathologists may not have a diagnosis report.

Table 2. Results for the retrieval task, * denotes cases with multimodal queries.

Method	MAP	GM-MAP	P@10	P@30
Image Retrieval [8]	0.5113	0.3921	0.4500	0.4600
Text Retrieval [8]	0.4092	0.3561	0.4913	0.3775
Multimodal Retrieval* [8]	0.5404	0.4196	0.5217	0.4884
KLSE* [6]	0.6263	**0.4843**	0.5667	**0.6326**
Visual TF-IDF	0.4390	0.3486	0.3717	0.3667
Text TF-IDF	0.3574	0.3143	0.3848	0.3377
V-LSE	0.5881	0.3966	0.5000	0.4949
M-LSA	**0.6450**	0.4187	**0.5752**	0.5500

The proposed methodology represents an important opportunity for clinical translation, in fact, a CAD system can include M-LSA to provide a second opinion or retrieve similar cases. Contrary to other multimodal approaches, it does not require the text information during the prediction phase, which is important during uncertain diagnostics where the findings may not be clear and the annotations may be erroneous or cognitively biased.

5   Concluding Remarks

We present a novel information fusion strategy for improving image representations using weak semantic supervision from diagnostic reports. The method uses the text information of diagnostic reports attached to histopathology cases as a source of weak supervision during training. During prediction it only uses visual information, same as unimodal visual methods, however the experimental results showed that the use of multimodal information during training greatly improves the performance when compared to unimodal approaches. The proposed methodology shows that it is possible to exploit the multimodal information in medical databases that currently is not being fully exploited, considering a realistic environment in which pathologists may only have a WSI as input query.

Acknowledgments. This work was supported by COLCIENCIAS with the research project "Detección Temprana de daño ocular en Diabéticos usando un sistema de Inteligencia Artificial en Imágenes de Fondo de Ojo" number 1101-807-63563 and the Universidad Nacional de Colombia with the 2017–2018 national call for the project "Clasificación de retinopatía diabética y edema macular diabético en imágenes de fondo de ojo mediante redes neuronales convolucionales" number 202010029118. Sebastián Otálora has received funding from the European Union's Horizon 2020 research and innovation programme under grant agreement No 825292 (ExaMode, http://www.examode.eu/) and from Minciencias through the call 756 for PhD studies.

References

1. Arevalo, J., et al.: Gated multimodal networks. Neural Comput. Appl. **1**, 10209–10228 (2020)
2. Caicedo, J.C., Vanegas, J.A., Páez, F., González, F.A.: Histology image search using multimodal fusion. J. Biomed. Inform. **51**, 114–128 (2014)
3. Cao, Y., Steffey, S., Jianbiao, H., Xiao, D., Tao, C., Chen, P., Müller, H.: Medical image retrieval: a multimodal approach. Cancer Inform. **13**, 125–136 (2014)
4. Chang, H., Loss, L., Parvin, B.: Nuclear segmentation in H&E sections via multi-reference graph cut (MRGC). In: International Symposium on Biomedical Imaging (ISBI), pp. 1–4 (2012)
5. Cheerla, A., Gevaert, O.: Deep learning with multimodal representation for pan-cancer prognosis prediction. Bioinformatics **35**(14), i446–i454 (2019)
6. Contreras, V., et al.: Supervised online matrix factorization for histopathological multimodal retrieval. In: International Symposium on Medical Information Processing and Analysis, vol. 10975, pp. 1–8 (2018)

7. Jiménez del Toro, O., et al.: Convolutional neural networks for an automatic classification of prostate tissue slides with high-grade Gleason score. In: SPIE Medical Imaging, pp. 1–9 (2017)
8. Jimenez-del-Toro, O., Otálora, S., Atzori, M., Müller, H.: Deep multimodal case–based retrieval for large histopathology datasets. In: Wu, G., Munsell, B.C., Zhan, Y., Bai, W., Sanroma, G., Coupé, P. (eds.) Patch-MI 2017. LNCS, vol. 10530, pp. 149–157. Springer, Cham (2017). https://doi.org/10.1007/978-3-319-67434-6_17
9. Komura, D., Ishikawa, S.: Machine learning methods for histopathological image analysis. Comput. Struct. Biotechnol. J. **16**, 34–42 (2018)
10. Mourão, A., Martins, F., Magalhães, J.: Multimodal medical information retrieval with unsupervised rank fusion. Comput. Med. Imaging Graph. **39**, 35–45 (2015)
11. Nagpal, K., et al.: Development and validation of a deep learning algorithm for improving Gleason scoring of prostate cancer. NPJ Digital Med. **2**(1), 1–10 (2019)
12. PCEC: Gleason Score, Prostate Cancer Grading & Prognostic Scoring (2020). https://www.prostateconditions.org/about-prostate-conditions/prostate-cancer/newly-diagnosed/gleason-score
13. Ren, J., Hacihaliloglu, I., Singer, E.A., Foran, D.J., Qi, X.: Unsupervised domain adaptation for classification of histopathology whole-slide images. Front. Bioeng. Biotechnol. **7**, 102 (2019)
14. Ström, P., et al.: Artificial intelligence for diagnosis and grading of prostate cancer in biopsies: a population-based, diagnostic study. Lancet Oncol. **2045**(19), 1–11 (2020)
15. Vanegas, J.A.: Large-scale Non-linear Multimodal Semantic Embedding. Doctoral thesis, Universidad Nacional de Colombia (2017)
16. Vanegas, J.A., Escalante, H.J., González, F.A.: Semi-supervised online kernel semantic embedding for multi-label annotation. In: Mendoza, M., Velastín, S. (eds.) CIARP 2017. LNCS, vol. 10657, pp. 693–701. Springer, Cham (2018). https://doi.org/10.1007/978-3-319-75193-1_83
17. WCRF: Worldwide cancer data. Global cancer statistics for the most common cancers (2018). https://www.wcrf.org/dietandcancer/cancer-trends/worldwide-cancer-data

Opthalmology

GREEN: a Graph REsidual rE-ranking Network for Grading Diabetic Retinopathy

Shaoteng Liu[1,2], Lijun Gong[1(✉)], Kai Ma[1], and Yefeng Zheng[1]

[1] Tencent Jarvis Lab, Shenzhen, China
lijungong@tencent.com
[2] Northwestern Polytechnical University, Xian, China

Abstract. The automatic grading of diabetic retinopathy (DR) facilitates medical diagnosis for both patients and physicians. Existing researches formulate DR grading as an image classification problem. As the stages/categories of DR correlate with each other, the relationship between different classes cannot be explicitly described via a one-hot label because it is empirically estimated by different physicians with different outcomes. This class correlation limits existing networks to achieve effective classification. In this paper, we propose a Graph REsidual rE-ranking Network (GREEN) to introduce a class dependency prior into the original image classification network. The class dependency prior is represented by a graph convolutional network with an adjacency matrix. This prior augments image classification pipeline by re-ranking classification results in a residual aggregation manner. Experiments on the standard benchmarks have shown that GREEN performs favorably against state-of-the-art approaches.

Keywords: Diabetic retinopathy grading · Graph convolutional network

1 Introduction

Diabetic retinopathy (DR) is a common chronic disease leading to visual loss and blindness [6]. According to the severity of retinopathy lesion, DR is normally graded into five stages.[1] Medical treatments for DR varies according to different DR grades [5]. In practice, DR grading is an empirical process executed

---

This work was done when S. Liu was an intern in Tencent Jarvis Lab.

[1] The five stages are defined as none, mild, moderate, severe and proliferative stages according to the International Clinical Diabetic Retinopathy scale [3].

Electronic supplementary material The online version of this chapter (https://doi.org/10.1007/978-3-030-59722-1_56) contains supplementary material, which is available to authorized users.

© Springer Nature Switzerland AG 2020
A. L. Martel et al. (Eds.): MICCAI 2020, LNCS 12265, pp. 585–594, 2020.
https://doi.org/10.1007/978-3-030-59722-1_56

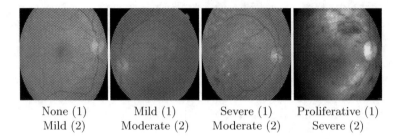

| None (1) | Mild (1) | Severe (1) | Proliferative (1) |
| Mild (2) | Moderate (2) | Moderate (2) | Severe (2) |

Fig. 1. Inconsistent labels from two physicians (i.e., 1 and 2) for the same DR fundus images. Class correlation causes this inconsistency and could limit the network classification accuracy.

by physicians, which requires sufficient expertise and time-consuming identifications. Therefore, there is a need to develop automatic DR grading systems to benefit both patients and physicians for efficient diagnosis.

The convolutional neural networks (CNNs) have improved the grading performance of DR [8]. Existing methods [8,11,12] formulate the DR grading as an image classification task where each predefined category represents one stage of DR. Li et al. [11] proposed two attention modules (i.e., disease specific and disease dependent models) which were integrated into the CNN to automatically grade DR. A number of randomly augmented images were generated in [12] for each sample and the CNN predictions of generated images were fused for final diagnosis. CNN predictions of fundus images captured from paired eyes (i.e., the corresponding left and right eyes) could be fused together for final predictions as well. These DR grading systems typically use off-the-shelf CNNs (i.e., VGG [13] and ResNet [9]) which are designed for natural image classifications where the categories of natural images (i.e., ImageNet [7]) usually do not correlate with each other. Differently, fundus images of DR dataset are visually similar. Besides, one stage/category of DR correlates with others, which brings difficulty for physicians to produce one-hot labels.[2] Figure 1 shows four examples of DR which were labeled differently by two physicians. Moreover, a physician may label the same fundus image differently at different time. When using the challenging training data to learn a classification network, we observe that the inter-class correlation is not effectively modeled and the classification performance is limited.

Soft labels are intuitively considered to model inter-class correlations. Bagherinezhad et al. [4] proposed a label refinery approach to iteratively update ground truth labels during the training process. A label embedding network was designed in [14] to learn soft distributions of network predictions. To the best of our knowledge, all existing methods tend to dynamically transform the one-hot label into a discrete probability distribution during the training process, and taking advantage of the inter-class correlation information, while leaving the

---

[2] In each one-hot label, there is only one element whose value is 1 while the remaining elements are all 0.

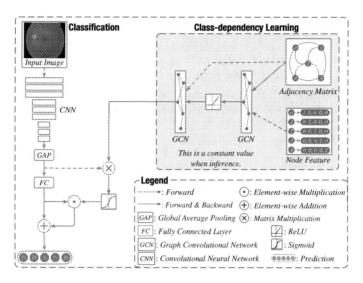

Fig. 2. Overview of the proposed framework. Besides the image classification network which consists of a feature backbone and a classifier, we propose a class-dependency module to model class correlation. The proposed module benefits image classification via residual aggregation to re-rank network prediction results.

structure of the classification network fixed. However, the inter-class correlation is implicitly modeled within the classification network, which may hamper the network's convergence or bring limited improvement as shown in Table 1.

In this paper, we propose a Graph REsidual rE-ranking Network (GREEN) to explicitly model the class correlation for significant DR grading improvement. GREEN consists of a standard image classification network and an extra class-dependency module. In this class-dependency module, we use a Graph Convolutional Network (GCN) [10] to integrate the class-dependency prior into the classification network. The graph structure formulates each class as one node and models the relationship between different nodes via an adjacency matrix. The adjacency matrix is learned to represent the dependencies of different classes in the CNN feature space. The class-dependency module is trained end-to-end together with the image classification network. The output of this module is kept fixed during inference and re-ranks classification results via residual aggregation. To this end, the class-dependency is learned offline and functions as a constant prior when we classify DR images. Experiments demonstrate that the proposed method improves original classification accuracy and performs favorably against state-of-the-art approaches.

2   Proposed Method

We illustrate the proposed Graph REsidual rE-ranking Network (GREEN) in Fig. 2 as an overview. The input of GREEN is a fundus image and the output is the corresponding grade of DR. The image classification network follows existing structures [9,15] which includes a feature extraction backbone and a classifier. On the other hand, the class-dependency module formulates class dependency as prior information to re-rank classification results via residual aggregation. In the following, we first show how the class-dependency module improves network prediction via residual re-ranking. Then, we illustrate the details of the proposed module including architectures and training details.

2.1   Image Classification with Residual Re-ranking

The training data with label uncertainty diminishes CNNs' discriminative capability when grading DR. To mitigate this effect, we propose a class-dependency module to reweigh network predictions. The proposed module is learned offline and kept fixed during online inference. It provides constant values to fuse with input CNN features for classification re-ranking. We illustrate the original image classification network in the following and show how the proposed module re-ranks in details.

Image Classification. A typical image classification network consists of a feature extraction backbone and a classifier. After extracting the CNN feature maps of an input fundus image, we apply a global average pooling (GAP) layer to the extracted feature maps and pass the output to the classifier (i.e., fully connected layers). The advantage of using GAP is that it effectively maps an input vector with arbitrary dimension to a fixed one. As such, we do not need to resize input images to a fixed resolution (e.g., 256×256), which is often a required preprocessing step of natural images. This benefits the severity estimation process which is akin to fine-grained image classification where the input fundus images are similar to each other. We keep the input images in high resolution to avoid potential detail missing to reduce misclassification.

Residual Re-ranking. For an input fundus image I, the output of GAP is a vector with fixed dimension d. We denote this vector as $G \in \mathbb{R}^{1 \times d}$. The class-dependency module produces a learned matrix $C \in \mathbb{R}^{n \times d}$ where n is the number of output categories. We generate the instance re-ranking weight by fusing these two inputs. The fusion process is a matrix multiplication operation followed by a sigmoid activation, which can be written as:

$$R_{\mathrm{I}} = \sigma \left(G \times C^T \right) \tag{1}$$

where C^T is the transpose matrix of C, σ is the sigmoid function and R_{I} is the instance re-ranking weight. This operation projects G into C along the direction of each output category, and measures the corresponding correlation values. After computing R_I, we re-rank the classification results via residual aggregation as follows:

$$P_I = \text{Softmax} \left(R_I \odot S_I + S_I \right) \tag{2}$$

where P_I is the probability of output classes, S_I is the class prediction score from the fully connected (FC) layer and $\odot$ is the element-wise multiplication operation. Along with the original prediction S_I from the FC output, we set the re-rank weights on it to adjust the prediction scores. The $R_I \odot S_I$ term functions as an auxiliary prediction from the perspective of class-dependency prior on the current input.

2.2   Graph Convolutional Network

The proposed class-dependency module consists of a graph convolutional network (GCN). GCN is introduced in [10] to perform semi-supervised classification, where the output of GCN is the probability of each class. Differently, we offline train the GCN to predict a constant class dependency prior to fuse with CNN features for final predictions.

The graph structure formulates each class as one node and constructs the relationship between different nodes via an adjacency matrix. As shown in Fig. 2, the adjacency matrix, together with node feature, is the input of GCN. The output is a learned projection matrix that contains the representation of each class in the CNN feature space. The dimension of this feature space is same as that of GAP output. For each input image, the corresponding feature representation after GAP output is multiplied with the projection matrix. The multiplication results indicate the correlation values between input features and each class.

Following [10], the GCN adopted in the proposed module consists of two matrix multiplication layers with a ReLU activation function. We denote the adjacency matrix as A, node features as X, and the weight of the first layer as W_1. The output of the first layer can be written as:

$$\mathcal{C}_1(A, X, W_1) = A \times X \times W_1 \tag{3}$$

where each row of $A \in \mathbb{R}^{n \times n}$ is initialized following the Gaussian distribution with the peak set on the diagonal position, $X \in \mathbb{R}^{n \times n}$ is an identical matrix and represents there are n nodes in the graph. $W_1 \in \mathbb{R}^{n \times h}$ maps dimension from n to h (the hidden layer). We send $\mathcal{C}_1(A, X, W_1)$ to the remaining GCN structures and obtain the output as:

$$C = A \times \text{ReLU} \left(\mathcal{C}_1 \right) \times W_2 \tag{4}$$

where $C \in \mathbb{R}^{n \times d}$ is the prior knowledge of the class dependency and $W_2 \in \mathbb{R}^{h \times d}$ maps dimension from the hidden layer to output class. Thus, we can learn the complex inter-class correlations by stacking two GCN layers. We refer interested readers to [10] for more details. During the training stage, we fuse C with G via Eq. (1) for forward computation. The gradients via back propagation are passed into both GCN and image classification network. When learning GCN, we update both adjacent matrix A and GCN parameters (i.e., W_1 and W_2) as they constitute the class-dependency prior. This class-dependency module is trained end-to-end together with the image classification network and the output is kept fixed as a constant prior during inference.

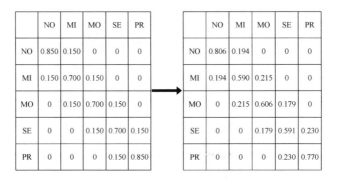

	NO	MI	MO	SE	PR
NO	0.850	0.150	0	0	0
MI	0.150	0.700	0.150	0	0
MO	0	0.150	0.700	0.150	0
SE	0	0	0.150	0.700	0.150
PR	0	0	0	0.150	0.850

	NO	MI	MO	SE	PR
NO	0.806	0.194	0	0	0
MI	0.194	0.590	0.215	0	0
MO	0	0.215	0.606	0.179	0
SE	0	0	0.179	0.591	0.230
PR	0	0	0	0.230	0.770

Fig. 3. Variations of elements in adjacency matrix before and after training. The abbreviation NO, MI, MO, SE and PR indicate corresponding five stages of DR. The learned matrix is fixed during testing to consistently provide class dependency priors for DR grading.

Adjacency Matrix Visualization. Figure 3 shows the adjacency matrix representing class-dependency. The matrix shown on the left is the initial matrix where the abbreviation NO, MI, MO, SE and PR correspond to none, mild, moderate, severe and proliferative stages respectively. The elements along the diagonal are initialized with large values while their neighbors are set to relatively small values. The values of neighboring elements indicate the class dependency between different categories. After training, we observe that in the matrix shown on the right part of Fig. 3, the values with distant categories are 0 (e.g., the adjacent value between NO and MO, or MI and PR). This shows that there exists a clear boundary between distant categories. Furthermore, the adjacent values between MI and MO, SE and PR are higher than others. It complies with the empirical observation from clinicians that the boundary of mild and moderate stages is not obvious, so as the severe and proliferative stages.

3   Experiments

In this section, we evaluate the proposed method on two DR benchmark datasets: Diabetic Retinopathy Detection (DRD) [1] and APTOS 2019 Blindness Detection (APTOS2019) [2]. There are 35,126 and 3,662 fundus images in DRD and

APTOS2019, respectively. We split each dataset into five folds for cross validation and use weighted kappa, weighted accuracy, and weighted F1 score as evaluation metrics.

We use EfficientNet-b0 [15] as image classification baseline with ImageNet pretraining [7]. When training with fundus images, we utilize SGD as the optimizer and set the initial learning rate as $1e^{-3}$. The batch size is set as 128 and the training procedure ends at the 60th epoch. More results are provided in the supplementary file. We will make our implementation code available to the public.

3.1 Ablation Study

The contribution of GREEN is to use a class-dependency module for classification reweighing. In this ablation study, we show how this module improves baseline classification accuracies. Meanwhile, training with soft labels (i.e., LEN [14] and LRN [4]) and training with fixed adjacency matrix [10] are also employed with the baseline network for comparisons. The evaluations are conducted on both datasets.

Table 1 shows the experimental results on the DRD dataset with EfficientNet-b0 [15] as the backbone for experimental efficiency. Compared to the baseline performance, the soft label learning schemes (i.e., LEN and LRN) bring limited improvement under all metrics. On the other hand, training GREEN with a fixed adjacency matrix (as shown in the left part of Fig. 3) does not robustly outperform soft label learning schemes (e.g., 0.773 v.s. 0.776 of F1 score). Nevertheless, by training the proposed class-dependency module with the adjacency matrix end-to-end, we consistently improve the baseline and perform favorably against other learning configurations under all metrics. Similar performance on APTOS2019 dataset is shown in supplementary file where GREEN performs favorably against other configurations on baseline improvements.

Table 1. The ablation study with different training schemes on the DRD dataset. GREEN performs favorably against other methods on baseline improvements.

Method	Backbone	Evaluation Metrics		
		Kappa	Accuracy	F1 score
Base	EfficientNet-b0	0.583	0.803	0.754
Base + LRN [4]	EfficientNet-b0	0.619	0.810	0.776
Base + LEN [14]	EfficientNet-b0	0.623	0.808	0.764
Base + GREEN (fixed adjacency matrix)	EfficientNet-b0	0.683	0.811	0.773
Base + GREEN	EfficientNet-b0	**0.700**	**0.816**	**0.782**

3.2 Comparisons with State-of-the-Art Approaches

We also compare GREEN with state-of-the-art approaches including DLI [12] and CANet [11]. DLI fuses multiple sources (i.e., randomly augmentation images and paired eyes if possible) while CANet involves deep CNN attentions. For a fair comparison, we follow CANet to use ResNet-50 as the feature extraction backbone. Besides, we also validate the effectiveness of GREEN by using prevalent backbones (i.e., EfficientNet-b0 and Se-ResNeXt50).

Table 2 shows the results on the DRD dataset. GREEN consistently outperforms other methods under all the evaluation metrics by using ResNet-50. Furthermore, the results show the effectiveness of GREEN of EfficientNet-b0 and Se-ResNeXt50 backbones. In Table 3, the evaluation results are similar on the APTOS2019 dataset. With the same CNN backbone, GREEN performs favorably against DLI and CANet. By using other CNN backbones, GREEN is shown to be effective as well. The evaluations on these two datasets indicate that GREEN suits prevalent backbones for effective DR grading and performs favorably against existing methods.

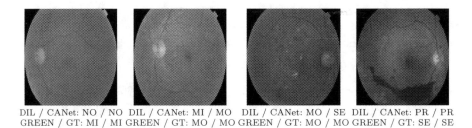

DIL / CANet: NO / NO DIL / CANet: MI / MO DIL / CANet: MO / SE DIL / CANet: PR / PR
GREEN / GT: MI / MI GREEN / GT: MO / MO GREEN / GT: MO / MO GREEN / GT: SE / SE

Fig. 4. Visual evaluations on the APTOS2019 dataset. GREEN is compared to DIL, CANet, and the ground truth (GT). The abbreviation NO, MI, MO, SE, PR correspond to the five DR stages illustrated in [3]. The results show GREEN is effective to perform DR grading.

Table 2. Comparison with state-of-the-art on the DRD [1] dataset.

Method	Backbone	Evaluation Metrics		
		Kappa	Accuracy	F1 score
DLI [12]	ResNet50	0.620	0.809	0.765
CANet [11]	ResNet50	0.649	0.816	0.774
GREEN	ResNet50	0.693	0.820	0.780
GREEN	EfficientNet-b0	0.700	0.816	0.782
GREEN	Se-ResNeXt50	**0.727**	**0.826**	**0.790**

Table 3. Comparison with state-of-the-art on the APTOS2019 [2] dataset.

Method	Backbone	Evaluation Metrics		
		Kappa	Accuracy	F1 score
DLI [12]	ResNet50	0.895	0.825	0.803
CANet [11]	ResNet50	0.900	0.832	0.813
GREEN	ResNet50	0.908	0.844	0.836
GREEN	EfficientNet-b0	0.910	0.848	0.835
GREEN	Se-ResNeXt50	**0.912**	**0.857**	**0.852**

Figure 4 shows the visual evaluation results. We compare GREEN with DIL and CANet on the APTOS2019 dataset. In general, DIL and CANet is not effective to accurately grade DR over all stages. This is due to a lack of class-dependency modeling during CNN classification. In comparison, by formulating class-dependency with GCN and integrating it into the CNN for end-to-end training, we achieve favorable results when grading DR of all the stages.

4   Concluding Remarks

In this work, we proposed to model class correlations for DR grading via a class-dependency formulation. In the proposed model, we integrated GCN into the original classification network and trained the whole network end-to-end. This model was kept fixed during online inference to consistently produce class dependency priors, which re-ranked the original classification results via residual aggregation. Experiments on the benchmark datasets showed the effectiveness of the proposed method by using prevalent CNN backbones. Meanwhile, the proposed method performed favorably against state-of-the-art approaches.

Acknowledgments. This work was funded by the Key Area Research and Development Program of Guangdong Province, China (No. 2018B010111001), National Key Research and Development Project (2018YFC2000702) and Science and Technology Program of Shenzhen, China (No. ZDSYS201802021814180).

References

1. Diabetic Retinopathy Detection (2016). https://www.kaggle.com/c/diabetic-retinopathy-detection/data
2. APTOS 2019 Blindness Detection (2019). https://www.kaggle.com/c/aptos2019-blindness-detection/data
3. Association, E.M., et al.: International clinical diabetic retinopathy disease severity scale, detailed table (2002). http://www.icoph.org/dynamic/attachments/resources/diabetic-retinopathy-detail.pdf
4. Bagherinezhad, H., Horton, M., Rastegari, M., Farhadi, A.: Label refinery: improving ImageNet classification through label progression. arXiv preprint arXiv:1805.02641 (2018)

5. Chakrabarti, R., Harper, C.A., Keeffe, J.E.: Diabetic retinopathy management guidelines. Expert Rev. Ophthalmol. **7**(5), 417–439 (2012)
6. Cho, N., et al.: IDF diabetes atlas: global estimates of diabetes prevalence for 2017 and projections for 2045. Diabetes Res. Clin. Pract. **138**, 271–281 (2018)
7. Deng, J., Dong, W., Socher, R., Li, L.J., Li, K., Fei-Fei, L.: ImageNet: a large-scale hierarchical image database. In: IEEE Conference on Computer Vision and Pattern Recognition, pp. 248–255. IEEE (2009)
8. Gulshan, V., Peng, L., Coram, M., Stumpe, M.C., Wu, D., Narayanaswamy, A., Venugopalan, S., Widner, K., Madams, T., Cuadros, J., et al.: Development and validation of a deep learning algorithm for detection of diabetic retinopathy in retinal fundus photographs. J. Am. Med. Assoc. **316**(22), 2402–2410 (2016)
9. He, K., Zhang, X., Ren, S., Sun, J.: Deep residual learning for image recognition. In: IEEE Conference on Computer Vision and Pattern Recognition, pp. 770–778 (2016)
10. Kipf, T.N., Welling, M.: Semi-supervised classification with graph convolutional networks. arXiv preprint arXiv:1609.02907 (2016)
11. Li, X., Hu, X., Yu, L., Zhu, L., Fu, C.W., Heng, P.A.: CANet: cross-disease attention network for joint diabetic retinopathy and diabetic macular edema grading. IEEE Trans. Med. Imaging **39**, 1483–1493 (2019)
12. Rakhlin, A.: Diabetic retinopathy detection through integration of deep learning classification framework, p. 225508. bioRxiv (2018)
13. Simonyan, K., Zisserman, A.: Very deep convolutional networks for large-scale image recognition. arXiv preprint arXiv:1409.1556 (2014)
14. Sun, X., Wei, B., Ren, X., Ma, S.: Label embedding network: learning label representation for soft training of deep networks. arXiv preprint arXiv:1710.10393 (2017)
15. Tan, M., Le, Q.V.: EfficientNet: Rethinking model scaling for convolutional neural networks. arXiv preprint arXiv:1905.11946 (2019)

Combining Fundus Images and Fluorescein Angiography for Artery/Vein Classification Using the Hierarchical Vessel Graph Network

Kyoung Jin Noh[1], Sang Jun Park[2], and Soochahn Lee[3(✉)]

[1] StradVision, Inc., Seoul, Korea
kyoungjin.noh@stradvision.com
[2] Department of Ophthalmology, Seoul National University College of Medicine,
Seoul National University Bundang Hospital, Seongnam, Korea
sangjunpark@snu.ac.kr
[3] School of Electrical Engineering, Kookmin University, Seoul, Korea
sclee@kookmin.ac.kr

Abstract. We present a new framework for retinal artery/vein classification from fundus images and corresponding fluorescein angiography (FA) images. While FA seem to provide the most relevant information, it is often insufficient depending on the acquisition conditions. As fundus images are often acquired by default, we combine the fundus image and FA within a parallel convolutional neural network to extract the maximum information in the generated features. Furthermore, we use these features as the input to a hierarchical graph neural network to ensure that the connectivity of vessels plays a part in the classification. We provide investigative evidence through ablative and comparative quantitative evaluations to better determine the optimal configuration in combining the fundus image and FA in a deep learning framework and demonstrate the enhancement in performance compared to previous methods.

Keywords: Fundus images · Fluorescein angiography · Artery/vein classification · Convolutional neural network · Graph neural network

1 Introduction

Close observation and assessment of retinal vessels are required to diagnose various retinal diseases. For degenerative diseases including diabetic retinopathy [3],

This work was supported by the National Research Foundation of Korea (NRF) grants funded by the Korean government (MSIT) (NRF-2018R1D1A1A09083241 and NRF-2020R1F1A1051847).

This work was done while K. Noh was with Seoul National University Bundang Hospital.

© Springer Nature Switzerland AG 2020
A. L. Martel et al. (Eds.): MICCAI 2020, LNCS 12265, pp. 595–605, 2020.
https://doi.org/10.1007/978-3-030-59722-1_57

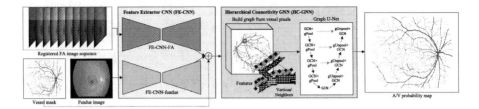

Fig. 1. Visual overview of the proposed method with integrated feature extractor CNN for combined fundus image and FA input (FE-CNN) and hierarchical connectivity GNN (HC-GNN).

cerebral disorders [9], and hypertension [18], there are differences in the alterations of arterial and venular structures. Thus accurate extraction and separation of arteries and veins from retinal imagery are of great clinical interest.

Many methods have been proposed for artery/vein (A/V) classification and segmentation based on fluorescein angiography (FA) and fundus images. FA provides the most relevant information to classify arteries and veins because they are highlighted separately at different time frames due to the flow of the fluorescent dye in the vessels. After early work using Bayesian analysis on pixel intensities [20], not many methods have been proposed for FA input. Rather, more focus has been on fundus images, which are much more easily achieved. Classification based on GMM color features [17] and texture features [24], graph based methods such as Dijkstra's search [10], graph cut on Markov random field [4], tree topology estimation [5], and dominant set clustering [26] have been proposed. Different variants of convolutional neural networks (CNN) [2,7,12,13, 23] have also been proposed.

While these works have advanced the technology, they are yet to be widely applied clinically. Further improvements must be made towards improving the performance and completeness of the assessed arteries and veins. While methods based on optical coherence tomography angiography (OCTA) are showing promise [1], its limited field of view is a major drawback.

Previous works has shown that the FA sequence and the fundus image can be combined to improve upon results based only on either modality for high quality vessel segmentation [14,15]. FA sequences can often have extremely low and irregular frame rates, making clear delineation of artery and vein very difficult. Fundus images serve as a good complement for FA because of their clarity and high resolution.

In this paper, we present an extension of the framework of [14,15] for A/V classification, where the synergy from combining both the FA image sequence and fundus image as input leads to significant improvements in the output. The proposed method comprises two main components, the feature extractor CNN (FE-CNN) for the fundus image and FA input and the hierarchical connectivity graph neural network (HC-GNN) for incorporating higher order connectivity into classification. For the FE-CNN, we empirically determine the optimal configuration, with the scale-space approximated CNN (SSANet) [16] as the backbone network. For the HC-GNN, we apply the graph U-net [6]. The proposed method, that we term the fundus-FA hierarchical vessel graph network (FFA-HVGN), is illustrated in Fig. 1.

There have been several works combining CNN and GNN [6,19,25]. In these methods, the nodes in the GNN were from sub-sampled pixel or voxel grids to reduce the size of the adjacency matrix. The GNN recursively learns the connectivity within this fixed node resolution using single-scale GNNs such as the graph convolution network (GCN) [11] or the graph attention network (GAT) [22]. In the proposed framework, hierarchical connectivity in multiple scales is learned through the node clustering by the node pooling layers in graph U-nets [6].

Our main contribution is the development of a highly accurate novel A/V classification framework. It combines fundus image and FA sequence as input, with a customized feature extraction CNN configuration. An integrated hierarchical GNN learns the high-level connectivity of vascular structures. We believe our method can be used to generate ground truth (GT) A/V masks with little manual editing. This can lead to a drastic increase in the training data for supervised learning of CNNs for fundus image inputs, thereby maximizing the potential of deep learning.

We present extensive quantitative evaluations to support the effectiveness of the proposed method. Ablative analysis on a private dataset comprising five hundred fundus image-FA pairs supports the combined use of FA and fundus images, the FE-CNN, and the HC-GNN all contribute to performance improvement. Comparative evaluations on the public RITE A/V label DB [8], based on DRIVE [21], demonstrate the performance improvement compared to previous methods.

2   Methods

2.1   Feature Extraction CNN for Fundus Image-FA Input

The proposed structure for the FE-CNN is illustrated in detail in Fig. 2. The main configurations pertain to i) preprocessing, ii) input of fundus images and FA, iii) backbone CNN structure, and iv) output features. Details are described below.

Pre-processing: Registration must be performed for combined analysis of the fundus image and the FA. Vessel segmentation must be performed either prior to A/V classification or concurrently, in order to generate artery and vein maps. As the results of vessel segmentation is one main criterion of registration, we perform both these tasks together, using the method by Noh et al. [14,15]. While concurrent multi-task segmentation methods such as the method by Ma et al. [12] might enhance accuracy for fundus image inputs, it is not suitable for combined fundus image and FA inputs because of the required registration.

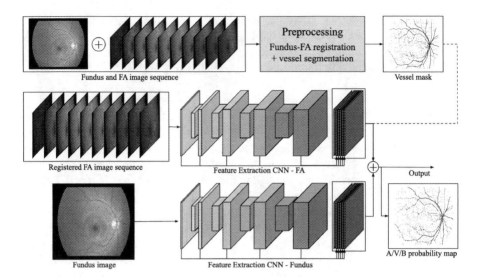

Fig. 2. Structural details of the parallel feature extraction CNN (FE-CNN) comprising the FE-CNN-fundus for fundus image input and the FE-CNN-FA for combined fundus image and FA input, with the SSANet [16] as the backbone CNN.

Input: There can be various ways to feed the combined input of fundus image and FA sequence into a CNN, including a) concatenation of FA frames and the fundus as image channels in the input (FE-CNN-Concat), b) cascade connection of two networks for FA and fundus image, respectively (FE-CNN-Cascade-FA-Fundus), c) cascade connection with reversed order (FE-CNN-Cascade-Fundus-FA), and d) parallel connection of two networks (FE-CNN-Parallel). Based on the experimental evaluations in Sect. 3.2, we empirically determine the optimal configuration as FE-CNN-Parallel. We note that this optimal configuration may vary depending on the vessel segmentation mask used within the framework, and that FE-CNN-Parallel was deemed optimal within this particular configuration using the vessel segmentation results of [14].

Backbone CNN: We use the SSANet [16] for the networks for fundus image (FE-CNN-Fundus) and FA (FE-CNN-FA) inputs, respectively. Particularly, we apply our implementation of the SSANet-3, with three scale space approximation layers. For the final layer of both FE-CNN-Fundus and FE-CNN-FA, the sigmoid layer is replaced with a softmax layer to handle three-class classification of artery, vein, and background.

Output: We concatenate the feature vectors of the FE-CNN-Fundus and the FE-CNN-FA to form the FE-CNN output. Both are 40-dimensional multi-scale feature vectors that are fed into the inference layers of respective SSANets. In order to extract graph nodes, the vessel segmentation mask is passed on together with these input features as the output.

2.2 Hierarchical Connectivity Graph Neural Network

GNNs are neural networks (NN) defined on graphs $\mathbb{G} = (V, E)$ comprising a set of vertices V and edges E, and can deal with input data with irregular structure. NN layers on the graph are stacked to learn hierarchical combinatorial relations. Similarly to CNNs, the extent to which these relations are learned depends on the receptive field of the GNN. More stacking will increase the receptive field.

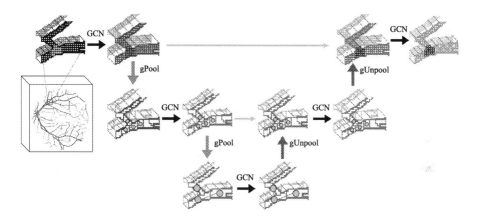

Fig. 3. A visual description of the hierarchical connectivity graph neural network (HC-GNN) based on graph U-nets [6].

But stacking layers also increases storage use. This is exacerbated in graphs because vertex neighborhoods must be defined individually. Storage requirement can become much higher than CNNs for same number of nodes, depending on the edge connectivities. Thus, a specialized scheme is necessary to increase the receptive field in GNNs. This is particularly crucial for the articulated structure of vessels, where pixels on a continuous vessel branch may have large geometric distance.

The graph pooling (gPool) and graph unpooling (gUnpool) operations defined within the graph U-nets [6] are quite suited to handle these problems. In gPool, a trainable projection vector $\mathbf{p}$ is defined to compute the retained information $\mathbf{y}$ from vertex features X as $\mathbf{y} = X\mathbf{p}/\|\mathbf{p}\|$. The $\mathbf{y}$ is a scalar for each vertex feature and can be sorted. For each pooling layer, the vertices with the k highest $\mathbf{y}$ values are sampled from the graph, similar to the max-pooling layer in CNNs. To ensure that information in the features of unsampled vertices is not lost, graph U-nets are structured so that features are aggregated by GCN layers [11] before gPool operations. The gUnpool operation is defined as the inverse of a gPool operation, which means the features of the sampled vertices are restored to the corresponding vertices is the graph prior to the gPool. Since the vertices that were not sampled in gPool would not have features to gUnpool, they are left with empty features. Again, GCN layers are placed after gUnpool, this time to generate interpolated features for these empty-feature vertices.

We apply graph U-nets to the output features of the FE-CNN as our HC-GNN. We gather pixel-wise features only for vessel regions, based on the vessel segmentation mask. All vessel pixels are defined as vertices with edges constructed with existing vessel pixels within an $\mathcal{N} \times \mathcal{N}$ local patch. gPool and gUnpool are both performed 4 times, respectively, so that the HC-GNN has a maximum depth of 4. A visual description of the HC-GNN is illustrated in Fig. 3 (with depth 3 rather than 4, due to restriction in space).

2.3   Training

Training the FFA-HVGN is done in three steps. First, the FE-CNN is trained with pixel-wise A/V classification cross entropy loss with the GT. Then, the HC-GNN is trained with its input as the output of FE-CNN fixed. Third and finally, both pre-trained networks are combined and fine-tuned in an end-to-end fashion. Below are details of each step.

For initial training of the FE-CNN, the loss function is defined as the sum of cross-entropy functions of the FE-CNN-Fundus and the FE-CNN-FA, both compared with the three class labels of artery, vein, and background of the GT, respectively. If the GT contains separate labels for vessel crossings, we omit those pixels when computing the loss. We use the ADAM optimizer with initial learning rate 0.0005, $\beta_1 = 0.5$, and $\beta_2 = 0.999$, with no scheduled learning rate decay. We perform a fixed number of 30,000 iterations. For initial training of the HC-GNN, all conditions are identical with the FE-CNN training, except that only two class labels for A/V of GT are considered since only vessel pixels are gathered, and with an initial learning rate of 0.001 which is decayed by one tenth every 10,000 iterations. For fine-tuning, the initial learning rate is set as $1e^{-6}$ with all else identical to HC-GNN training.

3   Experimental Results

3.1   Dataset and Experimental Environment

To the best of our knowledge, there are no public datasets with corresponding fundus images and FA. We thus construct a private dataset comprising 56 cases of FA and fundus image pairs from 51 patients. The training/test set was randomly split into 46 and 10 images, respectively. The training set and test set are split so that cases from the same patient are assigned as either training or test set, and not used in both sets. Fundus images and FA were acquired using Canon CF60Uvi, Kowa VX-10, and Kowa VX-10a cameras. FA frames with no visible dye were manually excluded. The FA channel number was set to the maximum number of frames, which was 20, and zero-padding was applied to FA sequences with frames fewer than that. Image resolutions originally varying from 1604×1216 to 2144×1424 were all normalized to 1536×1024. GT was constructed by manual expert annotation of A/V classes on vessel segmentation results constructed by the method of [14].

For comparative evaluation, we also use on the public RITE A/V label DB [8], for images of the DRIVE [21] DB. Because FA are unavailable, we remove the FE-CNN-FA and present results for the Fundus-HVGN – the HVGN with only fundus image input.

In all evaluations pixel-wise measurements are computed based on GT artery/vein pixels with arteries as positives and veins as negatives. Only pixels classified as vessel in the vessel mask are considered. Experiments were performed on a system with a 2.2 GHz Intel Xeon CPU and 4 nVidia Titan V GPUs. Training time was around 10, 18, and 33 h for the FE-CNN, HC-GNN, and fine-tuning, respectively. Inference time for the whole FFA-HVGN was on average 3.04 s for one image.

3.2   Results

We first present comparative and ablative results on our private DB in Table 1. Results for the various configurations of the FE-CNN are provided, as well as the results of FE-CNN with FA input only (FE-CNN-FA), FE-CNN with fundus image input only (FE-CNN-Fundus), and FE-CNN-Parallel combined with GCN rather than graph U-net (FE-CNN+GCN). For comparative evaluation, we provide results of our implementation of the multi-task method of Ma et al. [12], which takes only the fundus image as input, without their multi-channel input. These results demonstrate that each component of the proposed method actually helps to improve the performance.

Table 1. Quantitative results on our private DB. Results of our implementation of the multi-task method of Ma et al. [12] are provided for comparison. Sensitivity (Se), specificity (Sp), accuracy (Acc), and area-under-curve for the precision-recall curve (AUC-PR) and the receiver-operating-characteristic curve (AUC-ROC) are presented.

Method	Acc	Se	Sp	AUC-PR	AUC-ROC
Multi-task CNN on fundus only [12]	0.886	0.882	0.891	0.957	0.952
FE-CNN-FA-Only	0.908	0.918	0.894	0.979	0.972
FE-CNN-Fundus-Only	0.890	0.907	0.866	0.972	0.962
FE-CNN-Concat	0.895	0.914	0.870	0.974	0.965
FE-CNN-Cascade-FA-Fundus	0.926	0.922	0.931	0.982	0.975
FE-CNN-Cascade-Fundus-FA	0.894	0.911	0.871	0.974	0.963
FE-CNN-Parallel	0.931	0.943	0.916	0.986	0.982
FE-CNN+GCN, with fine-tuning	0.943	0.946	0.937	0.987	0.989
FFA-HVGN, no fine-tuning	0.942	0.953	0.945	0.987	0.989
FFA-HVGN (Proposed)	**0.944**	**0.957**	**0.950**	**0.989**	**0.990**

Next, we present comparative results on the public RITE A/V label DB [8] for images of the DRIVE [21] DB in Table 2, as a reference of the validity of our combined CNN-GNN approach. Because FA sequences are not provided in the DRIVE DB, we present results for Fundus-HVGN. We can see that our approach demonstrates comparable performance with the recent state-of-the-art.

Table 2. Quantitative results on RITE A/V label DB [8]. Sensitivity (Se), specificity (Sp), accuracy (Acc) are presented.

Method	Acc	Se	Sp
Multi-task CNN (as reported in [12])	0.9258	0.9218	0.9298
Fundus-HVGN	0.9264	0.9301	0.9219

Finally, Fig. 4 illustrates qualitative results of four sample cases from our private dataset. We can see that the combination of fundus images and FA, and the inclusion of the HC-GNN to form the FFA-HVGN, helps to generate more accurate classifications. Portions where the proposed method clearly improves upon results based only on the fundus image are highlighted by an arrow.

4   Discussion

We present a new method for A/V classification based on fundus images and FA sequences. We have observed that the accuracy of A/V classification from FA or fundus image alone is still often insufficient despite the great advances made in retinal segmentation and classification based on deep learning.

For future works, we plan to construct a new training dataset for A/V classification that can be used for supervised learning of retinal A/V vessel segmentation from fundus images. Our aim is to achieve datasets that are orders of magnitude larger than previous public datasets, which currently all have fewer than one hundred images.

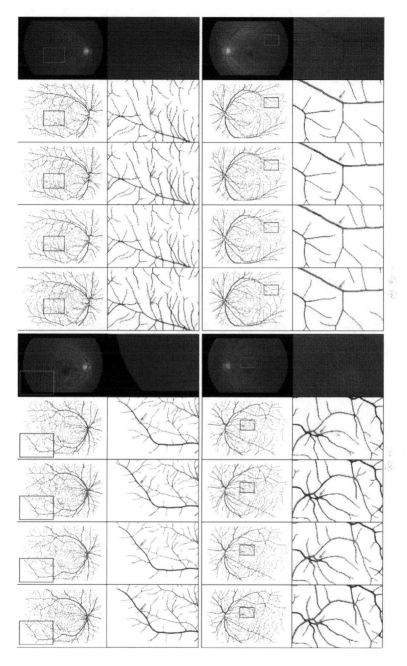

Fig. 4. Qualitative results. Four sample cases from our private DB are shown in 2 × 2 formation, with top to bottom rows illustrating (1) the original image, (2) GT, and results of (3) FE-CNN-Fundus (fundus image input only), (4) FE-CNN-Parallel (combined fundus-FA input), and (5) FFA-HVGN (proposed). Left and right columns show the images in full and zoomed resolution, respectively.

References

1. Alam, M., Toslak, D., Lim, J.I., Yao, X.: Color fundus image guided artery-vein differentiation in optical coherence tomography angiography. Invest. Ophthal. Vis. Sci. **59**(12), 4953–4962 (2018). https://doi.org/10.1167/iovs.18-24831
2. Badawi, S.A., Fraz, M.M.: Multiloss function based deep convolutional neural network for segmentation of retinal vasculature into arterioles and venules. BioMed Res. Int. **2019**, 1–17 (2019). https://doi.org/10.1155/2019/4747230
3. Cunha-Vaz, J.G.: Pathophysiology of diabetic retinopathy. Br. J. Ophthalmol. **62**(6), 351–355 (1978). https://doi.org/10.1136/bjo.62.6.351
4. Eppenhof, K., Bekkers, E., Berendschot, T.T., Pluim, J., ter Haar Romeny, B.: Retinal artery/vein classification via graph cut optimization. In: Proceedings of the Ophthalmic Medical Image Analysis Second International Workshop, OMIA 2015, Held in Conjunction with MICCAI 2015, pp. 121–128 (2015). https://doi.org/10.17077/omia.1035
5. Estrada, R., Allingham, M.J., Mettu, P.S., Cousins, S.W., Tomasi, C., Farsiu, S.: Retinal artery-vein classification via topology estimation. IEEE Trans. Med. Imaging **34**(12), 2518–2534 (2015). https://doi.org/10.1109/TMI.2015.2443117
6. Gao, H., Ji, S.: Graph u-nets. In: Chaudhuri, K., Salakhutdinov, R. (eds.) Proceedings of International Conference on Machine Learning (ICML). Proceedings of Machine Learning Research, Long Beach, California, USA, 09–15 June 2019, vol. 97, pp. 2083–2092. PMLR (2019). http://proceedings.mlr.press/v97/gao19a.html
7. Hemelings, R., Elen, B., Stalmans, I., Keer, K.V., Boever, P.D., Blaschko, M.B.: Artery-vein segmentation in fundus images using a fully convolutional network. Comput. Med. Imaging Graph. **76**, 101636 (2019). https://doi.org/10.1016/j.compmedimag.2019.05.004
8. Hu, Q., Abràmoff, M.D., Garvin, M.K.: Automated separation of binary overlapping trees in low-contrast color retinal images. In: Mori, K., Sakuma, I., Sato, Y., Barillot, C., Navab, N. (eds.) MICCAI 2013. LNCS, vol. 8150, pp. 436–443. Springer, Heidelberg (2013). https://doi.org/10.1007/978-3-642-40763-5_54
9. Ikram, M.K., et al.: Retinal vessel diameters and cerebral small vessel disease: the Rotterdam Scan Study. Brain **129**(1), 182–188 (2005). https://doi.org/10.1093/brain/awh688
10. Joshi, V.S., Reinhardt, J.M., Garvin, M.K., Abramoff, M.D.: Automated method for identification and artery-venous classification of vessel trees in retinal vessel networks. PLoS ONE **9**(2), 1–12 (2014). https://doi.org/10.1371/journal.pone.0088061
11. Kipf, T.N., Welling, M.: Semi-supervised classification with graph convolutional networks. In: Proceedings of International Conference on Learning Representations (ICLR) (2017)
12. Ma, W., Yu, S., Ma, K., Wang, J., Ding, X., Zheng, Y.: Multi-task neural networks with spatial activation for retinal vessel segmentation and artery/vein classification. In: Shen, D., et al. (eds.) MICCAI 2019. LNCS, vol. 11764, pp. 769–778. Springer, Cham (2019). https://doi.org/10.1007/978-3-030-32239-7_85
13. Meyer, M.I., Galdran, A., Costa, P., Mendonça, A.M., Campilho, A.: Deep convolutional artery/vein classification of retinal vessels. In: Campilho, A., Karray, F., ter Haar Romeny, B. (eds.) ICIAR 2018. LNCS, vol. 10882, pp. 622–630. Springer, Cham (2018). https://doi.org/10.1007/978-3-319-93000-8_71
14. Noh, K.J., Kim, J., Park, S.J., Lee, S.: Multimodal registration of fundus images with fluorescein angiography for fine-scale vessel segmentation. IEEE Access **8**, 63757–63769 (2020)

15. Noh, K.J., Park, S.J., Lee, S.: Fine-scale vessel extraction in fundus images by registration with fluorescein angiography. In: Shen, D., et al. (eds.) MICCAI 2019. LNCS, vol. 11764, pp. 779–787. Springer, Cham (2019). https://doi.org/10.1007/978-3-030-32239-7_86

16. Noh, K.J., Park, S.J., Lee, S.: Scale-space approximated convolutional neural networks for retinal vessel segmentation. Comput. Methods Programs Biomed. (2019). https://doi.org/10.1016/j.cmpb.2019.06.030

17. Relan, D., MacGillivray, T., Ballerini, L., Trucco, E.: Retinal vessel classification: sorting arteries and veins. In: Proceedings of 35th Annual International Conference of the IEEE Engineering in Medicine and Biology Society (EMBC), pp. 7396–7399 (2013). https://doi.org/10.1109/EMBC.2013.6611267

18. Ritt, M., Schmieder, R.E.: Wall-to-lumen ratio of retinal arterioles as a tool to assess vascular changes. Hypertension **54**(2), 384–387 (2009). https://doi.org/10.1161/HYPERTENSIONAHA.109.133025

19. Shin, S.Y., Lee, S., Yun, I.D., Lee, K.M.: Deep vessel segmentation by learning graphical connectivity. Med. Image Anal. **58**, 101556 (2019). https://doi.org/10.1016/j.media.2019.101556

20. Simó, A., de Ves, E.: Segmentation of macular fluorescein angiographies. A statistical approach. Pattern Recogn. **34**(4), 795–809 (2001). https://doi.org/10.1016/S0031-3203(00)00032-7

21. Staal, J., Abramoff, M.D., Niemeijer, M., Viergever, M.A., van Ginneken, B.: Ridge-based vessel segmentation in color images of the retina. IEEE Trans. Med. Imaging **23**(4), 501–509 (2004). https://doi.org/10.1109/TMI.2004.825627

22. Veličković, P., Cucurull, G., Casanova, A., Romero, A., Li, P., Bengio, Y.: Graph attention networks. In: Proceedings of International Conference on Learning Representations (ICLR) (2018). https://openreview.net/forum?id=rJXMpikCZ

23. Welikala, R., et al.: Automated arteriole and venule classification using deep learning for retinal images from the UK biobank cohort. Comput. Biol. Med. **90**, 23–32 (2017). https://doi.org/10.1016/j.compbiomed.2017.09.005

24. Xu, X., Ding, W., Abrmoff, M.D., Cao, R.: An improved arteriovenous classification method for the early diagnostics of various diseases in retinal image. Comput. Methods Programs Biomed. **141**, 3–9 (2017). https://doi.org/10.1016/j.cmpb.2017.01.007

25. Zhai, Z., et al.: Linking convolutional neural networks with graph convolutional networks: application in pulmonary artery-vein separation. In: Zhang, D., Zhou, L., Jie, B., Liu, M. (eds.) GLMI 2019. LNCS, vol. 11849, pp. 36–43. Springer, Cham (2019). https://doi.org/10.1007/978-3-030-35817-4_5

26. Zhao, Y., et al.: Retinal vascular network topology reconstruction and artery/vein classification via dominant set clustering. IEEE Trans. Med. Imaging **39**(2), 341–356 (2020). https://doi.org/10.1109/TMI.2019.2926492

Adaptive Dictionary Learning Based Multimodal Branch Retinal Vein Occlusion Fusion

Chen Huang[1], Keren Xie[2], Yuhan Zhang[1], Mingchao Li[1], Zhongmin Wang[2], and Qiang Chen[1(✉)]

[1] School of Computer Science and Engineering, Nanjing University of Science and Technology, Nanjing, China
chen2qiang@njust.edu.cn
[2] Department of Ophthalmology, The First Affiliated Hospital with Nanjing Medical University, Nanjing, China

Abstract. Multimodal imaging can provide complementary information for branch retinal vein occlusions (BRVO) visualization. We proposed an adaptive dictionary learning based multimodal BRVO fusion method for color fundus photography (CFP), Fluorescein angiography (FA) and optical coherence tomography angiography (OCTA) images. First, the contrast of lesion areas in CFP and FA images was enhanced by using a local contrast enhancement algorithm based on standard deviation, and meanwhile a Frangi filter based algorithm was adopted to enhance vessels in OCTA images. Then, the local energy and multi-scale spatial frequency of image patches were calculated as brightness and gradient features respectively. The K-singular value decomposition algorithm was performed to train and generate the brightness and gradient sub-dictionaries, which were merged together to obtain the final adaptive dictionary. Finally, the orthogonal matching pursuit algorithm was adopted to calculate the sparse representation coefficient, and the maximum absolute value fusion strategy was applied to combine multimodal information. Experimental results demonstrate that the proposed method is more effective for BRVO visualization than the single-modality image, because our method can combine complementary information from multimodal images. It is useful for the clinical evaluation of BRVO.

Keywords: Branch retinal vein occlusions · Image enhancement · Adaptive dictionary learning · Multimodal image fusion

1 Introduction

Retinal vein occlusion (RVO) is the second most common retinal vascular disease affecting retina and is an important cause of visual loss [1]. Retinal vein occlusions are divided into central (CRVO), hemi, and branch retinal vein occlusions (BRVO) [2]. Among RVOs, BRVO is considered to be the most common with an incidence of 0.5% to 1.2%. The visual acuity loss after BRVO commonly occurs due to macular edema, but may also

A. L. Martel et al. (Eds.): MICCAI 2020, LNCS 12265, pp. 606–615, 2020.
https://doi.org/10.1007/978-3-030-59722-1_58

result from macular ischemia or neovascular complications such as vitreous hemorrhage and neovascular glaucoma [3].

Multimodal imaging can provide the optimal approach for clinicians to monitor patients with BRVO. The preliminary diagnosis of BRVO is based on fundus exami-nation, because color fundus photography (CFP) can determine the existence of retinal hemorrhage and retinal exudates [4]. Fluorescein angiography (FA) is often performed to confirm the diagnosis (delayed filling of the occluded retinal vein) and to identify mac-ular and peripheral nonperfused areas and other complications such as macular edema, neovascularization, and associated artery occlusions [5]. FA enables detection of the presence or extension of nonperfused areas. Spectral domain optical coherence tomog-raphy (SD-OCT) can assist the clinician in identifying the appearance of subretinal fluid, hyperreflective dots, epimacular membrane, or vitreomacular traction [6]. Recently, the introduction of optical coherence tomography angiography (OCTA) has provided a novel method for imaging the capillary network in a noninvasive manner [7, 8]. OCTA uses the split-spectrum amplitude–decorrelation angiography algorithm [9] to detect erythro-cyte movement at the microcirculation level. OCTA enables accurate measurement of flow, nonflow, and flow area density. Moreover, OCTA shows its superiority in visualiz-ing the neovascularization and primary capillary plexus in BRVO. Multimodal imaging can provide multifaceted information for the clinical diagnosis of BRVO. Therefore, it is valuable to fuse the complementary information of BRVO provided by multimodal imaging modalities, as it may improve the ability of ophthalmologist to evaluate BRVO and the therapeutic effect of different treatments.

There have been ample publications on clinical and pathological analysis of BRVO, and they mostly centered on efficacy assessment and index quantification. Alexandre et al. [10] conducted qualitative and quantitative evaluation during follow-up of patients with RVO treated with antivascular endothelial growth factor (anti-VEGF). Vogl et al. [11] presented and evaluated two different data-driven machine learning approaches to predict if BRVO will recur within the covered interval followed over one year. These literatures have systematically introduced the classification, epidemiology, pathogenesis, risk factors, clinical features, and complications of BRVO. However, we are not aware of any studies that described the multimodal fusion of BRVO images. Therefore, the aim of our study is to display multifaceted characteristics of BRVO in a single fundus image by multimodal fusion.

In past decades, various research efforts have been made to develop an effective medical image fusion technique [12]. Multi-scale transform (MST) based image fusion methods have been widely studied due to their simplicity, feasibility, and effectiveness in implementation [13, 14]. However, these methods cannot adaptively express the image content. Neural network (NN) based methods [15, 16] have been proposed to obtain an encouraging fusion performance. But these methods mostly rely on data size and manual parameter setting. In recent years, sparse representation (SR) based methods, especially adaptive dictionary learning based methods, have been rapidly developed and applied owing to their self-adaptability and stability. Kim et al. [17] employed a joint clustering technique to classify image patches according to their similar structures, and the overcomplete dictionary can be obtained by combing principal components. Zhou et al. [18] proposed a dictionary learning method based on the brightness and detail clustering for brain images to address the shortcomings of low-learning efficiency and weak dictionary expression ability.

Considering the complementarity of different modalities with BRVO, we present a novel multimodal fusion strategy for BRVO visualization based on CFP, FA and OCTA images. According to the image quality and pathological characteristics of BRVO images, the proposed method mainly consists of image enhancement and adaptive dictionary learning to provide valuable information for clinical diagnosis. Our fused images can simultaneously display complementary characteristics of BRVO from multimodal images.

2   Method

2.1   Materials

The experimental data sets contain 10 sets of CFP, FA and OCTA images from 10 patients with BRVO from Jiangsu Provincial People's Hospital. Figure 1 shows the data structure under these three modalities.

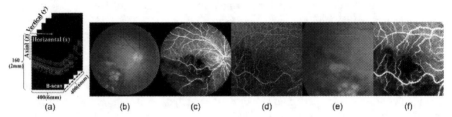

Fig. 1. Data structure of multimodal images. (a) OCTA cube. (b) Original CFP image. (c) Original FA image. (d) Maximum projection image of (a) along the axial lines. (e) Registered CFP image. (f) Registered FA image.

OCTA data was collected using a commercial 70 kHz spectral domain OCT system with a center wavelength of 840 nm (RTVue-XR, Optovue, CA). Each OCTA cube (Fig. 1(a)) consists of $400 \times 400 \times 160$ voxels corresponding to a 6 mm $\times$ 6 mm $\times$ 2 mm volume centered at the macular region of the retina in the horizontal, vertical and axial directions, respectively. The OCTA projection image (Fig. 1(d)) was generated with the maximum of flow projection of OCTA cube along the axial lines. CFP images (Fig. 1(b)) were collected with a Canon device and each CFP image contains 2736×1824 pixels. FA images (Fig. 1(c)) were obtained with a Topcon device with the size of 768×868 pixels. CFP and FA images were registered and cropped to accord with OCTA projection images. Each registered CFP (Fig. 1(e) and FA (Fig. 1(f)) images were resized to 400×400 pixels.

2.2   Overview of Our Method

In this paper, we propose a multimodal fusion method for BRVO visualization based on adaptive dictionary learning, as shown in Fig. 2. The proposed method consists of three main steps: image enhancement, dictionary construction and image fusion. The details of our proposed method will be described in the following sections.

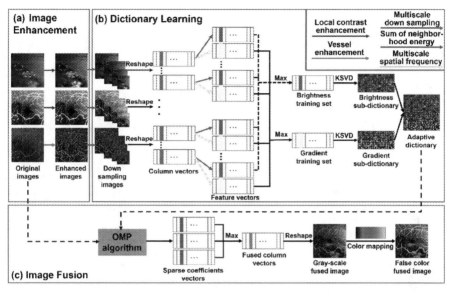

Fig. 2. Overview of the developed multimodal fusion method for BRVO visualization. The dashed blue ovals indicate retinal hemorrhage regions. The dashed green, yellow and red ovals represent the retinal exudates regions, the low contrast regions and the regions with capillary plexus, respectively. (Color figure online)

2.3 Image Enhancement

Owing to that the green channel of CFP images commonly hold the most contrast [19], we utilized the green channel for further processing. For CFP and FA images, we adopted an adaptive contrast enhancement method [20] to highlight lesion areas. We first extracted detail information through high-pass filtering, and then allocated corresponding enhancement coefficients according to the standard deviation of local regions. In this way, abnormal lesion regions with more detail information can adaptively obtain higher enhancement coefficients than normal regions. For OCTA images, we used a Frangi filter based method [21] to enhance retinal vessels and capillary plexus. Frangi filter based methods were frequently applied to segment OCTA images, which utilized the ratio of eigenvalues of Hessian matrix to distinguish tubular structures (e.g., vessels) from other structures. In the implementation, we conducted multiscale filtering on OCTA images and enhanced the parts with the maximum response. Figure 2(a) shows the comparison of original images and enhanced images.

2.4 Dictionary Learning

Our dictionary learning schematic diagram is illustrated in Fig. 2(b). To integrate the advantages of each patch with different sizes, we adopted multiscale down sampling on multimodal enhanced images to obtain a stronger training set. Multiscale down sampling can not only improve multi-scale properties of the training set but also reduce the dictionary training time. The down sampling rate ranges from 1 to 4 in this paper.

After down sampling operation, we extracted brightness and gradient features from multiscale enhanced images. Considering the energy correlation between pixels in medical images, the sum of neighborhood energy (SNE) is developed to evaluate the brightness of the central pixel, which can be calculated as follows:

$$E(i,j) = \sum_{m=-(M-1)/2}^{(M-1)/2} \sum_{n=-(N-1)/2}^{(N-1)/2} I(i+m,j+n)^2 \tag{1}$$

where $E(i,j)$ represents the SNE of image I centered at pixel (i,j); $I(i+m,j+n)$ denotes the intensity value of I at pixel $(i+m,j+n)$; M and N indicate the size of neighborhood.

Meanwhile, we calculated the multiscale spatial frequency (MSF) [18] of image patches as gradient features. MSF can be used to express the richness degree of the image gradient information, which is defined as:

$$MSF_I(i,j) = \alpha_1 \left| SF_I^{r_1}(i,j) - SF_I^{r_2}(i,j) \right| + \alpha_2 \left| SF_I^{r_1}(i,j) - SF_I^{r_3}(i,j) \right| \tag{2}$$

$$SF_I^r(i,j) = \sum_{m=-(r-1)/2}^{(r-1)/2} \sum_{n=-(r-1)/2}^{(r-1)/2} \left[I(i+m,j+n) - I(i,j) \right] \tag{3}$$

where $r(r = r_1, r_2, r_3)$ is the scale factor; $r \times r$ indicates the size of neighborhood; α_1 and α_2 are weighting factors (both α_1 and α_2 were set to 0.5 in this paper); $SF_I^r(i,j)$ denotes the r-scale spatial frequency of image I at pixel (i,j); $MSF_I(i,j)$ is the MSF of image I at pixel (i,j).

Then, we constructed a brightness training set by selecting the image patches containing the largest SNE value among multiscale image patches. Similarly, a gradient training set was generated by choosing the image patches with the largest MSF value. K-singular value decomposition (K-SVD) algorithm was adopted to obtain the brightness sub-dictionary and gradient sub-dictionary. Finally, the final adaptive dictionary was constructed by combining these two sub-dictionaries.

2.5 Image Fusion

During image fusion, multimodal source images were first divided into a series of image patches of size 8×8 pixels with an overlapping step length of 2 pixels, and then rearranging them into column vectors. The Orthogonal Matching Pursuit (OMP) algorithm was adopted to calculate the sparse coefficient vectors by the following underdetermined equation:

$$\hat{\alpha} = \arg\min_{\alpha} \left\{ \| y - D\alpha \|_2^2 + \| \alpha \|_1 \right\} < \varepsilon \tag{4}$$

where $\hat{\alpha}$ indicates the sparsest of the sparse coefficient vectors α; y denotes the original column vectors; D is the adaptive dictionary; $\varepsilon > 0$ is an error tolerance.

The max-absolute choosing rule was employed to obtain the fused sparse vectors. After that, the column vectors were reshaped into image patches, and then plugged into its corresponding original position. To enhance the visualization of the obtained grayscale fused image, a false color mapping was adopted to generate the false color fused image.

3   Experiment

3.1   Qualitative Evaluation

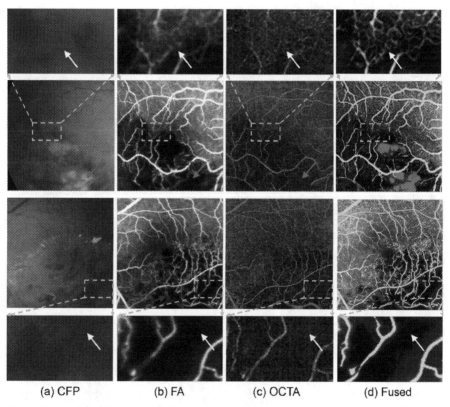

(a) CFP   (b) FA   (c) OCTA   (d) Fused

Fig. 3. Comparison of single-modality images and our fused images. From left to right are CFP, FA, OCTA projection and our fused images, respectively. The first and last rows devote the detail views of the dashed rectangles in the second and third rows, respectively. The blue, yellow, red and white arrows represent regions containing retinal vessels, retinal hemorrhage, retinal exudates and capillary plexus, respectively. (Color figure online)

Two set of experimental results are presented in Fig. 3. Through comparative analysis, the following major findings can be obtained.

(1) Our fused images can provide richer characteristics of BRVO than single-modality images. CFP images can visualize retinal hemorrhage (marked with yellow arrows in Fig. 3) and retinal exudates (marked with red arrows in Fig. 3). FA images can display non-perfusion regions. OCTA projection images enable observation of retinal capillary plexus (marked with white arrows in Fig. 3). These characteristics are of great significance in clinical diagnosis. Our fused images, as their combination, can simultaneously provide multimodal information for the clinicians.

(2) Our fused images perform better in displaying retinal vessels than traditional single-modality images. As indicated by the blue arrows in Fig. 3, our fused images not only contain more vascular details but also have higher vessel contrast. Besides, our fused images can also display vascular pattern of retinal capillary plexus, which may benefit the measurement of vascular density.

(3) Our fused images have higher contrast of lesion areas than CFP images. Retinal hemorrhage and retinal exudates in CFP images have weak contrast. While in our false color fused images, these lesion regions clinically concerned can be visualized more clearly, which were coded black and purple.

3.2 Quantitative Evaluation

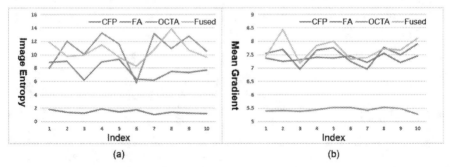

Fig. 4. Quantitative comparison of the CFP, FA, OCTA projection and fused images in 10 sets of data using information entropy (a) and mean gradient (b).

For a quantitative evaluation, we adopted information entropy [22] and mean gradient [23] as criterions. Figure 4 shows the quantitative evaluation of CFP, FA, OCTA projection and fused images. Table 1 indicates the average results of two criterions. From Fig. 4 and Table 1, we can find that our fused images have the second largest image entropy value only to OCTA projection images. This suggests that the fused images contain richer information than CFP and FA images, which can also be demonstrated from visual comparison. OCTA projection images commonly contain ample vascular details and noise, which leads to its superiority in criterion calculation. Such information provides limited valuable information. By contrast, our fused images enhance the visualization of lesion regions and weaken the noise. In terms of mean gradient, our fused images get the largest value, which indicates that our fused images have the highest definition.

Table 1. Average information entropy and mean gradient in CFP, FA, OCTA projection and fused images.

	CFP	FFA	OCTA	Fused
Image entropy	1.4119	7.7172	10.7958	**10.5783**
Mean gradient	7.3532	7.4967	5.4348	**7.7094**

4 Discussion

In order to simultaneously provide multifaceted information of BRVO from multimodal imaging for clinicians, we present a multimodal fusion method for CFP, FA and OCTA projection images. The main contributions of our method are: (1) We employed different image enhancement strategy for different multimodal images. These enhanced images can highlight the unobvious but significant information, and express them into patches, which could be beneficial to constructing a strong training set. (2) In order to comprehensively describe image information, we constructed brightness sub-dictionary and gradient sub-dictionary, which is necessary to produce encouraging fusion results. Figure 3 indicates that both brightness characteristics (marked with green arrows) and detail characteristics (marked with white arrows) retained in our fused images. (3) We took advantages of multiscale technique to improve the informative ability of the training set. Generally, large scale features can illustrate the shape and location of object, but the description about the details are insufficient, and vice versa. In our fused images, except from large lesion regions, small vessels even the vascular pattern of retinal capillary plexus can also be clearly visualized.

The fused images in Fig. 3 perform better than the traditional images on BRVO visualization for the following three reasons. (1) The fused images can provide clinicians with richer information of BRVO. CFP can determine the appearance of retinal hemorrhage and retinal exudates. FA provides rich vascular information and clear display of non-perfusion regions. Meanwhile, OCTA can supplement multilevel vascular network centered at the macular region of the retina. All of these multimodal pathological information is of great significance of clinical diagnosis. Our fused images enhanced valuable information and suppressed redundant information based on clinical prior. (2) The fused images are more suitable for clinic observation. Abnormal lesion regions were coded with high contrast colors, which may assist the clinicians in the rapid measurement of the range and the size of lesion regions. Moreover, retinal hemorrhage and retinal exudates regions contain few vessels in the fused images, which is accordant with clinical prior [24]. (3) Our proposed method costs 43.17 s (Intel Xeon CPU, E5-2683, 2.0 GHz) for one set of CFP, FA and OCTA projection images. To improve time efficiency, we constructed the adaptive dictionary based on three grayscale images instead of color images.

In conclusion, we propose a multimodal fusion method for BRVO visualization based on CFP, FA and OCTA projection images. The proposed method mainly employed image enhancement and adaptive dictionary learning techniques. Experimental results demonstrate that the fused images are more effective for BRVO visualization than single-modality images. This may be helpful to the clinician in the rapid assessment of BRVO and its response to treatment.

Acknowledgements. This study was supported by National Natural Science Foundation of China (61671242, 61701222), and in part by Key R&D Program of Jiangsu Science and Technology Department (BE2018131).

References

1. Rogers, S., McIntosh, R.L., Cheung, N., et al.: The prevalence of retinal vein occlusion: pooled data from population studies from the United States, Europe, Asia, and Australia. Ophthalmology **117**(2), 313–319 (2010)
2. Hayreh, S.S., Zimmerman, M.B., Podhajsky, P.: Incidence of various types of retinal vein occlusion and their recurrence and demographic characteristics. Am. J. Ophalmology **117**(4), 429–441 (1994)
3. Clarhson, J.C.: Natural history and clinical management of central retinal vein occlusion. A.M.A. Archives of Ophthalmology **115**(4), 486–491 (1997)
4. Jaulim, A., Ahmed, B., Khanam, T., et al.: Branch retinal vein occlusion epidemiology, pathogenesis, risk factors, clinical features, diagnosis, and complications. An Update Lit. Retina **33**(5), 901–910 (2013)
5. Hayreh, S.S., Zimmerman, M.B.: Fundus changes in central retinal vein occlusion. Retina **35**(1), 29–42 (2015)
6. Patel, M., Kiss, S.: Ultra-wide-field fluorescein angiography in retinal disease. Curr. Opin. Ophthalmology **25**(3), 213–220 (2014)
7. Tokayer, J., Jia, Y., Dhalla, A.H., et al.: Blood flow velocity quantification using split-spectrum amplitude-decorrelation angiography with optical coherence tomography. Biomed. Opt. Express **4**(10), 1909–1924 (2013)
8. Huang, D., Wilson, D.J., Campbell, J.P., et al.: Projection-resolved optical coherence tomographic angiography. Biomed. Opt. Express **7**(3), 816–828 (2016)
9. Jia, Y., Tan, O., Tokayer, J., et al.: Split-spectrum amplitude decorrelation angiography with optical coherence tomography. Opt. Express **20**(4), 4710–4725 (2012)
10. Alexandre, S., Agnes, G.B., Florence, C., et al.: Qualitative and quantitative follow-up using optical coherence tomography angiography of retinal vein occlusion treated with anti-vegf: optical coherence tomography angiography follow-up of retinal vein occlusion. Retina **37**(6), 1176–1184 (2017)
11. Vogl, W.D., Sebastian, M.W., Bianca, S.G., et al.: Predicting macular edema recurrence from spatio-temporal signatures in optical coherence tomography images. IEEE Trans. Med. Imaging **36**(9), 1773–1783 (2017)
12. Li, S., Yang, B., Hu, J.: Performance comparison of different multi-resolution transforms for image fusion. Inf. Fusion **12**(2), 74–84 (2011)
13. Ellmauthaler, A., Pagliari, C.L., da Silva, E.A.: Multiscale image fusion using the undecimated wavelet transform with spectral factorization and nonorthogonal filter banks. IEEE Trans. Image Process. **22**(3), 1005–1017 (2012)
14. Du, J., Li, W., Xiao, B., et al.: Medical image fusion by combining parallel features on multi-scale local extrema scheme. Knowl.-Based Syst. **113**(dec.1), 4–12 (2016)
15. Palsson, F., Sveinsson, J.R., Ulfarsson, M.O.: Multispectral and hyperspectral image fusion using a 3-D-convolutional neural network. IEEE Geosci. Remote Sens. Lett. **14**(5), 639–643 (2017)

16. Huang, W., Jing, Z.L.: Multi-focus image fusion using pulse coupled neural network. Patt. Recogn. Lett. **28**(9), 1123–1132 (2007)
17. Kim, M., Han, D.K., Ko, H.: Joint patch clustering-based dictionary learning for multimodal image fusion. Inf. Fusion **27**(C), 198–214 (2016)
18. Zhou, F., Li, X., Zhou, M., et al.: A new dictionary construction based multimodal medical image fusion framework. Entropy **21**(3), 267–275 (2019)
19. Niemeijer, M., van Ginneken, B., Staal, J.: Automatic detection of red lesions in digital color fundus photographs. IEEE Trans. Med. Imaging **24**(5), 584–592 (2005)
20. SomorjeetSingh, S., Tangkeshwar, S.T., Mamata, D.H., et al.: Local contrast enhancement using local standard deviation. Int. J. Comput. Appl. **47**(15), 39–44 (2012)
21. Frangi, A.F., Niessen, W.J., Vincken, K.L., Viergever, M.A.: Multiscale vessel enhancement filtering. In: Wells, W.M., Colchester, A., Delp, S. (eds.) MICCAI 1998. LNCS, vol. 1496, pp. 130–137. Springer, Heidelberg (1998). https://doi.org/10.1007/BFb0056195
22. Nunez, J.A., Cincotta, P.M., Wachlin, F.C.: Information entropy. Celest. Mech. Dyn. Astron. **64**(1–2), 43–53 (1996)
23. Pan, B., Lu, Z., Xie, H.: Mean intensity gradient: An effective global parameter for quality assessment of the speckle patterns used in digital image correlation. Opt. Lasers Eng. **48**(4), 469–477 (2010)
24. Sun, Z., Zhou, H., Lin, B., et al.: Efficacy and safety of intravitreal conbercept injections in macular edema secondary to retinal vein occlusion. Retina **37**(9), 1723–1730 (2017)

TR-GAN: Topology Ranking GAN with Triplet Loss for Retinal Artery/Vein Classification

Wenting Chen[1,2], Shuang Yu[1(✉)], Junde Wu[1], Kai Ma[1], Cheng Bian[1],
Chunyan Chu[1], Linlin Shen[2], and Yefeng Zheng[1]

[1] Tencent Healthcare, Tencent, Shenzhen, China
shirlyyu@tencent.com
[2] School of Computer Science & Software Engineering, Shenzhen University,
Shenzhen, China

Abstract. Retinal artery/vein (A/V) classification lays the foundation for the quantitative analysis of retinal vessels, which is associated with potential risks of various cardiovascular and cerebral diseases. The topological connection relationship, which has been proved effective in improving the A/V classification performance for the conventional graph based method, has not been exploited by the deep learning based method. In this paper, we propose a Topology Ranking Generative Adversarial Network (TR-GAN) to improve the topology connectivity of the segmented arteries and veins, and further to boost the A/V classification performance. A topology ranking discriminator based on ordinal regression is proposed to rank the topological connectivity level of the ground-truth, the generated A/V mask and the intentionally shuffled mask. The ranking loss is further back-propagated to the generator to generate better connected A/V masks. In addition, a topology preserving module with triplet loss is also proposed to extract the high-level topological features and further to narrow the feature distance between the predicted A/V mask and the ground-truth. The proposed framework effectively increases the topological connectivity of the predicted A/V masks and achieves state-of-the-art A/V classification performance on the publicly available AV-DRIVE dataset.

Keywords: Retinal imaging · Artery/Vein Classification · Generative adversarial network · Topology ranking

1 Introduction

Morphological changes of retinal arteries and veins have been reported to be associated with potential risks of various systemic, cardiovascular and cerebral diseases [2,17]. For example, it is reported that narrowing of arteries and widening of veins are associated with the increased risk of stroke [7]. In addition, research has also found that the narrowing of retinal arteriolar caliber is related to the risk of hypertension and developing diabetes [2,11]. Therefore, accurate A/V classification is of strong clinical interest.

© Springer Nature Switzerland AG 2020
A. L. Martel et al. (Eds.): MICCAI 2020, LNCS 12265, pp. 616–625, 2020.
https://doi.org/10.1007/978-3-030-59722-1_59

Automatic A/V classification has been actively investigated in recent years. Previous works are generally performed in a two-stage manner [3,4,12,18,20,21], which requires vessel segmentation in the first stage and then classifies individual pixels on the vessel or centerline into either A/V. Depending on whether topological structure is used in the procedure, those works can be further categorized into pure feature based methods [12,18] and graph based methods [3,4,20,21]. The graph based methods first reconstruct the graph tree structures for individual vessels, and then take advantage of the topological connection/crossover relationship to further refine the A/V classification results, which have been proved to be effective in boosting A/V classification performance [3,4,20,21].

Very recently, deep learning has been introduced to the A/V classification task, which enables the end-to-end A/V classification and eliminates the pre-requirement of vessel segmentation in the first place. For example, Xu *et al.* [19] first proposed to adopt the U-Net framework to segment arteries and veins from the background. AlBadawi and Fraz [1] performed pixel-wise A/V classification with an encoder-decoder based fully convolutional network. Ma *et al.* [9] proposed to perform retinal vessel segmentation and A/V classification simultaneously with a multi-task framework, which achieved the state-of-the-art performance on the publicly available AV-DRIVE dataset.

Deep learning based methods, although achieved high A/V classification accuracy, still suffer from the problem of limited connectivity for the obtained arteries and veins, which should be connected naturally. As aforementioned, the topological connection relationship of individual vessels can be adopted to mitigate this issue. To the best of our knowledge, however, integrating the vessel topological connectivity into the deep learning based A/V classification framework was rarely investigated. There is still a research gap of how to increase the topological connectivity of the predicted arteries and veins.

In order to fill this gap, a Topology Ranking Generative Adversarial Network (TR-GAN) is proposed in this paper, which tries to increase the topological connectivity of arteries and veins, and further improves the A/V classification performance. This paper is the first work trying to increase topology connectivity for the A/V classification task with a deep learning based framework. Three major contributions are made with this paper. Firstly, instead of using a general discriminator in adversarial learning that distinguishes the ground-truth (real) mask from the generated (fake) mask, a topology ranking discriminator based on ordinal regression is proposed to rank the topological connectivity of the real mask, the fake mask and the intentionally shuffled mask. The ranking loss is further back-propagated to encourage the segmentation network to produce A/V masks with higher topological connectivity. Secondly, a topology preserving module with triplet loss is also proposed to extract the high-level topological features from the generated mask, based on which further to narrow the feature distance between the generated mask and the ground-truth mask. Last but not least, the proposed framework achieves the state-of-the-art performance on the publicly available AV-DRIVE dataset for the A/V classification, surpassing the most recent approaches with a remarkable margin.

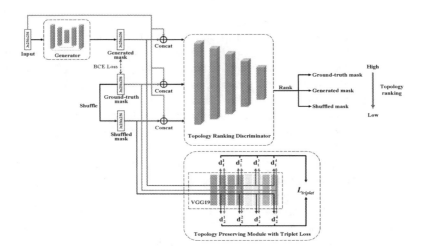

Fig. 1. Architecture of the proposed framework, including a generator based on U-Net, a topology ranking discriminator and a topology preserving module with triplet loss.

2   Method

Figure 1 shows the architecture of the proposed Topology Ranking GAN (TR-GAN) framework for the retinal A/V classification task. The overall architecture consists of three parts: (1) the segmentation network as the generator, (2) the topology ranking discriminator and (3) the topology preserving module with triplet loss. For the segmentation network, we adopt the widely used U-Net [14] architecture with a pretrained ResNet-18 as the encoder, and the decoder outputs a three-channel probability map for artery, vein and vessel segmentation. The generated mask is then concatenated with the original input image and fed to the topology ranking discriminator to evaluate the topological connectivity, similar for the ground-truth mask and the shuffled mask. A topology ranking adversarial loss is then calculated and back-propagated to update the generator.

Moreover, these three masks are also fed to the topology preserving module, which extracts the high-level topological features with a pretrained VGG-19 backbone [15]. The extracted features are further used to construct a triplet loss that tries to narrow the feature distance between the ground-truth mask and the generated mask.

2.1   Topology Ranking Discriminator

In this paper, the discriminator adopts the PatchGAN structure [8] and contains six convolutional layers. Input to the discriminator is conditioned by concatenating the input images and the A/V masks, so as to ensure that the generated masks are relevant to the corresponding original image content.

Instead of using a typical discriminator which distinguishes the real masks (ground-truth) from the fake ones (the segmented masks), we propose a topology

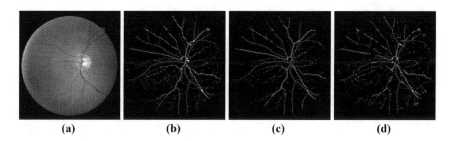

Fig. 2. Different levels of topology connectivity for artery/vein classification. Red denotes arteries, blue for veins and green for the cross-overs. (a) Original color fundus image; (b) ground-truth mask with highest level of topology connectivity; (c) model prediction with median level of topology connectivity; (d) shuffled ground-truth mask with lowest level of topology connectivity. (Color figure online)

ranking discriminator to rank the level of topology connectivity for the masks. In order to enrich potential connectivity levels and synthesize a mask with low topology connectivity, we intentionally shuffle the ground-truth mask by removing part of the vessels, shifting the position of vessel segments or exchanging the A/V labels for randomly selected regions. This random shuffle procedure is repeated until 5–25% of the vessel pixels shuffled away from the ground-truth vessels, so as to ensure that the shuffled mask has a lower level of topology connectivity compared with the generated mask. Afterwards, we have three different levels of topology connectivity ranked in descending order as: the ground-truth mask, the generated mask and the shuffled mask, as demonstrated in Fig. 2.

In order to preserve the ranking information contained in the three different classes, ordinal classification [5] is adopted to rank the three categories. For a simple yet effective implementation of the ordinal classification, the ordinal labels can be transferred to a multi-label classification problem with two individual labels: shuffled mask $y_1 : [0, 0]$, generated mask $y_2 : [1, 0]$ and ground-truth mask $y_3 : [1, 1]$. The first element indicates whether the mask topology is better than the shuffled mask, and the second denotes whether the mask topology is better than the generated mask. The discriminator can then be optimized with:

$$
\begin{aligned}
\mathcal{L}_{adv}^{D} = \ &\mathbb{E}_{L_s, y_1}[-y_1 \cdot log D(x, L_s)] \\
&+ \mathbb{E}_{G(x), y_2}[-y_2 \cdot log D(x, G(x))] \\
&+ \mathbb{E}_{L, y_3}[-y_3 \cdot log D(x, L)],
\end{aligned}
\tag{1}
$$

where x denotes the input image, and $L_s, G(x), L$ represent the shuffled mask, generated mask and ground-truth mask, respectively. By minimizing this objective, the discriminator D learns to rank the topology connectivity levels.

When updating the generator, the optimization target is to encourage the generated mask to have the highest level of topology and fool the discriminator, with the adversarial loss as below:

$$
\mathcal{L}_{adv}^{G} = \mathbb{E}_{x, y_3}[-y_3 \cdot log D(x, G(x))].
\tag{2}
$$

2.2   Topology Preserving Module with Triplet Loss

Pixel-wise losses, including the binary cross entropy loss and L1/L2 loss, can only measure the low-level pixel-wise difference between the segmented mask and the ground-truth, which often fail to measure the high-level topology difference. Therefore, we propose to calculate the distance of features extracted by a pretrained model, which is expected to contain high-level topological information [10]. In this paper, a VGG-19 backbone pretrained on ImageNet is adopted to extract the feature maps. A triplet loss is further proposed to narrow the feature distance between the ground-truth mask and the generated mask.

For the triplet loss configuration, the ground-truth mask L is selected as the anchor exemplar, the generated mask $G(x)$ as the positive exemplar and the shuffled mask L_s as the negative exemplar. The triplet loss is defined as:

$$L_{triplet} = \frac{1}{N} \sum_{i=1}^{N} max\left(d_1^i - d_2^i + \alpha, 0\right),\tag{3}$$

where α is the margin hyper-parameter and set to 1 by default in this research; N denotes the total number of network layers where we extract feature maps from. In this paper N is 4 and feature maps are extracted from the ReLU layers of the $2^{nd}, 4^{th}, 6^{th}$ and 8th convolutional blocks. d_1^i and d_2^i represent the distance of anchor-positive and anchor-negative pairs for the ith layer of the feature extraction network, and can be obtained with:

$$d_1^i = \frac{1}{C_i W_i H_i} ||\mathcal{F}_i(L) - \mathcal{F}_i(G(x))||_2^2,\tag{4}$$

$$d_2^i = \frac{1}{C_i W_i H_i} ||\mathcal{F}_i(L) - \mathcal{F}_i(L_s)||_2^2,\tag{5}$$

where C_i, W_i, H_i denote the channel number, width and height, respectively, for the feature maps of the ith layer; $\mathcal{F}_i$ denotes the mapping function for the ith model layer.

2.3   Generator Loss Function

In order to optimize the generator, the widely adopted cross entropy loss is utilized to optimize the pixel-level difference between the generated mask and the ground-truth mask. Meanwhile, the adversarial loss and triplet loss are also used to optimize the high-level topological information for the generated mask. The final loss for the generator network is the weighted combination of all three losses:

$$L_G = L_{BCE} + \lambda_1 L_{adv}^G + \lambda_2 L_{triplet},\tag{6}$$

$$L_{BCE} = -\sum_{c=1}^{3} \mu_c L_c \log(G(x)),\tag{7}$$

where c denotes the cth class of the output; the weights of vessel, artery and vein are denoted as μ_c and empirically set as 0.4, 0.3 and 0.3, respectively; λ_1 and λ_2 are the hyper-parameters to control the relative importance of each loss compared to the binary cross entropy loss and empirically set as 0.2 and 0.1, respectively.

3   Experimental Results

The proposed model is trained and tested on the publicly available datasets, including the AV-DRIVE dataset [6] and INSPIRE-AVR dataset [13]. The AV-DRIVE dataset contains 20 training images and 20 test images with the dimension of 584×565 pixels and a field-of-view of $45°$. Pixel-wise annotation of artery and vein is provided by AV-DRIVE. Besides, we have also tested the model on the INSPIRE-AVR dataset, which contains 40 fundus images with the dimension of 2048×2392 pixels and a field-of-view of $30°$. Since only the A/V labels of vessel centerline are provided, we cannot train or fine-tune the model on the INSPIRE-AVR dataset. Result reported for INSPIRE-AVR in this paper is obtained by direct model inference for all of the 40 images.

During the training stage, patches with the dimension of 256×256 pixels are randomly extracted from the fundus images and fed to the network. In the test stage, we extract the ordered patches at the stride of 50 and then stitch the corresponding predictions together to obtain final results. All experiments are performed on an NVIDIA Tesla P40 GPU with 24 GB of memory. The generator and discriminator are optimized alternatively with the Adam optimizer for the maximum of 30,000 iterations and a batch size of 4. The initial learning rate is set as 2×10^{-4} and halved every 7,000 iterations.

3.1   Ablation Studies

Detailed ablation studies have been conducted to evaluate the effectiveness of different modules in the proposed framework, including the topology ranking discriminator (TR-D) and the topology preserving module with the triplet loss (TL). In addition, in order to better assess the advantage of the proposed topology ranking discriminator against general discriminators (GD) that distinguishes the real from fake masks, related experiments have also been performed. In order to compare the proposed model under the same criteria with other methods in the literature, A/V classification performance is evaluated on the segmented vessel pixels with three metrics, including accuracy (Acc), sensitivity (Sen) and specificity (Spec). By treating arteries as positives and veins as negatives, Sen and Spec reflect the model's capability of detecting arteries and veins, respectively. Although the existing methods evaluated the A/V classification performance on the segmented vessels only, we evaluate the performance on all the ground truth artery/vein pixels, which is a relatively stricter criterion than that on the segmented vessels, since the classification of major vessels is comparatively an easier task if capillary vessels are not segmented.

Table 1. The ablation study results of artery/vein classification (%).

GD	TR-D	TL	Acc	Sen	Spec
			91.61	90.94	92.25
✓			94.01	93.83	94.25
	✓		94.84	94.33	95.40
		✓	94.73	94.30	95.25
	✓	✓	**95.46**	**94.53**	**96.31**

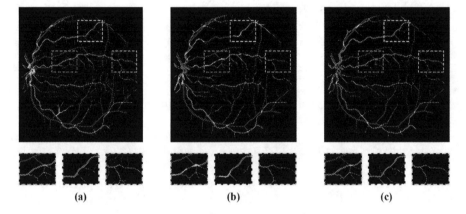

(a)   (b)   (c)

Fig. 3. Comparison of model performance of the baseline and the proposed method. (a) Ground truth; (b) baseline model; (c) proposed method.

As listed in Table 1, general discriminator improves the accuracy of A/V classification by 2.4%, indicating the effectiveness of adversarial learning for the A/V classification task. Compared with the general discriminator, the topology-ranking discriminator exploits the ranking information in three different levels of topological connectivity maps by using ordinal classification. When the topology-ranking discriminator is adopted, the accuracy of A/V classification is improved by 3.23%, which is higher than the general discriminator. This indicates the advantage of the proposed topology ranking discriminator over the general discriminator for the A/V classification task. Moreover, when integrating the topology preserving module with the triplet loss, the accuracy of A/V classification is increased by 3.12% over the baseline. Finally, the proposed method with the topology ranking discriminator and the triplet loss module achieves the best performance for A/V classification with an accuracy of 95.46%.

Figure 3 shows a representative result of the proposed model against that of the baseline. The proposed method has remarkably improved the topological connectivity of the arteries and veins, and thus achieved much better A/V classification result, as manifested in the enlarged views in the bottom row.

Table 2. Performance comparison (%) of A/V classification on the AV-DRIVE and INSPIRE-AVR datasets.

Methods	Type	AV-DRIVE			INSPIRE-AVR		
		Acc	Sen	Spec	Acc	Sen	Spec
Dashtbozorg et al. (2014) [3]		87.4	90.0	84.0	84.9	91.0	86.0
Estrada et al. (2015) [4]		93.5	93.0	94.1	90.9	91.5	90.2
Zhao et al. (2019) [21]	Graph	93.5	94.2	92.7	96.4	96.8	95.7
Srinidhi et al. (2019) [16]		94.7	**96.6**	92.9	**96.8**	**96.9**	96.6
Xu et al. (2018) [19]		90.0	-	-	79.2	-	-
Ma et al. (2019) [9]	DL	94.5	93.4	95.5	91.6	92.4	91.3
Proposed (GT)[a]		95.46	94.53	96.31	-	-	-
Proposed[b]		**96.29**	95.28	**97.14**	93.40	89.05	**97.29**

[a]: A/V classification performance is evaluated on the ground-truth vessel pixels;
[b]: A/V classification performance is evaluated on the segmented vessel pixels;

3.2   Comparison with State-of-the-Art

Table 2 lists the A/V classification performance comparison between the proposed framework and related methods in the literature for both AV-DRIVE and INSPIRE-AVR datasets. Among the compared research works, the methods proposed by Xu et al. [19] and Ma et al. [9] are deep learning based, which predict the artery and vein maps simultaneously; meanwhile the rest [3,4,16,21] are graph based methods, which extract the individual vessel tree structures first and then classify vessels into arteries and veins via a multi-step strategy. When evaluating under the same criteria with existing methods, the proposed method achieves an A/V classification accuracy of 96.29% for the AV-DRIVE dataset, with a remarkable margin of 1.59% over the current state-of-the-art method [16].

For the INSPIRE-AVR dataset, when comparing with deep learning based methods under the same evaluation criteria without fine-tuning, the proposed framework surpasses the methods proposed by Xu et al. [19] and Ma et al. [9], with an accuracy improvement of 14.2% and 1.8% respectively, indicating the generalization capability of the proposed model. However, when compared to the graph based methods, the performance of the proposed method is not as good as that of Zhao et al. [21] and Srinidhi et al. [16]. This is primarily resulted by the fact that both of the two aforementioned methods are trained and tested on the INSPIRE-AVR dataset, meanwhile the proposed method is only trained on AV-DRIVE and then predicts on INSPIRE-AVR without further training or fine-tuning. Since the INSPIRE-AVR dataset is quite different from the AV-DRIVE dataset in terms of image color, resolution and field-of-view, it is reasonable that the performance is not as good as that on the AV-DRIVE dataset.

4   Conclusion

In this paper, we proposed a novel framework with topology ranking GAN and topology preserving triplet loss for the retinal artery/vein classification task. The proposed framework takes advantage of the topological connectivity of arteries and veins, to further improve the A/V classification performance. Detailed ablation and comparison studies on two publicly available datasets validated the effectiveness of the proposed method, which has achieved state-of-the-art performance on the AV-DRIVE dataset with a remarkable margin over the current best method. To the best of our knowledge, this is the first research that tries to exploit topology information for A/V classification with deep learning based frameworks.

On the basis of the current research, future work will continue to explore the feasibility of a fully automated vascular parameter quantization system, which is expected to facilitate the clinical biomarker study of how various cardiovascular and cerebral diseases affect the retinal vessels.

Acknowledgment. This work was funded by the Key Area Research and Development Program of Guangdong Province, China (No. 2018B010111001), National Key Research and Development Project (No. 2018YFC2000702), National Natural Science Foundation of China (No. 91959108), and Science and Technology Program of Shenzhen, China (No. ZDSYS201802021814180)

References

1. AlBadawi, S., Fraz, M.M.: Arterioles and venules classification in retinal images using fully convolutional deep neural network. In: Campilho, A., Karray, F., ter Haar Romeny, B. (eds.) ICIAR 2018. LNCS, vol. 10882, pp. 659–668. Springer, Cham (2018). https://doi.org/10.1007/978-3-319-93000-8_75
2. Chew, S.K., Xie, J., Wang, J.J.: Retinal arteriolar diameter and the prevalence and incidence of hypertension: a systematic review and meta-analysis of their association. Curr. Hypertens. Rep. **14**(2), 144–151 (2012)
3. Dashtbozorg, B., Mendonça, A.M., Campilho, A.: An automatic graph-based approach for artery/vein classification in retinal images. IEEE Trans. Image Process. **23**(3), 1073–1083 (2014)
4. Estrada, R., Allingham, M.J., Mettu, P.S., Cousins, S.W., Tomasi, C., Farsiu, S.: Retinal artery-vein classification via topology estimation. IEEE Trans. Med. Imaging **34**(12), 2518–2534 (2015)
5. Frank, E., Hall, M.: A simple approach to ordinal classification. In: De Raedt, L., Flach, P. (eds.) ECML 2001. LNCS (LNAI), vol. 2167, pp. 145–156. Springer, Heidelberg (2001). https://doi.org/10.1007/3-540-44795-4_13
6. Hu, Q., Abramoff, M.D., Garvin, M.K.: Automated separation of binary overlapping trees in low-contrast color retinal images. In: International Conference on Medical Image Computing and Computer Assisted Intervention, pp. 436–443 (2013)
7. Ikram, M.K., de Jong, F.J., Vingerling, J.R., Witteman, J.C., Hofman, A., Breteler, M.M., de Jong, P.T.: Are retinal arteriolar or venular diameters associated with markers for cardiovascular disorders? The Rotterdam Study. Investigat. Ophthalmol. Visual Sci. **45**(7), 2129–2134 (2004)

8. Isola, P., Zhu, J.Y., Zhou, T., Efros, A.A.: Image-to-image translation with conditional adversarial networks. In: Proceedings of the IEEE Conference on Computer Vision and Pattern Recognition, pp. 1125–1134 (2017)

9. Ma, W., Yu, S., Ma, K., Wang, J., Ding, X., Zheng, Y.: Multi-task neural networks with spatial activation for retinal vessel segmentation and artery/vein classification. In: International Conference on Medical Image Computing and Computer Assisted Intervention. pp. 769–778. Springer (2019)

10. Mosinska, A., Marquez-Neila, P., Koziński, M., Fua, P.: Beyond the pixel-wise loss for topology-aware delineation. In: Proceedings of the IEEE Conference on Computer Vision and Pattern Recognition, pp. 3136–3145 (2018)

11. Nguyen, T.T., Wang, J.J., Islam, F.A., Mitchell, P., Tapp, R.J., Zimmet, P.Z., Simpson, R., Shaw, J., Wong, T.Y.: Retinal arteriolar narrowing predicts incidence of diabetes: the Australian diabetes, obesity and lifestyle (AusDiab) study. Diabetes **57**(3), 536–539 (2008)

12. Niemeijer, M., van Ginneken, B., Abràmoff, M.D.: Automatic classification of retinal vessels into arteries and veins. In: Proceedings of SPIE Conference on Medical Image: Computer-Aided Diagnosis. vol. 7260, p. 72601F (2009)

13. Niemeijer, M., Xu, X., Dumitrescu, A.V., Gupta, P., Van Ginneken, B., Folk, J.C., Abramoff, M.D.: Automated measurement of the arteriolar-to-venular width ratio in digital color fundus photographs. IEEE Trans. Med. Imaging **30**(11), 1941–1950 (2011)

14. Ronneberger, O., Fischer, P., Brox, T.: U-Net: Convolutional networks for biomedical image segmentation. In: International Conference on Medical Image Computing and Computer Assisted Intervention. pp. 234–241. Springer (2015)

15. Simonyan, K., Zisserman, A.: Very deep convolutional networks for large-scale image recognition. In: International Conference on Learning Representations (2015)

16. Srinidhi, C.L., Aparna, P., Rajan, J.: Automated method for retinal artery/vein separation via graph search metaheuristic approach. IEEE Trans. Image Process. **28**(6), 2705–2718 (2019)

17. Wong, T.Y., Hubbard, L., Klein, R., Marino, E., Kronmal, R., Sharrett, A., Siscovick, D., Burke, G., Tielsch, J.: Retinal microvascular abnormalities and blood pressure in older people: the Cardiovascular Health Study. Br. J. Ophthalmol. **86**(9), 1007–1013 (2002)

18. Xu, X., Ding, W., Abràmoff, M.D., Cao, R.: An improved arteriovenous classification method for the early diagnostics of various diseases in retinal image. Comput. Methods Programs Biomed. **141**, 3–9 (2017)

19. Xu, X., Wang, R., Lv, P., Gao, B., Li, C., Tian, Z., Tan, T., Xu, F.: Simultaneous arteriole and venule segmentation with domain-specific loss function on a new public database. Biomed. Opt. Express **9**(7), 3153–3166 (2018)

20. Zhao, Y., Xie, J., Su, P., Zheng, Y., Liu, Y., Cheng, J., Liu, J.: Retinal artery and vein classification via dominant sets clustering-based vascular topology estimation. In: International Conference on Medical Image Computing and Computer Assisted Intervention, pp. 56–64 (2018)

21. Zhao, Y., Xie, J., Zhang, H., Zheng, Y., Zhao, Y., Qi, H., Zhao, Y., Su, P., Liu, J., Liu, Y.: Retinal vascular network topology reconstruction and artery/vein classification via dominant set clustering. IEEE Trans. Med. Imaging **39**, 341–356 (2019)

DeepGF: Glaucoma Forecast Using the Sequential Fundus Images

Liu Li[1], Xiaofei Wang[1], Mai Xu[1,2(✉)], Hanruo Liu[3], and Ximeng Chen[4]

[1] School of Electronic and Information Engineering, Beihang University,
Beijing, China
maixu@buaa.edu.cn
[2] Hangzhou Innovation Institute, Beihang University, Beijing, China
[3] Beijing Tongren Hospital, Capital Medical University, Beijing, China
[4] Air Force General Hospital, Beijing, China

Abstract. Disease forecast is an effective solution to early treatment and prevention for some irreversible diseases, e.g., glaucoma. Different from existing disease detection methods that predict the current status of a patient, disease forecast aims to predict the future state for early treatment. This paper is a first attempt to address the glaucoma forecast task utilizing the sequential fundus images of a patient. Specifically, we establish a database of sequential fundus images for glaucoma forecast (SIGF), which includes an average of 9 images per eye, corresponding to 3,671 fundus images in total. Besides, a novel deep learning method for glaucoma forecast (DeepGF) is proposed based on our SIGF database, consisting of an attention-polar convolution neural network (AP-CNN) and a variable time interval long short-term memory (VTI-LSTM) network to learn the spatio-temporal transition at different time intervals across sequential medical images of a person. In addition, a novel active convergence (AC) training strategy is proposed to solve the imbalanced sample distribution problem of glaucoma forecast. Finally, the experimental results show the effectiveness of our DeepGF method in glaucoma forecast.

Keywords: Glaucoma forecast · SIGF database · DeepGF method.

1 Introduction

The early prediction of disease deterioration plays an important role in supporting clinicians, as an approximated 11% of deaths in hospital follow a failure of promptly recognization and treatment [18]. Therefore, forecasting the potential deterioration ahead of time has become an urgent demand in medical diagnosis,

---

Liu Li and Xiaofei Wang contribute equally to this paper.

Electronic supplementary material The online version of this chapter (https://doi.org/10.1007/978-3-030-59722-1_60) contains supplementary material, which is available to authorized users.

© Springer Nature Switzerland AG 2020
A. L. Martel et al. (Eds.): MICCAI 2020, LNCS 12265, pp. 626–635, 2020.
https://doi.org/10.1007/978-3-030-59722-1_60

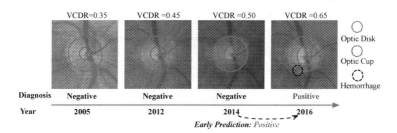

Fig. 1. Sequential fundus images of a patient transferring from negative to positive glaucoma between the year of 2005 and 2016.

especially for the incurable disease like glaucoma, which is the leading causes of irreversible blindness [2].

Different from the existing disease detection methods that predict the current status of the patient, disease forecast aims to predict the potential of contracting a disease in the future, utilizing the variation tendency from the historical data, which is even more important for glaucoma treatment. An example is shown in Fig. 1. As shown, the patient changes from negative to positive glaucoma in 2016 with a disc hemorrhage. Using glaucoma detection methods, this patient cannot be detected until 2016 with the hemorrhage. However, in 2014, glaucoma forecast with sequential fundus images can predict the deterioration in 2016, since the vertical cup-disc ratio (VCDR) increases from 0.35 to 0.5 during 2005–2014. As such, prevention and treatment can be conducted ahead of time. In this paper, we propose a deep learning method for glaucoma forecast (DeepGF), with an attention-polar convolution neural network (AP-CNN) and a variable time interval long-short term memory (VTI-LSTM) model to learn spatio-temporal transition for glaucoma forecast.

To our best knowledge, no previous works have focused on the glaucoma forecast task. While recently, a few works have been proposed for the early prediction of some other diseases, e.g., kidney injury [19] and chronic lung disease [5], based on the electronic health records (EHR). However, these EHR-based forecast methods faces the challenges by the trait of EHR: high-dimensionality, sparsity and irregularity [5,10]. Different from the EHR-based methods, in this paper, we address glaucoma forecast by utilizing the sequential fundus images, which can capture the subtle changes of glaucoma pathologies [6]. Specifically, we first establish a large-scale sequential fundus image database for glaucoma forecast, called SIGF, which includes an average of 9 images per subject, corresponding to 3,671 fundus images in total. Besides, our DeepGF model is trained and validated with the sequential images.

Apart from leveraging the spatio-temporal features for glaucoma forecast, there are still two challenges due to the data limitation: (1) Data imbalance problem; (2) the irregular sampling intervals of the sequential data. Firstly, the data imbalance between positive and negative samples is a widely concerned problem in medicine [3,16,19], e.g., the morbidity of glaucoma is only 3.5%

among people over 45 years old [17]. General solution to this problem is data augmentation [3,12], however, it may also lead to the overfitting problem [13]. In this paper, we solve such a data imbalance problem from both aspects of the network design and training strategy. Specifically, the attention mechanism is considered in the AP-CNN subnet highlighting the key features, so that less positive samples are needed for training our DeepGF model. Then, a novel active convergence (AC) training strategy is proposed to actively choose the hard samples, which increases the sensitivity rate while simultaneously keeps the high specificity rate.

Secondly, it is hard to regularize patients to take medical examinations with a fixed time interval, which may vary from months to years, bringing the difficulties to predict the status transition across times. Different from the traditional LSTM-based methods for forecast that simplify the variant sampling intervals [1,15], we propose a novel VTI-LSTM in the DeepGF, which can learn the temporal transition at different time intervals. Note that the input of the VTI-LSTM is the spatial features from AP-CNN.

To the best of our knowledge, our work is the first attempt for glaucoma forecast. The main contributions are concluded as follows. (1) We establish the SIGF database with sequential fundus images. (2) Based on the SIGF, we propose the DeepGF structure with AP-CNN and VTI-LSTM to predict the risk of glaucoma. (3) The attention mechanism and the AC training strategy are proposed in our DeepGF method to solve the imbalance sample distribution problem for glaucoma forecast.

2   Method

2.1   Framework

For glaucoma forecast, we develop a novel deep neural network (DNN) architecture that includes AP-CNN and VTI-LSTM. The architecture of our DeepGF is shown in Fig. 2. As shown, the input is an RGB-channel fundus image $\mathbf{I}_t \in \mathbb{R}^{224 \times 224 \times 3}$ at time step t, and the output at the time step t is the binary label $\hat{l}_{t+1}$ ($\in \{0, 1\}$) of being glaucomatous or not at the next time step $t+1$. Mathematically, the problem of glaucoma forecast can be formulated by

$$\hat{l}_{t+1} = f(\mathbf{I}_{t+1} | \mathbf{I}_1, \mathbf{I}_2, \cdots, \mathbf{I}_t), \tag{1}$$

where $f(\cdot)$ is the glaucoma forecast function to be learned.

In the DeepGF, the AP-CNN structure is composed of 2 subnets: the attention subnet and the polar subnet, inspired by the characteristics of glaucoma fundus images. Due to the characteristic that large redundancy exists in glaucoma detection [14], the attention subnet is proposed to remove the redundant regions on the fundus images by masking an attention map $\mathbf{A}_t \in \mathbb{R}^{224 \times 224 \times 1}$ on both the input fundus images and the extracted feature maps. As a result, the key features for glaucoma forecast can be highlighted. Besides, the polar subnet is introduced, because the positive glaucoma has larger VCDR [7,9]. The fundus

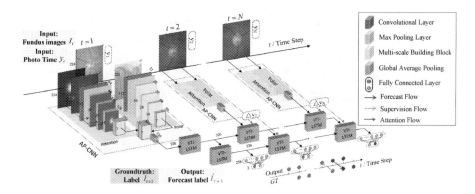

Fig. 2. Architecture of DeepGF.

images mapped in polar coordinates, i.e., $\mathbf{I}_t^r(\rho, \theta) \in \mathbb{R}^{224 \times 224 \times 3}$ can enlarge the optic cup regions, which is effective in finding the larger VCDR. Note that ρ and θ denote the radius and angle in the polar coordinates, respectively. Finally, the features extracted by the attention and polar subnets are concatenated and further reduced to a vector $\mathbf{f}_t \in \mathbb{R}^{1 \times 320}$ as the final spatial feature.

Subsequently, the 2-layer VTI-LSTM is designed to learn the dynamic glaucoma transition, in which features $\{\mathbf{f}_t\}_1^T$ (T denotes the total number of time steps) from the AP-CNN serve as the input. In contrast to the traditional LSTM [8], the length of variant time interval $\triangle y_t$ is further encoded into the forget gate f_t of the VTI-LSTM. Finally, the output from the second VTI-LSTM layer $\mathbf{h}_t^2 \in \mathbb{R}^{1 \times 320}$ at time step t is fed into the fully connected (FC) layers, outputting the probability of $\hat{l}_{t+1}$ at the next time step $t + 1$. Note that the AC training strategy is adopted in our DeepGF to solve the imbalance data problem.

2.2 Attention and Polar Based CNNs

Attention Subnet. In our AP-CNN, an attention subnet is designed for extracting the salient spatial features from the fundus images. As shown in Fig. 2, the architecture of the AP-CNN is followed by one convolutional layer with a kernel size of 7×7, a max-pooling layer and four multi-scale building blocks [14]. Note that all convolutional layers in AP-CNN are followed by a batch normalization layer and an ReLU layer for increasing the nonlinearity of AG-CNN. Then, to remove the redundancy on the fundus images, the attention map $\mathbf{A}_t \in \mathbb{R}^{224 \times 224 \times 1}$ is weighted on each channel of its input fundus image $\mathbf{I}_t$ and the corresponding feature maps $\{\mathbf{F}_t^k\}_{k=1}^4$ at layer k, as shown in Fig. 2. Note that, the attention map of each fundus image $\mathbf{A}_t$ is predicted by [14], as shown in Fig. 3 left. For the detailed structure of AP-CNN, refer to Table 1 in Supplementary Materials.

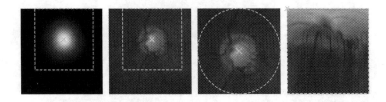

Fig. 3. An example of the input to the DeepGF. (Left): Attention map. (Middle-left): Original fundus images. (Middle-right): ROIs. (Right): ROIs in polar coordinates.

Polar Subnet. A polar subnet is proposed in the AP-CNN to extract features from the fundus images in polar coordinates (ρ, θ). The architecture of the polar subnet is similar to the attention subnet, and the input to the polar subnet is the ROIs of the fundus images mapped into polar coordinates, i.e., $\mathbf{I}_t^r(\rho, \theta) \in \mathbb{R}^{224 \times 224 \times 3}$. Consequently, the optic cup regions can be enlarged to effectively detect the larger VCDR, as illustrated in Fig. 3. To be specific, the ROIs in the polar coordinates $\mathbf{I}_t^r(\rho, \theta)$ are generated by the ROIs in rectangular coordinates $\mathbf{I}_t^r(u, v)$. Note that the ROI $\mathbf{I}_t^r(u, v)$ is cropped with the center of the optic cup center from original fundus image $\mathbf{I}_t(u, v)$. Mathematically, given $\mathbf{I}_t^r(u, v)$, ρ and θ of $\mathbf{I}_t^r(\rho, \theta)$ are calculated by

$$\begin{cases} \rho = \sqrt{(u - \frac{U_p}{2})^2 + (v - \frac{V_p}{2})^2}, \\ \theta = \tan^{-1}(\frac{v-v_0}{u-u_0}), \end{cases} \tag{2}$$

where U_p and V_p are the width and height of $\mathbf{I}_t^r(u, v)$, and (u_0, v_0) is the center coordinates of $\mathbf{I}_t^r(u, v)$.

Finally, the features $\mathbf{F}_t^a (\in \mathbb{R}^{7 \times 7 \times 256})$ extracted by attention subnet and $\mathbf{F}_t^p (\in \mathbb{R}^{7 \times 7 \times 64})$ extracted by the polar subnet are concatenated along with channels to obtain $\mathbf{F}_t (\in \mathbb{R}^{7 \times 7 \times 320})$, which is then down-sampled by global average pooling and reshaped to a vector $\mathbf{f}_t (\in \mathbb{R}^{1 \times 320})$. Note that the parameters ω_c of AP-CNN are shared across time steps.

2.3   VTI-LSTM

In addition to the AP-CNN, we propose a novel VTI-LSTM to learn transition across time steps. Mathematically, the VTI-LSTM can be formulated as:

$$i_t = \sigma(\mathbf{W}_{x_i} x_t + \mathbf{W}_{h_i} h_{t-1} + b_i), \tag{3}$$

$$\tilde{f}_t = \sigma(\mathrm{p} \triangle y_t + \mathrm{q}), \tag{4}$$

$$f_t = \sigma(\tilde{f}_t(\mathbf{W}_{x_f} x_t + \mathbf{W}_{h_f} h_{t-1}) + b_f), \tag{5}$$

$$c_t = f_t \circ c_{t-1} + i_t \circ \tanh(\mathbf{W}_{x_c} x_t + \mathbf{W}_{h_c} h_{t-1} + b_c), \tag{6}$$

$$o_t = \sigma(\mathbf{W}_{x_o} x_t + \mathbf{W}_{h_o} h_{t-1} + b_o), \tag{7}$$

$$h_t = o_t \circ \tanh(c_t), \tag{8}$$

where $\sigma(\cdot)$ is the sigmoid function, and "$\circ$" denotes the Hadamard products. For time step t, we have the input $\boldsymbol{x}_t$, the cell state $\boldsymbol{c}_t$, the hidden state $\boldsymbol{h}_t$ and the gates of input $\boldsymbol{i}_t$, forget $\boldsymbol{f}_t$ and output $\boldsymbol{o}_t \in \mathbb{R}^{1\times320}$. In addition, $\mathbf{W}_{x_\sim}$ and $\mathbf{W}_{h_\sim} \in \mathbb{R}^{320\times320}$ are the corresponding parameters to be learned. In (4), $\triangle y_t (\in \mathbb{N})$ is the time length from time step $t-1$ and t, and $\tilde{f}_t$ ($0 < \tilde{f}_t < 1$) denotes to the variable time interval (VTI) gate, which further controls the forgetting rate with the time interval. Besides, p and q($\in \mathbb{R}$) are the parameters of the VTI gate. As such, different from the traditional LSTM, the VTI-LSTM capably encodes the variant length between time steps.

2.4   Imbalance Sample Training Strategy: AC Strategy

To train the DeepGF, we supervise the training process with the labels of the next time step l_{t+1} by the forecast loss function $\mathcal{L}_f$ as follows:

$$\mathcal{L}_f = -\frac{1}{T}\sum\nolimits_{t=1}^{T} \left(l_{t+1}\log p_{t+1} + (1 - l_{t+1})\log(1 - p_{t+1})\right), \tag{9}$$

where T is the maximum time step of the image sequence, and p_{t+1} is the forecast probability of positive glaucoma at time step $t+1$. Note that $p_{t+1} = \frac{1}{1+e^{-z_t}}$, where z_t is the output of the second FC layer at time step t. Given the trained DeepGF, the forecast binary label $\hat{l}_{t+1}$ ($\in \{0,1\}$) is decided by $\hat{l}_{t+1} = \mathbb{1}(p_{t+1} \geq \xi)$, where $\mathbb{1}(\cdot)$ is a conditional binary indicator and ξ is the probability threshold.

However, the morbidity of glaucoma is 3.5% among people over 45 years old [17], leading to the imbalance data distribution problem. To address this problem, we propose a novel AC training strategy to self-update the distribution of the training set actively and adaptively. The AC strategy is consisted of 2 steps, as summarized in Algorithm 1 in the Supplementary Materials. (1) $\mathcal{L}_f(\omega)$ is calculated and the parameters ω of the DeepGF are updated by decreasing with the gradients $\nabla_\omega\mathcal{L}(\omega)$. (2) Some training samples are dynamically removed from the training set $\{\mathbf{I}^s\}_{s=1}^{S}$ according to $\mathcal{L}_f(\omega)$, where S is the total number of the training sequences, and $\mathbf{I}^s = \{\mathbf{I}_t^s\}_{t=1}^{T}$ represents a fundus image sequence. To be specific, a number of βS sequences, the training loss of which (i.e., $\mathcal{L}_f(\omega)$) ranks the lowest, are discarded from the training set every δ epochs. Note that the discarding terminates until reaching the maximum abandon epoch N. As a result, the training set $\{\mathbf{I}^s\}_{s=1}^{S}$ can be actively updated, remaining the hardest samples to be further learned.

3   SIGF Database

For training and testing our DeepGF model, we establish a database of sequential fundus images for glaucoma forecast, called SIGF[1]. To our best knowledge, SIGF is the first database consisting of sequential fundus images. Our SIGF database

---

[1] The database is available at https://github.com/XiaofeiWang2018/DeepGF.

contains 405 image sequences from different eyes, and each eye has at least 6 fundus images captured at different years (ranging from 1986 to 2018), with an average of 9 images per eye, corresponding to 3,671 images in total. An example of the SIGF database is shown in Fig. 1 in the Supplementary Materials

In the SIGF database, all fundus images are annotated with binary labels of glaucoma, i.e., positive or negative glaucoma. The samples are labeled to positive glaucoma when they satisfy any of the three criteria, i.e., retinal nerve fibre layer defect, rim loss and optic disc hemorrhage. Consequently, all the fundus images are labeled and the sequences can be divided into 2 types: time-variant (37 sequences change from negative to positive glaucoma) and time-invariant (368 sequences keep negative glaucoma). Note that no sequence changes from positive to negative glaucoma, since glaucoma is irreversible. Our work is conducted according to the Declaration of Helsinki. As the fully anonymous usage of fundus images, we are exempted by the medical ethics committee to inform the patients.

4   Experiment

4.1   Setting

In the experiment, the 405 image sequences of our SIGF database are randomly divided into training (300), validation (35) and test (70) sets, and the proportion of the time-variant and time-invariant sequences keeps invariant in the training (27 and 273), validation (3 and 32) and test sets (7 and 63).

Specifically, we temporally segment the 405 sequences into 1,146 clips, with each clip containing $T(= 6)$ time steps. An overlap of 5 frames is allowed in cutting the sequence clips, for the purpose of data augmentation. Before feeding into the DeepGF, the fundus image are resized to 224×224. In training AP-CNN and VTI-LSTM, we learn the parameters using Adam optimizer [11], and the hyper-parameters are tuned over the validation set, as provided in Table 2 in the Supplementary.

4.2   Evaluation

Glaucoma Forecast. In this section, we compare the glaucoma forecast performance with two other methods [4,14]. To our best knowledge, there is no method for glaucoma forecast. Therefore, we convert [4,14] to be glaucoma forecast methods by supervising their CNN models with the labels at the next time step. Table 1-left lists the results of accuracy, sensitivity and specificity. As shown in this table, our DeepGF achieves 80.7%, 85.7% and 80.6% in accuracy, sensitivity and specificity, respectively, which are considerably better than other two methods [4,14]. Then, Fig. 4(b) plots the ROC curves of our and other methods, for visualizing the trade-off between sensitivity and specificity. As shown, our ROC curve is closer to the upper-left corner than other two methods [4,14]. This indicates that given a referable specificity, our method has better performance in forecasting positive glaucoma than [4,14]. Similar results can be found from the AUC metrics in Table 1. In a word, our DeepGF method is effective in forecasting glaucoma, significantly outperforming the state-of-the-art methods.

Network Interpretability. An additional visualization experiment is conducted by the CAM-based method [20] for glaucoma forecast. As shown in Fig. 4 (a), the visualization result focuses on the potential pathological rim-loss regions and the optic cup regions (the biomarkers for glaucoma in clinic [6]), which verifies the interpretability of our DeepGF method for glaucoma forecast.

Table 1. Performance of glaucoma forecast over SIGF database.

Method	Glaucoma forecast, %			Ablation study (W/O), %				
	Ours	Chen [4]	Li [14]	Attention	Polar	VTI gate	LSTM	AC
Accuracy	**80.7**	67.6	66.0	76.0	77.8	73.2	67.1	58.4
Sensitivity	**85.7**	62.2	68.9	73.8	73.8	73.8	69.0	66.7
Specificity	**80.6**	67.8	65.9	76.0	77.9	73.1	67.1	58.2
AUC	**87.0**	71.8	70.0	80.9	81.6	80.8	74.9	64.8

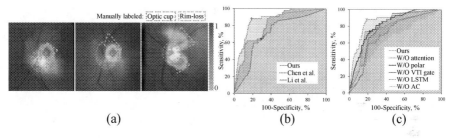

Fig. 4. (a): Visualization results of DeepGF for glaucoma forecast. (b): ROC curves of glaucoma forecast methods. (c): ROC curves of ablation experiments.

4.3   Results of Ablation Experiments

AP-CNN. In our ablation experiments, we first investigate the impact of the attention and polar subnets in the AP-CNN. To this end, we simply remove the attention and polar subnets, respectively, and then compare the performance of glaucoma forecast. The quantitative results are shown in Table 1-right. As shown, the attention subnet can improve the accuracy, sensitivity, specificity and AUC by 4.7%, 11.9%, 4.6% and 6.1%, respectively, and the polar subnet can also increase 2.9%, 11.9%, 2.7% and 5.4%, respectively. Also, the ROC curves of removing the attention or polar subnet are shown in Fig. 4-c. These results indicate the necessity of our AP-CNN model for glaucoma forecast.

VTI-LSTM. Additionally, we evaluate the impact of VTI-LSTM in the DeepGF by 2 stages. First, we replace the VTI-LSTM by a standard LSTM to show the impact of VTI gate encoding the variable time intervals. The result is shown in Table 1-right. We can see that the VTI gate improves the performance of glaucoma forecast in terms of accuracy by 7.5%. Similar results can be found for sensitivity, specificity and AUC. Second, we further remove the LSTM in our DeepGF, such that the temporal features are not considered. As shown in Table 1-right, all metrics decrease at least 12.1%. Such performance degradation is considerably more than that of the AP-CNN, also validated by the ROC curves in Fig. 4(c). Hence, the VTI-LSTM is vitally important for glaucoma forecast.

AC Strategy. We further evaluate the effectiveness of our AC training strategy, by replacing the AC training strategy with a data augmentation strategy [3], which is the common solution to the imbalance problem. As shown in Table 1-right, the performance of training the DeepGF with [3], instead of our AC strategy, decreases in all metrics, , i.e., the reduction of 22.3%, 19.0%, 22.4% and 22.2%, for accuracy, sensitivity, specificity and AUC, respectively. Similar results can be found from the ROC curves on Fig. 4(c). These ablation results validate the effectiveness of the AC training strategy proposed in this paper.

5   Conclusion

Glaucoma forecast refers to predicting whether a person will suffer from glaucoma in the future. Since glaucoma is an irreversible blindness disease, glaucoma forecast is even more important than glaucoma detection that aims at diagnosing glaucoma at the present stage. To achieve glaucoma forecast, both the current and previous fundus images are useful, as the temporal tendency of glaucoma can be learned. Input with the sequence of the present and previous fundus images, DeepGF has been proposed in this paper as a novel deep learning method for glaucoma forecast. In our DeepGF method, we proposed two new DNN structures: AP-CNN and VTI-LSTM. The AP-CNN mainly focuses on extracting the spatial features of fundus images by taking into account the attention mechanism and polar projection. The VTI-LSTM was developed to learn the temporal features across fundus images at different time steps. Consequently, the spatio-temporal features can be obtained for glaucoma forecast. Finally, the experiment results show that our DeepGF is superior to other state-of-the-art methods in glaucoma forecast.

Acknowledgement. This paper is supported by BMSTC project under grant Z181100001918035, and by the NSFC project under grant 61922009 and 61876013.

References

1. Amirkhan, R., Hoogendoorn, M., Numans, M.E., Moons, L.: Using recurrent neural networks to predict colorectal cancer among patients. In: SSCI, pp. 1–8. IEEE (2017)
2. Bourne, R.R.A., et al.: Causes of vision loss worldwide, 1990–2010: a systematic analysis. Lancet GH **1**(6), e339–e349 (2013)

3. Chen, J., et al.: Detecting hypoglycemia incidents reported in patients' secure messages: using cost-sensitive learning and oversampling to reduce data imbalance. JMIR **21**(3), e11990 (2019)
4. Chen, X., Xu, Y., Wong, D.W.K., Wong, T.Y., Liu, J.: Glaucoma detection based on deep convolutional neural network. In: EMBC, p. 715 (2015)
5. Cheng, Y., Wang, F., Zhang, P., Hu, J.: Risk prediction with electronic health records: a deep learning approach. In: ICDM, pp. 432–440. SIAM (2016)
6. Fan, X., Wu, L.L., Ma, Z.Z., Xiao, G.G., Liu Jr., F.: Usefulness of frequency-doubling technology for perimetrically normal eyes of open-angle glaucoma patients with unilateral field loss. Ophthalmology **117**(8), 1530–1537 (2010)
7. Fu, H., et al.: Disc-aware ensemble network for glaucoma screening from fundus image. IEEE TMI (2018)
8. Gers, F.A., Schmidhuber, J., Cummins, F.: Learning to forget: continual prediction with LSTM (1999)
9. Harizman, N., et al.: The ISNT rule and differentiation of normal from glaucomatous eyes. Arch. Ophthalmol. **124**(11), 1579 (2006)
10. Jin, B., Che, C., Liu, Z., Zhang, S., Yin, X., Wei, X.: Predicting the risk of heart failure with EHR sequential data modeling. IEEE Access **6**, 9256–9261 (2018)
11. Kingma, D.P., Ba, J.: Adam: a method for stochastic optimization. arXiv preprint arXiv:1412.6980 (2014)
12. Krawczyk, B., Galar, M., Jeleń, Ł., Herrera, F.: Evolutionary undersampling boosting for imbalanced classification of breast cancer malignancy. ASC **38**, 714–726 (2016)
13. Le, T., Vo, M.T., Vo, B., Lee, M.Y., Baik, S.W.: A hybrid approach using oversampling technique and cost-sensitive learning for bankruptcy prediction. Complexity (2019)
14. Li, L., Xu, M., Wang, X., Jiang, L., Liu, H.: Attention based glaucoma detection: a large-scale database and CNN model. In: IEEE CVPR, pp. 10571–10580 (2019)
15. Lipton, Z.C., Kale, D.C., Elkan, C., Wetzel, R.: Learning to diagnose with LSTM recurrent neural networks. arXiv preprint arXiv:1511.03677 (2015)
16. Liu, H., et al.: Development and validation of a deep learning system to detect glaucomatous optic neuropathy using fundus photographs. JAMA Ophthalmol. **137**(12), 1353–1360 (2019)
17. Tham, Y.C., Li, X., Wong, T.Y., Quigley, H.A., Aung, T., Cheng, C.Y.: Global prevalence of glaucoma and projections of glaucoma burden through 2040: a systematic review and meta-analysis. Ophthalmology **121**(11), 2081 (2014)
18. Thomson, R., Luettel, D., Healey, F., Scobie, S.: Safer Care for the Acutely Ill Patient: Learning from Serious Incidents. National Patient Safety Agency, London (2007)
19. Tomašev, N., et al.: A clinically applicable approach to continuous prediction of future acute kidney injury. Nature **572**(7767), 116 (2019)
20. Zhou, B., Khosla, A., Lapedriza, A., Oliva, A., Torralba, A.: Learning deep features for discriminative localization. In: IEEE CVPR, pp. 2921–2929 (2016)

Single-Shot Retinal Image Enhancement Using Deep Image Priors

Adnan Qayyum[1(✉)], Waqas Sultani[1], Fahad Shamshad[1], Junaid Qadir[1], and Rashid Tufail[2]

[1] Information Technology University of the Punjab, Lahore, Pakistan
adnan.qayyum@itu.edu.pk
[2] Wajahat Surgical Hospital, Attock, Pakistan

Abstract. Retinal images acquired using fundus cameras often contain visual artifacts due to imperfect imaging conditions, refractive medium turbidity, and motion blur. In addition, ocular diseases such as the presence of cataract results in blurred retinal image. The presence of these visual artifacts reduces the effectiveness of the diagnosis process followed by an expert ophthalmologist or a computer-aided detection/diagnosis system. In this paper, we put forward a single-shot deep image priors (DIP)-based approach for retinal image enhancement. Unlike typical deep learning-based approaches, our method does not require any training data. Instead, our DIP-based method can learn the underlying image prior using a single degraded image. We show that the architecture of the convolutional neural network imposes a strong image prior that is sufficient for capturing the retinal image statistics to generate an enhanced image using a degraded version of it. We evaluate our proposed framework on five datasets and show that the enhanced images using our proposed method perform significantly better on the retinal image enhancement and synthesis tasks as compared to several competitive baselines.

Keywords: Retinal image enhancement · Retinal image generation · Single image analysis

1 Introduction

In ophthalmic clinical practice, retinal images obtained through fundus photography (which shows retinal blood vessels) are routinely used in the diagnosis and treatment of diseases such as diabetic retinopathy, hypertensive retinopathy, and age-related muscular degeneration [4,17]. Such images are routinely used by various computer-aided detection/diagnosis systems to detect glaucoma [21] and diabetic retinopathy [11]; and perform classification of retinal arteries and veins [18] and blood vessel segmentation [20].

Electronic supplementary material The online version of this chapter (https://doi.org/10.1007/978-3-030-59722-1_61) contains supplementary material, which is available to authorized users.

© Springer Nature Switzerland AG 2020
A. L. Martel et al. (Eds.): MICCAI 2020, LNCS 12265, pp. 636–646, 2020.
https://doi.org/10.1007/978-3-030-59722-1_61

However, retinal images acquired in practice are often low quality for diverse reasons such as the use of low-resolution fundus camera, uneven illumination, blurring, incorrect focus, imperfect imaging conditions, and refractive medium turbidity [3], which results in hazy and blurred images. Eye diseases can also affect the quality of the fundus image—e.g., the presence of cataract results in visually blurred retinal images [19], with the blurriness increasing with cataract severity [27]. These artifacts affect the sensitivity of detection, diagnosis, and prognosis of the progressive ophthalmological diseases due to the difficulty of analyzing vascular structure in visually blurred images [17].

In the literature, different approaches have been proposed for retinal image enhancement including methods that focus on image transformation [17]; contrast adjustment [31] and normalization [9]; and deep learning (DL) [28,30]. These DL-based methods operate in supervised learning fashion and are typically data-driven. Such techniques require huge amounts of training data which is inconvenient in realistic settings because obtaining high quality (representative or paired) medical data is very difficult and expensive.

In contrast to the data-driven DL approaches, we present a new DL approach for the deblurring of retinal fundus images which does not require any training data (paired or unpaired images). Our approach is inspired by the recent successes of Deep Image Prior (DIP) techniques [10,26], which uses a single degraded image for recovering a faithful estimate of the true enhanced image without resorting to supervised learning. More specifically, our DIP-based method utilizes the structure of the deep network itself as the regularizer for the inverse problem of recovering the original unblurred image.

We formulate the problem of retinal fundus image enhancement as an ill-posed inverse problem in which our aim is to find a clean retinal image from a degraded one without having any prior knowledge of the clean image. Our interest in this approach is motivated by our desire to leverage the network's structure as a regularizer to solve the inverse problem of recovering the original image x. We strive to leverage coupled multiple DIP networks to decompose the blurred image into its basic layers (i.e., the blurry layer and the clean image layer). Our approach promises to be useful for the enhancement of medical images because good quality representative medical imaging datasets are not available for training of DL models. Moreover, it eliminates the strong underlying assumption of data stationarity assumed by DL that implicitly posits that both training and testing data comes from the same distribution. *To the best of our knowledge, this paper is the first attempt towards the development of a non-learning based method that exploits the structure of the convolutional neural network (CNN) for retinal fundus image enhancement.*

The following are the specific contributions of this paper: (1) We present a single-shot DL framework for retinal image enhancement that employs only degraded image during training; (2) We have formulated the problem of retinal image enhancement as a layer decomposition problem in which we aim to decompose a degraded image into different layers, mainly to model the blurriness effect and the clean retinal image; (3) We further augment the capacity of coupled DIP networks with dark channel prior; and (4) We perform extensive performance evaluation of the proposed framework on five different datasets, qualitatively and quantitatively and have obtained competitive results.

2   Related Work and Background

Retinal Image Enhancement: Over the past years, substantial research attention has focused on retinal image enhancement with the broad deployment of conventional image processing techniques—e.g., luminosity and contrast adjustment [31]; low-pass filtering and α-rooting [3]; contrast stretching and intensity transfer [2]. In more recent works, researchers have explored the use of DL-based methods. Samailagic et al. [24] trained a U-Net model for transmission map estimation that was integrated with a shadow removal layer of retinal fundus images. Xiong et al. [27] proposed a method for retinal image enhancement using the image formation model. Recently, Zhao et al. [30] proposed a DL-based approach employing generative adversarial networks (GAN) for fundus retinal image enhancement. Two GANs were trained for deblurring of retinal fundus images using a training set of 1100 images (550 normal and 550 blurred images) in a weakly supervised fashion using two sets of unpaired blurry/high-quality images. They used a training set of 949 images with 4× data augmentation, i.e., a total of 3796 images were used for the training. Our proposed approach is distinct from the DL-based approaches proposed in [24, 28, 30] since (1) our method does not require any training data, instead requiring only a single degraded image; (2) our method is capable of estimating atmospheric light $A(x)$ along with estimating transmission map $t(x)$, whereas the previous work assumed $A(x) = 1$.

Deep Image Priors (DIP): DIP was recently proposed in [26], where authors demonstrated that the architecture of CNN is biased towards natural images and structure of the CNN model is sufficient to capture the low-level image statistics before any training. The authors used a randomly initialized (i.e., untrained) CNN based generative model as a handcrafted prior for solving various inverse problems such as denoising, superresolution, and inpainting. Instead of training the complete CNN model, they only fitted the parameters of the generative network to a single degraded image. To restore the degraded image, the randomly initialized weights were optimized to maximize their likelihood given a specific input image and a task-specific observation model. Image statistics are then captured directly by the convolutional image generator's structure rather than through concepts learned through data. Several variations of DIP has been presented recently [1,10]. Inspired by [26], Gandelsman et al. [10] proposed to decompose an image into its layers—such that the distribution of the *"image elements"* within each layer is simple. They show that coupling multiple DIP networks is a potent tool for decomposing images into their basic layers for various inverse problems including image foreground/background segmentation, image dehazing, transparency separation in images and videos, and watermark removal.

The mathematical expression for solving inverse problems is given by energy minimization of the type

$$x^* = \operatorname*{argmin}_{x} E(x; x_0) + R(x), \qquad (1)$$

where, E is task-specific function, x and x_0 denote generated image and input image, respectively and $R(x)$ is the regularizer function. DIP removes the explicit regularization term $R(x)$ by assuming that the unknown image x should be an image generated from the generator network such that

$$\theta^* = \operatorname*{argmin}_{\theta} E(f_\theta(z); x_0), \quad x^* = f_{\theta^*}(z), \qquad (2)$$

where, $E(f_\theta(z); x_0)$ is a task specific data term (i.e., specified by the application, such as denoising), x and x_0 denote the enhanced image and the degraded image, respectively, and $f_\theta(z)$ is the generator that maps the random code vector z to an image x, i.e., $x = f_\theta(z)$. To obtain the minimizer θ^* from randomly initialized parameters, an optimizer (e.g., gradient descent) can be used and the result of the restoration process for given θ^* is given by $x^* = f_{\theta^*}(z)$.

3   Methodology

We formulate our problem as an image decomposition problem and utilize the approach of multiple DIPs, which has been very successful in solving inverse problems that aim at decomposing an image into its basic layers. The proposed method is described below.

3.1   Image Decomposition Using Coupled DIP Models

The concept of coupling multiple DIP is based on the fact that various computer vision applications aim to decompose an image into its constituent layers—e.g., in image segmentation the interest is in separating an image into foreground and background layers; in transparent layer separation, the interest is in separating into reflection and transmission layers; and in image dehazing, the interest is in separating into a clear image and a haze map.

Illumination Compensation via Coupled DIPs: It is well established that illumination compensation can be interpreted as an haze removal problem and the model to describe the hazy image $I(x)$ can be given as [8,13]:

$$I(x) = t(x)J(x) + (1 - t(x))A(x), \qquad (3)$$

where, $t(x)$ is transmission map (t-map), $J(x)$ is the recovered (*haze free*) image, and $A(x)$ is the atmospheric map. We formulate the problem of retinal image enhancement as a layer decomposition problem, where we are interested in decomposing a blurred or hazy image $I(x)$ into three layers, i.e., clean (*haze*

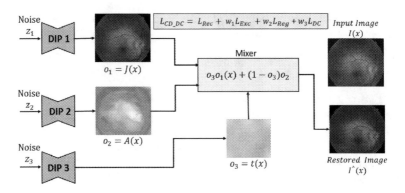

Fig. 1. The pipeline of retinal image enhancement using coupled deep image prior (DIP) networks. The input image $I(x)$ is decomposed into three layers $o_1 = J(x)$ (*the enhanced image*), $o_2 = A(x)$ (*the atmospheric light*), and $o_3 = t(x)$ (*the transmission map*) by DIP_1, DIP_2 and DIP_3, respectively. To reconstruct the recovered image ($\hat{I} \approx I$), o_1 and o_2 are mixed with o_3. The figure depicts the actual results.

free) image ($o_1(x) = J(x)$), atmospheric map ($o_2 = A(x)$), and the mixing mask, i.e., t-map ($o_3 = t(x)$). Therefore, the Eq. 3 can be expressed as

$$\hat{I}(x) = o_3 o_1(x) + (1 - o_3) o_2(x). \qquad (4)$$

The pipeline of the proposed method is depicted in Fig. 1. As shown in the figure, each DIP network (i.e., DIP_i) takes randomly sampled uniform noise z_i and produces a different layer o_i of the input image $I(x)$. The reconstructed image is obtain by mixing the output of each DIP (i.e., o_1 and o_2,) and learned mask o_3 (i.e., transmission map $t(x)$) for current image by DIP_3, as depicted in Eq. 4. The optimization loss for retinal image enhancement using coupled DIPs is given as $L_{CD} = L_{Rec} + w_1 L_{Exc} + w_2 L_{Reg}$ where L_{Rec} denotes the reconstruction loss i.e., $||I - \hat{I}||_2$, L_{Exc} forces DIP_1, DIP_2 and DIP_3 to capture different information by minimizing the correlation between the gradients of output layers o_1, o_2 and o_3, respectively. L_{Reg} is regularization loss of DIP_3 and enforces the weighted mask o_3 to be smooth and finally, L_{CD} represents the overall loss of coupled DIP architecture.

Augmenting the Capacity of Coupled DIPs: To further boost the power of coupled DIP networks in recovering a clean image, we propose to incorporate dark channel prior (DCP). DCP is a well known for single-image dehazing of natural images [13]. DCP is a popular method used for the estimation of $t(x)$, which is based on the observation that in most of the local patches of haze-free color images, pixels have very low intensity in one of the color channel, which is called the dark channel. The dark channel for an image $I(x)$ is computed using the following formulation.

$$I^{Dark}(x) = \min_{C \in \{R,G,B\}} \left(\min_{y \in \Omega(x)} (I^C(y)) \right), \qquad (5)$$

Table 1. Performance of the proposed method on different databases in terms of the average peak signal to noise ratio (PSNR) and the structural similarity index (SSIM).

Dataset	Total Images	PSNR	SSIM
Messidore	1200	40.3888	0.9396
STARE	397	38.8671	0.9928
DRIVE	40	38.9583	0.9559
DIARET DB0	130	41.5616	0.9835
DIARET DB1	89	41.2076	0.9714

where $I^C(y)$ is the color channel of image $I(x)$ and $\Omega(x)$ is local patch centered at x. Finally, the updated loss function of coupled DIP augmented with dark channel loss is given as:

$$L_{CD\_DC} = L_{Rec} + w_1 L_{Exc} + w_2 L_{Reg} + w_3 L_{DC}, \tag{6}$$

where $L_{DC} = \sum_{j=1}^{W \times H} |dark(\hat{I}(x))_i|$ is loss of dark channel prior, and W and H denotes width and height of the generated image, respectively. The function $dark(.)$ computes the dark channel of the generated image $\hat{I}(x)$ using Eq. 5 and w_1, w_2, and w_3 are optimization hyperparameters.

4   Experiments and Results

4.1   Setup and Dataset Description

We perform extensive experiments on the five publicly available fundus image datasets having different number of images and dimensions—namely, (i) DRIVE [25], (ii) STARE [14], (iii) Messidor [7], and (iv and v) DIARET DB calibration level 0 and 1 [15]). We note here that DRIVE and STARE are the benchmark databases for *retinal blood vessel segmentation* while Messidor and DIARET DB (0 and 1) are the benchmark databases for *diabetic retinopathy classification*.

4.2   Implementation Details

We use the U-Net [22] as the generator network for synthesizing the enhanced retinal images. U-net is a deep CNN based generative model that was specifically developed for biomedical image segmentation [22]. The model having an hourglass-like architecture and with skip-connections between encoder layers and decoder layers. The same model architecture was used in DIP [26] and Double-DIP [10]. The optimization of the network is performed using ADAM optimizer [16] with a learning rate of 0.005 and default values of $\beta_1 = 0.9$, $\beta_2 = 0.999$, and $\epsilon = 1e^{-8}$. We use $w_1 = w_2 = w_3 = 1$ and each images of all dataset are processed for 3500 iterations.

4.3   Visual and Quantitative Evaluation of Enhancement

We quantitatively evaluate the proposed method in terms of the peak signal to noise ratio (PSNR) and the structural similarity index (SSIM) on five different state of the art retinal fundus image datasets. The results are summarized in Table 1. PSNR is relatively low for blood vessel segmentation databases (i.e., DRIVE and STARE), as these databases are much more challenging as compared to diabetic retinopathy classification datasets. The comparison of the proposed method with existing methods for retinal image enhancement and synthesis is presented in Table 2. The table demonstrates that the proposed method performed remarkably better than existing methods despite being trained on the only single degraded image. Note that we have compared our method with the

Table 2. The comparison of the proposed method with existing methods for retinal image enhancement and synthesis. (Legend: M = Messidor; D = DRIVE; S = STARE; D0 = DIARET DB0; D1 = DIARET DB1; GAN = Generative Adversarial Network; VAE = Variational Autoencoder)

Retinal image enhancement									
Paper	Method	Dataset						PSNR	SSIM
		M	D	S	D0	D1	Other[a]		
[30]	Two GANs are trained for deblurring	-	-	-	-	-	10 images	19.24	0.89
[31]	Luminosity and contrast adjustment	-	-	-	-	-	10 images	17.73	0.73
[19]	Histogram and intensity equalization	-	-	-	-	-	10 images	16.38	0.78
[27]	Use image formation model	-	-	-	-	-	10 images	17.26	0.87
Ours	Deep Image priors based method	√	√	√	√	√	-	**40.19**	**0.96**
Retinal image synthesis									
[29]	Tub-sGAN	-	√	-	-	-	-	-	0.8980
[6]	Adversarial autoencoder and GAN	-	√	-	-	-	-	-	0.8716
[5]	Deep residual VAE and GAN	-	√	-	-	-	-	-	0.74
[12]	Two GANs are trained	-	√	-	-	-	-	-	0.64
Ours	Deep image priors based method	-	√	-	-	-	-	**38.9583**	**0.9559**

[a]Dataset publicly not available.

synthesis methods because our method utilizes generative modeling to reconstruct enhanced images (without data-driven training).

The intermediate results generated by the proposed method for the shown image along with PSNR and SSIM are demonstrated in Fig. 2. The figure depicts that the proposed method generates a random noise at the first iteration and gradually optimizes network parameters to generate an enhanced image. Note that the generator network fits its parameters using a single degraded image, i.e., without data-driven training.

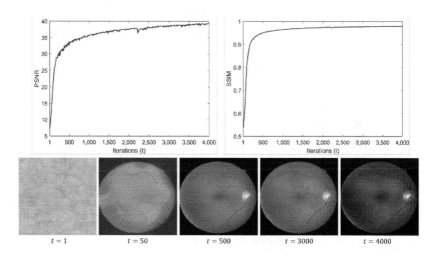

Fig. 2. The illustration of improvement in PSNR and SSIM over iterations t for a given input image, the intermediate results generated by our method at iteration $t = 1, 50, 500, 3000$, and 4000 are shown at bottom. Please see supplementary material for visualization.

The visual comparison of reconstructed (enhanced) images for different quality of blurry images is shown in Fig. 3. It can be clearly seen from Fig. 3 that the proposed method is able to recover good quality images in which retinal blood vessels are prominently highlighted. Note that it is done without any prior knowledge of the enhanced image.

To further evaluate the proposed approach, we perform separate experiments using blurred images and the enhanced images (generated by the proposed method) *diabetic retinopathy classification*. We use the Messidor dataset and VGG16 [23] model with pre-trained ImageNet weights. The model is trained for 100 epochs with a learning rate of 0.001. Our results show an accuracy of 91.18% for blurred input and 93.25% for enhanced input.

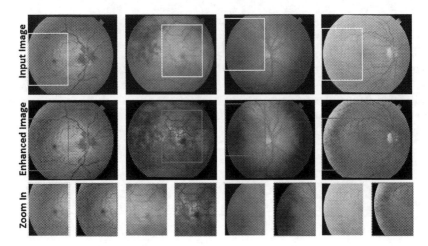

Fig. 3. Visual comparison of reconstructed (enhanced) images for different quality of blurry images. Blurry input images are shown in first row, second row contains enhanced version of the images in first row and selected zoom-in patches from blurry (yellow) and enhanced (red) are shown in the last row. Please see supplementary material for more examples. (Color figure online)

5   Conclusions

In this paper, we have presented a unified single-shot deep learning (DL) framework for the enhancement of retinal fundus images using deep image priors (DIP). The proposed method does not require any data-driven training and it recovers the enhanced image from a single blurry retinal image. Furthermore, we evaluate the proposed approach on five different retinal fundus image datasets in terms of average peak signal to noise ratio (PSNR) and average structural similarity index (SSIM). In addition, we performed experiments for a well-known computer-aided task, i.e., diabetic retinopathy classification. As paired clean and noisy medical images are scarcely available, this paper aims to instigate future research in developing unsupervised DL frameworks without data-driven training. In addition to enhancing degraded medical images, these can be augmented into the training set of data-driven pipelines to improve the efficacy of the DL systems.

References

1. Asim, M., Shamshad, F., Ahmad, A.: Blind image deconvolution using pretrained generative priors. In: British Machine Vision Conference (2019)
2. Cao, L., Li, H.: Enhancement of blurry retinal image based on non-uniform contrast stretching and intensity transfer. Med. Boil. Eng. Comput. **58**(3), 483–496 (2020). https://doi.org/10.1007/s11517-019-02106-7
3. Cao, L., Li, H., Zhang, Y.: Retinal image enhancement using low-pass filtering and α-rooting. Sig. Process. **170**, 107445 (2020)

4. Chen, B., Chen, Y., Shao, Z., Tong, T., Luo, L.: Blood vessel enhancement via multi-dictionary and sparse coding: application to retinal vessel enhancing. Neurocomputing **200**, 110–117 (2016)
5. Cheng, J., Li, Z., Gu, Z., Fu, H., Wong, D.W.K., Liu, J.: Structure-preserving guided retinal image filtering for optic disc analysis. In: Computational Retinal Image Analysis, pp. 199–221. Elsevier (2019)
6. Costa, P., Galdran, A., Meyer, M.I., Mendonça, A.M., Campilho, A.: Adversarial synthesis of retinal images from vessel trees. In: Karray, F., Campilho, A., Cheriet, F. (eds.) ICIAR 2017. LNCS, vol. 10317, pp. 516–523. Springer, Cham (2017). https://doi.org/10.1007/978-3-319-59876-5_57
7. Decencière, E., et al.: Feedback on a publicly distributed image database: the messidor database. Image Anal. Stereol. **33**(3), 231–234 (2014)
8. Fattal, R.: Single image dehazing. ACM Trans. Graph. (TOG) **27**(3), 1–9 (2008)
9. Foracchia, M., Grisan, E., Ruggeri, A.: Luminosity and contrast normalization in retinal images. Med. Image Anal. **9**(3), 179–190 (2005)
10. Gandelsman, Y., Shocher, A., Irani, M.: "double-dip": unsupervised image decomposition via coupled deep-image-priors. In: IEEE CVPR, vol. 6, p. 2 (2019)
11. Gargeya, R., Leng, T.: Automated identification of diabetic retinopathy using deep learning. Ophthalmology **124**(7), 962–969 (2017)
12. Guibas, J.T., Virdi, T.S., Li, P.S.: Synthetic medical images from dual generative adversarial networks. In: NIPS 2017 Workshops on Medical Imaging and Machine Learning for Health (2017)
13. He, K., Sun, J., Tang, X.: Single image haze removal using dark channel prior. IEEE Trans. Pattern Anal. Mach. Intell. **33**(12), 2341–2353 (2010)
14. Hoover, A., Kouznetsova, V., Goldbaum, M.: Locating blood vessels in retinal images by piecewise threshold probing of a matched filter response. IEEE Trans. Med. Imaging **19**(3), 203–210 (2000)
15. Kälviäinen, R., Uusitalo, H.: DIARETDB1 diabetic retinopathy database and evaluation protocol. In: Medical Image Understanding and Analysis, vol. 2007, p. 61. Citeseer (2007)
16. Kingma, D.P., Ba, J.: Adam: A method for stochastic optimization. In: 3rd International Conference for Learning Representations (ICLR) (2015)
17. Li, D., Zhang, L., Sun, C., Yin, T., Liu, C., Yang, J.: Robust retinal image enhancement via dual-tree complex wavelet transform and morphology-based method. IEEE Access **7**, 47303–47316 (2019)
18. Ma, W., Yu, S., Ma, K., Wang, J., Ding, X., Zheng, Y.: Multi-task neural networks with spatial activation for retinal vessel segmentation and artery/vein classification. In: Shen, D., Liu, T., Peters, T.M., Staib, L.H., Essert, C., Zhou, S., Yap, P.-T., Khan, A. (eds.) MICCAI 2019. LNCS, vol. 11764, pp. 769–778. Springer, Cham (2019). https://doi.org/10.1007/978-3-030-32239-7_85
19. Mitra, A., Roy, S., Roy, S., Setua, S.K.: Enhancement and restoration of nonuniform illuminated fundus image of retina obtained through thin layer of cataract. Comput. Methods Programs Biomed. **156**, 169–178 (2018)
20. Orlando, J.I., Prokofyeva, E., Blaschko, M.B.: A discriminatively trained fully connected conditional random field model for blood vessel segmentation in fundus images. IEEE Trans. Biomed. Eng. **64**(1), 16–27 (2016)
21. Raghavendra, U., Fujita, H., Bhandary, S.V., Gudigar, A., Tan, J.H., Acharya, U.R.: Deep convolution neural network for accurate diagnosis of glaucoma using digital fundus images. Inf. Sci. **441**, 41–49 (2018)

22. Ronneberger, O., Fischer, P., Brox, T.: U-Net: convolutional networks for biomedical image segmentation. In: Navab, N., Hornegger, J., Wells, W.M., Frangi, A.F. (eds.) MICCAI 2015. LNCS, vol. 9351, pp. 234–241. Springer, Cham (2015). https://doi.org/10.1007/978-3-319-24574-4_28

23. Simonyan, K., Zisserman, A.: Very deep convolutional networks for large-scale image recognition. arXiv preprint arXiv:1409.1556 (2014)

24. Smailagic, A., Sharan, A., Costa, P., Galdran, A., Gaudio, A., Campilho, A.: Learned pre-processing for automatic diabetic retinopathy detection on eye fundus images. In: Karray, F., Campilho, A., Yu, A. (eds.) ICIAR 2019. LNCS, vol. 11663, pp. 362–368. Springer, Cham (2019). https://doi.org/10.1007/978-3-030-27272-2_32

25. Staal, J., Abràmoff, M.D., Niemeijer, M., Viergever, M.A., Van Ginneken, B.: Ridge-based vessel segmentation in color images of the retina. IEEE Trans. Med. Imaging 23(4), 501–509 (2004)

26. Ulyanov, D., Vedaldi, A., Lempitsky, V.: Deep image prior. In: IEEE CVPR, pp. 9446–9454 (2018)

27. Xiong, L., Li, H., Xu, L.: An enhancement method for color retinal images based on image formation model. Comput. Methods Programs Biomed. 143, 137–150 (2017)

28. Xu, C., Cui, Y., Zhang, Y., Gao, P., Xu, J.: Image enhancement algorithm based on generative adversarial network in combination of improved game adversarial loss mechanism. Multimed. Tools Appl., 1–16 (2019)

29. Zhao, H., Li, H., Maurer-Stroh, S., Cheng, L.: Synthesizing retinal and neuronal images with generative adversarial nets. Med. Image Anal. 49, 14–26 (2018)

30. Zhao, H., Yang, B., Cao, L., Li, H.: Data-driven enhancement of blurry retinal images via generative adversarial networks. In: Shen, D., Liu, T., Peters, T.M., Staib, L.H., Essert, C., Zhou, S., Yap, P.-T., Khan, A. (eds.) MICCAI 2019. LNCS, vol. 11764, pp. 75–83. Springer, Cham (2019). https://doi.org/10.1007/978-3-030-32239-7_9

31. Zhou, M., Jin, K., Wang, S., Ye, J., Qian, D.: Color retinal image enhancement based on luminosity and contrast adjustment. IEEE Trans. Biomed. Eng. 65(3), 521–527 (2017)

Robust Layer Segmentation Against Complex Retinal Abnormalities for en *face* OCTA Generation

Yuhan Zhang[1], Chen Huang[1], Mingchao Li[1], Sha Xie[1], Keren Xie[2], Zexuan Ji[1], Songtao Yuan[2], and Qiang Chen[1(✉)]

[1] School of Computer Science and Engineering, Nanjing University of Science and Technology, Nanjing, China
chen2qiang@njust.edu.cn
[2] Department of Ophthalmology, The First Affiliated Hospital with Nanjing Medical University, Nanjing, China

Abstract. On *en face* optical coherence tomography angiography (OCTA), the vascular patterns from superficial vascular complex (SVC) and deep vascular complex (DVC) are distinguishable, while outer retina is normally avascular. To visualize *en face* OCTA images of different vascular patterns, it is inevitable to segment the three regions. However, the automated layer segmentation still faces huge challenge towards manifold advanced tissue lesions affected eyes. In this paper, we first design a region segmentation based augmented 3D U-Net network to fuse spectral domain optical coherence tomography (SD-OCT) structural information and OCTA vascular distribution. Subsequently, an innovative multitask layer-by-layer recoding module breaks up voxel-wise region segmentation probability maps into independent refinement task aiming at further weakening the influence of retinal abnormal regions on layer segmentation. In the end, a simple and effective layer surface encoding module converts the refined region segmentation result of each layer to its continuous surface vector, which advantages are that eliminates the outlier error segmentation in region segmentation tasks and guarantees the uniqueness and strict order constraint of each retinal layer surface in each column. The model validation is carried out on 262 eyes, including 95 normal eyes and 167 multifarious abnormalities affected eyes. The experimental results demonstrate that our method achieves higher segmentation accuracy and stronger ability to fight diseases compared with state-of-the-art segmentation methods.

Keywords: Deep learning · Layer segmentation · SD-OCT · OCTA

1 Introduction

Optical coherence tomography angiography (OCTA) is a novel OCT imaging modality, which can recognize the dynamic information of retinal blood flow with high resolution and is widely used in the diagnosis of blood-associated retinal diseases [1]. Based on the vascular distribution in retina, namely large vessels are located in superficial retina,

© Springer Nature Switzerland AG 2020
A. L. Martel et al. (Eds.): MICCAI 2020, LNCS 12265, pp. 647–655, 2020.
https://doi.org/10.1007/978-3-030-59722-1_62

capillaries with the exception of larger vessels that interconnect the plexuses are located in deep retina and outer retina is normally avascular, *en face* OCTA images with different vascular patterns (Fig. 1(c)) are generated by restricting the projection regions of retina [2]. In Fig. 1(b), superficial, deep and outer retina are separated by four retinal layer surfaces that are internal limiting membrane (ILM), lower surface of inner plexiform layer (IPL^{ls}), lower surface of outer plexiform layer (OPL^{ls}) and Bruch's membrane (BM). Thus the three regions can be obtained by segmenting the four retinal layer surfaces. However, retinal layer segmentation requires the aid of another corresponding OCT modality, namely spectral domain optical coherence tomography (SD-OCT), which shows retinal hierarchical structure with high resolution and are widely used as objects for layer segmentation tasks.

In the existing mainstream layer segmentation algorithms, graph theory based unsupervised layer segmentation algorithms [3–5] are mostly designed with established rules to segment retinal layer surfaces. These unsupervised methods have a good performance in the case of normal retinal structure, but they are difficult to perform well in complex retinopathy, such as edema and loss of layers. Machine learning based supervised layer segmentation algorithms [6–13] train the classifiers or neural networks by the supervised learning with manual annotations. The traditional machine learning methods firstly extract the effective features of layer surfaces and then classify each pixel into surface or not by trained classifiers [6, 7]. They show more robust performance than unsupervised layer segmentation methods. However, pixel-by-pixel classification is inefficient and hand-crafted features are not always comprehensive. With the rise of deep learning, its strong feature learning ability gains attention. The deep features extracted by neural networks are integrated to traditional machine learning frameworks to improve the performance of traditional machine learning based layer segmentation algorithms [8, 9]. However, their unamiable reproducibility hinders practical use. To improve the efficiency of layer segmentation algorithm, region segmentation based end-to-end deep learning models are introduced [10–13], which convert the local layer surface pixel classification tasks to global region segmentation tasks. These end-to-end deep learning models are easier to reproduce and have achieved excellent performance in terms of efficiency and accuracy in particular situations, but still have the following limitations: (1) model validations are carried out based on limited and specific diseases, as well as seldomly aim at severe advanced diseases affected eyes; (2) inherit the outlier error segmentation problem of region segmentation models; (3) neglect the inherent attribute of retinal layers, such as the continuity of layer surfaces and the order of layers from outside to inside.

In this paper, we present a deep learning model to segment superficial, deep and outer retina. The core of our proposed layer segmentation model is region segmentation, thus it remains the efficiency of region segmentation models. Besides, a multitask layer-by-layer recoding module is then developed to weaken the sensitivity of the layer segmentation model to abnormal regions. Finally, a layer surface encoding module converts the region segmentation result of each layer to its corresponding continuous surface vector, which purposes are to eliminate the outlier error segmentation and keep the inherent attribute of retinal layers. In our proposed model, OCTA vascular distribution information is regarded as supplement of SD-OCT retinal structural information. Another notice is that we take the continuity between adjacent slices into consideration, because our layer segmentation model is based on 3D convolution network. Although our layer segmentation targets are rough, the model is flexible to be extended to segment discretionary retinal layers.

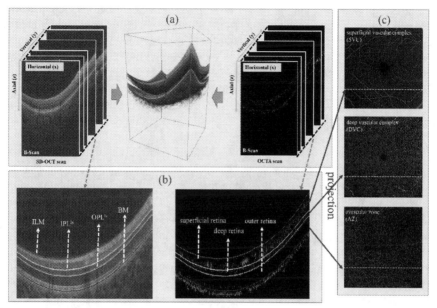

Fig. 1. (a) A full SD-OCT scan and corresponding OCTA scan. (b) A SD-OCT B-Scan and an OCTA B-Scan for visualization of four retinal layer surfaces. (c) False color *en face* OCTA images with different vascular patterns by restricting the projection regions of retina, where white dotted lines correspond to the selected B-Scan in (b).

2 Method

2.1 Materials

All SD-OCT images and corresponding OCTA images are from Jiangsu Provincial People's Hospital by using the RTVue XR Avanti OCTA instrument with center wavelength of 840 nm (Optovue, CA). Each full scan generates a SD-OCT cube (640 × 400 × 400 voxels) and corresponding OCTA cube (160 × 400 × 400 voxels), containing the corresponding trim size of 2 mm × 6 mm × 6 mm in the axial, horizontal and vertical directions respectively, shown in Fig. 1(a). We use bilinear interpolation to stretch the size of OCTA cube into 640 × 400 × 400 and suppress the projection artifact. Each slice along with vertical direction is referred to a B-Scan. The ground truth of four retinal layer surfaces in B-scans is manually delineated by ophthalmologists.

A total of 262 eyes (95 normal eyes and 167 abnormal eyes) are included in our experiment. According to the guide of ophthalmologists, the retinal abnormalities can be summarized as age-related macular degeneration (AMD), choroidal neovascularization (CNV), central serous chorioretinopathy (CSC), diabetic retinopathy (DR), optic atrophy

(OA) and "others". For the abnormalities less than 5 cubes, we arranged them into "others". The "others" includes a variety of abnormalities, such as retinal vein occlusion (RVO), etinitis pigmentosa (RP), retinoschisis (RS), preretinal hemorrhage (PH), retinal detachment (RD) and so on.

The construction of training set and testing set is based on the full scan instead of separated B-Scans, namely the B-Scans from the same scan do not appear in training set and test set simultaneously. In order to guarantee the rationality of data partitioning, we randomly select 80% scans of each category (Normal, AMD, CNV, CSC, DR, OA and "others") as training set and the remaining 20% scans as testing set. Then, we further randomly select 2 scans of each category from training set as validation set.

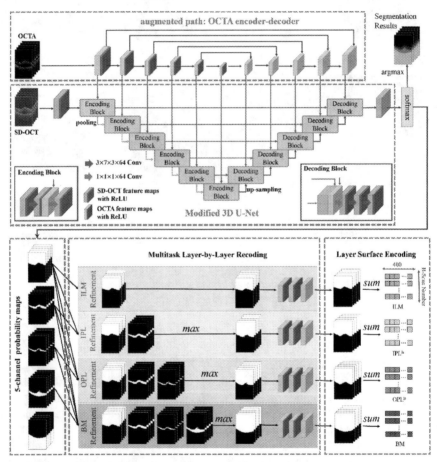

Fig. 2. The architecture of proposed model, including augmented 3D U-Net, multitask layer-by-layer recoding module and layer surface encoding module. The inputs are 3D SD-OCT cube and corresponding OCTA cube. The outputs are the four targeted layer surface vectors.

2.2 Model

The proposed layer segmentation model consists of augmented 3D U-Net, multitask layer-by-layer recoding module and layer surface encoding module (Fig. 2). As shown in Fig. 1(b), the B-Scan is divided into five regions by four retinal layer surfaces. The previous two modules (augmented 3D U-Net and multitask layer-by-layer recoding module) segment the five regions and try to get more refined segmentation results. The last layer surface encoding module converts the segmentation results into four targeted layer surfaces.

Augmented 3D U-Net Network

Most deep learning based layer segmentation methods were constructed based on 2D B-Scans [10–13]. Considering the model efficiency, 3D models are better able to take advantage of 3D OCT scan [14]. Thus, we directly use 3D volume data that is composed of n 2D consecutive B-Scans, as model input. Here, we choose $n = 5$ due to hardware limitation.

In the customized augmented 3D U-Net, an augmented path is used to exploit OCTA vascular distribution features, which is a 3D encoder-decoder network with residual connection. This augmented path only provides vascular distribution information for following U-shape path and does not output results.

The dominant U-shape path consists of 3D encoding blocks and 3D decoding blocks. Encoding blocks include two 3D convolutional layers, a concatenation layer used to cascade latent SD-OCT features with latent OCTA features and a $1 \times 1 \times 1 \times 64$ mapping layer used to compress the number of channels. In decoding blocks, the up-sampled feature maps are firstly cascaded with the features from the corresponding encoding block with same resolution and latent OCTA features, followed by a $1 \times 1 \times 1 \times 64$ mapping layer and two 3D convolutional layers. For the output of the last decoding block, we use a $1 \times 1 \times 1 \times 5$ mapping layer to obtain the probability maps of five regions. The probability maps of ith channel assign each voxel a possibility belonging to ith region. Finally, a softmax layer normalizes the probability maps along with channel dimension.

In the module, we use 3D separable convolution, which includes a $1 \times 1 \times 1 \times 16$ pointwise convolution and a $3 \times 7 \times 3 \times 64$ depthwise convolution, to replace 3D standard convolution to improve the model efficiency. It should be noted that the down-sampling operation and up-sampling operation are only performed along with the spatial dimension (height, width) of B-Scans and keep the number of sliced B-Scans the same.

Multitask Layer-by-Layer Recoding

This module is designed towards the refinement of regions affected by abnormalities. For normal eyes with smooth and differentiated layer structure, augmented 3D U-Net has achieved excellent segmentation results. Through augmented 3D U-Net, the difference of various abnormal regions is greatly inhibited as the voxels outside the targeted regions are assigned low probability values and voxels inside the targeted regions are assigned high probability values.

Specifically, we separate the output five-channel probability maps to four multitask branches corresponding to four layer surfaces. Each branch refines specific surface as a binary segmentation task, namely the region above the surface is positive and the region below the surface is negative. The four branches share the same network architecture, two 3D separable convolutional layers and a $1 \times 1 \times 1 \times 2$ mapping layer. The only difference among branches is the input. For each refinement branch, the selection strategies of five-channel probability maps are as follows:

(1) ILM branch input: select probability maps of $1st$ channel;
(2) IPL^{ls} branch input: select probability maps of the first two channels, and merge the probability maps to single channel using *max* operation;
(3) OPL^{ls} branch input: select probability maps of the first three channels, and merge the probability maps to single channel using *max* operation;
(4) BM branch input: select probability maps of the first four channels, and merge the probability maps to single channel using *max* operation.

Layer Surface Encoding

In a B-Scan, a specific retinal layer surface can be expressed as a vector:

$$S \in \mathbb{R}^{1 \times w} = [S_1, S_2, \dots, S_i, \dots, S_w]$$
$$S_i \in \{1, 2, \dots, h\} \tag{1}$$

where h and w are the height and width of each B-Scan respectively. For each branch, the refined binary region probability map divided by layer surface, namely the pixels above the targeted layer surface have high probability values (closed to 1) and the pixels under the targeted layer surface have low probability values (closed to 0), we directly sum each column to obtain the position vectors. Finally, a round operation restricts the position to be an integer. To guarantees the strict order of four retinal layers from top to bottom, we add the following constraint:

$$S_i^{ILM} \leq S_i^{IPL^{ls}} \leq S_i^{OPL^{ls}} \leq S_i^{BM}, i \in \{1, 2, \dots, w\} \tag{2}$$

Training Strategy and Loss Function

The Xavier initialization was used to initialize the model parameters. In order to train the full model more steadily, we optimized the model by joint hierarchical loss:

$$L = L^a + \lambda_1 \sum_{i=1}^{4} L_i^b + \frac{1}{2}\lambda_2 \sum_{j=1}^{4} \left\| V_k - \hat{V}_k \right\|_2^2 + \frac{1}{2}\lambda_3 \sum_{k=1}^{3} \left\| C_k - \hat{C}_k \right\|_F^2 \tag{3}$$

where L^a is the loss from augmented 3D U-Net, L_i^b is the loss of i th branch from multitask layer-by-layer recoding module, V_i and $\hat{V}_i$ are the real and the computed j th layer surface vectors, C_k and $\hat{C}_k$ are the real and the generated k th *en face* OCTA image. L^a and L_i^b are weighted combination of dice loss and cross-entropy (CE) loss:

$$L^{[a,b]} = \mu L_{CE} + L_{dice} \tag{4}$$

The hyper-parameters in loss function were empirically set as $\lambda_1 = 1$, $\lambda_2 = 0.05$, $\lambda_3 = 0.05$ and $\mu = 1$. The network parameters were optimized using an Adam optimization. The batch size was set to 3.

3   Experiment

3.1   Qualitative Evaluation

Our proposed model is qualitatively compared with state-of-the-art deep learning based layer segmentation models, BRU-Net [10], ReLay-Net [11], U-Net++ [15], DU-Net [16] and DeepLabv3+ [17], all of which directly segment the five regions. In Fig. 3, we use different colors to fill superficial, deep and outer retina regions for convenient qualitative comparison. Because ILM is the boundary between the vitreous and the retina that has sharp gradient change, thus most methods can obtain stable segmentation results. However, IPL^{ls}, OPL^{ls} and BM are sensitive towards retinal diseases. When the three layer surfaces are blurred or broken by retinal abnormal regions, the comparative methods show a highly unstable segmentation performance. In addition, in these comparative methods, there are not compensatory means to deal with the outlier error segmentation problem. Our result shows a better and more robust visual effect that eliminates the small error regions, keeps the integrity of layers and the continuity of layer surfaces.

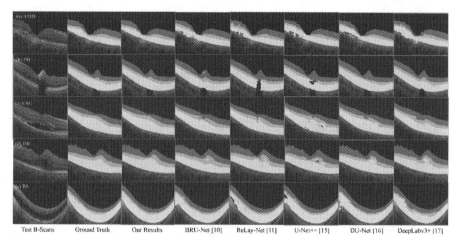

Fig. 3. Qualitative comparisons on AMD, preretinal hemorrhage (PH), CSC, DR and retinoschisis (RS). The superficial, deep and outer retina are marked with purple, yellow and glaucous, respectively.

3.2   Quantitative Evaluation

The quantitative comparison and analysis are conducted based on three evaluation metrics. The dice similarity coefficient (DSC) is used to estimate the accuracy of region segmentation. The mean absolute contour error (MACE) and the standard deviation (Std) are used to estimate the accuracy and stability of retinal layer surfaces respectively. For comparative methods, we select the edge pixels of adjacent regions as the layer surfaces to compute MACE and Std.

Table 1 summarizes the DSC of superficial, deep and outer retina segmentation. For the three regions, our model all achieved the highest DSC. Particularly for the most

Table 1. Comparison of our method and five other methods based on regions using DSC (%).

Layer region	BRU-Net [10]	ReLay-Net [11]	U-Net++ [15]	DU-Net [16]	DeepLabv3+ [17]	Our method
Superficial retina	98.06	98.35	96.65	97.24	96.79	**98.72**
Deep retina	94.76	95.43	91.18	91.94	93.01	**97.38**
Outer retina	98.03	98.20	96.40	97.28	97.66	**98.77**

difficult deep retina, our proposed model is higher about 2% than the second place ReLay-Net, which shows the ability of our model to fight against abnormalities.

Table 2 estimates the accuracy and stability of four retinal layer surfaces by MACE and Std. In general, ILM is more easily segmented than other retinal layer surfaces due to the stronger gradient change. Thus all segmentation methods achieve lowest MACE and Std than other three layer surfaces. Towards IPL^{ls}, OPL^{ls} and BM that are more difficult than ILM segmentation, the Std values from our proposed model are generally 2 pixels lower than comparative methods. It indicates that the layer surfaces segmented by our model is smoother and more continuous.

Table 2. Comparison of our method and five other methods based on surfaces using MACE ± Std (unit: pixel).

Layer surface	BRU-Net [10]	ReLay-Net [11]	U-Net++ [15]	DU-Net [16]	DeepLabv3+ [17]	Our method
ILM	1.1525±1.8494	1.1843±1.7166	1.2793±1.8291	1.2239±1.7315	1.2343±1.9518	**0.9522±0.4284**
IPL^{ls}	1.4306±3.0836	1.3734±2.7852	1.7932±3.2338	1.4744±3.1046	1.5735±3.1402	**1.1149±0.9883**
OPL^{ls}	1.5930±3.5651	1.5516±3.5441	2.2140±4.0551	2.3658±3.8431	1.7269±3.9078	**1.2786±1.1455**
BM	1.3182±2.9787	1.2934±2.9266	1.3384±3.2754	1.3372±3.3930	1.3178±3.3516	**1.0147±0.9421**

The quantitative evaluation results summarized in Tables 1 and 2 demonstrate that our method achieves the best segmentation performance than comparative methods.

4   Conclusion

Retinal layer segmentation for OCT images is a basic and essential task, which can assist ophthalmologists quantify retinal parameters and provide convenience for subsequent image processing tasks. However, severe retinal diseases destroy retinal layer structure and improve the difficulty of layer segmentation. In this paper, we propose a deep learning based model to segment three retinal layer regions for *en face* OCTA generation, which is more robust and high-accuracy facing retinal abnormal regions than state-of-the-art segmentation methods. The proposed model is flexible to be extended to perform the segmentation tasks of other retinal layers.

Acknowledgements. This study was supported by National Natural Science Foundation of China (61671242, 61701222), in part by Key R&D Program of Jiangsu Science and Technology Department (BE2018131), in part by Natural Science Foundation of Jiangsu Province under Grants No. BK20180069, and in part by Six talent peaks project in Jiangsu Province under Grant No. SWYY-056.

References

1. Jia, Y., Tan, O., Tokayer, J., et al.: Split-spectrum amplitude decorrelation angiography with optical coherence tomography. Opt. Express **20**(4), 4710–4725 (2012)
2. Campbell, J.P., Zhang, M., Hwang, T.S., et al.: Detailed vascular anatomy of the human retina by projection-resolved optical coherence tomography angiography. Sci. Rep. **7**, 42201 (2017)
3. Zang, P., Gao, S.S., Hwang, T.S., et al.: Automated boundary detection of the optic disc and layer segmentation of the peripapillary retina in volumetric structural and angiographic optical coherence tomography. Bio. Opt. Express **8**(3), 1306–1318 (2017)
4. Rathke, F., Desana, M., Schnörr, C.: Locally adaptive probabilistic models for global segmentation of pathological OCT scans. In: Descoteaux, M., Maier-Hein, L., Franz, A., Jannin, P., Collins, D.L., Duchesne, S. (eds.) MICCAI 2017. LNCS, vol. 10433, pp. 177–184. Springer, Cham (2017). https://doi.org/10.1007/978-3-319-66182-7_21
5. Oliveira, J., Pereira, S., Goncalves, L., Ferreira, M., Silva, C.A.: Multi-surface segmentation of OCT images with AMD using sparse high order potentials. Biomed. Opt. Express **8**(1), 281–297 (2017)
6. Montuoro, A., Waldetein, S.M., Gerendas, B.S., Schmidt-Erfurth, U., Bogunovic, H.: Joint retinal layer and fluid segmentation in OCT scans of eyes with severe macular edema using unsupervised representation and auto-context. Biomed. Opt. Express **8**(3), 1874–1888 (2017)
7. Liu, Y., Carass, A., He, Y., et al.: Layer boundary evolution method for macular OCT layer segmentation. Biomed. Opt. Express **10**(3), 1064–1080 (2019)
8. Liu, X., Fu, T., Pan, Z., et al.: Automated layer segmentation of retinal optical coherence tomography images using a deep feature enhanced structured random forests classifier. IEEE J. Biomed. Health Inform. **23**(4), 1404–1416 (2018)
9. Xiang, D., Tian, H., Yang, X., et al.: Automatic segmentation of retinal layer in OCT images with choroidal neovascularization. IEEE Trans. Med. Imaging **27**(12), 5880–5891 (2018)
10. Apostolopoulos, S., De Zanet, S., Ciller, C., Wolf, S., Sznitman, R.: Pathological OCT retinal layer segmentation using branch residual U-shape networks. In: Descoteaux, M., Maier-Hein, L., Franz, A., Jannin, P., Collins, D.L., Duchesne, S. (eds.) MICCAI 2017. LNCS, vol. 10435, pp. 294–301. Springer, Cham (2017). https://doi.org/10.1007/978-3-319-66179-7_34
11. Roy, A.G., Conjeti, S., Karri, S.P.K., et al.: ReLayNet: retinal layer and fluid segmentation of macular optical coherence tomography using fully convolutional networks. Biomed. Opt. Express **8**(8), 3627–3642 (2017)
12. Shan, A., Zhou, L., Abramoff, M.D., Wu, X.: Multiple surface segmentation using convolution neural nets: application to retinal layer segmentation in OCT images. Biomed. Opt. Express **9**(9), 4509–4526 (2018)
13. Wang, J., Wang, Z., Li, F., et al.: Joint retina segmentation and classification for early glaucoma diagnosis. Biomed. Opt. Express **10**(5), 2639–2656 (2019)
14. Kiaee, F., Fahimi, H., Rabbani, H.: Intra-retinal layer segmentation of optical coherence tomography using 3D fully convolutional networks. In: IEEE International Conference on Image Processing (ICIP) (2018)
15. Zhou, Z., Rahman Siddiquee, M.M., Tajbakhsh, N., Liang, J.: UNet ++: a nested U-net architecture for medical image segmentation. In: Stoyanov, D., et al. (eds.) DLMIA/ML-CDS-2018. LNCS, vol. 11045, pp. 3–11. Springer, Cham (2018). https://doi.org/10.1007/978-3-030-00889-5_1
16. Jin, Q., Meng, Z., Pham, T.D., Chen, Q., Wei, L., Su, R.: DU-Net: A deformable network for retinal vessel segmentation. Knowl.-Based Syst. **178**, 149–162 (2019)
17. Chen, L.-C., Zhu, Y., Papandreou, G., Schroff, F., Adam, H.: Encoder-decoder with atrous separable convolution for semantic image segmentation. In: Ferrari, V., Hebert, M., Sminchisescu, C., Weiss, Y. (eds.) ECCV 2018. LNCS, vol. 11211, pp. 833–851. Springer, Cham (2018). https://doi.org/10.1007/978-3-030-01234-2_49

Anterior Segment Eye Lesion Segmentation with Advanced Fusion Strategies and Auxiliary Tasks

Ke Wang[1], Xiaohong Liu[1], Kang Zhang[2], Ting Chen[1], and Guangyu Wang[1(✉)]

[1] Department of Computer Science and Technology and BNRist,
Tsinghua University, Beijing, China
`wangguangyu@tsinghua.edu.cn`
[2] Faculty of Medicine, Macau University of Science and Technology, Macau, China

Abstract. Anterior segment diseases of the eye cover a wide range of pathologies that occur at the front part of the eye such as conjunctival hemorrhage, corneal neovascularization and cataract. A tool for fast and accurate segmentation of anterior eye lesions can greatly benefit research and clinical care. However, the majority of current studies only pay attention to retinal-related diseases such as retinal diabetic retinopathy or macular degeneration and hence overlook this area. To enhance and boost research interest in this field, we construct the first anterior eye lesion segmentation dataset with pixel level annotations of four categories of lesions as well as the underlying eye structures. We propose a novel simultaneous eye lesion and structure segmentation model with two advanced feature fusion strategies and two auxiliary tasks. The fusion strategies enable knowledge gained from eye structure segmentation branch to be effectively transferred to the lesion segmentation branch, utilizing the intrinsic relationship between lesion and eye structure. The auxiliary tasks, which do not require extra manual annotations, are set to encourage the model to learn more general representations of features, thus improving the segmentation performance. Experimental results on the newly constructed dataset indicate that our model can exceed baseline models consistently and significantly. The source code and the newly constructed dataset are made public to benefit future research.

Keywords: Anterior eye diseases · Fusion strategy · Auxiliary task

1 Introduction

Anterior segment generally refers to the front structures of the eye including the conjunctiva, cornea, iris and lens, where many commonly seen disorders can occur such as pinguecula, corneal neovascularization, iris nevus and cataract. The segmentation of eye lesions plays an important role in the diagnosis and

© Springer Nature Switzerland AG 2020
A. L. Martel et al. (Eds.): MICCAI 2020, LNCS 12265, pp. 656–664, 2020.
https://doi.org/10.1007/978-3-030-59722-1_63

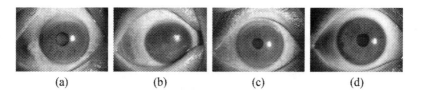

Fig. 1. Visual illustration of our constructed dataset with four categories of lesions including pinguecula (a), corneal neovascularization (b), pupil deformation (c) and iris nevus (d).

further surgery planning. However, manual segmentation of eye lesion area is labor-intensive and time-consuming, and it can only be done by experienced ophthalmologists.

With the development of artificial intelligence, many automatic lesion segmentation methods have been proposed and have been applied to many tasks such as brain tumor segmentation [5], lung nodule segmentation [12] and skin cancer segmentation [6]. These methods are generally built upon Convolutional Neural Networks (CNN), and follow a classic network framework approach such as the encoder-decoder structure in UNet [9] and spatial pyramid pooling in DeepLabv3 [3].

Eye-related disease segmentation has become a hot research field for decades, with the current research focus placed on retinal vessel segmentation [4], retinal layers and fluid leakage segmentation [10] and diabetic retinopathy lesion segmentation [7]. It's clear that the current research in this field has been focused more on the retinal area, with less attention to another equally important segment eye area. The reason for the lack of researchers' attention is mainly due to the lack of publicly available anterior eye disease segmentation dataset. To boost research in this field, we manually collect and construct the first anterior eye disease segmentation dataset. Four categories of lesions and eye structure, including eyelid, sclera, iris and pupil, are annotated at the pixel level by experienced ophthalmologists. A visual illustration of our constructed dataset can be seen in Fig. 1.

As one of the first research group working on the anterior eye lesion segmentation task, we propose a novel simultaneous eye lesion and structure segmentation model with two advanced feature fusion strategies and two auxiliary tasks. The framework of our model is a mixture of the encoder-decoder structure and spatial pyramid pooling, which possesses the ability to capture long range information and extract context features at multiple ranges at the same time. To exploit the intrinsic relationship between eye structure segmentation and eye lesion segmentation, we propose two advanced fusion strategies that can transfer meaningful information gained from eye structure segmentation to eye lesion segmentation. Two attention mechanisms are applied to improve the effectiveness of feature fusion. To enable the model to learn more general representations of features and improve feature fusion performance, we design two auxiliary tasks, which

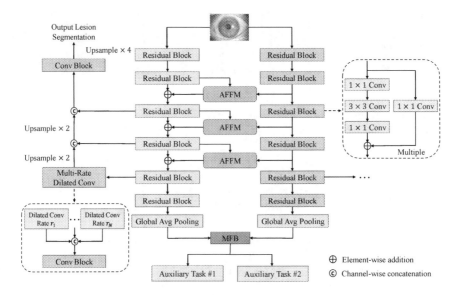

Fig. 2. Overview of our eye lesion and structure segmentation model. The left part is the lesion segmentation branch and the right part is the structure segmentation branch (we omit its decoder part for simplicity). The dashed box is the illustration of a certain module in our model. Conv is short for convolution and avg is short for average.

do not require additional annotations. Experimental results on our newly constructed dataset demonstrate that our model is superior to all baseline in all metrics with a great margin, which proves the effectiveness and robustness of our model. The source code and the newly constructed dataset can be found in https://github.com/kaisadadi/Anterior-Segment-Eye-Lesion-Segmentation.

2   Method

An overview of our proposed eye lesion and structure segmentation model is shown in Fig. 2. We use two separate branches to conduct eye lesion and structure segmentation (eyelid, sclera, iris and pupil), which share the same network structure. We design two feature fusion strategies, the first is Attention-based Feature Fusion Module (AFFM), which is for lesion segmentation, and the second is Multi-modal Factorized Bilinear Pooling (MFB), which is for auxiliary tasks. The segmentation branch structure, AFFM, MFB and two auxiliary tasks will be explained in details in the following parts. It is noticeable that we do not fuse information from the lesion segmentation branch to the structure segmentation branch because the structure segmentation task is much easier and can reach promising performance without feature fusion.

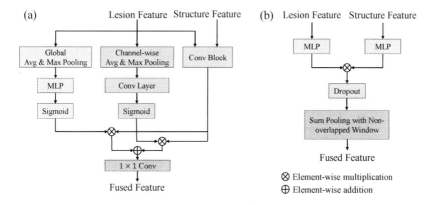

Fig. 3. Illustration of the internal mechanisms of AFFM (a) and MFB (b). MLP stands for multi layer perceptron.

2.1 Segmentation Branch Structure

We combine the encoder-decoder structure and spatial pyramid pooling as our basic segmentation branch structure. The input image is first encoded and down-sampled by several residual blocks until the multi-rate dilated conv module. It is noticeable that the global avg pooling and the residual block ahead of it are set for auxiliary tasks and are not part of the segmentation network. The multi-rate dilated conv module consists of several dilated convolutions with dilation rates of $1, 2, 3, 7$ and 11. The greatest common divisor of these dilation rates is 1, which is set on purpose to avoid the gridding problem [11]. The up-sampling operation and feature map aggregation from multiple layers mimic the skip-connection in [9] to capture long range information and recover local feature in a finer manner.

2.2 Attention-Based Feature Fusion Module

The Attention-based Feature Fusion Module (AFFM) is designed to fuse the information from structure segmentation branch to lesion segmentation branch efficiently. We use AFFM block at multiple places in the encoding process to encourage in-depth feature fusion. An illustration of AFFM is shown in Fig. 3(a). We apply two attention mechanisms, namely channel attention and spatial attention, to locate important channels and regions in the lesion feature map.

In channel attention, we first apply global avg pooling and max pooling followed by a multi layer perceptron to generate attention weight for each channel. In spatial attention, we first apply channel-wise avg pooling and max pooling. The pooling results are summed element-wisely and are further encoded by a conv layer to generate the attention map. The weights from both channel attention and spatial attention are normalized by sigmoid activation function.

The structure feature and lesion feature are concatenated channel-wisely and are fed into a conv block to extract their feature and mine their inter-relationship as a whole. The output of the conv block is multiplied with channel attention map and spatial attention map element-wisely, and the results are concatenated channel-wisely. To reduce the computation cost, we apply a 1×1 conv layer at last to reduce the output channel number of the fused feature.

2.3 Auxiliary Tasks

To alleviate the potential over-fitting problem and enable the model to learn more general representations of features, we design two auxiliary tasks that require the model's understanding of joint information from lesion segmentation and structure segmentation. The auxiliary tasks do not require extra annotations as all the labels can be generated from segmentation ground truth directly. We design two auxiliary tasks, the first is the multi-label classification task of lesion categories (4 categories in total), and the second is the binary classification task on whether the lesion exists in each four different regions of the eye structure. We have also attempted to take the regression of the area ratio of lesions in four different regions of the eye structure as the third auxiliary task, but we find it hard to converge and has negative effects on lesion segmentation.

Multi-modal Factorized Bilinear Pooling (MFB). To conduct auxiliary tasks, we use MFB [14] to fuse the final feature vector of eye lesion and structure segmentation after the global avg pooling operation. We choose MFB rather than a simple feature concatenation operation because MFB possesses greater capacities in feature fusion. An illustration of MFB is shown in Fig. 3(b). MFB utilizes two low-rank matrices (MLPs in Fig. 3(b)) to replace the original large projection matrix in bilinear pooling [8], which reduces the number of parameters drastically. The reduction of the parameters in the feature fusion layer is essential since we aim to use auxiliary tasks to adjust weights in the segmentation branch. The final sum pooling in Fig. 3(b) is done on the feature vector after element-wise multiplication, with non-overlapped sliding window of size k, where k is the rank of the low-rank matrices.

2.4 Loss Function

We train our propose model in an end-to-end way with loss $\mathcal{L}$ as follows:

$$\mathcal{L} = \mathcal{L}_{L-seg} + \mathcal{L}_{S-seg} + \lambda_1 \mathcal{L}_{AUX_1} + \lambda_2 \mathcal{L}_{AUX_2} \tag{1}$$

where $\mathcal{L}_{L-seg}$ and $\mathcal{L}_{S-seg}$ are weighted cross entropy loss for lesion segmentation and structure segmentation respectively. $\mathcal{L}_{AUX_1}$ and $\mathcal{L}_{AUX_2}$ are the binary cross entropy loss for the two auxiliary tasks. λ_1 and λ_2 are two hyper-parameters for tuning in the training procedure.

3 Experiment

3.1 Dataset Descriptions

We collect a total of 380 anterior segment photographs from patients diagnosed with pinguecula, corneal neovascularization, pupil deformation or iris nevus.

There are in total 158 images with pinguecula, 107 images with corneal neovascularization, 96 images with pupil deformation and 51 images with iris nevus. There are images with more than one category of lesions. Each image is annotated with lesion and eye structures by experienced ophthalmologists at the pixel level. All images are resized to 512×512 to balance computation cost and model performance.

3.2   Implementation Details

As the first research in anterior eye lesion segmentation, there is no model specifically designed for this field for comparison. Therefore, we adopt several state-of-the-art models in semantic segmentation including DeepLabv3 [3], PspNet [15] and UperNet [13], and medical image segmentation including UNet [9], R2U-Net [2] and LadderNet [1] as baselines.

We conduct five-fold cross validation to fully evaluate our model as well as baselines. In each fold of validation, we randomly split the data into training, validation and testing dataset with the ratio 0.7:0.1:0.2. We adopt SGD optimizer with an initial learning rate at 0.01 with momentum at 0.9. The learning rate decays by a factor of 0.9 for every 5 epochs and weight decay is 0.0001. We set hyper-parameters λ_1 and λ_2 to 0.3 and 0.1 respectively.

3.3   Results and Discussions

We adopt mean Jaccard Similarity Coefficient (mJSC), mean Dice's Coefficient (mDC) and mean Pixel Accuracy (mPA) as evaluating metrics for both lesion and structure segmentation. The results of segmentation performance are shown in Table 1.

Table 1. Evaluation of segmentation performance on eye lesion and structure segmentation. The values are averaged across the five-fold cross validation.

Model	Lesion			Structure		
	mDC	mJSC	mPA	mDC	mJSC	mPA
DeepLabv3	0.669	0.543	0.732	0.943	0.900	0.945
PspNet	0.665	0.541	0.719	0.944	0.900	0.944
UperNet	0.658	0.538	0.709	0.943	0.889	0.942
UNet	0.631	0.510	0.688	0.941	0.888	0.939
R2U-Net	0.649	0.525	0.705	0.945	0.900	0.944
LadderNet	0.655	0.536	0.712	**0.946**	0.900	0.945
Ours	**0.682**	**0.558**	**0.750**	0.945	**0.901**	**0.946**

We can see from Table 1 that our model can outperform all baselines in all metrics in the lesion segmentation task. Our model outperforms the best baseline DeepLabv3 by 1.3% in mDC, 1.5% in mJSC and 1.8% in mPA, which demonstrates that the advanced feature fusion strategies and auxiliary tasks we design can truly improve segmentation performance. It's noticeable that all models share similarly good performance in structure segmentation because this task is a relatively easy and can reach very good segmentation performance with very basic model such as valina UNet. The true and only problem we aim to solve is eye lesion segmentation (left part in Table 1), the right part in Table 1 is just used to show the simplicity of eye structure segmentation. This is also the reason we do not fuse information from lesion segmentation branch to structure segmentation branch.

To get a better understanding of the segmentation performance, we visualize the segmentation results in Fig. 4 as follows and compare with the best baseline DeepLabv3.

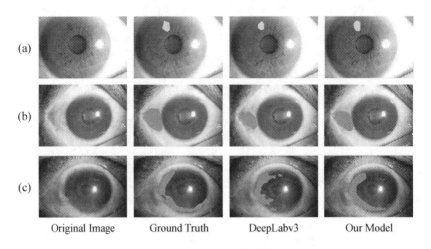

Fig. 4. Visualization of segmentation results on three categories of lesions, including iris nevus (a), pinguecula (b) and corneal neovascularization (c).

From Fig. 4 we can observe that our model can generate promising results on various categories of eye lesions. It's also noticeable that the anterior eye lesion segmentation task is difficult and challenging, and more research should be conducted in this field.

Ablation Analysis. We conduct ablation analysis to study the respective effects of AFFM, MFB and auxiliary tasks on our model. If we remove AFFM from the model, mDC, mJSC and mPA will drop by 0.7%, 0.5% and 1.0%. If we replace the MFB module with a simple feature concatenation operation, we will find the training of auxiliary tasks becomes tricky and the loss of auxiliary tasks become higher. We believe this is because a simple concatenation operation lacks the ability to fuse information from two different resources effectively. The auxiliary tasks are also important in our model, and we will see a 0.4% to 0.6% drop in mDC, mJSC and mPA if we remove the two auxiliary tasks.

Influence of Hyper-parameters. Both λ_1 and λ_2 are important hyper-parameters in our model. We find that our model is not very sensitive to λ_1, as the loss of the first auxiliary task drops fast and steadily in the training process. However, if we increase λ_2 to be larger than 0.2, it will bring negative effects to segmentation performance. We think this is due to the fact that the second auxiliary task is harder and requires complex reasoning ability of our model. If our model pay too much attention to the second auxiliary task, it will distract the focus of our model from lesion segmentation.

4   Conclusion

In this paper, we propose a novel simultaneous eye lesion and structure segmentation model with advanced fusion strategies and auxiliary tasks. The fusion strategies can transfer important information gained from structure segmentation branch to lesion segmentation branch. Two attention mechanisms and multi-modal bilinear pooling is applied to improve feature fusion efficiency. The auxiliary tasks we design require no extra annotations and can improve segmentation performance with clear margin. We also construct the first anterior eye disease segmentation dataset, and make it public to benefit future researches in this field.

Acknowledgements. This work is supported by the National Key R&D Program of China (2019YFB1-404804), the National Natural Science Foundation of China (grants 61906105, 61-872218, 61721003 and 61673241), Tsinghua-Fuzhou Institute of Digital Technology, Beijing National Research Center for Information Science and Technology (BNRist), and Tsinghua University-Peking Union Medical College Hospital Initiative Scientific Research Program. The funders had no roles in study design, data collection and analysis, the decision to publish, and preparation of the manuscript.

References

1. Laddernet: Multi-path networks based on U-Net for medical image segmentation. arXiv preprint arXiv:1810.07810 (2018)
2. Alom, M.Z., Hasan, M., Yakopcic, C., Taha, T.M., Asari, V.K.: Recurrent residual convolutional neural network based on U-Net (R2U-Net) for medical image segmentation. arXiv preprint arXiv:1802.06955 (2018)
3. Chen, L.C., Papandreou, G., Schroff, F., Adam, H.: Rethinking atrous convolution for semantic image segmentation. arXiv preprint arXiv:1706.05587 (2017)
4. Fu, H., Xu, Y., Wong, D.W.K., Liu, J.: Retinal vessel segmentation via deep learning network and fully-connected conditional random fields. In: 2016 IEEE 13th International Symposium on Biomedical Imaging (ISBI), pp. 698–701. IEEE (2016)
5. Havaei, M., et al.: Brain tumor segmentation with deep neural networks. Med. Image Anal. **35**, 18–31 (2017)

6. Jafari, M.H., et al.: Skin lesion segmentation in clinical images using deep learning. In: 2016 23rd International Conference on Pattern Recognition (ICPR), pp. 337–342. IEEE (2016)

7. Köse, C., Şevik, U., İkibaş, C., Erdöl, H.: Simple methods for segmentation and measurement of diabetic retinopathy lesions in retinal fundus images. Comput. Methods Programs Biomed. **107**(2), 274–293 (2012)

8. Lin, T.Y., RoyChowdhury, A., Maji, S.: Bilinear CNN models for fine-grained visual recognition. In: Proceedings of the IEEE International Conference on Computer Vision, pp. 1449–1457 (2015)

9. Ronneberger, O., Fischer, P., Brox, T.: U-Net: convolutional networks for biomedical image segmentation. In: Navab, N., Hornegger, J., Wells, W.M., Frangi, A.F. (eds.) MICCAI 2015. LNCS, vol. 9351, pp. 234–241. Springer, Cham (2015). https://doi.org/10.1007/978-3-319-24574-4_28

10. Roy, A.G., et al.: Relaynet: retinal layer and fluid segmentation of macular optical coherence tomography using fully convolutional networks. Biomed. Opt. Express **8**(8), 3627–3642 (2017)

11. Wang, P., et al.: Understanding convolution for semantic segmentation. In: 2018 IEEE Winter Conference on Applications of Computer Vision (WACV), pp. 1451–1460. IEEE (2018)

12. Wang, S., et al.: A multi-view deep convolutional neural networks for lung nodule segmentation. In: 2017 39th Annual International Conference of the IEEE Engineering in Medicine and Biology Society (EMBC), pp. 1752–1755. IEEE (2017)

13. Xiao, T., Liu, Y., Zhou, B., Jiang, Y., Sun, J.: Unified perceptual parsing for scene understanding. In: Ferrari, V., Hebert, M., Sminchisescu, C., Weiss, Y. (eds.) ECCV 2018. LNCS, vol. 11209, pp. 432–448. Springer, Cham (2018). https://doi.org/10.1007/978-3-030-01228-1_26

14. Yu, Z., Yu, J., Fan, J., Tao, D.: Multi-modal factorized bilinear pooling with co-attention learning for visual question answering. In: Proceedings of the IEEE International Conference on Computer Vision, pp. 1821–1830 (2017)

15. Zhao, H., Shi, J., Qi, X., Wang, X., Jia, J.: Pyramid scene parsing network. In: Proceedings of the IEEE Conference on Computer Vision and Pattern Recognition, pp. 2881–2890 (2017)

Cost-Sensitive Regularization for Diabetic Retinopathy Grading from Eye Fundus Images

Adrian Galdran[1(✉)], Jose Dolz[2], Hadi Chakor[3], Hervé Lombaert[2], and Ismail Ben Ayed[2]

[1] University of Bournemouth, Poole, UK
agaldran@bournemouth.ac.uk
[2] ETS Montréal, Montreal, Canada
{jose.dolz,herve.lombaert,ismail.benayed}@etsmtl.ca
[3] Diagnos INC, Brossard, Canada
hchakor@diagnos.ca

Abstract. Assessing the degree of disease severity in biomedical images is a task similar to standard classification but constrained by an underlying structure in the label space. Such a structure reflects the monotonic relationship between different disease grades. In this paper, we propose a straightforward approach to enforce this constraint for the task of predicting Diabetic Retinopathy (DR) severity from eye fundus images based on the well-known notion of Cost-Sensitive classification. We expand standard classification losses with an extra term that acts as a regularizer, imposing greater penalties on predicted grades when they are farther away from the true grade associated to a particular image. Furthermore, we show how to adapt our method to the modelling of label noise in each of the sub-problems associated to DR grading, an approach we refer to as Atomic Sub-Task modeling. This yields models that can implicitly take into account the inherent noise present in DR grade annotations. Our experimental analysis on several public datasets reveals that, when a standard Convolutional Neural Network is trained using this simple strategy, improvements of 3–5% of quadratic-weighted kappa scores can be achieved at a negligible computational cost. Code to reproduce our results is released at github.com/agaldran/cost_sensitive_loss_classification.

Keywords: Diabetic retinopathy grading · Cost-sensitive classifiers

1 Introduction

Diabetes is regarded as a global eye health issue, with a steadily increasing worldwide affected population, expected to reach 630 million individuals by 2045 [1]. Diabetic Retinopathy (DR) is a complication of standard diabetes, caused by damage to vasculature within the retina. DR shows early signs in the form of

© Springer Nature Switzerland AG 2020
A. L. Martel et al. (Eds.): MICCAI 2020, LNCS 12265, pp. 665–674, 2020.
https://doi.org/10.1007/978-3-030-59722-1_64

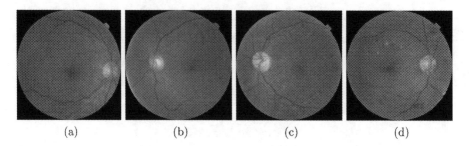

(a)   (b)   (c)   (d)

Fig. 1. Images from the Messidor-2 dataset illustrating the progressive behavior of DR. (a) Grade 1 (Mild NPDR): only few microaneurysms can be found (b) Grade 2 (Moderate NPDR): Presence of multiple microaneurysms, blot hemorrhages, venous beading, and/or cotton wool spots (c) Grade 3 (Severe NPDR): Micro-aneurysms if 4 quadrants of the retina, cotton wool spots, venous beading, severe intra-retinal microvascular abnormalities. (d) Grade 4 (PDR): Neovascularization, vitreous hemorrhages.

swelling micro-lesions that destroy small vessels and release blood into the retina. Advanced DR stages are characterized by the appearance of more noticeable symptoms, *e.g.* proliferation of neo-vessels, leading to the detachment of the retinal layer and eventually permanent sight loss.

Retinal images acquired with fundus cameras are the tool of choice for discovering these early symptoms, representing an effective diagnostic tool suitable for automatic diagnostic systems [19]. In this context, and with the advent of Deep Learning in the last decade, a wide set of techniques has been proposed in recent years [2,6,9]. However, the vast majority of these works are designed for the screening task, *i.e.* distinguishing healthy individuals from patients at any stage of risk. Due to its difficulty, fewer works have addressed the task of DR grading, consisting of classifying an eye fundus image into one of the five categories proposed by the American Academy of Ophthalmology [21], illustrated in Fig. 1. In addition, most recent DR grading techniques [11,12,16] have focused on scaling up existing Convolutional Neural Networks by considering larger/better databases, but only a few works addressed the design of customized loss functions that are more suitable for this task, which is the goal of this paper.

Cost-Sensitive classifiers are known to be useful for addressing two of the main challenges related to DR grading. First, they allow to model the underlying structure of an heterogeneous label space [7,13,15]. Second, they are beneficial for dealing with severely class-imbalanced scenarios [17,24]. Despite this, to the best of our knowledge, no previous work has explored Cost-Sensitive loss minimization approaches in the context of DR grading from eye fundus images.

In this paper, we present a straightforward approach for integrating Cost-Sensitive classification constraints in the task of DR grading from retinal images. We choose to introduce these constraints by attaching an auxiliary Cost-Sensitive loss term to popular miss-classification error functions, and by analyzing the impact of this process in the training of a standard CNN. In addition, we illustrate how to adapt our method to the modeling of label noise in each of the sub-problems associated to DR grading, an approach we refer to as *Atomic Sub-Task modeling*. We conduct a series of careful experiments demonstrating that expanding well-known loss functions with a Cost-Sensitive term brings noticeable performance increases, and that sub-task modeling leads to learning models that behave more similarly to human annotators.

2 Methodology

In this section we first describe our approach to build Cost-Sensitive (CS) classifiers, and the loss functions we select as baselines, to which we will add a CS-regularizing term. We then show how CS can be employed to model label noise for DR grading problems, and detail the training process we followed to optimize the parameters of our models.

2.1 Cost-Sensitive Regularization

In order to induce a different penalty for each kind of error, let us first consider the case in which a model U produces a prediction $U(x) = \hat{y} \in [0,1] \times \ldots \times [0,1]$. Such prediction is to be compared with the corresponding label y. For the sake of readability, in the following we will abuse notation and refer by y indistinctly to an integer label $y \in \mathbb{L} = \{1,2,3,4,5\}$ and its one-hot-encoded counterpart $y \in \{0,1\} \times \ldots \times \{0,1\}$, which takes a value of 1 in the position corresponding to y and 0 elsewhere.

Standard loss functions like the cross-entropy error, described by:

$$\mathcal{L}_{CE}(\hat{y}, y) = -\sum_{i=1}^{n=5} y_i \log(\hat{y}_i) \tag{1}$$

are insensitive to any underlying structure in the label space $\mathbb{L}$. This means that for a particular example (x, y_j), if any permutation is applied on $\mathbb{L} \setminus \{y_j\}$, the resulting error will remain the same. In order to modify that behavior, we consider a cost matrix M that encodes a null cost for a prediction such that $\hat{y} = y_j$, but cost that increases along with the distance $\|y - \hat{y}\|$.

A simple approach to achieve such increasing label-dependent penalty is by encoding in each row of M those costs, and then computing the scalar product of $\hat{y}$ with the row of M corresponding to y, i.e. $\mathcal{L}(y, \hat{y}) = \langle M(y, \cdot), \hat{y} \rangle$. However, due to the high imbalance of the DR grading problem (with typically few examples of classes DR1, DR3, and DR4) in our experiments we noted that simply minimizing such quantity would lead to models remaining stuck in local minima and classifying all images into DR0 and DR2 classes. For this reason, we prefer to combine a CS term with a base loss as follows:

$$\mathcal{L}^{cs}(\hat{y}, y) = \mathcal{L}^{base}(\hat{y}, y) + \lambda \langle M^{(2)}(y, \cdot), \hat{y} \rangle, \quad M_{ij}^{(2)} = \|i - j\|_2^2. \tag{2}$$

In the above equation, we have selected the L^2-based ground cost matrix $M^{(2)}$, since it fits nicely with the goal of maximizing quadratic-weighted kappa score, but other cost matrices could be easily implemented if previous knowledge of the problem is available to be embedded in the loss function. We give an example of how to build different penalties in the next section.

As for the base loss, in this paper we consider three different alternatives, namely the above Cross-Entropy loss together with the Focal Loss and Non-Uniform Label Smoothing Loss functions. The Focal Loss was introduced for object detection tasks in [14], but it has become widely popular in classification tasks due to its ability to penalize wrongly miss-classified examples during training. In a multi-class setting, it is given by the following equation:

$$\mathcal{L}_{FL}(\hat{y}, y) = -\sum_{i=1}^{n=5} y_i \alpha (1 - \hat{y}_i)^\gamma \cdot \log(\hat{y}_i), \qquad (3)$$

being α a weighing factor and γ the so-called focusing parameter that penalizes errors in wrongly classified examples more than errors in correctly classified ones.

Non-Uniform Label Smoothing Loss is a straightforward modification of the popular Label Smoothing technique in which neighboring labels receive more probability mass than farther-away ones. This process is described by the following formula [8]:

$$\mathcal{L}_{NULS}(\hat{y}, y) = \mathcal{L}_{CE}(\hat{y}, G_\sigma(y)), \qquad (4)$$

where actual labels are manipulated by means of convolution with a Gaussian kernel G_σ resulting in the introduction of lower penalty in neighboring grades and greater loss value for far away predictions. Differently from the Cross-Entropy and the Focal loss, the Non-Uniform Label Smoothing strategy is sensitive to the label space structure. Yet, we hypothesize that further imposing greater penalty on farther away grades could bring benefits training based on this loss, as well as the other two above functions. In our experiments, described below, we train several models by considering $\mathcal{L}^{base}$ to be $\mathcal{L}_{CE}$, $\mathcal{L}_{FL}$, and $\mathcal{L}_{NULS}$ and varying the λ hyper-parameter from $\lambda = 0$ (no CS regularization whatsoever) to greater CS penalty, and observe the resulting performance.

2.2   Atomic Sub-Task Modeling

Annotating retinal images regarding the level of DR severity is know to be a noisy process, with high rates of inter-observer disagreement [11,20]. In this paper we propose to leverage available data regarding the structure of that disagreement to improve DR grading accuracy. Our hypothesis is that if the kind of noise affecting labels in the training data can be estimated, we can make a model aware of such noise via a CS mechanism similar to the one described in Eq. (2).

Specifically, we consider the confusion matrix M_{opht} from the left hand side of Eq. (5). This matrix contains information collected in [11] regarding inter-observer disagreement between retinal specialists and an adjudicated consensus during the grading process of their clinical validation dataset. Interestingly, this matrix conveys not only information about which grades are most likely to be subject of expert disagreement, but it also tells us which grades are more often mistaken by which other grades.

To formalize the above, we refer to the task of categorizing an image of actual DR grade i image into the j-th grade as t_{ij}, and we refer to this process as *atomic sub-tasks*. For a given grade D_i, the amount of images actually belonging to that grade is $s_i = \sum_{j=1}^{n=5} t_{ij}$, and normalizing t_{ij} by s_i provides an estimate of $t_{ij} = P(D_j|D_i)$, which denotes the likelihood that an annotator diagnoses an image as grade D_j when it actually was of grade D_i, as shown in the right hand side of Eq. (5):

$$M_{opht} = \begin{bmatrix} 1469 & 4 & 5 & 0 & 0 \\ 58 & 62 & 5 & 0 & 0 \\ 22 & 3 & 118 & 1 & 0 \\ 0 & 0 & 13 & 36 & 1 \\ 0 & 0 & 0 & 1 & 15 \end{bmatrix} \quad M_{opht}^* = \begin{bmatrix} 0.994 & 0.003 & 0.003 & 0 & 0 \\ 0.464 & 0.496 & 0.040 & 0 & 0 \\ 0.153 & 0.021 & 0.819 & 0.007 & 0 \\ 0 & 0 & 0.260 & 0.720 & 0.020 \\ 0 & 0 & 0 & 0.06237 & 0.937 \end{bmatrix} \quad (5)$$

We assume below that matrices are indexed starting from 0, *i.e.* $0 \le i, j \le 4$. By observing M_{opht}^* we can draw several conclusions, for example:

- Annotators are likely to be greatly accurate when grading D_0 and D_4 images, as derived from $t_{0,0} \approx 1$ and $t_{4,4} \approx 0.94$.
- Around 50% of D_1 images are likely to be incorrectly labeled ($t_{11} \approx 0.5$).
- Only 8% of incorrectly labeled D_1 images are likely to be labeled as D_2.
- Approximately 93% of those incorrectly labeled D_1 images are likely to be labeled as D_0.

Under the hypothesis that in a dataset labeled by a single annotator the reliability of the annotations will follow a distribution similar to the above, we can assume, for instance, that such dataset will contain reliable labels concerning D_0 grades. However, we may also assume that when an image has been annotated as of grade D_1, this is quite likely to be incorrect, and it may well be the case that such image is actually of grade D_0, since the corresponding atomic sub-task $t_{10} = P(D_0|D_1)$ holds value comparable to $t_{11} = P(D_1|D_1)$.

Our goal is to impose in our models a penalty on erroneous predictions that takes into account all the above information. That is, we want to penalize incorrect predictions when the label is likely to be reliable, but we are willing to be more *tolerant* with erroneous predictions if we know the associated label is unreliable. Embedding this knowledge into a loss function is easily accomplished using the CS loss formulation as developed in the previous section: we consider $I - M_{opht}^*$ in Eq. (2), being I the identity matrix. Higher values of t_{ij} will result in lower penalties, whereas lower values lead to a greater penalty.

Note, however, that for grades such that $t_{ij} = 0$, M_{opht}^*, there is no useful information in terms of relative reliability of these grades, e.g. $t_{03} = t_{04} = 0$ does not convey the information that it is harder to misdiagnose a D_0 images as D_3 than it is to misdiagnose it as D_4. In those situations it might be better to rely on the penalty imposed by M_{ij}^2 from Eq. (2). For this reason, we suggest to implement an averaged Cost-Sensitive regularizer as:

$$\mathcal{L}^{cs}(\hat{y}, y) = \mathcal{L}^{base}(\hat{y}, y) + \lambda \langle \hat{y}, M(y, \cdot) \rangle, \quad M = (M^{(2)} + I - M_{opht}^*)/2 \quad (6)$$

We now describe the remaining training specifications aside of the loss functions.

2.3   Training Details

For analyzing the impact of minimizing CS-regularized loss functions in the problem of DR grading, we follow the process of varying the λ hyper-parameter in Eq. (2). For each base loss function, we train a Convolutional Neural Network (CNN) by setting $\lambda = 0$ (no regularization), $\lambda = 0.1$, and $\lambda = 1$. If the best performance of these three experiments results from employing $\lambda = 1$, we set $\lambda = 10$ and train the CNN again. This process is repeated until performance does not improve anymore.

As for the CNN, we select the Resnext50 architecture based on its excellent classification accuracy in other multi-class problems [22], and weights are initialized from training in the ImageNet dataset. We use Stochastic Gradient Descent with a batch size of 8, and the learning rate is set to 0.001. Performance (quadratic kappa score) is monitored in an independent validation set. The learning rate is decreased by a factor of 10 whenever performance stagnates in the validation set, and the training is stopped after 10 epochs of no further improvement. In addition, to mitigate the impact of class imbalance, we oversample minority classes [5].

3   Experimental Validation

In this section we describe the experimental setting we follow in order to validate our approach: considered datasets, comparing techniques, and numerical results.

3.1   Experimental Details

We consider as our primary dataset the Eyepacs database[1] the largest public dataset with DR grading labels for DR grading labels. It contains around 80,000 high resolution retinal fundus images (approximately 35,000 are assigned to the training set, from which we employ 10% for validation, and 55,000 are held out for testing purposes). The Eyepacs dataset contains a considerable amount of low quality images and label noise [20]. Therefore, it represents an interesting test-bed to observe the robustness of DR grading algorithms.

As a secondary test set, we also consider the Messidor-2 dataset [2], which contains 1748 images corresponding to 874 patients. In this case, we employ the ground-truth labels released by [11], available online[2]. These labels are extracted from a process of consensus adjudication of three retinal specialists, and they are therefore of much better quality than the Eyepacs dataset ground-truth.

For performance assessment, we apply as the main metric of interest the quadratic-weighted kappa score (quad-kappa), which is typically used to assess inter-observer variability, and is very popular metric in this task. As further measures of correlation, we also analyze Average of Classification Accuracy (ACA,

---

[1] https://www.kaggle.com/c/diabetic-retinopathy-detection.
[2] https://www.kaggle.com/google-brain/messidor2-dr-grades.

Table 1. Performance comparison when training without regularization, with CS regularization as in Eq. (2), and with Atomic Sub-Task modeling (AST) as in Eq. (6), for the three considered loss functions. Statistically significant results are marked bold.

	quad-kappa	mAUC	ACA	Kendall-τ
CE	75.76 ± 0.31	87.35 ± 0.14	51.32 ± 0.44	67.35 ± 0.31
CE-CS	77.27 ± 0.30	88.42 ± 0.14	53.26 ± 0.42	**69.89 ± 0.30**
CE-AST	**77.39 ± 0.29**	88.49 ± 0.13	**54.12± 0.44**	69.25 ± 0.30
Focal Loss	74.72 ± 0.34	86.63 ± 0.16	51.90 ± 0.44	65.38 ± 0.32
FL-CS	77.38 ± 0.31	88.58 ± 0.14	54.11 ± 0.45	69.45 ± 0.30
FL-AST	**77.94 ± 0.29**	**88.90 ± 0.13**	**54.71 ± 0.43**	**70.45± 0.29**
NULS	77.09 ± 0.30	88.44 ± 0.14	53.02 ± 0.46	69.47 ± 0.29
NULS-CS	77.91 ± 0.30	88.82 ± 0.14	54.55 ± 0.44	70.14 ± 0.30
NULS-AST	**78.71 ± 0.28**	**89.05 ± 0.13**	54.57 ± 0.46	**71.0 ± 0.30**

the mean of the diagonal in a normalized confusion matrix [23]) and the Kendall-τ coefficient. We also report the mean Area Under the Receiver-Operator Curve in its multi-class extension, after considering each possible class pair [10]. For statistical testing, expert labels and model predictions in each of both test sets (Eyepacs and Messidor-2) are bootstrapped [4] (n=1000) in a stratified manner with respect to the relative presence of DR grades. Performance differences for each metrics are derived in each bootstrap and p-values are computed for testing significance. The statistical significance level was set to $\alpha = 0.05$ in each case.

For comparison purposes, we select three other recent techniques that introduce methods specifically developed to solve the DR grading task: *DR|graduate* [3], Bilinear Attention Net for DR Grading (Bira-Net) [23], and Quadratic-Weighted Kappa Loss (QWKL) [18].

3.2 Numerical Results

After training a CNN by minimizing each of the three considered base losses (Cross-Entropy, Focal Loss, and Non-Uniform Label Smoothing) with different degrees of regularization, we select the best model and compute results first on the Eyepacs test set. We denote the unregularized models by CE, FL, and NULS respectively, and their regularized counterparts as CE-CS, FL-CS, and NULS-CS.

We then select the best hyperparameter setting for each regularized model ($\lambda = 10$ in all cases), and retrain the same model but this time using our proposed Atomic Sub-Task modeling, denoted by an *AST* suffix in each case. We compile in Table 1 the obtained results in terms of quadratic κ-score, mean AUC, ACA and Kendall-τ, for all the described options.

Finally, we report in Table 2 the performance of our best model (using as a base loss NULS and Atomic Sub-Task modeling) in comparison with the techniques proposed in [3,18], and [23], in the test set of both Eyepacs and Messidor. We also provide confusion matrices for the Eyepacs test set in Fig. 2.

Table 2. Performance comparison in terms of quad-kappa/ACA for different methods when tested on the Eyepacs and Messidor-2 datasets. Models were trained on Eyepacs and tested on Eyepacs and Messidor (without retraining/fine-tuning).

	$DR|graduate$ [3]	QWKL [18]	Bira-Net [23]	NULS-AST
Eyepacs	74.00/53.6	74.00/n.a	n.a./54.31	**78.71 $\pm$ 0.28/54.57 $\pm$ 0.46**
Messidor-2	71.00/59.60	n.a./n.a	n.a./n.a	**79.79 $\pm$ 1.03/ 63.41 $\pm$ 1.99**

T/P	DR0	DR1	DR2	DR3	DR4
DR0	81	16	3	0	0
DR1	35	48	17	0	0
DR2	11	25	49	14	1
DR3	2	5	34	55	4
DR4	2	8	22	33	35

(a)

T/P	DR0	DR1	DR2	DR3	DR4
DR0	79	6	15	0	0
DR1	51	19	30	0	0
DR2	16	4	69	9	2
DR3	3	1	43	47	6
DR4	0	1	22	19	58

(b)

T/P	DR0	DR1	DR2	DR3	DR4
DR0	97	2	1	0	0
DR1	68	24	8	0	0
DR2	26	13	50	10	1
DR3	4	2	39	52	3
DR4	7	1	18	24	50

(c)

Fig. 2. (a)–(c): Normalized confusion matrices corresponding to: (a) the method of Araújo et al. [3], (b) Zhao et al. [23], (c) NULS-AST.

4   Discussion and Conclusion

Results on Table 1 clearly show that introducing Cost-Sensitive regularization results in noticeable improvements, particularly when measuring performance in terms of quadratic κ-score. This is meaningful since the considered cost matrix was selected so as to quadratically penalize distance in the label space for erroneous predictions. Quadratic κ-score experimented an improvement ranging from 3.5% when regularizing the Focal loss to 1% for NULS. This could also be expected, since NULS already introduces some asymmetry in the way DR grades are treated. If Atomic Sub-Task modeling is considered, these improvements are even greater when compared with unregularized counterparts: from an increase of κ score of 4.3% for the Focal Loss to an increase of 2% for NULS. It is also worth noticing that the confusion matrix resulting from training with Atomic Sub-Task modeling shows certain similarity with respect to the inter-observer disagreement matrix in the left-hand side of Eq. (5), specially when compared with the confusion matrices produced by other techniques, as shown in Fig. (2).

It should be stressed that performance on Table 1 is not comparable to results of the competition that published the data. There are several reasons for this: the heuristics for ranking optimization common to these competitions, or the fact that participants were allowed to submit predictions on 20% of the testing data during the competition. In addition, the lack of cross-dataset experimentation complicates evaluating generalization ability. In contrast, the approach proposed here is a general improvement over standard techniques, not limited to the DR grading problem, and which generalizes to other datasets, as Table 2 shows.

References

1. Diabetes Report, WHO. Technical report. https://www.who.int/news-room/fact-sheets/detail/diabetes
2. Abràmoff, M.D., et al.: Improved automated detection of diabetic retinopathy on a publicly available dataset through integration of deep learning. Invest. Ophthalmol. Vis. Sci. **57**(13), 5200–5206 (2016)
3. Araujo, T., et al.: DRGRADUATE: uncertainty-aware deep learning-based diabetic retinopathy grading in eye fundus images. Medical Image Analysis (accepted) (2019). http://arxiv.org/abs/1910.11777, arXiv: 1910.11777
4. Bertail, P., Clémençcon, S.J., Vayatis, N.: On bootstrapping the ROC curve. In: Koller, D., Schuurmans, D., Bengio, Y., Bottou, L. (eds.) Advances in Neural Information Processing Systems, pp. 137–144. Curran Associates, Inc., New York (2009)
5. Buda, M., Maki, A., Mazurowski, M.A.: A systematic study of the class imbalance problem in convolutional neural networks. Neural Networks **106**, 249–259 (2018)
6. Costa, P., Galdran, A., Smailagic, A., Campilho, A.: A weakly-supervised framework for interpretable diabetic retinopathy detection on retinal images. IEEE Access **6**, 18747–18758 (2018)
7. Frogner, C., Zhang, C., Mobahi, H., Araya, M., Poggio, T.A.: Learning with a Wasserstein loss. In: Cortes, C., Lawrence, N.D., Lee, D.D., Sugiyama, M., Garnett, R. (eds.) Advances in Neural Information Processing Systems 28, pp. 2053–2061. Curran Associates, Inc., New York (2015)
8. Galdran, A., et al.: Non-uniform label smoothing for diabetic retinopathy grading from retinal fundus images with deep neural networks. Trans. Vis. Sci. Technol. **9**(2), 34–34 (2020)
9. Gulshan, V., et al.: Development and validation of a deep learning algorithm for detection of diabetic retinopathy in retinal fundus photographs. JAMA **316**(22), 2402–2410 (2016)
10. Hand, D.J., Till, R.J.: A simple generalisation of the area under the ROC curve for multiple class classification problems. Mach. Learn. **45**(2), 171–186 (2001)
11. Krause, J., et al.: Grader variability and the importance of reference standards for evaluating machine learning models for diabetic retinopathy. Ophthalmology **125**(8), 1264–1272 (2018)
12. Li, F., et al.: Automatic detection of diabetic retinopathy in retinal fundus photographs based on deep learning algorithm. Trans. Vis. Sci. Technol. **8**(6), 4–4 (2019)
13. Lin, H., Lu, Y., Han, X., Sun, L.: Cost-sensitive regularization for label confusion-aware event detection. In: Proceedings of the 57th Annual Meeting of the Association for Computational Linguistics, pp. 5278–5283. Association for Computational Linguistics, Florence, Italy (2019)

14. Lin, T.Y., Goyal, P., Girshick, R., He, K., Dollár, P.: Focal loss for dense object detection. IEEE Trans. Pattern Anal. Mach. Intell. **42**(2), 318–327 (2020)
15. Mensch, A., Blondel, M., Peyré, G.: Geometric losses for distributional learning. In: International Conference on Machine Learning, pp. 4516–4525 (2019)
16. Sahlsten, J., et al.: Deep learning fundus image analysis for diabetic retinopathy and macular edema grading. Sci. Rep. **9**(1), 1–11 (2019)
17. Thai-Nghe, N., Gantner, Z., Schmidt-Thieme, L.: Cost-sensitive learning methods for imbalanced data. In: The 2010 International Joint Conference on Neural Networks (IJCNN), pp. 1–8 (2010)
18. de la Torre, J., Puig, D., Valls, A.: Weighted kappa loss function for multi-class classification of ordinal data in deep learning. Pattern Recogn. Lett. **105**, 144–154 (2018)
19. Bellemo, V., et al.: Artificial intelligence using deep learning to screen for referable and vision-threatening diabetic retinopathy in Africa: a clinical validation study. Lancet Digit. Health **1**(1), e35–e44 (2019)
20. Voets, M., Møllersen, K., Bongo, L.A.: Reproduction study using public data of: development and validation of a deep learning algorithm for detection of diabetic retinopathy in retinal fundus photographs. PLOS One **14**(6), e0217541 (2019)
21. Wilkinson, C.P., et al.: Proposed international clinical diabetic retinopathy and diabetic macular edema disease severity scales. Ophthalmology **110**(9), 1677–1682 (2003)
22. Xie, S., Girshick, R., Dollar, P., Tu, Z., He, K.: Aggregated Residual Transformations for Deep Neural Networks, pp. 1492–1500 (2017)
23. Zhao, Z., et al.: BiRA-Net: Bilinear attention net for diabetic retinopathy grading. In: 2019 IEEE International Conference on Image Processing (ICIP), pp. 1385–1389 (2019). iSSN: 1522–4880
24. Zhou, Z.H., Liu, X.Y.: Training cost-sensitive neural networks with methods addressing the class imbalance problem. IEEE Trans. Knowl. Data Eng. **18**(1), 63–77 (2006)

Disentanglement Network for Unsupervised Speckle Reduction of Optical Coherence Tomography Images

Yongqiang Huang[1], Wenjun Xia[1], Zexin Lu[1], Yan Liu[1], Jiliu Zhou[1], Leyuan Fang[2], and Yi Zhang[1]($\boxtimes$)

[1] Sichuan University, Chengdu 610065, China
yzhang@scu.edu.cn
[2] Hunan University, Changsha 410082, China

Abstract. Optical coherence tomography (OCT) has received increasing attention in the diagnosis of ophthalmic diseases due to its non-invasive character. However, the speckle noise associated with the low-coherence interferometric imaging modality has considerably negative influence on its clinical application. Moreover, the lack of clean and corresponding noisy OCT image pairs makes it difficult for supervised learning-based approaches to achieve satisfactory denoising results. Therefore, inspired by the idea of disentangled representation and generative adversarial network (GAN), we propose an unsupervised OCT image speckle reduction algorithm which firstly disentangles the noisy image into content and noise spaces by corresponding encoders. Then the generator is used to predict denoised OCT image only with the extracted content features. In addition, the pure noise patches which are cut from the noisy image are utilized to ensure a purer disentanglement. Extensive experiments have been conducted and the results suggest that our proposed method demonstrates competitive performance with respect to other state-of-the-art approaches.

Keywords: Unsupervised learning · Optical coherence tomography · Disentangled representation

1 Introduction

Non-invasive imaging modality, depth capacity and cross-sectional view of tissue structures make OCT a safe and effective tool for the diagnosis of various ocular diseases [1,2], such as age-related macular degeneration (AMD) and diabetic macular edema (DME). However, OCT images inevitably suffer from heavy speckle noise during the low coherence interferometry imaging procedure

Electronic supplementary material The online version of this chapter (https://doi.org/10.1007/978-3-030-59722-1_65) contains supplementary material, which is available to authorized users.

A. L. Martel et al. (Eds.): MICCAI 2020, LNCS 12265, pp. 675–684, 2020.
https://doi.org/10.1007/978-3-030-59722-1_65

[3], which significantly degrades imaging quality and impedes its application in clinics. Therefore, efficient OCT image denoising methods are highly required.

In recent years, many efforts have been made for OCT denoising. These methods can be roughly divided into two categories: the hardware-based and software-based approaches [4]. Hardware-based methods [5,6] can reduce the noise of the detector and the scanner by improving the light source and structure of the imaging system, but the speckle or white noise is still remaining. Software-based approaches are the mainstream of OCT image denoising. Filtering-based methods usually depend on local or global statistical modeling of the speckle noise within OCT images [7]. Representatively, the non-local means method (NL-Means) uses a predefined searching window to perform the non-local weighted averaging over the noisy images [8] as well as the block-matching and 3D filtering method (BM3D) performs the collaborative filtering over stacked 3D similar patches extracted from the noisy image [9]. However, these methods need laborious procedure of parameter tuning for different noise levels [10]. Transform-based methods [11,12] can reduce the speckle noise partly but also may introduce extra artifacts. Sparse representation based methods, such as nonlocal weighted sparse representation (NWSR) [13], can achieve impressive performance, but the vectorization operation destroys the intrinsic structure of the images.

Deep convolutional neural networks (CNNs) show a great power for image denoising tasks [14,15] over the past few years. For OCT image speckle reduction, different GAN-based methods have been proposed recently [16–18]. In spite of remarkable denoising results, a large number of paired images are needed. Injecting noise into the clean images is a reasonable solution to augment the training set [19]. However, these methods may not work well in practice, since the noise in OCT images does not obey any specific statistical distribution.

In this paper, we present an unsupervised learning method for OCT image speckle reduction based on Disentangled Representations and GAN (OCT-DRGAN). The proposed method can predict the clean counterparts of the input noisy OCT images in an end-to-end manner. Moreover, in order to guarantee that only noise features would be extracted by the noise encoder, the pure noise patches (See supplementary material Sect. 1 for details) are cut from the noisy OCT image and forward to the noise encoder, constraining the extracted noise features to keep consistent with the ones encoded from the noisy OCT image.

2   Method

2.1   Problem Formulation

Let $\mathcal{I}^n$ represent the noisy image domain and $\mathcal{I}^c$ be the clean image domain. Our goal is to learn a denoising mapping from $\mathcal{I}^n$ to $\mathcal{I}^c$ with unpaired data $\{(x, y) | x \in \mathcal{I}^n, y \in \mathcal{I}^c\}$. As depicted in Fig. 1, we assume that a noisy image can be disentangled into a noise space and a content space, while the clean image only can be transformed to the content space. Specifically, the content encoder (E_C) and noise encoder (E_N) are utilized to extract content features (F_C) and noise features (F_N) of OCT image respectively:

$$F_C^x = E_C(x), F_N^x = E_N(x), F_C^y = E_C(y) \tag{1}$$

Then, noisy image generator (G_N) is used to generate the noisy OCT image y_{noisy}, while clean image generator (G_C) produces clean OCT image x_{clean} as:

$$y_{noisy} = G_N(F_C^y, F_N^x), x_{clean} = G_C(F_C^x) \tag{2}$$

In addition, the input image x and y are reconstructed as:

$$x_{recon} = G_N(F_C^x, F_N^x), y_{recon} = G_C(F_C^y) \tag{3}$$

Moreover, in order to handle unpaired data, we also perform disentanglement to the generated images x_{clean} and y_{noisy}, and the cycle noisy image x_{cycle} and the cycle clean image y_{cycle} are obtained by G_N and G_C respectively:

$$F_C^{x_{clean}} = E_C(x_{clean}), F_C^{y_{noisy}} = E_C(y_{noisy}), F_N^{y_{noisy}} = E_N(y_{noisy}) \tag{4}$$

$$x_{cycle} = G_N(F_C^{x_{clean}}, F_N^{y_{noisy}}), y_{cycle} = G_C(F_C^{y_{noisy}}) \tag{5}$$

Once the model is trained, the clean OCT image can be obtained simply by feeding the original noisy OCT image into E_C and G_C sequentially.

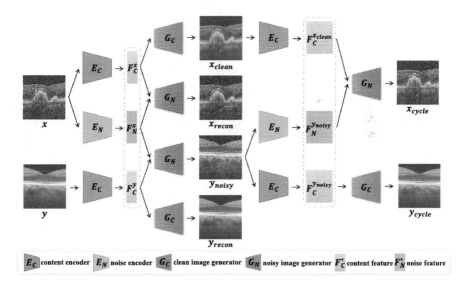

Fig. 1. The pipeline of our proposed OCT-DRGAN. In spired by CycleGAN [20], our encoder, including E_C and E_N, is consists of two convolutions and four residual blocks, while the generator contains four residual blocks and two transposed convolutions, and both G_C and G_N share the same architecture however has different parameters. As for discriminator, we employ the same architecture as that in [20].

2.2   Loss Functions

Cycle Consistence Loss. Inspired by the idea of CycleGAN [20], a cycle consistency loss is employed to ensure that the generated x_{cycle} and y_{cycle} are as close as possible to the original image x and y respectively:

$$L_{cycle} = \mathbb{E}\big[\|x - x_{cycle}\|_1\big] + \mathbb{E}\big[\|y - y_{cycle}\|_1\big] \tag{6}$$

where $\mathbb{E}[\cdot]$ denotes expectation operator and $\|\cdot\|_1$ is l_1 norm.

Reconstruction Loss. In order to generate accurate reconstruction results, the following reconstruction loss is utilized to facilitate the model training process:

$$L_{recon} = \mathbb{E}\big[\|x - x_{recon}\|_1\big] + \mathbb{E}\big[\|y - y_{recon}\|_1\big] \tag{7}$$

Adversarial Loss. Two kinds of discriminators, noisy image domain discriminator (D_N) and clean image domain discriminator (D_C), are employed to ensure the generated image is as similar as possible to that in the corresponding domain in an adversarial way. Therefore, the adversarial loss is defined as follows:

$$L_{adv}^{\mathcal{I}^c} = \mathbb{E}\big[\log\big(D_C(y)\big)\big] + \mathbb{E}\big[\log\big(1 - D_C(x_{clean})\big)\big] \tag{8}$$

$$L_{adv}^{\mathcal{I}^n} = \mathbb{E}\big[\log\big(D_N(x)\big)\big] + \mathbb{E}\big[\log\big(1 - D_N(y_{noisy})\big)\big] \tag{9}$$

$$L_{adv} = L_{adv}^{\mathcal{I}^c} + L_{adv}^{\mathcal{I}^n} \tag{10}$$

Disentanglement Loss. By introducing disentangled representation, the encoders perform a purifying procedure across the content space and the noise space, which means the features encoded by E_C should only have content information, while the E_N only extracts noise features. To further improve the performance, the pure noise patch n is also fed to E_C and E_N to extract the content feature F_C^n and the noise feature F_N^n, which can be formulated as:

$$F_C^n = E_C(n), F_N^n = E_N(n) \tag{11}$$

Then, we proposed to define a disentanglement loss as follows:

$$L_{disen} = \mathbb{E}\big[\cos(F_N^x, F_N^n)\big] + \mathbb{E}\big[\cos(F_N^{y_{noisy}}, F_N^n)\big] + \mathbb{E}\big[\|F_C^n - \mathbf{0}\|_1\big] \tag{12}$$

where $\cos(\cdot)$ represents cosine similarity and F_N^n is the noise feature of the pure noise patch while F_C^n denotes the content feature of the pure noise patch n.

Finally, the full loss function of our proposed OCT-DRGAN is:

$$L_{full} = L_{adv} + \alpha L_{cycle} + \beta L_{recon} + \gamma L_{disen} \tag{13}$$

where $\alpha = 20$, $\beta = 20$, $\gamma = 0.1$ are the weighting coefficients, respectively.

3 Experiments

3.1 Data

Two datasets [21,22] were combined to form the training and testing sets. For commercial scanners, the denoised OCT images are most commonly acquired by the sequential registering and averaging of several B-scans obtained at the same position of same subject [16]. However, it may lead to oversmoothed or artifact-affected results in the denoised images, which will degrade the image quality in the clean image domain in our experiments. Therefore, we manually removed some pairs of OCT images of which the clean counterpart was oversmoothed or the image details were destroyed during the registration and averaging operations. After that, there remained 26 image pairs and we randomly selected 10 as training set and the rest 16 as test set. More specifically, all the images were center-cropped to 450×900 (height $\times$ width) and the 10 training pairs were traversed with a window of 256×256, finally obtained total 9680 256×256 clean and noisy patch pairs. For the unsupervised training setting, we randomly shuffled the originally 9680 pairs and divided them into two parts, taking 4840 noisy patches in the first part as images in $\mathcal{I}^n$ and the 4840 clean patches in the other part are regarded as images in $\mathcal{I}^c$, while the size of the 16 test images was fixed to 450×900.

3.2 Compared Methods and Measurements

We quantitatively and qualitatively compared our proposed OCT-DRGAN with five classical algorithms: Median, NL-Means, Bilateral, Wavelet, and BM3D and three state-of-the-art learning-based denoising approaches: SNR-GAN [23], NWSR [13] and Edge-sensitive cGAN (ES-cGAN)[16]. SNR-GAN is based on unsupervised learning and the other two are supervised. Contrast-to-noise ratio (CNR), mean-to-standard-deviation ratio (MSR), signal-to-noise-ratio (SNR), and equivalent number of looks (ENL) were employed as the quantitative metrics. As common practice [13,22], we choose a region of interest (ROI) (the green rectangle #0) with no retinal or structure information in the background and four ROIs (red rectangles #1~4) at retinal layers or near the layers to calculate the metrics, since boundaries between retinal layers contained important information to detect the disease severity and pathogenicity. These ROIs are displayed in Figs. 2, 3.

3.3 Results

The quantitative results of our proposed OCT-DRGAN and the compared approaches are demonstrated in Table 1, listing the mean value of the four metrics computed on all 16 test images. It can be seen that our algorithm achieves the best results in terms of MSR, SNR and ENL, and is comparable in CNR with NWSR, which means that OCT-DRGAN could simultaneously suppress the speckle noise and maintain a high contrast for the testing set.

Table 1. Quantitative comparison with the state-of-the-art methods.

	CNR	MSR	SNR	ENL
Median	2.9756	4.6907	31.1694	135.2064
NL–Means	2.6380	4.3204	35.3789	303.5238
Bilateral	2.6020	4.1466	28.3219	61.1037
Wavelet	2.9034	4.4624	32.3159	175.5959
BM3D	2.7165	4.2996	37.7560	637.2720
SNR-GAN	2.6051	4.4118	36.6462	390.7385
ES-cGAN	2.6368	4.3516	32.3845	156.1844
NWSR	**2.9969**	4.8602	37.4616	584.8610
OCT-DRGAN	2.9750	**4.8805**	**41.1530**	**1645.3941**

Figure 2 shows the qualitative comparison of one representative case denoised by our proposed OCT-DRGAN and other classical and unsupervised approaches, from which we can see that our result are significantly better than those of the compared methods in both denoising and edge preservation. Specifically, it is obvious that there is still heavy speckle noise remaining in the images denoised by Median filtering and Bilateral filtering. More seriously, the median filtering blurs the edges. BM3D, Wavelet and NL-Means can suppress the noise in some extends, but they introduce extra unexpected artifacts. SNR-GAN achieves a better result, but it tends to destroy the edge structure near the retinal layers.

Figure 3 demonstrates the speckle reduction performance of our OCT-DRGAN compared with two state-of-the-art supervised methods. Both methods achieve impressive speckle reduction performance in the homogeneous region. However, ES-cGAN leads to blurred details as depicted in ROI #3. NWSR achieves a sharper result on retinal layer regions, but it seems to lose some layer information as indicated by the blue arrow in ROI #2 and #3 compared to the label.

3.4   Discussions

About Disentanglement Loss. We perform an ablation study to verify the effectiveness of our proposed disentanglement loss. The quantitative and qualitative comparisons of our proposed model with/without disentanglement loss are demonstrated in Table 2 and Fig. 4, respectively. We can see that the version containing disentanglement loss outperforms the other one in both denoising and edge preservation.

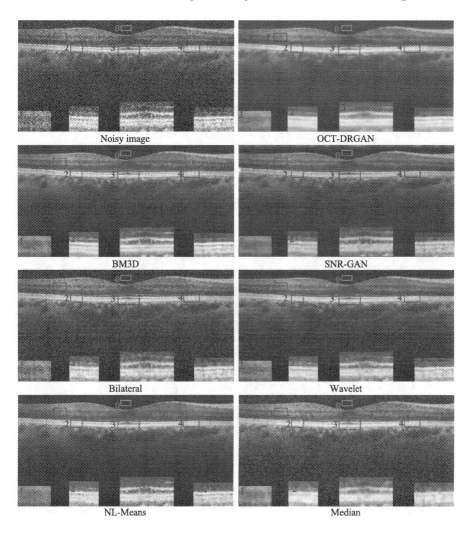

Fig. 2. Qualitative comparison with the classical and unsupervised approaches.

About Registered and Averaging Denoising. As aforementioned, the OCT denoising results in commercial scanners are achieved by registration and averaging. However, it is indicated in the orange rectangle in Fig. 4 that this commercial method loses some information of the clinical OCT image after processing, while our proposed method can maintain this detail well.

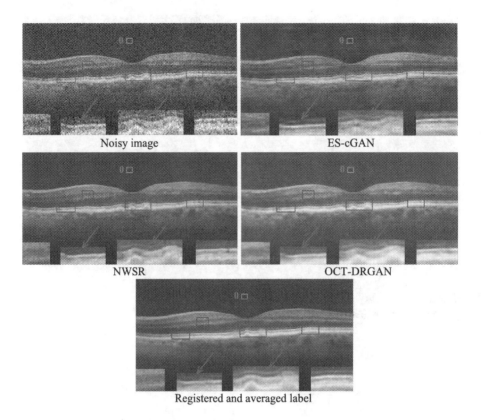

Fig. 3. Qualitative comparison with the state-of-the-art supervised approaches.

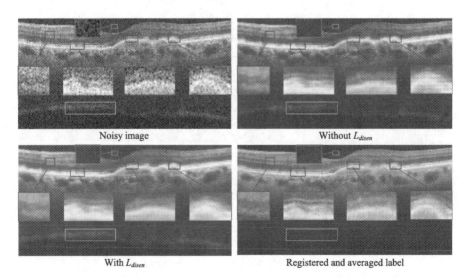

Fig. 4. Qualitative comparison w/o disentanglement loss.

Table 2. Quantitative comparison w/o disentanglement loss.

	CNR	MSR	SNR	ENL
Without L_{disen}	2.6311	4.3894	38.1356	717.9747
With L_{disen}	**2.9750**	**4.8805**	**41.1530**	**1645.3941**

4 Conclusion

In this paper, we proposed a novel unsupervised learning OCT image speckle reduction method based on the integration of GAN and disentangled representation. Thanks to the utilization of the corresponding encoder and generation mechanism of GAN, we can achieve competitive denoising results with unpaired data in terms of both noise suppression and detail preservation compared to other state-of-the-art OCT denoising approaches.

Acknowledgement. This work was supported by National Natural Science Foundation of China under Grant 61671312, 61922029.

References

1. Drexler, W., Morgner, U., Ghanta, R.K., Kärtner, F.X., Schuman, J.S., Fujimoto, J.G.: Ultrahigh-resolution ophthalmic optical coherence tomography. Nat. Med. **7**(4), 502–507 (2001)
2. Amini, Z., Rabbani, H.: Classification of medical image modeling methods: a review. Curr. Med. Imaging Rev. **12**(2), 130–148 (2016)
3. Gong, G., Zhang, H., Yao, M.: Speckle noise reduction algorithm with total variation regularization in optical coherence tomography. Opt. Express **23**(19), 24699–24712 (2015)
4. Xu, J., et al.: Wavelet domain compounding for speckle reduction in optical coherence tomography. J. Biomed. Opt. **18**(9), 096002 (2013)
5. Pircher, M., Götzinger, E., Leitgeb, R.A., Fercher, A.F., Hitzenberger, C.K.: Speckle reduction in optical coherence tomography by frequency compounding. J. Biomed. Opt. **8**(3), 565–570 (2003)
6. Klein, T., André, R., Wieser, W., Pfeiffer, T., Huber, R.: Joint aperture detection for speckle reduction and increased collection efficiency in ophthalmic mhz oct. Biomed. Opti. Express **4**(4), 619–634 (2013)
7. Adabi, S., et al.: Learnable despeckling framework for optical coherence tomography images. J. Biomed. Opt. **23**(1), 016013 (2018)
8. Aum, J., Kim, J., Jeong, J.: Effective speckle noise suppression in optical coherence tomography images using nonlocal means denoising filter with double Gaussian anisotropic kernels. Appl. Opt. **54**(13), D43–D50 (2015)
9. Chong, B., Zhu, Y.K.: Speckle reduction in optical coherence tomography images of human finger skin by wavelet modified BM3D filter. Opt. Commun. **291**, 461–469 (2013)
10. Li, M., Idoughi, R., Choudhury, B., Heidrich, W.: Statistical model for oct image denoising. Biomed. Opt. Express **8**(9), 3903–3917 (2017)

11. Mayer, M.A., Borsdorf, A., Wagner, M., Hornegger, J., Mardin, C.Y., Tornow, R.P.: Wavelet denoising of multiframe optical coherence tomography data. Biomed. Opt. Express **3**(3), 572–589 (2012)

12. Zaki, F., Wang, Y., Su, H., Yuan, X., Liu, X.: Noise adaptive wavelet thresholding for speckle noise removal in optical coherence tomography. Biomed. Opt. Express **8**(5), 2720–2731 (2017)

13. Abbasi, A., Monadjemi, A., Fang, L., Rabbani, H.: Optical coherence tomography retinal image reconstruction via nonlocal weighted sparse representation. J. Biomed. Opt. **23**(3), 036011 (2018)

14. Xie, J., Xu, L., Chen, E.: Image denoising and inpainting with deep neural networks. In: Advances in Neural Information Processing Systems, p. 1 (2012)

15. Zhang, K., Zuo, W., Chen, Y., Meng, D., Zhang, L.: Beyond a gaussian denoiser: residual learning of deep CNN for image denoising. IEEE Trans. Image Process. **26**(7), 3142–3155 (2017)

16. Ma, Y., Chen, X., Zhu, W., Cheng, X., Xiang, D., Shi, F.: Speckle noise reduction in optical coherence tomography images based on edge-sensitive cGAN. Biomed. Opt. Express **9**(11), 5129–5146 (2018)

17. Halupka, K.J., et al.: Retinal optical coherence tomography image enhancement via deep learning. Biomed. Opt. Express **9**(12), 6205–6221 (2018)

18. Huang, Y., et al.: Simultaneous denoising and super-resolution of optical coherence tomography images based on generative adversarial network. Opt. Express **27**(9), 12289–12307 (2019)

19. Devalla, S.K., et al.: A deep learning approach to denoise optical coherence tomography images of the optic nerve head. Sci. Rep. **9**(1), 1–13 (2019)

20. Zhu, J.Y., Park, T., Isola, P., Efros, A.A.: Unpaired image-to-image translation using cycle-consistent adversarial networks. In: Proceedings of the IEEE International Conference on Computer Vision, pp. 2223–2232 (2017)

21. Fang, L., Li, S., Nie, Q., Izatt, J.A., Toth, C.A., Farsiu, S.: Sparsity based denoising of spectral domain optical coherence tomography images. Biomed. Opt. Express **3**(5), 927–942 (2012)

22. Fang, L., et al.: Fast acquisition and reconstruction of optical coherence tomography images via sparse representation. IEEE Trans. Med. Imaging **32**(11), 2034–2049 (2013)

23. Guo, Y., et al.: Structure-aware noise reduction generative adversarial network for optical coherence tomography image. In: Fu, H., Garvin, M.K., MacGillivray, T., Xu, Y., Zheng, Y. (eds.) OMIA 2019. LNCS, vol. 11855, pp. 9–17. Springer, Cham (2019). https://doi.org/10.1007/978-3-030-32956-3_2

Positive-Aware Lesion Detection Network with Cross-scale Feature Pyramid for OCT Images

Dongyi Fan[1], Chengfen Zhang[1], Bin Lv[1], Lilong Wang[1], Guanzheng Wang[1], Min Wang[2], Chuanfeng Lv[1], and Guotong Xie[1(✉)]

[1] Ping An Technology (Shenzhen) Co., Ltd., Shenzhen, China
xieguotong@pingan.com.cn
[2] Department of Ophthalmology, Eye and ENT Hospital of Fudan University, Shanghai, China

Abstract. Optical coherence tomography (OCT) is an important imaging technique in ophthalmology, and accurate detection of retinal lesions plays an important role in computer-aided diagnosis. However, the particularities of retinal lesions, such as their complex appearance and large variation of scale, limit the successful application of conventional deep learning-based object detection networks for OCT lesion detection. In this study, we propose a positive-aware lesion detection network with cross-scale feature pyramid for OCT images. A cross-scale boost module with non-local network is firstly applied to enhance the ability of feature representation for OCT lesions with varying scales. To avoid lesion omission and misdetection, some positive-aware network designs are then added into a two-stage detection network, including global level positive estimation and local level positive mining. Finally, we establish a large OCT dataset with multiple retinal lesions, and perform sufficient comparative experiments on it. The results demonstrate that our proposed network achieves 92.36 mean average precision (mAP) for OCT lesion detection, which is superior to other existing detection approaches.

Keywords: Optical Coherence Tomography · Lesion detection · Cross-scale feature pyramid · Positive-aware

1 Introduction

Retinal diseases are among the leading causes of severe vision loss and blindness [1]. Optical coherence tomography (OCT) is widely used to observe retinal structures and their changes noninvasively. By means of OCT scan, many structural changes, namely retinal lesions such as pigment epithelial detachment (PED) and intraretinal fluid (IRF), can be identified to assist ophthalmologists in diagnosis of retinal diseases.

Recently, deep learning-based methods, such as image classification and segmentation, have been applied successfully in OCT images to solve various ophthalmic clinical

Dongyi Fan and Chengfen Zhang contribute equally and share the first authorship.

© Springer Nature Switzerland AG 2020
A. L. Martel et al. (Eds.): MICCAI 2020, LNCS 12265, pp. 685–693, 2020.
https://doi.org/10.1007/978-3-030-59722-1_66

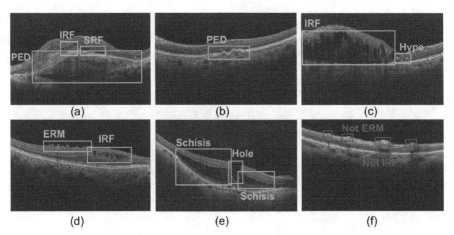

Fig. 1. Examples of various morphological OCT lesions and confusing tissues. The size and morph of the same type are distinctive. (a–d) show the contrast of size for PED and IRF. (d–e) shows the blurred border of macular hole (Hole) and epiretinal membrane (ERM) as well as lesions like Retinoschisis (Schisis). And some normal tissues (e.g. retinal vascular acoustic shadow and protuberance in (f)) are easily detected as lesions which are similar to IRF and ERM.

tasks [2, 3]. OCT image classification can achieve disease and lesion screening providing recommendation for urgent referral [4]. However, classification method cannot identify the detailed location information about the retinal lesions. OCT image segmentation can achieve retinal layer segmentation and provide quantitative information by estimating the boundary of lesions [5, 6]. Nevertheless, some retinal lesions, such as epiretinal membrane (ERM) and macular hole (Hole) as shown in Fig. 1(d, e), have blurred boundaries with normal structures which are not suitable for segmentation. It is crucial to detect more retinal lesions and provide location information for computer-aided diagnosis. Yet there is a lack of relevant works on OCT lesion detection currently.

Object detection with deep learning attracted much research attention in natural images [7–10], and has been gradually applied to lesion detection in medical images [11–14]. Compared to one-stage object detector, two-stage methods (e.g. Faster RCNN [9]) have advantages in the accuracy of detection, which are more suitable for medical requirements. To detect pulmonary nodule from CT images, Ding et al. [11] presented a two-stage framework with candidate screening and false positive reduction. Dou et al. [12] designed a hybrid-loss residual network which harnessed the location and size information as important cues to tackle the severe hard and easy sample imbalance problem. Compared with pulmonary nodule, retinal lesions in OCT images have more categories and more complex morphologies. Many lesions are obvious but not typical, such as intraretinal fluid (IRF) and PED shown in Fig. 1(a–d). And some normal tissues are easily misidentified as lesions shown in Fig. 1f. Due to the uncertainty of such tough candidates, it is meaningful to improve the detection results by identifying whether these candidate objects are positive lesions.

In addition, omission of small objects is a critical problem in lesion detection as well. To solve this problem, feature pyramid networks (FPN) [8] was proposed by extracting

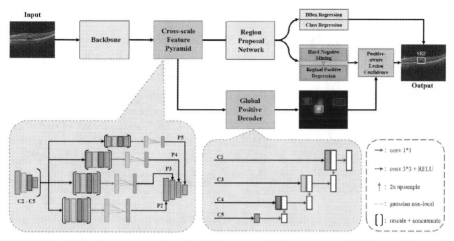

Fig. 2. Overview of our proposed method. The cross-scale feature pyramid (CFP), global positive decoder (GPD) and regional positive regression block (RPR) are designed for retinal lesion detection.

the feature hierarchy from backbone at all scales for natural image object detection. Shao et al. [14] proposed a multi-scale booster with channel and spatial attention to improve the detection performance of small lesions on CT images. However, these methods transfer the semantic information from high-scale to low-scale indirectly, which make the information obtained by different scales unilateral during region proposal. Lesions in OCT images like IRF and retinal pigment epithelium (RPE) atrophy vary significantly in size and shape as shown in Fig. 1. The approach is still lacking to promote the detection performance of lesions with large scale changes. It is necessary to enhance the feature representation through cross-scale direct connection.

In this paper, we propose a positive-aware lesion detection network with cross-scale feature pyramid to detect retinal lesions on OCT images. A cross-scale feature booster module enhanced by non-local network is constructed after backbone which fully obtains the information cross different scales to predict the proposals. Meanwhile, positive-aware lesion confidence is generated at global level and regional level. A positive-aware branch is constructed to improve the lesion detection results by predicting the positive and negative attributes at regional level. The activation response on global feature map and positive proposal confidence are integrated into the final detection score. Finally, a large OCT dataset with multiple retinal lesions is established to verify the effectiveness of our proposed lesion detection method.

2   Method

The overview of our proposed method is shown in Fig. 2. The whole framework includes backbone network, cross-scale feature pyramid (CFP), region proposal network (RPN), bounding box regressor and classifier, and positive-aware lesion confidence. Among them, CFP and positive-aware lesion confidence are our special designs for retinal lesion detection on OCT images, which are described in detail below.

2.1 Cross-scale Feature Pyramid

The features extracted by backbone network have the characteristics of rich semantic information in high-level features and accurate location information in low-level features. Different from traditional parallel feature fusion methods (e.g. FPN [8]), we propose a novel CFP method which combines the information at all the scales. It consists of three steps: multi-level sampling, feature enhancement and feature integration.

For an input OCT image, the features are extracted from the last layer of each stage of the backbone. Then we adopt bilinear upsampling and downsampling by pooling to different feature scales, which are rescaled to the same resolution. After that, through concatenation and 1×1 convolution operation, the features from different scales are integrated to the feature of corresponding scale. Finally, we rescale the features to each resolution of the extracted original feature, so that all features at different scales obtain sufficient information from others.

The spatial connection is helpful to improve the prediction of lesion, since a lesion in OCT image is often related to the overall structural change of macula. Therefore, we use the embedded Gaussian non-local network [15] which considers the global correlation on the feature map when calculating the response of each point to further enhance the cross-scale features. For each integrated feature, the non-local network is added respectively, and the embedded Gaussian is adapted to calculate the relationship between pixels in the feature map. Such process can be expressed as:

$$y_i = \frac{1}{C_x} \sum_{\forall j} e^{x_i^T x_j} W_g x_j \tag{1}$$

where C_x is the normalization parameter, W_g represents the weighted matrix of x_j. After that, the enhanced feature representations by CFP are transmitted to RPN to extract candidate areas of lesions.

2.2 Positive-Aware Lesion Confidence

Our positive-aware lesion confidence includes a global positive decoder (GPD) and a regional positive regression block (RPR). GPD captures global pixel-wise complementary information including context, semantic segmentation of lesion and background. To avoid additional segmentation annotation, we obtain approximate pixel label for retinal lesion by shrinking from the maximum inscribed circle of annotated box by 0.2. This strategy obtains masks mainly covering the foreground and excluding the background pixels to great extent, which is commonly used in word detection as weakly supervised segmentation [16]. The decoder contains several upsampling and concatenation operation, which is approximate to common segmentation structure. The output of GPD is a response map activated by sigmoid. And the mean value for each detection proposal mapping on the response is regarded as the global positive score, which can promote the confidence of lesion proposals effectively because positive regions tend to have higher response.

Apart from GPD, RPR is implemented as auxiliary to learn discriminative feature together with lesion estimation, classification and position regression. The region proposals are all merged as positive samples by assigning to their corresponding ground truth boxes with given Intersection Over Union (IOU). In addition, we perform offline hard negative mining to restrain the false positive proposals. To be specific, we firstly train the baseline model for several epochs as a false positive extraction model, while no negative-labeled proposals are used for training. The extraction model is to roughly guide us in selecting regions which are likely to false positive. Subsequently it is used to select negative proposals which are not intersecting with labeled ground truth boxes over the entire training set. It is assumed that these misdetections on training set mainly contribute to reduce potentially fallible outputs. Therefore, the labels for lesion estimation head include normal background, hard false positive and positive object. And hard false positive category aims to reduce positive score on negative proposal due to the mutex relationship among 3 types. A separate detection head with localization and class information is constructed to learn these 3 labels. Two 1×1 convolution layers with 1024 channels are implemented after the outputs of the cross-scale feature pyramid.

Taking advantage of the above GPD and RPR, our lesion detection model is trained with multi-task loss function to reinforce the sensitivity and exclusion to false positives, which can be defined as:

$$
\begin{aligned}
L_{det} = \frac{1}{N} \sum_i L_{cls}\left(p_i, p_i^*\right) + \frac{1}{N} \sum_i L_{reg}\left(p_i, p_i^*\right) \\
+ \lambda_{pl} \frac{1}{N} \sum_i L_{pos}\left(p_i, p_i^*\right) + \lambda_{gl}(1 - Dice(p, q))
\end{aligned}
\tag{2}
$$

where N is number of proposals. p_i and p_i^* are the predicted and ground truth bounding boxes. $Dice$ is dice coefficient to estimate similarity between masks, while λ_{pl} and λ_{gl} are weight coefficients for each loss. The fused score of each proposal R_p is reassigned by 3 outputs: classification score C_c, regional positive confidence C_p and global semantic response C_g which can be defined as:

$$
C_{final} = \lambda_{gc} \frac{1}{M} \sum_{x,y \in R_p} C_{x,y}^g + \lambda_{cc} C_c + \lambda_{pc} C_p
\tag{3}
$$

where C_{final} is the final fused detection score, and λ_{cc}, λ_{pc} and λ_{gc} are weight coefficients for each score part. The mean value for each proposal mapping on the response map $\frac{1}{M} \sum_{x,y \in R_p} C_{x,y}^g$ is regarded as the global positive score C_g.

3 Experiments

3.1 Experimental Setup and Implementation Details

We evaluated the proposed method on a large OCT dataset. The experimental dataset was selected from a retrospective cohort, including 25832 lesions of 38489 OCT slices captured from 4813 eyes. This study was approved by the local institutional review board. All OCT images were collected by SD-OCT devices (iScan/iVue, Optovue), with the same intervals covering 8×7 mm range of macular region and the resolution of 1024×640. We randomly split 35134/3355 images for training and testing, making sure that no slice from the same eye was utilized in both sets. The distribution of lesions in the training and test set is listed in Table 1. A validation set (10%) was split from training set to adjust hyper-parameter.

Table 1. Definition and distribution of retinal lesion bounding boxes

Lesion type (abbreviation)	Training set	Test set
Epiretinal membrane (ERM)	5816	624
Macular hole (Hole)	340	56
Hyper-reflective foci (Hype)	2396	213
Intraretinal fluid (IRF)	4588	205
pigment epithelial detachment (PED)	2212	188
RPE atrophy (RPEAtro)	2476	283
RPE irregularity including drusen (Drusen)	1614	205
Subretinal fluid (SRF)	2922	218
Retinoschisis (Schisis)	1372	104
Overall	23736	2096

We used ResNet-50 as the feature extraction backbone for all experiments. The parameters from conv1 to conv5 were initialized from the model pretrained on ImageNet [17] and the remaining parameters were initialized randomly. The OCT images were rescaled to 512×320 pixels and padding to 512×512 pixels as the inputs to predict lesions. The anchor scales and the anchor ratios were set as (16, 32, 64, 128, 256), {1:2, 1:1, 2:1} respectively while training the RPN network. λ_{pl}, λ_{gl}, λ_{cc}, λ_{pc} and λ_{gc} used in Eq. (2, 3) were 0.5, 0.5, 0.7, 0.3 and 0.2. SGD Optimizer with initial learning rate $1e-3$ was applied to optimize the parameters. The model was trained on one NVIDIA Tesla P100 for 50 epochs.

3.2 Ablation Study

We ran a number of ablations to analyze the effectiveness of each proposed module, including CFP, GPD and RPR. The evaluation metrics included mean average precision (mAP), recall and precision of bounding box. The evaluation results were shown in Table 2.

Table 2. Performance of ablation study on our test set

Baseline	CFP	RPR	GPD	mAP	Recall	Precision
✓				85.02	82.07	82.20
✓	✓			88.78	85.36	86.07
✓	✓	✓		91.75	88.81	92.34
✓	✓	✓	✓	**92.36**	**91.56**	**93.19**

Table 3. The comparison results among proposed method and other methods

Method	mAP	mAP$_V$	Recall (bbox)	Precision (bbox)	Sensitivity (slice)	Specificity (slice)
Faster RCNN	83.60	80.22	81.01	79.11	91.33	96.90
FPN	85.02	79.47	82.07	82.20	92.31	95.02
MSB	88.59	81.67	85.97	83.70	94.67	96.15
Proposed	**92.36**	**88.83**	**91.56**	**93.19**	**97.85**	**98.50**

We gradually added CFP, RPR and GPD to compare the model performances of different modules. Compared with baseline, CFP improved three metrics by 1 to 2 percentage points. And these metrics were gradually enhanced by adding RPR and GPD shown in Table 2. To be more specific, RPR achieved the significant gain with 2.97 for mAP, 3.45 for recall and 6.27 for precision, while GPD brought more improvement with 0.61 for mAP, 2.75 for recall and 0.85 for precision. It demonstrated that CFP could make better use of location and category information in different scales of features, so as to provide better proposal prediction for lesion detector. And the positive lesion confidence could enable network to extract more discriminative features of lesion/non-lesion, and then reduce the number of false positive with weakly response on the global positive score.

3.3 Comparison with State-of-the-Arts

We compared our proposed method to some other two-stage object detection methods, including Faster RCNN [9], FPN [8] and MSB [14]. Besides mAP, recall and precision, we also demonstrated other evaluation metrics with sensitivity and specificity of each slice and mAP$_V$. mAP$_V$ was obtained by calculating the AP on specific categories uniquely which varies rapidly on lesion area, including IRF, RPE Atrophy and Hype.

As shown in Table 3, the proposed method obtained the best lesion detection results on all evaluation metrics and achieved most obvious improvement on mAP$_V$. This result clearly showed that our method with CFP could effectively improve the detection accuracy for lesions with diverse area changes. In addition, the specificity on each slice was 98.5%, which surpassed the results of FPN by 3.48%. Our method showed superiority on false positives suppression compared to prior arts. In Fig. 3, qualitative experimental results were visualized. Because FPN was better than Faster RCNN, we only showed the results of FPN, MSB and our proposed method here. In the first row, a small lesion of PED was detected by our proposed model with high confidence at 0.89. Atypical lesions existed in (f-l) and our proposed model successfully detected them, while other 2 detectors obtained lower sensitivity or even wrong results. When normal tissues existed (m-p), the proposed model was able to suppress false positives. These intuitively implied that our proposed cross-scale feature fusion and positive-aware modules including RPR and GFD helped the network to promote the sensitivity and specificity of lesion detection.

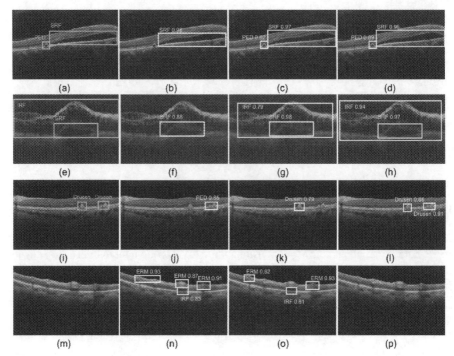

Fig. 3. Comparison examples among 3 detectors. (a) (e) (i) and (m) are annotated ground truth, (b) (f) (j) and (n) are from FPN, (c) (g) (k) and (o) are from MSB, (d) (h) (l) and (p) are from proposed method. The lesion name and detection score are illustrated on the picture. The green and yellow boxes are respectively ground truth and detection results. (Color figure online)

4 Conclusion

In this paper, a novel two-stage detection network is proposed to achieve multiple retinal lesions detection in OCT images. A CFP is used to solve the problem in detection of varied lesions by making full use of the information of all levels of features. Meanwhile, a positive-aware lesion confidence from both global and regional level is adopted to suppress false positives in lesion detection. The validation is performed on a large OCT dataset of 38489 OCT slices. Sufficient ablation experiments verify the effectiveness of the proposed method. And the experimental results show that our method has obvious advantages in different performance metrics compared with other state-of-the- art methods. Our proposed method can effectively detect multiple lesions in OCT images, even though the lesions vary greatly in size and morphology, which can provide important technical support for assistant diagnosis of retinal diseases.

References

1. Bourne, R.R.A., Flaxman, S.R., Braithwaite, T., et al.: Magnitude, temporal trends, and projections of the global prevalence of blindness and distance and near vision impairment: a systematic review and meta-analysis. Lancet Glob. Health **5**, e888–e897 (2017)

2. Ting, D.S.W., Peng, L., Varadarajan, A.V., et al.: Deep learning in ophthalmology: the technical and clinical considerations. Progr. Retinal Eye Res. **72**, 100759 (2019)
3. De Fauw, J., Ledsam, J.R., Romera-Paredes, B., et al.: Clinically applicable deep learning for diagnosis and referral in retinal disease. Nat. Med. **24**, 1342–1350 (2018)
4. Fang, L., Wang, C., Li, S., et al.: Attention to lesion: Lesion-aware convolutional neural network for retinal optical coherence tomography image classification. IEEE Trans. Med. Imaging **38**, 1959–1970 (2019)
5. Tennakoon, R., Gostar, A.K., Hoseinnezhad, R., et al.: Retinal fluid segmentation in oct images using adversarial loss based convolutional neural networks. In: 2018 IEEE 15th International Symposium on Biomedical Imaging (ISBI 2018), pp. 1436–1440. IEEE (2018)
6. Roy, A.G., Conjeti, S., Karri, S.P.K., et al.: ReLayNet: retinal layer and fluid segmentation of macular optical coherence tomography using fully convolutional networks. Biomed. Opt. Express **8**, 3627–3642 (2017)
7. Zhao, Z.Q., Zheng, P., Xu, S., et al.: Object detection with deep learning: a review. IEEE Trans. Neural Netw. Learn. Syst. **30**, 3212–3232 (2019)
8. Lin, T.Y., Dollár, P., Girshick, R., et al.: Feature pyramid networks for object detection. In: Proceedings of the IEEE Conference on Computer Vision and Pattern Recognition, pp. 2117–2125 (2017)
9. Ren, S., He, K., Girshick, R., et al.: Faster R-CNN: towards real-time object detection with region proposal networks. In: Advances in Neural Information Processing Systems, pp. 91–99 (2015)
10. Redmon, J., Farhadi, A.: Yolov3: an incremental improvement. arXiv preprint:1804.02767 (2018)
11. Ding, J., Li, A., Hu, Z., Wang, L.: Accurate pulmonary nodule detection in computed tomography images using deep convolutional neural networks. In: Descoteaux, M., Maier-Hein, L., Franz, A., Jannin, P., Collins, D.L., Duchesne, S. (eds.) MICCAI 2017. LNCS, vol. 10435, pp. 559–567. Springer, Cham (2017). https://doi.org/10.1007/978-3-319-66179-7_64
12. Dou, Q., Chen, H., Jin, Y., Lin, H., Qin, J., Heng, P.-A.: Automated pulmonary nodule detection via 3D convnets with online sample filtering and hybrid-loss residual learning. In: Descoteaux, M., Maier-Hein, L., Franz, A., Jannin, P., Collins, D.Louis, Duchesne, S. (eds.) MICCAI 2017. LNCS, vol. 10435, pp. 630–638. Springer, Cham (2017). https://doi.org/10.1007/978-3-319-66179-7_72
13. Li, Z., Zhang, S., Zhang, J., Huang, K., Wang, Y., Yu, Y.: MVP-Net: multi-view FPN with position-aware attention for deep Universal lesion detection. In: Shen, D., et al. (eds.) MICCAI 2019. LNCS, vol. 11769, pp. 13–21. Springer, Cham (2019). https://doi.org/10.1007/978-3-030-32226-7_2
14. Shao, Q., Gong, L., Ma, K., Liu, H., Zheng, Y.: Attentive CT lesion detection using deep pyramid inference with multi-scale booster. In: Shen, D., et al. (eds.) MICCAI 2019. LNCS, vol. 11769, pp. 301–309. Springer, Cham (2019). https://doi.org/10.1007/978-3-030-32226-7_34
15. Wang, X., Girshick, R., Gupta, A., et al.: Non-local neural networks. In: Proceedings of the IEEE conference on Computer Vision and Pattern Recognition, 7794–7803 (2018)
16. Zhou, X., Yao, C., Wen, H., et al.: EAST: an efficient and accurate scene text detector. In: Proceedings of the IEEE Conference on Computer Vision and Pattern Recognition, pp. 5551–5560 (2017)
17. Russakovsky, O., Deng, J., Su, H., et al.: Imagenet large scale visual recognition challenge. Int. J. Comput. Vis. **115**, 211–252 (2015)

Retinal Layer Segmentation Reformulated as OCT Language Processing

Arianne Tran[1,2(✉)], Jakob Weiss[1], Shadi Albarqouni[1,3], Shahrooz Faghi Roohi[1], and Nassir Navab[1,4]

[1] Computer Aided Medical Procedures, Technical University of Munich, Munich, Germany
arianne.tran@tum.de
[2] Computer Aided Surgery and Simulation, Ludwig-Maximilians-University Munich, Munich, Germany
[3] Computer Vision Lab, ETH Zurich, Zürich, Switzerland
[4] Computer Aided Medical Procedures, Johns Hopkins University, Baltimore, USA

Abstract. In the medical field, semantic segmentation has recently been dominated by deep-learning based image processing methods. Convolutional Neural Network approaches analyze image patches, draw complex features and latent representations and take advantage of these to label image pixels and voxels. In this paper, we investigate the usefulness of Recurrent Neural Network (RNN) for segmentation of OCT images, in which the intensity of elements of each A-mode depend on the path projected light takes through anatomical tissues to reach that point. The idea of this work is to reformulate this sequential voxel labeling/segmentation problem as language processing. Instead of treating images as patches, we regard them as a set of pixel column sequences and thus tackle the task of image segmentation, in this case pixel sequence labeling, as a natural language processing alike problem. Anatomical consistency, i.e. expected sequence of voxels representing retinal layers of eye's anatomy along each OCT ray, serves as a fixed and learnable grammar. We show the effectiveness of this approach on a layer segmentation task for retinal Optical Coherence Tomography (OCT) data. Due to the inherent directionality of the modality, certain properties and artifacts such as varying signal strength and shadowing form a consistent pattern along increasing imaging depth. The retinal layer structure lends itself to our approach due to the fixed order of layers along the imaging direction. We investigate the influence of different model choices including simple RNNS, LSTMs and GRU structures on the outcome of this layer segmentation approach. Experimental results show that the potential of this idea that is on par with state of the art works while being flexible to changes in the data structure.

The author was not affiliated with Ludwig-Maximilians-University Munich at the time of submission.

A. L. Martel et al. (Eds.): MICCAI 2020, LNCS 12265, pp. 694–703, 2020.
https://doi.org/10.1007/978-3-030-59722-1_67

Keywords: OCT · Retina segmentation · RNN segmentation · OCT language modelling

1   Introduction

Deep learning based image segmentation works have been so extensive over the recent years, that entire surveys have been written dedicated to this subject.

The predominant approach to recent research into image and medical image segmentation is the use of convolutional neural networks (CNN). Categories such as fully convolutional networks, encoder-decoder architectures, multi-scale and pyramid networks are well researched and many variants have been proposed [10]. The inherent ability of CNNs to extract features and learn abstract data representations makes them an obvious choice for image processing and segmentation.

Different to other approaches, however, the aim of this work is specifically to exploit the physical process of certain imaging modalities and show that the utilization of specific physical properties such as directionality can enable models with better regard for the image formation process. In this regard, we investigate the effects of reformulating semantic segmentation for imaging modalities following a directional imaging approach (OCT, Ultrasound, X-Ray) as a problem based on concepts predominantly used in natural language processing and focus specifically for the use-case of OCT imaging. We focus on the task of retinal layer segmentation in optical coherence tomography (OCT) to demonstrate how these concepts can be applied.

OCT reconstructs subsequent image columns (A-Scans) by a laser scanning across the region of interest. In retinal OCT, the imaging pathway always passes through the pupil, resulting in a restricted imaging direction and therefore consistent anatomical view. The directional quality of OCT imaging gives rise to specific characteristics which are particularly interesting for sequence modeling. Firstly, each A-Scan provides a consistent directional view along a line into the tissue. Due to the anatomical structure of a healthy retina, the succession of layers along the imaged line is highly regular. Strong variations in specific locations such as macula or fovea could occur, where some layers are thinned or nonexistent, but the order in which specific structures appear is largely consistent. Secondly, the imaging modality exhibits inherent directional effects: similar to ultrasound imaging, the modality measures the reflected signal along the depth of the path of the laser. This causes gradual signal loss with increasing depth through the tissue. Partial or total signal loss can also locally be caused by optically dense structures blocking more light, such as blood vessels, liquid bubbles or calcifications. Our approach therefore aims at making this a priori understanding of the physical and anatomical properties of retinal OCT apparent to the algorithm by following a directional processing within the network itself.

Recent OCT segmentation methods are mostly variants or extensions of UNet [12]: Orlando et al's U2-UNet [11] and Kiaee et al.'s 3D-UNet [7] focus on the segmentation of a varying number of the retina layers. Roy et al. [13] presented RelayNet, a modified UNet which replaces the deconvolutional decoder branch with unpooling layers. They show its effectiveness in the presence of anomalies such as fluid pockets.

Constraints to ensure preservation of the anatomical structure and ordering of the layers are introduced by methods such as He et al. [4]. They employ a two-step segmentation, a rough U-Net segmentation refined by a second network which forces the output towards a correct layer order, at a high computational cost. The use of RNNs in image processing has been largely restricted to processing videos or image captioning tasks [1]. Notable exceptions to this are ReNet [16] which applies RNNs to image classification, and its extension ReSeg-Net [15] which is applied for image classification by using a combination of convolutional and recurrent layers. Kugelmann et al. [8] have investigated a variety of network architectures for retinal layer boundary segmentation. They show that a patch-wise boundary classification can be achieved well by a ReNet-based architecture with patch-wise processing of 32×32 pixels. However, they rely on post-processing the probability maps with graph search [14] to extract the final layer boundaries which limits the applicability to healthy eyes with continuous boundaries.

By treating the image as an ordered sequence, we explore the effectiveness of recurrent neural networks (RNN), borrowing on concepts of the natural language processing (NLP) domain while considering the physics of image formation in OCT. By viewing the problem as a sequence labeling problem, we redefine the image as a sequence, thus exploiting the directionality of each an A-Scan. This allows us to transfer ideas and process schemes that are readily used in NLP processing and apply them to image segmentation. We test out concepts of language modelling which appear highly suited given the premise and a novel weighting schema that we adapt to our needs, inspired by known ideas from NLP text classifications [9]. Our competitive results highlight the advantages of our modeling, however we also report potential drawbacks of our method.

2   Methods

By exploiting the natural order of the retina layers as well as the physical properties of the OCT imaging modality, we redefine the image as a sequence following along the direction of an A-Scan. This layer order seen in Fig. 1 enables us to regard the image vertically as a sentence structure with n words which are the n subsequent rows of the image, starting from the top. To extend the analogy we can transform this segmentation problem into a sort of translation from image intensities "words" to label "words" which have the constraint of being dependent on the prior sentence elements due to the given anatomy. The semantic segmentation in terms of tissues types of individual retina layers is adapted in this concept in sentences which follow learn-able grammar structure. Anomalies interrupting the regular structure (c.f. R1) are not a general problem of our method, as the research field of NLP has been extensively dealing with discrepancies, inter language exceptions and errors. We are not limited to healthy examples as shown by our experiment with fluid pockets as anomalies. In medical cases we argue that we have an advantage as these anomalies do not occur completely randomly. They can be seen as a grammar variation which can be picked up by the network.

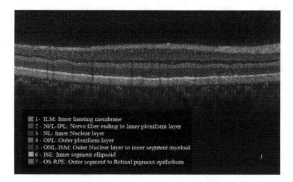

Fig. 1. The 7 layers of the retina

Pre-processing. By treating the image height as sequence and the width as context we can divide the image vertically into parts of equal width as shown in Fig. 2 to improve the model by learning on shorter simpler 'words'. Additionally we augment the data by creating overlapping splits of a fixed overlap size, which introduces a variety of word patterns into our data set. One could consider the sequential processing of every single A-scan independently as a sequence of letters. If we consider collection of neighboring A-modes, then we can consider every row as one word. In our experiments we have used a width of 30 px with an overlap of 20 px for an image of height 406 px. This means all words include 30 characters and each sentence 406 words and each image turns into an average of 60 sentences. Longer words greatly increase memory requirements while the number of sentences are dramatically reduced. This makes it harder for the network to learn the grammar. Shorter words increase the effects of noisy pixels therefore make it harder for the network to learn the vocabulary. In our experiments 30 px was the optimal length for each word.

We employ the standard split patient wise of 60%–20%–20% for train, validation and test set. The high variability of the data is dealt with by z-score normalization across the entire data-set using its average mean and average standard deviation. A small layer free portion of the image top and bottom, are cropped to reduce memory usage and equalize the sequence length across all inputs. Minor missing annotation parts are interpolated between the two last know locations to ensure an uninterrupted layer contour.

Architecture. The input to the network is size 12 batches of shuffled image splits. To deal with the unusual length of our input sequence, we use multi layer bi-directional GRU [3] network with variations between 3 and 4 layers and hidden units ranging from 128 to 256. This is followed by a drop-out layer, a fully connected dense layer and a log soft max to retrieve the probability map. We segment all 7 retina layers as well as the region above and below the retina which we distinguish from one another. Experiments show that the simpler GRU based network trains faster with slightly better results than a LSTM [5] based network, while a simple RNN is insufficient. The advantage of a LSTM lies in its performance of very long sequences with high variability, which are not required for retina layers where short history is sufficient due to the fixed order of the layers. The simplicity of this architecture leads to a straight forward implementation and a fast training and execution time due to the low number of parameters.

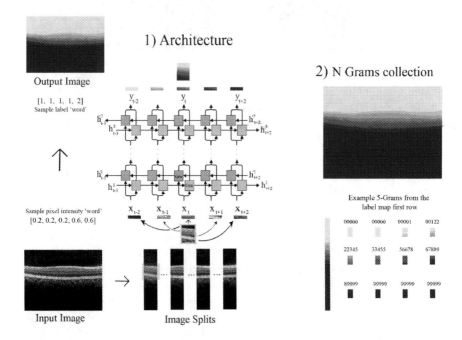

Fig. 2. 1) Shows the architecture and the reformulation of the image into sequences 2) Displays an example of N-Gram gathering along a row, for visualization's sake the row has been widened in this figure to cover several columns

N-Gram Inspired Counter Weighting. OCT images of the retina have a very high class imbalance, which stems from the significant region above and below the retina but also from the variability of layer thickness between the layers itself. We rely on the unique idea inspired by a well-known technique from NLP called n-grams, a principle which RNNs model closely. The intuition is that the probability $P(w_n|w_l^{n-1})$ of a word w can be approximated by the last n seen words rather than its entire history [6]. We take this idea, adapt and reverse it to calculate a pixel wise weighting map. We are not interested in the highest future word probability, instead we want to use the lowest probability for a word given a history of w_h words before and a future of w_f words after, forming an N-long mini sequence we refer to as n-gram. In order to obtain a pixel wise weight map, we use 5-grams of only one "letter"/pixel words. The 5-gram is a 1×5 pixel column, from which the weight is calculated for the center pixel, in this case the 3rd pixel. We assemble the bag of 5-grams by collecting the 1×5 pattern centered around each image pixel based on the ground truth label map as can be seen in on the right side of Fig. 2. Since the segmentation classes have a fixed order and limited number there are only a limited number of n possible patterns. Unique pattern occurrences such as in underrepresented layers have a low frequency which is even lower around layer boundaries. Because of the high imbalance within the sum of each unique pattern we normalize the n pattern frequencies $F_p = f_1, f_2.....f_n$ by mean and standard deviation. The weight map is obtained by finding the pattern to which each pixel belongs, and assigning its weight $1/f_x$, $f_x \in F_p$. For the upper and lower most pixels we mirror the frequencies by means of padding. The result is a weight map seen in Fig. 3 which favors underrepresented classes and layer borders as well as abnormal structures.

Fig. 3. From left to right: OCT Image, Annotation Label Map, Weight Map. Low weights are darker and high weights are brighter. Pixels with a common pattern have a lower weight while pixels occurring in an uncommon pattern have a higher weight

Smooth Probabilistic Output. The segmentation is performed similar to training on vertical image splits of a fixed width n. To obtain the segmentation over the entire image, predictions on overlapping slices are calculated. These slices are created in a sliding window fashion of step size 10. The probabilities of every overlapping image within an overlap region are combined through majority voting, before going through an arg max function to predict the final label. This smooths the results and prevents jagged edges and leads to an overall higher prediction accuracy.

3 Experiments

Our hypothesis is tested on two cases, first segmentation of 7 retina layers in absence of anomalies and second segmentation of 7 retina layers with fluid pockets within arbitrary layers. We use the Duke OCT retina dataset 2015 [2] and the

2014 dataset which each contain 10 patients, 10 slices per patient and two sets
of independent expert annotations. The established baseline to compare the different methods is a 3-layer deep bi-directional sequential GRU with 256 hidden
units per layer is employed trained on a pixel-wise weighted cross entropy loss.
Inputs use a batch size of 12 image slices of size 406×30. In addition to that
we use a dropout of 20% and a L2-regularization weight decay of 0.0002 while
learning on a rate of 0.001. We report the results on a k-fold cross validation
of 5 folds by splitting the dataset into non-overlapping subsets of patients, seen
in Table 2. This allows a more detailed understanding of the performance of our
own method. For fair comparison against other methods we use the same setting
of our first fold, which uses patient 2–6 for training, 7–8 for validation and 9–10
for testing, for all methods. We show all results based on expert 1 annotations
which are used for training and validation of all compared methods. Experiments
on expert 2 annotations showed similar results. We present the impact of our
weighting scheme by reporting results with and without weighting and showcase
the robustness of the network by evaluating on the second data set containing
anomalies in the form of fluid pockets. To evaluate the method against others,
3 metrics are computed: the mean dice score per class, the contour error (CE)
calculated by the mean absolute distance of two layer contour lines and the
mean absolute difference in layer thickness (MAD-LT). The layer abbreviations
are described in Fig. 1, RaR is the region above retina and RbR respectively the
region below retina. The comparisons are reported against RelayNet [13], which
is capable to also deal with anomalies, and Kugelmann et al. [8].

Table 1. Comparison on healthy retina image segmentation between two experts,
comparative methods and our own method. The best performance is shown in bold

| | Layers | | | | | | | | | | |
	Method	RaR	ILM	NFL-IPL	INL	OPL	ONL-ISM	ISE	OS-RPE	RbR	Mean	Std
DICE	Exp 1 vs 2	0.99	0.87	0.91	0.79	0.81	0.94	0.77	0.82	0.99	0.88	0.08
	RelayNet	0.66	0.91	**0.94**	0.87	0.83	0.94	0.92	0.93	0.77	0.86	0.09
	Kugelmann	0.99	0.74	0.63	0.83	0.57	0.60	0.75	0.56	0.98	0.74	0.16
	Ours	0.99	**0.92**	**0.94**	**0.89**	**0.87**	**0.96**	**0.93**	**0.95**	0.99	**0.94**	**0.04**
CE	Exp 1 vs 2	-	0.95	1.13	1.40	1.28	1.39	0.76	2.4	-	1.33	0.49
	RelayNet	-	NA	NA	NA	NA	NA	NA	NA	-		
	Kugelmann	-	1.48	2.08	2.125	2.11	2.03	1.78	0.68	-	1.75	0.49
	Ours	-	**0.49**	**0.92**	**0.73**	**0.89**	**0.87**	**0.34**	**0.46**	-	**0.67**	**0.22**
MAD-LT	Exp 1 vs 2	-	1.40	1.73	1.84	1.78	1.55	2.25	2.33	-	1.84	0.32
	RelayNet	-	1.14	1.30	1.44	1.70	1.47	0.75	0.98	-	1.25	0.29
	Kugelmann	-	1.13	1.58	1.43	3.14	1.35	0.80	1.01	-	1.49	0.72
	Ours	-	**1.05**	**1.20**	**1.19**	**1.22**	**0.97**	**0.65**	**0.81**	-	**1.01**	**0.20**

As can be seen in Table 1 there is a lot of ambiguity even among experts
even more so in the case of anomalies 4. The results of the presented methods
lie within the margin of the presented expert 1 vs 2 variation. Due to non-
continuous predictions in the relay-net method, it was not possible to reconstruct
a clean contour for comparison. As Kugelmann et al. predict layer boundaries,

Table 2. 5-Fold cross validation of our own method. The best performance is shown in bold

	Layers									
	Method	ILM	NFL-IPL	INL	OPL	ONL-ISM	ISE	OS-RPE	Mean	Std
DICE	Fold 1	0.92	0.94	0.89	0.87	0.96	0.93	0.95	**0.92**	**0.03**
	Fold 2	0.92	0.95	0.89	0.86	0.96	0.91	0.94	**0.92**	**0.03**
	Fold 3	0.89	0.90	0.83	0.77	0.91	0.88	0.91	0.87	0.05
	Fold 4	0.78	0.77	0.61	0.60	0.69	0.59	0.84	0.70	0.09
	Fold 5	0.92	0.94	0.87	0.86	0.96	0.90	0.93	0.91	**0.03**
CE	Fold 1	0.49	0.92	0.73	0.89	0.87	0.34	0.46	**0.67**	0.22
	Fold 2	0.65	0.73	0.70	0.85	0.99	0.40	0.60	0.70	**0.17**
	Fold 3	0.90	1.21	1.50	1.75	2.15	0.61	0.88	1.28	0.50
	Fold 4	1.50	2.18	3.44	3.75	3.91	0.76	1.71	2.46	1.14
	Fold 5	0.55	0.92	0.79	1.00	0.93	0.43	0.83	0.77	0.19
MAD-LT	Fold 1	1.05	1.20	1.19	1.22	0.97	0.65	0.81	**1.01**	0.20
	Fold 2	1.03	1.05	1.10	1.3	1.08	0.75	1.02	1.05	**0.14**
	Fold 3	1.52	1.65	1.23	1.51	2.76	1.07	1.28	1.57	0.52
	Fold 4	2.82	3.27	1.62	1.58	4.31	1.10	1.85	2.36	1.05
	Fold 5	1.05	1.27	1.19	1.45	1.06	0.93	1.05	1.14	0.16

Table 3. Experiment results on the fluid retina dataset comparing other methods with ours and between two experts

	Layers										
	Method	ILM	NFL-IPL	INL	OPL	ONL-ISM	ISE	OS-RPE	Fluid	Mean	Std
DICE	RelayNet	0.84	0.85	0.70	0.71	0.87	0.88	0.84	0.30	0.75	0.18
	Ours w/o weights	0.82	0.89	0.77	0.76	0.88	0.88	0.82	0.31	0.76	0.17
	Ours with weights	0.85	0.89	0.75	0.75	0.89	0.90	0.87	**0.39**	**0.78**	**0.16**
CE	RelayNet	2.86	2.99	3.04	2.30	7.61	1.24	1.47	-	3.07	1.97
	Ours w/o weights	2.12	1.38	1.80	1.60	4.13	1.14	0.89	-	1.87	1.00
	Ours with weights	0.97	1.48	1.86	1.73	3.66	0.79	0.90	-	**1.67**	**0.91**
MAD-LT	RelayNet	1.97	2.72	2.76	2.25	3.65	1.36	1.20	-	2.27	0.79
	Ours w/o weights	2.66	1.98	1.71	2.44	3.43	1.05	2.24	-	2.21	0.69
	Ours with weights	1.61	1.93	1.63	1.70	3.02	0.99	0.99	-	**1.69**	**0.63**

false predictions lead to a false intersection layer structure which hampers the reconstruction of a sensible label map in some cases, preventing a quantitative evaluation of the dice score. Consequently these datasets are omitted and dice scores are reported for cases where a comparison of all methods was achievable, respectively. We see stable performance throughout the folds but for one major exception, which reflects in the folds 3 and 4. We found that the data of patient 2 is an outlier from the rest in terms of inter-layer and overall intensity distribution. To come back to the language analogy, this would be similar to a dialect within a language. The 20% of data we use for testing consist of only two patients, therefore one outlier strongly skews the results. We assume that this effect will vanish when increasing dataset size. As additional stress test, the model is tested on retinal images with anomalies such as fluid pockets, which can appear in arbitrary layer locations. This shows how the model is able to deal with sudden grammar interruptions compared to a well ordered layer structure it has so

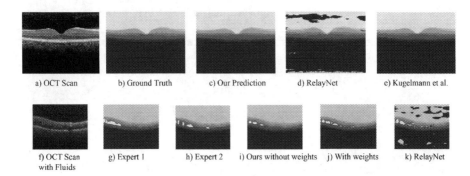

a) OCT Scan   b) Ground Truth   c) Our Prediction   d) RelayNet   e) Kugelmann et al.

f) OCT Scan   g) Expert 1   h) Expert 2   i) Ours without weights   j) With weights   k) RelayNet
with Fluids

Fig. 4. The upper row a) to e) shows a sample prediction of our method along with RelayNet und Kugelmann's method on a healthy retina, corresponding to Table 1. The second row demonstrates the effect of the weighting scheme under anomaly occurrence as presented in Table 3

far seen. We use the same settings that have been presented so far to train on the anomaly dataset. We can observe in Table 3 that the introduction of our weighting schema increases sensitivity towards fluid detection quite a bit (Fig. 4).

4   Discussion and Conclusion

In this paper we introduced a novel way of dealing with OCT retinal layer segmentation by strongly taking the physics of OCT image formation into consideration. Motivated by the natural direction of the A-Mode, which passes through the layers in a fixed order, we transform the problem from the image domain to a sequential labeling inspired by automatic language analysis. We advocate an approach of thorough analysis and understanding of the physics and anatomy of a problem to allow for the design of improved network architectures for specific problems. In the case of retinal OCT imaging this led us to consider its similarity to language processing, which are successfully handled by RNNs in NLP community. Our results are highly comparable to that of the state of the art. Modelling this problem in a sequential nature allows us to use a straightforward, simple architecture as a proof of concept. In fact, this work only investigated the stacking of equally-sized RNN blocks, the use of many architectural extensions such as RNN-based encoder-decoder structures could also be explored. The robustness of our approach was tested by training on a pathological data set, where anomalies disrupt the regular structure and therefore our sequential ordering hypotheses, and finding out that the proposed solution can still achieve good results. A highly interesting direction for future improvements will be to investigate how NLP methodologies deal with intra-language variations such as accents or dialects and with incomplete sentences to draw further inspiration from them to model solutions for layers segmentation in OCT in presence of more complex pathology.

References

1. Aafaq, N., Mian, A., Liu, W., Gilani, S.Z., Shah, M.: Video description: a survey of methods, datasets, and evaluation metrics. ACM Comput. Surv. (CSUR) **52**(6), 1–37 (2019)
2. Chiu, S.J., Allingham, M.J., Mettu, P.S., Cousins, S.W., Izatt, J.A., Farsiu, S.: Kernel regression based segmentation of optical coherence tomography images with diabetic macular edema. Biomed. Opt. Express **6**(4), 1172–1194 (2015)
3. Cho, K., et al.: Learning phrase representations using RNN encoder-decoder for statistical machine translation. arXiv preprint arXiv:1406.1078 (2014)
4. He, Y., et al.: Topology guaranteed segmentation of the human retina from OCT using convolutional neural networks. arXiv e-prints arXiv:1803.05120, March 2018
5. Hochreiter, S., Schmidhuber, J.: Long short-term memory. Neural Comput. **9**(8), 1735–1780 (1997)
6. Jurafsky, D., Martin, J.H.: Speech and Language Processing -. Pearson Education, Amsterdam (2014)
7. Kiaee, F., Fahimi, H., Rabbani, H.: Intra-retinal layer segmentation of optical coherence tomography using 3d fully convolutional networks. In: 2018 25th IEEE International Conference on Image Processing (ICIP), pp. 2795–2799. IEEE (2018)
8. Kugelman, J., et al.: Automatic choroidal segmentation in oct images using supervised deep learning methods. Sci. Rep. **9**(1), 1–13 (2019)
9. Li, B., Zhao, Z., Liu, T., Wang, P., Du, X.: Weighted neural bag-of-n-grams model: new baselines for text classification. In: Proceedings of COLING 2016, the 26th International Conference on Computational Linguistics: Technical Papers, pp. 1591–1600. The COLING 2016 Organizing Committee, Osaka, Japan, December 2016
10. Minaee, S., Boykov, Y., Porikli, F., Plaza, A., Kehtarnavaz, N., Terzopoulos, D.: Image segmentation using deep learning: a survey. arXiv e-prints arXiv:2001.05566, January 2020
11. Orlando, J.I., et al.: U2-net: a Bayesian u-net model with epistemic uncertainty feedback for photoreceptor layer segmentation in pathological OCT scans. In: 2019 IEEE 16th International Symposium on Biomedical Imaging (ISBI 2019), pp. 1441–1445. IEEE (2019)
12. Ronneberger, O., Fischer, P., Brox, T.: U-Net: convolutional networks for biomedical image segmentation. In: Navab, N., Hornegger, J., Wells, W.M., Frangi, A.F. (eds.) MICCAI 2015. LNCS, vol. 9351, pp. 234–241. Springer, Cham (2015). https://doi.org/10.1007/978-3-319-24574-4_28
13. Roy, A.G., et al.: ReLayNet: retinal layer and fluid segmentation of macular optical coherence tomography using fully convolutional networks. Biomed. Opt. Express **8**(8), 3627 (2017). https://doi.org/10.1364/BOE.8.003627. http://arxiv.org/abs/1704.02161. https://www.osapublishing.org/abstract.cfm?URI=boe-8-8-3627
14. Trucco, E., MacGillivray, T., Xu, Y.: Computational Retinal Image Analysis - Tools, Applications and Perspectives. Elsevier, Amsterdam (2019)
15. Visin, F., et al.: Reseg: a recurrent neural network-based model for semantic segmentation. In: Proceedings of the IEEE Conference on Computer Vision and Pattern Recognition Workshops, pp. 41–48 (2016)
16. Visin, F., Kastner, K., Cho, K., Matteucci, M., Courville, A., Bengio, Y.: Renet: a recurrent neural network based alternative to convolutional networks. arXiv preprint arXiv:1505.00393 (2015)

Reconstruction and Quantification of 3D Iris Surface for Angle-Closure Glaucoma Detection in Anterior Segment OCT

Jinkui Hao[1,5,6], Huazhu Fu[2(✉)], Yanwu Xu[1], Yan Hu[3,5], Fei Li[4,5], Xiulan Zhang[4,5], Jiang Liu[3], and Yitian Zhao[1,5(✉)]

[1] Cixi Institute of Biomedical Engineering, Ningbo Institute of Materials Technology and Engineering, Chinese Academy of Sciences, Ningbo, China
yitian.zhao@nimte.ac.cn
[2] Inception Institute of Artificial Intelligence, Abu Dhabi, UAE
hzfu@ieee.org
[3] Department of Computer Science and Engineering, Southern University of Science and Technology, Shenzhen, China
[4] State Key Laboratory of Ophthalmology, Zhongshan Ophthalmic Center, Sun Yat-sen University, Guangzhou, China
[5] Glaucoma Artificial Intelligence Diagnosis and Imaging Analysis Joint Research Lab, Guangzhou and Ningbo, China
[6] University of Chinese Academy of Sciences, Beijing, China

Abstract. Precise characterization and analysis of iris shape from Anterior Segment OCT (AS-OCT) are of great importance in facilitating diagnosis of angle-closure-related diseases. Existing methods focus solely on analyzing structural properties identified from an individual 2D slice, while accurate characterization of morphological changes of iris shape in 3D AS-OCT may be able to reveal in addition the risk of disease progression. In this paper, we propose a novel framework for reconstruction and quantification of 3D iris surface from AS-OCT volume. We consider it to be the first work to detect angle-closure glaucoma by means of 3D representation. An iris segmentation network with wavelet refinement block (WRB) is first proposed to generate the initial shape of the iris from single AS-OCT slice. The 3D iris surface is then reconstructed using a guided optimization method with Poisson-disk sampling. Finally, a set of surface-based features are extracted, which are used in detecting of angle-closure glaucoma. Experimental results demonstrate that our method is highly effective in iris segmentation and surface reconstruction. Moreover, we show that 3D-based representation achieves better performance in angle-closure glaucoma detection than does 2D-based feature.

Keywords: AS-OCT · 3D iris surface · Angle-closure glaucoma

1 Introduction

Anterior Segment OCT (AS-OCT) imaging is a non-contact and non-invasive method for cross-sectional viewing of anterior segment structure, as shown in

© Springer Nature Switzerland AG 2020
A. L. Martel et al. (Eds.): MICCAI 2020, LNCS 12265, pp. 704–714, 2020.
https://doi.org/10.1007/978-3-030-59722-1_68

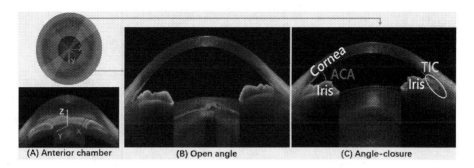

Fig. 1. For one AS-OCT volume (A), the open angle (B) and angle-closure (C) cases may appear in different sectors. A 3D volume is more suitable than a 2D image for supporting global analysis.

Fig. 1 (A). Anatomical structures, such as iris shape and anterior chamber angle (ACA), observed in AS-OCT play key roles in facilitating examination and diagnosis of angle-closure glaucoma [1–4]. Figure 1 (B, C) show two AS-OCT images revealing open angle and angle-closure glaucoma, respectively. However, manual identification of angle-closure glaucoma is time consuming and prone to human error. To this end, automated extraction of morphological features, e.g., ACA, iris and other anterior segment structures, would benefit both clinical diagnosis and any automated screening system [5–7].

Epidemiological studies [7–10] have established that quantitative iris parameters are independently related to narrow ACA, and an anteriorly-bowed iris may be related to the degree of angle-closure progression. Huang et al. [9] also suggest that morphological changes in the iris surface are an important sign, revealing and enabling the understanding of the pathogenesis of angle-closure glaucoma. As a result, automated extraction of the iris from the AS-OCT has become an active research area of significance for future diagnosis and prognosis. Ni et al. [11] assessed angle-closure glaucoma by computing mean iris curvature and the trapezoidal area of the iridocorneal angle, etc. Fu et al. [5] proposed a data-driven method of segmenting the cornea and iris, as well as measuring the clinical parameters essential to screen for glaucoma. Shang et al. [12] presented a curvilinear structure filter based on the local phase tensor to extract the iris region, so as to further assist the diagnosis of angle-closure glaucoma. However, all of the aforementioned methods rely on 2D slices of AS-OCT, which are less useful in distinguishing the stages of angle-closure glaucoma. This may stem from the fact that AS-OCT provides only a single cross-sectional slice view across the anterior segment and, in consequence, all other slices are irrelevant to the task of determining angle status [13,14]. In contrast, a comprehensive study of the global information provided by a 3D representation of the iris may improve measurement accuracy and robustness more significantly than conventional approaches that make use of only an individual 2D slice. Moreover, the occludable iridocorneal, or fully closed ACA leads to the presence of trabecular iris contact (TIC) and exacerbate the iris reconstruction problem [15].

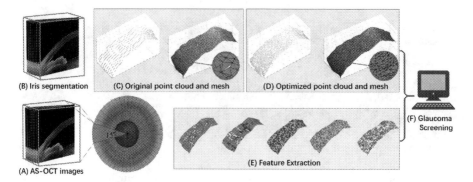

Fig. 2. Flowchart of the proposed approach. Given an AS-OCT sector in a 15° radiant area (A), the iris boundaries (B) are firstly identified by a segmentation network. We then convert the segmentation into a 3D point cloud and mesh (C). A constrained Poisson-disk sampling method is used to optimize the point cloud and mesh (D), so as to obtain a more accurate iris surface. Finally, different surface measurements (E) are computed for diagnosis of angle-closure glaucoma (F).

To this end, in this paper we propose an automated reconstruction and quantification framework for 3D iris surface. Inspired by the discrete wavelet transform, we introduce a novel wavelet refinement block (WRB) into a U-shaped architecture [16] with a view to reducing the redundancy while maintaining local details to the decoder, for extracting an initial iris segmentation. The detected iris boundaries are then utilized to reconstruct a 3D iris surface based on Poisson-disk sampling. Finally, we extract features from this 3D iris surface (e.g., principal curvatures, Gaussian curvature, mean curvature and shape index) to further assist the examination and diagnosis of angle-closure glaucoma. The experiments demonstrate that our proposed method has high effectiveness on iris segmentation and reconstruction.

2   Proposed Method

In this section, we introduce the proposed 3D iris reconstruction and quantification framework for angle-closure glaucoma detection in AS-OCT. Figure 2 illustrates the pipeline of our proposed method.

2.1   Iris Segmentation Network with Wavelet Refinement Block

In [16,17], high resolution features from an encoder are combined with decoder features using skip connection, which takes detailed information directly to the decoder to remedy information loss due to pooling and convolutional operations. However, this operation also imports massive quantities of irrelevant information into the decoder, which disturbs and weakens the learning ability of networks. To address this issue, we introduce a new network component into the segmentation network, which we call a wavelet refinement block (WRB). This is able to

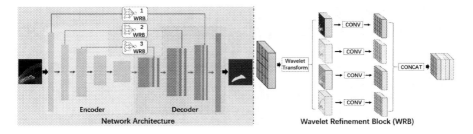

Fig. 3. Architecture of our segmentation model.

reduce the amount of redundant information, while preserving local details for the decoder. Figure 3 illustrates the architecture of our segmentation network.

Discrete Wavelet Transform: Given the input feature X, a 2D Discrete Wavelet Transform (DWT) with four convolutional filters - low-pass filter f_{LL}, and high-pass filters f_{LH}, f_{HL}, and f_{HH} are performed to decompose X into four subband features, Y_{LL}, Y_{LH}, Y_{HL}, and Y_{HH}. Taking the Haar wavelet as an example, the four filters are defined as:

$$f_{LL} = \begin{bmatrix} 1 & 1 \\ 1 & 1 \end{bmatrix}, f_{LH} = \begin{bmatrix} -1 & -1 \\ 1 & 1 \end{bmatrix}, f_{HL} = \begin{bmatrix} -1 & 1 \\ -1 & 1 \end{bmatrix}, f_{LL} = \begin{bmatrix} 1 & -1 \\ -1 & 1 \end{bmatrix}. \tag{1}$$

Note that all the convolutions above are performed with stride 2, yielding a subsampling of factor 2 along each spatial dimension. The DWT operation is defined as $Y_{LL} = (f_{LL} \otimes X) \downarrow_2$, $Y_{LH} = (f_{LH} \otimes X) \downarrow_2$, $Y_{HL} = (f_{HL} \otimes X) \downarrow_2$, and $Y_{HH} = (f_{HH} \otimes X) \downarrow_2$, where $\otimes$ denotes a convolution operator, and $\downarrow_2$ means the standard down-sampling operator with factor 2.

Network Architecture: We utilize U-Net [16] as the backbone, which consists of four encoder blocks which correspond to the first four blocks, as shown in Fig. 3. In order to restore boundary details, we insert three WRB after the first three blocks to take local detail information to the decoder. Specifically, we use a Haar wavelet in Eq. (1) to decompose the corresponding feature maps into four frequency subbands channel-wise, where each band is half-resolution of the input. It is worth noting that the low frequency band Y_{LL} stores local averages of the input data: correspondingly, the high frequency bands, namely Y_{LH}, Y_{HL}, and Y_{HH}, encode details that are significant in recovering boundaries. We then employ 1×1 convolution for each subband separately and cascade them with decoder feature maps. Allowing comparison with the skip connection that directly brings features from the encoder into the decoder in the general U-Net [16], our WRB reduces the introduction of redundant information while preserving details, which makes our network more accurate and robust in predicting details.

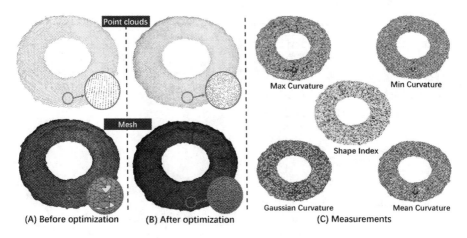

Fig. 4. Illustrative of iris 3D reconstruction and feature measurements. (A) Original point cloud and mesh generated by proposed 2D iris segmentation method. (B) Optimized point cloud and mesh. (C) Visualization of different measurements.

2.2   3D Iris Surface Reconstruction and Quantification

At present, the gold standard for diagnostic angle assessment is observation of ACA by gonioscopy. In simpler terms, ophthalmologists move the gonioscope counterclockwise, making an annotation every 15°. In a similar manner, the AS-OCT automated scan obtains multiple consecutive radiant slices within a 15° area, which can then be used to reconstruct a mesh of the iris surface in 3D.

Surface Reconstruction: Using the previously obtained segmentation results, the upper boundaries of the iris are used to produce a 3D point cloud of the iris surface. These point clouds are nonuniform and sparse: nevertheless, the mesh generated is coarse and deficient of lacking local details. As demonstrated by the representative patch shown in Fig. 4 (A), distortions of the mesh lead to mispresentation of the iris surface. In addition, the geometrical changes in some regions are more dramatic than in others due to the existence of iris frill. This leads to a higher point density than in smooth areas, which leads to a low quality mesh, as shown in Fig. 2 (C).

To this end, we adapted a constrained Poisson-disk sampling [18] of the coarse mesh to refine the surface. This method produces a more uniform and dense point cloud, while guaranteeing that objects of a certain size will be distributed according to the sampling scheme, without overlapping. In practice, an adaptive radius r was utilized, to obtain a more precise representation of the point cloud while being as uniform as possible. Specifically, if the maximum curvature of a given point was larger than the global average, r was set to r_1: otherwise, it was set to r_2. In our work, following empirical testing we set r_1 and r_2 to 6 and 10, respectively. Figure 2 (D) and Fig. 4 (B) demonstrate the optimized point cloud and mesh, which are more effective in revealing geometrical details.

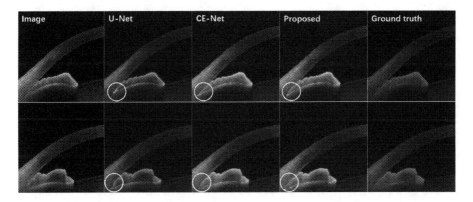

Fig. 5. Visualization of 2D iris segmentation results. From left to right: original image, and results as obtained by U-Net [16], CE-Net [17], our method, and ground truth.

Feature Extraction: As suggested by study [9], the quantitative iris parameters, such as iris curvature, were independently associated to the degree of angle-closure progression. In consequence, after the reconstruction of the iris surface, we calculated the following curvature-related measures for the later diagnosis of angle-closure related diseases: principal curvatures, Gaussian curvature, mean curvature and shape index [19].

It is worth noting that the *shape index* is introduced in order to capture the intuitive notion of 'shape' locally and globally. The shape index $\mathscr{E}$ of each point may be defined as

$$\mathscr{E} = \frac{2}{\pi} \arctan \frac{\mathscr{C}_2 + \mathscr{C}_1}{\mathscr{C}_2 - \mathscr{C}_1}, \tag{2}$$

where $\mathscr{C}_1$ and $\mathscr{C}_2$ are the maximum and minimum curvatures of a point, respectively, and $\mathscr{E} \in [-1, 1]$. Unlike the curvature, the shape index is invariant to scaling of the shape, and it could give a simple measurement of the local shape - it can present the flat concave and convex regions significantly [19].

3   Experimental Results

In order to validate the effectiveness and superiority of the proposed method, we evaluated its individual components separately: first 2D iris segmentation, and then angle-closure glaucoma detection in 3D iris quantification.

3.1   Evaluation of Iris Segmentation

Data and Metrics: A total of 100 AS-OCT images captured by CASIA-2 (Tomey Inc., Japan) from different subjects were collected. The iris regions were annotated by an image analysis expert and an ophthalmologist, and a consensus of their results was used as the final reference standard. The dataset was divided equally into training and testing sets. For a quantitative evaluation, we

Table 1. Performance in 2D iris segmentation of different methods.

Method	Region			Edge		TIC
	Sen(%)	Dice(%)	Acc(%)	RNMSE	HD	TIC Err.(Pixel)
FCN [20]	84.63	87.01	97.24	0.0601	6.60	21.77
U-Net [16]	88.19	91.84	99.26	0.0543	4.64	19.63
Segnet [21]	91.09	92.70	99.32	0.0619	**4.31**	17.65
CE-Net [17]	95.74	94.89	99.45	0.0512	4.41	14.43
Proposed	**96.46**	**95.21**	**99.48**	**0.0504**	4.32	**13.24**

employed the following metrics: accuracy (Acc), sensitivity (Sen) and dice coefficients (Dice) as region-level evaluation criteria; and root normalized mean square
error (RNMSE) and Hausdorff distance (HD) as edge-level evaluation criteria.
In addition, we also provided the trabecular iris contact (TIC) error score [5].

The segmentation performance of the proposed model was compared with
the following state-of-the-art segmentation methods: FCN [20], U-Net [16], Segnet [21], and CE-Net [17]. As shown in Table 1, our model achieved the best
performance in terms of all metrics, with a single exception: its HD score is 0.01
lower than that of Segnet. Figure 5 illustrates the iris segmentation results of the
different methods over two sample images. Overall, the proposed method demonstrated that it could correctly segment the iris region, when compared with the
corresponding manual annotations. From careful observation of the TIC regions,
it was clear from visual inspection that our method was better able to identify
the iris root than the competing methods. This is because our method introduces the wavelet refinement block to reduce redundancy in the image, so that
our network may then pay greater attention to the salient context than other
segmentation models.

3.2 Evaluation of Angle-Closure Glaucoma Detection

In this experiment, we first reconstructed 3D iris surfaces using different segmentation methods: FCN [20], U-Net [16], Segnet [21] and CE-Net [17]. We then
used measurements obtained in Sect. 2.2 and entire point cloud as the input of
a 3D classification model, PointNet [22], to classify the glaucoma subjects into
cases of open angle and angle-closure glaucoma types, respectively.

Data and Metrics: A total of 42 AS-OCT volumes were captured from 42
eyes, with each volume containing 128 AS-OCT images. A senior ophthalmologist made an annotation (determining open or angle-closure glaucoma) from
gonioscopic examination of every $15°$ segment ACA of each eye, yielding 24
annotations for a single eye, resulting in a total of 1008 annotations for each
dataset (504 open-angle and 504 angle-closure). In light of this, we partitioned
the 42 automatically-generated 3D iris shapes into 1008 sub-surfaces by dividing

each shape into twenty-four 15° segments. We trained using 80% of these sub-surfaces and reserved 20% for testing. We employed the metrics of *Acc, Sen, Spe*, and area under ROC curve (AUC) to measure the final angle-closure glaucoma detection performance.

Results: Table 2 reports the detection performances using features extracted from the 3D iris reconstruction by the different segmentation methods. It may be seen that clearly significant margins of improvement in detection results were achieved when the proposed method is compared with the other state-of-art segmentation models. For example, our method exhibits a large advantage over FCN by increases in *Acc* and *Sen* of about 8.33% and 10.5%, respectively. Comparatively, our method reduces noise and other redundancies in AS-OCT, thereby allows the decoder to concentrate on high-level context, such as the TIC region, which is more beneficial for disease detection.

Effectiveness of Optimization Step: In addition, we also demonstrate how the detection result benefits from the point cloud optimization process. We may observe that the generated 3D iris surface seen in Fig. 4 A, suffers from distortion without the subsequent optimization step optimization step (Fig. 4 B), and this scenario leads to incorrect curvature estimation, which will further compromise the accuracy of detection. This finding is evidenced in Table 2: without the point cloud optimization step, the detection results show decrements of 3.1%, 2.1%, and 4.2% for ACC, Sen and Spe, respectively.

Comparison of 2D and 3D Features: All existing angle-closure glaucoma detection methods are accomplished using 2D features obtained from a single AS-OCT slice. To further verify whether the features extracted from a 3D iris surface obtained by our method could improve detection performance, we compared the proposed method to the conventional approaches that use 2D feature representation: histograms of oriented gradients (HOG) features [23] with linear Support Vector Machine (SVM), AlexNet [24], VGG [25], and ResNet [26]. The detection performances of these methods are reported in Table 2. It may be seen that by enabling the use of features extracted from a reconstructed 3D iris surface, the 3D classification network, PointNet, achieved the best performances in terms of Acc, Spe, and AUC. This confirms that making use of 3D features is more helpful in improving the accuracy of angle-closure glaucoma detection than using 2D features alone.

Table 2. Angle-closure glaucoma detection results obtained by different methods.

Method	Acc(%)	Sen(%)	Spe(%)	AUC(%)
2D: HOG+SVM	85.01	74.33	95.90	91.92
2D: ResNet34	96.87	97.91	94.79	99.52
2D: AlexNet	92.18	90.62	84.37	93.81
2D: VGG16	94.18	96.48	93.75	98.50
3D: FCN + PointNet	90.10	88.54	91.66	97.55
3D: U-Net + PointNet	92.70	89.58	95.83	98.82
3D: Segnet + PointNet	94.79	96.87	92.70	99.01
Our WRB + PointNet	95.31	96.87	93.75	99.17
Our WRB + Optimization + PointNet	**98.43**	**98.95**	**97.91**	**99.83**

4   Conclusion

Existing methods to identify gonioscopic angle-closure have focused solely on the extraction of features from 2D slices, which are less satisfactory for the identification of angle-closure glaucoma subtypes. In this work, we have developed a novel framework for reconstruction and quantification of 3D iris surface from AS-OCT imagery. This is for the first time that a comprehensive surface-based framework has been applied to model and analyze 3D iris from AS-OCT. The high evaluation performance in segmentation experiments shows the ability and robustness of our models in extracting iris features from individual AS-OCT slices. Feature analysis and angle-closure glaucoma detection have then been performed based on 3D iris reconstruction, which shows the high effectiveness of our approach. The proposed framework opens the possibility for further investigation of AS-OCT from a new perspective. In our future work, we will focus on the development of a 3D representation based analysis and diseases detection framework including more anterior chamber structures.

Acknowledgment. This work was supported by Zhejiang Provincial Natural Science Foundation of China (LZ19F010001,LQ19H180001), Ningbo "2025 S&T Megaprojects" (2019B10033, 2019B10061).

References

1. Chansangpetch, S., Rojanapongpun, P., Lin, S.C.: Anterior segment imaging for angle closure. Am. J. Ophthalmol. **188**, xvi–xxix (2018)
2. Ang, M., Baskaran, M., et al.: Anterior segment optical coherence tomography. Progr. Retinal Eye Res. **66**, 132–156 (2018)
3. Xu, B.Y., Chiang, M., et al.: Deep learning classifiers for automated detection of gonioscopic angle closure based on anterior segment OCT images. Am. J. Ophthalmol. **208**, 273–280 (2019)

4. Zhao, Y., et al.: Automated tortuosity analysis of nerve fibers in corneal confocal microscopy. IEEE Trans. Med. Imaging **39**, 2725–2737 (2020)

5. Fu, H., Xu, Y., et al.: Segmentation and quantification for angle-closure glaucoma assessment in anterior segment OCT. IEEE Trans. Med. Imaging **36**(9), 1930–1938 (2017)

6. Fu, H., Baskaran, M., et al.: A deep learning system for automated angle-closure detection in anterior segment optical coherence tomography images. Am. J. Ophthalmol. **203**, 37–45 (2019)

7. Zhao, Y., et al.: Retinal vascular network topology reconstruction and artery/vein classification via dominant set clustering. IEEE Trans. Med. Imaging **39**(2), 341–356 (2019)

8. Wang, B., Sakata, L.M., et al.: Quantitative iris parameters and association with narrow angles. Ophthalmology **117**(1), 11–17 (2010)

9. Huang, J., Wang, Z., Wu, Z., Li, Z., Lai, K., Ge, J.: Comparison of ocular biometry between eyes with chronic primary angle-closure glaucoma and their fellow eyes with primary angle-closure or primary angle-closure suspect. J. Glaucoma **24**(4), 323–327 (2015)

10. Zhao, Y., et al.: Uniqueness-driven saliency analysis for automated lesion detection with applications to retinal diseases. In: Frangi, A.F., Schnabel, J.A., Davatzikos, C., Alberola-López, C., Fichtinger, G. (eds.) MICCAI 2018. LNCS, vol. 11071, pp. 109–118. Springer, Cham (2018). https://doi.org/10.1007/978-3-030-00934-2_13

11. Ni Ni, S., Tian, J., Marziliano, P., Wong, H.T.:Anterior chamber angle shape analysis and classification of Glaucomain SS-OCT images. J. Ophthalmol. **2014** (2014)

12. Shang, Q., Zhao, Y., et al.: Automated iris segmentation from anterior segment OCT images with occludable angles via local phase tensor. In: Annual International Conference of the IEEE Engineering in Medicine and Biology Society (EMBC), pp. 4745–4749. IEEE (2019)

13. Cho, H.k., Ahn, D., Kee, C.: Evaluation of circumferential angle closure using iridotrabecular contact index after laser iridotomy by swept-source optical coherence tomography. Acta Ophthalmol. **95**(3), e190–e196 (2017)

14. Zhao, Y., et al.: Automatic 2-D/3-D vessel enhancement in multiple modality images using a weighted symmetry filter. IEEE Trans. Med. Imaging **37**(2), 438–450 (2017)

15. Fu, H., et al.: A deep learning system for automated angle-closure detection in anterior segment optical coherence tomography images. Am. J. Ophthalmol. **203**, 37–45 (2019)

16. Ronneberger, O., Fischer, P., Brox, T.: U-Net: convolutional networks for biomedical image segmentation. In: Navab, N., Hornegger, J., Wells, W.M., Frangi, A.F. (eds.) MICCAI 2015. LNCS, vol. 9351, pp. 234–241. Springer, Cham (2015). https://doi.org/10.1007/978-3-319-24574-4_28

17. Gu, Z., Cheng, J., et al.: CE-Net: context encoder network for 2d medical image segmentation. IEEE Trans. Med. Imaging **38**(10), 2281–2292 (2019)

18. Corsini, M., Cignoni, P., Scopigno, R.: Efficient and flexible sampling with blue noise properties of triangular meshes. IEEE Trans. Vis. Comput. Graph. **18**(6), 914–924 (2012)

19. Zhao, Y., Liu, Y., et al.: Region-based saliency estimation for 3d shape analysis and understanding. Neurocomputing **197**, 1–13 (2016)

20. Long, J., Shelhamer, E., Darrell, T.: Fully convolutional networks for semantic segmentation. In: CVPR, pp. 3431–3440 (2015)

21. Badrinarayanan, V., Kendall, A., Cipolla, R.: Segnet: a deep convolutional encoder-decoder architecture for image segmentation. IEEE Trans. Pattern Anal. Mach. Intell. **39**(12), 2481–2495 (2017)
22. Qi, C.R., Su, H., Mo, K., Guibas, L.J.: Pointnet: deep learning on point sets for 3d classification and segmentation. In: CVPR, pp. 652–660 (2017)
23. Xu, Y., Liu, J., et al.: Anterior chamber angle classification using multiscale histograms of oriented gradients for glaucoma subtype identification. In: Annual International Conference of the IEEE Engineering in Medicine and Biology Society, pp. 3167–3170. IEEE (2012)
24. Krizhevsky, A., Sutskever, I., Hinton, G.E.: Imagenet classification with deep convolutional neural networks. In: Advances in Neural Information Processing System, pp. 1097–1105 (2012)
25. Simonyan, K., Zisserman, A.: Very deep convolutional networks for large-scale image recognition. arXiv preprint arXiv:1409.1556 (2014)
26. He, K., Zhang, X., Ren, S., Sun, J.: Deep residual learning for image recognition. In: CVPR, pp. 770–778 (2016)

Open-Appositional-Synechial Anterior Chamber Angle Classification in AS-OCT Sequences

Huaying Hao[1,5], Huazhu Fu[2(✉)], Yanwu Xu[1], Jianlong Yang[1,5], Fei Li[4,5], Xiulan Zhang[4,5], Jiang Liu[3,5], and Yitian Zhao[1,5(✉)]

[1] Cixi Institute of Biomedical Engineering, Ningbo Institute of Materials Technology and Engineering, Chinese Academy of Sciences, Ningbo, China
yitian.zhao@nimte.ac.cn
[2] Inception Institute of Artificial Intelligence, Abu Dhabi, UAE
hzfu@ieee.org
[3] Department of Computer Science and Engineering, Southern University of Science and Technology, Shenzhen, China
[4] State Key Laboratory of Ophthalmology, Zhongshan Ophthalmic Center, Sun Yat-sen University, Guangzhou, China
[5] Glaucoma Artificial Intelligence Diagnosis and Imaging Analysis Joint Research Lab, Guangzhou and Ningbo, China

Abstract. Anterior chamber angle (ACA) classification is a key step in the diagnosis of angle-closure glaucoma in Anterior Segment Optical Coherence Tomography (AS-OCT). Existing automated analysis methods focus on a binary classification system (i.e., open angle or angle-closure) in a 2D AS-OCT slice. However, clinical diagnosis requires a more discriminating ACA three-class system (i.e., open, appositional, or synechial angles) for the benefit of clinicians who seek better to understand the progression of the spectrum of angle-closure glaucoma types. To address this, we propose a novel sequence multi-scale aggregation deep network (SMA-Net) for open-appositional-synechial ACA classification based on an AS-OCT sequence. In our method, a Multi-Scale Discriminative Aggregation (MSDA) block is utilized to learn the multi-scale representations at slice level, while a ConvLSTM is introduced to study the temporal dynamics of these representations at sequence level. Finally, a multi-level loss function is used to combine the slice-based and sequence-based losses. The proposed method is evaluated across two AS-OCT datasets. The experimental results show that the proposed method outperforms existing state-of-the-art methods in applicability, effectiveness, and accuracy. We believe this work to be the first attempt to classify ACAs into open, appositional, or synechial types grading using AS-OCT sequences.

Keywords: Angle-closure glaucoma · Anterior chamber angles · AS-OCT

© Springer Nature Switzerland AG 2020
A. L. Martel et al. (Eds.): MICCAI 2020, LNCS 12265, pp. 715–724, 2020.
https://doi.org/10.1007/978-3-030-59722-1_69

1   Introduction

Glaucoma is one of the most significant causes of irreversible blinding worldwide, and primary angle-closure glaucoma (PACG) is the major cause of blindness in Asian populations [1]. Anterior Segment Optical Coherence Tomography (AS-OCT) imaging, as a non-contact and non-invasive tool, is widely used to observe cross-sections of the anterior segment structure, to assist ophthalmologists in early screening and accurate assessment of PACG [2], as shown in Fig. 1(a).

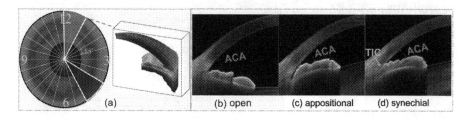

Fig. 1. (a) Visual demonstration of manual annotations by gonioscopy. ACA angles in the 12–1 o'clock region (red) viewed with synechiae, and 4–5 o'clock (blue) viewed with appositional ACAs, and a sequence of AS-OCT images in a random 15° radiant area. (b)–(d) Image samples of open-appositional-synechial ACA grading. (Color figure online)

According to the configuration of the anterior chamber angle (ACA), cases of glaucoma may first be classified into two types: primary open angle glaucoma (Fig. 1(b)); and angle-closure glaucoma (Fig. 1(c–d)). Drawing on epidemiological research [3], clinicians have suggested that angle-closure glaucoma may be further divided into different sub-stages: primary angle closure suspect (PACS), and primary angle-closure/primary angle-closure glaucoma (PAC/PACG). PACS denotes the eye with **appositional** but non-adhesive ACA, as shown in Fig. 1(c), while PAC/PACG denotes the eye with an occludable ACA, *a.k.a*, **synechiae**, which leads to the presence of trabecular iris contact (TIC) [4], as shown in Fig. 1(d). This secondary level of grading would benefit clinicians in better understanding the progression of the spectrum of angle-closure glaucoma types. Moreover, surgical treatment during PACS can open any non-firm adhesion between the peripheral iris and the trabecular meshwork, which may avoid or alleviate the permanent adhesion seen in the progression to PACG [5]. Therefore, the accurate identification of open-appositional-synechial ACAs is potentially important in guiding clinical management at different stages of angle-closure glaucoma.

Several methods have been proposed to enable automatic classification of open angle and angle-closure ACAs from AS-OCT images. Xu *et al.* [6,7] began by localizing the ACA region, and then classified the ACA into open angle or angle-closure based on visual features present in their AS-OCT images. Fu *et al.* [8] proposed a data-driven approach to integrate AS-OCT segmentation, clinical parameter measurements, and glaucoma screening. However, clinical measurement-based methods rely heavily on precise segmentation of the AS-OCT structure. Recently, deep learning-based methods have demonstrated superior performance in ACA classification [2,9–12]. Fu *et al.* [4] proposed a multi-context deep network, in which parallel convolutional neural networks are applied to ACA regions and at corresponding scales known to be informative for clinically diagnosing angle-closure glaucoma. Xu *et al.* [12] employed deep learning classifiers for automated detection of gonioscopic angle closure and primary angle closure. However, multi-level network learning is costly in terms of storage capacity, and slow to proceed to inference. In addition, it depends on a proper integration model, in the absence of which it is less effective than a single model.

All the aforementioned methods focus on the binary classification of open angle and angle-closure in a 2D slice. The open-appositional-synechial ACA classification based on an AS-OCT sequence has been rarely explored, despite its significance in understanding disease progression [13]. Inspired by the procedures of the dynamic gonioscopy examination, in which ophthalmologists move the gonioscope counterclockwise and make an annotation every 15° (see left row of Fig. 1(a)), we address the open-appositional-synechial ACA classification as an image sequence classification problem. The main contributions of this paper are summarized as follows. **(1)** We develop a sequence multi-scale aggregation deep network (SMA-Net) for discriminating the temporal dynamics of features in order to classify ACAs into the open-appositional-synechial grading, using AS-OCT sequences. To best of our knowledge, this is the first work in the area of automated open-appositional-synechial ACA classification. **(2)** A multi-scale discriminative aggregation (MSDA) block is designed to extract the multi-scale representations at slice level, and a ConvLSTM is employed to study the temporal dynamics of these representations at sequence level. **(3)** A new multi-loss function is used to combine slice-based and sequence-based losses, so as to extract spatial and temporal features from AS-OCT sequences. **(4)** Our proposed method outperforms existing state-of-the-art methods in applicability, effectiveness, and accuracy on two AS-OCT datasets (one public and one private dataset).

2   Methodology

Figure 2(a) illustrates the framework of our SMA-Net. Given an AS-OCT sequence, first, a coarse-to-fine method [13] is utilized to localize the ACA regions with sizes of 448×448 pixels for each AS-OCT slice, which is the most useful discriminative area for glaucoma classification. Then, a cropped ACA sequence with of size $224 \times 224 \times T$ is obtained and fed to MSDA blocks to extract a sequence of feature maps at slice level. Here T denotes the scan number of the AS-OCT within a 15° radiant area. Finally, a stacked 2-layer ConvLSTM is employed to study the temporal dynamics of these representations at sequence level, which produces the prediction of open-appositional-synechial ACA.

2.1   Multi-scale Discriminative Aggregation Block

In our method, each MSDA block consists of a depthwise separable convolutional module and an aggregation gate module. The structure of a depthwise

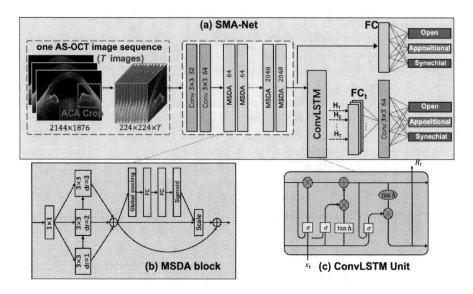

Fig. 2. Overview of our SMA-Net for open-appositional-synechial ACA classification based on an AS-OCT sequence.

separable convolutional module includes one 1×1 convolutional layer and three 3×3 atrous convolutional layers, as shown in Fig. 2(b). The separable convolution not only reduces the number of parameters, but improves feature learning ability of the network [14,15]. $\mathbf{x}$ denotes the output of the 1×1 convolution, and $\mathbf{f}_i$ corresponding to 3×3 atrous convolutional layers are used to enlarge the receptive field, with different dilation rates $i \in \{1, 2, 3\}$. Moreover, Batch Normalization and ReLU activation are used for each convolutional layer. The feature $\mathbf{x}$ is added to the output of $\mathbf{f}_{i-1}$, and then fed into $\mathbf{f}_i$, as

$$\mathbf{y}_i = \begin{cases} \mathbf{f}_i (\mathbf{x}), & i = 1 \\ \mathbf{f}_i (\mathbf{x} + \mathbf{y}_{i-1}), & i > 1 \end{cases}, \tag{1}$$

where $\mathbf{y}_i$ denotes the output of $\mathbf{f}_i$. Finally, multi-scale convolutional features are aggregated as the output of the depthwise separable convolutional module. Compared with existing multi-scale blocks, our block effectively reduces the number of parameters within the hierarchical aggregation structure.

In order to combine different scale representations more effectively, an aggregation gate is also introduced, using a Squeeze and Excitation (SE) module to obtain discriminative representation. With the output of the depthwise separable convolutional module, the SE module is used in our block followed the coarse fusion to the new output. More specifically, the SE module is composed of a global average pooling layer and a Multi-Layer Perceptron (MLP) with a ReLU-activated hidden layer, followed by the sigmoid activation. Note that the SE module follows a self-attention architecture, which can selectively enhance discriminative representation. In contrast to single feature addition fusion, this more discriminative fusion can achieve dynamic weighted distribution in the channels of multi-scale branches.

2.2   Open-Appositional-Synechial ACA Classification

In our method, Xception architecture [14] is used as the backbone. We replace the 3×3 convolution with our MSDA block, which can learn multi-scale representation and integrate the discriminative representation with the output. With the slice-based features from MSDA blocks, a stacked 2-layer ConvLSTM, with 1024 hidden units in each of the cells, is used to process feature maps and generate a sequence of ConvLSTM states $\{\mathbf{H}_1, \mathbf{H}_2, \cdots, \mathbf{H}_T\}$, which can learn spatial and temporal information by spatial dependencies, as shown in Fig. 2(c). At each position t, the output state $\mathbf{H}_t$ is fed into a global average pooling and a fully connected (FC) layer that computes the estimated probabilities $\{\mathbf{Y}_1, \mathbf{Y}_2, \cdots, \mathbf{Y}_T\}$.

In this work, we consider a multi-level loss function to combine slice-based and sequence-based losses. To optimize the SMA-Net and avoid gradient disappearance, we propose to use cross entropy loss as our slice-based loss. To be specific, we use global average pooling and an FC layer to generate estimated probabilities $\mathbf{Y}_t^s$ from each slice t. To this end, the slice-based loss is defined as:

$$\mathcal{L}_{2\mathrm{D}} = \sum_{t=1}^{T} \{\mathcal{L}_{CE}\left(\mathbf{Y}_t^s, \mathbf{Y}^*\right)\}, \tag{2}$$

where $\mathcal{L}_{CE}$ represents cross entropy loss, and $\mathbf{Y}^*$ denotes the ground truth of the input AS-OCT sequence. Note that in our method, all AS-OCT slices have the same labels within the whole sequence.

To improve performance, we use a weighted ensemble (WE) method to optimize the final result by these estimated probabilities. We first concatenate a sequence of estimated probabilities to obtain a new descriptor with dimension $T \times 3$. We then perform a 1-D convolution operation with on the new descriptor, and feed the result to the FC layer for final classification $\mathbf{Y}_f$, which can weight predictions of T state. Finally, we define a new loss-based cross entropy as our sequence-based loss function:

$$\mathcal{L}_{3\mathrm{D}} = \sum_{i=1}^{t} \{\mathcal{L}_{CE}\left(\mathbf{Y}_i, \mathbf{Y}^*\right)\}. \tag{3}$$

Therefore, the overall loss function of our network is as:

$$\mathcal{L}_{\mathrm{SV}} = \mathcal{L}_{2\mathrm{D}} + \lambda \mathcal{L}_{3\mathrm{D}}, \tag{4}$$

where λ is the balance weight ($\lambda = 1$ in our experiment).

3   Experimental Results

The proposed architecture was implemented using the publicly available Pytorch Library. In the training phase, we employed an Adam optimizer to optimize the

Table 1. Classification of the open-appositional-synechial ACAs by different methods on the private dataset.

Methods	kappa	F1	B-Acc	Sen	Spe
ResNet-34 [16]	0.6766	0.7527	0.8188	0.7485	0.8891
MSCNN [13]	0.6773	0.7498	0.8171	0.7455	0.8887
Xception [14]	0.7252	0.7835	0.8393	0.7752	0.9035
MA-Net	0.7477	0.8121	0.8600	0.8063	0.9137
C3D [17]	0.7489	0.8115	0.8532	0.8048	0.9136
I3D [18]	0.7662	0.8171	0.8619	0.8073	0.9166
S3D [19]	0.7431	0.8007	0.8567	0.8016	0.9119
Our SMA-Net	**0.7931**	**0.8459**	**0.8829**	**0.8371**	**0.9282**

deep model. We used a gradually decreasing learning rate, starting from 0.0001. In addition, online data enhancement was employed to enlarge the training data, which includes brightness, color, contrast and sharpness transformations, and we set a random seed from 1 to 4 for enhancement.

3.1 Performance of Open-Appositional-Synechial ACA Classification

Private Dataset: All AS-OCT volumes in our dataset were captured by a CASIA-2 machine (Tomey Inc., Japan) from 66 eyes with open-appositional-synechial grading (human expert annotations of images derived from by dynamic gonioscopic examinations). Each volume contains 128 AS-OCT images, and each slice in a volume is 2144×1876 pixels. A senior ophthalmologist annotated each $15°$ segment of the ACAs of an eye, yielding 24 annotations for each single eye, and resulting in a total of 1584 annotations for this dataset. In light of this, we formed the AS-OCT slices ($T = 11$ slices) in each $15°$ region as one sequence. Finally, a total of 1584 image sequences are generated, in which 504 sequences are annotated with open ACA, 742 sequences are with appositional ACA, and 338 sequences contain synechial ACA. In our experiments, the dataset was equally and randomly divided into training and testing sets, taking into account the integrity of data from each eye, so that two ACAs from the same eye would not be separated between the training and testing sets.

In order to demonstrate the superiority of the proposed method for classification of open-appositional-synechial angle, we carry out a comprehensive comparison between the proposed method and the following state-of-the-art methods: (1) 2D deep models: Multi-Scale Regions Convolutional Neural Networks (MSCNN) [13]; Resnet-34 [16]; Xception [14]; and MA-Net (Xception with our MSDA block). 3D deep models: C3D [17]; I3D [18]; and S3D [19]. Following the standard performance assessment protocol for multi-class classification [20,21], we use weighted sensitivity (Sen), specificity (Spe), and balanced accuracy (B-acc). In order to reflect the trade-offs between Sen and Spe and evaluate the quality of our classification results, the kappa analysis [22] and F1 [23] score were also provided. Table 1 reports the classification performance of different methods. It may be observed that our SMA-Net yields best performance in terms

Table 2. Classification performance of the open-appositional-synechial ACAs by different module combinations on private dataset.

Methods	kappa	F1	B-acc	Sen	Spe
Xception [14]	0.7252	0.7835	0.8393	0.7752	0.9035
MA-Net	0.7477	0.8121	0.8600	0.8063	0.9137
Xception+ConvLSTM	0.7705	0.8238	0.8664	0.8135	0.9194
MA-Net+ConvLSTM	0.7820	0.8377	0.8780	0.8310	0.9250
MA-Net+ConvLSTM+$\mathcal{L}_{SV}$	**0.7931**	**0.8459**	**0.8826**	**0.8371**	**0.9282**

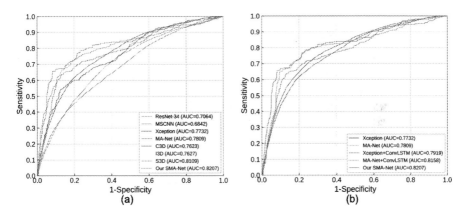

Fig. 3. AUC curves of different approaches in classifying appositional, and synechial ACA. (a) Comparison of state-of-the-art 2D and 3D deep networks. (b) Ablation study of our model.

of all metrics when compared to either 2D or 3D deep learning-based methods. The probable reason for this is that the proposed networks can learn rich and discriminative representation from both local features (2D image features) and global geometry (image sequence).

Because binary open angle and angle-closure classification is a relatively straightforward and easy task, our method and other networks achieve similar high performances (AUC=0.998). Therefore, only the AUC curves in distinguishing appositional and synechial angles are illustrated in Fig. 3(a). As expected, our method still produced the best performance on the classification of appositional and synechial angles, with AUC=0.8207. Overall, all 3D networks achieved relatively higher performances than 2D networks, since a 3D deep network can learn spatial representation from an image sequence.

To evaluate the effectiveness of each module in our network, we provide an ablation study, and the results are reported in Table 2 and Fig. 3(b). Results show that the Xception+ConvLSTM and MA-Net+ConvLSTM method clearly outperformed the and Xception and MA-Net alone, with improvement of about 4.53% and 3.43% in kappa, and about 1.87% and 3.49% in AUC. This demonstrates that the ConvLSTM learns discriminative representations from

Table 3. Performance of compared methods on AGE dataset.

Methods	AUC	*Sen*	*Spe*
Resnet-34 [16]	0.990959	0.859375	0.999219
Inception-V3 [24]	0.999285	0.918750	0.998438
Xception [14]	0.999347	0.950000	0.996094
MCDN [25]	0.999604	0.959375	0.998438
MSCNN [13]	0.999727	0.978125	0.996875
SMA-Net	**1.000000**	**1.000000**	**1.000000**

an AS-OCT image sequence, and is capable of preserving the spatial information, so memorizing the change in appearance that corresponds to motion information (neighboring slices), thereby improving performance in separating appositional angle and fully closed angle. Table 2 and Fig. 3(b) also reveal that after $\mathcal{L}_{SV}$ was applied, classification performance of our SMA-Net (MA-Net+ConvLSTM+$\mathcal{L}_{SV}$) improved significantly, with an improvement of approximately 4.53% in *kappa* and 0.49% in AUC, respectively. This is because with $\mathcal{L}_{SV}$, the ConvLSTM explores the temporal dynamics of appearance features of an AS-OCT sequence, and these features are further aggregated for classification purposes.

3.2   Performance of Open Angle and Angle-Closure Classification

We also evaluated our method for binary ACA classification, i.e., open angle and angle-closure cases. The public AS-OCT dataset, Angle-closure Glaucoma Evaluation (AGE) dataset [26] was used, which includes 3200 AS-OCT images with resolution of 2130×998 pixels. These images were divided into two sets: 1600 training and 1600 testing.

In this experiment, we changed the output of our method to binary classification. We carried out a comprehensive comparison between the proposed and the state-of-the-art methods: Multi-Context Deep Network (MCDN) [25], Multi-Scale Regions Convolutional Neural Networks (MSCNN) [13]; Resnet-34 [16]; Inception-V3 [24]; and Xception [14]. Table 3 shows that our SMA-Net outperforms all competing methods in terms of all metrics (AUC, *Sen* and *Spe*). To be more specific, it can be seen that our SMA-Net outperforms the Xception (our backbone network) alone, with improvement of 5.00% in *Sen*. Interestingly, all the methods achieved remarkable AUC scores. This is because, as we suggested above, the binary classification of open or angle-closure is relatively easy, and this finding is also evidenced by the leader board of AGE challenge - the task of open angle and angle-closure classification by means of AS-OCT has attained remarkably high standards of performance by using state-of-the-art deep networks, with AUC scores higher than 0.98 across the board. Another reason is that AGE dataset was motivated for the classification of explicit open and closed ACA.

4 Conclusion

Most of the existing automated methods are only able to classify the ACA as either open or angle-closure. In this paper, we proposed an automated ACA classification framework, which is not only able to classify open angle and angle-closure, but is also capable of grading the three-class open-appositional-synechial ACA from AS-OCT imagery, so as to further guide clinical management at different stages of glaucoma. To be more specific, we introduced a novel block, named the MSDA block, with a view to learning multi-scale discriminative representations over AS-OCT volumes. In addition, a new multi-loss function is used to combine the slice-based and sequence-based losses, as thus to extract spatial and temporal features from AS-OCT image sequences. The results demonstrate that the proposed method outperforms other state-of-the-art 2D and 3D deep networks. It may be expected that the proposed model could be a powerful tool for diagnosing the presence, and analyzing the progression of angle-closure glaucoma.

Acknowledgements. This work was supported by Zhejiang Provincial Natural Science Foundation of China (LZ19F010001, LQ19H180001), Ningbo "2025 S&T Megaprojects" (2019B10033, 2019B10061).

References

1. Tham, Y.C., Li, X., Wong, T.Y., Quigley, H.A., Aung, T., Cheng, C.Y.: Global prevalence of glaucoma and projections of glaucoma burden through 2040: a systematic review and meta-analysis. Ophthalmology **121**(11), 2081–2090 (2014)
2. Fu, H., et al.: A deep learning system for automated angle-closure detection in anterior segment optical coherence tomography images. Am. J. Ophthalmol. **203**, 37–45 (2019)
3. Foster, P.J., Buhrmann, R., Quigley, H.A., Johnson, G.J.: The definition and classification of glaucoma in prevalence surveys. Br. J. Ophthalmol. **86**(2), 238–242 (2002)
4. Fu, H., et al.: Angle-closure detection in anterior segment OCT based on multilevel deep network. IEEE Trans. Cybern. **50**(7), 3358–3366 (2019)
5. Shang, Q., et al.: Automated IRIS segmentation from anterior segment OCT images with occludable angles via local phase tensor. In: IEEE EMBC, pp. 4745–4749 (2019)
6. Xu, Y., et al.: Anterior chamber angle classification using multiscale histograms of oriented gradients for glaucoma subtype identification. In: IEEE EMBC, pp. 3167–3170 (2012)
7. Xu, Y., et al.: Automated anterior chamber angle localization and glaucoma type classification in OCT images. In: IEEE EMBC, pp. 7380–7383 (2013)
8. Fu, H., et al.: Segmentation and quantification for angle-closure glaucoma assessment in anterior segment OCT. IEEE Trans. Med. Imaging **36**(9), 1930–1938 (2017)
9. Zhao, Y., et al.: Automatic 2-D/3-D vessel enhancement in multiple modality images using a weighted symmetry filter. IEEE Trans. Med. Imaging **37**(2), 438–450 (2017)

10. Zhao, Y., et al.: Intensity and compactness enabled saliency estimation for leakage detection in diabetic and malarial retinopathy. IEEE Trans. Med. Imaging **36**(1), 51–63 (2016)

11. Zhao, Y., et al.: Retinal artery and vein classification via dominant sets clustering-based vascular topology estimation. In: Frangi, A.F., Schnabel, J.A., Davatzikos, C., Alberola-López, C., Fichtinger, G. (eds.) MICCAI 2018. LNCS, vol. 11071, pp. 56–64. Springer, Cham (2018). https://doi.org/10.1007/978-3-030-00934-2_7

12. Xu, B.Y., Chiang, M., Chaudhary, S., Kulkarni, S., Pardeshi, A.A., Varma, R.: Deep learning classifiers for automated detection of gonioscopic angle closure based on anterior segment OCT images. Am. J. Ophthalmol. **208**, 273–280 (2019)

13. Hao, H., et al.: Anterior chamber angles classification in anterior segment OCT images via multi-scale regions convolutional neural networks. In: IEEE EMBC, pp. 849–852 (2019)

14. Chollet, F.: Xception: deep learning with depthwise separable convolutions. In: IEEE CVPR, pp. 1251–1258 (2017)

15. Yu, F., Wang, D., Shelhamer, E., Darrell, T.: Deep layer aggregation. In: IEEE CVPR, pp. 2403–2412 (2018)

16. He, K., Zhang, X., Ren, S., Sun, J.: Deep residual learning for image recognition. In: IEEE CVPR, pp. 770–778 (2016)

17. Tran, D., Bourdev, L., Fergus, R., Torresani, L., Paluri, M.: Learning spatiotemporal features with 3D convolutional networks. In: IEEE CVPR, pp. 4489–4497 (2015)

18. Carreira, J., Zisserman, A.: Quo vadis, action recognition? A new model and the kinetics dataset. In: IEEE CVPR, pp. 6299–6308 (2017)

19. Xie, S., Sun, C., Huang, J., Tu, Z., Murphy, K.: Rethinking spatiotemporal feature learning: speed-accuracy trade-offs in video classification. In: Ferrari, V., Hebert, M., Sminchisescu, C., Weiss, Y. (eds.) ECCV 2018. LNCS, vol. 11219, pp. 318–335. Springer, Cham (2018). https://doi.org/10.1007/978-3-030-01267-0_19

20. Annunziata, R., Kheirkhah, A., Aggarwal, S., Hamrah, P., Trucco, E.: A fully automated tortuosity quantification system with application to corneal nerve fibres in confocal microscopy images. Med. Image Anal. **32**, 216–232 (2016)

21. Zhao, Y., et al.: Automated tortuosity analysis of nerve fibers in corneal confocal microscopy. IEEE Trans. Med. Imaging. **39**(9), 2725–2738 (2020)

22. https://en.wikipedia.org/wiki/Cohen%27s_kappa/

23. https://en.wikipedia.org/wiki/F1_score/

24. Xia, X., Xu, C., Nan, B.: Inception-v3 for flower classification. In: IEEE ICIVC, pp. 783–787 (2017)

25. Fu, H., et al.: Multi-context deep network for angle-closure glaucoma screening in anterior segment OCT. In: Frangi, A.F., Schnabel, J.A., Davatzikos, C., Alberola-López, C., Fichtinger, G. (eds.) MICCAI 2018. LNCS, vol. 11071, pp. 356–363. Springer, Cham (2018). https://doi.org/10.1007/978-3-030-00934-2_40

26. Fu, H., Li, F., Sun, X., et al.: AGE challenge: angle closure glaucoma evaluation in anterior segment optical coherence tomography. arXiv (2020)

A Macro-Micro Weakly-Supervised Framework for AS-OCT Tissue Segmentation

Munan Ning[1,2], Cheng Bian[1(✉)], Donghuan Lu[1], Hong-Yu Zhou[1], Shuang Yu[1], Chenglang Yuan[1], Yang Guo[2], Yaohua Wang[2], Kai Ma[1], and Yefeng Zheng[1]

[1] Tencent Jarvis Lab, Tencent Shenzhen, China
tronbian@tencent.com
[2] National University of Defense Technology, Changsha, China

Abstract. Primary angle closure glaucoma (PACG) is the leading cause of irreversible blindness among Asian people. Early detection of PACG is essential, so as to provide timely treatment and minimize the vision loss. In the clinical practice, PACG is diagnosed by analyzing the angle between the cornea and iris with anterior segment optical coherence tomography (AS-OCT). The rapid development of deep learning technologies provides the feasibility of building a computer-aided system for the fast and accurate segmentation of cornea and iris tissues. However, the application of deep learning methods in the medical imaging field is still restricted by the lack of enough fully-annotated samples. In this paper, we propose a novel framework to segment the target tissues accurately for the AS-OCT images, by using the combination of weakly-annotated images (majority) and fully-annotated images (minority). The proposed framework consists of two models which provide reliable guidance for each other. In addition, uncertainty guided strategies are adopted to increase the accuracy and stability of the guidance. Detailed experiments on the publicly available AGE dataset demonstrate that the proposed framework outperforms the state-of-the-art semi-/weakly-supervised methods and has a comparable performance as the fully-supervised method. Therefore, the proposed method is demonstrated to be effective in exploiting information contained in the weakly-annotated images and has the capability to substantively relieve the annotation workload.

Keywords: Primary angle-closure glaucoma · Weakly-supervised learning · Segmentation · As-OCT

1 Introduction

Glaucoma is the leading cause of irreversible vision loss world-widely that is predicted to affect more than 100 million people by year 2040 [19]. Primary angle

Electronic supplementary material The online version of this chapter (https://doi.org/10.1007/978-3-030-59722-1_70) contains supplementary material, which is available to authorized users.

© Springer Nature Switzerland AG 2020
A. L. Martel et al. (Eds.): MICCAI 2020, LNCS 12265, pp. 725–734, 2020.
https://doi.org/10.1007/978-3-030-59722-1_70

closure glaucoma (PACG), as a major subtype of glaucoma, develops when the angle between the iris and cornea is closed or narrowed, resulting in the blockage of drainage canals and sudden rise in intraocular pressure [16]. In the clinical practice, the anterior segment optical coherence technology (AS-OCT) [14] is widely utilized to obtain both quantitative and qualitative information on the anatomical structures of cornea and iris for the PACG diagnosis [6,10–12]. However, manual analysis of each image is laborious and requires professional knowledge. Although the rapid development of deep learning technologies reveals the feasibility of fully automatic anatomical structure segmentation with high accuracy [5], it still requires a large quantity of images with pixel-wise annotations for the related structures, which is time-consuming and expertise-demanding.

To alleviate the intensive annotation workload of clinicians, a lot of efforts have been made on semi-/weakly-supervised segmentation [3,8,9,13,17,18,20]. The semi-supervision based methods aim to extract information from a large amount of unlabeled images with the assistance of some fully-annotated images or samples. For example, Perone *et al.* [13] proposed a semi-supervised teacher-student framework, which leveraged the supervised knowledge learned from the teacher model to improve the segmentation performance of the student model. Yu *et al.* [20] further adopted the uncertainty information to the teacher-student model to fully exploit the information of the unlabeled data by following the prediction consistencies under different perturbations. Hung *et al.* [8] proposed an adversarial based strategy, which introduced a new discriminator to predict the confidence map for utilizing the information of unlabeled images. However, current semi-supervised methods still require a considerable quantity of fully-annotated images for a satisfactory performance. Another strategy is to improve the workload efficiency by adopting weak annotations[1] for training. For example, Kervadec *et al.* [9] introduced a differentiable term into the proposed loss function to impose the soft size constraints extracted from the weak annotations on the target region. Tang *et al.* [17,18] proposed to attain better performance by jointly optimizing the normalized cut with a deep learning model and CRFs for the weakly-supervised task. Although these weakly-supervised methods might relieve the annotation workload to some extent, their segmentation could be error-prone due to the lack of sufficient pixel-wise annotation information. In the clinical practice, apart from a large number of weakly-annotated samples, there is also a small number of full annotations, which might be combined together and employed to improve the model's performance.

To address the above issues of semi-/weakly-supervised learning, an intuitive solution is to integrate both the fully-annotated images and the weakly-labeled samples into the training process, so that the former images can provide accurate pixel-wise tutorial while the latter ones offer more high-level region proposals for segmentation.

In this paper, we propose an uncertainty-aware macro-micro (UAMM) framework for the segmentation of the cornea and iris with a few fully-annotated data

---

[1] For the rest of paper, full annotation refers to manual label of each pixel, while weak annotation refers to circles, dots, or scribbles denoting the region of interest.

and a relatively large number of weakly-labeled samples. The network of the proposed UAMM approach consists of two main components with two flows: the macro model with the microscopic flow and the micro model with the macroscopic flow. Unlike the teacher-student framework in which only the teacher model provides guidance to the student model, the macro model and the micro model in the proposed framework offer information for each other to achieve better segmentation performance. Specifically, the macro model utilizes the weakly-labeled samples to learn segmentation proposals to induce the semantic clues for the optimization of the micro model (a.k.a, microscopic flow), while the micro model employs fully-annotated images to present pixel-wise tutorial to guide the learning process of the macro model (a.k.a, macroscopic flow). The main contributions of this study are four folds:

1) We propose a novel weakly-supervised methodology for the segmentation of cornea and iris in the AS-OCT images, which outperforms state-of-the-art semi-/weakly-supervised methods and achieves comparable performance as the fully-supervised network.
2) Besides the informative features distilled from the weakly-labeled samples, we propose to add the macroscopic flow from the micro model to provide pixel-wise guidance for the optimization of the macro model.
3) Other than pixel-wise annotation information learned from the fully-annotated images, the microscopic flow from the macro model is designed to offer more high-level semantic information for the training of the micro model.
4) We propose to introduce uncertainty guidance strategies into the microscopic flow and macroscopic flow for more accurate and stable guidance.

2   Method

Figure 1 displays the diagram of the proposed UAMM framework, which consists of the micro model and the macro model. Both models have the same network architecture, $i.e.$, DeepLabV3+ [2], with different parameters. The proposed framework is optimized via a two-stage training strategy. In the first stage, the two models are trained individually using the fully-annotated images and weakly-labeled samples, i.e., the individual training stage, marked as ① and ② in Fig. 1. In the second stage, the two models are trained jointly using only the weakly-labeled samples, $i.e.$, the joint training stage marked as ③ in Fig. 1, which provide guidance (the macroscopic and microscopic flows, marked as ④ and ⑤) for each other to achieve better segmentation performance. To prevent potential misleading of the incorrect information, uncertainty guidance strategies are proposed to provide more accurate and stable guidance for the model training procedure. To clarify notations, $x \in \mathbb{R}^{H \times W \times 3}$ denotes the input image, where H, W and 3 represent the height, width and three channels of the input RGB image, respectively; $y^s, y^w \in \{0, 1\}^{H \times W \times C}$ stand for the C-way full and weak annotations, respectively; f, θ and m indicate the non-learning transformation of DeepLabV3+, the model parameters and model output, respectively.

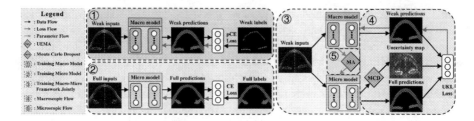

Fig. 1. The framework of our uncertainty-aware micro-macro framework. We only use full annotations in stage ②, while weakly-labeled images in the other.

2.1   Loss Functions for the Macro and Micro Model

In the first stage, the macro model and micro model are trained separately, *i.e.*, the macro model is optimized with the weakly-labeled samples, while the micro model is trained with the fully-annotated images. Specifically, suppose there are N fully-annotated images denoted as $\mathcal{D}_s = \{(x_i, y_i^s)\}_{i=1}^{N}$, and M weakly-labeled samples represented by $\mathcal{D}_w = \{(x_j, y_j^w)\}_{j=1}^{M}$. The loss function for each model in the individual training stage is defined as:

$$\mathcal{L}_{micro}(x_i) = -\frac{1}{K \times C} \sum_{k=1}^{K} \sum_{c=1}^{C} y_i^s(k, c) \log m_i^s(k, c) \tag{1}$$

$$\mathcal{L}_{macro}(x_j) = -\frac{1}{\sum_{k=1}^{K} s_j(k) \times C} \sum_{k=1}^{K} \sum_{c=1}^{C} s_j(k) \cdot y_j^w(k, c) \log m_j^w(k, c) \tag{2}$$

where $s_j \in \{0, 1\}^{H \times W \times 1}$ is the binary indicator denoting the weakly-annotated pixels; k iterates over all locations with $K = H \times W$ and c iterates over C classes; $m_i^s = f(x_i; \theta^s)$ and $m_j^w = f(x_j; \theta^w)$ represent the outputs of the micro model and macro model, respectively.

Equation 1 represents the vanilla cross-entropy loss [17] for the micro model, while Eq. 2 denotes the partial-cross-entropy (pCE) loss [17] for the macro-model. The pCE loss only considers the weak label proposals and the relevant regions during the training process, and thus can discourage the probability of mistakenly classifying the unlabeled pixels as the background.

2.2   Uncertainty-Aware KL Loss for the Macroscopic Flow

Because pixel-wise labels are not available for the weakly-labeled images, the macro model trained on them can hardly deliver satisfactory segmentation performance. In the second stage, to further improve the accuracy, we utilize the output of the micro model to guide the optimization of the macro model.

Specifically, we adopt the KL-divergence loss between the output of the two models to fine-tune the macro model. Despite the capability of KL-divergence to align the distributions of two models, the potential mistake of the micro model can result in inaccurate tutorials and mislead the optimization of the macro model. Therefore, we propose to use the uncertainty map to select the reliable pixels for guidance. By using the Monte Carlo dropout (MCD) method [7], the uncertainty map can be easily inferred, which serves as an indicator of the reliability of the model's prediction. Specifically, we modify the micro network with several dropout layers, and then repetitively perform the forward pass T times to obtain T Monte Carlo samples $\{p_t\}_{t=1}^T$, where $p_t^c \in \mathbb{R}^{H \times W \times C}$ denotes the softmax probability map of the cth class at the tth forward pass. Because the variance of Monte Carlo samples can be treated as an approximation of the epistemic uncertainty [15], the uncertainty map U of the micro model can be formulated as:

$$\mu_c = \frac{1}{T} \sum_{t=1}^{T} p_t^c \quad \text{and} \quad U = \frac{1}{T \times C} \sum_{t=1}^{T} \sum_{c=1}^{C} (p_t^c - \mu_c)^2. \tag{3}$$

Furthermore, an empirical threshold τ is applied on the uncertainty map to obtain a binary indicator map, in which the positive values represent the reliable pixels. Then, the element-wise multiplication is performed between the KL-loss and the binary indicator map to select the reliable loss for back-propagation. Therefore, for the microscopic flow in the joint training stage, the macro model can be updated via the uncertainty guided KL loss, as defined below:

$$
\begin{aligned}
\mathcal{L}_{UKL} &= \frac{\mathbb{I}(U < \tau) \cdot \mathcal{L}_{KL}\left(m_j^w \| m_i^s\right)}{\sum \mathbb{I}(U < \tau)} \\
&= \frac{1}{\sum_{k=1}^{K} \mathbb{I}(U(k) < \tau) \times C} \sum_{k=1}^{K} \sum_{c=1}^{C} \mathbb{I}(U(k) < \tau) \cdot m_j^w(k,c) \log\left(\frac{m_j^w(k,c)}{m_i^s(k,c)}\right).
\end{aligned}
\tag{4}
$$

where U denotes the uncertainty map, $\mathbb{I}(\cdot)$ represents the binary map and the threshold τ is set to 0.5 for all the experiments. Note that only weakly-labeled images are used in this step, because the micro model has extremely high confidence for the fully-annotated images, which has already been used to train the model in the first stage.

2.3   Uncertainty-Aware EMA as the Microscopic Flow

As previously stated, the micro model is first trained with the fully-annotated images. Despite the fact that the fully-annotated images contain informative pixel-wise annotation, optimization with a limited number of samples can easily result in overfitting and deteriorate the generalization capability of the model. Therefore, in the second stage, we use the segmentation proposals learned from the macro model to induce the semantic clues for the micro model.

Unlike in the macroscopic flow where the output of the micro model can be directly used as the tutorial, the output of the macro model trained with weakly-labeled samples may not be accurate enough to be used for guidance. Yu *et al.* [20] proposed an asynchronous updating solution for two collaborative models, *i.e.*, the exponential moving average (EMA) mechanism, based on the idea that the weights of the model would contain implicit information of the inference evidence. In this work, the weights of the macro model contain critical information learnt from the weakly-labeled regions and could be useful for the training of the micro model. However, adopting the classic EMA strategy to partially update the micro model with the weights of the macro model requires a predefined updating rate, which may not be the optimal solution. Instead, we propose an uncertainty-aware exponential moving average (UEMA) mechanism for the microscopic flow. θ^s and θ^w are used to represent the weight parameters of the micro and macro model, respectively. The proposed UEMA in the joint training stage can be summarized as:

$$\theta^s = \alpha\theta^s + (1-\alpha)\theta^w \qquad \text{and} \qquad \alpha = \frac{\sum_{k=1}^{K} \mathbb{I}\left(U(k) < \tau\right)}{\sum_{k=1}^{K} \mathbb{1}}, \qquad (5)$$

where the $\mathbb{1} \in \{1\}^{H \times W}$ denotes the unit map with the same shape as U. Note that U represents the uncertainty map the same as in Eq. 4. The updating rate α is calculated by dividing the sum of uncertainty binary map $\mathbb{I}(U(k) < \tau)$ with the sum of $\mathbb{1}$. It is used to control the updating rate of UEMA. The less certain the micro model is, the more its parameters are going to be affected by the macro model. Through this asynchronous updating strategy, the segmentation proposal learnt by the macro model can effectively guide the micro model towards better generalization ability with adaptive updating rates.

3   Experiment

Experimental setup. The proposed method is evaluated on a publicly available dataset: the Angle closure Glaucoma Evaluation (AGE) Challenge [4], which provides 3200 AS-OCT images with the dimension of 998×2130 pixels. The original challenge dataset provides annotation for the angle closure classification label and location of the scleral spur. In order to further realize the quantitative analysis of iris and cornea, we have the two key tissues manually re-annotated by experienced ophthalmologists, and offered two types of annotations, *i.e.*, the full annotation and the weak annotation. Pixel-wise masks of iris and cornea are provided by the full annotation, meanwhile, for the weak annotation, line strokes inside the tissues are marked. It is worth mentioning that the original PACG classification problem is reformulated to the tissue segmentation problem, therefore we do not use the original annotation in this work.

We randomly select 60% of the images for training, 20% for evaluation and 20% for test (only full annotations are used for evaluation and test). All the images and the corresponding annotations are resized to 240×512 pixels, and the image intensities are normalized into the range of $[-1, 1]$. The framework is implemented with PyTorch on an NVIDIA Tesla P40 GPU. We utilize the SGD optimizer with *weight decay* $= 0.0005$ and *momentum* $= 0.9$ to update the network parameters. The batch size is set to 4 for both micro and macro models. Dice coefficient (Dice, represented with percentage) and average distance of boundaries (ADB, represented with millimeter) [1] are used as the evaluation criteria. Higher Dice and lower ADB imply better segmentation performance. For convenience, we denote Dice1/ADB1 and Dice2/ADB2 as the evaluation metrics of the cornea and the peripheral iris in this work.

Table 1. Ablation studies on the proposed modules and annotation partition.

Methods	Combination				Annotation Composition		Ave Metric	
	Micro	Macro	Macro Flow	Micro Flow	Full Annotation	Weak Annotation	Dice	ADB
Module ablations	✓				1%	99%	82.13	2.85
	✓	✓			1%	99%	83.55	1.87
	✓	✓	*		1%	99%	86.70	1.15
	✓	✓	✓		1%	99%	89.35	0.66
	✓	✓	✓	*	1%	99%	90.12	0.43
	✓	✓	✓	✓	1%	99%	**91.64**	**0.30**
Annotation compositions	✓	✓	✓	✓	5%	95%	92.48	0.27
	✓	✓	✓	✓	10%	90%	92.60	0.26
	✓	✓	✓	✓	25%	75%	93.06	0.22
	✓	✓	✓	✓	50%	50%	**93.42**	**0.20**

*: The same flow being adopted in this study without uncertainty assistance.
Macro Flow: adding macroscopic flow with our uncertainty-aware KL loss.
Micro Flow: adding microscopic flow with our uncertainty-aware EMA mechanism.

Ablation study. To demonstrate the effectiveness of the proposed modules, we conduct ablation studies as well as experiments with different annotation composition. As shown in Table 1, the performance has improved around 5.80% and 2.29% in average Dice by adding the macroscopic and microscopic flow, respectively. In order to evaluate the effect of the proposed uncertainty strategies, the results of flows without uncertainty are presented as well, *i.e.*, marked by the asterisk symbol. To be more specific, we use the conventional EMA for the macroscopic flow and the KL-loss for the microscopic flow directly. As expected, the result without uncertainty shows inferior performance (2.65% lower for macroscopic flow and 1.52% lower for microscopic flow, respectively), demonstrating that the proposed uncertainty strategies can improve the effectiveness of the tutorials. To evaluate the stability of the proposed method, we conducted additional experiments with different percentages of fully-annotated images. As expected, the more fully-annotated images we utilize, the better performance the method achieves, indicating that the proposed method can exploit the information from full annotations as well.

Comparison with State-of-the-Art. As illustrated in Table 2, the two columns within the annotation composition represent the percentages of fully-annotated and weakly-labeled images used for training. The results of state-of-the-art semi-/weakly-supervised methods, including WACT [13], UAMT [20], AdvSemi [8], and CRF-rloss [18], are presented for comparison. In the training set for the proposed UAMM method, only 1% images are fully-annotated

Table 2. Quantitative comparison with the state-of-the-art semi-/weakly-supervised learning algorithms.

Method	Annotation Composition		Metric					
	Full Annotation	Weak Annotation	Dice			ADB		
			Dice1	Dice2	Ave	ADB1	ADB2	Ave
Oracle	100%	0%	**95.71**	**91.59**	**93.65**	**0.13**	**0.21**	**0.17**
	0%	100%	55.14	35.03	45.09	9.30	13.62	11.46
	1%	0%	78.83	68.64	73.73	5.79	6.29	6.04
	1%	99%	83.71	80.55	82.13	2.58	3.11	2.85
WACT [13]	1%	0%	51.63	25.89	38.76	9.74	19.97	14.86
	1%	99%	84.74	83.13	83.94	1.19	0.77	0.98
UAMT [20]	1%	0%	86.59	64.23	75.41	2.53	5.79	4.16
	1%	99%	88.58	85.06	86.82	0.47	0.73	0.60
AdvSemi [8]	1%	0%	84.02	69.49	76.75	2.88	6.11	4.50
	1%	99%	88.36	83.33	85.85	3.19	2.02	2.6
CRF-rloss [18]	0%	100%	86.37	83.97	85.17	1.09	0.87	0.98
	1%	99%	93.44	83.26	88.35	0.32	0.92	0.62
UAMM	1%	99%	**93.68**	**89.60**	**91.64**	**0.27**	**0.32**	**0.30**

while the rest 99% samples are weakly-labeled. For the semi-supervised methods, *i.e.*, WACT, UAMT and AdvSemi, generally weakly-annotated samples will not be utilized in their studies. Similarly, the full-annotated samples are not used in the weakly-supervised studies, *i.e.*, CRF-rloss, either. For a fair comparison, both of full and weakly-annotated samples will be integrated in the training procedure and provide two versions of results, so as to keep the model comparison under the same evaluation criteria. Oracle indicates using only the micro model, *i.e.*, a single DeepLabV3+ network [2]. As the baseline method, Oracle has been applied on four training sets with different percentages of fully-annotated images and weakly-labeled samples, as denoted in Row 2. With the same training data setup, the proposed UAMM method has achieved the best performance among these methods, with 91.64% in average Dice score and 0.3 in ADB. Furthermore, the evaluation metrics of UAMM are close to the metrics of fully-annotated trained Oracle (only 2.01% lower on average Dice), demonstrating that the proposed method can exploit segmentation guidance from the weak annotations. The visualization of representative examples is displayed in Fig. 2.

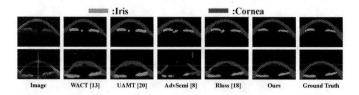

Fig. 2. Visualization of the segmentation results by different methods and ours.

4 Conclusion

In this work, we proposed a macro-micro weakly-supervised framework to tackle the problem of cornea and iris segmentation for the AS-OCT images. Specifically, an uncertainty-aware KL loss is designed for the macroscopic flow to assist the training of the macro model by the prediction priors from the micro model. Then, the microscopic flow is obtained with an uncertainty-aware moving average mechanism, which updates the micro-model by gradually involving the weights of the macro model. Our approach outperformed state-of-the-art semi-/weakly-supervised methods on the cornea and iris segmentation task for AS-OCT images. In addition, it achieved comparable performance by using only 1% of fully-annotated data with that of DeepLabV3+ using all fully-annotated images.

Acknowledgment. This work was funded by the Key Area Research and Development Program of Guangdong Province, China (No. 2018B010111001), National Key Research and Development Project (No. 2018YFC2000702) and Science and Technology Program of Shenzhen, China (No. ZDSYS201802021814180).

References

1. Bian, C., et al.: Pyramid network with online hard example mining for accurate left atrium segmentation. In: Pop, M., et al. (eds.) STACOM 2018. LNCS, vol. 11395, pp. 237–245. Springer, Cham (2019). https://doi.org/10.1007/978-3-030-12029-0_26

2. Chen, L.C., Zhu, Y., Papandreou, G., Schroff, F., Adam, H.: Encoder-decoder with atrous separable convolution for semantic image segmentation. In: Proceedings of the European Conference on Computer Vision (ECCV), pp. 801–818 (2018)

3. Cui, W., et al.: Semi-supervised brain lesion segmentation with an adapted mean teacher model. In: Chung, A.C.S., et al. (eds.) IPMI 2019. LNCS, vol. 11492, pp. 554–565. Springer, Cham (2019). https://doi.org/10.1007/978-3-030-20351-1_43

4. Fu, H., et al.: AGE: angle closure glaucoma evaluation challenge (2019). 10.21227/petb-fy10

5. Fu, H., et al.: Multi-context deep network for angle-closure glaucoma screening in anterior segment OCT. In: Frangi, A.F., Schnabel, J.A., Davatzikos, C., Alberola-López, C., Fichtinger, G. (eds.) MICCAI 2018. LNCS, vol. 11071, pp. 356–363. Springer, Cham (2018). https://doi.org/10.1007/978-3-030-00934-2_40

6. Fu, H., et al.: Segmentation and quantification for angle-closure glaucoma assessment in anterior segment OCT. IEEE Trans. Med. Imaging **36**(9), 1930–1938 (2017)

7. Gal, Y., Ghahramani, Z.: Dropout as a bayesian approximation: representing model uncertainty in deep learning. In: International Conference on Machine Learning, pp. 1050–1059 (2016)

8. Hung, W.C., Tsai, Y.H., Liou, Y.T., Lin, Y.Y., Yang, M.H.: Adversarial learning for semi-supervised semantic segmentation. arXiv preprint arXiv:1802.07934 (2018)

9. Kervadec, H., Dolz, J., Tang, M., Granger, E., Boykov, Y., Ayed, I.B.: Constrained-CNN losses for weakly supervised segmentation. Med. Image Anal. **54**, 88–99 (2019)

10. Li, H., Jhanji, V., Dorairaj, S., Liu, A., Lam, D.S., Leung, C.K.: Anterior segment optical coherence tomography and its clinical applications in glaucoma. J. Curr. Glaucoma Pract. **6**(2), 68 (2012)
11. Niwas, S.I., et al.: Automated anterior segment OCT image analysis for angle closure glaucoma mechanisms classification. Comput. Meth. Programs Biomed. **130**, 65–75 (2016)
12. Nolan, W.P., et al.: Detection of primary angle closure using anterior segment optical coherence tomography in Asian eyes. Ophthalmology **114**(1), 33–39 (2007)
13. Perone, C.S., Cohen-Adad, J.: Deep semi-supervised segmentation with weight-averaged consistency targets. In: Stoyanov, D., et al. (eds.) DLMIA/ML-CDS - 2018. LNCS, vol. 11045, pp. 12–19. Springer, Cham (2018). https://doi.org/10. 1007/978-3-030-00889-5_2
14. Radhakrishnan, S., et al.: Real-time optical coherence tomography of the anterior segment at 1310 nm. Arch. Ophthalmol. **119**(8), 1179–1185 (2001)
15. Smith, L., Gal, Y.: Understanding measures of uncertainty for adversarial example detection. arXiv preprint arXiv:1803.08533 (2018)
16. Sun, X., et al.: Primary angle closure glaucoma: what we know and what we don't know. Prog. Retinal Eye Res. **57**, 26–45 (2017)
17. Tang, M., Djelouah, A., Perazzi, F., Boykov, Y., Schroers, C.: Normalized cut loss for weakly-supervised CNN segmentation. In: IEEE Conference on Computer Vision and Pattern Recognition, pp. 1818–1827 (2018)
18. Tang, M., Perazzi, F., Djelouah, A., Ben Ayed, I., Schroers, C., Boykov, Y.: On regularized losses for weakly-supervised CNN segmentation. In: European Conference on Computer Vision, pp. 507–522 (2018)
19. Tham, Y.C., Li, X., Wong, T.Y., Quigley, H.A., Aung, T., Cheng, C.Y.: Global prevalence of glaucoma and projections of glaucoma burden through 2040: a systematic review and meta-analysis. Ophthalmology **121**(11), 2081–2090 (2014)
20. Yu, L., Wang, S., Li, X., Fu, C.W., Heng, P.A.: Uncertainty-aware self-ensembling model for semi-supervised 3D left atrium segmentation. In: Shen, D., et al. (eds.) MICCAI 2019. LNCS, vol. 11765, pp. 605–613. Springer, Cham (2019). https:// doi.org/10.1007/978-3-030-32245-8_67

Macular Hole and Cystoid Macular Edema Joint Segmentation by Two-Stage Network and Entropy Minimization

Lei Ye[1], Weifang Zhu[1], Dengsen Bao[1], Shuanglang Feng[1],
and Xinjian Chen[1,2(✉)]

[1] School of Electronics and Information Engineering, Soochow University,
Suzhou, China
xjchen@suda.edu.cn
[2] State Key Laboratory of Radiation Medicine and Protection, Soochow University,
Suzhou, China

Abstract. The co-occurrence of macular hole (MH) and cystoid macular edema (CME) indicates the serious visual impairment in ophthalmology clinic. Joint segmentation and quantitative analysis of MH and CME can greatly assist the ophthalmologists in clinical diagnosis and treatment. Benefitting from the advancement of computer digital image processing technology, deep learning has shown remarkable performance in assisting doctors to diagnose diseases. In this paper, we propose a two-stage network for the segmentation of MH and CME, the MH auxiliary network and the joint segmentation network, in which the output of the Linknet based auxiliary network is used as the input of the joint segmentation network. The MH auxiliary network is designed to solve the problem that the top boundary of the MH is difficult to be discriminated by the joint segmentation network. In the joint segmentation network, we add a mixed downsampling module to retain more fine feature information during the downsampling. Furthermore, a new self-entropy loss function is proposed, which can pay more attention to the hard samples and reduce the uncertainty of the network prediction. Experimental results show that our method achieved an average Dice of 89.32% and an average IOU of 81.42% in segmentation of MH and CME, showing extremely competitive results.

1 Introduction

Cystoid macular edema(CME) is a common symptom that mostly occurs in retinal diseases such as age-related macular degeneration (AMD), diabetic retinopathy(DR), cataract, etc [10]. Macular hole(MH) is a full-thickness defect of retinal tissue in the macular area, thereby affecting central visual acuity [4]. Benefitting from non-invasive, radiation-free and high-resolution, optical coherence tomography(OCT) is widely used in ophthalmic clinics [12]. Ophthalmologists can judge

---

L. Ye and W. Zhu—Equal contribution.

A. L. Martel et al. (Eds.): MICCAI 2020, LNCS 12265, pp. 735–744, 2020.
https://doi.org/10.1007/978-3-030-59722-1_71

the degree of retinopathy according to the sizes of MH and CME through OCT images, but manually quantitative analysis of CME and MH from each image is time-consuming and labor-intensive. Therefore, the automatic CME and MH joint segmentation can greatly assist the ophthalmologists in clinical diagnosis and treatment.

In recent years, many methods have been proposed for the segmentation of MH or CME, including traditional algorithms and deep learning based methods. Zhu et al. [12] used graph cut and Adaboost classifier to improve the segmentation accuracy of CME with co-existence of MH. Wu et al. [9] combined Gaussian mixture model and active contour model to segment CME. Wilkins et al. [8] proposed a bilateral filter and thresholding based method to perform CME segmentation.

Some deep learning based methods have also been applied for the CME segmentation problem. Bai et al. [1] combined conditional random fields(CRF) and fully convolutional networks(FCN) [6] to refine the results of FCN in CME segmentation. On the basis of FCN, the U-Net [7], a more powerful and widely used network was proposed. Girish et al. [3] applied U-Net to the segmentation of intra-retinal cysts and achieved excellent results. To the best of our knowledge, there are no deep learning based methods for MH segmentation or CME and MH joint segmentation.

In this paper, we propose a two-stage encoder-decoder network for the joint segmentation of CME and MH. Our main contribution includes: (1) A MH auxiliary network is proposed to segment the top boundary of the MH, which can effectively improve the overall performance of the proposed network. (2) A mixed downsampling module is adopted to reduce the false positives of CME segmentation. (3) A self-entropy loss based loss function is proposed to improve the performances of CME and MH segmentation.

2 Method

2.1 Overall Architecture

The overall structure of the proposed two-stage network is shown in Fig. 1, which consists of MH auxiliary network and joint segmentation network. The original image is processed by the MH auxiliary network to generate an auxiliary line on the top of MH, which represents the top boundary of MH. Then the output of the MH auxiliary network is used as the input of the joint segmentation network. The characteristics of MH and CME lesions have high similarity in some aspects such as intensity value. If these two kinds of lesions are segmented separately, it is easy for the model to mistake CME as MH or MH as CME. Joint segmentation can use their relative position information to better distinguish these two types of lesions. Our baseline is composed of a shared encoder and two independent decoder branches. Similar as U-Net, each block is constructed by two convolution layers, and the number of feature channels is shown in Fig. 1(ii).

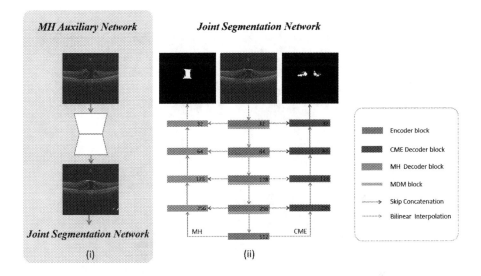

Fig. 1. Overview of the architecture of two-stage network.

2.2 MH Auxiliary Network

When the neural network model is used to segment the MH, it is prone to produce false positive or false negative in the top area of MH, shown as the second image in Fig. 3. It is very difficult for the model to learn the definition of the top boundary of MH directly from the OCT image because of the high similarity of intensity between the inner and outer region of MH, which is shown as the red line in Fig. 2(iii). According to the definition of top boundary of MH in medicine, we designed a MH auxiliary network as shown in Fig. 2(i). First, we feed the original image into a Linknet [2] based location network to find the highest point on both sides of the MH, which is shown as white dots in Fig. 2(iii). The location network outputs two Gaussian maps. The maximum likelihood estimation(MLE) method is used to estimate the center point of the Gaussian map as the predicted highest point. The auxiliary line of MH is generated by these two location points, which will be fused with the original image and finally sent it to the segmentation network. We will discuss different fusion options in the following ablation experiments.

2.3 Joint Segmentation Network

The structure of the joint segmentation network is shown in Fig. 1(ii). The network also adopts the classical encoder and decoder structure. Each block has two convolution layers and the number in block represents the amount of feature channels. Different from U-Net, the joint segmentation network proposed by us has two decoding paths and one encoding path. The outputs of the two decoder branches correspond to MH and CME respectively. We replace max

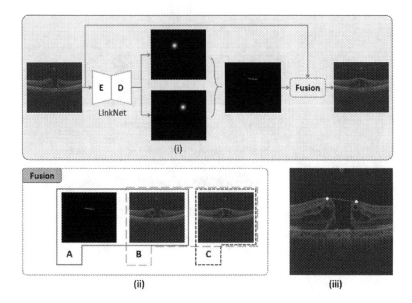

Fig. 2. Illustration of the MH auxiliary network. (i) Auxiliary line generator, we use Linknet as the backbone of our location network. (ii) A, B and C represent different fusion ways between the auxiliary line and original image. (iii) The enlarged view of lesions.

pooling with a mixed downsampling module(MDM), and propose a new loss function named as self- entropy(SE) loss.

MDM. Pooling is a very important operation in neural network models, which has the functions including feature dimension reduction, network parameter reduction, effective receptive field expansion and overfitting relief. Max pooling preserves texture features, while average pooling preserves overall features. Max pooling is the most widely used pooling method in neural network. Although max pooling can effectively reduce the computation, it inevitably loses some important features, which is disastrous for small targets such as CME, and cannot be recovered. In order to retain more features during the downsampling process, inspired by [5], we use a MDM that combines max pooling and average pooling. The MDM can be summarized as follows:

$$F_H = \alpha \cdot f_{avg}(F_L) + \beta \cdot f_{max}(F_L) \tag{1}$$

Where F_L means the low level features, while the F_H means the high level features. f_{avg} denotes the average pooling operation and f_{max} denotes the max pooling operation. α and β are the weights of two pooling methods respectively, which are both set as 1 in this paper.

SE. In order to enhance the generalization of the network, we propose a joint loss function, which is composed of binary cross entropy (BCE) loss, Dice loss and SE loss. The motivation of the SE loss function can be summarized as follows. First, when designing the loss function, we tend to narrow the distribution between the predicted image and the ground truth, but often ignore the constraint on the prediction image of the network. For a label, its entropy is 0, while for the prediction image, its entropy is not certain. Second, similar to focal loss for the description of hard samples, the SE loss can automatically pay more attention to those hard samples, because according to the definition of SE loss, the closer the predicted value is to 0.5, the higher is the loss. Dice loss can effectively alleviate the problem of data imbalance in image segmentation, which is beneficial to CME segmentation. But Dice loss makes the training of the model unstable, which will be relieved by the addition of BCE loss. The joint loss can be expressed as:

$$
\begin{aligned}
L_{\mathrm{joint}} &= w_0 L_{Dice} + w_1 L_{BCE} + w_2 L_{SE} \\
&= w_0 \left(1 - \frac{2 \sum_{i=1}^{C} g_i \times p_i}{\sum_{i=1}^{C} g_i + p_i} \right) - w_1 \left[\frac{1}{C} \sum_{i=1}^{C} g_i \log p_i + (1 - g_i) \log (1 - p_i) \right] \\
&\quad - w_2 \left[\frac{1}{C} \sum_{i=1}^{C} p_i \log p_i + (1 - p_i) \log (1 - p_i) \right]
\end{aligned}
$$

$$(2)$$

Where w_0, w_1 and w_2 are weights of these three loss functions respectively, which are all set as 1 in our experiments. $g \in \{0, 1\}$ is the ground truth, and $p \in [0, 1]$ is the predicted probability. C is the sum of the pixels of the output results.

3   Experimental Results

3.1   Dataset, Evaluation Metrics and Implementation Details

The collection and analysis of image data were approved by the cooperative hospital and adhered to the tenets of the Declaration of Helsinki. Because of its retrospective nature, informed consent was not required from subjects. 240 images from 20 subjects (Topcon OCT-2000, radial scan model) were acquired as our experimental dataset. The corresponding ground truth were all annotated by professional ophthalmologists. It should be pointed out that the medical significance of this paper is to help doctors find the relationship between MH and CME, so there will be no case without MH. In order to make the experiment more representative, we split data into training and test set according to the subject and the strategy of 3-fold cross validation is adopted. All the experimental results are the average of the 3-fold cross validation results. The original image size is 1024×885, we resize to 512×448. For data augmentation, we apply a random horizontal flip, random vertical flip and random rotation between 0 and 45 degrees in our dataset. During training, batch size is set to 6 and the poly learning rate scheduling is adopted, decay coefficient is 0.9. The initial learning rate is 0.01 and 60 epochs are trained per fold. All the models are based on the pytorch framework and a NVIDIA GeForce RTX 2080Ti with 11 GB memory.

The evaluation metrics include Intersection-over-Union (IoU), Dice, Accuracy (Acc), Sensitivity (Sen) and Specificity(Spec) are adopted, among which, IoU is regarded as the most important evaluation metric. The epoch of all other metrics is the same as the epoch corresponding to the maximum IoU.

3.2 Ablation Experiments

MH Auxiliary Network. For the MH auxiliary network, we not only perform ablation experiments, but also discuss the fusion methods. We design three methods to fuse the original image and the auxiliary line (shown in Fig. 2(ii)). In scheme A, we concatenate the auxiliary line and the original image in the channel dimension, while in scheme C, these two images are directly merged into one image. In solution B, we concatenate the original image and the image generated by scheme C.

Table 1. The performance comparison of different fusion methods in MH segmentation

Methods		IoU(%)	Dice(%)	Acc(%)	Sen(%)	Spec(%)
Baseline	MH	86.04	92.36	99.70	93.26	99.83
A	MH	88.00	93.50	99.75	91.00	**99.92**
B	MH	88.72	93.92	99.77	**93.37**	99.90
C	MH	**89.36**	**94.30**	**99.79**	93.26	99.91

The experimental results show that no matter which kind of fusion method is used, it can greatly improve the performance of MH segmentation (shown in Table 1). Among them, scheme C is the best, which can improve about 3.3% in IoU compared with the baseline. The visualization of experimental results in Fig. 3 show that the auxiliary network can significantly improve the segmentation performance of the top boundary of MH(indicated by white arrows).

MDM and SE. The detailed ablation experiment results of MDM and SE loss function are presented in Table 2. As can be seen from Table 2, the addition of MDM and SE loss function significantly improves the segmentation performance of CME and improves the segmentation of MH relatively small, which is in line with our idea. CME lesions have a large number of hard samples with high degree of uncertainty due to the characteristics of big differences in size and spatial distribution. In the downsampling process of the network, MDM helps to retain more feature information about small CME lesions, while the SE loss can pay more attention to hard samples. For IoU index, the addition of MDM and SE loss improves by 1.26% and 1.18% in CME segmentation, respectively. As shown in Fig. 3(green arrow), MDM and SE loss can effectively reduce the false positives of CME.

Fig. 3. Examples results of ablation experiments. From left to right: original image, baseline, baseline+MH auxiliary network, baseline+MH auxiliary network+MDM, baseline+ MH auxiliary network +MDM+SE. Magenta, red and blue represent the true positive, false positive and false negative for MH, while yellow, green and cyan represent true positive, false positive and false negative for CME. (Color figure online)

3.3 Comparison Experiments

The details of the comparison experiments are shown in Table 2, where Aux represents the MH auxiliary network. As can be seen from Table 2, the proposed two-stage method achieves significant improvements in IoU, Dice, accuracy and

Table 2. The performance of different segmentation models on MH and CME.

Methods		IoU(%)	Dice(%)	Acc(%)	Sen(%)	Spec(%)
FCN8s [6]	CME	39.47	54.22	99.35	52.49	99.71
	MH	74.03	84.32	99.47	80.00	99.84
	AVG	56.75	69.27	99.41	66.24	99.78
U-Net [7]	CME	63.10	76.54	99.57	83.00	99.70
	MH	78.96	87.87	99.53	85.86	99.82
	AVG	71.03	82.21	99.55	84.43	99.76
U-Net++ [11]	CME	70.95	82.59	99.70	86.26	99.81
	MH	88.41	93.78	99.75	**94.50**	99.86
	AVG	79.68	88.19	99.72	90.38	99.83
Baseline	CME	70.20	82.05	99.68	88.15	99.78
	MH	86.04	92.36	99.70	93.26	99.83
	AVG	78.12	87.32	99.69	**90.67**	99.80
Baseline+Aux	CME	70.53	82.31	99.69	87.09	99.80
	MH	89.36	94.30	99.79	93.26	99.91
	AVG	79.95	88.31	99.74	90.17	99.86
Baseline+Aux+MDM	CME	71.79	83.22	99.71	**90.67**	99.81
	MH	89.49	94.36	99.78	93.33	**99.92**
	AVG	80.64	88.79	99.75	90.33	99.86
Baseline+Aux+MDM+SE	CME	**72.97**	**84.06**	**99.73**	86.30	**99.84**
	MH	**89.87**	**94.59**	**99.79**	93.96	99.91
	AVG	**81.42**	**89.32**	**99.76**	90.13	**99.87**
	CME_ONLY	69.66	81.60	99.67	86.55	99.78
	MH_ONLY	83.81	90.93	99.66	87.06	**99.92**

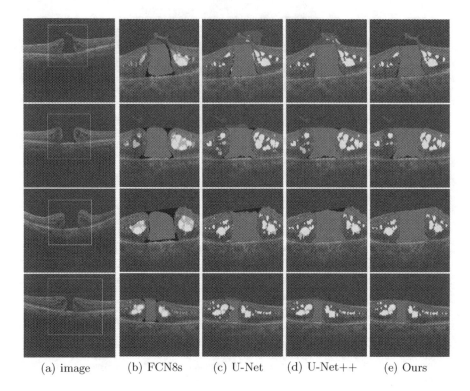

(a) image   (b) FCN8s   (c) U-Net   (d) U-Net++   (e) Ours

Fig. 4. MH and CME segmentation results with different models. Magenta, red and blue represent the true positive, false positive and false negative of MH respectively, while yellow, green and cyan represent the true positive, false positive and false negative of CME respectively. (Color figure online)

specificity compared with other models, such as FCN8s, U-Net and U-Net++ [11], which are popular in medical image segmentation.

Compared with U-Net++, our method improves average IoU by 1.74% and Dice by 1.13% respectively. We use the best model (Baseline+Aux+MDM+SE) to segment MH and CME separately. The corresponding experimental results prove the necessity of joint segmentation. For the sake of fairness, all models were trained and tested under the same set of hyperparameters.

Figure 4 shows the MH and CME segmentation results with different methods. It is obvious that our method achieves an impressive segmentation performance. For those models that have not been preprocessed by the MH auxiliary network, they are easy to produce serious false positives or false negatives in the top boundary of the MH, which indicates that the MH Auxiliary network plays an important role in MH segmentation. The addition of the MDM and SE loss effectively improves the segmentation performance on the hard CME samples.

4   Conclusion

In this paper, we propose a new two-stage encoder-decoder network for the joint segmentation of MH and CME in retinal OCT images. The overall network consists of two parts, the MH auxiliary network and the joint segmentation network. The MH auxiliary network is used as a pre-processing to help the segmentation network determine the top boundary of the MH. In the joint segmentation network, MDM can effectively retain more fine features, which is beneficial to the segmentation of CME. The SE loss function can automatically pay more attention to the hard samples and reduce the uncertainty of the network prediction. Experiment results show that the proposed network has compelling performance and great potential in the segmentation of MH and CME.

References

1. Bai, F., Marques, M.J., Gibson, S.J.: Cystoid macular edema segmentation of optical coherence tomography images using fully convolutional neural networks and fully connected crfs. arXiv preprint arXiv:1709.05324 (2017)
2. Chaurasia, A., Culurciello, E.: Linknet: exploiting encoder representations for efficient semantic segmentation. In: 2017 IEEE Visual Communications and Image Processing (VCIP), pp. 1–4 IEEE (2017)
3. Girish, G., Thakur, B., Chowdhury, S.R., Kothari, A.R., Rajan, J.: Segmentation of intra-retinal cysts from optical coherence tomography images using a fully convolutional neural network model. IEEE J. Biomed. Health Inform. **23**(1), 296–304 (2018)
4. Ho, A.C., Guyer, D.R., Fine, S.L.: Macular hole. Surv. Ophthalmol. **42**(5), 393–416 (1998)
5. Lee, C.Y., Gallagher, P., Tu, Z.: Generalizing pooling functions in cnns: mixed, gated, and tree. IEEE Trans. Pattern Anal. Mach. Intell. **40**(4), 863–875 (2017)
6. Long, J., Shelhamer, E., Darrell, T.: Fully convolutional networks for semantic segmentation. In: Proceedings of the IEEE Conference on Computer Vision and Pattern Recognition, pp. 3431–3440 (2015)
7. Ronneberger, Olaf: Invited talk: U-net convolutional networks for biomedical image segmentation. Bildverarbeitung für die Medizin 2017. I, pp. 3–3. Springer, Heidelberg (2017). https://doi.org/10.1007/978-3-662-54345-0_3
8. Wilkins, G.R., Houghton, O.M., Oldenburg, A.L.: Automated segmentation of intraretinal cystoid fluid in optical coherence tomography. IEEE Trans. Biomed. Eng. **59**(4), 1109–1114 (2012)
9. Wu, J., Niu, S., Chen, Q., Fan, W., Yuan, S., Li, D.: Automated segmentation of intraretinal cystoid macular edema based on gaussian mixture model. J. Innov. Opt. Health Sci. **13**(1), 1950020 (2019)
10. Zhang, L., Zhu, W., Shi, F., Chen, H., Chen, X.: Automated segmentation of intraretinal cystoid macular edema for retinal 3d oct images with macular hole. In: 2015 IEEE 12th International Symposium on Biomedical Imaging (ISBI), pp. 1494–1497 IEEE (2015)

11. Zhou, Z., Rahman Siddiquee, M.M., Tajbakhsh, N., Liang, J.: Unet++: a nested u-net architecture for medical image segmentation. In: Stoyanov, D., et al. (eds.) DLMIA/ML-CDS -2018. LNCS, vol. 11045, pp. 3–11. Springer, Cham (2018). https://doi.org/10.1007/978-3-030-00889-5_1

12. Zhu, W., et al.: Automated framework for intraretinal cystoid macular edema segmentation in three-dimensional optical coherence tomography images with macular hole. J. Biomed. Opt. **22**(7), 076014 (2017)

Retinal Nerve Fiber Layer Defect Detection with Position Guidance

Fei Ding[1], Gang Yang[1,2(✉)], Dayong Ding[3], and Gangwei Cheng[4]

[1] AI & Media Computing Lab, School of Information, Renmin University of China, Beijing, China
yanggang@ruc.edu.cn
[2] MOE Key Lab of DEKE, Renmin University of China, Beijing, China
[3] Vistel AI Lab, Visionary Intelligence Ltd., Beijing, China
[4] Peking Union Medical College Hospital, Beijing, China

Abstract. The retinal nerve fiber layer defect (RNFLD) provides early diagnostic evidence for many irreversible disabling or blinding diseases. This paper aims for automated RNFLD detection based on fundus images. Different from previous works that only consider the local contexts, we are the first to propose to detect RNFLD with position guidance, which senses both the physiological position and global dependencies with ease. Our solution consists of a position-consistent data preprocessing, a Position Guided Network, and a weakly supervised learning strategy. In the position-consistent data preprocessing, the optic disc region is evenly divided into several sectors according to the distribution regularity of RNFL. To detect RNFLD in sectors, the proposed Position Guided Network highlights the significant region with a position-aware attention module and captures the global dependencies with a bidirectional GRU module. The dataset about RNFLD suffers from noise labels, which is verified in our created dataset containing 4,335 fundus images. Thus the weakly supervised learning strategy, which jointly optimizes network parameters and label distributions, is proposed to reduce the impact of noise labels. Tested on a clinical dataset of 750 images, our solution achieves outstanding performance, attaining the F1 score of 81.00% that outperforms the baseline by 13.71%.

Keywords: RNFLD · Fundus image · Cnn · Position · Dependency

1 Introduction

The retinal nerve fiber layer (RNFL) is an important clinical diagnostic evidence in many kinds of optic neuropathy, such as *Glaucoma* that ranks as the second most disabling and blinding disease worldwide. The degeneration of RNFL provides the earliest evidence of glaucoma much before the actual visual field

G. Cheng—This work is supported by the Beijing Natural Science Foundation (No. 4192029, No. 4202033).

A. L. Martel et al. (Eds.): MICCAI 2020, LNCS 12265, pp. 745–754, 2020.
https://doi.org/10.1007/978-3-030-59722-1_72

defect begins [1,16,21]. Compared with other techniques that require expensive infrastructure or skilled clinicians (e.g., optical coherence tomography (OCT)), detecting RNFLD in fundus images is cost-effective.

In fundus images, the retinal nerve fiber appears as the arc radiating from the optic disc. The very subtle intensity difference between the RNFLD region and background makes RNFLD detection very challenging, even for skilled clinicians. Besides the local intensity difference, a clinician also considers the physiological position (i.e., he knows where he is looking at.) and the global dependencies to recognize RNFLD, e.g., the ISNT rule that the thickness of RNFL decreases in the order inferior (I) > superior (S) > nasal (N) > temporal (T) in normal eyes. However, current methods only consider the local intensity difference.

A few researchers focus on the research of RNFLD detection in fundus images. Some of them propose to detect the RNFLD boundaries [11–15]. But many types of RNFLD do not show clear boundaries (e.g., the suffusive RNFLD and RNFL thinning), and the uneven distribution of RNFL in normal eyes also forms the intensity difference similar to the RNFLD boundaries. Others follow a patch classification strategy to decide whether a selected patch contains RNFLD [9,10]. Like those methods of boundary detection, they both only consider the local contexts and ignore the physiological position and global dependencies.

As clinicians are easily confused by the very subtle intensity difference between the RNFLD region and background in fundus images, the dataset about RNFLD suffers from noise labels, which is verified in our created dataset containing 4,335 fundus images. We believe every clinician made a serious diagnosis based on his clinical experiences, and collecting such a large scale dataset is expensive and time-consuming, so these inconsistent annotations should be used efficiently rather than discarded simply. However, the noise labels will lead deep neural networks to exhibit large generalization error, i.e., the difference between "training error" and "testing error" [8,20]. Unfortunately, none of the existing methods have thought about this problem.

To address the above problems, we propose a novel solution for RNFLD detection, which distinguishes whether there is RNFLD in each of the sectors along the optic disc center. This paper makes contributions as follows.

– We propose to preprocess input images by referencing a consistent coordinate system to make the absolution position of pixels meaningful, where there is a consistent match between the content and the position in all fundus images.
– We propose a Position Guided Network (PGN) designed for sector classification, which models both physiological position and global dependencies of RNFL in fundus images.
– To address the noise labels, we introduce a weakly supervised learning strategy that jointly optimizes network parameters and label distributions.
– Extensive experiments on a clinical dataset of 750 fundus images show the advantages of our solution, which achieves the F1 score of 81.00% and the accuracy of 98.99% when detecting RNFLD in sectors, and the F1 score of 92.42% and the accuracy of 97.33% when detecting RNFLD in images.

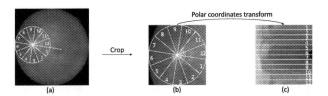

Fig. 1. An illustration of the position-consistent data preprocessing in our solution. The optic disc region is evenly divided into 12 sectors based on a consistent polar coordinate system (a). In this polar coordinate system, the line from the optic disc center to macula fovea is the original axis and the inferior temporal direction is positive. Sectors in (b) are transformed from cartesian coordinates to polar coordinates, which correspond to rectangular areas with the same numbers in (c).

2   Methodology

Given a color fundus image, we evenly divide the optic disc region into several sectors according to the distribution regularity of RNFL, and our goal is to automatically recognize whether there is RNFLD in each of sectors. The proposed solution consists of three parts, i.e., a position-consistent data preprocessing, a Position Guided Network (PGN), and a weakly supervised learning strategy to train the network with noise labels.

2.1   Position-Consistent Data Preprocessing

As shown in Fig. 1, the optic disc region is evenly divided into 12 sectors by referencing the optic disc center and the macula fovea. The optic disc center and macula fovea are located via the CenterNet [3], a state-of-the-art CNN for object detection. According to the suggestion of clinicians, the optic disc region is cropped out using a radius of the seven-tenths of the distance between the optic disc center and macula fovea (about 2 times Papillary Diameter). Transformed from cartesian coordinates to polar coordinates, sectors of the cropped optic disc region are unfolded to form corresponding rectangular areas with the same numbers, just like the process from Fig. 1(b) to Fig. 1(c). This transformation drives the sectors more adaptive to the rectangular receptive field of CNNs. The polar coordinate transformed image is fed into the PGN for RNFLD detection.

2.2   Position Guided Network

As shown in Fig. 2, our Position Guided Network (PGN) consists of three important parts, i.e., a backbone followed by a position-aware attention module and a bidirectional GRU (biGRU) module. The backbone, which is dismounted from ImageNet pretrained ResNext50 [18] that has less parameters and shows better performances than its ResNet counterpart, extracts feature maps $\hat{x}$ from a polar coordinates transformed image $x \in \mathbb{R}^{384 \times 384 \times 3}$, and it is trained with other modules. We replace the convolution within the last residual block of the backbone

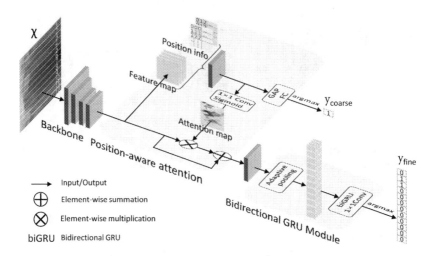

Fig. 2. A diagram of the proposed position guided network for RNFLD detection. The input image is first fed into the backbone to extract semantic features. By injecting the absolution position (e.g., the upper left corner is $(0, 0)$.), the position-aware attention module generates an attention map to highlight the features of significance and detects RNFLD in the image (image-level RNFLD). Finally, The biGRU captures the dependencies among regions and detects RNFLD in sectors (sector-level RNFLD).

by a dilated convolution, so the output stride is 16. The position-aware attention module guides PGN to focus on the significant area by sensing the absolute position. Similar to [5], it also detects the image-level RNFLD y_{coarse} for providing supervision to optimize the attention map. The biGRU captures the dependencies among sectors and detects the sector-level RNFLD $\{y_{fine}^j \mid 1 \leq j \leq n\}$, where n is the number of sectors divided from the optic disc region, and we set n to 12. Notably, the RNFL thickness around the optic disc is related to the position, so our PGN, which utilizes position information, has a great advantage in detecting RNFLD.

Position-aware Attention Module. Let c be the number of channels of the feature map $\hat{x} \in \mathbb{R}^{h \times w \times c}$. We inject the absolute position information $p \in \mathbb{R}^{h \times w \times 2}$ into $\hat{x}$ and obtain the position-aware embedding of shape $h \times w \times (c + 2)$, where two additional channels denote the x-axis position and y-axis position respectively. Information concerning absolute position is inherently useful for CNNs [7], especially for our proposed PGN whose input is processed based on our position-consistent data preprocessing. Then the position-aware embedding is convoluted by a 3×3 convolution to aggregate a $h \times w \times 2$ feature map, which represents the activation map for each of two classes. On the one hand, the $h \times w \times 2$ feature map is down-sampled by a global average pooling (GAP) and outputs the image-level class probability $y_{coarse} \in \mathbb{R}^2$ by passing through a fully-connected layer with the *softmax* function. On the other hand, the $h \times w \times 2$ feature map is transformed by a 1×1 convolution layer with the *sigmoid* function to generate an attention map $g(\hat{x} \| p) \in \mathbb{R}^{h \times w \times 1}$, where $\|$ denotes channel-wise concatenation. The attention mechanism performs as bellow:

$$\tilde{x} = f(g(\hat{x} \| p) \cdot \hat{x} + \hat{x}) \tag{1}$$

in which f is a convolution block that has the same structure as the last residual block of the backbone. The features at the peak of the attention map are highlighted and the attention map shows the evidence of diagnosis.

Modelling Global Dependencies with biGRU. Since there is a consistent one-to-one match between the content and position of sectors in all input images, we consider the sector classification as a sequence modeling problem. The bidirectional GRU (biGRU) [2], which is known to be effective for making use of both past and future contextual information of a given sequence, is used for modeling the global dependencies. Before applying the biGRU, the $\tilde{x}$, which is the output of the attention mechanism, is transformed by an adaptive average pooling (AAP) to generate features of dimension $n \times 2048$, which corresponds to the semantic vector of the n sectors around the optic disc center. Let $\overrightarrow{h_t}$ and $\overleftarrow{h_t}$ be the forward and the backward hidden state at a specific time step $t \in \{1, ..., n\}$, respectively. They are generated by the biGRU as below:

$$\left\{ \overrightarrow{h_t}, \overleftarrow{h_t} \mid t = 1, ...n \right\} = biGRU(AAP(\tilde{x})) \tag{2}$$

Concatenating $\overrightarrow{h_t}$ and $\overleftarrow{h_t}$, we obtain the biGRU output $h_t = \left[\overrightarrow{h_t}, \overleftarrow{h_t} \right]$ of dimension $n \times 1024$. The classification results of n sectors are obtained by applying a 1×1 convolution layer with $Softmax$ function on h_t.

2.3   Learning with Noise Labels

To address the noise labels, we propose a novel weakly supervised learning strategy, which optimizes both network parameters and label distributions. Deep label distribution learning [6,17,19] is conducted in the soft-label space by converting a categorical label into a label distribution (i.e., a normal distribution whose mean is the categorical label). For our strategy, the image label y_{coarse} is concatenated with sectors label y_{fine}, thus we obtain a one-hot label $y \in \mathbb{R}^{(n+1) \times 2}$ for label optimization. Our learning strategy consists of three stages as below.

Learning Initial Network Parameters. The network is first trained with the traditional strongly supervised way to learn the easy samples. The classic Kullback-Leibler (KL) loss is used to calculate the distance between the initial label distributions y and the prediction distributions $\hat{y}$.

$$L_{stage1} = KL(y \| \hat{y}) = \frac{1}{n+1} \sum_{j=1}^{n+1} \sum_{c=1}^{2} y_{j,c} \log(\frac{y_{j,c}}{\hat{y}_{j,c}}) \tag{3}$$

Minimizing the L_{stage1}, the network is trained with a fixed high learning rate.

Joint Optimization. After learning the initial network parameters in the first stage, the network parameters and label distribution are jointly optimized in the second stage. We maintain a label distribution $\tilde{y}$ for every image, which models the unknown noise-free label. The $\tilde{y}$ is used as the pseudo-label, which is initialized with the noise label y and continuously updated by the moving average of network prediction $\hat{y}$:

$$\tilde{y} = \rho \cdot \tilde{y} + (1 - \rho) \cdot \hat{y} \tag{4}$$

where ρ is the momentum. With label optimization, the noise is gradually corrected while the useful part is retained. The network parameters are optimized by an objective function which is constructed by three terms:

$$L_{stage2} = KL(\tilde{y}||\hat{y}) + \alpha KL(\tilde{y}||y) - \beta \frac{1}{n+1} \sum_{j=1}^{n+1} \sum_{c=1}^{2} \hat{y}_{j,c} \log \hat{y}_{j,c} \tag{5}$$

in which α and β are two hyperparameters. The first term calculates the deviation between the pseudo-label and the network prediction, which guides how the network parameters should be updated. The second term constrains that the estimated label distribution $\tilde{y}$ should not be completely different from the original noise label y and the useful part of y is kept. As discussed in [17,19], the third term is an entropy loss which forces the network to peak at only one category rather than being flat. The label distribution $\tilde{y}$ and network parameters are updated using Eq. (4) and Eq. (5) respectively in every training iteration.

Fine Tuning. Fixing the pseudo-label $\tilde{y}$, we fine-tune the network with only the KL-loss $KL(\tilde{y}||\hat{y})$, where the learning rate is gradually reduced.

3   Experiments

3.1   Experimental Setup

Dataset. There is no public dataset available for RNFLD detection. We collect 4,335 color fundus images from the Department of Ophthalmology, Peking Union Medical College Hospital, where each image is annotated by two to five experienced ophthalmologists who have at least three years of clinical experience. In the dataset, 1,387 images are annotated as RNFLD by one to five clinicians, but only 323 images are annotated as RNFLD by two or more clinicians (i.e., only annotations of 323 images are consistent). The testing set, consists of 125 images with RNFLD and 625 normal images, is created with manual data cleaning (i.e., clean label). The training set consists of 1,262 images with RNFLD and 2,323 normal images, in which the label of each sector is the union of all annotations about it (i.e., noise label). We retain 10% of the training data for validation.

Settings and Metrics. We implement our network with PyTorch on TITAN Xp GPU. The Stochastic Gradient Descent with momentum of 0.9 and weight decay of $1e-4$ is used as the optimizer. For the proposed learning strategy,

Table 1. Comparison between the strongly supervised learning strategy using cross-entropy loss and our weakly supervised learning strategy. (a) The effect of learning rate when using cross entropy loss. (b) Performance of our proposed learning strategy.

(a)

LR	F1	Se
0.001	0.4787	0.4350
0.01	0.6224	0.6667
0.02	**0.7102**	**0.7073**
0.03	0.6650	0.5569

(b)

Method	F1	ACC	Se	Sp
Cross-Entropy Loss	0.7102	0.9842	0.7073	0.9920
Our method	**0.8100**	**0.9899**	**0.7886**	**0.9955**

Table 2. Ablation study of components in PGN. These components are the attention mechanism without position information (Att), the attention mechanism with position information (PAtt), and biGRU. The baseline contains none of these components.

Method	F1	ACC	Se	Sp
Baseline	0.7371	0.9859	0.7236	0.9933
Baseline+Att	0.7725	0.9882	0.7317	0.9954
Baseline+PAtt	0.7826	0.9889	0.7318	0.9961
Baseline+biGRU	0.7439	0.9860	0.7439	0.9928
Baseline+Att+biGRU	0.7763	0.9887	0.7195	**0.9962**
Baseline+PAtt+biGRU (PGN)	**0.8100**	**0.9899**	**0.7886**	0.9955

we set the momentum in Eq. (4) ρ=0.9, and use 0.8 for α and 0.1 for β in Eq. (5). Using a fixed learning rate of 0.02, the network is trained for 10 epochs in the first stage and trained for 20 epochs in the second stage. In the fine-tuning stage, the base learning rate is set to 0.05 and is multiplied by 0.1 at the tenth epoch of 20 epochs. We present the results by the Accuracy (ACC), F1 score (F1), Sensitivity (Se), and Specificity (Sp).

3.2   Results and Analysis

Generalization. We compare the proposed weakly supervised learning strategy with the traditional strongly supervised learning that uses the cross-entropy loss function. We first examine the effect of the learning rate when training PGN with only the cross-entropy loss. Table 1(a) lists the results of four learning rates, which is consistent with the previous study [17,19] that a high learning rate prevents the network from overfitting noise labels. Using the learning rate of 0.02, we train PGN with the proposed learning strategy. Table 1(b) shows our method is more robust for noise labels.

Ablation Study for Position Guided Network. To examine the contribution of each component in PGN, we conduct an ablation study. Given varied combinations of the components, six models are trained with the proposed

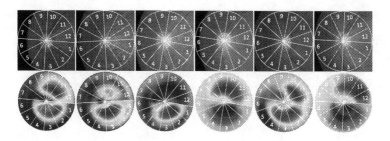

Fig. 3. Visualizing the attention map, which is used to highlight the significant regions for RNFLD detection. We transform the attention map back to the cartesian coordinates.

Table 3. The performance of PGN trained with images that are preprocessed with different methods, i.e., whether using the consistent coordinate system.

Method	Sector classification				Image classification			
	F1	ACC	Se	Sp	F1	ACC	Se	Sp
Inconsistent position	0.6279	0.9801	0.6138	0.9904	0.8152	0.9360	0.8320	0.9568
Consistent position	**0.8100**	**0.9899**	**0.7886**	**0.9955**	**0.9242**	**0.9733**	**0.9760**	**0.9728**

learning strategy. All models are initialized with the same random seed. Table 2 summarizes the results. Between the attention modules, PAtt, which injects absolute position information into feature maps, turns out to be the most effective. After adding the biGRU, the overall performance goes up. For the PGN which combines all components, it significantly outperforms other combinations. This suggests that PAtt and biGRU are complementary to each other and they are necessary for the advantages of PGN.

Position-consistent Data Preprocessing. We conduct experiments to study our position-consistent data preprocessing (i.e., Sector 1 is always below the line from the disc center to the macula fovea). Following the common way [4], the compared position-inconsistent data preprocessing uses the horizontal axis as the original axis of the polar coordinates system. Table 3 shows that our position-consistent data preprocessing contributes to PGN's success a lot.

Visualization. Figure 3 shows our consistent coordinate system and attention maps. The fourth image shows the RNFLD without obvious boundaries, where the correct diagnosis of sectors 8–11 can only be made when considering the global dependencies rather than the local intensity difference (e.g., normally, the RNFL in sectors 8–11 is similar to the RNFL in sectors 2–5 and thicker than the RNFL in sectors 1, 12, 6, and 7). In addition to guiding the network to focus on the significant area, the attention map also shows the evidence of diagnosis.

4   Conclusion

This paper proposes a novel solution to detect RNFLD with position guidance in fundus images. By fitting with a position-consistent data preprocessing, the proposed position guided network (PGN) senses both the physiological position and global dependencies. Concerning the noise labels found in our dataset with 4,335 fundus images, we develop a weakly supervised learning strategy, which jointly optimizes network parameters and label distributions. A clinical dataset of 750 images verifies the effectiveness of the proposed solution. Notably, our position-consistent data preprocessing improves the F1 score from 62.79% to 81.00%. Our solution that senses position in both input data and network is very helpful for RNFLD detection, which can also be extended to other position-related diseases.

References

1. Chen, X., Xu, Y., Yan, S., Wong, D.W.K., Wong, T.Y., Liu, J.: Automatic feature learning for glaucoma detection based on deep learning. In: Navab, N., Hornegger, J., Wells, W.M., Frangi, A.F. (eds.) MICCAI 2015. LNCS, vol. 9351, pp. 669–677. Springer, Cham (2015). https://doi.org/10.1007/978-3-319-24574-4_80
2. Cho, K., et al.: Learning phrase representations using rnn encoder-decoder for statistical machine translation. EMNLP (2014)
3. Duan, K., Bai, S., Xie, L., Qi, H., Huang, Q., Tian, Q.: Centernet: keypoint triplets for object detection. In: ICCV, pp. 6569–6578 (2019)
4. Fu, H., Cheng, J., Xu, Y., Wong, D.W.K., Liu, J., Cao, X.: Joint optic disc and cup segmentation based on multi-label deep network and polar transformation. TMI **37**(7), 1597–1605 (2018)
5. Fukui, H., Hirakawa, T., Yamashita, T., Fujiyoshi, H.: Attention branch network: learning of attention mechanism for visual explanation. In: CVPR, pp. 10705–10714 (2019)
6. Gao, B.B., Xing, C., Xie, C.W., Wu, J., Geng, X.: Deep label distribution learning with label ambiguity. IEEE Trans. Image Process. **26**(6), 2825–2838 (2017)
7. Islam, M.A., Jia, S., Bruce, N.D.: How much position information do convolutional neural networks encode?. ICLR (2020)
8. Jiang, L., Zhou, Z., Leung, T., Li, L.J., Fei-Fei, L.: Mentornet: learning data-driven curriculum for very deep neural networks on corrupted labels. In: ICML (2018)
9. Joshi, G.D., Sivaswamy, J., Prashanth, R., Krishnadas, S.R.: Detection of peripapillary atrophy and RNFL defect from retinal images. In: Campilho, A., Kamel, M. (eds.) ICIAR 2012. LNCS, vol. 7325, pp. 400–407. Springer, Heidelberg (2012). https://doi.org/10.1007/978-3-642-31298-4_47
10. Lamani, D., Manjunath, T., Mahesh, M., Nijagunarya, Y.: Early detection of glaucoma through retinal nerve fiber layer analysis using fractal dimension and texture feature. Int. J. Res. Eng. Technol. **3**, 158–163 (2014)
11. Muramatsu, C., et al.: Detection of retinal nerve fiber layer defects on retinal fundus images for early diagnosis of glaucoma. J. Biomed. Opt. **15**(1), 016021 (2010)
12. Oh, J.E., Yang, H.K., Kim, K.G., Hwang, J.M.: Automatic computer-aided diagnosis of retinal nerve fiber layer defects using fundus photographs in optic neuropathy. Invest. Ophthalmol. Vis. Sci. **56**(5), 2872–2879 (2015)

13. Panda, R., Puhan, N.B., Rao, A., Mandal, B., Padhy, D., Panda, G.: Deep convolutional neural network-based patch classification for retinal nerve fiber layer defect detection in early glaucoma. J. Med. Imaging **5**(4), 044003 (2018)
14. Panda, R., Puhan, N.B., Rao, A., Padhy, D., Panda, G.: Recurrent neural network based retinal nerve fiber layer defect detection in early glaucoma. In: ISBI, pp. 692–695 IEEE (2017)
15. Panda, R., Puhan, N.B., Rao, A., Padhy, D., Panda, G.: Automated retinal nerve fiber layer defect detection using fundus imaging in glaucoma. Comput. Med. Imaging Graph. **66**, 56–65 (2018)
16. Sedai, S., Mahapatra, D., Hewavitharanage, S., Maetschke, S., Garnavi, R.: Semi-supervised segmentation of optic cup in retinal fundus images using variational autoencoder. In: Descoteaux, M., Maier-Hein, L., Franz, A., Jannin, P., Collins, D.L., Duchesne, S. (eds.) MICCAI 2017. LNCS, vol. 10434, pp. 75–82. Springer, Cham (2017). https://doi.org/10.1007/978-3-319-66185-8_9
17. Tanaka, D., Ikami, D., Yamasaki, T., Aizawa, K.: Joint optimization framework for learning with noisy labels. In: CVPR, pp. 5552–5560 (2018)
18. Xie, S., Girshick, R., Dollár, P., Tu, Z., He, K.: Aggregated residual transformations for deep neural networks. In: CVPR, pp. 1492–1500 (2017)
19. Yi, K., Wu, J.: Probabilistic end-to-end noise correction for learning with noisy labels. In: CVPR, pp. 7017–7025 (2019)
20. Zhang, C., Bengio, S., Hardt, M., Recht, B., Vinyals, O.: Understanding deep learning requires rethinking generalization. ICLR (2017)
21. Zhao, R., Liao, W., Zou, B., Chen, Z., Li, S.: Weakly-supervised simultaneous evidence identification and segmentation for automated glaucoma diagnosis. AAAI **33**, 809–816 (2019)

An Elastic Interaction-Based Loss Function for Medical Image Segmentation

Yuan Lan🆔, Yang Xiang🆔, and Luchan Zhang$^{(\boxtimes)}$🆔

Department of Mathematics, The Hong Kong University of Science and Technology,
Hong Kong SAR, China
`ylanaa@connect.ust.hk`, `{maxiang,malczhang}@ust.hk`

Abstract. Deep learning techniques have shown their success in medical image segmentation since they are easy to manipulate and robust to various types of datasets. The commonly used loss functions in the deep segmentation task are pixel-wise loss functions. This results in a bottleneck for these models to achieve high precision for complicated structures in biomedical images. For example, the predicted small blood vessels in retinal images are often disconnected or even missed under the supervision of the pixel-wise losses. This paper addresses this problem by introducing a long-range elastic interaction-based training strategy. In this strategy, convolutional neural network (CNN) learns the target region under the guidance of the elastic interaction energy between the boundary of the predicted region and that of the actual object. Under the supervision of the proposed loss, the boundary of the predicted region is attracted strongly by the object boundary and tends to stay connected. Experimental results show that our method is able to achieve considerable improvements compared to commonly used pixel-wise loss functions (cross entropy and dice Loss) and other recent loss functions on three retinal vessel segmentation datasets, DRIVE, STARE and CHASEDB1. The implementation is available at https://github.com/charrywhite/elastic_interaction_based_loss.

Keywords: Medical image segmentation · Deep learning · Elastic interaction

1 Introduction

The medical image segmentation task is to automatically extract the region of interest, such as organs and lesions in medical images. Segmentation plays a critical role in medical image analysis since the information of the segmented region (such as length, width, angles) can be used for further diagnosis and treatment of related diseases. How to locate the region of interest in an exact manner is a major challenge.

In recent years, convolutional neural networks (CNNs) have shown ground-breaking effects to medical image segmentation task and different approaches have been proposed [11, 12, 17, 18]. The widely adopted choice of the loss function in CNN methods

Electronic supplementary material The online version of this chapter (https://doi.org/10.1007/978-3-030-59722-1_73) contains supplementary material, which is available to authorized users.

© Springer Nature Switzerland AG 2020
A. L. Martel et al. (Eds.): MICCAI 2020, LNCS 12265, pp. 755–764, 2020.
https://doi.org/10.1007/978-3-030-59722-1_73

is pixel-wise loss functions such as cross entropy. Pixel-wise loss functions classify each pixel of an image individually by comparing the corresponding ground truth and learning each pixel in an image equally. As a result, this type of loss functions are not necessarily robust in detecting the details and small structures which are critical in medical image analysis. For instance, in the retinal vessel segmentation task, the long, thin and weak vessels can be disconnected easily or even missed under the supervision of a pixel-wise loss function.

Before the flourishing of CNNs, variational image segmentation approaches [1, 16, 23] based on intensity or textural information were widely used in dealing with the segmentation task. Among them, the active contour methods define an evolving curve under the force derived by some energy functional, and this evolving curve moves to minimize this energy. Different energy functionals have been proposed in the active contour methods, such as the balloon force model [8], region-based methods [2, 13], gradient vector flow method (GVF) [22] and elastic interaction model [20, 21]. Compared to the pixel-wise loss functions in CNN models, the curve evolution based on energy functionals in the active contour methods considers the topological or physical properties of the target objects rather than learning each pixel individually. However, these methods can only process one image at a time and cannot handle massive images in a collective way as in CNN methods.

Recently, methods have been proposed [3, 9, 10] to train a CNN by minimizing curve-evolving energy functionals. In [3] and [10], the image segmentation task was represented as a minimization problem of the Mumford-Shah functional. While in [9], an objective minimization function based on boundary integral was defined. Despite these efforts, developing robust medical image segmentation methods, especially for long, thin structures in medical images, is still a challenging task.

In this paper, we propose an elastic interaction-based loss function in a deep learning framework specifically for the long, thin structures that are commonly seen in medical images. Under the supervision of this loss function, the predicted region will be attracted strongly by the object boundary through a global elastic interaction. Moreover, the self-interaction of the boundary of the predicted region will tend to smooth its own shape and will keep the predicted boundary connected. Due to these properties, this new loss function shows great advantages in tackling the segmentation of thin, long structures, such as vessels, in medical images. Also, one of the difficulties for most of the energy functional-based loss functions during training is the unstable performance in early steps, because the random initial guess in CNN may cause instabilities. Due to the long range nature, the minimization of the elastic interaction energy functional is not sensitive to the initialization. As a result, the proposed new CNN method with this elastic interaction-based loss function has demonstrated stable performance in the early stage of the training, as shown by the results of experiments in supplementary material.

The proposed elastic interaction-based loss function can be implemented efficiently using the Fast Fourier Transform (FFT), making it easy to incorporate in CNN. We examine our new loss function on three retinal image datasets, DRIVE, STARE and CHASEDB1, and the results indicate that our method is able to achieve a considerable improvement compared to commonly used pixel-wise loss functions (cross entropy and dice loss) and other recent loss functions.

2 Methodology

2.1 Review of the Framework of Deep Neural Network

In this section, we will briefly review the framework of deep neural network (DNN) under supervised learning. In supervised learning, the objective function (i.e. the loss function) that we want to minimize is a function between the output of DNN and ground truth. The output of DNN is generated by forward propagation of the input, i.e. the input of DNN is processed by each hidden layer and activation layer in this network in the forward direction. Then the parameters within each hidden layer are updated by gradient descent in back propagation. The entire process of DNN is as follows,

$$
\begin{cases}
\min_{\theta} \ \mathcal{L}(\theta) = \sum_i f\left(u_N^{(i)}, u_{gt}^{(i)}\right) \\
\text{Forward inference: } u_N^{(i,t)}(\theta) = \mathbf{W}_N^{(t)} \sigma \circ \left(\mathbf{W}_{N-1}^{(t)} ... \sigma \circ \left(\mathbf{W}_2^{(t)} \sigma \circ \left(\mathbf{W}_1^{(t)} u_0^{(i)}\right)\right)\right) \\
\text{Back propagation: } \mathbf{W}_k^{t+1} = \mathbf{W}_k^t - \lambda \cdot \frac{\partial \mathcal{L}}{\partial u_N} \cdot \frac{\partial u_N}{\partial \mathbf{W}_k}
\end{cases}
\tag{1}
$$

where $\mathcal{L}$ is the loss function to be minimized. u_0, u_N, u_{gt} are input and output of network and ground truth, respectively, i denotes the number of data and t is the number of iterations, $\theta = \{\mathbf{W}_1, \mathbf{W}_1, \ldots, \mathbf{W}_N\}$ are the parameters to be trained, σ is nonlinear scalar function, $\circ$ means element-wise operation, and λ is step size in gradient descent. In this work, we will proposed a new objective function for this DNN process.

2.2 Elastic Interaction-Based Loss Function

Our elastic interaction-based loss function is inspired by the elastic interaction between dislocations, which are line defects in crystals [5]. These dislocations are connected lines and the elastic interaction between them is long-range. Inspired by this interaction energy, in deep learning segmentation task, we consider the boundary of the ground truth and that of the prediction as two curves with their own energies, during training process, the evolution of the boundary of predicted region is under the supervision of their elastic interaction energy.

Consider a parameterized curve $\gamma(s)$ in the xy plane, which represents the boundary of a region. The curve has an orientation that could be either clockwise or counterclockwise. The elastic energy of the curve γ is

$$
E = \frac{1}{8\pi} \int_\gamma \int_{\gamma'} \frac{d\boldsymbol{l} \cdot d\boldsymbol{l'}}{r},
\tag{2}
$$

where γ' is the curve γ with another parameter s', vector $d\boldsymbol{l} = \boldsymbol{\tau} dl$ with $\boldsymbol{\tau}$ being the unit tangent vector and dl being the line element of the curve γ, and same for $d\boldsymbol{l'}$ of γ', $\boldsymbol{r} = (x - x', y - y')$ is the vector between the points (x, y) on γ and (x', y') on γ', and the distance between these two points is $r = \sqrt{(x - x')^2 + (y - y')^2}$. This is the elastic energy stored in three dimensional space of a dislocation line γ in the xy plane. (Note that this is a simplified version of the dislocation interaction energy [5]. Prefactor of the energy has also been omitted in this formulation.)

The notation γ in Eq. (2) can also be understood as a collection of curves. Especially, for a system of two curves γ_1 and γ_2, the total elastic energy is

$$
\begin{aligned}
E &= \frac{1}{8\pi} \int_{\gamma_1 \cup \gamma_2} \int_{\gamma_1' \cup \gamma_2'} \frac{dl \cdot dl'}{r} \\
&= \frac{1}{8\pi} \int_{\gamma_1} \int_{\gamma_1'} \frac{dl_1 \cdot dl_1'}{r} + \frac{1}{8\pi} \int_{\gamma_2} \int_{\gamma_2'} \frac{dl_2 \cdot dl_2'}{r} + \frac{1}{4\pi} \int_{\gamma_1} \int_{\gamma_2} \frac{dl_1 \cdot dl_2}{r}.
\end{aligned}
\tag{3}
$$

In this expression, the first two terms are the self-energies of the two curves, respectively, and the last term is the interaction energy between them. Note that this total energy of two curves γ_1 and γ_2 depend on their orientations.

For a system of two coincident curves with opposite orientations, i.e., $\gamma_2 = -\gamma_1$, the total energy in Eq. (3) vanishes. This means a perfect segmentation result if curve γ_1 is the boundary of the object (the ground truth) and γ_2 is the evolving boundary of prediction [21].

Using an artificial time t, we describe the evolution of a curve γ by minimizing the total energy in the steepest descent direction, which is $\gamma_t = f = -\frac{\delta E}{\delta \gamma}$, where γ_t is the velocity of the curve γ and f is the force on it. (This is essentially the dynamics of dislocations with mobility 1 in its unit.) The obtained velocity of the curve γ is

$$
\gamma_t(x, y) = f = \left(-\frac{1}{4\pi} \int_{\gamma} \frac{r \times dl}{r^3} \right) \times \tau = \left(\frac{1}{4\pi} \int_{\gamma} \frac{r \cdot n_\gamma}{r^3} dl \right) n,
\tag{4}
$$

where $r = (x - x(s), y - y(s))$ is the vector between the point (x, y) and a point $(x(s), y(s))$ on γ, and $r = \sqrt{(x - x(s))^2 + (y - y(s))^2}$ is the distance between the two points. τ and n are the unit tangent vector and unit normal vector of γ at the point (x, y), respectively, and τ_γ and n_γ are the unit tangent vector and unit normal vector of γ at the point $(x(s), y(s))$. In the derivation of this equation, we have used $dl = \tau_\gamma dl$, $\hat{z} \times \tau = n$, $\hat{z} \times \tau_\gamma = n_\gamma$, where $\hat{z}$ is the unit vector in the $+z$ direction. Note that in Eq. (4), γ could be a collection of curves.

Therefore, in the image space, derived from (2) by using $\nabla G_t = -\delta(\gamma_1)n$ for the ground truth G_t whose boundary is γ_1, and $\nabla H(\phi) = -\delta(\gamma_2)n$ for the moving curve, where $\delta(\gamma_1)$ and $\delta(\gamma_2)$ are regularized Dirac delta functions of curves γ_1 and γ_2, the proposed loss function in CNN is,

$$
L_{en} = \frac{1}{8\pi} \int_{\Omega} dx dy \int_{\Omega} \frac{\nabla (G_t + \alpha H(\phi))(x, y) \cdot \nabla (G_t + \alpha H(\phi))(x', y')}{r} dx' dy',
\tag{5}
$$

where ϕ is the level set representation of the moving curve γ_2 [14], and α is a hyperparameter. Here $H(\cdot)$ is a smoothing Heaviside function which controls the width of the contour by regularization parameter β,

$$
H(\phi) = \begin{cases} 0 & \text{if } \phi \leq -\beta \\ \frac{1}{2}\left(\sin\left(\frac{\pi \phi}{2\beta} \right) + 1 \right) & \text{if } -\beta < \phi < \beta \\ 1 & \text{if } \phi \geq \beta. \end{cases}
\tag{6}
$$

The parameter α and the Heaviside function $H(\cdot)$ control the strength of the elastic energy generated by the moving curve γ_2 compared with that generated by the object boundary γ_1. In CNN context, we applied HardTanh activation function whose range is $[0, 1]$ instead of using the above $H(\cdot)$ for convenience. The level set representation ϕ can be computed by $Prob - 0.5$, where $Prob$ is the softmax output of target class.

Similarly, we describe the velocity of curve γ_2 (the boundary of predicted region) derived from (4) as,

$$v = -\frac{\partial L_{en}}{\partial \phi} = -\frac{1}{4\pi} \int_{R^2} \frac{\mathbf{r} \cdot \nabla (G_t + \alpha H(\phi)) (x', y')}{r^3} dx' dy' \tag{7}$$

The velocity of curve γ_2 is the gradient of loss L_{en} with respect to the level representation of predicted curve ϕ, and it will be used in back propagation for training.

2.3 Efficient Computation for Loss Function and the Backward Gradient

In order to compute the loss function (5) and gradient (7) efficiently in CNN, we reformulate them by Fast Fourier Transform which reduces the computational complexity from $O(N^2)$ to $O(N \log N)$.

Assume the Fourier transform of $\nabla (G_t + \alpha H(\phi))$ in Eq. (5) is d_{mn}, where m, n are the frequencies in Fourier space. It can be calculated that out the fourier transform of $\frac{1}{R} = \frac{1}{\sqrt{x^2 + y^2}}$ is $\widehat{\frac{1}{R}} = \frac{1}{2\pi \sqrt{m^2 + n^2}}$. Therefore, by Parseval's identity, the loss function L_{en} can be expressed in the Fourier space as

$$L_{en} = \sum_{m,n} \sqrt{m^2 + n^2} \cdot |d_{mn}|^2. \tag{8}$$

From Eq. (7), the Fourier transform of the gradient of L_{en} with respect to the output ϕ is

$$\widehat{\frac{\partial L_{en}}{\partial \phi}} = \frac{\sqrt{m^2 + n^2}}{2} d_{mn}. \tag{9}$$

According to this equation, we obtain the gradient for back propagation by inverse Fourier transform

$$\frac{\partial L_{en}}{\partial \phi} = \mathcal{F}^{-1} \left(\frac{\sqrt{m^2 + n^2}}{2} d_{mn} \right) \tag{10}$$

2.4 Discussion on Connectivity and Fast Convergence Due to the Strong Long-Range Attractive Interaction

The elastic interaction between two curves γ_1 and γ_2 is strongly attractive when the two curves have opposite orientations, as can be seen from the interaction energy given by the last term in Eq. (3). When the moving curve γ_2 (the predicted boundary) is set to have an opposite orientation with that of the object boundary γ_1 (ground truth), the moving curve will be attracted to the object boundary to minimize the total energy in Eq. (3), see Fig. 1(a); and when the two curves coincide, the energy minimum state is reached and the object is identified perfectly by the moving curve.

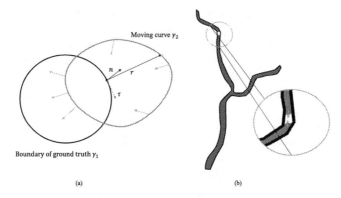

Moving curve γ_2

Boundary of ground truth γ_1

(a)   (b)

Fig. 1. (a) Elastic interaction between the moving curve (the predicted boundary) γ_2 and the ground truth (object boundary) γ_1. Arrows on the moving curve γ_2 show schematically the directions of the interaction force acting on the moving curve γ_2. (b) Schematic illustration of recombination of a disconnected moving curve under elastic interaction in vessel segmentation. The black contour represents the true vessel, and the blue region represents the prediction. The boundaries of the disconnected parts of the prediction will be attracted to each other and recombine under the elastic interaction. Red arrows show the directions of the interaction force. (Color figure online)

This interaction between two curves is long-range because the energy density is inversely proportional to the distance between two respective points on them, which decays very slowly as the distance approaches to infinity, see the last term in Eq. (3).

It can be shown that near a curve γ_1, the interaction force experienced by a point on another curve γ_2 given in Eq. (4) has the asymptotic property [5,21]

$$f \sim \frac{1}{r}, \tag{11}$$

where r is the distance from the point on curve γ_2 to the curve γ_1. Therefore, the elastic interaction provides a strong attractive force to recombine a disconnected moving curve. See a schematic illustration in vessel segmentation in Fig. 1(b). (Here γ_1 and γ_2 are the two branches of the moving curve.)

Moreover, the force generated by the moving curve on itself is proportional to $\kappa \log \frac{1}{\beta}$, where κ is the curvature of the curve, and β is the half width of the smooth Heaviside function $H(\cdot)$ [5,21]. This self-force has the effect to smooth the moving curve.

3   Experiment

3.1   Dataset

DRIVE: The Digital Retinal Images for Vessel Extraction (DRIVE) dataset [19] is provided by a diabetic retinopathy screening program in the Netherlands. This dataset includes 40 images ($3 \times 565 \times 584$ pixels) which are divided into a training set and test set, both containing 20 images and the corresponding ground truth. In our experiment, we split 5 images from training set as validation set. We train the DNN for vessel segmentation on 15 training data and evaluate our algorithm with 20 test images.

STARE: STARE dataset [6,7] consists of 20 color retinal images with size 700×605 pixels. 15 images were used for training and the remaining were used for validation. The hand labeled ground truth are provided for all images in this dataset.

CHASEDB1: This dataset [4] includes 30 color images with size 999×960 pixels. We split 5 images for validation, 25 images for training. The ground truth is provided for each image.

3.2 Implementation Details

Data Preprocessing: Since the retinal images are low contrast usually, we selected the green channels of images for training because the green channels have higher contrast than the red and blue channels. Then all values in images are normalized into $[0, 1]$.

Architecture and Training: In our experiment, we employed U-Net [17] as the end-to-end convolutional neural network architecture on our experiment. Based on this architecture, we trained our model 50 epochs with a batch size equal to 6 on training dataset. Adam optimizer was used to optimize this model with learning rate of 0.001. For our elastic interaction loss function in Eq. (5), we set hyperparameter $\alpha = 0.35$, and $\beta = 0.25$ in the Hardtanh (smoothing Heaviside) function. We implemented our model based on Pytorch [15] and ran all the experiments by the machine equipped with an TESLA P100 with 16 GBs of memory.

Evaluation Metrics: To evaluate the performance of segmentation, sensitivity, specificity, f1 score and AUC (the area under the receiver operating characteristics curve) were calculated.

3.3 Results

Quantitative Evaluation: We evaluated our model with the elastic interaction-based loss function (EL) on three datasets comparing to models with cross entropy loss function (CE), the dice coefficient loss (DICE), active contour loss (AC) [3] and surface loss [9]. The quantitative results of our proposed loss on three datasets are shown in Table 1. The experimental results show that our proposed loss function has better performance than other loss functions by achieving highest Sensitivity, Specificity, F1 scores and AUC on DRIVE and STARE, highest AUC and Specificity on CHASEDB1. We show the practical running time of the above-mentioned models in supplementary material.

Qualitative Evaluation: Figure 2 shows the qualitative results of different loss functions. From Fig. 2, we can see that the results under the proposed loss outperform other loss functions because our method can segment the much more details of vessel among all of the mentioned loss functions. Specifically, in the first row of Fig. 2, the result

Table 1. Results of the proposed elastic loss function (EL) and other loss functions on DRIVE, STARE and CHASEB1. Sen, Spec, F1 score, AUC in the table are Sensitivity, Specificity, F1 score and the area under the receiver operating characteristics curve, respectively.

Dataset	Method	Sen	Spec	F1 score	AUC
DRIVE	CE	0.9667	0.7721	0.8025	0.8694
	DICE	0.9615	0.7287	0.7658	0.8451
	AC [3]	0.9647	0.7682	0.7921	0.8664
	SL [9]	0.9660	0.7940	0.8043	0.8800
	Proposed EL	**0.9664**	**0.8067**	**0.8093**	**0.8866**
STARE	CE	0.9564	0.7296	0.7214	0.8430
	DICE	0.9403	0.6588	0.6212	0.7996
	AC [3]	0.9419	0.6461	0.6144	0.7940
	SL [9]	0.9540	0.7434	0.7146	0.8487
	Proposed EL	**0.9576**	**0.7449**	**0.7304**	**0.8513**
CHASEDB1	CE	0.9526	0.8408	0.8245	0.8967
	DICE	0.9276	0.7243	0.7186	0.8259
	AC [3]	0.9506	0.8215	0.8145	0.8861
	SL [9]	**0.9545**	0.8207	**0.8258**	0.8876
	Proposed EL	0.9526	**0.8428**	0.8248	**0.8977**

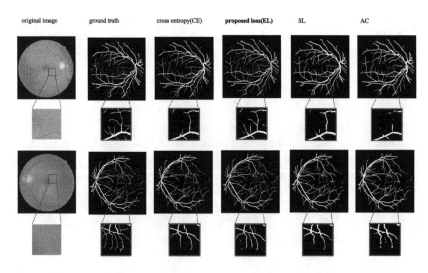

Fig. 2. The example test results obtained by our proposed loss and other loss functions. From left to right, original images, ground truth, segmentation result by cross entropy (CE), our proposed loss (EL), surface loss (SL), active contour loss (AC). (Color figure online)

under the supervision of cross entropy can not extract the thin and long vessel within red box and the prediction is disconnected, thus this segmentation lost a lot of details. While in the prediction from our proposed loss (EL), we can see that it segments the full vessels successfully and the predicted vessels are connected. Therefore, we conclude that the elastic interaction loss function has better performance than other three loss functions in extracting details of images (especially for thin and long structures). Same for the second row.

4 Conclusions and Discussion

In this paper, we propose a new elastic interaction-based loss function that can connect the whole segmented boundary strongly, thus it has great advantages in the segmentation of details of images in medical image datasets. Experimental results show that the proposed loss function indeed enhances the ability of CNN to segment medical images with complex structures and is able to achieve better performance comparing to the commonly used loss functions and other energy functional based loss functions. We would like to remark that the proposed loss function is developed to detect the details of long, thin structures such as vessels in medical images. When it applies to general images without these structures, the proposed method may not necessarily have obvious advantages.

Acknowledgement. This work was supported by The Hong Kong University of Science and Technology IEG19SC04.

References

1. Chan, T.F., Shen, J., Vese, L.: Variational PDE models in image processing. Notices AMS **50**(1), 14–26 (2003)
2. Chan, T.F., Vese, L.A.: Active contours without edges. IEEE Trans. Image Process. **10**(2), 266–277 (2001)
3. Chen, X., Williams, B.M., Vallabhaneni, S.R., Czanner, G., Williams, R., Zheng, Y.: Learning active contour models for medical image segmentation. In: Proceedings of the IEEE Conference on Computer Vision and Pattern Recognition, pp. 11632–11640 (2019)
4. Fraz, M.M., et al.: An ensemble classification-based approach applied to retinal blood vessel segmentation. IEEE Trans. Biomed. Eng. **59**(9), 2538–2548 (2012)
5. Hirth, J.P.: Theory of Dislocations, 2nd edn. Krieger Pub. Co., Malabar (1992)
6. Hoover, A., Kouznetsova, V., Goldbaum, M.: Locating blood vessels in retinal images by piecewise threshold probing of a matched filter response. IEEE Trans. Med. Imaging **19**(3), 203–210 (2000)
7. Hoover, A., Goldbaum, M.: Locating the optic nerve in a retinal image using the fuzzy convergence of the blood vessels. IEEE Trans. Med. Imaging **22**(8), 951–958 (2003)
8. Kass, M., Witkin, A., Terzopoulos, D.: Snakes: active contour models. Int. J. Comput. Vision **1**(4), 321–331 (1988). https://doi.org/10.1007/BF00133570
9. Kervadec, H., Bouchtiba, J., Desrosiers, C., Granger, E., Dolz, J., Ayed, I.B.: Boundary loss for highly unbalanced segmentation. arXiv preprint arXiv:1812.07032 (2018)
10. Kim, B., Ye, J.C.: Mumford-Shah loss functional for image segmentation with deep learning. IEEE Trans. Image Process. **29**, 1856–1866 (2019)

11. Litjens, G., et al.: A survey on deep learning in medical image analysis. Med. Image Anal. **42**, 60–88 (2017)
12. Milletari, F., Navab, N., Ahmadi, S.A.: V-Net: fully convolutional neural networks for volumetric medical image segmentation. In: 2016 Fourth International Conference on 3D Vision (3DV), pp. 565–571. IEEE (2016)
13. Mumford, D., Shah, J.: Optimal approximations by piecewise smooth functions and associated variational problems. Commun. Pure Appl. Math. **42**(5), 577–685 (1989)
14. Osher, S., Sethian, J.A.: Fronts propagating with curvature-dependent speed: algorithms based on Hamilton-Jacobi formulations. J. Comput. Phys. **79**(1), 12–49 (1988)
15. Paszke, A., et al.: Automatic differentiation in pytorch. In: NIPS (2017)
16. Pham, D.L., Xu, C., Prince, J.L.: Current methods in medical image segmentation. Annu. Rev. Biomed. Eng. **2**(1), 315–337 (2000)
17. Ronneberger, O., Fischer, P., Brox, T.: U-Net: convolutional networks for biomedical image segmentation. In: Navab, N., Hornegger, J., Wells, W.M., Frangi, A.F. (eds.) MICCAI 2015. LNCS, vol. 9351, pp. 234–241. Springer, Cham (2015). https://doi.org/10.1007/978-3-319-24574-4_28
18. Shen, D., Wu, G., Suk, H.I.: Deep learning in medical image analysis. Annu. Rev. Biomed. Eng. **19**, 221–248 (2017)
19. Staal, J., Abràmoff, M.D., Niemeijer, M., Viergever, M.A., Ginneken, B.V.: Ridge-based vessel segmentation in color images of the retina. IEEE Trans. Med. Imaging **23**(4), 501–509 (2004)
20. Xiang, Y., Chung, A.C., Ye, J.: A new active contour method based on elastic interaction. In: 2005 IEEE Computer Society Conference on Computer Vision and Pattern Recognition (CVPR 2005), vol. 1, pp. 452–457. IEEE (2005)
21. Xiang, Y., Chung, A.C., Ye, J.: An active contour model for image segmentation based on elastic interaction. J. Comput. Phys. **219**(1), 455–476 (2006)
22. Xu, C., Prince, J.L.: Snakes, shapes, and gradient vector flow. IEEE Trans. Image Process. **7**(3), 359–369 (1998)
23. Zhao, F., Xie, X.: An overview of interactive medical image segmentation. Ann. BMVA **2013**(7), 1–22 (2013)

Retinal Image Segmentation with a Structure-Texture Demixing Network

Shihao Zhang[1,2], Huazhu Fu[3], Yanwu Xu[4(✉)], Yanxia Liu[1],
and Mingkui Tan[1(✉)]

[1] South China University of Technology, Guangzhou, China
mingkuitan@scut.edu.cn
[2] Pazhou Lab, Guangzhou, China
[3] Inception Institute of Artificial Intelligence, Abu Dhabi, UAE
[4] Cixi Institute of Biomedical Engineering, Ningbo Institute of Materials Technology
and Engineering, Chinese Academy of Sciences, Ningbo, China
ywxu@ieee.org

Abstract. Retinal image segmentation plays an important role in automatic disease diagnosis. This task is very challenging because the complex structure and texture information are mixed in a retinal image, and distinguishing the information is difficult. Existing methods handle texture and structure jointly, which may lead biased models toward recognizing textures and thus results in inferior segmentation performance. To address it, we propose a segmentation strategy that seeks to separate structure and texture components and significantly improve the performance. To this end, we design a structure-texture demixing network (STD-Net) that can process structures and textures differently and better. Extensive experiments on two retinal image segmentation tasks (*i.e.*, blood vessel segmentation, optic disc and cup segmentation) demonstrate the effectiveness of the proposed method.

Keywords: Retinal image · Optic disc and cup · Vessel segmentation

1 Introduction

Retinal image segmentation is important in automatic disease diagnosis [1,2]. For example, retinal vessels are correlated to the severity of diabetic retinopathy, which is a cause of blindness globally [1]. Moreover, the optic disc (OD) and optic cup (OC) are used to calculate the cup-to-disc-ratio (CDR), which is the main indicator for glaucoma diagnosis [2]. However, retinal image segmentation is often extremely challenging because retinal images often contain complex texture and structure information, which is different from general natural images.

Recently, deep neural networks (DNNs) have shown a strong ability in image segmentation with remarkable improvements [3–7]. However, existing methods are strongly biased toward recognizing textures rather than structures [8] since they handle the two types of information jointly. As a result, tiny structures that

© Springer Nature Switzerland AG 2020
A. L. Martel et al. (Eds.): MICCAI 2020, LNCS 12265, pp. 765–774, 2020.
https://doi.org/10.1007/978-3-030-59722-1_74

are very similar to textures will be misclassified. Therefore, separately processing the structure and texture information in a retinal image is necessary. Structure-texture demixing is an essential operation in image processing that has been extensively utilized in many computer vision tasks, including image enhancement [9], optical flow [10] and image stylization [11]. However, the application of a structure-texture demixing operation in retinal image segmentation remains an open question.

Existing structure-texture demixing methods cannot adequately distinguish the boundary structures from textures, because they may have similar statistical properties [12,13]. The texture component will inevitably contain structure information. Therefore, the structure information is not fully exploited by these methods, which produces inferior segmentation results.

In this paper, we propose a **Structure-Texture Demixing Network (STD-Net)** that decomposes the image into a structure component and a texture component. Note that, the structure and texture components have different properties and need to be treated differently. We exploit two types of networks to treat them differently. The structure component mainly contains smooth structures, while the texture component mainly contains high-frequency information. Thus the structure component is suitable for processing by representative networks, and the texture component is easily overfitted, a shallower network is a better choice. We conduct extensive experiments for two tasks: vessel segmentation using the DRIVE dataset, and optic disc and cup segmentation using the ORIGA and REFUGE datasets. The results demonstrate the effectiveness of our method.

The contributions of this paper are listed as follows: 1) We propose a segmentation strategy that demix a retinal image into structure and texture components. This strategy can be applied to any segmentation framework to improve its performance. 2) We design a structure-texture demixing network (STD-Net) that can process structures and textures differently and better. 3) Extensive experiments for two retinal image segmentation tasks demonstrate the effectiveness of the proposed strategy.

2 Methodology

We illustrate the overview of our proposed STD-Net in Fig. 1. STD-Net decomposes an input image to a structure component and texture component. The structure component corresponding to the main object (smoothed part), and the texture component contains fine-grained details (almost periodic textures, noise). The segmented object's primary information is contained in the structure component. We choose M-Net [14] to process the structure component. The segmented object's detailed information is contained in the texture component, such as the boundaries. We propose a texture block to process the texture component. Details are provided in the following section.

2.1 Structure-Texture Demixing Loss Function

The structure-texture demixing module decomposes an image into a structure component and texture component by two types of loss functions, namely the

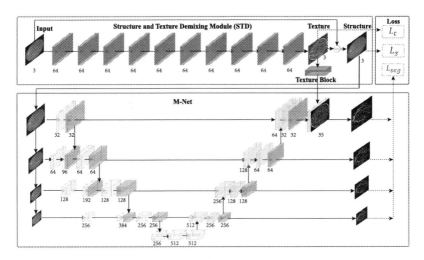

Fig. 1. Overview of the proposed STD-Net. Built on the M-Net [14] as a backbone, STD-Net decomposes the input image into structure and texture components. The structure component serves as the input of M-Net to recover the boundary structures using the texture information extracted by a *texture block* (refer to Fig. 2). The operator ⊖ represents the minus operation. The functions $\mathcal{L}_t$, $\mathcal{L}_s$ and $\mathcal{L}_{seg}$ represent the texture loss, structure loss, and segmentation loss, respectively.

structure loss and the texture loss. The structure and the texture loss demix images by penalizing structures and textures differently. The different penalizes are based on statistical priors that structures and textures receive different penalty under some loss functions.

Given the input image $\mathbf{I}$, the structure-texture demixing (STD) module aims to decompose $\mathbf{I}$ into two components: $\mathbf{I} \to \mathbf{S} + \mathbf{T}$, where $\mathbf{S}$ and $\mathbf{T}$ represent the structure component and texture component, respectively. This decomposition can be formulated as the following optimization problem:

$$\min_{\mathbf{S},\mathbf{T}} \lambda \mathcal{L}_s(\mathbf{S}) + \mathcal{L}_t(\mathbf{T}), \qquad (1)$$

where $\mathbf{S} = \mathbf{I} - \mathbf{T}$, $\mathcal{L}_s$ is the structure loss function and $\mathcal{L}_t$ is the texture loss function, which leads $\mathbf{S}$ and $\mathbf{T}$ to different statistical properties, that is, for the structure component $\mathcal{L}_s(\mathbf{S}) \ll \mathcal{L}_t(\mathbf{S})$ and for the texture component $\mathcal{L}_s(\mathbf{T}) \gg \mathcal{L}_t(\mathbf{T})$. The constant λ is the balancing parameter.

The total variation (TV) [15] is one of the most popular structure priors; we exploit it as the structure loss function $\mathcal{L}_s$:

$$\mathcal{L}_s(\mathbf{S}) = \sum_{i,j} ||(\nabla \mathbf{S})_{i,j}||_2, \qquad (2)$$

where ∇ is the spatial gradient operator. Using the TV, various demixing methods have been proposed, e.g., TV-$\triangle^{-1}$ [16], TV-L2 [15], and TV-L1 [17]. The

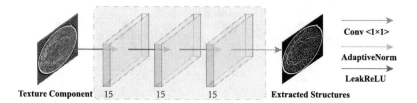

Fig. 2. Architecture of the texture block. The texture block is utilized to recover the falsely demixed structures and reduce the texture influence.

L1-norm is more suitable for structure-texture demixing [16]. Specifically, the texture loss function can be defined as follows:

$$\mathcal{L}_t(\mathbf{T}) = ||\mathbf{T}||_1. \tag{3}$$

We employ the cross-entropy function $\mathcal{L}_{seg}$ as the segmentation loss function. The final loss function $\mathcal{L}_{total}$ is defined as:

$$\begin{aligned}
\mathcal{L}_{total}(\mathbf{I}, \mathbf{T}, \mathbf{R}) &= \mathcal{L}_{seg}(\mathbf{R}) + \mu(\mathcal{L}_t(\mathbf{T}) + \lambda\mathcal{L}_s(\mathbf{S})) \\
&= \mathcal{L}_{seg}(\mathbf{R}) + \mu(\mathcal{L}_t(\mathbf{T}) + \lambda\mathcal{L}_s(\mathbf{I} - \mathbf{T})),
\end{aligned} \tag{4}$$

where μ and λ are trade-off parameters, and $\mathbf{R}$ is the segmentation result.

2.2   Structure-Texture Demixing Module

We show the architecture of the proposed Structure-Texture Demixing (STD) Module in Fig. 1. First, we apply STD to extract the texture component. Second, we obtain the structure component by subtracting the texture component from the input image. In this way, we confirm that $\mathbf{I} = \mathbf{S} + \mathbf{T}$. The STD consists of 10 convolutional layers with Leak ReLU to extract texture features. The extracted texture features are also serves as the input of the texture block.

Texture Block: The texture block is a component of STD. Because some structures, especially the boundary structures, may receive similar penalties from the structure loss and texture loss, they may be misclassified as the texture components. While these structures in texture component are important for segmentation, the textures and noises will affect the segmentation performance. To address it, the texture block is designed to extract boundaries and reduce the influence of textures and noises. Considering the limited amount of information in the texture component and a deep model may overfit, we design a very shallow network as the texture block. Figure 2 shows the architecture of the texture block, which contains two convolution layers, an adaptive normalization layer [18] and a leaky ReLU layer.

Figure 3 shows the visualization of the demixed structure, demixed texture, and E-structures extracted by the texture block. To help observe more clearly, we only display the green (G) channels (RGB image). The extracted structure component mainly contains smooth structures and the texture component

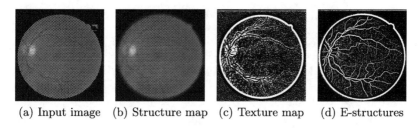

(a) Input image   (b) Structure map   (c) Texture map   (d) E-structures

Fig. 3. Visualization of components in STD. Comparing (a) and (b), using texture loss, the demixed structure component maintains most of the smooth structure information and filters out many high-frequency texture noises. As shown in (c), the texture component mainly contains high-frequency information, which is a mixture of textures and boundary structures. Comparing (c) and (d), the texture block clearly helps to extract structures in the texture component, while filtering out high-frequency textures.

mainly contains high-frequency information. With the proposed texture block, we strengthen the structure information in the texture component and reduce the high-frequency textures.

3   Experiments

In this paper, we evaluate our method in vessel segmentation and optic disc/cup segmentation from retina fundus images. We train our STD-Net using Adam with a learning rate of 0.001. The batch size is set to 2. The balancing parameters λ and μ are set to 1 and 0.001 respectively.

3.1   Vessel Segmentation on DRIVE

We conduct vessel segmentation experiments with DRIVE to evaluate the performance of our proposed STD-Net. The Digital Retinal Images for Vessel Extraction (DRIVE) dataset [19] contains 40 colored fundus images (20 training images and 20 testing images), which are obtained from a diabetic retinopathy screening program in the Netherlands. We resize the original images to 512×512 as inputs. Following the previous work [20], we employ Specificity (Spe), Sensitivity (Sen), Accuracy (Acc), intersection-over-union(IOU), and Area Under ROC (AUC) as measurements.

We compare our STD-Net with several state-of-the-art methods, including Li [21], Liskowski [22], MS-NFN [23],U-Net [3], M-Net [14], and AG-Net [20]. Li [21] redefines the segmentation task as cross-modality data transformation from a retinal image to a vessel map, and outputs the label map of all pixels instead of a single label of the center pixel. Liskowski [22] trains a deep neural network with samples that were preprocessed with global contrast normalization and zero-phase whitening and augmented using geometric transformations and gamma corrections. MS-NFN [23] generates multi-scale feature maps with an 'up-pool' submodel and a 'pool-up' submodel. U-Net [3] applies a contracting

Table 1. Quantitative comparison of segmentation results with DRIVE

Method	Acc	AUC	Sen	Spe	IOU
Li [21]	0.9527	0.9738	0.7569	0.9816	–
Liskowski [22]	0.9535	0.9790	0.7811	0.9807	–
MS-NFN [23]	0.9567	0.9807	0.7844	0.9819	–
AG-Net [20]	0.9692	0.9856	0.8100	0.9848	0.6965
U-Net [3]	0.9681	0.9836	0.7897	0.9854	0.6834
M-Net [14]	0.9674	0.9829	0.7680	**0.9868**	0.6726
STD-Net	**0.9695**	**0.9863**	**0.8151**	0.9846	**0.6995**

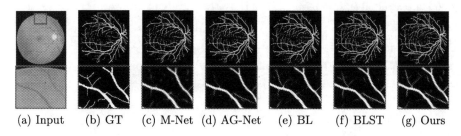

(a) Input   (b) GT   (c) M-Net   (d) AG-Net   (e) BL   (f) BLST   (g) Ours

Fig. 4. Example results for DRIVE. M-Net, AG-Net, and BL disregard some edge structures, which are very similar to textures. Conversely, by decomposing structures and textures, BLST gains better discrimination power and detects more tiny structures. Comparing (f) and (g), when adding the texture block, more tiny boundary structures are detected.

path to capture context and a symmetric expanding path to enable precise localization. M-Net [14] introduces multi-input and multi-output to learn hierarchical representations. AG-Net [20] proposes a structure sensitive expanding path and incorporates it into M-Net.

Table 1 shows the performances of different methods for DRIVE. Based on the results, for the four metrics AUC, Acc, Sen, and IOU, the proposed STD-Net achieves the highest value. STD-Net outperforms the backbone M-Net by 0.0021, 0.0034, 0.0471 and 0.0269 in terms of Acc, AUC, Sen, and IOU, respectively. Note that the proposed STD-Net achieves a much higher Sen score than M-Net, which shows that our structure-texture demixing mechanism improves the structure detection ability of models.

We remove the texture block, structure loss $\mathcal{L}_s$, and texture loss $\mathcal{L}_t$ from STD-Net and name the baseline model as **BL**. The model **BLST** is formed by adding the structure-texture loss into BL. Figure 4 shows a test example, including the ground truth vessel (GT) and segmentation results obtained by M-Net, AG-Net, BL, BLST, and the proposed STD-Net. The experimental results of BL and BLST are shown in Table 3.

Table 2. Comparisons of different methods with ORIGA and REFUGE

	ORIGA			REFUGE		
Method	OE_{disc}	OE_{cup}	OE_{total}	OE_{disc}	OE_{cup}	OE_{total}
ASM [24]	0.148	0.313	0.461	–	–	–
SP [25]	0.102	0.264	0.366	–	–	–
LRR [26]	–	0.244	–	–	–	–
U-Net [3]	0.115	0.287	0.402	0.171	0.257	0.428
AG-Net [20]	**0.061**	0.212	0.273	0.178	0.220	0.398
M-Net [14]	0.071	0.230	0.301	0.204	0.231	0.435
STD-Net	0.063	**0.208**	**0.271**	**0.168**	**0.217**	**0.385**

3.2   Optic Disc/Cup Segmentation on ORIGA

Optic Disc/Cup Segmentation is another important retinal segmentation task. In this experiment, we employ the ORIGA dataset, which contains 650 fundus images with 168 glaucomatous eyes and 482 normal eyes. The 650 images are divided into 325 training images and 325 testing images (including 73 glaucoma cases and 95 glaucoma cases, respectively). We crop the OD area and resize it to 256×256 as the input. We compare STD-Net with several state-of-the-art methods, including ASM [24], Superpixel [25], LRR [26], U-Net [3], M-Net [14], and AG-Net [20]. The ASM [24] employs the circular hough transform initialization to segmentation. The superpixel method [25] utilizes superpixel classification to detect the OD and OC boundaries. The method in LRR [26] obtains satisfactory results but only focuses on OC segmentation. AG-Net [20] also strengthens the structure information but is easily influenced by the textures.

Following the setting in [20], we localize the disc center with a pre-trained LinkNet [27] and then enlarge 50 pixels of bounding-boxes in up, down, right and left directions to crop the OD patch as the input image. The polar transformation is also exploited to improve the segmentation performance. We employ overlapping error (OE) as the evaluation metric, which is defined as $OE = 1 - \frac{A_{GT} \bigcap A_{SR}}{A_{GT} \bigcup A_{SR}}$. A_{GT} and A_{SR} denote the ground truth area and segmented mask, respectively. In particular, OE_{disc} and OE_{cup} are the overlapping error of OD and OE. OE_{total} is the sum of OE_{disc} and OE_{cup}.

Table 2 shows the segmentation results. Our method outperforms all the state-of-the-art OC segmentation algorithms, which demonstrates the effectiveness of our model. For OD segmentation, the proposed STD-Net is slightly lower than AG-Net, but STD-Net achieves the best performance on OC segmentation and better performance when considering OC and OD segmentation. Our STD-Net performs much better than the original M-Net, which further demonstrates that our structure-texture demixing method is beneficial for the segmentation performance.

We obtained similar results with the REFUGE dataset [28], which are shown in Table 2. The training set and validation set of REFUGE have distinct appearances due to different shooting equipment, which requires a high generalization

Table 3. Ablation study with DRIVE and ORIGA

	DRIVE					ORIGA		
Method	Acc	AUC	Sen	Spe	IOU	OE_{disc}	OE_{cup}	OE_{total}
BL	0.9678	0.9829	0.7776	**0.9864**	0.6785	0.065	0.217	0.282
BL+$\mathcal{L}_s$	0.9684	0.9842	**0.8236**	0.9827	0.6948	**0.063**	0.211	0.274
BL+$\mathcal{L}_t$	0.9687	0.9841	0.8167	0.9837	0.6951	0.064	0.213	0.277
BLST	0.9691	0.9859	0.8201	0.9837	0.6984	**0.063**	0.210	0.273
STD-Net	**0.9695**	**0.9863**	0.8151	0.9846	**0.6995**	**0.063**	**0.208**	**0.271**

ability to reduce overfitting. Therefore, the results with REFUGE can better demonstrate the ability of structural texture decomposition.

3.3   Ablation Study

We conduct an ablation investigation to further verify the effectiveness of the structure-texture demixing mechanism and texture block. The results for DRIVE are presented in Table 3. We note several interesting observations. First, when BL considers the structure loss $\mathcal{L}_s$ or the texture loss $\mathcal{L}_t$, the results are improved with metrics other than Spe. With the structure loss, BL achieved the highest Sen score, which shows that more vessel structures are detected. Second, when BL considers both the structure loss $\mathcal{L}_s$ and the texture loss $\mathcal{L}_t$, it achieves higher Acc, AUC and IOU scores, which demonstrates the superiority of the structure-texture demixing strategy. Last, when BL further incorporates the texture block (STD-Net), it achieves the highest scores for Acc, AUC, and IOU. This finding demonstrates the effectiveness of the texture block. As shown in Table 3, similar results are obtained for ORIGA.

4   Conclusion

In this paper, we have proposed a trainable structure-texture demixing network (STD-Net) to decompose an image into a structure component and texture component and separately process them. In this way, the segmentation model focuses more on structure information and reduces the influence of texture information. We have also proposed a texture block to further extract the structural information from the texture component, which substantially improves the segmentation results. Extensive experiments for two retinal image segmentation tasks (*i.e.*, blood vessel segmentation, optic disc and cup segmentation) demonstrate the effectiveness of our proposed method.

Acknowledgments. This work was partially supported by National Natural Science Foundation of China (NSFC) 61836003 (key project), Program for Guangdong Introducing Innovative and Enterpreneurial Teams 2017ZT07X183, Guangdong Provincial Scientific and Technological Funds under Grant 2018B010107001,

Grant 2019B010155002, Tencent AI Lab Rhino-Bird Focused Research Program (No. JR201902), Fundamental Research Funds for the Central Universities D2191240.

References

1. Jelinek, H., Cree, M.J.: Automated Image Detection of Retinal Pathology. Crc Press, Boca Raton (2009)
2. Hancox, O., Michael, D.: Optic disc size, an important consideration in the glaucoma evaluation. Clin. Eye Vis. Care **11**(2), 59–62 (1999)
3. Ronneberger, O., Fischer, P., Brox, T.: U-net: convolutional networks for biomedical image segmentation. In: International Conference on Medical Image Computing and Computer-Assisted Intervention. Springer (2015)
4. Gu, Z., Cheng, J., et al.: Ce-net: context encoder network for 2d medical image segmentation. IEEE Trans. Med. Imaging **38**(10), 2281–2292 (2019)
5. Zhang, Z., Fu, H., Dai, H., Shen, J., Pang, Y., Shao, L.: Et-net: a generic edge-attention guidance network for medical image segmentation. In: Shen, D., et al. (eds.) MICCAI 2019. LNCS, vol. 11764, pp. 442–450. Springer, Cham (2019). https://doi.org/10.1007/978-3-030-32239-7_49
6. Zhang, Y., et al.: From whole slide imaging to microscopy: deep microscopy adaptation network for histopathology cancer image classification. In: Shen, D., et al. (eds.) MICCAI 2019. LNCS, vol. 11764, pp. 360–368. Springer, Cham (2019). https://doi.org/10.1007/978-3-030-32239-7_40
7. Zhang, Y., Wei, Y., et al.: Collaborative unsupervised domain adaptation for medical image diagnosis. IEEE Trans. Image Process. **29**, 7834–7844 (2020)
8. Geirhos, R., Rubisch, P., et al.: Imagenet-trained cnns are biased towards texture; increasing shape bias improves accuracy and robustness. International Conference on Learning Representations (2019)
9. Guo, X., Li, Y., Ling, H.: Lime: low-light image enhancement via illumination map estimation. IEEE Trans. Image Process. **26**(2), 982–993 (2016)
10. Revaud, J., Weinzaepfel, P., et al.: Epicflow: edge-preserving interpolation of correspondences for optical flow. In: Proceedings of the IEEE Conference on Computer Vision and Pattern Recognition (2015)
11. Gastal, E.S., Oliveira, M.M.: Domain transform for edge-aware image and video processing. ACM SIGGRAPH 2011 papers (2011)
12. Xu, L., Yan, Q., et al.: Structure extraction from texture via relative total variation. ACM Trans. Graph. **31**(6), 1–10 (2012)
13. Kim, Y., Ham, B., Do, M.N., Sohn, K.: Structure-texture image decomposition using deep variational priors. IEEE Trans. Image Process. **28**(6), 2692–2704 (2018)
14. Fu, H., Cheng, J., et al.: Joint optic disc and cup segmentation based on multi-label deep network and polar transformation. IEEE Trans. Med. Imaging **37**(7), 1597–1605 (2018)
15. Rudin, L.I., Osher, S., Fatemi, E.: Nonlinear total variation based noise removal algorithms. Physica D **60**(1–4), 259–268 (1992)
16. Aujol, J.-F., Gilboa, G., et al.: Structure-texture image decomposition modeling, algorithms, and parameter selection. Int. J. Comput. Vis. **67**(1), 111–136 (2006). https://doi.org/10.1007/s11263-006-4331-z
17. Alliney, S.: A property of the minimum vectors of a regularizing functional defined by means of the absolute norm. IEEE Trans. Signal Process. **45**(4), 913–917 (1997)

18. Ogasawara, E., Martinez, L.C., De Oliveira, D., Zimbrão, G., Pappa, G.L., Mattoso, M.: Adaptive normalization: a novel data normalization approach for non-stationary time series. In: The 2010 International Joint Conference on Neural Networks. IEEE (2010)
19. Staal, J., Abràmoff, M.D., et al.: Ridge-based vessel segmentation in color images of the retina. IEEE Trans. Med. Imaging **23**(4), 501–509 (2004)
20. Zhang, S., et al.: Attention guided network for retinal image segmentation. In: Shen, D., et al. (eds.) MICCAI 2019. LNCS, vol. 11764, pp. 797–805. Springer, Cham (2019). https://doi.org/10.1007/978-3-030-32239-7_88
21. Li, Q., Feng, B., et al.: A cross-modality learning approach for vessel segmentation in retinal images. IEEE Trans. Med. Imaging **35**(1), 109–118 (2016)
22. Liskowski, P., Krawiec, K.: Segmenting retinal blood vessels with deep neural networks. IEEE Transactions on Medical Imaging (2016)
23. Wu, Y., Xia, Y., Song, Y., Zhang, Y., Cai, W.: Multiscale network followed network model for retinal vessel segmentation. In: Frangi, A.F., Schnabel, J.A., Davatzikos, C., Alberola-López, C., Fichtinger, G. (eds.) MICCAI 2018. LNCS, vol. 11071, pp. 119–126. Springer, Cham (2018). https://doi.org/10.1007/978-3-030-00934-2_14
24. Yin, F., Liu, J., et al.: Model-based optic nerve head segmentation on retinal fundus images. In: 2011 Annual International Conference of the IEEE Engineering in Medicine and Biology Society. IEEE (2011)
25. Cheng, J., Liu, J., et al.: Superpixel classification based optic disc and optic cup segmentation for glaucoma screening. IEEE Trans. Med. Imaging **32**(6), 1019–1032 (2013)
26. Xn, Y., et al.: Optic cup segmentation for glaucoma detection using low-rank superpixel representation. In: Golland, P., Hata, N., Barillot, C., Hornegger, J., Howe, R. (eds.) MICCAI 2014. LNCS, vol. 8673, pp. 788–795. Springer, Cham (2014). https://doi.org/10.1007/978-3-319-10404-1_98
27. Chaurasia, A., Culurciello, E.: Linknet: exploiting encoder representations for efficient semantic segmentation. In: 2017 IEEE Visual Communications and Image Processing. IEEE (2017)
28. Orlando, J.I., Fu, H., et al.: REFUGE challenge: a unified framework for evaluating automated methods for glaucoma assessment from fundus photographs. Med. Image Anal. **59**, 101570 (2020)

BEFD: Boundary Enhancement and Feature Denoising for Vessel Segmentation

Mo Zhang[1,2,3], Fei Yu[1], Jie Zhao[2], Li Zhang[2(✉)], and Quanzheng Li[4(✉)]

[1] Center for Data Science, Peking University, Beijing 100871, China
[2] Center for Data Science in Health and Medicine, Peking University,
Beijing 100871, China
zhangli_pku@pku.edu.cn
[3] Laboratory for Biomedical Image Analysis, Beijing Institute of Big Data Research,
Beijing 100871, China
[4] Center for Advanced Medical Computing and Analysis, MGH/BWH Center for
Clinical Data Science, Department of Radiology, Massachusetts General Hospital,
Harvard Medical School, Boston, MA 02115, USA
li.quanzheng@mgh.harvard.edu

Abstract. Blood vessel segmentation is crucial for many diagnostic and research applications. In recent years, CNN-based models have leaded to breakthroughs in the task of segmentation, however, such methods usually lose high-frequency information like object boundaries and subtle structures, which are vital to vessel segmentation. To tackle this issue, we propose Boundary Enhancement and Feature Denoising (BEFD) module to facilitate the network ability of extracting boundary information in semantic segmentation, which can be integrated into arbitrary encoder-decoder architecture in an end-to-end way. By introducing Sobel edge detector, the network is able to acquire additional edge prior, thus enhancing boundary in an unsupervised manner for medical image segmentation. In addition, we also utilize a denoising block to reduce the noise hidden in the low-level features. Experimental results on retinal vessel dataset and angiocarpy dataset demonstrate the superior performance of the new BEFD module.

Keywords: Boundary enhancement · Feature denoising · Vessel segmentation

1 Introduction

The precise segmentation of blood vessel plays an important role in the diagnosis of related diseases. For example, the morphological changes of retinal vessel may indicate some relevant diseases (eg. glaucoma, diabetes and hypertension), and the quantitative analysis of coronary arteries in digital subtraction angiography (DSA) is commonly used in the assessment of myocardial infarction and coronary

© Springer Nature Switzerland AG 2020
A. L. Martel et al. (Eds.): MICCAI 2020, LNCS 12265, pp. 775–785, 2020.
https://doi.org/10.1007/978-3-030-59722-1_75

atherosclerotic disease. Moreover, some pathophysiological changes of retinal vessel caused by prolonged hyperglycemia are related to the smallest vessels [2], so it is vital to extract the thin vessels. In the past decades, many automatic approaches have been proposed to segment the blood vessel, such as tracking based models [8], filtering based models [5] and deformable models [9].

Recently, deep learning based methods have significantly improved the performance of vessel segmentation. For example, Hu *et al.* [11] presented a multi-scale convolutional neural network (CNN) with an improved cross-entropy loss for vessel segmentation, outperforming the traditional unsupervised algorithms. However, although CNN has tremendous power to extract high-level representative features, it is inevitable that spatial information is partly lost in the downsampling layers. Further, the lost information mainly belongs to the high-frequency components in the image, such as object boundary which contains essential cues for localization. This is consistent with the observation in [24], where they found that most mispredicted pixels by UNet are located in the edges of blood vessels. Therefore, it is very necessary to strengthen the network capability to capture edge information in vessel segmentation.

There have been presented a variety of related methods, which can be roughly divided into four categories: 1) Many works reused the low-level features with rich spatial information by a "skip connection" structure to maintain more edge details, such as SegNet [3], UNet [18] and DeeplabV3+ [7]; 2) Some approaches employed post-processing techniques (eg. conditional random fields (CRFs) [6], active contour models [19]) to refine the segmentation results; 3) Some researchers exploited an additional branch for edge detection to enhance the segmentation task, which can be regarded as a multi-task framework [10,17,27]; 4) Some studies proposed a boundary-aware loss function [25] or labeled the object contours as an independent class [24], thus paying more attention to the border pixels.

In this paper, we provide a novel solution to boost the accurate delineation of borders in blood vessel segmentation, which serves as an insertable module called Boundary Enhancement and Feature Denoising (BEFD). By applying the traditional edge detection operator to the raw image, BEFD can gain an edge attention map in an unsupervised way. This pixel-wise attention map assigns higher weights to the pixels around the object boundary, which would be multiplied (element-wise product) by certain intermediate feature maps in the encoder part. In this way, the prior knowledge about vascular edges are transferred to the neural networks, enhancing the boundary information in semantic segmentation. In addition, in order to avoid amplifying noise at the same time, BEFD also conducts feature denoising in the process of skip connection via a denoising block.

We evaluate the proposed BEFD module on both retinal vessel images and angiocarpy images. The experimental results demonstrate the effectiveness of the BEFD module. Compared to existing state-of-the-art models for vessel segmentation, UNet integrated with BEFD module achieves the highest score in accuracy, AUC, sensitivity and specificity on DRIVE dataset.

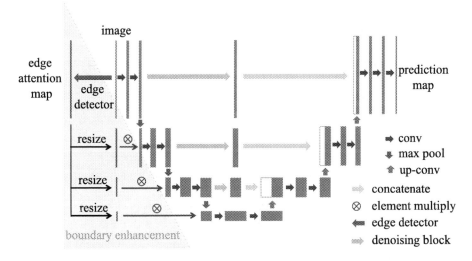

Fig. 1. Architecture of BEFD-UNet. It consists of three parts: 1) the basic UNet; 2) the boundary enhancement (BE) part in the gray triangle, which employs an edge detector to provide boundary localization for the encoder path of UNet; 3) the feature denoising (FD) part, formed by three denoising blocks in the phase of skip connection.

The contributions of this work are summarized as follows:

1) We propose an innovative module (BEFD) to boost boundary feature extraction in semantic segmentation, which can be easily incorporated into any encoder-decoder framework in an end-to-end manner. Moreover, the proposed BEFD module applies the unsupervised edge detector to provide edge prior knowledge for CNNs in medical image segmentation.
2) We use the denoising block to eliminate the noise existing in the low-level feature maps, preserving the indeed required spatial information for segmentation.
3) Our approach obtains remarkable performance for blood vessel segmentation, actually, it can also be easily generalized to deal with other segmentation tasks.

2   Method

2.1   The Architecture of BEFD-UNet

In this section, we choose U-Net as baseline, to elaborate how the BEFD module can fit into it. The incorporated model is named as BEFD-UNet, and its structure is illustrated in Fig. 1. The baseline UNet consists of an encoder path and a decoder path. In the encoder path, each step includes two 3×3 convolutions followed by a 2×2 max pooling with stride of 2 for downsampling, which doubles the number of feature map channels. In the decoder path, each layer contains a deconvolution for upsampling followed by two 3×3 convolutions, where the channel number is halved. Additionally, the skip connection between encoder and decoder combines the low-level features in the shallow layers with the high-level abstract features, preserving more spatial information for better localization.

As for the BEFD module, it is composed of two parts: the Boundary Enhancement (BE) part and Feature Denoising (FD) part. In the BE part, edge detection is firstly conducted on the raw image to get a pixel-wise edge attention map, whose values indicate the importance of the corresponding pixels, in this setting, edge pixels are assigned with greater weights. Then, this attention map is incorporated into the last three layers in the encoder path via element-multiplication, before which the attention map has been resized to be consistent with the corresponding feature maps by bilinear interpolation. Benefiting from the edge prior produced by the unsupervised edge detection, the boundary information is enhanced with little extra computation.

In the FD part, the skip connection structure is modified by adding a denoising block before the simple concatenation. The low-level features in the encoder path contain not only rich spatial details, but also background noise which is undesirable for the decoder path, so it is necessary to make feature denoising in the process of skip connection. On the other hand, edge detector may misidentify image noise as boundary, thus enhancing the unexpected noise simultaneously, in this view, feature denoising is also indispensable. Furthermore, the denoising block [23] is a typical method to restrain the noise in the intermediate feature maps, so we apply it to the low-level features. In addition, more details about the edge detection and feature denoising are described in the next sections.

2.2   Unsupervised Edge Detection

Edge detection aims to locate the object boundaries in the image, which is an important step towards extracting image features. In this paper, we utilize Sobel edge detector [13] to obtain this goal. Sobel edge detector calculates the first derivatives of the raw image for the horizontal direction and vertical direction separately, then combines these two components together via the absolute magnitude of gradient. It can be expressed as follow:

$$G_x = \begin{bmatrix} -1 & 0 & 1 \\ -2 & 0 & 2 \\ -1 & 0 & 1 \end{bmatrix} * I, G_y = \begin{bmatrix} -1 & -2 & -1 \\ 0 & 0 & 0 \\ 1 & 2 & 1 \end{bmatrix} * I, G = \sqrt{G_x^2 + G_y^2} \qquad (1)$$

where I is the raw image, $*$ denotes the convolution operator, G_x, G_y are the gradient components of x axis and y axis respectively, and G denotes the Sobel edge map. In order to obtain the final edge attention map which emphasizes the boundary pixels in a suitable and adjustable way, we apply the thresholding method as well as linear transformation to the Sobel edge map as follows:

$$G_{final}(x,y) = \begin{cases} 1, & \text{if } G(x,y) > \lambda_{max} \text{ or } < \lambda_{min} \\ (1 - \frac{G(x,y) - \lambda_{min}}{\lambda_{max} - \lambda_{min}}) \cdot \alpha + \beta, & \text{otherwise} \end{cases}$$

$$(2)$$

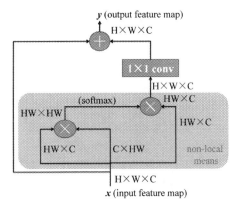

Fig. 2. Architecture of the feature denoising block [23].

Here $G(x, y)$ denotes the Sobel gradient value at pixel (x, y), and $\lambda_{min}, \lambda_{max}, \alpha, \beta$ are tunable parameters to regulate the scope of weights. Note that in the setting of $1 - \frac{G(x,y)-\lambda_{min}}{\lambda_{max}-\lambda_{min}}$, weak edges are emphasized with higher weights than the strong ones, as the key challenge in vessel segmentation is the detection of micro vessels with low contrast.

2.3 Feature Denoising

The concept of feature denoising [23] is proposed to improve adversarial robustness in image classification, based on the observation that adversarial perturbations on images result in noise in the features. At the same time, segmentation networks always make efforts to maintain more high-frequency components for sake of restoring more details (eg. skip connection in UNet [18]), providing an opportunity for the introduction of noise in the feature maps. Hence, it is also necessary to conduct feature denoising in image segmentation as we do in this work.

Non-local means [4] is widely used for the task of image denoising, which calculates a weighted mean of all locations in the image. It is defined as:

$$\mathbf{y}_i = \frac{1}{\mathcal{C}(\mathbf{x})} \sum_{\forall j} f(\mathbf{x}_i, \mathbf{x}_j) \cdot \mathbf{x}_j, \tag{3}$$

where $\mathbf{y}_i$ is the output value at location i, $\mathbf{x}_i$ is the input value at location i, and j denotes all possible positions. f is a weighting function and $\mathcal{C}(\mathbf{x})$ is a normalization factor. Following the idea of non-local means [4] and non-local neural networks [21], the work [23] presented a denoising block to make feature denoising. As shown in Fig. 2, except for the non-local means part, the denoising block also contains a 1×1 convolution and residual connection for feature fusion. In this work, we use this denoising block to eliminate the feature noise in segmentation networks, where the pairwise function f is set to dot product

$f(\mathbf{x}_i, \mathbf{x}_j) = \mathbf{x}_i^T \mathbf{x}_j$ and $\mathcal{C}(x) = N$ (N is the number of locations in $\mathbf{x}$). More information about the denoising block can be found in [21,23].

3   Experiments

To evaluate the effectiveness of the BEFD module, we compare two models: 1) the baseline UNet; 2) BEFD-UNet, which integrates BEFD module into UNet.

Data Description. We evaluate the new approach on two datasets of blood vessel: DRIVE and HEART. The DRIVE dataset is a public resource including 40 fundus images and corresponding labels of retinal vessel (the first manual annotation). The resolution of each image is 565 × 584, and the whole set has originally been divided into two parts: 20 images for training and the rest 20 images for testing. Apart from the fundus images, we also collect 1092 digital subtraction angiographies (DSA) of coronary (546 for train, 218 for valid and 328 for test). All images are resized to the same dimension 256 × 256, and this dataset is named as HEART. Moreover, both datasets are preprocessed by Contrast Limited Adaptive Histogram Equalization (CLAHE) and normalization. To avoid overfitting, data augmentation is used by horizontal and vertical flip.

Evaluation Metrics. To quantify the performance of our approach, we use several metrics consisting of sensitivity (Sen), specificity (Spe), accuracy (Acc), and F1-score (F1), the formulas are shown below:

$$Acc = \frac{TP + TN}{TP + TN + FP + FN}, Sen = \frac{TP}{TP + FN},$$
$$Spe = \frac{TN}{TN + FP}, F1 = \frac{2TP}{2TP + FP + FN}, \tag{4}$$

Table 1. Quantitative analysis of different methods on DRIVE dataset.

Methods	Year	Sen	Spe	F1	Acc	Auc
Hu [11]	2018	0.7772	0.9793	-	0.9533	0.9759
Zhuang [28]	2018	0.7856	0.9810	0.8202	0.9561	0.9793
Alom [1]	2019	0.7792	0.9813	0.8171	0.9556	0.9784
Jin [12]	2019	0.7963	0.9800	0.8237	0.9566	0.9802
Mou [16]	2019	0.8126	0.9788	-	0.9594	0.9796
Wu [22]	2019	0.8038	0.9802	-	0.9578	0.9821
Lyu [15]	2019	0.7940	0.9820	-	0.9579	0.9826
Wang [20]	2019	0.7940	0.9816	**0.8270**	0.9567	0.9772
Zhou [26]	2019	0.8135	0.9768	0.8249	0.9560	0.9739
Li [14]	2020	0.7791	0.9831	0.8218	0.9574	0.9813
UNet	2020	0.7887	**0.9861**	0.8140	0.9686	0.9836
BEFD-UNet	2020	**0.8215**	0.9845	0.8267	**0.9701**	**0.9867**

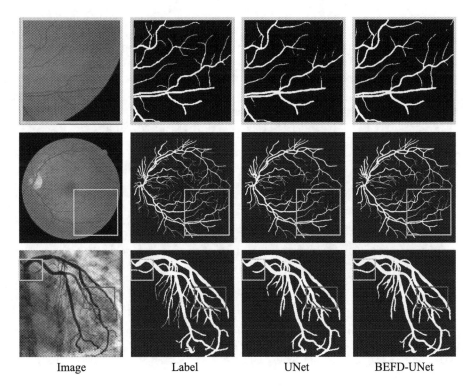

| Image | Label | UNet | BEFD-UNet |

Fig. 3. Segmentation results of different models. The top two rows: prediction maps on DRIVE dataset; The bottom row: prediction maps on HEART dataset.

where TP,TN,FP,FN denote the numbers of true positives, true negatives, false positives and false negatives respectively. In addition, we also calculate the AUC metric (the area under the ROC curve) for evaluation.

Implementation Details. All networks are implemented in TensorFlow 1.2.1 (https://www.tensorflow.org) on a single NVIDIA GTX1080ti GPU. We use the Adam algorithm to minimize the cross entropy loss, which is trained for 30k iterations with batch size of 8. In order to accelerate convergence, batch normalization is followed by each convolutional layers. In the UNet architecture, we set the channel number in the first layer to 64. The parameters $\lambda_{min}, \lambda_{max}, \alpha, \beta$ in edge detection are set to 0.8, 5.0, 2.0 and 1.0 respectively.

4   Results

Evaluation of the Performance of the BEFD Module. Table 1, 2 report the qualitative results of retinal vessel segmentation on DRIVE dataset and cardiac vessel segmentation on HEART dataset respectively. Compared to the baseline UNet, BEFD-UNet obtains better performance in four of the total five metrics with a considerable margin on both datasets, only Spe (specificity) is

Table 2. Quantitative analysis of different methods on HEART dataset.

Methods	Sen	Spe	F1	Acc	Auc
UNet	0.9186	0.9839	0.9073	0.9750	0.9938
BE-UNet	**0.9411**	0.9779	0.9030	0.9730	0.9935
FD-UNet	0.9234	**0.9849**	0.9140	0.9767	0.9939
BEFD-UNet	0.9333	0.9835	**0.9141**	**0.9767**	**0.9947**

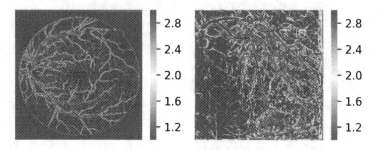

Fig. 4. Example of edge attention map on DRIVE dataset (left) and HEART dataset (right). Boundary pixels (mostly white) have higher values than background pixels (blue), while noise (red points) is widely distributed on the map, requiring feature denoising to restrain it. (Color figure online)

a bit lower. Moreover, BEFD-UNet provides a significant improvement in Sen (sensitivity) from 0.7887 (0.9186) to 0.8215 (0.9333) on DRIVE dataset (HEART dataset), indicating that our approach yields a lower false negative (FN) ratio. This can also be demonstrated by the segmentation results shown in Fig. 3, where BEFD-UNet successfully captures the extremely thin retina vessels and identifies the coronary arteries with low contrast to background. Besides the evaluation of the whole image, we also evaluate the models on small vessels (with a width of 1 or 2 pixels) only. In such a setting, BEFD-UNet makes a significant improvement in F1 score from 0.7163 (UNet) to 0.7628 (BEFD-UNet) on DRIVE dataset, indicating that our method has strong ability to capture the thin vessels.

On the other hand, we also compare the results with recent state-of-the-art models on DRIVE dataset as listed in Table 1. It shows that the proposed BEFD-UNet ranks first in four metrics except for F1 score. More specifically, it achieves the highest accuracy (1.05% higher than the second best [16]), the optimal AUC (0.41% higher than the suboptimal result [15]) as well as the best sensitivity (0.80% higher than the previous highest score [26]). Additionally, it is worth mentioning that the F1 score (0.8267) of our method is relatively close to the best score (0.8270) [20]. The above comparisons demonstrate the strong capacity of the new BEFD module to tackle semantic segmentation.

Discussion About the Mechanism of the BEFD Module. To explore the effect of the BEFD module, we show an example of edge attention map on both datasets in Fig. 4. It can be observed that boundary pixels have higher values, making it possible to pay more attention to the object contours. When the feature maps in the encoder path are multiplied (element-wise) by such attention map, the object boundaries are enhanced accordingly. At the same time, maps contain lots of noise due to the emphasis on weak vessels, for which it requires introducing the feature denoising block. In addition, we also conduct experiments using the boundary enhancement (BE) part or feature denoising (FD) part independently, which are shown in Table 2. The results indicate that using either BE or FD part would produce an unbalanced result. BE-UNet tends to generate high Sensitivity with low Specificity, because the BE part may misidentify image noise as boundaries, thus amplifying the undesirable noise. On the other hand, FD-UNet performs oppositely (high Specificity with low Sensitivity), since the FD block may make excessive denoising, which eliminates some fine structures. Therefore, we apply both BE and FD blocks jointly in BEFD-UNet, which leverages the advantages of both the BE and FD blocks.

5 Conclusion

In this paper, we propose a novel BEFD module to boost the boundary localization in the encoder-decoder framework for blood vessel segmentation. The integrated BEFD-UNet outperforms the baseline UNet as well as most of state-of-the-art approaches, resulting from its powerful ability to detect extremely tiny vessels. More broadly, the BEFD module provides a novel solution to leverage the advantage of traditional image processing algorithm, which can compensate for the defects of CNNs in an unsupervised way. This mechanism is worth investigating further in the future work.

Acknowledgments. This work was supported by Natural Science Foundation of China (NSFC) under Grants 81801778, 71704024, 11831002; National Key R&D Program of China (No. 2018YFC0910700); Beijing Natural Science Foundation (Z180001).

References

1. Alom, M.Z., Yakopcic, C., Hasan, M., Taha, T.M., Asari, V.K.: Recurrent residual u-net for medical image segmentation. J. Med. Imaging **6**(1), 014006 (2019)
2. Archer, D.B.: Diabetic retinopathy: some cellular, molecular and therapeutic considerations. Eye **13**(4), 497–523 (1999)
3. Badrinarayanan, V., Kendall, A., Cipolla, R.: Segnet: a deep convolutional encoder-decoder architecture for image segmentation. IEEE Trans. Pattern Anal. Mach. Intell. **39**(12), 2481–2495 (2017)
4. Buades, A., Coll, B., Morel, J.M.: A non-local algorithm for image denoising. In: 2005 IEEE Computer Society Conference on Computer Vision and Pattern Recognition (CVPR 2005), vol. 2, pp. 60–65. IEEE (2005)
5. Chaudhuri, S., Chatterjee, S., Katz, N., Nelson, M., Goldbaum, M.: Detection of blood vessels in retinal images using two-dimensional matched filters. IEEE Trans. Med. Imaging **8**(3), 263–269 (1989)

6. Chen, L.C., Papandreou, G., Kokkinos, I., Murphy, K., Yuille, A.L.: Deeplab: semantic image segmentation with deep convolutional nets, atrous convolution, and fully connected crfs. IEEE Trans. Pattern Anal. Mach. Intell. **40**(4), 834–848 (2017)
7. Chen, L.-C., Zhu, Y., Papandreou, G., Schroff, F., Adam, H.: Encoder-decoder with atrous separable convolution for semantic image segmentation. In: Ferrari, V., Hebert, M., Sminchisescu, C., Weiss, Y. (eds.) ECCV 2018. LNCS, vol. 11211, pp. 833–851. Springer, Cham (2018). https://doi.org/10.1007/978-3-030-01234-2_49
8. Chutatape, O., Zheng, L., Krishnan, S.M.: Retinal blood vessel detection and tracking by matched Gaussian and Kalman filters. In: Proceedings of the 20th Annual International Conference of the IEEE Engineering in Medicine and Biology Society, Vol. 20 Biomedical Engineering Towards the Year 2000 and Beyond (Cat. No. 98CH36286), vol. 6, pp. 3144–3149. IEEE (1998)
9. Dizdaro, B., Ataer-Cansizoglu, E., Kalpathy-Cramer, J., Keck, K., Chiang, M.F., Erdogmus, D.: Level sets for retinal vasculature segmentation using seeds from ridges and edges from phase maps. In: 2012 IEEE International Workshop on Machine Learning for Signal Processing, pp. 1–6. IEEE (2012)
10. Hatamizadeh, A., Terzopoulos, D., Myronenko, A.: End-to-end boundary aware networks for medical image segmentation. In: Suk, H.-I., Liu, M., Yan, P., Lian, C. (eds.) MLMI 2019. LNCS, vol. 11861, pp. 187–194. Springer, Cham (2019). https://doi.org/10.1007/978-3-030-32692-0_22
11. Hu, K., et al.: Retinal vessel segmentation of color fundus images using multi-scale convolutional neural network with an improved cross-entropy loss function. Neurocomputing **309**, 179–191 (2018)
12. Jin, Q., Meng, Z., Pham, T.D., Chen, Q., Wei, L., Su, R.: Dunet: a deformable network for retinal vessel segmentation. Knowl.-Based Syst. **178**, 149–162 (2019)
13. Kittler, J.: On the accuracy of the sobel edge detector. Image Vis. Comput. **1**(1), 37–42 (1983)
14. Li, L., Verma, M., Nakashima, Y., Nagahara, H., Kawasaki, R.: Iternet: retinal image segmentation utilizing structural redundancy in vessel networks. In: The IEEE Winter Conference on Applications of Computer Vision, pp. 3656–3665 (2020)
15. Lyu, J., Cheng, P., Tang, X.: Fundus image based retinal vessel segmentation utilizing a fast and accurate fully convolutional network. In: Fu, H., Garvin, M.K., MacGillivray, T., Xu, Y., Zheng, Y. (eds.) OMIA 2019. LNCS, vol. 11855, pp. 112–120. Springer, Cham (2019). https://doi.org/10.1007/978-3-030-32956-3_14
16. Mou, L., Chen, L., Cheng, J., Gu, Z., Zhao, Y., Liu, J.: Dense dilated network with probability regularized walk for vessel detection. IEEE Trans. Med. Imaging **39**, 1392–1403 (2019)
17. Qin, X.: Transfer learning with edge attention for prostate MRI segmentation. arXiv preprint arXiv:1912.09847 (2019)
18. Ronneberger, O., Fischer, P., Brox, T.: U-Net: convolutional networks for biomedical image segmentation. In: Navab, N., Hornegger, J., Wells, W.M., Frangi, A.F. (eds.) MICCAI 2015. LNCS, vol. 9351, pp. 234–241. Springer, Cham (2015). https://doi.org/10.1007/978-3-319-24574-4_28
19. Sun, Y., Zhang, X., Zhao, X., Xin, Q.: Extracting building boundaries from high resolution optical images and lidar data by integrating the convolutional neural network and the active contour model. Remote Sens. **10**(9), 1459 (2018)
20. Wang, B., Qiu, S., He, H.: Dual encoding u-net for retinal vessel segmentation. In: Shen, D., et al. (eds.) MICCAI 2019. LNCS, vol. 11764, pp. 84–92. Springer, Cham (2019). https://doi.org/10.1007/978-3-030-32239-7_10

21. Wang, X., Girshick, R., Gupta, A., He, K.: Non-local neural networks. In: Proceedings of the IEEE Conference on Computer Vision and Pattern Recognition, pp. 7794–7803 (2018)
22. Wu, Y., et al.: Vessel-net: retinal vessel segmentation under multi-path supervision. In: Shen, D., et al. (eds.) MICCAI 2019. LNCS, vol. 11764, pp. 264–272. Springer, Cham (2019). https://doi.org/10.1007/978-3-030-32239-7_30
23. Xie, C., Wu, Y., van der Maaten, L., Yuille, A.L., He, K.: Feature denoising for improving adversarial robustness. In: Proceedings of the IEEE Conference on Computer Vision and Pattern Recognition, pp. 501–509 (2019)
24. Zhang, Y., Chung, A.C.S.: Deep supervision with additional labels for retinal vessel segmentation task. In: Frangi, A.F., Schnabel, J.A., Davatzikos, C., Alberola-López, C., Fichtinger, G. (eds.) MICCAI 2018. LNCS, vol. 11071, pp. 83–91. Springer, Cham (2018). https://doi.org/10.1007/978-3-030-00934-2_10
25. Zhen, M., Wang, J., Zhou, L., Fang, T., Quan, L.: Learning fully dense neural networks for image semantic segmentation. In: Proceedings of the AAAI Conference on Artificial Intelligence, vol. 33, pp. 9283–9290 (2019)
26. Zhou, Y., Chen, Z., Shen, H., Peng, P., Zeng, Z., Zheng, X.: A symmetric equilibrium generative adversarial network with attention refine block for retinal vessel segmentation. arXiv preprint arXiv:1909.11936 (2019)
27. Zhu, Q., Du, B., Yan, P.: Boundary-weighted domain adaptive neural network for prostate MR image segmentation. IEEE Trans. Med. Imaging **39**, 168–178 (2019)
28. Zhuang, J.: Laddernet: Multi-path networks based on u-net for medical image segmentation. arXiv preprint arXiv:1810.07810 (2018)

Boosting Connectivity in Retinal Vessel Segmentation via a Recursive Semantics-Guided Network

Rui Xu[1,2,3], Tiantian Liu[2,3,4], Xinchen Ye[1,2,3(✉)], Lin Lin[1,2,3], and Yen-Wei Chen[5,6]

[1] DUT-RU International School of Information Science and Engineering, Dalian University of Technology, Dalian, China
{xurui,yexch}@dlut.edu.cn
[2] DUT-RU Co-Research Center of Advanced ICT for Active Life, Dalian, China
[3] Key Laboratory for Ubiquitous Network and Service Software of Liaoning Province, Dalian, China
[4] College of Software, Dalian University of Technology, Dalian, China
[5] College of Information Science and Engineering, Ritsumeikan University, Kusatsu, Japan
[6] Research Center of Healthcare Data Science, Zhejiang Lab, Hangzhou, China

Abstract. Many deep learning based methods have been proposed for retinal vessel segmentation, however few of them focus on the connectivity of segmented vessels, which is quite important for a practical computer-aided diagnosis system on retinal images. In this paper, we propose an efficient network to address this problem. A U-shape network is enhanced by introducing a semantics-guided module, which integrates the enriched semantics information to shallow layers for guiding the network to explore more powerful features. Besides, a recursive refinement iteratively applies the same network over the previous segmentation results for progressively boosting the performance while increasing no extra network parameters. The carefully designed recursive semantics-guided network has been extensively evaluated on several public datasets. Experimental results have shown the efficiency of the proposed method.

Keywords: Vessel connectivity · Semantics · Recursive refinement · Retinal vessel segmentation

1 Introduction

Retinal vessel segmentation is a fundamental and crucial step to develop a computer-aided diagnosis (CAD) system on retinal images [10]. Although a lot

This work was supported by National Natural Science Foundation of China (NSFC) under Grant 61772106, Grant 61702078 and Grant 61720106005, and by the Fundamental Research Funds for the Central Universities of China.

ⓒ Springer Nature Switzerland AG 2020
A. L. Martel et al. (Eds.): MICCAI 2020, LNCS 12265, pp. 786–795, 2020.
https://doi.org/10.1007/978-3-030-59722-1_76

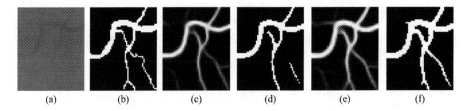

Fig. 1. Examples for retinal images and corresponding segmentation results. (a): retinal image. (b): ground truth for vessel segmentation. (c)–(d): predicted probability map and binary segmentation for the work [7], which achieves relatively high AUC (0.982) but brings breakpoints on segmented vessels. (e)–(f): probability map and binary segmentation for the proposed method, which largely boosts the vessel connectivity. (Otsu's thresholding method [8] is applied for the probability maps to obtain the binary segmentation results.)

of deep learning based works have been devoted to precise retinal vessel segmentation, few of them have paid attention to the connectivity of segmented vessels. In these methods, deep networks are developed to predict dense probability maps indicating how probable each pixel belongs to retinal vessels or not, and then retinal vessels are segmented by thresholding these maps. Many works have evaluated their methods by calculating some segmentation metrics, such as the area under the ROC curve (AUC). However, these metrics can not quantify the topology or connectivity of segmented vessels. Even if high values are achieved for them, breakpoints still exist on the binary segmentation results (see Fig. 1). In this paper, we propose a novel deep network to improve the connectivity on retinal vessel segmentation and evaluate it by using some metrics that quantify the topology of segmented vessels.

The U-net architecture is widely adopted in many previous works for retinal vessel segmentation [2]. The original U-net progressively connects high-level layers to shallow layers, which makes the semantics information embedded in the high-level layers to be gradually diluted. Semantics information is important for retinal vessel segmentation. It can not only provide more robust features to boost the segmentation of weak vessels while eliminating the effects of abnormal lighting and retinal pathology, but also give holistic cues for recognizing whole vessel trees. Thus, semantics information is valuable for removing the breakpoints in segmented vessels. Several previous works try to solve this problem by adding more semantics information into the U-net. Wang et al. [12] design a dual encoding U-Net with a context path to capture more semantic information. Xu et al. [16] improve U-net by introducing carefully designed semantics and multi-scale aggregation blocks. These works are devoted to designing a complicated network architecture by either adding a large number of connections [16] or inserting an extra sub-network that is relatively large [12]. Different from these efforts, we apply several widely-used network block or operation to design a simple but efficient module, which can not only fully extract semantics information from high-level layers but also guide the network to learn powerful features for better vessel connectivity.

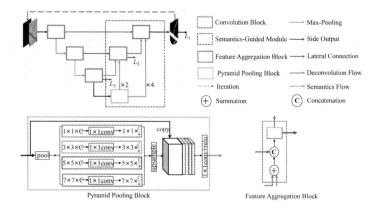

Fig. 2. The architecture of the proposed recursive semantics-guided network.

Besides, refinement is a usual manner to enhance segmentation in literatures and has been adopted to improve vessel segmentation in previous works [1,14]. Wu *et al.* [14] refine the vessel segmentation by using an extra multi-scale based network that is cascaded to a preceding network. Ara *et al.* [1] have claimed that the connectivity of segmented vessels can be improved by stacking another variational auto-encoder based network after a previous one. The cascaded manner adopted in these approaches introduces lots of extra network parameters, which demands much more labelled data for training. In this paper, we adopt a different refinement that uses a single network and recursively refines its output. This refinement does not increase extra network parameters while enhancing the connectivity of segmented vessels.

Our contribution of this paper can be summarized as follows. 1) A simple but efficient network is proposed to boost connectivity in retinal vessel segmentation. 2) A semantics-guided module, which exploits semantics information to guide the network to learn more powerful features, is introduced to enhance the capacity of U-net. 3) A recursive refinement that requires no extra network parameters are exploited to iteratively refine the results.

2   Recursive Semantics-Guided Network

2.1   Network Architecture

We propose a recursive semantics-guided network to enhance the connectivity in retinal vessel segmentation. Figure 2 illustrates the detailed network architecture, which is designed to address the semantics dilution problem of the original U-net. Semantics information is crucial for retinal vessel segmentation. It is usually embedded in high-level layers of deep network and less suffered from the effect of some abnormalities, such as non-uniform lighting and retinal pathology. It can also provide the holistic cue that is helpful for recognizing the whole blood vessel tree. Thus, it is required that semantics information should be fully exploited for boosting the vessel segmentation and connectivity. In this paper, we design a semantics-guided module that distills the semantics information for guiding the network to produce more powerful and robust features. Besides, we adopt a recursive refinement for further boosting the connectivity of segmented vessels. Different from the stacked or cascaded refinement, our method re-uses the proposed network that iteratively takes the previous results as the input to produce better output. We find that this refinement increases no extra network parameters while gradually boosting the connectivity of segmented retinal vessels.

The top part of Fig. 2 shows the whole structure of the proposed network, which is based on a 3-layered encoder-decoder architecture. The encoder on each layer is a convolutional block comprised by two stacked convolutional layers with 3×3 filters and the rectified-linear unit (ReLU) activation function. These convolution blocks are serially connected by max-pooling that halves feature map sizes to produce hierarchical features in different levels. We carefully design the decoder part by introducing a semantics-guided module that can fully exploiting semantics information of the deep network. Besides, at the end part on the 2nd and 3rd layers, there is a side output path that uses upsampling and 1×1 convolution to obtain a prediction for deep supervision. In the following subsections, we describe the semantics-guided module, the recursive refinement and network training in details.

2.2 Semantics-Guided Module

The semantics-guided module is indicated by the red dash block in Fig. 2. It is mainly comprised by a pyramid pooling block [17] and two feature aggregation blocks. The pyramid pooling block is fed with feature maps generated on the 3rd layer. As pointed by some previous works [4,17], the receptive field of a deep network is not wide enough, even on the deepest layers. For retinal vessel segmentation, semantics information from a wider region can give more holistic cues to identify the global profile of a vessel tree for preventing breakpoints. In order to extract more holistic semantics information, we connect the pyramid pooling block to the deepest layer. The detailed structure of the pyramid pooling block is given in the left bottom part in Fig. 2. At first, feature maps are fed into four parallel adaptive pooling layers to produce feature maps with the spatial sizes of 1×1, 3×3, 5×5 and 7×7 respectively. Then 1×1 convolution followed by upsampling is used to compress channels to be $C/4$ and match their spatial sizes. Finally, they are concatenated with the original feature maps and passed to a 1×1 convolution with a ReLU activation function to produce the final holistic semantics information, which is provided for the feature aggregation blocks.

The structure of feature aggregation blocks is given in the right-bottom part in Fig. 2. They exploit semantics information to guide the aggregation of more powerful features. Semantic information is inserted via semantics flows that utilize upsampling and convolution to match the feature maps coming from a deconvolution flow. An element-wise summation is used for fusion and then the results are concatenated with feature maps from the lateral connection. Finally, a convolution block consisting of two stacked 3×3 convolution is used to learn more powerful feature representation.

2.3 Recursive Refinement and Network Training

The semantics-guided module can improve the connectivity of segmented vessels, however the results can be further improved by using a recursive refinement, which gradually boosts weak vessels and eliminates break points. In our refinement, predicted vessels together with the original image patch are iteratively fed into the same deep network to successively obtain a better result. A similar iterative approach is also advocated in previous works [5,6], showing that previous results can always be iteratively improved when Lipschitz continuity is assumed. Besides, this refinement is less demanding of labeled data, since it increases no extra network parameters for training. Our recursive refinement can be formulated as $\hat{y}^{i+1} = F(x \copyright \hat{y}^i)$ $i = 0, 1, \ldots, I - 1$, where x denotes input image patch, $\hat{y}^i$ denotes the predicted results of a network F in the i-th iteration, $\copyright$ denotes channel concatenation and I is the total iteration number. The refinement is initialized with $\hat{y}^0 = 0$, which is an empty prediction, and the final result is $\hat{y}^I$.

Due to the less training data of fundus images, our network uses image patches cropped from training images as inputs. Our network can be trained in an end-to-end manner by minimizing a weighted sum of loss functions in all iteration. In each iteration, there are a master L_1 for predicted results and two auxiliary losses (L_2 and L_3) for deep supervision. Thus, the total loss in the i-th iteration can be formulated as $L_t^i = \sum_{j=1}^{3} L_j^i$. For all of these losses, we adopt a weighted binary cross-entropy [15], which penalizes more on false negatives than false positives [1]. The final refinement loss can be expressed by $L_r = \frac{1}{Z} \sum_{i=1}^{I} i \cdot L_t^i$, where Z is the normalization factor $Z = \sum_{i=1}^{I} i$. We give more weight for the loss in a later iteration to increase numerical stability for network training. In practice, we initially train the network without the refinement, which is $I = 1$. Then, we increase I to start the training with the refinement. In experiments, we set I to be 3.

3 Experiments and Results

3.1 Databases and Evaluation Protocol

We evaluate the proposed method and other methods by using three publicly available datasets, which are DRIVE [11], STARE [3], and CHASE_DB1 [9]. The DRIVE dataset consists of 40 images, 7 of which show retinal pathology. The STARE dataset contains 20 images, 10 of which belong to sick individuals. The CHASE_DB1 dataset includes 28 images that are collected from both eyes of 14 children. The DRIVE dataset is officially divided into the training and testing sets that respectively contains 20 images. For the STARE and CHASE_DB1 datasets, we randomly select 10 images for testing, and use the rest for training.

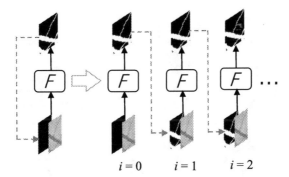

$i = 0 \qquad i = 1 \qquad i = 2$

Fig. 3. In our recursive refinement, previously predicted results together with the original input are fed into the same network to gradually obtain better results without increasing extra network parameters.

Table 1. Ablation study of the proposed method with different network configurations for retinal vessel segmentation on the DRIVE dataset. (A smaller value of INF means better performance.)

Methods	Semantics	Refine	AUC	SE	SP	INF	COR
baseline			0.980	0.884	**0.958**	0.350	0.564
method-a	√		0.981	0.900	0.953	0.313	0.599
method-b		√	0.980	0.894	0.954	0.322	0.589
method-c	√	√	**0.981**	**0.912**	0.947	**0.274**	**0.633**

We evaluate all methods by calculating three widely-used metrics for segmentation and two metrics that can quantify the connectivity of segmented vessels. The metrics for segmentation include the area under the receiver operating characteristic curve (AUC), sensitivity (SE), and specificity (SP). The metrics for quantifying vessel connectivity are previously used for measuring how well the topology of a road network is [13], and recently adopted to measure the connectivity of segmented vessels in [1]. Their calculation requires to randomly select two points which lie both on the ground-truth and binary segmentation result. Then, check whether the shortest path between the points has the same length. This is repeated many times to record the percentages of correct and infeasible paths. Large correct (COR) while low infeasible (INF) percentage indicates good connectivity on segmented vessels. In experiments, we find 1000 times repetition per testing image is enough to obtain converged percentages. Besides, binary segmentation results are produced apply the Otsu's thresholding method [8] on predicted probability maps for all methods in experiments.

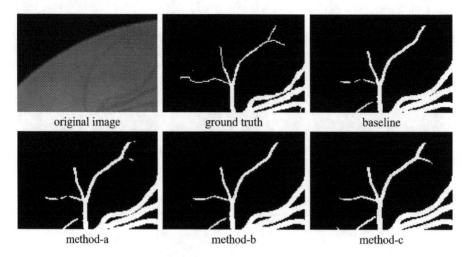

original image   ground truth   baseline

method-a   method-b   method-c

Fig. 4. Visualization results of segmented vessels for different network configurations in the ablation study.

3.2   Ablation Study

We perform the ablation study to check whether the proposed semantics-guided module and recursive refinement are effective or not. This study is performed by evaluating different network configurations on the DRIVE dataset. Detailed results are summarized in Table 1. The baseline method is only a 3-layered U-Net trained by deep supervision, when neither the semantics-guided module nor the recursive refinement is used. The method-a and method-b respectively denote that either the semantics module or the recursive refinement is utilized, while the method-c denotes that both of them takes effect. Just from the three segmentation related metrics, the four methods achieve the similar results, though the method-c has achieved the highest values on AUC and SE. However, they quite differ in the metrics related to vessel connectivity. It can be seen that both INF and COR become better when either the semantics-guide module or recursive refinement is activated. The best performance for vessel connectivity is achieved when both of them take effect. Compared with the baseline method, the INF is decreased by 21.7% while the COR is increased by 12.2% for the method-c. Therefore, these results quantitatively demonstrate that the connectivity of segmented vessels can be enhanced by using the proposed recursive semantics-guided network.

Besides, we also give the visualization results in Fig. 4 to show how these methods are visually different on binary segmentation results. Compared with the baseline, the semantics-guided module improves the connectivity slightly and makes more capillary vessels be extracted. The refinement strategy can significantly avoid the breakpoints in segmented vessels. By using the semantics-guided module together with the refinement, not only the vessel extraction becomes more accurate but also the connectivity is largely enhanced.

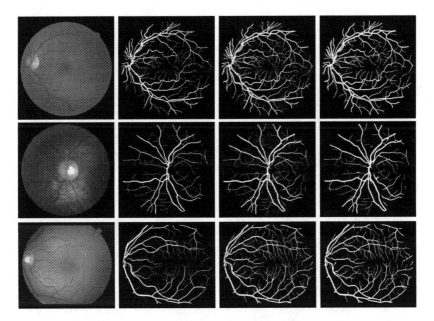

Fig. 5. Retinal vessel segmentation results for the proposed method on the DRIVE, CHASE_DB1 and STARE datasets. From the column in left to right, the retinal images, the ground truth, the predicted probability maps and the corresponding binary segmentation of the propose method are given respectively.

3.3 Comparison with Other Leading Methods

We compare the proposed method with three leading methods by evaluating them on the DRIVE, CHASE_DB1 and STARE datasets. Ara *et al.* [1] propose a stacked variational auto-encoder based network to improve the connectivity of segmented vessels, which could be the only work that is targeted for boosting vessel connectivity and published in recent years, according to our knowledge. The other two methods are specifically aimed for improving the retinal vessel segmentation. Oliveira *et al.* [7] propose a multiscale fully convolutional network

Table 2. Comparison of the proposed method with other leading methods for retinal vessel segmentation. (A smaller value of INF means better performance.)

Methods	Year	DRIVE					CHASE_DB1					STARE				
		AUC	SE	SP	INF	COR	AUC	SE	SP	INF	COR	AUC	SE	SP	INF	COR
Oliveira *et al.* [7]	2018	**0.982**	0.804	0.980	0.437	0.489	0.986	0.778	**0.986**	0.709	0.254	**0.991**	0.832	**0.986**	0.295	0.635
Ara *et al.* [1]	2019	0.979	0.897	0.953	0.291	0.612	0.980	0.898	0.956	0.480	0.456	0.986	0.901	0.968	0.231	0.692
Xu *et al.* [16]	2020	0.980	0.795	**0.981**	0.539	0.387	**0.986**	0.846	0.977	0.653	0.302	0.987	0.895	0.978	0.319	0.627
Proposed	-	0.981	**0.912**	0.947	**0.274**	**0.633**	0.985	**0.923**	0.954	**0.388**	**0.526**	0.986	**0.928**	0.954	**0.212**	**0.727**

for vessels segmentation, which combines the multiscale analysis provided by the stationary wavelet transform. Xu *et al.* [16] improve vessel segmentation by introducing a carefully designed semantics and multi-scale aggregation network. The results are summarized in Table 2. If only evaluating these methods by the AUC, SE and SP, one might consider that the performance of our method were roughly equal to the others. However, the difference becomes obvious when they are compared by using the INF and COR, which can quantify the connectivity of segmented vessels. Especially for the CHASE_DB1 dataset, our method can decrease the INF by 19.1% while increase the COR by 15.4%, compared with the 2nd ranking method. These results show that the proposed method outperforms the three leading methods and achieves the best performance on vessel connectivity. Finally, we give examples of our method for retinal vessel segmentation on the three public datasets in Fig. 5.

4 Conclusion

In this paper, we propose a recursive semantics-guided network for better connectivity on retinal vessel segmentation. It is featured by a semantics-guided module that can fully exploit semantics information for guiding the network to learn more powerful features, and a recursive refinement that can iteratively enhance the results while saving network parameters. Its efficiency is demonstrated from extensive experimental results.

References

1. Araújo, R.J., Cardoso, J.S., Oliveira, H.P.: A deep learning design for improving topology coherence in blood vessel segmentation. In: Shen, D., et al. (eds.) MICCAI 2019. LNCS, vol. 11764, pp. 93–101. Springer, Cham (2019). https://doi.org/10.1007/978-3-030-32239-7_11
2. Fraz, M.M., et al.: Blood vessel segmentation methodologies in retinal images-a survey. Comput. Methods Programs Biomed. **108**(1), 407–433 (2012)
3. Hoover, A., Kouznetsova, V., Goldbaum, M.: Locating blood vessels in retinal images by piecewise threshold probing of a matched filter response. IEEE Trans. Med. Imaging **19**(3), 203–210 (2000)
4. Liu, J.J., Hou, Q., Cheng, M.M., Feng, J., Jiang, J.: A simple pooling-based design for real-time salient object detection. In: Conference on Computer Vision and Pattern Recognition (CVPR) (2019)
5. Mosinska, A., Marquez-Neila, P., Koziński, M., Fua, P.: Beyond the pixel-wise loss for topology-aware delineation. In: Conference on Computer Vision and Pattern Recognition (2018)
6. Newell, A., Yang, K., Deng, J.: Stacked hourglass networks for human pose estimation. In: Leibe, B., Matas, J., Sebe, N., Welling, M. (eds.) ECCV 2016. LNCS, vol. 9912, pp. 483–499. Springer, Cham (2016). https://doi.org/10.1007/978-3-319-46484-8_29
7. Oliveira, A., Pereira, S., Silva, C.A.: Retinal vessel segmentation based on fully convolutional neural networks. Expert Syst. Appl. **112**, 229–242 (2018)

8. Otsu, N.: A threshold selection method from gray-level histograms. IEEE Trans. Syst. Man Cybern. **9**(1), 62–66 (2007)
9. Owen, C.G., et al.: Measuring retinal vessel tortuosity in 10-year-old children: validation of the computer-assisted image analysis of the retina (CAIAR) program. Invest. Ophthalmol. Vis. Sci. **50**(5), 2004–2010 (2009)
10. Srinidhi, C.L., Aparna, P., Rajan, J.: Recent advancements in retinal vessel segmentation. J. Med. Syst. **41**(4), 70 (2017)
11. Staal, J., Abràmoff, M.D., Niemeijer, M., Viergever, M.A., Van Ginneken, B.: Ridge-based vessel segmentation in color images of the retina. IEEE Trans. Med. Imaging **23**(4), 501–509 (2004)
12. Wang, B., Qiu, S., He, H.: Dual encoding u-net for retinal vessel segmentation. In: Shen, D., et al. (eds.) MICCAI 2019. LNCS, vol. 11764, pp. 84–92. Springer, Cham (2019). https://doi.org/10.1007/978-3-030-32239-7_10
13. Wegner, J.D., Montoya-Zegarra, J.A., Schindler, K.: A higher-order CRF model for road network extraction. In: Conference on Computer Vision and Pattern Recognition (CVPR) (2013)
14. Wu, Y., Xia, Y., Song, Y., Zhang, Y., Cai, W.: Multiscale network followed network model for retinal vessel segmentation. In: Frangi, A.F., Schnabel, J.A., Davatzikos, C., Alberola-López, C., Fichtinger, G. (eds.) MICCAI 2018. LNCS, vol. 11071, pp. 119–126. Springer, Cham (2018). https://doi.org/10.1007/978-3-030-00934-2_14
15. Xie, S., Tu, Z.: Holistically-nested edge detection. In: International Conference on Computer Vision (ICCV) (2015)
16. Xu, R., Ye, X., Jiang, G., Liu, T., Li, L., Tanaka, S.: Semantics and multi-scale aggregation network for retinal vessel segmentation. In: 2020 IEEE International Conference on Acoustics, Speech, and Signal Processing (ICASSP 2020) (2020)
17. Zhao, H., Shi, J., Qi, X., Wang, X., Jia, J.: Pyramid scene parsing network. In: Conference on Computer Vision and Pattern Recognition (CVPR) (2017)

RVSeg-Net: An Efficient Feature Pyramid Cascade Network for Retinal Vessel Segmentation

Wei Wang[1], Jiafu Zhong[1], Huisi Wu[1(✉)], Zhenkun Wen[1], and Jing Qin[2]

[1] College of Computer Science and Software Engineering, Shenzhen University, Shenzhen, China
hswu@szu.edu.cn
[2] Centre for Smart Health, School of Nursing, The Hong Kong Polytechnic University, Hung Hom, Hong Kong

Abstract. Accurate retinal vessel segmentation plays a critical role in the diagnosis of many relevant diseases. However, it remains a challenging task due to (1) the great scale variation of retinal vessels, (2) the existence of a large number of capillaries in the vascular network, and (3) the interactions of the retinal vessels and other structures in the images, which easily results in the discontinuities in the segmentation results. In addition, limited training data also often prohibit current deep learning models from being efficiently trained because of the overfitting problem. In this paper, we propose a novel and efficient feature pyramid cascade network for retinal vessel segmentation to comprehensively address these challenges; we call it RVSeg-Net. The main component of the proposed RVSeg-Net is a feature pyramid cascade (FPC) module, which is capable of capturing multi-scale features to tackle scale variations of retinal vessels and aggregating local and global context information to solve the discontinuity problem. In order to overcome the overfitting problem, we further employ octave convolution to replace the traditional vanilla convolution to greatly reduce the parameters by avoiding spatial redundancy information. We conducted extensive experiments on two mainstream retinal vessel datasets (DRIVE and CHASE_DB1) to validate the proposed RVSeg-Net. Experimental results demonstrate the effectiveness of the proposed method, outperforming start-of-the-art approaches with much fewer parameters.

Keywords: Retinal vessel segmentation · Feature pyramid cascade network · Retinal fundus image analysis

1 Introduction

Retinal blood vessels are related to many diseases, such as diabetes, hypertension, arteriosclerosis, and so on. Clinical studies show that the thickness and curvature of blood vessels are related to hypertension and diabetes to a certain

© Springer Nature Switzerland AG 2020
A. L. Martel et al. (Eds.): MICCAI 2020, LNCS 12265, pp. 796–805, 2020.
https://doi.org/10.1007/978-3-030-59722-1_77

extent while diabetic retinopathy and macular mutation are the main causes of vision loss [5]. With the rapid development of medical imaging, many high-quality and high-resolution retinal fundus images have been generated. However, it would be a very laborious and time-consuming process to rely on the previous visual inspection [6]. In this regard, implementing an effective and accurate retinal vessel segmentation algorithm is highly demanded in clinical practice; such an algorithm can not only help ophthalmologists better evaluate and analyze complex fundus images but also can be embedded into more complex systems or pre-screening methods to deal with a large amount of images.

However, accurate retinal vessel segmentation remains a challenging task for the following reasons. (1) Retinal vessel size, shape and local intensity vary widely. For example, the size of the blood vessels usually vary between 1 and 20 pixels wide [15], which makes the segmentation of fine vessels extremely difficult. (2) Various structures appear in retinal images, including optic disk, pathologies, and the retinal boundary, often resulting in severe discontinuities problem. (3) Relatively small datasets easily lead to overfitting problem in training deep models; in our experiments, both two datasets only had 20 images available for training.

A lot of effort has been dedicated to overcoming these challenges. In early studies, artificially designed features are usually used for feature selection [16–18,24]. For example, Faraz Oloumi et al. [17] design a set of of directionally sensitive Gabor filters by analyzing of the vessel architecture of the retinal for elongation parameters. Niemeijer et al. [16] extracted a feature vector consisting of a Gaussian matched filter and its first and second derivative response waves at multiple scales in each pixel, and enhanced it by the green channel of the color image. Although these methods achieved good segmentation results in some specific situations, the hand-crafted features are insufficient in representing the complicated characteristics of retinal vessels and hence fail in relatively large dataset with many complex cases.

Recently, deep convolutional neural networks (CNNs) have shown impressive results in image segmentation [2,3,12]. Since the milestone networks, FCN [14] and U-Net [19], for image segmentation have been proposed, many variant methods based on them have been developed for retinal fundus image segmentation [1,7,10,26]. Alom et al. [1] employed a recurrent residual convolution neural network to train a patch-level classifier on image patches to achieve satisfactory performance without adding extra parameters. To address the low contrast between retinal vessels and the background in fundus image, Zhang et al. [25] utilized U-Net with residual connection and introduced an edge-aware mechanism to detect vessels.

While these methods made significant progress in retinal vessel segmentation, they are still incapable of meeting the challenges of large vessel variation and severe discontinuity. To address these challenges, we propose a novel and efficient feature pyramid cascade network for retinal vessel segmentation; we call it RVSeg-Net. The main component of the proposed RVSeg-Net is a feature pyramid cascade (FPC) module, which is capable of capturing multi-scale features to tackle scale variations of retinal vessels and aggregating local and globe context information to solve the discontinuity problem. In addition, to avoid the overfitting problem under limited training dataset and improve the training and inferencing efficiency,

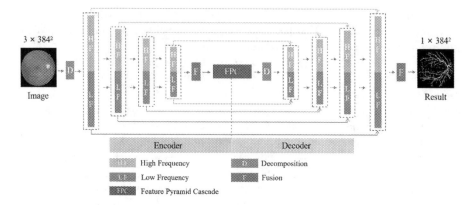

Fig. 1. The architecture of the proposed RVSeg-Net, where the backbone is based on the U-shape structure. A Feature Pyramid Cascade (FPC) module is designed to fuse image features at different scales for multi-scale context information extracting. Moreover, we replace the vanilla convolution with an octave convolution to reduces the amount of calculation. The yellow and blue arrows denote the skip connections that copy and concatenate the high- and low-frequency feature maps, respectively. D and F mean features decomposition and fusion. (Color figure online)

we replaced vanilla convolution with octave convolution [4] to reduce the redundancy parameters. We conducted extensive experiments on two mainstream retinal vessel datasets (DRIVE and CHASE_DB1) to validate the proposed RVSeg-Net. Experimental results demonstrate the effectiveness of the proposed method, outperforming start-of-the-art approaches with much less parameters.

2   Methodology

The architecture of the proposed RVSeg-Net is shown in Fig. 1, where U-Net [19] is utilized as the backbone network. In the following, we shall introduce the the proposed feature pyramid cascade (FPC) and the multi-frequency convolution (MFC) in details.

2.1   Feature Pyramid Cascade Module

In semantic segmentation, context information and multi-scale fusion are necessary to improve segmentation accuracy. Due to the variations of the vessel size, how to capture and fuse image features in different scales is important for retinal vessel segmentation, and the size of receptive field roughly determines how much context information we can harness.

The structure of the proposed FPC module is illustrated in Fig. 2. Given a high-level input feature map $X_{in} \in \mathbb{R}^{C \times H \times W}$, which is obtained by the encoder network, like [27], we first employ a pyramid pooling structure with a size of 2 × 2, 3 × 3 and 4 × 4, respectively, to divide the original feature map into three

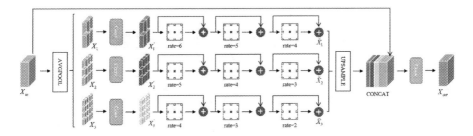

Fig. 2. Illustration of the proposed feature pyramid cascade (FPC) module. Conv indicates the convolutional layers. Each convolution layer is followed by batch normalization and Relu nonlinear activation. Rate represents the atrous rate.

different subregions and generate three new feature maps $X_1 \in \mathbb{R}^{C \times H/2 \times W/2}$, $X_2 \in \mathbb{R}^{C \times H/3 \times W/3}$ and $X_3 \in \mathbb{R}^{C \times H/4 \times W/4}$, respectively. The type of pooling operation is average pooling, which is able to abstract different sub-regions by adopting varying-size pooling kernels in a few strides.

Second, we fed these three feature map X_1, X_2, and X_3 into a convolution layer at the same time to enhance the characteristic representation and get the corresponding mapping feature X'_1, X'_2, and X'_3. Considering sizes of different sub-regions feature maps, we designed dilated convolution with different atrous rates for the feature maps of each sub-region and gradually merged the extracted features step-by-step. The fusion of information at different scales can help the model to extract multi-scale features, thereby better adapting to blood vessels of different thicknesses. Meanwhile, we can get the output feature map $\tilde{X}_1$, $\tilde{X}_2$ and $\tilde{X}_3$, respectively.

Finally, the feature maps of different subregions are directly up-sampled by bilinear interpolation to obtain feature maps of the same size as the original feature map. Then the origin feature map and the output feature maps of the three branches are connected. The output of FPC module can be simplify described as follows:

$$X_{out} = F \left(X_{in} \oplus \sum_{j=1}^{3} \text{Upsample} \left(\tilde{X}_j \right) \right) \tag{1}$$

where $F(\cdot)$ refers to the convolution function, the $\tilde{X}_j$ represents the output of jth branch and $\oplus$ mean the concatenate operation, respectively.

2.2 Multi-Frequency Convolution Module

As stated in [4], vanilla convolution is simply a mapping of the input and output of the feature maps, which results in a large amount of spatial redundancy in the mapped feature maps. In order to overcome the disadvantages of low network computation efficiency, we therefore replace the vanilla convolution with a multi-frequency convolution to reduces the amount of calculation. We decompose the feature map into high- and low-frequency features by channel. Considering the

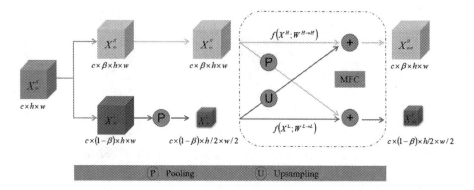

Fig. 3. An overview of the multi-frequency convolution (MFC) module. The hyper-parameter $\beta \in [0,1]$ denotes the ratio of high frequency part. (Color figure online)

low-frequency feature map has a lot of redundant background information, we further compress the feature map of the low-frequency part. Apart from this, the MFC module also carries out information interaction between low-frequency features and high-frequency features, which plays a role in feature fusion to a certain extent. As show in Fig. 3, let X_{in}^H, X_{in}^L denote the input high-frequency and low-frequency feature maps, respectively, illustrating by the yellow cube and the blue cube in the figure, the output can be figured out by:

$$X_{out(i,j)}^H = X_{out(i,j)}^{H \to H} + X_{out(i,j)}^{L \to H} = f^{H \to H}(X_{in}^H) + f^{L \to H}(X_{in}^L) \tag{2}$$

$$X_{out(i,j)}^L = X_{out(i,j)}^{L \to L} + X_{out(i,j)}^{H \to L} = f^{L \to L}(X_{in}^L) + f^{H \to L}(X_{in}^H) \tag{3}$$

where (i, j) denotes the location coordinate. The high-frequency and low-frequency feature maps of the output denoted as $X_{out} = \{X_{out}^H, X_{out}^L\}$.

3   Experiments and Results

3.1   Data Description and Implementation Details

We conduct extensive experiments on two famous datasets: DRIVE [20] and CHASE_DB1 [9], to validate the proposed RVSeg-Net. The DRIVE dataset contains 40 retinal fundus images with a size of 565 × 584 while the CHASE_DB1 dataset contains 28 retinal fundus images with a size of 999 × 960. The 40 images in DRIVE dataset has been divided into a training and a test set with both containing 20 images. Like many previous methods [11,21,23], we take 20 samples on the CHASE_DB1 dataset for training and the remaining 8 images for testing. We implemented our method based on the Pytorch framework. During the training, we employ a NVIDIA RTX 2080Ti and use the Adam algorithm with the learning rate of 0.001 and set a mini-batch size of 2. Each image is resized to 576 × 576 (DRIVE) and 960 × 960 (CHASE_DB1), and 4 patches of size

384×384 are crop from it randomly. We adopt the dice loss as the loss function to be minimized. We employ Accuracy (ACC), Sensitivity (SE), Specificity (SP), F1-score (F1), Area Under ROC (AUC), Parameters (Params) and GFLOPs as measurements.

3.2 Results

We compare the proposed RVSeg-Net with several state-of-the-art methods, including Liskowski [13], MS-NFN [22], R2U-Net [1], and CE-Net [8]. The classical U-Net [19] is also included for comparison. Table 1 shows the results of these methods on DRIVE dataset. It is observed that the MS-NFN [22], which used cascaded U-Net to capture features of different sizes, and fused the details of different sizes with each other between upsampling and downsampling, achieved good segmentation performance, reaching 79.44% and 98.07% on SE and AUC, respectively. The R2U-Net [1] and the CE-Net [8] also achieve good results, outperforming the U-Net in terms of AUC. The proposed RVSeg-Net achieves 96.81%, 81.07%, 98.17% in ACC, SE, and AUC respectively, outperforming other methods. In addition, it is observed that the U-Net [19] consumes approximately 1.8 times as much computation as RVSeg-Net. Moreover, RVSeg-Net requires only 5.2 million network parameters, which reduces the amount of parameters by about 25% compared with the U-Net. Table 2 shows the experimental results on the CHASE_DB1 dataset. RVSeg-Net also achieved best results with lower computational complexity, further demonstrating the effectiveness of the proposed RVSeg-Net.

Table 1. Quantitative comparison of segmentation results on DRIVE dataset.

Method	ACC (%)	SE (%)	SP (%)	AUC (%)	Params (M)	FLOPs (G)
Liskowski et al. [13]	95.35	78.11	98.07	97.90	–	–
MS-NFN [22]	95.67	79.44	98.19	98.07	–	–
R2U-Net [1]	95.56	77.92	98.13	97.84	–	–
CE-Net [8]	96.77	79.38	**98.62**	97.81	15.1	305.3
U-Net [19]	96.62	78.47	98.50	97.78	7.7	215.4
RVSeg-Net	**96.81**	**81.07**	98.45	**98.17**	**5.2**	**119.0**

We further visualize some typical segmentation results in Fig. 4. In Fig. 4(b) and Fig. 4(c), we can observe that the shapes of some vascular trees are extremely complicated, which exist many tiny vessels, and some of them are entangled with each other. Moreover, there exist many capillaries that are difficult to be directly observed by the naked eye at the borders of retinal images or in areas with dark intensity values. These examples demonstrate the difficulties in accurate retinal vessel segmentation. We can see in Fig. 4(d), due to its limitation, the U-Net is not able to segment the fine vessels well. Although CE-Net combines a DAC module and an RMP module to capture multi-scale features, its ability to

Table 2. Quantitative comparison of segmentation results on CHASE_DB1 dataset.

Method	ACC (%)	SE (%)	SP (%)	AUC (%)	Params (M)	FLOPs (G)
Liskowski et al. [13]	95.81	75.07	97.93	97.16	–	–
MS-NFN [22]	96.37	75.38	98.47	98.25	–	–
R2U-Net [1]	96.34	77.56	98.20	98.15	–	–
CE-Net [8]	96.92	78.48	**98.75**	98.05	15.1	848.0
U-Net [19]	96.81	78.07	98.48	98.08	7.7	598.2
RVSeg-Net	**97.26**	**80.69**	98.36	**98.33**	**5.2**	**330.4**

extract thin blood vessels is much worse than the proposed RVSeg-Net, as shown in Fig. 4(e) and Fig. 4(f). In addition, it is worth mentioning that the proposed RVSeg-Net can extract more detailed vessels than U-Net and CE-Net in some regions that are not easily segmented. Particularly, the proposed RVSeg-Net is able to obtain a more refined result at the boundaries and in the areas with dark intensity values, demonstrating its effectiveness in dealing with challenging cases.

We also conduct an ablation study to demonstrate the effectiveness of the proposed components. In terms of time consumption, we trained 200 iterations on a single NVIDIA RTX 2080Ti GPU. As can be seen from Table 3, by applying MFC, our training time has been greatly reduced while the inference speed increased from 14 FPS to 23 FPS, which is about 2x faster than the vanilla convolution (VC). To confirm the effectiveness of the FPC module, we apply a lightweight version of U-Net with MFC as our backbone. Table 4 shows the segmentation results. It is observed that by adopting the proposed FPC module, the segmentation performance is much better than that of the backbone network.

Table 3. Quantitative comparison of the time consumption.

Method	Train time (s)	Inference time (FPS)
UNet with VC	1526	14
UNet with MFC	**1165**	**23**

Table 4. Ablation study for vessel segmentation on DRIVE dataset.

Method	ACC (%)	SE (%)	SP (%)	AUC (%)
Backbone	96.30	77.75	**98.51**	97.72
Backbone+FPC	**96.81**	**80.07**	98.45	**98.17**

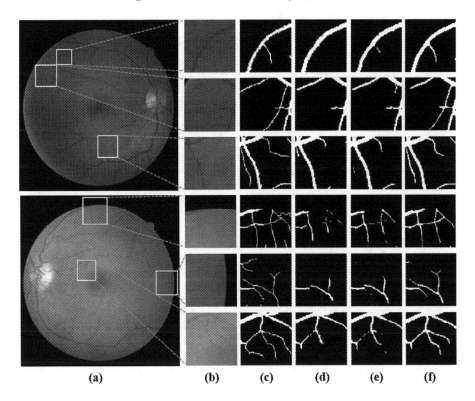

Fig. 4. Visualization of the results of retinal vessel segmentation, from left to right: (a) fundus images, (b) magnified view, (c) ground truth, results of (d) U-Net, (e) CE-Net, and (f) RVSeg-Net.

4   Conclusions

We present a novel network, namely RVSeg-Net, with a feature pyramid cascade (FPC) module and a multi-frequency convolution (MFC) module to address the challenging problem of retinal vessel segmentation. The FPC module can not only capture multi-scale features but also make better use of local and global context information to produce more representative features for better segmentation results. On the other hand, by applying the MFC in our network, we can reduce the redundancy parameters to improve computing efficiency and avoid overfitting. Experimental results demonstrate that the proposed RVSeg-Net achieved state-of-the-art performance without excessive computing resource consumption. Further investigations include validating it on more datesets and integrating it into clinical systems.

Acknowledgement. This work was supported in part by grants from the National Natural Science Foundation of China (No. 61973221), the Natural Science Foundation of Guangdong Province, China (Nos. 2018A030313381 and 2019A1515011165), the Major Project or Key Lab of Shenzhen Research Foundation, China (Nos. JCYJ2016060 8173051207, ZDSYS201707311550233, KJYY201807031540021294 and JSGG201 805081520220065), the COVID-19 Prevention Project of Guangdong Province, China (No. 2020KZDZX1174), the Major Project of the New Generation of Artificial Intelligence (No. 2018AAA0102900) and the Hong Kong Research Grants Council (Project No. PolyU 152035/17E and 15205919).

References

1. Alom, M.Z., Yakopcic, C., Hasan, M., Taha, T.M., Asari, V.K.: Recurrent residual U-Net for medical image segmentation. J. Med. Imaging **6**(1), 014006 (2019)
2. Badrinarayanan, V., Kendall, A., Cipolla, R.: Segnet: a deep convolutional encoder-decoder architecture for image segmentation. IEEE Trans. Pattern Anal. Mach. Intell. **39**(12), 2481–2495 (2017)
3. Chen, L.-C., Zhu, Y., Papandreou, G., Schroff, F., Adam, H.: Encoder-decoder with atrous separable convolution for semantic image segmentation. In: Ferrari, V., Hebert, M., Sminchisescu, C., Weiss, Y. (eds.) ECCV 2018. LNCS, vol. 11211, pp. 833–851. Springer, Cham (2018). https://doi.org/10.1007/978-3-030-01234-2_49
4. Chen, Y., et al.: Drop an octave: reducing spatial redundancy in convolutional neural networks with octave convolution. In: The IEEE International Conference on Computer Vision (ICCV), October 2019
5. Cunha-Vaz, J.: The blood-retinal barrier in the management of retinal disease: euretina award lecture. Ophthalmologica **237**(1), 1–10 (2017)
6. Dachsel, R., Jöster, A., Breuß, M.: Real-time retinal vessel segmentation on high-resolution fundus images using laplacian pyramids. In: Lee, C., Su, Z., Sugimoto, A. (eds.) PSIVT 2019. LNCS, vol. 11854, pp. 337–350. Springer, Cham (2019). https://doi.org/10.1007/978-3-030-34879-3_26
7. Dai, J., et al.: Deformable convolutional networks. In: Proceedings of the IEEE International Conference on Computer Vision, pp. 764–773 (2017)
8. Gu, Z., et al.: CE-NET: context encoder network for 2D medical image segmentation. IEEE Trans. Med. Imaging. **38**(10), 2281–2292 (2019)
9. Hoover, A., Kouznetsova, V., Goldbaum, M.: Locating blood vessels in retinal images by piecewise threshold probing of a matched filter response. IEEE Trans. Med. Imaging **19**(3), 203–210 (2000)
10. Jin, Q., Meng, Z., Pham, T.D., Chen, Q., Wei, L., Su, R.: Dunet: a deformable network for retinal vessel segmentation. Knowl.-Based Syst. **178**, 149–162 (2019)
11. Li, Q., Feng, B., Xie, L., Liang, P., Zhang, H., Wang, T.: A cross-modality learning approach for vessel segmentation in retinal images. IEEE Trans. Med. Imaging **35**(1), 109–118 (2015)
12. Lin, G., Milan, A., Shen, C., Reid, I.: Refinenet: multi-path refinement networks for high-resolution semantic segmentation. In: Proceedings of the IEEE Conference on Computer Vision and Pattern Recognition, pp. 1925–1934 (2017)
13. Liskowski, P., Krawiec, K.: Segmenting retinal blood vessels with deep neural networks. IEEE Trans. Med. Imaging **35**(11), 2369–2380 (2016)
14. Long, J., Shelhamer, E., Darrell, T.: Fully convolutional networks for semantic segmentation. In: Proceedings of the IEEE Conference on Computer Vision and Pattern Recognition, pp. 3431–3440 (2015)
15. Mo, J., Zhang, L.: Multi-level deep supervised networks for retinal vessel segmentation. Int. J. Comput. Assist. Radiol. Surg. **12**(12), 2181–2193 (2017). https://doi.org/10.1007/s11548-017-1619-0

16. Niemeijer, M., Staal, J., van Ginneken, B., Loog, M., Abramoff, M.D.: Comparative study of retinal vessel segmentation methods on a new publicly available database. In: Medical Imaging 2004: Image Processing, vol. 5370, pp. 648–656. International Society for Optics and Photonics (2004)

17. Oloumi, F., Rangayyan, R.M., Oloumi, F., Eshghzadeh-Zanjani, P., Ayres, F.J.: Detection of blood vessels in fundus images of the retina using Gabor wavelets. In: 2007 29th Annual International Conference of the IEEE Engineering in Medicine and Biology Society, pp. 6451–6454. IEEE (2007)

18. Ricci, E., Perfetti, R.: Retinal blood vessel segmentation using line operators and support vector classification. IEEE Trans. Med. Imaging **26**(10), 1357–1365 (2007)

19. Ronneberger, O., Fischer, P., Brox, T.: U-Net: convolutional networks for biomedical image segmentation. In: Navab, N., Hornegger, J., Wells, W.M., Frangi, A.F. (eds.) MICCAI 2015. LNCS, vol. 9351, pp. 234–241. Springer, Cham (2015). https://doi.org/10.1007/978-3-319-24574-4_28

20. Staal, J., Abràmoff, M.D., Niemeijer, M., Viergever, M.A., Van Ginneken, B.: Ridge-based vessel segmentation in color images of the retina. IEEE Trans. Med. Imaging **23**(4), 501–509 (2004)

21. Wang, B., Qiu, S., He, H.: Dual encoding U-Net for retinal vessel segmentation. In: Shen, D., et al. (eds.) MICCAI 2019. LNCS, vol. 11764, pp. 84–92. Springer, Cham (2019). https://doi.org/10.1007/978-3-030-32239-7_10

22. Wu, Y., Xia, Y., Song, Y., Zhang, Y., Cai, W.: Multiscale network followed network model for retinal vessel segmentation. In: Frangi, A.F., Schnabel, J.A., Davatzikos, C., Alberola-López, C., Fichtinger, G. (eds.) MICCAI 2018. LNCS, vol. 11071, pp. 119–126. Springer, Cham (2018). https://doi.org/10.1007/978-3-030-00934-2_14

23. Yan, Z., Yang, X., Cheng, K.T.: Joint segment-level and pixel-wise losses for deep learning based retinal vessel segmentation. IEEE Trans. Biomed. Eng. **65**(9), 1912–1923 (2018)

24. You, X., Peng, Q., Yuan, Y., Cheung, Y.M., Lei, J.: Segmentation of retinal blood vessels using the radial projection and semi-supervised approach. Pattern Recogn. **44**(10–11), 2314–2324 (2011)

25. Zhang, Y., Chung, A.C.S.: Deep supervision with additional labels for retinal vessel segmentation task. In: Frangi, A.F., Schnabel, J.A., Davatzikos, C., Alberola-López, C., Fichtinger, G. (eds.) MICCAI 2018. LNCS, vol. 11071, pp. 83–91. Springer, Cham (2018). https://doi.org/10.1007/978-3-030-00934-2_10

26. Zhang, Z., Fu, H., Dai, H., Shen, J., Pang, Y., Shao, L.: ET-Net: a generic edge-attention guidance network for medical image segmentation. In: Shen, D., et al. (eds.) MICCAI 2019. LNCS, vol. 11764, pp. 442–450. Springer, Cham (2019). https://doi.org/10.1007/978-3-030-32239-7_49

27. Zhao, H., Shi, J., Qi, X., Wang, X., Jia, J.: Pyramid scene parsing network. In: Proceedings of the IEEE Conference on Computer Vision and Pattern Recognition, pp. 2881–2890 (2017)

Author Index

Printed in the United States
By Bookmasters